THE LETTERS OF
T. S. ELIOT
VOLUME 6

By T. S. Eliot

THE POEMS OF T. S. ELIOT
Volume 1: Collected and Uncollected Poems
Volume 2: Practical Cats and Further Verses
edited by Christopher Ricks and Jim McCue

THE COMPLETE POEMS AND PLAYS

verse
COLLECTED POEMS 1909–1962
PRUFROCK AND OTHER OBSERVATIONS
THE WASTE LAND AND OTHER POEMS
FOUR QUARTETS
SELECTED POEMS
THE WASTE LAND:
A Facsimile and Transcript of the Original Drafts
edited by Valerie Eliot
INVENTIONS OF THE MARCH HARE:
Poems 1909–1917
edited by Christopher Ricks
THE ARIEL POEMS
THE WASTE LAND
OLD POSSUM'S BOOK OF PRACTICAL CATS

plays
MURDER IN THE CATHEDRAL
THE FAMILY REUNION
THE COCKTAIL PARTY
THE CONFIDENTIAL CLERK
THE ELDER STATESMAN

literary criticism
THE SACRED WOOD
SELECTED ESSAYS
THE USE OF POETRY AND THE USE OF CRITICISM
THE VARIETIES OF METAPHYSICAL POETRY
edited by Ronald Schuchard
TO CRITICIZE THE CRITIC
ON POETRY AND POETS
FOR LANCELOT ANDREWES
SELECTED PROSE OF T. S. ELIOT
edited by Frank Kermode
THE COMPLETE PROSE OF T. S. ELIOT: THE CRITICAL EDITION
Volume 1: Apprentice Years, 1905–1918
edited by Jewel Spears Brooker and Ronald Schuchard
Volume 2: The Perfect Critic, 1919–1926
edited by Anthony Cuda and Ronald Schuchard
Volume 3: Literature, Politics, Belief, 1927–1929
edited by Frances Dickey, Jennifer Formichelli, Ronald Schuchard

social criticism
THE IDEA OF A CHRISTIAN SOCIETY
NOTES TOWARDS THE DEFINITION OF CULTURE

letters
THE LETTERS OF T. S. ELIOT
Volume 1: 1898–1922
Volume 2: 1923–1925
edited by Valerie Eliot and Hugh Haughton
Volume 3: 1926–1927
Volume 4: 1928–1929
Volume 5: 1930–1931
edited by Valerie Eliot and John Haffenden

THE LETTERS OF
T. S. Eliot

EDITED BY

VALERIE ELIOT

AND

JOHN HAFFENDEN

VOLUME 6
1932–1933

Yale

UNIVERSITY PRESS

New Haven & London

First published in the
United States in 2016 by Yale University Press.
First published in
Great Britain in 2016 by Faber and Faber Limited.

Yale University Press books may be
purchased in quantity for educational, business, or
promotional use. For information, please e-mail sales.press@yale.edu
(U.S. office) or sales@yaleup.co.uk (U.K. office).

Typeset by Donald Sommerville.
Printed in the United States of America.

Library of Congress Control Number: 2016933960
ISBN 978-0-300-21180-1 (hardcover: alk. paper)

A catalogue record for this book is available from the British Library.

This paper meets the requirements of
ANSI/NISO Z39.48-1992 (Permanence of Paper).

10 9 8 7 6 5 4 3 2 1

CONTENTS

ILLUSTRATIONS

ACKNOWLEDGEMENTS

For help and advice in many capacities, including copyright permissions, the publishers and editors would like to thank the following individuals and institutions. (Sadly, a number of those named below are now deceased, but we wish still to put on record our gratitude to them.) Dr Donald Adamson; Barry Ahearn; Ruth M. (Beth) Alvarez; The American Jewish Archives, Cincinnati, Ohio; Dr Norma Aubertin-Potter, Librarian in Charge, Codrington Library, All Souls College, Oxford; Camilla Bagg; Joan Bailey; Ruth Baker; Susan Bank, Secretary to Rev. Carl Scovel, Minister, King's Chapel, Boston, Massachusetts; Owen Barfield; Buona Barnes; Tansy Barton, Special Collections Administrator, Senate House Library, University of London; H. Baugh; Denison Beach; T. O. Beachcroft; Anne Olivier Bell; Mrs W. J. Bender; Robert J. Bertholf, Curator, The Poetry/Rare Books Collection, University Libraries, State University of New York at Buffalo; Bibliothèque Nationale, Paris; Kenneth Blackwell, Mills Memorial Library, McMaster University; Michael Harry Blechner, McFarlin Library, University of Tulsa; Mary Boccaccio, McKeldin Library, University of Maryland; Maxwell Bodenheim; John Bodley; William H. Bond; University of Bonn Library; J. M. L. Booker, Archivist, Lloyds Bank; Ann Bowden, Harry Ransom Humanities Research Center, University of Texas at Austin; David Bradshaw; The British Library; Valerie Brokenshire; Jewel Spears Brooker; Robert Brown, Archivist, Faber & Faber Ltd; Sally Brown; Richard Buckle; Penelope Bulloch, Balliol College Library; Dr R. W. Burchfield; Professor P. H. Butter; William R. Cagle and Saundra Taylor, Lilly Library; Herbert Cahoon, The Pierpont Morgan Library; Anne Caiger, Manuscripts Librarian, University of California, Los Angeles; Douglas Campbell; Kathleen Cann, Department of Manuscripts and University Archives, Cambridge University Library; Humphrey Carpenter; François Chapon, Bibliothèque Littéraire Jacques Doucet; Mrs Charlton; Christopher M. Cherry; Joseph Chiari; Mary Clapinson, Keeper of Western Manuscripts, Bodleian Library; Alexander P. Clark, Firestone Library, Princeton University; Alan Clodd; Marguerite Cohn; Dorothy Collins; Henri Colliot, Fondation Saint-John Perse; John Constable; Joyce Crick; Peter Croft; Arthur Crook; Tanya Crothers; Tony Cuda; Charles T. Cullen, President and Librarian, The Newberry Library; Rexi Culpin;

Dr Robin Darwall-Smith, Archivist, University College, Oxford; Roy L. Davids; Carolyn A. Davis, Reader Services Librarian, The George Arents Research Library for Special Collections, Syracuse University Library; Dr A. Deiss, General Secretariat, Swiss Medical Institutions; Giles de la Mare; the Literary Trustees of Walter de la Mare; Rodney G. Dennis; Herbert Dieckmann; Valentine Dobrée; E. R. Dodds; David Doughan, Fawcett Library; Kenneth W. Duckett, Morris Library, Southern Illinois University at Carbondale; Ellen S Dunlap, Harry Ransom Humanities Research Center; Peter du Sautoy; Donald D. Eddy, Department of Rare Books, Cornell University Library; Professor Charles W. Eliot; Sarah Ethier, University of Wisconsin-Milwaukee Libraries; Matthew Evans; Sir Richard Faber KCVO; Toby Faber; Tom Faber; Elizabeth A. Falsey; Patricia Fanshawe; Christopher Farley; David Farmer, Harry Ransom Humanities Research Center (and Warren Roberts, Mary Hirth, Sally Leach, and many other members of staff); Donald Farren, University of Maryland Libraries; Barbara Fehse, Secretary in Manuscripts, University of Virginia Library; Anton Felton, Continuum Ltd; Dominique Fernandez; James Fergusson Books and Manuscripts; Mrs Harry Fine; Mrs Burnham Finney; Christopher Fletcher; Barbara Floyd, Director of the Ward M. Canaday for Special Collections, University of Toledo; Angel Flores; Henri Fluchère; Fondren Library; Jennifer Formichelli; Donald Gallup; Special Collections, Isabella Stewart Gardner Museum, Boston, Mass.; K. C. Gay, Lockwood Memorial Library, State University of New York, Buffalo; Herbert Gerwing, University of Victoria; Mrs Ghika; Catherine Gide; M. A. M. Gilbert; Robert Giroux; Dr Peter Godman; Emile Goichot; Estate of Enid Goldsmith; Adrian M. Goodman; Philip Goodman; Warwick Gould; Nicollette Gray; Herbert T. Greene; Ernest G. Griffin; J. C. Hall; Dr Michael Halls; Saskia Hamilton; Bonnie Hardwick, Manuscripts Division, The Bancroft Library, University of California, Berkeley; Sir Rupert Hart-Davis; Harvard University Archives; Professor E. N. Hartley, Institute Archives, MIT; Michael Hastings; The Library, Haverford College; Desmond Hawkins; Cathy Henderson, Research Librarian, Harry Ransom Humanities Research Center; Robert Henderson; David Higham Associates Ltd; Roger Highfield; Robert W. Hill, New York Public Library; Aurelia Bolliger Hodgson; Michael Hofmann; Michael Holroyd; Hornbake Library, University of Maryland; Lélia Howard; Penelope Hughes-Hallett; J. W. Hunt, Royal Military Academy, Sandhurst; Jeremy Hutchinson; Lord Hutchinson; Elizabeth Inglis (Special Collections, The Library, University of Sussex); Carolyn Jakeman; Robin Jackson, The British Academy; William A. Jackson, Houghton Library;

P. D. James; Revd Martin Jarrett-Kerr, CR; Dorothy O. Johansen, Reed College, Portland, Oregon; Gregory A. Johnson, Alderman Library, University of Virginia; William Jovanovich; William L. Joyce, Princeton University Library; Michael Kammen; Paul Keegan; Professor John Kelly, St John's College, Oxford; Dr Paul Kelly, National Library of Scotland; Mary Kiffer, Assistant Secretary, John Simon Guggenheim Memorial Foundation, New York; Modern Archives Centre, King's College, Cambridge; Monique Kuntz, Bibliothèque Municipale, Vichy; Dr L. R. Leavis; Major N. Aylward Leete; Mrs Dorothy Milburn Léger, Lockwood Memorial Library; Paul Levy; Kenneth A. Lohf, Librarian for Rare Books and MSS, Butler Library, Columbia University; London Library; Pat Lowe; Richard Luckett; Richard M. Ludwig, and Howard C. Rice Jr., Princeton University Library; Jim McCue; Mary C. McGreenery, Harvard Alumni Records; Patricia McGuire, Archivist, and Peter Monteith, Assistant Archivist, King's College, Cambridge; Charles Madge; Ed Maggs; Lady Marshall; Professor R. B. Martin; Professor B. K. Matilal; Francis O. Mattson, Berg Collection, New York Public Library; R. Russell Maylone, Special Collections Department, Northwestern University Library; Bernard Meehan, Keeper of Manuscripts, Trinity College Dublin; Erik Mesterton; Wim van Mierlo; Marvin A. Miller, Director of Libraries, University of Arkansas; Mrs Edward S. Mills; University Library, Missouri History Museum; Joe Mitchenson; Kate Mole, Librarian/Archivist, The British Academy; Glen E. Morgan; Frank Vigor Morley; J. D. I. Morley; Leslie A. Morris, Houghton Library, Harvard University; Lewis Morris; Tim Munby; Katherine Middleton Murry; Mary Middleton Murry; Richard Murry; The Bursar, New College, Oxford; Jeanne T. Newlin, Harvard Theatre Collection; Richard Ollard; Richard D. Olson, Curator of Rare Books and Special Collections, The University Library, Northwestern University; Jessie Orage; Dr James Marshall Osborn; Anne Owen; Martin Page; Stephen Page; Stephen R. Parks, Curator, The James Marshall and Marie-Louise Osborn Collection, Yale University; Alasdair Paterson, University of Exeter Library; Fondation Saint-John Perse; C. G. Petter, Archivist Librarian, Special Collections, University of Victoria; Robert Phillips; Sir Charles Pickthorn Bt; Charles E. Pierce, Jr., Director, The Pierpont Morgan Library; Jean F. Preston, Princeton University Library; Lord Quinton; Mary de Rachewiltz; Craig Raine; Lawrence S. Rainey; Wanda M. Randall; Graham Wallas and Angela Raspin, London School of Economics; Benedict Read; Real Academia de la Historia, Madrid; Dr R. T. H. Redpath; Joseph Regenstein Library, University of Chicago; Stanley Revell; Howard C. Rice, Jr., Associate Librarian for

Rare Books & Special Collections, Princeton University Library; I. A. and Dorothea Richards; Glyn Richards; Canon Pierre Riches; Helene Ritzerfeld; Alain Rivière; Sir Adam Roberts; Galleria Nazionale d'Arte Moderna, Rome; Rosenbach Museum & Library; Anthony Rota; Bertram Rota; Mme Agathe Rouart-Valéry; Carol Z. Rothkopf; A. L. Rowse; Royal Literary Fund; Lord Russell; Mrs N. Ryan; Professor Alfred W. Satterthwaite; Marcia Satterthwaite; Sean Sayers; Schiller-Nationalmuseum, Marbach am Neckar; Gerd Schmidt; David E. Schoonover, Yale University Library; Susan Schreibman; Rev. Karl Schroeder, SJ; Ronald Schuchard; Grace Schulman; Timothy and Marian Seldes; Miranda Seymour; Christopher Sheppard, Brotherton Collection, Leeds University Library; Ethel C. Simpson, Trustee, John Gould Fletcher Literary Estate; G. Singh; Samuel A. Sizer, Curator, Special Collections, University Libraries, University of Arkansas; Janet Adam Smith; Theodora Eliot Smith; Susanna Smithson; Virginia L. Smyers, Harvard University Archives; Revd Charles Smyth; Natasha Spender; Sir Stephen Spender; Tom Staley; Jayme Stayer; Dom Julian Stead; Alix Strachey; James Strachey; Jenny Stratford; Kendon L. Stubbs, University of Virginia Library; Barbara Sturtevant; University of Sussex Library; Michael Sutton; Lola L. Szladits, Berg Collection, New York Public Library; Allen Tate; Elizabeth Stege Teleky, The Joseph Regenstein Library, University of Chicago; David S. Thatcher, University of Victoria, British Columbia; Alan G. Thomas; Willard Thorp; Dr Michael J. Tilby; Kathleen Tillotson; Trinity College, Cambridge; François Valéry; Judith Robinson-Valéry; The Paul Valéry Collection, Bibliothèque Nationale, Paris; Julian Vinogradoff; University of Virginia Library; Michael J Walsh, Heythrop College; J. Waterlow; Dr George Watson; John Weightman; John Wells, Cambridge University Library; Richard Wendorf; Gretchen Wheen; James White, National Gallery of Ireland; Brooke Whiting, Department of Special Collections, University Research Library, University of California, Los Angeles; Widener Library, Harvard University; Helen Willard; David G. Williams; Dr Charlotte Williamson; George Williamson; Julia Ross Williamson; Patricia C. Willis, Beinecke Rare Book and Manuscript Library, Yale University; Joan H. Winterkorn; Melanie Wisner; Harriet Harvey Wood; Woodson Research Center, Rice University; Dr Daniel H. Woodward, Huntington Library; C. J. Wright; Yale University Archives; Michael Yeats.

For permission to quote from copyright material: Letters by W. H. Auden are used by kind permission of Edward Mendelson, the Estate of W. H. Auden. Letters by James Joyce are used by kind permission of Stephen Joyce. Letters by F. R. Leavis are used by kind permission of

Robin Leavis. Unpublished letters by Ezra Pound – Copyright © by Mary de Rachewiltz and Elizabeth S. Pound – are used by permission of New Directions Publishing Corp. Unpublished letters by Stephen Spender are used by kind permission of Matthew Spender and Lizzie Spender.

Special thanks go to Judith Hooper and Clare Reihill, trustees of the Estate of T. S. Eliot, for their generous support, faith and friendship; my editor Matthew Hollis of Faber & Faber Ltd; Nancy Fulford, Project Archivist – T. S. Eliot Collection; Donald Sommerville for expert copy-editing and type-setting; Iman Javadi for swift, authoritative help with translations; David Wilson for proof-reading; Douglas Matthews for indexing; Mrs Valerie Eliot's personal assistant Debbie Whitfield for her commitment and long hard work; and the Institute of English Studies, University of London, for hosting the T. S. Eliot Editorial Project funded by the Arts and Humanities Research Council. John Haffenden is grateful above all to Jemma Walton for her good humour, love and kindness.

PREFACE

We have few demonstrable facts about the personal relationship of T. S. Eliot and Vivien Haigh-Wood. The same cannot be said for opinions on their marriage, and especially for judgements of Eliot. Unsurprisingly, Virginia Woolf's reflections on the state of Eliot's first union, in the summer of 1932, are as acidly acute as any: 'Behold Tom & Vivienne . . . – she wild as Ophelia – alas no Hamlet would love her, with her powdered spots – in white satin, L[eonard] said; Tom, poor man, all battened down as usual, prim, grey, making his kind jokes with her . . . Then her chops and changes . . . all of which he bears with great patience: feeling perhaps that his 7 months of freedom draw near.'

Tortured by life with his volatile, erratic wife, Eliot, at forty-four, resolves to secure an abrupt separation. It is an excruciating decision for him; a matter of overwhelming shock and bewilderment for her.

Eliot met and promptly married Vivien, only daughter of the minor artist and middle-class absentee landlord Charles Haigh-Wood (he owned a few modest domestic properties near Dublin), in mid-1915. By 1932, when this volume of letters opens, Vivien's fluctuating mental state has left Eliot feeling so desolatingly 'battened down' that it comes as a relief to him to be travelling to a temporary academic appointment in the USA for the seven months referred to by Woolf. The business of managing Vivien's increasingly distressed and alarming behaviour – she is given to imagining slights and making embarrassing scenes, periods of withdrawal, aggression and intense neediness – has become for Eliot a matter of unbearable sufferance. The couple go out as much as Vivien's precarious mental condition will allow, and even attempt entertaining at home. However, few guests are in their company for long without registering the intolerable strain between husband and wife. Elizabeth Bowen finds that witnessing the couple in their flat was 'very sinister and depressing' – all because of the spectacle of 'two highly nervous people shut up together in grinding proximity'. The one person in whom both Eliot and his Vivien take delight is the whimsical, kind-hearted poet Ralph Hodgson, who is visiting London on leave from his university in Japan, with his American girlfriend Aurelia Bolliger (they will marry in 1933). Hodgson brings cheer into the Eliots' otherwise distraught world:

they love spending time together and taking day trips into the country; and they adore Hodgson's pet mastiff. (Other friends, for the most part, feel merely pity for the staunchly suffering Eliot, and little more than apprehension and exhausting anxiety in the company of Vivien.) But it ends all too soon, and too abruptly. In August 1932 Hodgson and Bolliger are bound to return to Japan, just weeks before Eliot has to depart for the USA. Vivien feels at once deserted and bereaved. 'I was very nearly insane . . . with the Cruel Pain of losing Tom,' she writes early in September. She feels 'haunted' by horrors.

'He looks like a sacerdotal lawyer – dyspeptic, ascetic, eclectic. Inhibitions. Yet obviously a nice man and a great poet.' Harold Nicolson spoke for perhaps a majority of people who met Eliot during this period of his life. However, despite Eliot's polite, prim personality (as it seemed to many on first acquaintance), he is assiduous in cultivating contacts and nurturing talent – sooner or later, everyone in whom he expresses an interest is taken for lunch or given tea at the office – and his kindness is manifest. 'If it had not been for him, I would not . . . have had a chance,' says George Barker. Eliot is the greatest talent-spotter of the age, commissioning for the *Criterion* contributions by young writers including Michael Roberts, Maurice Bowra, Louis MacNeice, Hugh MacDiarmid, L. C. Knights and Peter Quennell, as well as pieces by his contemporaries including Hermann Broch and Ezra Pound. He publishes James Joyce's proud, poignant poem 'Ecce Puer', on the birth of his grandson; and at Faber & Faber, W. H. Auden's *The Orators: An English Study* (1932) – hailing it as 'the only recent satire worth reading'. Not in the least jealous of the position he has earned over the last decade as the major arbiter of creative and critical taste (through his dual editorial role at Faber & Faber Ltd and the *Criterion*), Eliot is happy also to offer a helping hand when he learns of the 'project of *Scrutiny*', as he terms it, writing to the critic F. R. Leavis: 'If I can be of any use in interesting possible contributors and subscribers I shall be very glad.' (By way of poor return, when launching *Scrutiny* Leavis is openly rude about the calibre of recent contributors to the *Criterion*.)

In terms of Eliot's own output, the period is largely devoted to essays and talks with an ethical, specifically Christian, bias. He writes a preface to a translation of Charles-Louis Philippe's *Bubu de Montparnasse*, praising it for evoking 'an intense pity for the humble and oppressed'; a gracious obituary of the poet and critic Harold Monro, proprietor of the Poetry Bookshop, London; an essay on George Herbert; an article entitled 'Building up the Christian World'; and four talks in a radio series on 'The Modern Dilemma', choosing as his topic the requisite place of Christianity in the current world order. Then in September 1932, just before leaving for the USA, he brings out his *Selected Essays 1917–1932*. Later in the year he will publish (in the USA only) *John Dryden: The Poet, The Dramatist, The Critic* (BBC talks), and his savagely funny and menacing theatre-experiment: *Sweeney Agonistes: Fragments of an Aristophanic Melodrama*.

Home for Eliot means a 'futile life', and a 'hideous farce' (to use his own terms) – but it is not just for the sake of absenting himself from the domestic melodrama that he works so hard at his paid employment. He relishes the absorption of work at the office – as a member of the mutually cooperative Faber & Faber family – and prefers its purposeful routine, even at times of high pressure, to almost anything else. He reveals, rather surprisingly: 'I don't think I like writing . . . it's not a regular occupation. Thank God, I have a regular job.'

'My year in America . . . was the happiest I can ever remember in my life,' he declares to his brother Henry in the summer of 1933, on returning to England after his extraordinarily energetic eight months as Charles Eliot Norton Lecturer at Harvard. That trip sees him adopt a gruelling work schedule: he gives around eighty talks or lectures; his eight formal Harvard lectures, written under fierce time constraints, will be published as *The Use of Poetry and the Use of Criticism* (1933); and in spring 1933 he delivers the Page-Barbour Lectures at the University of Virginia (published as *After Strange Gods*, 1934).

In Cambridge, Massachusetts, Eliot finds it 'strangely comfortable . . . to be among a society which consists largely of one's own relatives . . . I like to be with people who were fond of me before the malady of poetry declared itself.' He makes close friends with his colleagues Theodore Spencer and F. O. Matthiessen, and with an Englishman, Gerald S. Graham, who is teaching history at Harvard. For a man who normally guards his privacy, Eliot is remarkably sociable. At Christmas 1932 he travels across country to pass a few days with his old friend Emily Hale in California; and he goes on to give talks across the USA – California, Missouri, Minnesota, Chicago, New York. His letters describing encounters with F. Scott Fitzgerald, Marianne Moore and Edmund Wilson brim with gossip. High points of the excursion include the première at Vassar College of his comic melodrama *Sweeney Agonistes*, produced by the brilliant experimental director Hallie Flanagan.

Before returning to England, he writes to Vivien via his solicitor to advise her of his decision to live apart. Upon his return, he hides out for some weeks with friends in Surrey: he has reason to fear her reaction. The months of happiness, and the kindness of friends and family that he has relished in America, have enabled him to see his marriage from a new perspective. But one of the especially striking features about the letters referring to his wife at this period is the unprecedented vehemence of his feelings. For a man of a predominantly charitable frame of mind, his expressions of resentment and even anger are frank to the point of being shocking. He has given 'the best years' of his life to an impossible relationship, he says; now he wishes to remove himself from 'the poison of uncongeniality and pretense'. The last eighteen years – from his late twenties to his mid-forties – have been a 'nightmare . . . like a bad Dostoievski novel'. And yet, he readily concedes in the same letter, 'I have nothing to complain of: I think that (so long as I can keep free of any illusions about my own importance) that I have got about what I deserved, both ways, and (to put it romantically) the vulture on the liver.' (He was thus comparing himself bleakly to the Titan Prometheus, interminably tortured for his crime.) He feels emotionally annihilated. Over the years he has taken pains to ensure that his wife should be cared for by the best consultants and psychiatrists, to spend time in specialist treatment centres, including the reputable Sanatorium de la Malmaison outside Paris, and to meet the heavy costs involved. He has stood by her, and stood up for her, at all times; and he has suffered with her through terrible days and nights. He can take no more.

A split, but not a divorce, ensues – as a devout Anglo-Catholic, Eliot will never countenance divorce – leaving Eliot married to Vivien until her death, aged fifty-nine, in 1947. He has taken a personal vow of celibacy, and means to abide by it. In terms of financial support, he is willing to make her a decent allowance – and in the event he helps to support her for the rest of her days. All he asks in return is that his personal possessions, including books, papers and heirlooms, should be given back. His determination to behave as properly as he can manage under the circumstances is appreciated by members of Vivien's family. Eliot's brother-in-law Maurice Haigh-Wood remains on respectful and affectionate terms with him even until Eliot's demise in 1965.

For her part, Vivien buries herself in denial. She refuses to accept a deed of separation. She seems to comprehend nothing of the negativity amounting to a despair that her husband has experienced for many months. Thus it is perhaps the most painful irony of their separation that she will never actually understand why it has come about.

In addition to the letters by Eliot in this volume, Vivien's voice is also to be heard at numerous moments. This fullness is a testament to Eliot's second wife, Valerie, who spent her widowhood pouring her considerable energies into sourcing, acquiring and annotating her husband's letters with the explicit purpose of making them public. Valerie hoped that, while facts relating to her husband's first relationship were scarce, the public could at least have knowledge of all his thoughts relating to the period. Valerie was also adamant that Vivien's point of view should be given air. To this end, this volume includes many letters from Vivien, addressed both to Eliot and to close friends.

There are almost as many interpretations of the first Eliot marriage as there were days of their relationship. Valerie Eliot hoped that the publication of this volume would allow the reader to truly, as Virginia Woolf put it, 'behold Tom & Vivienne'. In beholding the first Mr and Mrs Eliot, it is tempting to suggest that the main observation one could decently make regarding their relationship is a very simple one. The marriage of T. S. Eliot and Vivien Haigh-Wood was profoundly, ineffably, sad for the man and woman involved.

JOHN HAFFENDEN[1]

2015

1–I must own up to an error. In *L5*, 96, a review of E. A. Baker's *History of the English Novel* (*TLS*, 17 July 1930) was attributed to TSE; it was in fact written by the writer and critic Harold Child. My apologies for the mistake.

BIOGRAPHICAL COMMENTARY

1932–1933

1932 3 JANUARY – Vivien tells Mary Hutchinson, 'I have had a sort of breakdown, & have felt very ill in every way.' 4 JANUARY – TSE writes to James Joyce, on the death of his father: 'I know something about such things, as I had meant to return to Boston to visit my mother, and allowed one thing after another to delay me . . . I think, however, that the death of my father, ten years earlier, pained me more deeply; it was just at the end of the war, so that I could not have gone to see him; but he died still believing, I am sure, that I had made a complete mess of my life – which from his point of view, and possibly quite rightly, I had done. I cannot forget him sitting in the railway station before my last departure, looking completely broken. Whereas my mother lived long enough to take an immoderate pride in my accomplishment and to feel that I had done the best for myself: that may or may not be so, but I am glad that she believed it. So when I suggest that possibly your father felt his life to be fulfilled in the recognition of your fame and greatness, it is not merely a conventional piece of consolatory chatter.' 8 JANUARY – TSE and Vivien take tea with Ottoline Morrell. 12 JANUARY – the Eliots throw a party, attended by Morrell, Alida Monro and Robert Sencourt. Morrell notes that guests were seated on rows of chairs like at a prayer meeting; an exotic lady sang, and TSE recited some verses. It struck her as being very 1870s: 'no talk, only readings, pianoforte records & recitations', and with VHE talking wildly in the street. For the next six months, TSE and his wife make friends with the poet Ralph Hodgson: Vivien feels a deep affection for Hodgson's companion Aurelia Bolliger. Both TSE and VHE feel a great sense of loss when the other couple return to Japan in August. TSE reviews a book called *This Unemployment*, expressing satisfaction in having a job apart from the business of poetry. 'A certain amount of routine, of dullness and of necessity seems inseparable from work; and for myself, I am too sceptical of my own abilities to make a whole-time job of writing poetry, even if I had the means.' 14 JANUARY – TSE publishes *Charles Whibley: A Memoir* (English Association Pamphlet No. 80). 18 JANUARY – issues a contract for W. H. Auden's *The Orators*. 10 FEBRUARY – TSE submits his 'Preface' to Charles-Louis Philippe's *Bubu of Montparnasse* (trans. Laurence Vail), declaring that *Bubu* 'stood for Paris as some of Dickens' novels stand for London': it evokes 'an intense pity for the humble and oppressed'. Publishes *Poems* by Clere Parsons. 19 FEBRUARY – rejects Eric Blair's manuscript 'A Scullion's Diary', the original of *Down and Out in Paris and London*. 24 FEBRUARY – TSE tells F. R. Leavis, 'I am much interested in the project of *Scrutiny*, and if I can be of any use in interesting possible contributors and subscribers I shall be very glad.' 29 FEBRUARY – TSE admires and accepts for publication in the *Criterion* Joyce's poem on the birth of his grandson, 'Ecce Puer'. 2 MARCH – TSE lunches with Jim Barnes (brother of Mary Hutchinson) and Harold Nicolson – who notes in his diary, of Eliot: 'Very yellow and glum. Perfect manners. He looks like a sacerdotal lawyer – dyspeptic, ascetic, eclectic. Inhibitions. Yet obviously a nice man and a great poet.' 12 MARCH – TSE publishes 'George Herbert', *The Spectator* 148 (the seventh in a series on 'Studies in Sanctity'); and contributes four talks to a BBC radio series on 'The Modern Dilemma' published in the *Listener*: 'Christianity and Communism' (16 Mar.); 'Religion and Science: A Phantom Dilemma' (23 Mar.); 'The Search for Moral Sanction' (30 Mar.); 'Building up the Christian World' (6 Apr.). He stresses his own vital need for chastity, austerity, humility, sanctity: without these, he would perish. When complimented on his talks by Sir John Reith, TSE tells his producer: 'I could not help feeling that if I had given him so much satisfaction I could not have said quite what I ought to have said.' TSE contributes to the expenses of an appeal by Geoffrey de Montalk against his imprisonment for 'obscene libel'. 'I do not see how any reputable publisher, or any reputable author, could refuse to support the cause of reform.' He considers the judgment against Montalk a 'deplorable piece of brutality'. 17 MARCH – writes an obituary, 'Harold Monro: A Poet and His Ideal', in *The Times*, and – as a matter of honour – declines to be paid for it. 21 MARCH – attends Monro's funeral at Golders Green Crematorium, along with Alida Monro, Ralph Hodgson, F. S. Flint, and Edith Sitwell, who relates: 'I saw Tom Eliot, for one moment only, and he looked broken.' 28 MARCH – Sitwell gossips: 'We had a very exciting time yesterday. A certain lady (Osbert will tell you who I mean) came to tea without her husband. As she entered, a strange smell, as though four bottles of methylated spirits had been upset, entered also, followed, five minutes afterwards, by Georgia [Sitwell] and her mother. Nellie (the maid) who was once what is known as an Attendant, enquired if she might speak to me on the telephone, and, as soon as she got me outside, said (looking very frightened): "If she starts anything, Miss, get her by the wrists, sit on her face, and don't let her bite you. Don't let her get near a looking glass, or near the window." I said "What *do* you mean?" and she replied that what I thought was an accident with the [methylated spirits] was really the strongest drug given by Attendants when the patient is so violent that nothing ordinary has any effect!! She concluded, gloomily: "Often, it has taken six of us to hold one down." – You can imagine my feelings. And when I got back into the room, I found that Mrs Doble had offered the lady a cigarette, and had been told that the lady *never* accepted anything from strangers. It was too dangerous. Poor Mrs D. was terrified, as she thought that the Patient was going to spring at her throat. Georgia was terrified too, and tea was undiluted hell.' 1 APRIL – Mario Praz publishes an Italian translation of 'Triumphal March' in *Nuova Antologia*. 6 APRIL – TSE publishes 'Building up the Christian World' in the *Listener*; and prints in the *Criterion* an essay 'The Categories of T. E. Hulme' by Michael Roberts; 'Mr Articularis' by Conrad Aiken; two poems by Lyle Donaghy; and C. M. Bowra's essay 'The Position of Alexander Blok'. After dining with the Eliots this month, Elizabeth Bowen 'wrote that she found their flat very sinister and depressing. Not that there was anything wrong with the flat itself; it was the atmosphere of "two highly nervous people shut up together in grinding proximity". As for Eliot himself, "he is so very funny and charming and domestic and nice to be with, besides being so great. I love knowing him".' 5 MAY – TSE tells his brother, 'it will be some years before I am on the right side of the Income Tax account. I imagine that I am some hundreds of pounds in debt to them, covering some years back. That is partly due to exceptional expenses at times in past years, to having taken a house because I thought Vivienne wanted it and then finding that she did not like it – it was about the worst small house in London, and I have had to carry it for two years and only get rid of it in September. And partly because things being as they are in my private life I find it impossible to live below a certain scale, and V. is not a very economical housekeeper. I am hoping to clear a good bit of my takings next winter [in the USA], towards paying off debts. It will be expensive keeping V. in England during my absence, but it would be still more expensive to take her with me, besides the fact that it would cripple me and prevent me from doing the extra lecturing. And finally, I do very much need a rest; and even the most active life will be restful if I am alone.' He admires the detective novel, *The Rumble Murders*, that his brother has published in New York under the pseudonym 'Mason Deal': 'I could never write a detective story myself; my only possible resource for adding to my income would be to write children's verses or stories, having had a little success in writing letters to children (and illustrating them of course).' He becomes a member of the committee of the Old Vic and the Sadler's Wells Society and publishes the essay-review 'John Ford', in the *TLS*. 18 MAY – writes for the first time to Louis MacNeice, rejecting his poems as a volume but expressing his willingness to publish some of his work in the *Criterion*. 19 MAY – publishes Auden's *The Orators: An English Study* – hailing it as 'the only recent satire worth reading'. He also publishes *Rooming House*, by the American poet Horace Gregory. Vivien confides to Aurelia Bolliger: 'Mr Eliot is playing on the Wireless and driving me *MAD*.' F. R. Leavis launches his Cambridge periodical *Scrutiny* with a disparaging declaration: 'Let us . . . express now the general regret that the name of *The Criterion* has become so dismal an irony and that the Editor is so far from applying to his contributors the standards we have learned from him.' 31 MAY – TSE participates in a discussion convened by C. A. Siepmann of the BBC to discuss guidelines for religious broadcasting. 8 JUNE – Vivien remarks to Mary Hutchinson: 'I could not stay *here* all the 8 months that Tom will be away. I've never left for *one night* for 2 years & 2 months. I could be so happy – & so could Tom, in those rooms. I could spend the winter making them all perfect for *Tom's return*. I can't stay here, I really hate it.' TSE exchanges letters with the poet George Barker, who will later say of him: 'He was kind to me . . . If it had not been for him, I would not (to speak too much of myself) have had a chance.' 9 JUNE – TSE tells Spender: 'I can't agree that religion provides such an effective escape as you seem to think . . . I know that there are plenty of material injustices to be set right, and I want them to be set right; nevertheless I believe that the world will always be an unpleasant place, a place of trial for individual souls, and that the vast majority of its population will always be a compound of knave and blockhead . . . and I believe that the man who thinks himself virtuous is in danger of damnation, *whatever* line of conduct he adopts.' 12 JUNE – the Eliots consider taking rooms – the top floors – at the Stracheys' house, 51 Gordon Square, Bloomsbury; Vivien tells Mary Hutchinson, 'Tom very *much* likes the rooms & knows he would be happy there. Poor Tom, let him have *somewhere* to work in that he likes *before* he dies.' The plan does not take off. 29 JUNE – TSE commiserates with Grace Hart Crane, on the death of her son: 'I must take the opportunity of expressing both my personal sympathy and my regret at the death of a poet, much of whose work I admired very much. There are very few living poets in America of equal interest to me.' JULY – The *Criterion* includes a poem by Hugh McDiarmid, 'Second Hymn to Lenin'; 'Harold Monro' by Ezra Pound; 'Education and the Drama in the Age of Shakespeare' by L. C. Knights; 'Climacteric' by Peter Quennell'; 'Disintegration of Values' by Hermann Broch (sections from the novel *The Sleepwalkers*), trans. Edwin and Willa Muir. 11 JULY – TSE tells Morrell of his 'appreciation of your kindness to Vivienne throughout this past year especially. She is so much a creature of environment that it is a vital matter – especially when she is in a very sociable phase – what company she frequents; and you have not only given your own influence, but have helped her to add a number of desirable people to her acquaintance. I am especially glad of this because I shall be so long absent.' Mario Praz publishes an Italian translation of *The Waste Land* – *La Terra Desolata* – in *Circoli* 2 (Genoa). Edith Sitwell relates this piece of gossip, from the summer of 1930: '"Hullo, Vivienne!" she called to her. Vivienne looked at her suspiciously and sadly, and replied, "Who do you think you are addressing? I don't know you." "Don't be silly, Vivienne: you know quite well who I am." Vivienne regarded her with profound melancholy for a moment, and then said, "No, no: you don't know me. You have mistaken me again for that terrible woman who is so like me . . . She is always getting me into trouble."' AUGUST – Frank Morley sometime recalls: 'As to V's health . . . she was sometimes in quite equable form – TSE and V. visited Pike's Farm [the Morleys' home in Surrey] together for Susanna [Morley]'s christening in August 1932, were there for lunch and tea (TSE driving his small Morris) and happy day for all.' T. S. Matthews notes: 'Vivienne noted remorsefully in her diary that Tom had a hard time getting her up and dressed and ready to leave, but that he had been very patient and gentle with her, only reminding her that they were keeping two old people (Frank Morley's parents) waiting, and that the old lady had come out of the London Clinic that very day.' 2 SEPTEMBER – while staying at the Lansdowne Hotel, Eastbourne, TSE and Vivien drive over to call on the Woolfs at Monk's House, Rodmell. Virginia Woolf recorded: 'behold Tom & Vivienne . . . she wild as Ophelia – alas no Hamlet would love her, with her powdered spots – in white satin, L[eonard] said; Tom, poor man, all battened down as usual, prim, grey, making his kind jokes with her . . . Then her chops & changes. Where is my bag? Where – where – then a sudden amorous embrace for me – & so on: trailing about the garden – never settling – seizing the wheel of their car – suddenly telling Tom to drive – all of which he bears with great patience: feeling perhaps that his 7 months of freedom draw near.' Vivien was later to recall in her diary: 'I drove Tom over . . . When we arrived at Rodmell both Virginia & Leonard *seemed pleased*. I took *several snapshots* . . . We had tea, & as I was *very nearly insane*, already with the Cruel Pain of losing Tom, & as they *both must* have *known* that, I paid very little attention to the conversation (*as usual*). . . When we got back to the Lansdowne I felt *very ill* and *was in a fever*. Tom also *seemed very strange*. I remember *all* he said. And I also remember having a faint uneasy feeling that the Wolves were in *some* way *against* Tom, just as I now, looking back see that I was always haunted by that horror in recent years. The only way I cld. have stopped it for *good* would have been to go to *America with Tom* & stick it out & *bring him safely back. I had not the courage to do that & so am damned for ever* – but it does not matter what I do, ever again.' 15 SEPTEMBER – TSE publishes (simultaneously in the UK and the USA) *Selected Essays 1917–1932* – having posted an advance copy to Emily Hale on 6 September. Farewell party at home; guests include the Morrells; Richard de la Mare and his wife; and John Hayward ('*Only old & tried friends* are invited,' says Vivien). Vivien writes too: 'I *wanted* to make it the *kind* of *gathering* together of people which Tom would *like to remember*. All wishing the same thing & *genuinely* desiring his *absolute safety* & *ultimate good* in every possible way – above all spiritually.' 17 SEPTEMBER – TSE departs for the USA. In Cambridge, Massachusetts, he stays first with his sister Ada Sheffield at 31 Madison Street, before moving into a suite at Eliot House – 'infinitely luxurious, and even very handsome' – overlooking the Charles River. 'I am rather dazed with new impressions.' Makes friends with his new colleagues Theodore Spencer and F. O. Matthiessen. Hugh Ross Williamson's study *The Poetry of T. S. Eliot* is published. OCTOBER – TSE's brother visits him for a few days. 17 OCTOBER – TSE gives a poetry reading at Wellesley College. 18 OCTOBER – TSE relates, 'The actual performance of lectures does not bother me much yet, as I have only 4 to give at Harvard before Christmas, but I must sit here and sweat over writing them and also over the odd lectures I expect to give elsewhere later on.' *John Dryden: The Poet, The Dramatist, The Critic* (reprints of BBC talks) is published in New York by Terence and Elsa Holliday. TSE publishes in the *Criterion* two poems by MacNeice. 4 NOVEMBER – opens his series of Charles Eliot Norton lectures at Harvard: he gives eight lectures in all, to be published as *The Use of Poetry and The Use of Criticism* (1933). Among his more memorable observations is the pronouncement that poetry is 'a mug's game'. 15 NOVEMBER – lectures to the Radcliffe Club. He is visited by the poet Ronald Bottrall. 1 DECEMBER – TSE publishes *Sweeney Agonistes: Fragments of an Aristophanic Melodrama*; 'Difficulties of a Statesman' in *Hound & Horn*; 'Apology for the Countess of Pembroke', *Harvard Graduates' Magazine*, reprinted in *The Use of Poetry and the Use of Criticism*. Just after Christmas he leaves for a tour encompassing New York, California, Missouri, Minnesota, Chicago, Buffalo, Baltimore. 27 DECEMBER – arrives at Claremont, California, where Emily Hale, 41, is Head of House, Eleanor Joy Toll Hall, and Assistant Professor of Oral English, Scripps College. Ahead of TSE's visit, Hale gives a talk on TSE and reads from his poetry. 'Miss Hale . . . presented him not only as a well-known literary figure, but as a man, and a product of many influences . . . A man of extremes, a man of undoubted faults and highest virtues.' Hale 'spoke of him often, always as "Tom", and was obviously much in touch with him, and wore a ring that he had given her'. Lorraine Havens remarks that TSE seemed 'somewhat reserved and formal, but very courteous, and obviously devoted to Emily'. He inscribes a copy of *Sweeney Agonistes* 'For Emily Hale from the author T. S. Eliot'. It transpires in January 1933 that VHE was not told in advance about TSE's trip: he wrote to her only on 11 Jan.

1933 JANUARY – TSE publishes 'Five-Finger Exercises' in the *Criterion*. 6 JANUARY – lectures at the University of California on 'The Formation of Taste'. 11 JANUARY – TSE lectures in Mudd Hall of Philosophy on 'Edward Lear and Modern Poetry'. 'I don't like California much,' he reports; 'no *country*, only *scenery*': the place is 'a nightmare'. 16 JANUARY – visits St Louis, Missouri, where he lectures in Graham Memorial Chapel on 'The Study of Shakespeare Criticism'. TSE is stunned at a lecture at Washington University to find his audience running to more than 600; he had expected a modest turnout of English Faculty members, and jokes about having to use a microphone: 'It's the first time I've talked to so many people at once by telephone.' He remarks to a newspaper reporter: 'I don't think I like writing . . . it's not a regular occupation. Thank God, I have a regular job.' He journeys on to St Paul, Minnesota, Chicago, Buffalo, and finally Baltimore. After dinner one day, he meets H. L. Mencken, who notes of him: 'An amiable fellow, but with little to say. He told me that his father was a brick manufacturer in Missouri. No talk of religion. We discussed magazine prices . . . I drank a quart of home-brew beer, and Eliot got down two Scotches. A dull evening.' 19 JANUARY – Stephen Spender's *Poems* is published by F&F. 27 JANUARY – TSE returns to Cambridge, Massachusetts, when he and Theodore Spencer ('of whom I became very fond') teach English 26b, a twice-weekly lecture course for fifteen undergraduates 'with a B-plus average' on 'Contemporary English Literature (1890 to the present time)', and where he continues with his series of public lectures. William Burroughs, who attends TSE's fifth Norton lecture, 'Shelley and Keats', hears TSE deplore the excesses of English Romantic poets and question the notion that people ought to be taught to think for themselves. While disagreeing with TSE's views, Burroughs thinks the lecture humorous and well delivered. One of his students in English 26b, C. L. Sulzberger, later a noted journalist and author, would recall: 'Even in 1933 [Eliot] forecast that Hemingway would be regarded as the Kipling of his time . . . Timid and withdrawn as Eliot was in class, [TSE] had a talent for banging the piano and singing a huge number of limericks, some of which I suspect he had written himself. I liked him despite the fact that he gave me a poor mark on my term paper. Its subject was "The Undergraduate Poetry of T. S. Eliot".' In Cambridge and Boston, TSE finds it 'strangely comfortable . . . to be among a society which consists largely of one's own relatives' – although he otherwise longs for peace and anonymity. He makes friends with a young Englishman, Gerald S. Graham (1903–88), an instructor in history at Harvard (ultimately to become Rhodes Professor of Imperial History, King's College, London). LATE JANUARY – lectures at the University of Buffalo on 'Edward Lear and Modern Poetry'. 30 JANUARY, 1 FEBRUARY, 3 FEBRUARY – delivers three lectures, 'The Varieties of Metaphysical Poetry', as 29th Percy Graeme Turnbull Memorial Lecturer, at the Johns Hopkins University: individual topics are 'Toward a Definition of Metaphysical Poetry', 'The Conceit in Donne and Crashaw', 'Laforgue and Corbière in our Time'. 2 FEBRUARY – lectures on obscurity in modern poetry, at the Poetry Society of Maryland, and reads from his work. 'My chief reason for being a critic at present is the fact that you can make a little money out of an essay on criticism.' Asked about his life in England, he remarks: 'I think that London, being the largest city in the world, is the best place in the world to lose yourself . . . In London you can always find some place where you can be alone.' 5 FEBRUARY – back in Cambridge, Mass., TSE completes his preface to the collected poems of Harold Monro. 19 FEBRUARY – gives a poetry reading at Brown University, Providence, Rhode Island. 'The critic's task, he said, is to bring works of real merit to the attention of the public . . . Literary greatness remains constant, though greatness can be attributed to different factors in different eras.' 23 FEBRUARY – speaks on 'English Poets as Letter Writers', under the auspices of the Lamont Memorial Foundation, to an audience of 500 in Sprague Hall, Yale University. A report of the lecture is given in *Yale Daily News*, 24 Feb. '"No other form of communication can ever supplant the letter," Mr Eliot said. "Letter-writing permits us to forget ourselves and to express the worthwhile things that come spontaneously. It can be a provocation of and a consolation for solitude. Our minds should be left to wander when writing a letter, and a good letter will focus the reader's attention on what the letter is getting [at], rather than the letter itself." . . . "A poet can be judged by his letters," Mr Eliot said . . . Other poets whose letters appeal to Mr Eliot are D. H.

Lawrence and Virginia Woolf, whose epistles he termed "master-pieces of the letter-writing art".' 24 FEBRUARY – lectures on 'Edward Lear and Modern Poetry' at Smith College, Northampton. 25 FEBRUARY – gives an informal talk and a reading at Mount Holyoke College. By FEBRUARY his plans for a permanent separation from VHE are well formulated. He has given 'the best years' of his life to a situation from which he wishes to be utterly extricated. 26 FEBRUARY – having consulted Geoffrey Faber and Francis Underhill, Dean of Rochester (his spiritual adviser), TSE tells Alida Monro that the time has come for a sudden 'complete break' from the 'futile life' he has been leading in London. 'I do not believe that there is any affection deep enough to consider, but there will be the emotion of fear . . . I have of course no feeling of affection myself to wound; this is a step which I have contemplated for many years; I should feel nothing but relief, and should prefer not to see V. again. (I have no doubt that all sorts of ulterior motives will be alleged in order to discredit my real, only and obvious motive of getting peace for work and throwing off the poison of uncongeniality and pretense).' His life with VHE was a 'hideous farce', he declares. 14 MARCH – he tells Ottoline Morrell: 'I have been very happy [in the USA], for me; primarily because of being near my sisters, and not very far away from my brother . . . [O]f course, outside of Boston I am simply T. S. Eliot, but here I am an Eliot. There is a pleasure in anonymity – and that I am better able to enjoy in London than here, where I am still a news item; but after eighteen years of being merely oneself there is a pleasure in being just a member of one's family . . . I like to be with people who were fond of me before the malady of poetry declared itself.' Of Bertrand Russell: 'Bertie, because at first I admired him so much, is one of my lost illusions. He has done Evil, without being big enough or conscious enough to Be evil. I owe him this, that the spectacle of Bertie was one contributing influence to my conversion. Of course he had no good influence on Vivienne. He excited her mentally, made her read books and become a kind of pacifist, and no doubt was flattered because he thought he was influencing her . . . Unfortunately, she found him unattractive . . . For my part, I should prefer never to see [Vivien] again; for hers, I do not believe that it can be good for any woman to live with a man to whom she is morally, in the larger sense, unpleasant, as well as physically indifferent.' He confides his intentions also to

Paul Elmer More, whom he visits in Princeton. He anticipates spending the remainder of his life in 'solitude': as an Anglo-Catholic – 'a rather fanatical Catholic,' as he calls himself – he holds that divorce is 'impossible', only permanent separation. 14 MARCH – reads his poetry at Eliot House, Harvard. Matthiessen notes: '[T]he excruciating poignancy of his voice brought tears springing to my eyes.' 17 MARCH – Vivien writes to Henry Eliot: 'I wish to make it certain that the rest of Tom's life is happier and easier and more secure than his life has ever been up till now.' 23 MARCH – TSE delivers the Spencer Trask Foundation Lecture, 'The Bible and English Literature', at Princeton University. 24 MARCH – lectures on 'The Development of Shakespearean Criticism' at Haverford College. 31 MARCH – Vivien claims to Ottoline Morrell that she is in a shocking physical condition: she has bathed only two or three times since TSE's departure; she has washed her hair only twice; her nails and teeth are bad. 'Children in the street do not look so dreadful.' 6–7 APRIL – TSE participates, with Theodore Dreiser, in an event at the Institute of Modern Literature at Bowdoin College, Maine, lecturing on 'The Poetry of Edward Lear' and joining in a round-table discussion. 20–23 APRIL – stays with brother Henry at 315 East 68th Street, New York. 21 APRIL – talks on 'The Verse of John Milton' at Columbia University, under the auspices of the Institute of Arts and Sciences. The *Evening Sun* (23 Apr.) reports his judgement that the most promising of the young British poets are W. H. Auden, Stephen Spender, Louis MacNeice, and Ronald Bottrall. 24 APRIL – participates in a symposium at the Classical Club at Harvard. 27 APRIL – talks at the New School for Social Research, New York, where his friend Horace Kallen is on the faculty. Edmund Wilson relates to John dos Passos: 'I heard Eliot read his poems the other night. He did them extremely well – contrary to my expectation. He is an actor . . . He gives you the creeps a little at first because he is such a completely artificial, or rather, self-invented character . . . but he has done such a perfect job with himself that you often end up admiring him.' Despite finding TSE's personality 'really rather incoherent', Wilson concludes that he was 'the most highly refined and attuned and chiselled human being' he had ever met. Another auditor notes that TSE 'looked for all the world like a highly bred Anglican cleric'. 28 APRIL – TSE speaks at Bryn Mawr on 'Modern Poetry', describing *The Waste*

Land as 'a piece of rhythmical grouching'. MAY – makes a recording of *The Hollow Men* and *Gerontion* for Harvard University Phonograph Records – the 'Harvard Vocarium'. His 'Critical [Note]' is published in *The Collected Poems of Harold Monro*. 6 MAY – Hallie Flanagan ('I regarded her as a very intelligent producer') mounts the first production at Vassar College of TSE's '*croquis* of a play' *Sweeney Agonistes* – 'our tragic feelings are best expressed not through "tragedy" but through farce,' he says – which he stipulates should be 'stylised as in the Noh drama', and with the characters in masks – with a supplementary scene written for the occasion by TSE. Later he remarks of it, 'the interpretations of the meaning of the play – the meaning of a play which was never written – are in a sense original creations of the interpreter. I think that if I had been able to finish, it would have turned out very differently from any interpretations of the fragment that I have seen, but I must confess that I simply don't know what it would have been like, and what the thing as a whole would have meant.' 7 MAY – at a poetry reading, TSE declares 'My poetry is simple and straightforward' – and looks pained when the audience laugh. One student, 'referring to the lines – "Every man has to, needs to, wants to / Once in a lifetime do a girl in" – asks hopefully, "Mr Eliot, did you ever do a girl in?" Mr Eliot looked apologetic and said, "I am not the type."' 10–12 MAY he delivers the three Page-Barbour lectures, under the working title 'Tradition and Contemporary Literature', at the University of Virginia ('a beautiful place'): the individual titles are 'The Meaning of Tradition', 'Modern Poetry', 'Three Prose Writers' – to be published as *After Strange Gods* (1934). He is vehemently critical of D. H. Lawrence ('a very sick man indeed', whose works were notable for 'the absence of any moral or social sense') and Thomas Hardy. In a later year, when William Empson asks him about *After Strange Gods* (which proclaims *inter alia* that the USA is 'worm-eaten by Liberalism'), TSE says that he himself had been 'very sick in soul' when he wrote the lectures – which he disavowed. He meets F. Scott Fitzgerald (who 'liked him fine' even though he thought him 'very broken and sad and shrunk inside'). MID-MAY – TSE addresses the Boston Association of Unitarian Clergy on the topic 'Two Masters': 'Would it not be better, people may ask, if the standard set were not that of an ideal asceticism, but rather that of the highest natural human life; for then, perhaps, more people would live up to it? An unattainable ideal, they may say, makes for dishonesty . . . Perhaps the simplest retort is to ask what is the alternative. What happens when you trim your ideals down to fit the behaviour of the nicest people? Instead of compromising practice you have compromised the ideal . . . When you think that you are getting rid of hypocrisy, you are merely descending to complacency and self-conceit: an ideal which can be attained is one of the most dangerous of booby-traps, for its attainment leads to spiritual pride . . . We must have an ideal so high that measured by it the purest and most devout feels that he is indistinguishable from the greatest sinner . . . Ideals *are* inhuman, but we are only human, instead of being animals, by our capacity to transcend humanity.' 18 MAY – TSE tells Elmer More: 'My life seems like Alice and the glass table: there is something I want here (domestic affection) and something I want in England, and I can't have both; fortunately the time of choice is long since past. One side of life suffers from dullness, the other from nightmare – the last eighteen years like a bad Dostoevski novel. One of my most constant temptations is to a feeling of exasperation with human beings – not for their faults & vices, I can sympathise with those – but for their tepidity; their pettiness is somehow more awful than their evil – not many are alive enough to be evil. The materialism of the virtuous is what baffles me especially in this country.' At the end of May, TSE stays with Edmund Wilson in New York, and meets Marianne Moore. 'Marianne is a real Gillette blade she doesn't skip anything and she talks all the time but I love her the more for that.' He later describes her to Ezra Pound as a 'captivating creetur', with an 'Eye like a Auk and a brain like a Gimblet'. (In 1944 he will say: 'I took a great fancy to her: she and Bunny Wilson were the two people I liked best of those whom I met in New York in 1933.') 6 JUNE – awarded the honorary degree of Doctor of Letters, Columbia University. EARLY JUNE – participates in a family vacation, which includes Emily Hale, at Mountain View House in Randolph, New Hampshire: *vide* the poem 'New Hampshire'. ('A most lovable person,' his brother Henry writes of him on 28 June.) 17 JUNE – TSE gives the Prize-Day address at his old school, Milton Academy, with Emily Hale and members of his family in attendance – taken down in shorthand without TSE's knowledge, the uncorrected talk is published in *Milton Graduates Bulletin* (Nov. 1933) – the last of his public engagements. He reckons that over the course of the year he had spoken in public between seventy and eighty times. LATE JUNE – TSE returns to England, passes one night at the Oxford and Cambridge Club, London, calls on his solicitor to discuss his separation from Vivien, and then travels south to the village of Lingfield, Surrey, where he is to spend the next three months lodging with Mr and Mrs Jack Eames (foreman of the East Surrey Brick Company) – in 'Uncle Tom's Cabin' (he has two rooms, at a cost of 25/- per week), just a few steps from the property called 'Pike's Farm' inhabited by the Morley family with whom he dines daily. Jack Eames was to recall TSE as 'a funny man really. He was very quiet and so engrossed in what he was doing that you could almost touch him and he wouldn't realise that you were there.' He enjoys life with the Morleys and their children: picking fruit, making bread, 'playing Patience, observing the habits of finches and wagtails, composing nonsense verses,' as he tells Virginia Woolf on 16 Aug. 7 JULY – VHE writes that she has been feeling 'insane with anxiety for 2 weeks' – though she had in fact been informed of TSE's decision to separate from her. 9 JULY – TSE tells his brother: 'My year in America . . . was the happiest I can ever remember in my life.' It has been 'a successful and amusing year'. 12 JULY – attends a formal separation interview with Vivien, in the offices of his solicitors. It is reported that Vivien said of the meeting: 'he sat near me & I held his hand, but he never looked at me.' She will write in August: 'I have had 2 years of terrible strain – ending with a very great shock.' TSE is distressed when any of their friends turns 'against' Vivien. He will write in August to Lady Ottoline Morrell: 'I am anxious to be able to feel that Vivienne will not lose any friends through my action, or cease to see any of the people whom I have liked her to see in the past.' He chooses to become 'socially invisible' for several weeks. However, TSE would say, much later, that he also considered the year 1933 a good year – 'as that is the year in which I broke into Show Business. In that year I was commissioned to write the text for a mammoth Pageant to advertise the need for 45 new churches in the outer suburbs of London.' This grand enterprise is to eventuate in a 'revue' (as he called it): the historical pageant-play *The Rock* – to be produced in 1934. TSE tells Elmer More that he is engaged upon 'the writing of some verse choruses and dialogues for a sort of play . . . If I have a free hand I shall enjoy it. I am trying to combine the simplicity and immediate intelligibility necessary for dramatic verse with concentration, under the inspiration of, chiefly, Isaiah and Ezekiel.' His fee is £100: profits from the first edition to go to the Fund. 'I could not think of it as a personal production.' 25 JULY – delivers the opening address on 'Christianity and International Order' to the Anglo-Catholic Summer School of Sociology, Keble College, Oxford: published in *Christendom* (Sept. 1933). 'I have no objection to being called a bigot myself,' he says. MID-AUGUST – enjoys a break in Gloucestershire. 21 AUGUST – visits Rochester. 31 AUGUST–4 SEPTEMBER – visits the Faber family at their holiday home in Ciliau Aeron, Cardiganshire. 8–17 SEPTEMBER – visits the Society of the Sacred Mission, Kelham, Nottinghamshire. 9 SEPTEMBER – visits the Woolfs at Monk's House, for a day and a night. Virginia notes: 'He is 10 years younger: hard, spry, a glorified boy scout in shorts & yellow shirt. He is enjoying himself very much. He is tight & shiny as a wood louse (I am not writing for publication). But there is well water in him, cold & pure. Yes I like talking to Tom . . . He's settling in with some severity to being a great man . . . At 46 he wants to live . . . He has seen nothing, nobody, for the last 10 years. We had it out about V. at breakfast. Some asperity on Tom's part. He wont admit the excuse of insanity for her – thinks she puts it on; tries to take herself in . . . I thought him a little resentful of all the past waste & exaction.' 21 SEPTEMBER – TSE writes to brother Henry: 'My affairs at the moment are in a state of deadlock. After a period of apparent capitulation, Vivienne again begs that I return to her "on any conditions that I may impose" – which is of course a meaningless phrase. The next step is to try to find people who can convince her that I mean what I say and do not propose to go back on my intentions. As her lawyer himself remarked in conversation, I have had my fair share; and I'll never get those seventeen years back.' 10 OCTOBER – visits York for two days. 11 OCTOBER – Janet Adam Smith, literary editor of *The Listener*, invites TSE to write a report on the poetry published in the periodical, consequent upon the Poetry Supplement published on 12 July alongside an editorial leader on Modern Poetry. Sir John Reith wanted to be told about the principles of selection, and the justification, for printing such poetry – especially Auden's supposedly shocking poem, in twenty-nine verses, entitled 'The Witnesses'. 16 OCTOBER – TSE tells VHE he will give her £5 a week (fixed during the lifetime of her mother), and will pay the rent of 68 Clarence Gate Gardens until the expiry of the lease in June 1934 – 'more than by law I could be compelled to do'. (VHE responds by pressing him for a meeting; and as late as 22 Jan. 1934, she is still declining to sign a separation agreement, and persists in demanding that TSE should come back to her.) 17 OCTOBER – TSE visits John Hayward at his flat in Bina Gardens. 18 OCTOBER – submits his report on poetry in *The Listener*: 'Of all the younger poets, Auden is the one who has interested me the most deeply, though I feel that it is impossible to predict whether he will manifest the austerity and concentration necessary for poetry of the first rank, or whether he will dissipate his talents in wit and verbal brilliance.' 19 OCTOBER – publishes 'The Modern Dilemma' – a version of an address he had delivered to a gathering of Unitarian clergymen in Boston – in *Christian Register* (Boston, Mass.). 2 NOVEMBER – publishes *The Use of Poetry and the Use of Criticism*, of which he will say in a later year: 'They are . . . largely drivel, but amongst them, I am still persuaded (but I cannot bring myself to read them) are imbedded a few paragraphs in which I was talking about what I knew and saying something fresh.' 9 NOVEMBER – entertains Ronald Bottrall at the Oxford & Cambridge Club. 13 NOVEMBER – following a two-day trip to Scotland, with Frank Morley and the American publisher Donald Brace, TSE travels with Morley to Paris, where they spend an evening with James Joyce. TSE also meets Henri Massis. MID-NOVEMBER – starts looking for permanent lodgings (two rooms); recruits Virginia Woolf to help. 'Clerkenwell is all right,' he reports to Ezra Pound, 'but there aren't any bathrooms there.' He moves into 'a polite boarding house' – 33 Courtfield Road (three guineas a week) – in South Kensington. 3 DECEMBER – visits I. A. Richards and his wife in Cambridge. 8 DECEMBER – solicits poems from Marianne Moore. 9 DECEMBER – writes to his brother: 'It is impossible, as it always has been, to gauge the amount and rate of [Vivien's] mental deterioration; but it is possible that eventually – perhaps not for years – she will have to be looked after in a home.' MID-DECEMBER – seeks to publish Joyce's *Ulysses* in the UK, now that Judge Woolsey has lifted the ban in the USA.

ABBREVIATIONS AND SOURCES

PUBLISHED WORKS BY T. S. ELIOT

ASG	*After Strange Gods* (London: Faber & Faber, 1934)
AVP	*Ara Vos Prec* (London: The Ovid Press, 1920)
CP	*The Cocktail Party* (London: Faber & Faber, 1930)
CPP	*The Complete Poems and Plays of T. S. Eliot* (London: Faber & Faber, 1969)
EE	*Elizabethan Essays* (London: Faber & Faber, 1934)
FLA	*For Lancelot Andrewes: Essays on Style and Order* (London: Faber & Gwyer, 1928)
FR	*The Family Reunion* (London: Faber & Faber, 1939)
Gallup	Donald Gallup, *T. S. Eliot: A Bibliography* (London: Faber & Faber, 1969)
HJD	*Homage to John Dryden: Three Essays on Poetry of the Seventeenth Century* (London: The Hogarth Press, 1924)
IMH	*Inventions of the March Hare: Poems 1909–1917*, ed. Christopher Ricks (London: Faber & Faber, 1996)
KEPB	*Knowledge and Experience in the Philosophy of F. H. Bradley* (London: Faber & Faber, 1964; New York: Farrar, Straus & Company, 1964)
L	*Letters of T. S. Eliot* (London: Faber & Faber, Vol. 1 [rev. edn], 2009; Vol. 2, 2009; Vol. 3, 2012; Vol. 4, 2013; Vol 5, 2014)
MiC	*Murder in the Cathedral* (London: Faber & Faber, 1935)
OPP	*On Poetry and Poets* (London: Faber & Faber, 1957; New York: Farrar, Straus & Cudahy, 1957)
P	*Poems* (London: The Hogarth Press, 1919)
P 1909–1925	*Poems 1909–1925* (London: Faber & Gwyer, 1925)

POO	*Prufrock and Other Observations* (London: The Egoist Press, 1917)
SA	*Sweeney Agonistes: Fragments of an Aristophanic Melodrama* (London: Faber & Faber, 1932)
SE	*Selected Essays: 1917–1932* (London: Faber & Faber, 1932; 3rd English edn, London and Boston: Faber & Faber, 1951)
SW	*The Sacred Wood: Essays on Poetry and Criticism* (London: Methuen & Co., 1920)
TCC	*To Criticise the Critic* (London: Faber & Faber, 1965; New York: Farrar, Straus & Giroux, 1965)
TUPUC	*The Use of Poetry and the Use of Criticism: Studies in the Relation of Criticism to Poetry in England* (London: Faber & Faber, 1933)
TWL	*The Waste Land* (1922, 1923)
TWL: Facs	*The Waste Land: A Facsimile and Transcript of the Original Drafts*, ed. Valerie Eliot (London: Faber & Faber, 1971; New York: Harcourt, Brace Jovanovich, 1971; reissued, with corrections, 2011)
VMP	*The Varieties of Metaphysical Poetry*, ed. Ronald Schuchard (London: Faber & Faber, 1993; New York: Harcourt Brace, 1994)

PERIODICALS AND PUBLISHERS

A.	*The Athenaeum* (see also *N&A*)
C.	*The Criterion*
F&F	Faber & Faber (publishers)
F&G	Faber & Gwyer (publishers)
MC	*The Monthly Criterion*
N.	*The Nation*
N&A	*The Nation & The Athenaeum*
NC	*New Criterion*
NRF	*La Nouvelle Revue Française*
NS	*New Statesman*
NS&N	*New Statesman and Nation*
TLS	*Times Literary Supplement*

PERSONS

CA	Conrad Aiken
RA	Richard Aldington

WHA	W. H. Auden
RC-S	Richard Cobden-Sanderson
BD	Bonamy Dobrée
CWE	Charlotte Ware Eliot, TSE's mother
EVE	(Esmé) Valerie Eliot
HWE	Henry Ware Eliot (TSE's brother)
TSE	T. S. Eliot
VHE	Vivien (Haigh-Wood) Eliot
GCF	Geoffrey (Cust) Faber
MHW	Maurice Haigh-Wood
JDH	John Davy Hayward
MH	Mary Hutchinson
AH	Aldous Huxley
JJ	James Joyce
GWK	G. Wilson Knight
DHL	D. H. Lawrence
FRL	F. R. Leavis
WL	Wyndham Lewis
HM	Harold Monro
FVM	Frank (Vigor) Morley
OM	Ottoline Morrell
JMM	John Middleton Murry
EP	Ezra Pound
HR	Herbert Read
IAR	I. A. Richards
BLR	Bruce Richmond
ALR	A. L. Rowse
BR	Bertrand Russell
ES	Edith Sitwell
SS	Stephen Spender
WFS	William Force Stead
CW	Charles Whibley
OW	Orlo Williams
LW	Leonard Woolf
VW	Virginia Woolf
WBY	W. B. Yeats

ARCHIVE COLLECTIONS

Arkansas	Special Collections, University Libraries, University of Arkansas

BBC	BBC Written Archives, Caversham
Beinecke	The Beinecke Rare Book and Manuscript Library, Yale University
Berg	Henry W. and Albert A. Berg Collection of English and American Literature, the New York Public Library
Bodleian	The Bodleian Library, Oxford University
BL	The British Library
Brotherton	The Brotherton Collection, Leeds University Library
Buffalo	Poetry Collection, Lockwood Memorial Library, State University of New York, Buffalo
Butler	Rare Books and Manuscripts Division, Butler Library, Columbia University, New York
Caetani	Fondazione Camillo Caetani
Cambridge	Cambridge University Library
Colby College	Special Collections, Colby College, Waterville, Maine
Cornell	Department of Rare Books, Olin Library, Cornell University
Bib Jacques Doucet	Bibliothèque littéraire Jacques Doucet, Paris
Exeter	Exeter University Library
Faber	Faber & Faber Archive, London
Harcourt Brace	Harcourt Brace & Company
Harvard	University Archives, Harvard University
Houghton	The Houghton Library, Harvard University
House of Books	House of Books, New York
Howard	Lelia Howard
Huntington	Huntington Library, San Marino, California
King's	Modern Archive Centre, King's College, Cambridge
Lambeth	Lambeth Palace Library
Lilly	Lilly Library, Indiana University, Bloomington
Magdalene	Old Library, Magdalene College, Cambridge
Marshall	Marshall Library, University of Cambridge
Morgan	Pierpont Morgan Library, New York
National Gallery of Ireland	National Gallery of Ireland, Dublin
NHM	Natural History Museum Archives

Northwestern	Special Collections Department, Northwestern University Library, Evanston, Illinois
Princeton	Department of Rare Books and Special Collections, Princeton University Library
Reading	Special Collections, University of Reading
Renishaw	Sitwell Papers, Renishaw Hall, Derbyshire
Rosenbach	Rosenbach Museum and Library, Philadelphia, PA
Southern Illinois	Southern Illinois University Library, Carbondale
Sussex	Manuscript Collections, University of Sussex Library
Syracuse	Syracuse University Library, Syracuse, New York
TCD	The Library, Trinity College, Dublin
Templeman	Templeman Library, University of Kent at Canterbury
Texas	The Harry Ransom Humanities Research Center, University of Texas at Austin
UCLA	University of California at Los Angeles
VE Papers	Vivien Eliot Papers, Bodleian Library, Oxford
Victoria	Special Collections, McPherson Library, University of Victoria, British Columbia
Wellesley	Wellesley College Library
Williamson	Mrs M. H. Williamson (Dr Charlotte Williamson)
Wyoming	University of Wyoming

CHRONOLOGY OF *THE CRITERION*

The Criterion

Vol. 1. No. 1. 1–103, Oct. 1922; No. 2. 105–201, Jan. 1923;
No. 3. 203–313, Apr. 1923; No. 4. 315–427, July 1923.

Vol. 2. No. 5. 1–113, Oct. 1923; No. 6. 115–229, Feb. 1924;
No. 7 231–369, Apr. 1924; No. 8 371–503, July 1924.

Vol. 3. No. 9. 1–159, Oct. 1924; No. 10. 161–340, Jan. 1925;
No. 11 341–483, Apr. 1925; No. 12. 485–606, July 1925.

The New Criterion

Vol. 4. No. 1. 1–220, Jan. 1926; No. 2. 221–415, Apr. 1926;
No. 3. 417–626, June 1926; No. 4. 627–814, Oct. 1926.

Vol. 5. No. 1. 1–186, Jan. 1927.

The Monthly Criterion

Vol. 5. No. 2. 187–282, May 1927; No. 3. 283–374, June 1927.

Vol. 6. No. 1. 1–96, July 1927; No. 2. 97–192, Aug. 1927; No. 3.
193–288, Sept. 1927; No. 4. 289–384, Oct. 1927; No. 5. 385–480,
Nov. 1927; No. 6. 481–584, Dec. 1927.

Vol. 7. No. 1. 1–96, Jan. 1928; No. 2. 97–192, Feb. 1928;
No. 3. 193–288, Mar. 1928.

The Criterion

Vol. 7. No. 4. 289–464, June 1928

Vol. 8. No. 30. 1–183, Sept. 1928; No. 31. 185–376, Dec. 1928;
No. 32. 377–573, Apr. 1929; No. 33. 575–772, July 1929.

Vol. 9. No. 34. 1–178, Oct. 1929; No. 35, 181–380, Jan. 1930;
No. 36, 381–585, Apr. 1930; No. 37, 587–787, July 1930.

Vol. 10. No. 38. 1–209, Oct. 1930; No. 39. 211–391, Jan. 1931;
No. 40. 393–592, Apr. 1931; No. 41. 593–792, July 1931.

Vol. 11. No. 42. 1–182, Oct. 1931; No. 43. 183–374, Jan 1932;
No. 44. 375–579, Apr. 1932; No. 45. 581–775, July 1932.

Vol. 12. No. 46. 1–174, Oct. 1932; No. 47. 175–338, Jan. 1933; No. 48. 339–548, Apr. 1933; No. 49. 549–722, July 1933.

Vol. 13. No. 50. 1–178, Oct. 1933; No. 51. 179–352, Jan. 1934; No. 52. 353–536, Apr. 1934; No. 53. 537–716, July 1934.

Vol. 14. No. 54. 1–180, Oct. 1934; No. 55. 181–350, Jan. 1935; No. 56. 351–546, Apr. 1935; No. 57. 547–730, July 1935.

EDITORIAL NOTES

The source of each letter is indicated at the top right. CC indicates a carbon copy. Where no other source is shown it may be assumed that the original or carbon copy is in the Valerie Eliot collection or at the Faber Archive.

del. deleted

MS manuscript

n. d. no date

PC postcard

sc. *scilicet*: namely

ts typescript

< > indicates a word or words brought in from another part of the letter.

Place of publication is London, unless otherwise stated.

Some obvious typing or manuscript errors, and slips of grammar and spelling, have been silently corrected.

Dates have been standardised.

Some words and figures which were abbreviated have been expanded.

Punctuation has been occasionally adjusted.

Editorial insertions are indicated by square brackets.

Words both italicised and underlined signify double underlining in the original copy.

Where possible a biographical note accompanies the first letter to or from a correspondent. Where appropriate this brief initial note will also refer the reader to the Biographical Register at the end of the text.

Vivienne Eliot liked her husband and friends to spell her name Vivien; but as there is no consistency it is printed as written.

'Not in Gallup' means that the item in question is not recorded in Donald Gallup, *T. S. Eliot: A Bibliography* (1969).

THE LETTERS
1932–1933

1932

TO *Howard Morris*[1]   TS Morgan Library

1 January 1932   *The Criterion*, 24 Russell Square,
                                  London W.C.1

My dear Howard,

Many thanks for your letter of the 16th December, and for your offer of hospitality from the Harvard Club in New York. So far my plans are quite inchoate, and as a matter of fact I have not even had any official notification from Harvard.[2] I shall no doubt have to come to New York sooner or later, but I had rather come for the pleasure of spending a weekend with yourself and your family at Easthampton than to plunge into the vortex of the metropolis.[3] I am particularly anxious to keep out of the way of publishers, agents, editors, authors and poetesses, the last of whom I understand abound in New York. Your account of the liquid refreshment is about as depressing as it could be, and I think the best thing I can do, if it is within my powers, is to train myself to be able to live on orange juice.[4] I wonder if that is possible, however, for seven or eight months. Incidentally my term does not begin until October 1932, and lasts until May 1933 so there is plenty of time.

---

1 – Howard Morris (b. 1887), from Milwaukee, Wisc., who had been TSE's contemporary and friend at Milton Academy, Mass., and at Harvard, was a successful dealer in investment bonds.

2 – The official notification from the Office of the President and Fellows of Harvard College was to be dated 6 Jan. 1932, and signed by the secretary: 'I beg to inform you that on the ninth day of November you were elected by the President and Fellows Charles Eliot Norton Professor of Poetry, to serve for one year from September 1, 1932, and that this election was duly confirmed by the Board of Overseers at their meeting of November 23, 1931' (Houghton MS Am 2560).

3 – Morris spent weekends in East Hampton, Long Island; weekdays at the Harvard Club, NYC.

4 – 'Better get in training for the alcoholic junk you will find here. All gin is synthetic – and of course raw. The Scotch for the most part is expensive & green – not to say something worse. The rye is all of Canadian manufacture & without mellowness. The wine is practically non-existent, & the beer horrible. I suggest a daily ration of raw alcohol to get your innards in tune with the American spirit.'

With a happy New Year to you,

from

Tom

TO *J. B. Trend*[1]

1 January 1932   [*The Criterion*]

My dear Trend,

I am very sorry indeed that you will not be able to come to the next meeting, but hope that you will be back in March. Meanwhile I return your handsome and well-deserved New Zealand compliment, and hope that Mr Lindsay will continue to read the *Criterion* for your sake if for none other.

With best wishes for the New Year,

Yours ever,

[T. S. Eliot]

1–J. B. Trend (1887–1958), journalist, musicologist, literary critic – he wrote the music chronicles for C. – was to become Professor of Spanish at Cambridge, 1933–52. Works include *Alfonso the Sage & Other Spanish Essays* (1926), *Manuel de Falla and Spanish Music* (1928), *The Origins of Modern Spain* (1934). See Margaret Joan Anstee, *JB: An Unlikely Spanish Don: The Life & Times of Professor John Brande Trend* (2013).

1 January 1932   *The Criterion*

Dear Mr Spencer,

Thank you very much for your letter of the 16th December, and for your kind offer of assistance in finding lodgings.[2] Your suggestion sounds very attractive, but unless it is necessary to make reservations at once, I should prefer to wait a month before settling. Naturally if I decided that I should like to occupy a don's apartments I should be very glad to be under your protection in the house which I believe you rule. I am wondering if I ought to address you as 'Master'?

With many thanks and looking forward to seeing you in the autumn.

Yours sincerely,

T. S. Eliot

Please remember me and my wife most cordially to your Aunt.[3]

---

1 – Theodore Spencer (1902–49), poet and critic, taught at Harvard, 1927–49; as Boylston Professor of Rhetoric and Oratory from 1946. Co-editor of *A Garland for John Donne 1631–1931* (1931), for which TSE wrote 'Donne in Our Time'; author of *Shakespeare and the Nature of Man* (Lowell Lectures on Shakespeare, 1951); *Selected Essays*, ed. Alan C. Purves (1966). TSE told J. S. Barnes, 18 Jan. 1937, that Spencer was 'a delightful person'. He advised T. R. Henn, 30 May 1939 – Spencer had applied for a Cambridge University lectureship – 'I imagine that Theodore Spencer is so well-known to most of the English lecturers in Cambridge that any testimonial from me should be superfluous. Also, it is only fair to say that Spencer is a close personal friend of mine, and that I may be biased in his favour . . . I have a very high opinion indeed of Spencer's abilities. I did not meet everyone even in the English department at Harvard, but I have no reason to believe that there was anyone there of greater ability or greater gifts for teaching. I saw enough of his relations with the students whom he tutored (that was before he had been made an assistant professor) to say that no one could have devoted more zeal than he to work with individuals, or with better effect. He was very popular with the undergraduates, and it was by his initiative and under his direction that the members of Eliot House started their productions of Elizabethan plays, which became a rather important college event.

'I have a high opinion, also, of Spencer's appreciation of literature, both new and old.'

2 – Spencer recommended TSE to take a suite (study, two bedrooms, bathroom) in Eliot House, at a cost of approx. $50 a month, for the period of his stay at Harvard.

3 – Katherine Spencer, who had been a neighbour of TSE's mother, had visited London in 1931 – 'a most jolly and cultivated woman whom we liked immensely'. Postscript added by hand.

TO *Mary Butts*[1]   TS BL/Mrs Camilla Bagg

1 January 1932   *The Criterion*

Dear Miss Butts,

Indeed I remember having met you often in what are beginning to seem distant days. It is quite true that I liked *Ashe of Rings*, or rather I very much liked what I saw of it, for I only read several parts which were serialized, and the published book never came my way.[2] I certainly am very happy to hear that a long delayed English edition will be published. But as for a prefatory note by myself, I am afraid that I must be quite consistent with the principles I have adopted, and decline, except for very special reasons – as when I wrote an introduction to a selection of Ezra Pound's poems – ever to introduce in this way a living author. As for the value of such prefaces in helping a book there are two opinions, and I think myself that the value of prefatory commendations is over-rated. But the real point is, that if I did agree, as I should like to do, I should find it exceedingly difficult ever to refuse less welcome tasks of the same sort, particularly from people whose claim upon me would be rather personal than due to my admiration for their work. But in expressing my regret I must say again how glad I am that the book is to be made accessible.[3]

Yours sincerely,
T. S. Eliot

1–Mary Butts (1890–1937), writer, was married to the poet and publisher John Rodker (1894–1955) from 1918 to 1926, and to the artist Gabriel Aitken/Atkin (1897–1937) from 1930 to 1934. She lived in France, 1925–30. Her works include *Speed the Plough and Other Stories* (1923), *Ashe of Rings* (1925), *Imaginary Letters*, illustrated by Jean Cocteau (1928), *The Macedonian* (1933), *Several Occasions* (1932). Butts remarked on 25 Dec. 1927: 'T. S. Eliot, with his ear on some stops of english speech which have not been used before, the only writer of my quality, dislikes me & my work, I think' (*The Journals of Mary Butts*, ed. Nathalie Blondel [2002], 275). See further Nathalie Blondel, *Mary Butts: Scenes from the Life* (1998); *A Sacred Quest: The Life and Writings of Mary Butts*, ed. C. Wagstaff (1995).
2–Butts asked TSE on 29 Dec. 1931 to write a preface for the British edition of *Ashe of Rings* (Desmond Harmsworth). The novel had so far appeared only in the USA and in France.
3–Blondel writes: '[TSE] declines Butts's request for him to write an introduction to a British edition of *Ashe of Rings*, which Desmond Harmsworth . . . is interested in publishing. Despite his apparent enthusiasm for the novel, Eliot refuses (which presumably leads to Harmsworth's loss of interest in the republication) – on the grounds that he does not provide introductions to living authors, except for Pound. This must have made his introduction to Djuna Barnes' *Nightwood* (1936) all the more galling to Butts' (*Journals*, 369).

TO *Desmond Harmsworth*[1]

1 January 1932   [Faber & Faber Ltd]

Dear Harmsworth,

I do not know *Ashe of Rings* quite as well as you suppose inasmuch as my interest, though keenly aroused by several parts which I saw in serial form, was never gratified by reading the whole book.[2] The point is, however, that I prefer not to write introductions to the work of other living authors except in very special circumstances. If I did I should be embarrassed by people whose claim upon me was purely personal and was not reinforced by my admiration for their work. I can only say that I am very glad that you should have the enterprise to publish the book in England.

If I am going to Harvard it will not be until next September, and then for seven months only, so you must not be surprised to see me about before and after.[3]

Yours very sincerely,
[T. S. Eliot]

FROM *TSE'S Secretary* TO *Jean Paulhan*[4]

1 January 1932   [*The Criterion*]

Dear Sir,

Mr Eliot asks me to say that he will be writing to you personally early in the New Year, but meanwhile he wishes to put in a word with you on behalf of his young friend Edouard Roditi, who he believes will be coming to see you about some translations he had made of poems by

---

1–Desmond Harmsworth (1903–90), British painter, publisher and poet. Son of the 1st Baron Harmsworth (he succeeded to the title in 1948), he published, in the early 1930s, works by writers including JJ, EP, Roy Campbell, and Norman Douglas.

2–Desmond Harmsworth was thinking of publishing a new edition of *Ashe of Rings*, by Mary Butts, and wondered whether TSE, 'as (I believe) a particular admirer of her work, could be persuaded to write an introduction' (28 Dec. 1931).

3–'I hear from Pound that you may perhaps be going to Harvard. I sincerely hope, for the good of the rest of us, that this is not so.'

4–Jean Paulhan (1884–1968), editor of *Nouvelle Revue Française* (in succession to Jacques Rivière), 1925–40, 1946–68. He was active in the French Resistance during WW2. His works include *Entretiens sur des fait-divers* (1930); *Les Fleurs de Tarbes, ou, La Terreur dans les lettres* (1936); *On Poetry and Politics*, ed. Jennifer Bajorek et al. (2010). See William Marx, 'Two Modernisms: T. S. Eliot and *La Nouvelle Revue Française*', in *The International Reception of T. S. Eliot*, ed. Elisabeth Däumer and Shyamal Bagchee (2007), 25–33.

Stephen Spender. Mr Eliot wishes me to say that you will of course be much better able to judge the quality of the translations than he is himself, but he knows Mr Roditi to be a young man of considerable abilities who is practically bi-lingual, and also that he is very much assured of the merit of Mr Spender as a poet. The firm of Faber and Faber will probably be publishing a volume of Mr Spender's poems next autumn.

Yours faithfully,
[Pamela Wilberforce]
Secretary.

TO *Edouard Roditi*[1]

1 January 1932   *The Criterion*

Dear Roditi,

I have gladly written to Paulhan about you and about Spender, and hope that you will succeed in persuading him. I will only add that I shall not be leaving England until September next, and then for seven months only, so I hope to see more of you during the coming year.

Yours in haste,
T. S. E.

TO *Virginia Woolf*[2]

CC

1 January 1932   [Faber & Faber Ltd]

Dear Virginia,

I am very sorry indeed for your decision and hope and believe that you are wrong about the possibility of arousing a 3/6 appetite for your work.[3] But your decision is really what I expected after our talk the other day, and now your refusal of Chatto's overture makes it impossible to raise the matter again for a long time. I still hope that in a few years you will relent.

1–Edouard Roditi (1910–92), poet, critic, biographer, translator: see Biographical Register.
2–Virginia Woolf (1882–1941), novelist, essayist and critic: see Biographical Register.
3–F&F offered to bring out VW's novels in a 'cheap edition'; but she replied on 8 Dec. that there seemed to be little point in transferring her works to another publisher 'as theyve only been in our five shilling edition a year or two and are at present selling briskly'. She was grateful for GCF's 'flattering offer' but had turned down a similar offer from Chatto & Windus.

According to this morning's *Times* Lytton has picked up a little, but that is not very reassuring in itself.[1] At best it appears to be a long and dangerous illness. Do let me know as soon as you return to London.[2]

Affectionately yours,

[Tom]

TO *Stephen Spender*[3]

TS Northwestern

1 January 1932   *The Criterion*

Dear Spender,

<Might we not now drop the 'Mr'?>[4]

I have been meditating a letter to you for a long time, but the fact is that one of the points you raise in your last letter has been germinating in my mind into an article which I have not yet finished. An article is hardly a satisfactory answer to a personal letter, and I should like to write to you more fully very soon. Meanwhile I must answer your letter of the 29th December.

1. I am ashamed to say that I have not yet read 'The Colleagues', but I will do so at once and get it back to you in a few days.[5] I assume that you are settled in Berlin until further notice.

2. I should not like to stand in your way with regard to the Hogarth Press Anthology, but I should like to know whether the poems you propose to give them are poems which have already appeared in periodicals or are unprinted, and also what proportion of our book, in number of pages, will these eight poems represent.[6]

In haste, but with all good wishes for the New Year.

Yours sincerely,

T. S. Eliot

---

1 – 'A slight improvement was reported yesterday in the condition of Mr Lytton Strachey' ('Invalids', *The Times*, 1 Jan. 1932, 10).

2 – Strachey was to die of cancer, 21 Jan. 1932.

3 – Stephen Spender (1909–95), poet and critic: see Biographical Register.

4 – Handwritten in the margin.

5 – Spender had asked for the return of Edward Upward's story 'The Colleagues', submitted on 21 Oct. 1931. 'I am so much in the dark as to what has happened about the story that I only assume it has reached you: because although it was never acknowledged by Faber's, I suppose that, if you have not received it, you would have written saying so in answer to one of the subsequent letters in which I have referred to it.'

6 – The Hogarth Press had asked Spender to submit eight poems for an anthology that they were bringing out in March: he referred the matter to TSE in case of any 'breach of faith'.

TO *Harold Monro*[1]   TS Gallup

1 January 1932   *The Criterion*

Dear Harold,

What a pork-pie that was! It was a capital pork-pie, and I thank you from the bottom of my heart and the pit of my stomach, which passed the examination with perfect marks. Our saturnine servant from Saffron Walden told me that one was not intended to eat the crust and she was so darkly ominous about what would happen to me if I did eat the crust that I obeyed her injunction. But I was sorry to omit the crust and wonder if she was right.[2]

I hope that you are making a rapid recovery, but it seemed to me better on the whole to put the next *Criterion* meeting as late as possible, and so I suggest for your approval Wednesday February 3, <That suits Bumbaby, I find>[3] the Wednesday before Lent. That is, if it needs to be a Wednesday, and I believe that Wednesday is slightly more convenient for Morley.[4] Although I suppose it would be impossible to get Herbert[5] I should like to have as full a roll of the inner circle as possible with a view to a preliminary discussion of the conduct of the *Criterion* while I am in America.

With thanks, and all best wishes for a better year.

Yours ever,

T. S. E.

P. S. In any case I want to have a private talk with you before the next *Criterion* meeting. One point I want to discuss is Frank's Chronicle. It did not turn out as I had hoped, and I am not satisfied now that Frank is the right man in the right frame of mind for reviewing the work of new poets.[6]

1–Harold Monro (1879–1932), poet, editor, publisher, bookseller: see Biographical Register.
2–Monro (19 Jan.): 'Ridiculous about that Pork Pie crust – of course it was meant to be eaten.'
3–Bonamy Dobrée.
4–Frank Morley (1899–1980), editor and publisher; a founding director of Faber & Faber Ltd: see Biographical Register.
5–Herbert Read (1893–1968), English poet and literary critic: see Biographical Register.
6–Monro replied on 13 Jan., 'I can decide nothing. I'm laid up here [Castlemere, Broadstairs, Kent] with a high temperature – ulcerative colitis, jolly. I'll dictate a letter to you after Alida joins me on Friday, & best not fix *Criterion* till after then. I want very much to talk to you about [Frank] Flint's view of poetry: it has appalled me for some time. I have aching eyes & arms & head & – I'll stop.' F. S. Flint (1885–1960): English poet and translator and civil servant.

TO *J. Lyle Donaghy*[1]   CC

1 January 1932   [*The Criterion*]

Dear Mr Donaghy,

It is I who must offer an apology because it has been on my mind to write to you for a very long time.[2] I hope that you are now very well, and send you my most cordial wishes for the New Year. I am just on the point of considering the manuscript which I have with a view to selecting a poem for the next number, and you shall hear from me shortly.

                          Yours very sincerely,
                          [T. S. Eliot]

FROM *Vivien Eliot*[3] TO *Mary Hutchinson*[4]   MS Texas

3 January 1932[5]   68 Clarence Gate Gardens,
                                     Regents Park, London N.W.1

My dear Mary

Thank you for your charming Christmas present. It is very sweet & dainty, & just what I love. Thank you *very much*.

Forgive me for not having written sooner. I have had a sort of breakdown, & have felt very ill in every way. So have not been out – for a week.

I hope you have kept well over Christmas, & that all 4 of you are well & happy.

I send you my best wishes in every possible way, for 1932.

I hope to see you very soon. Will you ring me up if you ever want it?

                          With my love
                          Yrs. ever
                          Vivienne Haigh Eliot

1–John Lyle Donaghy (1902–49), Irish poet and teacher, was educated at Larne Grammar School, County Antrim, and Trinity College, Dublin. His early poetry was published by the Yeats family's Cuala Press; and he was a friend of Samuel Beckett. His works include *At Dawn over Aherlow* (1926) and *Into the Light, and Other Poems* (1934).

2–Donaghy wrote from the Down County Mental Hospital, Downpatrick, on 28 Dec. 1931, that he had written a letter 'some time ago for which, as it must obviously have reflected ill-health, I shall not offer any further apology.' He asked for a decision about the article and poems that TSE had had 'for a long time now'.

3–Vivien Eliot, *née* Haigh-Wood (1888–1947): see Biographical Register.

4–Mary Hutchinson (1889–1977), a half-cousin of Lytton Strachey; prominent hostess, author: see Biographical Register.

5–VHE mistyped '1931'.

TO *Sydney Schiff*[1]   TS British Library

4 January 1932   *The Criterion*

My dear Sydney,

It is very pleasant to hear from you at Christmas time, and I must answer your letter in order to send you and Violet our most cordial wishes for the New Year in which I hope we may again meet.[2] I have no particular change to mark in my affairs with the exception of this appointment, which however is not to Cambridge in Cambridgeshire but to Cambridge in Massachusetts. It is a visiting professorship which is granted to each incumbent for a year only and means an absence of about seven months from next September. I do not expect that you are likely to spend the whole winter in England even in these times, but I should be glad to know what your plans are.

I have read with great interest the paper by John Cornford which you sent me.[3] He is obviously a boy of whom much may be expected, but at present alarmingly precocious. On principle I should never wittingly publish anything by a boy at school or even by an undergraduate at college, because I feel that nowadays there is a tendency for young talents to blossom before they have taken deep root. I doubt if I should have accepted this even if I had not known the age of the author because it seems to me that he has not yet learned to manage the English language with great ease, and he is inclined to use cumbrous words and cumbrous constructions. But I do not suppose that you yourself wished to see this particular performance in print, and I can sincerely say that I am very much impressed by the boy's abilities and I should like to be kept in touch from time to time with his development.

Yours always affectionately,
T. S. E.

1–Sydney Schiff (1868–1944), British novelist and translator (illegitimate child of a stockbroker), patron of the arts and friend of WL, JMM, Proust, Osbert Sitwell, published fiction under the name Stephen Hudson. Works include *Richard, Myrtle and I* (1926); and he translated Proust's *Time Regained* (1931). In 1911 he married Violet Beddington (1874–1962), sister of the novelist Ada Leverson (Oscar Wilde's 'Sphinx'). See AH, *Exhumations: correspondence inédite avec Sydney Schiff, 1925–1937*, ed. Robert Clémentine (1976); Richard Davenport-Hines, *A Night at the Majestic: Proust and the Great Modernist Dinner Party of 1922* (2006); Stephen Klaidman, *Sydney and Violet: Their life with T. S. Eliot, Proust, Joyce, and the excruciatingly irascible Wyndham Lewis* (2013)

2–Schiff sent affectionate greetings at Christmas 1931.

3–Schiff sent a short essay by the sixteen-year-old John Cornford (1915–36), son of the Cambridge professor Francis Cornford and of the poet Frances Cornford, who was still at Stowe School.

TO *James Joyce*[1]

4 January 1932   Faber & Faber Ltd,
                                                  24 Russell Square, London W.C.1

Dear Joyce,

I was very sorry to hear your news and much moved by your letter.[2] I know something about such things, as I had meant to return to Boston to visit my mother, and allowed one thing after another to delay me; and I had warning enough, as her writing became feebler, and for several months she had not the strength to write at all. I think, however, that the death of my father, ten years earlier, pained me more deeply; it was just at the end of the war, so that I could not have gone to see him; but he died still believing, I am sure, that I had made a complete mess of my life – which from his point of view, and possibly quite rightly, I had done. I cannot forget him sitting in the railway station before my last departure, looking completely broken. Whereas my mother lived long enough to take an immoderate pride in my accomplishment and to feel that I had done the best for myself: that may or may not be so, but I am glad that she believed it.

So when I suggest that possibly your father felt his life to be fulfilled in the recognition of your fame & greatness, it is not merely a conventional piece of consolatory chatter.

My wife is anxious that I should add her expressions of sympathy and will write herself when she is well enough to do so.

My appointment to Harvard, by the way, is only for seven months; I shall leave England in September next and return in the following May.[3] So I hope there is some chance of our seeing you and Mrs Joyce here during the coming summer.

The printers will begin on Part 1 as soon as you can let us have it.[4]

---

1 – James Joyce (1882–1941), Irish novelist, playwright, poet: see Biographical Register.

2 – Joyce's father had died in Dublin on 29 Dec. 1931. JJ wrote to TSE on 1 Jan.: 'Excuse me if I am backward in my work and correspondence. I have been through a bad time telephoning and wiring to Dublin about my father. To my great grief he died on Tuesday. He had an intense love for me and it adds anew to my grief and remorse that I did not go to Dublin to see him for so many years . . . I have been very broken down these last days & I feel that a poor heart which was the one faithful to me is no more' (*Letters of James Joyce*, ed. Stuart Gilbert [1957, 1966], I, 311).

3 – 'I have heard about your Harvard appointment. I offer my congratulations if the appointment is pleasant for you and I hope Mrs Eliot and yourself will have all luck and happiness this year.'

4 – 'I will prepare the end of Pt I after a few days' rest.' JJ's 'Work in Progress, which TSE fostered through the coming years, would ultimately become *Finnegans Wake* (F&F, 1939).

I hope that your eyesight has improved to such an extent as to obviate another visit to Zurich. I was glad to see Monsieur Gillet, whom I liked, for a few minutes; had his visit not been so brief I should have asked him to have lunch with me.[1] I was sorry that he was unable to give me any recent report of you.

With all cordial wishes to Mrs Joyce and your family from my wife and myself,

Yours sincerely,
T. S. Eliot

TO *C. M. Grieve*[2]   CC

6 January 1932   [Faber & Faber Ltd]

Dear Mr Grieve,

Thank you very much for your letter of the 5th with its good wishes, which I reciprocate. I am not likely to leave England until next September, and shall return the following May.

1–Louis Gillet (1876–1943), literary editor of the *Revue des deux Mondes* (in which he had recently published an article about JJ's 'Work in Progress', and earlier a piece on *Ulysses*) had called on TSE in the last week of 1931, with an introduction from JJ dated 23 Dec. 1931. (See Joyce, *Letters*, I, 309–10.)

2–Christopher Murray Grieve (1892–1978): pseud. Hugh MacDiarmid – poet, journalist, critic, cultural activist, self-styled 'Anglophobe', Scottish Nationalist and Communist; founder member of the Scottish National Party, 1928; founder of the Scottish Centre of PEN. His works include *A Drunk Man Looks at the Thistle* (1926), *To Circumjack Cencrastus* (1930), *'First Hymn to Lenin' and Other Poems* (1931), *In Memoriam James Joyce* (1955), *Hugh MacDiarmid: Complete Poems, 1920–1976* (2 vols, 1978). See further Alan Bold, *MacDiarmid, Christopher Murray Grieve: A Critical Biography* (1988); *The Letters of Hugh MacDiarmid*, ed. A. Bold (1984); and *Dear Grieve: Letters to Hugh MacDiarmid (C. M. Grieve)*, sel. and ed. John Manson (2011).

Grieve remarked to the novelist Neil M. Gunn (1891–1973), 3 May 1928: 'Now as to Eliot, I believe (vide *Drunk Man*) he's a Scotsman by descent – but it's a damned long descent: and mentally he certainly fills the role you seem to have cast him for in your papers. He is pure Boston – ultra-English classicist in criticism: that's what makes him so unintelligible to mere English conventionalists – they can't follow their own ideas to their logical conclusions well enough to recognise their own supporters' (MacDiarmid, *Letters*, 222).

When invited by Albert Mackie of the *Edinburgh Evening Despatch* to a celebration in Edinburgh of MacDiarmid, TSE responded with this tribute (15 Aug. 1948): 'As I cannot be present, I should like to send my greetings to Hugh MacDiarmid and to the Makars assembled to do him honour. There are two reasons why I should have wished to be present on this occasion. The first is my respect for the great contribution of the Poet to Poetry – in general – in my time; the second is my respect for his contribution to Scottish Poetry – in particular. I value the latter also for two reasons. While I must admit that Lallands is a language which I read with difficulty – rather less fluently, in fact, than German – and a

I did approach Richmond some time ago, and he told me at the time that he had no vacancies whatever for review work.[1] I can do no more than raise the subject again at a later date. Meanwhile I daresay you have other means of introduction to other editors, but if there are any with whom I can help, please let me know. I hope before long to be able to return one of your luncheons.

Yours sincerely,
[T. S. Eliot]

TO *Elizabeth Manwaring*[2]   TS Wellesley College Library

6 January 1932   *The Criterion*

Dear Miss Manwaring,

Very many thanks for your kind letter of the 23rd December.[3] I should of course be very happy to produce a reading at Wellesley College, and the remuneration offered seems to me as much as I am worth. I have not, however, had any official notification from Harvard University. Furthermore I am not certain whether I should make any engagements

---

language the subtleties of which I shall never master, I can nevertheless enjoy it, and I am convinced that many things can be said, in poetry, in the language, which cannot be expressed at all in English. The second reason follows from the first: I think that Scots poetry is, like that of other Western European languages, a potentially fertilising influence upon English poetry; and – speaking as an English regionalist – I hold that it is to the interest of English poetry that Scots poetry should flourish. It is uncontested, and now everywhere recognised, that Hugh MacDiarmid's refusal to become merely another successful English poet, and his pursuing a course which at first some of his admirers deplored and some of his detractors derided, has had important consequences and has justified itself. It will eventually be admitted that he has done more for English poetry, by committing some of his finest verse to Scots, than if he had elected to write exclusively in the Southern dialect.'

TSE wrote to Richard Church, 21 Aug. 1963: 'I am delighted to know that you and I see eye to eye about C. M. Grieve, otherwise Hugh MacDiarmid. My own feeling about the modern synthetic Lallans is that it has produced a group of second-rate versifiers.' Joseph Chiari noted, in *T. S. Eliot: A Memoir* (1982): 'Strange as it will appear to some, [Eliot], the self-proclaimed royalist and conservative, liked and respected the rebellious, ever explosive anti-monarchist Hugh MacDiarmid, whose poetry he admired and whose efforts to raise the Scots language to the level of a mature medium for all aspects of literature he applauded.'

1 – Grieve reminded TSE that when they had met at TSE's club, TSE had kindly promised to approach BLR to see if Grieve might undertake some reviewing work for the *TLS*.

2 – Elizabeth W. Manwaring (1879–1949), Professor of English at Wellesley College, was author of a pioneering study, *Italian Landscape in Eighteenth Century England: a study chiefly of the influence of Claude Lorrain and Salvator Rosa on English Taste, 1700–1800* (1925). She was given an introduction to TSE by his brother-in-law A. D. Sheffield in the summer of 1931 when she paid a visit to London.

3 – Not found.

for speaking until I know how much work they will want me to do at Harvard, and at what hours. Perhaps you know more about this than I do, but it seems to me that I ought to make enquiries there before engaging myself even for one Monday afternoon. I shall make such enquiries and will write to you again.

The other question is what you mean by a reading. If you want me to read my own poetry – which I do not particularly like doing, but will if desired – it seems to me that if I read for a whole hour I should have to read nearly everything that I have written. I have never read poetry aloud for more than half an hour, and certainly if it is longer I should really prefer to read other people's rather than my own.

I look forward with much pleasure to renewing our acquaintance.

Yours sincerely,
[T. S. Eliot]

TO *Stephen Spender*   TS Northwestern

6 January 1932   *The Criterion*

Dear Spender,

I have now read Upward's story, and although it hardly seems to me clearly finished enough for publication, it is sufficient to interest me in his work, and I should very much like to see more of what he writes.[1]

I saw Auden today at lunch, and he seems to think as I do that it is time you returned to England. After all South Wales can hardly be more expensive, I should think, than Berlin at the present time.[2] I look forward with some hope, however, to a possible Anglo-Scandinavian economic understanding which might permit Britons to sojourn in those northern countries without serious loss of exchange.

1–Spender had submitted on 21 Oct. 1931 a story by Edward Upward entitled 'The Colleagues'. On 29 Dec. 1931 he asked TSE to return it 'at the first possible opportunity . . . as the other editor to whom I can submit The Colleagues is leaving England in the middle of January.' Edward Upward (1903–2009): English novelist and short-story writer; schoolteacher; friend of Christopher Isherwood, WHA and SS; member of the Communist Party of Great Britain, 1932–48. His novels include *Journey to the Border* (1938) and a trilogy, *The Spiral Ascent* (1962–77).
2–Spender had been purposing in Sept. 1931 to spend 'a fortnight in S. Wales to see what it is like, as I want to live in a mining district'. But he wrote on 21 Oct., 'I have had to abandon my South Wales project for the time being, and I am returning to Berlin on the 29th.' Then on 2 Nov. he reported from Berlin, 'I am experiencing the restricted standard of living imposed on policemen, teachers and all the worthiest members of English social life by the writers of the May report . . . At the moment the value of the £ is declining at the rate of 2d . . . a day.'

Sincerely yours,
T. S. Eliot

A letter from you comes this morning but [I] cannot answer this for a day or two.[1]

TO *Rose Holmes Smith*[2]   CC

6 January 1932   [Faber & Faber Ltd]

My dear Aunt Rose,

Thank you very much for your kind note of the 21st December. I doubt whether Vivienne will be strong enough to be able to come with me, but it is impossible to decide so far ahead.[3] In any case I shall of course

---

1–Added by hand. Spender's letter, dated 4 Jan., was answered by TSE on 3 Feb.

2–Rose Greenleaf Eliot (1862–1936) – Mrs Holmes Smith – invited TSE to stay at 5440 Maple Avenue, St Louis, Missouri. 'I hope Vivian will be able to come with you,' she wrote on 21 Dec. 1931; 'you will be more than welcome to make our home your abiding place.' TSE was to be 'received' at Washington Univ. on Mon. 16 Jan. 1933.

3–Nearly three months later, Edith Sitwell was to gossip about the state of VHE's health, in a letter to David Horner (Osbert Sitwell's lover), on 28 Mar.: 'We had a very exciting time yesterday. A certain lady (Osbert will tell you who I mean) came to tea without her husband. As she entered, a strange smell, as though four bottles of methylated spirits had been upset, entered also, followed, five minutes afterwards, by Georgia [wife of Sacheverell Sitwell] and her mother [Mrs Doble]. Nellie (the maid) who was once what is known as an Attendant, enquired if she might speak to me on the telephone, and, as soon as she got me outside, said (looking very frightened): "If she starts anything, Miss, get her by the wrists, sit on her face, and don't let her bite you. Don't let her get near a looking glass, or near the window." I said "What *do* you mean?" and she replied that what I thought was an accident with the [methylated spirits] was really the strongest drug given by Attendants when the patient is so violent that nothing ordinary has any effect!! She concluded, gloomily: "Often, it has taken six of us to hold one down." – You can imagine my feelings. And when I got back into the room, I found that Mrs Doble had offered the lady a cigarette, and had been told that the lady *never* accepted anything from strangers. It was too dangerous. Poor Mrs D. was terrified, as she thought that the Patient was going to spring at her throat. Georgia was terrified too, and tea was undiluted hell' (*Selected Letters of Edith Sitwell*, ed. Richard Greene [1997, revised edn, 1998], 133–4).

John Pearson (*Façades: Edith, Osbert and Sacheverell Sitwell* [1978], 278) relates the following exchange, when Edith Sitwell ran into VHE in Oxford Street in the summer of 1932:

'Hullo, Vivienne!' she called to her.

Vivienne looked at her suspiciously and sadly, and replied, 'Who do you think you are addressing? I don't know you.'

'Don't be silly, Vivienne: you know quite well who I am.'

Vivienne regarded her with profound melancholy for a moment, and then said, 'No, no: you don't know me. You have mistaken me again for that terrible woman who is so like me . . . She is always getting me into trouble.'

take the first opportunity of visiting Saint Louis, which will probably be directly after Christmas. I should like to be there for New Year's Day. It is very kind of you to ask me to be your guest for the few days of my visit, and I shall be very happy to accept; but as I feel diffident about it I should be grateful if you would write to me again at Harvard as the time approaches.[1]

With best wishes to you and Uncle Jack.

Affectionately your nephew

[Tom]

TO *Anthony Blunt*[2]   CC

6 January 1932   [*The Criterion*]

Dear Mr Blunt,

I have your letter of the 30th and remember reading your article on Baroque and thinking that it would have done excellently as a review.[3]

---

1 – Aunt Rose undertook (24 Jan. 1932) to write again 'as the time approaches . . . We have all been very sorry that Vivienne is and has been so much of an invalid. I hope she doesn't suffer.'

2 – Anthony Blunt (1907–83), art historian and spy, was a Fellow of Trinity College, Cambridge, 1932–6, before joining the Warburg Institute, 1937–9. From 1939 he was Reader in the History of Art, London University, and Deputy Director of the Courtauld Institute of Art. He was Professor of the History of Art, and Director of the Courtauld, 1947–74; Surveyor of the Queen's Pictures, 1952–72; Advisor for the Queen's Pictures and Drawings, 1972–8. He was Slade Professor of Fine Art, Oxford, 1962–3; Cambridge, 1965–6. He was awarded the KCVO in 1956 (but the award was annulled in 1979 following his exposure as a Soviet spy during WW2); Commander of the Order of Orange Nassau (Holland), 1948; Commandeur de la Légion d'Honneur, 1958. His publications include *The Drawings of Nicolas Poussin* (1939), *Artistic Theory in Italy* (1940), *The Nation's Pictures* (1951), *Art and Architecture in France, 1500–1700* (1953), *Nicolas Poussin: Catalogue Raisonné* (1966), *Nicolas Poussin* (2 vols, 1967) and *Picasso's Guernica* (1969).

3 – Blunt wrote, 30 Dec. 1931: 'I am writing to you on the recommendation of Mr Rylands who sent you recently an article of mine on Sacheverell Sitwell & the Baroque. In your letter, written when you sent back this article, you spoke of the possibility of my doing some reviewing for you. I should in general very much like to review books on painting, especially Italian or French. If you have not already published a review of [R. H.] Wilenski's book on French Painting (Medici Society) I should particularly like to write about this, or indeed about any of the other books which have been produced in connexion with the French Exhibition.

'In the same connexion would you perhaps also be prepared to consider an article on Poussin either as an artist or as a theorist on painting. I have done a certain amount of research on French XVIIth century theories of painting in the course of my work at Cambridge.'

(George Rylands [1902–99] was a Fellow of King's College, Cambridge, from 1927.)

The only difficulty about books on painting is that they go normally to our art editor, Mr Roger Hinks, and only in exceptional cases elsewhere. But if I can find an opportunity I will keep you in mind.

I should certainly be prepared to consider an article on Poussin as theorist, but you will understand that I cannot possibly commission such an article.

Yours sincerely,
[T. S. Eliot]

TO *Edward W. Titus*[1]   CC

6 January 1932[2]   [Faber & Faber Ltd]

Dear Mr Titus,

I have under weigh [*sic*] an essay which I think might do for your collection of *Contemporaries*. It is concerned with the relation of the poet at the present time, on the one hand to his limited public, and on the other to his own political and religious beliefs. Nowadays when nearly everyone who thinks at all is more or less compelled to attend to political matters, it seems to me opportune. I am not discussing personalities nor am I advocating any particular political or social or economic policy in this paper. I should like to know whether you consider the subject suitable.

If the answer is in the affirmative, I should like to know whether payment is to be upon receipt (though this was stated by Mr Drake in his letter of October 29th);[3] and also whether it is understood that I may use the article in any other way after publication of the volume; and finally whether it is understood that in the event of the volume not appearing by June 30th next I am then at liberty to use the article in any other way I choose.

Sincerely yours,
[T. S. Eliot]

1–E. W. Titus (1870–1952), publisher; proprietor of the Black Manikin Press, 1926–32. A Polish-born American, in 1924 he set up a bookshop in Paris called 'At the Sign of the Black Manikin'. He was married to Helena Rubinstein, 1908–37, and profits from her cosmetics business supported his press. Titus published twenty-five books (including a version of *Lady Chatterley's Lover*, 1929); and he was owner–editor of the magazine *This Quarter*, 1929–32.
2–Mistyped '1931'.
3–Lawrence Drake (writing on behalf of Titus) had promised the sum of twenty guineas (£21) for an article he had discussed with TSE; payment was to be made on receipt of the piece, which would appear in *Contemporaries 1931* – 'the first of a yearly collection of previously unpublished stories, poems, essays and plays by American and British writers'.

TO *St Clair Donaldson*[1]

7 January 1932   [Faber & Faber Ltd]

My dear Lord Bishop,

I thank you for your kind letter of 29th December, in which you make a suggestion which would be very attractive to me even without the offices of the Warden of All Souls.[2] It would give me very great pleasure to come and give such a talk as you propose, but I am afraid that my other engagements preclude acceptance. The most of my spare time from the present moment must be given to preparing four broadcast talks to be delivered in March, and as the subject of these is everything in general but nothing in particular, I know that I shall have to expend much time in their preparation.[3] Furthermore if I have the time left during February or March to give a talk out of London I am really pledged to go to Kelham for that purpose at the first opportunity. So I am afraid that there is little possibility of my being able to undertake such a responsibility – which is rendered greater by the standing of your other contributors as well as by the seriousness of the subject – until I return from America in the spring of 1933.

With very many thanks and regrets,

I am,

Your Lordship's obedient Servant,

[T. S. Eliot]

1–St Clair Donaldson (1863–1935), who had been the first Anglican Archbishop of Brisbane, 1905–21, was Bishop of Salisbury from 1921.

2–Donaldson invited TSE to give a talk at Salisbury in Lent, on 12 Feb. or 11 Mar., on an issue relating to their faith and obligations as Christians. He hoped that TSE might 'take a text' from the last page of *Thoughts After Lambeth*, where he remarked: 'The world is trying the experiment of attempting to form a civilized but non-Christian mentality.'

3–TSE contributed four talks to the series 'The Modern Dilemma' (Mar. 1932). See further Michael Coyle, '"This rather elusory broadcast technique": T. S. Eliot and the Genre of the Radio Talk', *ANQ* 11 (Fall 1998); Coyle in *T. S. Eliot and the Turning World*, ed. Jewel Spears Brooker.

TO *Francis W. Pember*[1]   CC

7 January 1932   [Faber & Faber Ltd]

My dear Warden,

Thank you for your note of December 31.[2] It was a pleasure to hear from you after so many years, and it would have been an added pleasure if I could have accepted the Bishop of Salisbury's kind invitation which is a very attractive one. I have had, however, to write to him to explain that four broadcast talks in March will consume most of my time and energy, and that I have another tentative engagement during that period to speak out of London, to which I should be obliged to give priority if I can go anywhere at all.

I am flattered by your opinion of my very elementary pamphlet on Dante,[3] which is not, I fear, of a scholarship calculated to impress the author of *Musa Feriata*, of which I have, by the way, a review for the next *Criterion*.[4] I hope you will be interested in it.

Yours sincerely,

[T. S. Eliot]

TO *H. B. Parkes*[5]   CC

7 January 1932   [*The Criterion*]

Dear Mr Parkes,

I have now read the very interesting essay on Puritanism enclosed with your letter of November 7th.[6] It strikes me as extremely able. What I

---

1 – Francis Pember (1862–1954); lawyer and academic; Warden of All Souls, Oxford, 1914–32.

2 – Pember, who had met TSE when he visited All Souls as a guest of GCF, wrote to petition TSE to accept an invitation from the Bishop of Salisbury to give an address or talk at Salisbury.

3 – 'I have read it twice, & shall read it again. My only quarrel with it was that it was not longer.' (See Stuart Y. McDougal, 'T. S. Eliot's Metaphysical Dante', in *Dante Among the Moderns*, ed. McDougal [1985], 57–81).

4 – See D. O. Malcolm's review of Pember, *Musa Feriata*, in *C.* 11 (Apr. 1932), 523–5.

5 – Henry Bamford Parkes (1904–72), English-born academic and author; Professor of History at New York University from 1930.

6 – Parkes wrote on 2 Nov. (not 7 Nov.): 'In the enclosed essay I have attempted to define the differences between Calvinism and Catholicism more clearly than has previously been done, and to show how Calvinism ended inevitably in the death of all religion and the loss of the Christian tradition. You may not find it *Criterion* material; but I am hoping that it may interest you, especially as the ideas on which it is based are derived so largely from the writings of yourself and of Dawson and Maritain.'

do not feel, however, is that this is a subject particularly apposite for presentation to an English public. It would be more accurate to say that it is not quite suitable or effective in this form. There is of course a parallel generation in England, and the history of New England theology gives a very good view of the rapidity with which heresy spreads. But, however, people are very slow to apply to their own history lessons drawn from foreign or colonial material. A smaller essay on the development of liberal theology in England might be extremely valuable. I should very much like to see more of your work especially such as might primarily interest the English public.

Yours sincerely,
[T. S. Eliot]

TO *Bonamy Dobrée*[1]
TS Brotherton

7 January 1932   *The Criterion*

Dear Bonamy, +,

I had not read the review of H.D. until I heard from you, and even then was able to read it with an unclouded mind. Owing to your handwriting I did not appreciate that you were the author until a second reading of your note.[2] It struck me in reading as a review distinctly above the level on which the *T.L.S.* ordinarily reviews poetry, and obviously by someone who knew what he was talking about. I have not seen the book but think that in the main I should be quite in agreement. It only struck me that one or two sentences were a bit hurriedly constructed and needed reading more than once in order to get their sense, but perhaps this was a defect of type-reading.

'I am an Englishman, 26 years old; but have lived in America (solely for financial reasons) since I left Oxford in 1927. I have spent the best part of the last four years studying the religious history of New England, and expect to have a long book on this subject ready within the next year. I have previously published a biography of Jonathan Edwards (in the fall of 1930; a potboiler, which however sold badly and had undeservedly good reviews); and have contributed articles to *New England Quarterly*, *Dictionary of American Biography*, etc.' Other works included 'New England in the Seventeen-Thirties', *The New England Quarterly* 3: 3 (July 1930), 397–419; *Marxism: An Autopsy* (1939).

1 – Bonamy Dobrée (1891–1974), scholar, editor and critic: see Biographical Register.

2 – 'Poems by H. D.' – on *Red Roses for Bronze* – *TLS*, 31 Dec. 1931, 1052: 'Hers is a bold talent but it must not be stretched too far; and so long as she is content to remain within its limitations, her poems give great pleasure as the expression and communication of a delightful mood.' BD had requested on 31 Dec. 1931, 'It's the first time I have even done a serious review of poetry since 1913! I *really* want your criticism of this.'

There is one matter, about which I have written to Harold as he is away at the moment, on which I should like your own confidential opinion, as it obviously cannot be discussed openly in that way at the meeting. I wish you would let me know from your own reading of the specimen in the current number of the *Criterion* whether F.S.F. is likely to be a good reviewer of verse.[1] I have a feeling that his summary dealing with young poets is not quite what we want. I have already received a letter to the Editor from our friend Leavis, the opponent of Summers [Gummers][2] on this point, which I shall publish.

Yours ever,
Thomas+

+ I omit variants.

FROM *Vivien Eliot* TO *Ralph Hodgson*[3]　　　　　MS Beinecke

10 January 1932　　　　　　68 Clarence Gate Gardens

Dear Mr Hodgson,

We hope you have not forgotten that you agreed to come to dinner here on Friday next 15th at 7.30 & we are looking forward to seeing you & Miss Bullinger [*sic*] here. It will be a great treat.

With kindest regards, & please bring your *nice puppy*.

Yours sincerely,
Vivienne Haigh Eliot

TO *C. A. Siepmann*[4]　　　　　　　　　　TS BBC

10 January 1932　　　　　　Faber & Faber Ltd

Dear Siepmann,

I am writing to ask whether you will be so gracious as to let me have complete copies of Macmurray's talks, as you did of Dawson's.[5] I do not

---

1 – F. S. Flint, 'Verse Chronicle', C. 11 (Jan. 1932), 278–81.

2 – Montgomery Belgion: see TSE to him, 2 Mar. 1932.

3 – See TSE to Hodgson, 17 Mar. 1932.

4 – Charles Arthur Siepmann (1899–1985), radio producer and educationalist: see Biographical Register.

5 – 'The Modern Dilemma: A Symposium' was a series of twenty-four talks broadcast by the BBC on Sundays, with contributions by TSE, John Macmurray, Christopher Dawson and others. Macmurray (1891–1976), British moral philosopher, was at this time Professor of the Philosophy of Mind and Logic at University College, London.

expect to be able to hear all of them – Sunday afternoon one is usually out or else has visitors – and even if I do, I shall want the text, and not the truncated text of *The Listener*. I expect more to bite on than from Dawson – not that I did not like what Dawson said; but as you know, I felt that another method of arranging the problems was wanted.

If you should still be in want of another man to fill the gap, I think that I might induce Kenneth Pickthorn,[1] if that appealed to you; but if you can get Smyth,[2] I should not suggest having Pickthorn too.

Sincerely yours,
T. S. Eliot

FROM *Vivien Eliot* TO *Ottoline Morrell*[3] MS Texas

Monday 11 January 1932 68 Clarence Gate Gardens

Dearest Ottoline

I do hope you have kept well over the weekend. The party is arranged to begin at 8.30 tomorrow. I *do hope* you will feel able to come. It would be horrible if you do not. Alida Monro is coming, I hope & trust, & Robert Gordon George[4] will be here, but I do not think there will be anyone else that you know, although they are all charming & entertaining people. Perhaps you would like Alida Monro to come *with* you?[5]

Yours with *much love*. (I personally *adored* your last tea party.[6] But everything at your house is always perfect. I intended to write at once to you, but have had a *most* worrying and wretched weekend.)

Ever yrs. affectly.
Vivienne Haigh Eliot

1–See TSE to Pickthorn, 15 June 1932.
2–See TSE to Smyth, 23 Jan. 1932.
3–Lady Ottoline Morrell (1873–1938), hostess and patron: see Biographical Register.
4–Robert Esmonde Gordon George – better known as Robert Sencourt (1890–1969) – critic, historian and biographer: see Biographical Register.
5–OM noted at the Eliots' party that the guests were seated on rows of chairs like a prayer meeting; an exotic lady sang, and TSE recited some verses. It struck her as being very 1870s: 'no talk, only readings, pianoforte records & recitations' (Journal of OM: Goodman Papers).
6–VHE had been to a party at OM's house, in company with L. A. G. Strong and Ralph Hodgson – and presumably TSE?

13 January 1932   [Faber & Faber Ltd]

Dear Mr Greenslet,

Thank you very much for your kind letter of the 4th instant. I am not at all sure that du Bos's diary is a book which could be expected to have much general sale in England in translation.[2] It has already, I understand, had considerable currency here in French. Nevertheless we should certainly be interested to see Bandler's translation and to know what parts of the book and how much he is using. Personally it is more because I have a high opinion of Bandler's abilities and know that he has gone into the subject very conscientiously that I am interested. So I should like to go further into the matter with you. Is there any of the material ready which we could see?

As for the second paragraph of your letter, I now understand from Hughes Massie and Co. that you wish me to take it up with them on your behalf so I will not advert upon it in this letter.[3]

I am very much honoured and pleased by the invitation to become a guest of the St Botolph Club while in Boston. I shall certainly hope to make use of the club and to make your acquaintance. When I had to leave Germany rather hurriedly in 1914 one of the books among other articles which I had to leave behind in my flight was your essay on Walter Pater.[4]

Yours sincerely,

[T. S. Eliot]

1 – Ferris Greenslet (1875–1959), author and literary adviser; director of Houghton Mifflin Co., Boston. His books include *James Russell Lowell: His Life and Work* (1905), *Under the Bridge: An Autobiography* (1943), *The Lowells and Their Seven Worlds* (1946).
2 – Houghton Mifflin Company was considering a translation by Bernard Bandler of excerpts from the diary of Charles du Bos; but it could not move forward except by importing sheets from Britain. 'Is there any chance that your house would be willing to pull the laboring oar?'
3 – Houghton Mifflin hoped to be able to issue next fall, to coincide with TSE's appointment as Norton Lecturer, a new edition of *TWL*, a collection of recent poems, 'or whatever'.
4 – Greenslet responded (28 Jan.) to this remark by TSE: 'It is quite a kick, as the saying is, to hear that my rather precious WALTER PATER was among your German *vestigia* in 1914 . . . If I were to write on him now, the result, I am afraid, would be a horse of a very different hue.'

TO *A. L. Rowse*[1]   TS Exeter

13 January 1932   *The Criterion*

My dear Rowse,

Many thanks for your letter of the 9th.[2] I don't mind in the least your having been furious with me for giving your book to Smyth so long as you acquit me of any personal malice or even mere love of mischief. Please reflect at any rate upon my declaration that had Smyth written a book about politics I should have asked you to review it. The most you can say is that I am a stirrer-up of strife, although I cannot say like Bertrand de Born in respect of yourself and Smyth *'perch'io partii cosi giunte persone, partito porto il mio cerebro lasso'*.[3]

The serious matter of the moment is, however, your letter to the Editor.[4] Of course I naturally consider myself obliged to print any letter of protest

1–A. L. Rowse (1903–1997), historian; Fellow of All Souls, Oxford: see Biographical Register.

2–ALR wrote on 9 Jan., of Charles Smyth's review of his *Politics and the Younger Generation* (C. 11 [Jan. 1932], 304–13), 'I was furious with you for sending him the book to review, for one might have known what would happen. One can't really be annoyed with him, for he's such an ass that he wouldn't know any better. But you ought to have done. (I shall talk myself into a fury of indignation again, you can see!)

'Several people, like [J. M.] Murry and [E. L.] Woodward [Bursar of All Souls], have written and protested to me about it; I told them that their protests might more suitably have been directed to you.

'I dare say you wd agree now that it was a wretched piece of work, with hardly a single argument in it directed to what I said, and ending up in a sort of sermon about Holy Baptism and Penance!

'But the only serious point worth considering is this; that you missed the opportunity of securing a really valuable criticism of the book. I shouldn't have minded how damning it was, if good. In point of fact, what wd have interested me most of all, wd have been a criticism by a real pucker Marxist, if possible a Communist. He wd have excommunicated me all right, but it is only arguments from that quarter that concern me, & which I really fear. I don't care a damn what ordinary bourgeois critics think . . . I sat down and wrote a letter of pure invective against the Revd Chas. Smyth. I think I'll send it on with this for the *Criterion*; all my friends tell me Mr Smyth is not worthy of notice. (They know him.) So don't consider it a serious production. If it's not amusing, don't print it; on the other hand, if it's libellous, don't print it.

'But I gather from your essay [on Whibley], you are rather sympathetic to invective!'

3 – 'Perch'io partii così giunte persone, / partito porto il mio cerebro, lasso! / dal suo principio ch' è in questo troncone' (*Inferno* 28: 139–40): 'Because I parted persons thus united, I carry my brain, ah me! parted from its source which is in this trunk' (Temple Classics edn, 1900, 1932).

4–ALR had despatched this undated draft Letter to the Editor from St Austell, Cornwall: 'In the best academic circles, to which your reviewer refers me, the Rev. Charles Smyth is known to be a buffoon. I am therefore the more disappointed, though I cannot be surprised, that you should have seen fit to let him review my book on politics. It does not matter to me,

from an outraged author, which is not either blasphemous, obscene or libellous. I do not consider your letter either obscene or libellous, and not particularly blasphemous; and as for the matter of libel, in any case I should prevent Smyth from being such a fool as to take any action beyond writing a similar letter in the style of which you are both masters. But seriously I don't think the present letter is calculated to do your own cause any good, and I think you could write a much better one. I have often written angry letters to Editors in the evening, and I have always found it better to keep them until the morning, when I either wrote a fresh letter or none at all. It seems to me that in controversy as in boxing the man who loses his temper is lost. So I return your letter (as it is in manuscript) merely to ask you to re-read it, and see if you cannot do better in your

---

still less to any of the causes which I advocate, what this person may or may not think. It only seems to me desirable in the interest of the good name of the *Criterion* as a serious and reputable journal, that a protest should be recorded against the employer of such a reviewer on these subjects.

'For what is one to think – I hope I am regarding his work as impersonally as may be – of a long review in which not an argument is advanced against any of the positions which the reviewer so heartily dislikes? It is fairly obvious that he either fails to understand them, or is unwilling to do them justice.

'The review may be divided into three parts. The first is given up to a long examination of the style in which the book is written. Fancy devoting two whole pages to such a subject! Only a solemn ass could have failed to see that the book's usage of grammar was deliberate; and there were not wanting plenty of people to point out its solecisms, even if I hadn't recognised them for myself. I set myself in this book of abstract argument the difficult aim of keeping as near as possible to the colloquial – I believe that in any case to be a good principle for a living prose style, and more than ever necessary to be held in view, since so many current books on politics and economics are written in a jargon of their own, divorced from living speech. And far more subtle and discerning intelligences than Mr Smyth have recognized the aim I had in mind, and testified to the effectiveness, in general, of the result.

'The second part was taken up by a travesty of the book's argument. But since I do not regard Mr Smyth as competent to judge any of the subject-matter, from the first page to the last, I would not specify any complaint.

'The third part of his review is hortatory and has nothing to do with my book. God knows what it has to do with; I recognize only the familiar sermon-style, the meaningless clamour of the resounding pulpit.

'But why couldn't my book have been sent at least to an intelligent person like Father D'Arcy? – Since the circle of possible reviewers is so restricted to parsons – I had almost said, to priests, – when I remembered a certain little difference between Mr Smyth and Father D'Arcy in this respect too. And perhaps the Rev. Charles Smyth might be confined to dealing with Holy Baptism and the Divine Right of Kings, and to that "political philosophy that begins with the Nunc Dimittis, and ends in this world with the Agnus Dei, to find its consummation in the Adoration of the Lamb", – all subjects with which he is as familiar and perhaps qualified to deal in. – So long as your readers and I are delivered from the terrors of his views on political and social questions.'

own interest. If, however, on reflexion you still wish the letter to appear in its present form, I will print it.[1]

Ever yours affectionately,
T. S. Eliot

TO *Geoffrey Faber*[2]

13 January 1932   [Faber & Faber Ltd]

Dear Geoffrey,

I am sorry to bother you, though it is merely to consult you on a matter of decorum. I wish you would read the enclosed letter to the Editor from A. L. Rowse and tell me whether you agree with the attitude I have adopted. I showed Rowse's letter to Morley, Blake and de la Mare, and they were all of the opinion that it would do Rowse no good. Blake and de la Mare both thought that I should refuse to print it. Morley thought that I ought to print it because otherwise I should merely inflame Rowse's sense of grievance. So I have taken a middle course. I think it would be a good thing if Rowse would try to write a reasonable letter against Smyth, but he will never become a real master of invective until he learns to keep his temper.[3]

Yours ever,
[T. S. E.]

1 – ALR replied to this letter (n.d.): 'Of course I acquit you of any malice or mischief-making in the matter: in fact, it never entered my head. But I do accuse you of having very uncertain academic standards: or else you wd have known the opinion rightly entertained of the Rev. C. Smyth at Cambridge as well as at Oxford: anywhere else, e.g., here, he is not known at all.

'The whole point of my letter evidently escaped you. I didn't expect you to think it good . . . For it wasn't intended as a reply: I do not consider Mr Smyth's opinions worth taking any notice of. My letter was only intended as a deliberate insult.'

Rowse's atrabilious 'Letter to the Editor' did not appear in C.

2 – Geoffrey Faber (1889–1961), publisher and poet: see Biographical Register.

3 – No reply found.

TO *Douglas Jerrold*[1]

13 January 1932   [Faber & Faber Ltd]

My dear Jerrold,

An able young historian of my acquaintance would be interested to write a book on Charles I, and I gather would approach the problem from an extreme High Tory point of view. But he says that he has heard a rumour that you are doing, or are going to do very much the same thing (I believe also that he is a member of your church, but I am not sure). The point is that if you have begun or have in mind to write such a book he does not wish to compete with you, but would prefer to turn to other subjects. Is it asking too much to beg you to let me know whether you have any such intention? I don't want the lad to take so much trouble in vain.

Yours ever,

[T. S. Eliot]

TO *Cyril Clemens*[2]

14 January 1932   [Faber & Faber Ltd]

Dear Mr Clemens,

I thank you for your letter of the 24th December, and for the kind thought of the Society and yourself.[3] I hope that I may be able to make your acquaintance when I visit St Louis as I confidently hope to do.

Yours very sincerely,

[T. S. Eliot]

1–Douglas Jerrold (1893–1964): publisher and author; director of Eyre & Spottiswoode, 1929–59, Chairman from 1945; editor of *The English Review*, 1931–6 – the organ of 'real Toryism' – revived after WW2 as the *New English Review Magazine*. A fundamentalist Roman Catholic, convinced of the moral void of contemporary life and arguing for the restitution of a Christian social order, on occasion his ideals and inclinations ran to the right of the Conservative Party: he came to praise Mussolini's methods and to sympathise with the British Union of Fascists. Though by no means a racist, he confused political rigour with moral righteousness. TSE grew increasingly sceptical towards Jerrold's attitudes. Jerrold's works include *Georgian Adventure* (1937), *The Necessity of Freedom* (1938) and *Britain and Europe, 1900–1940* (1941).

2–Cyril Coniston Clemens (1902–99) was born in St Louis, Missouri, and graduated from Washington University. A distant cousin of Samuel Langhorne Clemens, in 1930 he was founder and president of the International Mark Twain Society; founder-editor of the *Mark Twain Quarterly*, 1936–82. Works include biographies of Twain and President Harry Truman.

3–Clemens congratulated TSE on his appointment as Norton Professor – 'a post which you will honor far more than it can honor you'.

TO *John Middleton Murry*[1]   TS Northwestern

14 January 1932   Faber & Faber Ltd

Dear John,

I read *The Fallacy of Economics*[2] with enjoyment and was very largely in agreement. I was only slightly disappointed in one respect. I mean that it seemed to me that the occasion justifies much greater ferocity than you have adopted. But perhaps you have your own reasons for deliberate quietness of tone. There are one or two smaller points which I will take the liberty of querying when I send proofs, but the only question I raise before the manuscript goes to the printer is whether the note on profit should be included. For my part I am all for leaving it out as a matter of pamphlet tactics. For pamphlet purposes it seems to me that a note like this added at the end merely weakens the effect, and whereas you have made a very good finish on page 43, you seem to me, whether right or wrong in your subsequent reasoning, to effect merely an anti-climax by adding a note which tends to bring the plane down to that of ordinary professional economists, any one of whom could, I am sure, knock you or me through the ropes the moment we consented to accept their own sphere of discourse. My main point, however, is that I think an appended note superfluous unless it is essential, and the effect of your pamphlet is much more impressive without it.

I return the note as I presume you have not made a copy, but alternatively if you really consider it essential, could it not be in some way interpolated rather than put at the end?

Affectionately yours,

Tom

TO *Geoffrey Curtis*[3]   TS Houghton

14 January 1932   Faber & Faber Ltd

My dear Curtis,

I was very glad to get your letter of the 12th November, far more glad than my delay in replying might lead you to think. Many thanks for telling me more about your brotherhood. I wish that I might come down and

1–John Middleton Murry (1889–1957), writer, critic, editor: see Biographical Register.
2–JMM, *The Fallacy of Economics* (Criterion Miscellany 37, 1932).
3–The Revd Geoffrey Curtis (1902–81): Vice-Principal, Dorchester Missionary College, Burcote, Abingdon, Oxfordshire.

visit you in the beautiful country about St. Ives. You have my frequent thoughts about your vocation, whether to Lichfield or elsewhere.[1]

But meanwhile what exactly are you doing? Is it regular parochial cure of souls or some more specialized work?

About the piece of prose which you enclose. I think that it is qua story or sketch rather slight. The centre of the piece is of course the sermon itself which is good, but I don't feel that you have made the setting for it sufficiently solid and dense. I don't quite get, before the sermon, worked up to the proper feeling of awe and doom. Such an occasion would surely have one of two effects upon individuals according to their temperaments. They would either be numbed into a dull anaesthesia or their mind and senses would be more sharply stimulated than ever before in their lives. I should like to see more clearly the contrast between the two types.

About your Lyra Apostolica I should like to encourage you to pursue the hope of getting these published. I must tell you frankly that it would not make a type of book for which my firm would be the most suitable publishers, and I am trying to think where else it might do better. Is there ever any prospect of your having to be in London for a day or two? If so I should like to talk the matter over with you.[2]

Yours ever affectionately,

T. S. Eliot

1 – Curtis wrote, 12 Nov. 1931: 'Christa Seva Sangha . . . is a very real attempt to let the gospel come alive in India released from its European graveclothes. The brotherhood has a Franciscan spirit but no scrupulosity about ransacking all the riches of Eastern metaphysical and devotion . . . I enclose under separate cover (1) an undergraduate prose outpouring (2) a poem which I've just written. I thought that the first might be a prelude, the second a concluding item in a little anonymous autobiographical volume called "Lyra Subapostolica". Some of the items seem to have wings, to have a certainly apologetic value for strays such as I once was.' 'Paschal Christmas' (*Philippians* III: 12–16) opens: The harassed soul her pride still quite unhealed / Cheered herself jadedly how she would come / In garments newly purpled Lord from Bozrah's field / Having trod the winepress solitarily home.' He added to his letter: 'Pray that I may be guided aright as to whether to return to theological teaching. I have been asked to go as vice-principal to Lichfield, a college that has almost, perhaps quite, touched bottom as regards reputation. There is a new principal who is striving to reconstitute it into soundness.'

2 – Curtis responded on 17 Jan.: 'It is a joy to me [to] think of you and a greater joy to be writing to you . . . There is none among a multitude of friends with whom I can so freely share part of my deepest experience.'

TO *I. A. Richards*[1]

TS Magdalene

14 January 1932   *The Criterion*

My dear Richards,

I have just received a book by Max Eastman called *The Literary Mind* which I beg you to review for the *Criterion*. He seems to condemn every living writer who has any connection with literature whatever, including yourself. But there are two reasons why you should review the book. One is that Eastman allows you and no one else a little merit for having attempted to introduce scientific method into literature, though he seems to consider that beyond that you have made a pretty hopeless mess of it. The other is that he has an elaborate appendix attacking your views. But of everybody who might suitably review the book you are the only person whose name will carry any authority.[2]

When are you coming up to London again?

Yours in haste,
T. S. Eliot

TO *Michael Sadleir*[3]

CC

14 January 1932   [*The Criterion*]

Dear Mr Sadleir,

Several years ago you will remember that your firm published a second series of Tudor translations arranged by Charles Whibley. At Whibley's invitation I wrote an introduction to the *Ten Tragedies of Seneca*. I had no negotiations with your firm about the matter. I think that Whibley and myself both disliked anything in the nature of business-like methods. The arrangement was entirely private between him and myself. I sent him the manuscript and received his personal cheque, and that closed the matter. I now propose to include this essay with acknowledgments in a new volume of collected essays which I am preparing. It seemed to me no more than courtesy to notify you of the fact. I hope that the Seneca sold well, but

1–I. A. Richards (1893–1979), theorist of literature, education and communication studies: see Biographical Register

2–IAR agreed on 15 Jan. to write on Eastman – 'another expert at misunderstanding everybody though not as bad as Belgion' (*Letters*, 63). See review of Eastman, *The Literary Mind: Its Place in an Age of Science* (1931): C. 12 (Oct. 1932), 150–5; collected in *Complementarities*.

3–Michael Sadleir (1888–1957), author, publisher, bibliographer; director of the publishers Constable & Co.

I fear that there was not the same demand for the second series as there was for the first, and no doubt in both series the profits were reaped by the second-hand booksellers.

Yours very truly
[T. S. Eliot]

TO *J. D. Aylward*[1]   CC

14 January 1932   [Faber & Faber Ltd]

My dear Aylward,

I am in arrears with you to the extent of two letters. I first apologise for never having acknowledged your tempting invitation to take a land cruise with you on a Sunday. The truth about that is that my domestic obligations usually engross my weekends, and as my wife has a microscopic car somewhat similar to yours, differing only in that it will carry four people in a state of suffocation and extreme discomfort instead of carrying two people airily and comfortably, I have very little excuse for scooting about the country in someone else's car on a Sunday, although I should have liked to have the excuse of meeting Mr Fothergill in your company.[2]

1 – James de Vine Aylward (1870–1966) had been a colleague and close friend at Lloyds Bank; author of *The Small-Sword in England, its History, its Forms, Its Makers, and its Masters* (1946); *The House of Angelo: A dynasty of swordsmen, with special reference to Domenica Angelo and his son Henry* (1953). On 8 Dec. 1955 TSE would tell Simon Nowell-Smith, Secretary and Librarian, London Library, that Aylward was 'an old man of well over eighty, who was at one time a colleague of mine in Lloyds Bank in the City. Before the First World War he had been a painter, and had made his living as a kind of minor Munnings – the resemblance applies only to their occupations as portrait painters of people's horses. Not being a Munnings, his means of livelihood vanished after 1914, and he took a job in the Bank, from which he is now retired on a small pension. Since his retirement he has made himself an authority on swords and swordsmanship, and knows more about 18th century small swords than anyone in England, and up to the age of about eighty was a very active fencer. He has already written one or two books on swords, and now appears to be concerned in writing about a Frenchman who established the first and last academy of equitation, deportment and swordsmanship in the time of Charles II.

'I give you all this information merely to explain that my friend is somewhat of an oddity, but that I know him very well.'

2 – Aylward had written, 23 Nov. 1931: 'Yesterday I was down the road in the fog, and on the way had a breather and a "glass of sherry wine" chez the one and only John Fothergill, now mine host of the Spread Eagle at Thame [Oxfordshire]. Conversation with John brought up the name of one Eliot, and John admitted to his shame that he was about the only lithery cyarkter of repute that he didn't know. You ought to meet the great John, who is one of the characters of the day . . . so why don't you come one Sunday – next Sunday if you like provided it be fine – and let me run you down there in the Bug . . . Nothing to report,

Now for your question of good English, not that I know any more about the subject than you do.[1] I agree wholeheartedly with you that 'craft and mystery' is to be treated as a single concept, and must therefore be used with a singular verb, and as you say that assumption rests upon the fact that you can correctly talk about 'craft and mystery' instead of 'The craft and the mystery'.

I have a good mind to walk into your den in Gracechurch Street one day and hail you out for a city lunch. At what time do you lunch nowadays? And I hope that you have now been elevated from the position which we once occupied together in a dark and foetid basement.

Yours ever sincerely
[T. S. Eliot]

TO *Hugh Macdonald*[2]

14 January 1932   [Faber & Faber Ltd]

Dear Macdonald,

You will remember that a couple of years ago we had some discussion about the length of time to be allowed for the Dryden volume before I reprinted my dialogue elsewhere, and that I declined a suggestion from some

---

[Lloyds] Bank more pestilential than ever, of course, and will certainly meet the fate of Sodom and the other show as soon as the Almighty has time to give it the whack it deserves.'
1–On 31 Dec 1931 Aylward posed a question about good English usage: 'Recently I wrote an article for the *Motor*, to which they gave a full page, and while I know that my casual scribblings are only journalism and not literature in any sense of the word, I really do like to write something resembling the language I was taught in my younger days.

'One of the town pests, however, seized upon the occasion to address a letter to me, in which he rebuked me for a grammatical error in language which, charitably, I suppose to have been intended for humour, but which was really distinctly uncouth.

'The sentence that raised his wrath was this:–
"The craft and mystery of the Road is . . . . . ."
'I thanked him profusely, and admitted that he was probably right, but took my stand on Fowler's *English Usage*, which says that compound words like "bread and butter" take the singular verb.

'It was (and is) my view that a "craft and mystery" is an indivisible unit, and therefore entitled to the singular. The phrase is obsolete, I know, but I think it is still kept alive by the City Companies. Further, the "craft and mystery" of anything is not two things, but one, the mystery implying (as I think) a further degree of initiation.'

'Do rebuke or comfort me, according to your conscience!'
2–Hugh Macdonald (1885–1958), who trained as a solicitor, went into partnership with Frederick Etchells to produce fine editions under the imprint of The Haslewood Books, 1924–31. His own works include *England's Helicon* (1925), *The Phoenix Nest* (1926), *John Dryden: A Bibliography of Early Editions and of Drydenianae* (1939), and *Portraits in Prose* (1946)

American periodical to reprint it by itself. I have not been up to now put to any inconvenience, because I have not wanted to reprint the paper until now; but at present I have in preparation a new volume of collected essays for the autumn, and I am anxious to include this dialogue. So I should like to hear from you, and perhaps we may lunch together before long.[1]

Yours ever,

[T. S. Eliot]

TO *G. B. Harrison*[2]   CC

14 January 1932   [Faber & Faber Ltd]

My dear Harrison,

I am proposing to include in a new volume of collected essays the 'Shakespeare and the Stoicism of Seneca' which I prepared several years ago for the Shakespeare Association, and which the Shakespeare Association published as a pamphlet.[3] I do not suppose for a moment that the Shakespeare Association can have any legal or moral objections to an enterprise which can hardly interfere with any demand there may be for the original pamphlet, but I should be very much obliged if you would let me know the official sanction of the Council, and at the same time might I have three more copies of the pamphlet with invoice.[4]

I am extremely sorry that I was unable to attend the last two meetings of the Council, and particularly that I could not be present at Granville Barker's inauguration.[5] When is there to be another meeting?

Yours sincerely,

[T. S. Eliot]

1 – Macdonald replied (n. d.); 'By all means make any use of your dialogue as soon as you wish. I have sent two copies of the book to you & charged the price to your firm. I wouldn't have charged you anything but for the fact that we are winding up the business with a heavy loss.'

2 – G. B. Harrison (1894–1991), literary scholar, wrote many studies of Shakespeare and his contemporaries, and would become renowned as general editor of several series of popular editions of Shakespeare. Having been taught at Queens' College, Cambridge, by E. M. W. Tillyard, Mansfield Forbes and I. A. Richards (he was proud to have been IAR's first pupil in English), he was at the time of this letter Assistant Lecturer in English at King's College, London, and Hon. Secretary of the Shakespeare Association.

3 – See Phillip L. Marcus, 'T. S. Eliot and Shakespeare', *Criticism* 9: 1 (Winter 1967), 63–78; Jason Harding, 'T. S. Eliot's Shakespeare', *Essays in Criticism* 62 (2012), 160–77.

4 – Harrison relayed the permission of the Council on 2 Feb.

5 – Granville Barker delivered his inaugural address as President of the Shakespeare Association, 'Associating with Shakespeare', on 25 Nov. 1931: published by the Association in 1932.

TO *W. Victor Ranford*[1]   CC

15 January 1932   [Faber & Faber Ltd]

Dear Father Ranford,

I am very glad to have your letter of the 13th January and it is as well that you wrote when you did, although I should have written to you this week in any case.[2] I have had regretfully to come to the conclusion that with the other work I have in hand I cannot possibly find time to lecture either in or out of London during the period in question. Apart from arrears of various sorts I have to prepare four broadcast talks to deliver on the successive Sundays in March and I anticipate considerable difficulty in the preparation. It might just be possible for me to do something in April or May, but this falls outside of your programme, and in any case I shall have so much to do between then and September that I should prefer not to make any further engagements until I return from America in May 1933.

I hope that you will not consider me much to blame for having flirted so long with the prospect of speaking to you at Kelham and holding out hopes which I am unable to gratify. I trust that you will perceive that my delay was due partly to my warm desire to pay a visit to Kelham and establish an acquaintance both with the place and its inmates. I trust that I may be permitted to think that for me this is merely a hope deferred.

Yours very regretfully
[T. S. Eliot]

TO *Michael Sadleir*   CC

19 January 1932   [*The Criterion*]

Dear Mr Sadleir,

Thank you for your letter of January 16th.[3] I must admit, however, that it causes me some surprise.

---

1 – The Revd William Victor Ranford, SSM (1902–61), wrote the entry on 'Sociology' in the *Encyclopaedia Britannica*, vol. 20 (1949).

2 – Ranford enquired whether TSE would be available to give a talk in Feb. or Mar.

3 – Sadleir maintained: 'We regard the introductions of the second series of the TUDOR TRANSLATIONS as being as much our copyright as though we had paid fees direct to their authors . . . Constable's were considerably out of pocket on the whole venture, and are naturally for that reason the less inclined to let such proprietary rights as they possess in the series go by the board.'

On every other occasion on which I have provided an introduction to a reprinted text I have stipulated to use my own contribution in any other way that I thought fit after the expiry of two years from the publication of the book, and in no case has this right been contested. I may mention among other such pieces of work my introduction to the Everyman Library Edition of Pascal's *Pensées*.

The only reason why I made no explicit stipulation at all in the case of my introduction to the *Ten Tragedies of Seneca* was that I was dealing entirely with a personal friend. As I observed in my previous letter I had no negotiations with your firm whatever. If your firm had in view that any possible loss on the series might be partially recouped by possession of the rights over the introductory notes, it seems to me that this should have been made explicit. The arrangement between Mr Whibley and yourselves, whatever it may have been, did not seem to me to concern myself as I had no cognizance of it.

I have discussed the matter with a friend who has considerable knowledge of copyright law, and I have also looked at the sixth edition of Copinger's *Law of Copyright*, and cannot find anything applicable to the present situation. If you maintain your present point of view in the matter perhaps you will be so kind as to let me know on what authoritative statement or legal ruling it is based. You will understand that unless I can be convinced that my position is mistaken I cannot consider making application to you for a right which I believe to be my own.

Yours very truly
[T. S. Eliot]

TO *Erik Mesterton*[1]

TS Erik Mesterton

20 January 1932   *The Criterion*

Dear Mr Mesterton,[2]

I have your long letter of the 14th and as you say that you are rather pressed for time I will hasten to answer it although briefly. I am very glad of course to hear that you have decided to translate the whole poem.

---

1 – Erik Mesterton (1903–2004): Swedish author, critic, translator; editor during the 1930s of the poetry magazine *Spektrum*, founded in 1931. With the poet and novelist Karin Boye (1900–41), he translated *TWL*. See *The Waste Land: Some Commentaries*, trans. Llewellyn Jones (1943): from a prefatory essay to *Dikter i Urval* (1942); and Mesterton, *Speglingar: Essäer, brev, översättningar*, ed. Lars Fyhr and Gunnar D. Hannson (1985).
2 – This letter was first published in Mesterton's *Speglingar*, 235–8.

Most of your corrections of Curtius and Menasce are quite justified. I will refer to them as you did by lines.[1]

Line 35. You are right about the word 'first'. One might have said 'd'abord' in French but certainly 'pour la première fois' would have been more natural, and I understand the impossibility of putting it in one word.

Line 49. You can give either the equivalent for 'rock' or for 'cliff'. There is no particular intention of referring to either use of the word 'rock' in the poem. Here it is definitely 'sea-rocks', i.e. a siren.

Line 70. I see no great loss in omitting the ships if there are metrical difficulties.

---

1 – Mesterton wrote: 'I wish you would let me consult you on some points regarding the translation. Compared with Curtius and Menasce, we are at a disadvantage in not being able to get the Swedish text corrected by the author.

Line 35. You gave me hyacinths first a year ago. Both Menasce and Curtius leave out the word "first" (which I take to mean "for the first time")' we have also left it out, as else the line would be too long: for the one syllable in English there would be five in Swedish.

49. the Lady of the Rocks. I do not understand ll. 49–50. Is the same word to be used for "Rocks" here as for "rock" in Part V.?

70. in the ships at Mylae. This phrase is one of the very few which we have not translated quite literally, for metrical reasons. Is the mention of the ships essential? Are we taking too great a liberty by saying instead: "You who were with me when we fought at Mylae"?

94. Huge sea-wood fed with copper . . ., which I understand as oak wood from a wrecked or waterlogged copper-bottomed ship; it burned green because of being saturated with copper hydroxide.

96. carved dolphin. If, as I suppose, "the coloured stone" of the fireplace is porphyry, would it be permissible to substitute, again for metrical reasons, "porphyry" for "carved"?

102. and still the world pursues. Curtius (mis)translates "pursues" by "fährt fort", which can only mean "continues" – I take the verb in the transitive sense of pursuing a prey.

128. Shakespeherian Rag. Curtius: dieser Fetzen Shakespeare. But "Rag" being spelt with a capital R, I take the word, not in the sense of scrap, but of ragtime. As ragtime is not in common use in Swedish, we would put "jazz", simply.

273. The barges wash etc. Curtius: Die Kähne *streifen* Treibende Scheiter. The German verb is transitive and means "graze", "touch"; I take "wash" as intransitive: to be carried or driven along, by waves or stream. There was a comma, I remember, in the text first printed in *The Criterion* and *The Dial*. However, there seems to exist no such sense of "wash" as that given by Curtius.

276 and 300. the Isle of Dogs – Margate Sands. Curtius and Menasce have translated both of these, but is it right to translate proper names? Margate Sands, with capital letters, indicating a place-name in this case also.

372. Cracks and reforms and bursts etc. Are these words nouns or verbs? Curtius and Menasce both take them as nouns (C. renders "reforms" by "Neubildungen – " – if a noun, the word in such a sense is itself a Neubildung, isn't it?) I hesitate as I have seen this line quoted by an American critic who evidently took the three words as verbs, having "the city over the mountains" as their subject.

404. an age of prudence. "age" is to me "time", "period" – our time; Curtius and Menasce both have "era", in that sense. But Mrs Boye prefers the sense of "life", "lifetime"; I promised her to ask you.

Line 94. You are quite correct.

Line 96. Porphyry will do.

Line 102. You are correct.

Line 128. ditto.

Line 273. By 'Wash' I mean both to be carried along by the stream and swayed from side to side by the varying gusts of wind in land-locked waters.

Line 276 & 300. It is better to leave these place names in English.

Line 372. The three words are intransitive verbs, the city being the subject.

Line 404. 'age' means any long period of time with the suggestion of bringing one into old age.

As to your next paragraph I do not think that any more difficulties are presented in translation than in the original.[1]

Line 198. Refers certainly to the Sweeny [*sic*] poems, but not by intention to the dialogues which I have renamed *Sweeny Agonistes*, because they were not written at the time. A reference to it is suitable, however, although the dialogue is only obtainable in back numbers of *The Criterion*.

Line 182. You seem to have missed the quotation from Spenser's *Epithalamion*. There is no reference to Byron or Shelley. I do not seem to remember any antecedent for 'City, City' in the Old Testament* <*but cf.

---

1 – 'As to the *Notes*,' Mesterton remarked, 'I wish I could persuade you to give a few more notes and references.' In particular, he hoped for elucidation of Belladonna and of *red rock* in Part I. He went on: 'Would you permit me to add, as did M. de Menasce, a few supplementary notes, to be distinguished from your own by being put within brackets? "Jug jug", for instance, ought to be explained as being the conventional transcription used in old English poetry, of which no Swedish equivalent exists. Line *198*, a reference to the Sweeney poems and to "Wanna Go Home, Baby?" L. *172*, the reference to Hamlet. L. *182*: the allusion to the rivers of Babylon etc. needs of course not to be pointed out; but is there no particular reference to any individual line or poem by Byron or Shelley here? L. *259*: O City, City, I associate with a similar phrase in one of the Prophets; but I forget where it occurs, and only know it in Swedish. "London Bridge is falling down" etc. Menasce calls a "chanson populaire": I thought it was rather a children's game or nursery rhyme. I have only heard of "London Bridge is broken down" – is that another version, or did you alter the rhyme? L. *428*: O swallow swallow – is there an allusion to Swinburne here? L. *431*: Why then ile fit you etc. (mistranslated by Menasce (Or donc, je *te rapiécerai*) I think, if "fit you" means "furnish you" with what you want). "Hieronymo's mad againe", this quotation I have not been able to find in the Temple Dramatists text, although I have read the drama several times. The significance of these two quotations from Kyd, in the context of your poem, is quite obscure to me. But I do not imagine it can be explained.'

Our Lord's prophecy over Jerusalem.>[1] There is of course the reference given to Baudelaire.

'London Bridge etc.' is a children's game, and my version is probably merely a variant of yours.

Line 428. The reference is not particularly to Swinburne though I had that in mind, but to the whole history of the swallow in literature since the affair of Procne and Philomela. The swallow of course is also a reference to the nightingale.

Line 431. You are right. It is 'furnish'.

'Hieronymo's mad againe' is not as I remember a quotation though I have not time to verify this, but was either an alternative title sometimes given to the *Spanish Tragedy* or the title of a similar play, I forget which. I think it would be as well to leave out the rather lengthy passage from Ovid.[2]

Yours sincerely,

T. S. Eliot

You make me realise that I let down both C. & M. badly: I saw their translations in ms. & should have spotted these errors.[3]

TO *Harold Monro* CC

20 January 1932   [*The Criterion*]

Dear Harold,

Thank you for your letter of the 19th. I am sorry to hear your report of yourself, but I suppose as your illness was really very long so also must your convalescence be.[4] I had a word with Frank Morley this morning about the *Criterion* meeting, and we both felt that it would be better to

---

1 – Handwritten in the margin.

2 – 'If space allows, I am supplying some of the passages you only refer to, seeing that the works of Webster, Marvell etc. are not accessible to more than a very few of our readers. On the other hand, if space is lacking, you will perhaps allow me to cancel *one* quotation which you give, the Tiresias passage from Ovid, and only give the reference. If it is not necessary to exclude it, I should wish to give the passage in the classical Swedish verse translation, instead of in Latin.'

3 – Added by hand.

4 – HM wrote from his rest home in Broadstairs, Kent: '[M]y condition has been so uncertain that I hardly knew how to write. I am still in bed, & my temperature is not quite steady yet so plainly I have a long & weary time before me.

'It is absolutely certain that I cannot be present at a *Criterion* meeting on the 3rd February . . . By March I am bound to be much fitter . . . But if you want to have a meeting on the 3rd February, of course do not fail to do so in spite of my absence. I'd like to hear your views.'

have a meeting in February in order to keep the continuity. Now, if it is inconvenient for you to have us meet at the Poetry Bookshop in your absence I believe that we could arrange with the housekeeper here to provide for us. Other things being equal it seems to me desirable to keep the continuity, so to speak, of place as well as time, but I wish you would let me know candidly whether it is asking too much of Mrs Monro and incidentally of your housekeeper. As Bonamy wants to come up for the 3rd February I think we had best keep to that date. We will have, I trust, a preliminary discussion of the arrangements to be made for the *Criterion* during my absence and a fuller discussion at the meeting in March when you will be present.

I don't feel quite so strongly as you do about Frank.[1] In any case he is not due to provide another chronicle until the June number so there will be plenty of time to discuss it. I think that his arrangement of the chronicle with a list of books at the end, many of which he did not touch upon at all, and with no references for quotations is bad and irritating, and I think he could avoid giving the impression that there is no good contemporary verse at all. At any rate there will be, by June I think, several new books which I shall call to his attention and which really deserve a good word.

Let me know what you think best about the February meeting.[2] I should like to have lunch with you privately before we meet again in March.

Yours ever,
[Tom]

TO *Bonamy Dobrée*   CC

20 January 1932   [*The Criterion*]

Dear Bonamy,

Morley and I have come to the opinion that it is best to have a February meeting although I have just heard from Harold that he is still very low and does not expect to return from Broadstairs until March. I have just written to Harold to say that I think we had better keep to the 3rd

1–HM had written on 13 Jan.: 'I want very much to talk to you about Flint's view of poetry: it has appalled me for some time.' On 19 Jan.: 'With regard to the question of Frank I feel very strongly that he is not a suitable reviewer of current books of verse. During past years I have watched his taste becoming more & more jaded for poetry.'
2–'Between you & me, & for no one else to know,' wrote Monro (22 Jan.), 'I don't much like Criterions [i.e. *Criterion* gatherings at his premises] in my absence, but I yield absolutely to public necessity, & please have the room on the 3rd without fail.'

February in spite of his absence, and that if it is inconvenient for him or for Mrs Monro to have us use the Poetry Bookshop we will try to arrange to have it here, but unless you hear to the contrary the meeting will be at the Poetry Bookshop.

Yours ever,
[T. S. E.]

TO *John F. Lehmann*[1]   TS Reading/cc

20 January 1932   Faber & Faber Ltd

Dear Mr Lehmann,

I must apologise for my delay in answering your letter of the 13th.[2] I have discussed the matter with the directors and with Spender, and we have come to the conclusion that we have no objection for our part to your including the eight poems selected in an anthology to be published during this coming spring, especially as it now appears that these eight poems will form a smaller proportion of the book which we intended to publish than was at first supposed. Will you accordingly arrange your terms for anthology rights with Spender.

Yours very truly,
T. S. Eliot

1 – John Lehmann (1907–87), author, editor, publisher; founder-editor in 1935 of the twice-yearly *New Writing* (later *Penguin New Writing*); Managing Director of the Hogarth Press, 1938–46 (he bought Virginia Woolf's share of the firm); founder of the publishing house of John Lehmann Ltd, 1946–54; founder-editor of *The London Magazine*, 1954–61. His writings include volumes of autobiography, among them *The Whispering Gallery* (1955), *I Am My Brother* (1960), *Thrown to the Woolfs* (1978), and studies of VW, Rupert Brooke and Lewis Carroll. See further Adrian Wright, *John Lehmann: A Pagan Adventure* (1998).

2 – The compiler of an anthology of poems to be published by the Hogarth Press in the spring wished to include eight recent poems by Spender, who was 'very keen to come into the book'.

TO *E. R. Curtius*[1]   CC

20 January 1932   [Faber & Faber Ltd]

My dear Curtius,

Very many thanks for your letter of the 10th January.[2] It is indeed refreshing to hear that you are again writing. I should like very much to see your book itself and particularly the chapter on Humanism. I am rather doubtful whether I shall have room for it in the April number, but its prior appearance does not really matter, and as it would have appeared in Germany before April anyway I should like very much to have it with a view to publication in the July if not in the April number. I hope you will let me have a copy as soon as ever you can.

Yours ever cordially,
[T. S. Eliot]

TO *F. McEachran*[3]   CC

20 January 1932   [*The Criterion*]

Dear McEachran,

I like your paper on 'Church and Empire in Dante' and will use it as soon as I can.[4] Meanwhile I am returning your essay 'The Wholly Other in Shakespeare' chiefly for the reason that I had rather give Shakespeare a rest for a time.[5] Have you, by the way, ever read Wilson Knight's books on Shakespeare, *The Wheel of Fire* and *The Imperial Theme*?

1 – Ernst Robert Curtius (1886–1956), German scholar of philology and Romance literature: see Biographical Register.

2 – Curtius had written a small book, *Deutscher Geist in Gefahr* (published in Feb.), and wished to offer TSE the 'last and most important chapter' entitled 'Humanismus': 'However, it would no longer be an *inédit* in April, and I would therefore perfectly understand if you rejected it.'

3 – Frank McEachran (1900–75), schoolmaster, classicist, author, was to become a friend of TSE and contributor to C. In the 1920s he taught at Gresham's School, Holt, Norfolk (where WHA was a pupil); then at Shrewsbury School (where Richard Ingrams, later editor of *Private Eye,* was a student). Alan Bennett has acknowledged that the eccentric, charismatic Hector, in *The History Boys* (2004), is based on McEachran (Dave Calhoun, 'Alan Bennett: interview', *Time Out,* 2 Oct. 2006). On TSE's recommendation, F&F brought out McEachran's first books, *The Civilised Man* (1930) and *The Destiny of Europe* (1932). See John Bridgen, 'Sometime Schoolmasters All: Frank McEachran and T. S. Eliot . . . and a few others', *Journal of the T. S. Eliot Society (UK)* 2010, 21–40.

4 – McEachran, 'The Eagle and the Cross', C. 12 (Jan. 1933), 200–5.

5 – McEachran wrote, 10 Feb.: 'I am venturing to send you the enclosed essay on "The Wholly Other in Shakespeare", being an attempt to apply the ideas of Otto to some of

And don't forget about the review for the March number.[1]

Yours sincerely,

[T. S. Eliot]

TO *Leonora Eyles Murray*[2]   CC

20 January 1932   [Faber & Faber Ltd]

Dear Mrs Murray,

I have been far too busy to do more than glance at the book by your friend, but I have had it read carefully.[3] My report is distinctly for the author though not, so far as we are concerned, to the book. It appears that the book is much too large an attempt for the scale of the material presented, and that it tends to diffusion, and finally that we are doubtful whether a novel of such length, dealing with this subject in this way would be likely to have any success. Our reader felt sure, however, that the book ought to be examined impartially by other good publishing houses, and suggested for instance that it might be forwarded to Jonathan Cape.

Yours sincerely,

[T. S. Eliot]

Shakespeare's plays. I am not sure that I haven't spun a myth to my own satisfaction, but I think it may interest you.' He added: 'Mr Robert Schafer has been good enough to publish a very good review of "the Civilised Man" in the *Bookman*, which I hope will sell a few copies over there. I have not, as yet heard from Babbitt.'

1–Review of four titles in the series 'Essays in Order', and of *José Ortega y Gasset*: C. 11 (Apr. 1932), 532–6.

2–Leonora Eyles (1889–1960), author, was the wife of D. L. Murray, editor of the *TLS* from 1938. Her works include *Women's Problems of To-day* (1926) and *Shepherd of Israel* (1929).

3–Mrs Murray submitted on 1 Jan. a novel, *Winter Discontent*, by a friend, Alexander Knox: 'The author is Canadian, who is now in England acting. He has just written a play also and published some very unusual poems in American magazines before he came over. He is only 24 but I think you will agree that his work shows no immaturity. The novel is mainly placed in Canada and Boston, but it should interest English readers in these days when the Dominions are so much in everyone's mind; also, it deals with Canadian town life whereas most Canadian novels are set in the prairie or in the North; Mr Knox finds since he came to England that people have little idea that Canada has a "civilisation" and a culture of its own at all.' (P. Wilberforce was the reader.)

20 January 1932   *[The Criterion]*

Dear Mr Leavis,

I have read your pamphlet with care and with general interest and satisfaction.[2] There are a few small points, however, which I should like to raise and which I think involve alterations which would make the pamphlet more effective.

1. The title. This is a small matter, but for a popular pamphlet I suggest dropping 'Quis Custodiet?' and entitling it 'Culture and Authority' with perhaps a fuller sub-title giving some fuller indication of the subject matter.

2. It seems to me that it would be more effective if you began with some general remarks of your own, stating the subject matter and your attitude toward it at once, and then proceeded to the quotation from an American paper. And as the quotation is so long I think it would probably be better to give the name of the author and references to the publication.

3. Then after this illustration of American folly proceed to some parallel illustration of English folly so as to make a gradual ascent toward the more elegant and dignified forms of stupidity with which you are really concerned. Gosse is all right in his place when you get to him.

4. On page 8 you quote me as giving a kind of testimonial to the *Times Literary Supplement*. Surely you observe in its context my phrase has a slightly ironic flavour. Not that I wish this to be underlined either but your use of quotation seems to clothe me in the most orthodox solemnity.

5. I feel that the amount of attention concentrated on Harold Nicholson [*sc.* Nicolson][3] as an individual is excessive and slightly distorts the proportions of your essay. I mean that you slightly defeat your own end by concentrating attention on an individual rather than on a mass attitude.

6. Finally I think that it is a mistake to make so many references to myself. I say this not out of modesty sincere or false, but with an eye on

---

1–F. R. Leavis (1895–1978), literary critic: see Biographical Register.
2–Leavis had submitted the ts of his pamphlet, which he proposed to title *Quis custodiet? or, Culture & Authority*, on 12 Jan. 1932. He said he hoped TSE would not object to the 'propagandist note. I'm bent on getting a momentum going, so that things may carry on if I'm ejected from Cambridge. It sounds portentous, but it's true, when I say that there are a number of young men, here & in schools & elsewhere, who will take the pamphlet as a manifesto.'
3–Harold Nicolson (1886–1968) relinquished in 1930 a thriving career in the Diplomatic Service to work as a journalist for the *Evening Standard*. In Mar. 1931 he left the *Standard* to join Sir Oswald Mosley's New Party and soon became editor of the New Party's journal *Action*.

policy. It would give the impression to many people that you are speaking not so much in the name of culture and commonsense in general as of a particular clique real or imaginary, and people find it easy to ignore what they can construe as the expression of a small ambitious group. I wonder if you realize how easily people fall into the belief in cliques. I once saw in some elegant periodical, I think it was the *New Statesman*, a reference to the *Criterion* as the organ for the views of Messrs Eliot, Read, Richards and Fernandez,[1] and I remember writing a letter to assert that the four persons named were in accord chiefly on what they considered important problems, and differed very widely in their various solutions.

I hope that these suggestions will not appear to you quite beside the point or else impossible of alteration. It is because I think the pamphlet so good and the subject so important that I should like to see it in its most effective form.[2]

Yours sincerely,
[T. S. Eliot]

TO *Der Neue Geist Verlag* CC

20 January 1932   [*The Criterion*]

Dear Sirs,

I beg to acknowledge your Post-card of the 13th instant, and to apologise for my delay in writing to you about the small book of Professor Scheler's, *Die Idee des Friedens und der Pazifismus.*[3] I would gladly have used in the *Criterion* the section which was first under discussion and which appeared, as I remember, in the *Neue Schweizer Rundschau*, except

1–Ramon Fernandez (1894–1944), philosopher, essayist, novelist, was Mexican by birth but educated in France, where he contributed to *NRF*, 1923–43. Works include *Messages* (1926) – which included an essay on 'Le classicisme de T. S. Eliot' – and *De la personnalité* (1928).
2–Leavis responded (22 Jan.) by accepting the majority of TSE's suggestions, including the change of title he proposed. Leavis would also revise his piece with a view to being 'more politic' and avoiding accusations of cliquishness. As to TSE's item 4, however: 'I must confess that there was some malice in my use of your "testimonial" to the *T.L.S.* Am I unforgivably impertinent if I say that it seemed to me that you wouldn't much mind its being taken as a testimonial, as it has been, I believe, by all but very few of your readers, & if I add that I was, perhaps crudely, indignant? You see, none of the considerable number of people who have brought the passage in triumph to me would accept my explanation that it was ironical. – Not that there could in any case be any question of my being reluctant to emend my reference.'
3–Max Scheler (1874–1928): German philosopher specialising in ethics, value theory, phenomenology, philosophical anthropology; Professor of Philosophy and Sociology at Cologne, 1919–28; a notable influence on Karol Wojtyla, the future Pope John Paul II, who

that I found your terms impossible. Our rates are £2 per 1000 words and in the case of material which has to be translated from a foreign language we deduct 15/- per 1000 as fee for the translator. In no circumstances have I ever paid higher rates and we could not possibly consider any negotiations in foreign currency.

We have gone very seriously into the question of translating the whole work as a separate brochure but we finally decided with regret that it was not a subject which was likely to arouse any great interest. In principle, however, we are still interested in all of the late Professor Scheler's work and should like to find a suitable mode of introducing it more widely in England.

Yours faithfully,
[T. S. Eliot]

TO *A. W. Dodd*   CC

20 January 1932   [Faber & Faber Ltd]

Dear Mr Dodd,

I have at last found time to read and consider your fantasy 'The Soul Within'.[1] It seems to me that the title is very suitable in this sense that your conception of what you wish to say is much better than the execution of it. The prelude does not seem essential to the dialogue itself and it suffers to my mind from the use of the ancient image of foliage as a symbol of mortality which is not revivified by original phrasing. Again in the body of the work I found an excellent conception and a partially successful communication of tone and atmosphere marred by worn phrasing and rather rheumatic construction. For instance in your line 'Many are the salt tears that I have drunk of' the phrase 'salt tears' illustrates the first defect, and the construction 'Many etc' the second. I think that you need a great deal more practice in expressing a variety of moods in a more easy and colloquial modern style, and I think it is worth your while to persist in writing.

Yours truly
[T. S. Eliot]

---

wrote his *Habilitation* (1954) on Christian ethics in the light of Scheler. His works, including *Nation und Weltanschauung*, are gathered in *Gesammelte Werke* (Bern, 1963).
1–A. Wm Dodd (aged 28), from Birmingham, had posted his fantasy story to TSE on 30 Sept. 1931; he had not received it back by 1 Dec. 1931. 'I now feel that I can start again on the right track, thanks to your help and your last inspiring comment,' he responded on 23 Jan. 1932.

20 January 1932   [*The Criterion*]

Dear Quennell,

I have read your three stories and like them, but particularly 'Climacteric' which I want to use in the *Criterion*. I am therefore keeping that one, and sending the other two back.

I should like to publish 'Climacteric' in the April number, but I find that I have another longish story accepted for that number about which I had forgotten; but if not in April this story will appear in July so that it will not affect the collected book of stories disadvantageously.

The only point which seems to me a blemish in the story is the name of Paradine. It seems to me, if I may say so, a peacock sort of name, intruding in a story which is not at all peacock, and it seems to me that a more ordinary English name which might be borne by any real baronet would do better.[2]

                                   Yours ever,
                                   [T. S. Eliot]

TO *C. A. Siepmann*   TS BBC

21 January 1932 [misdated 1931]   Faber & Faber Ltd

Dear Siepmann,

I return herewith the six examination tests together with Macmurray's notes.[3] I am wholly in agreement with him <ex. of course that I am much more in sympathy with Smyth than he is>. Barry's is a real find, from the point of view of form and striking the right note; whether one agrees with him does not matter. Smyth will be a little too impersonal

---

1–Peter Quennell (1905–93), biographer, essayist, editor. Though rusticated from Balliol College, Oxford, he was to become a noted man of letters (encouraged by figures including Harold Monro, Edward Marsh and Edith Sitwell). Works include *Baudelaire and the Symbolists* (1929); *Four Portraits* (1945); *Alexander Pope: The Education of Genius 1688–1728* (1968); *Samuel Johnson: His Friends and Enemies* (1972); and works of autobiography including *The Marble Foot* (1976) and *The Wanton Chase* (1980). He edited *The Cornhill Magazine*, 1944–51; co-edited (with Alan Hodge) *History Today*, 1951–79.

2–'Climacteric', *C.* 11 (July 1932), 626–41. The name was changed to 'Paradigm'.

3–Siepmann had sent TSE 'the summaries of possible talks' for the BBC series on 'The Modern Dilemma'. He added (25 Jan.), 'I have now shown these to Sir John [Reith] who feels very doubtful about [John E.] Barry.'

and rigid, but will be a good & independent talk.[1] Hanson is the greatest disappointment: his covering letter is promising and his paper so meagre. Stewart is hopelessly commonplace; Rowse at his worst would be much better than this. In short, I should say: Barry & Smyth can be trusted to go ahead; I think Stewart and Hanson should be dropped overboard; Wilson I think will just do. There remains the dialogue. It is promising; in its present form the two seem merely to be chasing each other round in circles and then just stop, like the caucus race.[2] But as they seem to have some perception of its weakness, I should say let them do it if there is time to help them a bit.

Yours in haste,
T. S. Eliot

TO *Kenneth B. Murdock*[3]

cc

22 January 1932   [Faber & Faber Ltd]

Dear Dr Murdock,

Thank you very much for your letter of January 6th.[4] The duplicate official notice reached me at the same time, and the original two days later. It had been addressed to a flat which I occupied about three years

---

1 – Siepmann had written on 13 Jan. that Charles Smyth 'has given me an excellent summary. I was just a little doubtful of his effectiveness at the microphone.' Smyth related to TSE, 7 Jan.: 'Thanks so much for mentioning my name tp the BBC. I had an interview with Siepmann who seemed to like my line (I argued that the Modern Dilemma is Hamlet's graveyard soliloquy – "What a piece of work is man! &" – and the solution, Institutional Christianity)'. For Smyth, see TSE's letter to him, 23 Jan. 1932.

2 – See Lewis Carroll, *Alice's Adventures in Wonderland*, iii: 'A Caucus-Race and a Long Tale'.

3 – Kenneth B. Murdock (1895–1975): Associate Professor of English, Harvard University, 1930–2, Professor, 1932–64; Dean of the Faculty of Arts and Sciences, 1931–6; Master of Leverett House, 1931–41. Works include *Increase Mather* (1924), *Literature and Theology in Colonial New England* (1949), *The Notebooks of Henry James* (with F. O. Matthiessen, 1947).

4 – Murdock asked, *inter alia*: 'Have you yet decided whether Mrs Eliot will come with you to this country? . . . Also, would you be interested in giving any formal instruction in addition to the six lectures which the terms of the Professorship require? In the Department of English we have a half-course on Contemporary English Literature which can be taken only by students of high honor grade. It meets two hours a week . . . [T]here is no obligation of any sort upon you even to consider this. If you did it, it would have to be simply because you felt like doing it and not because you imagined it was in any way any part of your duty . . . If there is the slightest hesitation or doubt in your mind about it, please cable me that you do not wish to consider it.'

ago, opened by the present tenant, and apparently forgotten for a good many weeks.

It is unlikely that my wife will be coming with me. I am considering whether I shall accept or not Mr Spencer's kind offer to a set of rooms in Eliot House.

I wish that I might have a few more particulars about what would be expected in a course on contemporary English literature. I am a little doubtful as to whether it would be possible for me to handle this subject tactfully and at the same time honestly. There are so many contemporary authors whose works I have never read, and my ignorance of fiction is almost complete. And what attitude should I be expected to adopt towards such writers as Lawrence and Joyce? Unless one discusses these men, and pretty fully and frankly, any course on contemporary literature would seem to me a farce. Finally would I be expected to stay until June in giving such a course or could it be completed by the beginning of May?

With many thanks for your letter,

Yours very sincerely,
[T. S. Eliot]

TO *I. A. Richards*   CC

22 January 1932   [Faber & Faber Ltd]

Dear Richards,

I wish that you came to London oftener than you do, because a good deal accumulates that I should like to discuss. However, as I have no immediate hope of seeing you I must ask your counsel now on two particular points in connection with Harvard. The first is that I am offered a suite of rooms in Eliot House at fifty dollars a month. I had the impression that you found living in College, or whatever they call it, unsatisfactory. If so what better arrangement could I make? I shall probably not be taking my wife with me. And is 50 dollars a month a reasonable price? Maclagan[5] told me that dinner in hall has to be at six o'clock or half past so that the waitresses (sic)[6] can get to the pictures punctually by eight o'clock. Was that your experience? He said he found it disturbed his digestion especially as when he dined out, which appeared to be a frequent necessity, dinner

5 – Eric Maclagan (1879–1951), Director of the Victoria & Albert Museum, London, 1924–45. Charles Eliot Norton Lecturer, 1927–8: his lectures were published as *Italian Sculpture of the Renaissance* (1935).
6 – TSE's 'sic'.

was always at a quarter past eight. Anyway I should very much like your views as to the most suitable form of housing.

The second point is that they want me to give a half year course for honour students on contemporary English literature. This would be a very depressing subject if conducted with academic propriety, but if one could say what one likes it might be pleasant. Should I be permitted, for instance, to mention *Ulysses*? The other difficulty is that it might be impossible to say exactly what one thinks about contemporary literature without hurting the feelings of a number of amiable people if ever it came to their ears. I had thought of a course on criticism as an alternative but am deterred from suggesting that as I should be overshadowed by your reputation there.

Yours in haste,

[T. S. E.]

TO *Charles Smyth*[1]

CC

23 January 1932   [*The Criterion*]

My dear Smyth,

This note is merely to ask whether you would be able to review Penty's *Means and Ends*[2] for our next number. I know that Penty would be very much pleased if you would, and I think it is a book which on the whole you will like. In any case I am sending you a copy as we published it ourselves.

1–Charles Smyth (1903–87): ecclesiastical historian and preacher in the Anglican communion. In 1925 he gained a double first in the History Tripos at Corpus Christi College, Cambridge, winning the Thirlwell Medal and the Gladstone Prize, and was elected to a fellowship of Corpus (R. A. Butler was elected a fellow on the same day). He edited the *Cambridge Review* in 1925, and again in 1940–1. He was ordained deacon in 1929, priest in 1930; and in 1946 he was appointed rector of St Margaret's, Westminster, and canon of Westminster Abbey. (On 28 Apr. 1952 TSE expressed the view, in a letter to Janet Adam Smith, that Smyth should be 'moved up to where he so eminently belongs, an episcopal see'.) Smyth's works include *Cranmer and the Reformation under Edward VI* (1926); *The Art of Preaching (747–1939)* (1940); and a biography of Archbishop Cyril Garbett (1959).

Smyth wrote to EVE, 21 May 1979: 'Your husband was one of the best and kindest friends that I have ever had. – He was also a friend of our Siamese cat, Angus (long since departed this life), who was ordinarily terrified of men (particularly bishops in gaiters!), but took to your husband at sight. I have a treasured copy of the *Book of Practical Cats*, inscribed to "Charles and Violet Smyth, and Angus", by "OP" . . . It was under his auspices that I broadcast from BBC Savoy Hill (!) in 1932, which is now an uncommon distinction of which to boast . . . He had a great sense of fun.'

2–F&F, 1932. For Penty, see TSE to him, 5 July 1932, below.

I shall be writing to you at greater length in a few days about your essay on Education which is very much to my taste, but about which I shall have a few suggestions to make.[1]

Yours ever,
[Pamela Wilberforce, p.p. T. S. Eliot]
Secretary

TO *Frederic Manning*[2]   CC

23 January 1932   [Faber & Faber Ltd]

My dear Manning,

This is just a hurried note to remind you that you were going to speak to Peter Davies about the suggestion I made to you.[3] As I have not heard from him I am wondering whether you found an opportunity to mention it. In either case what should my next step in the matter be?[4]

Yours ever,
[T. S. Eliot]

1–Smyth hoped his essay 'The Education of an Officer Class' (7 Jan.) might be suitable for the Criterion Miscellany; it was 'primarily an attack on Dr Norwood's theories of public school education on their most vulnerable side'. He wrote on the 'Feast of Charles, K. & M.': 'I am relieved that it is to your taste.'

2–Frederic Manning (1882–1935), Australian writer who settled in 1903 in England, where he came to know artists and writers including Max Beerbohm, William Rothenstein, Richard Aldington and Ezra Pound; author of *Scenes and Portraits* (1909; 2nd edn, revised and enlarged, 1930). Despite being an asthmatic, he served in the ranks (Shropshire Light Infantry) in WW1, being involved for four months in heavy fighting on the Somme: this experience brought about his greatest achievement, a novel about the Western Front, *The Middle Parts of Fortune* (privately printed, 1929; standard text, 1977; expurgated as *Her Privates We*, credited pseudonymously to 'Private 19022', 1930; republished in full, with intro. by William Boyd, 1999) – 'the best book to come out of the First World War', Eliot is said to have said of it.

3–TSE had hoped to be able to secure permission to print a cheap edition of Manning's *Her Privates We* in the Faber Library.

4–Manning replied on 25 Jan. that he had mentioned the proposal to Davies – but 'I do not think he will agree.'

23 January 1932   [*The Criterion*]

My dear Demant,

   Would you be inclined to review for the next *Criterion* Douglas's small book on the Monopoly of Credit? Say 1000 words. We should have to have the copy by February 12th. I know this is short notice but the book has only just come in and I should like to have some notice of it in the April number, particularly as he seems to be regularly ignored by nearly every periodical. I do hope you can find time to do this.[2]

Yours sincerely,

p.p. T. S. Eliot

Secretary

1–The Revd Vigo Auguste Demant (1893–1983) trained as an engineer but embraced a wholly different career when he converted to Christianity and became a deacon in 1919, priest in 1920. Following various curacies, he became, while working at St Silas, Kentish Town, London, Director of Research for the Christian Social Council – the Council of Churches in England for Social Questions – 1929–33. As noted in the *ODNB*, he was 'the major theoretician in the Christendom Group of Anglican Catholic thinkers, whose concern was to establish the centrality of what they termed "Christian sociology", an analysis of society fundamentally rooted in a Catholic and incarnational theology'. The Group's quarterly, *Christendom,* ran from 1931 to 1950. He was vicar of St John-the-Divine, Richmond, Surrey, 1933–42; Canon Residentiary, 1942–9, at St Paul's Cathedral. He was Canon of Christ Church and Regius Professor of Moral and Pastoral Theology, Oxford, 1949–71. His works include *This Unemployment: Disaster or Opportunity?* (1931), *God, Man and Society* (1933), *Christian Polity* (1936) and *The Religious Prospect* (1939).

   On 8 Aug. 1940 TSE was to write this unsolicited recommendation to Sir Stephen Gaselee (Foreign Office): 'My friend the Reverend V. A. Demant, whom I have been associated with intellectually for some years, has been recommended by the Bishop of Bath and Wells for a vacant canonry at Westminster. Demant is, in my opinion, one of the most brilliant, or perhaps the most brilliant, of the younger theologians in England, and I also consider him thoroughly sound both in theology and politics. His book, *The Religious Prospect,* was one of the very few important books of last year. He is a very conscientious parish priest, with a large straggling parish in Richmond, and if he is to make the most of his gifts and do what he should do for Anglican theology in the future, he ought to be freed from this routine.'

   Demant remarked at the Requiem Mass for TSE at St Stephen's Church, 17 Feb. 1965: 'The Revd Frank Hillier, to whom Eliot used to go for confession and spiritual direction after the death of Father Philip Bacon [at St Simon's, Kentish Town, London], writes to me: "Eliot had, along with that full grown stature of mind, a truly child-like heart – the result of his sense of dependence on GOD. And along with it he had the sense of responsibility to GOD for the use of his talents. To his refinedness of character is due the fact that like his poetry he himself was not easily understood – but unbelievers always recognized his faith"' (*St Stephen's Church Magazine,* Apr. 1965, 9).

2–Untitled review by Demant: C. 11 (Apr. 1932), 552–4.

TO *Evelyn Underhill*[1]   CC

27 January 1932   [Faber & Faber Ltd]

Dear Mrs Stuart Moore,

Excuse me for not having answered immediately your letter of the 19th January.[2] I had not forgotten my promise or your previous reminder and though I shall find the contract difficult to execute as I am involved in a series of peculiarly difficult broadcast talks, yet I hope to fulfil the engagement. Also I am happy to say that I am not leaving for America until September and therefore hope very much that we may see you again.

Yours very sincerely,

[T. S. Eliot]

1–Evelyn Underhill (1875–1941): esteemed spiritual director and writer on mysticism and the spiritual life. Compelled by deep study and the counsel of Baron Friedrich von Hügel, she became an Anglican in 1919 and dedicated her kindly life to religious writing and guidance, notably as a retreat director. She wrote or edited 39 books and over 350 articles and reviews; among her other activities, she was theological editor for *The Spectator* and wrote too for *Time and Tide*. Her works include *Mysticism: A Study of the Nature and Development of Man's Spiritual Consciousness* (1911) and *Worship* (1936). In 1907 she married Hubert Stuart Moore (1869–1951), a barrister. TSE wrote to Sister Mary Xavier, SSJ, 1 Aug. 1962: 'I . . . wish that I could tell you more about the late Mrs Moore, otherwise Evelyn Underhill. I did not know her intimately and knew [her] I think in the first place through her cousin, Francis Underhill, who was my spiritual director and later Bishop of Bath and Wells. I remember her, however, with affection and regret. I do not know whether you would call her a mystic though she was certainly an authority on mysticism. She was a very cosy person to meet and have tea with in her home in [no. 50] Campden Hill Square and was also very fond of her cats. I should not call her a mystic whether qualified by the adjective Anglican or not, but I should call her an authority on mysticism and indeed would accept your phrase for her "deep spirituality". She was, I am sure, an admirable spiritual director herself and I am pretty sure was a great help to many young women . . . I think that any correspondence we had would have been merely to do with social engagements and I never remember having had any long correspondence with her on spiritual or other matters. I remember her not at all as an intimate friend, but as a very highly valued and regretted acquaintance.'

In an unpublished note to *The Times*, 1941, he wrote too: 'She gave (with frail health and constant illness) herself to many, in retreats, which she conducted and in the intercourse of daily life – she was always at the disposal of all who called upon her. With a lively and humorous interest in human beings, especially the young. She was at the same time withdrawn and sociable. With shrewdness and simplicity she helped to support the spiritual life of many more than she could in her humility have been aware of aiding.'

See further Donald J. Childs, 'T. S. Eliot and Evelyn Underhill: An Early Mystical Influence', *Durham University Journal* 80 (Dec. 1987), 83–98.

2–Underhill sought gently to remind TSE of his undertaking to write an article on George Herbert for *The Spectator*. 'You will remember that . . . the object was to treat George Herbert from the point of view of personal sanctity as expressed in his work.'

TO *Michael Sadleir*   CC

27 January 1932   [*The Criterion*]

Dear Mr Sadleir,

Thank you for your letter of the 21st.[1] I am very sorry to hear that you found my first letter off-hand or, as you say, very airy, and I trust that you will attribute my tone to innocence rather than arrogance. You see it had not occurred to me for a moment that your firm would take such a keen interest in the copyright of my introduction, and you must remember that I had assumed from the beginning that the copyright was my own. I am, however, extremely appreciative of your conciliatory behaviour.

Yours very truly,
[T. S. Eliot]

TO *C. A. Siepmann*   TS BBC

27 January 1932   Faber & Faber Ltd

Dear Siepmann,

Thank you for your note of the 25th.[2] Meanwhile I have prepared a rough draft of my first talk which I enclose herewith for perusal return and comment. You will observe that I have already made a few deletions on page 10 of personal references which might be unwise. Furthermore I do not want you to fear from page 10 that I am going to rush in and talk nonsense about sciences of which I am ignorant. So far as I deal with them at all it will be only to try and put them in their general relation to principles. Ruskin, by the way, is a good respectable name to give credit to views which might be considered subversive when attached to other names. I am not at all satisfied with page 2, and think that I can remove it and put in something different and more vigourous [*sic*], but I should

---

1–'Do not think that we are raising anything like a legal point. We were however a little surprised at the very airy note of your first communication, seeing that there was – to say the least of it – as good a case for our claiming the copyright of the essay as for your doing so . . . Of course now that Whibley is dead and has left no written record of his transactions as Editor of the second series of TUDOR TRANSLATIONS, we are not in a position to refute your reading of the position, even if we seriously wished to. So by all means go ahead, and do what you have always intended to do, merely registering the fact that the procedure seems to us a little high-handed and that we should have thought our position in the matter merited rather more consideration than you have felt disposed to give.'
2–Not found.

like to know your general impression of the start I have made before I go
further.[1]

Yours sincerely,
T. S. Eliot

TO *James M. Murphy*   CC

27 January 1932   [Faber & Faber Ltd]

Dear Mr Murphy,

   Thank you very much for your letter of the 4th January which I was
unable to answer quickly as I had to discuss your suggestion with several
of my colleagues.[2] We are indeed interested by your suggestion that we
should publish a comprehensive book of Professor Planck's essays, and
should like to go into the matter thoroughly. Would it be possible to
let us have a synopsis of the contents and a few of the papers, either
or preferably both, in German or in English? I can assure you that the
proposal is one which we take very seriously.

   With many thanks

Yours sincerely,
[T. S. Eliot]

1–R. A. Rendall, who had taken over adult education at the BBC, wrote in reply (1 Feb.)
that while he found TSE's draft 'very interesting', he was given pause by one remark, viz.,
'It is hardly the purpose of a symposium such as this series has been, to aim at any final
explanation of the problem or solution of it.' Rendall observed: 'We do very definitely
want you to indicate your personal idea of where the solution lies . . . Otherwise I have no
comments to make except to suggest that you may be in danger of becoming a little difficult
and using too many long words. I realise your difficulty here, but I think perhaps it would
be a good plan if you could keep this in mind in making your final draft.'
2–James Murphy, editor of *The International Forum*, asked in his letter (misdated 4 Jan.
1931) if F&F might be interested in 'a large book' containing 'all of Professor Planck's essays
on physical science and its relation to philosophy and so on . . . The book in question would
run to perhaps 125 or 150 thousand words and the translations would be done here [in
Berlin] in consultation with the author.'

TO *Walter de la Mare*[1]   TS De La Mare Estate

27 January 1932   Faber & Faber Ltd

My dear de la Mare,

So far as I remember, when you were so kind as to invite me to collaborate in the Royal Society of Literature's volume on the Eighties it was agreed

---

1–Walter de la Mare (1873–1956), poet, novelist, short-story writer, worked for the Statistics Department of the Anglo-American Oil Company, 1890–1908, before being freed to become a freelance writer by a £200 royal bounty negotiated by Henry Newbolt. He wrote many popular works: poetry including *The Listeners* (1912) and *Peacock Pie* (1913); novels including *Memoirs of a Midget* (1921); anthologies including *Come Hither* (1923). He was appointed CH, 1948; OM, 1953. See TSE's poem 'To Walter de la Mare'; and Theresa Whistler, *Imagination of the Heart: The Life of Walter de la Mare* (1993).

In Oct. 1956 TSE opened an evening of readings (by readers including Christopher Hassall and Margaret Rutherford). The next day, he sent the following 'preliminary draft' of his spoken remarks to Richard de la Mare (Walter's son, a director of F&F): 'I should have been incredulous, if some fortune teller had prophesied, in say 1917, that in 1956 I would be invited to open an evening of readings in memory of Walter de la Mare. I should have been surprised also to be told that I would accept . . .

'When one is a young poet, as I was in those years, one is intolerant of any kind of poetry except the kind one wants to write oneself. As one gets older, and the shadows lengthen, and one's work is done, one becomes more appreciative of work that is very different from one's own. Schools and movements disappear, and a few good poets, very different from each other, are left each in his own isolation. Of course, in each of these cases there are, I think, objective reasons for my change of mind also. Yeats, as we all know, underwent some surprising mutation, so that the minor epigone of the nineties became a great poet, the celtic twilight gave way before a more powerful source of illumination. Pound, I think, gradually taught himself a modern idiom. De la Mare, on the other hand, has always been essentially the same, but developing in power and range so that, like Yeats, he may almost be said to have reached his maturity in old age – for "The Traveller" is astonishing evidence of increased power and undiminished vitality.

'There is another point, too, to be made about the evolution of Walter de la Mare. The Georgian Anthologies served a useful purpose in their day, and the comprehensive term "Georgian Poetry" served its turn also. But anthologies which appear to present the work of a "school" of poetry, or at least of poets who have a common idiom, can have disadvantages also. I for one, in those days, thought of Walter de la Mare merely as one of a number of poets who wrote some very charming lyrics in a manner which seemed to me to render them superfluous. It was some years before I was aware that De la Mare, if it would be unfair to others to call him the only stayer on the course, was the one who would keep on the longest and go the farthest. Furthermore, as the years went on, and incidentally one's own judgment ripened, the differences between De la Mare's work and that of his contemporaries emerged more and more clearly. I recognised him at last as not simply the most eminent of a group, but as not belonging to any group at all; as a poet who had done something different from the work of any other poet – and unless you can say that of a poet, you cannot feel sure of his permanence.

'I remember my surprise on first hearing De la Mare read some of his own poetry. It was during the war, at a poetry reading for the benefit, I think, of some Red Cross organisation, at which there were a number of other poets reading, among them two or three who have made a reputation as good readers of their own verse. De la Mare's style of reading was

that I should have the right to reprint my contribution in any volume of collected essays of my own. We are expecting to bring out a volume of my collected essays in the autumn and I want to include this paper. I have not yet had time to look up this correspondence, but in any case I should have written to you again to acquaint you with my intention, and to ask you to confirm my understanding of the arrangement.[1]

I have been seeing something lately of Ralph Hodgson and like him immensely. What a pity that he has apparently given up writing for good![2]

Yours sincerely,
T. S. Eliot

---

different from that of any of us. It was not, perhaps, best suited to a large auditorium; he read as if he had before him not a public audience but a small select company of friends in a drawing room; and his voice was very low. But he managed to put into his reading a more *conversational* tone than that of any of the other [*sic*] of us. It was De la Mare, so to speak, talking to a few friends, but talking poetry. It was a chamber concert, not a brass band. But we know that as great music has been written for a few stringed instruments as for the full orchestra. I am glad that this room does not accommodate more than this small company of listeners; it is I am sure, the proper setting for what you are about to hear.'

He followed up with this personal letter to Richard de la Mare, 20 Oct. 1956: 'I should have made it clear that the points I failed to make were not so much in the draft I sent you, as indicated in the notes I had in my hand. I wanted to say something, for example, about the lighter poems and "children's poems" – as it seems to me that these are sometimes overrated relatively to your father's other work, and can also be underrated – the point being that they are, in a way peculiar to himself, integral with all his poetry – so that you need to know each kind for a full appreciation of the other. But this would have been longwinded and difficult to follow, and better developed on paper. Another point was that the term "Georgian Poetry" and the anthologies had for a long time obscured the fact that he was both superior to and different from the others, and that the term had in fact been misleading. Perhaps it was as well that I omitted this too, as Christopher Hassall was such a friend of Eddie Marsh, and as comparisons are odious.'

TSE wrote to Mrs Lawrence (Theresa) Whistler, 21 Nov. 1962: 'I have your letter of November 12th and will ask my secretary to look out any letters to me from Walter de la Mare. This will be a tedious business as my correspondence from this office goes back to 1925 and my letters from Walter de la Mare are not numerous. I should not be able to give you any lengthy reminiscences as I did not know him intimately and saw him on very few occasions but I have at least one memory of a visit to him which is worth recording and will let you have it in due course.'

1–De la Mare confirmed (27 Jan.) that TSE was free to reprint his essay on Pater.

2–De la Mare responded, 27 Jan.: 'Do use all the influence you have to persuade R. H. to write again. The best book – I believe – about England & Englishness (quite apart from the poetry that must be there too) is in *his* head, & heart. There are few writers one can charge with writing too little. But there'd be no possible appeal in his case. Give him my love, but don't repeat this – I've said it too often & he just points his pipe at me!' See also TSE to Hodgson, 17 Mar. 1932.

TO *Peter Davies*[1]   CC

27 January 1932   [Faber & Faber Ltd]

Dear Davies,
   I should like very much to have the opportunity of discussing with you
a project which I took up with Fred Manning a week or so ago. It would
be a pleasure also if you would have lunch with me one day soon. Is there
any day during next week that would suit you to lunch with me at the
Oxford and Cambridge Club at 1.15.[2]

                                   Yours sincerely,
                                   [T. S. Eliot]

TO *Bruce Richmond*[3]   CC

27 January 1932   [Faber & Faber Ltd]
                     Private and Confidential
Dear Richmond,
   I am asked by my friend the German critic Professor Ernst Robert Curtius
to convey a message to you.[4] As the message is a singular one and also
rather embarrassing inasmuch as it concerns another London publisher I
take no responsibility in the matter and should certainly not even convey
the message in any but a confidential way. Curtius is extremely incensed
with Allen & Unwin over their treatment of the translation of his book
The Civilisation of France which they have just published. He claims that
he had no voice in choosing the translator who is a lady unknown to him

---

1 – Peter Llewelyn Davies (1897–1960), publisher, felt plagued for life after being identified
by J. M. Barrie as the original of Peter Pan. After dreadful and distinguished war service, for
which he was awarded the Military Cross, in 1926 he founded the publishing house Peter
Davies Ltd – he would publish his cousin Daphne du Maurier's volume about her renowned
grandfather, *The Young George du Maurier, letters 1860–1867* (1951). See Andrew Birkin,
J. M. Barrie & the Lost Boys (1979); *Finding Neverland* (film, 2004); John Logan, *Peter and
Alice* (play, 2013).
2 – Davies wrote later (11 Feb. 1932): 'I have come to the conclusion that it is definitely
unsuitable from my point of view that your people should issue a cheap edition of any of
Frederic Manning's works. I think I more or less explained to you the reasons when we had
lunch together the other day, and nothing has occurred to me since to alter my view. At the
same time, I am still open to persuasion, and should be delighted if you would say what you
can to persuade me while lunching with me one day next week.' Manning was not published
by F&F.
3 – Bruce Richmond (1871–1964), editor of the *Times Literary Supplement*: see Biographical
Register.
4 – Curtius conveyed these sentiments in a letter to TSE of 22 Jan. 1932.

and to his English friends, and who incidentally is unknown to me. He says that she asked him only one question about the translation, when she sent him a post-card and asked him what the word 'Kraftwagen' means. (Certainly that does not suggest a very intimate acquaintance with the language.) He compares his treatment very unfavourably with the treatment he has received from the publishers of the French translation. He has had no opportunity to read or criticize a single [word] of the translation.

This is the message which he wishes conveyed to the Editor of the Literary Supplement of the *Times*. Please understand that I am not conveying it to the Literary Editor of the *Times* but to B. L. Richmond Esq.

Yours ever,
[T. S. E.]

TO *E. R. Curtius* CC

27 January 1932   [*The Criterion*]

My dear Curtius,

Many thanks for your letter of the 22nd.[1] I shall await receipt of your book[2] with great interest.

Your London publishers have sent a review copy of *The Civilisation of France* as they call it, but I have not yet had time to examine it or compare it with the original with a view of forming an opinion of the translation. In any case their behaviour to you certainly seems to me incorrect. Of course in many cases a foreign author is not interested to see the translation of his work, but it should have been obvious to them that in your case it was clearly both a matter of courtesy and of conscientiousness toward the translation to have sent you the proof for your comment and revision. I should say that the responsibility in this matter lay far more with the publisher than with the translator. As you say the one

---

1 – Curtius said his book would be appearing in mid-Feb., when TSE could judge for himself whether to print a chapter in C. He was very unhappy about the English edition of his book on France: the translator (Olive Wyon) had contacted him only once, by postcard, to ask about the meaning of the word '*Kraftwagen*' (motor vehicle), which did not inspire any confidence in the translation; whereas for the French edition, published by Grasset, he had been able to review the translation page by page. He hoped TSE would be able to use his good offices to advise the *TLS* of the likely inadequacies of the English edition: he regarded this as a 'literary–political matter'.
2 – *Deutscher Geist in Gefahr*.

question which your translator had to ask does not inspire confidence in the accuracy of the translation. When I have had a chance to look at a few pages of the book carefully I will write again. Meanwhile I have written at once to the Editor of *The Times Literary Supplement*. You will understand that it would have been of doubtful propriety for me to have written impersonally because it would hardly have been correct for one publisher to criticize the behaviour of another in such a matter. But the Editor happens to be a personal friend of mine and I have written to him as such to convey your message.

In so far as the question of biographical material is concerned that is quite a usual request for publishers to make, but as an author I share your disinclination for such advertisement and I should have responded in the same way as you.

> With all sympathy,
> Always yours,
> [T. S. Eliot]

TO *H. G. Leach*   CC

27 January 1932   [Faber & Faber Ltd]

Dear Mr Leach,

Thank you very much for your kind letter of the 13th.[1] It is quite possible that I may be in New York for a short time and in that event I shall look forward to seeing you again.

Your suggestion is very interesting. Of course it is impossible to predict what I shall want to write when I return to London, but I shall certainly keep your proposal in mind and am very much obliged to you.

> Yours sincerely,
> [T. S. Eliot]

1–H. G. Leach, editor of *The Forum* (NY) congratulated TSE on his Harvard appointment. 'It has occurred to me that after lecturing to American undergraduates you may find that you have material for an article, and if so, I hope you will let THE FORUM see it . . . Any aspect of American education, provided it was not too specialized and academic for our rather general audience, would interest us. We should perhaps be even more interested, if you were at all sympathetic with the idea, in a more personal paper – an analysis, say, of the United States today as it appears to one who was born here and has since taken up his residence abroad. A suggested title, "America Revisited" may give you some indication of what I mean.'

TO *Leonard Woolf*[1]   CC

27 January 1932   [Faber & Faber Ltd]

My dear Leonard,

I am proposing to bring out a volume of collected essays in the autumn, among which I propose to include the three which you published under the title of *Homage to John Dryden*. I do not know whether you have kept the pamphlet in print, or what stock you have on your hands. I should be very glad to know this point, but I do not suppose that my volume could conflict in any way with what slender interest the pamphlet may still have. These three articles will be only a very small part of what promises to be much bulkier than I expected. So far as I am concerned there is no reason why the pamphlet should not be reprinted indefinitely, but I imagine that there is now hardly any demand for it.[2]

I was very sorry to miss you the last time I came to tea, and hope that I may come again soon when you can be at home.

                                                    Yours ever,
                                                    [T. S. E.]

TO *Ezra Pound*[3]   TS Beinecke

27 January 1932   *The Criterion*

Honourable Rabbit,

In reply to several communications of varying length, and with apologies for the delay.

    1. Could you tell me approximately when the Guido is to appear? It is not much use trying to settle on a reviewer until I know the date. Do you mean that Gilson would be more satisfactory to you than anybody else you can think of? If so I will try to get him.[4] I don't know him personally and don't know whether you do. I can't see why on earth you should think of J. B. S. Haldane for this purpose. I always thought of him as a popular biologist distinctly superior to Julian Huxley but that is not

1–Leonard Woolf (1880–1969), writer and publisher: see Biographical Register.
2–LW (28 Jan.) happily granted permission. Even though the Hogarth Press was still selling 'quite a number of copies every year' of the second impression of TSE's work, LW did not anticipate that its inclusion in a collection would harm the original publication.
3–Ezra Pound (1885–1972), American poet and critic: see Biographical Register.
4–See Etienne Gilson's review of EP's *Guido Cavalcanti, Rime*: C. 12 (Oct. 1932), 106–12; repr. in *Ezra Pound: The Critical Heritage*, ed. Eric Homberger (1972), 273–9.

saying much, and I believe he is a brother or something like that of Naomi Mitcheson [*sic*], and a World Leaguer for Sexual Reform; but what all that can have to do with the text of Guido Cavalcanti I can't imagine. Do you know Raffaello Piccoli here in Cambridge (in Cambridgeshire) who seems to me rather intelligent? He is supposed to be recuperating from lung trouble at present in Switzerland, but ought to be back here in a few months.[1] But I am open to reason about Haldane if you *have* any reasons.

2. Your letter to the Editor about Whitewashed Tombstones seems to me to contain matter which is worth exposing, or linen which is worth washing in public, and it also shows a good heart.[2] The trouble is 1). It deals with two matters which I think would be more effectively dealt with in two separate letters. The British public might get roused a bit over the Golden Treasury <Note>, but would hardly stir an eyelash to read about Guggenheim fellowships. Not that the second is not worth considering in the *Criterion*, but I think it would weaken your case against Macmillan or the Oxford Press or whoever it is to whom you refer, if tacked on to the same letter. 2). The whole exposition seems to me so obscure, or shall we say on such a high intellectual plane that the aforesaid British public would probably not know what you are talking about. It is quite beyond my capacity to re-write any of your correspondence without losing ~~some~~ all of that peculiar personal idiom which is one of the secrets of your own typewriting machine, and one of the outstanding virtues of your correspondence. In other words would you consider the question and write two separate letters to the Editor?

I am not quite sure, but I think that the case against the publishers could be put a little more clearly without yet over-stepping the bounds of libel. Have I succeeded in conveying any meaning?

I don't know Elias Low of Corpus, but I should think that a man who could only pronounce on palaeography would be a last resource. When I know the date, or have the book, still better, I will tackle Gilson.

Indice I believe goes to my Italian specialist colleague for the *Criterion* or at least it ought to. Did I tell you I am here till September next and back

1–Raffaello Piccoli (1886–1933): Professor of Italian, Cambridge University. His works include *Astrologia Dantesca* (1909) and *Benedetto Croce: An Introduction to His Philosophy* (1922). He translated plays by Shakespeare, Robert Greene, George Peele and Christopher Marlowe; and poems by Shelley; and he was a Dante scholar. In the 1920s he contributed some 'Letters from Italy' to *The Dial*. His translation of 'Perch' Io non Spero', entitled 'Le Ceneri', appeared in *Cambridge Review* 51 (week of 9 June 1930), 492. In 1939 TSE would refer to Piccoli as 'my regretted friend . . . whose death a few years ago was a great loss to Cambridge'.
2–Not published: not found.

again in May? *Criterion* will be carried on in some form during absence, but machinery not yet assembled.

> Yrs. etc.
>
> T.

TO *T. F. Burns*[1]

27 January 1932   [*The Criterion*]

Dear Burns,

I have read Don Luigi Sturzo's article which you kindly sent with your letter of the 17th, but I cannot feel that it is quite suitable for the *Criterion*.[2] Candidly it seems to me rather vague maundering, and I am disappointed in an author from whom I should have expected much more. I should like to get you to lunch with me soon. Would any day next week be possible for you? My friend Gordon George, otherwise Robert Sencourt, may be in London, and if so I should like you to meet him. In any case I should like to see you and also to talk about *l'Esprit*.[3]

> Yours,
>
> [T. S. Eliot]

1–Tom Burns (1906–95), publisher and journalist, was educated at Stonyhurst (where he was taught by Fr Martin D'Arcy) and worked with the publishers Sheed & Ward, 1926–35. From 1935 he worked for Longmans Green – where he arranged to finance Graham Greene's mission to enquire into the persecution of the Catholic Church in Mexico – and he became a director of the Tablet Publishing Co., 1935–85. During WW2 he was press attaché to Sir Samuel Hoare, British Ambassador to Spain: see Jimmy Burns, *Papa Spy: A True Story of Love, Wartime Espionage in Madrid, and the Treachery of the Cambridge Spies* (2011). He was chairman of Burns & Oates, the premier Catholic publishing house, 1948–67; editor of *The Tablet*, 1967–82.

2–Burns wondered whether TSE would consider Luigi Sturzo's essay 'a satisfactory meditation on how the "dreams cross"'. (FVM, to whom TSE showed the piece, wrote on Burns's letter: 'seems very turgid to me: can't catch on to it properly, perhaps'.)

3–Burns said he had 'been landed with the job of finding English contributions for *L'Esprit*.'

TO *Basil Bunting*[1]

27 January 1932   [*The Criterion*]

Dear Mr Bunting,

Thank you for your letter of the 21st.[2] I have not yet seen the February number of *Poetry*, and did not know that you have mentioned me. I am quite used to being attacked and am even accustomed to personal attacks, but I cannot see why anyone should be offended by destructive criticism of his work unless it is also an attack on his character and private life. I can't see any reason why I should feel hurt by your pitching into my political or ecclesiastical opinions. In any case I will read your article if it comes my way with interest and with your kind letter in mind.

With many thanks,

Yours sincerely,

[T. S. Eliot]

1 – Basil Bunting (1900–85), Northumberland-born poet, lived in Paris in the early 1920s, working for Ford Madox Ford at the *Transatlantic Review*. From 1923 he was mentored by EP, whom he followed to Rapallo; and it was through EP that he became acquainted with JJ, Zukofsky and WBY. EP published his work in *Active Anthology* (1933); but his enduring fame came about after WW2 with the publication of *Briggflatts* (1966). *Collected Poems* appeared in 1968. TSE wrote of him to J. R. Ackerley, 17 Aug. 1936: 'He is a good poet and an intelligent man'; and in a reference for the John Simon Guggenheim Memorial Foundation, 30 Dec. 1938: 'Bunting . . . is a very intelligent man and an able poet. I say "able", because I am still doubtful whether he will ever accomplish anything of great importance as an original author. I think he has just the qualities to qualify him as a translator of poetry . . . I back him strongly for the sort of work that he proposes to do [translations from Persian] – work, also, which is in itself worth doing.' See Bunting, 'Mr T. S. Eliot', *New English Weekly*, 8 Sept. 1932, 499–500; R. Caddel and A. Flowers, *Basil Bunting: A Northern Life* (1997); Richard Burton, *A Strong Song Tows Us: The Life of Basil Bunting* (2013).

2 – 'I am afraid my article in the February number of *Poetry* Chicago contains some phrases that might easily be misread into a personal attack on you. This is due partly to overhasty clumsy journalism and partly to Harriet Monro's habit of cutting bits out of articles sent in. The proofs reached me here [Rapallo] too late for correction. I have sent a letter for publication as soon as possible to put my meaning beyond doubt. I do want to be as rude as possible about royalism anglo-catholicism etc, but that is a very different matter from personal bitterness. My words in the article dont strictly bear such a construction, but a not-very-careful reader might easily get the impression that they did. I am very sorry about it.

'If after seeing the article and the letter you think it is still too bad, please thunder; and that will give me an opportunity of stating more explicitly etc etc.'

See 'Muzzle and jowl and beastly brow', *Poetry* 32: 5 (Feb. 1932), 251. See also another rude piece by Bunting, 'Mr T. S. Eliot', *The New English Weekly* 1: 21 (8 Sept. 1932), 499–500: 'The alleged anachronism of Pound consists in assuming a reader better acquainted with history and literature than readers usually are. Eliot's, in his devotional verse, is more fundamental. He writes as though from conditions that have vanished, as a contemporary of George Herbert. He has his reward. What is antique enough is notoriously harmless, is supine, and the ruling powers can encourage its circulation without uneasiness.'

TO *Jean Stewart*   CC

27 January 1932   [Faber & Faber Ltd]

Dear Miss Stewart,

I was sorry not to see you when you called.[1] Indeed I remember you very well in a sense. That is to say I remember that when I was in Cambridge in 1926 and had the pleasure of your parents' hospitality you were in Paris.

I sincerely hope that you will get the Commonwealth Fellowship, though I confess I do not know just what they are, and that you will go to Harvard especially as you will have there the opportunity of Babbitt's supervision. Contemporary American literary criticism is a large and rather disorderly field and I am by no means well acquainted with it. I take it that you know the work of Irving Babbitt[2] and some of Paul More's Shelburne essays,[3] and that you have looked at the younger humanists, one of the best of whom is G. R. Elliott[4] and about the worst of whom is named Gass.[5] Van Wyck Brooks[6] had a certain influence ten or twelve years ago, especially with his books on Henry James and Mark Twain, but I believe that his work and that of a contemporary, Randolph Bourne,[7] are rather in eclipse. Among the younger critics both Lewis Mumford[8] and Goram

1–Jean Stewart – daughter of Dr H. F. Stewart, Trinity College, Cambridge – wrote on 21 Jan. at the suggestion of IAR: 'I want to apply for a Commonwealth Fellowship to go to America this autumn. I am thinking of writing on American literary criticism from Poe to the present day, (having worked on French & English criticism in my "Hogarth Lecture") & I find my knowledge of recent critical movements extremely vague. I should be infinitely grateful if you could advise me as to what to read? the barest outline, so that I can show up a convincing plan of work when I apply. Dr Richards advises me to try for Harvard, & Professor Irving Babbitt has promised to "supervise" my studies if I go there.'
2–Irving Babbitt (1865–1933), Professor of French at Harvard, where TSE took his course on literary criticism in France; author of *Rousseau and Romanticism* (1919). See TSE, 'The Humanism of Irving Babbitt' (SE).
3–Paul Elmer More (1864–1937), critic, scholar and writer, author of *Shelburne Essays*: see Biographical Register.
4–G. R. Elliott taught at Amherst College, Mass.; author of *The Cycle of Modern Poetry: A Series of Essays toward Clearing our Present Poetic Dilemma* (1929)
5–Sherlock Bronson Gass (b. 1878), Professor of English at the University of Nebraska; author of *A Lover of the Choir* (1919), *A Tap on the Shoulder* (1929), contributed an essay 'The Well of Discipline' to *Humanism and America* (1930), 268–84.
6–Van Wyck Brooks (1886–1963), critic, biographer, historian; author of *The Ordeal of Mark Twain* (1920).
7–Randolph Bourne (1886–1918), progressive essayist: see *The Radical Will: Selected Writings of Randolph Bourne* (1977).
8–Lewis Mumford (1895–1990), historian, literary critic, sociologist, philosopher of technology; sometime associate editor of *The Dial*; author of *Herman Melville: A Study of His Life and Vision* (1929); later renowned for his work on cities and urban architecture,

B. Munson[1] have some reputation, though neither I think seems to me yet quite first-rate. I wish I could give you something more orderly and comprehensive than this, and if the names of any books that you ought to read occur to me I shall write to you again. As a matter of fact I should think that Dr Richards probably was better informed on contemporary American literature than I am.

Yours sincerely,
[T. S. Eliot]

TO *Norreys Jephson O'Conor*[2]
CC

27 January 1932   [Faber & Faber Ltd]

My dear O'Conor,

Thank you very much for your kind note of the 23rd which gave me much pleasure.[3] Is there any chance of your being in America yourself during part of that time? I have only seen Conrad Aiken once for ten minutes since he has been in England, but he tells me that he is likely to be in Cambridge during the winter so it seems to me possible that I may in America see something of the people whom I never see in London. And by the way how is the Seven Norreys Brothers book getting on?

With many thanks
Yours sincerely,
[T. S. Eliot]

---

including *The City in History* (1961; National Book Award) and *The Myth of the Machine* (2 vols, 1967, 1970).
1 – Gorham B. Munson (1896–1969), critic and editor, taught at the New School from 1927.
2 – Norreys Jephson O'Conor (1885–1958), American author, graduated from Harvard and taught at various universities, including Harvard, Grinnell and Bryn Mawr, before undertaking a period of independent research and writing in England, 1927–39. Publications include *Celtic Memories and Other Poems* (1913), *Songs of the Celtic Past* (1918), *Battles and Enchantments* (1922), and *Memoir*, with letters of Maarten Maartens (1930).
3 – O'Conor was delighted by the news. 'Harvard seems to me to have made its wisest and most fitting choice . . . One thing I am sure you will accomplish during your incumbency of the Norton chair, namely, to remind your colleagues and your students that, though the shield of Harvard bears the word "Veritas", that shield is surrounded by the legend "Christo et Ecclesiae".'

TO *Georges Cattaui*[1]   MS Bib Jacques Doucet

Candlemas [2 February] 1932   Faber & Faber Ltd

Dear Mr Cattaui

It will give me much pleasure if you can lunch with me, and one or two friends, on *Tuesday next* the 9th (Shrove Tuesday) at the *Oxford & Cambridge* Club at 1.15.

Sincerely yours,
T. S. Eliot

TO *Theodora Eliot Smith*[2]   CC

3 February 1932   [Faber & Faber Ltd]

My dear Theodora,

Thank you very much for your letter of the 17th January.[3] I think that there is a possibility of my being invited to lecture in Baltimore, and as I have never been there and should like to see the place, I shall certainly accept. I suppose that I shall see you in Boston at Christmas time, but it is more satisfactory to know that I shall at least see you in Baltimore. I am told by several people that the school in which you are teaching is considered one of the best in that part of the world, and the other day I met at lunch a lady who had been at school there herself. But I hope to have the opportunity of forming my own opinions.

I do not believe that Vivienne will be able to come with me. Her own health makes it unlikely and probably undesirable, and I am sorry to say that Mrs Haigh Wood has become very feeble lately.

Always affectionately,
Your uncle
[Tom]

1–Georges Cattaui (1896–1974), Egyptian-born (scion of aristocratic Alexandrian Jews, and a cousin of Jean de Menasce) French diplomat and writer; his works include *T. S. Eliot* (1958), *Constantine Cavafy* (1964), *Proust and his metamorphoses* (1973). TSE wrote to E. R. Curtius, 21 Nov. 1947: 'I received the book by Cattaui [*Trois poetes: Hopkins, Yeats, Eliot* (Paris, 1947)] and must say that I found what he had to say about myself slightly irritating. There are some personal details which are unnecessary and which don't strike me as in the best taste.'

2–Theodora Eliot Smith (1904–92) – 'Dodo' – daughter of George Lawrence and Charlotte E. Smith (TSE's sister). A graduate of Vassar College (AB, 1926), she studied too at Radcliffe College, 1926–7. She taught at Bryn Mawr School, Baltimore, from 1931, and attended summer school sessions at Cambridge University (1929, 1931, 1936, 1939); Oxford University (1937); London Speech Institute (1938); Harvard (1940, 1941, 1942).

3–Not found.

TO *John Middleton Murry*

3 February [1932]   [Faber & Faber Ltd]

Dear John,

Herewith is your manuscript and two copies of the page proof.[1] We are very anxious to get this pamphlet out on Thursday the 25th of this month which means that we cannot give very much time for revision. I hope that it is not asking too much of you to return a corrected proof by Monday next, the 8th. If that is absolutely impossible please drop me a line to say when we can have it, but I do hope that it is not beyond the bounds of possibility.

Yours in haste,
[Tom]

P.S. Could you please at the same time provide a very brief statement, if possible in one sentence, to be printed on the front flap of the pamphlet. I mean what is known in the trade as 'blurb'. I think it would be better to have such a statement from you rather than to prepare it in the office.

TO *I. A. Richards*

3 February 1932   [Faber & Faber Ltd]

Dear Richards,

Many thanks for your letter of the 26th which is very useful. On the strength of what you say I think I will accept Spencer's invitation.[2]

As for the rumour that I want to work very hard at Harvard, this is grossly exaggerated.[3] I have no notion of how it came to your ears. But

---

1 – *The Fallacy of Economics*, Criterion Miscellany 7, 1932.

2 – IAR had responded on 26 Jan. to TSE's enquiry of 22 Jan.: 'I'd be inclined myself, if I were going back again, to get into a House if I had the chance. It's true that dinner is early there. The doors used to shut by 7.0 at Dunster [House]. But that did not take a great deal of getting used to for me. Equally I used to dine out about 3 times a week at 8.15 as a rule – but my digestive habits are between those of an ostrich and a camel.

'The great point in favour of a House is that you lose the minimum of time by going into one. It's all organised for you, no arrangements to make. I've never done so much work in three months anywhere else.

'Another great advantage is the House libraries . . .

'I don't think $50 is excessive. I doubt whether you could make a much better bargain outside, all things considered. The other expenses inside a House are slight and the meals reasonably priced.'

3 – IAR wrote, 26 Jan.: 'I've heard a rumour that you don't feel 8 lectures is enough. They are rather obscure rumours – all that is clear is the consternation behind them. I found that

what I did tell them was that I thought I ought to do more for the money than deliver six public lectures which attract, I understand, an audience of old ladies from Boston. I merely wanted to have something to do with the more intelligent undergraduates (and from my experience there I should prefer the more intelligent undergraduates to the graduate students). I don't think it is excessive to give two informal lectures a week during the second half-year, but after what Maclagan told me I wrote cautiously to enquire about the work of correcting papers, setting examinations etc. and drudgery of that sort which I don't want to do. I don't think that the English department will be able to complain of me setting too high a standard of industry.

I gather, however, that you yourself gave a course, possibly the same course, on contemporary English literature, and that again makes me rather shy of the subject. I wish that I might see you to find out more exactly what you did with this course as I don't want merely to attempt to duplicate it.[1]

Review the book when you can, but what I am more anxious to have is an essay of some sort from you. Perhaps that is not very urgent, but I do certainly wish very much to have an article from you for publication while I am away.[2]

With many thanks,
Yours ever,
[T. S. E.]

lecturing Mon. Tues. Wed Thurs & duplicating them at Radcliffe left me quite sufficiently prostrated. In fact I used regularly to go to bed after giving two consecutive hours. I was glad enough to take Fri. & Sat. as holidays and get on with *Mencius on the Mind*. I fancy some of the best of the faculty (who think the students are overlectured as a general rule) would be very glad if you didn't do an hour's more work than you need.'

1–'As to Contemporary English Literature,' replied IAR (26 Jan.), 'I found I could be very free. I was asked, it is true, not to list *Ulysses* or *Lady Chatterley* in my prescribed reading, but in revenge I could read and talk about = e.g. the Scylla-Charybdis Library Doorway passage in *Ulysses*. Indeed I spent two or three very lively hours over it and found it a most diverting book to lecture about. Eliot House has some very pleasant young people in it [–] Ted Spencer and young Ellery Sedgwick. They would make everything beautifully untroublesome.'

2–IAR, review of Max Eastman, *The Literary Mind, Its Place in An Age of Science*, C. 12 (Oct. 1932), 150–5.

TO *J. H. Oldham*[1]

3 February 1932   [Faber & Faber Ltd]

My dear Oldham,

Thank you for your note of the 1st enclosing your memorandum.[2] I am writing at once to say that I shall be willing and able to attend such a meeting during one of the first two periods, though preferably not at the very week-end. I am afraid that if it takes place in September I should be unable to come as I shall be leaving for America.

As for the supplementary names out of the list you have given I only feel in principle that the larger proportion of laymen the better. For this reason I should certainly be glad to see the Master of Balliol[3] and Joseph Needham.[4] I am not quite sure whether Christopher Dawson[5] would add a great deal or not. Fawcett I do not know, and to judge from what I have read and heard of his I fear that if he spoke at all he might be very wordy. On the other hand he is representative of a contemporary attitude which does not otherwise appear. I should suggest him, however, only as an alternative to Lawrence Hyde[6] whom you have already invited. Father Thornton impresses me very favourably, and Raven[7] also might be a very

---

1–Joseph ('Joe') Oldham (1874–1969): indefatigable missionary, adviser and organizer for national and international councils and mission boards. Travelling all over the world to confer with missionary educators and colonial administrators, he worked closely with governments and public policy makers. From 1912 to 1927 he was editor of the *International Review of Missions*; and in 1921 became secretary of a new International Missionary Council (IMC). He was also Administrative Director of the International Institute of African Languages and Cultures, 1931–8. From 1934 he was Chair of the Research Committee for the Universal Christian Council for Life and Work, ably preparing the ground for the establishment in 1948 of the World Council of Churches. In 1939 he launched the fortnightly *Christian News Letter*, to which TSE became a faithful contributor, and he set up too an intellectual discussion group called The Moot, to which TSE also eagerly contributed. His works include *The World and the Gospel* (1916), *Christianity and the Race Problem* (1924), *The New Christian Adventure* (1929), *White and Black in Africa* (1930), *Real Life is Meeting* (1941), *Life is Commitment* (1953), and *New Hope for Africa* (1955). He was appointed CBE in 1951. See further Kathleen Bliss, 'J. H. Oldham, 1874–1969: from "Edinburgh 1910" to the World Council of Churches', in *Mission Legacies*, ed. G. H. Anderson et al. (1994); and K. Clements, *Faith on the Frontier: The Life of J. H. Oldham* (1999).
2–Oldham in his letter said he was enclosing 'a memorandum about a meeting of a group to consider the present religious situation, which I have already discussed with you and others'. The memorandum has not been found.
3–Dr Alexander Lindsay (1879–1952), Master of Balliol College, Oxford, 1924–49; Vice-Chancellor, 1935–8.
4–See TSE to Needham, 10 Mar. 1932.
5–Christopher Dawson (1889–1970), cultural historian: see Biographical Register.
6–Author of *Prospects of Humanism*.
7–Charles Earle Raven (1885–1964), theologian; Dean of Emmanuel College, Cambridge,

useful contributor. I should rather like to see on the list someone who is primarily an economist. Some time ago you suggested Josiah Stamp,[1] but I have no doubt you have thought this over since. What does have a bearing on the meeting, at least so far as the three persons responsible are concerned is the broadcast series on the Modern Dilemma to which MacMurray and Dawson have already made their contributions, and in which I am to take my part in March.[2] I am sure that MacMurray, Dawson and myself would all be glad if any other members had read or heard our remarks.

Have you thought of Victor Demant? His book on Unemployment struck me as very good so far as it goes.[3]

Yours ever,
[T. S. Eliot]

---

and residentiary canon of Liverpool Cathedral, 1924–31. From 1932, Regius Professor of Divinity at Cambridge; Master of Christ's College, Cambridge, 1939–50. His publications include *Christian Socialism, 1848–1854* (1920) and *Apollinarianism* (1923)

1 – Josiah Stamp (1880–1941), civil servant, industrialist, economist; author of *British Incomes and Property* (1916), *The Christian Ethic as an Economic Factor* (1926).

2 – TSE's broadcast was scheduled for 20 Mar.: 'Religion and Science: a Phantom Dilemma', *The Listener*, 23 Mar. 1932, 428–9. 'It is not science that has destroyed religious belief,' suggests Mr Eliot, 'but our preference of unbelief that has made illegitimate use of science.'

3 – Vigo Auguste Demant, *This Unemployment: Disaster or Opportunity?: An Argument in Economic Philosophy Submitted to the Christian Social Council by its Research Committee* (1931).

TO *Elsie Elizabeth Phare*[1]

3 February 1932   [*The Criterion*]

Dear Miss Phayre [*sic*],

I have your letter of the 26th ultimo.[2] Mr Richards did write to me some weeks ago about your novel, and I am extremely disappointed to hear that you do not want to publish it. This I feel is very much in its favour, and perhaps you will re-consider your decision or at least allow us to look at the manuscript.[3]

I noticed some of your published work while you were at Cambridge, and I have heard of you from others besides Mr Richards. I shall certainly keep your name in mind for reviewing. I have nothing particular on hand which I want reviewed for the next number, and in any case it is always a help if reviewers will write to me from time to time and suggest the names of books which they would like to review.

Yours sincerely,

[T. S. Eliot]

1–Elsie Phare (1908–2003) is better known by the surname Duncan-Jones: in 1933 she was to marry Austin Duncan-Jones (1908–67), who became Professor of Philosophy at Birmingham. She read English at Newnham College, Cambridge, where she was taught by IAR, FRL and Enid Welsford; she took a starred First with Special Distinction in both parts of the Tripos. As President of the Newnham College Arts Society, she invited VW (whom she found 'haughty') to give the talk that would become *A Room of One's Own* (1929). She went on to teach at Southampton University, 1931–4; Birmingham University, 1936–75. Her works include *The Poetry of Gerard Manley Hopkins: A Survey and Commentary* (1933); articles on subjects including TSE (1946); a British Academy Warton Lecture, 'A Great Master of Words: some aspects of Marvell's poems of praise and blame' (1976); and the third edition (with Pierre Legouis) of H. M. Margoliouth's *The Poems and Letters of Andrew Marvell* (2 vols, 1971).
2–'I don't know whether Mr I. A. Richards wrote to you some weeks ago about a novel which I then very much wanted you to look at & which I now don't want to publish: I should be very glad if you would take his recommendation as a reason for giving me a little reviewing for the *Criterion*.'
3–Phare responded, 13 Feb., 'Since you were so kind as to say that you would like to look at my novel I have sent it to you . . . I ought perhaps to say that Mr Richards had not seen this work when he recommended me – I expect he said so anyhow.' (IAR wrote in his diary, 30 Sept. 1932: 'She wrote on Eliot while in Paris & Hopkins later which have missed her a Fellowship.')

TO F. McEachran

CC

3 February 1932   [*The Criterion*]

Dear McEachran,

Thank you for your note of the 31st enclosing your review which does not seem to me to be too long.[1]

I should be delighted to sign a copy of my poems for yourself, but I am afraid that I cannot sign a copy for anyone who is a stranger to me.[2] You see there was also a limited signed edition of the poems at a higher price, and whatever one's opinion of the policy of issuing signed editions at all, I feel that it would be unfair to the silly people who have bought that edition to sign copies except for my own friends. I hope you will understand and agree with my feeling in the matter, and I would apologise to your friend. Were there no limited edition to the book it would give me great pleasure to sign the book for him.

Yours sincerely,

[T. S. Eliot]

TO *David Higham*[3]

CC

3 February 1932   [Faber & Faber Ltd]

Dear Higham,

Thank you for your letter of the 15th January.[4] I am favourably inclined to the proposal of the Holliday Bookshop, and will write to you again

---

1–'I am enclosing a review of the Sheed and Ward books and the Modern Theme of Ortega y Gasset, the latter of which rather disappointed me . . . [I]t could be shortened by detaching the paragraph on Ortega y Gasset . . .' See his review of four titles in the series 'Essays in Order' – E. I. Watkin, *The Bow in the Clouds*; M. de la Bedoyère, *The Drift of Democracy*; Carl Schmitt, *The Necessity of Politics*; Nicholas Berdyaev, *The Russian Revolution* – published by Sheed & Ward, and of José Ortega y Gasset, 532–6. TSE did dock the paragraph on Ortega y Gasset.

2–'A friend of mine here [Gresham's School], Mr A. D. Thomson and myself, both being admirers of your poems, would be very grateful if you would sign our copies of your collected poems . . . We are both actively engaged in popularizing *The Waste Land* among the more receptive elements in this school!'

3–David Higham (1896–1978), literary agent, worked for Curtis Brown Ltd, 1925–35; then for David Higham Associates; author of *Literary Gent* (memoir, 1978). FVM told Helen Jacobs, 20 May 1935, of Higham: 'He is an ebullient young man with a curly moustache, and an eager but not very accurate tennis player'; and he wrote to Joseph Chiari, 7 Feb. 1953 (when Higham was a director of Pearn, Pollinger, & Higham): 'Higham is a very active and pushing agent.'

4–Not found.

after I have looked through the material to decide whether I think it really fit for the purpose.[1]

With many thanks,
Yours sincerely,
[T. S. Eliot]

TO *Ranjee G. Shahani*[2]   CC

3 February 1932   [Faber & Faber Ltd]

Dear Sir,

We have read with interest your collection of stories entitled 'Children of Siva', and it is reluctantly that we have come to the conclusion that we cannot consider their publication.[3] While we recognize their merit we must face the fact that even in the best of times it is very difficult to sell volumes of short stories, and in the present conditions we feel that we should be wholly unjustified.

With many regrets,
Yours faithfully,
[T. S. Eliot]

TO *Dilys Powell*[4]   CC

3 February 1932   [Faber & Faber Ltd]

Dear Miss Powell,

Thank you very much for sending me the copy of *Life and Letters* with your very careful article.[5] I had heard about it from several friends, and was very glad indeed to be able to read it. I am probably the worst

---

1 – Contract for TSE's *John Dryden: The Poet, The Dramatist, The Critic* (reprints of BBC talks to be published by the Holliday Bookshop (New York, 1933), sent to TSE by Curtis Brown literary agency on 27 May 1932.
2 – Ranjee G. Shahani (1904–68), who had a DLitt from Paris, was author of *Shakespeare through Eastern Eyes*, intro. by JMM (1932); *Indian Pilgrimage* (1939); and various articles.
3 – Submitted on 24 Dec. 1931; recommended by J. M. Robertson.
4 – Dilys Powell (1901–95), journalist, author, film critic, BBC radio celebrity, wrote for the *Sunday Times* from 1928 and was film critic, 1939–79. Works include *Descent from Parnassus* (1934), *An Affair of the Heart* (1957) and *The Golden Screen: Fifty Years at the Films* (1989).
5 – 'The Poetry of T. S. Eliot', *Life and Letters* 7 (Dec. 1931), 386–419. Powell sent her article to TSE on 29 Jan., at the suggeston of OM (for whom Powell had worked as assistant until 1928).

possible judge of such criticism, and cannot possibly return you any criticism in detail, but your article seems to me on the whole extremely fair and just. I cannot help wishing that you had made a little more of the fragment of *Sweeny* [*sic*] *Agonistes* for which I have a particular affection, but that is merely an expression of taste on my part. By the way do I infer from a sentence of yours on page 415 that any remedy for the diseases of civilisation, in order to be a good remedy must also be a new one?[1]

With many thanks,
Yours sincerely,
[T. S. Eliot]

TO *Dilys Bennett*[2]

CC

3 February 1932   [Faber & Faber Ltd]

Dear Miss Bennett,

I must apologise for having kept your poems for so long without acknowledgment.[3] To begin with, although I had not the original with me to compare with, your translation from Musset struck me as quite a brilliant accomplishment in its kind. On some of the other poems I have taken the liberty of pencilling comments. In some places I think you have been tempted to use the wrong word merely to make a right rhyme, which is not quite so pardonable as using a wrong word to make a right rhythm. The long poem which you now call 'Rameh' seems to me a little strained in its effort to reach the grandiose, but your work interests me, and I should be glad to see more of it from time to time.

Yours sincerely,
[T. S. Eliot]

1–Powell replied on 5 Mar.: 'With regard to my remark about the diseases of civilisation . . . I am sorry if I implied that a remedy in order to be a good one must be new. I did not mean to make any judgment on any remedy, new or old. I merely wanted to say that the importance of your work to the present generation did not lie in the exposition of a hitherto untried remedy: whereas many people, I think, imagine that in Lawrence, for instance, they have found a new road to salvation. I spoke of him because my article was intended to be one of a series in which his work also should be discussed.'

2–Dilys Bennett (1906–60), poet and author. Born in Wales, she married in 1936 Alexander Laing, an academic at Dartmouth College, and became an American citizen. Works include *Another England* (1941) and *The Collected Poems of Dilys Laing* (1967).

3–Bennett, who was living in Seattle, Washington, was an acquaintance of Emily Hale who had introduced her work to TSE in 1931. 'Rameh' included this verse: 'And this I say in prophesy, – the rod / Of life shall blossom when the soul hath trod / The way of imperfection, and the world / Reweaves by love the broken web of God.'

TO *Harry H. Clark*[1]

3 February 1932   [*The Criterion*]

Dear Mr Clark,

I have read your essay on Nationalism in American Literature with much interest and appreciation.[2] My reason for rejecting it is simply that I do not think it would have the right moral effect on British readers, who would merely thank God that they are not as these people are, instead of being inspired to detect the same vice when it appears in England. I hope, however, that I may see more of your work.

Yours sincerely,
[T. S. Eliot]

TO *Stephen Spender*

3 February 1932   *The Criterion*

Dear Spender,

I ought to have written to you sooner to let you know that I heard from Lehmann of the Hogarth Press, and replied to tell him that we had no objection to his publishing eight of your poems in an anthology in the spring, and told him to make his arrangements with you irrespective of Faber & Faber. No doubt you have settled the choice of poems and the terms by now.

I think it would indeed be a good thing if you had a few more poems for our volume than were originally intended, though there is no reason to fix the number at forty. Anyway I hope you will let me know say by June how much material you have that you want to include in the volume so that we may make our plans for the autumn.[3]

1–Harry H. Clark (b. 1901), Assistant Professor of American Literature, University of Wisconsin – author of an essay published in *Humanism in America* – was working in Paris as a Guggenheim Fellow on a book, *Thomas Paine and Eighteenth Century Radicalism*.

2–Clark had submitted his essay, 'Nationalism and American Literature' (given as a lecture at the State University of Iowa) on 25 Nov. 1931.

3–Spender wrote on 4 Jan. that the eight poems requested by the Hogarth Press represented a quarter of the poems he had prepared for his Faber book. 'My poems don't vary much in size, so it would also be about a quarter of the number of pages in the book . . . But I suggest . . . that it might be better anyhow for me to wait until I had nearly fifty poems for my volume, and then the Hogarth Press Anthology wouldn't matter so much, and also my own volume would look better.' He wrote on 9 Feb.: 'I shall try and let you have forty poems by June for the volume.' John Sutherland remarks, 'Of the many hundreds of poems he wrote in these years, only thirty-three would reach print in *Poems, 1933*' (*Stephen Spender: The Authorized Biography*, 115–16).

I read Murry's article[s] in December and January with much interest, and [think] that they need dealing with seriously. I quite agree that his criticism of Russian Communism is a brilliant summary.[1] I wish that I was sure that his alternative was equally clear. That remains to be seen, and I am not encouraged by his approval of Rowse's book, which seemed to me wordy, vague and dangerously conservative. It also remains to be seen how much positive is left when you take out of Communism all that the Russians have put into it.

I am very glad to hear that you are getting a lot of work done. I look forward to hearing about German politics when you return.[2]

Yours ever,

T. S. Eliot

TO *Geoffrey Curtis*   TS Houghton

3 February 1932   Faber & Faber Ltd

My dear Curtis,

Thank you very much for your letter of the 17th January. You slightly abate my pleasure in it by your apologetic tone at the end for your 'unreserve'. That seems to me rather silly for what is the use of any correspondence between friends if one is in effect exchanging apologies for the friendship?

1 – 'By the way,' asked Spender (on 4 Jan.), 'did you read an article by Murry in the January *Adelphi*? I usually detest his stuff, but I think this is far the most brilliant short comment on contemporary party Communism that I've ever read. He's come to a conclusion about the relationship of Russia to the Communist Parties in Europe which is fully borne out by what [Christopher] Isherwood and I have seen of Communists here, although I could never have expressed my feeling so clearly as he has done.'

2 – 'I am working a lot now, mostly at poetry. I take a great deal of interest in politics, but things are so depressing at present that they don't bear any comment.' On 10 Mar. he reported: 'The presidential election is in full swing here, and the most terrific propaganda for Hindenburg is going on. I have an uneasy feeling that perhaps people will be sensible enough to realize that he is a complete puppet, and that the only motive for voting for him is one of blue funk at what the other candidates might do if they came into power. It is quite possibly insanely stupid of the middle parties not to have put up a young and active man instead of someone who is a puppet whose only qualification is the quite superstitious reverence everyone has for him. Heaven knows what will happen here if he is not elected. Hitler is so passionately hated that it is even possible the moderates will put in the Communist at the second vote rather than him. However almost as soon as this letter reaches you the results will be known. Also the idea that Hitler might be elected at the first vote has only occurred to me very recently as being a disturbing possibility.'

I was sorry that I missed you when you came up to London. I wish that you would explain to me what you mean by saying that the S.C.M. are the publishers for your poems. Of course I shall be delighted to write a line to the Secretary about the poems, and are you suggesting that I should provide a preface to them?[1] If so we shall have to discuss the matter carefully. I have not time to write more at the moment, but you are constantly in my thoughts.

Affectionately yours,

T. S. Eliot

P.S. I daresay that you might meanwhile find it useful to have these copies of some of your poems which I have kept for a long time.

TO *The Secretary, Student Christian Movement*   CC

3 February 1932   [Faber & Faber Ltd]

Dear Sir,

I understand that a volume of Devotional verse entitled 'Lyra Subapostolica' by a young friend of mine, the Reverend Geoffrey Curtis of Lichfield Theological College is likely to be sent to you with a view to publication. I trust that you will not take it as an impertinence on my part if I express the hope that the volume may receive favourable attention as I have been warmly interested in Father Curtis's poetry for several years.

Yours faithfully,

[T. S. Eliot]

TO *James Joyce*   CC

3 February 1932   [Faber & Faber Ltd]

My dear Joyce,

I return to you herewith two sheets of copy of correspondence[2] which has reached me, I imagine through the offices of Miss Weaver,[3] though

---

1–Curtis had visited London on 16 Jan., but failed to make contact. 'I noticed that S.C.M. house is near your premises. I think that they are the publishers for the poems. Would you write (1) a note to the reader encouraging perusal (2) in the event of publishing a line of preface?'

2–Not found.

3–Harriet Shaw Weaver (1876–1961), English editor and publisher: see Biographical Register, *L* 4, 5.

as I did not see the envelopes in which they were contained and there was no covering letter I cannot be sure. I am extremely sorry to learn of this new exasperation, but cannot for the life of me see what is to be done about it. Mr Rosenfeld's letter was no doubt well meant, but hardly seemed to me likely to accomplish anything.[1] I wish that I knew of a reliable lawyer in New York, but my own experience in an affair which was extremely irritating though of far less moment than yours, was very unsatisfactory, and I dropped my lawyer there altogether. I, however, am not in the position of having very much that is worth pirating. Thank you for letting me see the correspondence, and if I can be of the slightest use please let me know. Meanwhile I hope that you and your family are well and that you are able to work again.

Yours always sincerely,
[T. S. Eliot]

TO *Edgar Foxall*[2]   CC

3 February 1932   [*The Criterion*]

Dear Sir,

I have considered your letter of the 15th July and your enquiry about the confection of new words.[3] It is not a device which particularly commends itself to me. The idea, of course, is not a new one, and an argument in its favour may be found in *Alice in Wonderland*. Of course I admit that a similar technology has been extensively employed by Mr James Joyce, but you must remember that Mr Joyce has only arrived at it after a very long process of literary toil; that his use of it, though it may be justified by his own genius, is not necessarily a warrant for further experiment along these lines. Furthermore I think that in the verses you have shown,

---

1–Not identified, but possibly a letter from Paul Rosenfeld (1890–1946), American critic of music and letters.

2–Edgar Foxall (1906–90) left school at fourteen and worked in a variety of jobs (clerk, foreman, journalist) before becoming a teacher. His works include *Poems* (1938) and *Water Rat Sonata* (1940); and his poetry is represented in *Poetry of the Thirties* (1964).

3–Foxall (Ellesmere Port, Wirral) had written: 'I venture to ask your opinion upon three poems enclosed, in which I have used words I have coined. My reason for making this attempt at finding words to express sensations I have felt, is that I feel that, in reading, I am apt to pass familiar words without grasping their essential meaning in relation to the passage in which they have place. I thought that, by finding words which could be understood almost at first sight, I might, by startling readers into notice, get my points and sensations conveyed more readily.'

the composite words stand out far too conspicuously. I should advise you to spend ten or fifteen years seeing what you can do with the ordinary vocabulary of the language before pursuing these experiments. My own experience has been that forcing experimentation has sometimes tended to conceal from myself a poverty of what I had to communicate, and I have destroyed a fair number of my verses for this reason.[1]

Yours faithfully,
[T. S. Eliot]

TO *Theodore Spencer*   TS Houghton

10 February 1932   Faber & Faber Ltd

Dear Mr Spencer,

Thank you for your note of the 23rd January. I now think that I should very much like to join you in Eliot House, even though you are not Master, and send my respects to Merriman whom I remember though I do not think I have ever met him.[2] I hope that you will be able to detail for my service a nice negro scout whose name ought to be George.[3] I look forward to having your company during the winter.

Yours sincerely,
T. S. Eliot

---

1 – Foxall responded to this letter on 9 Feb., 'I agree that the coinages do not justify themselves . . . I have to struggle against my environment, which is a singularly bleak one. This industrial town, the little office in the steel works where I am employed, seem to conspire against me. I hate the damnation of genteel poverty.'

On 22 July 1970, Foxall would write from Penrhyn Bay, Llandudno, to the *TLS*: 'Turning up some old correspondence, I came across a letter from T. S. Eliot dated some thirty-eight years ago. The circumstances which preceded its receipt are still a source of amusement to me.

'In my early years I had the notion of creating composite words to fit into some poems I was then writing. These I made by beheading and disembowelling little used words which attracted me. The results were thoroughly bad in themselves, but appalling when set in the "poems".

'However, at that time of life, when ambition far outstripped talent, such considerations meant little in the way of lost sleep. Accordingly I sent them to T. S. E. in the hope of publication in *The Criterion* . . .

'Since the re-discovery of this letter, I have found myself more than once speculating upon the nature of those lost verses, which will never fall into the hands of the scholar.'

2 – Spencer had advised TSE that the Master of Eliot House was R. B. Merriman, 'whom you doubtless remember from your time'. See TSE to Merriman, 23 June 1932.

3 – Spencer replied, 22 Mar.: 'As for getting you a black servant named George, that will be perhaps more difficult, but you will have 3 porters or janitors, all named Jim who will – if my experience is any criterion – make you very comfortable.'

TO *Herbert Read*[1]   CC

10 February 1932   [*The Criterion*]

Dear Herbert,

I would have answered your note by return but that I was waiting
for Frank to make up his mind whether he could afford to interrupt his
excavations at Ur of the Chaldees in order to lunch with us.[2] Apparently
they have got to a point at which they cannot be left, so will you lunch
on Saturday? I forgot to ask Vivienne whether it would be convenient at
home, because I am sure she would like to see you and also Mrs Read if
she is coming with you; but unless you hear to the contrary by tomorrow
will you come [to] Clarence Gate Gardens for Saturday lunch?

                                        Yours ever,
                                        [T. S. E.]

TO *Caresse Crosby*[3]   CC

10 February 1932   [Faber & Faber Ltd]

Dear Mrs Crosby,

I sent you my note on Monday and am now returning the *bonne feuille*
of *Bubu*. As my note is so short it seems properer to call it Preface rather
than Introduction, but I think it is about the same length as Aldous
Huxley's, and about the length that you want. After all I don't suppose
many people read these introductions. All that is really useful is the name
of an introducer.[4]

1–Herbert Read (1893–1968), English poet and literary critic: see Biographical Register.
2–HR said (6 Feb.) he was coming to London, and hoped to meet TSE for lunch.
3–Caresse Crosby (1892–1970), née Jacob (her parents were wealthy New Yorkers),
married in 1922 the poet Harry Crosby, with whom she set up in Paris an imprint called
Editions Narcisse, which became the Black Sun Press: they published writers including JJ,
DHL, Hart Crane and EP. Following Harry Crosby's suicide in Dec. 1929, she continued
to expand the Black Sun Press – publishing works including Crane's *The Bridge* (1930) and
editions of her husband's writings – before returning to the USA. In later years she took
initiatives in various fields: she opened the Crosby Gallery of Modern Art, Washington, DC;
she launched a quarterly journal, *Portfolio: An Intercontinental Review*; and she became
active in the international peace movement, co-founding both Citizens of the World and
Women Against War. Writings include *The Passionate Years* (memoir, 1953).
4–TSE remarked in his 'Preface' to Charles-Louis Philippe, *Bubu of Montparnasse*, trans.
Laurence Vail (Paris: Crosby Continental Editions, 1932), that *Bubu*, which he had read on
his first visit to Paris in 1910, 'stood for Paris as some of Dickens' novels stand for London
. . . Philippe . . . has an intense pity for the humble and oppressed, a pity still more akin
to that of Dickens' Russian disciple Dostoievski; and a pathos which as in Dickens and

The translation seems to me on the whole adequate but not highly polished, and I think it could do with a little revision. For instance there are places where the translator seems to me to have contented himself with the literal equivalent rather than the word in current use. For instance 'fonctionnaire' is hardly 'functionary' in either English or American. The word is more comprehensive of course than 'Civil Servant' because it can include people of authority in banks or industries, so I should suggest 'Head of a department'. There are other translations of the same kind. As for the slang, practically no slang is translateable at all. The difficulty is that to anyone who knows both languages the nearest English or American equivalent seems more grotesque than a literal translation. But after all translations are meant for people who do not know the original language, and I daresay that they get a closer approximation out of their own slang. There are other places, however, where something not quite slang is in question. For instance 'la gueule en avant' is very feebly translated by 'the jaw thrust forward' and I wish that your translator could have found a more forcible equivalent for 'tu t'emerdes torcher tes frères'. I hope that the Preface will be satisfactory, but I am quite ready to alter it if desirable.[1]

Yours sincerely,

[T. S. Eliot]

TO *John Middleton Murry*

TS Morgan Library

10 February 1932   [Faber & Faber Ltd]

Dear John,

I must apologise for the delay in considering the essay about Katherine which you sent me.[2] I agree that it has a good deal of merit, and I think that the author has noticed some very important things which have usually

---

Dostoievski trembles on the edge of the maudlin. He differs from both of the greater men by the absence of any religious or humanitarian zeal: he is not explicitly concerned with altering things. And in that he is perhaps the most faithful to the point of view of the humble and oppressed themselves, is more their spokesman than their champion. You can look towards Christianity or towards communism, according to your predisposition, but Philippe himself is no propagandist.'

1 – Crosby responded on 16 Feb. that TSE's piece was 'more than I hoped for . . . I am delighted that we can publish it with BUBU for I know that it will make a great deal of difference to English and American readers . . . I have written to Laurence Vail about the suggestions you made in the translation; I am sure he will be glad to have your opinion and hope he will find something better for the one or two expressions you cite.'

2 – Not identified. Katherine is presumably Katherine Mansfield, JMM's late wife.

been overlooked, but I am not quite satisfied that the essay as a whole is quite what is wanted, so I am returning it.

Yours with thanks,
Tom

TO *I. A. Richards*   CC

10 February 1932   [Faber & Faber Ltd]

Dear Richards,

Many thanks for your letter of the 5th.[1] I wish very much that I might come down to your Pepys dinner especially if Ponsonby[2] is not to give his after-dinner causerie this year. But I am afraid that it is very unlikely that I shall be able to get away, so you had better make your arrangements and ask some other guest. I hope, however, that you will be up in London before very long.

I should very much like to have for the *Criterion* the paper you are reading in Oxford. What I have to set about now is to accumulate as many good articles by the best people that I can, in order to provide effective numbers while I am away, but if your paper is ready, and you would prefer to have it brought out sooner I could use it in June or September.[3]

With many regrets,
Yours ever,
[T. S. E.]

P.S. I still feel very doubtful about contemporary English literature, but I suppose somebody will give this course if I don't, so I might as well do it as anyone else. After all I shall not be speaking to the same pupils that you did.[4]

1–IAR invited TSE to attend the Pepys Dinner at Magdalene College on 23 Feb.

2–Possibly Colonel Sir Charles Edward Ponsonby, 1st Bt (1879–1976).

3–IAR was to give a paper, on 'Science Value and Poetry', at Oxford on 28 Feb., and said he might be able to let TSE have it 'perhaps as an article. It will deal with *Eastman* partly perhaps. The same views (as far as I can tell) as before but since nobody has yet, for me, got near seeing what the old views were, it would, if I could make them clearer, seem a novelty of opinion.' IAR's review of Max Eastman's *The Literary Mind: Its Place in an Age of Science* (1931), C. 12 (Oct. 1932), 150–5, was collected in his *Complementarities* (1990).

4–IAR had written, 5 Feb.: 'I did, roughly, De la Mare, Hardy, Bridges, Yeats, Joyce, Lawrence & yourself as a course. Probably the same course as you are asked for (I fancy they called it *English 26* or something of that sort. I found I had a quite free hand and could be as [?arbitrary] and unsystematic and incomplete as I liked.'

TO *Edmund Cork*

10 February 1932   [Faber & Faber Ltd]

Dear Sir,

I must apologise for my delay in answering your letter of the 13 January.[1] I should, of course, always be interested to consider publication with a firm of the standing of the Houghton Mifflin Company, but it happens that at the time you wrote and now the only things which I am likely to want to publish have already been arranged for. I shall be glad, however, to keep your suggestion in mind for some future book.

Yours very truly
[T. S. Eliot]

TO *Charles Smyth*

10 February 1932   [Faber & Faber Ltd]

Dear Smyth,

I am afraid Thursday afternoon is impossible for me as I have a committee for the whole afternoon.[2] In any case I think it would be better for me to send you a draft of our suggestions first for your consideration, and then, if you could manage a half-day in town in a week or so, so much the better.

I listened to your Dilemma on Sunday and liked it very much.[3] In fact I have very few criticisms to make. It does strike me that the phrase 'Institutional Religion' which recurred several times is rather an

---

1 – W. Edmund Cork (London representative of Hughes Massie & Co., Copyright Agents; literary agent for Agatha Christie) wrote on behalf of the Houghton Mifflin Company to ask whether they might publish TSE in the USA.

2 – Smyth had written on 8 Feb., in response to a (now lost) letter from TSE: 'I have this *Thursday* afternoon free, and could come up by the 1.- which gets to L'pool St at 2.19 if that would be of any use to you. Or by a later train, for I have nothing on that night. I hope my Dilemma was up to scratch. Could you let me know by return if Thursday will do?'

3 – Smyth wrote ('Feast of Charles, K & M'): 'the Modern Dilemma as seen by Me [in his radio broadcast] is the fact that man's increasing control over nature does not seem to have diminished in the least his fundamental impotence (which, of course, isn't peculiarly modern), and the solution, also as seen by Me, is institutional religion. But I am left shuddering at my own impudence.' On 7 Feb., he spoke of 'the age-old problem of how to reconcile the value of all human achievement with its ultimate futility. How is it that man can do so much and yet so little? How comes it that he is at once so self-reliant and so dependent. It is this combination of man's amazing potentialities with his no less amazing limitations that constitutes the Modern Dilemma as I see it.'

unnecessary periphrasis for the Church simply. After all Bolshevik Russia is an Institutional Religion, and some of what you said might be used to defend that cause as well as our own, and I don't see why one needs to use a phrase which would also comprehend Shinto and Tibetan Buddhism. Otherwise I was very highly pleased.[1]

Yours ever,

[T. S. Eliot]

P.S. Let me know if you can see any day next week or the week after when you might come to London. On the other hand it seems a pity to bring you up just for this purpose. Are you coming up, for instance, to see the French pictures?

TO *Charles B. Blanchard*   CC

12 February 1932   [Faber & Faber Ltd]

Dear Mr Blanchard,

Thank you for your letter of the 28th ultimo.[2] I am pleased that Mr Van Doren should wish to include some of my work in the anthology which you are about to publish. I feel, however, although with regret, that the number of items of my verses which he wishes to use form rather too high a proportion of my total production. I should be quite willing to allow you to use the poems listed in your letter with the exception of J. Alfred Prufrock and the Hollow Men, and if Mr Van Doren were willing to omit one of the other six poems then perhaps one of the more recent Ariel poems could be included.

Perhaps we may leave the question of terms until the list of poems has been agreed upon.

Yours very truly,

[T. S. Eliot]

1–Smyth responded on the '1st Sunday of Lent': 'I accept your criticism of my Dilemma, but my defence of institutional religion as such seemed to me the necessary prolegomena to a defence of the Church as *the* one institution, – I hadn't time for both.'
2–Blanchard, Little, Brown & Company was planning to publish, in the autumn of 1932, an anthology of American poetry edited by Mark Van Doren, and requested permission to reprint no fewer than eight poems from *Poems 1909–1925*: 'The Love Song of J. Alfred Prufrock', 'Rhapsody on a Windy Night', 'Portrait of a Lady', 'Morning at the Window', 'Gerontion', 'The Hippopotamus', 'Sweeney Among the Nightingales' and 'The Hollow Men'.

TO *Douglas Jerrold*   CC

12 February 1932   [Faber & Faber Ltd]

My dear Jerrold,

I have read your appeal to Conservative members with much interest.[1]
I am still, however, far from clear as to what you have in mind. So I hope
that you will allow me to make a few comments before going any further.

You say 'What has to be done is what has been done for the Socialists by
the Fabian Society during the past forty years'. I understand the pertinence
of the analogy, but it seems to me in more than one way misleading. It
is misleading in so far as it suggests that all that Conservatism has to
do today is to build up a body of thought and research in opposition
to Fabianism, and forty years behind the times, because it seems to me
that what Conservatism or Toryism has to do, if it has anything to do
at all, is much more serious than that. You have no longer merely to
compete with the pinhead philosophy of populist peers or the perpetual
pamphleteering of an irresponsible Irish mountebank. Fabianism, in other
words, is no longer of the slightest account. Marx and his German and
Russian disciples are infinitely more serious and important people.

The parallel with Fabianism seems to me misleading in another respect.
The Fabians began in quite different, and in some ways much more
advantageous conditions. A very small body of intellectuals wrote and
lectured for a good many years in only very distant relation to Parliamentary
activities. The Fabians were not bothered by nominal alliance with an
enormous mass of people in nominal accord with their ideas, but had to
a large extent the opportunity to create their own following. But people
who wish to promulgate Conservative ideas today must be up against a
very serious obstacle indeed, that is to say the Conservative party and its
followers.

You say further 'to expound and to popularize Conservative doctrines
is, to-day [*sc.* to us], the supreme task of Conservatism to-day'. It may be
the supreme task but it does not seem to me the primary task, because it
seems to me of first importance to have doctrines and to understand them

---

1 – Jerrold sent TSE on 9 Feb. a two-page document entitled 'An Appeal to Conservative
Members of the House of Commons for Organised Propaganda in the country on behalf of
Conservative Principles', and asked if he would allow the organisation to use his name 'as
a provisional signatory' to it. '[George] Lloyd, [Jack] Squire and myself are approaching a
number of more or less key people simultaneously with a view to getting their signatures
and enlisting their co-operation generally.' Jerrold, who wished to become an MP, was a
High Tory.

and of only secondary importance to popularize them. If I knew myself what other Conservatives think in so far as they think at all, I should know with greater certainty whether I am really a Conservative. Now the definition and elaboration of doctrine seems to me a task which can only be performed by a small number of people in active collaboration, with no immediate concern with Parliamentary affairs, and with a very long view of present difficulties. I do not yet see what can be accomplished by an appeal to Conservative members of the House of Commons to expound and to popularise Conservative doctrines. There are a great many Conservatives in the House of Commons. One might even say a great many too many, and I should question how many of these people have any but the vaguest notion of what Conservatism is. I can see no advantage, in other words, in inviting to collaboration a rabble of louts and blockheads whose usefulness only begins after other people have done some thinking.

Finally, your leaflet. Although I agree cordially with a great deal which is positive so far as it goes, it seems to me to avoid one of the principal issues. I doubt whether agreeable phrases such as 'Church and State', 'Home and Family', and so on will take many tricks. In any case, before people use them, as they'll want to do, they ought to be made to understand to what they are committing themselves. One great question to me is whether Conservatism can recover from being what it has tended to become all through the last century – merely a Conservative wing of Industrial Liberalism. In other words how far is Conservatism committed to Capitalism? So many of the people who call themselves Conservatives today are people who owe whatever social position they have (and their Conservatism is a function of their social position) to the purchasing power gained through the industrialization of Britain. In any sort of Conservatism to which I can myself subscribe I should have to hold myself free for what from the industrial point of view might be the grossest economic heresy.

I affirm finally that the recommendation to take as a model the Fabian Society as it was first formed is a confession of weakness, but that if it is really meant then other suggestions in the leaflet should forward this design.

Yours sincerely,
[T. S. Eliot]

TO *J. S. Barnes*[1]

TS Buona Barnes

17 February 1932   Faber & Faber Ltd

Dear Jim,

I am very sorry too about Friday. I found that I had a lunch engagement that day, and would have rung you up on Thursday but was told that you were already out of town. Your not coming in the morning did not put me out in the least, but I am extremely sorry to learn the reason. Your wife has my sympathy in her difficulty in adapting herself to this climate, particularly at this time of year, and I hope that she will soon be restored. You have certainly had a very difficult time.[2]

1–James Strachey Barnes (1890–1955): son of Sir Hugh Barnes. Brought up in Florence by his grandparents, Sir John and Lady Strachey, he went on to Eton and King's College, Cambridge. During WW1 he served in the Guards and Royal Flying Corps. Enamoured by Italy, he came in time to forge a friendship with Mussolini; and as a Roman Catholic he sought to credit the notion that Fascism and Catholicism were compatible. TSE was to write to HWE, 7 Jan. 1937: 'There is a man whom I have known for some years named Jim Barnes, otherwise Major James Strachey Barnes . . . Jim is rather a queer bird. He is a cousin of the Stracheys and I think his father is a head of the Anglo-Persian Oil Company or something of the sort. He is very correct, having been to Eton, Cambridge, in the Blues and ended the War in the Air Force. He is a violent Italophile, a pal of Mussolini, and wrote a couple of books about Fascism in its early stages. He is also some kind of honorary valet to the Pope, being a R. C. convert.' To Sir Robert Vansittart, 12 Jan. 1939 (when Barnes was applying to be Assistant Director of the British Institute in Florence): 'James Strachey Barnes is the younger brother of an old friend of mine, Mrs St John Hutchinson, and I have known him, in this way, off and on for a good many years. He wrote two books on Fascism . . . and was one of its earliest champions in this country. He was brought up in Italy (before going to Eton: he was subsequently in the Blues, then a Major in the Air Force, and at King's after the War), has an Italian wife, and is the most convinced pro-Italian and pro-Fascist that I know. He is a Roman Catholic convert, and has or had some honorary appointment at the Vatican; but manages to combine this with a warm admiration for Mussolini, from which it follows that he has disapproved of British policy whenever that policy did not favour Italian policy. He was for a time a correspondent of Reuter, and in that capacity was with the Italians in Abyssinia. He has since lectured in America on international politics, and I believe took the opportunity of defending Italy. In private life he is rather a bore, and talks more than he listens, somewhat failing to appreciate that the person to whom he is talking may have other interests and other engagements.

'I would not encumber you with these details – which for aught I know may be all in his favour – but that my conscience is uneasy if I give a recommendation in which I do not say all that I know which may be relevant . . .'

See also David Bradshaw and James Smith, 'Ezra Pound, James Strachey Barnes ("the Italian Lord Haw-Haw") and Italian Fascism', *Review of English Studies* 64 (2013), 672–93
2–Barnes had been unable to get up to town from Westcott, near Dorking, because his wife was down with the flu; and his telephone had been out of order.

The subject of your letter is very interesting, but needs a good deal of conversation.[1] Curiously enough I had had a communication, I suppose

1 – Barnes wrote (undated): 'What I wanted to see you about was this:- I have been talking to Mosley and been telling him that you must have a movement for a party to represent. He must go ahead as best seems to him; but what seems to me essential to supplement anything he may be doing in the way of "activist" groups & political organizations on party lines, is an intellectual movement promoted much in the same kind of way as the Fabian Society prepared the Socialist movement. He agrees – and plans are on foot.

'Well, my idea is to make it a non-party organization, a thing round which young people of all parties and no parties might rally for the purpose of study and discussion and vulgarization on the basis of a certain ideology.

'Now I am convinced you agree on most points with my point of view and I am very anxious to keep at a distance those who do not agree on the essentials. This may not be possible altogether, but it should be possible to load the dice with the essentials. The essentials to my mind are the necessity of moral leadership and a real catholicity of ideas. After which, it is largely a matter of pragmatism.

'We want to make an end of this civilization based on [illegible word] ego-centric principles & pure rationalism. The doctrinaire liberal regime (whether implied or acknowledged consciously) under which we live now represents conservatism in the sense of inertia and resistance to change. On the other hand, we do not want to move to the middle class paradise of robots towards which both American capitalism & socialism seem to be pushing us. We need universal ideas & enhanced personality. The state must be organized, but organized to allow for personality to flourish, a harmony in variety. Wealth must go with responsibility. We must cease to regard technical questions as matters on which to take sides – and nearly all practical questions are such. Call this Fascism if you like, as I do – or not. It depends on how you weigh up that phenomenon. Mosley can pursue Fascism as a party man. I want to get down to the nameless essence of a right attitude & right principles & get people to think along these lines, till the professors begin teaching it & the young become formed by it.

'I haven't the time here to tell you [?easily] what I mean, but you know me & my views well enough to guess – and what is suggested is this:-

'On the one hand, a jolly big comfortable room where we can get people together to talk; and an energetic organizing secretary and sufficient funds to give the new Fabian Society a start on modest lines. On the other hand, the publication of a book of essays by a group of carefully chosen persons (8 or 10 persons writing 8 or 10 thousand words each), each tackling the ideology of the movement from his own angle. Round this book will rally all those who approve – the book to come out in July or the early Autumn. It is a book which we can be certain will be taken notice of, if we choose the right contributors. Its effect may be the beginning of what will prove decisive in the destinies of this country.

'I don't want Mosley to write, because I don't want the public to identify the Society with the New Party – and the people I want are:-

    Myself
    Yourself
    Christopher Dawson
    Sir Theodore Chambers (the great town planning architect)
    perhaps Douglas Jerrold

These would set the right tone.

'Aldous Huxley might strike the right tone too. I think he would if I asked him.

'Harold Nicolson would probably have to contribute & if he kept himself (or if we kept him) out of his silly lapses, he might do something v. good too. Any other suggestions would be welcomed.

confidential, from Douglas Jerrold on similar lines only a few days ago. I objected to Jerrold's project on two grounds. (1) That the principles were not made clear enough and (2) that the method of procedure seemed to me mistaken, and I now find myself involved in an elaborate correspondence with him. Between ourselves one of my objections to Jerrold's scheme is that he is involved with Jack Squire whom I do not much like,[1] and with George Lloyd,[2] of whose judgement I am not at all sure. Also his scheme is essentially on party lines, and I think that one such as you suggest which would have no party affiliation would be much more hopeful. One of the great difficulties at the inception of such a plan is not merely whom to get in but, what is still more important, whom to keep out. It seems to me a little premature to discuss rooms etc. Your first job would be of course to get a small and reliable nucleus of people, and it would be better to take a great deal of time over that rather than admit even one undesirable person.

I think perhaps the best thing is to wait until you can come up to London when we can have a talk about it, and I could tell you more about Jerrold's notion. Perhaps by that time you will have worked out in more detail your scheme for a book of essays.[3]

Yours ever,
T. S. E.

'Anyhow I want your consent to the idea in principle – for I attach great importance to your contribution. Christopher Dawson will help, if he is given till the late summer.

'If you will say "yes" in principle, I can put up a concrete scheme to Mosley and then I shall endeavour to get him to raise the means for the finance – just the minimum required for a fair start (£10,000 would be more than sufficient and I am sanguine of getting that, provided I can get you & one or two A1 others).

'Please let me have your answer as soon as possible, as I shall be seeing Mosley on Monday 22nd & want to lay things before him in writing soon after that.'

1 – J. C. Squire (1884–1958), poet and critic, literary editor of NS 1913–19; founding editor of The London Mercury, 1919–34. Squire scorned TWL: 'Mr. Eliot believes the poem to be about the decay of Western civilisation and his own utter sickness with life . . . A grunt would serve equally well' (London Mercury, Oct. 1923).

2 – George Lloyd (1879–1941), Conservative politician, Anglo-Catholic, opponent of the National Government, whom Tories of the radical right (like Jerrold) wished to replace Baldwin.

3 – Barnes replied on 18 Feb.: 'I agree with your remarks entirely. Jerrold's idea might be able to be worked in with mine, if he doesn't stand out on reactionary lines. I don't think George Lloyd is our kind of sponsor.'

Harold Nicolson wrote on 2 Mar. 1932: 'Lunch with T. S. Eliot and Jim Barnes at the Spanish restaurant in Swallow Street. We discuss the making of a symposium on modern politics. I say that unless we tell our contributors that the book is New Party or fascist in tendency we are not playing fair. And that if we do tell them this we shall not get good contributors. I thus propose that Jim should write an Introduction showing where Tom [Mosley] has

TO *Paul Léon*[1]   CC

17 February 1932   [Faber & Faber Ltd]

Dear Sir,

I thank you for your letter of the 9th instant, and [I] am extremely
pleased to hear that Mr Joyce has recovered his ownership of the world
rights of *Ulysses*. I note what you say further about an American edition
of *Ulysses*, and the conditions laid down, all of which are perfectly
reasonable.[2]

In the present circumstances I desire to inform Mr Joyce that we are
still interested in the proposal which was made to him last summer, that
one or more of the sections of *Ulysses* should appear in the Criterion
Miscellany. I am writing to Mr Joyce to this effect.

                                        Yours sincerely,
                                        [T. S. Eliot]

---

made mistakes, that he should send Tom that Introduction, and that on the basis of that
Introduction he should invite Keynes etc. to contribute. Eliot agrees. He is very yellow
and glum. Perfect manners. He looks like a sacerdotal lawyer – dyspeptic, ascetic, eclectic.
Inhibitions. Yet obviously a nice man and a great poet. My admiration for him does not flag.
He is without pose and full of poise' (*Diaries and Letters 1930–1939*, ed. Nigel Nicolson
[1966] 111).

1–Paul Léon, né Paul Léopoldovich (1893–1942?): cultured multilingual Jewish émigré
from the Bolshevik revolution who had settled in Paris; he met JJ in 1928, when JJ was forty-
seven and Léon thirty-five. He became JJ's unpaid assistant and amanuensis from 1930, and
protected his papers even after the Nazis took over Paris. Léon was eventually seized by the
German authorities and despatched to a camp where he died in unknown circumstances.
See *The James Joyce–Paul Léon Papers in the National Gallery of Ireland: A Catalogue*,
compiled by Catherine Fahy (1992); John Naughton, 'Arm in arm with a literary legend'
(interview with Alexis Léon), the *Observer*, 13 Jan. 1991.

2–'I am acting as lawyer for Mr Joyce in Paris and according to his wishes I am to inform
you that I am in the possession of a letter from Miss Beach containing a declaration annulling
the contract which existed between her and Mr Joyce and a recognition of his ownership of
the world rights for *Ulysses*. This letter is, according to French law, a valid deed of transfer
so that at present Mr Joyce is the owner of the world rights for *Ulysses*.

'In view of the fact that Mr Joyce is to receive within the next fortnight a proposal for an
American edition of *Ulysses* I am directed to draw your attention to the fact that it is urgent
to obtain any other offers for such an edition in the meantime in order to have a basis for
discussion.

'There are four preliminary conditions which Mr Joyce wishes me to state to you as
follows:

      1. There will not be any preface.
      2. The text is to be published unabridged and unaltered.
      3. The publication is to be made as soon as possible.
      4. The text of the 11th Paris edition is to be read by an expert proof reader.'

17 February 1932   [Faber & Faber Ltd]

My dear Joyce,[1]

I have your letter of the 13th, and also the copies of your correspondence with Hamish Miles[2] which reached me a few days earlier, and which I return to you herewith. I had also a letter from Monsieur Paul Léon of the 9th instant, to which I have replied.[3]

I am delighted to hear that you have recovered the rights of *Ulysses*, and I hope that you can now arrange an American edition on satisfactory terms. Should you not be able to come to an agreement with Mr Bennett Cerf, I believe that there are one or two other American publishers who would be very much interested. But I will wait to hear from you after you see Mr Cerf on the 21st before making any suggestions.[4]

Your recovery of the *Ulysses* rights suggests our raising again the question which Morley and I discussed with you last summer, of publishing some of the sections of *Ulysses* in the Criterion Miscellany. As I believe you considered the suggestion rather favourably I should like to know how you feel about it now. One of the points in its favour would be that it would help to keep the pot boiling until *Work in Progress* appears, and would also provide the new book with a rather better educated public. We might merely use one or two of the sections as we have already done with *W.I.P.*, or alternatively we might proceed to print one by one all of the sections that can be published in England.

I am afraid from current indications that there is no immediate prospect of a relaxation of the censorship in this country, and possibly the tendency is even more obscurantist than ever. I am cordially in agreement with your dislike of a bowdlerized edition, and would never have contemplated making such a suggestion to you on behalf of my firm, but I do think that both of my suggestions avoid this kind of mutilation. I should very much like to know what you feel about it. According to the last return the total sales so far for *A.L.P.* are 6546 and for *H.C.E.* 3655,[5] and during the last week we sold 47 copies of the former and 10 copies of the latter.

1 – The first page of this letter, ending 'published in England' is missing from Buffalo and has been taken from the carbon copy.
2 – Hamish Miles (1894–1937), author and publisher's editor (Jonathan Cape Ltd).
3 – See TSE's letter to Léon, 17 Feb., above.
4 – JJ wrote on 13 Feb.: 'My daughter-in-law's brother [Robert Kastor], a N.Y. stockbroker, is bringing me a personal offer for the U.S. publication of *Ulysses* . . . from a friend of his, Mr Bennett Serf [*sic*], who has two books of mine in his *Modern Library* . . . I am at present owner of all the rights of *Ulysses*.'
5 – *Anna Livia Plurabelle* and *Haveth Childers Everywhere*.

I am keeping Terence Gray's letter to you[1] until I can get the information for you of the present situation in Cambridge.

The copy of the *Correspondent* arrived this morning, and I have not yet had time to read it.[2] Do you wish me to return it to you when I have finished it? I believe it is the first time that I have ever opened a copy of that periodical.

Desmond Harmsworth's publishing firm does not promise to amount to much.[3] I do not know anything about the Duff who has written the book about you. In any case we have no right to object to its publication and have no desire to do so. The main thing for us is that Gorman's book should have your nihil obstat, and that we should be allowed to say so. I will make enquiries again about his manuscript.

I am very glad to hear that you are rather better again, and hope that the first section of *W.I.P.* will soon be ready.

Yours ever sincerely,
T. S. Eliot

to *Marguerite Caetani*[4]   CC

17 February 1932   [Faber & Faber Ltd]

Dear Marguerite,

I succeeded in obtaining your twelve lottery tickets for the Grand National at a price of £6. 2s. 6d. including 2/6 for the messenger. I thought it better not to send you the tickets until I hear from you to that effect. Meanwhile I am lodging them in our office safe here. Please note that they are registered in the name of Aroma, 24 Russell Square, London. The numbers of the tickets are HM 73651, HM 73655, HM 73654, HM 73593, HM 73595, HM 73588, HM 73587, HM 73592, HM 73589, and MJ 45034 [*sic*]. I await your instructions.

1 – Terence Gray (1895–1986), Director of the Festival Theatre, Cambridge (where he promoted verse drama and expressionist plays), 1926–33. Gray's letter has not been traced.
2 – 'I send you an article [by the Catholic scholar and writer Daniel Rops] which has just come out in *Le Correspondent* which, as you probably know, is the oldest review in France.'
3 – JJ asked in his letter (13 Feb.): 'Desmond Harmsworth showed me a book "J. J. and the Common Reader" by – Duff, which he thinks of publishing if I do not object. I told him to go ahead but mentioned you. It would be well to find out from Gorman's N.Y. publishers what has become of him and his biography.' See Charles Duff, *James Joyce and the Plain Reader* (1932).
4 – Marguerite Caetani, née Chapin (1880–1963) – Princesse di Bassiano – literary patron and editor: see Biographical Register.

Yours affectionately,
[Tom]

TO *Alexander McKechnie* CC

17 February 1932   [Faber & Faber Ltd]

Dear Sir,

Thank you for your letter of the 12th instant which has had our consideration.[1] It has of course been my view that such a series as the Great Languages[2] ought eventually to comprehend a volume on Gaelic, which should deal with Irish and Scottish Gaelic, and possibly also with Welsh and its relation to Breton and Cornish. But we have not approached any scholar on the subject. A series like this, which although it expects a steady sale cannot look for a great immediate sale, has to be developed very slowly, and it will at best be several years before we contemplate such a volume. Meanwhile I can only thank you for your suggestion, and for your interest.

Yours faithfully,
[T. S. Eliot]
Director

1–McKechnie asked if F&F would consider a volume on Gaelic in their projected 'Great Languages' series. He had an Oxford B.A. Hons in Modern Languages; had been a Scottish Delegate at the Celtic Congress; and had translated two Italian books. For the last six years – having 'an intense love of my ancestral tongue' – he had been studying Irish and Scots Gaelic.

2–A series on the 'Great Languages', under the general editorship of G. E. K. Braunholtz, Professor of Comparative Literature at the University of Oxford, had been launched by F&F in 1932 with the volume *The Greek Language* by B. F. C. Atkinson (Under-Librarian, University Library, Cambridge). TSE wrote in a related (undated) internal memo: 'I like the notion of a History of English Literature, though I like it less if Jake Spingarn is tied on to the tail of it. The notions of D. MacC. (?not Desmond MacCarthy I hope?) are excellent, but a little diffuse, too much *symposistisch*. I do not think it a *better* idea than the Great Languages; but it might be a more popular and striking one; and I think it is worth exploring before we are committed to the other. I am not sure that it does not require three rather than two publishers collaborating. It means finding an editorial committee. It is a more difficult task than any of its predecessors; partly because nowadays there is no one of any importance who would dare to cover so much ground as Gosse etc. I do think that it [is] worth having several conversations with Bell about the work. The danger is of getting merely a collection of university officials to write it, or else of getting merely a collection of fashionable literary dilletantes [*sic*]. It ought to be scholarly and critical, but at the same time should be admittedly representative of the opinions and researches of our own time, and not, like most histories, pretend to be done for all time: should be a document of contemporary taste and judgment at the same time that it is a history.'

TO *Algar Thorold*[1]   CC

17 February 1932   [*The Criterion*]

My dear Thorold,

I have your card of the 11th. I should be very glad to have an article from you on Maine de Biran, about whom I have always had some curiosity, and on whom I have always wanted to publish an essay.[2] I should like it either for next summer or for one of the numbers of the coming winter. In fact it is particularly important that I should as soon as possible get hold of good articles for the winter numbers during the period when I am out of England. I shall be away from the beginning of September to the middle of May, and there will be three numbers which I shall not be able to supervise on the spot. I hope to see you several times before I leave, as well as in the future. Perhaps when the weather moderates and your lumbago with it you will be up for lunch one day.

Yours ever,

[T. S. Eliot]

1 – Algar Thorold (1866–1936), diplomat, author, journalist, son of Bishop Anthony Wilson Thorold of Winchester, was editor of the *Dublin Review*, 1926–34. TSE wrote in a memorial note in C. (Oct. 1936, 68) that Thorold 'had been a frequent contributor since very early in our history: his knowledge, especially of modern French philosophy and theology, was invaluable. Having written very few books – his [*Six*] *Masters of Disillusion* has been out of print for many years – he was not known to a very wide public, and another generation will not be aware that *The Dublin Review*, under his editorship, was one of the most distinguished periodicals of its time. Being half-French by birth [his mother was Emily Labouchère], and at the same time thoroughly English, with the culture of the past and the curiosity of the present, he held a position as a man of letters such that we could say of him, that he was the sort of man whom we could ill afford to lose.' On 24 Nov. 1954, when Dom Michael Hanbury, OSB (St Michael's Abbey, Farnborough), asked TSE to recall Thorold for the *Dublin Review*, TSE responded (1 Dec.): 'I certainly remember the man himself not only with regard and respect, but affection.'
2 – 'I have recently acquired his works and am much interested in him. He was I fear not a particularly good Catholic, 1766–1824 was a difficult period! But he is in the line of the great . . . moralists & . . . had much in common with Pascal. His interior life was of prodigious intensity.' On 20 Apr., Thorold wrote further of the French philosopher Maine de Biran (1766–1824): 'A charming melancholy creature. I shd have liked to know him.' And on 10 May: 'He is incredibly important, historically speaking, & it seems extraordinary that there shd be nothing at all in English (as far as I can find out) about him.' See 'Maine de Biran', C. 12 (Apr. 1933), 441–53.

TO *Ferris Greenslet*

17 February 1932   [Faber & Faber Ltd]

Dear Mr Greenslet,

Thank you for your letter of the 28th, and for the copy of Bandler's selections which I have looked at with much interest and approval.[1] I am afraid, however, that from what you say there is very little prospect of our being able to sell enough copies between us to justify undertaking it. Whatever market there may be in America should be, I think, two or three times greater than that in England. When you first wrote I formed the impression that you were thinking in terms of from 750 to 1000 sheet copies. We should not be able to count upon selling more than 150–200 copies in England, and even that is perhaps an exaggeration. But if you thought that you could dispose of 750 or 1000 the project would be worth our while to consider merely as one of producing a valuable book with a minimum loss to ourselves.

As you quote a minimum of only 200/250 I suppose that it is unlikely that you would advance that figure sufficiently to make it possible for us to take up the proposal seriously. Nevertheless I will retain the typescript here until I hear from you again. As I think I said before in other words I should very much like to forward such a commendable project, but I fear that the majority of the people who would be interested in the book in England have already read it in the original French.

I have had a high opinion of MacLeish's verse and I am always interested personally in anything that he brings out, but I fear that the sale of a narrative poem such as described in your memorandum would be quite negligible, especially as the author is not very well known here.[2] Furthermore to sell it at all we should have to produce it for a few shillings and your sale price of 2.50 dollars suggests that it would be impossible for

1 – Greenslet (Houghton Mifflin Company) had sent over the manuscript of Bernard Bandler's translation of Charles du Bos's Diary. 'If Faber & Faber were to undertake it, we could take a minimum of 200/250 at a feasible price.'

2 – Greenslet enclosed an advertising flyer about Archibald MacLeish's narrative poem *Conquistador*: would F&F like 'first option'? MacLeish (1892–1982), poet and playwright, studied at Yale and at Harvard Law School (he abandoned the practice of law and took up poetry in 1923), then lived in France for a while in the 1920s. *Conquistador* (1933) won a Pulitzer prize; and for his *Collected Poems, 1917–1952* (1953) he won three awards: a second Pulitzer, the Bollingen Prize, and the National Book Award. His verse play *J. B.* (1957) won the Pulitzer Prize for Drama and a Tony Award. During WWII, at President Roosevelt's bidding, he was Librarian of Congress, and he served with the United Nations Educational, Scientific and Cultural Organization. He was Boylston Professor of Rhetoric and Oratory, Harvard, 1949–62.

you to offer sheets at anything remotely approaching the cost in relation to our sale price. In poetry we are confining our attention at present almost entirely to very low priced volumes each season.

With many thanks,
Yours sincerely,
[T. S. Eliot]

TO *George Bell*[1]   Lambeth Palace Library

17 February 1932   Faber & Faber Ltd

My dear Lord Bishop,

Your letter of the 12th makes me feel like the famous man, I have forgotten who it was, who apologized to his friends for being so long

---

1–Rt Revd George Bell, DD (1883–1958): Dean of Canterbury, 1924–9; Bishop of Chichester, 1929–58; President of the Religious Drama Society of Great Britain from its foundation in 1929; chairman of the Universal Christian Council for Life and Work, 1934–6; President of the World Council of Churches from 1954 – he has been called both a true 'world churchman' and 'the father of modern religious drama'. Though shy, modest and soft-spoken, with a high voice, he was a man of uncompromising conscience, courage and energetic commitment, especially to the work of international ecumenism and the place of the Church in public life. 'Not for me', he said, 'a fugitive and cloistered Church, which refuses to face the problems and crises of the modern world.' In 1944 his denunciation in the House of Lords of the Allied policy of bombing cities and civilian homes in Germany caused much resentment: his stance was believed to have wrecked his chances of succeeding William Temple as Archbishop of Canterbury later that year. His works include *Randall Davidson, Archbishop of Canterbury* (2 vols, 1935), *Christianity and World Order* (1940) and *The Church and Humanity* (wartime speeches, 1946). While at Canterbury he had invited John Masefield to write for the Festival: *The Coming of Christ* (nativity play, 1928), with music by Gustav Holst and settings by Charles Ricketts, was the first play to be performed in the Cathedral for 400 years. Building on that success, in 1934 Bell commissioned TSE to write *MiC*. Other verse dramatists to produce work for the Chapter House during the annual Festival included Charles Williams, Dorothy Sayers and Christopher Fry. See further Ronald C. D. Jasper, *George Bell: Bishop of Chichester* (1967); G. Rupp, *I Seek My Brethren: Bishop George Bell and the German Churches* (1975); K. Slack, *George Bell* (1971).

See TSE, 'Bishop Bell', *The Times*, 14 Oct. 1958: 'I hope it is not too late for a reader who had been abroad and has just returned to England, to add a personal postscript to your obituary notice of Bishop Bell, and to Sir Charles Tennyson's tribute to his services to the arts.

'On a summer afternoon in 1934, walking in the garden of his Palace, Dr Bell proposed to me that I should write a play for the next Canterbury Festival. I accepted the invitation and wrote *Murder in the Cathedral*. To Dr Bell's initiative (and subsequently, Mr Ashley Dukes's enterprise in bringing the play to London) I owe my admission to the theatre.

'I am only one among other artists and poets who have benefited from the patronage of Bishop Bell, and who have reason to remember him with gratitude and affection.'

On 30 Dec. 1958 TSE recorded a contribution for the programme 'The Way of Life' (broadcast on the Home Service, 18 Jan. 1959): 'In my memories of Bishop Bell, four meetings stand out. The first memory is of a weekend, which must have been in 1930 or 1931 [actually Dec. 1930, when TSE had recited *Ash Wednesday* to a party which was at once impressed and bewildered], when I was a guest at the Palace in Chichester. Mr Martin Browne had been appointed by the Bishop [in 1930] his Adviser on Religious Drama for the diocese, and Mr and Mrs Browne dined with us: out of that meeting came the invitation in 1933 to write the Church Pageant which became "The Rock". I remember also that Dr Bell travelled up to London with me on the following Monday; not having consorted much with bishops in those days, I found it strange to be journeying with a bishop in a third-class railway carriage. On that journey, the Bishop spoke to me about Dr J. H. Oldham and his work for the Church and the World: and so that weekend brought about my acquaintance with two men, Mr Browne and Dr Oldham, with whom I was later to be closely associated in quite different activities. The second of those four meetings which are clearest in my memory was also to have important consequences for me: it was on a summer afternoon in 1934 walking in the garden of the Palace that Bishop Bell proposed that I should write a play for the Canterbury Festival, the Festival which he had originated when Dean of Canterbury and in which he retained a warm interest. The result was "Murder in the Cathedral". A third meeting was in Stockholm in 1942: the Bishop arrived on the day on which I was to leave. We all know now, what I did not know then, why Dr Bell had come to Sweden: it was no fault of his that the conversations he had there led to nothing. [While lecturing in Sweden for the Ministry of Information, Bell had been made privy to a German plot to assassinate Hitler: when he conveyed this information to the Foreign Office no credence was given to his report – but it turned out two years later that the names he had vouchsafed to the British authorities turned out to be those of officers executed by Hitler after the attempt on his life.] And the fourth meeting was at a conference which he had assembled in Chichester, I think also during the War, to discuss the place of the Arts in the life of the Church: among others present, I remember Mr Henry Moore, Sir Edward Maude, and Miss Dorothy Sayers.

'These four meetings, chosen by my memory from among others, illustrate the varied interests and activities of the Bishop, outside of the regular duties of a diocesan which he carried out so faithfully: his interest in the service which Art could perform for the Church, and no less in the inspiration and employment which the Church could give the artist; his interest in the Oecumenical Movement, of which there is ample documentary evidence; his interest in foreign affairs and his sense of the international responsibility of the Church and of churchmen. He and another of my friends, Duncan-Jones the late Dean of Chichester, were men of very different type, but in two respects in which they were both outstanding, they had much in common. The Dean made the Cathedral the musical centre of the diocese; the Bishop, by his patronage and encouragement of drama and of the plastic arts, made his diocese an exemplar for all England. And both Bishop and Dean, during the 1930s, were tirelessly outspoken in their protests against the religious and racial persecution taking place in Germany.

'My first impulse, in speaking of the impression which George Bell has left upon me, is to say that he was a "loveable man". On reflection, I find that in applying this adjective, I am making it a compendium of all the qualities for which I loved and admired him. These include a dauntless integrity: no ambition could ever have deflected him from whatever course he felt to be right, no fear of the consequences to himself could ever have prevented him from speaking the truth as he saw it. With this went modesty and simplicity of manner, the outward signs, I believe, of inward humility. A friendly man, and a man of genuine piety – in short, a good man and an honest man.'

a-dying.[1] Your condolences and others I have received make me almost apprehensive of my reception on my return to England. My appointment is an ordinary visiting professorship. You probably know Eric Maclagan who held it a few years ago, and H. W. Garrod.[2] I am leaving in September and returning in May, and one of my friends is lending me a fur-coat.[3]

The *Manchester Guardian* article was brought to my attention, and I took steps to have a correction printed, but usually only a small number of the people who read a piece of misinformation ever see the correction. A somewhat misleading notice appeared in the *Times*, and when I wrote to that paper about it they merely printed three lines in very small type under the heading 'Telegrams in Brief'.

I was amused to hear of your telephone conversation with Sir John Reith, because I had heard from a source within the B.B.C. itself that Reith has a great admiration for you and that he was more upset by your name than by those of all the other signatories put together.[4]

With very many thanks,

> I am, my Lord,
> Yours very sincerely,
> T. S. Eliot

I hope I may see you before I leave.

1–King Charles II in 1685 apologised for being 'such an unconscionable time a-dying'.

Bell had read in the *Manchester Weekly Guardian* of TSE's appointment at Harvard – 'Mr Eliot goes home' – and understood from it that he was 'going to live in USA; for I had hoped it might be a case of a visiting professorship – with roots still in London, and Faber & Faber! . . . It has been a pleasure very much appreciated by me to get to know you: and I hope you will let me count you as a friend, on whichever side of the Atlantic you may be.'

2–H. W. Garrod (1878–1960), classical scholar and literary critic; Tutor and Fellow of Merton College, Oxford, from 1904; Oxford Professor of Poetry, 1923–8. His publications include *Wordsworth: Lectures and Essays* (1923), *The Profession of Poetry* (1929), *Keats: A Critical Appreciation* (1926), the *Oxford Book of Latin Verse* (1912); and his Norton Lectures were published as *Poetry and the Criticism of Life* (1931).

3–Gordon George/Robert Sencourt.

4–'I had, by the way, a tremendous tussle on the telephone with Sir John Reith [Director-General of the BBC, 1927–38] the day the joint letter on BBC talks came out in the *Times*. I know Reith very well, and he was startled by my signature! but I stick to it.'

TO *C. M. Grieve*   CC/TS

17 February 1932   [*The Criterion*]

Dear Mr Grieve,

Thank you for your letter of the 11th. I like your 'Second Hymn to Lenin' very much indeed, and want to publish it. The only point is that I do not feel that I have the right to commit the *Criterion* to the sixth quatrain on page 2 (I take it that you have a typescript copy). It is a good stanza, and must be restored when the poem appears in a book, but I have to take into account other considerations for the *Criterion*. Could you modify it or would you omit the stanza altogether?

My only *personal* criticism of the stanza is that I do not like the phrase 'win through' unless it is used sardonically, and in that case it seems to me that it ought to be in quotes. You may have observed that it is a favourite phrase of the Prince of Wales and Sir John Simon, as well as of other politicians.[1]

I should like to use the poem in the June number.

Yours sincerely,
[T. S. Eliot]

1–Grieve responded, 18 Feb.: 'I quite see your point about the quatrain to which you take editorial exception and I am, of course, quite prepared that it should be omitted from the poem as it appears in the *Criterion*. I also agree with you with regard to the personal criticism you make of the phrase "win through" and am greatly obliged to you for the useful suggestion that it might be put in quotes with the implication of being used sardonically.' 'Second Hymn to Lenin' was to appear in C. 11 (July 1932); and the quatrain that TSE queried was retained:

Gin I canna win through to the man in the street.
The wife by the hearth,
A' the cleverness on earth'll no' mak' up
For the damnable dearth.

TO *H. J. Massingham*[1]   CC

17 February 1932   [Faber & Faber Ltd]

Dear Mr Massingham,

I have carefully thought over your kind and flattering suggestion.[2] I have come to the conclusion that I do not want to write again about Matthew Arnold, and that there is no one of the other possible figures, including Pusey about whom I could write anything satisfactory to myself without a great deal more labour of reading and thought than I have time to give it. I have thought over very carefully the things which I have already undertaken to do, and the times at which they have to be done, and I am convinced that it would be very foolish for me to undertake even to begin such a serious piece of work before June of 1933.

With many regrets, and all best wishes,

I am,
Yours sincerely,
[T. S. Eliot]

TO *Paul Elmer More*   TS Princeton

17 February 1932   Faber & Faber Ltd

My dear More,

Thank you for your kind letter of the 27th January.[3] It certainly came to my mind in accepting the appointment that I might look forward to a visit to Princeton, and to seeing you there, and I shall now look forward also to being your guest. I have already received one invitation from Princeton to which I have replied evasively and on which I should like your advice. I have been asked to deliver a lecture on what they call the Spencer-Trask Foundation, and the fee offered is a hundred dollars. Now I may appear grasping but I have need to earn as much money as I can in America, and at the same time not to over-work. I do not know what the return fare

1 – Harold John Massingham (1888–1952), writer and journalist devoted to rural traditions; his works include *Downland Man* (1926), *Wold without End* (1932), *Country Relics* (1939) and *Remembrance: An Autobiography* (1941).
2 – Massingham wrote on 9 Feb. to remind TSE that they had spoken about the suggestion that TSE should write on Pusey for *The Great Victorians*. 'From what you told me of the press of work that confronts you, the importunacy of this letter is a little inconsiderate.'
3 – More invited TSE to visit him 'for several days' during his time at Harvard. Professor J. D. Spaeth, chair of the lectureship committee, was keen to invite TSE to give an address at Princeton University.

from Boston to Princeton would cost, but I should imagine that it would come to twenty-five dollars anyway, and it is a question whether it is worthwhile to take the time and energy, including the writing of a special paper, for what would be left out of 100 dollars after my expenses. But if you consider that this is fair pay, with my expenses in mind, then I shall be inclined to accept, and if that is the best invitation to Princeton to accept I shall accept it for the pleasure of a visit to you.

I have read your new book *The Catholic Church* [*sic*]with great enthusiasm tempered by irritation. On the whole it seems to me one of the finest things that you have done, but I still detect traces of heresy. I think that I can show that you eliminate eternal damnation entirely out of the kindness of your heart, and for no other reason, (I will not accuse you of being a humanitarian) but that you are forced surreptitiously to reintroduce it. And your preference for the Apostles Creed over the Nicene does not seem to me wholly justified. But perhaps the best subject for discussion which we could begin when you come over here in the spring is St John of the Cross. I really feel that you are over-bold in your criticism of one who is crowned with so much authority. But that is a long subject to discuss in a letter![1]

Yours ever sincerely,
T. S. Eliot

1 – More replied, 4 Mar.: 'Your "enthusiasm" over *The Catholic Faith* honours me and your "irritation" rather amuses me. My dear fellow, I am rank with heresies; but the whole point of the book is to show how much heresy a man may carry and still be a good Catholic. Or, to speak more seriously, I would say that the book lays no claims to authority and is not written from within the Church . . .

'As for hell, my only serious objection to that cheerful doctrine is based on the orthodox notion of a man's eternal fate being determined *in articulo mortis* . . . In fact the whole theory of a static eternity of happiness or misery resulting from this present life of ours is repugnant to me. I can't believe that many of us are big enough to merit such a judgement one way or the other . . . I admit that I have dealt rather cavalierly with the Nicene Creed. It is magnificent as rhetoric; but it is also, for me, too tightly dogmatic in some of its articles, and I miss grievously "the communion of saints".

'As for St John of the Cross, I chose him for criticism because of his greatness, and my estimate of mysticism demanded just such a man . . . There is a very dark side to the lives of the Christian mystics, a deep taint of confusion in their practices.'

17 February 1932   [*The Criterion*]

Dear Mr Leavis,

Ian Parsons has sent me a copy of your book, which I read immediately and naturally with great interest.[1] I have only three criticisms to make.

1. That the word 'impinge' ought to be left to Aldous Huxley who likes that word, so he might as well have it.[2]

2. 'Cerebral muscle' seems to me a metaphor which would be rather much even for Crawshaw [*sic*].[3]

3. You use the phrase 'vestigial habit' twice on one page without making it quite clear that the repetition is intentional and the use identical.[4] Otherwise I of course like the book very much. At any rate I can say that your criticisms of other people, for instance Yeats and de la Mare, seem to me to put them exactly in their place, and the word 'vulgarity' is just all the criticism of Rupert Brooke that is needed.[5] I am particularly delighted by your praise of 'Hugh Selborne Moberley' [*sc.* 'Hugh Selwyn Mauberley'] which is as you say a great poem. I admit that I think much more highly of the Cantos than you do, but there we may both be wrong, and time and the completion of that poem, if it is ever completed, will

1–*New Bearings in English Poetry* (1932).

2–Leavis notes 'the peculiar importance of Mr T. S. Eliot. For, though there is, inevitably, a great deal of snobbism in the cult he suffers from, mere snobbism will not account for his prestige among the young. Having a mind unquestionably of rare distinction he has solved his own problem as a poet, and so done more than solve the problem for himself. His influence has been the more effective in that he is a critic as well as a poet, and his criticism and his poetry reinforce each other . . . He has made a new start, and established new bearings.

'To justify these contentions . . . it will be necessary first to make a closer survey of the situation as it was just after the war, before Mr Eliot impinged' (28).

3–'Arnold . . . shares with his age a prejudice against recognizing as poetry anything that is not, in the obvious sense of Milton's formula, "simple, sensuous, and passionate" . . . Wit, play of intellect, stress of cerebral muscle had no place' (16). 'It is possible to consider [Browning] as a philosophical or psychological poet only by confusing intelligence with delight in the exercise of certain grosser cerebral muscles' (24).

4–'*The Testament of Beauty* was a best seller . . . But it is plain that its sales show mainly with what success adroit journalism can exploit even a vestigial habit . . . It does indeed look . . . as if respect for poetry were mainly a vestigial habit' (170–1).

5–'[Brooke] energized the Garden-Suburb ethos with a certain original talent and the vigour of prolonged adolescence. His verse exhibits a genuine sensuousness rather like Keats's (though more energetic) and something that is rather like Keats's vulgarity with a Public School accent . . . And Brooke's "complexity" amounts to little more than an inhibiting adolescent self-consciousness in an ironical disguise. In its extremer forms it is painfully embarrassing' (57).

show. But I confess I did feel bewildered by what seems to be a lack of any central conviction or even the search for a conviction in Pound's work.

I had today a letter from Joyce in which he says that he has heard that *Ulysses* is on the programme for Cambridge examinations and that the professors (sic) lend copies to the students. He is very curious to know just what circulation *Ulysses* has in Cambridge and under what conditions.[1] Perhaps you would be so kind as to give me a hint or two. I am afraid that he is anything but familiar with the present state of British liberty.

Yours ever sincerely.

[T. S. Eliot]

TO *Harold Monro*

TS Beinecke

17 February 1932   *The Criterion*

My dear Harold,

I must apologise for my delay in sending the enclosed cheque, which includes the collection made by Morley and myself. However, if I had sent it sooner it would have been 10/- less, as I had completely forgotten the further debt of 10/- of which you remind me. No formal acknowledgment is necessary.[2]

The evening was a very quiet one – only three inner members present, Morley, Bonamy and myself, and no news of Flint. I can't say that any very important issue was discussed, but I think that the small number of guests enjoyed themselves. There was a rumour that Oswald Mosley was coming, but by 10.15 when I left he was only represented by two of his subalterns.

It is rather difficult to discuss *Criterion* arrangements until you are set up again in London. Fortunately there is no hurry about it, as I know from observation that colitis is not a malady that can be hurried, but I

1–JJ had commented on 13 Feb.: 'It is said here that *Ulysses*, though banned for sale in England, is on the programme for some Cambridge examinations and that the professors lend copies to the students' (*Letters of James Joyce*, I, 314).

2–Monro had asked, 15 Feb.: 'I hope the *Criterion* evening was successful & I do hope that in the preceding discussion you stuck to one or two points & arrived among you at a few conclusions, but I doubt this particularly if (in my absence) the sherry was opened too early.

'Will you send me a business-like little account with a cheque as previously? And will you kindly add to the letter the 10/- you owe me from a former occasion as I need every penny I can raise.'

imagine that lying in bed in Broadstairs becomes pretty trying.[1] I wish I could get off for a day and come down to see you.

Yours ever,
Tom

TO *G. B. Harrison*CC

17 February 1932   [Faber & Faber Ltd]

Dear Harrison,

    Am I a member of the Publications Sub-committee of the Council of the Shakespeare Association? My impression is that I am not, and I do not see any reason why I should be, but I just wanted to know whether the formal notice I received today is meant to apply to me or not.[2] In any case I am doubtful whether I can be present because it happens again that I have a Board meeting here on the same day.

Yours sincerely,
[T. S. Eliot]

TO *Eric Blair*[3]CC

19 February 1932   [Faber & Faber Ltd]

Dear Mr Blair,

    I am sorry to have kept your manuscript. We did find it of very great interest, but I regret to say that it does not appear to me possible as a publishing venture. It is decidedly too short, and particularly for a book of such length it seems to me too loosely constructed, as the French and English episodes fall into two parts with very little to connect them.

---

1 – 'I haven't been allowed to get up yet, nor really have I wanted to. Colitis is a trying & a persistent illness . . . I simply can't tell how much longer I am going to be kept here.'

2 – 'Shakespeare Association: There will be no meeting of the full Council on February 26th, but the Publications Sub-Committee will meet in Professor Read's room at 4 p.m., when Miss B. M. White will explain her proposals for the Index to Sir E. K. Chamber's Works.'

3 – Eric Blair – George Orwell (1903–50) – novelist and essayist, was educated at Eton College and worked for the Burma Police, 1921–7, before resolving to endure periods of slumming in London and Paris. From Feb. 1941 to Nov. 1943 he worked for the Far Eastern Section of the BBC, based at Oxford Street, London. His publications include *Down and Out in Paris and London* (1933), *The Clergyman's Daughter* (1935), *Keep the Aspidistra Flying* (1936), *The Road to Wigan Pier* (1937), *Homage to Catalonia* (1938), *Coming Up for Air* (1939), *Animal Farm* (1945), *Nineteen Eighty-Four* (1949). See *The Complete Works of George Orwell*, ed. Peter Davison (20 vols, 1986–98).

I should think, however, that you should have enough material from your experience to make a very interesting book on Down-and-out life in England alone.[1]

With many thanks for letting me see the manuscript.[2]

I am,
Yours faithfully,
[T. S. Eliot]

TO *James Joyce*   CC

19 February 1932   [Faber & Faber Ltd]

Dear Joyce,

I have your letter of the 16th this morning. I know all about the matter of the enclosed correspondence, which I return herewith; and I am in touch with Leonard Woolf. I think that everything possible is being done. It is quite true that Leonard Woolf has given £5 and guaranteed £20 further so that the solicitors may go forward, and I have told him that I will contribute myself. There ought not to be the slightest difficulty in collecting the money and it seems to me better from every point of view that you should not be among the contributors. It will be far better, I think, if the sum can be made up, as I think it can, by contributions from outside people who are not themselves creative writers. So I beg that you will withhold your financial support until further notice. I do not know Mr Douglas Glass, but I believe that he is quite a young man who is a friend and contemporary of this Montalk.[3]

---

1 – *Down and Out in Paris and London* was to be published by Gollancz on 9 Jan. 1933.

2 – Orwell told Leonard Moore, 26 Apr. 1932, that his MS had been seen by TSE – 'who is a reader to Faber and Faber. Eliot said the same as Cape's – i.e. that the book was interesting but much too short . . . If by any chance you *do* get it accepted, will you please see that it is published pseudonymously, as I am not proud of it' (*The Collected Essays, Journalism and Letters of George Orwell, 1: An Age Like This 1920–1940*, ed. Sonia Orwell and Ian Angus [1968], 101; Orwell, *A Life in Letters*, ed. Peter Davison [2010], 14).

3 – On 8 Feb. 1932, Geoffrey Wladislas Potocki de Montalk, a British subject born in New Zealand in 1904 (his grandfather was a Polish count, and it seems he was entitled to be styled 'count'), was convicted at the Central Criminal Court of 'uttering and publishing an obscene libel'. (As it happens, Montalk had written to TSE on 24 July 1929, claiming to be 'anglo-catholic' and seeking an audience; he had met Walter Lowenfels, Edward Dahlberg and RA during a year in Paris – which he hated – and he knew Humbert Wolfe; and TSE had talked with him in Aug. 1929.) Montalk had sought to publish through a firm of printers called Comps a collection of his poems – some of which, as he explained in the witness box, were translated from Rabelais.

I will write about the other matter and return the letter in a few days. Meanwhile I must congratulate you very cordially on the birth of your grandson.[1]

Yours ever sincerely,

[T. S. Eliot]

TO *James F. Courage*[2]

19 February 1932   [Faber & Faber Ltd]

Dear Mr Courage,

I must apologize for our having kept the manuscript of 'The Wanklins'[3] for what must have seemed a long time, but we wanted to have as many readings, and as many shades of opinion as possible. I must say frankly that after the promise of 'The Promising Years' we were disappointed with the subject and with the tone of 'The Wanklins'. There are, as we were all very well aware, certain very good touches in the book, but I felt

---

The Times reported his evidence on 9 Feb.: 'The manuscript in question was intended as a literary experiment for publication among his friends, who were literary people. He had not the slightest intention of publishing it to the general public.'

His defence counsel submitted that this was a case of 'a poet writing for a small circle of poets and literary experimenters to test words. Serious-minded writers like D. H. Lawrence and James Joyce used words regarded as objectionable in order to make them respectable.

'The Recorder [Sir Ernest Wild, KC], summing up, said that a man must not say he was a poet and be filthy. He had to obey the law just the same as ordinary citizens, and the sooner the highbrow school learnt that the better for the morality of the country.

'The jury, without leaving the box, found de Montalk Guilty, and the Recorder . . . said that no decent-minded jury could have come to any other decision than that the defendant had attempted to deprave our literature.' He was sentenced to six months in prison.

Montalk's friend Douglas Glass had first approached LW to organise the appeal.

See further Stephanie de Montalk, *Unquiet World: The Life of Count Geoffrey Potocki de Montalk* (2001); and Ian MacNiven, *Lawrence Durrell: A Biography* (1998), 83: 'Among Larry's stranger acquaintances on the margins of literary London were a pair of Polish royalists, Geoffrey and Cedric Potocki de Montalk, claimants to the throne of Poland . . . Both were pale, slender, blue-eyed and gentle-looking. The elder brother went by the title and name of Count Geoffrey Wladislaw Vaile, and he sometimes dashed about Bloomsbury in kilts. Nancy would recall going with Larry to their tiny flat near Lamb's Conduit Street. On the door was a sign, "Communists and racial enemies please abstain from calling." . . . They were right-wing to the point of fascism, anti-Semitic and intolerant, but Larry cherished them as true eccentrics.'

1–Stephen James Joyce was born on 15 Feb. 1932.

2–James F. Courage (1903–63), New Zealand-born novelist, was educated at Christ's College, Christchurch, and St John's College, Oxford. His works include *Our House* (1933), *The Fifth Child* (1948), *Desire Without Content* (1950) and *Fires in the Distance* (1952).

3–A novel submitted on 17 Dec. 1931.

clearly that the characters lacked the distinctness and conviction of even minor characters in the New Zealand episodes of *The Promising Years*, and this vagueness of the small county society is not compensated by any compelling movement of the plot.

I believe, however, that there may be many people who would say that I was wrong, and I am sure that those who disagree with me would be likely to disagree very strongly. I had thought at first of suggesting some other publisher, but as I feel that there are a number of good publishers, any one of whom might reverse my opinion, I am inclined to advise you to put both books in the hands of one of the best agents.

With many regrets,
Yours sincerely,
[T. S. Eliot]

FROM *Vivien Eliot* TO *Aurelia Bolliger*[1]   MS Beinecke

21 February 1932   68 Clarence Gate Gardens

Dear Miss Bolinger [*sic*],

We did enjoy our evening with you on Friday.

Dont forget that you & Mr Hodgson have promised to come on next *Friday week, March 4th* at 7 o'clock, will you? And Pickwick also.[2]

We had some discussion about a lunch on Tuesday, but on looking up my Diary I find that I should not have suggested that day as I have already an engagement.

As you know I am not very well, & shall be very busy for this next week, but let us, please, make another lunch engagement for the following week, & do not forget that you are to *bring some music* & play the piano. I suggest *Tuesday March 1st*, at 1 o'clock. I do hope that day will suit you. If not, please write & suggest another.

Yours very sincerely,
Vivienne Haigh Eliot

1–Aurelia Bolliger (1898–1984): born in Pennsylvania, studied at Heidelberg College, Ohio; taught in Wisconsin before journeying to teach at a mission school in Tokyo, 1922–3, and for the next seven years at the Women's College of Sendai, where she met and fell in love with Ralph Hodgson. She was to marry Hodgson in 1933.
2–Hodgson's mastiff bitch puppy.

TO *Seán Ó'Faoláin*[1]   CC

24 February 1932   [*The Criterion*]

Dear Mr O'Faolain,

I have your letter of the 19th, and must apologise for my delay in answering your letter of the 29th January.[2] I discussed your suggestion with our Sales Manager, but it did not appear that there was much more that I could do than to let you have a copy of our catalogue immediately on publication, and I send you a copy of our spring list herewith. Possibly you may be interested in some of the new books and if you will ask me about any of these I will give you any further information that I have, if any.

I will try to get AE's new book of poetry for you.[3]

Yours sincerely,
[T. S. Eliot]

1 – Seán Ó'Faoláin (1900–91): novelist and short-story writer. Brought up in Ireland (where he was born John Francis Whelan), he attended University College, Cork – for a while in the early 1920s he was an ardent nationalist and joined the Irish Volunteers (later the IRA) – and he was a Commonwealth Fellow at Harvard University, 1926–8. Founder-editor of the Irish periodical *The Bell* – see Kelly Matthews, *The Bell Magazine and the Representation of Irish Identity* (2013) – he also served as Director of the Arts Council of Ireland, 1957–9. Following his first book, *Midsummer Night Madness and Other Stories* (1932), he wrote a wealth of short stories. See *Collected Stories of Seán Ó'Faoláin* (1983); Maurice Harmon, *Seán Ó'Faoláin: A Life* (1994); M. Arndt, *A Critical Study of Seán Ó'Faoláin's Life and Work* (2001)

2 – Ó'Faoláin was 'angling' for 'some regular American literary hack-work', and hoped TSE could help him acquire 'inside information' on publicity material relating to F&F's Spring lists.

3 – Ó'Faoláin wished to review Æ's new book *Song and its Fountain*. 'He has been in London last week and I missed him. His wife died on the 3rd after a long illness and he has been very troubled and muddled. If you cannot let me write a note on his book may I be so bold as to hope you can save him from some rash young man unsympathetic to mystical psychology. It is very bold of me to write this but I love the old man and he has a nobility that few people recognise in his own land and few have time to give its due outside it – except, strangely, in America.' (Æ: pseud. of George William Russell [1867–1935], Irish poet, painter, nationalist, mystic.)

TO *Francis Underhill*[1]   CC

24 February 1932   [Faber & Faber Ltd]

Dear Father Underhill,

I have been invited, apparently at the instigation of Percy Dearmer,[2] to join something called the Westminster group. I feel that I have nearly reached the limit of effective grouping and joining for my limited time and abilities, and I do not like to be a merely nominal joiner of anything; but the list of officials of the Westminster group includes your name, and I imagined that you might have had something to do with the proposal. In short is this something I ought to join or not?[3]

Sincerely yours,
[T. S. Eliot]

TO *F. R. Leavis*   CC

24 February 1932   [*The Criterion*]

Dear Mr Leavis,

Thank you very much for your very full and instructive letter of the 21st instant which I have forwarded to Joyce for inspection and return.[4]

1–Revd Francis Underhill, DD (1878–1943) – TSE's spiritual counsellor – Anglican priest and author; Warden of Liddon House and priest in charge of Grosvenor Chapel, Mayfair, London, 1925–32; later Dean of Rochester, 1932–7; Bishop of Bath and Wells from 1937. His works include *The Catholic Faith in Practice* (1918) and *Prayer in Modern Life* (1928). TSE would notify the Revd D. V. Reed on 30 Mar. 1961 that he 'continued to be a penitent of Father Underhill during his period as Dean of the Cathedral' – i.e. Rochester, 1932–7. TSE went to Underhill (Liddon House, 24 South Audley Street, w.1) for his weekly confession, on Fridays.

2–Percy Dearmer (1867–1936): priest and liturgist best known as the author of *The Parson's Handbook*, a liturgical manual for Anglican clergy.

3–Underhill replied, 25 Feb. 1932, 'I do not really think you need bother about the Westminster Group . . . I am on it because I think it helps in keeping Anglo-Catholics in touch with the more official side of the Church of England, and vice versa.'

4–FRL wrote in response to TSE's letter of 17 Feb.: 'Dear Mr Eliot, / I imagine that my little brush with authority was the ultimate occasion of the rumours that have reached Joyce. At any rate, it has been immortalized in a saga, current in a variety of preposterous forms that, to my disadvantage, passes as secret history at Cambridge. These are the facts:

'Some years ago – it must have been 1926 – my very respectable bookseller (chairman of the Rate-payers' Association) was complaining to me about the prudery of the Americans: they had stopped a parcel from him containing, I think, "Ovid's Love Books". 'Well, Mr P[orter]," I replied, "we can't afford to crow. There are books you can't get me." "What, for instance?" – "Ulysses, by James Joyce."

'Mr P.'s pride was piqued: he has framed licences in his office, permitting him to import German books during the War. "What do you want it for?", he asked. "I want to lecture on

111

it," I replied (it was a prompting of the moment). "Is that course down on the list?" It was, or one that would do well enough. "Shall I write to the Home Office asking permission to import a copy?" "Yes" I replied, – "if you'll let me dictate the letter." So I there and then dictated a letter, asking permission to import a copy of *Ulysses* for purposes of illustration and comment in a course of lectures for the English Tripos on Prose.

'I knew, of course, that I was asking for trouble. But I thought it was time someone took a risk, and it seemed a good opportunity. Anyway, I had little to lose (and I was not married in those days).

'I heard nothing for some weeks. Then I got a letter from the Vice-Chancellor: "I have received a letter from the Public Prosecutor about a book which you have recommended for the English Tripos. I shall be glad if you will call on me . . ."

'When I called, the Vice-Chancellor handed me a type-script of a dozen pages, which started with an account of my application, and went on to give a report of an inquiry conducted by the local police, at Home Office instructions, into my career, my lectures, the number of women who attended them, etc. The letter ended on a hortatory note: "The book is indescribably filthy. We do not suppose you have seen it but will, if you like, send you a copy for inspection." And there followed an exhortation to put me down.

'I asked the Vice-Chancellor if he had read "the book". He hadn't. So I described it to him, and why it was considered important by students of English literature. "As for recommending it, I'm just as much recommending it – and just a little – as the *Times Literary Supplement*, that stronghold of institutional respectability, was, when, on the front page last March, it quoted a passage for approval." And I gave him the names of various eminent critics, of both sexes, who had written on *Ulysses* in the most respectable journals.

'I could have got a copy, I pointed out, without any trouble by the ordinary channels. But I objected to the glamour of clandestine circulation which seemed to me the only unwholesome thing about the cult. "Anyone who wants to read it can, you know. It's freely worn – It's the Oxford trousers of the intellectuals."

'It ended by the Vice-Chancellor's virtually asking me what to reply to the Public Prosecutor.

'I was lucky in my V.-C. It was [Professor A. C.] Seward of Downing, a decent and intelligent scientist. I heard no more, directly, about the affair, but I know that Seward reported to Quiller-Couch [Professor of English Literature], and the legend got under way. It has never, I believe, been used against me formally, but it has been a most useful and potent confidential argument: – "you know, that man with the unsavoury temperament." Echoes reach me continually; and, of course, that kind of reputation can never be overtaken and pinned down.

'It was, however, a great triumph. I had announced my intention of lecturing for the Tripos on *Ulysses*, and, in spite of the Public Prosecutor, was not forbidden. Actually, I hadn't time to deal at length with the book, though I examined a passage as prose-texture. But when Forster (giving the Clarke [*sic*] Lectures) raised in my hearing the question whether it was permissible to speak about *Ulysses* to a University audience I was able to settle his doubt authoritatively. And Forster did lecture on *Ulysses*.

'That's the story. The clandestine cult retains its glamour for the very naïve, but the book circulates freely. College servants know that it is valuable, so a man has to take care of his copy.

'Yes, I'm following the de Montalk case, and it has been much talked about here. I'm hoping that someone (I'm clearly not the right person) will institute a protest in Cambridge.

Many thanks for the curiosites [*sic*]. The *Bookman* anthology will be useful for elementary laboratory work with my pupils. As for the Caravan, I'm too close to the Bronowski troupe to be merely amused. I do very much regret that you let them into the *Criterion*.

I am interested in your remark about the *Experiment* group. I had not taken it, however, that they had been 'let in' to the *Criterion*. I merely tried out Bronowski on Belgion's book, and I am not very much impressed by his performance.[1] It succeeded in annoying Belgion, but then almost any review could have done that, and it does not seem to have given pleasure to anyone else. Of whom else does the group consist at present beside Bronowski? He came to see me once and I was not very highly impressed by that either.

I am much interested in the project of *Scrutiny*, and if I can be of any use in interesting possible contributors and subscribers I shall be very glad. In starting a review of this sort it seems to me that the best way of enticing subscribers is by encouraging them to believe that they may sooner or later become contributors – so far as one can honestly hold out this inducement.[2]

'I enclose an announcement of *Scrutiny*. I hope it's plain that it won't be at all like *Experiment*. I didn't write the announcement, though I suppose it bears pretty obvious traces of my influence. The project has behind it a group of unusually good and mature people – no exhibitionists. It's a serious thing, and I hope that a movement among schoolmasters will be associated with it.

'Yours sincerely, / F R Leavis'

See further FRL, 'Freedom to Read', *TLS*, 3 May 1963, 325; Ian MacKillop, *F. R. Leavis: A Life in Criticism* (1995), 88–91; Kevin Birmingham, *The Most Dangerous Book: The Battle for James Joyce's 'Ulysses'* (2014), 263–6.

1 – See Bronowski's review of Montgomery Belgion, *The Human Parrot, and other essays*, C. 11 (Jan. 1932), 322–4.

2 – TSE was consistent in his support for the place and importance of *Scrutiny*, despite the fact that FRL was often his antagonist over the years; on 3 July 1942 he would write to the Rt Hon. Sir Malcolm Robertson at the British Council, London: 'When I approached Desmond [MacCarthy] with regard to the preservation of the review *Scrutiny*, it was with a view to his being one of a number of signatories of a letter which I proposed to address to you later, begging that the British Council should appeal for the continuation of sufficient paper supply to make it possible to maintain the review in its present form. Desmond, however, has anticipated this by writing to you personally at once. I have not meanwhile had the chance to approach other people, except a few whom I have seen personally such as Herbert Read, Major Bonamy Dobrée (professor of English literature at Leeds) and Michael Roberts, all of whom I found as perturbed as myself by the prospect of *Scrutiny* coming to an end. I am sure that I. A. Richards of Magdalene would [support] such an appeal strongly, but he is in America. I have written to him on the matter. I may also mention, as being still more to the point, that I know that Ronald Bottrall is anxious to make use of *Scrutiny* in Stockholm and I am sure that Frederick Tomlin, who is now in your office in Ankara, would take the same view.

'While I have often had occasion to criticise *Scrutiny* and its Editor, Dr Leavis of Downing College, I should consider its disappearance as a grave misfortune. It is the only serious and heavyweight literary and general periodical left, and if we are to direct any cultural propaganda toward the highest intellectual layer of foreign countries we must be able to show evidence of our own cultivation of art and thought, under whatever difficulties. I think

Your revised pamphlet seems to me a vast improvement on its first form. I am showing it to two other directors, one of whom is at the moment in bed with a cold, so you may not hear from me again for a week or so.

Yours ever sincerely,

[T. S. Eliot]

to *Messrs J. P. Allen & Co.*[1]   cc

24 February 1932   [Faber & Faber Ltd]

Dear Sirs,

I have your letter of the 22nd instant and am pleased to recommend to you Mr M. H. Haigh-Wood of 42 Eaton Terrace. Mr Haigh-Wood is my brother-in-law, and to the best of my belief is highly respectable.[2]

I advised him to come to you as I thought that he had a figure which you would appreciate and to which you would do better justice than any other tailor I have known.

Yours ever,

[T. S. Eliot]

to *James Joyce*   cc

24 February 1932   [Faber & Faber Ltd]

Dear Joyce,

I promised to write to you again when I had made enquiries about the Cambridge situation. I wrote to F. R. Leavis, who I imagined would know more about it than anyone else, and here is his reply which I thought might interest you. Will you please let me have it back when you have read it. I also return herewith your letter from Terence Gray.

Scrutiny is particularly suitable for a serious folk like the Swedes who might find a magazine like *Horizon* a little light and frivolous. The point is that the Paper Control, for some reason, has given notice of such an extreme reduction in the quantity allowed in the future that it would not be worth while to continue the review at all, inasmuch as such a reduction must completely change its character. I apologise for raising this matter before I was quite ready to do so, but I do consider the matter a grave and urgent one.'

1 – Tailors, 32 Old Burlington St, Burlington Gardens.

2 – MHW wished to open an account with the firm.

I return also the letter to yourself from Frank Budgen(?).[1] You are better able to judge than I am whether this is likely to be a good book, as I know nothing about the author. But I will say at once that it cannot bother us in the least. So far as we are concerned the more books that appear about you, if they are reasonably good books, the better; and the more books about you there are published by other firms the better for us in publishing your own works. So this is entirely a matter for your own opinion of the particular writer. If the book is a good book we should be glad to see Grayson's publishing it.

Yours ever,
[T. S. Eliot]

TO *I. A. Richards*

TS Magdalene

24 February 1932   Faber & Faber Ltd

Dear Richards,

I looked forward to seeing you if only for a short time on Monday afternoon, but no doubt you found it too much out of your way to be possible. I do hope that you may be able to give me a whole afternoon or evening in town before very long.

One thing which I wanted to talk about is that our Montgomery Belgion has just sent me an essay for the *Criterion* on the subject of Belief.[2] In this essay he is entirely concerned with you and Martin D'Arcy, and is as usual the bright boy asking questions, and not, so far as I can see, answering any questions himself. I do not think that it is a very good essay but I should like to use it if there is any prospect of it starting you and D'Arcy off on a further exposition of your views, and if possible arguing with each other rather than with Belgion. What I propose to do is to have the article set up and then send proof to you and to D'Arcy. If you cared to discuss it between you, so much the better. Then I should like to use Belgion's article as the start off for an article or so each by yourself and D'Arcy, the whole to be staged during my absence in America. I hope that you will not think unfavourably of this. Belgion, after all, is extremely useful as an irritant and for provoking other people to develop their own theories on important subjects.[3]

---

1 – Frank Budgen (1882–1971), English painter and writer who befriended JJ in Zurich; author of *James Joyce and the Making of 'Ulysses'* (1934); *Myselves When Young* (1970).
2 – Not published in C.
3 – IAR replied, 25 Feb.: 'I am *very* hesitant about promising anything in connection with anything that Belgion might do. I don't in the least agree with you about his utility – he is

I very much regret your Pepys dinner although I am not sorry to miss Sir John Simon. Do you always have the perfect after dinner speaker for these occasions?

Yours ever,
T. S. E.

TO *Marguerite Caetani*   Photocopy of TS

24 February 1932   Faber & Faber Ltd

Dear Marguerite,

Thank you for your note of the 18th and your cheque for £6 in payment of the tickets. You will have received meanwhile my letter following the telegram, and I shall expect to get from you your instructions about the disposition of the tickets which repose in the safe here.

I look forward to the forthcoming issue of *Commerce*. I hope that you will soon be publishing something by Spender or Roditi.

About the picture gallery in London.[1] Well, I do not want to be discouraging, but I hardly know of anybody at present who is in a position to buy good pictures. The few who are at the moment are likely to be the sort of people who would obey the injunction to Buy British, – not that I have noticed the imperial movement having any favourable effect on the fortunes of our native painters.

However, let me have a lot more information before you take any steps.

Ever affectionately,
Tom

---

irritating as a stupid child crying "look at my fingers; *arnt* they sticky!" is irritating. D'Arcy seemed to agree thoroughly with me about him . . .

'Sorry to be so unfavourable to the proposal – but one doesn't 'develope [*sic*] one's theories' by bothering over such stuff as Belgion's. D'Arcy might be better to argue with; but argument is clearly as obsolete an intellectual exercise as horoscopy . . . I shan't be much help. But I'll send you my Oxford Paper before long – which shows how Croce and Watson can be translated into one another without loss or gain!'

1–Caetani wrote, 18 Feb., 'What would you think of my having a tiny picture Gallery in London? I might.'

TO *C. M. Grieve*

24 February 1932   [*The Criterion*]

Dear Mr Grieve,

Thank you for your letter of the 18th. I am very glad to hear that I may publish 'Hymn' in our June number.[1]

I have thought over carefully your suggestion about a book on Charles Doughty[2] and discussed it with one or two others; but the fact is that we have already two or three more books in this series commissioned which may turn up at any time, and the prospects are not bright enough to encourage us to take on any more just yet; and although it would be useful to have a good short book on Doughty I do not feel that the probable interest would justify it until the series is very much more firmly established than it is now.

Yours ever sincerely,
[T. S. Eliot]

TO *Christopher Dawson*[3]

24 February 1932   [Faber & Faber Ltd]

My dear Dawson,

This letter is to introduce my friend Mr J. H. Oldham, a member of my communion, whose name is very likely known to you, and who is very actively engaged both speculatively and practically in the sort of interest which you and I have in common. Mr Oldham also knows Macmurray. I think it would be a very useful thing if you could meet each other and discuss these matters, and I am writing this letter with that hope.

Sincerely yours,
[T. S. Eliot]

1–Hugh McDiarmid, 'Second Hymn to Lenin', C. 11 (July 1932), 593–8.
2–Grieve said (18 Feb.) he had been making 'an intensive study' of the poetry of Charles Doughty, and proposed a volume for the Poets on Poets series (MacDiarmid, *Letters*, 443–4).
3–Christopher Dawson (1889–1970), cultural historian: see Biographical Register.

TO *W. Fraser Mitchell*[1]   CC

24 February 1932   [Faber & Faber Ltd]

Dear Mr Mitchell,

Thank you for your interesting letter of the 16th, and for letting me
see your manuscript.[2] It is quite true that Dr More mentioned you to
me while he was in England last summer, and I look forward with great
interest to the appearance of your book which the S.P.C.K. is to produce.
It is for every reason a book in which I shall be especially interested.

I have considered very carefully the manuscript of your poems, both
with a view to publication by Faber & Faber and in consultation with one
of the directors of the Porpoise Press.[3] I am not myself really competent
to judge the poems in Scots, but I fully appreciate the merit of the
classical adaptations. I feel, however, regretfully, that this is the sort of
verse, however perfect in its kind, which at the present time can only be
considered by private presses for small limited editions. In any case, as the
publication of poetry is in my experience always attended with loss we
are obliged to ration ourselves to a very small number of volumes a year,
and it would be impossible for us to consider another volume of verse for
some time to come.

                              Sincerely yours,
                              [T. S. Eliot]

1–W. Fraser Mitchell, Lecturer in Education, University of Reading.
2–Mitchell, who had met More in the summer of 1931, was to publish *English Pulpit
Oratory from Andrewes to Tillotson: A Study of Its Literary Aspects* (1932); he had earlier
brought out a broadsheet of poems entitled *Cobweb and Mustardseed* (1928), and hoped
now that TSE would take over his poems for F&F. Humbert Wolfe and John Masefield, he
reported, had expressed admiration for the 'classical' pieces.
3–See Alistair McCleery, *The Porpoise Press 1922–39* (1988); McCleery, 'The Porpoise
Press, 1930–1939', *Publishing History* 21 (1987), 69–92.

TO *C. H. Douglas*[1]

CC

26 February 1932   [Faber & Faber Ltd]

Dear Major Douglas,

I have discussed your letter of the 20th instant with several of my colleagues and we are very much interested in your suggestion.[2] Would it be possible for you to suggest a morning next week when you could come to see us at 11.30 or 12? If you could bring one or two of your most important books with you it would be an advantage, as I do not think that the others are very familiar with them.

In any case I had been hoping to see you before very long, and should be very glad if you cared to lunch with me one day in the following week.

Yours sincerely,
[T. S. Eliot]

TO *Edwin Muir*[3]

CC

29 February 1932   [*The Criterion*]

My dear Muir,

I must apologize for having delayed such a very long time before writing to you about the extracts from the book of Broch's.[4] I found what

---

1–C. H. Douglas (1879–1952), British engineer and economic theorist, proponent of 'social credit': his notion was that prices for goods might be kept lower than actual costs by supplying more money to consumers, or else subsidies to producers: a debt-free credit to support purchasing power. The Labour Party discountenanced the theory in the 1920s, but it was promulgated in the 1930s, in the *New Age* and *New English Weekly*, in Douglas's own organ *Social Credit*, as a panacea for the Depression. Major works are *Economic Democracy* (1920), *Credit-Power and Democracy* (1920) and *Social Credit* (1924). See also David Bradshaw, 'T. S. Eliot and the Major: Sources of literary anti-Semitism in the 1930s', *TLS*, 5 July 1996, 14–16; Meghnad Desai, *The Route of All Evil* (2006).
2–'I am desirous of transferring the publication of my books now published by Messrs Cecil Palmer, and I should be glad to know if you would be interested in the matter. These books have a steady sale all over the world, but are not, in my opinion, being properly handled.'
3–Edwin Muir (1887–1959), Scottish poet, novelist, critic, translator: see Biographical Register
4–Hermann Broch (1886–1957): Austrian writer. TSE was to write to Alvin Johnson, The New School for Social Research, New York, 30 Mar. 1951: 'I should like to feel that I could support the candidature of Hermann Broch, because I do believe that he is an author who has to be most seriously considered for a Nobel Prize, but this belief is not one which I could defend from adequate knowledge of Mr Broch's writings. I have read a good deal of his *Death of Virgil*, but only in the English translation, and I hope that you will understand that it is not lack of goodwill on my part, but merely conscientiousness, that makes me feel that to know only a part of one work by a man, and that only in a translation, is an insufficient

I understood of them very interesting though inconclusive. But the point was that I shall not be able to use any in the April number. I could use some in the June number if that is not too late. If it is too late I can only express my regret. Will you please let me know, and will you come up to lunch with me one day before long.[1]

Yours ever,
[T. S. Eliot]

TO *Mrs Rowan*   CC

29 February 1932   [Faber & Faber Ltd]

Dear Mrs Rowan,

Mrs Haigh-Wood has shown me your letter to her about your daughter's friend. If there were any possibility at all of an opening of the sort, I would suggest that the girl should come and see me, but I know that it would only [be] a disappointment to her. I get applications myself fairly frequently, and our chairman receives them without number. On the one hand there are a large number of well-qualified people wanting such work, and on the other hand it is not a time when publishing houses are likely to be increasing their staff. The only possibility would be of someone leaving us to take up another position elsewhere, but even so I am doubtful whether we should like to take on a girl so young as your daughter's friend, even though she be extremely well suited for such a post.

With many regrets,
Yours sincerely,
[T. S. Eliot]

---

qualification for a sponsor, and I also feel a responsibility towards the Swedish Academy, all the greater because of their generosity to me.'

1 – Muir said (7 Mar.) that TSE might use 'whatever of Broch's speculations' he chose, since the book would not now be published until the autumn. See 'Disintegration of Values' (two sections from *The Sleepwalkers*), trans. Edwin and Christina [*sc.* Willa] Muir, C. 11 (July 1932), 664–75.

TO *James Joyce*

29 February 1932   [Faber & Faber Ltd]

My dear Joyce,

Thank you for your letter of the 22nd. If you say that the Budgen book is not likely to be a good one it alters the matter.[1] All I wanted to say was that it is entirely a matter between you and myself.

Thank you very much for the poem which I like extremely.[2] We have as a matter of fact decided to discontinue the publication of our Ariel series.[3] It was of its kind extremely successful, but the returns show a diminishing sale during the last few years and we feel that it is wisest not to publish any fresh numbers. What I suggest is this. I should very much like to publish the poem in the *Criterion*, but as for that you can only get two guineas I suggest trying to place it with some American magazine first both to protect the American rights and to get the maximum return from it. There are at least one or two American magazines which ought to pay 50 and possibly even up to 100 dollars for even a very short poem by you. If you say yes I will take it up with one of the American magazines.[4]

I dare say you are quite right about fragments of *Ulysses* in the Criterion Miscellany.[5] I was not myself really in favour of publishing *all* of the

1 – JJ had written on 22 Feb.: 'I have not yet replied to [Frank] Budgen but he wants me to do so and I think the inclusion of letters invades Gorman's ground. Moreover counting Jordan Smith [*Key to Ulysses*], Stuart Gilbert, Gorman's two books, Louis Golding and Charles Duff, Budgen's would be the seventh book, in the field. I should like to see his illustrations and he could do a good text if he chooses a line different from the others' (*Letters* I, 314).

2 – 'Some time ago some member of your firm wrote to ask me if I had a poem to be published separately in a leaflet series. I replied that I had not. A few days ago however I wrote the enclosed, the first piece I have inflicted on anybody for eight years, a short poem about the birth of my grandson. Would it suit?' (*Letters* I, 315). 'Ecce Puer' appeared in C. 12 (Jan. 1933), 184.

3 – See Peter de Sautoy to Marjorie Reed, 6 Dec. 1973: 'In the years before the last war Faber & Faber published a series of "Ariel Poems", by a number of different poets, each with a specifically designed illustration by an appropriate artist. They were like rather elaborate Christmas cards . . . The series was given the name "Ariel" simply because the name has a suggestion of poetry about it. It is nothing whatever to do with the B.B.C. and the poems were not in any way prepared for broadcasting. They were, as I say, more in the nature of special publications for small presents and they gave an opportunity for matching poet and artist in an interesting way. A part of each edition was signed by the poet concerned and a few of those signed copies, if the poet became especially famous, would be valuable if they could be found today.'

4 – JJ responded to this passage on 4 Mar.: 'Many thanks indeed for your kind words about my little poem. By all means dispose of it as you say though really it is Pinker [his literary agent] who should do this . . . The chief point is that you like the verse' (*Letters* I, 316).

5 – JJ opposed the proposal to publish episodes of *Ulysses* in the Criterion Miscellany: 'First it implies that I have recognized the right of any authorities in either of Bull's islands to

publishable fragments in that form because that would, I am sure, have exactly the effect which you do not wish to produce. But it did seem to me, and still does, that one or two might help the readers of *W.I.P.* and would not expose us to this objection. However, I will not press the point.

Yours ever cordially,
[T. S. Eliot]

TO *William Rothenstein*[1]   TS Houghton/CC

29 February 1932   Faber & Faber Ltd

My dear Rothenstein,

I think that the man you mean is one George Edward Woodberry.[2] I am not quite sure about that, and I am not sure whether he is still living or not. He was a man of considerable academic reputation as a literary critic. I do not remember whether he was also a professor or not, but I think that he was at some time or other. I have never read anything of his or met him. I imagine him as an oldfashioned American critic of the James Russell Lowell order 'Among my books' and that sort of thing, and probably a member of the Century Club.

Yours ever sincerely
T. S. Eliot

P.S. The American *Who's Who* says that he is 78, has been a professor at the University of Nebraska, and at Columbia, and has written or edited countless books on or by Poe, Emerson, Swinburne, Hawthorne, Shelley, Tennyson, Lamb and Rupert Brooke. He lives at Beverly, Mass.

---

dictate to me what and how I am to write. I never did and never will. Secondly the episodes are of unequal length, thirdly I think that at least seven of the eighteen episodes would not pass the censor . . . Fourthly *Ulysses* is a book with a beginning, middle and an end and should be presented as such. The case is quite different with *W.i.P.* which has neither beginning nor end' (*Letters* I, 315).

1 – Sir William Rothenstein (1872–1945), artist and administrator: see Biographical Register.
2 – Rothenstein asked, 24 Feb.: 'When I was in New York 20 yrs ago I met an essayist – Woodberry? There was a Woodberry Society, so he must have been a man of reputation. Can you give me his correct names?' George Edward Woodberry (1855–1930), prolific critic and poet; Professor of Comparative Literature at Columbia University, 1891–1904.

TO *Michael Sayers*[1]　　　　　　　　　　　TS Sean Sayers

29 February 1932　　　　　　　Faber & Faber Ltd

Dear Mr Sayers,

I have been meaning to write to you for some time. I am very glad indeed to hear that you have had the opportunity to go to Trinity, and I hope that the surroundings and the work will prove congenial. You were very badly in need of suitable conditions in which to improve your physical health which seemed very low when I last saw you. So I hope you will stay at Trinity as long as you can and if possible take a degree there, as I am convinced that this sort of interlude in life, coming at this time, may be in the highest degree beneficial to your work.

I have read your novel and have given a good deal of thought to it.[2] It is of course unprintable as you must have known, but I daresay that in two or three years you will no longer feel any desire to see it in print, as it is a work which I am sure you will out-grow. I think there is very considerable merit in it, and in parts a considerable intensity and depth of pathos. I am not, however, moved by some of the passages which perhaps seemed to you the most moving. In the purple bits addressed to the reader you have attempted something very difficult, and I feel that your control of the language fails at this sort of thing. Unless it is handled with great mastery and held very tight, it is at best verging on the maudlin. It is not, however, a question of offering you suggestions for improving this book. I do not think that this book can be sufficiently improved. My suggestions are meant to bear upon your future work. What does vitiate this narrative

1–Michael Sayers (1911–2010), Dublin-born writer of Jewish-Lithuanian ancestry, had been taught French at Trinity College, Dublin, by Samuel Beckett. In the 1930s he was drama critic of the *New English Weekly,* and for a while shared a flat in Kilburn, London, with George Orwell and Rayner Heppenstall. Some of his stories were included in *Best British Short Stories,* ed. Edward O'Brien; but in 1936 he left London for New York, where he worked as dramaturge for the designer and producer Norman Bel Geddes. During WW2 his interests and writings pursued a pro-communist direction, for which he was later blacklisted by the House Un-American Activities Committee (having enjoyed much success as a writer for NBC Television). In later years he wrote plays for the BBC, and contributed episodes to TV series including *Robin Hood* and *Ivanhoe.* He worked too on the screenplay of *Casino Royale* (1967).

2–In an undated letter from London, posted before leaving for Trinity College, Dublin (where he was to read Philosophy), Sayers said of his piece: 'It seems to me a novel literary medium is developing out of the old autobiographical form, allowing an address at once more subtly personal and . . . lyrical. I look on my short volume as the merest stammerings in this new form . . . [T]his poor bitter impure stuff is all I have, yet even it like a primitive physic may do some good, as indeed it is intended to do, for many a boy and girl bewildered with tangled values. In this moral light my prentice practice is put before you.'

is the morbidity of the point of view which I think will disappear with better physical health and better conditions in which you can do work which you like and feel worthwhile. I am not of course speaking from an ordinary prudish point of view, but more profoundly I think that a distorted vision muddles the values.[1]

I shall hope to hear from you more about your work at Trinity.

Yours sincerely,
T. S. Eliot

TO *Viscount Halifax*[2]   cc

29 February 1932   [Faber & Faber Ltd]

Dear Lord Halifax,

Thank you very much indeed for sending me the copy of *The Good Estate of the Catholic Church*.[3] I have of course read the book and possess a copy, but I am very happy indeed to have one inscribed by you.

It has been a disappointment to me that I have been unable to take you at your word and suggest myself for a night at Hickleton, but it has been extremely difficult for me to get away from London, and I have not been out of town for a long time.

Yours very sincerely,
[T. S. Eliot]

1 – Sayers replied: 'what . . . vitiates any work I produce is not so much, as you suggest, a muddled vision of values as a complete deficiency in any sense of values . . . That book was meant . . . to be nothing less than a blasphemy, a total repudiation of all that seemed good & true & beautiful in life.' And yet he allowed: 'My health is improving. I am living a regular life.'
2 – Charles Lindley Wood, 2nd Viscount Halifax (1839–1934): Anglo-Catholic ecumenist: President of the English Church Union, 1868–1919, 1927–34.
3 – C. L. Wood, Viscount Halifax, *The Good Estate of the Catholic Church* (1930).

TO *C. M. Bowra*[1]

29 February 1932   [Faber & Faber Ltd]

Dear Mr Bowra,

    Probably you will have heard from Geoffrey Faber by now, but I should naturally have written to you in any case.[2] I do not as a rule read very

---

1–C. M. Bowra (1898–1971), educated at New College, Oxford (DLitt, 1937), was a Fellow and Tutor of Wadham College, Oxford, 1922–38; Warden of Wadham, 1938–70; Oxford Professor of Poetry, 1946–51; Vice-Chancellor, 1951–4. President of the British Academy, 1958–62, he was knighted in 1951; appointed CH in 1971. Publications include *Tradition and Design in the Iliad* (1930), *Greek Lyric Poetry* (1936), *The Romantic Imagination* (1950), *The Greek Experience* (1957), *Memories, 1898–1939* (1966). See further Leslie Mitchell, *Maurice Bowra: A Life* (2009).

TSE wrote rhetorically to JDH, 23 June 1944, of Bowra: 'was there ever a more vulgar little fat Head of a House than he?' And to Hope Mirrlees, Christmas 1944:

> Mr Maurice Bowra
> Gets sourer and sourer,
> Having been in a hurry
> To succeed Gilbert Murray
> And is now (poor soul) at the bottom:
> I.e. Warden of Wadham.

To Theodore Spencer, 5 June 1948 (when Bowra was appointed Eliot Norton Professor): '*If* you don't know him, I may mention that he is extremely social, a very amusing talker, with a trained palate (it is well known that he has at Wadham the best chef in Oxford) and a keen interest in people and their humours . . . He likes wealth and fashion as well as intelligence and wit.'

2–TSE had invited Bowra to review B. F. C. Atkinson's *The Greek Language* (F&F, 1931), a volume in the series 'The Great Languages' edited by Prof. G. E. K. Braunholtz. (Dr Basil Atkinson [1895–1971] was Under-Librarian of the University of Cambridge, 1925–60.) The review, which TSE had promptly set up, was damning: Bowra complained of 'lack of method and scholarship . . . Dr Atkinson combines history with literary criticism, and both are harmed in the process . . . There are . . . too many hasty generalizations and unfounded or inaccurate statements . . . His knowledge of the Greek language is partial and hazardous . . . The study of the classics may be limited and sterile, but its standards are too high and the competition in it too great for there to be any place for slipshod workmanship and imperfect knowledge.'

Bowra wrote to GCF on 22 Feb. 1932: 'Goronwy Rees tells me that you are worried about a review I have written for the Criterion about Atkinson's book, and as the situation is difficult I hope you will forgive me for writing to you about it. I had doubts about sending the review as I dislike being merely destructive and normally review with kindness. But unfortunately the book is really very bad – much worse than any such book ought to be. There are many more howlers which I have not mentioned and the man who is reviewing it for the Classical Review is trouncing it harder. If Atkinson wishes to reply, by all means let him, but he must expect to be smashed worse in return.

'I feel that Braunholz [*sic*] is very much to blame for not going through the book and correcting the howlers – or perhaps he is not capable of recognizing them. Even apart from these the book is very inferior to much shorter works such as Meillet's Aperçu de la langue Grecque [Antoine Meillet, *Aperçu d'une histoire de la lange grecque* (1913)].'

carefully the reviews by people whom I know and trust in their subjects when they first come in; I usually send them off to the printer and defer reading them with care until I have the galley. That was what happened in this case. Indeed I had already had the galley for some days before I settled down to reading it with care. Hence the delay in raising any question.

When I finally read your review thoroughly I found it so damaging to the book – and so convincing to anyone of my limited and old-fashioned scholarship – that I thought it necessary to show it at once to Faber and he saw immediately the difficulties which I believe he has put to you. In this I entirely concur, but it is better that he should put them to you, both as the head of the publishing firm and as the original instigator of the series in question.

I do not suppose that I have reviews in the *Criterion* of one out of ten of the books that Faber and Faber publish. I have always, I think, kept to the principle of complete impartiality except that on the whole I have tended to keep down the number of our own books reviewed rather than to increase it. Whenever I thought it necessary I have reminded reviewers that they are to consider our books with at least as severe standards of criticism as they would those of any other publisher. *The Greek Language* was a book which there was no particular necessity for reviewing at all;

'I am sorry to be so intransigent, but the classics are so well worn that no book is worth consideration unless it satisfies the ordinary standards of scholarship, and this Atkinson fails to do.'

GCF responded to Bowra, 26 Feb. 1932: 'Naturally I am distressed by your verdict. But, though my own scholarship is at once too limited and too out-of-date to allow me to form my own judgment, I fully recognize the impossibility in matters of scholarship, of tempering justice with mercy.

'At the same time, it would be very difficult for us to publish your review in the Criterion. I should explain that it was Eliot who first perceived this, and showed me your review in proof. You see, the series was planned by us (by me, to be exact); we invited Braunholtz to edit it; and we agreed to his selection of the author. If, then, we publish an uncompromising attack upon the Greek volume in our own periodical, we put ourselves into an extremely uncomfortable position.

'I have never interfered with the reviews in the Criterion, though it has more than once unfavourably reviewed a book which we have published. But on this occasion I felt obliged to put these considerations to Eliot. He agrees with me that we cannot very well stultify ourselves by publishing your review. We both feel that its exclusion will not damage the cause of truth, since the book is to be reviewed from an angle similar to yours in the Classical Review.

'I expect you will hear from Eliot himself. But in the meantime I am anxious that you should understand my own attitude; and particularly that you shouldn't think either (a) that we wanted or want you to tone down your review or (b) that we are at all influenced by the possible effect of your review on the sales of the book. It is a personal, not a commercial, decision.'

I thought that a certain number of our readers would be interested in it but I should not have chosen to review it except for believing that you were exactly the person to make an interesting review of it. My expectation was certainly justified though in an unexpected way.

There was a further oversight on my part which would have made it necessary to postpone the review in any case, and that is that I had been under the impression that I was going to use your Blok in the June number, and then discovered both that I had said I would use it and that I in fact wanted to use it in the April number, and I have made a rule from which I have only occasionally departed by bad management, never to publish a review and a leading article by the same author in the same number.[1]

With my humble apologies,

> I am,
> Yours sincerely,
> [T. S. Eliot]

FROM *Vivien Eliot* TO *Aurelia Bolliger*   MS Beinecke

29 February 1932   68 Clarence Gate Gardens

Dear Miss Bullinger,

Please come to lunch *here* – do you mind? At 1.30? I am still so ill & chilled to *death*. So come here to lunch & bring Pickwick, because I really do not feel *up* to going *out* to *lunch*.

> Yours most sincerely,
> Vivienne Haigh Eliot

TO *Evelyn Underhill*   CC

1 March 1932   [Faber & Faber Ltd]

Dear Mrs Stuart Moore,

Thank you very much for your kind letter.[2] I hope indeed that my note on Herbert[3] is as satisfactory as you believe it is. I found it more difficult to

---

1–Bowra, 'The Position of Alexander Blok', C. 11 (Apr. 1932), 422–38.
2–Underhill (*The Spectator*) wrote, 17 Feb.: 'Thank you so much for your beautiful study of George Herbert. I feel greatly honoured by being able to include it in the series ['Studies in Sanctity']. It interested me enormously, & gave me an entirely fresh view of G. H. as a poet for all of which I am most grateful.'
3–'George Herbert', *Spectator* 148 (12 Mar. 1932), 360–1.

write than I had anticipated in order to keep it from being merely a piece of literary criticism, and by emphasis on the human character. A young friend of mine, Geoffrey Curtis, Vice-Principal of Lichfield College, tells me that he has sent you some of his poems to ask you for your opinion and advice about publication. I like some of them very well indeed, and hope that you also will like them, and will be able to help him to get them published. I do not feel that it would make a book of verse suitable for the public which my own firm can expect to reach.[1]

Yours very sincerely,
[T. S. Eliot]

TO *Ian Parsons*[2]

CC

2 March 1932   *The Criterion*

Dear Parsons,

Thank you very much for sending me Leavis's book.[3] I like the book very much indeed and have written to Leavis about it. Of the value of a large part of the book I am of course not in a position to judge, but from what I can judge I am delighted that such sensible criticism should be written and published.

With many thanks,
Yours sincerely,
T. S. Eliot

1–Underhill answered, 5 Mar.: 'I had a very kind and charming letter from your friend, Mr Curtis, enclosing his MS, but the dreadful thing is that unfortunately I do *not* like his poems at all! Without holding any brief for conventionality, I do feel in these a desperate attempt to be unusual at all costs, which is always rather distressing, and perhaps specially so where poems on spiritual subjects are concerned.'

2–Ian Parsons (1906–80), who read English at Trinity College, Cambridge, was editor of *The Cambridge Review*. On graduation he joined Chatto & Windus, initially as a typographer but presently as a junior partner under the chairmanship of Harold Raymond. His successes included Empson's *Seven Types of Ambiguity* (1930) and Leavis's *New Bearings in English Poetry* (1932). In 1954 he became chairman of Chatto & Windus (which had taken over the Hogarth Press in 1946); and he was President of the Publishers' Association, 1957–9. Later years saw Chatto & Windus merge with Jonathan Cape, 1969, and with the Bodley Head, 1973: Parsons became joint chairman. His publications include *The Progress of Poetry: An Anthology of Verse from Hardy to the Present* (ed., 1936), *Men Who March Away* (ed., 1965) and *The Collected Works of Isaac Rosenberg* (1979). He was made a CBE in 1971.

3–*New Bearings in English Poetry* (1932).

TO *Frederick May Eliot*[1]   CC

2 March 1932   [*The Criterion*]

Dear Frederick,

I find that I never answered your letter of last July which gave me much pleasure. I want first to apologize to you and to your friend Miss Boie for not having seen her again when she passed through London.[2] I wish that you would explain to her that I was very preoccupied at the moment and misread her letter, so that when I was about to write and ask her to come and see us I discovered that she had already gone. I hope that I shall have the opportunity of repairing the omission on her next visit to London. She struck me as extremely intelligent and sympathetic and I thought that the success which she appeared to have had in London journalism was quite exceptional.

I had heard from other sources of your having adopted a child and was very glad indeed to hear it.[3] The latter part of your letter interested me and makes me hope that we may be able to arrange to meet sometime or other while I am at Harvard next winter. I expect to have a certain amount of time to travel about and see more of the country.[4]

Yours ever,

[Tom]

1–The Revd Frederick May Eliot (1889–1958), a cousin of TSE's, educated at Harvard Divinity School and Carleton College, Minnesota, was Minister of Unity Church, St Paul, Minnesota, 1917–37; from 1937 President of the American Unitarian Association. He married in 1915 Elizabeth Berkeley Lee. Works include *Fundamentals of Unitarian Faith* (1927), *Toward Belief in God* (1929) and *Samuel McCord Crothers, Interpreter of Life* (1930).

2–Frederick had written from Camp Magog, Canada, 21 July 1931, thanking TSE for having been kind to Mildred Boie while she was in London: they had known her for several years, 'and in our judgment she has at least a touch of real ability'.

3–Elizabeth and Frederick had adopted an eight-week-old child named Richard ('Ricky'). 'He is as entrancing and as time-absorbing as any baby.'

4–Frederick and family were enjoying Camp Magog, which was 'very much as it was in the old days, though the trees are a lot bigger and a few of the modern conveniences have intruded upon us. The hermit thrushes still sing, however, and the sense of being happily remote from the busy world has not been lost.' Frederick hoped some day to talk at length with TSE. Camp Maple Hill was a summer retreat, with fifty-four acres of forest, on the northeastern shore of Memphremagog (an extensive lake straddling the Vermont–Canada border), which the family had purchased in 1903. TSE had stayed at the camp with his cousins in the maiden season of 1904: see Cynthia Grant Tucker, *No Silent Witness: The Eliot Parsonage Women and Their Unitarian World* (2010), 175–9.

TO *Thomas Dawes Eliot*[1]   CC/Reed College

2 March 1932   [Faber & Faber Ltd]

Dear Tom,

I find that I never replied to your letter of August 20th,[2] but I will try
to repair my omission now by writing to let you know that I have seen
Professor Scott Buchanan[3] and was much interested in him and in his
subjects of research. I should have been able to do more for him perhaps
had he been able to be in London for some time or to go to Paris, but
when I saw him last I was sorry to learn that his mother who is a member
of his party had been very seriously ill indeed in Cambridge.

I hope that I may have the opportunity of seeing you during the next
summer.

Yours,
[Tom]

TO *A. L. Morton*[4]   CC

2 March 1932   [*The Criterion*]

Dear Morton,

I have your letter of the 28th.[5] The second part of the article in question

---

1 – TSE's cousin Thomas Dawes Eliot (1889–1973) was a Professor in the Dept. of Sociology
and Anthropology, College of Liberal Arts, Northwestern University, Evanston, Illinois.
2 – Thomas D. Eliot had sent TSE on 20 Aug. 1931 a note of introduction for Scott Buchanan.
3 – Scott Buchanan (1895–1968), scholar and educator, was educated at Amherst College,
as a Rhodes Scholar at Balliol College, Oxford, and at Harvard. At the time of this letter he
was a professor of philosophy at the University of Virginia, 1929–36; thereafter Chairman
of the Liberal Arts Committee at Chicago – where he worked to establish the influential
'Great Books' programme – and from 1937 Dean of St John's College, Annapolis. Writings
include *Poetry and Mathematics* (1929), *Symbolic Distance in Relation to Analogy and
Fiction* (1932) and *Tragedy and the New Politics* (1960). See further *Scott Buchanan: A
Centennial Appreciation of His Life and Work, 1895–1968,* ed. Charles A. Nelson (1995).
4 – A. L. Morton (1903–87), Marxist historian; in the 1930s he worked for the *Daily
Worker*; from 1946 he chaired the Historians Group of the Communist Party of Great
Britain. *A People's History of England* (1938) is a modern classic. Later works include
The Everlasting Gospel: A Study in the Sources of William Blake (1958) and *The World
of the Ranters: Religious Radicalism in the English Revolution* (1970). See *Rebels & Their
Causes: Essays in Honour of A. L. Morton,* ed. Maurice Cornforth (1978); *History and the
Imagination: Selected Writings of A. L. Morton,* ed. Margot Heinemann (1990).
5 – Morton had been reading the first part of the article, by Gallox, i.e. Aline Lion, on
Poetry and Property: 'it seems to be based on a quite incorrect idea of the Marxist attitude
to property and of the kind of society we expect. As a result of this, for example, [she]
completely misses the point of Stalin's speech.

appears in the next number which will be out some time in this month. I should be very glad to see any reply that you may care to make up to about 3000 words with a view to publishing it in the following issue.

Yours sincerely,

[T. S. Eliot]

TO *Willard Thorp*[1]

TS Princeton

2 March 1932

The Criterion

Dear Thorp,

Thank you very much for your note of the 29th.[2] I had had a letter from More in which he mentioned the matter. As a matter of fact I was rather confused about it and should of course have written to you before to ask for information. I had had an invitation already to deliver what I think was called a Spencer-Trask lecture but did not immediately identify it with what More was talking about. Knowing nothing of the foundation I wrote evasively asking to postpone the decision if possible as I wanted to take advice in the meantime. One question in my mind was this – that the fee offered was 100 dollars and I wanted to find out how much of that sum would be consumed in travelling expenses from Boston to Princeton and back. You see I have to consider seriously two things: to make all the money I decently can while in America, and at the same time to get some needed rest and recreation out of the visit, so I want to choose carefully the most desirable suggestions. But if this Trask lecture of which I have had an invitation is the one recommended by both More and yourself

---

'Would you be interested in a short reply, of a couple of thousand words say, from the point of view of myself as a Marxist who regards the writing of poetry as a matter of real importance?'

1 – Willard Thorp (1899–1990), scholar and author, taught in the English Department at Princeton for forty-one years until retirement in 1967, becoming a full professor in 1944; chair of the Department, 1958–63; Holmes Professor of Belles Lettres, 1952–67. He co-founded and chaired the American Civilization Program. Works include the *Oxford Anthology of English Poetry* (with Howard Lowry, 1935), *A Southern Reader* (1955), *American Writing in the Twentieth Century* (1960), *American Humorists* (1964); a pioneering annotated edition of Herman Melville's *Moby-Dick* (1947); *The Princeton Graduate School: A History* (with Minor Myers Jr. and Jeremiah Finch, 1978); and he co-edited, and contributed to, the *Literary History of the United States* (first published in 1948). See further the special Willard Thorp issue of *Princeton University Library Chronicle* 54: 2 & 3 (Winter–Spring 1993).

2 – 'I have just received a letter from Dr Spaeth of my department telling me that the University Lecture Committee is asking you to give the Trask Lecture at Princeton next winter. May I add my humble petition? . . . There are so many Eliot "fans" among our undergraduates that your lecture would be as crowded as a foot-ball rally (in the old bad days)!'

I think that I ought to accept it. I have never visited Princeton and should much like to go there.

We hope to see you and Mrs Thorp again on Thursday evening.

Yours sincerely,
T. S. Eliot

TO *Charles Harris*[1]

cc

2 March 1932   [Faber & Faber Ltd]

Dear Harris,

I suppose I ought to have replied at once to your circular of the 15th February about the Harton book; but of course from what little I have heard of the book I am cordially in agreement with the proposal.[2]

Yours sincerely,
[T. S. Eliot]

1–The Revd Charles Harris, DD (1865–1936): Prebendary of Hereford Cathedral from 1925; Vicar of South Leigh, Witney, Oxfordshire, 1929–34; Chairman of the Book Committee of the (English) Church Union from 1923; Assistant Editor of *Literature and Worship*, 1932. His works include *Creeds or No Creeds?* (1922); *First Steps in the Philosophy of Religion* (1927).

See TSE, 'Dr Charles Harris', *Times*, 13 Aug. 1936, 12: 'The death of Charles Harris removes the most powerful force in the publication of theological literature in the Church of England. I say "publication", because in spite of his considerable learning, his wide interests, and his fertility of ideas, Harris always put his own writing second to his great enthusiasm, which was the work of the Book Committee of the Church Union. Of his work in Convocation, to which he gave equal attention so long as health permitted, I cannot speak with such intimate knowledge. But I have always thought that if he had been a layman, and if he had chosen such a profession, he might have become the most successful publisher in London: he would either have made or lost a fortune. He was, however, indifferent to money and celebrity. His aims were on a grand scale, and sometimes gave pause to the more cautious: some of his most ambitious remain unrealized. But one believed that if anyone could realize them, it was he. Enthusiasm sometimes made him a little tactless, but few men have had a greater power of communicating their enthusiasm. During his last years he lived in continuous discomfort between periods of acute physical suffering, but at all times, even just before or after a serious operation, his cheerfulness, serenity, and zeal were undiminished. He was sometimes misjudged by those who knew him only superficially; but no one could know him at all well without regarding him with great affection and admiration.'

2–The proposal was for F. P. Harton's book *The Elements of the Spiritual Life: A Study in Ascetical Theology* to be published by SPCK and The Sheldon Press in association with the English Church Union.

TO *Aline Lion*[1]   CC

2 March 1932   [*The Criterion*]

Dear Miss Lion,

I must apologise for my delay in answering your letter[2] and also for the fact that as I am rather pressed for time I am answering in English. The important point is to decide first whether Paulhan – that is to say the Editions NRF – is the best publisher to which to send it. I am quite ready to send a word to Paulhan about the essay though I should have thought that Marguerite's influence in that quarter would be much more potent than mine. But it has struck me that the NRF under Paulhan and since the secession of Claudel has been moving more and more to the left, and that possibly some other publisher might be more suitable. Have you thought for instance of Plon or even of Grasset? If you would like to discuss the matter I should be very glad to see you any morning by arranging a few days ahead.

                                        Yours very sincerely,
                                        [T. S. Eliot]

TO *I. A. Richards*   TS Magdalene

2 March 1932   *The Criterion*

Dear Richards,

Your remarks about Belgion are certainly put in a most convincing manner. I should be inclined to protest in general, but I must admit that this particular article, which you have not seen, entirely justifies them and I have come to the conclusion that it would not be [a] profitable way of introducing the subject. So I will drop that suggestion and hope to have your other essay as soon as possible.

                                        Yours ever,
                                        T. S. E.

1–Aline Lion, DPhil (Oxon), who lived in France from 1913 to 1927, was teaching at Roedean School; author of *The Pedigree of Fascism: A Popular Essay on the Western Philosophy of Politics* (1927), which TSE discussed in 'The Literature of Fascism', C. 8 (Dec. 1928), 280–90.
2–Not found.

Lines to a Persian Cat[1]

The songsters of the air repair
To the green fields of Russell Sq.
Beneath the trees there is no ease
For the dull brain, the sharp desires
And the quick eyes of Woolly Bear.[2]
There is no relief but in grief.
O when will the creaking heart cease?
When will the broken chair find ease?
Why does the summer day delay?
When will Time flow away?

Composed in the
Underground.
Too obvious Blake
+ Hopkins to be
useful.[3]

P.S. Please tell me what you know about *Rolf Gardner*?[4]

1 – See *CPP*, 135. Poem written on 28 Feb. 1932. Aurelia Hodgson's notes on TSE: 'During the spring he wrote two short poems, one Lines to a Cat, the other To a Dog. Vivienne told me he had written the former the day before, and after dinner she asked him to read it to me. He found it and said, "I will if you'll stay in the room. The more people there are, the easier it is to read." I felt very honoured. When R. was present a few days later we asked him to read it again. By then he had the two, and he felt the latter <former> was the better. R. said, "Read both, and we can see." He did, tho after the first he opened Blake and read a poem about the three nuns, which was remotely suggestive. T. S. E. said, "A poem is nothing, if it isn't unique, and this one isn't." The second one came to him while he was in a tube train, and he passed up his station in his haste to put it on paper' (Bryn Mawr).
2 – Years later, when TSE's friends Commander Hugh Standley and his wife Mary wrote (29 Sept. 1952) that they had acquired 'two little half Siamese kittens' – 'Mother is a most aristocratic Siamese, with a pedigree a yard long' – which they named Prince Krapotkin ('Potkin for short') and Mr Possum, TSE replied on 6 Nov. 1952 that if their Siamese was 'one of the aristocrats of that race, she may turn out to be a more or less near connection of our own Siamese, who is also reputed to belong to one of the best families. At the time when I kept Yorkshire terriers, and was interested in their pedigrees, it seemed that all Yorkshires were descended from a distinguished ancestor named Lord Richard. At another time, when I had a Persian cat, it seemed that all the distinguished Persian cats were descended from some magnificent animal of the name of Woolly Bear. It may be the same with the Siamese.'
3 – IAR responded on 3 May: 'It is months ago since you sent me the Wooleybear verses – which were much enjoyed and still are. I like authors to burlesque themselves and thought there was more of your manner in it than Hopkins – tho' Blake was openly alluded to. How is the Triumphal March series going on? – a seriously concerned inquiry.' (*Letters*, 64) In a later, undated letter, which for some reason he did not post, IAR repeated that '*Wooly Bear*' 'is more derivative, I think, from you than from Hopkins. Blake, yes! I like it very much & think it is a good thing for poets to parody themselves slightly – they do it so much better than other folk.'
4 – IAR wrote (unposted letter), of Rolf Gardiner: 'Charming, enthusiastic, inflated . . . He used, about 1922, to have swallowed D. H. Lawrence in such quantities as to reek of it. Then he became *Rolf the Ranger* a member of some camping–"youth-movement"–fascisty–self-help–primitivist–"Rebuild Civilisation in the Backwoods" Association . . . Later, being half-German (or rather, Finnish mother & born in Berlin – father editor of the big Berlin Dictionary of Hieroglyfics) he got much into the German Youth Movement (post-War revival, of course) . . . I think he is a rather fine creature.

TO *Montgomery Belgion*[1]   CC

2 March 1932   [Faber & Faber Ltd]

My dear Belgion,

I should have written to you sooner but after reading your paper on Belief I felt that I must read it through again with some care and ponder the matter. Frankly I am disappointed in this essay. The questions no doubt are of interest to Richards and D'Arcy respectively though no doubt they will merely say you have misunderstood their meaning; but I cannot feel that an article in this form can have very much interest for even the limited public for such questions. Your article assumes that its reader will be familiar with both Richards and D'Arcy's books and even so I think the reader would be tempted to say 'If you have these questions to ask of Richards and D'Arcy why don't you just write to Richards and D'Arcy and try to settle them', for there is no point in making a public controversy of it unless you are opposing them with a positive theory of your own which the reader can contrast with the others. Your method seems to me admirable when applied to established figures such as those to whom you referred in *Our Present Philosophy of Life*, but in the present context you are not concerned with pricking bubbles of reputation but in contributing to disinterested enquiry. I do not see how you can treat Richards or D'Arcy as you would treat André Gide or Bertrand Russell and I do not see what good can come of asking private questions in a public place. I do not feel *a priori* that either Richards or D'Arcy could be aroused to interest in replying unless you had some views of your own to attract their attention. I wish you would think this question over.

Yours ever,
[T. S. Eliot]

'I used to know his sister Margaret Gardiner well – you may remember meeting her.' See also TSE to Gardiner, 23 Mar. 1932.
1–Montgomery ('Monty') Belgion (1892–1973), author: see Biographical Register.

TO *William Greenleaf Eliot*[1]   CC

2 March 1932   [Faber & Faber Ltd]

Dear Will,

   Thank you very much for your note of December which reached me the other day.[2] It was very kind of you to write. I hope very much that I may be able to see you and Minna while I am in America next winter.

                              Very cordially your cousin
                              [Tom]

TO *Vivien Eliot*[3]   MS Bodleian

4 March 1932   68 Clarence Gate Gardens,
                                    Regents Park, London N.W.1.

My dear Vivienne,

   I have been appointed Charles Eliot Norton Professor at Harvard University, Cambridge Mass., U.S.A, for the academic year 1932–1933. I subjoin duplicate of the official notification. I shall leave England in September next and return the following May. For this period of lecturing at Harvard I shall receive 10,000 dollars, out of which I must pay my expenses, and on which I must pay income tax in America and England.

   I shall remain a Director of Faber & Faber Ltd and Editor of the *Criterion*, which periodical is to continue uninterrupted during my absence. I shall forego [*sic*] my salary and director's fees for the period of my absence: that is to say that I shall receive no salary or fees for the quarters ending December 31 next, March 31 1933 and June 30 1933. Upon my return I shall resume my active editorship of the *Criterion* and directorship of Faber & Faber Ltd.

   I shall also remain a member of the Standing Committee of the Literature Committee of the English Church Union.

   I wish to make quite clear that my appointment at Harvard is for the period stated above only, and is not renewable.

1–Dr William Greenleaf Eliot, Jr (1866–1956), who was born in St Louis, Missouri, and studied at Harvard Divinity School, was minister of the Church of Our Father, Portland, Oregon, 1906–34. He married in 1894 Minna Sessinghaus (1868–1944), who taught at the Mary Institute, St Louis, 1890–4, and was active in educational and philanthropic work.
2–'Will' had spoken to TSE by phone on 13 Dec. 1931 – 'though unfortunately there was "line trouble" and we were cut off when you had spoken for a few minutes'.
3–Presumably intended to give formal information and reassurance to his wife, this copy of the letter, which is not signed, was pasted by VHE into her diary.

I am,
Affectionately yours,
your husband
SIGNED:

TO *Theodore Spencer*   TS Harvard

10 March 1932   Faber & Faber Ltd

Dear Spencer,

I had last week a letter from my sister Mrs Sheffield telling me of a discussion her husband had had with you about the arrangement for my housing. I am writing therefore to express my appreciation of your suggestion and to say that I shall be very glad to accept it – that is to take my lodgings in Eliot House for the first half-year, leaving it open until I have had some experience of life in Cambridge to decide whether I shall continue there or to remove myself to the Sheffields.[1] It is very good of you and of them to have given such consideration to my welfare.

With many thanks,
Yours sincerely,
T. S. Eliot

TO *Kenneth B. Murdock*   CC

10 March 1932   [Faber & Faber Ltd]

Dear Dr Murdock,

Thank you for your useful letter of February 4th.[2] The sort of course that you suggest is one which I think that I could handle especially if it could be restricted to a small enough number of students to be conducted rather informally. If the course were in the second half-year it would I am

1 – The Sheffields lived at 31 Madison Street, Gray Gardens, Cambridge, Mass.
2 – Murdock explained that TSE could teach a course running for just two hours a week for some fifteen or twenty of 'our best students'; and he could make the course 'just what he wants it to be'. Very often, one of the students would be expected to lead the class each week, so the instructor would function as 'a kind of moderator'. Such a half-year course would conclude with an examination or 'an essay or thesis of considerable length'; for the first half-year the examination would take place the following January; for the second half-year, it would normally be conducted during June. But if TSE were to opt for examination by essay, the essays could be handed in by the beginning or middle of May – so that he could do his grading before departure.

afraid have to be arranged in the matter of papers and examinations so that I could leave before the end of May. On the other hand it seems to me from every other point of view better to give it in the second half than in the first. I shall understand the situation by then and will have had more time in which to organize a programme. At the same time I should be quite ready to meet and advise during the first half-year any particular students to whom my advice and criticism might possibly be of use.[1]

Yours sincerely,

[T. S. Eliot]

TO *Bonamy Dobrée*   TS Brotherton

10 March 1932   *The Criterion*

My dear Bonamy,

Yours of the 6th received. It is far better that you should be whitewashing apple-trees than listening to my hog-wash.[2] I have sent you a copy of my paper on Whibley and have ordered one or two of the books for you. I don't quite understand your references to my functions as a publisher.[3] I am glad that I shall be on the spot to boost the sales of Penn <Penn, not Benn>[4] when it appears.[5] As for your book on modern prose I'd rather you made a selection yourself and then submitted it for my approval.[6] As for fees, if it [is] merely a long quotation as in Herbert's book on prose and if there is no resemblance to an anthology I don't see why I or any other author should have a fee.

1 – J. Tucker Murray (Dept. of English) replied on 28 Mar., for Dean Murdock, that Dr Theodore Spencer would look after his examining if TSE elected to do his course in the second half-year.

2 – 'Damn it all, I missed you this afternoon. I didn't discover you were performing (were you preaching) till eight o'clock this evening. Had I known, I would have torn myself away from whitewashing my apple trees.'

3 – 'I have been reading Don Quixote (aloud) for the first time in my life. What an astonishing thing it is. It seems impossible for anyone nowadays to invent a form in which they can say everything. Still, we live in an age of abounding genius, if we are to believe people like you (I refer to your functions as a publisher).'

4 – Added by hand in the margin: TSE had mistyped 'Benn'.

5 – 'Penn [BD's book on William Penn] is dead, and very nearly buried. You will be in America to share the vast enthusiasm for it when it appears.'

6 – 'I am doing a book on modern prose for Oxford, and propose to quote a passage from you (at present unselected; you can choose it yourself if you like). What are your views on a fee?'

The news about Harold vary. A week ago he was almost given up, but my wife heard from Alida yesterday that he had taken a turn for the better.

Yours ever,
T. S.E.

TO *Joseph Needham*[1]

10 March 1932   [*The Criterion*]

Dear Needham,

I have read your paper with great interest and I must say with much dissatisfaction.[2] Contrary apparently to your expectations I do not differ so very radically from your political views as I do from your theological views. Very likely I am quite mistaken as to your design, but certainly the impression given me is that of the usual foggy but indigestible substance called religion which is always being offer[ed] to us. Don't think that I put you on a level with drivellers like Julian Huxley but that seems to me the kind of thing to which you tend to lead us. Am I quite wrong in believing that a very radical attitude towards the political and economic structure can be associated with religious orthodoxy? And even if I am wrong I don't see how a union can be effected by compromise. I should be very grateful for your reply to this objection.

Yours sincerely,
[T. S. Eliot]

1 – Joseph Needham (1900–95), biochemist, historian of science and civilisation in China, and Christian socialist, was educated at Gonville and Caius College, Cambridge (a Fellow for life, he served as Master for ten years from 1966). His early works included *The Sceptical Biologist* (1929) and *Chemical Embryology* (3 vols, 1931); but his major project – conceived during WW2 when he established the Sino-British scientific cooperation office and served as scientific counsellor at the British Embassy, Chongqing – was a comprehensive history of Chinese science, technology and medicine. A polymath and a pro-Chinese witness (he was for some years declared *persona non grata* by the USA), he was ultimately regaled with honours. In 1992 he was made a Companion of Honour, and in 1994 received the Einstein Medal from UNESCO.

2 – Needham sent his paper on 6 Mar. 'I am sure you will not be in agreement with my political position, but the admiration which we share for the English divines of the 17th century may make it of some interest to you.' See 'Laudian Marxism? Thoughts on Science, Religion and Socialism', C. 12 (Oct. 1932), 56–72.

TO *H. C. Crofton*[1]   CC

10 March 1932   [*The Criterion*]

My dear Crofton,

Thank you very much for your kind note about my talk.[2] It is the first word I have had and was all the more welcome because I had been feeling extremely dissatisfied with my performance. It is no doubt an impossible subject. Either I risk being vague and verbose or else playing the fool with subject of which one is ignorant [*sic*].

After this nightmare is over, that is to say after Easter, I hope that you will come and lunch with me one day early in April.

Yours ever,
[T. S. Eliot]

TO *Montgomery Belgion*   CC

10 March 1932   [*The Criterion*]

Dear Belgion,

Thank you very much for your long and considerate letter of the 4th.[3] I can only repeat that I do not think that even the quite superior and

---

1–H. C. Crofton (d. 1938) had been a colleague and friend at Lloyds Bank. Crofton was the senior of the four managers of the Colonial and Foreign Department. Crofton's son John told the Archivist of Lloyds Bank, 1 Aug. 1980: 'I have memories of my father inviting T. S. for several week-ends to our home. My mother . . . used to speak of him and of how much they enjoyed his visits. (If I may add that in those days it was a little unusual for the Chief Foreign Manager to invite "a clerk" for week-ends!!!) I do know that the object of the visits from my father's side, was to persuade T. S. to give up the Bank and devote himself to his obvious real calling.'

2–Crofton wrote on 8 Mar., 'I want to tell you how intensely I appreciated your talk on "The Modern Dilemma".

'I have listened to your precursors but you are the first man who approached the subject from, to my mind, the only sound point of view. I agree with every word you said and am greatly looking forward to your development of the subject on the next three Sundays.'

3–Belgion sought to defend the article he had submitted. 'It is only fair, I think, to point out that there is a case for the article in its present form. The "positive theory" which you say [letter to Belgion, 2 Mar.] the reader should be able to contrast with the others is there all right, but it is only implied . . . It is quite true, as you say, that the article assumes its reader will be familiar with Richards's *Principles* and D'Arcy's *Nature of Belief*. In fact, it is so written that it can only be read properly with these two books at hand.' All the same, TSE's response had made him reconsider his position; and he now proposed '(1) An article stating directly my views on belief either (a) in contrast to those of Richards and D'Arcy, or (b) without mention of any one else at all, or (2) Something quite different, i.e. the appendix I am adding to the French translation of *Our Present Philosophy of Life* and which deals with Gide's objections and my reply thereunto.'

industrious reader will get from your essay any definite suggestion of your own positive views, so I am ready to accept one of your other proposals. I should like very much for instance to see your appendix dealing with Gide, and I suggest that that might be used first[1] and that you do another article on Belief, the one which you call 1B, at your leisure.

With all best wishes,

Yours ever,

[T. S. Eliot]

TO *N. H. Rubin*[2]   CC

10 March 1932   [Faber & Faber Ltd]

Dear Sir,

We have your letter of the 24th February to which we have given consideration.[3] Although I am not sure that there is room for another book on *Ulysses* at the moment I think that we are more interested than any other publisher is likely to be and I myself should very much like to see what you have written. If, therefore, you will send me a copy of the manuscript we shall consider it with a prejudice in its favour.

Yours sincerely,

[T. S. Eliot]

TO *Geoffrey W. Rossetti*[4]   CC

10 March 1932   [Faber & Faber Ltd]

Dear Mr Rossetti,

Thank you for your letter of the 26th February and for sending me your brother's essay on the League of Nations which we have considered.[5]

---

1 – 'A Postscript on Mr André Gide', C. 12 (Apr. 1933), 404–20.

2 – Nathan Harold Rubin (b. 1907, New York), a graduate of Washington Square College (1931), was co-author, as 'Peter Galinet', of a play entitled *Garbo and Dietrich can have it!* (1932).

3 – Rubin wished to submit a 375-page study, 'Brick and Mortar: Index Studies in the Form and Development of Joyce's *Ulysses*', aiming to show the work as a psychological novel – 'to explain its form and psychology' – and as a complement to Stuart Gilbert's book.

4 – Geoffrey Rossetti worked in administration at the University of London, South Kensington.

5 – Rossetti had come down from Cambridge in 1931 'after reading rather more widely than what is normal in International Law and kindred matters'.

Although we have found it interesting it does not appear to us quite suitable for a pamphlet, and our suggestion is that it would appear much better in some weekly periodical. For that purpose it would have to be reduced of course, but my suggestion is that it be sent in its present form to one of the weekly papers such as the *Week End Review* or the *New Statesman*, and that you ask them whether they would be interested in publishing a shorter version.

I am sorry that your investigations into the Renaissance have been disappointing, and I should be glad to hear more of what you are doing now.

Yours sincerely,
[T. S. Eliot]

TO *Richard Faber*[1]

TS Sir Richard Faber

Thursday [Postmark 10 Mar. 1932] London

Dear Dick:

I got up this Morning and Went into the Bathroom; and there I found the Plumber Man Working; and When he Saw me he turned over and Said:

Why don't you Sit down & Write a letter to Dick?

So Then

I went into the Next room and There I Found the Window-Cleaning Man, and He said: WHY don't you Sit down & Write a letter to Dick?

1–Richard Faber (1924–2007), diplomat and writer. Elder son of GCF, Dick was educated at Westminster School and won a scholarship to Christ Church, Oxford, where he was President of the Union and graduated with a first in Greats (he just failed to win a Fellowship of All Souls). After a wartime period in the Royal Navy, in 1950 he joined the Foreign Service (later the Diplomatic Service), serving as Head of the Rhodesia Political Department, 1967–9; Counsellor, The Hague, 1969–73; Counsellor, Cairo, 1973–5; Assistant Under-Secretary of State, Foreign and Commonwealth Office, 1975–7; Ambassador to Algeria, 1977–81 (being appointed KCVO on the occasion of the Queen's State Visit in 1980).

So then I Went into the Kitchen
and There I Found the

COOK
And She Said:
While I'm Frying these Eggs
WHY don't you sit Down and
Write a Letter to Dick?

So then I thought very hard, and I
got my Shiny Hat and Brushed It,
and then

I Sat Down and I wrote a Letter to Dick. It said

Dear Dick,

Thank you very much for your Nice Letter and For the Pixtures You
have drawn for Me. I was very glad to Hear from You Agin, & Hope
you are very Well. I wonder whether You are having Good weather in
Hampstead. Here it is very Nice but It is too Warm to go Skating & Too
Cold for Swimming and Too Wet to Play Cricket and Too dry to Play
Frogs, but Otherwise it is very Nice Weather Indeed.

Your fexnite Unccle
Tom

Mulling over his career choices in 1950 – whether to join F&F or to go in for diplomacy
– he chose the latter on the grounds that it would be a worthwhile job 'working more or
less for international peace', and that it might be 'a little easier to combine some writing'
with it: his works include *Beaconsfield and Bolingbroke* (1961); *The Vision and the Need:
Late Victorian Imperialist Aims* (1966); *Proper Stations: Class in Victorian Fiction* (1971);
A Chain of Cities (autobiography, 2000).

то W. Hamilton Fyfe

10 March 1932   [Faber & Faber Ltd]

Dear Mr Hamilton Fyfe,

Thank you for your letter of the 24th February.[1] I knew that you had gone to Queen's University in Canada so you will see that I am better informed, though in no more detail, about you than you are informed about me. I am not going to Harvard until September and I shall be there only for seven months and am then returning to London, and I very much dislike being addressed as Professor, and do you remember by the way once coming to lunch with me in my flat in the year 1916?

I am flattered by your request of a contribution to the *Queen's Quarterly*. The copy has not arrived but in any case I cannot undertake any fresh commissions until I have the Harvard job off my hands and am back in London. Meanwhile I hope that while I am in America I shall be able to pay a visit to Canada as well and I look forward to the possibility, however remote, of meeting you again.

Yours sincerely,
[T. S. Eliot]

то *James Joyce*

10 March 1932   [Faber & Faber Ltd]

Dear Joyce,

Thank you for your letter of the 4th. Lady Ottoline Morrell's address is 10 Gower Street, W.C.1. and Sidney Schiff's is 32 Porchester Terrace, W.2. I do not know where Schiff is at the moment. At this time of year he is usually in Switzerland, but I am pretty sure that letters will be forwarded from that address.[2]

I hope you can give me a few days grace as we want to look thoroughly into the question of the practicability of bringing out an edition of *Ulysses* in England.[3] So far as I know the case has no precedent as I do

---

1–W. Hamilton Fyfe (1878–1965), Principal of Queen's University, Kingston, Ontario, Canada – who had known TSE at Merton College, Oxford (where Fyfe held the office of 'Principal of the Postmasters') – addressed him as 'Professor T. S. Eliot, c/o Department of English, Harvard University', with the request that he would contribute an article to *Queen's Quarterly*.

2–JJ hinted at his reason for wishing to contact OM and Sidney Schiff: 'It is really for my daughter I want it or rather for her publisher!!!' (*Letters* I, 316)

3–Bennett Cerf (Random House) had offered £700, with royalty of 15%, for the rights to an American edition of *Ulysses* – 'text unabridged and unaltered' – and an offer was

not suppose that the book of Proust in question had ever been banned in England before Chatto published a limited edition. It is I believe quite true in general that limited editions are less liable to censorship than ordinary editions, but I doubt for instance whether it would be possible now to publish *Lady Chatterley's Lover* in England in this way. But if the book can be published at all we would naturally rather do it ourselves than see any other publisher have it; so that we want to make as sure as possible of the ground by private enquiry before going further.

I will make fresh enquiries about Gorman from his New York publisher.[1] When I sent you the cutting from the *Observer* I had not seen the *New Statesman* which has since been sent me. I liked your ode to Sullivan very much indeed.[2]

Yours sincerely,
[T. S. Eliot]

TO *B. E. Nicolls*[3] CC

10 March 1932   [Faber & Faber Ltd]

Dear Mr Nicholls,

I must apologize for my delay in answering your kind letter of the 22nd February.[4] I had to wait a few days in order to think the matter over, but I really should have written to you a week ago.

---

coming from Harcourt Brace. JJ asked, 'If there is no prospect of your firm doing a high priced private edition of *Ulysses* as was suggested that evening have you any objection if I ask Pinker to offer it in this way to Chatto and Windus who McGreevi [*sic*] tells me did something like this for a book of Proust's? He says the Home Office took no steps against it.' (*Letters* I, 316)

1 – Gorman and his wife were divorced – 'and this will leave him at the mercy of journalism which is very regrettable in the circumstances as he will probably shelve his book on me'.

2 – 'From a Banned Writer to a Banned Singer', *NS&N*, 27 Feb. 1932, 260–1: extracted from a letter sent by JJ to Sullivan: 'Hats off, *primi assoluti*! Send him canorious, long to lung over us, high toseasoarious! Guard safe our Geoge!' 'I hope you got my jottings about Sullivan, the bit you sent from the Observer was copied from the New Statesman.'

3 – Basil E. Nicolls (1893–1965) was educated at Christ Church, Oxford (Slade Prize Exhibition), and served in the army in Gallipoli, Mesopotamia, India and Afghanistan. After joining the BBC in 1924 he was successively Manchester Station Director, London Station Director, General Editor of Publications, Controller of Administration, and Controller of Programmes. From 1944 he was Senior Controller; from 1947 Director of Home Broadcasting. He retired in 1952 as Acting Director-General. He was made CBE in 1945; knighted in 1953.

4 – The Double Crown Club, founded in London in the early 1920s, is a dining club and society of printers, publishers, book designers and illustrators. Nicolls, secretary of the club, renewed the invitation: might TSE be free for dinner on 21 Apr.?

When I last wrote there seemed no reason why I should not have ample time to accept the honour of being the guest of the club toward the end of April, but since then I received my appointment to Harvard which very much alters matters. It means that I shall have to devote myself during the spring to several pieces of work which might otherwise have waited till midsummer, because I must spend some weeks in outlining my Harvard lectures before I leave England. I have therefore refused every other invitation to speak this year, and now feel that I must also, although with the greater regret because of its postponement, decline yours. I do not feel that I can honestly undertake anything new until I return to London in May 1933. I can only hope that by that time you or your successor and the Double Crown Club will be kindly disposed to renew the invitation.

With many regrets,
Yours sincerely,
[T. S. Eliot]

TO *Ada Sheffield*[1]   cc

12 March 1932   [Faber & Faber Ltd]

My dear Ada,

I was very much touched by your kind letter of the 14th February and by all the trouble you and Shef have taken on my behalf.[2] It had not

1–Ada Eliot Sheffield (1869–1943): eldest of the seven Eliot children; author of *The Social Case History: Its Construction and Content* (1920) and *Social Insight in Case Situations* (1937). TSE considered her 'a very exceptional woman' – the Mycroft to his Holmes – and 'an authority on Organized Philanthrophy'. FVM informed Helen Gardner, in 1978: 'she and he, when he was a child, had the habit of communicating with each other, as they sat on the steps of their home in St Louis, in lengthy and happy communications by rhythms. Throughout life Tom relied on Ada's understanding.' TSE told JDH, 20 Feb. 1943: 'Being nearly twenty years older than I, and having no children of her own, she came to occupy a quasi-parental relation with me (my mother would be 100 this year!) Also she and I have always had more in common than with the rest of our family. She has far more brains than any of the others, and with my grandfather's organising and executive ability combined a more reflective mind, and a capacity of abstraction, coming from the other side of the family. Without being "masculine" in any way to suggest psychological distortion, she has a capacity for impersonal thought, and for detaching herself from emotion and prejudice, which I have never found in any other member of her sex. So I have always felt a tacit understanding with her, and a more satisfactory relationship, than I have ever found in those of either excitement or friendship with women – in the long run' (King's).
2–Alfred Dwight ('Shef') Sheffield (1871–1961), husband of Ada, taught English at University School, Cleveland, Ohio, and was an English instructor, later Professor, of Group Work at Wellesley College. His publications include *Lectures on the Harvard Classics: Confucianism* (1909) and *Grammar and Thinking: a study of the working conceptions in*

occurred to me that you would care to take on such a burden as having me to live with you in Cambridge, knowing how much you both have to do and how difficult a matter American housekeeping must be. Your suggestion conjointly with Theodore Spencer is a very agreeable one. I should not in any case like to impose myself on you until I have some notion of the sort of life I shall have to live. It may turn out for the best that I should remain at Eliot House for the whole time, but if not nothing would give me greater happiness than to spend the rest of the season with you if, as you say, you have the room for me. So I shall write to Spencer accepting his rooms to the mid-year provisionally. I hear from Richards that Eliot House has some pleasant society and the Master is Roger Merriman. After that we will see. Meanwhile I should like indeed if it proves possible to have a regular arrangement such as Sunday dinner, but I should naturally want to contribute my regular share to the expenses.

About public lectures outside of the University. I had already had a talk with Eric Maclagan on the subject, and his notion is the same, that it is best to postpone making such engagements until one is on the spot. In any case I shall not make any series of engagements with a lecture agency. It would hardly seem fair to the University to lecture on such a scale as that and as I am and shall be rather tired I want to reserve as much leisure time as possible.

With many thanks,
Your affectionate brother
[Tom]

---

syntax (1912). 'Shef' had discussed arrangements at Harvard with Theodore Spencer, who advised that TSE might do best to take the suite (sitting room, bedroom, bathroom) at Eliot House for the first six months, and then move in with the Sheffields for the final weeks of his visit. The Sheffields lived at 31 Madison Street, Gray Gardens, in a newly developed area about a mile from Harvard. But Shef, being a nervous person, was sensitive to noise, so that lodging with them might inhibit TSE from inviting many guests over to their house. Still, staying with them would be much cheaper for him. 'We are eagerly looking forward to renewing our old congeniality with you.'

TO *E. Gordon Selwyn*[1]   CC

14 March 1932   [Faber & Faber Ltd]

My dear Selwyn,

My firm has received with a view to publication a book entitled *Catholicism: the Idea and the Actuality* by the Revd. J. L. Beaumont James whose name is unfamiliar to me.[2] The duty of considering this book devolves upon me, and as I notice that Mr Beaumont James refers to you as having recommended him to us I should be very grateful if you could find time while I am reading the book to let me have any information about him that you think fit. How old a man is he?

I have so far only dipped into the book which appears interesting, but I am rather hesitant about a book of this kind in view of the number and variety of centenary literature which is certain to be published next year.[3] No doubt you know yourself about the various projected volumes of the E.C.U. and the S.P.C.K.[4]

Yours sincerely,
[T. S. Eliot]

1–The Revd Edward Gordon Selwyn (1885–1959): editor of *Theology: A Monthly Journal of Historic Christianity*, 1920–33. Educated at Eton and King's College, Cambridge (Newcastle Scholar; Porson Scholar and Prizeman; Waddington Scholar; Browne's Medallist; 2nd Chancellor's Medallist), he was Rector of Redhill, Havant, 1919–30; Provost in Convocation, 1921–31; Dean of Winchester, 1931–58. His writings include *The Approach to Christianity* (1925); *Essays Catholic & Critical by Members of the Anglican Communion* (ed., 1926).
2–J. L. Beaumont James: educated at Magdalene College, Cambridge; later Steel University Student and Lady Kay Scholar of Jesus; Proctor in Convocation for the Diocese of Winchester; Rector of Millbrook, Southampton; he told TSE (27 Feb. 1932) that his book included 'a searching analysis . . . of the position of the English Church both in relation to its separation from Mediaeval Catholicism and to its gradual return to Catholic ideals. This leads to a justification of Anglo-Catholicism.' The typescript had been read – '& I think I may say highly approved' – by the Vice-Chancellor of Cambridge, the Dean of King's, and the Senior Tutor of Magdalene; and he submitted it 'on the express suggestion of the Dean of Winchester'.
3–Centenary of the Oxford Movement.
4–Selwyn replied (17 Mar.) that Beaumont James was his exact contemporary at Cambridge, which meant that he was about forty-six. 'I have not read his manuscript . . . but I gather that [Will] Spens has seen it, or part of it, and thought it of considerable interest and value . . . [B. J.] is a little bit inclined to be *cacoethes loquendi*, and this may possibly extend itself to his pen; but I dare say he could to some extent curtail what he has written if length proves to be a difficulty.'

TO *Charles du Bos*[1]

14 March 1932   [*The Criterion*]

CC

My dear du Bos,

This letter is to introduce to you Dr Aline Lion, and I should be very grateful to you if you could have a talk with her while she is in Paris. Mademoiselle Lion, who has done much work at Oxford in philosophy and economics and who is at present a lecturer at Roedean School, has written a long and very interesting essay on Property and Poetry which I have published in the last number and the current number of the *Criterion*. She has now re-written this essay at greater length in her native language, which is French, and is anxious to find a publisher in Paris who would produce it as a small book. She has been recommended to the *NRF* but I was anxious that she should see you before settling on a publisher. Mademoiselle Lion is a Catholic and I think you would find her views sympathetic, and I hope that you may perhaps be able to suggest a more suitable publisher for a book of this kind.

With all best wishes to yourself and Madame du Bos,

I am,

Yours sincerely,

[T. S. Eliot]

TO *Charles B. Blanchard*

CC

16 March 1932   [Faber & Faber Ltd]

Dear Mr Blanchard,

I have your letter of the 3rd instant and confirm the arrangements made therein.[2] It will be satisfactory to me if payment is made in November, but I should be obliged if you will take note that my address at that time will be Eliot House, Cambridge, Mass.

Yours sincerely,

[T. S. Eliot]

1–Charles du Bos (1882–1939), French critic of French and English literature (his mother was English, and he studied for a year at Oxford), contributed one review to C., in 1935. He wrote essays on Shakespeare, Shelley, Byron, Flaubert, Goethe, Mérimée and Mauriac, and was admired for his posthumously published journals (6 vols, 1946–55).

2–Little, Brown & Company agreed to omit 'Prufrock' and 'The Hollow Men' from their original wish-list of eight poems; a fee of $75 would be paid on publication, probably in Nov.

TO *Ferris Greenslet*   CC

16 March 1932   [Faber & Faber Ltd]

Dear Mr Greenslet,

Thank you for your letters of March 1st and 2nd.[1] About Du Bos's
Byron I know that this is a very good book.[2] I have discussed it with my
colleagues but I am afraid that we feel too much as you do to venture to
undertake the translation and publication ourselves. As you may know
we are very chary of publishing translations of French books, especially
when as in this case the books themselves are for a rather select public.
Furthermore I am sorry to say Du Bos is not yet well known in England.
Finally I think that Byron is now a bad publishing subject in view of
the recent works that you mention. So I am very sorry that I must again
decline.

                                       Yours cordially
                                       [T. S. Eliot]

TO *James Joyce*   CC

16 March 1932   [*The Criterion*]

My dear Joyce,

This letter is merely to ask whether there is any likelihood of our soon
having the first part of *W.I.P.* to send to the printers. You will remember
that we originally expected it at about Christmas time. I imagine that you
have had various distractions and disturbances and I don't want to hurry
you but I should like to have some idea of when we may have part of the
work for setting up.

I hope to be able to let you know more about the question of publishing
Ulysses within a few days.

1–Greenslet reported on 1 Mar. that he had been reading du Bos's *Byron* with 'a good deal
of interest. There have been so many recent books on that subject that I am rather too fearful
of the financial result to feel like . . . arranging for translation and publication in English. If,
however, it could be done in Great Britain, I think we could at least take a fair sized edition
of the sheets.' On 2 Mar., in response to TSE's letter of 17 Feb., he added: 'Apparently your
position is very much the same as ours. We certainly couldn't use more than 350 copies at
the outside.'
2–*Byron et le besoin de la fatalité* (1929).

I have received from Miss Beach[1] the proof of Herbert Read's introduction to the Duff book[2] and I am posting it to Miss Weaver. My only objection to Read's preface is that I am rather tired of the Freud business. The Unconscious seems to include, to most people, everything conscious which previous writers have chosen to ignore.

I have also received from Mr Herbert Hughes[3] a notice of the recital of your songs, but as it is tomorrow I am afraid it is probable that I shall be unable to go. I am very sorry and wish that I had had longer notice.

Yours sincerely,
[T. S. Eliot]

TO *Bonamy Dobrée*   CC

16 March 1932   [Faber & Faber Ltd]

Dear Bonamy,

Yours of the 10th instant to hand. I had been waiting in the hope that your publishers would have the sense and good taste to send a copy of the work[4] here, but as they have not done so I think that a note from you to them on the subject would be more effective than an application from here. If you are disposed to fall in with this suggestion could you think of anybody, barring John Hayward, who is fit to review it? Do you think Willie King is up to it?[5]

1-Sylvia Beach (1887–1962), American expatriate who in Nov. 1919 opened (with Adrienne Monnier) Shakespeare & Company, a bookshop and lending library, at 8 rue Dupuytren, Paris, moving two years later to 12 rue de l'Odéon. Her customers included JJ (she published *Ulysses*), Gide, Maurois, Valéry, EP, Hemingway and Stein. TSE wrote in tribute ('Miss Sylvia Beach', *The Times*, 13 Oct. 1962): 'I made the acquaintance of Sylvia Beach, and . . . Adrienne Monnier, on a visit to Paris early in the 1920s, and thereafter saw them frequently during that decade. Only the scattered survivors of the Franco-Anglo-American world of Paris of that period, and a few others like myself who made frequent excursions across the Channel, know how important a part these two women played in the artistic and intellectual life of those years.' See further *The Letters of Sylvia Beach*, ed. Keri Walsh (2010); *James Joyce's Letters to Sylvia Beach 1921–1940*, ed. Melissa Banta and Oscar A. Silverman (1987).

2-Charles Duff's book on Joyce, forthcoming from Desmond Harmsworth.

3-Herbert Hughes (1882–1937), Irish composer, music critic, and collector of folk songs.

4-*Lord Chesterfield's Letters*, ed. BD (6 vols, 1932).

5-William King (1894–1958), who worked at the Victoria & Albert Museum (his areas of expertise were British and European glass and ceramics), was ultimately to become Deputy Keeper of the Department of British and Medieval Antiquities.

I hope that your last paragraph but four refers to the actual winter and not to next winter,[1] and that you will be seen in London in the immediate future.

[T. S.E.]

TO *Stephen Spender* TS Northwestern

16 March 1932   Faber & Faber Ltd

Dear Spender,

Thank you for your letter of the 10th and for your new address. I hope that your change means at least that the semi-stabilization of the pound is at a point at which life in Germany is still tolerable for you. This is a business letter, and I am writing primarily to ask you when you expect to have your volume of poems ready. It is not the sort of book one wants to hurry, and we are equally prepared to do it in the autumn or in the very early spring, and if you have it ready we will do it in the autumn. I should just like a word from you as to your plans and expectations for it.

I am interested to hear that you are re-writing your novel although as you may imagine still suspecting that you are wasting your abilities in this antiquated form of literature.[2] But may I be allowed to see it when it is finished?

I like Goethe's poetry too.[3] I am bored by most of his prose that I have read, with the exception of one magnificent book. Do you know the invaluable *Conversations with Eckermann*? What I chiefly dislike about Goethe is the fact that he is having a centenary. I always dislike everybody at the centenary moment. I am, however, sending a book which may amuse you and on which please write a note or not according to your opinion of it.[4]

1–'I have accepted an invitation to lecture once a week to Westfield College, a female annexe of the University of London, during the winter.'
2–Spender wrote (10 Mar.): 'I am completely re-writing my novel [*The Temple*], as it keeps on bothering me, so I decided about three weeks ago that I had better re-write the thing at once and be done with it. I have worked so hard that I have already completed half of the new version, and I hope to have it all done in another three weeks.'
3–'I've been reading all I can about and by Goethe, as someone sent me a book on him to review. Rather to my surprise I like his poetry very much. He seems to have had a very considerable and entirely beneficial influence on Tennyson.'
4–SS wrote brief notices of Barker Fairley's *Goethe* and *Goethe's Tragedy of Faust Translated with Notes and a Life of Goethe*, by G. Fillingham Coxwell, C. 11 (July 1932), 757–8.

The essay that I spoke of[1] has only reached about the third or fourth page, for the reason that the man who commissioned it has disappeared in vagueness and I don't want to finish it unless I have some hope of being paid. So it will probably return to the form of a letter to yourself which I hope to write as soon as Easter is over. I will explain that the last sentence refers to a series of broadcast talks I am giving which finish at Easter.

Yours ever sincerely

T. S. E.

TO *Kenneth Ingram*[2]   CC

16 March 1932   [Faber & Faber Ltd]

My dear Ingram,

Long ago when you were discussing with me your plans for the Grecian Club in which I was so unhappily unable to take part, you mentioned to me a youngish Jewish Rabbi of ability who I believe was to be a member.[3] Could you be so kind as to tell me a little more about him. Whether he is a man who writes well, and in what direction his special scholarship lies. I have been thinking of the possibility of a history of the Jews and I wondered whether at least he would be able to tell me whether there is a vacancy for such a book, and if so who might be a good man to write it, either himself or someone else known to him. If you think he is a suitable man to help or advise I should be extremely grateful if you would put me in touch with him.[4]

And may I take this occasion for suggesting that we should meet again for lunch some time after Easter?

Yours sincerely,

[T. S. Eliot]

P.S. I want to come down to St. Mary's again for the Holy Saturday offices. I suppose they are, as usual, at ten o'clock?

---

1 – 'You may remember that you wrote to me some weeks ago saying you had been meaning to write to me at length about something I had said in one of my letters, and that your thoughts were crystallizing into an essay. I have been wondering ever since what you were referring to.'

2 – Kenneth Ingram (1882–1965), author, founded and edited *Green Quarterly* (Society of SS Peter & Paul, Westminster House, London) in 1924. His works include *Why I Believe* (1928) and *Has the Church Failed?* (1929).

3 – See TSE's letter to Rabbi Israel I. Mattuck, 23 Mar. 1932.

4 – Ingram replied (17 Mar.) 'that the Rabbi of whom I spoke to you would answer to most of the qualifications you mention. He is an exceptionally brilliant man.'

17 March 1932   Faber & Faber Ltd

Dear Hodgson,

~~I am~~ We are looking forward to the refreshment of your company and Miss Bolliger's (& Pickwick) tomorrow evening. 7 o'clock. We are sad & need your company.

I do not know whether you saw the notice of Harold Monro's death (which I wrote) in *The Times* today.[2] I am sure it would be a gratification

---

1–Ralph Hodgson (1871–1962), Yorkshire-born poet; author of *The Last Blackbird* (1907); winner of the 1914 Edmond de Polignac Prize of the Royal Society of Literature; lectured in English at Sendai University, Japan, 1924–38. He was awarded the Order of the Rising Sun, 1938; Annual Award of the Institute of Arts and Letters (USA), 1946; the Queen's Gold Medal, 1954. Other publications include *A Song of Honour* and *The Skylark*. Robert Sencourt said of Hodgson: 'his accent was homely, his figure portly and his manners hearty'. TSE and Hodgson were introduced by OM at home on 11 Dec. 1931. See further Stanford S. Apseloff, 'T. S. Eliot and Ralph Hodgson Esqre', *Journal of Modern Literature* 10: 2 (June 1983), 342–6; Vinni Marie D'Ambrosio, 'Meeting Eliot and Hodgson in Five-finger Exercises', *Yeats Eliot Review* (2005); John Harding, *Dreaming of Babylon: The Life and Times of Ralph Hodgson* (2008). TSE was to write to Colin Fenton, 22 Oct. 1963: 'I took great delight in his company and saw a great deal of him during that one year . . . Hodgson well deserves a biographical record.'

2–'Mr Harold Monro: A Poet and His Ideal', *The Times*, 17 Mar. 1932, 16: 'Mr Harold Monro, a distinguished poet and man of letters, died on Tuesday, the day after his fifty-third birthday, at a nursing home at Broadstairs. His death will be mourned not only by admirers of his own verse, but by all in England who have cared seriously, during the last 30 years, for serious poetry.

'Both his father and his maternal grandfather were engineers. He was born at Brussels, and was educated partly abroad, so that he spoke French, German, and Italian fluently, and at Radley, whence he went up to Caius. After taking his degree at Cambridge he spent much time on the Continent for several years. One of the results was "The Chronicle of a Pilgrimage" (1909), the prose account of a walking tour from Paris to Milan; but he had already published a volume of poems in 1906 and two in 1907. His importance in the literary life of London dates from 1911, when he founded, in conjunction with the Poetry Society, the *Poetry Review*, in the first number of which (January, 1912) he affirmed that "Poetry should be, once more, seriously and reverently discussed in its relation to life, and the same tests and criteria applied to it as to the other arts." Difficulties arose, and Monro retired at the end of a year. In March, 1913, Monro issued the first number of another periodical to be entirely under his own direction, entitled *Poetry and Drama*, which survived with distinction until December, 1914. In the first number are contributions by Rupert Brooke, Edward Thomas, Sir Henry Newbolt, Maurice Hewlett, James Elroy Flecker, and Lascelles Abercrombie; and in other numbers there was hardly any young poet or man of letters who was not a contributor.

'Monro's enthusiasm next led him to found the Poetry Bookshop, for which he took an old house in a small street off Theobald's-lane. It was discovered by most readers of poetry in London, and became also a place of pilgrimage for American visitors; and its removal to the more commonplace neighbourhood of Willoughby-street, Great Russell-street, was regretted. Monro then started the series of Poetry Readings which have continued almost

to Alida if you would come on Saturday at 11.30 to the interment at Golders Green Crematorium. There will be very few friends; only, so far as I know, myself & Frank Flint.

'The poor procession without music goes . . .'[1]

And it would give satisfaction to me if you come.[2]

Yrs. aff.

T. S. Eliot

---

without interruption. Of the poets who were well known when the Readings began, and of those who have become known since, there can be few who have not given readings of their own poetry, or of their favourite poets, either at the first or the present dwelling of the Bookshop. Monro's own taste was sympathetic both to the "Georgian" poetry, which flourished just before the War, and to the more modern poetry which has risen since. His own verse had something of this mediating character. He had – what is none too common among verse writers – a steady capacity for improvement; and his latest poems are considered by good judges to be his best. The development is already evident in "Strange Meetings" (1917); it continues in "Real Property" (1922) and in "The Earth for Sale" (1928); and a poem published recently in the *Criterion* indicates that his development had not reached a climax. Throughout, however, there is a quality peculiar to himself: a way of giving to the familiar and commonplace a dreamlike, sometimes nightmarish character which is unlike the mode of either his earlier or his later colleagues.

'While his poetry will remain to justify itself, his importance in the literary life of London in his time may be overlooked. As editor, as publisher, and as the proprietor of the Poetry Bookshop his efforts were wholly disinterested, and indeed meant much sacrifice of his private means. He was more concerned that other people should write poetry, that able writers in difficulties should be helped to write, and that a larger public should read and enjoy poetry, than he was concerned with what he wrote himself. One of the causes dearest to his heart was the instigation of sociability among men of letters, and to this he devoted his own social gifts. In the few years before the War he was active in keeping poets of different gifts in friendly contact; among them the group – including Ezra Pound, F. S. Flint, Richard Aldington, and H. D. – who produced "The Imagist Anthology", and in his circle was included T. E. Hulme, who, after his death in action in 1917, has had a great influence upon the philosophical and critical theory of the present time. After the War he resumed his efforts, with what was left of his own generation, and with recruits from the younger generation. He had a great gift of hospitality, and was happiest when providing a fireside at which writers with common sympathies could sit and talk until late hours of the night. Such devotion to such an ideal as his – the ideal of poetry and of fraternity among poets – is rare always, and nowadays difficult to pursue. Even in the last year or two, when crippled by increasing ill-health and pain, Monro never lost faith in his ideal. He was twice married, and had one son by his first marriage. His second wife was Miss Alida Klemantaski.

'The funeral will be at Golders Green on Saturday at 11.30.'

1 – Quoted from Lionel Johnson, 'Dead', l. 3.

2 – Dominic Hibberd relates, in *Harold Monro: Poet of the New Age*, 259: 'The congregation at Golders Green Crematorium on 21 March 1932 numbered scarcely thirty people, conspicuous among them the tall, melancholy figures of Edith Sitwell, Eliot and Flint . . . Alida . . . was touched to see her old friend Ralph Hodgson, who happened to be on leave from Japan.' Edith Sitwell wrote, in a letter to Alida Monro ('Wednesday'), of TSE's response to the news of HM's death: 'I saw Tom Eliot, for one moment only, and he looked broken' (MS BL Add MS 83366).

18 March 1932   Faber & Faber Ltd

Dear Leonard,

Here is my cheque.[1] Having been very busy for the last two or three weeks I was ignorant of what was happening, relying upon you to let me know if there was anything I could do. I am thoroughly shocked by the result. I suppose that there is nothing for it but that the lad should do his stretch; but could not some small body of people be formed, which would be prepared to work for years if necessary, to have the law altered? I am always sceptical of committees etc., but there ought to be some concerted and persistent action. It is incidentally a matter of serious practical interest to every publisher; and I do not see how any reputable publisher, or any reputable author could refuse to support the cause of reform. (Some will refuse, no doubt). We had to have a directors' meeting of over three quarters of an hour a couple of days ago to deal with fuck and bugger in a book of verse.[2]

I hope you and Virginia are both well. I have been broadcasting, and the work on that has taken all my time and energy; I suppose you will be at Rodmell for Easter; but I want to see you both as soon as you return.

Yours ever,

T. S. E.

FROM *Stephen Spender*   MS Valerie Eliot

18 March [1932]   Lützoplatz 10, (bei Voss),
                                   Berlin W.62

Dear ~~Mr~~ Eliot,

Thank you very much for your letter.

I'm afraid that my poems cant possibly be ready before the summer. I have not enough poems in the first place, and in the second place I am dissatisfied with what I have been writing. I put aside two months for the writing of my novel, largely because I felt this would provide a gap, so that I could make a new start with my poetry in April. Partly also because

---

1–LW said (16 Mar.): 'As you know, de Montalk's appeal failed. You were good enough to say that you would subscribe to the expenses if necessary. I have settled the solicitors' bill which comes to about £90, so that if you could let me have the £5, I should be very grateful.' Montalk's appeal, with St John Hutchinson, KC, appearing for the defence, failed on 7 Mar.
2–This remark is presumably related to WHA's *The Orators*; see TSE to him, 6 Apr. 1932.

the novel provides an essentially poetic problem to me, and I dont feel I can get on with any work properly until I have solved that problem.

I will have the novel ready and also typed out in four weeks time. Will you be in England then? If so, I will send you the 2nd copy which is meant for the American branch of Curtis Brown before I send it to them. If you have already gone to America, I will have another typescript copied for you, and send it to you separately. So can you let me know?

Unfortunately I have to submit the new version of my novel to Cobden-Sanderson before I send it to anyone else. Honour seems to require that, and also I cant afford to give up their contract by which I get £75 down. With that I would be able to afford to take a nice room alone in London in the Autumn, which is what I want to do.

Thank you very much for sending me the book on Goethe. I have already written a short unsigned review of this for the *Listener*. But, unless this prevents me, I would be glad to do another note for the *Criterion*. I'm afraid I could not trust myself to do a long review of this book, as I dont know enough about Goethe, nor what is the standard of Goethe criticism.

I was deeply interested in your essay in the *Listener* (enshrining a poem of mine which must have seemed rather tactless under the circumstances).[1]

---

1 – 'Christianity and Communism', *The Listener* 7 (16 Mar. 1932, 382–83), is run alongside SS's 'After They Have Tired', which proclaims this faith: 'Comrades, in this time when grief pours freezing over us / When the obvious light of pain gleams at every street corner / . . . / our strength is now the strength of our bones / Clean and equal like the shine from snow / And the strength of famine and of our enforced idleness, / And it is the strength of our love for each other.' TSE argues in his talk against the 'experiment' of Russian communism – 'a religion which is not mine' – and in favour of 'the organisation of the world in a Christian way'. Far from being a 'medievalist', he contends that 'the Christian organisation of society is an ideal towards the realisation of which non-Christians can co-operate': 'It is possible that in some respects we have now too much liberty – or, I would say, too much licence . . . I have no expectation and no desire to enforce the non-Christian to obey rules of life in which he cannot believe; I should only wish to persuade him, by practical results, that that rule of life is better than his own, if he has any.' He readily owns that the Christian scheme can never work perfectly; but he bears witness to his own conversion – of having being 'borne gradually' towards a 'profound conviction' – whereby 'a kind of crystallisation occurs, in which appears an element of faith not strictly definable from any reason or combination of reasons . . . [T]here are some interesting remarks on the subject of conversion in a book by the great French novelist Stendhal entitled *On the Subject of Love*. In my own case, I believe that one of the reasons was that the Christian scheme seemed to me the only one which would work. I hasten to add that this is not a reason for believing . . . That was simply the removal of any reason for believing in anything else, the erasure of a prejudice, the arrival at the scepticism which is the preface to conversion . . . Among other things, the Christian scheme seemed the only possible scheme which found a place for values which I must maintain or perish (and belief comes first and practice second), the belief, for instance, in holy living and holy dying, in sanctity, chastity, humility, austerity' (p. 383). He was alluding to the devotional works of Bishop Jeremy Taylor (1613–67): *The Rule and Exercises of Holy Living* (1650) and *The Rule and Exercises of Holy Dying* (1651).

Your essay conveyed much more to me than your pamphlet on the Lambeth Conference because it advances to what is for me the very central problem, the organization of society. It has always seemed to me that the objection to religion is that it provides people with an escape from the organization of society, and from all materialistic problems, and that it also offers them an unreal consolation for material injustices that could be altered, and often too for injustices to other people and to the lower classes of society which would seem intolerable if it were not for this escape into a sentimental dreamland. The same difficulty also applies to art, and I often think how I will try and write in a way that provides no romantic consolation for people, but which will present bare problems to people, and in which the art will only be used as a frame to make those problems memorable, and to emphasize the fact that evil is intolerable. However in your essay you really give the reply to this point of view, and I dare say I would be converted if conversion by argument was possible. If I did not seem to feel in my bones that nothing can ever be done with that old English Church, and if I had not had all belief in it knocked out of me during my adolescence, and by being confirmed, and by being specially blessed by the Bishop of London, and by what I discovered afterwards about the Bishop of London, etc. etc.

Your use of the word 'licence' seems to me only to have the value of official blackmail. When I read it, I think at first 'oh yes, of course, that's what I am – licentious', simply because I have been brought up to secretly believe that. But it isn't really true, although I sleep often with boys. Nor is it true that as a movement the new sexual behaviour of the young people in Russia is licentious. All that has happened is that the old rules of life in those matters have broken down, or rather it has been revealed that they were corrupted by our fathers long ago, and the young people are trying to evolve new rules. A lot of people exercise real liberty and show an admirable moral courage in being what you call 'licentious'. In your essay on Baudelaire you showed admirably how he for moral reasons chose evil, and these young people are also making another deliberate moral choice.[1]

---

1 – TSE, 'Baudelaire': 'The sexual act as evil is more dignified, less boring than the natural "life-giving," cheery automatism of the modern world. For Baudelaire, sexual operation is at least something not analogous to Kruschen Salts.

'So far as we are human, what we do must be either evil or good; so far as we do evil or good, we are human; and it is better, in a paradoxical way, to do evil than to do nothing: at least, we exist. It is true to say that the glory of man is his capacity for salvation; it is also true to say that his glory is his capacity for damnation' (SE, 429).

The point is that all the words you use, 'chastity, humility, austerity, discipline', convey to me (and hundreds of other people like me, I think) the feeling of staying in a cold schoolroom-chapel unheated by a metal stove and doing nothing but be as consciously miserable as possible.

All these words are associated too deeply with our education and our childhood.[1] When I was a child, or an adolescent, rather, I used to wash

---

1 – In the last of his BBC talks on 'The Modern Dilemma' – 'Building up the Christian World' (*The Listener*, 6 Apr. 1932, 501–2) – TSE was to make unattributed use of this sentence, and passages from the three preceding paragraphs, of Spender's letter (and he would apologise for so doing in his letter to Spender of 9 June, below): 'There is a common complaint and one of long standing – I have heard it from the young and recently from correspondents . . . the complaint that the Church – or, I should say, Churches . . . which have proved so pliant to various forms of government, and so indifferent to the root causes of social injustice and oppression, are unworthy to speak in the Name of Christ, or, if they are worthy, then Christianity is condemned. And the craving, which exists in nearly all of us, for some religion which shall demand a better society on earth, drives many towards Communism. For even as a perfect organisation of society, without a religion to transfigure it, is destitute of energy, hope and ecstasy; so a perfect religion, which has no relation to the affairs of this world, lacks reality. The first thing to do, to convert people in the mass to being "Christians so far as they are anything", is to convince them that the Christian faith really has something to say on these matters [in] which they are intensely interested . . . To remove, in short, the ancient prejudice that Christianity is, or has become, merely the parasitic supporter of things as they are. I want to quote at this point from a private letter from a young man, who I think has put on paper what many feel:

"'It has always seemed to me that the objection to religion is that it provides people with an escape from the organisation of society and from all materialistic problems, and that it also offers them an unreal consolation for material injustices that could be altered, and often, too, for injustices to other people and to the lower classes of society which would seem intolerable if it were not for this escape into a sentimental dreamland."

'He is wrong, of course, in confounding "religion" with the history of the Churches during the last two or three centuries; in assuming that the consolation is unreal; and in refusing to recognise that for the individual, when *he* can do nothing about the injustices to himself or to others, this "escape", as he calls it, is right and proper. I quote him because I think many others feel the same way. He continues:

"All the words you use, 'chastity, humility, austerity', convey to me (and hundreds of other people like me, I think) the feeling of staying in an old school-room chapel, unheated by a metal stove and doing nothing but be as consciously miserable as possible. All these words are associated too deeply with our education and our childhood."

'There, I think, we are up against something very serious: the power of association. It is so difficult to talk to people about things of which they have no knowledge, when they have been made sordidly familiar with the *names* for the things: when they have heard repeated so many words belonging to Christian theology, and have never heard anything of Christian theology itself! I am not nearly so frightened of communism as I am of the "Christianity" that many Englishmen have learnt at school; that Christianity which is merely one of the finishing processes of that over-produced commodity, the gentleman.

'So I always say to such people: "Because you have never seen real Christianity in theory or in operation, because your early years were enveloped in a Christianity which I can hardly

in freezing water and lie on the hard floor and be as miserable as I could, because I imagined that that is what the Church wanted. And it *is* what the Church wanted. And most people of my upbringing who go on being Churchy after their adolescence only do so because they are retarded adolescents. So these words you use make me shiver, and want to go for a walk in the sun again.

———

describe as much better than an imposture, an imposture associated with all that was most unpleasant in your early youth – and I am quite well aware how unpleasant early youth can be or how few sensitive men were happy in it – do not suppose that you are in a position to judge the Christian faith. I have more right to judge Marxism on insufficient knowledge than you have to judge Christianity on insufficient knowledge. For I can judge Marxism because I know, from its own evidence, that it is incompatible with that in which I already believe; but you, I am sure, became a Marxist because you previously did not believe in anything. I sympathise with your desire to believe something; but unless you are content to be a mere creature of environment, you are not yet in a position to deny the truths of Christianity. We are all partly creatures of environment, for good or bad, and of heredity and hereditary environment. But consider this. Suppose yourself existing a hundred, or two hundred, or any number of years ahead, and suppose that by that time communism had long since become the established religion, the established government and the established society. Is it not quite likely that if you were to be born into such a period you would be brought up in the same imposture, the same claptrap, the same diluted, adulterated and standardised sentiment, the same parroting of words which have lost their meanings, as afflicted the childhood you remember? The words would be different, because they would come out of communist theology and not out of Christian; but they would give you the same nausea and aversion from communism that you now have from Christianity. I should not like to think that then you would become a Christian, or anything else, simply by reacting from communism as you knew it. I am perfectly aware, in these matters, that we have not to do simply with intellectual conviction, but with the whole man and his desires. I dare say that you, and people like you, have no desires, no aspirations, which cannot be fulfilled in a communist society. You will have no doubt your own "chastity", your own "humility" and your own "austerity", for which you will use different words, and which will give you different rules of behaviour than mine. If you are in the majority, well for you. But in that event, I only hope that I, and my like, may be allowed to expiate our intransigence quickly with our blood; and in any case I and my life shall expect little sympathy, either from the pagan society into which we and you were born, or from the communist society which you hope to construct. Mr Middleton Murry, in a little book *The Necessity of Communism*, pictures a gentle advance into communism which, like every programme offered to British voters, involves no violence or great discomfort – "the inevitability of gradualness" again ... The Church – by which I think he has in mind not only our Anglican Church, but all Churches – is to be tolerated, as the persons of retarded development who will continue to patronise the Church will be tolerated. But for my part, I prefer to hope that I shall be untolerated, intolerant and intolerable."

'That ends my little piece of parenthetical oratory. But I must add and repeat, for your own benefit, first that I do not wish to be named among the usual antagonists of communism. I have tried to make clear, throughout, that I and any who agree with me are in what is called a "hopeless minority"; we loathe communism and we loathe the world as it is, and if this is the dilemma, if these are the only alternatives, then our strongest objection to communism is that it is a waste of time, of brains, of resources, and a great provocation to still more humbug, to change over from one bad system to another.'

Of course this is irrelevant to your main argument. But I thought it might interest you as showing you what, in one case at all events, you were up against.

Yours sincerely,

Stephen Spender.

Thank you very much – I am much better off now, chiefly because I have learnt to manage within my means.

There is a new opera here by Weill called the *Bürgschaft*.[1] It is so wonderful, I keep on thinking about it and cannot get over it at all.

TO *Joseph Needham*   CC

23 March 1932   [*The Criterion*]

Dear Needham,

Many thanks for your interesting letter of the 15th which deserves and shall have a full reply.[2] Unfortunately through an oversight on my own part your manuscript was returned to you. I had intended to keep it until having your reply as I thought probably that you would, if you had time, advance your opinions, and I cannot very well advance my own objections without having the manuscript in front of me. Would it be making too great a claim upon your patience to ask if I might have it back in order to reply to your letter? It is of course possible that you may convince me that I am wrong, and in that case I shall of course want to

1–Kurt Weill, *Bürgschaft* (*The Hostage*), from a ballad of 1798 by Schiller.
2–Needham wrote on 15 Mar. in response to TSE's letter of 10 Mar.: 'I am glad that you dissociate me in your mind from Julian Huxley, for I differ from him exceedingly, the difference consisting in the fact that I do, as I think, understand what religion is about from the inside, while he doesn't, and never has ... The religious experience itself, by which I mean not only the mysticism of St Teresa or George Herbert, but the divination of the numinous which the Church evokes in ordinary people by liturgical means – seems to me much more important and valuable than the ever-changing formulae which the theologian invents to systematise the deposit of faith ... Marx's acceptance of the anthropological arguments against religion may or may not have been a mere historical coincidence due to the fact that he was writing at the time of the nineteenth-century "push" in that direction; but in any case there was nothing in the aspect of Eastern Christianity to suggest to Russian Marxists that Christianity might have a social–economic tendency similar to their own ... I chose the curious title of "Laudian Marxism" in order to indicate the possibility that the English Marxism which is now developing may have an attitude towards religion, entirely different from Russian Marxism ... As for religion itself, I doubt, as you have read in the paper I sent you, whether either its external forms as we know them, or the greater part of its theology as we know it, can survive the upheavals which lie before us. For my own part, I earnestly hope that these things will survive.'

print your essay. I hope that I shall be seeing you at Oldham's conference on the 4th and 5th of April. In that case perhaps you could bring the essay with you, and if you are staying in London for a few days we could have lunch and a private talk.

Yours sincerely,
[T. S. Eliot]

TO *Robert Fitzgerald*[1]   TS Beinecke

23 March 1932   *The Criterion*

Dear Mr Fitzgerald,

Thank you for sending me your recent poems which I am interested to see and which I should like to discuss with you. I am afraid, however, that I can hardly find any time this week. I have already had to crowd in a good deal before Easter. I hope that you will be stopping in London for a few days on your way back to Cambridge and that you will let me know as soon as you get here if not before.

Yours sincerely,
T. S. Eliot

1 – Robert Fitzgerald (1910–85), poet, critic, translator of Greek and Latin classics including Euripides, Sophocles and Homer, studied at Harvard, 1929–33, and worked in the 1930s for the *New York Herald Tribune* and *Time*. He was Boylston Professor of Rhetoric and Oratory, Harvard, 1965–81; Consultant in Poetry to the Library of Congress, 1984–5. TSE wrote to Henry Allen Moe, The John Simon Guggenheim Memorial Foundation, 22 Dec. 1939: 'Fitzgerald I saw something of during 1932–33 while he was an undergraduate at Harvard. I am at present slightly out of touch . . . but at that time I was more interested in the work of Fitzgerald than in that of any other young poet in America; and I should regard [Dudley] Fitts [1903–68] as a very worthy but not quite so interesting poet. In any case, their translation of the *Alcestis* seemed to me admirable, and indeed my approval as well as that of my colleagues was shown by the fact that Faber & Faber published the book in England. The *Antigone* I have not seen . . .'

TSE would later write this blurb for *Oedipus Rex*, trans. Fitzgerald (1951): 'The reader who knows the masterpieces of Greek tragedy only in the translations of an older generation, is astonished to find how living, how contemporary they become when translated by a modern poet into the idiom of modern speech and the metres of modern verse. What happens when a significant modern poet who is also a scholar turns his hand to translation was shown by Mr Louis MacNeice's *Agamemnon*. And Mr MacNeice proved also that a translation into modern English verse can be as accurate and literal as any translation in an older fashion.

'Mr Fitzgerald's translation of *Oedipus Rex* is comparable. The author is a well-known American poet and scholar, who has devoted much of his time, during many years, to translation from the Greek. His translation of Euripides' *Alcestis*, published some years ago, was highly commended; in translating a greater play he has made a greater contribution, and has reinforced Mr MacNeice's proof of the relevance of the Greek classics to modern English poetry and the value of modern verse for interpreting the classics.'

TO *Israel I. Mattuck*[1]   CC

23 March 1932   [Faber & Faber Ltd]

Dear Sir,

It is through the courtesy of my friend Mr Kenneth Ingram, who has often spoken of you and who has given me the permission to use his name in introducing myself, that I am writing.

My firm has been considering the possibility of there being a place for a book on the History of the Jews since the Dispersion, and my friend Mr Ingram thought that you would be as likely to be able to advise me first whether there might be a place for such a book, and second how the book should be written. I do not know whether the subject falls within your own particular scholarship, but in any case it is our opinion that such a book ought to be written by someone who is himself a practising Jew in touch with modern thought.

I should be very grateful if you could give me an opportunity to talk this over in the near future, either here or at your own house, or I should be very pleased if you would lunch with me one day.[2]

I was myself an original member of the Grecian Club, but unfortunately never found an opportunity to attend a meeting.

Yours sincerely,
[T. S. Eliot]

TO *R. Ellis Roberts*[3]   CC

23 March 1932   [Faber & Faber Ltd]

Dear Mr Roberts,

I am writing to express my appreciation of the article in the *New Statesman* summing up the results of the Montalk case, which I imagine

---

1–Rabbi Israel I. Mattuck (1884–1954) was born in Lithuania and taken as a child to the USA, where he studied at Harvard and was ordained at the Hebrew Union College. On removing to London, he became Rabbi of the Liberal Synagogue, 28 St John's Wood Road, 1911–47. He was the first chairman of the World Union for Progressive Judaism, 1926–54, and edited the Liberal prayer book (3 vols, 1923–6). Other works include *The Essentials of Liberal Judaism* (1947), *What Are the Jews?* (1949) and *Jewish Ethics* (1953).

2–Mattuck answered on 29 Mar. that the topic proposed 'has both a personal and larger interest for me': he invited TSE to discuss it at his home on Hampstead Heath.

3–Richard Ellis Roberts (1879–1953), author, editor, critic; literary editor of the *New Statesman & Nation*, 1932–4; of *Life and Letters To-day*, 1934; biographer of Stella Benson (1939).

was written by yourself.[1] My first impulse was to write a formal note for publication if you wished to use it, but then I reflected that a letter from one individual to another is of very little use except at the beginning, in order to call people's attention to some scandal of which they are ignorant. Furthermore as my firm are the publishers of James Joyce in England, so far as he is able to have any, I felt that it was hardly in Joyce's interest for me to draw attention to my own views by myself.

Why I am writing, however, is to ask whether you have thought of any steps that might be taken by a body of suitable persons to be organized for the purpose, in order to influence public opinion, if there is any, and with the aim of securing a more civilized law on the subject – a law which should incidentally have some reasonable relation to the law of copyright. Such a body of people ought of course to be prepared to work for many years before hoping to accomplish much. But the question is, is there any work which they can be doing? If something could be done, then this deplorable piece of brutality will not have been in vain.[2]

Yours sincerely,

[T. S. Eliot]

1 – 'Obscene Libel', *The New Statesman & Nation*, 12 Mar. 1932, 320, questioned the decision of the three judges in the Court of Criminal Law, that very week, to uphold the cruel sentence of six months' imprisonment on a charge of obscene libel which had been handed down to Geoffrey de Montalk by the Recorder of London – even though the supposed obscenity had not in fact been published but only shown to a printer. The decision 'means that any individual who writes an indecent limerick and gives it to a friend is liable to imprisonment if it happens to fall into the hands of the police . . . There was no suggestion or, indeed, possibility that anyone except the printer could have been corrupted by Mr Montalk's action. The crime was, in fact, purely technical. In brief, the law is that to show an obscene word to one other person . . . is to publish an obscene libel . . . It was obvious that Montalk had done harm to no one. Yet the judges . . . who as men of the world knew, of course, that in fact Montalk had done nothing more heinous than any of us who tell our friends dirty stories, felt compelled by the law to keep this harmless individual in prison until his six months' sentence is completed . . . [W]e must now assume that intention to corrupt public morals, which was certainly not present in this case, is not a necessary element in obscene libel . . . It is clear that this is an intolerable state of affairs.'

2 – Ellis Roberts replied on Maundy Thursday: 'I began the Montalk protest in the *Statesman*, but am not responsible for the leader. I am glad you suggest that something practical might be done in the matter. I was talking on Tuesday to St John Hutchinson & he confirmed my own impression – it was not unfortunately emphasized in our leader – that the judges of appeal were wrong in their law. Samuel, who has been privately approached, defends his inaction by saying that the poem had no literary merit – "dreadful stuff, not like Joyce or Lawrence": if the implications of this remark were followed, most of the Covent Garden porters, whose expletives are not of much literary value, would be in jail . . . As any common informer can proceed under the law by which Montalk was caught, we might inform against the University Presses . . . who print classics in which "obscene" words occur, & provoke, thro' ridicule, a reaction. But one never knows – perhaps the times are big with a new Bowdler!'

TO *Rolf Gardiner*[1]

23 March 1932   Faber & Faber Ltd

Dear Mr Gardiner,

I have read your pamphlet, *World without End* with great interest, and at many points in warm agreement.[2] I do not feel, however, that the matter contained in it is quite suitable for the pamphlet form, or that it appears in this form to advantage. The pamphlet form of writing is really only suitable for making some one point which shall be very clear even though it be crude. (At least even if one makes a great many more points one should give the reader the impression that there is only one.) A pamphlet is not the kind of literature which people pore over and re-read. If they don't grasp the meaning which is to be forced upon them simply by one straight reading they will drop it altogether. I feel that the matters you dealt with are of such magnitude and so many and diverse that they are only really suitable for a book of some length.

I should much like to see you again and talk to you about these and other matters and about the book of which you told me, and I hope you will let me know when you are next in London.

Yours very sincerely,

T. S. Eliot

P.S. Have you thought of the Minority Press as a possible means of publicity?[3]

1 – Rolf Gardiner (1902–71), a graduate of St John's College, Cambridge, was in the 1920s a youth leader, influenced by DHL (whom he visited in Switzerland in 1928), with concomitant interests in fields including folk dance, guild socialism, rural revivalism and Social Credit; but by the early 1930s he was evincing approval of the *Jugendbewegung* (German Youth Movement), a leaning which led him towards pro-Nazi, anti-Semitic sentiments and writings.

Gardiner's publications include *World Without End: British Politics and the Younger Generation* (1932), *England Herself: Ventures in Rural Restoration* (1943), *Water Springing from the Ground: An Anthology of the Writings of Rolf Gardiner*, ed. Andrew Best (1972).

2 – Gardiner wrote on 5 Mar. that his pamphlet-essay *World without End: British Politics and the Younger Generation* was 'largely an argument for British allegiance to Europe as against any Imperial System, or divorce of economics from culture'. He intended by June 1933 to complete a bigger book called *Phoenix of Ygdrasil: Wisdom and Action in Northern Europe*.

3 – The Minority Press was run by Gordon Fraser in Cambridge.

23 March 1932   Faber & Faber Ltd

Dear Curtis,

   Very many thanks for your kind letter of the 20th which gave me much pleasure. I believe that I quite agree with you about Francis Thompson.[1] If I omitted him it was probably because I do not know his poetry very well, and if I do not know it very well it is probably because I do not like it very much. But I agree that there is nothing specifically religious about his poetic gift, and I am not sure that in his religious poetry he ever reaches a spirit of pure devotion. The only poem I remember at the moment is certainly a very good one, the lines 'To the Dead Cardinal [of Westminster]', but as I remember that, it is rather fine rhetoric than piety.

   With affectionate good wishes for Eastertide,

Yours ever,
T. S. Eliot

1 – Curtis was grateful for TSE's article on George Herbert in *The Spectator* which, he said, lifted Herbert 'from the ranks of the conventionally & solidly pious into the number of the saints. A spiritual gain – the Devil loses thereby.' Curtis went on: 'I only wish that you had included Francis Thompson in your comparisons. Do you feel as I do that he (for a different reason than Fr. Hopkins) does not belong to the Tree of Jesse, the royal lineage of evangelical poets? He seems to me to be a mystic who remained satisfied with the honeydew of Parnassus which is only a subsidiary sister-peak to Mount Zion. But of course a most considerable poet. A great Christian poet? I would reserve the term for those who climb higher and sing simpler.'

TO *Eleanor Hinkley*[1]

23 March 1932   Faber & Faber Ltd

Dear Eleanor,

I have your letter of the 28th February.[2] Of course I shall be delighted to go to see Miss Fassett or to see anybody else and do whatever I can. I find that the London Play Company is still at the same address, but I do not know whether Miss Fassett is still connected with it. I hope that she is as I have a small claim upon her, having known her niece very well. But as you were so tiresome as not to send the play with your letter I am only writing now to tell you to send it on at once.

> In haste,
> Yours ever affectionately,
> Tom

P.S. MS. just arrived this morning – will read first and then try Miss Fassett.[3]

TO *Scott Buchanan*

23 March 1932   [Faber & Faber Ltd]

Dear Buchanan,

I was glad to get your note of the 20th.[4] I am afraid my time will be quite full up this week, but if you are staying over the Tuesday before

---

1 – Eleanor Holmes Hinkley (1891–1971): TSE's cousin, second daughter of Susan Heywood Stearns (1860–1948) – TSE's maternal aunt – and Holmes Hinkley (1853–91), a scholar 'of rare modesty and delicacy of temperament', who died before Eleanor was born. She studied at Radcliffe College, Cambridge, Mass. Among the advanced courses she took was Professor George Baker's '47 Workshop'. She went on to act with Baker's group as well as to write a number of plays for it (see *Plays of 47 Workshop*, 1920). She wrote in all seven one-act and nine full-length plays: they included *A Flitch of Bacon* (1919) and *Mrs Aphra Behn* (1933). *Dear Jane*, a romantic comedy in three acts about Jane Austen, was to be produced by Eva Le Gallienne in Nov. 1931 at the Civic Repertory Theater, New York, where it ran for eleven performances. Other works included *The Parsonage* – a play about Charlotte Brontë and her family. It was through amateur theatricals held at her family home, 1 Berkeley Place, Cambridge, that in 1912 TSE met and fell for Emily Hale (see Biographical Register).

2 – Eleanor had just finished a play about Charlotte Brontë which she liked 'so much better than anything I have ever done. I have sent it to five important offices . . . But I do think it is highly important to give it to a London agent, because it is more an English play than American really.' She asked TSE if he would take it to Dorothea Fassett, Managing Director of the London Play Company, 51 Piccadilly.

3 – Postscript written by hand.

4 – Buchanan was to visit London for a week, and hoped he could arrange a meeting with TSE and D'Arcy. 'I am feeling a bit more intelligent about the things I am working on and

Easter I should be delighted to see you at any time that day. D'Arcy, I am sorry to say, has gone to Dublin for Easter and I do not suppose he will be back before the latter part of next week. I wish that you could stay longer.

I hope that you will be able to give me a more hopeful report of your mother's illness.

Yours sincerely,

[T. S. Eliot]

FROM *Vivien Eliot* TO *Aurelia Bolliger*   MS Beinecke

Good Friday 25 March 1932   68 Clarence Gate Gardens

Dear Miss Bullinger,

I found this handkerchief in the bathroom, & as it may belong to you I am sending it on the chance. If it is not yours it will be my Aunt's. My Mother & Aunt liked meeting you so much today & were so pleased to meet you that Mother will be glad if you will go to tea at her house one day soon with me. Do ring me up on Tuesday about lunch time, so that we can arrange it. I hope you found Mr Hodgson & Picky quite well when you got home. We are both looking forward to having you both here to *dinner next Friday*, one week from today.

It was good of you to go with me to Marylebone Church today, & I shall not have gone, I think, but for you. It is something to remember. They think I am not strong enough to motor to Eastbourne at *present*, but when the warmer days come we must do that together, & also we both continue to look forward to a day in the country with you & Mr Hodgson.

In the meanwhile, can you listen to my husband's talk on the Wireless on Sunday at 5 o'clock? If you want to ring me up about it tomorrow, *Saturday*, please do. I am sorry I forgot the *Salt*!

With many thanks.

Affectly yours,

Vivienne Haigh Eliot

I think some mutual cross-examination with someone who really knows would help.' He went on: 'I have also just read Weston's *From Ritual to Romance* as you suggest. I am glad you wrote a poem about it; I should be tempted if you hadn't. As it is I am tempted to write a magazine article about it and the movies. I think I ought to consult you first and perhaps be dissuaded.'

FROM *Vivien Eliot* TO *Ralph Hodgson*   MS Beinecke

Easter Sunday 27 March 1932   68 Clarence Gate Gardens

Dear Mr Hodgson,

If you & Miss Bolliger do come, you will find here Mrs & Miss Lockyer, friends of my Mother's & mine. They are coming in to listen as they have no Wireless.

Will you please sit in the warm, & wait until we return.

Yours very sincerely,

V. H. Eliot

TO *M. C. D'Arcy*[1]   cc

30 March 1932   [*The Criterion*]

My dear D'Arcy,

I owe you a double apology. First because I did not answer your letter of the 16th before you left for Dublin, and secondly because I meant to write to you on the evening after my first broadcast talk[2] for the reason that on that evening I listened to the service, having noticed that you were to preach, and was extremely impressed by your sermon (or should it be called talk?) which seemed to me wholly admirable and quite suited to the purpose, neither too mild nor too severe. I very rarely listen to Sunday evening services, but of those I have heard only yours and one by Reeves[3] made any impression on me.

Please let me know as soon as you are back in London. I know that my wife would like to see you, and also I have an enquiring young American philosopher interested in the Trivium and Quadrivium.[4] I have a note

1 – Martin D'Arcy (1888–1976), Jesuit priest and theologian: see Biographical Register.
2 – D'Arcy had written on 16 Mar. that he had just read TSE's talk in *The Listener*, '& I thought it so good I must write & tell you. I thought the ways you put the issues admirable.'
3 – Reeves was, as Buchanan was to report to TSE on 17 July, 'the Dominican in London who has been studying the Trivium and Quadrivium, the man Father D'Arcy told me about. ... It is unfortunate that his book on the Seven Arts is going to be held up by the more immediate task of interpreting the new physics and social theory in terms of Thomism, a good enough thing in itself but hardly the fundamental thing that the Arts represent, as he himself says.'
4 – The trivium (Lat.: 'three ways') comprised the three preliminary subjects – grammar, logic, rhetoric – of the medieval liberal arts education. The more advanced quadrivium consisted of geometry, arithmetic, astronomy, music. See Sister Miriam Joseph, *The Trivium: The Liberal Arts of Logic, Grammar, and Rhetoric* (2002); Caroline Winterer, *The Culture of Classicism: Ancient Greece and Rome in American Intellectual Life, 1780–1910* (2002).

from him saying that he is coming up on Monday next, the 4th, to listen to an address by you. I am sorry that I have an engagement for the whole of that afternoon and evening, but if it is true that you are giving an address or reading a paper would it be possible for you to lunch and meet him on the following day?[1]

Yours ever,
[T. S. Eliot]

TO *Scott Buchanan*   CC

30 March 1932   [Faber & Faber Ltd]

Dear Buchanan,

I have your note of the 24th.[2] I have just written a line to D'Arcy to ask him if he will be free for lunch on Tuesday the 5th, and if he says Yes I shall write again and ask you to join us.

Many thanks for your book which I look forward to reading, but Routledge ought to send me a review copy as well.[3]

Yours sincerely,
[T. S. Eliot]

1–D'Arcy replied (1 Apr.) that he was giving a talk not on 4th Apr. but in the week after that.
2–Buchanan was planning to return from Cambridge to London, 'to hear D'Arcy's paper before the Aristotelian Society', and hoped to be able to meet up with TSE again in a week or so.
3–*Symbolic Distance in Relation to Analogy and Fiction* (1932).

TO *Julian Morrell*[1]   cc

30 March 1932   [Faber & Faber Ltd]

Dear Julian,

   Please excuse me for not having answered your letter of the 20th sooner.[2] I have been extremely busy over what are called the Easter Holidays. I am glad to know that your house will be available for the summer season. The point at the moment is, since I saw Madame de Bassiano in the autumn I have not heard a word from her about her plans of taking a house in London, and from another source I am told that she probably doesn't now intend to come at all. So I think the best thing I can do is to write to her myself and ask whether she is still likely to want a house, and if she thinks that she does I will then suggest that you should write to her. Otherwise it might be giving you unnecessary trouble.

                                        Yours ever,
                                        [T. S. Eliot]

TO *Marguerite Caetani*   cc

30 March 1932   [Faber & Faber Ltd]

Dear Marguerite,

   In the autumn you expressed an intention of taking a house in London for May and June for Lélia and yourself. Sometime later Vivienne mentioned your suggestion to our friend Lady Ottoline Morrell. I have had a letter from Lady Ottoline's daughter, Mrs Goodman, to say that they want to let their house which is in Chelsea near Cadogan Square for part of the summer season. It struck me, as you have not mentioned the subject in writing since, that you may have altered your plans, but if you are still, as we hope, contemplating coming to London for a month or

---

1–Julian Goodman, née Morrell (1906–90), only surviving child of Philip and Lady Ottoline Morrell. In 1926 Julian had fallen in love with the Russian-born Igor Vinogradoff (1901–87), son of Sir Paul Vinogradoff (1854–1925), Professor of Roman Law at Oxford. But Philip Morrell and OM so disapproved of the engagement – they thought Igor wild and penniless, albeit the brilliant young man had taken a first in Modern History at New College, Oxford – that it was called off. In 1928 Julian married Victor Goodman (1899–1967), later to become Clerk of the Parliaments, but the marriage was dissolved after WW2 – whereupon Julian at long last married her true love, Igor.

2–'I hear from Mummy that your cousin, Princess Bassiano, might possibly want to take a house in London this summer. We very much want to let this one, & I wondered if I could get in touch with her? . . . It's really a very comfortable well-furnished house.'

two, please let me know whether a house in that part of town would suit you, and I will go and look it over and tell you what I think of it.

In haste,
Yours affectionately,
[Tom]

TO *Ottoline Morrell*

30 March 1932   Faber & Faber Ltd

My dear Ottoline,

I meant to answer your letter from Tunbridge Wells[1] although you told me not to. I will certainly try to get hold of the book on Burke that you recommend. I have indeed seen Wilson Knight's second book.[2] I have not read the whole book, but read some parts of it which he showed me in manuscript. I think it is quite as good a book as the first although of course not quite so exciting for anyone who has read the first volume, and I was surprised at the inadequacy of the reviewing considering the attention which the first book received.

I hope very much to see you soon. I am sorry that Thursday afternoon is impossible for me, but I have a special committee on that day of indefinite length. We are very anxious to find out about Alida's prospects and to see what can be done.[3] My friend Flint is one of Harold's executors and I shall try to see him next week to find out what Alida's financial position will be.

Affectionately,
Tom

1–Not found.
2–*The Imperial Theme* (1931).
3–Alida Monro was the recent widow of Harold Monro.

TO *Orlo Williams*[1]   CC

30 March 1932   [*The Criterion*]

Dear Williams,

Thank you for your note of the 27th.[2] As soon as Morley returns
from his Easter holidays we will try to arrange a *Criterion* meeting at the
beginning of May. I see no reason why we should not arrange it for a date
that will suit Angioletti and we ought to do so. The meeting will have to
be arranged here, at 24 Russell Square.

It is just possible that Mrs Monro, who I know is very anxious to keep
on the Poetry Bookshop as a kind of memorial to Harold, may want us
to continue to have meetings in Harold's old rooms. I certainly shall not
make the suggestion to her, but if she makes it to me and appears really
keen on the matter I think we ought to fall in with her wishes although it
will be rather dismal for some of us. In any case I think we may certainly
arrange this May meeting at Russell Square.

I am sending you a few more miscellaneous books. Any novels I may
send are as a matter of course, that is to say if they don't fit in with
your chronicle ignore them. The Italian books are at your discretion. I
should rather like to have a short note on the Everyman volume if possible
because Rhys is on the whole doing very good work with that library.

Yours ever,
[T. S. Eliot]

TO *A. L. Rowse*   TS Exeter

30 March 1932   Faber & Faber Ltd

My dear Rowse,

Since I saw you others beside myself have read and considered your
essay on Keynes. It is extremely interesting and to the point, but none
of us feels that it is quite suitable for a pamphlet. The pamphlet market
is not a large one at best, and the pamphlet public expects to be dealt
with in very large terms and not minute particulars. For the purposes of

---

1 – Orlando (Orlo) Williams (1883–1967), Clerk to the House of Commons, scholar, critic:
see Biographical Register.
2 – Thr Italian writer G. B. Angioletti would probably not arrive in London till the last week
in Apr., and was probably going to Spain first (said OW). OW had told TSE on 27 Mar.,
'Angioletti says he will now be here from April 30 to May 7. I think we may take it as fixed.
Can we get up a meeting of Criterionists for his benefit, with any sideshows you like.'

a pamphlet Keynes is a minute particular, and I am pretty sure that not enough people are interested in a critique of his views to pay a shilling for them. A pamphlet by Keynes might be saleable as also a pamphlet by yourself; but not, I am sure, a pamphlet *on* Keynes whether by yourself or by anyone else. Your essay is really a Review article in form. I should have been ready to take it for the *Criterion* but for the fact that I had already accepted, as I told you, and have now published a criticism of Keynes by Penty.[1] Even the *Criterion* cannot carry very much Keynes as it can only float even Shakespeare at carefully determined intervals. But I think that you ought to try to get it off on some other Review. Do you think that Reggie Harris would be willing to use it either at its present length or abbreviated?[2]

I want you to do something about Wells's book[3] for the next *Criterion* if you can. What I should like to do would be what I once before did with Bernard Shaw – to get four people of different opinions to review it independently, the whole to make a leading article. The difficulties are to choose the other three people and to provide enough copies of the book to go round. Have you read the book or have you a copy in your possession or can you borrow one? If not I will send you our review copy directly. Secondly can you suggest anyone of more extreme Left than yourself and who could also write well on the subject? I have thought of Boothroyd who knows friends of mine. I have another man in mind for a third angle and must also try to think of a competent Tory if there is any.[4]

Yours affectionately,

T. S. Eliot

1 – Arthur J. Penty, 'The Philosophy of J. M. Keynes' – a review-essay on *Essays in Persuasion* – C. 11 (Apr. 1932), 386–98.

2 – ALR wrote against this paragraph: 'Macmillan did publish.' See *Mr Keynes and the Labour Movement* (1936). He replied on 3 Apr.: 'I quite agree about the Keynes article: I thought before sending it, it won't do for a pamphlet, but wanted you to see it all the same. It was a pity that Penty should have got in first, – perhaps you are right and have, as you said the other day, an unfortunate inclination towards cranks. The views of people like Mr Devant [*sc.* Demant] on economics are hardly worth taking seriously by serious people. Why not get into touch with a really first-class young man like Douglas Jay – do you know him? He would rather like to write for you; he's an economist on *The Times* (for God's sake, inhibit your usual infantile reaction at that point) . . . he's extremely clever and has something good to say.'

3 – H. G. Wells, *The Work, Wealth and Happiness of Mankind*.

4 – 'I am willing to take part in your Wells symposium, and in fact think well of the idea.'

P.S. I apologise for my so numerous and frivolous pencilled notes on your manuscript. I trust that you can rub them out or instruct your typist to ignore them.[1]

1–ALR replied (3 Apr.): I confess many of your remarks on my mss annoyed me: it's a relief to know you think them frivolous. You must know by this time that on the question of grammar, I am determined to follow as free a habit as may be without flagrant mistakes. I regard that as by far the better course and much more likely to conduce to a living style than the dead, dry as a bone accuracy of academically-inclined writers. Nor are the last as subtle even as grammarians as they might be: take e.g. your questioning this sentence of mine:

'"It is not dissimilar, as we have seen, *with* his attitude to Socialism in England."

You suggest "*from*" in place of "*with*". But you are entirely mistaken: "with" here means, of course, "*in the case of*". I am not directly comparing the first with the second: I am merely connecting them as cases of the same attitude of mind. The meaning of the sentence is clearly "It is not dissimilar *in the case of* his attitude to Socialism etc"; or "The case is not dissimilar when you consider his attitude to Socialism" etc.

'However, this is mere pedantry; and any fool can do this sort of thing, who thinks it a sort of thing worth doing. Some day I should be most interested to set down my general ideas about style and the wider implications the literary problem has.

'But you are definitely immoral when you question my view of the necessity of avoiding the wreckage of Revolution, & comment "behold the British Conservative speaking", and "who cares about wreckage anyway?" For the point is clear that in bringing about a change in society it is desirable to have *less* suffering rather than more; and it might well be that the thing would involve so much suffering as not to justify any change at all. Mere wreckage, as such, doesn't so much matter: it's the suffering it bears witness to that is important, and any responsible politician *must* seek to diminish that, always and at every point in his activities.

'You see that there are moral standards implied by my view of politics. Any one could have seen that, without pointing out that I haven't as yet said anything about religion and what I hold on the subject. For in the first place, it is possible in my view to have moral standards that hold, without implying a religious basis. And in the second, I do not regard it as very respectful to the claims of religion to drag it in at every point whether it means anything in the particular context or no. It is so easy, and not at all helpful, at any essential point in the argument to shove in "Oh the Nicene creed will do very well". For if you look into yourself you will find that the phrase absolves you from the necessity of thinking the argument out any further for yourself. Not that I mind people attaching themselves to authority as such, – I think it the only solution open to most people. But I have not yet come to the necessity of succumbing to it myself; and if ever I were to, it would be less from a sense of helplessness in my own power to think my way through, than in a sense of the hopelessness of other people outside me.

'I have not yet expressed myself publicly on the subject of religion & religious belief, because the time has not come to do so . . .

'You do not recommend your comments any the more by instancing the Rev. Mr Smyth. He may be all very well in his sphere; but from my point of view the man is no better than a fool, & anything he says can have no importance . . .

'Forgive all the above scrawl: but I thought it sincerer not to disguise the fact that I was annoyed no less by this than by your Smith [*sic*] review. To think that I am misunderstood arouses my worst complexes; but the fact remains that one is *not* understood, at least not in the least clearly.'

TO *M. Judson*   CC

30 March 1932   [Faber & Faber Ltd]

Dear Sir or Madam,

I have your letter of the 13th March.[1] It is very difficult to recommend reading to anyone whom one does not know personally, and it would have been unsuitable for me to have recommended books to the general public in my talks. I have, however, discussed your letter with a friend and suggest your reading W. R. Matthews's *God in Christian Thought and Experience*. I think also that the late Baron von Hügel's *Letters to his Niece* (Gwendolen Green) which is published I think by Dent, is a very helpful and more personal introduction to Christian thought and experience.

Yours faithfully,
[T. S. Eliot]

TO *Dorothea Fassett*[2]   CC

30 March 1932   [Faber & Faber Ltd]

Dear Mrs Day,

My only reason for writing to you personally is that you may have heard my name from your brother or from your niece Irene who was my secretary, as you may remember, up to the time of her last illness.[3] I am writing, however, purely on a matter of business. An American cousin of mine, Miss Eleanor Hinkley, has confided to my charge the manuscript of a new play which she would like to place if possible with a London producer. I believe that Miss Hinkley called upon you or had some communication with you when she was in London last summer. She is the author of several plays, some of which have been produced in New York, but none, I think, here.

May I call upon you one day early next week and bring the manuscript and discuss its possibilities with you? I have a cable from Miss Hinkley

1 – Judson had heard TSE's talk on 'The Modern Dilemma': 'you said that there was a very strong case, requiring careful study, for Christianity, on intellectual grounds. I do not know if you would find it possible, or think it desirable, to spare time in another talk to mention any books which could be studied with this end in view.'
2 – Dorothea Fassett, Managing Director, The London Play Company (who acted for Bram Stoker among others).
3 – Irene Pearl Fassett (1900–28), born in Paddington, London, had been TSE's secretary at the *Criterion*. She died of pulmonary tuberculosis on 28 July 1928, aged twenty-seven.

yesterday which suggests that she has an introduction to some London manager unnamed and is anxious to refer that manager to an agency as quickly as possible.[1]

Yours sincerely,
[T. S. Eliot]

TO *John Maynard Keynes*[2]   TS Marshall

30 March 1932   *The Criterion*

Dear Keynes,

I am sending you a copy of the current *Criterion* which contains an article on yourself by a friend of mine.[3] If it should goad you to the point of any sort of rejoinder I should be only too glad. I must add that even within my small sphere of editing activity you are now a very general target, and the article I have published is only the best one that I have received.[4]

Yours sincerely,
T. S. Eliot

1–Fassett replied on 5 Apr. that she had arranged with TSE's secretary for TSE to call on her at 3.15 on 6 Apr., 'unless I hear that this is not convenient for you'.

2–John Maynard Keynes (1883–1946): economist and theorist of money (expert on macro-economics); pamphleteer; patron of the arts (begetter and financier of the Arts Theatre, Cambridge), government adviser and negotiator; editor of *The Economic Journal*, 1912–45; columnist for *N&A* (of which he was chairman from 1923); intimate of the Bloomsbury circle; Trustee of the National Gallery; author of *A Treatise on Probability* (1921), *A Treatise on Money* (2 vols, 1930) and *The General Theory of Employment, Interest and Money* (1936). He married in 1925 the ballet dancer Lydia Lopokova (1892–1981). TSE declared in an obituary notice that *The Economic Consequences of the Peace* (1919) was 'the only one of his books which I have ever read: I was at that time occupied, in a humble capacity, with the application of some of the minor financial clauses of that treaty' ('John Maynard Keynes', *The New English Weekly*, 16 May 1946, 47).

3–Arthur J. Penty, 'The Philosophy of Mr J. M. Keynes', *C.* 11 (Apr. 1932), 386–98.

4–Keynes responded on 5 Apr.: 'I have enjoyed reading Mr Penty's article. But I am much too much in sympathy with his general state of mind to be goaded into any rejoinder! Indeed, my rejoinder would have to be that he had gone out of his way to pick quarrels with me instead of trying to discover the more sympathetic passages. And my comment would be that whilst I have great sympathy with his general state of mind, I think he is extravagant, or even silly, about details, – Free Trade, for instance. Also he does not seem very clear as to whether he considers it impossible or undesirable to relieve poverty.

'He will get a little further light on my state of mind, if that interests him, in a short contribution on "The Dilemma of Modern Socialism" which I have contributed to the current *Political Quarterly*.'

TO *Elsie Elizabeth Phare*   CC

30 March 1932   [*The Criterion*]

Dear Miss Phayre,

I am sorry that I have had to keep your manuscript so long in order to wait for the comparative leisure of Bank Holiday to read it. But as you had already told me before I urged you to send it that you had abandoned all intention of publishing it, I felt, perhaps wrongly, that there was no haste. In short I quite agree with you and very much respect your integrity, as it is in fact very much better than most novels of the same sort which people want to publish. It is, if I may say so without offence, highly intelligent, but intelligence and sensibility, however acute, are not alone an indication that a writer has a real vocation for writing novels, although it is obvious that you have some vocation for writing. I know that if you want to write novels you will go on doing so, but in the meanwhile I hope soon to have some books to send you for reviewing.

Yours sincerely,
[T. S. Eliot]

TO *Geoffrey West*[1]   CC

30 March 1932   [*The Criterion*]

Dear Mr West,

I shall be very glad to have you review Arnold Bennett's *Journal* when it appears if I can get a copy.[2] The only qualifications are, first, that if it is published in April it probably means too late to appear in the June number, and secondly that Cassell's is one of the two or three publishers who seem inclined to grudge review copies to the *Criterion*. If you have any influence with the firm yourself I should be glad if you would suggest that they send us a copy as soon as it appears.

Yours sincerely,
[T. S. Eliot]

1–Geoffrey West was author of biographies of H. G. Wells and Annie Besant, and a book on the *Future of Literary Criticism*; he reviewed for the *TLS* and *Adelphi*.
2–Vol. 1 of Bennett's *Journal*, covering 1896–1910, was due out in April. West was writing a 'short critical volume on Bennett's works'. No review of Bennett's *Journal* appeared in *C*.

TO *Will Spens*[1]

30 March 1932   [Faber & Faber Ltd]

Dear Spens,

I want to trouble you about a manuscript which has been sent to us by the Revd. J. L. Beaumont James of Millbrook. In his letter he said that it was Selwyn who had advised him to send it to us. I wrote to Selwyn, but although he spoke highly of the author he said he had not read the book. I gather that you have read it (it is called 'Catholicism in Idea and Actuality'). So before putting the question to my board of directors I should very much like to know your candid opinion of its value and of its practicability. I enjoyed reading the book very much. My doubt is whether it is a book which general publishers like ourselves can sell – that is to say whether it is a book which any but Anglo Catholics can be induced to read, and secondly whether it will not be swamped by the mass of literature in preparation for the Oxford Movement Centenary.

I do not like to trespass on your time and I hope you will understand that it is just a matter of conscience on my part to write to you.[2]

Yours sincerely,
[T. S. Eliot]

1 – Will Spens (1882–1962), educator and scientist, was Master of Corpus Christi College, Cambridge, 1927–52. Early in his career he gave a course of lectures on *Belief and Practice* (1915); he wrote on the Eucharist in *Essays Catholic and Critical by Members of the Anglican Communion*, ed. E. Gordon Selwyn (1926), and on birth control in *Theology* (1931). He was a member of the commission on Christian doctrine appointed by the Archbishops of Canterbury and York, 1922–38. He was knighted in 1939.
2 – Spens replied on 1 Apr. 1932 that Beaumont James's brother and sister-in-law were friends of his – '& through his brother he asked me to read the MS. I thought B. J. had overweighted the book badly & that it wanted re-writing so as to give (i) a much less heavy general discussion of his thesis in a short book & (ii) a number of articles, published separately, on particular people, points etc . . . Perhaps naturally he didn't like the criticism &, I think, didn't take the advice. I very much doubt whether as it stands the book has a public but there is very good stuff in it.'

TO *Ezra Pound*   TS Beinecke

30 March 1932   *The Criterion*

Dear Rabbit,

Thanks for your undated letter.[1] I had feared that I should have to do the obituary for Harold in the *Criterion* myself, but if you feel up to it, i.e. if you feel sufficient and not over critical enthusiasm for his work I should be glad if you would have a whack at it for the June number. Are you in possession of all his numbers up to June last? If not I will procure them for you. My own points were put very briefly in the obituary which I wrote for the *Times* which you may have seen. That is, so far as his work goes I feel that it did on the whole improve steadily up to the last (which is a poem in the *Criterion* a few months ago), that it has a character which clearly distinguishes it both from the Georgian work on the one hand and our own on the other, and finally that he received very little appreciation in his life-time either for the poetry or for his social work. If you agree in the main with these theses please go ahead. I should want about 4000 words by May 1st.[2]

I must postpone answering other correspondence for a few days.

                                        Yours in haste,
                                        T.

TO *James Joyce*   TS Buffalo

31 March 1932   Faber & Faber Ltd

Dear Joyce,

I have the copy of your letter of the 25th to Pinker which you sent me and I am waiting to hear from him on the matter.[3] I am afraid that we have

---

1–EP wrote, 'In looking for Harold's woiks I have dug up the Cawflik [Catholic] Anfology.

'I rather doubt if H. DID very much progress, at least sfar as style is concerned. Howeffer . . . thass not the point. I leave yr/ supposition. The obit ought to say the best possible, with only enough retraction to keep it from failing. I mean, one cant claim too much and get anything . . .

'Re Harold . . . oh well . . . personal flavour, but "character" perhaps a bit strong. The George/wordsworfian etc/ combed out a bit at time Yeats was combing out under "new" infloonz. Later H. M. becomes a bit Eliotic, but "clearly defined".

'apart from his little undercurrent . . . I am afraid is just what it AINT. BUT I see no use in telling the pubk. that. They'll honour him little enough, without being given discriminations and dissociations far beyond their comprehension.'

2–EP, 'Harold Monro', C. 11 (July 1932), 581–92.

3–JJ informed his agent (in a letter copied to TSE) that Robert Kastor, his son's brother-

no control over Knopf with regard to making excision of quotations from the American edition of Gilbert's book which Knopf set up themselves, so I shall have to suggest that Pinker take the matter up with Knopf himself. As for the hoped for English edition ~~we would defer that for a time and go into the matter more fully when publication is more imminent.~~ may we defer this question until it is known whether an English edition is possible?[1]

Personally I do not believe that Gilbert's book even with the very full quotations is likely to interfere in the least with the sale for the complete text and I feel that the book might lose some of its value if very much quotation were excluded. <But of course we should want to meet your wishes.>[2] I do not know of course at what price *Ulysses* will be offered in America. We agreed I think that publication here would have to be at a pretty high price which is all the more reason for doubting whether there would be any conflict with Gilbert's book.

I am very sorry to hear that you have been in poor health and hope that your health has improved since you wrote.

Yours ever sincerely
T. S. Eliot

TO *William Butler Yeats*[3]

TS Michael Yeats

1 April 1932   68 Clarence Gate Gardens

Dear Mr Yeats,

I am venturing to ask for your advice.

My wife's family have some house property in Dun Laoghaire, of which I and my brother-in-law are trustees. One or the other of us will probably

---

in-law, had negotiated for Bennett Cerf (Random House) to publish *Ulysses*, 'substantially unchanged', in return for $1,000 advance, and so recommended JJ to sign the contract. 'In view of this,' JJ went on, 'I think you should inform Faber and Faber and say that any American re-edition of Gilbert's book should be curtailed by the exclusion of quotations and this also applies to the English re-edition as soon as *Ulysses* becomes accessible to the reading public in England.' On the copy of the letter forwarded to TSE, JJ added: 'Please excuse me. I have not been very well.'

1 – Deletion, and the final part of the sentence, added by hand.

2 – Sentence added by hand.

3 – W. B. Yeats (1865–1939): Irish poet; Nobel laureate: see Biographical Register. EVE to Francis Warner, 21 Sept. 1966: 'There is very little correspondence between the two poets in my files and, curiously enough, in more than fifteen years I only heard my husband speak of Yeats occasionally and he said that no particular meeting remained in his mind. They had, of course, met many times – and there was the vicarious association when Pound was acting as the Irishman's

be going over to Dublin quite soon for the usual semi-annual inspection, and discussion with the Agent and the Solicitors of the Estate.

Some time ago, when I was expecting to go over, I procured introductions to various people of importance in Dublin. Unfortunately, all the introductions were to people in your late Government. (Desmond FitzGerald, also, was very obliging and helpful on one or two occasions.)[1]

Now, to put it simply, do you know anyone in the new Government whom it might be desirable or useful – however indirectly – for us to know? And if so, would you be willing to give a line of introduction either to my brother-in-law or me (whichever happened to be going)? If you could I should be very grateful.[2]

It is so rare that you are in London, and such a pleasure, that I wish that we might see you again before you leave. Should you happen to be free tomorrow (Saturday) evening, and have nothing better to do, my wife and I would be very happy if you cared to come in after dinner for coffee.[3]

Sincerely yours,
T. S. Eliot

P.S. I met De Valera[4] years ago in London, but he would not remember me.

———
secretary – but it was a formal friendship, due partly, perhaps, to the difference of age.' See also Michael Butler Yeats, 'Eliot and Yeats: A Personal View', in *The Placing of T. S. Eliot*, ed. Jewel Spears Brooker (1991), 169–84.

1–Desmond Fitzgerald (1888–1947): Irish nationalist politician; poet. See L 4.

2–Yeats replied by return ('Saturday' [?2 Apr.]), from the Savile Club, London: 'The two parties have not mixed socially. If I can think of anybody who could help you I will let you know. Desmond Fitzgerald could advise you better than I.'

3–'Alas I am engaged tonight. I wish I could see more of you but this seems impossible.'

4–Éamon de Valera (1882–1975), a leader in Ireland's struggle for independence from the UK, founded Fianna Fáil in 1926; President of the Executive Council, 1932–48, 1951–4, 1957–9.

1 April 1932   Faber & Faber Ltd

My dear John,

Thank you for your letter and for inscribing the copy of your book for me.[1] I was able to read it at once and did in fact mention it in my last talk.[2] You will understand that in a series of talks which have to be so elementary in character and hortatory in tone it was impossible to do more. I found the same difficulty with your theory of Knowledge that I found with *Jesus* and *God*, but that would take considerable working out.

You have no need to assure me that your recent conversion brings no worldly advantage, especially as one of your chief tasks will be I imagine to convert the Communists themselves.

Yours ever affectionately,

Tom

1–JMM sent TSE a copy of *The Necessity of Communism* (1932), inscribed 'For T. S. Eliot / and particularly for him / March 16 1932' (TSE Library). His blurb proclaimed, in a manner designed to be a red rag to TSE's bull: 'One is, in the fullest sense of the word, *converted* to communism. It is a religion, precisely as Roman Catholicism is a religion; it has a philosophy, a morality, a dogma. In the author's view Communism is the religion of the future. Through Communism the skeptical mind may enter a new world . . . Karl Marx believed that England was the only country in Europe where Communism *might* come to pass peacefully. Communism itself arose out of Marx's devoted and life-long study of *English* conditions. London, not Moscow, is the birthplace of Communism; England, not Russia, its Galilee. England has the chance to lead the world once more, but only through Communism. And Communism, if it is not to come through collapse and undreamed-of misery, must be prepared for by an intellectual and moral revolution in a dedicated minority of individual men. Revolution is inevitable. Where will you have it? In yourselves, or in the world about you. You must choose, and choose *now*.'

JMM challenged TSE in his covering letter, 15 Mar. 1932: 'I see in *The Listener* this morning that you are giving a series of BBC talks on "Christianity & Communism". This morning also, the copies of my little book *The Necessity of Communism* have arrived. Not the first example of odd coincidence between us.

'So I send you the book. I hope that you will give it some attention in one of your talks. You will acquit me of any desire to seek self-advertisement: manifestly it is a book by which I have nothing to gain, and a great deal to lose. But, if you are tackling your own subject, "Christianity & Communism", *seriously*, it is this little book of mine you have to meet. And I think you ought to meet it – I mean that, if you do not meet it, you will be judged by me as guilty of an evasion – an evasion not of me, but of the fundamental question itself.'

TSE scorned a number of passages in JMM's tolerant tome, which he thought a wholly misbegotten manifesto: for instance, against JMM's remark 'We English Communists will, at any rate, be objective enough not to treat Communism and bloody revolution as identical', TSE commented in the margin: 'But it isn't the bloody revolution that I mind, it's the communism.'

2–See note to SS to TSE, 18 Mar. 1932, above.

TO *John Reith*[1]   CC

1 April 1932   [Faber & Faber Ltd]

Dear Sir John Reith,

   Thank you for your kind note of the 31st which goes some way toward
relieving the extreme dissatisfaction which I myself have felt about my
talks.[2]

                                   Yours sincerely,
                                   [T. S. Eliot]

TO *Willard Thorp*   TS Princeton

1 April 1932   Faber & Faber Ltd

Dear Thorp, (it seems to me that we might drop the Mr)

   Very many thanks for your letter of the 31st.[3] To have given you so
much trouble in the matter makes me feel ashamed of my avarice. I had
in any case written to Princeton, not to Dr Spaeth himself but to a Mr
Tomlinson who originally wrote to me, to say that I should be very glad
to accept the invitation.

   So I shall look forward to seeing you and Mrs Thorp in Princeton at
some time next winter as well as I trust in the near future.

                                   With many thanks,
                                   Yours sincerely,
                                   T. S. Eliot

1 – John Reith (1889–1971), knighted in 1927, was Director-General of the BBC, 1927–38.
2 – 'I have listened to your four talks with great interest, and satisfaction – for want of
a better word. I should like particularly to mention the last one, which I thought most
impressive. I hope it will have some real effect among those who listened to it.' He went on:
'Some time I should rather like to have a talk with you about our religious policy; I am not
satisfied with it.'
3 – 'After our conversation here [in Lincoln's Inn] . . . about the possibility of your lecturing
in Princeton next year, I wrote Dr Spaeth, the chairman of the lecture committee, saying that
in view of the fact that the fee is so small I thought they should add the bill for expenses too.

   'Dr Spaeth has just replied that they will be glad to do so. It is no more than they should
do, but I am glad they have so decided, if it makes it certain that you can come to Princeton.'

1 April 1932   [Faber & Faber Ltd]

Private & Personal

Dear Rendall,

Very many thanks for your kind letter of the 30th March which gives me so much pleasure,[2] and also a feeling of chagrin at not having written to you as I intended to express my appreciation of the trouble you took over the talks and especially in your attempts to improve my delivery. I was feeling rather down in the mouth about it and especially this morning when I received a letter from the great man himself expressing his satisfaction; and I could not help feeling that if I had given him so much satisfaction I could not have said quite what I ought to have said.

About your last paragraph, let us meet again for lunch in a few weeks and perhaps I will have a few suggestions.[3]

With many thanks,
Yours sincerely,
[T. S. Eliot]

FROM *Vivien Eliot* TO *Aurelia Bolliger*   MS Beinecke

3 April 1932   68 Clarence Gate Gardens

Just a line, as I promised, to say that I am feeling a little better, but of course have not been able to go out yet.

---

1 – Richard A. Rendall (1907–57), educated at Winchester and Trinity College, Cambridge, joined the BBC as an announcer, progressing in 1929 to the Talks Department. In later years he was Assistant Director of Television; Director of Empire Services from 1940; Acting Controller, Overseas Services; Controller of the Talks Division, 1945–50. CBE, 1951.

2 – 'I want to thank you very much for all the trouble you took with your talks in "The Modern Dilemma" series. I think the series on the whole was definitely a success and quite a few people who have spoken to me stressed particularly your contribution. It was very long-suffering of you to subject yourself to my attentions on Sunday afternoon. I realise, of course, that I was asking you to do all sorts of things of which you probably don't approve, but . . . I am convinced that such meretricious aids must be brought in to produce really successful broadcasting.'

3 – 'If at any time you have any ideas about speakers or subjects for broadcasting I would be awfully grateful if you would let me know. You know our conditions here and what we are trying to do pretty well now, I think, and I should very much value your advice at any time.'

It *was so very* good of you to come to see me on Saturday, & I appreciated it more than I can tell you. Do give me a call *before* Saturday evening (9th).

Yours very sincerely,

Vivienne Haigh Eliot

TO *W. H. Auden*[1]   TS Pierpont Morgan Library

6 April 1932   [Faber & Faber Ltd]

Dear Auden,

The modifications of the few passages which I discussed with you the other day have been agreed upon.[2] As for the preface I felt myself from

1–W. H. Auden (1907–73), poet, playwright, librettist, translator, essayist, editor: see Biographical Register.

2–In the draft of an undated 'Foreword' (?Aug. 1965) for the 1966 edition of *The Orators*, WHA cast his mind back to 1932: 'One incident connected with the book seems worth relating. I had used the phrase *A fucked hen*. In 1932 publishers still boggled at the four-letter words and a substitute had to be found. The solution was provided by Eliot. He suggested *A June Bride*. When I asked him why he thought the phrase equivalent in meaning to mine, he told me the following story. After a hotly contested election, the defeated candidate was asked how he felt about the voting figures. "Like a June bride," he answered, "sore but satisfied." To the same question the successful candidate gave a similar reply: "Like a June Bride. I knew it would be big, but I didn't think it would be that big."'

Charles Monteith, poetry editor at Faber, commented to WHA on 29 Sept. 1965 (apropos 'that spiffing preface to the new edition'): 'The June Bride story is an absolutely superb piece of uncollected Eliotiana.' A few weeks later, however, he wrote again: 'Dick de la Mare, our Chairman, thinks there's just a chance – though not a very big one – that Valerie Eliot might be slightly fussed by the June Bride story – at any rate, if it appeared without her having been told about it first. And he wondered if you'd mind writing to her about it and clearing it with her, as it were. If you would, he'd be most tremendously grateful to you – as indeed we all would. And forgive us, please, for bothering you about it.'

WHA responded to Monteith's request on 4 Nov. 1965: 'If you think there's the slightest chance of Valerie minding about that story, then cut it.

'I don't like to ask her myself because, judging from personal experience, I can imagine the possibility that she might feel she had no right to forbid publishing it, yet be personally upset all the same; and, naturally, I wouldn't upset her for the world.'

Monteith reported his decision in a letter of 11 Nov.: 'I think perhaps we had better cut the June Bride story. There's a chance it might upset Valerie; and, like you, I wouldn't want to do that for the world. A pity, though – it's a very good story; and it must see print one day.'

The lady was less prim than they anticipated. In 1980 Humphrey Carpenter posted to EVE passages from the draft of his *W. H. Auden: A Biography* (1981), including (124): 'When *The Orators* was being prepared for publication, Eliot asked Auden to delete "the fucked hen", and suggested "the June bride" as a substitute, which Auden accepted. According to Auden, the form in which Eliot offered this emendation was "like a June bride, sore but satisfied".' EVE responded to Carpenter, 8 May 1980: 'The anecdote about TSE and the June bride is delicious!'

the beginning that it was not really desirable and I find my own opinion confirmed by two other directors who feel as I do that there is no need to apologize for obscurity.[1] I hope to send you a copy of page proof before long.

Yours ever,
T. S. Eliot

TO *Padraic Colum*[2]   CC

6 April 1932   [*The Criterion*]

Dear Colum,

I am going to publish Joyce's poem,[3] but what I told him was that I would try to get it published simultaneously in America as he could obviously get much more money for it there. It has been suggested to me that a magazine like *Harper's* might pay 50 or even 100 dollars for a new poem by Joyce. If that is likely I suppose that it is much more than the *New Republic* would be able to pay. What do you think? You know much more about conditions and prices than I do and I am sure that you could place the poem better than I. My only interests are, first to get as much money for Joyce as possible without the intervention of an agent, and second to see that American publication and English publication in the *Criterion* should be as nearly simultaneous as possible. I can publish the poem either in September or in December, whichever suits the American publisher best, but I should not object if publication in America were slightly earlier. I should like to know where you think it could be placed to best advantage, and if you have not a copy of the poem I will send one to you.

Yours sincerely,
[T. S. Eliot]

---

1 – WHA had submitted (undated) this attempt at a Preface for *The Orators*: 'I feel that this book is more obscure than it ought to be. I'm sorry, for obscurity, as a friend once said to me, is mostly swank. The central theme is the revolutionary hero. The first book describes the effect on him and of his failure on those whom he meets; the second book is his own account; and the last some personal reflections on the question of leadership in our time.' (Quoted in *The English Auden: Poems, Essays and Dramatic Writings 1927–1939*, ed. Edward Mendelson [1977], xv.)

2 – Padraic Colum (1881–1972) was associated with WBY and Lady Gregory at the beginning of the Irish Theatre movement in 1902. Following periods in the USA and Hawaii (where he surveyed myths and folklore), he wrote poetry, novels, books for children and essays. Works include *Collected Poems* (1932) and *Our Friend James Joyce* (with Mary Colum, 1959).

3 – 'Ecce Puer' – on the birth of Joyce's grandchild Stephen – submitted from Paris by Padraic Colum, was to be published in C. 12 (Jan. 1933), 184.

TO *J. B. Pinker & Sons*[1]   CC

6 April 1932   [Faber & Faber Ltd]

Dear Pinker,

Mr Morley received your letter of the 29th March[2] but I am answering it myself as I had already been in communication about the matter with Joyce who sent me a copy of his letter to you. I told Joyce that I had not yet heard from you. I added that Stuart Gilbert's book had been set up in America by Knopf and it did not seem to me that we were in a position to intervene with Knopf in the matter of excision of passages from any further edition. I suggest in short that that was a matter which might best be discussed with Knopf by you and Joyce himself, possibly in conjunction with Gilbert.

The possibility of an edition of *Ulysses* in this country being tolerated appears so slight that I suggest that the question of a revised edition of Gilbert's book should be left open until publication of *Ulysses* was definite.

I added, however, as my own opinion, that I think it would be a pity to alter Gilbert's book in this way as I am sure, at least for Great Britain, that the continued circulation of Gilbert's book would in no way restrict the sales of *Ulysses* itself. Our private enquiries have not yet quite brought us to the final opinion that publication of *Ulysses* in this country is impossible, but in any case it is agreed that it could hardly be a trade edition and would have to be a limited edition at a rather high price.

Yours sincerely,

[T. S. Eliot]

---

1 – (James) Ralph Pinker (1900–59) was a partner, with his brother Eric (b. 1892) in James B. Pinker & Sons, Literary, Dramatic and Film Agents – founded by their father James Brand Pinker (1863–1922) – representing authors including John Galsworthy, H. G. Wells, Henry James, Jack London, Arnold Bennett, Joseph Conrad and JJ.

2 – Pinker wrote to FVM: 'I think you will be interested to know that we have arranged for *Ulysses* to be published in a proper trade edition in America, and I think perhaps I had better quote you a paragraph from a letter from Joyce with regard to Gilbert's book:-

"I think that any American re-edition of Gilbert's book should be curtailed by the exclusion of quotations and this also applies to the English re-edition as soon as *Ulysses* becomes accessible to the reading public in England."

'Is it possible to us to take any further steps with regard to a trade edition of *Ulysses* in this country?'

TO *William L. Sollory*[1]   cc

6 April 1932   [Faber & Faber Ltd]

Dear Mr Sollory,

I am glad to have your letter of the 4th, but very much surprised and shocked to learn of the interpretation of the law given by your Labour Exchange.[2] I cannot understand how this can be and am taking the liberty of writing to my solicitors to ask them to try to find out the truth about the matter. I will write to you again as soon as I hear.

Yours truly
[T. S. Eliot]

1 – William Sollory was a working man in his early fifties, from Bushey, Hertfordshire. He had three daughters: one was married and lived with her husband; the younger ones, with low-income jobs, still lived at home. The married daughter was knocked down by a car in Jan. 1932 and had to spend some time in hospital – she 'had a rare smashing up', as Sollory put it to TSE – which compounded his cares. Sollory was married to the Eliots' former servant Ellen Kellond. Previously employed in the metal industry (which was now 'beyond the pale', as he said in one of his letters), early in 1932 he secured a short-term job, ending at Easter, stoking the boilers at a girls' academy, St Margaret's, Bushey. His labouring day was long and hard, since he had to work a short week and then a longer one – the long week meant that he had to be on duty from 7 a.m. until 9 p.m. – and he had time off only every second Sunday. He earned just over fifty shillings a week, and he had to buy his own unemployment stamp at a cost of 1/8d. His accumulated debts were a huge worry: at times he felt he would have to sell off his furniture in order to pay the bills. It is not known how Sollory's plight came to TSE's notice. But TSE, recognising the deserving nature of the man, his manifest honesty and hard-working, responsible character, would help him out with parcels of clothes – the clothing he despatched included a used Burberry coat, some boots in pretty good repair ('The boots are a size too large but they will do me a good turn in the stoke hole,' said Sollory), and even some underwear ('I can picture you trying to get into those pants. They have shrunk haven't they?') – and TSE would afford him financial succour too. 'I feel rather troubled at times,' he told TSE in one undated letter, 'because I have been unable to cancel my liabilities to you.' In a letter of 28 Jan. 1932 he wrote, 'I can quite understand how you are feeling when you mention worry, it takes the vitality out of one more so than all the hard work. Yes, I did begin to wonder what had become of you, although I couldn't visualise your "dropping" me. When that happens I lose the only *friend* I have left . . . Now do take care of yourself and try not to worry any more than you can help.' TSE exchanged letters with Sollory, and sent him alms (clothes and financial help), for many years.

2 – The heating was turned off at St Margaret's School at the end of March. Sollory wrote, 'I am again on the unemployed list. I finished a week last Saturday. Of course that was expected, although I was hoping to be kept on at something else after the fires were down . . . But the trouble is I am afraid I have forfeited my right to any unemployment pay, because, so they tell me at the Labour Exchange, all schools, Hospitals, and Institutions, are exempt from paying the stamps. I have been buying the stamps myself but *they* have to put them on my card, but it appears that I can only get my money refunded. This isn't final but I shall know how I stand on Wednesday. If I can't get any work or money off them very quickly I am afraid it is Amen.'

TO *Messrs James & James*   cc

6 April 1932   [Faber & Faber Ltd]

Dear Sirs,

I should be very much obliged if you could investigate for me a situation arising under the Unemployment Act. A friend of mine, a Mr W. R. Sollory of Bushey was on the dole for a considerable time, and last autumn succeeded in getting a very small post as furnace stoker at a school near Watford. His job has now come to an end as apparently the school is to enjoy no further central heating until the autumn. He has written to inform me that he is told at the local Labour Exchange that he has forfeited his right to any further unemployment pay because schools, hospitals and institutions are exempt from buying the stamps. He tells me that he has been buying the stamps and that the school authorities have been stamping his card, but he is told that all he can expect is to have his stamps money refunded. This situation seems to me so preposterous that a man should have forfeited his right to unemployment pay merely by taking a temporary job in a school that I am writing to ask whether the local Labour Exchange is not ill-informed.

Mr Sollory was formerly a skilled non-ferrous metal worker and up to the time when that trade began to decline had been some years foreman, earning very good wages in a substantial business. He is an old-fashioned type of non-union worker, Liberal in politics, and I know that his motive in taking the very humble job that he took was not so much a slight increase of remuneration under the dole as a dislike of being out of work. He has three daughters, one of whom is married, another in service, and the youngest, who is about 16 has been looking after her father at home.

Yours faithfully,
[T. S. Eliot]

TO *The Contributions Department,* The Times   cc

6 April 1932   [Faber & Faber Ltd]

Dear Sirs,

I have received from you a cheque for £1 12s. 6d. for contributions during March last. As the only contribution which I have made to the *Times* during that period appears to be an Obituary notice I am returning the cheque with thanks.

Yours faithfully,
[T. S. Eliot]

TO *Hugh Massingham*[1]

7 April 1932   [Faber & Faber Ltd]

Dear Mr Massingham,

Thank you for your kind letter of the 4th April.[2] It would certainly
have been somewhat easier for me to do Bradley than Pusey although I
think that Bradley is so near to being a contemporary that he ought to be
done by somebody with a little personal recollection of him. I am afraid
that my original difficulty still holds its force, and is indeed, if anything,
stronger than when I wrote to your brother. I simply have not the time
and energy to undertake any fresh commission for another year, and the
fact that your book will be, as I hope, an important one, makes me all the
more wary of the undertaking.

> With very many regrets,
> Yours sincerely,
> [T. S. Eliot]

TO *Leonard Woolf*

7 April 1932   [*The Criterion*]

Dear Leonard,

From the receipt of a cheque for £5. 17. 3d. I infer that you have
returned to London. I hope that Virginia is well enough to be able to see
me soon, and I am sure that Vivienne would like to come in also. Is there
any afternoon when you would be in too as I should like to have a few
words about the future of the Montalk situation? My difficult afternoons
as you know are Monday and Thursday.

> Yours ever,
> [T. S. E.]

1–Hugh Massingham (b. 1905), journalist and author. See *The Great Victorians* (1932), ed.
Hugh Massingham and H. J. Massingham (his brother). See also *An Englishman Abroad*
(1962).
2–'My brother, H. J. Massingham, has already told me . . . that you found yourself unable
to do Pusey for *The Great Victorians* . . . I happened last night to pick up again *For Lancelot
Andrewes*, and it occurred to me that we might be able to persuade you to do a very short
appreciation of F. H. Bradley.'

TO *Ezra Pound*   TS Beinecke

7 April 1932   Faber & Faber Ltd

Dear Rabbit,

Yours of the 2nd inst.[1] I agree that the personal note is the one to blow loudest. There is no need to run to 4000. I only put that in to prevent your running on at greater length. I think you ought to have Harold's last few volumes which I will send tomorrow to the address you quote. Your last paragraph finds me in agreement.

I wish I could feel happy about Bunting as he seems to be an admirable character and we heard the story of his life with many highly improbable details from Yeats last week. I have racked my brains over the manuscript but so far I can't see that it is much more than a rather fuzzy imitation of the cantos.[2] At what period of his life, by the way, was Basil in Japan?

Yours,

T.

TO *R. E. Gordon George*[3]   CC

7 April 1932   [Faber & Faber Ltd]

My dear Robert,

Many thanks for your letter of the 3rd.[4] I sent you the book only on a venture taking it for granted that you would, as you have done, report if you considered it not worth the trouble. So will you just hang on to it in the possibility that some other book might turn up to review to which it might be worth appending?

About the two books you mention. I have heard of Maeztu for years in terms of high commendation. I gather that the book has appeared in Spain. How could I get hold of a copy? The German book doesn't sound so promising and I feel also that my firm happens to have a rather large proportion of German books on its list at present.[5]

1–Not found.
2–EP to FVM, 8 Jan. 1933: 'An interest in Bunting's poems. He is about THE white hope of yr/ adopted country, and considerably more interesting than the oter [*sic*] new poets on yr/ list.'
3–Robert Esmonde Gordon George – better known as Robert Sencourt (1890–1969) – critic, historian and biographer: see Biographical Register.
4–TSE had sent a book on El Greco and Cervantes, which George did not think worth a review.
5–George recommended *Don Quixote: Don Juan y la Celestina: Ensayos de simpatia*

I will drop a line to Smyth about the 'Spanish Crown'.[1]

I hope that you will be firm with yourself and make up your mind to act decisively when the time comes, as I am sure it will come soon, when you will have to absent yourself from Hyères again. After all you know as well as I do that beyond a certain point of fatigue one ceases to be useful when present.[2]

I am not sure yet about Mrs Dixon Davies.[3] She has been extremely kind and persistent and it seems to me to have worked very well so far. I am only afraid that she may have the hope of accomplishing more than she can; but in any case I am grateful to you for having established the connection as I am for many other things.

Ever affectionately,

[T. S. Eliot]

TO *C. H. Douglas*   CC

8 April 1932   [Faber & Faber Ltd]

Dear Major Douglas,

I am very sorry to have to say that I have not been able to obtain a favourable decision from my Board.[4] The chief argument is that when a book has been on the market for some years a mere change of publisher does not at all stimulate the rate of sale, and that according to your figures Cecil Palmer have enough stock to supply the market for some little time. I cherish the hope of reopening the question at a later date, unless meanwhile you have made arrangements with some other firm. Meanwhile we should of course be extremely happy to entertain the

---

(1926), by his friend Ramiro de Maeztu; also, 'a new comedy, a light satire, very readable, on feudalism in East Prussia'.

1 – 'I have just heard from Benn that they have sent Charles Smyth a copy of my new book, suggesting to him to review it for the *Criterion*, and perhaps it might be added to the Empress and called "Studies of Monarchy", if you like the idea.'

2 – 'Life here presents its usual difficulties: all so intangible, yet so exhausting. There is nothing more to say about it than what you know already, except that I gratefully remember your warning not to stay too long . . . [M]y sister quietly stifles any suggestion of anything being done.'

3 – 'Mrs Dixon Davies writes to me at length about Vivienne: whether she is herself the best person for V. I think is doubtful, but she may be a means of helping towards something being done.' (Mrs Dixon Davies was possibly to be retained as a companion for VHE during TSE's absence in the USA.) In a later letter (15 June), Sencourt reported, 'I often hear from Mrs Dixon D.; she has become very fond of V.'

4 – See TSE's letter to Douglas, 26 Feb. 1932, above.

suggestion of publishing any further work that you may write. I must add that for personal reasons I am of course disappointed.

> Yours sincerely,
> [T. S. Eliot]

TO *Montgomery Belgion*

CC

8 April 1932   [*The Criterion*]

My dear Belgion,

Many thanks for your kind letter of the 5th.[1] I am glad that you are of the same opinion as myself about 'Triumphal March'. As for that old paper in the *NRF* that is extremely kind of you.[2] I will have another look among old papers to see if I have a copy of the original text. I am afraid I really feel too tired and lazy and the time is too short for me to bother about translating it back into English from the French, and I have another article still to write to go into this volume.

I hope that my wife will be coming to Paris before very long and if so I shall certainly let you know.[3]

> Yours ever,
> [T. S. Eliot]

TO *T. F. Burns*

CC

13 April 1932   [Faber & Faber Ltd]

Dear Burns,

Many thanks for your kind note of the 7th.[4] I am glad to hear that Dawson's talks are to appear in the Essays in Order, which is where they should be. As for my own I have been rather averse to publishing them at all in their present form, but the question has already been raised here in

---

1 – Belgion thanked TSE for sending the issue of *Commerce*: 'On rereading the poem I continue to think it is better than *Triumphal March*. "Démission" must be right.'

2 – 'By the way, I think you should very seriously consider including in the volume of essays you mentioned to me that paper you sent the N.R.F. on English Prose Style – Newman the last stylist, &c . . . The paper is one of the most interesting you have ever done, I am sure.' See TSE, '*Le roman anglais contemporain*', *NRF* 28: 164 (1 May 1927), 669–75.

3 – 'If your wife comes to France, you'll let me know, won't you.'

4 – 'I've just come across two of your talks in the *Listener* . . . Would you consider adapting them for an Essay in Order? Dawson's four talks are going into the series.' 'Essays in Order' was a series published by Sheed and Ward.

Faber & Fabers, and if I do publish them I am certainly committed to my own firm. Otherwise I should certainly have preferred to see them among the Essays in Order than anywhere else.

With many regrets,
Yours ever,
[T. S. Eliot]

TO *Maurice B. Reckitt*[1]

CC

13 April 1932   [Faber & Faber Ltd]

Dear Mr Reckitt,

We have carefully considered your MS., and I at least was sufficiently interested to neglect other duties for the pleasure of reading it thoroughly and with much profit. After collation of opinions however we do not feel that this is a book for our firm to publish.

It seems to me that in its present form it would be extremely useful to those of your own way of thinking, and who are already closely associated with the social work of one Christian organisation or another. What I do not feel is that it is a book adapted to convert or persuade the general public. While the considerable historical part of the book is extremely interesting to me, and to a limited number of others, it would, I feel, weary the general reader and incline him to form the conclusion that a great deal of benevolent energy has been exerted in order to produce very small results. Whether the last and more constructive parts of the book, in which you ally yourself to Credit Reform, could be made into a small volume by itself is a question which I am not able to answer, and which depends partly on the aims you have in view. As the book stands, and perhaps even were it revised or condensed, I cannot help feeling that it is more suitable for a more specialised publishing house which would be more closely in touch with the public already formed for it.

1–Maurice Reckitt (1888–1980) was editor of *Christendom: A Quarterly Journal of Christian Sociology*, and primary organiser of the Oxford Summer School of Sociology. He was a dogmatically outspoken contributor to Christian policy conferences; and at his bidding, numerous Christian thinkers and strategists – including TSE, Dorothy L. Sayers, Philip Mairet – were to participate in the discussion groups he promoted. 'The Christendom group stood for autochthonous thought and activity and was once denounced as "the rudest group in the Church of England"' (*ODNB*). His other works include *Faith and Society* (1932), *Maurice to Temple* (Scott Holland memorial lectures, 1947), *Prospect for Christendom* (ed., 1945). See further Reckitt, *As It Happened: An Autobiography* (1941); V. A. Demant, *Maurice B. Reckitt: A Record of Vocation and Versatility* (1978); J. S. Peart-Binns, *Maurice B. Reckitt: A Life* (1988).

I hope that we may continue our acquaintance; and I should be very pleased if you could lunch with me one day in the near future, whenever it suits you to be in London.

Yours sincerely,

[T. S. Eliot]

TO *James Joyce*   CC

13 April 1932   [Faber & Faber Ltd]

Dear Joyce,

I must apologise for my delay in returning to you Rubin's letter herewith. My Secretary searched everywhere for it but was unable to find it as it was in my pocket the whole time.

Meanwhile I have had two letters from Rubin himself, one saying that he was sending off the MS. at once, and the other explaining that he could not send it because it was his only good copy and he could not afford the fifty dollars demanded for insuring it. He has promised to send it if possible by a friend who may come to England this summer. As we can hardly ourselves pay fifty dollars to inspect an MS. by an unknown author, I am leaving the matter over.

Yours ever sincerely,

[T. S. Eliot]

TO *Keith Feiling*[1]   CC

13 April 1932   [*The Criterion*]

Dear Sir,

I am writing to ask whether you would be willing to review for the *Criterion* the edition of *Lord Chesterfield's Letters* edited by Bonamy Dobrée, and published by Eyre & Spottiswoode in six volumes. I hope

1–Keith (later Sir Keith) Feiling (1884–1977), was from 1928 a Fellow of Christ Church, Oxford; Lecturer in Modern History. He was to be Chichele Professor of Modern History at All Souls, 1946–50. His publications include *A History of the Tory Party, 1640–1714* (1924), *What Is Conservatism?* (Criterion Miscellany 14, 1930), *The Second Tory Party, 1714–1832* (1938), *The Life of Neville Chamberlain* (1946) and *Warren Hastings* (1954; James Tait Award). See *Essays in British History presented to Sir Keith Feiling*, ed. Hugh Trevor-Roper (1964); A. L. Rowse, *Historians I Have Known* (1995); and Reba N. Soffer, *History, Historians, and Conservatism in Britain and America: From the Great War to Thatcher and Reagan* (2009).

that you will be able to do so as I know of no one whose review of this book would interest me more. As the book is so voluminous I shall wait for your reply before sending it to you.[1]

Faithfully yours,
[T. S. Eliot]

TO *Mario Praz*[2]   CC

13 April 1932   [*The Criterion*]

Dear Praz,

I am very interested to hear that you have completed your translation of *The Waste Land*.[3] I understand that you mean the text and translation to appear in the *Nuova Antologia* or some other periodical, and I have not the slightest objection. If, however, you intend to publish it as a book I should like to hear from you further, as in this case I ought to reserve certain rights, though I should hardly expect any royalties.

I have been busy with many things lately and I am sorry to say that I have not yet dealt with your translation.[4] I am glad that you reminded me and hope to write to you again next week.

Yours ever,
[T. S. Eliot]

1–See Feiling on Chesterfield: C. 12 (Oct. 1932), 118–21.
2–Mario Praz (1896–1982), scholar and critic of English literature: see Biographical Register.
3–Praz reported (Apr. 1932) that he had completed a translation of *TWL*: 'would Faber & Faber allow me to reprint the English text side by side without royalties?' he asked. 'La Terra Desolata' appeared in *Circoli* (Genoa), 2: 4 (July/Aug. 1932), 27–57.
4–Praz had submitted for consideration on 24 Feb. a choice of contemporary Italian poetry he had translated into English – his selection included works by Montale, Carazzini, Ungaretti and Sbarbaro – which he hoped might make up a small anthology in F&F's series of Ariel Poems.

TO *Derek Verschoyle*[1]

13 April 1932   [Faber & Faber Ltd]

Dear Mr Verschoyle,

Thank you for your letter of the 11th.[2] I do indeed remember you very well, though I did not know that you had joined the staff of *The Spectator*.

I am interested in your suggestion and should like to think of it further, but I am more than doubtful whether I shall be able to undertake any further commissions for articles until my return from America a year hence. I imagine that your space would be limited to about 2,000 words, and it is really more difficult to say anything valuable about a great poet in that space than it is in 5 or 6,000 words. I think on the whole that I had better decline your invitation.

> With regrets,
> Yours sincerely,
> [T. S. Eliot]

TO *Gloria Goddard*[3]

14 April 1932   [Faber & Faber Ltd]

Dear Miss Goddard,

Thank you for your kind letter of the 12th March, and for sending me your novel, *These Lords' Descendants*, which is extremely interesting.[4] I am sorry that I have found it necessary to make a strict rule against

---

1–Derek Verschoyle (1911–73), writer and editor, was literary editor of *The Spectator*, 1932–9. Educated at Arnold House Prep School in Wales (where he was taught by Evelyn Waugh) and Malvern College; he took degrees at Trinity College, Dublin, and Trinity College, Oxford. After distinguished service during WW2 in the RAF (wing commander), he was First Secretary at the British Embassy, Rome, 1947–50; and for four years he ran his own publishing house, Derek Verschoyle Ltd, 1952–6.

2–Verschoyle, who had been introduced to TSE by F. W. Bain in May 1931, wrote that *The Spectator* was shortly to run a series of articles on important English poets, written by living poets. 'I very much hope that you will be able to see your way to doing one of the articles. For subject, may I tentatively suggest Milton, Dryden, or Vaughan? I am writing to Mr Pound to ask him for an article and am hoping to get Mr Yeats to write (perhaps on Spenser).'

3–Gloria Goddard (1897–?1978), author; born in Pennsylvania.

4–Goddard (New York City) asked whether TSE might write a preface to her biography *Don John of Austria: The Last Knight of Europe*. 'The story of this prince holds all the glamor, all the religious fervor, all the dedication to a high purpose that are so lacking today.' She enclosed a copy of her recent novel, to illustrate both her skill as a writer and her seriousness of manner.

writing prefaces or introductions to books by living authors, except where there is some strong personal reason. Furthermore I very much doubt whether such prefaces are of much importance in assisting the sales of books. In any case I am sure that for your biography of Don John of Austria the most suitable introducer, if you can prevail upon him, would be Mr G. K. Chesterton.

With grateful thanks for the compliment, and with many regrets,

I am,

Yours truly,

[T. S. Eliot]

TO *Rolf Gardiner*   TS Cambridge University Library

14 April 1932   Faber & Faber Ltd

Dear Mr Gardiner,

Thank you for your letter of the 11th.[1] I ought to have written to you before. I found that the Woolfs are just going off for a holiday to Greece and will not be back until the middle of May. Woolf tells me that in any case he could not consider the MS. for publication earlier than the autumn. So I think that unless you want to try some other publisher, with a view to immediate publication, the best thing is for you to write to Leonard Woolf about the middle of May and remind him that I have spoken to him about you and let him read your MS. then.

I am not quite sure whether I should be able to get into the next number a review of the book you mention,[2] but in the case of foreign books the lapse of three months hardly matters, and I should be very glad if you cared to send a review of a thousand words or so on approval, with a view to either the June or September number.

With all best wishes,

T. S. Eliot

1–Gardiner asked whether TSE had been able to contact LW about his proposed book 'World without End, Politics and the Younger Generation'.

2–Gardiner wished to review *Die Europaeischen Revolutionen, Volkskaraktere und Staatenbildung* – 'the most important German work published since Spengler's *Untergang des Abenlandes* [*The Decline of the West*]' – by Eugen Rosenstock, Professor of Law at Breslau University and one of the leading sociologists of Germany. Gardiner wrote that he had worked with Rosenstock 'for many years, particularly in Silesia and in the Arbeitslager movement'.

FROM *TSE's Secretary* TO *Lucienne Southgate*[1] CC

14 April 1932 *The Criterion*

Dear Madam,

Mr Eliot has asked me to thank you for your letter of the 11th, and to express his regret for the repetition in the *Criterion* of the remark attributed to *Mr Wells*.[2] He wishes me to add, however, that he cannot consider that his reviewer is in any way at fault in quoting a statement made in a Russian periodical. Mr Eliot proposes to publish your letter in the next number of the *Criterion*, but I am writing to inform you in case Mr Wells prefers to have the correction made in some other form.[3]

Faithfully yours,
[Pamela Wilberforce]
Secretary

FROM *Vivien Eliot* TO *Mary Hutchinson* Notecard MS Texas

18 April 1932 68 Clarence Gate Gardens

When can I see you? Please write or telephone at once.

Yours ever,
Vivienne Haigh Eliot

1 – Secretary to H. G. Wells.
2 – 'Mr H. G. Wells follows the new fine critical methods of the younger school of literary brilliance with respectful attention. He notes that in your April issue you resort to a translation from a Moscow article in which Mr Lunacharski said among other things what after an interval of forgetfulness he imagined Mr Wells said to him about Mr Galsworthy. This tiresome fragment of retranslated gossip was served up in America last year and it was then repudiated by Mr Wells. Mr Wells had hoped that he was a sufficiently copious writer to escape from judgments based on hearsay and personal chatter. His relations with his friend Mr Galsworthy remain unruffled.'
3 – Southgate replied to this letter on 15 Apr.: 'I have shown this to Mr Wells and he says he would like to make an alteration in my letter of the 11th before it is printed. I enclose a copy showing the correction and shall be glad if you will kindly see that it appears in this form.'

TO *Joseph Needham*   CC

20 April 1932   [*The Criterion*]

Dear Needham,

Thank you for the review which has gone to press and for the revised edition of Laudian Marxism[1]. It is rather late for the June number which is already pretty full, and I shall want to print it in the September number.

I agree with you about the value of the work Oldham is doing.[2] As for Berdiaev's work I think that most of it exists in German, but rather more has been translated into French than into English.[3] There is a long book published by Plon in the Roseau d'Or series called *Un Nouveau Moyen Age*. I am glad you find Smyth interesting. He is, I believe, to be in some London slum next winter and I think he would be a useful addition to the group. As you say, one or two more scientists are desirable.[4]

                              Yours sincerely,
                              [T. S. Eliot]

1 – Needham submitted on 10 Apr. a revised version of his paper 'Laudian Marxism', having removed 'the two or three pages at the end, which I think were the ones you took exception to. I do not in the least mind doing this as it leaves the main thesis of the paper quite untouched, namely that a purely scientific society is just what we want to avoid, that religion is an essential factor in our being able to do this, and that Marxism, most of the elements of which seem to be very justifiable, need not necessarily be, in its English form, antagonistic to religion and so an obstacle rather than a help to attaining the ideal society of the future.' 'Laudian Marxism: Thoughts on Science, Religion and Socialism', C. 12 (Oct. 1932), 56–72. Needham reviewed C. E. M. Joad, *Philosophical Aspects of Modern Science*, and F. R. Tennant, *Philosophy of the Sciences*, in C. 11 (July 1932), 719–22.

2 – 'Since our meeting,' wrote Needham (10 Apr.), 'I have written to Oldham expressing to him my sense of its great value from every point of view, and thanking him for organizing it.'

3 – 'I have ordered the little book of [Nikolai] Berdiaev [*The End of Our Time*], but I believe that he has written other books or essays. Do you know what these are, and whether they are worth reading?'

4 – 'I have lately seen Charles Smyth of C.C.C. [Corpus Christ College, Cambridge]. Although his political opinions differ toto caelo from mine, I think most highly of him. I hear he is leaving us soon and going to some parish to a cure of souls . . . He has a subtle mind, and if Oldham asks me at any time to suggest new members of the group I shall suggest him. Although I also think we want another scientific representative.' (Smyth was set to go, on 1 Jan. 1933, to the parish of St Clement's, Barnsbury, London, close to the Caledonian Market and to Pentonville Prison.)

TO *Gilbert Seldes*[1]   TS Timothy and Marian Seldes

20 April 1932   *The Criterion*

My dear Seldes,

I was surprised and pleased to hear from you after such a very long time during which I supposed you had completely lost interest in the *Criterion*.[2] It is true that I am coming to Harvard in the autumn for seven months, so I hope that we may meet. I should be glad to have another American chronicle of the usual chronicle length in the autumn for the September number, but it occurs to me that you might find it more convenient according as events and the publication of books fall out to provide it for the December number. Please let me know which suits you better.

Yours sincerely,
T. S. Eliot

TO *Padraic Colum*   CC

20 April 1932   [*The Criterion*]

Dear Colum,

Thank you for your note of the 13th.[3] Please understand, however, that the main purpose is to sell the poem for Joyce in America at the highest possible price, and that if the necessity of delay in publication here hampered you in bargaining I should want the *Criterion* to stand aside. Waiting to hear from you further.

Yours ever sincerely
[T. S. Eliot]

1–Gilbert Seldes (1893–1970), influential journalist, critic and editor, wrote several 'New York Chronicles' for C. Works include *The Seven Lively Arts* (1924) and *The Stammering Century* (1928). See Michael Kammen, *The Lively Arts: Gilbert Seldes and the Transformation of Cultural Criticism in the United States* (1996).

2–After a gap of three years, Seldes offered on 6 Apr. to send an American Chronicle. 'I have done a variety of things since I saw you last – perhaps too great a variety. But some of them have been entertaining and one, a vulgarization of Lysistrata, at least temporarily profitable.' He spent his time, he said, 'partly on a daily column of more or less intellectual comment for the Hearst press and in writing plays'. (He was Managing Editor of the *New York Evening Journal*.)

3–'Now that I know Joyce's poem is not to be published until September or December I see that there isn't much reason for offering it to the New Republic. I suggested N.R. because early publication could be arranged in it. Harper's or Scribner's would give far more. I'll send a copy to Harper's . . . and will find out from them approximate date of publication.'

20 April 1932   [Faber & Faber Ltd]

My dear Oldham,

Thank you for yours of the 18th.[1] About the autumn meeting I think that the first weekend in September is the only one of which I could be at all sure. I expect to leave by the 15th. On the other hand I ought to remind you that several other members said they would find it difficult or impossible to attend any meeting in that month, and furthermore I shall have so much to do before leaving that I might find it difficult to give so much time just then. So I really think that it would be much better to arrange the meeting without regard to me, but merely consulting the convenience of the other members. I shall very much regret missing the meeting and hope that you will make progress and arrange another soon after my return. I am looking forward to lunching with you on Thursday.

                         Yours sincerely,
                         [T. S. Eliot]

to *Herbert Read*   cc

20 April 1932   [*The Criterion*]

Dear Herbert,

Thank you for your note of the 11th as well as for your previous letter of the 16th March which I think I never answered.[2] I am putting in the review notes and am glad to see that your interest in poetry is reviving. I don't think that I shall have room for 'The Innocent Eye' in the June number though I shall use it if I possibly can.[3] I would certainly use it in the September number but I imagine that you would rather give it to the *Listener* than wait till then. So may I at least hang on to it for another fortnight or so?

We are going to have a *Criterion* meeting here on Tuesday the 3rd of May. I do not suppose that the date will be possible for you even were there longer notice. We fixed the date because Angioletti is to be in town. There will be a plain supper, but I believe rather more wholesome than

---

1–Oldham asked for dates in Sept.–Oct. for 'the proposed further meeting of the Group'.
2–HR wrote on 16 Mar.: 'I've got an idea for a long poem, but as you know, such ideas don't bear discussion until they are at least in part realised.' On 11 Apr. he sent 'The Innocent Eye'.
3–'Two Poems: The Innocent Eye. Schwermut', C. 12 (Oct. 1932), 43–4.

we used to have, at the Board Room of 24 Russell Square at 6.30. In any case we shall make another attempt in June, so please let me know when you can come up.

Yours ever,
[T. S. E.]

TO *G. Wilson Knight*[1]   CC

20 April 1932   [Faber & Faber Ltd]

Dear Knight,

Thank you very much for your letter of the 2nd April and for sending me the copy of your broadcast talk.[2] The latter seemed to me from my point of view quite admirable considering the extreme difficulty which I have experienced myself of saying anything worth saying on the wireless in fourteen minutes. I mean that your most difficult problem was to get the proportion just, and in this it seems to me that you have succeeded. Thank you very much. I am glad to hear that you are likely to be in England this summer when I look forward to an opportunity of discussing with you the work you had in hand, and in more detail your interesting suggestion

---

1–G. Wilson Knight (1897–1985) served in WWI and took a degree in English at St Edmund Hall, Oxford, in 1923. He held teaching posts in secondary schools before being appointed Chancellors' Professor of English, Toronto University, 1931–40. In 1946 he was made Reader in English Literature at the University of Leeds, where he became Professor, 1955–62. His publications include *The Wheel of Fire: Five Essays on the Interpretation of Shakespeare's Sombre Tragedies* (1930) – for which TSE wrote the introduction – and *The Imperial Theme: Further Interpretations of Shakespeare's Tragedies including the Roman Plays* (1931). See also Wilson Knight, 'T. S. Eliot: Some Literary Impressions', *Sewanee Review* 74: 1 (Winter 1966), 239–55; Phillip L. Marcus, 'T. S. Eliot and Shakespeare', *Criticism* 9: 1 (Winter 1967), 63–72; Wilson Knight, 'Thoughts on *The Waste Land*', *Denver Quarterly* 7: 2 (Summer 1972), 1–13.

2–Wilson Knight, who had taken up in autumn 1931 a post at Trinity College, Toronto, had sent a copy of a recent fourteen-minute radio broadcast. 'T. S. Eliot and the Spirit of Modern Poetry' closes: 'These poems are typical of our generation. Typical of its despair, its sense of futility. But typical too of the stirring which today heralds a revival to dispel our consciousness of death. That Mr Eliot's most positive poetic statements should be presented in terms of Christian orthodoxy is extremely significant. It is equally significant that his most recent, and perhaps his most exquisite, happy poem [*Marina*] should be directly related to one of Shakespeare's supreme acts of paradisal vision . . . [I]f we regard Mr Eliot's work as a whole, we find a small, but intense, poetic world of the same quality as Shakespeare's and Dante's. It has its visions of darkness; its progress towards paradisal radiance. Starting from the Old Testament of cynicism and death, it is moving now towards the New Testament of victorious life.'

about Middleton Murry.[1] Had you not been coming to England I should still have hoped to see something of you on the other side of the Atlantic in the winter, and perhaps that will be possible too.

In haste,
Yours ever sincerely,
[T. S. Eliot]

TO *J. B. Pinker & Sons*   CC

20 April 1932   [Faber & Faber Ltd]

Dear Pinker,

We have gone into the question of the publication of *Ulysses* as thoroughly as possible and we are sorry to say that the balance of opinion is emphatically not only that we should render ourselves liable to prosecution and serious penalties, but that in all probability such prosecution would take place. The judgement in appeal on the Montalk case of course makes matters a great deal worse than ever before. The opinion also is that there would be no distinction and no more immunity in publishing an expensive limited edition than an ordinary popular edition.

We are therefore forced with the greatest regret to stand aside in this matter. Of course it is possible that some other publisher might take a different view of the prospects.

Yours sincerely,
[T. S. Eliot]

1 – 'I have lately seen very clearly where Mr Murry goes wrong. What he says would be right if put in poetry or fine prose, but is false altogether as it stands – that's how I see it. I thought his review of my book [*The Imperial Theme*] in [the] *T.L.S.* really amazing. It's that partly that makes my second book a financial failure – as the O.P. [Oxford University Press] seem to think it. (They say it has lost a lot of money.) Partly, of course, the depression too, I expect.'

TO *Alfred Kreymborg*[1]   CC

20 April 1932   [Faber & Faber Ltd]

Dear Krimmie,

Thanks for your line of the 1st March, but I am afraid I have nothing on hand and no time to undertake anything this year.[2] I suppose I shall be in New York off and on, and look forward to seeing you.

                                    Yours ever,
                                    [T. S. Eliot]

TO *Jacob Bronowski*[3]   CC

20 April 1932   [*The Criterion*]

Dear Mr Bronowski,

I did not reply to your letter of February for the reason that I was waiting till I could let you know that I had received payment from Brewer and Warren.[4] I have just received a cheque for three guineas from Mr Samuel Putnam and am writing at once to let you know.

1–Alfred Kreymborg (1883–1966): poet, playwright, puppeteer (who also supported himself for some years as a chess player). His works include *Puppet Plays* (1923) – which TSE found fascinating – and *Lima Beans* (1925); and *Troubador* (1925), which includes an account of his meetings with TSE in London. In 1915–19 he edited *Others* (which took TSE's 'Portrait of a Lady') – see Suzanne Churchill, *The Little Magazine Others and the Renovation of American Poetry* (2006) – and he was co-editor, with Van Wyck Brooks, Lewis Mumford and Paul Rosenfeld, of *American Caravan*, an annual anthology of new writing.

2–Kreymborg sent TSE on 1 Mar. a flyer put out by *Theatre Arts Monthly* (of which he was a co-editor), promulgating a comprehensive project: 'An investigation prompted by the varied, original and opposing opinions held by people in the theatre today, offers you an opportunity of expressing your most obstinate and special belief as it pertains to the art of theatre and drama, and would be pleased to have that expression in not more than 5,000 words for publication.' He requested of TSE in his covering letter: 'We'd love to have you join us in this investigation.'

3–Jacob Bronowski (1908–74) – Polish-born scientist, humanist, writer and broadcaster, whose family came to the UK in 1920 – read mathematics at Jesus College, Cambridge. After gaining his doctorate in 1933, he taught at the University College of Hull, 1934–42; and after WW2 he became scientific deputy to the British Joint Chiefs of Staff mission to Japan (where he wrote a report on the effects of the atomic bombs on Hiroshima and Nagasaki). From 1950 he was Director of the Coal Research Establishment of the National Coal Board, working on the development of smokeless fuel; and in 1964 he became Senior Fellow at the Salk Institute for Biological Studies in San Diego, California. Works include a critical study of William Blake (1944). In later years he won acclaim for his thirteen-part TV series *The Ascent of Man* (1973).

4–Bronowski said on 10 Feb. he had sent TSE two copies of *European Caravan*: 'I regret to say that, as you will have noticed, the mis-statement I made in the biographical notes

I quite took it for granted that you had endeavoured to rectify the mistakes and that the fault occurred on the other side of the Atlantic. It doesn't really matter very much.

Yours very sincerely,
[T. S. Eliot]

TO *James Joyce*   CC

20 April 1932   [Faber & Faber Ltd]

My dear Joyce,

We have gone into the question of the publication of *Ulysses* in England as thoroughly as possible, and have taken every opinion available on the prospects. Of course, as you know, the fact of the judgement in appeal on the Montalk case is such as to make matters very much worse in England than ever before, and we are advised that we should certainly be liable to prosecution and heavy penalties, with the possibility of the chairman's having to spend six months in gaol, which in itself would be disastrous for the business. The opinion further is that such prosecution would certainly take place.

Of course it is possible that some other publishing firm may take a different view of the prospects, and in that case I very much hope that *Ulysses* will be published, although it would of course be a matter of great regret to feel, if another publisher succeeded in getting away with it, what we had lost by our caution. I have written to Pinker, and I hope that he will try other publishers. In fact I should not like to feel that you had been dissuaded from the attempt merely by the opinions of one firm.

Meanwhile I hope that you have been able to pick up the threads of *Work in Progress* and will soon send us something for the printer.

Yours ever sincerely,
[T. S. Eliot]

---

prefacing your poems has survived, together with the mass of mistakes which I corrected throughout the English section – Messrs Brewer & Warren now simply informing me that they had to rush the book through the press and could not wait for the return of my proofs . . . Will you let me know whether Messrs Brewer & Warren have made you the copyright payment which we arranged?'

TO *Charles Smyth*   CC

20 April 1932   [*The Criterion*]

Dear Smyth,

I must apologize for the delay in reporting to you about 'The Education of an Officer Class', but it has taken Morley and myself a good deal of time to clear up our minds about its troubles. In the end we have both come to feel that there is in it, (1). the material for a good chronicle, (2). some of the material for a good book, but that it is unlikely to make its mark as a pamphlet.

One of the difficulties is that a fair part of the matter is likely to alienate rather than persuade a considerable number of wavering persons of indefinite religious faith who ought in this matter to be gained for your side. Another trouble is that it treats of several matters which from the point of view of the general public do not necessarily unite into one subject. One is the whole question of whether an officer class should be trained, and if so, how, and this is really related to one's fundamental assumptions as to what Social Organization and Political Constitution should be. The second theme is the general inefficiency and sloppiness of the public schools, and third and most important here is the need for a genuine theological education in the public schools which are nominally Church of England, and finally you touch upon the general necessity of a church.

I hope that you will have the patience to endure my suggestions. One is that you should take one heading, perhaps merely to show up the essential unchristianity of public schools and make an article for the *Criterion*. The other suggestion is more tentative. Has it ever occurred to you that there might be a place for a book not so much critical of the present methods as constructive on the teaching of theology in the school curriculum? Do you even think that there might be an opportunity for a textbook on theology applying your principles for use in the upper forms of schools? I should be very much interested to know what you think about this, because I am convinced that your ideas on this subject ought to be pursued thoroughly.[1]

Yours ever,
[T. S. Eliot]

1–Smyth responded ('Feast of SS. Philip and James'): 'I think you are absolutely right, and you tempered the blow very nicely . . . I shall . . . weigh your suggestions again, later on. The only disadvantage is that I don't know any theology . . . I don't regret writing The Officer Class.'

TO *Frederick May Eliot*   CC

20 April 1932   [*The Criterion*]

Dear Frederick,

   Thank you very much for your kind letter of the 4th.[1] It would be a very
great pleasure to me to spend a night or two with you and Elizabeth in St
Paul, and I should be very [glad] of the excuse of a lecture engagement. I
have thought it advisable not to make any definite arrangements of dates
or engagements for distant places until I arrive in Cambridge at the end
of September, and I hope that will not make it too late to be possible
for me to come to St Paul. In fact, I should like very much, as I had
purposed going to St Louis in any case, to get as far as the West Coast and
possibly visit Portland. In any case I am happy to know that you will be in
Cambridge during part of April as I shall certainly be there until the first
of May. I hope that Elizabeth will be coming with you.

                                   With many thanks,
                                   Yours affectionately,
                                   [Tom]

1–Frederick hoped TSE might visit them. He could arrange for TSE to lecture at the
University of Minnesota or at Carleton College (where he had studied). However, he would
be away in late Apr. 1933, when he would be on duty at Appleton Chapel in Boston.

TO *Samuel Eliot Morison*[1]   CC

20 April 1932   [Faber & Faber Ltd]

My dear Morison,

I find that I failed to answer your kind note of the 2nd February[2] and I apologize. I have been and shall be extremely busy this spring, and rather tired, and I do not want to do any more writing than I can help, beyond preparing my lectures. If the delay is not too great I should prefer it if you could keep the Winthrop Papers until I get to Cambridge where I hope it will be easier for me to do the job. If on the other hand that would make the review too late, do send the volume along now, and I will try to let you have something in the summer.

Looking forward to seeing you in Boston,

I am,

Yours sincerely,

[T. S. Eliot]

TO *Maurice B. Reckitt*   CC

20 April 1932   [Faber & Faber Ltd]

Dear Mr Reckitt,

Thank you for your kind letter of the 15th.[3] I do indeed much hope that you will be successful in arranging the production of your book

1–Samuel Eliot Morison (1887–1976), American historian, was for thirty years from 1925 Professor of History at Harvard. He was a cousin of TSE. In 1922 he became the first Harmsworth Professor of American History at Oxford. His publications include *The Maritime History of Massachusetts* (1921), *The Oxford History of the United States* (1927), *The Growth of the American Republic* (1930), the history of Harvard University (5 vols, 1930–6), the history of the American navy in WW2 – *History of United States Naval Operations* (15 vols) – which is rated by many historians his finest achievement, the *Oxford History of the American People* (1965), and *The European Discovery of America* (1972). A Fellow of the Society of Antiquaries and of the American Philosophical Association, he served too as President of the American Historical Association; and his awards included the Bancroft Prize (twice), the Pulitzer Prize (twice), the Alfred Thayer Mahan Award of the Navy League, the Gold Medal for History, National Institute of Arts and Letters, and the President's Medal for Freedom. See also 'The Dry Salvages and the Thacher Shipwreck', *The American Neptune* 25: 4 (1965), 233–47.

2–Morison invited TSE to review for the *New England Quarterly* vols I and II of the *Winthrop Papers*.

3–Reckitt conceded that his book MS was 'addressed to a Christian constituency, and I suppose a narrow one at that'. He expressed the hope that TSE might at some time contribute something to *Christendom* – albeit they had 'neither funds nor circulation to reward our contributors'.

with a suitable publisher. I should like very much indeed to contribute to *Christendom*. I have nothing on my hands at present that I can offer and I have so much to do here during the next few months that I want to avoid undertaking any further commissions. I should be very glad if I could do something for you on my return from America next spring. I hope also that I shall have the pleasure of seeing you before I leave next September.

Yours sincerely,
[T. S. Eliot]

TO *Gordon Bottomley*[1]　　　　　　　　　　　　　　　　　CC

20 April 1932　　　　　　　　　　*[The Criterion]*

Dear Mr Bottomley,

Thank you for your kind note of the 15th April.[2] I have thought over carefully your question about a footnote, but it does not seem to me desirable to add any footnote to a short poem published by itself. In a book among other poems it would be another matter, but I do feel that in this place it would be a disfigurement.

It is a great pleasure to me to be able to have this poem for the *Criterion*.

Yours sincerely,
[T. S. Eliot]

TO *Bonamy Dobrée*　　　　　　　　　　　　　　　　　　　CC

20 April 1932　　　　　　　　　　[Faber & Faber Ltd]

Dear Bonamy,

Very many thanks for your letter and enclosure of the 15th.[3] I had already seen the outside of your book and was hoping that I might be

1–Gordon Bottomley (1874–1948), author, was awarded the Femina Prize, Paris, 1923, and the Benson Medal of the Royal Society of Literature, 1925. His publications include *Poems of Thirty Years* (1925), *Scenes and Plays* (1929), *Lyric Plays* (1932), *A Stage for Poetry* (1948).

2–'Thank you for . . . the proofs of my poem about the mountains of Rhum . . . I wonder if you think it might be necessary to insert a foot-note saying that Bride is pronounced Breedjé? I am not anxious to do it, for the phonetic version looks so eccentric, not to say unsightly; but I should be docile if it were thought necessary.' See 'Maisie's Song', *C.* 11 (July 1932), 662–3.

3–'I send you this [*Lord Chesterfield's Letters*] in the hope that it may amuse an idle ten minutes or so some time; at any rate, it can do no harm, as you are under no obligation.'

honoured with a copy from the author which I am glad to have. I shall read it.

We have arranged a *Criterion* meeting at rather short notice for Tuesday the 3rd of May. Light supper at 6.30 in the Board Room here. I am afraid it will be very poorly attended as it is at such short notice, and I wish that you could come. We arranged that date because Angioletti is to be in London at that time and wants to meet as many *Criterion* people as he can. We hope to arrange another *Criterion* meeting in June, and if you cannot possibly come now we will try to fix a date to suit you then, on the 15th, 16th, 17th whichever you like best.

Yours ever,
[T. S. E.]

TO *Bonamy Dobrée* TS Brotherton

20 April 1932   Faber & Faber Ltd

Dear Bonamy,

Eyre & Spott. have sent the Chesterfield (in plain vans) and Keith Feiling is delighted to review it, but that wont be in time for this number, not until the September no.

I hope you will try to come on the 3d. The Characters in their Order of Appearance:

F. V. Morley	An honest downright farmer
T. S. Eliot	A student
F. S. Flint	A roaring boy
O. Williams	An Italianate gallant, newly returned from his travels
J. B. Trend	A phantasticall master of Arts
B. Dobrée	A needy half-pay captain in the train bands

Yours etc.
T. S. E.

TO *R. B. McKerrow*[1]

CC

20 April 1932   [Faber & Faber Ltd]

Dear Sir,

I thank you for your letter of April 14th inviting me to review books for the *Review of English Studies*.[2] I should be very glad to do so in principle, but at present I have so much work to do here in the next few months that I have decided not to undertake any writing that I can possibly avoid, until my return from America in May of next year.

> With many thanks,
> Yours faithfully,
> [T. S. Eliot]

TO *Christopher Eliot*[3]

CC

20 April 1932   [Faber & Faber Ltd]

Dear Uncle Chris,

I must apologize for having failed to answer immediately your kind letter of the 6th February, but I have been extremely busy and rather

---

1–R. B. McKerrow (1872–1940), educated at King's College, London, and Trinity College, Cambridge (Chancellor's English Medal, 1895), was from 1925 editor of *The Review of English Studies*; editor of *The Library*, 1934–7; and a director of the publishers Sidgwick & Jackson. After lecturing in Tokyo and at King's College, London, he was from 1928 Sandars Reader in Bibliography at Cambridge. His publications include an edition of the works of Thomas Nashe (5 vols, 1904–10), editions of various plays for the Malone Society; *Introduction to Bibliography for Literary Students* (1927), *Prolegomena for the Oxford Shakespeare* (1939).

2–McKerrow invited TSE to review *The Essential Shakespeare*, by J. Dover Wilson, and *Revaluations*: essays by several hands.

3–The Revd Christopher Rhodes Eliot (1856–1945). 'After taking his A.B. at Washington University in 1876, he taught for a year in the Academic Department. He later continued his studies both at Washington University and at Harvard, and received two degrees in 1881, an A.M. from Washington University and an S.T.B. from the Harvard Divinity School. He was ordained in 1882, but thereafter associated himself with eastern pastorates, chiefly with the Bulfinch Place Church in Boston. His distinctions as churchman and educator were officially recognized by Washington University in granting him an honorary Doctorate of Laws in 1925' ('The Eliot Family and St Louis': an appendix prepared by the Department of English to TSE's 'American Literature and the American Language' [Washington University, 1953], 38).

tired.[1] I look forward very much to seeing you and Abigail[2] frequently during the winter, and I hope to be able to see Martha too.[3] I have just had a letter from Frederick suggesting that I should visit St Paul, and this I should like to do if possible. In any case I am happy to hear from him that he is to be the University preacher at Harvard for several weeks in the spring. I wish indeed that I might come in time to visit your camp before you return for the winter, but I am afraid I shall be unable to get away from London until the middle of September.

Affectionately your nephew
[Tom]

TO *Raymond W. Postgate*[4]　　　　　　　　　　CC/TS Texas

20 April 1932　　　　　　　　[Faber & Faber Ltd]

Dear Mr Postgate,

Thank you for your note of the 15th.[5] I really should have written to you some time ago about this matter I suppose, but I had quite forgotten that you might be expecting to hear from me further. I have made a satisfactory arrangement with Harcourt Brace to bring out a volume of selected essays in the autumn. As for the question of collected poems, that is still open, but at present, particularly as meanwhile we are to publish here a cheap edition of the old volume, I feel that I prefer to postpone

1–Uncle Chris ('emeritus') extended a welcome to TSE on his appointment at Harvard. 'How I wish your visit might be early enough to include a visit to Camp again. You wouldn't recognize it, but the Lake and the hills are the same, and could make you have a good time, I know.'

2–Abigail Adams Eliot (b. 1891?). See *A Heart of Grateful Trust: Memoirs of Abigail Adams Eliot*, transcribed and ed. Marjorie Gott Manning (n.d.); Cynthia Grant Tucker, *No Silent Witness: The Eliot Parsonage Women and Their Unitarian World* (2010).

3–Martha May Eliot (1891–1978), a cousin resident in Boston.

4–Raymond Postgate (1896–1971), journalist and author, was European representative of Alfred A. Knopf, 1930–49. A rebel and left-winger in his youth – in 1920 he was a founder member of the Communist Party of Great Britain, though his affiliation lasted only for a few months – he gained a reputation as a writer of labour and radical history: early works included *The International (Socialist Bureau) during the War* (1918), *The Bolshevik Theory* (1920) and *Robert Emmet* (1931). Later he worked for the Board of Trade, 1942–50. But his claim to fame came about when he launched in 1951 the annual volumes of the *Good Food Guide*, which he would edit until 1968. Other works include *The Plain Man's Guide to Wine* (1951). See J. Postgate and M. Postgate, *A Stomach for Dissent: The Life of Raymond Postgate* (1994).

5–Postgate reported that Knopf was 'anxiously pressing me to know whether I can get any further information from you about your feelings of Collected Poems and a Collected Prose: what can I say to him?'

the matter for a year or so in the hope that I may have something more substantial to include in a new collection.

With many regrets,
Yours sincerely,
[T. S. Eliot]

FROM *Vivien Eliot* TO *Mary Hutchinson*　　　　MS Texas

Thursday 21 April 1932　　　　68 Clarence Gate Gardens

My dear Mary,

I did love seeing you again. Dont ever think again that 'Vivienne does'nt mind'. She does. But she does not want to *show* it.

And dear, when you speak of these losses, & of the outside world being able to force its way in upon us – do look through the Past & you will see that there are many people, wonderful people getting *old* now, & *full* of marvels, who we have never really had *time* for, or never realised, & when they die, like Harold Monro, & one realises one has only seen them once or twice in 20 years or so. This should not happen. I know you will agree. I send you my card which I forgot to leave, & also my brother's card. Simply that you should know where he is.

Tom is interested that you wish to become Secretary to the Friends of Sadler's Wells. And will put it to Philip Morrell.

I send you the notice of Harold Monro's death, which please do keep for me as it is the last I have. Tom wrote it.

We look forward to seeing you here on May 4th at 7 p.m. I will ask a nice Proffessor [*sic*].

Tom is going to America next September until the following May – & it is all of our duties to keep things going for him *here*.

Your loving friend
Vivienne Haigh Eliot

22 April 1932   [Faber & Faber Ltd]

Dear Mr Sollory,

I am much relieved to hear from you that it was all a mistake of the school and that the Labour Exchange are now paying up.[1] In any case it is little enough to keep a man going. I do hope that something also will turn up before long, and shall be especially glad if it is something in your own line. Let me know if there is any more trouble.

Yours ever sincerely

[T. S. Eliot]

1–Sollory had written ('Friday'): 'I have just come from the Labour Exchange. I am glad to be able to tell you my unemployment pay has come through. I have just been paid 10/2 at the rate of 15/3 per week. It was very kind of you to go to the trouble of writing your solicitor on my behalf, for which I thank you. I couldn't send him my cards as one (the unemployment book) was already lodged and if I had withdrawn it my pay would have been shorter still. The muddle came about through the School people I had been working for classing me as a gardener. (I had to do a bit in my spare time from the fires.) They don't pay any unemployment contributions for anyone. I had to buy my own stamps. I hope it wont be long before I am in work again.'

He was to write again on 22 May: 'I am getting in a bad way. When I have paid the rent I have 9s/9d left on which to live and find a fare here and there in search of work. If it wasn't for my two Girls giving me 10/- between them I should be done for. You can just imagine what it feels like to have to hang about idle and wait for ones youngsters to have to bring one a little for sustenance . . . It is only the thought that everything happens for the best that keeps a little faith in me. I begin to feel very small in my own eyes so I may do so in other peoples.'

Two days later again, in reply to a (now lost) letter from TSE: 'Yours to hand. Thanking you very much. You are not alone in wondering when the tide is going to turn. But when it does I shall know that I have been kept afloat by the best (pal) & whitest man that it is possible for one to meet. My little girl has got a job near home and comes in to meals & bed. They give me 12/- per week between them. So you can guess the kind of struggle I am having with the "Wolf". I should be glad of the suit. I am not badly off for clothes on the whole but I have no working clothes. It is boots that wear out first. I have a sort of a hunch that something will turn up soon. If I could get a job away I can place the girls alright. But it is a bit of a wrench after keeping a roof over one's head for nearly 30 years to have to make a break. Still there it is and it is ordained by One that knows best.'

TSE promptly sent him some money that week, for Sollory acknowledged the gift on 26 May: 'I am more than grateful to you. You have been a *God send* to me . . . I feel much better for the time being having got rid of a few debts. But I have not lost sight of the fact that it is you and not me who has paid. I only wish I could be of some service to you in return.'

TO *J. L. Beaumont James*

22 April 1932 [Faber & Faber Ltd]

Dear Sir,

I am afraid it may appear to you that we have kept your book on Catholicism an unduly long time, but I am sure you will understand that its length and the seriousness of its character necessitated many and careful readings. It has now been fully discussed by our Board, and all its chances of success have been exhaustively examined. The Board was unanimous in its view that your book contained a very great deal that was most valuable and important, but the final verdict was that it was too great a proposition for a general publishing house like ourself to undertake. In view of the approaching centenary of the Oxford Movement there is likely to be an enormous number of books more or less of this character thrown on the market, and, unless sponsored by some specially equipped firm such as S.P.C.K., we feel that your book could not justify the very great risk entailed in its publication.

I am therefore returning it to you with many regrets that we can go no further in the matter, but also with many thanks for giving us this opportunity of seeing the book.

Yours faithfully,
[T. S. Eliot]

TO *D. S. Mirsky*[1]

22 April 1932 [*The Criterion*]

Dear Mirsky,

In the hope that you are still in London I am writing first to ask if you can lunch with me one day within a week or two, and secondly to say that

---

1–Dmitri S. Mirsky (1890–1939): son of Prince P. D. Svyatopolk-Mirsky, army officer and civil servant (on his mother's side he was descended from an illegitimate son of Catherine the Great). Educated at the University of St Petersburg, where he read Oriental languages and classics, he served as an army officer and was wounded during WW1 while fighting on the German front; later he served in the White Army. In 1921, he was appointed lecturer in Russian at the School of Slavonic Studies, London (under Sir Bernard Pares), where his cultivation and command of languages brought him to the attention of a wide literary circle. His works include *Contemporary Russian Literature* (2 vols, 1926) and *A History of Russian Literature from the Earliest Times to the Death of Dostoevsky, 1881* (1927). In 1931 he joined the Communist Party of Great Britain ('Why I became a Marxist', *Daily Worker*, 30 June 1931), and in 1932 returned to Russia where he worked as a Soviet literary

I have just received a copy of the December number of *Echanges*.[1] I had to write to you to tell you how good I think your article about my poetry is. I am hardly a judge of such articles, but to me at least this was about the most interesting thing that I have ever read, and short of being a Marxist myself I am very much in agreement with it. I wish that you might even do a book about contemporary English literature from your own point of view.

Thirdly would you consider contributing to the September *Criterion* a note of 2000–2500 words on H. G. Wells's last book, *The Work, Wealth and Happiness of Mankind*? What I want is to get four people from very different points of view to contribute their opinions on the same book. A. L. Rowse will write one, and I have yet to find two representatives of other forms of orthodoxy or heresy. The note might, or might not, as the writer prefer, be limited to a criticism of this book, or might deal more largely with the total value of Wells's compendious works and of his significance for the present time. I should be extremely grateful if you would take part.[2] I hope that I may be able to see you soon, and I should very much regret it if we could not meet again before you leave England.

Yours ever sincerely
[T. S. Eliot]

TO *Algar Thorold* CC

22 April 1932   [*The Criterion*]

Dear Thorold,

Thank you for your card of the 20th. I shall be glad to have a note

---

critic (and met Edmund Wilson and Malcolm Muggeridge). In 1937 he was arrested in the Stalinist purge, found guilty of 'suspected espionage', and sentenced to eight years of correctional labour: he died in a labour camp in Siberia. See G. S. Smith, *D. S. Mirsky: A Russian–English Life, 1890–1939* (2000).

1–Of Mirsky's article, '*Eliot et la fin de la poésie bourgeoise*', TSE would later write that it 'considerably exceeds the importance of the nominal subject' ('Commentary', C. 11 [July 1932], 678). TSE glosses in his 'Commentary' the 'modern theory of art' to which Mirsky addressed himself: 'It is (to put it crudely) that art is entirely a form of social expression, that it is determined in its forms by social and economic conditions, that it is wholly relative to these conditions and has no meaning beyond them. I cannot, of course, hold this view myself: it seems to me that this would reduce all art, once the society which produced it had passed away, to mere archæological remains or at best, object-lessons or obscure prophecies. And anyone who is committed to religious dogma must also be committed to a theory of art which insists upon the permanent as well as the changing.'

2–Mirsky, 'H. G. Wells and History', C. 12 (Oct. 1932), 1–9.

from you, preferably a couple of pages about Lossky's book for the June number.[1] I have not kept a copy of the *Listener*, but I have ordered a few more, and I shall be able to lend you one when they come.[2] I have not yet had time to read the current *D.R.*, not even Belgion's article, but will write to you again when I have looked through it.[3]

By the way may I count upon Maine de Biran for my December number? You know I am anxious to collect a set of first rate articles for the three numbers which will appear while I am out of England. In fact I am particularly anxious to have some good stuff in *The Criterion* then.

Yours ever,
[T. S. Eliot]

TO *Tom Faber*[4]   TS EVE

[?23 April 1932][5]   [Faber & Faber Ltd]

Dear Tom,

This morning I got Up and I Thought to myself: 'It must be Almost Tom's Birthday, so I must Write Him a Letter. What Shall I Do? So I went to Speak to Cook, because she is Clever; and I Said to her: 'It must be almost Tom's Birthday, So I Must write Him a Letter. What shall I Do?' So Cook said:

'Let me Make you a nice Cuppatee'.

So I had a Nice cuppatee, and then I Felt better, and then I Knew What to Do, So

---

1–Thorold considered N. O. Lossky's *Freedom of Will* 'very interesting. It depends entirely . . . on his general philosophy & particularly on his "The World as an Organic Whole". Plotinus & Solovyov are his masters. The Russian anti-Soviet philosophers in exile are very important in my opinion based on what I have read of them in translation.' See C. 12 (Oct. 1932), 124–31.

2–'Cd you lend me a copy . . . of your last "dilemma" talk – the one given on Easter Sunday.'

3–'The Values of Contemporary Apologetics: A Symposium 1': Montgomery Belgion, *Dublin Review* 190: 381 (Apr., May, June 1932), 211–24. 'Will you tell me frankly what you think of current *D.R.*? I have tried to make it rather "lighter", but fear I may have made it too light!?'

4–Tom Faber (1927–2004), physicist, publisher – TSE's first godchild – was to take a double first in physics at Trinity College, Cambridge; thereafter he became a Fellow of Corpus Christi College, Cambridge, 1953–2004; Lecturer in Physics, 1959–93, specialising in superconductivity, liquid metals and liquid crystals; he wrote *Introduction to the Theory of Liquid Metals* (1972) and *Fluid Dynamics for Physicists* (1995). From 1969 he was a director of Faber & Faber, and served as Chairman of Geoffrey Faber Holdings, 1977–2004. TSE paid tribute to the young Tom in his preface to *Old Possum's Book of Practical Cats* (1939).

5–Tom Faber's birthday was 25 Apr.

I put on my Roller Skates –
(to Save Time) –

And I SPED to Woolworth's –

AND I Bought a Typewriter –

And a Useful Table –

AND a Practical Chair –

AND then I Sat down to
Write a Letter to Tom. It
said:

Dear TOM,

I Beeleaf it is Somewhere Just About your Birthday, and you will Feel that You are Getting very Old, so I Want to write you a letter. I hope that the Sloop Yacht Estelle sails Proppaly, and that the Weather at Ty Glyn Aeron has been Good, & not Too many Squalls & Hurricanes & Un-favour-able Winds, so that She (that means Estelle) has been able to Cruise. If Not, then We must go Up to the Pond in Hampstead when You come Back, and see what's Wrong.

Your fexnight Uncle,
TOM.

P.S. The Porpentine Cat has been in Bed with Ear Ache, so the Pollicle Dog stopped at Home to Amuse it by Making Cats' Cradles; so That's why They did Not come to Woolworth's with me. But it is Nearly Well now.

TO *Elmer Edgar Stoll*[1]   CC

28 April 1932   [*The Criterion*]

Dear Professor Stoll,

I must apologise for keeping your essay so long.[2] I am sorry after all that I do not find it quite suitable for the *Criterion*, but I hope that you will have more material to offer me, perhaps some longer consideration of *Paradise Lost*

It is possible that I may have the pleasure of seeing you next winter. I have a cousin living in St Paul, and I may find it possible to stop there if I take a trip to the Far West.

Yours sincerely,
[T. S. Eliot]

TO *Michael de la Bedoyère*[3]   CC

28 April 1932   [*The Criterion*]

Dear Mr de la Bedoyère,

Thank you for your note of the 25th enclosing your essay on Censorship. It is an interesting essay and may provoke discussion and I should like to publish it. May I keep it for publication, probably in the December number? I am in the position of having to find good material in advance

---

1 – E. E. Stoll (1874–1959) was Professor of English at the University of Minnesota; author of works including *Poets and Playwrights* (1929) and *Art and Artifice in Shakespeare* (1933).
2 – An essay on Milton.
3 – Michael de la Bedoyère (1900–73) entered the Society of Jesus and gained first-class honours in philosophy, politics and economics at Campion Hall, Oxford, before a crisis of faith caused him to relinquish his noviciate. By birth a count in the French nobility, he worked as assistant editor to his uncle and father-in-law Algar Thorold on the *Dublin Review* before becoming editor of the *Catholic Herald*, 1934–62. Works include *The Drift of Democracy* (1931), *Lafayette* (1933), *Christian Crisis* (1940) and a study of Baron von Hügel.

for the numbers of the *Criterion* which will appear during my absence in America, and it would be a great help to me to have your essay among it.[1]

Yours sincerely,

[T. S. Eliot]

TO *Douglas Jerrold*   CC

28 April 1932   [*The Criterion*]

Dear Jerrold,

I have now received and read your revised version of 'Authority, Mind and Power',[2] and if I may say so without impertinence I think that I was right in feeling that it would be more effective in the form of an article than in that of a pamphlet. It seems to me very much improved and you will know without my telling you the extent to which I am in agreement with it.

I only wish to raise the question of the date of publication. I think that I told you at the time that I should be glad to use it in the June number. Since then I have discovered that I was committed to more publications in that issue than I had supposed, and what has made things the most difficult is that I have an article on the work of Harold Monro which I feel ought not to be postponed to a later issue because Monro was for a long time so closely associated with the *Criterion* and its work.[3]

Now, if it is of vital importance to you that your essay should be published in the June number I must manage to make room for it somehow. In that case, however, I shall be obliged to truncate it, or rather I shall have to omit the first nine pages and pages 29–34. It is rather a long paper. I should much prefer to publish it in full in September, but I must leave the decision to you. I should be very grateful if you could let me know immediately as I must very shortly arrange the final form of the June issue.[4]

Yours ever,

[T. S. Eliot]

1 – 'Censorship: More or Less', C. 13 (Jan. 1934), 252–69.
2 – David Higham submitted a revised version of the MS by Jerrold. Jerrold himself told TSE on 13 Apr. that he had 'taken out of the particular references to which [you] objected and have put them them back in a generalised form which will not create any heartbreakings'.
3 – Ezra Pound, 'Harold Monro', C. 11 (July 1932), 581–92.
4 – Jerrold responded (29 Apr.) that he was content for the article to appear in Sept.; all the same, he disagreed with TSE and proposed in due course to publish an enlarged version as a pamphlet. See 'Authority, Mind and Power', C. 12 (Jan. 1933), 223–43.

TO *Ernest Rhys*[1]   CC

28 April 1932   [Faber & Faber Ltd]

Dear Mr Rhys,

Thank you for your letter of the 22nd.[2] I brought up the question at our last committee meeting. It would be indeed a great honour to be able to publish a book of your verse, but as we have already several commitments for future volumes and as we find that any volume of verse nowadays is almost a complete loss to us, we regret that we cannot in the present circumstances contemplate taking any more poetry. I can only hope that the world may change at least enough for good verse to be able to pay for itself.

With many regrets,
I am,
Yours sincerely,
[T. S. Eliot]

TO *Montgomery Belgion*   CC

28 April 1932   [*The Criterion*]

My dear Belgion,

Thank you for your letter of the 20th and 23rd. First about Malraux. I have tried to get a copy of the French version of *Lady Chatterley's Lover*, to find that London booksellers are frightened and do not import it. So the only safe thing would be for him to tear out his introduction and send it to me separately, though I do not suppose that I should be liable to a criminal prosecution if he posted me the whole book. However, I have no idea whether I should prefer the introduction or a part of his novel, and if he is so inclined I should very much like to see a section of the latter as well.[3]

1–Ernest Rhys (1859–1946): author and editor; friend of WBY and Madame Blavatsky, and participant from 1890 in the Rhymers' Club. From 1906 he was editor of Everyman's Library (J. M. Dent & Sons), which brought 983 volumes into print by the date of his death.
2–'I wonder if Messrs Faber would care to consider a small book of poems, – "Rhymes & Unrhymes", – which I have written in the last 15 or 16 years. Here are two or three experimental pieces . . . I could secure a small edition against loss.' See Rhys's *Rhymes for Everyman* (1933).
3–Belgion wrote on 23 Apr.: 'Malraux thinks it is extremely decent of you to want to publish something of his. Unfortunately, he has nothing on hand and is fully taken up with finishing his novel, the second part of his trilogy. He wonders if you might not like to

I should like to know more about the man you mention – Thierry Maulnier.[1] My subscription to the *Action Française* lapsed just about the time when the pound fell, and I felt, as I am sure you will approve, too patriotic to export the equivalent of 190 francs for the purpose of renewing it, so I have never noticed anything that he has written. But if there is any book or pamphlet that he has written I should like to get hold of it.

Now about your Gide.[2] I am afraid it is too late for the June number. It is partly, however, that two contributions turned up unexpectedly, one of which at least, an essay on Harold Monro, will have to be used. I do not feel, however, that prior publication in French will affect its value and I should like to use it in September. I wish, if I may, to make a suggestion. The manuscript as it stands is suitable in the form of an appendix to your book. The first section, therefore, seems to me to take too much for granted to be quite suitable for a periodical, as it would give the impression that this is merely a personal squabble between you and Gide of no great interest to the general reader. What I do think is important is the thesis of Part 2 which seems to me to deserve further elaboration. Would you consider taking this part by itself and expanding it? The point that it is an enlarged and inordinate demand for what is called "experience" that is considerably responsible for the present situation for the world seems to me a very important one. Part 3 is also of importance but except as illustrating another of Gide's tergiversations is not very relevant to Part 2. I wish you would let me know whether you care to undertake this extra labour.

Yours ever,
[T. S. E.]

---

put into *The Criterion* a translation of the preface he has written to the French version of *Lady Chatterley's Lover*. This contains some of his views on "eroticism" which are very interesting.' 'Preface to the French Translation of *Lady Chatterley's Lover*', C. 12 (Jan. 1933), 215–19.

1 – Belgion (20 Apr.); 'I hear that a young member of the Action Française, Thierry Maulnier – he is only 23 or so – is looked upon as a very promising writer on the contemporary situation.'

2 – Belgion said of his article on Gide, 'I hope you will be able to run it in July so as to be sure it appears in *The Criterion* before it does so in French.' See 'A Postscript on Mr André Gide', C. 12 (Apr. 1933), 404–20.

28 April 1932   68 Clarence Gate Gardens

Dear Mr Hodgson,

This is just to remind you that Miss Bolliger & I have been so forward as to arrange between us that you & she are to come here to dinner tomorrow evening, & we look forward to having you *both*. Then after dinner Miss Bolliger & I intend to steal away to 3 Compayne Gardens so that she shall meet my brother at last, & to leave you with Mr Eliot.

I am *missing* Aurelia tonight, & I am sorry to hear you are feeling the weather today. It *is* depressing & horrid, isn't it? How do we survive it?

Until 6 p.m. tomorrow Friday – please leave A. B. with me for the weekend!

I do so appreciate her company, & it is such a treat to know you both.

Yours very gratefully
Vivienne Haigh Eliot

TO *William Rothenstein*   MS Houghton

2 May 1932   *The Criterion*

Dear Rothenstein

I should have written before now to tell you that Fred Manning is in a nursing home in St Johns Wood: Miss Muir's Nursing Home, 12 Merton Road. He was brought up from Bourne a week ago, apparently at the point of death, but the bronchitis did not turn to pneumonia; when I saw him a few days ago he was coughing violently and smoking cigarettes.

Anyway, he is likely to be there for some days, and asked me to let you know. Of course I don't know, nor did he, how you are at present, or whether you have either strength or leisure enough, but I know that he would like very much to see you, if you were able to visit him.

Yours ever sincerely,
T. S. Eliot

3 May 1932[1]   [Faber & Faber Ltd]

Sir,

I think that Professor Pear has missed the point of my brief remarks about modern psychology; but that, I perceive, is chiefly my own fault.[2] The phrase which I used, 'modern psychology or psycho-analysis', was a deplorable ellipsis. Although it is twenty years since I studied psychology seriously, I was quite aware that psycho-analysis is only one department, or perhaps one type, of psychological study. I should have said: 'modern psychology, which for the purposes of this talk is represented by psycho-analysis'. I was, as the context ought to have made clear, concerned only with psychology in so far as it infringes upon the domain of theology; and that psychologists do so infringe, Freud's *Future of an Illusion* and some of the popular works of Adler make abundantly evident.

I ought also to explain to Professor Pear the point of my joke about 'sublimation'. The joke is, of course, that, as he says, sublimation was invented 'in relation to the sexual instincts'. Professor Pear has not controverted my point that 'sublimation' means practically 'substitution'; or alternatively my contention that the theory of sublimation infringes upon the territory of Werttheorie. The *higher* values (not merely alternative values) exist (or if you prefer, subsist) already; and what we want is the

---

1 – 'What is Modern Psychology', *The Listener*, 7: 174 (11 May 1932), 698. Not in Gallup.
2 – Professor T. H. Pear, in a letter to *The Listener* ('What is Modern Psychology', 4 May 1932), challenged TSE's assertion, given in his talk 'The Search for Moral Sanction' (*The Listener*, 30 Mar.): '"*Modern psychology or psycho-analysis* received its impulse from work at the French School for mental disorders at Nancy, and from the great French psychiatrists, Charcot and Ribot and Janet . . ." (The italics are mine.) This assertion prepared me for the next, that "the psychologists tend to persuade us that we are all ill in mind."

'I think [Pear argued], if Mr Eliot will read a recent *résumé* of psychology, for the general public, Dr C. S. Myers' presidential address to the Psychology section of the British Association for the Advancement of Science (London meeting, 1931), he will not identify modern psychology with one of its branches, important as that branch is . . .

'I re-read Mr Eliot's view of "sublimation" with care, for it is humiliating to overlook a joke. But . . . I take him seriously. The concept of sublimation was originally formed . . . in relation to the sexual instincts . . . Mr Eliot was told by a priest who was told by an habitual thief that she was told by a doctor (name, age and training unspecified) that she had a "complex" which "made her do these things". If a priest told me that a psychoneurotic woman told him that a doctor told her (as he might) that her trouble was due to the thyroid gland, this communication would not make me forget the existence of physiologists or of the Medical Research Council. Nor should I lightly blame upon physiology a single therapeutic error made by a practitioner.'

science which tells us about them; and that science turns out to be theology.

I am, Sir,
Your obedient servant,
T. S. Eliot

TO *Gabriel Atkin*[1]   cc

3 May 1932   [Faber & Faber Ltd]

Dear Mr Atkin,

It has been a cause of great distress to me that your drawings should have been lost.[2] We have had several careful searches made throughout this office. I also saw Ross Williamson a few days ago, and had a further talk with him about the matter. The difficulty is that there is no assurance where the loss occurred. It is not even certain that the drawings left the *Bookman* office. Neither I nor any of the secretaries who might normally have dealt with the drawings when they came in has any recollection of having seen them. I only hope that they may turn up in some unexpected way. I have never known even a manuscript to be lost in this office, and it is extraordinarily unfortunate that such a loss whether in the *Bookman* office or in the post or here should have been of drawings which are irreplaceable.

With very many regrets,
I am,
Yours very truly,
[T. S. Eliot]

1–Gabriel Atkin/Aitken (1897–1937), artist and illustrator, studied at Armstrong College (Newcastle College), King Edward VII School of Art, London, and at the Slade, and lived in London for some years, painting landscapes and illustrating books. After several homosexual liaisons (his lovers included Siegfried Sassoon and J. M. Keynes), he met in 1928 the writer Mary Butts (1890–1937) and was married to her, 1930–4. See *Catalogue of the Loan Exhibition of Paintings and Drawings by Gabriel Atkin* (Newcastle: Laing Art Gallery and Museum, 1940).

2–Atkin (n.d.): 'I am more disappointed than I can say to learn, after all this time, that you have completely lost the drawings for the forthcoming publication of Mary Butts "Alexander" [*The Macedonian*]. Apart from their actual intrinsic value, they were the result of a careful and sympathetic study of the book, but also of the "period" rightness; and there is, as you will realise, no possibility of repeating them . . . I beg of you to have a further intensive search.'

TO *C. A. Siepmann*   TS BBC

3 May 1932   Faber & Faber Ltd

Dear Siepmann,

Thank you for your letter of the 30th[1]. I shall be very glad to be of as much use as I can as a member of your committee. Any week-day afternoon is usually possible for me except Mondays and Thursdays on which I have committee meetings. As I think I told you the afternoon suits me very much better than the evening.

Yours sincerely,
[T. S. Eliot]

TO *Ford Madox Ford*[2]   Cornell/CC

3 May 1932   [*The Criterion*]

My dear Ford,

I must apologize for my delay in answering your letter of the 2nd February, but the fact is that I lent your essay to someone to read, and he forgot to return it to me until recently.[3] I should like very much to use the essay if you will allow me to keep it for one of my winter numbers. You see I shall be at Harvard from September until May or June (not every year but only this year) and that means that three numbers of the *Criterion* must appear in my absence. So I am especially anxious to secure now good material to put into these numbers.[4]

1–'I have in mind . . . to call together a small group to discover the means of implementing our present service [*viz.* religious broadcasting] and of extending its appeal to that intelligent and sensitive section of the public for which the various denominational services carry no conviction. Will you help?' Other members of the proposed committee were to include Dr Moberly, J. H. Oldham, John Macmurray, Dr Micklem and Dr Lindsay. All of them consented to get together; and the first meeting duly took place at Broadcasting House on Tues. 31 May.

2–Ford Madox Ford (1873–1939), novelist, memoirist, critic and editor, joined the Welsh Guards in 1915, and fought on the Somme and at Ypres before being invalided out in 1917. The four novels of *Parade's End* (1924–8) drew on his experiences.

3–Ford had written an article, entitled 'Drinking Less Beer', for *XIX Century & After,* 'on England as she looks from abroad'; but then the magazine had refused to publish it 'because, said they: we must all be re-constructive now and I was too pessimistic. The article merely said in effect that if "we" drank less beer and paid some attention to the arts we should get on better.' Might TSE be interested in the piece? TSE agreed (in a now lost letter) to have a look at it, and Ford submitted it on 2 Feb.

4–'Certainly keep the article for any number you like,' replied Ford (22 May). 'Though I should imagine that it will be rather antiquated by the time you print it. You once, by the bye, said you would like to serialize any book I sent you.' Ford's article did not appear in C.

I have not yet come across anybody in London who would like to exchange for apartments in Paris for a month, but I should think that there ought to be plenty of people, and I will ask anyone who seems likely.[1]

Yours ever,

[T. S. Eliot]

TO *Hugh Ross Williamson*[2]　　　　　　　　　　　　　　CC

3 May 1932　　　　　　　　　　　[Faber & Faber Ltd]

Dear Mr Williamson,

Thank you for your letter of the 29th enclosing the pamphlet of the Festival Theatre. I read the programme of your play with interest which remained unsatisfied, and I hope that it may some day be revived at a place where I can see it.

By the way I have become a member of the committee of the Old Vic and Sadler's Wells Society which means that I am supposed to secure as many subscribers as possible. I hope to induce you to support a very worthy and needy cause. The subscription is £1 a year, and the arrangement is that subscribers get their tickets at a slightly reduced rate. So if you go to twenty performances a year you get your money back. I will send you the notices as soon as they are ready.

You are a rash man to want to do a book on me. For one thing my experience is that books about living men of letters, even when the subject is much more distinguished than myself, sell very badly. However, if you persist in the attempt I shall be very glad to give a hand.[3]

Yours ever sincerely

[T. S. Eliot]

---

1 – Ford (in Paris) wanted to exchange apartments with someone in London for a month or two.

2 – Hugh Ross Williamson (1901–78), author, historian, dramatist, journalist and broadcaster, worked on the *Yorkshire Post* (leader writer, drama critic) before becoming editor of *The Bookman*, 1930–4. Geoffrey Grigson would recall that Williamson 'worked hard to drag that tame old-fashioned literary journal from allegiance to the Squirearchy to support of Eliotry and Audenism [and] to conduct what we thought was the necessary game of harassing the Sitwells as pretenders to modernism' (*Times*, 21 Jan. 1978). Robert Waller wrote of him, in *Pilgrimage of Eros:* 'He was exuberant, witty and a bit of a dandy.' In 1943 he was ordained in the Church of England and was for twelve years an Anglo-Catholic curate before converting to Roman Catholicism in 1955. A prolific author, he wrote over thirty-five books, including *The Poetry of T. S. Eliot* (1932), biographies and histories. See too *The Walled Garden* (autobiography, 1956).

3 – Williamson, *The Poetry of T. S. Eliot* (Hodder and Stoughton, 1932).

TO *Gordon Fraser*[1]   cc

3 May 1932   [Faber & Faber Ltd]

Dear Fraser,

Thank you very much for your letter of the 23rd.[2] It is a great pleasure to me to know that you remember an essay which has remained for so long buried in the files of the *Criterion*. I should have accepted your suggestion without hesitation, but for the unfortunate fact that I am bringing out a big book of selected essays in the autumn including everything that I wish to preserve from *The Sacred Wood* on, and I am printing 'The Function of Criticism' in this volume. So I cannot feel that it is any good reprinting it as a pamphlet. Perhaps there might be something later on that might be possible for you to use.

With many regrets,
Yours sincerely,
[T. S. Eliot]

TO *Henry Eliot*[3]   TS Houghton

5 May 1932   Faber & Faber Ltd

My dear Henry,

It was very satisfactory to receive your *Rumble Murders*[4] (the title puzzled me at first until I found out that a rumble is the same thing as a dickey). And I am very glad to have your letter.[5] It has been on my mind and conscience that I have not written to you, although I did write in reply to yours about my broadcast talk, and you have not written since and do not allude to that letter.

I read any detective story with enjoyment, but I think yours is a very good one; I am simply amazed at any human mind being able to think out all those details. I am quite sure that I could never write a detective story myself; my only possible resource for adding to my income would be

---

1–Gordon Fraser (1911–81), book and greetings card publisher, established in 1930 an imprint called The Minority Press while a student at St John's College, Cambridge, issuing several pamphlets by FRL and others; and from 1935 he ran a bookshop in Portugal Place. He would later become world-renowned as a publisher of greetings cards.
2–Fraser asked with enthusiasm if he might reprint TSE's essay 'The Function of Criticism' (*Criterion*, Oct. 1923) as a Minority Press pamphlet.
3–Henry Ware Eliot, Jr (1879–1947), TSE's brother: see Biographical Register.
4–The story was published by Houghton Mifflin (1932), as by 'Mason Deal'.
5–Not found.

to write children's verses or stories, having had a little success in writing letters to children (and illustrating them of course). But apart from my astonishment at your skill in plot, I was especially interested by the book as a social document – I guessed that it was probably Winnetka.[1] The picture of that society is extremely interesting to me; there is nothing like it in England. For one thing, you would never get that combination of wealth, crudity and intellectual activity. 'County people', who form the stupidest, most intolerant and most intolerable part of society in England, would never collect incunabula or mention Proust; intellectual activity, and interest in art and letters, is found in isolated individuals all over the country, but otherwise is confined to a limited society, drawn from various natural classes, and most of the individuals composing which, I probably know.[2]

I am very sorry to hear of the state of your finances, and of Margaret's.[3] My own are none too healthy, and it will be some years before I am on the right side of the Income Tax account. I imagine that I am some hundreds of pounds in debt to them, covering some years back. That is partly due to exceptional expenses at times in past years, to having taken a house because I thought Vivienne wanted it and then finding that she did not like it – it was about the worst small house in London, and I have had to carry it for two years and only get rid of it in September. And partly because things being as they are in my private life I find it impossible to live below a certain scale, and V. is not a very economical housekeeper. I am hoping to clear a good bit of my takings next winter, towards paying off debts. It will be expensive keeping V. in England during my absence, but it would be still more expensive to take her with me, besides the fact that it would cripple me and prevent me from doing the extra lecturing. And finally, I do very much need a rest; and even the most active life will be restful if I am alone. Ada has very kindly offered to take me in during the second half year, and that would be a considerable saving in expense, though the terms she suggests are too absurdly low.

1 – A very prosperous community near Chicago.
2 – HWE made the first two paragraphs of this letter available for publication, in abbreviated form, in an article 'Book Marks for Today', *New York World-Telegram*, Tues. 31 May 1932, 23.
3 – Margaret Dawes Eliot (1871–1956), TSE's second oldest sister, resident in Cambridge, Mass; never married. In an undated letter (1952) to his Harvard classmate Leon M. Little, TSE wrote: 'Margaret is 83, deaf, eccentric, recluse (I don't think she has bought any new clothes since 1900).'

Probably before Christmas I am going to Bryn Mawr and Princeton, one lecture at each, and to give three lectures at Johns Hopkins;[1] I imagine that can all be done in one trip. I could stop over in New York either going or coming, or both – I should like a room at some small hotel near you[2] – I don't want to be in N.Y. very long at one time, because there must be a good many literary folk whom I don't want to see; but I very much want to see you as soon as possible. Then after Christmas (as I do not have to be back at Harvard till February) I mean to go to St Louis (stopping with Aunt Rose who has invited me); and if I can get an engagement or two to help pay the way I should like to get as far as the west coast, even; as I feel that this is the only opportunity of a lifetime to explore America a little at moderate cost.

I shall not sail to New York if I can help it. I may take a Boat to Boston, or preferably to Montreal and arrive in Boston by train. It is not yet settled how V. is to be looked after in my absence.

Harcourt Brace will publish a book of my *Selected Essays* – quite a big book – in the autumn, for which they promise 500 dollars advance; I am negotiating for the sale of three broadcast Dryden talks to another firm;[3] I may possibly revise and amplify the four talks on 'The Modern Dilemma' which I gave for the London B.B.C. in March; and I have my lectures to prepare.

I was pleased to see that Washington University honoured grandpa in the record of their 75th anniversary which they have sent me.[4]

Ever affectionately your brother
Tom

---

1 – See *VMP*, ed. Ronald Schuchard (1993).
2 – HWE was at 344 West 72nd Street, NYC.
3 – *John Dryden The Poet The Dramatist The Critic* (New York: Terence & Elsa Holliday, 1932).
4 – *Washington University 1857–1932: Seventy-fifth Anniversary of the Inauguration* (1932) saluted William Greenleaf Eliot (1811–87), one of the founders and third chancellor of the university.

HWE replied on 15 May: 'Your letter ... with its praise of the *Rumble Murders* has cheered and heartened me immensely. It is certainly the most sympathetic comment on the story that I have received. Houghton Mifflin were and seem still convinced that it is a good story, and a Unitarian minister in Brooklyn ... wrote me an enthusiastic letter telling me how he kept his whole family up in the evening until he had finished reading it aloud ... I have received $200 (less 10% agent's fee) but I think that is probably all that I shall receive ... I am writing another story (which I think is much better than the first), and without this activity I should become melancholic. The writing of detective stories is a better "escape" than the reading of them.

'I hope you will get to St Louis, in the course of your engagements. I also hope that you may give a lecture at Washington University; it would, to my mind, be a beautiful and

TO *Bernard Bandler*[1]

6 May 1932   *The Criterion*

Dear Mr Bandler,

Thank you for your letter of the 26th April. I doubt the advisability of publishing any of the Norton lectures in periodical form before their production as a book, even if that is permissible by the terms of the foundation. But I can offer you, if you would care to have it, a part of an unfinished poem which so far has only appeared in a French translation in *Commerce*.[2] I have not published it here and I doubt whether *Commerce* has any circulation in America.

Yours sincerely,
T. S. Eliot

TO *A. L. Morton*

6 May 1932   [*The Criterion*]

Dear Morton,

Thank you for your letter of the 23rd enclosing your reply to Gallox. Unfortunately I found that for special reasons the June number was already over-crowded, so that I have had to postpone two other articles until September. But I found your article very interesting and should like to use it then if I may. It is a pity that it could not follow immediately the second Gallox article. In view of the delay I should suggest that a new title might be found for it, and that a note should be included giving the reference to the Gallox articles. Your own, however, stands on its own

---

dignified gesture. It would please me very much also if they should give you some kind of honorary degree . . . I feel more sentiment about the family and appreciate our forebears more than I ever used to in youth. I received a copy of the memorial to W. G. E. [William Greenleaf Eliot] . . .

'You are wise to come by way of Montreal, and escape the "ship news" reporters and newsreel and camera men. Publicity is all right, but I imagine that one's utterances are sometimes badly garbled . . .

'Your visit here will do you immense good nervously and physically, and your welcome in intellectual circles will be most enthusiastic. I rejoice in it.'

1–Bernard Bandler II (1905–93), co-editor of *Hound & Horn*. Born in New York, he gained an MA in philosophy from Harvard University, where he taught for two years before enrolling in the College of Physicians and Surgeons at Columbia University: he was in practice for many years as psychiatrist and Boston University professor.

2–'Difficultés d'un homme d'état' (trans. Georges Limbour), *Commerce* 29 (Winter 1932), 79–87.

feet and it does not require a previous reading of the Gallox essay in order to be understood.[1]

Yours sincerely,
[T. S. Eliot]

TO *Lilian Donaghy*[2]   CC

6 May 1932   [*The Criterion*]

Dear Mrs Donaghy,

I was glad to have your letter of the 20th April as I had had no news of you and your husband for so long.[3] I trust that the slight relapse you mention was quite transient and that your husband's progress will continue to established good health. But I appreciate the heavy burden of anxiety as well as responsibility which you are obliged to bear. I have no objection to your having used my name. I have not heard from the *Evening Press* but if they write to me I shall be very glad to say all that I can to help you.

With renewed good wishes,
Yours sincerely,
[T. S. Eliot]

TO *Léon de Poncins*[4]   CC

6 May 1932   [*The Criterion*]

Dear Sir,

I must apologise for my delay in acknowledging your letter enclosing the manuscript of 'La France contre l'Americanisme' which was due to

---

1 – Morton, 'Poetry and Property in a Communist Society', C. 12 (Oct. 1932), 45–53. Reply by 'Gallox' (Aline Lion), C. 12 (Jan. 1933), 271.

2 – Lilian Donaghy, née Roberts: wife of the Irish poet John Lyle Donaghy.

3 – Lilian Donaghy wrote from Dublin that after a period when her husband Lyle was doing well in Dublin, he had again become 'very queer' and said 'that he wished to be free'. She understood that he had 'gone back to his people in County Antrim'; he was annoyed with her for becoming a Roman Catholic, but he had 'even said' that 'that was not the real reason he had left me'. She had hopes of becoming woman's editor of a new Dublin newspaper – the *Evening Press* – but wished to apologise to TSE for putting his name down as a referee without asking permission.

4 – Léon de Poncins (1897–1976), French Catholic journalist and author, was increasingly obsessed with a Masonic–Jewish conspiracy working to undermine Catholic doctrines and institutions. His several publications include *Les Forces secrètes de la Révolution* (1928):

my uncertainty about the date on which I could use it. I have not yet had the space available, but if you are willing to leave it with me, I can promise to use it at some time during the coming winter. When the time comes I will give you due warning, so that if you feel it is desirable you can make any alteration that may be needed to bring it up to date.[1]

Yours sincerely,

[T. S. Eliot]

TO *Montgomery Belgion*   cc

6 May 1932   [Faber & Faber Ltd]

My dear Belgion,

Thank you for your very useful letter of the 3rd instant. I hope that I may soon hear from Malraux. I have ordered Maulnier's book from Zwemmer.[2]

Perhaps I was rather confused about your meaning.[3] Anyway I think all that the article absolutely needs is that Part I should be reduced or omitted and that 2 and 3 should be put together a little more tightly. So when you have time to do this I shall be glad to have it back.[4]

I have been meaning to ask you about several French writers hitherto unknown to me. One is named Daniel Rops,[5] and there is another man

---

Freemasory and Judaism: The Secret Powers behind Revolution (1929) and *Judaism and the Vatican* (1967). He had met TSE in London in Nov. 1931.

1 – 'France's Fight Against Americanization', C. 12 (Apr. 1933), 339–54.

2 – Thierry Maulnier, *La Crise est dans l'homme*. A. Zwemmer (English and Foreign Books, Prints and Modern Pictures), 76–78 Charing Cross Road, London WC2: see Nigel Vaux Halliday, *More Than a Bookshop: Zwemmers and Art in the Twentieth Century* (2001).

3 – Belgion responded to TSE's letter of 28 Apr. above: 'Thanks very much for your interesting and kind comments on my Gide. Your words, however, "It is an enlarged and inordinate demand for what is called 'experience' that is considerably responsible for the present situation of the world", are not entirely clear to me . . . Be that as it may, the fact is that I do not think, and I do not say in my article, that the current emphasis on "experience" is responsible for any situation. What I do think, and say, is that the value we now attach to "experience" is reflected in the growth of class hostility and in the way national hatreds have become fiercer and deeper.

'This being so, I do not quite see how I could elaborate the article in the way you suggest. It would of course be easy to suppress Part 1. Also, while I do think Parts 2 and 3 are at present related, I could without difficulty knit them more tightly together, and in doing so I would no doubt take up a little more space in order to make myself clearer.'

4 – 'A Postscript on M. André Gide', C. 12 (Apr. 1933), 404–20.

5 – Daniel-Rops, pseud. of Henri Petiot (1901–1965), historian, novelist, biographer, essayist; Professor of History in Chambéry, then in Amiens, and finally in Paris; elected to the Académie française, 1955. His publications include *Notre inquiétude* (1926), *L'âme obscure* (1929), *Le peuple de la Bible* (1943) and *Histoire de l'Eglise du Christ* (1948–65).

whose name I have forgotten, but whose book I have at home called *Les Chiens de Garde*. Also can you tell me anything about the Comte du Plessis?

The manifesto which I return herewith seems all right to me and at least in its present form I think I can certainly support it. So I think it is safe to ask you to tell Dandieu that I should like to have his article.[1] I must repeat that I am very grateful to you for taking the trouble to make these suggestions. Your collaboration in connection with French writers should be very useful.

Yours ever,
[T. S. Eliot]

TO *Mary Swan*   CC

6 May 1932   [Faber & Faber Ltd]

Dear Madam,

Thank you for your interesting letter of the 26th April.[2] I should be much interested to see one of the books you mention.[3]

Yours sincerely,
[T. S. Eliot]

1 – Belgion had enclosed a manifesto by 'a group of Frenchmen of my own age or younger who propose to work for a revolution in favour of what may be called "improved Proudhon". The revolution is to be brought about by Fabian tactics and is to occur throughout the world.' Arnaud Dandieu – co-author of *Décadence de le nation française*, a work TSE had noticed in one of his 'Commentaries' – wished to submit to TSE an expository article on the lines of the manifesto.

2 – Mary Swan, Hon. Sec. of the Psychological Aid Society, remarked that TSE's broadcast on the 'Modern Dilemma' 'contained some remarkably apposite statements about the relation of Psychology to Religion'. The Psychological Aid Society 'holds firmly the belief that a correct understanding of the dream symbolism leads the enquirer to the same point of view as the teaching of Christ' – 'the belief that there is a process of spiritual regeneration going on within the interior consciousness of the subject which is related to the function of dreaming'. She offered to send TSE two textbooks written by the President of the Society, Miss J. Turner – *The Psychology of Self-Consciousness* and *Human Psychology as seen through the Dream* – setting out this new point of view 'which departs from the position of the well known dream psychologists in postulating that every element in the dream is (a) subjective & (b) symbolical'.

3 – Swan sent TSE both books on 9 May.

TO *Kenneth Clark*[1]   CC

10 May 1932   [*The Criterion*]

Dear Sir,

I am writing to ask whether you would be willing to review Adrian Stokes's *The Quattro Cento* for the *Criterion*. The book has only just appeared, but I am anxious to have it reviewed, if possible for the next number of the *Criterion* which is already in press. That means, unfortunately, that there is very little time in which to read the book and review it, but I am sending the review copy in the hope that you will be sufficiently interested to let me have a review of 1000 words by Monday 23rd, which would be the very last day possible. This is asking a great deal of you, but I do hope you will find it possible. I shall be grateful, in any case, if you will let me have a line to say whether you care to review the book, and whether you can attempt to review it within the time.[2]

                              Yours very truly,
                              [T. S. Eliot]

TO *Frances Wilkinson Gregg*[3]   CC

11 May 1932   [*The Criterion*]

Dear Mrs Gregg,

I must apologize for the length in time for which I have kept your stories and sketches sent on January 10th.[4] I do not feel that the more

---

1–Kenneth Clark (1903–83), art historian and patron.

2–Clark replied on 11 May, 'I have just come home from a month abroad, and have before me a pile of work, three lectures and two articles, as well as a book which I am writing, all of which are due in the next ten days. So I am afraid that I cannot possibly take on Stokes's book, which requires careful reading and reflection. Of course I might vamp up something but it would not be up to *Criterion* standard.' See Clark's review of *The Quattro Cento: Part 1: Florence and Verona* (F&F, 1932), C. 12 (Oct. 1932), 146–9.

3–Frances Gregg (1884–1941), American writer, was brought up in Philadelphia. Friend of EP and intimate of H.D. (Gregg wrote in her diary: 'Two girls in love with each other, and each in love with the same man. Hilda, Ezra, Frances'), she married in 1912 the writer Louis Wilkinson ('Louis Marlow') after breaking with H.D. (though she divorced him in 1923). She had contributed poems to *The Egoist* and *Others*. See Gregg, *The Mystic Leeway*, ed. Ben Jones (1995), which includes an account of Gregg by her son Oliver Wilkinson. Her career is well reviewed by Helen Carr, *The Verse Revolutionaries: Ezra Pound, H.D. and The Imagists* (2009).

4–Gregg worried (10 Jan. 1932) about some of the stories she had sent. 'I don't know whether it is permissible to invent a character who lives among real people like Hilda Doolittle and the Powys brothers, as I have, to a degree, invented my dwarfed onlooker.

biographical parts introducing H.D. and others are quite suitable for the *Criterion*, but I am keeping 'Little Goat' which I shall be happy to publish at the first opportunity.[1]

> Yours sincerely,
> [T. S. Eliot]

TO *James G. Leippert*[2]   cc

11 May 1932   [Faber & Faber Ltd]

Dear Mr Leippert,

Thank you for your letter of March 14th and for doing me the honour of asking me to contribute to *The New Broom*.[3] This would be a great pleasure to me only unfortunately I have nothing on hand at present which I could offer you, and I do not believe that I shall have time to undertake any more writing for another year. I should be very much interested to see a copy of the reorganized *The New Broom*.

> With many regrets,
> Yours sincerely,
> [T. S. Eliot]

They were all such interesting people and, I think, cannot fail to leave their mark upon this period. It seems a pity to lose my memories of them. It would not be a long series, like the novel.'

1 – 'Little Goat', C. 12 (Apr. 1933), 438–40.

2 – James G. Leippert (whose real name was Ronald Lane Latimer), editor and publisher, gained a reputation for producing signed limited editions of contemporary American poets under the imprint of The Alcestis Press, 1935–6. Latimer backed the press as an experiment in printing while he was editor of *Alcestis*, a short-lived poetry quarterly, Oct. 1934–July 1935. He edited two other periodicals under the name Leippert: *the new broom* and *Morningside* (Jan.–Apr. 1932), and also *The Lion and Crown* (Fall 1932–Winter 1933?).

3 – Leippert, then an undergraduate at Columbia University, founder of *the new broom*, an independent magazine, hoped to be able to print 'for the first time either a poem or a critical article by you'. He was keen to increase the prestige of his periodical by publishing 'a little work by one or two of the greatest living writers to first appear in the magazine'. An enthusiast for TSE's work (having won in 1931 the annual Philolexian Poetry Prize for an imitation of TSE's poetry), he would do everything he could to afford a fee for TSE.

TO *Herbert Henson*[1]   CC

11 May 1932   [*The Criterion*]

My dear Lord Bishop,

I do not suppose that you will remember me having met you long ago one evening at Lambeth, and I should have ventured to write to you at this moment even without any introduction. I wish to have Mr H. G. Wells's *Work, Wealth and Happiness of Mankind* discussed in the October number of the *Criterion* from four different points of view. I have already had a promise from an English Radical and a Communist and I am asking Mr Christopher Dawson if he will discuss it as a Roman Catholic. I should be most happy if Your Lordship were able and would consent to discuss the book, and should consider it a great distinction for the *Criterion*. With so many contributors to the same subject the space would of course be limited and I am allowing for from 2000–2500 words from each contributor.

If I receive an affirmative reply I shall forward a copy of the book.

In the hope that Your Lordship may both find the time and the interest to contribute to the discussion,[2]

> I remain,
> Your Lordship's obedient servant,
> [T. S. Eliot]

TO *A. L. Rowse*   TS Exeter

11 May 1932   Faber & Faber Ltd

Dear Rowse,

Many thanks for your note of suggestions.[3] Nothing on earth would induce me to invite Amery[4] for such a discussion, but Henson appeals to

---

1–Herbert Henson (1873–1955), priest, scholar, controversialist; Bishop of Durham, 1920–39.

2–Henson replied the next day that unfortunately he could not undertake the job: he was 'much pressed at the present time, and the sudden death of the Suffragan Bishop has indefinitely increased the pressure'.

3–Rowse wrote (undated): 'The very best suggestion I can think of for a real reactionary to contribute to the Wells symposium, is Henson, Bishop of Durham. I believe he might be prevailed on to do it, as he rather likes contributing to periodicals; & he might write something really brilliant . . . Failing him, what about Amery? He also writes; & it would be interesting to see what such an Imperialist thinks of Wells's ideological cosmopolitanism.

'Or what do you think of asking some nationalist Frenchman . . . For a Liberal point of view, what about Lippmann . . . I very much agree that it wd be good to ask Mirsky.'

4–Leo Amery (1873–1955), British Conservative Party politician.

me more and I have written to him. I may also have Christopher Dawson. I think, as the number of contributors must be limited it is better to confine the choice to Britons, though there are a few new men in France whom I am thinking of for other purposes.

I still seem never to find time to answer your previous long letter, though I have re-read it several times with much pleasure. I should be very glad if we could meet again for lunch before very long and continue the discussion. I am convinced that you are the most lovable prig that I have ever known.[1]

Yours ever affectionately,
T. S. Eliot

I have secured Mirsky.[2]

TO *Jacob Bronowski*   CC

11 May 1932   [*The Criterion*]

Dear Mr Bronowski,

Thank you for your letter of the 7th.[3] I should have been glad to let you review *Fiction and the Reading Public* for the *Criterion*, but the fact is that I want to say something about the book myself and am too selfish to give it up.[4] As for other books, the June number is now filled up, and I think it will be better to wait and see what there is before settling reviews for the September number. Let me have a card in case any other books appear in which you were interested.

Yours sincerely,
[T. S. Eliot]

1–Rowse responded to this remark, on 28 May: 'What nonsense about the lovable prig! You know it's strange to me people can say such things without thinking whether it isn't exactly what other people say about themselves! Anyway, I never expected a reply to my long letter – so long as you didn't mind receiving it.'
2–PS added by hand.
3–Bronowski was reviewing Q. D. Leavis's *Fiction and the Reading Public* for a Cambridge journal, but thought to offer his review to TSE instead. He asked also to review *Dorothy Wordsworth*, by C. M. Maclean.
4–See TSE's 'Commentary', C. 11 (July 1932), 676–83.

TO *P. Mansell Jones*[1]   CC

11 May 1932   [Faber & Faber Ltd]

Dear Mr Jones,

We have read and discussed your book with much interest and sympathy, and it is only after much discussion and hesitation that we have come to the conclusion that we cannot publish it.[2] The first part of the book, descriptive of childhood, is very charming and is what I think is the most effective, but we are doubtful whether the book as a whole would make upon the general public a clear impression of the kind at which you aim in your letter of the 4th April.

I hope, however, that the book may find another publisher, and also that our firm may remain in relations with you.

With many regrets,
Yours sincerely,
[T. S. Eliot]

TO *Christopher Dawson*   CC

11 May 1932   [*The Criterion*]

My dear Dawson,

Would you be willing to contribute to a symposium on Wells's *Work Wealth and Happiness of Mankind* in our October number? I have already secured A. L. Rowse and D. S. Mirsky and am anxious to have points of view more sympathetic to my own more strongly represented. I am also asking the Bishop of Durham but am doubtful whether he will have time. In that case I have several other people in mind. If you have not a copy of the book I will send you one.

1–P. Mansell Jones (1889–1968), educated at University College, Cardiff, and Balliol College, Oxford, was teaching at the University College of South Wales and Monmouthshire, Cardiff; he was later Professor of Modern French Literature, University of Manchester, 1951–6. His works include *Tradition and Barbarism* (1930), *French Introspectives* (1937), *Background of Modern French Poetry* (1951), *Baudelaire* (1951) and *The Oxford Book of French Verse* (ed., 1957).

2–Jones (who had published with F&F a work on the French anti-romantic critics) proposed: 'It is obvious that the nineteenth century systems of education and religion have been powerful agents in perpetuating the wrong tradition. I have had the temerity to attempt a critical account of our "Romantic Education" by tracing its effect upon an individual who has passed through most of its stages. The treatment is autobiographical and my story shows the intimate Bovarism which the system produces . . . [M]y explicit criticism is aimed at the system itself . . .'

With all good wishes,
Yours sincerely,
[T. S. Eliot]

P.S. Each contribution should be about 2000 words.[1]

FROM *Vivien Eliot* TO *Ralph Hodgson*   MS Beinecke

12 May 1932   68 Clarence Gate Gardens

Dear Mr Hodgson,

Aurelia has just told me, & I cannot express to you how much I feel for you.[2] And yet I know you will feel, as in such a case I should, the sooner it is over the sooner to sleep. But you had not looked for or expected this trouble in your year of rest & change. All the same how glad you must be that you were here.

Please accept my real sympathy & all the thoughts of a real friend if you will allow me to think of myself as being your friend.

You have brought so much into my life, & done so much for me in clearing up some things which I never understood, & you have seemed to me like some very solid tower of strength & reality in a world which had become a world of ghosts & shadows & unrealities.

I shall never cease to be grateful to you. Nothing is finished yet, or quite clear. But this is all beside the point. This letter is to tell you that I am with you in your trouble about your brother's death, & that I have seen all the time your courage & wonderful patience & kindness & tact.

Please let us see *you* during the Whitsun holidays. My husband is going to spend the 3 days in bed.

Yours with sincere sympathy & gratitude,
Vivienne Haigh Eliot.

FROM *Vivien Eliot* TO *Aurelia Bolliger*   MS Beinecke

12 May 1932   68 Clarence Gate Gardens

My dear Aurelia,

After you have gone I write this letter to say that I am sorry you did not have a happier evening with us this evening.

---

1 – Dawson agreed (17 May) to write on Wells's book; he submitted his piece on 28 July, but (for unknown reasons) it did not appear.
2 – Hodgson's brother had just died.

I am afraid, my dear girl, that we have come to look upon you as too much one of the family.

But that is in itself the greatest compliment, if you could only see it. I feel so much at ease with you that I can write my 19 letters while you are here, & Mr Eliot can read & grumble & you can arrange the books.

It is all very delightful if you look upon it in the right way. I hope you do.

Some day you & R. H. will come back & pick up all the old threads again.

Remember that you are coming with R. H. here on Sunday at 3.30, & on Monday let us all go down to the country in the car to see my Aunt Lillia at Hindhead.[1]

With my love & thanks,
V. H. E.

TO *F. R. Barry*   CC

12 May 1932   [Faber & Faber Ltd]

Dear Mr Barry,

Thank you very much for your kind letter.[2] I must apologize to you for not having answered immediately. I feel greatly honoured at being invited to give a University sermon, so to speak, but I am afraid that the date, May 28th 1933, makes it impossible for me to accept. I have to be lecturing in America between October and May, and although it is probable that I shall be back by that date, and certain that I shall be back by a few days later, nevertheless I do not feel that it is safe for me to make any engagements. Furthermore I should only just have returned, at best, and should not have the time to prepare an address worthy of the occasion. Otherwise I should certainly have accepted the proposal.

With many regrets,
I am,
Yours very truly,
[T. S. Eliot]

1 – MHW wrote of their maternal aunt, in an undated memoir: 'Aunt Lillia [Symes] was a clown and tremendous fun.'

2 – The Revd F. R. Barry (Balliol College, Oxford; vicar of St Mary-the-Virgin) wrote on behalf of the Committee of the University Church Union to invite TSE to give an address at St Mary's on 28 May 1933 on the topic of 'Organs of Public Opinion': 'As there are normally a thousand undergraduates in St Mary's on Sunday evening the speaker has really a magnificent opportunity and what he says can have a very far-reaching influence.'

TO *Arthur B. Thornhill*

12 May 1932   [Faber & Faber Ltd]

Dear Sir,

Thank you for your letter of May 7th. I was under the impression that I had replied to your previous letter, and if I have not done so I can only apologize for the oversight.[1]

While I am naturally in sympathy with the aims of the Westminster Group, I feel that I prefer not to join or associate myself with any movement in which I am unable to take an active part. If I felt that I had either the time to devote to the work, or that I were especially qualified to be useful to the group I should be very glad to join. But I have always had a dislike of forming a purely nominal connection.

I am,
Yours very truly,
[T. S. Eliot]

TO *The Vice Chancellor, University of Leeds*   CC

12 [or 13] May 1932   [Faber & Faber Ltd]

Dear Mr Baillie,

I am very much obliged to you for your kind letter of the 10th instant.[2] I should be very happy to deliver a lecture at the University at some time or other, but unfortunately I am this winter lecturing in America and must leave England some time during September, not returning until the end of May. I must therefore decline your kind invitation with much regret.

Yours sincerely,
[T. S. Eliot]

1 – The Revd Arthur Thornhill, Secretary of the Westminster Group, had invited TSE to join the Group in a letter of 7 Feb. 1932: 'The Group is not a "party". It seeks to unite people of all points of view who are willing to put "Church before party", in love for, & defence of, the Church.'

2 – J. M. Baillie, Vice Chancellor of Leeds University, invited TSE to lecture 'on some literary topic in which you are yourself particularly interested'. The honorarium would be 12 guineas.

TO *Gilbert Seldes*   TS Timothy and Marian Seldes

17 May 1932   *The Criterion*

My dear Seldes,

Thank you for your note of the 29th April. If I have your chronicle by
July 15th that will do nicely for the September number. Your suggestion of
the subject matter seems to me very good.[1] I wish you would let me know
how much you intend to say about Wilson's *Devil take the Hindmost*[2]
as I should rather like to arrange for a separate review if you only mean
to touch upon it. If your chronicle arrives just too late for the September
number I will certainly let you have proof back in time to correct it in time
for December.[3]

                         Yours sincerely,
                         T. S. Eliot

TO *J. H. Nelson*   CC

17 May 1932   [Faber & Faber Ltd]

Dear Professor Nelson,

Thank you for your letter of April 16th.[4] As for the selections you
suggest, I should prefer not to publish any of my prose writings, as I am
bringing out a volume of selected essays in the autumn. I should also
prefer not to publish 'The Hollow Men' in an anthology, but I should be
quite willing to have you use any one of the first four of my Ariel poems
that you care to choose.

                         Yours very truly,
                         [T. S. Eliot]

1 – 'About the chronicle, I want particularly to discuss the abandoning of literature by such
people as Edmund Wilson, the rise of a proletarian school, and general things of that sort.'
2 – Edmund Wilson, *Devil take the hindmost (The American Jitters): A Year of the Slump*
(1932).
3 – No further 'American Chronicle' by Seldes appeared in C.
4 – J. H. Nelson, Professor of English, University of Kansas, was editing for the Macmillan
Company an anthology – 'probably' to be entitled *American Literature since 1914* – of
'prose and verse from about seventy-five authors of the twentieth century'; he requested
permission to reprint in the volume, which was to function as a textbook for schools and
colleges, 'The Hollow Men' and 'The Humanism of Irving Babbitt'.

TO *Bonamy Dobrée*   CC

17 May 1932   [*The Criterion*]

My dear Bonamy,

Is [it] possible for you to let me know at once at what time or times
during June you could come up to London? I am writing to Herbert by
this same post to ask the same question. I should like especially to arrange
a *Criterion* meeting when both you and Herbert could be present, if it is
at all possible. After the June meeting it does not seem very likely that we
shall be able to have another full meeting during the summer, and I am
very anxious to have as full a meeting as possible of the original group
before I leave in September.

> Yours in haste,
> [T. S. E.]

TO *Herbert Read*   CC

17 May 1932   [*The Criterion*]

My dear Herbert,

Is it possible for you to let me know at once at what time or times
during June you could come up to London? I am writing to Bonamy by
this same post to ask the same question. I should like especially to arrange
a *Criterion* meeting when both you and Bonamy could be present, if it is
at all possible. After the June meeting it does not seem very likely that we
shall be able to have another full meeting during the summer, and I am
very anxious to have as full a meeting as possible of the original group
before I leave in September.

> Yours in haste,
> [T. S. E.]

TO *P. Mansell Jones*   CC

17 May 1932   [*The Criterion*]

Dear Mr Jones,

Thank you for your letter of the 12th and for reminding me about
the article on Ronsard which I have and which is certainly to be used.
The article has been delayed merely because it falls into that unfortunate

small category of good articles, very useful to an editor – that is to say which have no topical insistence and are therefore extremely comfortable to have in reserve for an emergency. But I promise you that it shall be used this winter.[1] It will be extremely useful to me as I have three numbers to prepare for publication during my absence in America.

With all good wishes,
Yours sincerely,
[T. S. Eliot]

P.S. You will of course receive proof in good time.

TO *George Williamson*[2]   CC

17 May 1932   [Faber & Faber Ltd]

My dear Mr Williamson,

I have wanted for a long time to see you again and am very sorry that day to day, and week to week engagements have had to interfere. I should be very glad if you could lunch with me one day next week, and if you would drop me a line I will write again toward the end of this week and suggest one or two days.

Yours sincerely,
[T. S. Eliot]

TO *Peter Neagoe*   CC

17 May 1932   [Faber & Faber Ltd]

Dear Mr Neagoe,

Thank you very much for your kind letter of May 13th.[3] I wish that I had something unpublished which I could offer you for your interesting anthology, but I am afraid that I have nothing whatever on hand and have

---

1 – 'The Approach to Ronsard', C. 12 (July 1933), 571–84.
2 – George Williamson (1898–1968) taught at Pomona College, Claremont, California, 1925–7; then at Stanford University, and subsequently at the University of Chicago (1936–68), where he was Professor of English from 1940. His works include *The Talent of T. S. Eliot* (1929), *The Donne Tradition* (1930), *A Reader's Guide to T. S. Eliot* (1953). TSE, in a letter to Theodore Silverstein (28 June 1962), called Williamson 'this distinguished scholar', and added: 'I . . . owe him a personal debt for his book about my own work.'
3 – Peter Neagoe, editor of *the New Review* and *New Review Publications* (Paris), pleaded with TSE to contribute 'something representative of your work' to *Anthology of American Artists Abroad* which he was editing: it was quite ready for the press.

not time to carry out any fresh engagements for at least another year.

With many regrets,
Yours sincerely,
[T. S. Eliot]

TO *W. H. Auden* CC

17 May 1932 [Faber & Faber Ltd]

My dear Auden,

Thanks for your note of the 15th.[1] I am very sorry indeed to hear your news. What sort of job do you want? I mean do you want to go on as a school-master or take up something else? I was very much surprised as I thought that you had settled down at Larchfields for some time, and when I last saw you, you spoke hopefully of the change of headmaster.

I am glad you like the production of the *Orators*.[2] I am very well pleased myself with the book, but was rather dissatisfied with the wrapper. It seemed to me very silly to repeat the same notice from the front on the inside flap, and I should like to see the Poems advertised more conspicuously. Is there any chance of seeing you in London at the end of the term?

Yours ever sincerely,
[T. S. Eliot]

1 – WHA wrote from Larchfield Academy, Helensburgh: 'I'm leaving this place at the end of the term. I don't like the future headmaster and anyway I think I've done all I can here. If you hear of any kind of a job for me, I should be most grateful if you would let me know . . . P.S. I've just had to withdraw "The Knight of the Burning Pestle" from school use. One of the governors was horrified at its indecency.'

2 – *The Orators* was published on 19 May. 'I like the get-up of the Orators immensely,' wrote WHA (15 May). And to Richard de la Mare (20 May): 'This is just to thank you very much for the way you got up *The Orators*. I thought it was awfully nice.' *The Orators* was to be favoured in *The Annual Register* 1932 as one of 'the 25 books of the year that really matter'. The blurb, printed on both front cover and inside flap, and in the F&F catalogue (Spring 1932) – it was almost certainly written by TSE – characterised the book thus: 'Of W. H. Auden's first volume of *Poems* (which we published last year) the most discerning readers remarked that the author was often very "obscure", but that he was unquestionably a poet, and one of the few poets of first rate ability who have so far appeared to voice the post-war generation, a generation which has its own problems and its profound difficulties. *The Orators* is not a collection, but a single work with one theme and purpose, partly in prose, and partly in verse in which the author continues his exploration of new form and rhythm. It will not disappoint those who have been excited by the unfamiliar metric and the violent imagination of the earlier book.'

TO *Harvey Foster*   CC

18 May 1932   [Faber & Faber Ltd]

Dear Mr Foster,
   Thank you for your kind letter which I should have answered sooner.[1]
If you should see any opportunity of our meeting while I am in Cambridge
next winter, I should be very happy to make your acquaintance.
                                   Yours sincerely,
                                   [T. S. Eliot]

TO *Louis MacNeice*[2]   CC

18 May 1932   [*The Criterion*]

Dear Mr MacNeice,
   I must apologize for having kept your poems for such a very long time,
but as you have since learnt they arrived in an envelope without any letter

---

1–Harvey Foster, from Hartford, Connecticut, hoped to meet TSE during his visit to the
USA. 'I should like to know you then. One of a thousand requests? And only an hundred
days. I cannot be at Cambridge to be in listening [*sic*]. And that would not be good. Shall I
reiterate the request. I would like to talk with you, say, in a booth at a restaurant, in a room
with lamps, if you will meet me half-way. If you cannot do this, there is nothing. I realize
the largeness of the request. I would feel deeply the largess [*sic*] if the request were granted. I
can make no sustained superficial conversation. Only more or less groping, inchoate, eager.
That is all.'
2–Louis MacNeice (1907–63), brought up in Carrickfergus, was educated at Marlborough
School and Oxford University. In the 1930s he taught Classics at Birmingham University
and Bedford College, London; and for twenty years from 1940 he worked for the BBC as
writer and producer of radio features and plays. His publications include *Autumn Journal*
(1939), *Solstices* (1961) and *The Burning Perch* (1963). TSE wrote of him on 30 May 1941,
to the General Establishment Officer of the BBC: 'Mr MacNeice is extremely well-known
both as one of the leading poets of his generation and as a prose writer. I should certainly
consider that his abilities are such as to make him a valuable addition to the staff of the
British Broadcasting Corporation and very much hope that you will be able to find a place
for him. He is, incidentally, a classical scholar of some distinction, and may be regarded as
belonging to that rather uncommon type, the well-educated man. He has also a very distinct
social charm and likeability.'
   He wrote in *The Times*, 5 Sept. 1963: 'There is little that I can add to the encomiums
of Louis MacNeice which have already appeared in the press, except the expression of my
own grief and shock. The grief one must feel at the death of a poet of genius, younger than
oneself, and the shock of his unexpected death just as my firm had ready for publication a
new volume of his verse [*The Burning Perch*].
   'MacNeice was one of several brilliant poets who were up at Oxford at the same time,
and whose names were at first always associated, but the difference between whose gifts
shows more and more clearly with the lapse of time. MacNeice in particular stands apart. If

from you, and without any indication of an address.[1] I have found them very interesting work. It does not seem to me that this lot quite forms the justification for a volume, but I think I could choose a few for publication in the *Criterion* if that interested you.

If you are ever in London it would be more satisfactory to have a talk about the matter. If there is no likelihood of that I will make a selection and consult you about it.

Yours sincerely,
[T. S. Eliot]

TO *J. de Lacy*   cc

18 May 1932   [Faber & Faber Ltd]

Dear Mr de Lacy,

Thank you for your letter of May 9th.[2] I have, however, considered for some time the proposal of making a new collected edition of my poems, but I still feel that the time has not come. There is not really enough new material yet to make people who possess the 1925 volume feel that they would get their money's worth. I must therefore postpone that consideration for several years.

Meanwhile Faber & Faber are just bringing out a new edition of the 1925 volume priced at 3/6 instead of 7/6.

---

the term "poet's poet" means a poet whose virtuosity can be fully appreciated only by other poets, it may be applied to MacNeice. But if it were taken to imply that his work cannot be enjoyed by the larger public of poetry readers, the term would be misleading. He had the Irishman's unfailing ear for the music of verse, and he never published a line that is not good reading. I am very proud of having published the first volume he had to offer after coming down from the university. [*Blind Fireworks* (1929), his first book, was published by Victor Gollancz while he was still an undergraduate.]

'As for the radio plays, no other poet, with the exception of the author of *Under Milk Wood*, has written works as haunting as MacNeice.'

1–MacNeice's missive had been mislaid (as he explained on 19 Apr. 1932). He added: 'As for the poems themselves I think that only a few of them stand on their own merits, but that as a collection and arranged in a certain order they would supplement each other and make an aggregate of some value. Whereas if I chose a dozen individuals, they would remain, perhaps, merely individuals. It seems to me (as far as I can see myself) that I am not sufficiently in a school for my poems to be readily significant; therefore they have to build up their own explanation' (*Letters of Louis MacNeice*, ed. Jonathan Allison [2010], 228).

2–J. de Lacy (proprietor of the Dunster House Bookshop, Cambridge, Mass.) wondered if Charles Scribner's Sons might be enabled to bring out a new collected edition of TSE's poems.

I look forward to visiting the Dunster House Bookshop next winter.

Yours sincerely,
[T. S. Eliot]

TO *Samuel E. Morison* CC

18 May 1932   [Faber & Faber Ltd]

Dear Morison,

Many thanks for your note of the 2nd.[1] It is very kind of you to be so lenient in the matter, but also very wise as I doubt whether anything I did in the stress of the moment would be worthy of the *Quarterly*. I will, however, be very happy to do some sort of article for you later on, the subject to be arranged when we meet.

I have put down Monday 21st November for the Colonial Society Dinner.

I will keep Volume 1 of the Winthrop papers here until you let me [know] where to send it.[2]

Yours sincerely,
[T. S. Eliot]

TO *Hugh Ross Williamson* CC

18 May 1932   [Faber & Faber Ltd]

Dear Mr Williamson,

Thank you for your note.[3] I have meanwhile sent you a subscription form of the Sadlers Wells Society and am very glad to hear that you will become a member. You will observe that though the Society is formed for

---

1 – 'I expect that we had better give up the idea of your reviewing the Winthrop Papers, for when you once get over here you are certain to find other and more interesting things to do. But may we bespeak anything you may care to write on Puritanism, or New England, for the *N. E. Quarterly*?'

2 – Kenneth B. Murdock, book review editor of *The New England Quarterly*, advised TSE on 8 June to hang on to vol. 1 of the Winthrop Papers; they had sent vols 1 and 2 to another contributor.

3 – Williamson had written (undated), 'I find that my suggestion to write a book on you has matured very rapidly. I spoke of it to one of my directors and – much to my surprise – he has asked me to begin it at once and do it as quickly as possible.

'So, in a few weeks, may I come to see you again and ask your help where my obtuseness stumbles? I really want it to be authoritative – "The Waste Land" is too important to be left any longer to the eccentricities of an individual interpretation (see MacGreevy).'

the benefit of Sadler's Wells the vouchers are available for either theatre. As for the book which you contemplate, I have come across in Walter de la Mare's *Lewis Carroll* a quotation from a letter which Carroll wrote about *The Hunting of the Snark*. 'I am very much afraid' he said, 'I didn't mean anything but nonsense . . . But since words mean more than we mean to express when we use them . . . whatever good meanings are in the book I am very glad to accept as the meaning of the book.'[1]

Yours sincerely,

[T. S. Eliot]

TO *Ezra Pound*   Photocopy of TS

18 May 1932   *The Criterion*

Dear Ezra,

Please confirm which Gilson it is that I am to approach. I was under the impression that it was Etienne, but somebody tells me that there is another one named Paul, and possibly a third named Pierre whom you might have meant. But I think you meant Etienne, and his address is merely Sorbonne, I suppose? I shall also approach your friend Elias of C.C.C. [Corpus Christi College] in any case.[2]

About Stokes, I am sorry, but this has already been offered to one Kenneth Clark whom I do not know, but who was recommended. I have no idea what he will make of it.[3] I think I agree about Stokes so far as I have read. There is a lot of meat, but I think a fair amount of suet as well.[4]

Yours,

T.

1–Williamson replied on 19 May that when he came to finish his commentary on *The Waste Land*, 'I'm going to send you the MS, if I may, because if my interpretation is right, your other commentators are wrong. I argued it with Mirsky yesterday. It's not the incidental explanation I'm worried about, but the attitude as a whole, and I should like to feel I was on the right track.'

TSE agreed in mid-June, in response to a specific request from Williamson dated 14 June, to read his draft section on *The Waste Land* and on 'Word Within Word'. 'I am most anxious', said Williamson, 'to feel that you will approve of my treatment of the religious poems and the general religious standpoint' (see Ross Williamson, *The Poetry of T. S. Eliot* [1932]).

Walter de la Mare, *Lewis Carroll* (1932), 53.

2–*Guido Cavalcanti, Rime* was reviewed by Etienne Gilson, C. 12 (Oct. 1932), 106–12.

3–*The Quattro Cento. Part 1. Florence and Verona*, by Adrian Stokes, was reviewed favourably by K. M. (later Lord) Clark in the same number, 146–9.

4–EP forwarded this letter to Stokes: 'Dear A/ An' thaats thaat. I offered to review it for *Crit.* am now writing to *Symposium* repeating the offer as what I have to say is too long for

TO *Frederick May Eliot*   CC

18 May 1932   [*The Criterion*]

Dear Frederick,

Very many thanks for your letter of May 3rd and for the trouble that you are disposed to take on my behalf.[1] My only question is whether I can arrange my visit at a time of year when the Universities will want lectures. I get a holiday from Christmas until February 1st and propose to make my western trip then; going to St Louis directly after Christmas, then perhaps to Chicago and St Paul, and thence to the Far West. Would it be possible or not to arrange lecture engagements during that period? My only purpose in arranging such engagements in the west is to help to pay the expenses of the journey.

With many thanks,
Yours ever affectionately,
[Tom]

TO *Thomas Dawes Eliot*   CC

18 May 1932   [Faber & Faber Ltd]

Dear Tom,

Thank you for your kind note of the 21st April.[2] It is quite likely that I shall come to Chicago. Indeed I hope to visit St Paul and spend a night or two with Frederick and possibly go out to the west coast. So I warn you that it is quite likely that I shall take you at your word and ask for shelter, though with the primary desire of renewing our acquaintance.

Yours ever,
[Tom]

---

a letter. Certainly a good job and worth doing.' EP's review appeared in *Symposium*, 3: 4 (Oct. 1923), 518–21.

1–Frederick wanted to approach the English Departments at the Univ. of Minnesota and Carleton College to arrange lecture engagements for TSE. 'Elizabeth and I will be simply overjoyed to have you with us, and we are prepared to defend our rights to some real measure of your time against all comers.'

2–Not found.

TO *Ronald Bottrall*[1]   TS Texas

18 May 1932   Faber & Faber Ltd

Dear Bottrall,

I have your letter of the 25th April with manuscript and this morning
your further note of the 10th May.[2] I have read the poem once and it
seems to me about the best thing you have done, but I will not make any
detailed criticisms until I receive the second version. If I may say so, your
metric owes much more to Ezra Pound's *Cantos* than to anything of mine,
and indeed the whole arrangement of the poem is strongly suggestive of
that work. It seems to me, however, to have been a good influence.[3] The

---

1-Ronald Bottrall (1906–89), poet, critic, teacher and administrator, studied at Pembroke
College, Cambridge, and taught in Helsinki, 1929–31, before spending two years at
Princeton University. He was Johore Professor of English at Raffles University, Singapore,
1933–7, and taught for a year at the English Institute, Florence, before serving as British
Council representative in Sweden, 1941–5; Rome, 1945–54; Brazil, 1954–7; Greece, 1957–
9; Japan, 1959–61. At the close of his career he was Head of the Fellowships and Training
Branch of the Food and Agricultural Organization of the United Nations in Rome. His
poetry includes *The Loosening* (1931) and *Festivals of Fire* (1934).
2-Bottrall (Graduate College, Princeton) submitted on 5 Apr. a long poem called 'Festivals of
Fire': 'I began it about five [months ago] and finished it (except for a few minor corrections)
about two months ago, at a time when I did not suspect that Communism would so soon
lead you and Mr Murry to public utterances. My attitude differs widely from your own, but
in this poem, I have pointed to Soviet Russia as a social order which views certain problems
much as I view them; I do not imply that I consider the Bolshevist political system suited to
England, or even to the rest of Europe.
   'The structure of *Festivals of Fire* owes much to the example of *The Waste Land*, but I
believe that I have succeeded in making my own poem personal, and that I am quite outside
any charge of being a parasite or plagiary. The anthropological method is, for me, the most
fruitful one possible, and the one great achievement in that style is your work. I have not
acknowledged my indebtedness to you in my prefatory Note, because the extent of that debt
should be sufficiently clear.'
   On 10 May he wrote that he had 'received from England some lengthy criticisms' of the
poem, and that he would send TSE a corrected version 'as soon as possible'.
3-Bottrall responded to TSE's remarks on 31 May 1932: 'I was most interested to have
your remark on the affinities of my poem with Pound's *Cantos*, because Leavis had already
written to say that he found the influence of the Cantos "fairly pervasive".
   'The strange thing is that I have never possessed a copy of any of the Cantos. About a
year ago I read the first seven Cantos and I naturally admired greatly the technical mastery
shown there, but I made no excerpts for future reference. The planning of *Festivals of Fire*
was done around Xmas and I wrote the first two sections, much as they stand at present, in
January–February. Then followed an interval of about a month during which I got hold of a
copy of the *XXX* Cantos which was borrowed for me by Princeton from Brown University.
I had only time to read the volume through once, carefully, and, again, I made no excerpts.
My memory is of a kind that recollects poetry imperfectly and fragmentarily, except after
long frequentation. I doubt if I could quote two lines from the Cantos correctly, or any two
consecutive lines at all. When I went on with sections III and IV of my poem in March I did

---

only comment I will make at present is that the explanatory note strikes me as an undesirable preface, at any rate for the poem's first appearance.[1]

Are you likely to remain at Princeton for another year? If so I shall expect to see you there at some time during the autumn.

Yours sincerely,
T. S. Eliot

TO *I. A. Richards*

CC

18 May 1932   [Faber & Faber Ltd]

Dear Richards,

Many thanks for your letter of the 3rd.[2] You needn't worry about hurrying the article for me. All I want to know is some date towards the

---

not therefore feel that I had been so greatly influenced by the Cantos, nor did I depart from the scheme I had formulated at Xmas.

'My opinion of the Cantos is that no poet since Pope has shown a greater mastery over his metric than Pound shows in them. But their influence upon my metric must have been almost unconscious and I do not see how they could have influenced the arrangement of my poem at all. I have never studied them as I studied *Hugh Selwyn Mauberley* at an early date in my writing.'

In a letter to the *TLS*, 24 Oct. 1980 – responding to a review of his *Reflections on the Nile* – Bottrall commented: 'I should perhaps mention that Noël Annan (now Lord Annan) thought the poem "Festivals of Fire" was too much influenced by *The Waste Land*. I asked Eliot if he agreed. He replied: "Your poem owes nothing to any work of mine. If it owes anything to anybody it is to Pound in his *Cantos*, but I am not at all sure about that." Faber and Faber, of course, published the book *Festivals of Fire* in 1934. My poetry may not be very good, but I am quite certain that I have written the poems myself, and not under the influence or instruction of anyone else.' The *Times* obituary remarked, 'Bottrall never thought Pound a great poet, but his early poetry is none the less modelled on the latter's *Hugh Selwyn Mauberley*' (27 June 1989).

TSE, in his blurb for *Festivals of Fire*, wrote emphatically of Bottrall: 'Although critics anxious to "place" him have commonly related him to Mr Eliot, actually it is Mr Pound – the Pound of *Mauberley* and the *Cantos* – who has influenced his technique. But his poetry is his own and highly individual, for his attitude to the problems of the contemporary world, his interests and his sensibility are as unlike Mr Pound's as his technique is unlike Mr Eliot's.'

1 – Bottrall responded on 31 May 1932: 'With your comment on the explanatory note I entirely agree. The note is either too specific or not specific enough. I did not think that the poem would ever require a full apparatus of notes, but I thought that some reference to *The Golden Bough*, Arnold and Rimbaud might be necessary. Do you think that the first paragraph might stand?'

2 – 'An article on something or other I will try to contrive fairly soon . . . The probable sort of subject for an article (as well as I can foresee it) might be *Metaphor* – or some analysis of thought & feeling transmutations' (*Letters of I. A. Richards*, 64). See 'Fifteen Lines from Landor', C. 12 (Apr. 1933), 355–70.

end of the year by which I may be sure of having it. As I told you I have to plan out as far as possible three numbers in advance.

I expect to leave England about the middle of September and am thinking of going by way of Montreal. Can you tell me anything about the C.P.R.[1] service? I still hope that I may see you before I leave but there is not much likelihood of my getting down to Cambridge.

By the way I have had a letter from the University of Buffalo asking me to give a lecture there, and mentioning your name. They ask what fee I should expect. Can you suggest a reasonable figure? I don't suppose that any of these institutions have much superfluous money in these times.

With kindest regards to Mrs Richards from both of us.

Yours ever,
[T. S. E.]

TO *F. R. Leavis*

TS L. R. Leavis

18 May 1932   *The Criterion*

Dear Mr Leavis,

I can do nothing but apologize for my delay over your pamphlet, and I am only too well aware that delay in dealing with a pamphlet is like delay in planting flower-beds.[2] I can only plead that I have been extremely busy and very tired and that I kept postponing writing to you in the hope of having more time in which to make my points clear and put them in a helpful way.

I still feel that the pamphlet is open to some of the objections which I raised to the first draft. I think that the greatest weakness for a pamphlet of this sort is the attempt toward the end to outline a constructive policy. In my opinion a pamphlet of this sort ought to be sudden and wholly destructive and leave it at that. You say on page 43 'these brief hints – this is no place for anything more'. I quite agree that this is no place for anything more, but I think that the hints are only enervated by being made so brief. They really belong to another pamphlet or preferably something different from or longer than a pamphlet. After all[,] the

---

1 – Canadian Pacific Railway.
2 – Leavis had written on 27 Apr., 'If my pamphlet "Culture & Authority", is unsuitable for your purpose I should like to have it back. The topical element has, I'm afraid, been going stale, but I might be able to do something with it for [Gordon] Fraser [at The Minority Press, Cambridge], who is worrying me for another pamphlet. Or I might cut an article out of it [for] *Scrutiny*.'

immediate practical possibilities which anyone can offer in opposition to such a tremendous social decay as your previous study indicates must appear but trifling when contrasted so directly with the situation.

My other comments are much as before. I still feel that for the purpose of a general pamphlet there is too much of Harold Nicholson [*sc.* Nicolson] etc.

It is possible, however, that we have been at cross-purposes. I mean that your pamphlet may be aimed and may have its point in being aimed at a more specific audience than that with which the *Criterion Miscellany* can deal. I had not thought of this until you mentioned it yourself in your last note, but it is possible that rather than go on tinkering with this piece of work for a bigger general public you might prefer to issue it with the Minority Press as it stands. Even for a Minority Press pamphlet I should be inclined to maintain my objection to your ending on a constructive note though I should no longer feel quite certain of my opinion. But otherwise the pamphlet would probably, for that purpose, for that Press, be better as it stands than with any alteration.

Do not think that I want in the least to slip out of publishing the pamphlet. I am merely thinking it over coolly and enquiring about your views.

Yours very sincerely,
T. S. Eliot

P.S. I have very much enjoyed reading Mrs Leavis's book, and hope to say something about it in the *Criterion*.[1]

Congratulations on *Scrutiny* No. 1.

1–TSE wrote in his next 'Commentary', discussing Q. D. Leavis, *Fiction and the Reading Public*: 'Mrs Leavis has attempted, not a history of the novel, but a history of the best-seller; a history, therefore, of the changes, and (as one would expect) the decline of taste in the last three hundred years . . . She describes her method as "anthropological"; and if she means by this term, as I suppose she does, that not only individual and social psychology, but also economics and sociology, are no longer to be ignored by literary criticism, then I am wholly in agreement . . . We may say that it was only to be expected that when the whole public had been taught to read, it would choose to read very poor stuff; that the taste of the mob can never be much elevated, because of its invincible mental laziness . . . But there is a good deal more to it than this. An *élite* which is only recognized by itself is in a bad way . . . One of the most interesting phenomena to which she calls attention is in the increasing stratification of literature into classes, each of which prefers to ignore the others. Thus the labour of the few at the top, their labour in developing human sensibility, their labour in inventing new forms of expression and new critical views of life and society, is largely in vain. A society which does not recognize the existence of art is barbaric. But a society which pretends that it recognizes art, by tolerating the Royal Academy and patronizing such novelists as Mr Thornton Wilder, Mr Hemingway and Mr Priestley (at best) is decidedly decadent . . . In a properly organized world the vast majority of novels such as are published to-day would not

TO *G. B. Harrison*

18 May 1932   [Faber & Faber Ltd]

My dear Harrison,

I am sending you herewith the circulars just issued by the Sadler's Wells Society. It occurred to me that some at least of the members of the Shakespeare Association might be interested. This is not merely on my part the perfunctory step of a member of a committee, but represents a desire to help something in which I am very keenly interested. I speak also as a practising member of the audience.

I should like your advice as to whether it would be possible, practicable and worthwhile to circularise the members of the Shakespeare Association. If so, how could the secretary of the committee have access to a list of the members?

And by the way, has the Shakespeare Association Council ceased to meet or have I been silently dropped from its membership?

Yours sincerely,

[T. S. Eliot]

---

be published, because there would be no market . . . For the great majority of novels do only as the great majority of films: their purpose is to provide day-dreams. We know well enough what day-dreaming means, and what it can lead to, in individual psychology. But it is now a disease of society . . . [T]he finest living novelists are those whose work demands of the reader far more of an attention akin to *poetic* appreciation than any previous novelists have asked. But poetry, in one form or another, will always be wanted . . . The drama, perhaps, is one form which might gain new life in a new age, and at the same time provide a fresh, and much-needed, vehicle for poetry . . . But . . . I cannot see any likelihood that either revolution or reform will, in itself, improve the quality of the produce . . . It may be only my own prejudice which makes me believe that a communist régime might merely perfect the work of the capitalist régime in stamping out any vestiges of art . . . But it is surely rational to maintain that we cannot expect any merely political or social change to raise the artistic sensibility of the public, to stimulate the flowering of artistic talent . . . For the present, no doubt commercial literature will continue to flourish and to pander, more and more severed from real literature. The latter will be produced by those who will not merely be content not to make a living by it, not merely content to have no career; but who will be resigned to a very small audience – for we all should like to think that our poetry might be read and declaimed in the public-house, the forecastle and the shipyard. What is required for the production of great art seems to be any one of many possible situations in which the ingredients are liberty, individuality, and community' (C. 11 [July 1932], 676–83).

Leavis responded to this letter on 19 May: 'I'm glad you like my wife's book. Again, Cambridge doesn't.'

FROM *Vivien Eliot* TO *Ralph Hodgson*   MS Beinecke

18 May 1932   68 Clarence Gate Gardens

Dear Mr Hodgson,

I hope Miss Bolliger told you that we have been trying to get up a theatre party to go once more to 'Wings Over Europe'.[1] She & I had arranged it for next Monday or Tuesday. Tonight we have been dining out & have heard that the play has *already* been *taken off*. This made me very miserable, & then I received a letter from the people we had invited to go with us to say they had already seen it & thought it very bad. I can hardly believe it is really off, and I *should* be so grateful if you will find out for me in the morning & if it is still on we shall go again at once. Miss Bolliger is to telephone me at lunch time.

About *one day in the country*, I find we are going *to a play* on *Sunday next* – so we could not go that day. But my husband says that *Monday & Tuesday 23rd & 24th* will suit him, so do let us make it one of those 2 days – can we? If you agree dont you think we might go towards Arundel? Although I think there are better places to go.

Anyhow, if Wings Over Europe is *still on*, I *must* go again, & shd. put *anything* aside for it.

Yours most sincerely,
Vivienne Haigh Eliot

FROM *Vivien Eliot* TO *Aurelia Bolliger*   MS Beinecke

19 May 1932   68 Clarence Gate Gardens

Dear Aurelia,

Just a line to remind you that *you & Mr Hodgson* are to come in on Saturday afternoon for us to arrange *definitely* about our days in *the country*. Mr Eliot wishes to go on next Monday & Tuesday. We also think it would be fun to go to the *Derby* – do tell Mr Hodgson – we could do it in our car, & what fun it would be! Wednesday June 1st. Do let's.

Keep *Saturday & Sunday afternoons* for me.

Mr Eliot is playing on the Wireless & driving me *MAD*

Yours ever,
Vivienne Haigh Eliot

1 – *Wings Over Europe*: a three-act play by Robert Nichols and Maurice Browne, first produced on Broadway in 1928.

TO *A. W. Dodd*   CC

19 May 1932   [Faber & Faber Ltd]

Dear Mr Dodd,

Excuse my delay in answering your letter of the 23rd.[1] It is a little difficult to advise you about the treatment of your manuscript after such a considerable time; but my memory leads me to suggest strongly that you should leave *The Soul Within* to one side for a time, and try your hand at some other piece of work. If you do this, I believe that by the time you return to *The Soul Within* you will be much better able to criticise it yourself and decide about its future.

Yours sincerely,

[T. S. Eliot]

TO *Horace Gregory*[2]   CC

19 May 1932   [Faber & Faber Ltd]

Dear Mr Gregory,

Thank you for your letter of April 20th.[3] I am afraid that the series in which *Rooming House* was published has not so far been a successful venture either from the point of view of sales or of reviews. We are, however, quite satisfied with ourselves for having made the attempt and with the volumes which we have produced, including your own.

I have looked up the cuttings, but I do not find any one which is acute enough to be worth sending you. One says that you are best when most

---

1–Dodd, from Birmingham, wished to know if his work of fantasy was worthy of 'total revision, if I try my best with a more modern treatment as you suggest? . . . Do you suggest a light, humorous treatment of the subject?'

2–Horace Gregory (1898–1982), poet and critic, majored in English at the University of Wisconsin before moving to New York City. His poetry includes *Chelsea Rooming House* (1930), *No Retreat* (1933), *Poems, 1930–40* (1941), *Medusa in Gramercy Park* (1961); prose writings include *The House on Jefferson Street* (memoir, 1971), *Spirit of Time and Place: The Collected Essays of Horace Gregory* (1973). He was awarded a Guggenheim Fellowship in 1951, and won the Bollingen Prize in 1965. His Russian-born wife, Marya Zaturenska, won a Pulitzer Prize for her second volume of verse, *Cold Morning Sky* (1937).

3–Gregory expressed 'delight' at the format of *Rooming House*: 'I felt at last that my poems had received topographical distinction. Here was the unpretentious accuracy that I admire.' The F&F Catalogue for Spring 1932 reads: 'This is the first book of poems by a young New York poet, who is as yet little known either here or in America. The poems are characterized by a bitter realism in treating the lives of the poor and oppressed in New York, but exalted by a rare lyric quality. They constitute a document upon our time which is as interesting and significant here as it is for America.'

---

simple and direct. The *Scotsman* says approvingly 'He says what he wants to and gets it over at times'. *The Aberdeen Press* says that the book has 'vigour and not a little music' and so on. I think that perhaps the local atmosphere of your book was a little foreign to some of the provincial reviewers.

I shall of course be much interested to read your new volume which Harcourt Brace are publishing. As I am coming to Harvard at some time during September it would be better to wait and let me see the proof or a copy then. I shall be at Harvard until the spring and hope that we may have an opportunity of meeting.

Yours sincerely,
[T. S. Eliot]

TO *Marià Manent*[1]   CC

19 May 1932   [*The Criterion*]

Dear Madam,

Thank you very kindly for your letter and for doing the honour of translating *Journey of the Magi* into Catalan.[2] I am of course totally incompetent to criticise such a version or to appreciate its merits, but I can, even though ignorant of Provencal, follow the translation with interest. The Catalan language certainly seems to have a distinct beauty of its own.

I fear that the *Criterion* would never be able to find space for any regular contribution on the subject of Catalan literature, but if at any time you cared to send me something you have written, I should be much interested. I should think after reading your letter that you should be as competent to translate your own work into English as any other translator.

With many thanks,
Yours very truly,
[T. S. Eliot]

1 – Marià Manent, poet (she wrote original poems in modern literary Catalan) and journalist, had contributed to *Commonweal* (New York) and *Hispania* (Paris); and she was in charge of the Foreign Letters section of the Barcelona newspaper *La Veu de Catalunya*.
2 – Manent sent a copy of her translation of 'Journey of the Magi' as published in the Barcelona newspaper *La Publicitat*; she was sorry to be behindhand in asking TSE's permission for it.

TO *B. Jocelyn Brooke*[1]   CC

19 May 1932   [Faber & Faber Ltd]

Dear Mr Brooke,

I have thought over your letter of May 10th.[2] I am afraid that there is hardly any likelihood of Faber & Faber having a vacancy for some time to come, and that conditions in other publishing houses are much the same. But if you care to call and discuss the general question with me I should be glad to see you almost any morning next week by appointment.

                                    Yours sincerely,
                                    [T. S. Eliot]

TO *Norreys Jephson O'Conor*   CC

23 May 1932   [Faber & Faber Ltd]

My dear O'Conor,

I find that I am supposed to go to the country for the day tomorrow, although I don't want to, and I very much hope for bad weather. However, as I shall probably have to go, could we make lunch Friday instead? I am very sorry if this puts you out.

                                    Yours ever,
                                    [T. S. Eliot]

TO *Siegfried Sassoon*[3]   CC

23 May 1932   [*The Criterion*]

My dear Sassoon,

I did not get your note[4] until Friday evening, and could not answer it until I returned to my office this morning, as I knew that I had some

---

1–Jocelyn Brooke (1908–66), British writer and novelist.
2–A friend of the late Clere Parsons, Brooke had come down from Oxford in 1928 and worked for a while at Messrs Simpkin Marshall. He was now in keen search of another post in publishing. His father would be willing to invest a certain amount of capital if the right opportunity afforded itself. Might TSE be able to advise Brooke on possible openings?
3–Siegfried Sassoon, MC (1886–1967), poet, writer and soldier. Initially known as a war poet and satirist, he won greater fame with his fictionalized autobiography *Memoirs of a Fox-Hunting Man* (1928, James Tait Black Award), which was followed by *Memoirs of an Infantry Officer* (1930) and *Sherston's Progress* (1936). He was appointed CBE in 1951.
4–Sassoon had written from the Reform Club, Pall Mall, on 19 May: 'R. Hodgson is lunching with me here on May 26th at 1.15. I very much hope that you can join us.'

engagement or other for Thursday lunch, and hoped that it might be one which I could postpone. But I find that it is William Force Stead[1] who is coming up just for the day by arrangement with me, and the engagement was made ten days ago, so I cannot possibly let him down. I shall be taking him to lunch at the Oxford and Cambridge, and if you were willing I should be very glad to bring him in for a few moments after lunch as you are almost next door. But I don't know whether he is even an acquaintance of yours, so I shall not bring him unless I hear from you. I shall be very sorry, however, to miss you, as you are so seldom visible.

Yours sincerely,
[T. S. Eliot]

TO *J. B. Trend*   CC

26 May 1932   [*The Criterion*]

Dear Trend,

I am afraid I may be unable to get to the General Meeting on Tuesday, as I have a committee at 2.30 and do not know when it will end. But if I can get it over in time I will certainly come up, and am of the same opinion as yourself.[2]

Yours ever,
[T. S. Eliot]

TO *Elmer Edgar Stoll*   CC

26 May 1932   [*The Criterion*]

My dear Professor Stoll,

Thank you very much for your letter of May 15th. I hope that it may be possible for me to come to Minneapolis and make your acquaintance.[3]

1–William Force Stead (1884–1967), poet and critic; Chaplain of Worcester College, Oxford: see Biographical Register.
2–Trend asked TSE (22 May) to come along to the General Meeting of the Oxford and Cambridge Club on 31 May, at 5 pm, as there was a proposal to allow smoking in the South Library. Trend wrote, 'I (as one of the people who use it constantly), hope that the proposal will be thrown out. I can think of lots of reasons; but I wont inflict them on you in writing!'
3–E. E. Stoll wrote from the College of Science, Literature, and the Arts, University of Minnesota, that his Department desired the university authorities to invite TSE to give a public lecture during the course of his forthcoming visit to the USA.

I believe that I never received a copy of your *Poets and Playwrights*. It is of course quite possible that it may have been mislaid here, but I am almost sure that if it had come I would not have overlooked it. It would be very kind of you to send me another copy.[1]

Yours very truly,
[T. S. Eliot]

TO *T. F. Burns*   CC

26 May 1932   [Faber & Faber Ltd]

My dear Burns,

Thank you for your letter of the 24th. The Gurian book has arrived this morning and I shall be very much interested to read it myself as soon as I can.[2] The two names which suggest themselves to me at once are J. H. Oldham, 2 Edinburgh House, Eaton Gate, s.w.1., and C. A. Siepmann, Broadcasting House. I suggest your writing to these two people mentioning my name and asking them to suggest the names of other Anglicans who would be interested, as they are both in touch with the right people. I think that Oldham especially would be interested. You might as well mention that you are sending copies anyway to the Archbishop of York and the Bishop of Chichester, as they are otherwise certain to suggest them themselves. I will write again when I have read the book.[3]

Yours ever,
[T. S. Eliot]

TO *Elsie Elizabeth Phare*   CC

26 May 1932   [*The Criterion*]

Dear Miss Phare,

Thank you for your note of the 17th.[4] I am sorry to have to tell you that I have incorporated Mrs Leavis's book into my commentary for the

---

1 – Stoll sent off a further copy of *Poets and Playwrights* (1930) on 20 June.
2 – Burns had sent a review copy of Waldemar Gurian's *Bolshevism: Theory and Practice*, and asked TSE to suggest other names – 'chiefly . . . Anglicans' – to whom he should send copies. A. J. Penty was to review the book in *C.* 12 (Jan. 1933), 285–7.
3 – No further letter on the subject by TSE has been found.
4 – Phare had asked (17 May) if she might review Q. D. Leavis's *Fiction and the Reading Public*, along with FRL's *Cross Currents in Modern Poetry*.

next number and therefore do not want a separate review. As for her husband's book, it may sound a little unfair but I am rather averse to having reviewed in the *Criterion* any book which devotes so much space to myself. Have you any other suggestions?

Yours sincerely,

[T. S. Eliot]

TO *F. R. Leavis*   TS Texas

26 May 1932   Faber & Faber Ltd

Dear Mr Leavis,

Thank you for your kind letter of the 19th.[1] I have returned your pamphlet and hope to hear from you shortly.

At the end of your letter you refer to Harding and Peacock.[2] Are these people who may have written to me or who were going to come and see me? I am afraid I cannot recall either of the names.

Yours sincerely,

T. S. Eliot

P.S. I want to subscribe to *Scrutiny*. I have left the circular at home. So pardon this cheque made out to yourself.[3]

1–Leavis had replied (19 May) to TSE's letter of 18 May: 'I am prepared to find, when I look at my pamphlet again, that it might have been criticized more heavily . . . The end of the pamphlet is obviously (I expect to find) in some ways inappropriate now, even if it wasn't so much so when I wrote it. I expect to find it in any case crude: a certain personal sense of urgency (which I can excuse myself for since I know the circumstances) tends, I realize, towards propagandist naïveté . . . If you send the typescript back I will, perhaps, nerve myself to look it over, though I had written it off when it became plain that it was too late for Fraser to bring it out this term (his is, of course, mainly a Cambridge public, & next term is too far away). Still, I will think about it. It will, if necessary, stay comfortably in the bottom drawer . . . My position is now such that I shall be hard put to it to make a living here at all, & shall have even less time & energy to spare for serious writing.

'Cambridge, by the way, (or that part of it which determines academic careers), doesn't like "destructive" pamphlets: I gather that it includes my book under that head.'
2–D. W. Harding (1906–93) read English and Psychology at Emmanuel College, Cambridge. He was co-editor, with FRL, of *Scrutiny*, 1933–47. After early years at the London School of Economics and at Liverpool University, he became the first Professor of Psychology at Bedford College, London, 1945–68. He edited the *British Journal of Psychology*, 1948–54. His works include *Experience into Words* (1963). Carlos Peacock, an undergraduate at St John's College, was an enthusiast for John Donne.

'I hope you liked Harding & Peacock. They seem to me real finds (they're both pupils of mine – or have been).' Leavis replied to TSE's question on 27 May: 'Harding & Peacock contribute to *Scrutiny* no. I. My mention of them was merely a polite acknowledgement of your kind reference [in TSE's letter of 18 May] to *Scrutiny* – though I do think they are good.'
3–'We shall try hard to keep *Scrutiny* going. There's plenty of help & enthusiasm: the difficulty will be making it pay its way. We need a couple of hundred more subscribers.'

TO *Algar Thorold*   CC

26 May 1932   [*The Criterion*]

My dear Thorold,

Thank you for your note of the 18th. I will send directly for the Bergson book and hope that a review copy will be sent. If not I will buy one. I take it for granted that it is published by Alkon [*sc.* Alcan] but would you mind letting me have the exact title? I should say twelve or thirteen hundred words for both.[1]

I don't think my Dilemma talks are substantial enough to be reprinted in their present form.[2] Perhaps after I get the American business off my hands I may set to work and re-write them. But by that time I daresay I may have turned to something different.

I will count upon Maine de Biran for February 1st.[3] That will be quite satisfactory.

Yours ever,
[T. S. Eliot]

TO *Montgomery Belgion*   CC

26 May 1932   [*The Criterion*]

My dear Belgion,

Thanks for your letter of the 19th. It's surprised me a little because I thought I had written you a letter which anticipated one or two of your remarks. But my Secretary tells me that I wrote no such letter so I suppose that I merely outlined it in my head and assumed that it had got on to paper.

I have received both enclosures from Malraux and when I have considered them I will write to him in your care.[4]

I have glanced at Nizan and the stuff strikes me as rather negative and getting nowhere, somewhat like Berne.[5]

---

1 – Review of *Les Deux Sources de la Morale et de la Réligion*, in C. 12 (Oct. 1932), 124–31.
2 – 'I hope you are bringing your "Dilemma" talks out in book form. The one you sent me in *Listener* [is] full of mistakes due to bad proof reader. But even so *Kolossal!*'
3 – 'Shall we say March . . . ? I think I can promise you something rather interesting. Anyhow it will be a *primeur* in London.' See 'Maine de Biran', C. 12 (Apr. 1933), 441–53.
4 – Malraux had sent both a copy of the French edition of *Lady Chatterley's Lover* with his preface, and a separate copy of the preface: see C. 12 (Jan. 1933), 215–19.
5 – Belgion wrote (19 May) of Paul Nizan, author of *Les Chiens de Garde*: 'About thirty, probably in l'Enseignement, and a Communist candidate somewhere in the South at the last elections, polling a few hundred votes. He is not quite such an out-and-out Communist in

As for your suggestion of a short review of Rops's book which I have now read and thought rather good.[1] What I thought I had suggested to you was that you might care to put it into the form of a kind of French Chronicle and round up a number of the people of the sort which we have been mentioning. It seems to me that this sort of French mental activity is still quite unknown in England. I have also read Maulnier's book which has good points in it, but which I find rather scrappy, as it is evidently merely a collection of journalistic articles.

I should imagine that Richmond's difficulties are that he has committed himself to assigning foreign reviewing to a small number of people and feels conscientiously that he ought not to go outside of this number. Perhaps the review you had in mind is much the same thing as the Chronicle I suggested and would probably be more in place though less influential in the *Criterion*.[2]

[Unfinished]

TO *Bonamy Dobrée*   CC

26 May 1932   [*The Criterion*]

My dear Bonamy,

The difficulty about fixing the date is that Herbert has disappeared into Germany. I have a card from his wife saying that he will not be back until the end of the month.[3] So let us fix the 15th provisionally and when I hear from Herbert I will make an attempt to induce him to come on that date.

---

his conversation, and between ourselves I am told that actually he is more than a little of an *arriviste*.'

1–*Le Monde sans âme*, by Henry Daniel-Rops [pseud. of Henri Petiot, historian, novelist and essayist], had been a success in France; the first edition of 5,000 copies being 'rapidly exhausted', Belgion wrote on 10 May. 'Rops is in with Massis, but he is not, as Maulnier is, a disciple. He indignantly rejects the suggestion of Marcel, Du Bos, and Maritain, that the book's logical outcome for the reader is that reader's conversion to Catholicism. He is working on behalf, not of Catholicism, but of "le spirituel", he says . . . Daniel-Rops is a little chap, under thirty I should say, and rather natty. He is a professor in the Lycée Pasteur at Neuilly.' See Belgion's 'French Chronicle', C. 12 (Oct. 1932), 80–90.

2–Belgion felt exasperated with Bruce Richmond at the *TLS*: 'I suggested to him an omnibus review of a number of such books, a review which would indicate the present trend of "young" thought in France. He replied that alas! he had no space for foreign books. Then today I see another column and two-thirds on *German* novels following on one only a few weeks ago!'

3–BD was trying to fix a date for the next Criterion Club gathering. Evelyn Read had written on 20 May that HR was in Holland till perhaps the end of May.

Professor Elmer Edgar Stoll Ph.D. is at the University of Minnesota, Minneapolis. I received the pamphlet too but have not read it. He is primarily an earnest and sometimes right-minded writer on Shakespeare etc.[1]

Yours ever,

[T. S. E.]

TO *E. Gordon Selwyn* cc

26 May 1932   [Faber & Faber Ltd]

My dear Selwyn,

I am sorry to trespass on your time to ask again for suggestions of suitable authors. But if you feel that the matter of this letter is too trivial you need not bother to reply at all.

It has been suggested to us that there is a possibility for a popular book on the Christian churches. When I say 'popular' I do not mean it in a derogatory sense, I merely mean a book for the general reader and not for the theological student or specialist. A book, in fact, which might have the same general interest and be in a way parallel to Hoskyn's [*sic*] and Davey's admirable *Riddle of the New Testament* which has been quite successful.[2]

The suggestion came from such an educated general reader who feels the lack of any brief convenient book which would give an account of the development of the various churches such as the Nestorians and the Coptic church, and the separation of the Eastern and Western churches, giving not only a history of events but a simple account of the dogmatic differences. I am not sure in my own mind to what date such a book could be carried without losing its unity. That is to say, whether it would be possible in one volume of such a sort, to deal with the complete history of the main Christian divisions down to the Methodist Schism (as the person who made the suggestion desires) or whether within the compass of one volume it would be necessary to stop, as does Paul More, with some such date as the Council of Chalcedon. I might as well admit that I do not envisage the book very clearly myself, and it is difficult to convey

1–BD wrote on 18 May: 'a certain Elmer Edgar Stoll has sent me a very dull pamphlet on Life and Literature ... Do you know where he is, and where I ought to send an acknowledgment?' *Art and Artifice in Shakespeare* was to be reviewed by BD in C. 13 (Jan. 1934), 326–8.
2–The Revd Sir Edwyn Hoskins and the Revd Francis Noel Davey, *The Riddle of the New Testament*, was reviewed by Paul Elmer More in C. 11 (Jan. 1932), 351–5.

to another an idea imperfectly apprehended by oneself. It struck me as quite possible that there might already be in existence something covering the subject.

So my first question is, what do you think of the possibility and desirability of such a book bringing the history down into the eighteenth century, and second, who could write it? It would have to be of course someone of pretty encyclopaedic scholarship, and at the same time having the imagination which could make the whole of the subject matter appear living and significant to the ordinary reader.

Yours ever sincerely
[T. S. Eliot]

FROM *Vivien Eliot* TO *Aurelia Bolliger*   MS Beinecke

27 May 1932   68 Clarence Gate Gardens

My dear Aurelia

Just a line to say that we expect you & Mr Hodgson to tea tomorrow, & are looking forward to seeing you *both*. We have never got over the beautiful day in the country – & I dont suppose you have either. It was *perfect* – & I shall never be able to say enough about it.

We have *missed* you these days – but of course you know that we expect you *and* Picky to spend the weekend here, I mean to come *tomorrow* & to *stay until Monday* – & again to *spend the week* which Mr Hodgson is staying with Mr Sassoon.

Until 4 o'clock tomorrow, then, *empty* handed.

With every kind thought,
Yours very sincerely,
Vivienne Haigh Eliot

TO *I. A. Richards*   TS

31 May 1932   Faber & Faber Ltd

Dear Richards,

I have not the least idea whether there is any German metaphysical poetry or whether there is any living authority on the subject in Germany.[1] (There was of course metaphysical poetry in Dutch). But I am sure that Mario Praz knows whatever there is to be known about Metaphysical poetry and scholarship on the continent and I do not think that your pupil could do [no] better than to consult him before making a decision. His address is 45 Bentley Road, Liverpool and your pupil could use my name in writing.

Yours in haste,
T. S. E.

TO *N. H. Rubin*   CC

31 May 1932   [Faber & Faber Ltd]

Dear Mr Rubin,

We have now read and considered *Brick and Mortar* carefully. I must say that you have performed a monumental labour and I very much admire your industry. It is therefore with very much regret that we have come to the conclusion that we cannot afford to publish this book. It would be a large and expensive book to produce and would have to be priced very high; and we have come to the conclusion that the state of the market at present is too bad for us to risk another expensive book on *Ulysses* even though, as you say, it does not by any means duplicate the work of Stuart Gilbert. There is, however, another reason which in the present state of things would make it impossible to produce the book in England. Among the passages which you quote are some of those of the type to which most objection has been taken and which [have] been the cause of the present anomalous and absurd position of *Ulysses* itself. Indeed it might be considered by the people who are so minded that the publication of these excerpts calls rather more attention to them than they would receive in their context. As you may now know the

---

1–IAR asked, in an undated card: 'I have a pupil who is thinking either of working under Mario Praz or of going to Germany to see if anything is being done there on Metaphysical Poetry. Do you happen to know if there really is any *German* Metaphysical Poetry?'

censorship in England has become much more stringent within the last six months. And on the other hand, to omit all such passages would mutilate your book directly.

I have thought it advisable to retain the MS here until we hear from you again. I do not believe that any other publisher in England would take a different view from ourselves, but you might like to consider offering it to Shakespeare & Co. or the Black Sun Press or any other Anglo-American publishing firm in Paris. When I hear from you again I will then forward the MS wherever you direct and will see that a receipt is obtained for it.[1]

With many regrets,
I am,
Yours sincerely,
[T. S. Eliot]

TO *E. Gordon Selwyn*   CC

31 May 1932   [Faber & Faber Ltd]

My dear Selwyn,

Thank you very much for your letter of the 30th.[2] I do not gather that the suggestion is one to proceed with, but I shall have a talk with Faber about it.

1–In 1933 Rubin would apply for a Fellowship from the John Simon Guggenheim Memorial Foundation: 'I wish to complete a study in the ethos and morphology of James Joyce's *Ulysses*; to annotate it, to write special studies of the "parody" and "Night-town" episodes, and to enlarge my critical introduction. I wish also to add one more index to the three already compiled which consist of material from *Ulysses*; an index which would objectively illuminate the book's relation to Homer's *Odyssey*.' Invited to support the application, TSE submitted this undated reference: 'All that I know of Mr Rubin is that he wrote to me some time ago about his book, as he proposed to offer it to my firm for publication. I could not give him much encouragement, as I was sure that a book of [on] such a subject and on such a scale would be expensive to produce and bring in little return. However, he sent the book over to me for inspection. While I cannot say that I read it thoroughly, it certainly struck me as an impressive piece of research, though here and there unnecessarily elaborated in detail. I can still hold out no hopes of publication, for the reasons which I have suggested. But Mr Rubin seems to be devoted to his self-imposed task, and I think it would be a great pity if he could not put it into a final and definitive form. The plan of work in Europe that he outlines strikes me as the right one for his purpose, and (although as I say I do not know him personally) I believe that he would carry it out' (J. S. Guggenheim Foundation).
2–Selwyn recommended two possible authors for the volume TSE was projecting: (i) the Revd C. P. S. Clarke, 'who has written an excellent and readable history of the Christian Church'; (ii) Mrs Duncan Jones, wife of the Dean of Chichester. 'My only fear is that both of them may feel that they have already written what they have to say.'

I should be very glad to lunch with you at the Royal Societies on the 15th.

With many thanks,
Yours sincerely,
[T. S. Eliot]

TO *W. B. Curry*   CC

2 June 1932   [Faber & Faber Ltd]

Dear Mr Curry,

I have your letter of the 1st June.[1] I have known Mr W. H. Auden ever since he came down from Oxford. I have been struck from the beginning, not only by his remarkable literary abilities, but by his general activity and curiosity of mind and variety of intellectual interests, such as biology and psychology. He has always struck me as a man of great promise and ability, and there are few young men in whose future I am so much interested. I have also a great liking for him personally and believe him to have both high principles and commonsense. For his qualifications by temperament and experiences as a schoolmaster he has no doubt given you better evidence than I can give; but it may not be irrelevant to add that in informal conversation when I have seen him from time to time, he has always given me the impression of enthusiasm in his teaching work and sympathy with small boys in their studies, in their sports and in their recreations.[2]

Yours sincerely,
[T. S. Eliot]

1–William Burnlee Curry (d. 1962), Headmaster of The School, Dartington Hall, Totnes, S. Devon, had received an application from WHA for the post of form master in the Junior School: 'the duties would consist in being in general charge of the group as guide, friend and philosopher, and in teaching the greater part of the academic work.' He asked TSE to furnish a reference.

'This is one of the so-called progressive schools, which means that we dispense almost entirely with purely formal discipline, and it follows that, if successful results are to be achieved, the staff must have unusual qualities of personality and enthusiasm as well as of learning . . . In considering a teacher coming into a community of this sort one is particularly interested in his ability to form satisfactory relationships with other people, both staff and children.'

2–Curry responded to his testimonial on 3 June: 'It is going to be very difficult to make a selection for this post, as several good men are applying, but Mr Auden is at any rate near the top and I am much obliged to you for your opinion.'

FROM *Vivien Eliot* TO *Mary Hutchinson*   Card MS Texas

2 June 1932   68 Clarence Gate Gardens

My dear Mary

Please excuse me & forgive me for not having written to thank you for your lovely necklace.

Thank you very *very* much dear Mary – & forgive the really bad negligence. I am very distracted. Tom says you have invited us to dinner on *Tuesday* next, but I have it down for *Wednesday*. Wld. you mind ringing up tomorrow Sunday? To say which. I am looking forward to coming to dinner. I shall be very tired because I am having an Inventory taken of the *whole* flat. It will take 2 days.

With much love, *apologies* & thanks.

Yours with love,
Vivienne Haigh Eliot

TO *Bonamy Dobrée*   TS Brotherton

3 June 1932   *The Criterion*

My dear Bonamy,

More trouble. More trouble. I finally heard from Herbert who explains that his visit to Germany was paid for by lectures and says that he is absolutely beggared.[1] He can't get down at all this month, but suggests Wednesday July 6th as he is going as far as Leeds on the 4th to collect a Litt. D. from his Alma Mater.

I am anxious to have as full a meeting as possible, because I do not expect we shall have another opportunity before I leave for America in the middle of September. Do you think you could be so sweet and kind as to come up for Wednesday July 6th? If not I do not know quite what to do. And if you come for July 6th, do by all means come up in the middle of this month as well.

Yours in haste,
T. S. E.

1–HR had written on 30 May: 'I'm sorry to be so helpless; but the inevitable expenses I incurred moving in here [Edinburgh], plus a sudden influx of income-tax (they got me on the change of employment dodge, which you have probably experienced, & now on the Clark Lectures, which I had kept dark) have left me floundering. I've just been to Holland, which does not sound like economy, but I had my expenses there paid in exchange for a lecture.'

TO *Messrs W. & G. Foyle*   TS Valerie Eliot

5 June 1932   68 Clarence Gate Gardens

Dear Sirs,

I should be glad to know whether you could arrange for one of your staff to come and make an inventory of the books in my private library at this address.

If so, it would no doubt be advisable for you to send a representative to look at the library and estimate the cost. If you could have me rung up here in the earlier part of the morning, or later at Museum 9543 (Faber & Faber) we could arrange an appointment.[1]

Yours faithfully,
T. S. Eliot

TO *Marguerite Caetani*   TS Lelia Howard

7 June 1932   [Faber & Faber Ltd]

Dear Marguerite,

I have been wondering why I have heard nothing from you for so long, and hope that no illness or other misfortune has intervened. I had lunch with Mirsky a little while ago; he had not much news of you, but mentioned that *Commerce* had suspended publication. I was very sorry to hear that, but was not surprised, as such enterprises are becoming more and more nearly impossible in modern society; I have been much worried myself about the collapse of America. I am all the more sorry for recent events in the world at large, as the prospect of ever seeing you again diminishes! We hardly expected you to come to London, as you thought of doing when we saw you last October; but now the possibility of seeing you in Paris seems to be removed; and I have no notion when I shall ever be able to afford a visit to Italy again.

I have heard recently (confidentially) from Jones and Evans, who, like all booksellers (and consequently all publishers) are having difficult and

---

1–The inventory, if it was made, is evidently distinct from the list pasted into a ledger by VHE (Bodleian MS Eng. lett. b. 20), which was compiled by Messrs Bird & Bird in Nov. 1934. A representative of W. & G. Foyle Ltd reports, 11 Nov. 2014: 'Regrettably, there is no Foyles archive. Some documents are held privately by individual members of the Foyle family, but they are not accessible to us and the family is unable to undertake searches for specific items.'

anxious times, and are concerned about your account.[1] I do hope that you can do something at once to reduce it, as I gave Mr Whittaker my verbal guarantee, and feel personally responsible.

My greatest anxiety at the moment is what to do with Vivienne while I am in America. I cannot afford to take her, as my chief excuse for going is that I hope to save enough money to pay arrears of income tax; furthermore, if I had to look after her there I simply could not do my work properly. It would really be cheaper to leave her in the Malmaison,[2] even now; but I do not think it advisable that she should be so far away from her family and friends while I am away; nor do I think that it would be good for her to stop as long as eight months in any sanatorium. I hope to persuade her to accept some paid companion, but she is rather refractory. Meanwhile I am feeling increasingly tired and look to the sea voyage for a little rest. (I suppose there is no prospect of your visiting America this winter?) Vivienne has continued in as normal condition as she is ever likely to attain, and has been able, though with dwindling resources, to keep her small car in which she gets about.[3]

1 – W. C. Whittaker (Jones and Evans Bookshop Ltd, Cheapside) had advised TSE on 11 May that the Princess's unpaid account stood at £170: much of it was for periodicals and journals.

2 – The Sanatorium de la Malmaison, where Vivien had been treated for several weeks in 1926, was housed in a mansion in Rueil, to the west of Paris, built in the early nineteenth century (the Empress Joséphine had died there); in 1911 it was transformed into a sanatorium specialising in 'des affections du système nerveux'. The dramatist Georges Feydeau (1862–1921) died there; and Mrs F. Scott (Zelda) Fitzgerald was to pass a few days there following a nervous breakdown in Apr. 1930 (Kendall Taylor, Sometimes Madness Is Wisdom: Zelda and Scott Fitzgerald: A Marriage, [2002]). See further M. de Brunhoff, Le Sanatorium de la Malmaison (1913).

3 – FVM was to write, in 'Notes on Sencourt's T. S. Eliot: A Memoir': 'As to V's health in 1932 she was sometimes in quite equable form – TSE and V. visited Pikes Farm together for Susanna's christening in August 1932, were there for lunch and tea (TSE driving his small Morris) and happy day for all' (Berg: Morley papers box 10, file 1). TSE stood as godfather to Susanna Morley. T. S. Matthews notes in Great Tom: Notes Towards the Definition of T. S. Eliot (1973, 1974), 108: 'Vivienne noted remorsefully in her diary that Tom had a hard time getting her up and dressed and ready to leave, but that he had been very patient and gentle with her, only reminding her that they were keeping two old people (Frank Morley's parents) waiting, and that the old lady had come out of the London Clinic that very day.'

FVM's full account of the occasion is in 'A Few Recollections of Eliot', 106–7: 'Rendezvous Oxted, where I was to meet them in my second-hand American Ford V-8 and blaze the trail – not more than 20 m.p.h. – for the Morris to follow through the twisty narrow lanes. Wonderful hot summer day. We met on time, we started sedately. I had forgotten that in a lane half way there was a bend and a slight rise which the Ford had never noticed. Before the spot I tooted to give warning fore and aft, went around the twist and up the rise, and waited. Don Quixote – almost I hesitate to tell it – was not prepared, had trouble, missed his gear-change, stalled, began to roll back – I draw a veil. Another thing I had forgotten was that in the back of the Morris there would be the heaviest of suitcases – Tom never journeyed without the *heaviest* of suitcases. Another thing I remembered was that Tom would intensely dislike any notice taken, any assistance. I went on waiting. Unveil now, and listen: at a third attempt and with unexampled gallantry Tom with the heart of a lion did charge to the top of the mountain. Vivien's nerves withstood the strain better than mine. And at the top, and all in an instant, the perspiring Knight of the Doleful Countenance turned into the Knight of the Lions, conformable to the ancient custom of knights-errant. The (though still perspiring) Knight of the Lions was hilarious with laughter and success and a happy memorable day was had by all, with lunch *al fresco*, small children quick now, here now, in the garden.'

FVM said of VHE, in his interview for *Omnibus*, 8 June 1970 (Berg): 'You must remember that I never knew her in her prime, but when I knew her it was quite obvious that she had been a person of immense charm and vivacity, and quickness of uptake, and I'm quite sure of one thing – that she, rather like Ezra, was of an immense help to Eliot as a poet, and her contribution (and indeed her courage) in encouraging the publication of *The Waste Land*, which many wives would have blanched from, is something which is worthy of tribute and memory.'

On 2 Sept. 1932, while staying at Eastbourne, the Eliots drove over to call on LW and VW at Monk's House, Rodmell. VW recorded: 'behold Tom & Vivienne: we cant buy our fish for dinner. But it was a friendly thought, – she wild as Ophelia – alas no Hamlet would love her, with her powdered spots – in white satin, L. said; Tom, poor man, all battened down as usual, prim, grey, making his kind jokes with her. "Oh but why didn't they tell me Adrian Stephen was your brother. Why? Nobody mentioned it. They kept it from me." Then her chops & changes. Where is my bag? Where – where – then a sudden amorous embrace for me – & so on: trailing about the garden – never settling – seizing the wheel of their car – suddenly telling Tom to drive – all of which he bears with great patience: feeling perhaps that his 7 months of freedom draw near' (*The Diary of Virginia Woolf*, IV: *1931–35*, ed. Anne Olivier Bell [1982], 123).

See too VW, letter to Ethel Smyth, 7 Sept. 1932: 'The other day in walked the T. S. Eliots – he's the poet, and she, poor raddled distressing woman, takes drugs. On a wild wet day she dresses in white satin, and exudes ether from a dirty pocket handkerchief. Also she has whims and fancies all the time – some amorous, some pornographic. Meanwhile he sits there, as trim as a bank clerk, making exact, but rather laboured, conversation – for instance about his motor car' (*Letters* V, 100). She had told OM on 22 June 1932, of VHE: 'The ether, the whistle, the dog – its too sinister and sordid and depressing . . . If she weren't so malodorous and tousled it would be more tolerable – No, nothing could make me see them again together' (ibid., 71).

VHE was to recall in her diary on 1 Apr. 1935: 'This is the paper which was stuck on the pot of Raspberry Jam given to me by Virginia Woolf at Monk's House Rodmell, nr. Lewes Sussex in August 1932. She had made the jam herself . . . Tom & I were staying together at The Lansdowne Hotel *Eastbourne* in the room on the *ground* floor *facing* the side of *The Grand Hotel*. I drove Tom over, in the Morris car which I had *then* & *afterwards* exchanged for the Ford V8 2 door saloon . . . When we arrived at Rodmell both Virginia & Leonard *seemed pleased*. I took *several snapshots* which are among my collection. We had tea, & as I was very nearly insane, already with the Cruel Pain of losing Tom, & as they both must have known that, I paid very little attention to the conversation (as usual) . . . When we got back to the Landsdowne I felt *very ill* and *was in a fever*. Tom also *seemed very strange*. I remember *all* he said. And I also remember having a faint uneasy feeling that the Wolves were in *some* way *against* Tom, just as I now, looking back see that I was always haunted by that horror in recent years. The only way I cld. have stopped it for *good* would have been to go to *America with Tom* & stick it out & *bring him safely back. I had not the courage to do*

I wish that I might have a word from you just to let me know how you and your family are.

Affectionately yours,
Tom

FROM *Vivien Eliot* TO *Mary Hutchinson*   MS Texas

Wed. 8 June 1932   68 Clarence Gate Gardens

My dear Mary –

I did not telephone at 7. because I was *too tired* then to bear a possible disappointment. I need what I asked you about *so much* – you don't suppose I don't need a change *too* – do you?

I could not stay *here* all the 8 months that Tom will be away. I've never left for *one night* for 2 years & 2 months. I could be so happy – & so could Tom, in those rooms. I could spend the winter making them all perfect for *Tom's return*. I can't stay here, I really hate it. We both *loved* our evening with you. Will you bring Barbara[1] to tea on *Wed. 15th.* at 4? And O please do not ring me up with any bad news. *Only good.*

Yr. lover –
Vivienne

TO *Charles Smyth*   CC

8 June 1932   [Faber & Faber Ltd]

My dear Smyth,

No, of course I don't mind in the least, and on the contrary shall be flattered.[2] But if you really understand my theory of royalism you are

---

that & so am damned for ever – but it does not matter what I do, ever again' (Bod: MS Eng lett c. 382). She had not seen TSE since 12 July 1933, and she wrote too: 'As I have never seen him again & as he gave me *no* token at the meeting I am *justified* in *doubting if it was actually T. S. Eliot* & in *doubting the word* of *all who say* they have seen him since that day.'

1 – The Hutchinsons' daughter Barbara (1911–89).

2 – Smyth wrote on 5 June: 'Here is an extract from the first draft of my Introduction to the York Anonymous: "It is perfectly true that the form in which the theory of the Divine Right of Kings was held by James I was not identically the same with that in which it has been maintained or admitted by the prophet Samuel, St Peter and St Paul, Alexander of Macedon, Gregory the Great, the Emperor Henry IV, Pope Gregory VII, the York Anonymous, King Richard, Sir Robert Filmer, Archbishop Sancroft, Dr Pusey, Mr T. S. Eliot, the natives of the Polynesian Archipelago, or myself: but why should the theory of the D. R. be confined to this particular interpretation of it in preference to any other?"'

cleverer than I am, because it has always been unformulated in my own mind.[1]

Yours ever,
[T. S. Eliot]

TO *George Barker*[2]   CC

8 June 1932   [Faber & Faber Ltd]

Dear Mr Barker,

I must apologize for not having answered your letter of the 28th

---

1–Smyth replied to this gnomic response by TSE on 9 June: 'Thanks: but that really was the point: that lack of formulation is the saving difference between your political theory and that of King James I of England and VI of Scotland.'

2–George Barker (1913–91), poet and author. His works include *Thirty Preliminary Poems* (1933), *Poems* (1933), *Poems* (1935), *Calamiterror* (1937), *The True Confession of George Barker* (1950), *Collected Poems*, ed. Robert Fraser (1987). With support from TSE, he became Professor of English Literature, Tohoku University, Sendai, Japan, 1939–40. His liaison with Elizabeth Smart is memorialised in her novel *By Grand Central Station I Sat Down and Wept* (1945). See Barker, 'A Note for T. S. Eliot', *New English Weekly*, 11: 3 (Mar. 1949), 188–92. Robert Fraser, *The Chameleon Poet: A Life of George Barker* (2001).

Barker told EVE, 5 Jan. 1965: '[TSE] was kind to me, as he was, I know, to many others. Most of all I think of the constant help he gave to me in matters of circumstance when I was young. If it had not been for him, I would not (to speak too much of myself) have had a chance.' (Fraser adds [397]): 'As the years passed, he would weave anecdotes portraying his erstwhile mentor as lounge lizard, footpad, Sweeney, nightbird, Mr Hyde. Eliot, he would grow accustomed to relating, had worn green eyeshadow. He had prowled the back streets of London after hours dressed as a policeman. He had kept a secret *pied-à-terre* in the Charing Cross Road, visitors to which were obliged to ask the porter for "the Captain".' (Fraser's source was Barker himself, 10 Oct. 1981.)

TSE wrote on 14 May 1936 to the University of Durham (where Barker had applied for a lectureship in English Literature): 'He is one of a very small number of younger poets whose work I consider important: I have been concerned with it both as editor and as publisher. His prose, both imaginative and critical, is also of great interest and merit. I believe that he has a wide knowledge of English poetry and some experience of lecturing; and I am sure that he would not fail to make any subject in which he lectured, interesting and stimulating to his pupils.' (Barker was not interviewed for the post.) TSE wrote on 15 Nov. 1945 to H. G. Wayment of the British Council: 'I have your letter of the 13th November about the application of Mr George Barker for the Byron Chair of English at Athens and the Chair of British History and Institutions at Salonica. I am afraid that I can only speak of Mr Barker in his capacity as a poet, of which, of course, I have a very high opinion. I have known him for some years and find him also a very charming and agreeable person. I must confess, however, that I simply have no knowledge of Mr Barker's administrative powers any more than I have of his ability as a lecturer. I should have thought that, while his name might be considered for a Chair of English Literature, a Chair of British History and Institutions was somewhat out of his scope. At least, I have no knowledge of his having made any special study of these subjects.'

May immediately.[1] I am afraid that this is a very bad time for anyone looking for a post in a publishing business. We have frequent applications ourselves, but there is no prospect in sight of increasing our staff, and the only possibility would be if some member of the staff left to better himself. The only meagre suggestion that I can make is that you should let me see some of your work, both prose and verse, with a view to the *Criterion*. Reviewing for the *Criterion* of course could only add a mite to anybody's income, and its chief use is as a stepping-stone to more popular and better paying periodicals.

Yours sincerely,
[T. S. Eliot]

P. S. I return herewith your letter from Mr Gerard Hopkins.

TO *Francis Underhill*   CC

8 June 1932   [Faber & Faber Ltd]

Dear Father Underhill,

I suppose that I may congratulate you on your preferment to the Deanery of Rochester, but I am much more inclined merely to express my great regret at hearing that we are to lose you from London.

Yours sincerely,
[T. S. Eliot]

TO *Mario Praz*   CC

8 June 1932   [*The Criterion*]

My dear Praz,

I must apologize for my shameful neglect. I have been very rushed and consequently very forgetful, and I must still beg a few days' grace about the Italian translations.

As for the book of translations of my own poetry which you flatter me by undertaking, I should of course be glad if it could be done, and should

---

1 – The nineteen-year-old Barker petitioned for 'work in any capacity' at F&F. 'I am in such a state that I have to mention that [JMM] has privately written to me that my work as a writer is what he calls "a good deal more than good" . . . I apologise for this begging, but I am not able to get work, and yet somehow I fancy I could do good work if I had secure money.'

hardly expect that such a book would be remunerative to the author.[1]
I think, however, that you will agree that I should be right in having some
contract merely to safe-guard my interests. What I suggest is that I should
be given a nominal royalty of, say, 10%, but that the royalty should not
commence until after the sale of a considerable number of copies. That
is to say, enough sale to cover all the expenses. I do not suppose that the
sale could ever amount to enough to bring me any royalty, but that does
not really matter. Do you think that your publishers would be prepared
to make a contract on this basis? If so, what figure would they suggest?

I look forward to seeing your translation in *La Nuova Antologia*.[2]

Yours in haste,

[T. S. Eliot]

TO *Harry H. Clark*   CC

8 June 1932   [*The Criterion*]

Dear Mr Clark,

Thank you for your letter of May 17th and for 'The Literary Theories
of Thomas Paine' which I have read with much interest. I am sorry to say
that I feel that this paper, interesting and valuable as it is, does not seem to
me to be quite in place in such a review as the *Criterion*. It really requires,
I think, the context of the complete book which you have promised and
which I look forward to seeing.[3]

1–Praz wrote on 28 May, 'Adriano Grande, the editor of CIRCOLI, the Italian poetry
review where my translation of the *Waste Land* is going to appear in the summer number
(without the original text, because of lack of space), asks me to prepare a little volume
of your poems transl. into Italian for a new series ... The volumes look very nice, but
unfortunately yield no royalties owing to the cost of production.' Might TSE consent to be
published without royalties?

2–Praz's translation of 'Triumphal March' appeared in the text of a critical article on
modern English poetry in *Nuova Antologia* (Rome), 1 Apr. 1932, 4–5.

3–Clark was working on a book entitled *Thomas Paine and Eighteenth Century Radicalism*.
He first broached his essay 'The Literary Theories of Thomas Paine' in a letter of 9 May:
'Authorities on political thought agree that ... Paine's great influence on two revolutions
and upon humanitarian reform generally, was due chiefly to his style. I have brought together
his scattered statements regarding literary theory, interpreting them in the light of his central
philosophy which I think stems from Newtonian science and deism.' He ventured further
on 17 May that his piece 'opens what seems to me, at least, an important but uninvestigated
subject, the theories underlying applied prose in Paine's era. And ... the attempt to correlate
religious and literary doctrines is, I think, in the case of Paine at least, entirely novel.' And he
asked where he might try to place 'Nationalism in American Literature'.

The only English magazine which I think might care to use your paper on Nationalism and American Literature is a new review entitled *Scrutiny*, at 13 Leys Road, Cambridge. I am afraid, however, that *Scrutiny* is unable to pay its contributors. It promises to be an interesting periodical.

Yours sincerely,

[T. S. Eliot]

TO *A. L. Morton*   CC

8 June 1932   [*The Criterion*]

Dear Morton,

Thank you for your letter.[1] I agree with you about the difficulty of finding another suitable title, but I think that 'Property and Poetry in a Communist Society' will do.[2]

Yours sincerely,

[T. S. Eliot]

TO *Michael Stuart*   CC

8 June 1932   [*The Criterion*]

Dear Sir,

I have your letter of May 6th enclosing your article entitled 'James Joyce Satirist'.[3] I do not feel quite satisfied with the title, but the article is interesting and I should like to publish it some time during the next year, but unfortunately cannot say just how soon. I think that the thesaurus at the end were best omitted in periodical publication. What I really want to know before accepting the contribution definitely is whether you have

---

1–Morton (30 May) found it hard to fix upon a title for his article (a reply). He suggested either 'Property and Poetry in a Communist Society' or 'Proletarian Dictatorship and Communist Tactics'. 'I quite frankly don't like either, but probably the first is the least unsatisfactory.'

2–'Poetry and Property in a Communist Society', C. 12 (Oct. 1932), 45–53.

3–Michael Stuart (Denver, Colorado) had published articles on Joyce in periodicals including *transition*, *This Quarter* and *The Symposium*. 'In regard to my article printed in "*la revue européene*" of Paris Mr Joyce wrote to me that "it is probably the best article that has yet been published on the subject of my last work . . ."

'You are at liberty to publish any part of the essay you see fit, but the enclosed fairly complete thesaurus of "The Mookse and the Gripes" examined and approved by Mr Joyce together with the first pages of that fable may also be of some interest to your readers.'

permission from the Black Sun Press to include the extract from 'The Mookse and the Gripes' with the article. It would add very much to the interest, as the *Tales of Shem and Sean* [*sic*] have not yet been widely circulated in England.[1]

Yours sincerely,
[T. S. Eliot]

TO *Lewis E. Upcott*[2]   CC

8 June 1932   [*The Criterion*]

Dear Sir,

I thank you cordially for your kindness in letting me see your interesting papers on *The Broken Heart* which I return herewith.[3] Though it seems to me to contribute something of distinct value to the study of Ford and makes me feel that my own cursory notes on *The Broken Heart* were rather superficial,[4] the papers were rather too minute and technical in form for a review like the *Criterion*, but I think it would be a great pity if they were not published in some suitable periodical of English studies.

With very many thanks,
Yours sincerely,
[T. S. Eliot]

1–'The Mookse and the Gripes': from *Finnegans Wake*, 152–9. Caresse Crosby, The Black Sun Press, granted permission on 26 July 1931 for Stuart to quote from JJ's *Tales Told of Shem and Shaun*. Stuart replied to TSE's letter with the suggestion that the piece might be called 'James Joyce, the Mookse and the Gripes'; it did not appear in C. (*Tales Told of Shem and Shaun* was to be published by F&F: Richard de la Mare of F&F sent it to Hamish MacLehose, printer, on 1 Nov. 1932.)

2–Author of *Introduction to Greek Sculpture* (1887).

3–Upcott had submitted on 14 May a short paper on John Ford's *The Broken Heart*, as read to the Literary Section of the Torquay Natural History Society. In an initial letter of 6 May Upcott had explained that he questioned TSE's interpretation of the character of Penthea as lunatic: 'To my thought she is not mad, but "wandering" (through physical weakness) and every word she speaks is pregnant with meaning. But though when *read* it all seems disjointed, if *acted* as I conceive it might be, the sense becomes clear: you must imagine Penthea "wandering" in her thoughts as in her action, she turns from one to another of the other persons on the stage.'

4–TSE, 'John Ford', *TLS*, 5 May 1932, 317–18; repr. in *SE* (1932).

TO *Peter Winckworth*[1]   CC

8 June 1932   [Faber & Faber Ltd]

Dear Mr Winckworth,

Please excuse me for having kept your poems for such a long time.[2]

I think that the first poem, although not quite satisfactory, as a whole is much the best, and I should say from internal evidence that it is the most recent. The others, if I may say so, seem to me to be rather immature exercises. I should like to see more of your work in a year's time.

Yours sincerely,

[T. S. Eliot]

TO *Henry Tonks*[3]   TS Texas

8 June 1932   Faber & Faber Ltd

Dear Professor Tonks,

I do not know whether you will remember having met me once or twice at the Hutchinson's [*sic*] years ago, when they were living on the Mall.[4] I only remind you of the fact because it is owing to my having remarked that I had met you some years ago that I am deputed to write to you now. It occurred to some of us that you might possibly be thinking of writing a volume of Memoirs and Reminiscences at some time, or that if you had not already thought of it you might be persuaded to think. You have probably seen Will Rothenstein's *Memoirs* which we published and which

---

1–Peter Winckworth was to be author of *Sensible Christians* (1935); *Does Religion Cause War?* (1934); *The Way of War: Verses* (1939); *A Simple Approach to Canon Law* (1951); *The Seal of the Confessional and the Law of Evidence* (1952); *A Verification of the Faculty Jurisdiction* (1953); *A History of the Gresham Lectures* (1966); and *Beware of the Archdeacon: A Commentary on the Ecclesiastical Jurisdiction Measure, 1963* (1972).

2–Sent at the suggestion of Kenneth Ingram. Winckworth was not to be published in *C.*

3–Henry Tonks (1862–1937), surgeon (Fellow of the Royal College of Surgeons, 1888), artist, art teacher and caricaturist, taught from 1892 at the Slade School of Art (where his pupils included Augustus John, WL, Stanley Spencer, Mark Gertler, Isaac Rosenberg); during WW1 he produced pastel drawings of facial war wounds, and served as a war artist in 1918. He was Slade Professor of Fine Art, 1918–30; and he is featured in Pat Barker's novels *Life Class* (2007) and *Toby's Room* (2012). See Joseph Hone, *The Life of Henry Tonks* (1939).

4–The Hutchinsons lived until 1928 at River House, Upper Mall, Hammersmith (by Kelmscott House). See Dixie Nichols, 'Tales from the river bank', *Weekend Telegraph*, 16 Feb. 1991, xxii.

have proved very successful. We should be most happy if we could persuade you to think about writing your own.

Yours sincerely,
T. S. Eliot

TO *Sally Cobden-Sanderson*[1]

CC

8 June 1932   [Faber & Faber Ltd]

My dear Sally,

I can't see any reason why I shouldn't make my arrangements through your agency although I don't want any domestic help either male or female at the moment. But, on the other hand, I warn you that I shall expect you or Richard to join Sadler's Wells Society of which I send you notice.

But you may regret it when you know what I want. I want to find the cheapest possible *decent* way of getting to Boston. I don't know anything about modern liners or the difference in accommodation or decorum between one class or another. I want to go if possible by the Canadian and Pacific to Montreal, and I want to know the price of a ticket through from London to Boston by that route. I also want to know whether I can save any money by taking a return ticket, and I want to know whether it is best to spend the night in Montreal and if so, where to go. I want to know how to arrange to have a *small* crate of books sent, and I want to arrive in Boston somewhere about the 25th September.

Now, if your agency can cope with all this, I shall think well of you, and pay you a visit in Regent Street. Perhaps one day we might all lunch together.

Yours ever affectionately,
[T. S. E.]

1–Sally Cobden-Sanderson (d. 1972) was working for Hutchinson's Agency ('for Domestic Help Male and Female'), Carlton Chambers, Regent Street – a firm which also catered for travel arrangements. 'Sally is a little too boisterous for my taste,' wrote TSE to HWE on 1 Jan. 1936 (Houghton).

TSE at forty-three

TO *Elsie Elizabeth Phare*

9 June 1932   [*The Criterion*]

Dear Miss Phare,

We dealt with the Byron book when it came out in French, and the others do not seem to me important enough to merit reviews so much later than their publication.[1] I am under the impression that Beevor's Catholic Sermons are all by contemporary preachers and in your letter you speak as if it were seventeenth century work; but if you are quite sure what the book is, and this is what you want, I will get it for you.[2]

Yours sincerely,
[T. S. Eliot]

TO *Bennett A. Cerf*[3]

TS Columbia University Libraries

9 June 1932   *The Criterion*

Dear Mr Cerf,

Thank you for your kind letter of the 20th May.[4] Your suggestion that I should do a new introduction to the translation of the *Divine Comedy* is a very attractive one, but I am afraid that it is quite out of the question for me to undertake any commission for writing until about a year from now.

With many regrets,
Yours sincerely,
T. S. Eliot

1–Phare wished (27 May) to review Desmond MacCarthy, *Selections from Remy de Gourmont*; *Criticism*; Charles du Bos, *Byron and the Need of Fatality*. In the event, she did not review them.

2–'I don't expect that you would trust me with them but I should like to review Humphrey Beevor's Catholic sermons. I couldn't consider them from an expert theological point of view but I have read quantities of sermons in the course of doing research on the survival of the English Church in Paris during the seventeenth century. I should like to make comparisons.'

On 16 Sept. 1932 Phare submitted the MS of 'a small book on Gerard Hopkins of which the aim is I suppose to make the poems more easily comprehensible to ordinary readers'. Unluckily, on 30 Sept. 1932 she was sent this note: 'Mr Eliot had unfortunately already left for America when your essay on Gerard Manley Hopkins arrived, but it has been very carefully considered by the other Directors of the Firm. Its merits were fully appreciated, and we should ordinarily very much like to be able to publish it, but I am afraid that it has been our bitter experience recently that there is absolutely no market at all for essays of this length.'

3–Bennett Cerf (1898–1971), founder with his friend Donald Klopfer of Random House, 1927. Author of *At Random: The Reminiscences of Bennet Cerf* (1977).

4–Cerf asked TSE to write an intro. to the Carlyle-Wicksteed prose translation of *The Divine Comedy*, for the Modern Library series: ten or twelve pages, for a fee of $100, delivery in Aug. 1932.

TO *George Boas*[1]   CC

9 June 1932   [*The Criterion*]

Dear Boas,

Thank you for your kind letter of the 20th May. I shall of course be delighted to stay with you and Mrs Boas when I come to Baltimore and hope that when the date is fixed it will not prove inconvenient to you. I look forward very much to renewing our acquaintance.[2]

Yours sincerely,

[T. S. Eliot]

1 – George Boas (1891–1980), who had known TSE since 1914, taught philosophy at Johns Hopkins University, 1921–56; author of *A Primer for Critics* (1937) and *Dominant Themes in Modern Philosophy* (1957).

2 – Boas invited TSE to stay with him and his wife Simone while delivering the Turnbull Lectures. T. S. Matthews, *Old Tom*, 114: 'He was in Baltimore for nearly a week that winter, to lecture at Johns Hopkins (the Metaphysical Poets) and to give a reading before the Poetry Society. He stayed at Baltimore with his old Harvard friend George Boas, who had become Professor of Philosophy at the Hopkins. (Eliot had a bad cold and asked Mrs Boas to refuse as many invitations for him as she could.) Boas was delighted to see his admired friend and mentor again. But soon afterward, when he read the lectures Eliot gave at the University of Virginia [*After Strange Gods* (1933)], he was deeply wounded by Eliot's statement about "free-thinking Jews". Boas's comment was "I felt that in that case I could relieve him of one of them and did."' E. H. Gombrich corroborates that story, as told to him by Boas himself, in *Tributes: Interpreters of our Culture* (1984), 77. See too James F. Loucks, 'The Exile's Return: Fragment of a T. S. Eliot Chronology', *ANQ: A Quarterly Journal of Short Articles, Notes, and Reviews*, 9: 2 (Spring 1996), 23.

TSE was to write to Leslie G. Fiedler, 14 Jan. 1948: 'Your letter is the third of its kind that I have received during the last eighteen months or so: they have all been from young Jews in America. I mention both the place and the generation; for I have not met, in England, the kind of sensitiveness that you exhibit, nor among my older Jewish friends and acquaintances in America. I think that it is certainly something peculiar to a generation much younger than mine: I do not know whether to call this phenomenon "Semitism" or "anti-anti-semitism", or what other name to find for it. You refer, for instance, to supposed evidences of anti-semitism in my poems. I suppose you mean poems in which the word "Jew" occurs. I would ask you to reflect upon the fact that these poems were all first published in this country by my friend Mr Leonard Woolf, himself a Jew, who never raised any objection. If you question his integrity or loyalty to his own origins, there are plenty of people from whom you can obtain confirmation of that. Incidentally, these same poems were first published in America by Mr Alfred Knopf and by Mr Horace Liveright. In short, the evidence on which you rely dates from many years ago; and the documents were not regarded at that time as anti-semitic, either by Gentiles or by Jews.

'I can only recall one sentence in any of my prose writings on which such a construction could be placed, and that only by a careless reader. It is an expression of regret that so many Jews have lost their religious faith; and of opinion that a Jew living in a society of Christian origin, who has lost his faith, is still more derelict than a Gentile in the same society. If there are other passages that you construe in an anti-semite sense, I should be glad to know what they are.

'I realise that it must be very difficult for a young man to realise that the mass emotions of his own time and generation did not exist at an earlier time, and that they may still be quite alien to older men still alive. I recommend it, however, as a point worth sober reflection. If you could succeed in understanding the difference, and the comparative novelty of both semitic and anti-semitic hysteria, you could render great service to the appeasement of the violent and irrational passions by which the world is now torn.

'Incidentally, and last, as you say that you are Jewish: I hope that you will not consider it an impertinence of me to express the hope that you are diligent in attendance at your synagogue (if you are so fortunate as to have one in Missoula), that you observe the Law and read the Scriptures, and that you cherish the faith of your fathers. I should naturally pray for the conversion of everyone to Christianity; but short of that, for the maintenance of all religion.'

When Fiedler returned to the fray, TSE responded on 22 Feb. 1949: 'Thank you for your long and interesting letter of the 30th January, in which there is much with which I am in sympathy. I feel rather sadly, however, that you still regard me as at least having been at one time an anti-semite. I am not aware that this is so. I wonder whether you include Shakespeare and Dickens in this category, as one sentence suggests that you are inclined to do. I wonder also why the few references to Jews in my early poems should be supposed to express a general antipathy to Jews, while it has never been suggested (even by those amongst my acquaintance who happen to be named Sweeney) that I am anti-Irish.

'I fear that we can get no farther along these lines.'

To Canon B. Iddings Bell, 13 Dec. 1951: 'It is a curious thing, but I cannot make clear to the anti-anti-Semitic zealots that for me, the interesting Jewish problem is not one of race at all, but one of religion. I think that the very few remarks that I have made in print, bear this out.'

Many years later TSE told an interviewer who cited that same passage: 'The quotation you have there was taken out of context. If that is used to prove that I'm anti-Semitic, there are plenty of other evidences that I'm not. I'm a Christian and therefore I'm not an anti-Semite. I did think on the whole I was rather pro-Semitic . . .' (Robert Herguth, 'Un-Beat T. S. Eliot Isn't Sure How World Will End: Poet Here For Reading', *Chicago Daily News*, 6 Nov. 1959, 12).

To Simon Weinberg, 27 Apr. 1962: 'I am interested in your mentioning in your letter the name of Rabinowich ['Sweeney Amongst the Nightingales']. The fact that I used the name at all was at one time taken by a few persons, to my astonishment, as evidence of anti-Semitic bias.

'I chose the name, of course, as I chose the name Sweeney, because it pleased me and seemed to me euphonious in its place.'

To Ezra Pound, 13 Aug. 1954: 'I do not see why I should continue to accept from you insults to my nationality or to my religion. The latter includes the Jewish religion.'

To Simon Weinberg, 7 June 1962: 'The fact that I was a friend, and a grateful friend, of Ezra Pound has never meant that I was influenced against people of Jewish race. Indeed, I think that Ezra's mind was living in an imaginary past in which all Jews were bankers and usurers. And I gather that he has more recently spoken to the effect that if he had been aware of the Nazi persecution in Germany he would have spoken very differently at the time.'

See also correspondence in the *TLS*, Aug.–Sept. 1957; Christopher Ricks, *Eliot and Prejudice* (1988), ch II: 'Anti-Semitism'; Anthony Julius, *T. S. Eliot, anti-Semitism, and literary form* (1995; new edition with a preface and a response to the critic, 2003); John Gross, 'Was T. S. Eliot a Scoundrel?', *Commentary* 102: 5 (Nov. 1996), 26–31; special issue of *Modernism/modernity* 10: 1 (2003), 'T. S. Eliot and anti-Semitism', 1–70, opening with Ronald Schuchard's essay 'Burbank with a Baedeker, Eliot with a Cigar: American

TO *William Force Stead*[1]

9 June 1932   *The Criterion*

My dear Stead,

I really wired because I thought we had fixed a day, and that a Thursday, and didn't remember whether it was today or today week. But if we didn't fix a day, that accounts for there being no record in my notebook. So as you are involved in a pageant, and I am not sure of all my days next week, please let me know what days of the week, if any, are better than others – what is the usual day from Oxford – and may we fix definitely a day in the week after next.

What a variety of activities you are pursuing at the moment. I thought Buchan was an old man with a moustache,[2] and I never could understand what Lord Crewe had to do with poetry.[3]

Yours ever affectionately,

T. S. E.

I sympathise with the Tooth.

TO *Ruth Grandison*

9 June 1932   [Faber & Faber Ltd]

Dear Miss Grandison,

I am honoured by your invitation of May 17th to address the Amy Lowell Memorial Poetry Club.[4] It is difficult for me so far ahead to know just what my engagements will be and how much leisure I shall have. If it is possible to leave the matter open I shall be very glad to consider it again after my arrival in Cambridge, but if it is necessary to make a fixture at once I am afraid I must decline.

Intellectuals, Anti-Semitism, and the Idea of Culture'; with responses by David Bromwich, Ronald Bush, Denis Donoghue, Anthony Julius, James Longenbach, Marjorie Perloff, and a 'Reply' by Schuchard.

1–William Force Stead (1884–1967), poet and critic; Chaplain of Worcester College, Oxford: see Biographical Register.

2–Stead was living at The Red House, Clifton Hampden, Abingdon, Berkshire. John Buchan (1875–1940) was a friend, living at Elsfield Manor (the family estate in Oxfordshire). Buchan, 1st Baron Tweedsmuir – Scottish novelist, historian, Unionist politician; Governor-General of Canada – was author of novels including *The Thirty-Nine Steps* (1915) and *Greenmantle* (1916).

3–Lord Crewe (1858–1945), son of Lord Houghton, was president of the Shelley–Keats Society.

4–Ruth Grandison wrote from the Bookshop for Boys and Girls, Charlestown, Mass.

With many thanks,
Yours sincerely,
[T. S. Eliot]

TO *L. C. Knights*[1]   CC

9 June 1932   [Faber & Faber Ltd]

Dear Mr Knights,

Thank you for your letter of the 6th June.[2] I am afraid that I must stick to my determination not to undertake any commissions whatever until my return from America. From now on I shall have to give all the time that I can spare to the preparation of my lectures there.

In any case I am not sure whether I should want to discuss contemporary poets. The only recent satire worth reading, if it could be called that, is, I think, Auden's *The Orators* and there again it is hardly etiquette for me to review books published by my own firm.

With all best wishes for the future of *Scrutiny*.

Yours sincerely,
[T. S. Eliot]

TO *Stephen Spender*   TS Spender

9 June 1932   Faber & Faber Ltd

My dear Spender,

I am ashamed of not having answered your very interesting letter of March 13,[3] but your postcard of May 27 encourages me to write now.

---

1 – L. C. Knights (1906–97), literary scholar and critic, held a Research Fellowship at Christ's College, Cambridge, 1930–1, and was founder-editor of *Scrutiny: A Quarterly Review*, 1932–53. He taught at Manchester University, 1933–47, and was Professor of English at Sheffield, 1947–53; Winterstroke Professor of English at Bristol; King Edward VII Chair of English at Cambridge, 1965–73. Works include *How Many Children had Lady Macbeth?* (a lecture published by Gordon Fraser's Minority Press, 1933); *Drama and Society in the Age of Jonson* (1937); *Explorations* (1946); *Some Shakespearean Themes* (1959). TSE to Helen Gardner, 20 Oct. 1956, refers to LCK as 'a former disciple of Leavis, who is, I think, very intelligent' (Bod. MS Eng. lett. d. 294, fol. 18).

2 – Knights invited TSE to write a Note on Modern Satire, for the third number of *Scrutiny* scheduled for 1 Dec. 'You will probably agree that there is very little contemporary satire of any value, and it would be useful if this were stated authoritatively and the reasons analysed.'

3 – Actually 18 Mar.

First of all, about the poems. For you to feel obliged to present them at any particular date – in fulfilment of a vague promise – would be spoiling the ship for a ha'p'orth of tar. The point is that we should be ready to publish the book when you are satisfied that it is ready. As for the novel, it is certainly best, as you have put so much work into it, that you should get it out of you and off your mind, especially if it means £75. I am afraid, however, that I shall have left England before you return, if you do return: I must leave by the middle of September – I shall be in London most of the time until then – and shall probably not get back until the beginning of next June.

Another reason why I should have written sooner is that I quoted without permission from your letter, in my last broadcast talk. The temptation was great, as you gave me an exact formulation of an attitude I wanted to deal with; nobody knew who my correspondent was, and I can't see that it would do any harm if they did: but I suppose that a gentleman would ask permission before quoting from any letter in public; and sometimes I suspect that I have come down in the world so far as to have become tainted with the conscience of a gentleman.[1]

I can't agree that religion provides such an effective escape as you seem to think. The great majority of people find their escape in easier ways; there are a great many unimaginative, selfish and lazy people who profess to be religious, but a vastly greater number who are not: and the real question seems to me not so much what can be done with the English Church but with the English people. All of the middle classes want to be gentlemen, and being a gentleman is incompatible with holding any strong religious convictions; with the latter, one must at least be prepared sooner or later to commit some ungentlemanly act. And for one person who escapes through religion into a 'sentimental dreamland', there are thousands who escape by reading novels, by looking at films, or best of all, by driving very fast on land or in air, which makes even dreams unnecessary.

My position is always a difficult one to maintain, or rather to defend effectively, because, if one doesn't like the new, one is naturally supposed to be a supporter of the old. The 'old', as it appears to me, is just one stage in the same progression of which your new is the next, and it is indifferent to me which stage is actual. What really matters is not what I think about the Church today, or about Capitalism, or military processions, or about

1 – 'Building up the Christian World', *The Listener*, 6 Apr. 1932, 501–2; see also TSE to Spender, 18 Mar. 1932, above.

Communism: what matters is whether I believe in Original Sin. I know that there are plenty of material injustices to be set right, and I want them to be set right; nevertheless I believe that the world will always be an unpleasant place, a place of trial for individual souls, and that the vast majority of its population will always be a compound of knave and blockhead, chiefly moved by vanity and fear, and kept quiet by laziness.

Do you really suppose that 'chastity, humility, austerity, and discipline', as I mean them, have anything whatever to do with what is taught in school-room chapels? If people really knew what the words mean, they would lock up or deport anyone who pronounced them. So my flesh does not creep at the thought of any 'new' morality – because it is just the same old decayed puritanism taking another form: I am not concerned with how people behave, but with what they think of themselves in their behaviour; and I believe that the man who thinks himself virtuous is in danger of damnation, *whatever* line of conduct he adopts.

This letter threatens to become more and more incoherent, so, as it is lunch time anyway, I will stop.

Yours ever,
T. S. Eliot[1]

TO *Willard Thorp*   TS Princeton

9 June 1932   *The Criterion*

My dear Thorp,

Here is the poem of your young man[2] which I forgot to bring home to hand you the other night. It seems to me that if he is only nineteen he is quite likely to outgrow his present very imitative stage, and produce something original. But the present poem strikes me as just an attack of distemper. I hope that we may see you both again before long.

Yours sincerely,
T. S. Eliot

1–Spender recollected, in *World Within World*: 'This letter I remember reading in the bright spring sunlight in the Hofgarten at Munich. There I felt sure that I did not believe in "Original Sin". I supposed, even, that it was wrong to do so. Nevertheless, I felt guilty and disturbed at the back of my mind when I read this letter, which was an answer to mine disputing his pamphlet, *Thoughts after Lambeth*, in which he maintained that what the young need is to be taught "chastity, humility, austerity, and discipline"' (148).

2–The poet was named Horton.

TO *John Maynard Keynes* TS Marshall

9 June 1932 *The Criterion*

Dear Keynes,

Can you tell me anything about a youthful economist named Geoffrey Biddulph? I am sure that I have heard of him – I think from some of the Mosley people. He has sent me in a reply to Penty's article on yourself[1] in which he defends your position very stoutly. I thought, therefore, that he might have been a pupil of yours at Cambridge. I can't possibly use this article which is hardly more than a long letter, because so much time has gone by, but if he is a youth of ability, I should be glad to put him on to something else.[2]

<Apologies for bothering you.>[3]

Yours sincerely,
T. S. Eliot

P.S. It does not seem to me that it was any very extreme praise for me to call Marx's work impressive.[4] Anything that has impressed so many people is at least impressive as a historical phenomenon. There is, I admit, a great deal that I can't understand, and the whole theory of historical materialism and economic determinism in the Marxian sense is just to me an incredible religious dogma.

1–Arthur J. Penty, 'The Philosophy of Mr J. M. Keynes', C. 11 (Apr. 1932), 386–98.
2–Keynes replied, 10 June: 'I do not know much about Geoffrey Biddulph . . . He is not a student of mine. I have seen a number of journalistic contributions of his and he also writes to me from time to time. From my point of view I find his stuff of a right tendency. But he is an amateur interested in these matters rather than a professional or academic economist.'
3–Added by hand in the margin.
4–Keynes had challenged TSE, 5 Apr.: 'I have been much enjoying your own series in *The Listener*. But why, on page 468 of *The Criterion*, do you allege that no one can fail to be impressed by the work of Marx? Have you read him? And are you impressed? I have just made another try in the last few weeks, and it absolutely beats me what people find in him.'

TSE had devoted his April 'Commentary' to the issue of 'what Péguy would have called *la mystique* of economics; the mixture, which may easily be a muddle, of economic theory, humanitarian enthusiasm, and religious fervour . . . [N]o one who is seriously concerned can fail to be impressed by the work of Karl Marx. He is, of course, much more cited than read; but his power is so great, and his analysis so profound, that it must be very difficult for anyone who reads him without prejudice on the one hand, or without any definite religious faith on the other, to avoid accepting his conclusions.

'But those who are in this way converted to Marxism must also become converts to the religion to which it has given rise . . . And it is exactly in its religious development that Communism seems to me to collapse and to become something both ludicrous and repulsive.'

TO *James G. Leippert*   CC

9 June 1932   [Faber & Faber Ltd]

Dear Mr Leippert,

Thank you for your letter of May 21st.[1] I should be very glad in principle to contribute to the *Lion and the Crown*, but I am afraid that it will have to be at least a year hence, as I cannot possibly find the time to do any work for periodicals between now and then.

Yours sincerely,
[T. S. Eliot]

TO *G. R. Elliott*   CC

9 June 1932   [*The Criterion*]

Dear Mr Elliott,

I must apologise for my delay in dealing with 'Two Anglican Qualities'.[2] I have hesitated over it a good deal, but have come to the conclusion that it is not quite suitable for the *Criterion*. I hope that you can offer me something else before long. Possibly you might submit this essay to a new review called *Scrutiny*, at 13 Leys Road, Cambridge.

Yours sincerely,
[T. S. Eliot]

TESTIMONIAL FOR *John Hayward*[3]   TS King's

10 June 1932   *The Criterion*

I have followed Mr John Hayward's work with interest ever since he came down from Cambridge to London. He has reviewed regularly for *The Criterion* and I have also read his contributions to *The Times Literary Supplement* and other papers.

---

1 – Leippert had urged TSE to reconsider his refusal. *The new broom* was to be 'reorganized (and revitalized!)' in the form of *The Lion and Crown* – the first issue being due in Oct. – with contributing editors including Mark van Doren and Irwin Edman. He 'would be glad to pay' at least $50 for the privilege of publishing 'some critical article' by TSE – 'out of my own pocket'.

2 – Elliott called his paper 'a piece of mock-Oratory with a grave idea in the background. The idea seemed to me too grave to be treated too gravely by me – or, perhaps, by any one writer.'

3 – John Davy Hayward (1905–65), editor and critic: see Biographical Register.

His scholarship is considerable, his criticism acute, and his style admirable. I have found his reviewing in certain departments indispensable; but I have often expressed the wish that he might use his abilities in writing more literary essays, rather than in reviewing and editing, so that they might secure a wider recognition and express themselves in a more permanent form.

T. S. Eliot

TO *Paul Elmer More*   TS Princeton

10 June 1932   *The Criterion*

My dear More,

I find I have not answered your letters of March 8th and April 22nd, for which I apologise. First of all it is a great disappointment to learn that you have postponed your visit until next year, and my wife wishes me to convey her regrets. But I look forward to spending a couple of evenings with you in Princeton. The authorities have written to me to say that they would like me to give the lecture on March 8th.

I was very much pleased with your review of Knox–Lunn.[1] That is to say I found myself wholly in agreement with it. The book seemed to me very unsatisfactory. At least Lunn raised a number of questions which to me are irrelevant or of small importance, and was incompetent to find his way quickly to the weakest point in Knox's position and stay there. The result seemed to me that Knox has much the best of the argument, but more through Lunn's weakness than through his own strength.

I was sorry on the other hand to see the extract which represents you in a book which we have published ourselves, called *Whom Do Men Say That I Am?*[2] It seems to me a bad book, but then I was never in sympathy

1–More reviewed *Difficulties: Being correspondence about the Catholic Religion between Ronald Knox and Arnold Lunn*, in C. 11 (July 1932), 739–44.
2–*Whom Do Men Say That I Am?*, chosen and ed. by H. Osborne (formerly scholar of Trinity College, Cambridge). The catalogue reads: 'Whatever views men may hold of the origin and destiny of mankind and of the individual, there is one figure in human history whose challenge none can ignore. To the orthodox Christian, Jesus is the answer to all problems. To the sceptic He is the problem which, left unanswered, will in the end undo all answers to all other problems.

'In this book Mr Osborne has brought together the different opinions which men of different creeds and schools of thought have uttered about Jesus. No collection of this kind can be entirely comprehensive. But the reader will find that the passages chosen are not only based on a very wide field of reading, but reflect a very wide variety of views. The writers laid under contribution are those of our own time or of the very recent past; and they include

with the project. But I really did not know that you were so unsound on the subject of the Virgin Birth. But I hope to have the opportunity of a discussion on the whole subject of the Incarnation when I see you.

May I keep the two reviews which you sent me? You seem indeed fortunate in having such intelligent reviewers. Burke especially impressed me.[1] I have heard nothing from P. S. Richards and am wondering whether to write to him or invite someone else.

Yours ever sincerely,
T. S. Eliot

TO *G. Wilson Knight*   CC

10 June 1932   [*The Criterion*]

Dear Wilson Knight,

Thank you for your letter of the 12th.[2] I imagine that you are now settled at Cheltenham again for the summer. It is very kind of you to suggest my coming down. I should very much like to be able to do so, but I am afraid that I cannot get away. I expect to be here until I sail in September. If I go away in the summer it will only be for a few days at a time, and I should be very glad to see you whenever it would suit you to come to town. My wife and I would be very glad to have you dine with us.

Yours sincerely,
[T. S. Eliot]

---

theologians, philosophers, scientists and artists.

'Here, then, is the composite answer which the modern world has so far made to the question which forms the title of the book.'

The passages taken from the works of Paul Elmer More (pp. 58–63) are: (i) 'The Definition of the Council of Chalcedon defended and explained by the Philosophy of Platonism. The Incarnation is essential to the Existence of Religion itself'; (ii) 'The Superficiality and Religious Poverty of "liberal" interpretations of Jesus'; (iii) 'Virgin Birth and Resurrection'.

1–Francis Burke, 'The Faith of Dr More', *The Commonweal*, 9 Mar. 1932, 516–18: a review of *The Catholic Faith*. More wrote to TSE, 8 Mar.: 'Burke is a very learned Jesuit of Georgetown University. He has, I think, hit the bull's eye quite in the centre by raising the fundamental question of faith in the Church rather than any subsidiary question of heresy. The last part of his paper suggests to me that the issue ought to be taken up by some Anglican. Can the Anglican Church give to its communicants any equivalent for the sort of assurance, with its mystical ethos and its power, which Burke holds out to the Romanist? . . . The issue is fundamental, as you will admit . . . I am writing to P. S. Richards [author of *Belief in Man*] and proposing the subject to him.'

2–12 May.

TO *Ruth Harrison*[1]   CC

10 June 1932   [*The Criterion*]

Dear Miss Harrison,

I must apologise for my delay in answering your enquiry of the 20th May.[2] I have thought over the problem of how your book on Péguy should be dealt with, as I am sure from what I have seen that it would be a pity if it could not be published. I am afraid that it is a book which could have but a very limited sale. A small number of people in England know something about Péguy, and a few may even have read a volume of *Morceaux Choisis*, but any real interest in him is something still to be aroused. I think that it is the sort of book which one of the University Presses ought to consider. I should be very glad to write to one of my friends in the Clarendon Press about it, and will do so whenever you like, but I feel that I can write with more conviction when I can say that I have seen the complete manuscript.

Yours sincerely,

[T. S. Eliot]

TO *Israel I. Mattuck*   CC

10 June 1932   [Faber & Faber Ltd]

Dear Mr Mattuck,

Thank you for your note of the 25th.[3] I think that we came to the conclusion, as we are often reluctantly compelled to do, that although

1–Following six years at the École Supérieure, Vevey, Switzerland, Ruth Harrison won a scholarship to Westfield College, London, where she gained a first class degree in French (with English subsidiary); she then took a six-month secretarial training course at Mrs Hoster's College. After a year of working in temporary posts at Girton College, Cambridge, she spent five years as Secretary to the Headmistress, Roedean School, Brighton. 'I have subscribed to the *Nouvelle Revue Française* and the *Criterion* ever since I discovered them,' she added to her CV.

2–Harrison had finished her study of Charles Péguy: it was to be put up for a PhD degree, but she was also anxious to get it published. Would F&F be interested, she asked? 'I cannot help thinking it is time Péguy was known in England. In some ways, he might be more acceptable to Englishmen than Frenchmen. The question of the exact nature of his orthodoxy – or lack of it – is less pressing, & idiosyncracies of form less distressing to us, I imagine. And the moment seems an opportune one, with the publication of Bergson's new book, which is surely one that would have rejoiced Péguy's heart. I even allow myself to trace touches of Péguy-action in it.'

3–'I wonder whether you have come to any decision about publishing such a book as you described in your first letter.'

there is no book fulfilling the requirements, there seem to be enough
somewhere near the subject to make the possibility of getting just the
right book and of selling it extremely doubtful. I should myself be much
more interested in a really exhaustive piece of scholarship on a large scale,
but such a work could of course only be handled by one of the University
Presses.

With many thanks for your helpful kindness.

Yours sincerely,
[T. S. Eliot]

TO *Kenneth Clark* CC

10 June 1932   [*The Criterion*]

Dear Mr Clark,

Here is *The Quattro Cento* again. If you can possibly find the time,
could you let us have 1000 words by August 1st? And I very much hope
that you will find something kind to say about it.

I did so enjoy last Sunday. Barbara, I am sorry to say, is feeling very
bitter about the R.I.B.A.[1] so I harangued her in my most sententious
manner, and told her how we must all start at the bottom . . . etc. . . . .

With best wishes to both of you,

Yours sincerely,
[T. S. Eliot]

TO *Etienne Gilson*[2] CC

10 June 1932   [*The Criterion*]

Sir,

I am writing to ask whether you would do me the honour of reviewing
for the October number of the *Criterion* a critical edition of the *Rime
of Guido Cavalcanti* which has just been published in Genoa under the
editorship of Mr Ezra Pound and Professor Manlio Dazzi. I do not suppose
that you are often inclined to review books for literary periodicals, but
I hope that the exceptional nature of this book will make you disposed to

---

1 – The Royal Institute of British Architects, London.

2 – Etienne Gilson (1884–1978), renowned philosopher and scholar of medieval philosophy;
taught at the University of Paris, 1921–32.

do it for me. The fact is that to the best of my knowledge and belief you are the only man in Europe with the mastery of mediaeval philosophy which is required in discussing Cavalcanti.[1]

In any case I should like to tell you how very much I have enjoyed and admired your books on Saint Thomas and Saint Bonaventura.[2]

I send a copy of the *Criterion* so that you may understand what kind of periodical it is.

I am, Sir,
Your obedient servant,
[T. S. Eliot]

TO *A. L. Rowse*   TS Exeter

10 June 1932   Faber & Faber Ltd

My dear Rowse,

I ought to have written before: but I think that I understood that you were going to ring again. I should like very much to meet Tawney;[3] but I rarely go out in the evening; and so I should be so grateful if you would arrange a lunch. We could arrange most evening [*sic*] if you could ring me up here one morning, or at Ambassador 1518 in the evening; but I am usually free for lunch a week or so ahead.[4]

Of course I know I have been called a prig, you goose; that's how I made my acquaintance with the word.[5]

Yours ever affectionately,
T. S. Eliot

1–Gilson reviewed EP's *Guido Cavalcanti, Rime*, in C. 12 (Oct. 1932), 106–12.
2–*Saint Thomas d'Aquin* (1925); *La philosophie de saint Bonaventure* (1924).
3–R. H. Tawney (1880–1962) – economic historian, social critic, ethical socialist, Christian socialist; President of the Workers' Educational Association, 1928–44 – was Professor of Economic History at the London School of Economics, 1931–49. Publications include *The Acquisitive Society* (1920) and *Religion and the Rise of Capitalism* (1926).
4–Rowse wrote on 28 May: 'There's such a charming French Professor at the School of Economics, Vaucher, – he's a very distinguished historian . . . I'd like you to meet both him & Tawney, & they'd like to meet you, if you can bear to come down to a meal at the School in the evening. Could you? It's rather squalid . . .' (Paul Vaucher [1887–1966], Professor of French History and Institutions at the University of London, 1922–42, was author of *Robert Walpole et la politique de Fleury (1731–1742)* (1924), *Le monde Anglo-Saxon au XIXe siècle* (1926). See John C. Rule, 'Paul Vaucher: Historian', *French Historical Studies* 5: 1 [Spring 1967], 98–105.)
5–See footnote to TSE's letter to ALR, 11 May, above.

Sunday, 12 June 1932	68 Clarence Gate Gardens,
3.30 pm	Regents Park

My dear Mary

I cant write very much now. As I am just going out.

I want to thank you *very very much* for having planned & arranged our interview at 51 Gordon Square.[1] We went, in good order & arrived at 12.30. as Tom had to go to Church *first*.

I must just tell you at once now, that the rooms & the house are more beautiful & desirable than even I had dreamed. Miss Strachey[2] is sweet, isn't she, & was so *kind* to us both.

You will have seen the rooms. On top there are 2 big & 1 little, also bathroom & good kitchen. Just the same number as we have here. Whereas *here* we have the *economy* & convenience of the constant hot water, (which is not in every way a real benefit) (*cont'd* at 8.30) at 51 Gordon Square we shd. have the rather higher gas bills. That is nothing at all. I have been interrupted 3 times in writing this letter. Yet it is of vital importance to me. I promised to write to Miss Strachey, – I will. Tom very *much* likes the rooms & knows he would be happy there. Poor Tom, let him have *somewhere* to work in that he likes *before* he dies. So *my idea* is to take the *top* flat, & to gradually decorate & furnish it beautifully, & to live there quietly & cultivate my mind. Then I would like, once having found out the *actual* price of Lytton's 2 rooms – to start a *Society*, or *Fund*, to keep them always perfect in memory of Lytton. And to let Tom have the use of them for writing, reading & thinking.

You would perhaps like to be the 'Curator' if they would let you. I mean you shd. have a big part in this. Now I must stop for tonight. Please think it over, & I beg you say no more to *anyone* until I see you.

Bring Barbara on Wednesday afternoon at 4. o'clock.

---

1 – MH had suggested that the Eliots might take rooms at the Strachey home; nearby were Adrian and Karin Stephen at no. 50; the Keyneses at no. 46; the Woolfs at 52 Tavistock Square.

2 – Philippa Strachey (1872–1968) – 'Pippa' – one of the many siblings of Lytton Strachey, was prominent in the movement for women's rights. As Secretary of the London National Society for Women's Suffrage she organised in 1907 the first mass feminist demonstration of the National Union of Women's Suffrage Societies, and during WW1 she organised the Women's Service (finding jobs for women and training them for skilled work). She was secretary of the London Society for Women's Service, 1918–51. See further Barbara Caine, *Bombay to Bloomsbury: A Biography of the Strachey Family* (2005).

With much love, & many thanks – say nothing until I see you. Do not mention it.

Yours ever,
Vivienne Haigh Eliot

I am worn out.

V. H. E.

TO *Sally Cobden-Sanderson* CC

13 June 1932   [Faber & Faber Ltd]

My dear Sally,

Many thanks for your impressive reply to my conundrums. I think that will do very well.

I take it that £40 covers the voyage both going and coming? That seems very cheap. And if I pay for the round trip I suppose I can come back at any time, on any boat, so long as I come via Cunard-Montreal? As I said, I return next May; but circumstances might make me come a few weeks earlier or later than May 15th.

Also, could the Cunard line (or yourselves) sell me a ticket straight through to Boston, or must I buy the rail ticket in Montreal? As I remember, Montreal is under a day, or about one night, from Boston. And finally, where does the customs and passport examination take place: on the train?

Will you please let me know if (I am typing this myself) you can secure a passage for me on the *Ausonia* for the 17th? and how many other people will be in the same cabin?

I think the books might as well go direct to Boston. I suppose the thing to do is to get somebody like Maple's to pack them.

With many thanks,
Yours ever affectionately,
[T. S. E.]

TO *Messrs James & James*   CC

14 June 1932   [Faber & Faber Ltd]

Dear Sirs,

Re 43 Chester Terrace

I have your letter of the 11th instant and return the enclosures herewith.[1] As for Gapp & Co. it seems to me that they have a reasonable claim on me for some commission. The situation is indeed rather an unusual one, and it hardly seems to call for the full commission. But on the other hand I recognise that I am escaping very lightly from the repairing and decorating clauses, so would you kindly negotiate with Messrs Gapp & Co. for what you consider a reasonable sum for me to pay.

Yours faithfully,
[T. S. Eliot]

TO *Charles du Bos*   TS Texas

15 June 1932   Faber & Faber Ltd

My dear du Bos,

Thank you very much for again remembering me with the new volume of *Approximations*.[2] I fell upon it instantly with some anxiety, to find out whether your essay on Baudelaire would be seriously upsetting to any of my own contentions in my own essay on the same subject. I do not think you have seen that and I will send to you in the autumn my new volume of selected essays in which it is included. I believe that though your essay is much more thorough and goes more deeply into the matter, there is no serious difference of opinion. I hope you will let me know what you think of it, and meanwhile look forward to the letter which you promised me.

I shall be in America between next September and next May, but I hope that I may get over to Paris after I am settled in London again.

With very many thanks,
Yours sincerely,
T. S. Eliot

---

1 – Enclosures not found.

2 – Charles Du Bos, *Approximations* (5th series, Éditions R.-A. Correa, 1932). 'For T. S. Eliot, in thanks for many valuable offerings and in anticipation of a second long letter (for him, not for Hodgson's!), from his faithful friend Charles Du Bos Thursday June 2nd 1932.'

15 June 1932 Faber & Faber Ltd

My dear Brother,

This is a very brief acknowledgement of your kind letter of the 15th May.[1] I should have waited until I could answer it more fully, but wish to return the letter from Merriman which you wanted back. I hope, by the way, that you have corrected his dates, as it ought to be 1843 instead of 1845.

I have no idea how soon I shall see you, but hope within a few weeks of my arrival. I certainly prefer coming down to New York by train to arriving there by water.

> With love to Theresa,
> Yours affectionately,
> Tom

TO *Charles K. Colhoun* CC

15 June 1932 [*The Criterion*]

Dear Colhoun,

Here is one of the French manuscripts which I mentioned to you. Could you let me have a translation as soon as possible, or rather will you let me know at once how soon you can get it done? As I explained to you, the point about this particular article is that Mauron especially asked me to translate it myself, and I want to be able to assure him that the translation has had my approval. So I shall ask you to send the original back with the translation, which indeed is the rule.[2]

> Yours sincerely,
> [T. S. Eliot]

1–See note to TSE's letter to HWE of 5 May 1932, above.
2–See Charles Mauron, 'The Cow', C. 12 (Apr. 1933), 454–67. No translator is credited.

15 June 1932   [*The Criterion*]

Dear Herbert,

Many thanks for agreeing to the 5th, as we shall then have both yourself and Bonamy. We shall expect you then at 6.30 at 24 Russell Square, where a very satisfactory supper is provided.

What is the position about 'Personality in Literature'? Is it still available for the *Criterion*? And if so will you want the manuscript back before it is set up in order to alter the preliminary lecture-room phrases?[1]

Yours ever,

[T. S. Eliot]

TO *Louis T. More*[2]   CC

15 June 1932   [Faber & Faber Ltd]

Dear Professor More,

I have your letter of the 25th May, and we have discussed the matter carefully.[3] I am afraid that the past year has forced us to alter our attitude toward many books in which under different circumstances we should be keenly interested. I want to make it quite clear that we are individually as much interested in your 'Life of Newton' as we were when we first discussed the matter with you. But the fact is, bluntly, that the margin of profit in the publishing business in London is now so very narrow that we cannot afford at present to consider any book which would lock up a considerable amount of capital. Your book would be, and indeed ought to be, an expensive book to produce, and while I should be confident of its future as the standard book on Newton, we should not expect to cover our expenses for several years.

I think that the only publishing houses which are likely to entertain such an enterprise are the University Presses, and one or the other, but

---

1–HR replied (21 June) that he had forgotten that TSE still had the manuscript of 'Personality in Literature': he regretted that it had already appeared in *Symposium* (USA).

2–Louis T. More (1870–1944) – physicist, humanist, critic of the Darwinian theory of evolution; Dean of the Graduate School, University of Cincinnati – was brother of Paul Elmer More. His works include *The Dogma of Evolution* (1925); *Isaac Newton: A Biography* (1934).

3–More reported on the progress of his biography of Newton, saying that it would now run to 300,000 words and would thus almost certainly become two volumes. Was F&F still interested?

specially the Cambridge Press, ought to undertake it. I cannot remember whether you had gone into the question with the Cambridge University Press before I saw you, though I believe that you had some discussion on the subject of subsidy with people at Trinity. But I should suggest that S.C. Roberts of the Cambridge University Press[1] is the man to approach, and Morley and myself would both be very glad to have you use our names.

We were disappointed to learn that Paul was not coming to England this summer, but I look forward to seeing him at Princeton in the winter and to seeing you here next summer if not in America.[2]

Yours very sincerely,

[T. S. Eliot]

TO *James Joyce* CC

15 June 1932   [Faber & Faber Ltd]

My dear Joyce,

It is such a long time since I have heard from you that I have begun to be rather anxious and am writing in the hope that if you do not feel up to writing yourself Mrs Joyce or your daughter may be so kind as to let me hear. I hope that nothing further has gone wrong with your affairs, and that *Work in Progress* is still in progress. I also hope to hear from Padraic Colum that he has succeeded in placing 'Ecce Puer' in New York as I should like to publish it in our December number.

---

1 – Roberts was Secretary of Cambridge University Press; author of *Dr Watson* (Criterion Miscellany 28, 1931).

2 – More responded to this letter only on 27 Sept. 1932: 'Your letter of June 15th I have not answered because, in the first place, it was a great disappointment to me, and . . . I thought I would have more accurate information to give you this autumn . . . I thought your intention was to have a combined publishing venture with an American house and I supposed that plan would divide the cost. In the next place, I have spent the summer revising the work and have so far finished eight chapters, ready for press. Not only have I very much improved the manuscript as a book, but I find that it can almost certainly be printed in one volume and if I remember rightly, that was your chief fear of an excessive cost.' TSE passed More's letter to FVM, who wrote to More on 19 Oct. 1932: 'The original notion had been to think of the life of Newton as a combined publishing adventure, but to work out such combination it generally means that one house takes the initiative and the other publishing house in the other country orders copies from the first . . . That was the situation at the time of our conversations in London, but after those talks the market began to get worse and worse until, thinking over our commitments, and our hopes, we felt the only fair thing to do would be to warn you that it did not look as if we could possibly take the initiative on the book.' Accordingly, he too advised More to contact S. C. Roberts of the Cambridge University Press, mentioning the names of TSE and FVM.

As you know I shall be going to America in the middle of September and shall not return to London until next May. Any business of yours in the meantime will be handled by Mr F. V. Morley whom you have met. Is there any possibility that you and Mrs Joyce may come to London again this summer?

Yours sincerely,
[T. S. Eliot]

TO *Henry Tonks*   TS Texas

15 June 1932   Faber & Faber Ltd

Dear Professor Tonks,

Thank you for your kind letter of June 11th.[1] We are of course deeply disappointed by your refusal to entertain the possibility of writing your Memoirs, but if at any time you should change your mind I hope that you will not forget our suggestion.

Yours sincerely,
T. S. Eliot

P.S. I do not think I have yet seen your painting of the Hutchinson family. Some time ago Mary showed me some delightful illustrations you had made depicting the adventures of McColl in Heaven.[2]

TO *Rolf Gardiner*   TS Cambridge University Library

15 June 1932   Faber & Faber Ltd

Dear Gardiner,

I have your letter of June 12, and I have discussed it with our Board.[3] While we do not generally undertake publications on such terms, we are

1 – Tonks replied to TSE's invitation by protesting that he had 'no capacity as a writer, no one knows better than you how difficult it is, even supposing you give your life to it. I intend as long as I can to paint which I firmly believe is a better way of finding pleasure in life than any other notwithstanding the disappointments.' He added that he had 'just painted a slightly comic dream of the Hutchinson family [who were close friends of his] which might amuse you for a time at Albert Rd where it is now.' (See Tonks's *Saturday Night in the Vale* [1929], Tate Gallery.)

2 – Dugald S. MacColl (1859–1948), writer and art critic; Keeper of the Tate Gallery, 1907–11, Wallace Collection, London, 1911–24. He was caricatured by Tonks in various guises.

3 – Gardiner (Baltic Festival Tour, 1932, c/o National Union of Students) asked F&F to publish *World without End* on a subsidised basis: his friends and colleagues would eagerly

inclined in the special circumstances to entertain your suggestion. First of all, however, it strikes me that the cost of printing an essay of 15,000 words could hardly be kept as low as £29. I suppose that your friends would be prepared to go higher than that. I should think that the cost would be somewhere in the neighbourhood of £40. The only way to let you have a definite figure is for us to have your manuscript back and make a proper estimate. The cheapest form of production would be similar to that of the *Criterion* miscellany, although your essay would not be uniform or be an item in that series.

It would have to be understood that the subsidy took the form of a cash payment as soon as the cost was known and upon signature of contract. I should like to know, furthermore, whether you would expect us to do anything in the way of distribution as this would naturally affect both our outlay and our overhead charges.

I understand that Mr Cobb is delivering it here today or tomorrow. We will accordingly go ahead with the estimate at once and meanwhile please let me know how many copies you are reasonably sure you can dispose of, and more definitely what you would expect us to do in the way of circulation of the pamphlet. I hardly think that we should be prepared to do any *advertising*, and if so that would of course have to be added on to the figures which I will give you.

I wonder whether you have received Lord Lymington's book on British Agriculture, called *Horn Hoof and Corn* which I had sent to your Wiltshire address. If you have time I should be very grateful if you would look at the book and if in your opinion it is sufficiently deserving write a short notice for the September *Criterion*. But I daresay that you will be too busy between now and your return to the continent.[1]

Yours sincerely,

T. S. Eliot

---

subscribe – 'provided that some firm of note and sufficiently interested to bring it before a greater public, will give it their imprint.' He hoped that the cost of printing the essay (*c.* 15,000 words) would amount to about £29, and that the work could 'be undertaken forthwith . . . The pamphlet will lose a great deal of its force if it is not issued during the time of the Ottawa Conference . . . My friends will do everything in their power to push the book, provided that Messrs. Faber & Faber are able to give their imprint and bring it to the notice of reviewers and the book-selling trade.' See *World Without End: British Politics and the Younger Generation* (Cobden-Sanderson, 1932).

1–See review of Viscount Lymington, *Horn, Hoof and Corn: The Future of British Agriculture*, in C. 12 (Oct. 1932), 134–6.

TO *Norman Foerster*[1]   CC

15 June 1932   [Faber & Faber Ltd]

My dear Foerster,

I have your letter of May 30th.[2] I am a little at sea because I cannot remember whether any of my poems were included in the previous edition of your anthology. It would take me some time to find out from my correspondence as I do not know when that edition appeared. But I cannot find that I possess a copy of the anthology. Could you please let me know which of my poems if any appeared in the previous edition?

Otherwise I should suggest that I should prefer not to have you include both 'Prufrock' and the Portrait. Choose whichever you prefer and make up with a few short poems. I suggest omitting the Portrait and putting in 'Gerontion'. You say Preludes. Do you mean all of them or only one? I had rather not include 'Because I do not hope' inasmuch as that is merely the first section of 'Ash Wednesday' and I had rather not have it appear again separately. I suggest that you might take any one of the five Ariel poems instead. The Ariel poems were all written in the year of publication. The dates of the others, so far as I can remember, are:

        Prufrock 1910–11
        Portrait of a Lady 1909–10
        Hippopotamus 1917
        Morning at the Window 1914
        Preludes 1909–1911

                            Yours sincerely,
                            [T. S. Eliot]

1–Norman Foerster (1887–1972) – a contemporary of TSE's at Harvard, though they did not meet there – taught at the University of North Carolina, Chapel Hill; then as Director of the School of Letters, University of Iowa, 1930–44. See Robert Falk and Robert E. Lee, 'In Memoriam: Norman Foerster 1887–1972', *American Literature* 44 (Jan. 1972), 679–80; J. David Hoeveler Jr, *The New Humanism: A Critique of Modern America, 1900–1940* (1977).
2–Foerster was reissuing his college anthology, *American Poetry and Prose* (Houghton Mifflin), and wished to include in it 'The Love Song of J. Alfred Prufrock', 'Portrait of a Lady', 'The Hippopotamus', 'Morning at the Window', 'Prelude', 'Because I do not hope'. 'This is a fair amount, but I do not wish to include anybody unless I can represent him pretty adequately.'

TO *D. S. Mirsky*   CC

15 June 1932   [*The Criterion*]

Dear Mirsky,

I am writing to ask if you will do a kindness for the *Criterion* either now or after you get to Moscow? A couple of years ago Miss Bertha Malnik[1] kindly arranged to have some of the more important Russian periodicals, such as are suitable for exchange with the *Criterion*, sent regularly from Moscow. Lately these appear to have been falling off, and I do not know why they have ceased to come. I attach a special importance myself to have the best Russian periodicals reviewed, and I shall be very much disappointed if we have to give up this item. The ones which my reviewer mentions are:

> *Novy Mir*,
> *Krasnaya Nov*,
> *Oktiabr*,
> *Proletarskaya Literature*,
> *Literature of the World Revolution*,
> *Sovremmeniya Zapiski (Les Annales Contemporaines)* published
>   in Paris.

I shall be very grateful for anything you can do.

Remember you promised to let me know before you leave England, as I shall be sorry not to see you once more before you go.

Yours sincerely,
[T. S. Eliot]

1–Lecturer at the School of East European Studies, University of London; translator.

TO *Kenneth Pickthorn*[1]   cc

15 June 1932   [*The Criterion*]

Dear Pickthorn,

I have your letter of the 11th.[2] I shall be very glad of course to have a talk with Richard Marriott, though I am afraid that the prospects of his getting a promising job in any publishing house at the present time are very slight. Perhaps he will write to me or telephone to arrange an interview as soon as he gets to London.

Yours sincerely,
[T. S. Eliot]

TO *R. F. Rattray*[3]   cc

16 June 1932   [*The Criterion*]

Dear Mr Rattray,

Indeed I remember you perfectly well, and the year that you spent at Harvard.[4] You were then agitating on behalf of Pan-Psychism, somewhat to the annoyance, as I remember, of the Neo-Realists who were flourishing at Harvard. The Neo-Realists apparently have now passed into oblivion and you have apparently taken up new interests.

I am afraid that I cannot use your essay, which is rather highly technical for the *Criterion*. A stronger reason is that I have recently had an essay in somewhat the same field by Christopher Dawson, and it is not a subject which the *Criterion* can make very much of. But I should be glad to see

1–Kenneth Pickthorn (1892–1975): historian and politician; Fellow of Corpus Christi College, Cambridge: see Biographical Register.
2–'Richard Marriott, who is just going down from this college, is rather thinking of trying to do something in the publishing line, and would be very grateful if he might see you and ask your advice. He came here from Uppingham, is in my judgment one of the nicest and ablest people we have had since the war, is taking quite a good degree although I do not think he has been lucky in his examinations; he has a little money of his own so that he would not mind how small a wage he were paid for the first year or two.'
3–Robert Fleming Rattray (1886–1967), teacher and writer on philosophy, and university adminstrator. Born in Glasgow, and educated at Glasgow University and Manchester College, Oxford, he spent two years at Harvard working on a PhD on Samuel Butler. On his return to England, he entered the Unitarian Ministry and become Pastor of the Great Meeting in Leicester, 1917. In 1921 he was appointed first Principal of the new Leicester, Leicestershire and Rutland College (later University College, Leicester); and after ten years at Leicester retired in 1931 to become Pastor of the Unitarian Memorial Chapel, Cambridge.
4–Rattray submitted on 18 May an article entitled 'Romance, Renaissance and Reformation'. He added, 'I think I am right in thinking that we were at Harvard together. If so, Greeting!'

anything you care to offer, and hope that if you are ever in London you may care to renew our acquaintance.

Yours sincerely,
[T. S. Eliot]

TO *Francis Birrell*[1]   CC

16 June 1932   [*The Criterion*]

My dear Birrell,

I have kept your essay on Diderot for an extremely long time without letting you know anything about it.[2] But during the past winter my delay has been intentional. I have [been] trying to collect enough good material by reliable people nearly to fill the three numbers of the *Criterion* which must appear in my absence in America. Will you be very kind and let me use this essay in one of the three numbers? I cannot tell yet just how I can best shuffle the material which I have accumulated.

I assume that you have not meanwhile arranged to publish this essay elsewhere, and am encouraged to that belief by the fact that several pages of it are in manuscript.

We shall be having a *Criterion* meeting here, at 24 Russell Square on the 5th of July. It is likely to be the last that we can have for some time to come, and I hope that you may care to join us as my guest any time after 8.15. We have fixed that date so that both Dobrée and Read will be able to come.

Yours sincerely,
[T. S. Eliot]

TO *Sherwood Trask*[3]   CC

16 June 1932   [*The Criterion*]

Dear Mr Trask,

I am very sorry that I have not found any of the poems quite suitable for

---

1 – Francis Birrell (1889–1935), critic; owner with David Garnett of a Bloomsbury bookshop; wrote for *NS&N*, and published two biographies: his life of Gladstone came out in 1933.
2 – Birrell submitted his essay on 20 Jan. 1931. 'I wonder whether these remarks on Diderot as a prose writer, not as a philosopher, could be of any interest.' Birrell, 'Things Diderot Could Do', *C.* 12 (July 1933), 632–41.
3 – Sherwood Trask (1890–1973), poet and teacher. A graduate of Dartmouth College, he

the *Criterion*.[1] I was much more interested in your play, but unfortunately it is impossible to find room in the *Criterion* for a play of such length. I should always be glad to see more of your dramatic work which I have found interesting, especially if you have anything more brief.

With continued interest,
Yours sincerely,
[T. S. Eliot]

TO *A. D. Peters*[2]   CC

16 June 1932   *[The Criterion]*

Dear Mr Peters,

I find that I have overlooked for a long time Mr T. M. Ragg's[3] story 'The Pond' which you sent me on the 9th September last. I very much regret not having been able to use it, but it is only by a very exceptional coincidence of a number of short articles that I am able to print such a long piece of fiction. I have come to the conclusion that it is hopeless to expect a number in which I may use this story and can only say that I should like to see more of Mr Ragg's work if of suitable length. A story of about two thirds of this length would be much more easy to find a place for.

Yours sincerely,
[T. S. Eliot]

---

taught at colleges including the Stelton Modern School and the Manumit School, Pawling, New York; and finally as a social science teacher at the Walden School, New York City. Publications include *The Interweaving Poetry of American History* (poems, 1967).

1 – Trask submitted 'several poems' on 2 Apr. 1931; the play in question cannot be identified. (His poem 'A Footnote of History' had appeared in *NC* 5 [Jan. 1927], 43–4.)

2 – A. D. Peters (1892–1973): Prussian-born literary agent (formerly August Detlef). Educated at St John's College, Cambridge, he worked in early years as a literary editor and drama critic before founding in 1927 a literary agency which came to represent authors including Hilaire Belloc, Edmund Blunden, Alec Waugh, J. B. Priestley, Rebecca West, Terence Rattigan, A. E. Coppard, Evelyn Waugh, C. Day-Lewis and Frank O'Connor. In the 1950s he worked with Norman Collins and Lew Grade in forming the Associated Television (ATV) company, which enjoyed considerable commercial success.

3 – T. M. Ragg (1897–1953), editor at Routledge & Co.; author of *The Emperor Charles V and the Rise of Modern Europe* (1928).

16 June 1932   [Faber & Faber Ltd]

Dear Professor Nelson,

Thank you for your letter of May 31st which somewhat alters my
attitude towards your previous suggestion.[1] I am willing to have you use
the 'Portrait of a Lady', 'Gerontion', 'Journey of the Magi' and 'Animula'
if that selection suits you.

Ordinarily I ask a nominal fee as a matter of principle for any anthology
use of my verse, but I understand that your anthology is an unremunerative
educational undertaking, and if you assure me that payment is impossible
I shall be glad to consider waiving the fee.

Yours sincerely,
[T. S. Eliot]

TO *Gertrude P. Kurath*[2]   TS British Library

16 June 1932   *The Criterion*

Dear Mrs Kurath,

I must apologize for the delay in returning the two volumes which you
sent for my inscription. I do not find, I confess, anything much to inscribe
in the books, but I have acknowledged for the first time my authorship of
the essay, by writing my name on the title page.[3] The pamphlet was really
written, as well as I can remember such a distant event, at the instance of
Mr Knopf who was publishing some new book of Mr Pound's and wanted

---

1–Nelson pleaded for 'a little fuller representation' of TSE's work in his forthcoming
anthology: to meet 'a serious gap'. The anthology in question was not aimed at the general
reading public but at the college market. 'It is not designed to make money; at least I don't
see how I can ever make a penny out of it, although the publishers probably will. My sole
reason for consenting to edit it is the hope of providing my classes in American literature,
and others like them, with a sound introductory guide to a literary period which they find
bewildering.' With this 'humble purpose' in mind, he asked: 'Would you on any account
consider allowing me to use "Portrait of a Lady" along with "Journey of the Magi" or
one of the others? Or if not that, might I not use two, possibly three, of the Ariel poems?
To reprint only one seems so pitifully inadequate that, if the Introduction did not show a
realization of the importance of your work, I should be concerned over what fellow-teachers
might think of my critical judgment.'
2–Gertrude Prokosch Kurath (1903–92), American dancer, researcher, author and ethno-
musicologist, Her husband was the Austrian-born linguist Hans Kurath (1891–1992).
3–*Ezra Pound, His Metric and Poetry* (New York: Alfred A. Knopf, 1917 [Jan. 1918]; repr.
in *TCC* (1965), 162–82.

an introductory essay for the uninitiated. The essay was anonymous merely because my name was entirely unknown and would not in any way have increased interest in the pamphlet.

As for *Ash Wednesday*, I am very glad that you like it. I feel that I am the last person to be qualified to compare this poem with *The Waste Land* and indeed I always find it more practicable, so far as it is possible, to put everything that I have previously written out of my mind.

Yours sincerely,
T. S. Eliot

TO *Bernard Windeler*[1]   CC

16 June 1932   [*The Criterion*]

Dear Windeler,

I had been hoping to arrange a meeting for lunch with you in the city for a long time, but feel that I must finally write. I am afraid that volumes of verse are pretty well out of the question at present, but I had been hoping to hear from you again about your short stories. What has happened to them, and can I see any of the stories which have not yet been published?

I shall be in England until early in September and hope that we can arrange a lunch during this month or next.

Yours sincerely,
[T. S. Eliot]

TO *G. Rostrevor Hamilton*[2]   CC

16 June 1932   [*The Criterion*]

Dear Mr Hamilton,

I am sorry that I have hesitated so long over my decision about your essay on Conrad Aiken,[3] but many other things have turned up, each of which has seemed more suitable at the moment for the *Criterion*, and I do not think we ought to hold the essay any longer, especially as it is of

---

1–Windeler worked for Windeler & Co., 20 Basinghall St., London, and wrote plays, songs and poems, using the pseudonym 'W. Bernard'.
2–George Rostrevor Hamilton (1888–1967), poet and critic, studied classics at Oxford and worked as a civil servant: he was knighted in 1951. *The Tell-Tale Article: A Critical Approach to Modern Poetry* (1949) includes a section on the achievement of TSE.
3–Submitted on 19 Dec. 1931.

considerable length. Have you thought of sending it to the *Hound and Horn* in America? That is the most likely review that I can think of as I do not suppose that the *London Mercury* could find room for anything of this length.

Yours sincerely,
[T. S. Eliot]

TO *Allen Tate*[1]   CC

16 June 1932   [*The Criterion*]

Dear Tate,

I ought to have written to you sooner about your essay on John Dewey.[2] I quite agree that the subject matter is important enough for publication anywhere, but the trouble is that very few people here are familiar with Dewey's work, and therefore I am afraid that your essay in its present form would fail in its effect. I do hope that you will have something new to offer me soon, and I hope that I may have a chance of seeing you somewhere while I am in America this winter.

Yours sincerely,
[T. S. Eliot]

FROM *Vivien Eliot* TO *Aurelia Bolliger*   MS Beinecke

20 June 1932   68 Clarence Gate Gardens

Dear Aurelia,

After your telephone call this afternoon I am writing to tell you that I understand that you & R. H. are going away to c/o John Drinkwater Esq. Pepys House – Brampton Huntingdonshire Ely – & that you will write me directly you *arrive*. I expect you back on *Friday* evening *before 8 p.m.* If you have to leave *before Friday*, you will bring Picky straight here to me, & stay till R. H. returns. You can come at any time, *without notice*. On Friday I shall be *here* until 8.30, & then at 7 Oak Hill Park N.W.3. Telephone – Ham. 4839. Please see if you can.

1–Allen Tate (1899–1979), American poet, critic and editor: see Biographical Register.
2–Submitted on 4 Dec. 1931: 'I am sending you a short article on a text out of John Dewey's *Philosophy and Civilization*. I'm not sure that he is much read over there, but his views of art are enough like I. A. Richards' to make the subject familiar to your readers.'

Telephone me from Huntingdon.

Yrs ever
V. H. E.

TO *T. F. Burns* CC

22 June 1932 [Faber & Faber Ltd]

Dear Burns,

I will discuss the question of Kierkegaard with my people, but I am under the impression that some of us talked of the matter some time ago and came to the conclusion that it was not likely to be a success. If, however, you are considering an Essay in Order on the subject that rather alters the matter and I will go into it afresh.[1]

I have just read the manuscript of a book or very long essay on Péguy by a young woman who I believe had a brilliant career at Girton and who is now teaching French somewhere.[2] It seemed to me to be more in your line than in mine, and I should be very glad if you were willing to look at it. If you found it impracticable as a book it seemed to me that she might boil it down for an Essay in Order.

Yours ever,
[T. S. Eliot]

TO *Rolf Gardiner* TS Cambridge University Library

22 June 1932 Faber & Faber Ltd

Dear Gardiner,

In reply to your letter of the 16th.[3] I hope to be able to provide an estimate for you within a few days. We shall naturally put the book forward through the usual channels and will send out copies for review.

---

1 – Burns wrote on 20 June: 'I have just read a couple of essays on [Sören Kierkegaard] by Theodor Haecker and they only make me wish the more that his works, or some of them, would get into translation . . . I am wondering whether Faber's would make a move. I have the outline of an "Essay in Order" on him which I would publish if they did. Can you give me any hope?'

2 – Ruth Harrison, Westfield College, London.

3 – Gardiner questioned TSE's declaration that the printing of 15,000 words would cost more than £29, and requested 'a proper estimate': 'I think I could safely dispose of 500 copies without difficulty, but would like to have a printing of 2000. Our last publication: In Northern Europe 1930 had an edition of 1500 and was sold out within three months.

If you know of any journals to which you would like review copies to be sent and which we might be likely to overlook, I shall be glad to have their names. I doubt, however, whether we could afford to do any advertising although, of course, we should be quite ready to advertise it at your expense. I am doubtful, however, whether this is the type of book which has much to gain from advertising.

As for the circular, it seems to me that it would be as well if we had it printed for you, and I am sure that we could have it done as cheaply as possible consistent with decent appearance. We would then send you the bulk of the copies for distribution purposes, and retain such as we could make use of ourselves. If this suits you I will get an estimate of the cost of printing the folder and let you know.

Yours sincerely,
T. S. Eliot

то *James Joyce*   cc

22 June 1932   [Faber & Faber Ltd]

My dear Joyce,

Thank you for your letter.[1] I am extremely sorry to hear your news of Lucia. You do seem to me to have had more misfortune within the last few years than any one man is entitled to have, and I do not wonder that you have found it impossible to work. I should have thought that in these

---

'I naturally hoped that any contract with Faber and Faber for publication with their imprint would include agreement on their part to push the book in the Trade, to secure reviews in the leading papers and to include the title in their advertising list. I would agree to cash payment on the signing of such a contract.'

1 – JJ reported from 2 Avenue S. Philibert, Passy, Paris, 20 June 1932, that his daughter Lucia had suffered a nervous breakdown and was spending time in a rest home: she was in the care of a nurse-companion, two doctors and a specialist neurologist. The effect on JJ was that he had been unable to carry on with his work for the last two months, and he did not know when he might pick up again. His wife too was perturbed and concerned. He went on: 'I cannot go to Zurich, of course, though Vogt sent me a message to come. A French cook took my London flat for 3 months. I am giving it up anyway. I worked all the winter and wish I could go on. Giorgio and family are in the south of France. Gorman seems to have vanished. Two Japanese pirated editions of *Ulysses* have appeared this spring and 13,000 copies have been sold to date. Is Japan a signatory to the Berne convention or not? *Ulysses* stands under French law. The pirates allege that European books become public property in Japan after 10 years. You remember somebody in your office advised me to ask certain terms. The Japanese found these terms and advance absurd as my lease had only 6 months to run. *U* was published 2/2/1922 and the first Japanese edition came out in Tokyo on 5/2/1932. No news from the American publishers . . .'

times French sanatoriums would be more accommodating in their prices. For instance the Sanatorium de la Malmaison at Rueil where my wife has been twice is extremely good, and specialises in that sort of trouble. They used to have a good many foreign patients and I should think that they must be suffering from the general depression, and would cut their prices. But I dare say you have looked into all this. At any rate I think that French doctors are as good as any in the world for this sort of trouble. I hope that she will soon recover. What worries me particularly is that this calamity is preventing you from going to Zurich, although to judge from your writing your eyes seem pretty strong.

Your news from Japan is also very depressing. I hope that the American engagement will be carried through satisfactorily, and also, of course, I shall be delighted if John Lane succeeds in publishing *Ulysses* without molestation, though from the result of our own enquiries I shall be very much surprised.

I am afraid, then, that there is no likelihood of our meeting until some time after I return from America next summer. In the circumstances it is no doubt out of the question for you to come to London this summer.

I am extremely glad to hear of the success of Lucia's illustrations.

Yours ever sincerely
[T. S. Eliot]

TO *Herbert Read*   CC

23 June 1932   [*The Criterion*]

Dear Herbert,

I enclose a copy of a letter which I have just received from Tom Burns. I believe you are almost the only person who knows anything about Kierkegaard, and I should like to have your opinion. I had a word with Martin D'Arcy on the subject last night. I don't think he knows very much about Kierkegaard either, but he was under the impression that he was an author who was bound to have a run in England sooner or later, and the

---

'The moment I have any good news I will send it. John Lane is "considering" *Ulysses* with the assistance of a Home Office man and a police solicitor. It is rather unfair and most un-English that the army and navy, the fire brigade and the Worshipful Fraternity of Frothblowers are not represented on their committee of public safety' (*Letters* I, 320).

Lucia Anna Joyce (1907–82) – trained as a dancer, talented as an illustrator – was diagnosed as suffering from schizophrenia and in consequence passed long stretches of her life in asylums. For her last thirty years she was in the care of St Andrew's Hospital, Northampton. See Carol Loeb Schloss, *Lucia Joyce: To Dance in the Wake* (2003).

only question is that of the right moment. Please let us know what you think.

Yours ever,

[T. S. E.]

TO *Etienne Gilson* CC

23 June 1932   [*The Criterion*]

Dear Sir,

Thank you for your kind letter of the 15th June and for your very interesting review of the *Rime* which has just arrived.[1] I am greatly obliged to you.

I will convey your message to Mr Bonamy Dobrée.[2]

Yours sincerely,

[T. S. Eliot]

TO *Bonamy Dobrée* TS Valerie Eliot

23 June 1932   *The Criterion*

Dear Bonamy,

Professor Etienne Gilson has asked me to convey to you the following message:

'That if he is right in telling that Frenchmen do not see that foreigners do not always relish being Frenchmen (p. 558) it is because of their radical inability to think that a man (French or not) is not a man. And, of course, it is an awful mistake for men (French or not) very seldom act and behave as men. There is nevertheless something to be said in favour

---

1–Review of *Guido Cavalcanti, Rime*, C. 12 (Oct. 1932), 106–12. 'This magnificent edition of *Guido Cavalcanti* will certainly be welcomed by all students of Italian literature. It seems to be his author's [EP's] desire to remain anonymous; whoever he may be, I want to assure him that I fully realize what a claim he has on the gratitude of his readers, even where they feel inclined to disagree with some of his interpretations. The text of the *Rime* in a critical edition, photostatic reproductions of the most important manuscripts, English translations of several poems, learned commentaries on their meaning, the whole enterprise carried on with a care and accuracy deeply rooted in the passionate love of the editor for his poet, all this is enough to put the book on a higher level than the ordinary reprint of an old text. I am not quite sure that *Guido Cavalcanti* "is not inferior to Dante in quality" (p. 9), but I am glad his editor and translator felt that way.'
2–See next letter.

of that attitude and the problem of humanism – once more – is involved in the question. The French revolution was behind Napoleon, and it was full of Greeks and Romans, crowded with humanistic memories. This is why Napoleon hailed the Egyptians as co-nationals and, at the same time declared that the French were just like the Egyptians. It is one and the same position, – and blunder; for besides being men, they were French, and Egyptians. With many apologies to Mr B. Dobrée, for I really enjoyed his review.'[1]

Yours ever,
T. S.

TO *Ezra Pound*   TS Beinecke

23 June 1932   *The Criterion*

Dear Rabbit,

Gilson's lengthy review of the *Rime* has now arrived. He does not mention your name and says at the beginning 'It seems to be the author's desire to remain anonymous'. As I sent Gilson the one copy which you sent me I can't check this now, but I don't remember any suggestion of anonymity. Please tell me what to say and I will alter the manuscript.

Yours in haste,
T.

1 – BD responded to Gilson's remarks, in a letter to TSE of 2 July: 'If I could speak to him frankly, I would ask, "But are you sure that what you claim as humanism is not really intolerance? an inability to understand how anybody can think differently from yourselves?" I myself, of course, being of the race that I am, prefer the English point of view, which seems to imply all the time a respect for the personality of others. It is not such a useful point of view politically, but to me it seems the better humanism to let other people differ from yourself, and to understand that they do differ, even if you do not understand why.

'I don't really believe that Napoleon was so humane as M. Gilson suggests. He wanted to make the Egyptians co-nationals for obvious reasons, and in his guile guilelessly supposed that he would make them so by flattering them with the appellation.'

TO *Willard Thorp*   TS Princeton

23 June 1932   *The Criterion*

My dear Thorp,

I must apologize for not having been able to reply at once to your letter
of the 16th. In any case I was not free for lunch any day this week.[1] I
am sorry as I understand that Penelope is leaving on Saturday. Perhaps,
however, we can arrange another day in the same neighbourhood.

The last *Criterion* meeting of the season will take place on the evening
of July 5th and will be here, at 24 Russell Square instead of at the Poetry
Bookshop. I shall be very glad if you care to look in any time after half
past eight.

Yours sincerely,
T. S. Eliot

TO *Francis Birrell*   CC

23 June 1932   [*The Criterion*]

Dear Birrell,

Thank you for your note.[2] I have put down your Diderot tentatively
for the March '33 number, though it may possibly be switched over to
December '32. I don't think that the appearance of two new volumes
affects the paper seriously, but if you care to add a paragraph or a note
you are quite welcome. If you like this might be done on the galley proof
if the additions were only slight.[3]

I am very glad that you can come on the 5th.

Yours sincerely,
[T. S. Eliot]

1–Thorp and his wife Margaret invited TSE to lunch with them and their friend Penelope
Noyes who was also visiting London. TSE's sister Ada wrote to him on 14 Jan. 1934:
'Penelope Noyes . . . said that one afternoon with V. [VHE] used her all up, and what must
it be to live with.'
2–Birrell asked (undated: 'Friday') whether he should add to his article some words about
the two volumes of Diderot's general correspondence that had just appeared.
3–Birrell, 'Things Diderot Could Do', C. 12 (July 1933), 632–41.

TO *Robert Fitzgerald*   CC

23 June 1932   [*The Criterion*]

Dear Fitzgerald,

I wish very much that I could use your review of Pound's *Cavalcanti*,[1]
but unfortunately I had already arranged for that to be done by Etienne
Gilson who has sent me a very long review indeed.

I am sorry to hear that I shall not see you again before you leave England,
but I hope you will pay me an early visit in Eliot House in October.[2]

Yours sincerely,
[T. S. Eliot]

TO *Kenneth Pickthorn*   CC

23 June 1932   [*The Criterion*]

Dear Pickthorn,

I shall be in London nearly all of the time until I leave in the middle
of September so I hope that you will be up for a week or two in London
before then. I am afraid it had not occurred to me that you would care to
bother about Dibdin's book, and I gave it to Smyth a week or two ago.
Incidentally you are on a select list of people who will receive a circular
letter asking them to suggest to the Secretary any books that they care
to review for the three numbers which will appear during my absence
in America. I hope that you will support me by a couple of long reviews
during that period.

If July 5th should happen to fit in with a visit to London we should be
very glad indeed if you could come to a *Criterion* evening here at any time
after 8 o'clock, with light refreshments.

Yours ever,
[T. S. Eliot]

1–Fitzgerald submitted a three-page review of *Guido Cavalcanti Rime*: 'I cannot pretend to
scholarship in Italian, nor to more scholarship in Cavalcanti than I could obtain from this
edition; if my piece has merit it is not a scholarly one. Anyway, I think you'd like to see it.'
2–Fitzgerald wrote on 15 June, 'I shall be leaving England in a hurry, and without being in
London again . . . I am very grateful for those two talks at Faber & Faber.'

TO *R. B. Merriman*[1]   CC

23 June 1932   [Faber & Faber Ltd]

My dear Master,
   I have to thank you cordially for your lines of June 8th,[2] and to express
my satisfaction and appreciation of the privilege of spending the winter in
Eliot House. I look forward also to making your acquaintance.
                                        Yours sincerely,
                                        [T. S. Eliot]

TO *Montgomery Belgion*   CC

23 June 1932   [*The Criterion*]

My dear Belgion
   About the Gide. I have had to collect as much material as I can in
advance and have worked out a tentative table of contents up to June
1933. At present I have the Gide down for the March number.[3] I expect
your French chronicle in time for September (August 1st)[4] and there is
a book for which you asked to review for the December number.[5] That
seems to me about the best that I can do.
   I have read with much interest the Flying Column which you have sent
me, and which is obviously, at least the important part of it, written by
your hand. I shall keep it by me in the hope that you may be over in
London this summer, and that we may have an argument about it, because
it does not seem to me to make sense. You are quite used to having people
assert roundly that you have completely misunderstood their meaning,

---

1 – Roger Bigelow Merriman (1876–1945): historian; first Master of Eliot House. Educated
at Harvard (PhD, 1902), Balliol College, Oxford, and in Berlin, he was appointed full
professor in 1918. Publications include *Life and Letters of Thomas Cromwell* (1902), *Rise
of the Spanish Empire* (4 vols, 1918–34). Fellow of the American Academy of Arts and
Sciences; vice-president of the Massachusetts Historical Society; Fellow of the American
Antiquarian Society; he received hon. degrees from Oxford, Glasgow and Cambridge.
2 – Merriman wrote on 8 June that he was pleased 'to extend you a formal invitation to
occupy the Visiting Professor's suite in Eliot House for the academic year 1932–33'.
3 – 'A Postscript on Mr André Gide', C. 12 (Apr. 1933), 404–20.
4 – 'French Chronicle', C. 12 (Oct. 1932), 80–90.
5 – Review of Lionel Robbins, *An Essay on the Nature and Significance of Economic Science*,
C. 12 (Jan. 1933), 292–5.

but in this case I think that you have also taken my remark rather too seriously.[1]

> Yours ever cordially
> [T. S. Eliot]

TO *Raymond D. Havens*[2]   CC

23 June 1932   [Faber & Faber Ltd]

Dear Mr Havens,

I am very much obliged to you for your kind letter of June 8th, and to the Poetry Society for doing me the honour of inviting me to address them.[3] I think the temptation is great, but I am unfortunately under the necessity of husbanding my strength as much as possible, and I feel that it would be imprudent for me to undertake any other public engagements for speaking in Baltimore beyond the Turnbull lectures. My chief responsibility after all is toward Harvard, and I feel that I must concentrate my energies. I am very sorry to have to come to such a decision, but I hope that I may at least have the opportunity of making your acquaintance and that of some of the other members.

> With many thanks,
> I am,
> Yours very truly
> [T. S. Eliot]

TO *R. E. Gordon George*   CC

23 June 1932   [Faber & Faber Ltd]

My dear Robert,

Very many thanks for your letter of the 15th. I had heard from Mrs Dixon Davis whom we are always delighted to see that you were on your

---

1 – Belgion responded on 30 June: 'I am not surprised you find I have not understood you, because I cannot understand you in this case. Concerning your fear that I must have taken your remark too seriously, the "Flying Column" must not be taken too seriously.'

2 – Raymond D. Havens, Department of English, School of Higher Studies, The Johns Hopkins University, Baltimore, Maryland.

3 – Havens hoped that TSE might be able to have time to speak to the Poetry Society when he came to Baltimore as Turnbull Lecturer. 'There will be no attempts to exploit you. The Society contains but few persons of social distinction and could probably pay you only $100.00.'

way to Paris and might possibly be expected in London. How good of you to remember the fur-coat which I am looking forward to protect me throughout the winter.[1] We also heard from Mrs Monro that she saw you in Hyères. Apparently she enjoyed her travels very much indeed and returned looking very much better.

I was beginning to think that you were staying too long at home, but I suppose that economy made it necessary.[2] Do write a line from Paris to let me know when you are to be expected in London. I shall be leaving for America about the middle of September and I hope that you can be in London long before then and discuss my plans with me.

I am afraid that *Albert the Good* will be rather out of date for the *Criterion* review. I am sorry that I missed it at the time, but the July number is practically ready and even the September number is already full, so that there is no opportunity for any more books until September. I will find out about the other book.[3]

Yours ever affectionately,
[T. S. Eliot]

TO *David Cecil*[4]   CC

24 June 1932   [*The Criterion*]

Dear Cecil,

Thank you very much for your note of the 20th and for the interesting essay on Victorian novelists. The only thing that bothers me is that you say that the book is to be published by Constable this year. My September number is already overflowing with material which I cannot possibly defer any longer and the earliest possible number in which I could publish your essay would be December. Can you let me know the approximate date of publication of the book?[5]

1–'[S]oon I must start for Paris . . . and when I do I shall have yr fur coat with me.'

2–'[M]y people have departed from Hyeres, and it has become a place of peace to me. To be in your home and unmolested is a joy almost unknown to me, and it has filled me with energy.'

3–George asked to review *Albert the Good*, by Hector Bolitho, and/or *The Works of Man*, by Lisle March Phillipps (with a preface by HR): he reviewed the latter in *C.* 12 (Jan. 1933), 305.

4–Lord David Cecil (1902–86), historian, critic, biographer; Fellow of Wadham College, Oxford, 1924–30; Fellow of New College, 1939–69; Professor of English, Oxford University, 1948–70; author of *The Stricken Deer* (1929), *Early Victorian Novelists: Essays in Revaluation* (1934), *Jane Austen* (1936), and studies of other writers including Hardy.

5–Orlo Williams was to write to TSE on 23 Dec. 1934 – 'Unless you very much desire it, I propose not to send you a review of Lord David Cecil's *Early Victorian Novelists*. I

I saw your sister[1] yesterday afternoon and she told me that you had sprained your ankle (or strained it, she wasn't sure which). But in the uncertainty I hope that the injury is not so serious as to prevent your coming to us on Monday.[2]

Yours sincerely,
[T. S. Eliot]

TO *R. Ellis Roberts*   CC

24 June 1932   [*The Criterion*]

Dear Roberts,

Ezra Pound has written to say that he is very anxious to review Adrian Stokes's *Quattro Cento* which we have recently published. Unfortunately I had already arranged for it to be reviewed for the *Criterion* by someone else. But Ezra is so anxious to write about the book and now knows the subject matter so thoroughly that I wish he might have the opportunity of reviewing it somewhere else. I trust you will not consider it professional indiscretion if I suggest that unless the book has already gone to someone else I believe Ezra might do it very well for the *New Statesman*.[3]

Yours sincerely,
[T. S. Eliot]

TO *Geoffrey Biddulph*[4]   CC

24 June 1932   [*The Criterion*]

Dear Mr Biddulph,

I have read your comments on Mr Penty's criticisms of Mr J. M. Keynes[5] with much interest. But in any case I should not be able to publish them

---

can find nothing to say about it but "painstaking and uninspired". And I don't think it is worth saying that in the *Criterion*' – and TSE replied on 27 Dec.: 'I take your word for it about David Cecil's book. He is a nice fellow, but he never struck me as having any very distinguished abilities.'

1 – Either Beatrice Ethel Mildred Cecil, or Mary Alice Gascoyne-Cecil, who married in 1917 Edward Cavendish, Lord Hartington (later 10th Duke of Devonshire).

2 – Cecil had accepted an invitation to tea on Mon. 27 June; in the event, he did not make it.

3 – Roberts (*NS&N*) replied on 27 June that regrettably the Stokes volume had already been assigned. See EP's review of Stokes, *Stones of Rimini*, C. 13 (Apr. 1934), 495–7.

4 – Biddulph reviewed C. H. Douglas's *The Monopoly of Credit*, in *The Economic Journal* 42: 166 (June 1932), 268–70.

5 – Penty, 'The Philosophy of J. M. Keynes', C. 11 (Apr. 1932), 386–98.

until the December number, and by then too much time would have elapsed since the publication of the Penty article, and your brief essay is hardly self-sufficient without reference to it. So I am afraid that I shall not be able to make use of it. But I should be much interested to see more of your work on similar subjects.

I understand from Keynes, by the way, that he feels considerable sympathy with the position taken up by Penty.

Yours very truly,
[T. S. Eliot]

TO *Ruth Harrison* CC

24 June 1932   [*The Criterion*]

Dear Miss Harrison,

When I read your essay it struck me that it might be more suitable for Sheed & Ward than for either of the University Presses. It is an R. C. firm of course, but quite unofficial and also enlightened, and they are the only people who have shown much intelligent interest in the propagation of continental thought. I have mentioned your book to Mr T. F. Burns of that firm and he would like to see it, but I am writing to ask for your permission before sending it to him.[1]

Yours sincerely,
[T. S. Eliot]

TO *John Gould Fletcher*[2] CC

24 June 1932   [*The Criterion*]

My dear Fletcher,

It is a very long time since I heard from you or have had news about you, and I have begun to be anxious. For aught I know you may be out of England, but if you are still in London can we not make an engagement? And will you not try to get to the last *Criterion* evening of the season which will be held here on July 5th? It is a very long time since you came to any of the *Criterion* parties, but wherever you are please let me hear

1 – Burns told Harrison on 5 July he had read her MS 'with the very greatest interest – I think it an excellent introduction to a very important and quite unknown figure' – but he did not think they 'would sell a sufficient number of copies to justify' publication (copied to TSE).
2 – John Gould Fletcher (1886–1950), American poet and critic.

from you when you get this. I shall be leaving for America in the middle of September and want to see you before I go.

Yours ever,
[T. S. Eliot]

TO *Barbara Whittingham-Jones*[1]   CC

24 June 1932   [*The Criterion*]

Dear Miss Whittingham-Jones,

The trouble is I have already filled up all the reviewing space in the October number, and I fear that the books you mention[2] are not sufficiently pertinent to the *Criterion* to justify our reviewing them so long after their publication next December. I have looked at the *Eighteen-Sixties*, and it struck me as a very slight affair. Perhaps you will have some other suggestion, or some recent book will present itself by the beginning of September.

Yours sincerely,
[T. S. Eliot]

TO *Kenneth B. Murdock*   CC

28 June 1932   [Faber & Faber Ltd]

Dear Dr Murdock

I should have written before to express my appreciation of the kind offices of your father in arranging for permission for Faber & Faber to publish my lectures in England.

In order to simplify my financial arrangements and to prevent my having to transfer money from one side to the other more than is necessary, I wonder if it would be possible for the University to pay in a part of my salary, say 1000 dollars, to my Boston Banker, The Old Colony Trust Company, 17 Cork Street, some time in September before my arrival. I am only known to the Trust Department there, but no doubt

1–Barbara Whittingham-Jones, later Oppenheim (d. 1947): journalist, who was to spend time in Malaya – becoming famous for her article 'Malaya Betrayed', *World Review*, May 1946

2–Whittingham-Jones (Liverpool) asked (15 June) to review Denis Gwynn, *Life of John Redmond*; Stanley Morison, *The English Newspaper*; *The Eighteen-Sixties*; Elizabeth Jenkins, *Lady Caroline Lamb*.

it would be quite easy for them to open a current account with cheque book to be given to me upon identification. If this can be done it will be a great convenience to me as I shall have current expenses on this side of the water simultaneously. I should be grateful if you could let me know whether it can be done or not.[1]

Yours sincerely,
[T. S. Eliot]

TO *Sally Cobden-Sanderson* CC

28 June 1932   [Faber & Faber Ltd]

My dear Sally,

I thought that I might be hearing from you again after your letter of June 15th. If you have got me a single berth cabin on the *Ausonia*, Southampton to Montreal, sailing September 17th, that will suit me to perfection. I also want the ticket to Boston. I am practically certain to return in May as I said, perhaps quite early in the month, and in fact I must do so. But in the case of illness or other unforeseen complications would be it be possible to make the return condition for either May or June 1933?

I should think that 50 books would be a generous allowance. I am told that the libraries are very good and I shall only need to take special working copies.

Please let me know what the total cost will be and when I have to pay the bill.

Yours ever affectionately,
[T. S. E.]

TO *Peter Davies* CC

28 June 1932   [Faber & Faber Ltd]

My dear Davies,

I do not know whether the recent expansion of your business gives any opportunity for a beginner, but I am writing to ask you to see Mr

---

1 – The Dean's Secretary wrote on 19 July: 'The Bursar will be glad to have $1000 of your salary deposited at the Old Colony Trust Co., as you request, as soon as the salary has been voted by the Corporation, which will be on or about September 26.'

Richard Marriott who has just come down from Cambridge very highly recommended by my friend Kenneth Pickthorn who was his tutor. As there is no prospect of our having a vacancy here of any sort I should be very grateful if you could at least see him and advise him.

Yours sincerely,
[T. S. Eliot]

TO *Richard Cobden-Sanderson*[1]   cc

28 June 1932   [Faber & Faber Ltd]

My dear Richard,

This is to introduce to you Mr Richard Marriott who has just come down from Cambridge and is anxious to get some sort of job in a publishing business if possible. Mr Marriott is very highly recommended to me by my friend Kenneth Pickthorn who was his tutor at Corpus, and as there is no possibility of our taking on anyone at present I am venturing to ask you to see him. At Cambridge he worked in history and modern languages. Unlike most applicants he does not seem to have many illusions about publishing. I talked to him for some time and I did not get the faintest impression that he wanted to write poetry. Everything is in his favour. I hope at least you can see him.

Yours ever,
[T. S. Eliot]

TO *Scott Buchanan*   ts Houghton

28 June 1932   *The Criterion*

My dear Buchanan,

I am terribly afraid that this will be too late – pressure of business and private affairs drove it clean out of my head for some days. If I am too late, please forgive me; I hope that you will have met Maritain in any case through Gilson. Please let me hear from you if this reaches you somehow

---

1 – Richard Cobden-Sanderson (1884–1964), printer and publisher, son of the bookbinder and printer T. J. Cobden Sanderson (1840–1922); grandson of the politician and economist Richard Cobden (1804–65). He launched his business in 1919 and was publisher of C. from its first number in Oct. 1922 until it was taken over by F&G in 1925. He also published three books with introductions by TSE: *Le Serpent* by Paul Valéry (1924); Charlotte Eliot's *Savonarola* (1926); Harold Monro's *Collected Poems* (1933).

and somewhere. I do hope that the voyage will be accomplished safely, and that your mother will be better when she gets home.

Yours sincerely, and with humble apologies,

T. S. Eliot

TO *Jacques Maritain*[1]   TS Houghton

28 June 1932   Faber & Faber Ltd

Cher ami,

Je me permets de vous présenter le Professeur Scott Buchanan, professeur de philosophie à la Université de Virginie en Amérique. Monsieur Buchanan s'interesse vivement à tous les problèmes de la philosophie chrétienne, et il s'occupe surtout à ce moment de l'instruction supérieure au moyen âge. Je vous serai bien reconnaissant si vous aurez le loisir de le voir pendant son bref séjour à Paris.

Mes amitiés sincères,

T. S. Eliot

J'espère vous revoir à Paris après mon retour de l'Amérique au mois de mai 1933.[2]

1–Jacques Maritain (1882–1973), philosopher and littérateur, was at first a disciple of Bergson, but revoked that allegiance (*L'Evolutionnisme de M. Bergson,* 1911; *La Philosophie bergsonienne,* 1914) and became a Roman Catholic and foremost exponent of Neo-Thomism. For a while in the 1920s he was associated with *Action Française,* but the connection ended in 1926. His works include *Art et scolastique* (1920); *Saint Thomas d'Aquin apôtre des temps modernes* (1923); *Réflexions sur l'intelligence* (1924); *Trois Réformateurs* (1925); *Frontière de la poésie* (1926); *Primauté du spirituel* (1927); *Distinguer pour unir ou les Degrés de savoir* (1932); *Humanisme intégral* (1936); *Scholasticism and Politics* (1940); *Creative Intuition in Art and Poetry* (1953). See Walter Raubicheck, 'Jacques Maritain, T. S. Eliot, and the Romantics', *Renascence* 46:1 (Fall 1993), 71–9; Shun'ichi Takayanagi, 'T. S. Eliot, Jacques Maritain, and Neo-Thomism', *The Modern Schoolman* 73: 1 (Nov. 1995), 71–90; Jason Harding, '"The Just Impartiality of a Christian Philosopher": Jacques Maritain and T. S. Eliot', in *The Maritain Factor: Taking Religion into Interwar Modernism,* ed. J. Heynickx and J. De Maeyer (2010), 180–91.

'The Jacques and Raïssa Maritain papers held at Kolbsheim include five letters and two Christmas cards from Eliot. That cannot however be the totality of their correspondence.' (James Matthew Wilson, '"I bought and praised but did not read Aquinas": T. S. Eliot, Jacques Maritain, and the Ontology of the Sign', *Yeats Eliot Review* 27: 1–2 [Spring–Summer 2010], 21).

2–*Translation:* Dear Friend, I take the liberty of introducing to you Professor Scott Buchanan, Professor of Philosophy at the University of Virginia in America. Mr Buchanan has a keen interest in all issues relating to Christian philosophy, and he is currently concentrating on higher education in the Middle Ages. I will be very grateful if you have the time to see him during his brief stay in Paris. Yours sincerely, T. S. Eliot.

I hope to see you again in Paris after my return from America in May 1933.

TO *David Cecil*   CC

29 June 1932   [*The Criterion*]

Dear Cecil,

Thank you for your note of the 28th. I am very sorry about the complications in your ankle. Had you been well enough to come the other day I should have suggested that we should be glad of your company at the last *Criterion* meeting of the year which will take place here next Tuesday evening from 8.15. I gather that you may not be about for some days to come. Otherwise we should have been very glad of your company.

I am very sorry about your essay and the book. In normal circumstances I should have said let me keep the essay and in the event of your book being delayed I will use it in December. But as I am leaving in September for seven months in America I have to arrange the body of the *Criterion* as completely as I can for three months in advance, and therefore I cannot leave matters in this way. But I hope that you may be able to send me something else later which I could use perhaps in March or June.

Yours sincerely,
[T. S. Eliot]

TO *Bennett A. Cerf*   TS Columbia University Libraries

29 June 1932   Faber & Faber Ltd

Dear Mr Cerf,

Thank you for your kind letter of June 20.[1] You are so amiably pressing in the matter that you make it all the more painful for me to refuse again. But the fact is that I cannot possibly undertake any piece of writing beyond the lectures which I have to prepare between now and the end of the year, and I doubt if I shall have time for anything but my lecture work until a year hence. I assure you that my reason for refusing is wholly that

---

1 – 'If we could persuade you to reconsider this matter, we would put off our publication of this book until late December of this year. This would mean that your introduction would not have to be in our hands until September 1st.

'Can't we tempt you with this change of plan? What we want is so close to the essay that you wrote for your Faber and Faber booklet, that you should be able to do the whole piece in a few hours time. And it is true that $100.00 commissions are not too plentiful in these worst of times for the publishing business. You see, I am trying to be as persuasive as ever I can, because we feel that your introduction to this book would be of inestimable value to us.'

I cannot possibly find the time to carry out even the simplest piece of work.

> With many regrets,
> Yours sincerely,
> T. S. Eliot

TO *Herbert Read*   CC

29 June 1932   [*The Criterion*]

Dear Herbert,

Many thanks for your letter of the 27th so neatly typed. If it is any saving of time on Tuesday will you go straight to the Oxford and Cambridge Club. Frank will bring Wheen with him.[1]

I see that we must look carefully into the Kierkegaard matter, but this is the worst possible time for starting such a venture. I think that if we went in for it we ought to do it thoroughly and get a translation made direct from the Danish if there is any competent translator.[2]

There is a book I have just received which I think you might like to possess – *Unpublished Letters of S. T. Coleridge,* published by Constable, two fat volumes, edited by Earle Leslie Griggs, who from his name I should judge to be an American professor. Yes, I see that he gives his address as

---

1–HR would arrive at King's Cross on 5 July, expecting to reach Russell Square by 1.15 p.m.

Arthur Wheen (1897–1971), librarian and translator, grew up in Sydney, Australia, and came to Europe with the Australian Expeditionary Force in WW1 (he received the Military Cross 'for some incredible act of valour in the last war, which provoked a temporary break-down,' as TSE said). A Rhodes Scholar at New College, Oxford, 1920–3, he worked in the Library of the Victoria & Albert Museum, becoming Keeper, 1939–62. He translated novels relating to WW1, winning praise for his translation of Erich Maria Remarque's *All Quiet on the Western Front* (1929); and he wrote one novella, *Two Masters* (1924, 1929). TSE wrote of him: 'He's completely honest, and one of the most silent men I know.' FVM thought his modest friend 'the best critic I know, bar none' (letter to Morley Kennerley, 5 July 1933). See *We talked of other things: The life and letters of Arthur Wheen 1897–1971,* ed. Tanya Crothers (2011).

2–'About Kierkegaard. The more I know about him the more I want to know, and I feel pretty sure he is the most important writer of his kind still to be translated into English. And the tide is with him. From what I know of him, I should say it is a case of all or nothing; his work is of a very personal nature, and one wants to follow his development from the beginning. I think the German translation of his complete works runs to about twelve volumes . . . But I think in a way it is a good enterprise for an English publisher. There is not the slightest doubt of his permanent value: I should put him considerably higher than Amiel, for example, and as high as Pascal, though that sounds like a rash statement . . . I strongly recommend you to go ahead.'

the University of Michigan.[1] I don't suppose that you would want to take the time to make it the peg for an article or a long review, but if you will at least do a short notice you may have the books.[2]

Yours ever,

[T. S. E.]

TO *Ferris Greenslet* cc

29 June 1932   [*The Criterion*]

Dear Mr Greenslet,

Thank you very much for your letter of June 15th.[3] A review copy of *Conquistador* was received and I am sending you a copy of our July number which is just out, where you will find the book discussed in the Poetry Chronicle.[4] But I am very glad to have a copy for myself. There is no living poet in America who seems to me to have greater technical accomplishment than MacLeish and I am always interested in his new work.

I expect to arrive in Boston about the 27th of September and shall be domiciled at Eliot House, Cambridge, and shall look forward to the pleasure of seeing you.

With many thanks,

Yours sincerely,

[T. S. Eliot]

1–Earl Leslie Griggs (1899–1975), a native of New York, worked at the Universities of Minnesota, Oregon, Michigan and Pennsylvania, before reaching the University of California as a Senior Professor in 1947. He published sixteen books and over forty scholarly articles, notably his acclaimed eight-volume edition of *The Collected Letters of Samuel Taylor Coleridge*.

2–Review of *Unpublished Letters of Samuel Taylor Coleridge*, ed. Griggs (2 vols, 1932), C. 12 (Oct. 1932), 164–5.

3–Greenslet sent TSE a copy of Archibald MacLeish's *Conquistador*.

4–John Gould Fletcher wrote in his 'Verse Chronicle' that *Conquistador* was 'one of the happy events of this half-year': 'Mr MacLeish is vigorous. The sun and air in his poem do not come out of books, and his Spaniards, though they may be too highly coloured for reality, have a real poetical existence. In short, Mr MacLeish has a style' (C. 11 [July 1932], 688).

29 June 1932   [Faber & Faber Ltd]

Dear Frederick,

Thank you very much for your letter of June 13th and for the pains you have taken in procuring an invitation for me to speak in Saint Paul.[1] I am, however, a little uncertain about the date of January 12th. As I think I told you I intend to go to Saint Louis privately for two or three days directly after Christmas, and immediately after that I want to go to California if I can secure one or two invitations to speak there. I am very anxious to cross the continent to the Pacific and I feel that I may never have another opportunity, and being so uncertain of any dates which I can make in California I cannot be positively certain that I can speak in Saint Paul on January 12th, though it might very likely fit in exactly.

As I imagine the University wants to arrange a speaker for this particular event before the autumn I am afraid that I had better ask for the alternative, the Women's City Club, if the date for that could be left open for a few months. I think I can be in Saint Paul at some time between the 10th and the 25th of January, certainly not later. I wish very much that I could say yes definitely for January 12th, but there is that possibility that it might interfere with my western visit.

With many thanks for your trouble and also for your hospitality, to which I look forward.

Yours ever affectionately,
[Tom]

1–Prof. Joseph Warren Beach wanted TSE to talk to the University of Minnesota Convocation on 12 Jan. 1933, for a fee of $100; and the Women's City Club were offering $100 for a lecture.

TO *Eleanor Farjeon*[1]   CC

29 June 1932   [*The Criterion*]

Dear Miss Farjeon,

Thank you very much for your kind letter.[2] I was unable to lay my hand
on any copy of the original transcript and therefore sent you three issues
of the *Listener* which I have. The talks had to be put [*sc.* cut] down, of
course, for the *Listener*, but I do not think that anything important was
omitted. I am sorry that I have not the 4th talk, but I understood from
you that you had heard that one. In my opinion it was the best of the lot.
As for the others I am only afraid that you will find on reading them that
the content is very much weaker than you supposed.

Yours sincerely,
[T. S. Eliot]

TO *Grace Hart Crane*   TS Butler Library

29 June 1932   *The Criterion*

Dear Madam,

I have your letter of June 7th and am having sent to you a copy of
a number of the *Criterion* in which is a poem by your son.[3] I imagine,
however, that this poem was also published in America, and that you
have already a copy of it. I am sorry to say that I have no manuscripts of
his at all.

1–Eleanor Farjeon (1881–1965), author of stories and plays for children, poetry, history
and satire; a friend of DHL, Walter de la Mare, Robert Frost and Edward Thomas, she
supported herself through poetry, journalism and broadcasting. Works include *Martin
Pippin in the Apple Orchard* (1921), *Martin Pippin in the Daisy Field* (1937), *The Little
Bookroom* (stories illustrated by Edward Ardizzone, 1955); and *Edward Thomas: The Last
Four Years* (1958); she also wrote the popular children's hymn 'Morning has Broken' (1931).
2–Farjeon asked on 25 June if TSE could spare a typed copy of his recent BBC talks on
'The Modern Dilemma', so she could read those she had missed and also share them with a
friend, Mr Earle, 'who lives with me' (Mr Earle had taught VHE at King Alfred's, he said):
'For those 2 or 3 weeks you mattered more to us than most things that were happening.'
3–Mrs Crane hoped to find 'enough unpublished poems to produce another book . . . I am
taking this opportunity to inquire of you concerning any writings of his, which in times past,
may have been published in your magazine.' Hart Crane (1899–1932) was author of *White
Buildings* (1926), *The Bridge* (1930): see *Complete Poems and Selected Letters*, ed. Langdon
Hammer (1997); Lee Oser, *T. S. Eliot and American Poetry* (1998). 'The Tunnel' appeared
in *MC.* 6 (Nov. 1927), 398–402.

I must take the opportunity of expressing both my personal sympathy and my regret at the death of a poet, much of whose work I admired very much. There are very few living poets in America of equal interest to me. I shall look forward to the book with great interest.

Yours very truly,
T. S. Eliot

to *Rolf Gardiner*   ts Cambridge University Library

29 June 1932   Faber & Faber Ltd

My dear Gardiner,

I am now able to inform you that our estimate for *World without End* comes to £41, 5d. without allowance for advertisement. I must add that if you dealt directly with the printer yourself it appears that you could get the pamphlet published for about £30, but we are obliged to add £10 for the overhead expenses in this office which of course include our name as publisher and our service of distribution. In the estimate no allowance is made for advertisement which is, as you probably know, an expensive matter, and in the case of a pamphlet of this sort hardly likely to justify itself. We should send our review copies to what seem to us the suitable papers and to whatever other papers you recommend, yourself. But as for advertising we should have to ask you to let us know where and how you wanted it advertised and charge you for the cost of the advertisement.

Will you let me know at once whether this is satisfactory?

Yours sincerely,
T. S. Eliot

P. S. Please let me know also about the circular.

to *C. K. Colhoun*   cc

30 June 1932   [*The Criterion*]

Dear Colhoun,

I am so very sorry about the delay over the Cambodia book. But as I think I explained earlier, the man who was reading it first was taken suddenly ill which delayed matters for several weeks. Although we found it individually extremely interesting and although it is in other times a book which we should have considered very seriously for publication, we came to the conclusion that in the present state of the market books of art and archaeology of this sort must almost certainly be published at a loss and we cannot afford to take the risk. I am therefore returning it to you with this and hope that you may find a more daring publisher.

Yours sincerely,
[T. S. Eliot]

P.S. Thank you very much for the Mauron translation which I have not yet had time to go through.[1]

TO *Willa Muir*[2]   CC

2 July 1932   [*The Criterion*]

Dear Mrs Muir,

I owe you my humble apologies for the unfortunate error which I had just discovered.[3] The instructions to add your names as translators emanated from myself, when I noticed their omission from the proof. We always do put the name of the translator, unless he requests us not to do so; and I have done just enough translation myself to know how much recognition the translator deserves. The names were added in rather a hurry, and the mistake was a deplorable, but natural error on the part of someone who thought they knew your name too well to need to verify it, and didn't.

I am extremely sorry, and will add a note of rectification to my next commentary if that commends itself to you.

Yours sincerely,
[T. S. Eliot]

1 – Mauron, 'The Cow', C. 12 (Apr. 1933), 454–67.

2 – Willa Muir, née Anderson (1890–1970), novelist and translator, was married in 1919 to the writer Edwin Muir (1887–1959). Her works include *Women: An Enquiry* (1925) and the novels *Imagined Corners* (1931) and *Mrs Ritchie* (1933). The Muirs' joint translations included works by Gerhart Hauptmann, Lion Feuchtwanger and Heinrich Mann ('I am a better translator than he is,' she reflected in 1953; 'Most of this translation, especially Kafka, has been done by ME. Edwin only helped'). See Willa Muir, *Belonging: A Memoir* (1968), Edwin Muir, *An Autobiography* (1953); Aileen Christianson, *Moving in Circles: Willa Muir's Writings* (2007).

3 – Willa Muir complained on 30 June that her name had been given incorrectly. The two sections from Broch's novel *The Sleepwalkers* – published as 'Disintegration of Values', C. 11 (July 1932), 664–75 – were credited as 'Translated by Edwin and Christina Muir'.

TO *P. G. L. Webb*   CC

4 July 1932   [Faber & Faber Ltd]

Dear Sir,

Thank you very much for your kind letter of June 17th.[1] I am much honoured by your invitation to become a member of the Keats–Shelley Memorial Association, and I shall have great pleasure in accepting.

Yours very truly,

[T. S. Eliot]

TO *Alistair Cooke*[2]   CC

4 July 1932   [Faber & Faber Ltd]

Dear Mr Cooke,

I am very doubtful whether we could do anything with an essay of that size on a subject which is not very popular in this country, but if you are able to finish it before you leave for America I should very much like to read it. If it is not likely to be finished by then, send me what you can.[3] I could at least suggest the names of other publishers. In normal times I should have said that such an essay would have much more chance of success in America than here, and perhaps I can recommend an American publisher too.

---

1 – P. G. L. Webb, Honorary Secretary, reported that at the most recent meeting of the Keats–Shelley Memorial Association he was requested to invite TSE to become a member.
2 – Alistair (Alfred) Cooke (1908–2004), broadcaster and writer, was brought up in Salford, Lancashire, and read English at Jesus College, Cambridge – where he founded the Mummers, the university's first dramatic group to admit women, and contributed to *Granta*, which in due course he also edited. From Cambridge he went in 1932 to the USA on a Commonwealth Fund fellowship which enabled him to study theatre at Yale and linguistics at Harvard. (He had long nurtured a passion for all things American including jazz music.) During his travels, he interviewed *inter alia* Charlie Chaplin, who hired him as a scriptwriter for a film about Napoleon that was never completed. From the mid-1930s, back in London, he made shift to begin a career with the BBC, while also working for the American network NBC on a London letter that was broadcast to New York every Sunday. In later years he wrote a great deal for the *Manchester Guardian*; and in 1946 he essayed a short series of radio talks entitled *Letter from America* which eventuated in a record run of fifty-eight years. In the 1970s he became ever more famous with a TV series entitled *Alistair Cooke's America* – the accompanying book sold two million copies – and a series on American music. Having taken US citizenship in 1941, he was made an honorary KBE in 1973. See Nick Clarke, *Alistair Cooke: The Biography* (1999).
3 – Cooke offered an essay of 40–50 pp. entitled 'A Preface to Theatrical Criticism': 'It fairly summarily dismisses the English criticism of the last three centuries as being appreciative writing by Literary Gentlemen and then goes on to adumbrate a method or predict a future in criticism more specifically dramatic.'

I am sorry to say I have booked a passage on another boat, but I hope to see you while you are at Yale.[1]

Yours sincerely,

[T. S. Eliot]

FROM *Vivien Eliot* TO *Ottoline Morrell*   MS Texas

Monday, 4 July 1932   68 Clarence Gate Gardens

Dearest Ottoline,

I hope you have enjoyed your weekend at Malvern. It has been perfect weather.

I was sorry to find that you would prefer to come to *tea* on *Monday* 11th *instead* of coming to dinner as we had hoped. But I do understand that it is tiring. And at the end of the summer, I know how you feel. But you will come to tea, won't you?

You have given us so many beautiful afternoons during this whole year, no-one could be grateful enough, whatever they might feel.[2]

I feel that the part of my life which is around you is the only part I can endure to contemplate. You *know* that it is entirely due to you that I have been able to keep up.[3]

---

1 – Cooke was booked to sail to the USA on the *Laconia*, out of Liverpool on 17 Sept., and wondered if TSE was to be on the same ship.

2 – VHE signed OM's Visitors' Book at 10 Gower Street eight times during 1932 (letter from Julian Vinogradoff to EVE, 3 Mar. 1985). In her diary for 12 Nov. 1934 VHE would remember such visits to Gower Street when she felt she had become '*as* inconspicuous & as inoffensive as possible, while Ottoline used to keep me by her which *was* kind of her, & all the literary & political gentlemen & all the literary & etc ladies talked, I suppose, & all the expensive cigarettes gave their smoke to scent the air & soothe & stimulate. However that all came to an end *either* when *T. S. Eliot* got his appointment at Harvard . . .' (Bod MS Eng. misc. e. 877). In her diary for 14 Mar. 1935 VHE would record: 'I wish I could see Bertie again (Earl Russell). I have not seen him for 10 or 11 or 12 years. . . . I mean only The [*sc.* that] Bertrand Russell seemed to understand me, as Ottoline Morrell does. They are both mad *fearless aristocrats.*'

3 – According to Victoria Glendinning, *Elizabeth Bowen 1899–1973: Portrait of a Writer* (1977), 80, OM had encouraged her friend: 'Do keep up with the Eliots. I feel it is such a pleasure and joy to Tom . . . it will give him life.' See Bowen to OM, 15 Aug. 1932: 'I saw the Eliots a good deal before leaving England, and dined there the night before I came over here, so sorry to think I should not see him again – for so long – I mean until after America. There is something about the atmosphere of the flat that I find exceedingly sinister and depressing: my spirits go down with a bump as I go in. Not that the flat itself is so bad, but it's the atmosphere of two unhappy and highly nervous people shut up together in grinding proximity. And that poor little Vivien's wild eyes! But it is a pleasure to see him anywhere: he is so very funny and charming and domestic and nice to be with, besides being so great.

Thursday, 7th, is your last tea party, so it will in a way be painful. Especially if you will *not* be back from your holiday before Tom leaves.

I will speak to you about *Monday* when I see you on Thursday.

Here are some photographs of Tom.

> With my best love,
> Your affect. friend,
> Vivienne

TO *Lawrence C. Powell*[1]   CC

5 July 1932   [Faber & Faber Ltd]

Dear Sir,

I have your letter of the 30th June.[2] I have never written any criticism of Mr Robinson Jeffers nor have I read much of his work. I believe him to be a first rate poet, but prefer to refrain as far as possible from expressing myself publicly about my contemporaries.

> Yours sincerely,
> [T. S. Eliot]

TO *Edouard Roditi*   TS UCLA

5 July 1932   *The Criterion*

Dear Roditi,

I should like to use a bit of 'Jehudah' in the *Criterion* as I am afraid it would be some time before I could print the poem in full, so will you tell me which part you are going to give to the *Spectator*? Why not give them Part 2 as you have already published Part 1?[3]

I love knowing him' (*The Mulberry Tree: Writings of Elizabeth Bowen*, ed. Hermione Lee [1986], 198). According to another account, TSE told Bowen that he drank alcohol to get into the mood for writing poetry (Patricia Craig, *Elizabeth Bowen* [1986], 80).

1 – Lawrence Clark Powell (1906–2001) joined the staff of UCLA Library in 1928 and became University Librarian, 1944–61; Director of the William Andrews Clark Memorial Library, 1944–66; founding Dean of the School of Library Service, 1959–66. He wrote fiction, non-fiction, autobiography and bibliography, including a study of Robinson Jeffers.

2 – Powell wondered whether TSE had issued 'any utterance' about Robinson Jeffers that he might cite in a thesis he was presenting at the University of Dijon. 'A part of the thesis is devoted to the opinions of Mr Jeffers' verse held by a few contemporary poets and critics.'

3 – Roditi replied from Berlin (14 July) that he would send part 2 to *The Spectator*. 'I think the fourth part of "Jehudah" would suit your purpose best – the one about the messianic myths.'

I should also like to use some of the Perse, but I must think about that as it would have to be a considerable time ahead.[1]

Yours ever,
T. S. Eliot

TO *Louis MacNeice*   CC

5 July 1932   [*The Criterion*]

Dear Mr MacNeice,

I have chosen three poems, namely 'Vitreamque Circen', 'Belfast', and 'Threnody', pages 40, 30, and 27 respectively.[2] I ought to have written to you before, but you said in your letter of June 16th [*sc.* 10th] that you might be in London at the end of that month. I hope you may still be coming. I am not returning the other poems until I know whether this choice has your approval. The choice has to be determined partly by considerations of space.

Yours sincerely,
[T. S. Eliot]

TO *Sally Cobden-Sanderson*   CC

5 July 1932   [London]

My dear Sally,

I can't see why a British subject should have to fill in a form merely because he wants to stop overnight in Canada. However, if it can't be helped I suppose I must go to the American Consulate and get their visa. I had not intended to do this until just before leaving as I understand that they will only give permission to remain in America for a limited time.

I will have the books ready for packing as early in September as you like.

---

1 – Roditi asked on 2 June, 'now that *Commerce* has been liquidated, I am wondering what to do with my translation of Perse's "La gloire de Rois". Would any of it interest you for the *Criterion*? I believe you have it in full.' See 'Trafalgar Square', *C.* 13 (Apr. 1934), 449–50.

2 – MacNeice responded to this letter on 8 July with the explanation that two of the poems chosen by TSE had appeared in *This Quarter*, and 'Threnody' in *Oxford Poetry 1930*; and six poems had appeared in *Oxford Poetry* (1929 and 1930). He therefore enclosed a copy of his latest poem – 'though it may seem fatuous to anyone other than myself' (*Letters of Louis MacNeice*, 230).

And shall I make out my cheque for £5 to you personally or to the Hutchinson's Agency for Domestic Help?

Affectionately yours,

[T. S. E.]

TO *Hugh Macdonald* CC

5 July 1932   [Faber & Faber Ltd]

Dear Macdonald,

I am doubtful whether any suggestions are likely to occur to my mind which would be helpful to you, but I should be very glad to lunch with you one day and discuss the matter.[1] I think Wednesday 13 or Friday 15 would be possible, if either of these suits you.

I am interested to have your news especially as it is a long time since I have seen those of my friends who could tell me much about you. I shall look forward to meeting your wife. As for any statement of mine, I am quite convinced that beyond a point it is intolerable to apply one's own views of conduct to people who do not accept the beliefs which alone justify them.[2]

Yours ever,

[T. S. Eliot][3]

P.S. I expect that in these times you are glad to be relieved of the Haslewood books, but I regret your disappearance as a publishing firm.

1–Macdonald (undated) was compiling 'a bibliography of Dryden's writings and contemporary literature relating to him': 'I should much like your advice . . . I am most anxious to find out what sort of information you would wish to find in the book if you picked it up.'

2–Macdonald wrote: 'Since I last saw you I have been divorced. I married again, &, as I think you know, I have a daughter . . . [V]arious opinions I have prevent my being a Christian in any strict sense of the word. It seems pointless to say one is a Christian unless one holds certain definite beliefs. Forgive my mentioning my personal affairs in this blunt way. I only do so because of your statements of your beliefs in print. My wife had an academic career. She took a first in English at Aberdeen & then at Oxford & was for 12 years a lecturer in English at Oxford. Can you spare time to lunch with us before the 15th of July? We will meet you anywhere . . . You really can be of assistance to me if you will give me an hour.'

3–Macdonald responded on 6 July, in connection with the work that would ultimately be published as *John Dryden: A Bibliography of Early Editions and of Drydenianae* (Clarendon Press, 1939): 'My wife has to go to Oxford on Thursday (*sc.* Friday) the 15th. Can you meet us on Wednesday the 13th? I ask you to endeavour to do this. The bibliography will be a long and laborious piece of work and the ground to be covered is so large that selection of the important material will be difficult . . . There are some specific points about which I want

TO *I. A. Richards*   CC

5 July 1932   [Faber & Faber Ltd]

Dear Richards,

I should consequently be glad if you would do some sort of note on Scott Buchanan's book or mention it as soon as possible in any way that you think best.[1]

I look forward to your comments on Eastman,[2] but am still more anxious to possess myself of your article. I expect to be here nearly all the time until September 17th, and hope you may manage to come up.

Yours ever,

[T. S. E.]

TO *A. J. Penty*[3]   CC

5 July 1932   [*The Criterion*]

My dear Penty,

I am afraid I have done nothing whatever to develop your interesting suggestion of a book of essays on Modernism. The principal reason is

---

to ask you. Grierson gives up theology when he reaches Dryden. A proper edition of Dryden must be done now or never, because no publisher will want to follow the Clarendon Press. I am doing the work without payment; because, unless Hayward is paid, he cannot possibly give the time. I am a Civil Servant and so am in a less uncomfortable position than most people . . . I hope to see [Herbert] Read tomorrow. I quite admit I shall go ahead with this job with more heart if I have your and his goodwill. I have a lot of almost unknown material . . . There are contemporary tracts & books about Dryden, which I doubt if anyone except (I suppose) Bredvold know of.' (Louis I. Bredvold was to be author of *The Intellectual Milieu of John Dryden* [1934].)

He remarked too, in his reply: 'I should like someday to study the Christian answer to Milton. I have found my Christian friends more tolerant and reasonable about divorce than my relations who would not like it suggested that they were not people of excellent religious views.'

1–IAR responded with a card (n. d.), 'Scott Buchanan's little book is, I think, really important; but damnably difficult to get the hang of. I don't mind doing a short review – or noticing it in the course of something, if you like. Shall be sending something on [Max] Eastman very soon.' In the event, he did not review Buchanan's book.

2–Max Eastman, *The Literary Mind: Its Place in an Age of Science*, was reviewed by IAR in *C.* 12 (Oct. 1932), 150–55. 'On reflection,' wrote IAR to TSE on 30 July 1932, 'I don't think Eastman is worth much, but his subject was near enough to being one that in better hands would be important just now, to seem reviewable.'

3–Arthur J. Penty (1875–1937), architect (he was involved in the development of Hampstead Garden Suburb, London) and social critic influenced variously by Ruskin, Carlyle, Matthew Arnold and Edward Carpenter, as well as in part by G. K. Chesterton and Hilaire Belloc,

that I have had far too much to do and must devote any spare time I have to the preparation of lectures in America. Another reason was that meanwhile a friend of mine had proposed a volume on very similar lines and I was waiting to see whether anything would come of this and if so whether the two books might be amalgamated.

I am leaving in the middle of September and shall not return to England till next May, so I shall be very glad if we could have lunch together again before I go.

Yours sincerely,
[T. S. Eliot]

TO *Edward Crankshaw*[1]

CC

5 July 1932   [*The Criterion*]

Dear Sir,

I have your letter of the 28th June and shall be glad to see you and

---

was an advocate of guild socialism, anti-modernism and anti-industrialism, agrarian reconstructionism and Anglican socialism. A regular contributor to periodicals including *The Guildsman, G. K.'s Weekly, The Crusader* and *C.*, his works include *Old Worlds for New* (1917), *A Guildsman's Interpretation of History* (1920) and *Towards a Christian Sociology* (1923). TSE noted in *The Idea of a Christian Society* (1939) that 'modern material organization . . . has produced a world for which Christian social forms are imperfectly adapted'; but there are simplifications of the problem that are 'suspect': 'One is to insist that the only salvation for society is to return to a simpler mode of life, scrapping all the constructions of the modern world that we can bring ourselves to dispense with. This is an extreme statement of the neo-Ruskinian view, which was put forward with much vigour by the late A. J. Penty. When one considers the large amount of determination in social structure, this policy appears Utopian: if such a way of life ever comes to pass, it will be – as may well happen in the long run – from natural causes, and not from the moral will of men' (New edn with Intro. by David L. Edwards [1982], 60).

1–Edward Crankshaw (1909–1984): writer, translator, commentator on Soviet affairs. Soon after leaving Bishop's Stortford College, he went to live in Vienna, teaching English at the Berlitz School, learning the language, and becoming absorbed by Austrian and German culture. On the outbreak of WW2 he was contacted by the British secret services and sent to work at the Military Mission in Moscow (where he also learned Russian). He later worked as a journalist for the *Observer*, 1947–68, writing authoritative commentaries on the USSR. His many publications include *Vienna: A Culture in Decline* (1938), *Gestapo* (1956), *Russia without Stalin* (1958), *The Fall of the House of Habsburg* (1963), *Maria Theresa* (1969), *The Shadow of the Winter Palace* (1976) and *Bismarck* (1981). In addition, he translated into English five plays by Ernst Toller (who had become a close friend while in Austria): *Nie Wieder Friede* he translated as *No More Peace! A Thoughtful Comedy*, with lyrics adapted by WHA (1937). In 1964 the Austrian government awarded him the Ehrenkreuz für Wissenschaft und Kunst; and he won both the Heinemann Award 1977, and the Whitbread Prize 1981.

discuss possible work.[1] As you are engaged in the day time I suggest that you might ring me up at the beginning of next week and suggest an evening to come in and see me. My private address is 68 Clarence Gate Gardens, which is close to you. My telephone number is Ambassador 1518.

Yours very truly,
[T. S. Eliot]

TO *Herbert Agar*[2]   CC

6 July 1932   [*The Criterion*]

Dear Mr Agar,

Thank you for your letter of July 5th.[3] I am very much afraid that it will be quite impossible for me to review Canon Sparrow Simpson's book for the *English Review*. I am leaving for America in the middle of September, and all my spare time between now and spring of next year will be taken up in the preparation of my lectures. I regret to say that this will also mean that I shall have to postpone writing the article I promised you on Von Hügel. I might be able to let you have it in the course of next winter, but I should prefer to leave it altogether until next spring.

With very many regrets,
Yours sincerely,
[T. S. Eliot]

1–The 23-year-old Crankshaw wrote from London that he had undertaken 'over three years of self-imposed apprenticeship', and had taught in a Berlitz School 'in Europe'; he had contributed to periodicals including *The Spectator*, *TLS*, *The Week-end Review* and *The Bookman*: his interests included German literature, the politics of south-eastern and central Europe, music, 'the true cinema' and theatre. A married man, he was passing his days writing advertising copy.

2–Herbert Agar (1897–1980), eminent conservative American journalist and author. Educated at Columbia and Princeton (PhD, 1922), he spent the years 1929–35 in England, where he was literary editor of Douglas Jerrold's *English Review* (he also wrote for Chesterton's periodical *G. K.'s Weekly*). On returning to the USA, where he edited the *Louisville Courier-Journal*, he won distinction as an author. *The People's Choice, From Washington to Harding: A Study of Politics* (1933) won the Pulitzer Prize 1934; and he edited (with Allen Tate) *Who Owns America? A New Declaration of Independence* (1936). Other major publications include *Land of the Free* (1935) and *The Price of Union: The Influence of the American Temper on the Course of History* (1950).

3–Agar, at the *English Review*, invited TSE to review Sparrow Simpson's *History of the Anglo-Catholic Revival* in 800–1,200 words by 15 Aug. or 15 Sept.

FROM *Vivien Eliot* TO *Mary Hutchinson*   MS Texas

6 July 1932   68 Clarence Gate Gardens

My dear Mary

Thank you for your card. I am *sorry* the *weekends* are nearly always impossible for you, because they are the best times for us to see our friends quietly.

So I am *sorry* about *Saturday*. I might be here all Friday doing nothing so I shd. like to know what you are doing on Friday?

If we *cannot* meet that day – Tom & I would like it so much if you would come out to supper with us on Monday evening (11th) & if so we would call for you at 7.30. Would you *like that*?

We should love it, so will you send me a card in return?

Yours, with much love,
Vivienne Haigh Eliot.

Anyhow I *must* see you, so if we can't fix anything else may I come round to you or you to me at 9. on Thursday?

TO *Maurice Haigh-Wood*[1]   cc

7 July 1932   [Faber & Faber Ltd]

Dear Maurice,

Your methods were certainly summary – I dare say that you were entirely justified – but I hope that no similar emergencies will arise during my absence. I was, as I said, in favour of selling the Conversion Stock; and I suppose that you had information to suggest that Central Electricity was likely to rise further in the immediate future. The difference of income is negligible. The justification of the purchase seems to lie in your spotting the right moment to sell; and I am quite in agreement about the probable desirability of reverting to Government Stock in nine months time, and of course of realising Central Electric (which I know nothing about) if it shoots upwards.

Affectionately,
[Tom]

1 – Maurice Haigh-Wood (1896–1980), brother of VHE: see Biographical Register.

7 July 1932   68 Clarence Gate Gardens

Dear Mr Hodgson,

I was terribly sorry to have to postpone my long looked-forward to lunch with you today, it was sickening but I was so tired yesterday that it was obvious that I shd. not be well enough to have lunch out & also go to Lady Ottoline's last tea party. And it turned out so, for I was very tired all day but just able to go to the tea party & enjoy it.

I asked Aurelia to ring me up *today* after lunch to tell me whether you can take us out to lunch *tomorrow* Friday – *instead* – (I do hope you can?) Aurelia did *not* telephone, & I am now writing to you, hoping that she is allright after her night here with Picky. He behaved very well indeed, I thought, & I had an *unusually* good night. I would gladly have him again – with Aurelia.

Will you, or Aurelia, please telephone me early tomorrow morning & just tell me what time you will fetch me & we will all go out to lunch in the car. I will try to go to bed early so as to get up earlier so as to be ready to start with you if you do feel inclined to come with Aurelia to fetch us. If you do not feel able to, Aurelia said that she & I would enjoy to go off for lunch together on our own. So please telephone me, one of you, in any case.

Yours ever,
Vivienne Haigh Eliot

TO *Henry Seidel Canby*[1]

8 July 1932   [Faber & Faber Ltd]

Dear Mr Canby,

Thank you very much for your kind letter of June 8th.[2] I hope to meet you in Cambridge.

It is true that there will be a number of essays in my volume which have not been published in America or in book form anywhere, but I am afraid Brace[3] is mistaken, and I hope he will not be disappointed to find that there is none which has not appeared in print. So I am afraid there is nothing in the volume which would be really suitable for the *Saturday Review*, and I imagine any of them would have to be cut down to fit into your columns. I hope that I may perhaps write something in the course of the year which would be suitable for you. Looking forward to making your acquaintance.

I am,
Yours very truly,
[T. S. Eliot]

TO *Rolf Gardiner*   TS Cambridge University Library

8 July 1932   Faber & Faber Ltd

My dear Gardiner,

It is a disappointment to me personally that we shall not be able to have our name on *World without End*, but as I think I suggested myself I knew

---

1–Henry S. Canby (1878–1961): critic and editor. Having taught for over twenty years at Yale, where he was the first professor to offer courses in American literature, and where he was assistant editor of the *Yale Review*, 1911–20, he was founder-editor of the literary review of the *New York Evening Post*, 1920–4, and co-founded and was first editor of the *Saturday Review of Literature*, 1924–36. In 1926 he became Chair of the newly founded Book-of-the-Month Club. His publications include *Classic Americans: A Study of Eminent American Writers from Irving to Whitman* (1931), *Thoreau: A Biography* (1939), *Walt Whitman, an American: A Study in Biography* (1943), *American Memoir* (1947) and *Turn West, Turn East: Mark Twain and Henry James* (1951); and he was co-editor of the *Literary History of the United States* (1948).

2–Canby, who was hoping to attend at least one lecture by TSE at Harvard, asked after the forthcoming *Selected Essays 1917–1932* which Donald Brace had advised him contained some unpublished pieces. Would it be possible for the *Saturday Review* to publish any such essay?

3–Donald Brace (1881–1955): publisher; see TSE to him 5 Sept. 1932.

---

348   TSE at forty-three

that you could get it done more cheaply by dealing direct with a printer.[1]

I am very glad that you like Lymington's book so much, and I am happy to have your review.[2]

I should be glad if it were possible to see you again before I leave for America. I am sailing on the 17th of September. Is there any likelihood of your being back in England before then? After that date, when your big book is ready will you please take the matter up with my colleague F. V. Morley in my absence? I shall not be back until next May.[3]

Yours sincerely,
T. S. Eliot

TO *Cyril E. Hudson* CC

11 July 1932 [Faber & Faber Ltd]

Dear Father Hudson,

I find to my regret that I had put aside your letter of the 2nd May together with the copy of the *Teaching Church Review* and had quite forgotten to answer it.[4] I must apologize for my tardiness. That does not, I am sorry to say, make any practical difference at the moment. I should be very glad indeed to help the *Review* out with an article, but I have been unable to undertake any writing this summer, and shall not be able to consider any articles for a year. I am going to America in September, returning the following May, and the preparation of lectures will take all my spare time. If you would still care for a contribution, please write to me next May on my return.

With many apologies,
Yours sincerely,
[T. S. Eliot]

---

1 – Gardiner replied on 7 July that his 'enquiries' had satisfied him that it 'is possible to issue the pamphlet appreciably more cheaply than your firm has been able to do'. (Cobden-Sanderson had undertaken to print the work at a lower price.)

2 – Review of Viscount Lymington, *Horn, Hoof and Corn: The Future of British Agriculture*, C. 12 (Oct. 1932), 134–6.

3 – Gardiner proposed to finish his big book, 'Phoenix of Yggdrasil', after taking part in the Baltic Festival Tour during Aug. and Sept.

4 – The Revd Cyril E. Hudson, Hon. Sec. of the Teaching Church Group for Adult Religious Education – editor of the *Teaching Church Review* – requested an article on 'something'.

TO *T. F. Burns*   CC

11 July 1932   [Faber & Faber Ltd]

My dear Burns,

I have dipped into *Die Anderen* myself and have read Dawson's admirable report and discussed it with Morley, and we both think that it is too risky an undertaking for us.[1] It might come off very well, but if it failed it would be an expensive luxury. Many thanks for letting me see it. One does not know what to venture upon publishing in these times, and it would not be worth any publisher's while to turn out more than six books a year if he could always guess the six right ones.

We are, however, quite seriously, going into the question of Kierkegaard and are going to get hold of the German edition which I understand is supposed to be complete. Could you meanwhile be so kind as to let me see the manuscript of the Essay in Order on him of which you spoke? It would be a great help as no one of us knows anything whatever about Kierkegaard beyond his reputation.

Yours ever,
[T. S. Eliot]

TO *E. W. F. Tomlin*[2]   TS Lady Marshall

11 July 1932   Faber & Faber Ltd

Dear Mr Tomlin,

I have read with much interest your essay on the Younger Generation

---

1 – Burns asked on 29 June whether F&F 'could do anything with this book "Die Anderen". I have had no less than three reports on it and have been driven to the conclusion that it is not quite my cup of tea. And [at] the same time I think it might be yours. Could you have it read in the ordinary way? I am enclosing Dawson's report on it.'

2 – E. Walter F. Tomlin (1914–88), writer and administrator. Educated at Whitgift School and Brasenose College, Oxford, he joined the British Council and served in Iraq, Turkey and France; also in Japan, on which he wrote three books. Anglo-Catholic in religion, he wrote a study of Simone Weil; a book about R. G. Collingwood; he edited volumes on WL, Arnold Toynbee and Dickens. He was President of the Dickens Fellowship, 1987–8, and served on the executive committee of international PEN. His memoir *T. S. Eliot: A Friendship* appeared in 1988. TSE was to write to Ashley Sampson, 31 May 1937: 'A young man as yet unknown to the public, and of whose abilities I have a high opinion, is E. W. F. Tomlin.' To W. E. Salt, Director of Extra-Mural Studies, Univ. of Bristol, 25 May 1939: 'I have known him for a number of years, indeed before he even went up to Oxford, and have always regarded him as a young man of very unusual promise . . . I consider him a young man of quite exceptional abilities, as well as of character and seriousness of purpose.'

and Politics.[1] Although I am more than doubtful of the possibility of such an essay from a publisher's point of view I was much impressed by your thinking and lucid gift of exposition. I should be very glad if you could find the time to call here and discuss it with me. I suppose that your school work will make this impossible until the end of July, but I expect to be in London throughout August. I will retain the manuscript until I hear from you.

Yours sincerely,
T. S. Eliot

TO *Herbert Read* CC

11 July 1932   [*The Criterion*]

Dear Herbert,

I was sorry not to see you again after the evening, but I hardly expected that I should. I hope they made you comfortable here, and that you got back without being over-fatigued. I thought that the evening was a fairly successful one.

We had a discussion about the Kierkegaard question yesterday, and I read the passage from your letter.[2] We finally decided to adopt an inspiration of Frank's and suggest that we should get the German edition, a review copy if possible, but if not we would buy it, present it to you on the condition that you wrote an article about him for the *Criterion* as soon as you possibly can. That seems to me a capital idea as I don't see how we are to learn anything about Kierkegaard unless you tell us. Can you give me the name of his German publisher and the years or year of publication? We shall also approach the Danish Legation and find out whether their government will cooperate.[3]

1–Tomlin wrote on 19 June 1932: 'In accordance with your letter some little time back in which you expressed the desire to see the Answer to Mr A. L. Rowse's "Politics and the Younger Generation" which I had proposed to write, I am now sending you the completed manuscripts for your perusal. . . . I shall be leaving school at the end of July and hope to go up to Oxford as an undergraduate in October.' According to Tomlin, TSE considered ALR's publication a 'bad book' (*T. S. Eliot*, 14, 19).

2–Cited in footnote to TSE to HR, 29 June 1932, above.

3–HR had suggested on 27 June, 'Incidentally, I believe there exists in Denmark a fund of the Academy or some such body which grants subsidies to translations of important Danish works. I don't know how you would find out about this, except through the Danish embassy.'

It is sad to think that I shall not see you again for a year, and I still hope that you may find another visit to London necessary this summer. Please give our regards to your wife.

Yours ever,
[T. S. E.]

TO *Mario Praz*

CC

11 July 1932   [*The Criterion*]

Dear Praz,

I must apologize for the very long delay in reporting on your translations of various poets. I think that I explained to you in one of our unfortunately rare and hurried conversations that the publication of another series of Ariel poems had been suspended for several reasons. The only one of the poems which definitely strikes on my box is Ungaretti's 'Moammed Sceab' and I should like to publish something by Ungaretti in the *Criterion*.[1] The trouble with translations of verse is that my funds are limited and if the fee has to be divided between translator and poet there is not very much for either. What shall we do about that?

I have not got any very definite impression from the poems of Montale, but I liked so much the one which you translated before that I want to go over these again and see whether they still fail to reach me.[2]

---

1 – Not published in C.

2 – Eugenio Montale, 'Arsenio', trans. Praz, C. 7 (June 1928), 342–3. Montale (1896–1981) was a poet, prose writer, translator, editor; winner of the Nobel Prize for Literature, 1975.

TSE told M. Jean Thomas, 2 Mar. 1948 (apropos an application by Montale for the post of administrative secretary of UNESCO): 'I have met Signor Montale only two or three times, but I have known him by correspondence and by reputation for a great many years. It should hardly be necessary to say that he is today certainly one of the two most distinguished living Italian poets, and in the opinion of some the most distinguished. I do not consider that I have sufficient knowledge of the Italian language to profess any opinion of relative distinction between Signor Montale and Signor Ungaretti. However that may be Signor Montale is a man of European reputation. I think that I was the first editor to introduce his work to English readers in the pages of *The Criterion* and that was a good many years ago.

'From all that I have heard of Signor Montale in Italy I believe that his political history is above reproach. I may add as a possible additional qualification for the post in view that he has an exceptionally good knowledge of the English language. I have never heard him speak it as I have only met him in company in which French was the language of communication but his letters show a very easy idiomatic command of the language.'

To the Academic Registrar, University of London (where Montale applied for the Chair of Italian at Bedford College), 11 May 1948: 'Signor Montale is undoubtedly in the opinion of his compatriots one of the two most distinguished living Italian poets. I have known him

Let me know if there is any book you would care to review for the December number. And when are you transferring yourself to Manchester?

Yours ever,
[T. S. Eliot]

TO *John Cournos*[1]

11 July 1932   [Faber & Faber Ltd]

Dear Cournos,

I was glad to hear from you with your letter of May 31.[2] I have looked into the matter of your two contributions, and unless the printer has made a mistake in computing the number of words I cannot find the error. The rates are the same as for body articles, that is to say considerably better than those for ordinary reviews. But I am distressed that you should have been spending your own money on periodicals, and I do not want this to happen again. I had a talk with Mirsky about it, and he has taken note of the periodicals you want, and promised to take the matter up when he reaches Moscow in August.

I hope that I may see you from time to time whilst I am in Cambridge. I shall get there from about the end of September, and my address will be Eliot House, Cambridge, Mass.

---

in a way for many years and published one or two of his poems many years ago in *The Criterion*. I have, however, met him only on a few occasions. I can only say that he is a very agreeable and cultivated person and that he has, I should think, quite a sufficient knowledge of English. But I do not know him intimately enough to be able to give more than this superficial impression, and I know nothing about his academic qualifications or his previous experience in teaching and lecturing. I can only say that he ranks as a man of letters of very high distinction.'

To the Italian Consul, Liverpool, 11 Dec. 1959: 'I have a very high respect for the poetry of Eugenio Montale and, though my knowledge of Italian is imperfect, feel a spiritual kinship with him. I know also that he has made what seemed to me very successful translations of several of my own poems into Italian. There is no Italian poet whom I would rank higher.'

See too Montale, 'Eliot and Ourselves', in *T. S. Eliot: A Symposium*, ed. Richard March and Tambimuttu (1948), 190–5.

1–John Cournos (1881–1966): US poet, novelist, essayist, translator: see Biographical Register.

2–'Has the *Criterion* cut fees for contributions? . . . [T]he cheque for the last article covering ten and a half pages amounted to Six Pounds and Twelve Shillings, whereas at the rates I had been previously paid I should have received a sum very close to Eight Pounds . . . Worse luck, the man who used to send me Russian periodicals from Moscow has let me down lately, – nor has your office been sending me any – and so I must pay for them out of my own pocket.'

With best wishes for you and your family.

Yours sincerely,

[T. S. Eliot]

TO *Geoffrey Biddulph*   CC

11 July 1932   [*The Criterion*]

Dear Mr Biddulph,

I have considered your essay on the Bank of England carefully. It is
very interesting and certainly ought to be published, but I am afraid that
it is slightly outside of the *Criterion*'s range. We laid it down long ago
that although we are anxious to have political articles we should confine
ourselves to discussions of first principles and the philosophy of politics
rather than include such questions of the time and every moment as are
handled in the other quarterly and monthly reviews.

This restriction, however, does not apply so closely to the department
of reviews, and I should be very glad if you would care to review for our
December number J. M. Kenworthy's new book *Our Daily Pay*. I had
never thought of Kenworthy as a specially thoughtful person, but I have
skimmed through this book and was surprised to find it both intelligent
and well-informed. This is merely the opinion of an ignoramus, *but* I
think you will find it worth reviewing.[1]

Yours sincerely,

[T. S. Eliot]

TO *Ottoline Morrell*   TS Texas

11 July 1932   Faber & Faber Ltd

My dear Ottoline,

Before you go away I must write to express my appreciation of your
kindness to Vivienne throughout this past year especially. She is so much

1–Joseph Montague Kenworthy (1886–1953), politician and author, served in the Royal
Navy, 1902–20, and entered Parliament as Liberal member for Central Hull. In 1926, when
Lloyd George became leader of the Liberal Party, Kenworthy joined the Labour Party and
held the same seat until 1931. In 1934 he succeeded his father as Lord Strabolgi. Biddulph
replied on 12 July that he had already been sent Kenworthy's book – '& haven't much to
say about it except that it's a bit repetitive & lengthy for the "man in the street", and that
the dictatorship chapter shows little sense of proportion'. The book was not reviewed in C.

a creature of environment that it is a vital matter – especially when she is in a very sociable phase – what company she frequents; and you have not only given your own influence, but have helped her to add a number of desirable people to her acquaintance. I am especially glad of this because I shall be so long absent.

Affectionately yours,
Tom

TO *David Higham*   CC

11 July 1932   [Faber & Faber Ltd]

Dear Higham,

Thank you for your letter of the 5th July about the Dryden essays.[1] I do not like to be ungracious, but I am afraid that I and my firm as well *do* object to the Holliday Bookshop exporting the essays to England. If I had wanted the essays to appear here we should naturally have published them ourselves, and I particularly do not want this volume to appear here at the same time as my big book of essays. I hope that Mr Holliday will appreciate my point of view.

Yours,
[T. S. Eliot]

FROM *Vivien Eliot* TO *Aurelia Bolliger*   MS Beinecke

Wednesday 13 July 1932   3 Compayne Gardens, N.W.3

My dear Aurelia,

I have not seen or heard of you & Mrs Hodgson since Sunday.

I am sitting here with Mother waiting for her to go away to the country at 4 p.m.

You remember on Sunday we mentioned meeting all together on Thursday. So this is to remind you, & I will look forward to seeing you *both*, & *Picky*, for tea on *Thursday* at 4.15 (tomorrow).

1–Higham had heard from New York about the Dryden essays [TSE, *John Dryden, The Poet, The Dramatist, The Critic*], as follows: 'Although Holliday has only the American and Canadian rights, has Eliot any objection to his filling orders in England? The volume is going to turn into a first edition item and English buyers will get hold of copies anyway. Holliday, of course, will not advertise or circularize, but wants to be able to ship when orders come in.'

If you cannot do this, be a *dear* & ring me up *early* tomorrow Thursday morning – or else ring up *this evening*. I shall be at *home* 68 Clarence Gate Gardens all the evening.

Yrs ever,
Vivienne Haigh Eliot

TO *David Higham*

CC

5 July 1932   [Faber & Faber Ltd]

Dear Higham,

Thank you for your letter of the 6th, enclosing the letter from Ray Everitt visaed by Holliday. I confirm the terms of the above mentioned letter of June 17th.[1]

It might be as well to remind Holliday that I am leaving for America in the middle of September. He had better get the sheets for signing to me here by the 12th September or otherwise hold them until I arrive at Harvard.

I am still of the opinion that I shall not want to do any general lecturing outside of Harvard. I have a few engagements with other universities and I hope to get two or three more to pay the expenses for some Christmas holiday travels across the country. But the number of lectures that I want is so few that I had best try to get the engagements direct.

Yours,
[T. S. Eliot]

1 – Ray Everitt, General Manager of the New York office of Messrs Curtis Brown, wrote on 17 June to Ted Holliday of The Holliday Bookshop, NYC: 'T. S. Eliot has agreed to sign a limited edition [of *John Dryden, The Poet, The Dramatist, The Critic*] for sale in America. According to our understanding, the arrangement is as follows:

'An edition of about one hundred fifty copies, the exact number depending on the number of subscribers; to be sold at not less than $7.50 per copy; the first signature will be sent to England for signing; and that you will pay a 15% royalty on the list price, this sum payable in advance on publication date in addition to the advance already arranged.

'If this meets with your approval, please Okay one copy of this letter and file the other.'

The subscription list for the signed edition was to be open until 15 July.

A statement sent from the T. E. Holliday Bookshop, New York, 25 Oct. 1933, to Curtis Brown Ltd, London, revealed that for the period ending 30 Sept. 1933, the ordinary edition had sold 41 copies, the limited edition 3 copies: the balance of royalties to be paid was $4.05.

(It was Everitt who, on 24 Feb. 1930, first mooted with FVM the possibility of putting out a volume of TSE's collected essays.)

TO *N. H. Rubin*

11 July 1932   [Faber & Faber Ltd]

Dear Mr Rubin,

Thank you for your letter of June 26.[1] I am glad to hear that you are able to publish your book. I am having it made ready for return to you, and my secretary will notify you on the day of its despatch. I shall be very glad to give any assistance, especially if in cooperation with Mr Edmund Wilson, but I cannot see why any form of advisory board is necessary if the duties are nominal. As for a prefatory note by myself I am uncertain whether that is desirable. For that point it would be much better from your point of view if you could get a prefatory note from Joyce himself, and I should want to consult him before going any further in the matter. Perhaps we may defer this question until I arrive in Cambridge in October.

> Yours sincerely,
> [T. S. Eliot]

TO *Sally Cobden-Sanderson*

11 July 1932   [Faber & Faber Ltd]

My dear Sally,

Thanks for your note of July 6. I enclose my cheque for £5 to reserve my passage. I never heard of a head-tax before, and it sounds like some early feudal custom. I shall be glad if you will book a sleeping reservation for the night you mention as I do not want to spend more than one night in Montreal. But will they get me up in the middle of the night to go to the baggage car and expose my belongings? If so I might do better to travel by

---

1 – Rubin had decided to publish *Brick and Mortar* by himself. 'I am satisfied, after consulting with Mr Clifton P. Fadiman [Simon & Schuster Inc.], that I can publish it without losing money. Briefly, I propose to get out an edition of 500 numbered copies . . . to sell at about $4; according to present estimates, if 250 copies will be sold, I shall have received sufficient money to cancel out all expenses . . . Mr Fadiman has consented to serve on the Advisory Board . . . if I can persuade both you and Mr Edmund Wilson . . . to do the same (the duties will be more paternalistic than actual, I simply feel that I need the cooperation you gentlemen can give me, if you feel I merit it.) I am also terribly anxious to get a prefatory note from you.' He had earlier reported (20 June) that he had discussed 'the pros and cons' of his work with Edmund Wilson: 'He tells me that the book is quite interesting and important, and that I might very well add an index on the Homeric parallelisms, inasmuch as he feels that there is much dead-weight in Gilbert's book. He also suggested that I might attempt to ferret out every allusion of any kind.'

day. I shall of course want a little American money, including the head-tax in question.

The great thing about Geoffrey T's[1] beard, from my point of view, is that we can longer be taken for each other. He certainly looks far more like a Rabbi than any Rabbi I have met.

Ever affectionately,

[T. S. E.]

TO *Richard Rees*[2]

12 July 1932   [Faber & Faber Ltd]

My dear Rees,

If you have not already arranged a review of Adrian Stokes's *Quattro Cento* which we published recently would you care to let Ezra Pound do a note on it? Ezra is very much interested in the book which deals with a period which he has been studying for some years, and is very anxious to write a review of it. Owing to a misunderstanding the *Criterion* review copy was sent to another reviewer. If you would care to have a review from Pound I am sure he would be very happy to do it. His address is Via Marsala, 12 int. 5, Rapallo, Italy, and he already has a copy.

I hope that the report that you are back in London is correct. I should be glad if we could meet again before I leave for America in September.

Yours sincerely,

[T. S. Eliot]

1 – Geoffrey Tandy.
2 – Sir Richard Rees, 2nd Baronet (1900–70) – diplomat, writer, artist, the original of Ravelston in George Orwell's *Keep the Aspidistra Flying* – was editor of *The Adelphi*, 1930– 6. His works include *Brave Men: A Study of D. H. Lawrence and Simone Weil* (1958), *George Orwell: Fugitive from the Camp of Victory* (1961) and *Simone Weil: A Sketch for a Portrait* (1966).

TO *Harley Granville-Barker*[1]   CC

12 July 1932   [Faber & Faber Ltd]

Dear Granville-Barker,

Thank you for your letter of the 7th.[2] I was much interested in Harrison's suggestion and only demurred on the ground that my American lectures would leave me no time for the preparation of such an essay; but he suggested that I could use it first as one of my odd lectures in America, and that caused me to reconsider. The book sounds very promising to me.

I am leaving for America in the middle of September and shall not be back until some [time] during the following May, but hope that we may meet next summer.

Yours very sincerely,
[T. S. Eliot]

TO *William Force Stead*   CC

12 July 1932   [Faber & Faber Ltd]

My dear Stead,

I am very glad that you can come on Friday, but I am afraid that it is impossible to allow you to be the host as we have asked Mrs Stuart Moore to meet you. So we shall expect you at 68 Clarence Gate Gardens, and I trust I may have the opportunity of lunching with you before I leave in September.

Affectionately yours,
[T. S.E.]

1–Harley Granville-Barker (1877–1946), actor, producer, director, playwright; manager from 1904 of the Royal Court Theatre; President of the British Drama League; author of *The Voysey Inheritance* (play, 1904) and *Prefaces to Shakespeare* (studies, 1927–48).
2–Granville-Barker was delighted to know that TSE would be joining their 'band' in putting together a 'Shakespeare Handbook'. 'We were more than commonly anxious to rope you in ... And you'll find, I imagine, that the review of Criticism will come happily to you.'

12 July 1932   [*The Criterion*]

Dear Mr Lowenfels,

In beginning a letter to you I feel rather discouraged. I was much interested in your elegy on Lawrence,[2] but it is very long for the *Criterion* and it would be at best a long time before I could use it. I wish that it were possible to publish poems of a length like this as separate pamphlets in England. Times have never been worse for the publication of poetry of any length and at any price than they are now. I kept your volume a long time hoping that we might be able to make you a proposal, but except when other types of publication are flourishing it is impossible to publish any poetry, because in publishing poetry we always reckon on a considerable loss. Except for one or two long standing commitments I doubt if we shall be able to publish any more verse for a long time to come.

If you intend to visit America next winter I hope that we may meet there.

Yours sincerely,
[T. S. Eliot]

1–Walter Lowenfels (1897–1976): American poet, journalist, author, activist; member of the Communist Party; editor of the *Daily Worker* from the late 1930s until 1953. After working for his father (a butter manufacturer), 1914–26, he lived in Paris, 1926–34, where he came to know expatriates including Ford Madox Ford and Henry Miller, and where he co-founded in 1930 the Carrefour Press. In 1953 he was arrested by the FBI and charged with conspiracy to overthrow the US government: his conviction in 1954 was overturned for lack of evidence. His works include *Episodes & Epistles* (1925) and *Steel, 1937* (1937). See too Hugh Ford, *Published in Paris: American and British Writers, Printers, and Publishers in Paris, 1920–1939* (1975).
2–Submitted from Paris on 8 June.

TO *Gerard Hopkins*[1]   CC

12 July 1932   [*The Criterion*]

Dear Hopkins,
   Would the Press be willing to consider a small book on Charles Péguy
written by a Miss Ruth Harrison who has made a study of the subject for
some years? I have a high opinion of Miss Harrison and think that the
book ought to be published; but like so many of the books that ought to
be published, it is quite certain not to make any money. But Péguy ought
to be a good deal better known in England than he is, and I do not see
how he is to become known unless people can read about him.[2]
                                   Yours sincerely,
                                   [T. S. Eliot]

TO *George Bell*   CC

12 July 1932   [Faber & Faber Ltd]

My dear Lord Bishop,
   I am gratified by your inviting me to be a member of your conference
at Chichester from October 1st to the 3rd.[3] Were I to be in England I
should make every effort to attend and should look forward to it with the
greatest interest. But unfortunately I am leaving for America on September
17 and shall not be back until next May. I hope that you will give me the
opportunity of seeing you again next summer.

1–Gerard Hopkins (1892–1961): publisher and translator. A nephew of Gerard Manley
Hopkins – whose poetry, letters and diaries he would put into print – he was educated at
Balliol College, Oxford (president of OUDS), and won the Military Cross during WW1. In
1919 he joined Oxford University Press, serving as publicity manager and later editorial
adviser. He became well known for his feats of translation: his output included vols 7–27 of
Jules Romain's *Men of Good Will;* biographies by André Maurois; Proust's *Jean Santeuil;*
and memoirs, broadcasts and plays. He was made Chevalier de la Légion d'Honneur, 1951.
2–Hopkins replied, 28 July: 'I am afraid we have had to say "No" to Miss Harrison.
Clearly there ought to be a book about Péguy, but since he is almost unknown here, even to
intelligent people, it ought to be a book with rather more superficial powers of attraction
than Miss Harrison's can boast. Obviously her knowledge and enthusiasm are great, but
her work bears rather too clearly the stamp of the thesis, for which, I must suppose, it was
originally intended.'
3–Bell (6 July) was organising a conference at The Palace, Chichester (1–3 Oct.), on the
subject of Religious Drama, and hoped TSE might be able to participate. Other notables
invited included Laurence Housman, Geoffrey Whitworth, E. Martin Browne and Kenneth
Ingram. In the event, the participants would include Lascelles Abercrombie, Robert Nichols
and Charles Williams.

With kindest regards to Mrs Bell,

Yours sincerely,

[T. S. Eliot]

TO *Robert Brittain* CC

15 July 1932   [Faber & Faber Ltd]

Dear Mr Brittain,

I must apologize for my long delay in answering your letter of February 22.[1] I am afraid that I have not been able to use any of your poems because I have so little space and such a vast quantity of material from which to choose. In any case I thought it was understood that you are perfectly free to place any of them elsewhere provided you notify me when you have done so.

I hope that your novel will be a success. You speak as if you would be likely to be in Princeton again next year, and if so I look forward to seeing you. I believe that they want me to come to Princeton on a date early in March.

With all best wishes,
Yours sincerely,
[T. S. Eliot]

TO *Wolfgang H. Clemen*[2] CC

15 July 1932   [*The Criterion*]

Dear Mr Clemen,

I am afraid I have kept your essay on Gundolf for an unpardonably long time. Indeed I was practically certain that I should not have space for it because of having had already a note on Gundolf by Rychner,[3] and I kept it merely because I was much interested to read it myself. I wish that you would send me something else later and of course if you should feel

---

1 – Brittain (Graduate College, Princeton, NJ) asked after his poem, 'Bottles in the Smoke', submitted at an earlier date: he had a 'pressing' money problem. His good news was that, thanks to an introduction by TSE, he had been commissioned by Mr Ballou to write a novel.
2 – Wolfgang H. Clemen (1909–90), German literary scholar, renowned for *Shakespeare's Imagery* (1951) – a work that began life as his doctoral dissertation in 1936. He taught at Cologne and Kiel, and was Professor of English at the University of Munich, 1946–74.
3 – Max Rychner, 'German Chronicle', C. 11 (Oct. 1931), 96–104.

yourself become a bit rusty in your English it would be quite welcome in German.

> With all best wishes,
> Yours sincerely,
> [T. S. Eliot]

TO *Louis MacNeice*   cc

15 July 1932   [*The Criterion*]

Dear Mr MacNeice,

Following the directions of your letter of July 8th I have now chosen 'The Creditor' and 'Trapeze'. Will you let me know if this suits you.[1] If you are coming to London give me as much warning as you can so that I shall be sure to have a time to see you.

> Yours sincerely,
> [T. S. Eliot]

TO *Eleanor Farjeon*   TS Texas

15 July 1932   *The Criterion*

Dear Miss Farjeon,

Thank you very much for your kind letter of the 9th.[2] I sometimes suspect that much clarity of writing is merely a kind of knack of style, and that the matter when examined is just as muddled as any other, and that this may be true of much I have written myself. However, it is a great pleasure to me that these papers have pleased you. You will of course be welcome to have them again at any time, if they are not lost

---

1 – 'I have nothing against your choice . . .' MacNeice responded (19 July), 'and am pleased that you have been able to make a choice after so many eliminations' (*Letters of Louis MacNeice*, 230). 'Two Poems: Trapeze, The Creditor', C. 12 (Oct. 1932), 54–5.

2 – 'These are as good to the eye as they were to the ear. I suppose it is because I begin by being in agreement with what you have to say that I find it said so satisfyingly; but I hope there is power of conversion too in these articles, for others who begin by disagreeing or half-agreeing. If change of spirit can occur by taking thought, this may have happened, for you make the thinking clear even to a rather hazy mind like mine . . . I wish the fourth paper were recoverable, for I remember that summing-up as the best of what I heard; and I am very glad of the opening one I missed, which seems to me as good. Lady Rhondda was here last night, and wanted to carry these off [for two weeks in Scotland] . . . We are taking the dates and trying to get back numbers for her; if we fail, may I, when she comes back, ask you to let her see them?'

meanwhile. But I think it is always possible to obtain back numbers of the *Listener*.

> With many thanks,
> Yours very sincerely,
> T. S. Eliot

TO *Alistair Cooke* CC

15 July 1932   [*The Criterion*]

Dear Mr Cooke,

I have read your letters to James with enjoyment, but candidly I cannot think of any English periodical for which I think they are likely to be suitable.[1] It seems to me, however, that a continuation of current comment of this sort might make a very suitable number for some foreign periodical or preferably some American newspaper. Unfortunately I have no relations with any of the American daily press, and as long ago I once tried to find such a connection for myself, I know that it is not too easy. Possibly you will be able to make enquiries in America, and if while I am there anyone asks me about a correspondent I will suggest your name. The difficulty there is of course that you could not be of any use to them until you returned to England. In the meantime possibly Orage[2] or someone like that might care to consider from you a more formal periodical letter commenting on life and events in America.

> Yours sincerely,
> [T. S. Eliot]

1–Cooke had written in response to TSE's letter of 5 July: 'I will certainly let you have as much of the essay ['A Preface to Theatrical Criticism'] as there is . . . before I sail.'

He ventured too – anticipating his radio series 'Letter from America' by several years – 'I hope you will not think it presumptuous of me to send along three essays in a form I had hoped to practise regularly . . . These letters are more careful, I hope not less spontaneous, write-ups of answers to a friend living first in Tours, then in Paris. They were provoked by his asking me actually to keep him "in touch with books, ideas, plays and so on" . . . My intention was to deal with one of these each week in the form attempted: these first three are on The Idiom of Letter-Writing, on Equating International Reputations, and on Popularisation via the B.B.C. . . . I could easily write about twenty or thirty . . . And continue them from America if necessary.'

2–A. R. Orage (1873–1934), owner-editor of the *New Age*, 1907–24; founder of the *New English Weekly*, 1932; disciple of G. I. Gurdjieff; proponent of C. H. Douglas's Social Credit.

TO *Herbert Read*   CC

15 July 1932   [Faber & Faber Ltd]

Dear Herbert,

I enclose two sets of poems. Would you be so kind as to take a few minutes to tell me whether you think they are any good?[1]

Yours ever,
[Tom]

TO *A. Humphry House*   CC

15 July 1932   [*The Criterion*]

Dear Mr House,

It is a long time now since you came to see me, but I have been meaning for some time to try to get into touch with you again. It would be very nice to hear from you again, and I should like to know if you would care to review some book for the December number of the *Criterion*.[2]

Yours sincerely,
[T. S. Eliot]

TO *Charles Harris*   CC

15 July 1932   [Faber & Faber Ltd]

Dear Harris,

Thank you for your letter of the 12th. I am disappointed to find that I have a lunch engagement for Wednesday 20th, or I should have been very happy to ask you to lunch with me. But in any case I shall look forward to a talk with you at 11.45.

I am going to buy a copy of Father Harton's book for myself, and I have got Lowther Clarke to send me a review copy which Evelyn Underhill is

---

1 – HR responded on 16 July: 'I don't feel very convinced by Miss [Emily Holmes] Coleman's poems. They show a morbid fancy, but no real poetic force. But I am inclined to like R. N. D. Wilson's "Equinox" . . . the poem as a whole seems to me to be good.' TSE declined Wilson's submission. (Wilson's 'Apollinaire in Classe' had appeared in *MC* 6 [Oct. 1927], 311.)

2 – House (Wadham College, Oxford) replied (18 July) that he would like to do a review. He added, 'Perhaps I should tell you that on finding myself unable to proceed to the priesthood I resigned my chaplaincy here last March, and wish to be counted for all purposes a layman. For the present I am retaining my fellowship as lecturer in English: but as there are few pupils a great deal of time is my own.'

going to review in the December number. I am very glad to hear that its sales are so cheerful in spite of the lack of reviews.[1] Could you tell me whether it has been reviewed in the *Times Literary Supplement*? I always get the *T.L.S.* but do not always open it. If not I will drop a line to the Editor whom I know very well.

I am delighted to hear of your success with the committee of Convocation, and it ought to be a very great satisfaction to yourself.[2]

I wish indeed that I could find a few more members of the sort that we want, and have always had the point in mind. Most of the people I know seem to be papists or atheists.[3]

Yours sincerely,
[T. S. Eliot]

TO *John Maynard Keynes*   TS Marshall

15 July 1932   *The Criterion*

My dear Keynes,

Someone told me that you had set afoot in Cambridge the theory that periods of great literary accomplishment always coincide with periods of inflation. If this rumour is true, as I hope it is, I suggest that the *Criterion* would very much like to have your views on paper for publication.

In case you refuse to take this suggestion seriously I will put it in another form and say that I am very anxious to keep the *Criterion* up at least to its level during my absence in America, and that this is difficult owing to my having to construct two numbers considerably in advance. Any contribution from you would not merely keep up the level of that issue, but raise it above.

Yours very sincerely,
T. S. Eliot

1 – 'Fr. Harton's book *The Elements of the Spiritual Life* is a *great* book, quite equal in excellence to the best ascetic treatises of the Roman Communion . . . It will be the standard Anglican treatise for many a long year. Northcote reviewing it in the forthcoming number of *Theology* calls it "the first Anglican manual of Ascetic Theology since Jeremy Taylor". Sales have gone up to 600 already.' See review by Evelyn Underhill, *C.* 12 (Jan. 1933), 282–4.
2 – 'I had a great personal triumph yesterday. The Joint Committee of Convocation on Unction finished its labours. It accepted (with very few amendments) the Introduction to the unction services which I laid before it, and the chairman (an evangelical) signed a *unanimous* report.'
3 – 'E.C.U. [English Church Union] "reconstruction" is proceed[ing] favourably. I wish you could rope in, and persuade to join, a few more intellectual Catholics. It would much strengthen my hands on the Council.'

TO *George Bell*   Lambeth

18 July 1932   Faber & Faber Ltd

My dear Lord Bishop,

I must apologise for my delay in answering your kind note of the 13th; but I was uncertain of my plans.[1] I now find that we are committed to a visit to my mother-in-law for that weekend, and so must regretfully decline your hospitality. In any case, I doubt whether my wife is strong enough, at the present time, for a weekend visit in a household strange to her. We hope that my absence for a time may have the effect of strengthening her nerves (and nerve), after she has been to some extent on her own feet. Therefore I hope very much that you and Mrs Bell will repeat your invitation next year. I wish that there were ever an opportunity of seeing you in London.

> With most regretful thanks,
> I am, my Lord,
> Yours very sincerely,
> T. S. Eliot

FROM *Vivien Eliot* TO *Mary Hutchinson*   MS Texas

Monday 18 July 1932   68 Clarence Gate Gardens

My dear Mary

Thank you for the lovely tea you gave me today. I was very happy to be with you – *alone*.

I find you are more *practical* than most of my friends, & it is *kind* of you to *interest* yourself in what I shall do this next year. I do appreciate that!!!

I just now want to say *that*, & then to say that I really do wish to move to 51 Gordon Square, & shall do that – & that I cannot endure my present servants much longer – will you tell me where you got Deal from? I think he is so nice. I should like now to get better service. I did try the Regina, but it was not very good.

You are going to ring me up & come one evening to see us before we go?

---

1 – TSE and VHE were invited to Chichester for the weekend of 23–5 July.

I was upset to hear that Philip Morrell has resigned, & Tom is really horrified.

With very much love,
Yours ever,
Vivienne Haigh Eliot

FROM *Vivien Eliot* TO *Aurelia Bolliger*   MS Beinecke

Monday Night [18 July 1932]   68 Clarence Gate Gardens

I had *hoped* you would telephone tonight – but you have not. *Please* telephone *tomorrow*! I am *free* on Wed. afternoon! Will you come? I have your stockings here for you.

Yrs. Affectly,
Vivienne

FROM *Vivien Eliot* TO *Ralph Hodgson*   MS Beinecke

Tuesday 19 July 1932   68 Clarence Gate Gardens

Dear Mr Hodgson

I am so sorry again to have to *bother* you, but I *wrote* last night to Miss Bolliger (c/o you) & reminded her that she had promised to *telephone* me. I have waited 2 days. I last saw her on Sunday night.

I asked her to telephone to say when she is coming.

I ask *you* – may she go once more to Hindhead – in the car, for 2 days – as before – to the same hotel where my Mother is?

My Eliot feels *too* tired to go *unless* she does. I do want to go once more, for as you know I get *little enough* fresh air.

Perhaps you will both look in tomorrow – if she could come to tea & you could come to fetch her?

But will she please telephone me during the morning as if she doesn't come I must go to see my *Aunt*.

This all cancels out because I have now spoken to ~~my~~ our dear Aurelia & she *will come* in to see me *at 6 tomorrow Wednesday*, & perhaps you will come too.

With love & *best best* wishes to you both.

Yrs.
Vivienne Haigh Eliot

TO *Reginald Tribe*[1]   CC

19 July 1932   [Faber & Faber Ltd]

Dear Father Tribe,

Thank you for your kind letter of the 18th.[2] It is an honour which I fully appreciate to be asked to take the chair at a meeting of this kind, and for such a cause. If I could accept it would also be a great pleasure to make my long deferred acquaintance with Kelham.

But unfortunately I am leaving for America in the middle of September, in order to deliver some lectures, and I shall be away until some time in the following May. Even were your meeting to take place before I left it would still be impossible for me to fulfil my engagements between now and my departure.

Perhaps I may have the pleasure of being of use to you in a year's time, and I still hope that after my return I may be able to spend a week or two at Kelham.

                    With many regrets,
                    I am,
                    Yours sincerely,
                    [T. S. Eliot]

TO *Paul Léon*   TS National Gallery of Ireland

19 July 1932   Faber & Faber Ltd

Dear Monsieur Léon,

Thank you for your letter of the 14th with enclosures.[3] I had already had a letter from Mr Joyce and was expecting the detailed report from

1–The Revd Reginald Tribe was Director of the Society of the Sacred Mission, Kelham Theological College, House of the Sacred Mission, Kelham, Newark, Nottinghamshire.
2–'A group of women tutors and students at Oxford supports an ordinand and a half at Kelham . . . And the members demand that they shall have a public meeting some time in the aurumn; & I want you to take the chair. Can you come down there . . . to do this?'
3–Léon sent an extract from the doctor's report on JJ's eyesight, along with a letter that Léon was sending (at JJ's suggestion) to JJ's London literary agent. 'Mr Joyce would like to have your opinion about the projected book of his daughter. I must add that she has actually developed a very original style and her illuminated letters are exceedingly beautiful.'

JJ reported that Prof. Vogt had determined that JJ's right eye was afflicted by 'total' cataract complicated by secondary glaucoma and partial atrophy of the retina. The doctor would have treated the other neglected eye but for the intervention of glaucoma and retinary atrophy resulting from interocular pressure. Vogt would decide within a few days, following further observations, said JJ, whether to let the eye go blind or to undertake two difficult

you. I am extremely distressed by these disasters. I shall be writing to Mr Joyce shortly but am going to have a word with his literary agents about his daughter's work first.

Yours sincerely,
T. S. Eliot

TO *J. H. Nelson*   CC

19 July 1932   [Faber & Faber Ltd]

Dear Professor Nelson,

Thank you for your letter of June 30.[1] In view of what you say I think that twenty-five dollars would be a reasonable fee. I should be obliged if you would instruct the publishers to send it to my Bankers, Lloyds Bank, 45 New Oxford Street, W.C.1. asking them to notify me of receipt.

Yours sincerely,
[T. S. Eliot]

---

operations in succession which would require him to stay in Switzerland for 5–6 months. 'This means a total cessation of work, a great deal of nervous tension and a considerable expenditure of money.'

See JJ's letter to Léon (12 July 1932) as copied by Léon to TSE (*Letters* III, 248).

Léon's letter (14 July) to JJ's literary agent Ralph Pinker spoke of Lucia's breakdown and proposed the idea of allowing her to develop confidence by using her talents in applied art. She had already decorated one book that was being launched in Paris; and JJ's idea was for Pinker to arrange – of his own accord, without any intervention by JJ himself – for 'a reputed English poet' to write a series of verses for children, each beginning with a letter of the alphabet; and Lucia would thereupon be commissioned to design the *lettrines* (*Letters* I, 322).

1–Nelson thanked TSE 'heartily' for permitting him to make use of the four poems in his forthcoming anthology. He declared too, in all honesty: 'This anthology is "an unremunerative educational undertaking" [TSE's phrase from his letter of 16 June] only in so far as I personally am concerned; the publishers expect to profit from it, and have authorized me to arrange for payment to authors . . . Otherwise I could not have brought myself to ask for the use of your poems. If you will state . . . what you feel the fee should be, I shall see to it that the Company sends you a cheque in payment promptly upon the publication of the book next spring.'

19 July 1932   *The Criterion*

Dear Mr Leavis,

Thank you for your note of the 17th.[1] I have been hoping to publish a part of the 'Festivals of Fire' in the *Criterion* some time next year. The whole poem would be much too long for periodical use. But if there is any possibility of the poem being published as a small book meanwhile, it is hardly worth while to hold it up for part publication in the *Criterion*. Therefore, so far as I am concerned you are free to do as you think best.

I am afraid that beyond one or two books already arranged for we are hardly likely to publish any new poetry for some time to come. It is a way of losing money in which we like to indulge as much as possible, but in these times we must walk very carefully.

I did not know that Bottrall had left Princeton. I hope that he did not find the place unsatisfactory. I had been expecting to see him when I pay a visit to Princeton.[2]

I commented to him on what I took to be his debt to Pound's *Cantos*. He told me that you had made the same criticism, but that he did not feel that he had been influenced by anything of Pound's subsequent to *Mauberley*. I still think, however, that he has assimilated something from Pound, even though unconsciously. There is a tendency to monotony in the poem, and I think he ought to learn to vary his metrical schemes still further. But I do think that the poem is worth publishing.[3]

Yours sincerely,
T. S. Eliot

---

1 – 'Bottrall asked me some time ago to see what I could do about getting his *Festivals of Fire* ... published. And now I've just had a hurried note from him which leads me to ask ... is there any prospect of the poem, or part of it, appearing in *The Criterion*? – or of Faber's bringing it out?

'I ask, because I don't know what step I ought to take at the moment, & don't want to cause a tangle ... I bother you, because Bottrall has left Princeton & gone over to the other side & exchange of letters is at the best going to take a long time.

'As for the poem, I criticized it a good deal at various stages of composition, & criticized the whole, &, in spite of Bottrall's altering it a great deal, have still a great deal of criticism to make. But I don't think it's any good his tinkering further & I think it would be best if he put it from him finally & that it's good enough to publish.'

2 – Leavis responded to this remark on 20 July: 'It was clumsiness that suggested he had left Princeton for good: he's only away for the vacation. He wrote from New Mexico.'

3 – Leavis replied (20 July): 'I hope you made to him the criticism about metrical monotony. I did, & he didn't like it, from which I conclude that it's a criticism to press. It's curious he should be so unaware of the debt to the *Cantos*. *Mauberley* he knows to have been his start.

TO *Bruce Richmond* CC

19 July 1932 [Faber & Faber Ltd]

Dear Richmond,

It may be an impertinence on my part, but in case Harton's *Elements of the Spiritual Life*[1] has been overlooked, I am writing to draw it to your attention. I have only glanced at the book, but it seems to me very good, and I am told by people far more competent than myself that it is an important work.

Don't forget the City Pilgrimage for some time in August.

Yours ever,

[T. S.E.]

TO *Alida Monro*[2] MS BL

19 July 1932 68 Clarence Gate Gardens

Dear Alida,

I have been wanting to write to you ever since Friday, because I felt that I did not half express my thanks & appreciation. It is the finest Mug Dog that ever was and its having belonged to Harold and stood in his room where I remember it makes it very precious to me.

Yours ever, gratefully,

Tom

I sent it to him (his first introduction to it) . . . three years ago, & he has developed steadily since, after most unpromising juvenilia.'

1 – F. P. Harton, *The Elements of the Spiritual Life: A Study in Ascetical Theology* (SPCK).

2 – Alida Klementaski (1892–1969) married Harold Monro on 27 Mar. 1920, having fallen in love with him in 1913. F. S. Flint wrote in 1933, of Alida: 'She was a young and beautiful woman who was earnestly bent on doing some good in the world, and who, to an equal degree with Harold, had a passion for poetry. She wanted to be a doctor, and to spend her life rescuing prostitutes; but Harold Monro persuaded her that, if she worked in the Poetry Bookshop, she would be doing as great a piece of social work as she would by the practice of medicine . . . She had an incisive mind and a keen sense of the ridiculous. Before the laughter in her cool, clear eyes, many of Harold Monro's phantasms and romantic illusions must have vanished, never to return again . . . For the rest of his life, Alida Klemantaski was at his side in the Bookshop, his chief help, assistant and guide. He himself said that, without her, he could not have carried on.'

TO *Mario Praz*   CC

19 July 1932   [*The Criterion*]

Dear Praz,

Many thanks for your letter of the 15th.¹ I will use Ungaretti's poem as soon as possible. We can only pay a guinea a page for short poems so that it will be all the more pleasant to be able to pay him the whole sum.

I shall be sorry if the book project falls through, but I know that in these days in England at least, the sale of even 100 copies of a book of translations from the work of a foreign poet is uncertain.² I regret it all the more if you have taken much trouble about it.

Thank you very much for your translation of 'Triumphal March' which seems to me to read very well. I look forward to the longer translation which you promise me.³

I am sorry that I shall not see you again as I leave for America in the middle of September. I am returning in the following May, and hope that we may meet during next summer.

Yours ever,
[T. S. Eliot]

TO *Georges Cattaui*   CC

21 July 1932   [*The Criterion*]

Dear Mr Cattaui,

I was very glad to get your letter and I hope that you will return from Switzerland very much strengthened. I am delighted to hear that you will be back by the middle of August. I shall not be leaving until the middle of September and my wife and I may therefore look forward to seeing you again before I go.⁴

1–'Your choice of Ungaretti's poem proves very sensible, as Ungaretti is likely to be proclaimed in the next few days the winner of a poetry prize given in Venice . . . Even the small amount you can give him for my translation will not be slighted, for I think his financial position is very precarious . . . As for myself, I do not want to receive any fee for the translation.' No poem by Giuseppe Ungaretti (1888–1970) was to come out in C.

2–The publisher of the projected Italian edition of *The Waste Land*, albeit 'very eager' to go ahead with the project, was anxious to have a guaranteed sale of at least 100 copies before proceeding with the printing. 'I am afraid the scheme is very likely to fall through,' wrote Praz.

3–Praz's translation of *The Waste Land* was to appear in *Circoli*: he would send a copy.

4–Cattaui wrote (16 July) to say he would be in London on 15 Aug., and to enclose his translation of *A Song for Simeon*. Incidentally, did TSE prefer 'Cantique' or 'Chant'?

I like your translation of the *Song for Simeon* (incidentally I think that 'Cantique' is preferable to 'chant') but I must look over it more at leisure before deciding whether I have any suggestions to make. Meanwhile I am writing to say that I cannot remember whether a French translation has appeared or not.[1] I have a vague impression that there was such a translation, but that if there was Maritain is more likely to know than anyone. It might have appeared in that periodical which came out successively under the title of *1929*, *1930* etc. Should you be communicating with Maritain any time you might ask him.

Looking forward to seeing you in August,

Yours very sincerely,

[T. S. Eliot]

to *Scott Buchanan* TS Houghton

21 July 1932 *The Criterion*

Dear Mr Buchanan,

Thank you for your kind letter of the 17th.[2] I am extremely sorry that my introduction to Maritain arrived too late, and can only apologize again for the delay. You were certainly anything but a nuisance to me. I enjoyed very much all our conversations and I am only sorry to have seen so little of you. I am also sorry that your year abroad should have been broken up by such distressing private anxieties.

Please let me hear from you as soon as you get home, and let me know how your mother stood the voyage. I am leaving in the middle of September and my address after that will be Eliot House, Cambridge, Mass.

Yours cordially,

T. S. Eliot

P.S. I wish that I could have been of more use to you.

---

1 – See *Cantique pour Simeon*, trans. Jean de Menasce, *Chroniques* 7 (1929), 69–71 (*Roseau d'or* IV. 3).

2 – Buchanan had not managed while in France to make contact with Maritain; and he regretted having been 'a nuisance' to TSE. 'My own life has been so strained and broken up that whatever I have hoped to accomplish has turned into some queer kind of self-torture and I am afraid I have allowed it to spread to the kind people that have tried to befriend me. If one is to have dark nights of the soul, one should arrange for some kind of hermetic isolation; I have learned that.'

TO *William Force Stead*   CC

21 July 1932   [Faber & Faber Ltd]

Dear Stead,

Thank you for your letter of Sunday. I am glad to say that our lunch was a great success.

We should very much like to come to enjoy your hospitality, but I am afraid that the dates put it out of the question. We could not possibly get away within the next week except for this week-end, when we have probably got to go to Hindhead.[1] So I can only express our joint regret.

I am seeing Gordon George tomorrow night and will ask him whether he has received your message and to let you know when he can come to see you. He intended to stay in London until the end of the month and then pay a few visits to the country. The address is 6 *Southwick* Crescent, w.2.

In any case I hope I may depend upon seeing you again before I leave in September.

Yours ever affectionately,
[T. S. E.]

TO *James Joyce*   CC

21 July 1932   [Faber & Faber Ltd]

Dear Joyce,

Thank you for your letter of the 13th, although I was very much saddened by your news.[2] I return Dr Coudet's [*sc*. Codet's] diagnostic

1–See VHE's letter to Ralph Hodgson, 19 July 1932, above.
2–JJ sent TSE from the Carlton Elite Hotel, Zurich, a copy of the neurologist's report on his daughter's condition, in confidence. He had arranged for his daughter to spend time in the Tyrol, in company with the Jolas family and a nurse. She was clear-headed and well-behaved; and had real talent as an artist.

He went on: 'Vogt saw me and you will get from Léon an account of the very unpleasant surprise that awaited me here. He is keeping me under observation.

'What am I to do about my book? Of course I can always refund the advance [£150 on *W.i.P.*] if I have to abandon it. But I want to finish it. Impossible to write in such circumstances. I may have to remain 4–6 months here. I hope you do not believe it is any bad faith on my part.

'And the money it all costs! Good Lord! And this place is so dear. I mean Switzerland. We stop at this hotel because my wife is exhausted by it all and must have a week or so rest and comfort . . .

'I really do not know what to do about *W.I.P.*' (*Letters* I, 322.)

herewith. Although I have very considerable respect for French methods of treatment I recognize in the statement a peculiarly French elaboration of uncertain opinion. French diagnoses seem to me very often an ingenious way of avoiding diagnosis. I therefore hope that the case may be very much less serious than one might suppose from this letter. I have had a talk with Pinker today and you or Léon will be hearing from him shortly about Lucia.

As for your own work, it is at the present time absurd to talk about refunding your advance, and we should not consider it. Let us wait until Vogt makes up his mind what to do, and I hope that you may be at work again within six months. Meanwhile, however, you will remember that you were going to let us have such part of the book as you considered completed in order that the printers might get ahead with the necessarily slow process of composition. Is there not any part ready that they could begin on? Once it was set up satisfactorily the plates could be kept until there *was* more. Anyway you are not to worry about us, but to do whatever is best for yourself and postpone thinking about work until Vogt allows you to begin again.

I shall hope to be kept posted about Vogt's opinions from time to time by Léon. We shall publish *WIP* when it is ready and you must not disturb yourself about it with the worries you have at present.

With kindest regards to Mrs Joyce and yourself,

Yours ever,

[T. S. Eliot]

TO *Mark Gertler*[1]

PC MS Luke Gertler

[Postmarked 23 July 1932]   68 Clarence Gate Gardens

We are more than sorry that this is your last Sat. evening, as we shall not be at home for this weekend again. Please let us have a p.c. when you get to the country, as we should like to *have your address* and to know how

---

1 – Mark – orig. Marks – Gertler (1891–1939), British artist of Polish Jewish descent, studied at the Slade School of Art (where contemporaries included Paul Nash, C. R. W. Nevinson, Stanley Spencer and Isaac Rosenberg); was supported variously by OM, Edward Marsh and Gilbert Canaan, and was for many years infatuated with Dora Carrington; suffered from tuberculosis for much of his adult life. See Sarah MacDougall, *Mark Gertler* (2002), David Boyd Hancock, *A Crisis of Brilliance: Five Young British Artists and the Great War* (2009).

yr. wife is.[1] & Please let us know when you expect to be back. Best wishes from both.

Tom.

FROM *Vivien Eliot* TO *Aurelia Bolliger* MS Beinecke

Sunday 24 July 1932   68 Clarence Gate Gardens

My dear Aurelia

All is forgiven! I have come back from Hindhead after a lovely day.

Will you be kind please & *bring Mr Hodgson* to dinner here on Tuesday, at *7.30*. ?? *R.S.V.P.*

Bring Picky too if he is back by then. Please *telephone* yr answer tomorrow morning.

Don't fail me!

With love,
Yrs. Ever,
Vivienne Haigh Eliot

TO *Eleanor Hinkley* TS Sturtevant/Houghton

25 July 1932   Faber & Faber Ltd

Dear Eleanor,

I was much pleased to get your letter of July 7, especially as I had had no news about your plays.[2] That is very bad luck indeed about the Brontës, although encouraging for the future. Is it not possible that if *Dear Jane* prove a success in New York, it may eventually be taken for London? To me, who knows nothing of theatre technique, *Dear Jane* seemed a more easily *actable* play than the Brontës. I mean simply that being closer knit, and requiring fewer characters and scenes, it should be

---

1 – Gertler was married in 1930 to Marjorie Greatorex Hopkinson, who would leave him in his last year.

2 – 'If . . . Eva Le Gallienne puts on "Dear Jane", and it isn't hooted off the boards, that in itself will be very satisfying. I have been thinking that if it opens on the proper day for you, you might go on for the opening? Even if everything went dreadfully it would be copy for you later! . . . [Y]ou did like the play, you remember . . . I must thank you for taking the Brontë play to Miss Fassett and sending me that cable . . . I heard from Miss Fassett the other day, some quite tantalizing news. There are some five plays on the Brontës now being peddled in London, and before mine even got there, Sir Barry Jackson had bought one for production in the autumn.'

377

much easier to produce. I can quite understand your feeling about trying to use your earlier work. If I start anything and have to leave it unfinished for a long time, I can never finish it; and if I do not publish a piece of writing as soon as it is written, I soon do not want ever to publish it at all. I am bringing out a big book of selected essays in the autumn, and have had the toil of reading the proof three times, and in consequence am thoroughly ashamed of everything in the book. Well, I hope you will succeed in getting a new play done in time; sometimes one can work very much better under the pressure and stimulus of a date.

Speaking of theatrical matters, I believe that I am to meet the notable producer, Mr Leon M. Lion, at tea this week.[1] Which reminds me that a few weeks ago I went to a small garden party where there were a number of stage people – they did a few turns – one sang Spanish songs to a guitar – Sara Allgood recited – and I was asked (much against my will) to read a section of *The Waste Land*. After it was all over an old lady came up to me and said earnestly: 'Please tell me, I have always wondered, do you pronounce your name Léon M. Lion in the French way, or Leon M. Lion in the English way?' I hated to undeceive her, especially as my own name seemed to convey nothing to her.[2]

I am relieved to hear that Spencer is giving 'my' course at Radcliffe – I was apprehensive lest I should have to give it myself, and I have never given a lecture exclusively to young women.[3] What it will be, I haven't the faintest idea; and I shall have to walk very warily not to offend literary friends and acquaintances. I really know very little about Modern English Literature, but that doesn't seem to me to matter much. May I formally invite you to come with me to the Yale football match, or if that is at New Haven, to the next best one at Cambridge?[4] A friend of mine is going to lend me a fur coat, so you will not be ashamed of me. I expect to arrive about the 26th or 27th of September. I shall be fearfully rushed at first, as I cannot find the time here to do much work on the lectures.

1–Leon Marks Lion (1879–1947), British actor, producer and manager; starred in Alfred Hitchcock's *Number 17* (1932).
2–TSE would write to Phyllis Woodliffe – who had played 'Mrs Bert' in *The Rock* – on 22 Aug. 1934: 'Now, *my* personal acquaintance with the stage, and what is much more important, with managers etc. is *very* limited; I was once mistaken for Leon M. Lion, that's about all.'
3–'I am planning to take the course you give at Harvard, at Radcliffe. Your Mr [Theodore] Spencer gives it at Radcliffe. He says the girls will feel terribly sold, and he doesn't know how they are to keep your course small, since there is already such an interest being taken in it.'
4–'Let's go to one foot-ball game, just for the fun of it . . . The crowds and the smell of tobacco and the remarks made by odd fat men who think they're funny, are so soothing.'

This *is* a dull letter, but I hope you will find my conversation rather brighter! With love to Aunt Susie,

Affectionately,

Tom

TO *W. McC. Stewart*[1]   CC

27 July 1932   [*The Criterion*]

Dear Mr Stewart,

I must apologize for the delay in dealing with your translation of 'Der Dichter in Zeiten der Wirren'[2] which you sent me on the 16th March. Your translation struck me as extremely skilful, and with all the prestige of George backed by your own authority I hesitated to use my own judgment. But I must confess that the poem still strikes me as intolerably generalized and dull. Perhaps it is hard for me to take the Poet so seriously as that. Perhaps one day you will have an essay of your own to offer.

With all best wishes,

Yours sincerely,

[T. S. Eliot]

TO *Ants Oras*[3]   CC

27 July 1932   [*The Criterion*]

Dear Dr Oras,

I have received and read with great interest your study of the *Critical Ideas of T. S. Eliot.* It is without the slightest irony that I can say that until

---

1–William McCausland Stewart (1900–89) was educated at Trinity College, Dublin. Resident Lecteur d'Anglais, École Normale Supérieure, Paris, 1923–6 (while studying at the Sorbonne), he taught too at the École des Hautes Études. He was Lecturer in French, University of Sheffield, 1927–8, and taught at St Andrews and Dundee before becoming Professor of French at Bristol, 1945–68. He was elected Chevalier de la Légion d'Honneur, 1950; Officier des Palmes Académiques, 1950; Commandeur, 1966. His works include translations of Paul Valéry's *Eupalinos, or, The Architect* (1932) and *Dialogues* (1956).

2–'The Poet in Times of Confusion', by Stefan George (from *Drei Gesänge*, 1921).

3–Ants Oras (1900–82): Estonian writer and translator; studied at Tartu University and at Oxford; taught at Tartu from 1928 (as Professor from 1934); and in his later years settled in Gainesville, Florida, where from 1972 he became Professor of English at Florida University. His writings include *The Critical Ideas of T. S. Eliot* (1932); a study of Milton; and translations from English into Estonian (including Shakespeare, Goethe, Pushkin, Molière) as well as translations of Estonian works into English, German and other languages.

I read your essay I had no notion how many critical ideas I had or how coherent they might appear to be. Naturally such an essay can hardly fail to give pleasure to the subject of it. Furthermore you have made a number of interesting suggestions which are quite new to me. I think, for instance, that you are quite right about Santayana, although the idea had never struck me before, and I admire your perspicacity. I always rather disliked Santayana personally, quite without justice. I dislike his style of writing which I find very hard to read, and I dislike his Post-Latin-Catholicism pretence. However he was very much of a figure in my time, and I read some of his books when I was very young and impressionable indeed, and the influence is more than likely.[1]

With many thanks and warm appreciation,

I am,

Yours sincerely,

[T. S. Eliot]

TO *Montgomery Belgion*   CC

27 July 1932   [Faber & Faber Ltd]

Dear Belgion,

Thank you very much first for sending the Aron and Dandieu article[2] which I have read with interest. Like so many French dissertations of the kind it seems to me to use more words than the matter really requires.[3] But still I think it is very interesting, and I am very much obliged to you

---

1 – TSE was to write to William B. Goodman (Associate Editor, Harcourt, Brace & World, Inc.), 12 Oct. 1961, with reference to Richard Blackmur's final revision of his essay on George Santayana: 'While Santayana's title *Three Philosophical Poets* did make a deep impression on me, I never regarded myself as to any degree a disciple of Santayana himself. As a matter of fact, I thought the man rather a poseur, who chose to look down upon New Englanders as provincial protestants. Most of his early books, *The Life of Reason*, seem to me very dull, and he was certainly much at his best on the borderline between philosophy and literary criticism.'

2 – 'Back to flesh and blood', an article especially adapted by Arnaud Dandieu and Robert Aron from the first chapter of their new book, was to be published in the Dec. *Criterion*. Belgion was to review the book in question, *La Révolution Nécessaire*, in C. 13 (Apr. 1934), 510–13.

3 – TSE's candidly outspoken secretary Pamela Wilberforce would later comment to her friend Mrs A. T. K. (Helen) Grant (30 Sept. 1932): 'Here are proofs of the Aron and Dandieu article, together with the French original. The trouble is that it is appallingly long, and as these Frenchmen seem to be surprisingly verbose and long-winded, I wonder if it would be possible for you to prune it down? Could you manage to eliminate, say, a galley and a half out of the total of six galleys? . . . [H]e or they are pretty sure to be troublesome about cuts!'

for bringing it our way. The only trouble is that I cannot possibly get it into the October number which is overflowing as things are. I should like very much to publish it in December, so much so that I can waive the objection of its appearing in Paris in October. I do not suppose that Aron and Dandieu will have any objection to that. You tell me furthermore that it is not quite the same as the French text.

Now about your chronicle. I found it extremely interesting and helpful and it is on the whole quite what it ought to be for its purpose. I feel, however, that I ought to have warned you about length, but I thought that you would have noticed the usual length of the other chronicles. The longest one I have had was that by Orlo Williams of which I made an exception as it was originally an article and had to be cut down. But the majority of chronicles have only been seven or eight pages. I know that this is very inadequate and that it is impossible to say much in seven pages, but space has to be limited by expense. Of course this chronicle could not be cut down as much as that, but I think I shall have to get it within the compass of, say, eleven pages. Will you try to reduce it yourself or would you prefer to leave it to my efforts? I am very sorry about this grim necessity, but it cannot be helped.

With many thanks,
Yours ever,
[T. S. Eliot]

TO *Peter Winckworth*   CC

27 July 1932   [Faber & Faber Ltd]

Dear Mr Winckworth,

Thank you for your letter of the 25th. It was very pleasant to hear from you again. I have discussed your suggestion of a pamphlet on the Boy Scout Movement[1] with other directors and we are all of the opinion that it would be an impossible undertaking at the present time. The market for such pamphlets has become a very poor one and we have not undertaken any new pamphlets for some time past. It can now I fear only be in the case of some subject of the very widest popular interest at the moment that we could contemplate new pamphlets. It is of course as it should be because a pamphlet form ought to be the proper vehicle for drawing

---

1 – Winckworth's title was to be simply 'The Boy Scout' – 'something on scouting that is critical, rather than statistically official or warmly propaganda in effect'.

public attention to [an] unfamiliar subject of importance. But it has to do partly no doubt with the general depression in the book trade.

I shall hope to see some more poems of yours when you have written any that satisfy you. I am very glad to hear that the examination has been passed and that you are likely to have more leisure.

Yours sincerely,
[T. S. Eliot]

TO *George Scott Moncrieff*[1] CC

27 July 1932 [London]

Dear Scott Moncrieff,

Thank you very much for sending me your book. I not only received it but read it immediately which is a rare thing for me to do; but I delayed writing to you in the hope that I might meantime receive your Scottish address which you promised me. I can only hope that this will reach you.

I enjoyed *Café Bar* very much, at least if it is not a book which one is meant to enjoy in the ordinary sense it seemed to me well written and well proportioned, and there were only one or two incidents such as that of Scottish Tommy and Cath which seemed to me out of scale. What I mean is that that one incident struck me as the sort which one does not expect to be introduced unless it is carried further. Nearly all the rest seemed to me to be of just the right kind and of just the right emphasis to be grouped naturally about the Café itself so that we see them in relation to the Café and expect to hear no more of them than we do. I hope that it will have a success. It seems to me that you have used that material so well as to have used it up, and I am wondering what the subject of your next book will be.

Do let me have your address and send a card from time to time if there are any books you would care for. And I should be very much interested to know how you get on in your fatherland. I presume you are too far away to have been one of the band of patriots who tore down the Union Jack at Stirling.

Yours sincerely,
[T. S. Eliot]

---

1 – George Scott Moncrieff (1910–74) – 'Scomo' – journalist, author, playwight and novelist. Educated in Edinburgh and at Aldenham School, England, he won praise for his first novel *Café Bar* (1932) – 'low-life vignettes of London'. His other works included *Scottish Country* (1935), *Lowlands of Scotland* (1938), *Edinburgh* (1946), *Death's Bright Shadow* (1948). See Morley Jamieson, *George Scott Moncrieff and a Few Friends: A Brief Memoir* (privately printed, 1987).

TO *W. M. Whiley*   CC

27 July 1932   [Faber & Faber Ltd]

Dear Father Whiley,

I have your letter of July 20 and am honoured by your invitation to join the General Committee of the Centenary.[1] Your circular letter says that this involves no work and I am taking you at your word because, as you probably know, I shall be absent from September to May of next year and could not be of more than nominal use.

Yours sincerely,
[T. S. Eliot]

TO *Charles Madge*[2]   TS Madge

27 July 1932   *The Criterion*

Dear Sir,

I must apologize for the delay in considering your manuscript on Blake and Bysshe.[3] I must confess to my ignorance in admitting that when I opened it I was under the impression that you were about to draw some comparison between Blake and Shelley and had chosen a somewhat capricious title. I found it extremely interesting, but I do fear that it is too long for the *Criterion* although the general conclusion to be drawn from it is of considerable interest. I am not at all keen on publishing papers in instalments as the intervals of a quarterly are so long. Possibly you might have some shorter essay to offer in connection with the same studies?

1 – The Revd Whiley, writing on behalf of the Executive Committee of the Oxford Movement Centenary (1933), chaired by the Rt Revd The Lord Bishop of Salisbury, had invited TSE to join 'the wider General Committee'.

2 – Charles Madge (1912–96), poet and sociologist, was a scholar at Magdalene College, Cambridge (which he left without taking his degree). In 1935–6 he was a reporter on the *Daily Mirror*: this was thanks to the help of TSE (who also published his first volume of verse, *The Disappearing Castle*, 1937). In 1937 he set up, with the anthropologist Tom Harrisson, the Mass Observation project: their output included *May the Twelfth* (1937) and *Britain by Mass Observation* (1939); and he was Professor of Sociology at Birmingham University, 1950–70. Other works include papers on social research and policy, as well as *Of Love, Time and Places* (poetry, 1994).

3 – Madge had written (5 May): 'I am sending you, on the suggestion of I. A. Richards, the typescript of an essay summarizing some work I did linking up Blake and Dryden. The argument requires a great deal of quotation, and this makes the essay probably too long for most papers to print. It might however be divided in two.'

Incidentally I wonder whether you sent me the complete article. The ending on page 48 seems very abrupt.

Yours sincerely,
T. S. Eliot

TO *Stephen Spender*   TS Northwestern

27 July 1932   *The Criterion*

Dear Spender,

Thank you for your letter of July 24.[1] I had given up all expectation, after what you had said about the subject from time to time, of getting your poems in time for this autumn. We had put them down pretty definitely for the beginning of next year, between seasons, and as this seemed to us probably the best time to publish, my mind was easy. I am afraid, too, that September 1 is too late for autumn publication, too late at least to get the book out before the time when the market is inundated.

In short, if you let us have the manuscript about the beginning of September that will be very convenient and will allow the book plenty of time to go through the press without being hustled. I should propose to bring it out in late January or early February, about the beginning of the term, and I still think that this is the best time. When Mr C. W. Stewart[2] returns next week I will ask him to draw up a contract for you.[3]

I have had a word with Faber about your novel, and I gather that it is very much changed since I read it.[4] I shall therefore read it again myself, and will let you hear within a week or ten days.

I am surprised that you did not receive a copy of the July *Criterion* as one was sent to you. I will have another sent. As for the proofs the trouble was that we received your manuscript too late for proofs to be possible. I hope that you will not find anything that you would have preferred to change.

1–SS had written (from Seeadler, Sellin auf Rügen, Ostsee, Germany) that he had only one more piece to write for a book of poems, and could 'quite easily' send the ts by 1 Sept.

2–C. W. Stewart, a director of F&F, was in charge of advertising. See GCF, 'Charles Stewart: A Personal Tribute', *The Bookseller*, 19 Apr. 1945.

3–Stewart had been away on honeymoon.

4–'I believe Faber have now the MS of my novel. If they should wish to take this, but to publish it after my poems, as you suggested they might do, I would be very willing to wait, and also to discuss with you and to make any changes in the novel which you may like.' He would send his Berlin address by Aug., he said. He added: 'Germany is getting very nasty just now.'

This is only a business letter so as I probably shall not have time to write in the next few days I shall be glad to have your Berlin address, and shall look forward to seeing you early in September.

Yours sincerely,
T. S. Eliot

TO *Ralph Hodgson*   TS Beinecke

28 July 1932   *The Criterion*

Dear Hodgson,

Miss Wilberforce has asked me to convey to you the knowledge that she has two photographs of her Stafford Terrier here in her room (very good ones too); but they are large and framed, so she cannot post them for you to see. But she would be delighted if you could find time to look in here any day and inspect them. I think she would also be glad to have your advice about breeding from him, which she is anxious to do.

I hope we may see something of you over the weekend.

Yours ever,
T. S. E.

FROM *Vivien Eliot* TO *Aurelia Bolliger*   MS Beinecke

Thursday 28 July 1932   68 Clarence Gate Gardens

My dear Aurelia

I heard today from T. S. that you & Mr Hodgson have taken tickets & that was bad news for me.

I got your postcard this morning about the canaries etc. so I hoped that would delay you!

As you have *not* telephoned to me, I suppose you will not run away without coming to see us again as you *promised*. Do not forget that I have certain things I want to *give* you, & one to show you.

Thank you dear Aurelia for the beautiful Kimono & scarf which you left here for me & which I shall always treasure. It is almost too much pleasure for me to have them.

Will you come *tomorrow evening* – or *Saturday* evening ? ?

I shall be here tomorrow until 2 p.m. & after 6 p.m.

Yours ever,
Vivienne Haigh Eliot

FROM *Vivien Eliot* TO *Mary Hutchinson*   MS Texas

Thursday 28 July 1932   68 Clarence Gate Gardens

My dear Mary.

I *was disappointed* at having such a flustered last meeting with you here. I have understood you to say you would come in to say good-bye *after dinner* one evening, so I did not expect you then.

I did ask my doctor about my doing some work, as you suggested. '*Getting a job*' I mean. His reply was that it would be very very *nice* & a very *good thing*. He told me he is going away for a month, & will help me on his return. I am sure he will.

I was *so much upset yesterday*, while I was with my doctor, & indeed all day, about Tom's affairs & all the worry connected with this business of Tom's 8 months in America, that it was not a good occasion for discussing the matter of work for myself.[1]

I understood you are going away tomorrow. Such *dismal* weather.

So now, I will say good-bye & *have a nice time*. Please write as you promised, & send yr. address, & let us know if we may come & see you there.

Yours ever,
Vivienne Haigh Eliot

FROM *Vivien Eliot* TO *Aurelia Bolliger*   MS Beinecke

Sunday 31 July 1932   68 Clarence Gate Gardens

Please *forgive* a post card, to remind you that *we are expecting* you both on Wednesday night to say Good-bye. We are *asking* one or two people *you have met here*, and who say they *must* see you both to say goodbye. Please be here by *8.30*.

Relying on you both & with best regards.

V. H. & T. S. Eliot[2]

1–Robert Sencourt believed that VHE was pushed 'beyond the confines of sanity' by TSE's decision to go to America without her (*T. S. Eliot: A Memoir*, 121).

2–TSE and VHE and friends including Mark Gertler enjoyed a 'merry' farewell dinner with Hodgson at the Three Arts Club (VHE was a member), 19A Marylebone Road, London NW1: see T. S. Matthews, *Great Tom*, 100.

VHE's mother wrote: 'Viv will miss you terribly for you have become quite a sister to her and I wish you could have remained until Tom comes back from the USA but the next best thing is for you to write often and cheer her up' (letter cited in Harding, *Dreaming of Babylon*, 154).

TO *The Editor,* The Glasgow News[1]   TS Valerie Eliot

[? July] 1932   *The Criterion*

Sir,

My attention has been drawn to an article in your issue of July 16th, entitled 'A Modernist Poet' by Mr W. K. Hamilton. The second paragraph of this article is seriously misleading as it suggests that I am to reside permanently in America; and I ask your courtesy for publication of the following correction.[2]

The Charles Eliot Norton Chair of Poetry is given for one year only. It has already been held by several incumbents, the first of whom was Professor Gilbert Murray. During the year of office, the Professor is required to be resident at Harvard from October 1st to May 1st.

I wish therefore to make clear that I am retaining my directorship of Faber & Faber Ltd; that during my absence from September next till May I shall continue publication of *The Criterion* with the assistance of my colleagues here; and that upon my return to London I shall resume all of my regular activities.

        I am, Sir,
        Your obedient servant,
        [T. S. Eliot]

Over thirty years later, TSE reminded Hodgson that he had 'admired [his] walking-stick, a Malacca stick with a leather-covered handle. On our next meeting you surprised me by the gift of a walking-stick, identical with your own. I hope you will remember, also, that during that year you and Aurelia were with us in London you and I exchanged walking-sticks on every occasion of meeting. Our last meeting has left me with the walking-stick which you bought for me. I should like you to know that it is still my principal walking-stick, and that I think of you whenever I use it, as well as on many other occasions. That was thirty years ago, and I remember your telling me one day that it was your 60th birthday. Thirty years have passed, but I can assure you though we have hardly ever communicated that my affection for you, and my admiration for your poems – and I am thinking above all of SONG OF HONOUR – remain undiminished.'

1 – This letter was probably not posted: the text is taken from an unsigned original.

2 – Hamilton announced that Harvard had appointed TSE to 'its Chair of Poetry': 'We are sorry that he is to leave Britain, where he has held a high place in the publishing house of Faber & Faber (intimately associated with our own Scottish "Porpoise Press"), but in the noble and beautiful New England city of Greater Boston, within whose confines the American Cambridge stands, his genius will have a setting worthy of a poet; and Quiller-Couch is no greater ornament to the Old Cambridge than he will be to the New – a vital force.'

TO *G. Wilson Knight*   CC

3 August 1932   [Faber & Faber Ltd]

My dear Knight,

I was very sorry to be obliged to wire to put off an engagement of such standing. My excuse is that you gave me no reason to believe that one day was less convenient than another, and this day was chosen rather at random. But it transpired yesterday that a great friend of mine is leaving suddenly on Thursday for Japan and is to be absent for three years, so I hope you will forgive the impertinence.[1] Please let me know what day in the near future will suit you – not a Thursday, and preferably not a Monday, and this Friday will be too late unless you wire. I shall have to change the place of meeting, as during this month my club is the guest of the United Universities Club in Suffolk Street.

> With many apologies,
> Yours sincerely,
> [T. S. Eliot]

TO *Edward Crankshaw*   CC

3 August 1932   [*The Criterion*]

Dear Mr Crankshaw,

Thank you for your letter of the 20th July, and for the various reviews and fragments of your novel which I return herewith. I remember taking notice of *The Times Literary Supplement* film book review at the time when it appeared.

It is very difficult to form any opinion of a novel from fragments, but I found myself interested, and should be glad to see it when it is completed.

I should be glad to give you a review to do at some time, but it is not very often that we have occasion to review the sort of books that you are much interested in. *The Criterion* has hardly taken cognizance of films and, as I told you, the musical side has been virtually in the hands of Mr J. B. Trend since the beginning. But if I notice anything that seems to suit you I will let you have it.

> With all best wishes,
> Yours sincerely,
> [T. S. Eliot]

1 – The farewell dinner with Hodgson and Bolliger.

TO *Wolfgang H. Clemen*   CC

3 August 1932   [*The Criterion*]

Dear Mr Clemen,

I was glad to hear from you and hope that you will have something more to show me when you have finished the work for your doctorate.[1] If you are working on Shakespeare's imagery might I commend to you two recent books published by the Oxford University Press by Mr G. Wilson Knight, entitled *The Wheel of Fire* and *The Imperial Theme*. You might find them of considerable use.

Yours sincerely,
[T. S. Eliot]

TO *Richard Thoma*[2]   CC

3 August 1932   [*The Criterion*]

Dear Mr Thoma,

I hasten to reply to your letter of the 30th July in order that you may understand the situation and not cast any blame on our friend Roditi.[3] When you wrote to me last I had completely forgotten his request to me to sign a book for a friend, and you have now recalled it to my memory. The point is that there was a signed limited edition of my *Dante*, and I make it a rule never to sign copies of the ordinary edition except of course when I am presenting the book to my friends. You see, it seems to me unfair to those who have bought the limited edition at a higher price. I know there are people who do not share this opinion, but my publishers concur. I am sorry not to be able to sign your *Dante* but I should be glad to sign any other of my books, of which there is not a signed limited edition.

I have not yet had time to look at your poems, but I will write to you about them at the earliest opportunity.[4]

Yours sincerely,
[T. S. Eliot]

1 – Clemen wrote (n.d.) that he expected to complete his 'doctor-dissertation' on Shakespeare's imagery within a year, and he would hope to send some other contribution after that.
2 – Richard Thoma (1902–74), American writer; associate editor of *The New Review*.
3 – Roditi had undertaken to ask TSE to autograph Thoma's copy of *Dante*; but when the copy in question found its way back to Thoma, he found it had not been signed.
4 – Thoma sent a book of poems called *Green Chaos*. He wrote from Paris (n.d.): 'If you would only "criticise" it for me I should be thoroughly happy. I have had, among others, Aldous Huxley's, Ezra Pound's and Stuart Gilbert's comments upon it, but of course they

TO *George Scott Moncrieff*   CC

3 August 1932   [Faber & Faber Ltd]

Dear Scott Moncrieff,

Thank you for your letter of the 31st.[1] Although you say you are off to the Isle of Skye I trust that this Edinburgh address will reach you. I also hope you feel better for breathing the free air of your native land. I am sending MacEwen's book to you at once. My friend George Malcolm Thomson who you know at least by name speaks well of it and of him. Will you write about 800 words on it for the December number, as the review list for September is already complete?[2]

Perhaps when I return from America I shall land in Glasgow and see a little of your country, although I fear I am committed to the Cunard Line which I believe goes no farther north than Liverpool.

With all best wishes,
Yours sincerely,
[T. S. Eliot]

TO *Betty Holter*   CC

3 August 1932   [*The Criterion*]

Dear Miss Holter,

Thank you for your note of July 18.[3] I have always been and shall be sympathetically interested in Mr Munson's work, but I doubt whether the enclosed is particularly appropriate for the *Criterion*. I should like to see something more of his, but I think an essay by him would be more effective in the *Criterion* if it dealt with someone rather better known in England than Carlos Williams.

Yours sincerely,
[T. S. Eliot]

---

know me, they know my life. I should like it reviewed by some one I do not know – especially if that some one be some one like you.'
1 – 'I have been amazed at the progress made by the National Cause in Scotland since my last visit. We are preparing for some sort of a push in the autumn. Young Moray Maclaren, whose *Return to Scotland* you may know, has a useful position on the BBC here and is a perfervid supporter. I am convinced that things will move shortly. Incidentally, I wonder if I could review for the *Criterion The Thistle & the Rose* by Sir Alexander MacEwen, a work by one of the older men that is expected to carry some weight in the "push". It is really extraordinarily thrilling to feel that there is even the possibility of helping in the making of a nation.'
2 – See review of A. A. MacEwen, *The Thistle and the Rose*, C. 12 (Jan. 1933), 308–9.
3 – Holter (*New English Weekly*) had submitted an essay by Gorham Munson, at his request.

TO *Katherine Norton* CC

3 August 1932 [Faber & Faber Ltd]

Dear Miss Norton,

The house in the New Forest of which I spoke to you which takes lodgers has the following address:

> Miss Ems,
> Karlton House,
> Queens Road,
> Lyndhurst, Hants.

The name and address sound improbable but I am assured that they are genuine and English. Lyndhurst itself is rather unattractive with boarding houses and some cheap hotels of the sort which ring dinner bells. But I am told that this house is a little outside and in a quiet place. I am informed, however, that it is not the most interesting residence for anyone who is unable to walk. It is pleasant for anyone who can walk seventy yards or so, and delightful for anyone who can walk a mile and back. Also it is rather primitive and can only supply tin baths in bedrooms. But if it should be of use the name to use of the person recommending it is Mr F. V. Morley.

I have heard of another pleasant quiet hotel near Oxted in Surrey, but I am told that everyone who goes there plays Bridge.

The only other places that I can think of near London are too high up in the Surrey hills. I should think that something out beyond Watford might be more convenient from your point of view.

Don't bother to acknowledge this. We are looking forward to seeing you next Tuesday.

Yours sincerely,
[T. S. Eliot]

TO *Bonamy Dobrée* CC

3 August 1932 [*The Criterion*]

Dear Bonamy,

I don't want to hurry you in the least – in fact there is no hurry, but I should like to know directly whether and when there is any prospect of your Macaulay article. My reason for putting the question at the moment is that I have had submitted another article on Macaulay[1] which I find just not good enough, and if I can say that I am expecting at some date an essay by you that will cover the matter.[2]

When are you coming up to town again before the middle of September?

Yours ever,

[T. S. E.]

TO *Marcel Aurousseau*[3]   CC

5 August 1932   *[The Criterion]*

Dear Mr Aurousseau,

Morley has shown me your interesting letter of the 2nd.[4] I should be very grateful to you if I might be allowed to take the first paragraph and rearrange it a little to stand by itself as a review of my book, which I should publish anonymously among the shorter notices in the *Criterion*. I hope you will let me do this, as the facts ought to be made known.[5]

Yours sincerely,

[T. S. Eliot]

1–By Ian L. Henderson.

2–BD replied on 5 Aug.: 'When you told me that you had 3 numbers made up, I thought Mac was off. However I am quite prepared to do him at any time. Give me a limit as far ahead as you can, & tell your *prétendant* that you have another.'

3–Marcel Aurousseau (1891–1983), Australian geographer, geologist and writer; President of the Geographical Society of New South Wales, 1959–61; member of the National Committee for Geography of the Australian Academy of Science, 1964–8; author of *Highway into Spain* (1930), *The Letters of F. W. Ludwig Leichhardt* (ed., 1968). See further Robert Freestone, *The Works of Marcel Aurousseau: A Bibliography* (1984).

4–Aurousseau wrote to FVM, 2 Aug. 1932: 'How about correcting Eliot's chemistry on pp. 17 & 18 of the *Selected Essays*? On p. 17, line 25, he takes oxygen and sulphur dioxide, and, on p. 18, line 9–11, he produces sulphur*ous* acid from them! $O_2 + 2SO_2$ do *not* equal $2H_2SO_3$ but only $2SO_3$, which *in the presence of water*, gives $SO_3 + H_2O = H_2SO_4$, sulphur*ic* acid. I haven't a text-book of inorganic chemistry handy, but reference to one would settle the point – there is, of course, a catalytic reaction involving platinum and one of the sulphur gases, but I've forgotten the exact terms and conditions of it.'

5–Aurousseau gave permission to TSE's recourse in a letter of 9 Aug. 1932: see unsigned review of TSE's *Selected Essays 1917–1932*, C. 12 (Oct. 1932), 167.

TO *Norman Foerster*

CC

5 August 1932   [Faber & Faber Ltd]

My dear Foerster,

Thank you for your letter of the 15th July.¹ It really does not matter whether you make acknowledgement to me or to Faber & Faber, but I think on the whole I prefer the latter. I return your enclosure with the date of Gerontion – at least I believe that is the date and it cannot be more than a year out.

I have consulted my colleagues as I always do on the matter of payment, and after some discussion I have persuaded them that twenty guineas is sufficient.² I shall be glad if you will arrange for your publisher to pay this sum direct to Faber & Faber.

Yours very sincerely,
[T. S. Eliot]

TO *Ruth Harrison*

CC

5 August 1932   [*The Criterion*]

Dear Miss Harrison,

I was very sorry to hear from the Clarendon Press people that although they appreciated your book they did not feel that they could afford to publish any book on such a subject. I am afraid that is the case throughout the publishing world at present and is a very depressing aspect of the business. We are constantly obliged to reject really first rate pieces of work because we are afraid of losing money on them. In ordinary times a publisher expects to produce a certain number of books at a loss and solely for their merit. That is one of the consolations of business which we have more and more to forgo. If I can think of any other suggestion I will write to you again.

With many regrets and good wishes,

Yours sincerely,
[T. S. Eliot]

1–In response to TSE's letter of 15 June, Foerster had decided to omit 'Portrait' and add 'Gerontion'; to omit *Ash-Wednesday* and add *Animula*. He would print the first 'Prelude'.
2–C. W. Stewart had initially suggested asking for a fee of $100.

TO *W. Symons*   CC

5 August 1932   [Faber & Faber Ltd]

Dear Mr Symons,

   Thank you for your letter of the 26th July. I have read *Wealth for Enjoyment*[1] with great interest and pleasure, for I think I am cordially in agreement with nearly all of what I understand. I liked it so much that it is very painful for me to have to tell you that after much discussion, my colleagues and I have been forced to the conclusion that in the present time we simply cannot afford to publish a book like this. That of course is part of the vicious circle, but it is unfortunately true that really sensible books on the economic situation are certain money losers. We are ourselves, of course, puppets of the system which is to be reorganized.

   I wish I had any suggestions to make for publication. I am looking forward keenly to seeing you again, I believe, next Friday, and perhaps we may get an opportunity to talk a little about the matter then.

                                        Yours very sincerely,
                                        [T. S. Eliot]

TO *J. D. Aylward*   CC

9 August 1932   [*The Criterion*]

My dear Aylward,

   I imagine you are back from your holiday now, so when can you come and lunch with me? I can at present manage any day next week except Monday and Thursday, and I hope one other day will suit you. Shall I pick you up in the City or will you come to the West End? Let it be whichever is the more convenient for you.

                                        Yours ever,
                                        [T. S. Eliot]

---

1 – The proposed work was compiled by the Chandos group, including [Maurice B.] Reckitt, Revd V. A. Demant, Revd J. F. Fletcher, Geoffrey Davies, Albert Newsome, and Symons himself.

9 August 1932   *The Criterion*

My dear Church,

I am very sorry indeed to hear about Abercrombie whom I have never known personally, and I have been thinking what I could do to help.[2] When it comes to the point it seems to me that I do not know any rich people or rather I do not know any very rich people well enough to be in a position to compel them to help a poet whose work they probably do not know very well. And I daresay any of the people whose names occur to me will already have been approached by Robert Trevelyan or someone else. I presume that Drinkwater has interested himself in the matter, and I suppose that someone has already tackled Siegfried Sassoon who I know is capable of great anonymous generosity. It is a pity that your letter did not reach me before Ralph Hodgson left for Japan, as he is a great friend of the Reginald McKennas[3] who are also very generous people, but it would still be worthwhile for you or Trevelyan to write to him and ask him whether he would be disposed to approach the McKennas on the matter. His address is Department of Arts and Letters, Imperial University, Sendai, Japan.

I am doubtful whether any of the younger people of wealth could be induced to take very much interest in an older poet like Abercrombie. We go out of date so quickly.

1–Richard Church (1893–1972), poet, critic, novelist, journalist and autobiographer, worked as a civil servant before becoming in 1933 a full-time writer and journalist. His first book of verse, *Mood without Measure*, was published by TSE at F&G in 1928. Church recalled, in his memoir *The Voyage Home* (1964), TSE's personality in the 1920s: 'its nervous intensity, its deliberate reserve . . . His voice was soft, with no trace of its American origin. The accent indeed was old-fashioned, in the Edwardian mode of such English precisionists as Max Beerbohm and Osbert Sitwell . . . Even though there was a cutting edge to this voice, a hint of merciless satire, I found myself attracted to the personality which it expressed.' Yet Church harboured misgivings about the nature of TSE's work: 'I share Eliot's temperamental attitude towards the demands and function of the art of poetry, both in society and as a discipline in the life of the individual. But I have distrusted the Montparnasse influence in his verse and doctrine, his sponsoring, even out of loyalty, of the writings of Ezra Pound. The dreadful self-consciousness of so many *déraciné* Americans, aping the hyper-civilised European decadents, have always given me the sensation of being in the presence of death' (69–71).

2–Church reported (3 Aug.) that the poet and critic Lascelles Abercrombie (1881–1938) was 'seriously ill with diabetes'. Since Abercrombie had three young sons, R. C. Trevelyan and Church were trying to get up 'a subscription among the people who was interested in Abercrombie either as a poet or as a man'. He did not expect TSE to subscribe ('we don't expect anything from fellow artists who all have their own burdens to bear'), but hoped he might be able to approach one or two wealthy persons.

3–Reginald McKenna (1863–1943), Liberal politician (Home Secretary, 1911–15; Chancellor of the Exchequer, 1915–18, under Asquith); from 1918 he was Chairman of the Midland Bank.

Other names have occurred to me, but they are likely to be people who have already been tackled by Trevelyan. I have one or two people in mind whom I will tackle if they are back in town before I leave in the middle of September.

I was glad that you were able to come to the last meeting at Russell Square. I hope that there may be meetings in my absence especially for the sake of continuity, but I shall not be able to attend another till next May.

Yours ever,

[T. S. Eliot]

TO *George Blake*[1]

CC

9 August 1932   [*The Criterion*]

Dear Blake,

I have read Rafferty's[2] poems. I think that the first is much the best. In fact the selection in the current number of the *Modern Scot* is a very

---

1–George Blake (1893–1961), novelist, journalist, publisher – author of *The Shipbuilders* (1935) – co-founded the Porpoise Press in hopes of refashioning a national publishing industry in Scotland. The Press was taken over by F&F in 1930. GCF wrote to H. M. Cohen, 14 Oct. 1930: 'We recently acquired the stock and good will of a small private business in Edinburgh called The Porpoise Press. The Porpoise Press exists for the purpose of publishing pamphlets, books and poems of Scottish national interest. It has hitherto been run in a very haphazard way by a single individual, and has just about paid its way. There are, however, considerable possibilities in it; and we are now working it up, with the assistance of two Scotchmen, named Blake and Thomson. Blake is one of our directors. Thomson is not. The arrangement with them is that they each take 25% of any net profits there may be arising from the Porpoise Press; and the management of the Press is entrusted to a sort of joint Committee consisting of Blake, Thomson and three of our own people. The whole of the business organisation is provided by us, and we put up all the money and collect all the income.' (See further Alistair McCleery, *The Porpoise Press 1922–39* [1988].) Blake was editor for four years of *John O' London's Weekly*, and for two years of *Strand Magazine*. On 20 June 1930 GCF wrote to offer him a Principal Directorship at F&F, starting on 1 Jan. 1931; but in the event he worked for F&F from 1 Aug. 1930. On 10 Oct. 1930 FVM told Henry S. Canby (editor of the *Saturday Review of Literature*) that 'my very good friend' was 'the recently appointed Fiction Editor to Faber and Faber . . . The fact that we have been able to snaffle him for Faber and Faber, shows the happy reputation which we have been establishing . . . There is a very interesting Scottish nationalistic movement; and it is really producing some brilliant writers.' FVM, in a letter to John Livingston Lowes, 12 Dec. 1930, wrote of the Porpoise Press as 'our new and lively subsidiary'. Blake was to take leave of F&F in 1932. On 22 Dec. 1951 TSE wrote to Harry Levin, of 'my old friend': 'George Blake's great-grandfather emigrated from Somerset to Scotland, and the Blakes have married Scotch [*sic*] wives ever since; and George Blake is about as Lowland-Scots as anyone can be.'

2–Seán Rafferty (1909–94), Scottish poet; see *Collected Poems*, ed. Nicholas Johnson (1995).

good one. I don't feel that the whole of this lot is good enough to justify publication, and I should be inclined to wait until he has done some better things. In the first poem he has followed very closely Pound's *Hugh Selwyn Mauberley*, but it is a good model, and he has used it well. Some of the other poems are rather poor pastiches of Donne, and he also has parroted my own style of about fifteen years ago. I should give encouragement, but I don't think that the present selection justifies itself for a Porpoise Press pamphlet.

Yours ever,

[T. S. Eliot]

TO *Katharine M. Day*   CC

9 August 1932   [Faber & Faber Ltd]

Dear Mrs Day,

Thank you very much for your kind letter of 23rd July, and for your invitation to address the Radcliffe Club of Boston.[1] I shall be very happy to do so, but you will understand that I am not in a position to fix a date until I arrive in Cambridge lest it should conflict with my duties at Harvard. I should suggest 150 dollars as a fee, and you will let me know if that is beyond the means of the Club.

Sincerely yours,

[T. S. Eliot]

P.S. I should think it extremely unlikely that I should have any official engagement on either the evening of November 8th or March 13th, but still I do not feel safe in making a definite promise. If you would be so kind as to remind me about the 1st of October we could settle the matter directly. My address will be Eliot House, Cambridge, Mass.

TO *H. C. Crofton*   CC

9 August 1932   [*The Criterion*]

My dear Crofton,

I shall be very disappointed if you cannot lunch with me before I leave in the middle of September. As I do not know when you are taking

---

1–Katharine M. Day (wife of Frederic L. Day, and a friend of TSE's cousin Abby Eliot) invited TSE to address the Radcliffe Club of Boston on 8 Nov. 1932 or 14 Mar. 1933. 'Also would you be so good as to tell me what your fee would be?'

your holidays or whether you are in London I should be glad of a word from you suggesting a date. It will have to be at the United Universities Club, as the Oxford and Cambridge Club is closed for August, but I expect that our hosts can provide at least a cold lobster and a bottle of hock at 12 o'clock if that time suits you best.

Yours ever,
[T. S. Eliot]

TO *Geoffrey Tandy*[1]   CC

9 August 1932   [Faber & Faber Ltd]

My dear Tandy,

   Will you come to lunch with me one day next week? It will have to be Tuesday Wednesday or Friday, and it is possible that I may find myself engaged for one of those three days, so if you have two of the three days open it will be better. I will try to get Frank to come also if he has returned to London. If next week does not suit you I am free all of the following week except Monday, Tuesday and Thursday.

Yours ever,
[T. S. Eliot]

---

1 – Geoffrey Tandy (1900–69), Assistant Keeper in the Department of Botany at the Natural History Museum, London, 1926–47, did broadcast readings for the BBC (including the first reading of TSE's *Practical Cats* on Christmas Day, 1937). During WW2 he served as a commander in the Royal Navy, working at Bletchley Park. He and his wife Doris ('Polly') were to become intimate friends of TSE. FVM would tell W. W. Norton on 1 May 1931 that Tandy was 'a very promising scientist . . . He has the possibilities of a Jennings or even of a Bateson.' Tandy was to write to Martin Ware (who had invited him to talk about TSE to a small literary society) on 20 Nov. 1935: 'I believe that anything I may be able to do to help anybody to a better understanding of Eliot's work will be a good work. Against that I have to set the fact that he is a pretty close personal friend (whatever that locution may mean) and my judgement may be vitiated in consequence. The text of "this side idolatry" may be used against me. However, having asked the man himself if he have any serious objection, I say yes and hope that you will not regret having asked me.' See Judith Chernaik, 'T. S. Eliot as "Tom Possum": The "good grey Poet" and the Tandy family', *TLS*, 1 Nov. 1991, 13–14; Miles Geoffrey Thomas Tandy, *A Life in Translation: Biography and the Life of Geoffrey Tandy* (thesis for the degree of MA in Arts Education and Cultural Studies, Institute of Education, University of Warwick, Sept. 1995).

TO *Kay Boyle*[1]   CC

10 August 1932   [London]

Dear Miss Boyle,

I have thought a good deal about the poems of Miss Coleman which you kindly sent me because I regard your recommendation very highly.[2] But I am afraid I cannot quite bring myself to see them in the same light as you do, and I return them with much regret.

Allow me to express my admiration of *Year before Last*.[3]

Yours sincerely,
[T. S. Eliot]

TO *John A. O'Neal*   CC

10 August 1932   [Faber & Faber Ltd]

Dear Sir,

Thank you for your letter of August 2nd.[4] I have returned the sheets signed, and regret that I was unable to make a more legible signature on the paper supplied.

1–Kay Boyle (1902–92): American author, editor, teacher and political activist, whose early novels, including *Plagued by the Nightingale* (1931), *Year Before Last* (1932) and *My Next Bride* (1934), were published by F&F. From 1923 to 1941 she lived primarily in France, marrying in 1932 Laurence Vail (ex-husband of Peggy Guggenheim) and enjoying friendships with artists and writers including Harry and Caresse Crosby (who published in 1929 her first fictions, entitled *Short Stories*, at their Black Sun Press), and Eugene and Maria Jolas; she also contributed to *transition*. See further Robert McAlmon and Kay Boyle, *Being Geniuses Together, 1920–1930* (1968); Jean Mellen, *Kay Boyle: Author of Herself* (1994).

2–Boyle submitted on 20 Mar. 1932 'some poetry of a young American woman: Emily Holmes Coleman. You have perhaps read her book entitled: *Shutters of Snow*. Her work seems to me very beautiful. I sincerely hope that you may find it so.

'In regard to the story of mine called *Three Little Men* which you were good enough to say you would like to print in the *Criterion*, I have advised my agent in N.Y. to send it to you at once. Nobody in America wants it! That's probably because it doesn't contain an Englishman in it.'

3–Published by F&F, 1932.

4–John A. O'Neal, assistant to Terence Holliday (who was ill), asked TSE to sign and return the 110 copies of the limited edition of his volume *John Dryden*. Only 100 of them were for sale: the other 10 were for TSE's personal use. The first ordinary edition of the book was to be limited to 2,000 copies. The printer's supply of type was insufficient to set the whole book at once: it would be printed in four or five sections, and they would appreciate it if TSE would correct the proofs only of the first section, leaving the remainder to be read in-house. If TSE was not willing to proceed on such a basis, they could not take full advantage of the autumn market.

I do not see any reason why you should decline to supply copies of John Dryden to English booksellers when they are ordered on behalf of particular clients. I merely did not wish the book to be stocked by booksellers or pushed in the English market in any way.

I understand your desire to market the book in September and will be quite satisfied to see the first fourth of it leaving the rest to your own responsibility.

Yours sincerely,
[T. S. Eliot]

TO *Harriet Monroe*[1]

10 August 1932   [*The Criterion*]

CC

Dear Miss Monroe,

Thank you for your letter of August 1st.[2] How very unfortunate that I could not have heard from you a little sooner. I have only one poem or part of a poem which I care to publish at the moment in any form, and I have given it to the *Hound and Horn* about six weeks ago. So now I am afraid there is literally nothing which I would care to offer to the readers of *Poetry*, and I cannot undertake to write anything for the purpose in time for your October number. I am very sorry indeed and should be glad if you would care [to] make known my expression of regret.

Yours very sincerely,
[T. S. Eliot]

TO *George Bell*

11 August 1932   Faber & Faber Ltd

Lambeth

My dear Lord Bishop,

Thank you for your letter of the 2nd, and for letting me see the charming poems.[3] Alas, the Ariel series has come to an end, or at least is postponed

---

1–Harriet Monroe (1860–1936), founder and co-editor of *Poetry: A Magazine of Verse* (Chicago). See Ann Massa, 'Harriet Monroe and T. S. Eliot: A curious and typical response', *Notes and Queries* 230 [32: 3], Sept. 1985, 380–2; *Dear Editor: A History of Poetry in Letters: The First Fifty Years, 1912–1962*, ed. and compiled by Joseph Parisi and Stephen Young (2002).

2–Monroe asked TSE on 1 Aug. to contribute a new poem to the Twentieth Birthday Number of *Poetry* (Oct. 1932).

3–Bell submitted four poems – including 'Troy' and 'Assisi' – in the hope they might make up a suitable volume for the 'Ariel' series.

indefinitely. The sales have shrunk considerably in the last few years, and what little demand there has been is for the earlier numbers of the series. Perhaps in more prosperous times we may be able to revive it. But it has also been a discouragement that the public for the Ariel poems seems to be wholly uninterested in any except the few stock poets whom they know already.

I cherish the hope of visiting you and Mrs Bell in Chichester next summer after my return.

I am, my Lord,
Yours very sincerely,
T. S. Eliot

TO *Terence Lawson*   CC

11 August 1932   [Faber & Faber Ltd]

My dear Mr Lawson,

I have read through your poems with some care and have scribbled a number of comments upon them.[1] Some of the comments may appear flippant in manner, but they are all meant very seriously. I think that if you work hard at self-criticism to make sure that you always know what you mean yourself, that you always know exactly what the words you use mean, and that the words mean what you want them to mean, you will be able to do a good deal better. I shall be glad to see more in nine months time.

Meanwhile I hope sincerely that you may find some more satisfactory occupation, but unless you are very sure of it I hope that for the present you will stick to Ford's.

Yours sincerely,
[T. S. Eliot]

1–Unable to afford to go to university, Terence Lawson had left his secondary school at sixteen and gone to work in the advertising department of the Ford Motor Co.; he wrote poetry and stories in his spare time. He wrote, 2 May 1932: 'I am now 18 and am still in the same place . . . I now spend some time of each day . . . preparing suggestions for business circulars. A poet composing business letters! The humour is becoming somewhat sinister . . . I am gradually drifting into the condition of contentment which seems to characterise the average "perfect clerk" . . . I am in the position of loathing myself utterly, and yet not being sufficiently strong to find the way out.' He accordingly petitioned TSE, 'Can you help me? Can you suggest a way out, a route of escape?'

TO *Cyril Strauss*

11 August 1932   [Faber & Faber Ltd]

Dear Mr Strauss,

I have read 'The Triumph of Job' and the miscellaneous poems with much interest but especially the first.[1] It is of course a very ambitious attempt, but I think to some extent you have succeeded at least in the management of the versification and the arrangement of the whole. The poem does of course reflect the Romantic Movement, chiefly Shelley and Byron more than Milton, although your versification is better when it is nearer to Milton than to the others. I think, however, that in a year or two's time you will regard this poem as an exercise which has been useful to you to make, but which you would not want to print. I shall be back in England next May and shall be delighted if you care to call on me at the end of term and show me what you have accomplished in the meantime.

Yours sincerely,
[T. S. Eliot]

TO *A. H. MacIntyre*

12 August 1932   [Faber & Faber Ltd]

Dear Mr MacIntyre,

Charlotte C. & Thomas S. Eliot
Trust. T-1388.

Thank you for your letter of August 2nd enclosing draft for regular quarterly remittance. I must point out, however, that heretofore these payments have by my instructions always been made direct to Lloyd's Bank, 45 New Oxford Street, London w.c.1., for my account, and it is a little disconcerting suddenly to have the remittance sent personally to

---

1 – Cyril Strauss (who was to be killed in action in 1944) had been introduced by Dr Reginald Miller, 110 Harley Street, London, on 24 July 1932: 'I have a young friend at New College, Oxford, who is taking his literary efforts extremely seriously & has begged me so hard to give him an introduction to you . . . He is a very clever boy of about 20, immensely solemn (Teutonic) & the son of a well-to-do banker. His father's name is Hermann Strauss, & the boy is Cyril & they live at 37 Grove End Road, N.W.8. I do not know what gifts he has, but I do know he is very anxious to submit a poem on the subject of Job & a few lyrics.' At some time he changed his name to Claude Vigée, and he made a French translation of *Four Quartets*. See too Claude Vigée, 'Les Artistes de la faim', *Comparative Literature* 9: 2 (Spring 1957), 97–117.

me, especially as I am leaving for Boston in a few weeks.[1] May I ask you to arrange that hereafter all payments to me shall be made direct to my Bankers, as I shall want these remittances for my expenses in London during the period when I am in Boston.

Yours very truly,
[T. S. Eliot]

TO *Conrad Aiken*[2]   CC

12 August 1932   [*The Criterion*]

Dear Conrad,

Thank you for your note.[3] I am sailing on September 17th from Southampton – the *Ausonia*, for Montreal – Tourist Third.[4] I should be delighted if you could secure a passage in the same class on the same boat.

Yours ever,
[Tom]

TO *Theodore Spencer*   Houghton

12 August 1932   Faber & Faber Ltd

My dear Spencer,

Thank you very much for your letter of July 29.[5] I am very much flattered by your writing an article about my poems, and I suppose that I ought to be even more flattered at being recognized finally by Ellery Sedgwick.[6] To have an article about myself published in *The Atlantic Monthly* strikes me as achieving complete respectability.

1–TSE was sent by A. H. MacIntyre, The Trust Officer, Old Colony Trust Company, Boston, on 2 Aug. 'a London draft for £63–17–6, the equivalent of $225, the amount of your regular quarterly remittance to which has been added the surplus income which has accumulated to date'.

2–Conrad Aiken (1889–1973), American poet and critic: see Biographical Register.

3–Aiken wrote on 11 Aug. to say that his proposed trip to the USA was 'still vaguish', but that he still hoped to go 'on a sort of financial raid' in Sept. 'When, and on what boat, do you sail? I might conceivably join you, at least to the extent of sailing in your steerage.'

4–The cheap tickets of 'Tourist Third' had been created in 1924 by the shipping companies of the North Atlantic Conference.

5–Spencer had sent his essay 'The Poetry of T. S. Eliot': Houghton MS Am 1691(23).

6–Ellery Sedgwick (1872–1960), American editor; editor of the *Atlantic Monthly* and President of the Atlantic Monthly Company, 1909–38; his wife was Mabel Cabot.

Seriously I have, I think, no criticism to make except one or two very small points which I have marked on the manuscript. I must admit that I am completely incompetent to criticize criticism of myself, but so far as I know you are right. There is another fragment of a poem about to appear in the *Hound & Horn* which I hope will interest you.

I had a formal invitation to Eliot House from Roger Merriman which I of course accepted. From everything I hear my suite of rooms there will be the last word in college luxury.[1] I expect to arrive on the 26th, and shall spend a night either with my sister or at a hotel. I trust that I shall find you in Cambridge when I arrive.

With many thanks,
Yours sincerely,
T. S. Eliot

TO *Michael Sayers*

TS Sean Sayers

12 August 1932   Faber & Faber Ltd

Dear Mr Sayers,

I am glad to hear from you again, and was very much interested both in your letter and in your piece of writing.[2] If it is not impertinent to say so I find them both very encouraging. Your letter is so interesting that it gives me the impression that it has been good for you to have something more comprehensive and objective to dislike than your previous immediate environment in Cricklewood. I have never visited Dublin though I have been on the point of doing so many times. But my impressions of Ireland

---

1 – The Eliot House suite allocated to TSE was on the third floor, facing the river.

2 – Sayers sent ('August 1932') a short story, and said he intended to send 'some pieces' of poetry 'very soon': 'I am still resident in Dublin, and I'm sick to the soul with it. With the bigotry, the slovenliness, the stunted growths, the mistrust, the hate. Above all the hate. Hate rules in Ireland. Children are reared in hate: another mouth to feed, another sin: the mother is blowsy, filthy; the father's a whiskeyed sot. Hate, hate, hate. Economic hate, social hate, religious hate, political hate. You are hated if you are educated; if you are young; if you are happy; or honest and truthtelling and enlightened. In a word because you are not stunted & superstitious, envious & ugly like themselves . . . Therefore, Mr Eliot, I believe & maintain that Irishmen don't want political honesty; they don't want clear political thoughts and clean political action. All they want is their strip of bunting & their faction-cry and their dreams of fairyland! But as for the society (the "ascendancy") into which I happen to have stumbled – why, it just clutches its shrinking acres of dirt and howls with the rest, – in a genteel accent of course. – Ireland is a burnt-out ashheap . . . But I sound hysterical . . .

'If I could find a job in London I'd run there as fast as the boat & train could take me. In London at least there is a sort of galvanic activity: "switch on the wireless; the electric lights!" Here there is nothing but dreams, dreams & hate & envy & madness.'

from a distance are very similar to those you have received through recent intimate acquaintance. That, however, is not necessarily a reason for your coming back to London as soon as you can. An environment against which you have such very healthy reactions may prove to have been extremely useful to you, and if you still have the opportunity of completing your course at Trinity, and taking a degree there, I don't believe that you will ever regret having stuck it out.

Your story seems to me a considerable improvement in dispassionate control of the material. Here and there are still some extravagances of the kind that I noticed from time to time in your book – e.g. 'All the birds carolled aubade' but these are only minor blemishes. The book you will remember I thought at its best where you were recording experienced facts, and at its worst where you were indulging in private verbal orgies such as might be induced by reading too much Walter Pater.

I look forward with much interest to the poems you promised to send. I am leaving England in the middle of September and shall not return until next May, but I shall be glad to hear from you if you care to write during my absence. My address in the interim will be Eliot House, Cambridge, Mass., U.S.A.

Yours sincerely,
T. S. Eliot

Postmark 16 August 1932[1]   London

How Delightful to Know Mr Hodgson!
  (Everyone Wants to Know *Him*).
With his Musical Sound
And his Baskerville Hound
    Who, moving Faster & Faster
    Will, just at a Word from his Master
Tear you Limb from Limb.
How DELIGHTFUL to know Mr Hodgson!
  (Everyone Wants to know *Him*).
Adored by all Waitresses
Upon his Palate (fine) he Presses
    The Juice of the Gooseberry Tart.
He has 99999999999999999999999 Canaries[2]
And around his Head the Finches & Fairies
    In jubilant Rapture Skim.
How Delightful to know Mr Hodgson!
  (Everyone Wants to Know *Him*).

1–According to Aurelia Hodgson, in a letter to EVE (19 Jan. 1965), these sets of verses 'were mailed to the ship when it was time to go back to Japan'. However, on 13 July 1981 she noted for EVE that the poems had actually been posted in separate envelopes to Sendai, Japan. Originals of both drawings in Beinecke: GEN MSS 245, Box 9, folder 167.
2–Aurelia Hodgson was to write from Sendai, Japan, to FVM and his wife, 11 July 1934: 'The canaries increase slowly – six for this year. But the total is now 23.'

How Unpleasant to Know Mr Eliot!
  With his Coat of Clerical Cut,
  And his Face so Grim
  And his Mouth so Prim
And his Conversation so Nicely
Restricted to What Precisely
  And If & Perhaps and But.
How Unpleasant to Know Mr Eliot!
  With a bobtailed Cur
  In a Coat of Fur
  And a Porpentine Cat
  And a Wopsical Hat.
How Unpleasant to know Mr Eliot!
  Whether his Mouth be Open or Shut.[1]

1 – See Robert H. Sykes, 'Eliot's "Lines to Ralph Hodgson Esqre"', *The Explicator* 9 (May 1972), no. 79.

TSE's fascination with Hodgson was reciprocated. Aurelia Bolliger took many notes from conversations with TSE in Jan.–July 1931 which were to be 'corrected' by Hodgson. Her observations, which she made available to EVE, include: 'I think there were eight children, six daughters, then a son, and eight years later the boy T. S. By that time some of the sisters were quite grown-up. "My parents were as indulgent as grand-parents are said to be".

'Meanwhile the "slum" (TSE's word) of the city was encroaching on the neighborhood where the Eliots had long been established. Just round the corner were the grandparents. The garden was big. So was the library. The neighborhood boys were a crude lot, and the little boy was afraid of them (Or: "They frightened me".) When he came home from school, he played about planting seeds or pulling them up; or reading. He had no playmates. At table he was quiet, listening: the older girls did most of the talking.

'"I don't believe my parents realized how poor the neighborhood had become. All their friends had moved away. We met at church. When I was about 10, there was the agony of dancing school, too. I had to go, but I was very shy. I used to wonder whether I could ever talk to a girl with the ease of the other boys" . . .

'He went off to prep school, but came back to spend the summers in the country . . . Birds had already nested and reared their young. It was a disappointment that he could never follow that development, but what there is to be seen in summer, he came to know very well.

'At the prep school, the rule was to take cold baths daily; actually the boys bathed one after another in the same tub of water. The last one could sleep longer and get the warmest

TO *Margaret Dawes Eliot*

17 August 1932   [Faber & Faber Ltd]

My dear Margaret,

This is merely a note to acknowledge your sweet letter of August 7th.[1] I am not yet sure what date I arrive, but I will send you a wire from Montreal. I shall be spending a night or two with Ada before going to Eliot House. Thank you very much for your birthday party invitation which I am very happy to accept. I have not mentioned your plans to anyone, and we will talk them over at leisure after I arrive.

I do not quite understand what your Mr Moriarty's intentions were, but you can let him know if you see him that Harcourt Brace & Co. are importing sheets of my poems, and will have the book on the market in September.

Looking forward keenly to seeing you,

I am, always,

Your affectionate Brother,

[Tom]

TO *T. O. Beachcroft*[2]

17 August 1932   [The Criterion]

My dear Beachcroft,

Your essay on Crashaw being in the patchwork state in which it is I think I ought to return it to you as quickly as possible. This or something like it would do excellently for a number of the *Criterion* some time next year if you are willing.

---

water. But TSE was the one who drew the water because "I was too fastidious to follow anyone."

'Ralph once mentioned how he's likely to relive repeatedly that moment of boyhood when he first discovered the curve of a girl's cheek. TSE could not agree: "It was too painful" . . .

'Ralph has the feeling that he carries his boyhood with him, and has carried it longer than most men. It explains the man. One is interested in it.'

1–Not found. TSE was due to arrive at Cambridge, Mass., in time for his forty-fourth birthday.

2–T. O. Beachcroft (1902–88), author and critic. A graduate of Balliol College, Oxford, he joined the BBC in 1924 but then worked for the Unilevers Advertising Service until 1941. He was Chief Overseas Publicity Officer, BBC, 1941–61; General Editor of the British Council series 'Writers and Their Work', 1949–54. His works include *A Young Man in a Hurry* (novel, 1934) and *Collected Stories* (1946).

I have allowed some days to elapse since I read it, and I daresay that I have now forgotten a few comments which occurred to me in reading. But it does seem to me first rate and extremely interesting. Furthermore this way of approaching the poetry of the period seems to me to have great possibilities. The only criticism that I can remember at the moment is that I think more highly of Ford's *Verses on the Nightingale* than you do. But in any case that does not affect your argument in the least. I do hope that you will not only put this essay into final shape but that you will persist in the project you have in mind.

I am, by the way, not in the least satisfied with my own note on Crashaw and am omitting it from my volume of *Selected Essays*.

Please let me have this back in its final form, unless you prefer to offer some other portion of the work in progress.[1]

Yours ever,

[T. S. Eliot]

TO *Ian L. Henderson*[2]   CC

17 August 1932   [*The Criterion*]

Dear Sir,

Our friend Mr Louis MacNeice has shown me your interesting essay on Macaulay. I have read it with much pleasure, but unfortunately Mr Bonamy Dobrée, one of our regular contributors, had already suggested to me some time ago that he should write an essay on Macaulay for the *Criterion*, and at the time I welcomed the suggestion. Since seeing yours I have naturally written to him to ask about his essay, and as I find that he is still interested and has actually done some work on the subject and expects to produce the essay in the spring I am regretfully unable to accept yours, as I should hardly be justified in using two such essays in the *Criterion*.

I should always be interested to see more of your work.

With many regrets,

Yours very truly,

[T. S. Eliot]

---

1 – 'Crashaw – and the Baroque Style', C. 13 (Apr. 1934), 407–25.
2 – British Consulate General, Antwerp.

TO *Ida Binder*

17 August 1932   [*The Criterion*]

Dear Madam,

I am obliged to you for your letter of August 16th.[1] I am afraid that our quarterly article on art is always done by our regular art critic, and there is not therefore space for any further contributions on that subject. Also, it is not our practice to commission articles; but if your husband should ever care to submit any of his work *in English* you may be sure that it will receive careful attention.

Yours faithfully,
[T. S. Eliot]
For *The Criterion*

TO *Geoffrey Biddulph*

17 August 1932   [*The Criterion*]

Dear Mr Biddulph,

Thank you for letting me have the revised version of your comments on Penty.[2] As I said I am not sure whether there will be any space left in the December number to make inclusion possible, but if I may be allowed to keep it I shall be very glad to publish it then if I can.

I am a little confused about your wishes for books to review. When I saw you, you mentioned Professor Cassell's forthcoming book and Gregory's *Mystery of the Trade Balances*, but in your last letter you mention neither of these nor a third book which you had in mind, but two other books published or to be published by Harper's.[3] What book or books do you really want most?

Yours sincerely,
[T. S. Eliot]

1 – 'My husband, Dr Bruno Binder, is a writer of distinction and a regular contributor to the principal German and Austrian periodicals . . . and is desirous of extending his English connection. Will you kindly say if you would be prepared to consider articles on any of the following subjects:- art, architecture, sculpture, etching, art history, the work of individual artists, Austrian towns, provinces, scenery and history.'

2 – Biddulph wrote on 18 July: 'Keynes, to whom I sent my reply to Penty, has written suggesting one important alteration, & saying he doesn't think Dec. would be too late for it to appear, so if you should care to reconsider your verdict on seeing the revised version I'll send it along.'

3 – Biddulph mentioned (18 July) *Is Capitalism Doomed?* by L. Dennis, and *Roads to Recovery* by Cyril James (both published by Harpers).

TO *Ada Sheffield*

17 August 1932   [Faber & Faber Ltd]

Dear Ada,

Very many thanks for your letter of August 5th. I should be very happy and grateful to be allowed to come direct to you for a night or two. I am not quite sure whether I arrive the 26th or 27th but will send you a wire from Montreal. Thank you for your directions which ought to enable me with the map to find your house. But I think perhaps I will take a taxi although I understand they are very expensive.

By all means make any arrangements for my meeting the English department that suit you. I will leave that entirely to you and no doubt shall have to consult you constantly about what social invitations to accept and which not.

I have had two long confidential letters from Margaret about her future plans, and shall want to discuss these with you when I see you.

                                 Your affectionate Brother,
                                 [Tom]

TO *H. L. R. Edwards*[1]

17 August 1932   [Faber & Faber Ltd]

Dear Mr Edwards,

I have your letter of the 12th August.[2] I should of course be glad to see you here if you are convinced that I could help you. But candidly I do not see how I could be of the slightest use to you as I know no more about the Latin Writings of the Tudor Period than anyone else does, and even if I have as you say perspective, that does not seem to me very useful when it comes to a subject of which I am ignorant. I suggest first as you are in London that you should write to Professor A. W. Reed of King's College, London University, who is extremely erudite, especially in the

---

1–Harold Llewelyn Ravenscroft Edwards was to be author of *Skelton: The Life and Times of an Early Tudor Poet* (1949), and co-editor of Skelton's *The Bibliotheca Historica of Diodorus Siculus* (1956), and he translated works by Stendhal and other writers.

2–A graduate of the University of Wales, Edwards was about to pursue research on the topic of 'Latin Writings of the Tudor Period in England'. His Professor, he claimed, knew 'nothing' of the subject, and the college library had no books; and indeed, he went on, his college (Cardiff) was 'an intellectual blank'. He earnestly desired TSE to help him compile a bibliography; and above all, he said, it was 'perspective (the most marked of your critical virtues) that I require'.

literature of the early Tudor period, and secondly you might get some valuable suggestions from the Revd. Charles Smyth of C[orpus] C[hristi] C[ollege], Cambridge, who has specialized in the historical literature of that time. As we are in the month of August I am not sure whether either of these gentlemen will be away, but I think it would be worth your while to approach them. If you can suggest any way in which you still think I might be useful to you I should be glad to hear from you.

Yours sincerely,
[T. S. Eliot]

TO *George Bell*

Lambeth Palace Library

17 August 1932

Faber & Faber Ltd

My dear Lord Bishop,

Very many thanks for having had sent to me your delightful broadsheet. Unless the public which it reaches is wholly insensible to all of the three arts I shall hope that it will do much toward forwarding your cause. Incidentally I should like to know more about the project for church building in Sussex.[1]

I am taking the liberty of asking you whether you would be willing to look, or at any rate to ask Martin Browne to look, at a Christmas Morality play *The Gate of Heaven* which has been submitted to me. I know very little about the lady who wrote it,[2] to whom I was introduced purely with a view to forwarding her designs. She is a cousin of a very lovely R.C. whom I know whose husband is the greatest authority on Railway Law, and she lives in Hampstead Garden Suburb. What she seemed to want was to get the play published, but I told her frankly that there was no chance and indeed no point in publication unless she could first get the play successfully produced. It does not seem to me the sort of manuscript on which my opinion is of much value. It ought to be judged by someone who is familiar with the actual production of Morality Plays, and judged from the point of view of produceability.

---

1 – Bell sent on 20 Aug. 'a copy of my Sussex Church Builders programme'.
2 – Mrs Tustain.

May I please submit it either to you or to Browne? If it has any merit*
I want to do anything for it that I can.[1]

> I am, my Lord,
> Yours sincerely,
> T. S. Eliot

* as it seems to me to have

TO *Leonard Woolf*   CC

17 August 1932   [Faber & Faber Ltd]

Dear Leonard,

I should be very grateful if you could find the time and would care to review Lowes Dickinson's lecture *The Contribution of Ancient Greece to Modern Life* for the December *Criterion*. In the circumstances I should have liked to have a review of it for the forthcoming number, but unfortunately there was neither space nor time. I am anxious to have a sizeable review – that is to say, to use the lecture as a pretext for a general appreciation of Dickinson and his work, and I cannot think of anyone whom I should like better to do this than yourself. Can you possibly manage it?[2]

> Yours ever,
> [T. S. E.]

TO *John Hayward*   TS King's

18 August 1932   Faber & Faber Ltd

THE CRITERION

Dear John,[3]

During my absence from England, from September 17th until some date in next May, I shall edit the numbers of the *Criterion* as far as is possible from abroad. The chief difficulty in editing from a distance is the department of reviews. The reviews for the *April* and *July* numbers must be arranged here.

---

1 – Bell (29 Aug.): 'With regard to the Christmas Morality Play, yes please do send it to Martin Browne . . . and tell him that I hope he will look at it and advise. It sounds attractive.'
2 – Goldsworthy Lowes Dickinson (1862–1932) had died just before his seventieth birthday on 3. Aug. His book was not reviewed in C.
3 – This same letter was sent to SS on 23 Aug.; and to other regular contributors.

I am therefore writing to you, as a regular contributor to the *Criterion*, to ask you to help by volunteering a review for either the April or the July number or both. I hope that you will kindly try to find some book or books, among the autumn and spring publications, which would interest you, and that you will send a postcard to Miss Wilberforce, the Secretary, asking that they be procured for you.

As I can see no other way in which the important review section of the *Criterion* can be carried on during this period, I depend upon our regular contributors to give their support in this way.

Yours sincerely,
T. S. Eliot

TO *J. R. Culpin*   TS Rexi Culpin/CC

19 August 1932   Faber & Faber Ltd

My dear Jack,

I am writing to you because I hear from Vivienne that Rexi is ill and about to have an operation. I hope that it will not be serious or expensive, and that her convalescence will soon be over. Anyway I shall try to ring you up tomorrow and learn your news.

Otherwise I should have written to Rexi herself about her manuscript.[1] But I should be glad if you would communicate the contents of this letter to her as soon as she is able to discuss such matters. I and another director have read the story and were both very much impressed by it. It is extraordinarily objective and controlled. She has written it at the right length for her purpose and has confined herself to the essentials of the matter where most writers would have spun it out to a futile length. It is, however, just the length which makes it awkward from the publisher's point of view. It is much too long for a periodical and much too short for an ordinary book. The only way in which it could be published is, I fear, some rather cheap series of short books. I thought first of Benn's

1–Rexi Culpin (née Regina Temunovich) submitted a story called *The Dead Image*. Years later, when she resubmitted the MS, TSE told her, 3 June 1959: 'I think that this version is a vast improvement over the one you showed me some years ago. You have become quite at home with the English language, and the advantage over a translation by another hand from the German is immense. The story has certainly a terrifying verisimilitude and it seems to me that if you can deal so well with the state of mind of a young man like your protagonist you ought to be able to cope in fiction with a considerable diversity of plots and creatures. But we do not feel that it is our book, and the short novel or extended short story, as this might be called, is not in our province.'

Ninepenny Library, but Rexi's story is, I think, very much above the level of the audience at which that library is aimed. We therefore want now to show it to Howard, one of the directors of Jonathan Cape Ltd in the hope that they might include it in their Florin Library. If this fails we must go farther afield. I have also thought of Desmond Harmsworth, but I know very little about the composition of his firm or its ability to market books, and I think it is worthwhile trying better known publishers first.

We are probably going away for a few days either next week or the following. When this is settled I want to fix a day with you for lunch. I suppose that it will suit you better if I call for you in the City.

Yours ever,
T. S. E.

TO *J. H. Oldham* CC

19 August 1932   [Faber & Faber Ltd]

My dear Oldham,

Thank you for your note of the 16th.[1] I should very much like to have another talk with you before I leave. It is probable that I shall be going away for three or four days, and I am not sure whether it will be this week or the week of the 29th, but I think I am pretty certain to be in London on Monday 29th, and shall be glad to lunch with you then at the Athenaeum. If anything makes it impossible I shall be able to let you know several days in advance.

With many thanks,
Yours sincerely,
[T. S. Eliot]

TO *Managing Director, Clarence Gate Mansions Co.* CC

22 August 1932   [Faber & Faber Ltd]

Dear Sir,

I shall be absent in America on business from the middle of September until next May. I have accordingly instructed my Bankers, Lloyds Bank Limited of 45, New Oxford Street W.C.1. to pay my rent to you direct.

1–Oldham hoped to be able to talk with TSE again before his departure for the USA, and suggested lunch at the Athenaeum on Mon. 29 Aug.

Mrs Eliot expects to be in residence in my flat No. 68 Clarence Gate Gardens.

For any other business matters, I will inform you that my Attorneys during my absence are Mr A. E. James and/or Mr T. Leigh-Hunt of the firm James & James, 23 Ely Place, Holborn Circus, E.C.I., who are also my solicitors.

Yours faithfully,
[T. S. Eliot]

TO *The Manager, Lloyds Bank* CC

22 August 1932   [Faber & Faber Ltd]

Dear Sir,

I have signed a power of procuration to my attorneys, Mr Alfred E. James and Mr Trevor Leigh-Hunt, which will entitle them to control my banking account from September 17th, when I leave for America, until my return at some time during May 1933.

Messrs. Faber & Faber Ltd will pay in to you £125 on September 29th, but no salary and fees thereafter until September 1933. They will be paying in to you for my account various sums on account of royalties. The Old Colony Trust Co. will continue to pay my American interest in to you.

Will you kindly take note that the quarterly payments of £37:10: – which you have been making for me to Mrs Haidee Powys Wilson are to cease *after* the September quarter, as my lease of the house in question lapses then. But will you please hereafter pay my quarterly rent of £55 (fifty-five pounds) to the Clarence Gate Mansions Co. Ltd of 190, Clarence Gate Gardens, beginning at the end of the September quarter.

You already are paying my dues to the Oxford & Cambridge Club, and I ask you to pay also the following in January and annually till further notice: £2:2 (two guineas) to the English Church Union, 24 Russell Square; £1:1 (one guinea) to the Catholic Literature Association. Also in December one guinea (£1:1) to the Warden of Liddon House, 24 South Audley Street, for the Christmas collection.

Yours faithfully,
[T. S. Eliot]

TO *Terence A. Holliday*   CC

23 August 1932   [Faber & Faber Ltd]

My dear Mr Holliday,

Thank you for your two letters of the 10th instant.[1] I assure you that I
have every confidence in your book production, and will leave the matter
entirely in your hands.

As for the matter of English orders for the book I hope that you understand that I merely did not want the book offered to English booksellers
or pushed in any way, but of course you may fill, and indeed could hardly
avoid filling orders from English booksellers for bona fide customers.

I am not unfortunately coming by way of New York, but I hope that
I may be there from time to time and can have the pleasure of accepting
your kind invitation.

Yours sincerely,
[T. S. Eliot]

TO *Stephen Spender*   TS Northwestern

23 August 1932   Faber & Faber Ltd

My dear Spender,

It is very good news to hear that you are back in London. I am afraid
that Thursday evening is impossible for me and my last weeks in England
are very crowded ones. But if possible I should like to get you to dine
with us one night before I go. Meanwhile I want to talk about the poems
and *The Temple*. Would it be possible for you to lunch at the United
Universities Club on Friday at a quarter to one?

Yours ever,
T. S. Eliot

1–Holliday (Holliday Bookshop) asked TSE to approve the typography and format of *John
Dryden*: 'We are most anxious that no pains be spared to make the book as exact and
attractive as possible.' In his second letter he invited TSE to dine with him and his wife if he
was travelling via New York.

to *T. O. Beachcroft*

CC

23 August 1932   [*The Criterion*]

My dear Beachcroft,

Some time ago I saw in the *Adelphi* a short story of yours which I liked, and I have heard word that there are others. I have been meaning on several occasions to speak to you about this. I am needing a story for next spring or summer and I should be very grateful if you have anything on hand which you would care to let me see.

Yours ever,
[T. S. Eliot]

to *Norreys Jephson O'Conor*

CC

23 August 1932   [Faber & Faber Ltd]

Dear O'Conor,

Thank you for your letter of August 21.[1] I had feared that you were out of England, and that I might have missed any opportunity of seeing you. Although I should like to see you before you go there is no occasion for your hurrying home. I am sailing on the 17th, and I fear that my last weeks will be pretty well filled up. If you are back and we could meet for a moment I should be very glad. Please let me know as soon as you return.

The other director whom I wanted you to meet is Frank Morley. He is to be away during that part of September, but will be back on the 26th. I have told him as much as I remember about your book, and he is very much interested, so that in any case I shall ask you to get in touch with him as soon as he returns. Hoping to see you, and trusting that your parents have benefited by their stay in France.

I am,
Yours sincerely,
[T. S. Eliot]

1–O'Conor wrote from France, where his parents were taking 'the cure', that he would be returning to London in Sept. He had been working on 'the Weston book', which he expected to run to about 30,000 words in length: 'I have completed the part about the attack on the house, i.e. the law suits I discovered, and have only to finish the book . . . [T]he end is clearly in sight.'

A sketch of TSE by Theresa Garrett Eliot, made from a snapshot, 1933.

Ralph Hodgson with Pickwick, his
bull terrier, and Eliot in London,
probably May 1932.

T. S. Eliot's passport photograph,
taken 2 September 1932.

Aurelia Bolliger with Pickwick,
Vivien with Polly, the Eliots'
terrier, and TSE.

Theresa Garrett Eliot and Henry
Ware Eliot, Jr., in 1930.

Eliot with Virginia Woolf and Vivien, 2 September 1932.
It is the last known photograph of him with his wife,
before their separation.

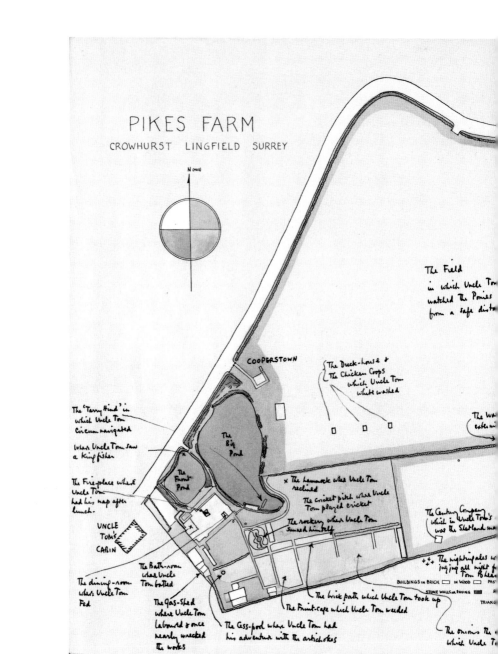

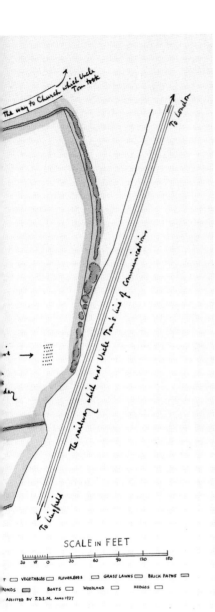

The way to Church which Uncle Tom took

To London

The railway which was Uncle Tom's line of Communications

To Lingfield

SCALE IN FEET

30   15   0   30   60   90   120   150

VEGETABLES   FLOWER BEDS   GRASS LAWNS   BRICK PATHS

PONDS   BOATS   WOODLAND   HEDGES

ASSISTED BY T.D.I.M. ANNO 1937

Eliot at Pike's Farm, holding a loaf of bread he baked himself, photographed by Frank Morley.

'Frank Morley's map of his ancestral county seat of Pike's Farm, Crowhurst, Lingfield, Surrey, whereon befell, in the Summer of 1933, sundry diverting, instructive, and comickall adventures and excursions of Thomas Stearns Eliot', drawn by Morley in the summer of 1933, when Eliot was staying in 'Uncle Tom's Cabin'.

Eliot in New York *c*. 1932–3.

Eliot in Baltimore, Maryland, 1933. Studio portrait by the society photographer Bachrach.

L to R, Laurette and Eleanor Murdock (wife of Professor Kenneth Murdock), Russell Cheney and F. O. Matthiessen, New Hampshire, early 1930s.

Emily Hale, visiting relatives in England, 1933–4.

Eliot with Professor Theodore Spencer on the Massachusetts shore,
1932–33.

'Comfortable in their rockers' on the porch of Mountain View House,
Randolph, New Hampshire; Eliot (third from left) with Professor Alfred
Dwight Sheffield, Ada Eliot Sheffield, Marian Cushing Eliot and Theresa
Garrett Eliot, photographed by Henry Ware Eliot, June 1933.

Eliot in white tie at the lecture given at the New School for Social
Research, New York, 20 April 1933. The photograph, by Acme News,
was reproduced in the *Herald Tribune*.

TO *Ronald Bottrall*   TS Texas

23 August 1932   *The Criterion*

Dear Bottrall,

I have your letter of the 6th from Los Angeles.[1] I am sorry that I have
been so long over 'Festivals of Fire'. My last few months in England
have been very busy ones. I had hoped to publish a section of the poem
in the *Criterion*, but had been unable to foresee any space for it until
some time in the spring. I should advise you therefore to allow *Scrutiny*
to publish Section 1, and if the whole poem could be published soon
after that, I think, would be the best course for you to pursue. The entire
poem I am sorry to say is much too long for the *Criterion*. As for Faber
& Faber we are publishing one book of poems in the spring and at the
moment simply dare not contemplate another until some time in the
autumn. All that I can say, therefore, is that if the Minority Press project
falls through, I should be very glad to raise the matter with my directors
next summer.

My address after the middle of September will be Eliot House,
Cambridge, Mass. and I should be very glad to hear from you there. Will
you be in Princeton again this winter?

Yours sincerely,

T. S. Eliot

TO *Algar Thorold*   CC

23 August 1932   [*The Criterion*]

My dear Thorold,

Thank you for your letter of August 20th. Meanwhile I have read your
review of Bergson with much interest. I don't know when I shall have space
for anything longer about his book, but I think that would do next year in
the form of an appraisal by someone of the whole Bergsonian philosophy
in the light of this latest book.[2] As for your projected essay, I should of

---

1 – 'I have been hoping to hear further from you regarding my revisions of *Festivals of Fire*
. . . The editors of *Scrutiny* are anxious to publish Section I of the poem.'
2 – Review of Henri Bergson's *Les Deux Sources de la Morale et de la Religion*: *C.* 12
(Oct. 1932), 124–31. 'In reading my proofs, I am painfully aware of the inadequacy of my
Bergson review. Of course the book needs a full-dress article & I hope you will have one
sometime – though not by Belgion! Couldn't you get one by Lévy-Bruhl – that would be
very interesting.'

course be delighted to have it, as I am using your Maine de Biran in the spring I could hardly use the other article for another six months. If you have not meanwhile published it elsewhere do let me have it.[1]

I find my last three weeks in England very crowded, and do not hope to see you again till next summer. My address will be Eliot House, Cambridge, Mass. and I should be delighted to hear from you there.

Yours ever,
[T. S. Eliot]

TO *E. Martin Browne*[2]

23 August 1932   [Faber & Faber Ltd]

Dear Mr Browne,

I hope that you will remember having met me at a very pleasant weekend at Chichester which is now nearly two years ago. I am writing at the suggestion of the Bishop to ask if you would be willing to look at a Christmas Morality Play which seems to me to have some merit. The author of the play is unknown to me, but was introduced to me in the hope that I might advise and assist her toward publication. My advice was that there was no point in or possibility of publishing such a play until it had been produced with some success, and after all a play is meant to be played, and not merely to be read. Would you look at it and let me know

1 – 'I have a notion of an article, really on Thomism, but to be called "Panegyric (or perhaps Portrait <Portrait is better>) of a Master". S. Thomas' name would not be mentioned, the idea being that he completely lost what moderns think is the soul & found it in the objective creation of his mind. It wd consist merely of the fundamental theses expressed as simply and limpidly as possible, with only absolutely necessary commentary and transitions . . . I need not say that there wd be no modern ecclesiastical controversy in it!'

2 – E. (Elliott) Martin Browne (1900–80), theatre director, read history and theology at Christ Church, Oxford, before working for the British Drama League and the Adult Education Movement; he then went to the USA as Assistant Professor of Speech and Drama at the Carnegie Institute of Technology, Pittsburgh, 1927–30, before being appointed in 1930, by Bishop George Bell, Director of Religious Drama for his diocese. He collaborated with TSE on *The Rock* (to raise funds for City of London churches), which was produced at Sadler's Wells Theatre, 28 May–9 June 1934; and thereafter he was to direct all of TSE's plays: see his *The Making of T. S. Eliot's Plays* (1969). He was director of a touring company called the Pilgrim Players, 1939–49; Director of the British Drama League (affording help to amateur productions), 1948–57; and in 1951 he directed the first revival since 1572 of the medieval cycle of York Mystery Plays. He was Visiting Professor of Religious Drama at Union Theological College, New York, 1956–62; Drama Advisor to Coventry Cathedral, 1962–5; and in 1967–8 he directed plays at the Yvonne Arnaud Theatre, Guildford. He was appointed CBE in 1952.

whether you think it has the necessary qualities for performance, and if so what could be done about it? I should be very grateful to you.

With best wishes to yourself and Mrs Browne.

Yours sincerely,
[T. S. Eliot]

TO *Ford Madox Ford*   Cornell/cc

23 August 1932   [Faber & Faber Ltd]

Dear Ford,

I have your letter of the 13th August. I did not know that Ezra's Cantos were to be published by Farrar and Rinehart, but I am extremely glad to do anything in my power to help.[1] Will you let me know more clearly what sort of thing you want, and especially by what time you want it. I am leaving for America in three weeks, and have hardly a moment to spare, so that if there were time for me to write my commendation on the voyage it would be much more possible.

Yours ever,
[T. S. Eliot]

TO *Leonard Woolf*   cc

23 August 1932   [Faber & Faber Ltd]

Dear Leonard,

Thanks for your note of the 18th.[2] I have taken your hint, and written to Forster who I believe knew Dickinson particularly well. But sometimes

---

1 – 'For me – as no doubt it is for you – this seems to be an event of primary importance in the tottering world. I am trying to organize in the United States – not in England from which Heaven defend me and where Orage says he's already active – a sort of campaign of log-rolling . . . What I want to do is to get together a number of tributes to Ezra in person and if possible to the CANTOS themselves. These I propose to print in a small pamphlet and to let Farrar and Rinehart send this out with review copies. If you would write a little – or indeed a lot – for this it would be of immense importance and use. I am thinking of brow-beating the American Reviewer into taking Ezra with the seriousness that ought to be accorded to him. I don't know what may be your opinion of the morality of this procedure but they do it for people like Conrad and Proust when they die and I don't see why poor Ezra should not get the benefit of this.'

2 – LW replied on 18 Aug.: 'I will do the review if you cant get any one better. The difficulty is that I do not know many of Lowes Dickinson's books. I should have thought Morgan Forster would have been better.' In the event, LW did not write on Lowes Dickinson for *C*.

it is more difficult for a close friend to write an obituary and if he declines I shall approach you again.

Yours ever,
[Tom]

TO *E. M. Forster*   CC

23 August 1932   [*The Criterion*]

My dear Forster,

I should be very grateful if you would be willing to write something for the December *Criterion* about Lowes Dickinson under the guise of a review of his recent lecture. I believe that you knew him perhaps better than any other man of our generation knew him, and it would be a great satisfaction to have something from you in his honour.[1]

Yours ever,
[T. S. Eliot]

TO *John Maynard Keynes*   TS Marshall

23 August 1932   *The Criterion*

My dear Keynes,

Thank you for your letter of the 20th.[2] I sympathize with your difficulties and indeed hardly expected that you would have the time to write anything specially. I merely wrote on the chance that you might at some time have written, or might at some time want to write, something in a leisure moment which might be more suitable in the *Criterion* than elsewhere.

I am leaving in three weeks time, and shall not be back until next May, but I should like very much to see more of you again when I get back.

Yours sincerely,
T. S. Eliot

1–Forster replied on 26 Aug. that he had already written on 'Goldie' for *The Spectator*. He recommended Roger Fry: failing him, J. T. Sheppard or Joe Ackerley. He added, 'If you can't arrange with any of them and don't think of anyone else, let me know, and I'll do the review.'
2–'I am sorry to be so disobliging about contributing to *The Criterion*. But I am always in a great perplexity about dividing my time between writing books and writing articles. It is fearfully easy to be lured by the latter into making the former impossible; and in so far as I can find time for articles, my energy is mainly taken up by contributions on what might be termed "urgent public affairs".'

TO *Marianne Moore*[1]   TS Rosenbach

23 August 1932   *The Criterion*

Dear Miss Moore,

During my absence from England, from September 17th until some date in next May, I shall edit the numbers of the *Criterion* as far as is possible from abroad. The chief difficulty in editing from a distance is the department of reviews. The reviews for the *April* and *July* numbers must be arranged here.

I am therefore writing to you, as a regular contributor to the *Criterion*, to ask you to help by volunteering a review for either the April or the July number or both. I hope that you will kindly try to find some book or books, among the autumn and spring publications, which would interest you, and that you will send a postcard to Miss Wilberforce, the Secretary, asking that they be procured for you.

As I can see no other way in which the important review section of *The Criterion* can be carried on during this period, I depend upon our regular contributors to give their support in this way.

                              Yours sincerely,
                              T. S. Eliot

1–Marianne Moore (1887–1972), American poet and critic: see Biographical Register. See too Moore, 'A Virtuoso of Make-Believe', in *T. S. Eliot: A Symposium*, compiled by Richard March and Tambimuttu (1948), 179–80.

TO *Cecil Day-Lewis*[1]

23 August 1932   [Faber & Faber Ltd]

Dear Mr Day-Lewis,

Thank you for your letter of August 17th.[2] I have not heard a word from Auden or anybody else about Warner's book, but should very much like to see it.[3] I am leaving England on the 17th September, and shall be

---

1 – Cecil Day-Lewis (1904–72), Anglo-Irish poet and novelist (author of an admired series of mystery novels under the pseudonym Nicholas Blake); Oxford Professor of Poetry, 1951–6; Norton Professor at Harvard, 1962–3; Poet Laureate, 1968–72. Educated at Sherborne School and Wadham College, Oxford, he edited with his friend and contemporary WHA the anthology *Oxford Poetry 1927*; and for a period in the mid-1930s he was a member of the Communist Party. After WW2 he worked as a director and senior editor of the publishers Chatto & Windus. His publications include *Beechen Vigil* (1925), *Transitional Poem* (1929), *From Feathers to Iron* (1932), *Word Over All* (1943) and *The Complete Poems of C. Day-Lewis* (1992); critical works including *A Hope for Poetry* (1934) and *The Poetic Image* (1947); *The Buried Day* (autobiography, 1960); and translations from Virgil. See further Sean Day-Lewis, *C. Day-Lewis: An English Literary Life* (1980); Peter Stanford, *C. Day-Lewis: A Life* (1998).

On 2 May 1933, GCF wrote to Day-Lewis: 'By the way, if you are not permanently associated with a particular publisher, I hope you will remember that we cast covetous glances in your direction. You and Auden ought surely to have the same imprint?'

2 – 'I don't know whether Auden has written to you about a prose allegory, "The Wild Goose Chase" by R. E. Warner, a friend of ours at present in Egypt: we both feel that it is a first rate piece of work & that you would be interested to read it . . . It is at present in the hands of a typist & being rather long will not be finished for a week or so. Would you be good enough to let me know whether you would care to read it; and if so, what is the latest date on which you could conveniently receive it. If it was not finished by then, I could have a part of it sent you.'

3 – WHA presently wrote to TSE, 31 Aug. 1932: 'I believe a ms of an allegory [*The Wild Goose Chase*] by a friend of mine Rex Warner has been sent to Faber's. I only saw half of it which I thought pretty good. I hope they will be able to take it as he is very hard up.'

Rex Warner (1905–86), novelist, classicist, translator, was educated in classics and English at Wadham College, Oxford – where his friends included WHA, SS and Day-Lewis – and taught for two years thereafter (1932–4) in Greece. In later years he was Director of the British Institute in Athens, 1945–7, and he also taught for some years in the USA (Bowdoin College, 1962–3; University of Connecticut, 1964–74). His publications included *The Wild Goose Chase* and *Poems* (both 1937), *The Professor* (1938), *The Aerodrome* (1941), and translations from the classics including Aeschylus, Euripides, Thucydides and Plutarch.

FVM told Day-Lewis, 4 Oct. 1932: 'I know that [TSE] was able to read only a little of the MS. and he left it with me as deputy . . . I have now read the typescript myself with steadily increasing interest, but publishing with us is a parliamentary affair, and I am afraid I shall have to ask a little more of your patience.'

GCF was to write to Warner on 27 July 1933, having sounded TSE's opinion of *Wild Goose Chase*: '[Eliot] was also adverse. He thought the end showed a considerable falling off. (Opinions differ there: I also much preferred the first to the second half, while Morley preferred the second to the first.) He also thought it wouldn't sell.' And on 22 Sept. 1933, GCF advised Warner of the final 'reluctant decision', taken with 'real regret', to reject his book.

very busy indeed up to that date, but if you can get the book to me as early as possible before then I will certainly have a look at it and will recommend it to my fellow directors for more careful consideration. If that is impossible I should be glad to see a portion of the book in advance.

Yours sincerely,
[T. S. Eliot]

FROM *Vivien Eliot* TO *Mary Hutchinson* MS Texas

23 August 1932   68 Clarence Gate Gardens

My dear Mary

I have just received your nice letter, & hasten to reply. I have been in fact wondering why you never wrote to us.

Thank you for asking us down for Friday or Saturday night. I should *love* it. But it is this way. Tom is now very tired by the long hot summer. He is also working very hard indeed at his Lectures & all the arrangements he must make. Perhaps you do not realise that there are only *3 weeks left before he goes.*

He is going to take me away, next week, because I am so run down myself. So that gives him even less time. He is really very worried, & so are we both.

How lovely for you all to be going off to Holland. You have so many chances! But then you deserve them for you never loose [*sic*] courage.

After September 4th, when you return from Holland – Tom will be really too rushed to go away any more. It is a pity. Yes, I *did* enjoy & *love* 'our heat'. The huge moons & the boiling days & the groaning & the shrieking. I only felt frightfully ill when the weather changed yesterday, & got chilly & changeable & in fact its old self again. Do send me a *post card* from *Holland*, & write to me again directly you return so that if there is *still a chance, we may take it.*

With my love,
Yours affectionate friend,
Vivienne

TO *Messrs James & James*   cc

24 August 1932   [Faber & Faber Ltd]

Dear Sirs,

I thank you for your letter of the 23rd instant and am returning herewith the draft with only a few corrections; one or two of these, however, are rather important.[1]

I shall be writing separately about the second paragraph of your letter.

Yours faithfully,
[T. S. Eliot]

TO *E. M. Harris*   cc

26 August 1932   [Faber & Faber Ltd]

Dear Mrs Harris,

I was very disappointed not to see Dr Harris the other day, and distressed to learn the reason.[2] I trust that his illness, which I suppose was brought about by overwork during the hot weather, will be of a very light duration. I agree that it will probably be impossible for us to meet again before I leave, but I shall be glad if you will tell him that I shall be out of town for the rest of next week, and after that shall be here until 17th September. Also that my address after that will be Eliot House, Cambridge, Mass. U.S.A.

I will let you have our report on the MS. in a few days time. I have had to send it for consideration to the Chairman who is, at present, in Wales.

With cordial sympathy,
Yours very truly,
[T. S. Eliot]

1–TSE had made a new Will with James & James. Alfred E. James wrote to him on 7 Sept. enclosing the draft of a Codicil 'regarding the trust fund which belongs to you absolutely . . . A clause embodying the Codicil could, of course, be included in your Will but if you get the terms of the trust altered or extended in the way you propose while you are in America the Codicil will not be wanted and you can then destroy it without affecting the Will.'
2–Mrs Harris said (23 Aug.) that the doctor had ordered her husband to take complete rest for a few days. TSE was to have had lunch with Harris at the Oxford & Cambridge Club.

TO *J. S. Barnes*   TS Buona Barnes

26 August 1932   Faber & Faber Ltd

Dear Jim,

I am glad to hear from you at last although you find me at an extremely busy moment.[1] I shall have to be out of town for the most of next week, and after that have only a fortnight before I sail for America and shall have a great deal to do in the time. If you could send me the essay this week I should be able to take it away with me to read. Otherwise there is no point in my having it at all the week after next. Will you suggest a meeting for that week?

Yours ever,
T. S. E.

My secretary has been ill & so this was not typed for two days. I leave on Tuesday & return on Saturday.[2]

TO *G. Wilson Knight*   TS Texas

26 August 1932   Faber & Faber Ltd

My dear Knight,

I have expedited the examination of your book on *The Christian Renaissance* as much as possible knowing your anxiety for making some arrangement about it before you leave England. You will admit, of course, that it is not a book to be read in a hurry and I fear that neither I nor the reader (who, by the way, has pencilled a few notes on the typescript) have had the time to do it merely justice. Had I the time and leisure I should have liked to comment in considerable detail.

We both feel that it is not only an interesting book, but a book of considerable importance. I cannot help saying that throughout you seem to me always to speak with very much more authority, as, evidently from a much more intimate knowledge, when you base your argument upon Shakespeare than elsewhere. I have a very definite impression that the book might be very much improved and made less laborious for the reader who approaches it without prejudice in its favour, if it were considerably

---

1 – Barnes wrote on 22 Aug. to say he had finished his essay and was having it typed. 'I have found it difficult to write & the result is rather long (about 18,000 words), & I doubt it will be congenial to a heretic like Harold Nicolson. But I shall be disappointed if *you* don't like it.'

2 – Postscript by hand.

reduced and concentrated. Here, of course, I ought to be able to give instances, but I am afraid that would require very much more time and two or three readings. Possibly one or two of the comments from the other reader may be illuminating, but I dare say you will disagree with me flatly on this point.

The immediate practical question however, is who is to publish such a book, and how are people to be induced to read it? Academic philosophy has always a certain limited sale in academic circles, but academic philosophy, especially when so original as yours, has a very hard time in making its way. Furthermore, it has not the claim upon a particular class of reader that, for instance, your Shakespeare books have. Every serious student of Shakespeare is obliged, or will be obliged in time, to acquaint himself with any Shakespeare criticism so original and important as yours, but there is no such class of students of philosophy or of literary criticism which will be obliged to read this book whether it wants to or not. I am, therefore, rather at a loss to suggest a publisher for it, and as no one firm comes very prominently in my mind I really think that the best you can do is to leave it in the hands of one of the better agents. You are quite at liberty, of course, to use my name in recommendation of it so far as that may be desirable from your own point of view. Among publishers I had thought both of Chatto & Windus and Allen & Unwin. These are merely guesses.[1]

I must add most cordial wishes also for your voyage and for a successful winter, and I hope that we may meet during the winter either in the United States on in Canada.

Yours ever,
T. S. Eliot

1–*The Christian Renaissance* was to be published by Macmillan in 1933.

TO *J. C. Perkins*[1]   cc

29 August 1932   [London]

Dear Mr Perkins,

Thank you for your kind letter of the 11th August.[2] It is quite true that I have accepted the honour of speaking at King's Chapel, and the date provisionally arranged was Thursday 1st of December.[3] I believe that your meetings of this kind take place in the afternoon. It will be a great pleasure to me, and I hope to prepare a satisfactory address. I look

---

1 – The Revd John Carroll Perkins (1862–1950): Minister of King's Chapel, First Unitarian Church of Boston – the oldest church (1717) in the USA.

TSE, in his letter of condolence to Edith Perkins (31 Dec. 1950), felt he could say only 'what you know already, and what must have been said already by many friends: what a good and beautiful person Uncle John [Perkins] was, and how much loved he was. Like every one else who knew him, I shall continue to cherish every memory of his very Christian soul, of essential integrity and innocence . . . His own patience and humility made one rather ashamed, and his readiness to see people at their best.'

2 – 'Emily Hale [Perkins's niece] tells me that you are good enough to come to the King's Chapel one day next winter and review with our Women's Alliance the poetry of the Bible, – if that is your subject. Although I am not a member of the Alliance I somehow assume responsibility enough in the church to be very grateful to you for your generosity.'

3 – TSE's address in King's Chapel House (at that time located at 13 Marlborough Street, Boston), delivered on 1 Dec. 1932, was entitled 'The Bible as Scripture and as Literature': 'As a matter of fact, from the point of view of literature there is no Bible . . . You will observe usually that those who talk about the Bible as literature choose most of their illustrations, unless they be merely a phrase or two, from the Old Testament. I suspect this to indicate, among other things, that it is easiest to enjoy as "literature" those parts of the Bible in which it is most easy to suspend definitely *Christian* belief . . . So far as actual borrowing and allusions go, my inclination is always to applaud those who have read the Bible as the Bible, and to frown at those who have read it as literature . . . But although I object to people talking about the Bible as literature, and although I object to their mining in the Bible for poetic material for purely secular purposes, I am still interested in the influence of the Bible upon English poetry.' Of his own experience as a writer: 'The influence of the Bible upon English literature in the future will be in direct ratio to the extent to which people read the Bible, and read it *not* as literature. I believe that I can defend any quotations and allusions that I have made, in this way . . . You cannot effectively "borrow" an image, unless you borrow also, or have spontaneously, something like the feeling which prompted the original image. An "image", in itself, is like dream symbolism, is only vigorous in relation to the feelings out of which it issues, in the relation of word to flesh. You are entitled to take it for your own purposes in so far as your fundamental purposes are akin to those of the one who is, for you, the author of the phrase, the inventor of the image; or if you take it for other purposes then your purposes must be consciously and *pointedly* diverse from those of the author, and the contrast is very much to the point; you may not take it merely because it is a good phrase or a lovely image.'

TSE also gave a talk, 'Two Masters', to the Boston Association of Unitarian Clergy, in Dec. 1932.

forward to renewing my acquaintance with Mrs Perkins and yourself
during my stay at Harvard.

Yours very sincerely,
[T. S. Eliot]

TO *J. T. Sheppard*[1]   CC

29 August 1932   [*The Criterion*]

Dear Mr Sheppard,

I should be grateful if you would be willing to write something for
the December *Criterion* about Lowes Dickinson under the guise of a
review of his recent lecture. I believe that you know him perhaps better
than any other man of our generation knew him, and it would be a great
satisfaction to have something from you in his honour.

Yours sincerely,
[T. S. Eliot]

TO *Sally Cobden-Sanderson*   CC

29 August 1932   [Faber & Faber Ltd]

My dear Sally,

Thank you for your letter of August 26. I can certainly have the books
ready by the 9th of September, but it does not now appear that I shall
want to take very many, and if I find there are too few to make a box
worthwhile I will let you know today week. I shall be away from Tuesday
to Friday of this week.

Thank you very much for your other information. As I practically
decided not to bother with a night in Montreal but to take the first
comfortable train I can get, shall I fill in that form which you sent me
or do I pay the head-tax here through yourselves? I have now got my
American visa.

I don't quite understand your suggestion about a meeting, as you say
you only return to London on the 17th which is the day I sail. But do you
mean that you and Richard might be available for lunch some day before
then?

---

1 – John Tressider Sheppard (1881–1968), classicist; Provost of King's College, Cambridge,
1933–54; knighted in 1950.

I should very much like to see a copy of your son's poem. It certainly starts off with a bang.

Yours ever affectionately,

[T. S. E.]

FROM *TSE'S Secretary* TO *Kay Boyle*   CC

30 August 1932   [*The Criterion*]

Dear Miss Boyle,

Mr Eliot has asked me to thank you for sending him your story 'Black Boy'.[1] He liked it very much indeed, and is therefore very disappointed to see that it has already appeared in the *New Yorker*. This means that American readers of the *Criterion* will have seen it already, and he regrets that he will not be able to use it. He hopes however that you will be able to let him see another story for which simultaneous publication could be arranged.

Yours very truly,

[Pamela Wilberforce]

TO *C. Platonoff*[2]   CC

30 August 1932   [Faber & Faber Ltd]

Dear Mr Platonoff,

I have read your essay on the Modern Crisis with great interest, and so far as I am qualified, close agreement. I have been puzzling over the question of the possibilities of publication. My own firm is not for the moment adding any new material to its collection of pamphlets. There are, however, two other firms to whom I should suggest your speaking: Wishart & Co.[3] and Desmond Harmsworth Ltd (in that order). Both of these are young firms who have taken to pamphlets, and yours might fit in very well in one or the other series. As, however, yours is still rather short for a pamphlet (10,000 words is the usual length) I suggest that in writing you indicate that this is the first draft, and that it might be expanded if necessary.

---

1 – Submitted on 25 Aug. 1932.
2 – Russian exile who had worked in London for five years at the Russian Commercial Bank: see *L* 5, 118–19.
3 – Directed by E. E. Wishart and C. H. Rickword.

I should strongly dissuade you from taking it merely to an ordinary printer. Printers are not as a rule in a position to give any circulation to what they print and I am afraid that you would merely have the expense without the satisfaction of knowing that your pamphlet reached any of the right people.

I am going away now for the rest of this week, and therefore am asking my Secretary to sign this letter. But I shall be back again for my last fortnight in London.

With all best wishes,
Yours sincerely,
[Pamela Wilberforce, pp T. S. Eliot]

TO *Ridgely Torrence*[1]   cc

30 August 1932   [*The Criterion*]

Dear Mr Torrence,

Thank you very much for your letter of August 23rd.[2] I am very glad that we may now consider the publication of Mr Joyce's poem in December as definitely settled. The January number of the *Criterion* appears on about December 16th, so I should be very grateful if you could arrange for American publication as near that date as possible.

Sincerely yours,
[T. S. Eliot]

TO *Donald C. Brace*[3]   cc

5 September 1932   [Faber & Faber Ltd]

Dear Mr Brace,

Thank you for your letter of August 23rd. The two copies of the book have arrived, and I am very well pleased by their appearance. I am very

---

1 – Ridgley Torrence (1874–1950), American poet and editor – friend of writers including E. A. Robinson and Robert Frost – was poetry editor of the *New Republic*, 1920–33.
2 – The *New Republic* had undertaken to publish JJ's poem 'Ecce Puer', and was happy for TSE to print it in the Dec. number of the *Criterion*.
3 – Donald Brace (1881–1955), publisher, founder in 1919 – with Alfred Harcourt, whom he befriended at Columbia College, New York: they graduated in 1904 – of the firm of Harcourt, Brace & Howe. See *The History of Harcourt Brace and Company: 75 Years of Publishing Excellence* (1994); *American Authors and Books: 1640 to the Present Day* (3rd edn).

glad that you have retained the other ten. I shall probably be sending you a list of names of people to whom I should like them despatched as soon as I arrive in Cambridge.

Yours sincerely,

[T. S. Eliot]

TO *D. S. Mirsky* cc

5 September 1932 [Faber & Faber Ltd]

Dear Mirsky,

Thank you for your letter of the 3rd. If I had known that you were going to be in London again for any length of time I should have suggested our lunching together again. I am afraid now that I shall be too rushed during my last two weeks here, but if there is any chance, and if I find any possibility I will drop you another line at the beginning of next week.

I am a little puzzled to know who the Harrison is about whom you ask. The only Harrison I can think of at the moment is G. B. Harrison of King's College, London, and I assume that you know him. But if he is the man you mean I always address him simply at King's College.[1]

I did get your article on Wells and enjoyed it very much and am using it in the September *Criterion*. I have been away for a week and my regular secretary started on her holiday before my return, but I understand that as your article was rather late, there was no time to send you a proof copy. The typescript was extremely clear, and I hope you will find no errors.[2]

TSE wrote in *The Times*, 27 Sept. 1955: 'The death of the New York publisher Donald Brace will be noted with sincere regret in the world of letters in this country. When, shortly after the First World War, Alfred Harcourt and Donald Brace founded the publishing house which bears their name, the task of establishing relations with British publishers, literary agents, and authors devolved upon the latter. Brace's acumen brought the firm *The Economic Consequences of the Peace*, a book which earned them both prestige and profit. By Maynard Keynes, Brace was put in touch with such authors as Virginia Woolf and Lytton Strachey.

'No American publisher was better known or better liked in the literary world of my generation. His English friends will remember his keen sense of humour, which, expressed in his very slow and deliberate speech, was at times irresistibly droll. And they will remember most gratefully the confidence which he inspired as a publisher, by his combination of Yankee shrewdness, loyalty to his authors' interests, and sweetness of temper.'

1–Mirsky replied (6 Sept.) that he had meant to ask after one 'Williamson' who was editing a historical series.

2–'H. G. Wells and History', C. 12 (Oct. 1932), 1–16.

With all best wishes for the coming year in case we do not meet again,

Yours very sincerely,

[T. S. Eliot]

P.S. My address in America will be Eliot House, Cambridge, Mass.

TO *Henry Eliot*

5 September 1932   [Faber & Faber Ltd]

My dear Henry,

Thank you very much for your two letters. The one of August 22nd arrived this morning. I am afraid that I shall not have time to answer them fully as they deserve. This is only a line to acknowledge receipt and say that I expect to reach Montreal on Monday, the 26th, and to take the night train arriving in Boston on the morning of the 27th. I hope that I may see you very soon.

Your affectionate brother,

[Tom]

TO *J. B. Trend*

5 September 1932   [*The Criterion*]

Dear Trend,

In Miss Wilberforce's absence I am answering your letter of the 4th. We have had only one of the books, that is *The Revolt of the Masses* which I gave to McEachran for a review. I will try to get the others and have them sent to you.[1]

I wish I might see you again before I leave England at the end of next week, but I have so much to do that I dare not make any engagements. If I have a spare lunch-time I shall come to the club and hope I may have the luck to find you there.

Yours ever,

[T. S. Eliot]

1–Trend asked after *Our Father San Daniel*, by Gabriel Míro, and *The Modern Theme* and *The Revolt of the Masses*, both by J. Ortega y Gasset.

5 September 1932   Faber & Faber Ltd

Dear Spender,

Thank you for your note of the 2nd. As for *The Temple*: it seems to me possible that the Alport[1] matter can be left over until I return in May.[2]

1–Dr Erich Alport (b. 1903), educated in Germany and at Oxford, was author of *Nation und Reich in der politischen Willenbildung des britischen Weltreiches* (1933). In the early 1930s GCF sought his advice about German books suitable for translation into English.

2–Spender wrote, 'I have thought a lot about *The Temple*, and I agree that sometime or other the MS must be shown to Alport by Faber & Faber. I doubt if he will make any difficulties, but if he does and they think it necessary, I will come home from wherever I am at that time and see him about it. It is a pity that you wont be in London as I feel sure you could be very reassuring to him. The point he must realize is that everyone (Curtius etc.) who, as far as he is concerned, would be affected by seeing my book, has already seen it, so its being published now cannot do him any harm.'

Spender's novel *The Temple* is based in part on his relationship with Alport, who is presented in the guise of the unpleasant and identifiable character of Dr Ernst Stockmann. F&F was therefore faced with the difficult question of whether they should seek to publish a fiction which was 'pornographic according to the law at that time' (as SS later put it) and potentially libellous. Spender had told Alport, 3 July 1931: 'My novel is now with the publishers. I do not think you will have cause to think I have done you any injustice in it' (BL Add MS 74771B). On 9 Aug. 1931: 'My novel seems impossible to publish in England. The first publisher took legal advice and rejected it, and the second (Cape) advise my publishing it in Paris, so I think I will withdraw it' (BL 74771B). On 20 Aug. 1931: 'I am going to withdraw the novel for a year at all events, and then I shall consider re-writing it. The American edition will have to go forward as it is, but that does not matter. I don't think the book is good enough in its present form to withstand the row that there will be if it is published in England. As Edward Garnett said, it is not only homosexual, it is pro-German homosexual, which is quite damning' (BL 74771B).

GCF was to write to Alport, 12 July 1933: 'With Stephen Spender's consent I am sending you to read the typescript of the finally revised version of his novel THE TEMPLE. I remember that you once expressed your interest in this book; but I have another reason for sending it, and it is as follows.

'I gather from Spender that, while the portrait of Ernst is really intended as a criticism of an aspect of Spender's own mind, some of its elements were suggested by his friendship with you. To me, Erich Alport and Ernst Stockman are such totally dissimilar persons that the idea of their being capable of identification seems grotesque. But, in view of what Spender said, I feel that you ought to be given the opportunity of reading the book before publication and of expressing your opinion about it.

'THE TEMPLE seems to us here to be an exceptionally interesting book. It doesn't conform to any accepted pattern; and it has obvious defects as a work of art. But it is at once a part of Spender and a valuable "document". I am really anxious to publish it.'

Alport (in a letter not found) objected to the novel, and asked GCF formally and firmly to tell Spender so. He wrote to GCF again on 28 July: 'Thinking the matter of "The Temple" over again I was wondering whether you had mentioned to S. in the letter you were going to write to him that I would do the necessary to protect myself against the publication of the book also in the case of another publisher taking it up. For, if you have not mentioned this part, I am not so sure if I am not going to write to him myself after all. In this case, could you

I am very rushed this week, but shall be here every day including Saturday morning. Could you not look in at some time between 11 and 12.30. on Saturday as that is always a quiet morning?

Yours ever,
T. S. Eliot

TO *E. L. Grant Watson*[1]   CC

7 September 1932   [*The Criterion*]

Dear Grant Watson,

I have read your essay on *Billy Budd* with much interest and considerable hesitation from the point of view of the *Criterion*, but I feel, on the whole, that it really is a kind of chapter which belongs in a fuller work about Herman Melville. I hope that some day I may see such a study completed.

---

possibly let me know the contents of your letter? It would be a help for me to know more or less accurately what you wrote, for I would not find it easy to write to him.'

GCF replied to his request, 31 July 1933: 'My dear Alport, I did not write at great length to Spender, but I think I wrote clearly. I said that I had seen you; that you were strongly opposed to the publication of THE TEMPLE, and that you had definitely said that you would be prepared to take any steps in your power to prevent publication – as nearly as I can remember the actual words I used. I added that I had not been able to produce any argument to shake that intention, and that I was very sorry – in these circumstances – that we couldn't publish.

'I did not specifically mention *other publishers*, since the last thing I wish to do is to encourage S. in the idea that he might go to another publisher.

'If I were you, I *think* I should write to Spender, but I am not sure. It is rather difficult to advise. It might be better to wait for the present. Spender's book is in the hands of an agent [David Higham at Curtis Brown Ltd], to whom I am writing to explain the situation; and I will let you know what, if anything results.'

Alport wrote again, 11 Aug.: 'I am very grateful to you for writing so comprehensively to Spender & to his agent; I disliked the idea of writing to S. myself, & I am now fully convinced that this will be unnecessary.'

Despite the efforts of GCF and TSE, the novel had to be abandoned *sine die*; and in due course SS would sell the manuscript to Texas, where it was rediscovered by the poet John Fuller only in 1985. *The Temple* (rewritten in part) was ultimately to be published by F&F in 1988.

1–E. L. Grant Watson (1885–1970): writer, geologist. After graduating from Trinity College, Cambridge (1st class Natural Sciences), he participated in an ethnological expedition to Western Australia and was enthralled by the country. A nomad by nature – he spent time in Fiji, Canada, Ceylon, Paris, Florence, London, New York, Paris, and cultivated writers including Joseph Conrad, DHL and Havelock Ellis – he wrote novels (including six 'Australian' fictions) and short stories, as well as scientific-philosophical works. See *But to What Purpose: The Autobiography of a Contemporary* (1946); *Descent of Spirit: Writings of E. L. Grant Watson*, ed. Dorothy Green (1990); Suzanne Falkiner, *E. L. Grant Watson and Australia* (2001).

I believe there is a book in existence by an American named Mumford, but I do not know how good it is.[1]

I shall be away for seven or eight months and if you want any books in my absence, please notify my secretary.

Yours sincerely,
[T. S. Eliot]

TO *E. L. Woodward*[2]   CC

7 September 1932   [*The Criterion*]

Dear Mr Woodward,

Faber has shown me a short story of yours which I have read with interest.[3] I like it very much, but to be quite frank, it does not seem to me quite a success. What I felt was that you are dealing with a situation which is as old as mankind and which, therefore, can only be given fresh significance, it seems to me, by being raised to a supreme degree of intensity. Nevertheless, I liked it very much and if you have more I should always like to see them.

Yours sincerely,
[T. S. Eliot]

TO *J. H. Oldham*   CC

7 September 1932   [Faber & Faber Ltd]

My dear Oldham,

Thank you for your letter of the 26th.[4] I have run through Wood's memorandum. My first impression is that he has too much to say about

1–Lewis Mumford, *Herman Melville: A Study of His Life and Vision* (1929).
2–Ernest Llewellyn Woodward (1890–1971): historian; Fellow of All Souls College, Oxford, 1919–44; lecturer at New College, 1922–39; Professor of International Relations and Fellow of Balliol College, Oxford, 1944–51; Research Professor, Institute for Advanced Study, Princeton, 1951–61. His works include *Three Studies in European Conservatism* (1929), *Great Britain and the German Navy* (1935) and *Short Journey* (1942).
3–GCF had written to TSE on 22 Aug., of Woodward's story: 'To please him, I am sending it on to you, but I have written that I do not think you will take it, and criticizing the story unfavourably. It is quite pleasant reading, & shows a nice donnish mind. Will you send it back to him satis longo intervallo?'
4–Oldham said he had been able to secure the Chichester Diocesan Retreat House for the meeting of the group on Sat. 1 Oct., and enclosed a document by H. G. Wood as a starting point for discussion. 'I hope to send you in about a week's time a copy of three articles in which I have tried to give the gist of Brunner's recent volume on Christian Ethics.'

Communism and not enough about Christianity, and if there is any danger of the meeting getting side-tracked, it seems to me to be along that line. I will take the memorandum with me and shall be interested to receive any reports of the meeting.

I am sending you three of the books I mentioned in conversation. Please don't bother to return them.

With all best wishes until we meet again,

Yours sincerely,

[T. S. Eliot]

TO *Norreys Jephson O'Conor* CC

7 September 1932   [Faber & Faber Ltd]

Dear O'Conor,

I am glad to have your note of the 1st September.[1] Unfortunately I find that I am rather overwhelmed with engagements during the last fortnight before I leave for America and I doubt whether I shall have time for lunch. But will you please ring me up on Monday morning and we must arrange certainly for at least a few minutes talk, preferably on Monday, Tuesday or Wednesday as I must keep the end of the week clear.

Yours ever sincerely,

[T. S. Eliot]

TO *Ezra Pound* TS Beinecke

7 September 1932   Faber & Faber Ltd

Dear Rabbit,

Yours of the 28th received.[2] The *Criterion* has no objection to publishing your communications in French, but it is impossible for me to promise publication without having the faintest notion what the joke is. If you want to send it let me have it at once as I leave this country on the 17th.

I have never heard of *Il Mare* before, nor seen the letter-paper. Will you send me a copy of Number 1? I am too gummed up with work until I leave to send a message to the Italians, but if you will let me have a copy

---

1–O'Conor, who was returning from Bruges by 10 Sept., invited TSE to have lunch with him at Dartmouth House.
2–Not found.

of your Supplemento Letterario I will see about it from the other side of the Atlantic. I don't know whether I can keep off religion and politics or not. I will try to find you a proof copy of Gilson, but if you have any rejoinder to make it must wait for the December number.

Yours ever,
Possum.

FROM *Vivien Eliot* TO *Ottoline Morrell*   MS Texas

11 September 1932   68 Clarence Gate Gardens

Dearest Ottoline

I hope you have come back perfectly well after your holiday.

If you please Ottoline, will you & Philip come to Tom's Good-bye party on Thursday 15th – from 8.30 p.m.? Please Do. He is really going next Saturday – 17th – from Southampton.[1]

Do *please* come.

Yours ever,
Vivienne

Very informal – only old friends.[2]

FROM *Vivien Eliot* TO *Ottoline Morrell*   MS Texas

Tuesday 13 September 1932   68 Clarence Gate Gardens

Dearest Ottoline,

– thank you for your beautiful card which I will give to Tom.

Yes I do know that you hate parties. There are a few people coming who I do know you care for, and I *wanted* to make it the *kind* of *gathering* together of people which Tom would *like to remember*. All wishing the same thing & *genuinely* desiring his *absolute safety* & *ultimate good* in every possible way – above all spiritually. That is why we should be very sorry indeed if *you* were not with us – even if only for a *very short time*. I will let you know *later* the best *time* to come in.

1 – MHW was to recall for Donald Adamson, 25 Feb. 1969: 'Vivien, my wife & I saw Tom off at Southampton when he sailed for America, & he & Vivien walked a little while on the liner's deck while my wife & I sat & waited' (Donald Adamson Collection).

2 – Other guests invited by VHE, at four days' notice, to Mr & Mrs T. S. Eliot's 'AT HOME' on Thurs. 15 Sept., from 8.30 p.m. ('Morning Dress') included Richard de la Mare and his wife.

On *Friday afternoon* – could you see Tom *alone* between 4.30 & 5.30? That he wld. *value* very much – & after that he will only see my Mother. Do, I *beg you* – do both these things.

Yours ever,
Vivienne

TO *Geoffrey Faber*

TS Valerie Eliot

13 September 1932   Faber & Faber Ltd

Dear Geofff#rey (This is to prove that I am typing myself)

Very many thanks for your letter received this morning. With all my rush I shall have to put it in my case and answer from the comparative leisure of Cambridge Mass. – you have started so many hares that the hounds do not know what path to follow. You may expect a long homily from me later.

I am delighted to have a beautiful new photograph of Tom. He looks to me both more grown, and more stout and robust than when he came here last. Vivienne succeeded in getting one very good photograph of Enid and the children, which she will send in due course.

I hope that you will be back on Monday. Paterson tells me that he has resigned again: probably it is not good for him to be too much alone with de la Mare and Stewart. Perhaps Frank had better come up from Dymchurch to wrestle with him.

I don't think any harm has been done, but I do think that there ought to be some rule, for a week like this, to prevent directors from accepting any book when there is not a quorum. <I don't mean that any has been accepted.[1]> I hope however that I shall be sufficiently refreshed in America to have more valuable suggestions to make than this. When I get back I hope to propose some programme for a Theological Department (popular).

If you see (when you see) Rowse will you ask him why he has dropped my acquaintance.

When you see Dermot Morrah[2] ask him whether he is descended from a remote ancestor of mine, Dermot Macmorrah King of Dublin.

1 – Sentence written by hand in the margin.
2 – Dermot Morrah (1896–1974), journalist; Fellow of All Souls College, Oxford; Arundel Herald Extraordinary of the College of Arms. FVM had written to Morrah (London) on 28 July: 'Your detective story [*The Mummy Case*] has given Faber and Eliot and me much pleasure, and if you are willing to accept our standard first novel terms of £25 advance against

I am going Bald (having an ancestor named Charles the Bald) but not reasonably like you; in Spots – a Spot the size of a Butter Dish behind my right Ear; the hairdresser (or Trichologist of Chiltern Court) says it is paralysis of a nerve, and the hair (with the assistance of his Lotion 7s.6d.) will come back White.

My love to Enid and the children, to whom I will write. I expect Vivienne to give me reports of them during the winter.

Yours aff.

Tom

FROM *Vivien Eliot* TO *John Hayward* MS King's

Wednesday 14 September 1932   68 Clarence Gate Gardens

Dear Mr Hayward[1]

We are asking a few friends to look in tomorrow evening to wish Tom good bye & we both hope particularly that you can manage to join us & feel that the party would be incomplete *without* you.

I rather hope no one will stay long as Tom is so tired – my idea is that people should simply come in & talk a little with Tom & have some refreshments & say Good-bye etc & go out again – *Only old & tried friends* are invited.[2]

---

royalties of 10% to 2,500 copies sold, 12½% to 5,000, and 15% after, we should be very glad to publish it . . . Aside from the question of title, which Faber may have discussed with you, there are a number of minutiae which the three of us would like to present. None of the suggestions are terribly serious, but a first-rate detective story nowadays calls for at least as much care in revision as a B.Litt thesis.'

1–VHE wrote 'Heywood'.

2–John Smart, *Tarantula's Web: John Hayward, T. S. Eliot and Their Circle* (2013), notes that when TSE and JDH lunched together in Jan. 1932, 'Eliot told Hayward that he had decided to accept the Charles Eliot Norton lectureship at his old university of Harvard in order to escape for a while from the impossible situation with Vivienne – and also to make some money. Hayward, always shrewd on financial matters, was very impressed by $10,000 – £2,700 according to his calculations – that his friend was to receive for seven months' work. He was surprised and pleased when Eliot began to take him into his confidence about his family and his American roots. Eliot recounted how his great-grandfather had gone to St Louis in the 1830s to preach the gospel, of "a very peculiar American brand", and talked of his sisters and his deaf brother who wrote detective stories under a pseudonym, having been implored by an old aunt not to disgrace the family' (83).

Smart notes too that soon after the tense and 'peculiar' farewell party, '[TSE's] wife had rung Hayward to ask him round to dinner at a few hours' notice. He could not go and so she had decided to pay him a visit in her new motor car which she could not drive. "And she insists on coming alone. What will happen?" Hayward wrote anxiously to Ottoline Morrell. Anything was possible as she was now "mad, quite mad".' (83)

Yrs.

V. H. E.

The time is from 8.30 – *Morning dress. V. H. E.*

TO *Algar Thorold*   CC

15 September 1932   [*The Criterion*]

My dear Thorold,

I am taking the liberty of sending you an essay on Richard Crashaw by a young American friend of mine, an Anglo-Catholic named Austin Warren who is a Professor of Literature somewhere.[1] He offered it for the *Criterion* and said that if I could not use it he would send it to the *Dublin*, so I think I am correct in sending it at once.

My own reason for not using it is simply that I have accepted an essay on Crashaw by Beachcroft which he has to put in order for me to publish next summer,[2] and I really cannot afford two essays on this subject within the same year. If you do not want the MS. will you please return it to Austin Warren, 36, Gardener Street, Beacon Hill, Boston, Mass.

See too JDH letter to Bunny Garnett, 23 Aug. 1932: 'If you are in town on the 8th of September – Thursday week – and have nothing better to do, will you come to dinner here? Tom Eliot is coming for a final meeting before he sails for America, and Peter and Nancy Quennell and, I hope, Frankie are coming in afterwards.'

JDH remarked to OM, Nov. 1932: 'I don't think Bertrand Russell was entirely correct in saying that Tom's manners were those of an Etonian. I should have thought that, at their best, Eton manners were characterized by an air of complete self-possession, a kind of ease which Tom has never quite attained. America is always breaking in! But he was certainly right about the window-dressing . . . I dare say this explains Tom's obsession with European tradition, his love of formality, bowler hats, stiff collars, Royalism, etc.' (King's).

1–Austin Warren (1899–1986), American critic and author, taught at the College of Practical Arts and Letters, Boston University; at the University of Iowa, 1939–48; and at the University of Michigan for twenty years from 1948; he was a Fellow of the Kenyon School of English, 1948–50; Senior Fellow of the School of Letters, Indiana University, 1950–64. Works include *Richard Crashaw: A Study in the Baroque Sensibility* (1939), *A Theory of Literature* (with René Wellek, 1949), and *Connections* (1970) which includes a chapter on TSE. See further *Teacher and Critic: Essays by and about Austin Warren,* ed. Myron Simon and Harvey Gross (1976). Warren was to write, in 'Some Periodicals of the American Intelligentsia', *New English Weekly* 1 (5 Oct. 1932), 595–7: 'Now the critic and the poet, both admirable in kind, in Mr Eliot consort ill together: the poet is a decadent and an Alexandrian, he [is a] singer of a dirge for dead men and waste lands; the critic is a philosopher, humanist (he still gives evidence of having once gone to school to Professor Babbitt), classicist, Anglo-Catholic. I take it that (despite "Ash-Wednesday") the poet in Mr Eliot is chronologically prior and is giving way to the critic and theologian in Mr Eliot.'

2–T. O. Beachcroft, 'Crashaw – and the Baroque Style', *C.* 13 (Apr. 1934), 407–25.

I hope that you keep well. I am sorry that I have not seen you again as I am leaving on Saturday, but I look forward to seeing you upon my return next May.

> With all best wishes,
> Yours,
> [T. S. Eliot]

P.S. My address will be Eliot House, Cambridge, Mass.

to *Charles Harris*   cc

15 September 1932   [Faber & Faber Ltd]

My dear Harris,

I have your card and should have been reporting to you today in any case about Mrs Thackray's MS. Perhaps we have been at cross purposes about this. I was under the impression when I got it from you, that you considered it as a possibility for a general publishing house and was, therefore, repassing it to Faber & Faber, and I read it and gave it to the chairman to read with this purpose in view.[1] But I now have the agenda of the E.C.U. Literature Committee Meeting for October 6th from which I find that I am expected to report on the MS. as if it were under consideration by the Committee and the S.P.C.K.

From whichever point of view I am to examine the MS. I find myself rather half-hearted. From a publisher's point of view I feel that it is doubly restricted in interest. First, it is not likely to have a wide appeal beyond Anglo-Catholic circles; secondly it can only interest those Anglo-Catholics who concern themselves with literary criticism and literary theory; and third, what is perhaps a more vital criticism, this essay, as is usually the case, does not escape the slightly musty smell which almost inevitably surrounds any piece of writing originally prepared as a dissertation for a prize or an academic degree. Mrs Thackray seems to me to be both a sensitive and intelligent critic, and to anyone who is already interested she offers help in the appreciation of Keble's poetry which, in itself, has

---

1–Harris had written on 13 Aug.: 'I am venturing to send you on Monday a 40,000 words MS on John Keble. It was awarded the Ripon Prize in English Literature in the University of Leeds in 1919. As it deals largely with literary criticism, it is more in your line than mine. Is there any possibility of your firm wishing to publish it?' He submitted the Keble MS on 15 Aug.: 'Personally I like it, and think it an extraordinarily mature piece of criticism for a young person.'

However, like TSE, GCF rejected the manuscript.

considerable merit. I was personally much interested in the account of Keble's literary views which was all quite new to me. Nevertheless the style hardly rises to distinction and I found the essay, as a whole, rather heavy going.

I think that from the point of view of the Literature Committee some other opinion ought to be taken, and perhaps Lowther Clarke will have a look at it if he has not already done so. Even if the essay is considered possible for publication I cannot see that there is anything to be gained by associating it with the Oxford Centenary. On the contrary, my own advice would be to withhold it for publication until some time after the Centenary, meanwhile concentrating on the few directly relevant books.

I was sorry not to see you again before leaving, and look forward to seeing you soon after my return in May. Meanwhile I hope that you will enjoy the best of health through the winter, and that all your projects will prosper. I shall, no doubt, be reporting to you from time to time from America.

Yours ever sincerely,
[T. S. Eliot]

TO *Karl Erdmann*[1]   cc

15 September 1932   [*The Criterion*]

Dear Mr Erdmann,

I must apologise for my long delay in writing to you about your essay on Burke. Meanwhile I have re-read it more than once and I still feel as I think I felt at first. The actual writing is very good and shows an admirable command of English, but there are obvious sentences and modes of statement, especially at the beginning and the end, which are appropriate for a paper read aloud, but not in print and which ought to be altered. What is much more important, however, is that I feel that the first part dealing with Burke in general is not, by any means, the important part. What I should like would be to have you revise somewhat the second part to make it an essay on the influence of Edmund Burke in Germany. This is, so far as I know, a new and extremely interesting subject.

I must apologise for postponing writing to you before my departure from England for some months. I should be very grateful if you would write to me at Eliot House, Cambridge, Mass. and let me know what you

1 – Heidelberg, Germany.

think of my suggestion, and if you care to present the second part of the essay in this way, I shall be very glad to publish it.

With all best wishes,
Yours sincerely,
[T. S. Eliot]

TO *Edwin Muir*   CC

15 September 1932   [*The Criterion*]

Dear Muir,

Thank you for your letter of 1st September. I have only had time to glance at your notes on Franz Kafka.[1] They look extremely interesting and I should have devoted more time to them except that you say they would have to appear in the October issue. The October issue was already made up when I heard from you, and I should hardly have had space even to consider them for December, so I return them with many regrets. I hope that you will have some else to send during the winter as I shall be in need of more material for next summer.

With all best wishes to Mrs Muir and yourself,

Yours sincerely,
[T. S. Eliot]

TO *Cyril Strauss*   CC

15 September 1932   [Faber & Faber Ltd]

Dear Mr Strauss,

I must apologise for the delay in answering your letter of September 7th. I had been intending to write to you as I had just heard from Dr Miller[2] of the death of your father. Please accept my sincere sympathy.

1–Muir wrote on 1 Sept.: 'I am enclosing herewith a collection of notes called "He", by Franz Kafka. This is from a volume recently published in Germany, a collection of fables, allegories and aphorisms left by Kafka at his death – a very extraordinary and beautiful book. My wife and I are translating it for Secker.'

2–Dr Reginald Miller (1879–1948), Consulting Physician to St Mary's Hospital and to the Paddington Green Children's Hospital, London; a general physician with a particular interest in children, he was a recognised expert in the problems of mental illness in children and in rheumatic diseases and heart diseases in childhood (on which he wrote several articles). He was the first editor, with Dr Hugh Thursfield, of the *Archives on Disease in Childhood*. Brought up in Hampstead, it seems very likely that he was a childhood friend of the Haigh-Wood family.

I especially hope that this misfortune will not in any way affect your career at Oxford.

I shall be back in London in May and shall be very glad to hear from you and see any of your more recent work on my return.

Yours sincerely,
[T. S. Eliot]

TO *Frank Morley*

15 September 1932   [*The Criterion*]

Dear Frank,

Yours of the 8th inst. I have never heard of Mrs Clifton.[1] You can probably imagine the first effect of Herbert's letter upon a temperament like mine. I am incorrigibly distrustful of enthusiasm. Nevertheless, and especially because I don't suppose I shall have to read 120,000 words myself, I am all for our getting hold of the book, and if it seems to you and others as good as it seems to Herbert, I should be on the side of taking a gamble, even if the immediate prospects are bad.

The fact that the lady is a descendant of William the Conqueror is not necessarily in her favour. Most of William's descendants are very dull people.

I was sorry you didn't come up last week, but I trust that you are enjoying the sunbathing at Dymchurch. The more skin you have the more good the sun will do you, if there is any.

Miss Evans[2] will have a few memoranda for you upon your return, and please interrogate Miss Wilberforce about the state of the *Criterion*. You will hear from me from Harvard before long. Meanwhile, give my love to Suzanna and the rest of the family.

Yours ever,
[Tom]

1 – 'Cast your eye over the enclosed: if so be as you know Mrs Clifton Queen of the Castle leave a note of what you know.'
2 – Margaret Evans, a Faber secretary.

TO *L. C. Knights*   CC

15 September 1932   [*The Criterion*]

Dear Mr Knights,

   Your paper on 17th Century Melancholy is very interesting and I should like to use it when I can. I am afraid that this is not likely to be before next summer. If, in the meanwhile, during my absence you find that you can place it more quickly elsewhere, please write to my secretary and ask for the MS. back. If not, you may be sure that I shall publish it sooner or later.[1]

                                 Yours sincerely,
                                 [T. S. Eliot]

TO *Herbert Read*   TS University of Victoria

15 September 1932   Faber & Faber Ltd

Dear Herbert,

   Thanks for your letter of the 7th.[2] I am sorry not to have seen you again. I had lunch with bon ami[3] and Frank last week and wished that you might have been there.

   I agree that the second poem is not quite up to the first, but I think that it is quite substantial enough to stand.[4] Incidentally it seems to me that occasional exercise in the statement of modes [*sc.* moods] is all to the good in helping the statement of convictions.

   I am quite convinced about *The Innocent Eye* as a whole. What seems to me the essential thing in this sort of research into the past is to adopt

1–'17th Century Melancholy', C. 13 (Oct. 1933), 97–112. Knights wrote to TSE on 25 Aug.: 'The larger part is concerned to show that the increase in educational activity in the late sixteenth century led many men to expect a higher position than they were able to obtain. "Intellectual unemployment" was largely responsible for the general discontent under James I.'

2–HR wrote from the Isle of Islay, where he was on holiday: 'I was rather surprised to get a proof yesterday including that second poem I sent you on the spur of the moment. I had rather regretted sending it, so I hope you did consider it disinterestedly. I have given it a less affected title & perhaps it will do. I suppose my objection to it is that it represents a mood rather than a settled conviction; but if a poet did not take advantage of his moods, he would have to exist on a very ascetic diet.

   'Morley told me that you have seen "The Innocent Eye" (prose version) & indeed, I've seen your queries & agreed with most of them. The word "innocent" does, of course, bear a heavy load & rather a special meaning, but I have taken it out in some doubtful places.'

3–Bonamy Dobrée.

4–HR, 'Two Poems: The Innocent Eye. Schwermut', C. 12 (Oct. 1932), 43–4.

one point of view and to stick to it and this, I think, with the exception of a few passages on which Wheen, Frank and myself seem to be in pretty close agreement, you have successfully done. Of course one wishes that it might be longer, but I think in this sort of thing one has to be completely obedient to memory and not search for what does not come of itself. Indeed, from any except a market point of view, it is of the right length, that is to say the reader feels that it could not have been of any other length than it is. Long ago I had the half formed opinion of trying something of the same sort myself which I was going to call 'The River and the Sea', but I think that my point of view would have been more definitely, or shall we say less subtly symbolical.[1]

I don't suppose I shall find Grierson on the boat as I am going by way of Montreal.[2] Please write to me some times or, at least send a post card to Eliot House, Cambridge, Mass.

Best wishes for the coming term,
Yours ever,
Tom

TO *C. A. Siepmann*   TS BBC

15 September 1932   Faber & Faber Ltd

My dear Siepmann,

Thank you for your letter of the 7th.[3] You need not have been concerned about your long silence because I had seen Oldham and he had told me how very busy and overworked you were. I am extremely sorry and also for your own sake, that you have not had the time to develop all your projects more fully, and I am sorry that we could not have had more meetings both privately and in Committee.

It is, I am afraid, impossible for me to be of much use to you at the present. I am leaving on Saturday to take up my work in America, and

---

1 – Herbert Read, *The Innocent Eye*: F&F catalogue 1933: '*The Innocent Eye* is an attempt to re-create the atmosphere of the early years of childhood on a remote farm in Yorkshire. The first impressions which the innocent eye conveys to the mind are those which determine the whole course of our emotional development, and life itself may be found to repeat the pattern of childhood. The recovery of these impressions in all their first vividness and in all their symbolic value is what Mr Read has achieved in this intimate revelation.'

2 – Read had written: 'Grierson leaves Edinburgh on the 16th. I wonder if by any chance you are going on the same boat.' (H. J. C. Grierson (1866–1960), Regius Professor of Rhetoric and English Literature, University of Edinburgh, 1915–35.)

3 – Not found.

shall not be back until next May, but I hope to have a certain amount of leisure while I am there, at least I shall not be affected by the daily worries of publishing, and if you have time to write to me, I shall be delighted to discuss any matters with you. My address will be: Eliot House, Cambridge, Mass., U.S.A.

So far as I have had time to consider your syllabus, it seems to me excellent. The only thing that I regret is that there does not seem to be room for a small number of speakers to give from two to four talks. I will take your letter with me and perhaps have more to say in a few weeks time.

With all best wishes until we meet again,

Yours sincerely,

T. S. Eliot

TO *David Higham*   cc

15 September 1932   [Faber & Faber Ltd]

Dear Higham,

Excuse me for not answering immediately your note about Spender's book, but I was seeing Spender on Saturday and I wanted to have a word with him first.[1]

He has told me in substance what he has written to you and what he has said is correct, except that I doubt if we can make our definite decision until the end of the month when Faber returns to London. I am personally in favour of publishing the book, but I do not think it is quite able to make its own way and am convinced that it ought not to be published until the Poems, which we expect to publish very early in the New Year, have had

---

1 – Spender had written to Higham: 'I have spoken to Eliot about the *Temple*. He says that he and Frank Morley are both in favour of publishing it & that I can say they are backed by Faber in the wish that it should appear in the Autumn of 1933. As you say in your letter, Fabers will make their definite decision this week. I had lunch with Eliot and Morley & they asked me if I was willing to wait till next Autumn. I am, as I think they are right in believing my poems should appear before the novel. So I assume that if the committee of Faber decide to accept the Temple, we will leave it at that, and then make the contract when it is necessary.

'With regard to the book of poems: I am very grateful to you for offering to make the arrangements with Fabers about them, but the fact is that I had arranged with Eliot that they should be published in the same format <& under the same conditions> as W. H. Auden's book of poems, two years ago. So I do not think it is necessary for a contract to be made out on any other terms, especially as I had made this arrangement with T. S. Eliot long before I first heard from Curtis Brown' (quoted by Spender in a letter to TSE, 11 Sept. 1932).

time to increase his reputation. Therefore there is no hurry about *The Temple*, and I sincerely hope that the rest of the Board will ratify my opinion. I am leaving London this week and hereafter all Spender matters will be under Frank Morley's jurisdiction.[1]

Yours ever,
[T. S. Eliot]

to *Edgar Foxall*

cc

16 September 1932   [*The Criterion*]

Dear Mr Foxall,

I have read your MS. on AGAMEMNON with much interest. It does seem to me that you have made considerable progress since the earlier small group of poems you sent me, and I think you may do still better.[2]

1–Spender's *Poems* was published on 19 Jan. 1933. Some irritation was aroused by the blurb:

> These thirty-three poems introduce to the general public a young poet whose work has already created unusual interest in a small circle. Some of them have appeared in various Reviews and Periodicals, and in the volume of *New Signatures* published by the Hogarth Press. Like W. H. Auden, who has already been recognised for a writer of great significance and originality, Stephen Spender comes from Oxford, and he is of almost the same generation as Auden.
>
> If Auden is the satirist of this poetical renascence Spender is its lyric poet. In his work the experimentation of the last two decades is beginning to find its reward. The poems are free, but they are rhythmical and musical; rhyme and assonance are used as they are needed, without selfconsciousness, by instinct rather than rule; the language is generally direct and simple, for all its frequent use of sensitive and subtle imagery; obscurities are rare. Technically, these poems appear to make a definite step forward in modern English poetry. Their passionate and obvious sincerity ranks them in a tradition which reaches back to the early Greek poets.

Christopher Isherwood commented to Spender, 22 Jan. 1933: 'portentous tripe – what idiot wrote it?' John Sutherland writes: 'The idiot was probably T. S. Eliot' (*Stephen Spender: The Authorized Biography* [2004], 147). In truth, in TSE's absence, it was more probably FVM. (The spelling of 'renascence' and the omission of a hyphen in 'selfconsciousness' were not usual with TSE.) Also, FVM wrote to James Hamilton, Harper & Brothers, London, 4 Jan. 1933: 'Eliot writes from Harvard that a good deal of interest is being expressed about Auden and Spender, the two young hopefuls of the present Oxford Poetry Movement. What I am wondering is whether you couldn't publish Auden and Spender in one volume? Auden is the satirist, Spender the lyrical leader of the liveliness?'

2–Foxall had written, 3 July: 'The enclosed poem concerns certain spiritual experiences, which I have attempted to relate to the Agamemnon image – a potent one with me. I have attempted to express dissatisfaction with former impulses towards popular philosophy and political antidotes like socialism.'

I am writing in rather a hurry as I am just leaving England for some months, but I hope that you will have some further experiments to show me when I return next summer.

Yours sincerely,
[T. S. Eliot]

TO *Siraj Din & R. Kapur* CC

16 September 1932   [Faber & Faber Ltd]

Dear Sirs,

Your letter duly reached me and I have been waiting merely for an opportunity to write and say that I shall be unable to see you.[1] I very much regret I have found so much to do in preparation for my voyage that I have been unable to keep any appointments at all this week, and it is impossible for me to see anyone before I go. I sincerely hope that you may both be here next year, and that I may look forward to meeting you after my return in May.

Yours very truly,
[T. S. Eliot]

TO *Theodore Spencer* TS Harvard

16 September 1932   Faber & Faber Ltd

Dear Spencer,

I shall, no doubt, see you almost as soon as you get this letter, but this is a hurried note to say that I should like to keep your interesting Marston essay for the *Criterion* although I probably shall not have the opportunity of using it before the autumn of next year.[2] If you wish to publish elsewhere meanwhile, you are, of course, at full liberty to withdraw it from us, but, at the moment, I am keeping the typescript here in London.

Yours ever sincerely,
T. S. Eliot
pp ME

1–Din and Kapur (Indian students who were studying TSE's work at Exeter College, Oxford) had asked on 25 Aug. for an interview; they wrote again on 4 Sept., and again on 14 Sept.

2–'John Marston', C. 13 (July 1934), 581–99.

16 September 1932   [Faber & Faber Ltd]

Dear Mr Barker,

I am extremely sorry for my long silence and also that I have not been able to see you before my departure, but you will understand, I hope, that as I am to be away from England for some months, I have had more to do this summer than I have been able to accomplish.[1] I have been interested by your poems for the *Criterion*. I shall be glad to see more.

Meanwhile, as you want to try some reviewing, will you at some time or other write to me at Eliot House, Cambridge, Mass., U.S.A. and suggest another book. I am sorry that *The Orators* had already been promised.

Yours sincerely,
[T. S. Eliot]

TO *Pamela Wilberforce*   TS Valerie Eliot

16 September 1932   Faber & Faber Ltd

Dear Miss Wilberforce,

I forgot to tell you that any cheques that may come for me (e.g. from American anthologies) as well as urgent business papers of a personal kind, such as Income Tax forms, should be sent to my attorneys, Messrs James & James of 23 Ely Place, Holborn Circus E.C.1. Should you have to ring them up about any affair of mine ask for Mr Shapcott. (Holborn 5312).

There are no doubt many points which I have failed to provide for, but it is difficult to remember everything at the last minute. I shall trust you to refer anything immediate to Mr Morley, and anything that is not immediate to me; and I hope that you will not find the *Criterion* too worrying.[2]

1–Barker had submitted in June some poems written when he was about seventeen. He had reviewed two books for the *Adelphi*, and would like to do more – perhaps Auden's *The Orators*? On 19 July he asked whether F&F might be able to publish a small book entitled 'Cycle of Eleven Poems' – 'which ought I think to sell almost as well as any recent verse, if advertised'. He wrote again on 22 Aug. to ask about the fate of his verses.
2–Pamela Wilberforce was to write to her friend Anne Fremantle, 29 Sept. 1932: 'The trouble is that I promised Mr Eliot to keep to the old gang while he was away. Of course he likes occasionally to try out new people, but in this case he does not want to unless he can take the full responsibility of possibly bad reviews. Besides I have the old gang more or less under my thumb and newcomers might not be so tractable! (Not that this would apply to

I trust that you will have acquired some Staffordshire puppies by next spring. With all best wishes for the winter,[1]

Yours sincerely,

T. S. Eliot

TO *William Force Stead*   CC

16 September 1932   [*The Criterion*]

My dear Stead,

I am very sorry indeed to hear that I missed you last week, especially as I am afraid now that there is such a rush for me to get off by Saturday morning, that I have no further chance of seeing anybody. Sally, who has been invaluable in making my travelling arrangements, suggested that we might all have lunch together one day, but I am afraid that I simply haven't time, so I can only look forward to seeing you upon my return in May unless, of course, you should happen to visit America this winter. (My address, by the way, will be Eliot House, Cambridge, Mass.)

We meet so very seldom and always, it seems, with so little time for intimate talk that I almost wish that you could cross the Atlantic so that we might have a long evening together.

With best wishes for your happiness and peace of mind during these months,

Yours ever affectionately,

[T. S. Eliot]

---

you, I am sure!) I am awfully sorry that there is nothing doing, but in any case you don't really miss very much, especially if you are wanting to make a little money. *Criterion* reviews require encyclopaedic knowledge, endless care and trouble, and only bring in a guinea or so when they are done.' Fremantle (1909–2002), a British-born graduate of Oxford and the London School of Economics, and a friend of WHA and Isaiah Berlin, was to become a distinguished author, art and book critic, essayist and literary editor: her works include *George Eliot* (1933), *The Medieval Philosophers* (1955), *The Protestant Mystics* (1964).

1 – Wilberforce reported this terrible news on 29 Sept. 1932: 'The Staffordshire treasure has been mercilessly attacked by another dog and is lying at death's door, which is very distressing.'

16 September 1932   [*The Criterion*]

My dear Windeler,

I am very much ashamed of myself and also very sorry for my own sake that I have had to be so neglectful and have been unable to come and pick you up for lunch in the city, but I had to go to the seaside with my wife for a short time, and during the rest of the time have had much more on my hands than I could deal with, and therefore I must postpone our lunch until I return in May.

I am afraid that the same difficulty applies to the short stories, from our point of view, as to the verse. The fact is that it is almost impossible to sell a volume of short stories however brilliant, unless the author has already established himself in some other form of writing. In more hopeful times we should, of course, take chances with books of short stories by new authors, merely for the sake of merit and in the hope of the writer's future work, but we simply cannot afford it at the present time.

I see that you ask quite justifiably, for a prompt reply to your letter of the 5th inst. and I apologise again for my negligence. I have thought the matter over, but I am convinced that this is the sort of work – production of a very limited number of copies on commission terms – which we ought not, and are not really very well equipped to undertake.[1] I do not recommend, of course, the publishers whom we have already discussed, but I should advise you to try the Hogarth Press who are personal friends of mine, and who have also done a considerable number of small books of verse. They have a first-rate reputation.

With best wishes for the coming winter, and hoping to see you next May,

Yours sincerely,
[T. S. Eliot]

1–Windeler (5 Sept.) had put together 'a new collection under the title "Ballet Suite" that I would like to have printed and published . . . I had it in mind to have 250/300 copies printed, to be retailed at say 4/- or $1 U.S.A. I think I have the means of disposing of about 150/200 copies myself, but this would be subject to the small book being out the first week of December.'

TO *Austin Warren*   CC

16 September 1932   [*The Criterion*]

Dear Mr Warren,

I am writing hurriedly to report on your Crashaw, although I hope
to see you before very long in Boston.[1] I should have liked to use it, but
the difficulty is that I have already accepted this summer an essay on
Crashaw by T. O. Beachcroft which he is revising for publication in the
June *Criterion*. Of course his treatment of the subject is very different
from yours, but still I do not feel that *The Criterion* can afford to publish
two essays on Crashaw in the same year or so. I have, therefore, taken
the liberty of sending it to Algar Thorold, the editor of the *Dublin Review*
personally, and have asked him to communicate with you.

    With many regrets, but looking forward to seeing you.

                                        Yours sincerely,
                                        [T. S. Eliot]

TO *Pamela Wilberforce*   MS Valerie Eliot

23 September 1932   Straits of Belle Isle[2]

Dear Miss Wilberforce,

    There are a few points which I ought to add before I forget them.

    1. You may have noted that Mirsky wants his payment sent to Vera
Somebody.

    2. Please keep the Tustain mystery play[3] in mind in case nothing is
heard from Martin Browne.

    3. The Poncins article can go to Colhoun, but please write to Colhoun
before you send it, as he is about to leave for Berlin for some months.[4]

    4. I have promised Dobrée to use his Stanhope (long) review in the
December number.[5]

---

1 – Warren had sent from Boston, Mass., a 'literary-theological essay' on the work of
Crashaw; he asked TSE, in the event that he could not accept it, to send it on to the *Dublin
Review*.
2 – Straits of Belle Isle: *détroit de Belle Isle* (Beautiful Island) is a waterway in eastern Canada
separating the Labrador Peninsula from the island of Newfoundland. TSE was en route for
Montreal, having sailed from Southampton on 17 Sept.
3 – A play by Phillipa Tustain (from Harpenden, Hertfordshire).
4 – 'La France contre l'Américanisme' was to be translated by Charles K. Colhoun: see
'France's Fight Against Americanization', C. 12 (Apr. 1933), 339–54.
5 – BD, untitled review of Basil Williams, *Stanhope: A Study in Eighteenth Century War and
Diplomacy*, C. 12 (Jan. 1933), 298–302.

5. Please remind Mr Morley about Mrs Culpin's (C. R. Temun)[1] mss of her Budapest story. I will write to her.

6. Will you please have a *Criterion* sent regularly to Mrs Eliot including the Oct. no.

7. Note provisional acceptance of two more articles: Spencer on Marston and Knights on Elizabethan unemployment.

8. If an article comes from Jim Barnes, it is not for the *Criterion* but is to be sent on *to me*.

9. Please send me addresses of *Cournos* and Joyce (both Paris & Zurich),

10. Please ask Pinker if he has any news of Joyce, or about Lucia.

11. Please ask Jones & Evans (that seems the simplest way) to take out a subscription to the *Times Lit. Supp.* for me, to go to Harvard.

I think that is all I remember. The pay sheet should be passed by Mr Morley before going to Mr Faber.

I hope you have not found many tangled knots upon your return.

Yours sincerely,
T. S. Eliot.

P.S. I think I left a note to ask you to try Morgan Foster again about Dickinson.[2]

TO *E. W. F. Tomlin*   TS Lady Marshall

28 September 1932   Faber & Faber Ltd

Dear Mr Tomlin,

I have looked over your MS., again, but I am very sorry to say that I have not had the leisure to study it carefully enough to make any suggestions. I am leaving for America tomorrow and am afraid, therefore, that I must return the MS. without further comment. I must add however,

---

1–Rexi Culpin's maiden name was Temunovich: she was born in Budapest.
2–In the event, TSE felt it incumbent upon himself to add to his 'Commentary': 'The death of Goldsworthy Lowes Dickinson must be commemorated in the *Criterion*, for it matters not only to his friends and colleagues and all the successive generations at King's, but to everyone who sympathized – without necessarily sharing his views – with his courageous, humane and civilized attitude towards public affairs, with which his classical scholarship was in happy combination. Death at his age is premature and painful for friends and admirers; but Dickinson always seemed – at least to one who knew him only casually over a period of some fifteen years – much younger than his age: he always was, and always would have been, so eagerly sympathetic and understanding towards young men and new writers. We hope to publish some appreciation in our next issue.'

that my opinion of it is in no way diminished on re-reading. If you have the time to adapt part of it in any way, or to write any other short essay, I hope you will let me see it. Please write to me direct at Eliot House, Cambridge, Mass., USA. I dare say that the first few terms in Oxford you will find yourself too busy with other matters, but remember that I shall be immensely interested and I hope you will come and see me after I am back next May.

Yours sincerely,

pp T. S. Eliot

P.S. This letter has had to be held over as I was doing Mr Eliot's work while his secretary was away, and was unable to obtain your address.

TO *John Hayward*   TS King's

Michaelmas Day [29 Sept.] 1932   [Eliot House, Harvard]

Dear John,

How very kind of you to send me a wire to the boat; I found it in my room after the ship was under weigh; it was the only missive of the sort which I received, and helped to raise my already sinking spirits.

I have given your remembrances to Ted Spencer, who has been – as indeed everyone whom I have seen so far – extremely kind to me. (He has presented me with a bottle of sherry, and offers to supply all the gin I may need). Eliot House is magnificent – I might even say gaudy; luxurious beyond the dreams of Oxford and Cambridge.[1] The grandeur of the high table is somewhat abated by the fact that the dais is occupied by undergraduates, and the dons (such as dine in hall) have an inconspicuous table in a corner of the lower hall; the coat of arms spread over everything – including the backs of chairs – is merely repulsive;[2] and my rooms would be perfect if it were not that I can hear the wireless, the gramophone, the typewriter, and all the conversation of two undergraduates next door. I may have to move. However, this address will always reach me.

Yours ever affectionately,

Tom

1 – Eliot House, an attractive redbrick hall of residence (one of the seven original houses of Harvard College) housing 294 students and 8 tutors, opened in 1931. It stands near the Charles River, at the intersection of Memorial Drive and John F. Kennedy Street (then Boylston Street).

2 – The omnipresent Eliot House shield – silver (the field) between gemels wavy azure (painted wavy blue lines) – is derived from the Devon and Cornwall branches of the family.

29 September 1932   Eliot House, Cambridge,
                                      Massachusetts, USA

My dear Mary,

I did not have time to thank you for your kind letter of farewell.[1] I was very sorry indeed not to see you again before sailing; but I simply did not have the time to take any more time out of town; and as it was, did not accomplish all I hoped to before I left. It is an aggravation that you should have returned to London so soon after I left.

I am still very dazed in the unfamiliar surroundings; at the moment I should very much like to be departing for London; but I expect to be busy enough to pass the next seven months without repining. I have found everyone – including customs officers – surprisingly polite & civil; but there is something very suffocating about the moral atmosphere; and I don't think I could ever become used to it again. Will you please write to me sometimes? I hope that Vivienne's affairs will go smoothly, but cannot conjecture. I do hope you will try to see her, and get her to come to see you, from time to time: it would be a kindness to me too.

With best wishes to Jack,
Yours always affectionately,
Tom

TO *Geoffrey Faber*   TS Valerie Eliot

29 September 1932   as from Eliot House,
                                      Cambridge, Mass.

My dear Geoffrey,

Being not yet settled in my new quarters – I am still lingering on at my sister's[2] – and dizzy and tired in mind by the effort of adaptation to new surroundings, I am relieving myself today by a first burst of letter writing. My impressions of Boston and Cambridge do not contradict my first impressions of the country on the journey down from Montreal. The mountains of Vermont are amazingly beautiful – more beautiful than I remembered – and would be so even if they were not now adorned by forest foliage of the most brilliant colours: every shade from light yellow

---

1 – Not preserved.
2 – The Sheffields lived at 31 Madison Street, Gray Gardens, Cambridge.

and brown through scarlet to deep heather purple, according to the species of tree. But the towns, the villages and the scattered homesteads are sordid and *mesquin*;[1] the country is almost a desert; and you [would] not believe that man could have inhabited a territory for a good three hundred years and made so shallow an impression upon it. He has not improved nature or in any way come to terms with it – as in England or in Italy you feel an intimate relation between the life of nature and the life of the race; he has merely scratched the surface; and you feel that every house and sign of human life might be swept away and leave exactly the same inhuman natural beauty that was there before. Cambridge, even with its tremendously solid and indeed beautiful buildings, seems an encampment; partly because some most costly and elaborate specimen of architecture may face a most squalid and temporary looking coffee-room or garage. The buildings, in fact, don't seem real; they seem to have as little relation to what goes on in them as the landscape does. Eliot House is infinitely luxurious, and even very handsome; and large trees have been planted in the quads to make it look as if it was there to stay; but it gives, by some inappropriateness, an effect of burlesque. It is not merely that there is a dais and no high table (the dais is used for undergraduates, and the dons, such as dine at all, dine obscurely at a small table in a corner), or that they have waitresses, or a Senior Common Room which no one ever enters. It is not either simply that having the family coat of arms sprawling over everything and even illuminated on the backs of armchairs gives me a feeling of distressing embarrassment, as if someone in the company had just made a joke in bad taste. It seems to go deeper than all that. The human life seems very insignificant. I have had a talk with President Lowell, and found him an affable, mediocre, uninteresting Boston business man, almost pathetically too small for the role he has to fill.[2] And everything seems like that: without importance.

I dare say that I shall become more reconciled, though the best I can hope is to see it in a more humorous light; and I know there are delightful people here and there, though not many together. But, as you can imagine, the first sense of alienation is painful – of an impassible [impassable] because invisible barrier – the feeling that there may be no one with whom I can wholly communicate; except the sister with whom I am staying.

Having relieved myself for the present, I hope to recover enough to write a letter to some purpose in a week or two. I hope the autumn programme

1 – 'Mean'.
2 – Abbott Lawrence Lowell (1856–1943), a brother of the poet Amy Lowell, succeeded Charles William Eliot as President of Harvard, 1909–33.

has started well, and that you now have a full roll at committees. My love to Tom.

Yours ever,

T. S. E.

TO *Pamela Wilberforce* TS Valerie Eliot

2 October 1932 [Eliot House, Cambridge]

Dear Miss Wilberforce,

Will you please have sent me (to my debit)

    2 copies   *Anna Livia Plurabelle*

    2 copies   *Haveth Childers Everywhere*

    1 copy   *In Retreat*[1]

Will you also kindly ask Jones & Evans to send me a copy of Edward Lear's Nonsense Books: not the illuminated edition, but the edition with Lear's own illustrations; and not the Limericks, but the complete text of his other poems, with also the Four Little People & the Quangle Wangle's Hat included.[2]

Sincerely yours,

T. S. Eliot

1–HR, *In Retreat* (1930): written 1919, first issued by the Hogarth Press, 1925.

2–At the close of the semester, TSE was to journey to visit his friend Emily Hale at Scripps College, Claremont, Calif. (Hale had been teaching there from 1 Sept. 1932), where he arrived on the Santa Fe Railroad just after Christmas 1932. On 5 Jan. 1933 he would lecture in Balch Hall on 'Edward Lear and Modern Poetry', a performance for which he took no fee (James F. Loucks, 'The Exile's Return: Fragment of a T. S. Eliot Chronology', *ANQ: A Quarterly Journal of Short Articles, Notes, and Reviews* 9: 2 (Spring 1996), 16–39 [18]). He would write to Professor Herbert B. Myron Jr., 2 Apr. 1953: 'I am flattered that you should retain any interest in the lecture I gave on Edward Lear, and am therefore sorry to say that I destroyed the script of this and of a number of occasional lectures which I delivered in the United States in 1932–33. Perhaps some day I shall return to the subject, and I hope, improve on my original effort' (Boston University Library). See William Baker, 'T. S. Eliot on Edward Lear: An Unnoted Attribution', *English Studies* 64: 6 (Dec. 1983), 564–6. See too TSE, 'The Music of Poetry' (3rd W. P. Ker Memorial Lecture, University of Glasgow, 24 Feb. 1942): 'the music of poetry is not something which exists apart from the meaning . . . The apparent exceptions only show a difference of degree . . . Take an apparently extreme example – the nonsense verse of Edward Lear. His nonsense is not vacuity of sense: it is parody of sense, and that is the sense of it. *The Jumblies* is a poem of adventure, and of nostalgia for the romance of foreign voyage and exploration; *The Yongy-Bongy-Bo* and *The Dong with a Luminous Nose* are poems of unrequited passion – "blues", in fact. We enjoy the music, which is of a high order, and we enjoy the feeling of irresponsibility towards the sense.' TSE was to write to Richard Jennings, '24th Sunday after Trinity' (Nov. 1947) – apropos his notice in the *Sunday Times* of *The Complete Nonsense of Edward Lear*, ed.

TO *Rose Holmes Smith*   Photocopy of TS o

3 October 1932   Eliot House, Cambridge

My dear Aunt Rose,

Very grateful thanks for your kind letter of the 28th, which Marion handed me when I went to dinner with her last Saturday night.[1] It makes me very happy to feel that I shall we welcomed in St Louis! I hope that, within a reasonable margin, it does not matter vitally to you if I leave the dates open for a few weeks. I must come at some time between the 20th December and the end of January, probably earlier rather than later, but the date must be fitted in with other Western plans which are unsettled. I will, however, write again as soon as possible.

I have not yet heard anything from Washington University. I imagine that if I have to come to St Louis very early in the holidays, it will be impossible to arrange a lecture. (I don't like either listening to lectures or delivering them, but the latter [*sc.* former] does not help to pay expenses!) But I shall of course visit St Louis, lecture or no.

I am very glad to hear – both directly and from other family sources – that you and Uncle Holmes keep so well. I was distressed to hear of your progressive deafness, but I am sure that we shall overcome the difficulties of communication.

> With many thanks,
> Gratefully & affectionately,
> your nephew,
> Tom

Holbrook Jackson (F&F, 1932) – 'Your review of Edward Lear prolonged the pleasure of the afternoon . . . I note in passing that you make no reference to the McTaggart Theory. You will remember that McTaggart of Trinity (Cambridge) held the preposterous view that *runcible* meant *tortoise-shell*. But the essay I have been intending for years to write – *The Concept of Runcibility, or McTaggart Refuted*, is still in the womb of time.'

1–Letter not found. Marion Cushing Eliot (1877–1964), fourth child of Henry Ware and Charlotte Eliot, had visited TSE in London with his mother in 1921. TSE wrote to Anna Selden, 15 May 1963: 'I remember when I was a small boy my sister Marion was the most regular and devoted church attendant of my generation in the family.'

3 October 1932   Eliot House, Cambridge, Mass

Dear Cournos,

I was very glad to hear from you.[1] I left England, as one always leaves anywhere when going on a long visit abroad, in a great rush at the last, and forgot many things; and I wrote to my secretary last week to ask for your address, which I forgot among other matters.

I hope confidently that I may see you sooner or later, and have the pleasure of meeting your wife at last. I am likely to be in New York from time to time – not for more than a night or two at a time – and *if* Yale asks me to give a talk there I shall certainly accept and will give you warning so that I may arrange to meet: but I do not know whether the ancient rivalry is so strong as to prevent Yale from inviting a lecturer from Harvard. I have by the way, left my wife in London. I have to save all the money I can to pay my debts, and it appeared to me much cheaper not to bring a wife; furthermore, her doctor did not advise her coming, in view of the climate and the conditions of life.

I am keeping my hand on the *Criterion* as firmly as possible, though the reviews will have to be run from the London office. Your suggestion of a Chronicle is a priori a good one, in the absence of periodicals; but has certain disadvantages. First, people take more interest in the 'Foreign Periodicals' than they do in the chronicles; second, the chronicles have to be uncomfortably short; and as you are paid at the same rate, you would get less out of it. What I shall do first is to stir up Mirsky, who should by this time have arrived in Moscow, and find out whether the periodicals can still be had. If nothing comes of this, we will reopen the question of a chronicle instead (if you hear of any new books, published in London, which sound worth notice, let me know). But so many people have mentioned the Russian periodicals review as of special interest that I am loath to abandon hope.

I am still rather dazed with new impressions of America – not that Cambridge Mass. is the best place from which to form notions about the country.

With all best wishes to your family and yourself,

Yours ever,

T. S. Eliot

1 – Cournos's letter has not survived.

3 October 1932   Eliot House, Cambridge

My dear Alida,

I am very grateful for your letter of the 22nd, and especially for your writing so promptly.[1] I confess that I was somewhat puzzled (though greatly relieved) by Vivienne's behaviour on my day of departure, up to the last.[2] I was not sure whether it was what is called 'bearing up', or a childlike distraction by the unfamiliar scene and the big ships which made her forget to adopt a more serious role. A letter received several days ago inclined me towards the diagnosis which you give.[3] This is, I am sure, the best of the situations which had seemed possible. Mrs Nelson seemed to me to play her part so perfectly, with such understanding and tact, that I rather wish that she was to stay permanently.[4] I am not so sure what the effect of the friend from America[5] – especially as they have not met for six

---

1 – Letter not found.

2 – See VW, letter to OM, 6 Sept. 1932: 'I hope the separation is complete and final, as it promised to be when I last had news. Poor V. was running amok all over London. Did she come to you? He is coming here [Monk's House, Rodmell, Sussex] one of these days – I mustn't say which, or where he is, for fear V. should put on her crazy old hat and follow after' (*The Sickle Side of the Moon: The Letters of Virginia Woolf* V: *1932–1935*, ed. Nigel Nicolson [1979], 99.) However, it seems unlikely that TSE had yet decided upon a formal and permanent separation.

3 – No letters from VHE to TSE during this period have been found.

4 – Sencourt notes that during the period when he was staying with the Eliots, two of his friends from New Zealand, Mabel Nelson and a son, lived nearby: 'Mabel . . . made friends with Vivienne – a friendship on which Vivienne came increasingly to depend . . . [S]he had a sensitive understanding of psychological abnormality' – even more so after TSE's departure for the USA. 'To avoid being alone, Vivienne . . . asked my friend Mabel Nelson to keep her company for a while, but soon Mabel . . . was feeling that she simply could not endure this situation any longer. Few of us are prepared to cope with mental illness' (*T. S. Eliot*, 118, 121–2).

5 – Lucy Ely Thayer (1887–1952), a cousin of TSE's old friend Scofield Thayer, had been a witness at the Eliots' wedding on 26 June 1915. VHE had written to EP in c.1925: 'Meanwhile damn Sco.' Cousin. But she has done me in. I think she hates Tom more than death. She came to my doctor's (Where I used to go every day to have my stomach punched which is now sed to have done me in) and told me her Pa was dead at larst & as she had already told me she ment to kill him it upset me. Then she nelt down beside me and asked me if I loved her, & made love. I could not get at anyone to help me & so nearly went mad. Helpless. Not dressed. Alone. So Tom afterwards removed her. He sent her a chit to say she should never see me againe. She then left England, to poison France' (Beinecke YCAL MSS. 43, box 1, folder 675). Clearly there had been some sort of reconciliation in the intervening years. (Donald Gallup wrote to EVE, 2 July 1984: 'Vivien's letter to Pound of c. 1925, telling of her seduction by Lucy Thayer [I think I showed this to you once when you were here], states that Lucy and Ellen were sisters and that both were cousins of Scofield. Vivien guessed that Ellen was about 41 then, which would seem to make her too old to be living now, or

years – will be; and I shall be very grateful if you will write again after you have had the opportunity of observing V. in relation to Miss Thayer. I do not know how quick her friend will be to understand V.'s condition and how able to handle it. In any case, I think it would be a misfortune for V. to devote herself to this friend and neglect to cultivate her other friends and acquaintances.

I should have written to you shortly in any case to thank you again for your heroic rescue of my suitcase – I should have had a very untidy time on the ship without it! And I should have been distressed if you had attempted a breakneck (and possibly futile) dash to Southampton.[1]

I found the voyage fairly restful, but the first week here rather fatiguing – not so much from activity, as I have been deliberately pretty idle, but from the effort of adjustment to an environment which is all the more strange from being a mixture of memory and novelty. I dare say I shall become sufficiently habituated to it, but I shall not be able to like it.

I do hope that the labours of the no doubt dilatory workmen will end in making you very comfortable: I shall look forward with much curiosity to seeing your new home.

Ever yours,
Tom[2]

---

even to have been living in the 1970–1975 period when Ellen Thayer gave Lucy's copy of the vellum *Ara Vos Prec* to Harvard.')

1 – See Sencourt, *T. S. Eliot*, 121: 'His departure . . . was dramatic. Vivienne and her brother Maurice and his wife accompanied him as far as Southampton, from which his liner was to sail to Montreal. Tom got his wife into a cab outside their flat in Clarence Gate Gardens, and the others followed in another cab containing his ample luggage. On the way to Waterloo Station, however, Eliot discovered that some of his important papers had been locked up by Vivienne in the bathroom. He stopped his taxi on Constitution Hill to speak to the devoted friend [Alida Monro] who was following, begging her to return to the flat and try to recover the papers with the porter's help. Her taxi drove back to Clarence Gate Gardens at top speed, a page boy was thrust through the bathroom window, and the friend managed to get the precious documents to Waterloo a few minutes before the boat train was due to depart.'

2 – Alida Monro pencilled this note at the foot of the letter: 'The suitcase which V had locked in the bathroom & which was not missed till we were 2/3 of the way to Waterloo (I was driving my luggage in my car, following Taxi in which T & V were travelling) contained all his papers & lecture notes, not clothes, as is suggested. AM.'

TO *Eleanor Hinkley*   TS Sturtevant/Houghton

6 October 1932   31 Madison Street,
                                  Gray Gardens, Cambridge[1]

Dear Eleanor,

I am sorry I did not reply to your letter at once.[2] But I was hoping to get my telephone in order and ring you up instead; and so far, nothing has been done, to my infinite vexation, though I spent the better part of yesterday morning over it. The trouble is that I had promised to go out into the country with the Spencers (I have not yet met Mrs S.) to lunch with some friends, and I now find that they had arranged to take supper there as well and return early (I hope) in the evening. I don't want to put them out, and if I mentioned coming back ahead they would be sure to insist upon bringing me; so I am afraid that I must postpone the Sunday supper with you – until next week, or whenever is convenient if you will have me. I am very sorry.

As soon as I can visit Sears Roebuck & procure a few thick cups and a teapot, and see about a small milk supply, I shall ask you to tea. It seems to be a rare beverage; I complained at breakfast of only being given one cup at a time (with a little bag of tea soaking in it) and was told that there was not a teapot in the whole kitchen.[3]

1 – Printed notepaper: the address is that of TSE's sister Ada and her husband 'Shef'.
2 – Letter not found.
3 – Loucks ('The Exile's Return') reports that TSE 'advertised in the [*Harvard*] *Crimson* that he would be at home to members of the university on Wednesdays at five. His teas drew mixed responses from undergraduates: William Burroughs, having heard they were awkward affairs, bypassed them (Morgan, 57–8); but Harry Levin, who discussed Auden's poetry one afternoon with TSE (Carpenter, 137), recalled the poet's "helpful benignity" (Ackroyd, 195). Once, embarrassed by a student's monologue about tea, TSE reportedly cracked his knuckles ("Tea", 11). On another occasion a pretty young woman distracted the male guests, prompting TSE to request that no ladies be invited to his at-homes (Fecher, 55).' (HWE insisted in a letter to the *New Yorker* that he had never known his brother to crack his knuckles ; and see Howard Derrickson, 'Reminiscences: with TSE at Harvard in '32', for his denial of the knuckle-cracking story: *T. S. Eliot Society News & Notes* no. 3, Fall 1987, 3.) Loucks relates too that 'TSE occasionally attended a literary salon at 53 Brattle Street in Cambridge as a guest of Olivia Saunders (later Mrs James Agee) and Mary Louise White (Bergreen, 97).' TSE must have become acquainted with James Agee (1909–55), author, poet, journalist, screenwriter, who entered Harvard in 1932 – his famous works included *Let Us Now Praise Famous Men* (1941) and *A Death in the Family* (1957: Pulitzer Prize 1958) – for in a later year he was asked by the Guggenheim Memorial Foundation to write in support of Agee.
   T. S. Matthews, *Great Tom*: 'In his study at Eliot House he held open tea parties. To one of them the Boston *Herald* sent a snide reporter, with small sympathy for this visiting expatriate:

I envy your spurt of work. I really hope that I shall be able to get to work myself next week.

Affectionately,
Tom.

TO *Elizabeth Manwaring* TS Wellesley College

7 October 1932 B-11 Eliot House, Cambridge

Dear Miss Manwaring,

Thank you for your kind letter of the 29th,[1] which I should have answered before, though I have sent messages to you through Mr Sheffield.

I have fixed October the 17th quite certainly, and I believe that my sister will be able to motor me out. As for your selection (which you gave Sheffield to give me) I am quite satisfied with it (I am naturally pleased that you should choose from my later work rather than from my earlier). Your computation is for 34 minutes. I should prefer not to read any *more* of my own work than you have chosen; and I thought that if a longer performance was wanted I might suggest reading a few more or less modern poems which the audience might not know. For instance, a poem of Gerard Hopkins, a bit of 'Hugh Selwyn Mauberley', and Auden's Pindaric Ode on a Football Match.[2]

If your programme needs such amplification will you let me know?

Looking forward with trepidation,
Sincerely yours,
T. S. Eliot

"His accent is an obvious pose. But it is not half-baked, like so many English accents: it goes the whole hog, and he nearly gets away with it . . .

"A discussion about what makes a good poem ended inconclusively. Good poetry has "something". Eliot's formula for making poetry is to catch that "something" and mix it with water. Water consists of images and words which your reader easily catches hold of. You use it according to what you think your reader can bear. Masefield is watery. Eliot's poetry is about 100 proof.

"Personally, Eliot seems to be all water. His manner is all a superimposed form and pose, which his special type of readers swallow with joy. But sometimes when he is silent he seems to enjoy watching them swallow."'

1–Not preserved.

2–Ode II ('To Gabriel Carritt, Captain of Sedbergh School XV, Spring, 1927'), *The Orators*, 89–92; repr. *The English Auden* (1977), 96–8.

TO *Frank Morley*   TS Faber

7 October 1932   B-11 Eliot House, Cambridge

Dear Frank,

Enclosed is the first ghost from Russell Square which has walked since my arrival. I have written a charming letter to Louis More saying that my sudden change to new surroundings has affected my memory and that I don't remember what approaches you made to New York publishers (leaving it open to you to say that you found no one interested); that I am sending you his letter; and that as I am not at present in touch with the affairs of the firm or the London book market, I am not in a position to influence the decision of the Board. But if you prefer, write to me about it and I will convey the decision to More.[1]

I have very comfortable rooms now – not too noisy – a spare bedroom for any visitor who deserves it – and a marble shower bath but no tub. Food not at all bad – I am getting used to tomato cocktails, fried pineapple, and strange salads, and have sampled the celebrated near-beer. Great hospitality – the Master of this House has some pretty good Scotch, but you have to take the ice out of it – and I have been presented with a bottle of real Booth's Gin. Wensleydale and Russian Stout are unobtainable, as you no doubt know. Mr Leach of the *Forum* has written to ask for my impressions of 'America Revisited', and a Widow in Watertown Mass. has written to offer me a home.

I should be glad to know what is happening to the *Criterion*. Love to Sukey.[2]

Yours ever,
T. S. E.

1–FVM replied, 19 Oct.: 'I have sent the enclosed tergiversation [copy not found] to the unsainted Louis with no more feelings of selfrespect than we had after our interview with him. The man is a catalytic agent for all the emotions of selfdisgust; for that reason I thought it more honourable to write him direct than to put it on you.'
2–The Morleys' daughter Susanna, who has told me (JH) that during her childhood she thought of TSE an an 'older brother'.

TO *Eleanor Hinkley*   TS Sturtevant/Houghton

11 October 1932   B-11 Eliot House, Cambridge

This is not my note paper, but a bit I found in the desk.
Dear Eleanor,

Thank you for your 2 notes.[1] I look forward to Sunday night supper
with you. I will cherish your general invitation to lunch; this week I find I
have to be out every evening, so I must keep the days as free as possible;
I had rather lunch one day when I do not have to dine out. I am eager to
learn the tytel [*sic*] of your play – but wasn't 'Dear Jane' good enough? It
sounded right to me. I am rather disappointed that the tickets are to be
Provided for the football match on Saturday (the 22nd) (I hope it is an
Important one, e.g. Holy Cross) but perhaps you will come to the Play
with me before long when there is something that you think worth seeing.
I suppose the 20th holds good for Miss Le Gallienne's.[2]

                    Affectionately,
                    Tom

TO *Hugh Ross Williamson*   TS Julia Ross Williamson

11 October 1932   B-11 Eliot House, Cambridge

My dear Mr Williamson,[3]

Your book has just reached me[4] – I read anything about myself with
a childish pleasure – and particularly, of course, I was eager to find out
what your views were. I of course am the last person to be able to express
any sound opinion on such a book: I cannot judge it in the gross but only
in detail – unlike Byron's Suwarrow.[5] There are numerous points which
give me satisfaction: such as the rejection of the facile distinction (made
originally I think by MacCarthy, but since repeated by others) between
the historically 'splendid' and the presently 'sordid'. In other places
you (like Dr Oras of Tartu, who wrote a treatise about my criticism)
overcredit me with knowledge and deliberate intent (e.g. the 'Dog' on

---

1 – Not found.
2 – Eva Le Gallienne (1899–1991), English-born actress, producer and director; founder of
the Civic Repertory Company, New York.
3 – This letter was first cited, in part, by Joseph Pearce, *Literary Converts: Spiritual
Inspiration in an Age of Unbelief* (2006).
4 – *The Poetry of T. S. Eliot* (1932).
5 – See Byron, *Don Juan*, canto vii.

p. 104).[1] I am not unnaturally content to be attributed a better and more conscious design than my memory tells me is correct! I regret the absence of my poor abortive fragment of 'Sweeney Agonistes', but that does not really fit in well (it comes chronologically between The Waste Land and The Hollow Men). It was to have been an Aristophanic ~~Morality~~ Miracle Play. But circumstance prevented me from continuing it, and circumstance and time changed me, and circumstance led me into shorter and less ambitious attempts; and perhaps it will always remain just a misfit. I feel the emphasis on 'Marina' (rather than 'Ash Wednesday') is right; whether 'Coriolan' will ever justify the hopes you may, I fear, raise, I must not think. But I do think that you have handled the religious problem with skill and sureness, and I am grateful for that.

I hope that the sales may justify you in the eyes of the Hodders and the Stoughtons, and the booksellers.

I am at present immersed in the preparation of lectures. Lectures, I suppose, will always be given and will always be listened to. But I hope that during the intervals I may be granted the grace of writing a little more verse worth writing.

With many thanks and best wishes,
Yours very sincerely,
T. S. Eliot

FROM *Pamela Wilberforce*   CC

11 October 1932   [London]

Dear Mr Eliot,

Thank you for your two letters. I have dealt with all the points you mention, and everything seems to be running fairly smoothly, though there are, as usual, far too many reviews.

The Tustain Play:[2] I found yesterday that Mr Brown [*sc.* Browne] reported on this on September 19th, but his letter and the play had been

---

1 – Williamson cites TSE's note that the line '"Oh keep the Dog far hence, that's friend to men . . ."' (*TWL*) derives from John Webster's dirge in *The White Devil*: 'But keep the wolf far hence, that's foe to men', and proceeds to remark as follows: 'The "Dog" of course is Sirius, the Dog Star, which in Egypt was regarded as the herald of the fertilising floods of the Nile. Its appearance, foretelling the rising of the waters, marked the Egyptian New Year, the feast of Isis, whose tears, they said, swelled the river in mourning for her slain husband, Osiris (the equivalent of the Phoenician-Greek Adonis).'

2 – The play by Philippa Tustain.

put away with the *Criterion* MSS which I have just been through.[1] I have now returned the play to Mrs Tustain with a digest of Martin Browne's letter, and have told him and her to communicate direct with each other in case a suitable parish for the production of the play turns up.

James Joyce's Zurich address as on his last letter to you was Hotel Carlton Elite, Zurich. Pinker has heard nothing, either of him or of Lucia, and is still trying to get hold of a copy of the forthcoming French edition of her illuminations.[2]

Lowes Dickinson: Sheppard [went off] to Monte Carlo, but said that the one person who ought to write about L. D. was Nathaniel Wedd of King's. So with Mr Morley's approval I approached him, and he is producing about 1500 words.[3]

I have dealt with Mirsky's payment, the Poncins article, and Jones & Evans, and will remember about Dobrée's review of Stanhope, Spencer on Marston, Knights on Elizabethan unemployment, and the E.C.U. file.

1–Browne agreed with TSE that 'the play *has* merits – it goes straight to the point . . . it embellished the story with a number of good conceits, new as well as old, and it is not precious. So I should like to see it performed . . . I will keep an eye open on its behalf. It must be done *well*, for it will certainly not stand a bad performance. A big parish is probably needed.'

2–A limited edition of *Pomes Penyeach* (25 copies), numbered and signed by JJ, with initial letters designed and illuminated by Lucia Joyce, and with the poems in facsimile of manuscript, was to be published by Jack Kahane at the Obelisk Press, Paris, and Desmond Harmsworth, London, in Oct. 1932. (JJ and S. Beach forfeited royalties: Lucia received 33% of the net profit.)

FVM was to write to John Wilson (John and Edward Bumpus, booksellers, London), 3 Dec. 1935, apropos the edition of *Pomes Penyeach* illuminated by Lucia Joyce: 'I had a letter on the 3rd November, 1932 from Joyce asking me to inspect a copy at your office; and on the 9th November, 1932 I reported to Joyce that I had called on you and seen the copy, but that we could not see what we could do with Miss Joyce's work in England. Apparently, the only reason for my seeing that copy was to get an impression of Miss Joyce's work, and I do not think, at least I don't find any record, of my having taken away the book itself. From his later correspondence, there are several other suggestions for his daughter, but no further suggestions about *Pomes Penyeach*.' (See JJ, *Letters*, vol. 3, 265–7, for JJ's exchanges with FVM.)

Pomes Penyeach was brought out by F&F in 1933 at one shilling: Spring Announcement 1933: 'The first publication in England of these famous Pomes. There are a baker's dozen of them, and the price of the little volume is as promised by the title.'

3–J. T. Sheppard (King's College, Cambridge) insisted (15 Sept.) that N. Wedd of King's – 'a life-long friend of GLD' – was the very best possible person to write about him. See N. Wedd, 'Goldie Dickinson: The Latest Cambridge Platonist', C. 12 (Jan. 1933), 175–83.

I believe that on your return you may look forward to the pleasant task of telling Alport about Stephen Spender's novel! But I hope that won't induce you to prolong your stay in America!

Yours sincerely,
[Pamela Wilberforce]

TO *Henry Eliot*

TS Houghton

12 October 1932 — B-11 Eliot House, Cambridge

My dear Henry,

It was a very great pleasure to have you with me for those few nights; and now that you know how easy it is for me to put you up, that the expense is trifling and the inconvenience nil (unless you stay out too late at Margaret's) I hope that you will make use of the room whenever you have an economical opportunity of coming up. I hope that you may be able to spend a few days at Thanksgiving, and bring Theresa with you. It is possible that for certain reasons I may want to go west directly the holidays begin, and not spend Christmas in the east, but you need not mention that possibility to anyone yet.

With love to Theresa,
Your affectionate brother,
Tom

TO *Tom Faber*

TS Valerie Eliot

12 October 1932 — Eliot House! Cambridge, USA

Dear Tom,

I have been Meaning to write you a Letter for quite-some-time O dear Me about 4 weeks, ever since I got to this Place, and I had to cross a lot of Water to get Here. I came in a Steam Boat; it was a Small boat, as you see from the Picture:

and when the Boat got to Montreal it stopped; I got out and Took a Train; and the Boat turned round and went back to England!

So after a While I got to this Place, and I have a House to live in; they call it Eliot House so that People will know where to come:

They go through a Court or Quad:

And Up a Staircase; and there they Find a Place with my Name on It:

But inside, There he Is, – Writing a Letter to TOM –

I shall write Soon again, & will Tell you more about America: you might like it, because there is Lots of Ice Cream; but you might Not like it, because there is no Jam or Honey for Tea.

Your fexchnite uncle
TOM

TO *John Cournos*   Photocopy of TS Satterthwaite

12 October 1932   Eliot House, Cambridge, Mass

Dear Cournos,

Thank you very much for your letter of the 8th.[1] I should like very much to be able to accept your kind invitation; but as I have here in Cambridge 3 sisters, 1 aunt, 2 uncles, and miscellaneous kin, you will understand that if I were to vanish from the family circle at the Thanksgiving Day festival, of all times, there would be bad blood.

Yes, I thought Mirsky first rate (though he used the word 'bouncing' too often).[2] I like your suggestion of a special chronicle of Russian émigré periodicals: of course you would make it clear at the beginning that you were rounding up *only* the émigré lot on this occasion; if you can do it in time for the December number I will write to Miss Wilberforce at once.

I should imagine that the depression had hit the literary income pretty hard. I should like to talk with someone who could tell me more about it; Cambridge Mass. does not seem to me to be the best place from which to view the American Scene as a whole.

Of course I should be delighted to give a lecture in New Haven. Especially nowadays when money is short for such purposes, it strikes me that the only way to net an appreciable profit from lecturing is to lecture at short distances from where one's centre is; the fees at long distances

1 – Not found.
2 – Mirsky, 'H. G. Wells and History', C. 12 (Oct. 1932), 1–16.

are eaten up by railway fares. I intend, however, to go at least as far as St Louis at Christmas (for sentimental reasons), and if I can get a few engagements, I should like to pay my way to the Pacific Coast and back, for once in my life. But I shall indeed be grateful if something can be arranged at Yale, and in that hope look forward to seeing you and Mrs Cournos.

Yours ever,
T. S. Eliot

TO *Rexi Culpin* TS Robert Craf

14 October 1932 B-11 Eliot House, Cambridge

Dear Rexi,

Some time ago, while you were in hospital, I wrote to Jack about your manuscript, but did not get any reply. You will know that we were very much impressed by your story, and the only difficulty whatever was that of its length – much too short for our own publishing purposes. Yet the story is quite complete and formed, and it would be a pity to add or subtract. I then suggested that we might try to interest one or two firms which do make a practice of publishing shorter books.

I should be very sorry to drop the matter, as I liked the story so much. I should like to hear from you, or you could write to Mr F. V. Morley, at 24 Russell Square, who was the other Director interested.[1]

I hope that you are very well again, and that everything goes well with you both, and that you may see Vivienne sometimes. The life here is

---

1 – Hamish Miles (Jonathan Cape Ltd) wrote to FVM, 8 Nov. 1932: 'Thanks for the untitled manuscript by Mrs Culpin . . . It is a very curious and horrifying affair which deserves to be published somewhere, but I fancy we feel very much as you do – that somebody else had better hold the baby!' FVM wrote to Allen Lane (John Lane & Sons), 23 Nov. 1932: 'I am sending on to you at the author's suggestion, an untitled MS by Mrs Culpin . . . Don't look on it with suspicion merely because another publisher sends it on. It is an exceptional piece of work, an extraordinary analysis, and I would say beautiful. T. S. Eliot liked it very much indeed. He and I both wanted to publish it. After much discussion we had to turn it down at Russell Square because we are jammed up with more commitments than we can handle. *The Criterion* brings us in more than one firm can deal with.' FVM told Cobden-Sanderson, 11 Jan. 1933: 'Our notion was to make a fine printing job of it at a fairly high price, and the reason we have not been able to put this over is that de la Mare is so thrutched up with our increased output that it is really unfair to hand him a proposition such as this which needs special thought.' Of Rexi Culpin, FVM wrote in the same letter: 'She is young, very intelligent and energetic.'

peaceful and pleasant; so far I have hardly stirred out of the college and the town. But I know I shall hate giving lectures and readings.

Ever yours cordially,

T. S. Eliot

TO *Howard Morris*

TS Morgan [Lewis Morris]

18 October 1932

B-11 Eliot House, Cambridge

My dear Howard,

I have been a long time answering your welcome letter;[1] but have been gummed up with preliminary affairs here, to say little of 3 sisters, 1 brother, 1 aunt, 2 uncles, 2 nieces etc.; and am still very far from sight of a visit to New York; I have dined once with Leon[2] but so far have seen no other survivals of the prehistoric or eolithic age of 1910. Harvard is not what it used to be; I can't say much about the undergraduates yet, I shall have a few piling up tomorrow afternoon to look me over. They don't seem to be the natty dressers that they were in our generation, and their mild and studious looks differ strangely from the hard & bestial faces of most of our old friends. But of course I may be misjudging on insufficient evidence. I see little evidence of alcoholism, which may be due to high prices; there is good whisky at $5.00 a bottle but I can't afford that myself: $25.00 a week is more than I can afford. I had to give a poetry reading at Wellesley,[3] and even the girls seemed to lack endocrines or something, as there was no rush to kiss me afterwards; only one lass (age about 14 I should think) came up and shouted in my ear 'I WAS AT MILTON TOO'.

1 – Not found.

2 – Leon M. Little (b. 1887) was a friend at Harvard (as 1910 Class Secretary he was to compile the *25th Anniversary Report*, 1935). By profession a banker, he worked for Parkinson & Barr and then, after wartime service in the Navy, for W. A. Harriman & Company. From 1921 he worked in the Trust Department of the First National Bank of Boston, and in 1927 became Vice-President of the New England Trust Company. He and his wife Eleanor Wheeler (married 1916) had five children (of whom one died young). He wrote, in 'Eliot: A Reminiscence', *The Harvard Advocate* 100: 3–4 (Fall 1966), 33: 'As a freshman T. S. Eliot was of the type that welcomes friendships but is too reserved to seek them. However, his scholastic brilliance and his charming personality quickly brought to him a circle of friends of two quite divergent types, the intellectuals on the one hand and, on the other, many of those who were not considered in that category. His requirements seemed to be a reasonable amount of brains but above all a happy, keen sense of humor. Within the circles of these friends he was a very gay companion.'

3 – TSE read his poetry in Billings Hall, Wellesley, at 4.30 p.m. on 17 Oct.

My wife, by the way, remains in London; I couldn't pay for two, and besides her doctor did not think she was up to the voyage. I should enjoy a Thanksgiving Festival at your home, but vide supra the miscellaneous relatives above expect me to a large dinner, and as I expect to go west at Christmas I dare not fail them. The actual performance of lectures does not bother me much yet, as I have only 4 to give at Harvard before Christmas, but I must sit here and sweat over writing them and also over the odd lectures I expect to give elsewhere later on.[1] I probably shan't get to New York before Christmas, but after that several times; and I should much like to drop down to Long Island for a night with you on one such occasion. Anyway, I'll let you know of any prospective visit. I hope that the Stock Exchange doesn't worry you to death and that you get enough to eat. I don't know whether football games ever attract you to Cambridge, and anyway I understand that the Yale game is at New Haven this year, but if you come this way you will be welcome at B-11.

Ever yours,
Tom

Give my regards to Mrs Morris, whom I haven't met yet.

TO *Pamela Wilberforce*   TS Valerie Eliot

18 October 1932   B-11 Eliot House, Cambridge

Dear Miss Wilberforce,

Thank you for your two letters of the 29th ult. and the 11th inst. I note the various points you mention.

First, the Holliday Bookshop have stupidly sent the (ten) author's copies of my Dryden essay[2] to Curtis Brown. So I have written to Brown's to send them to you; and I enclose a list of ten names and will ask you please to see that the copies are dispersed accordingly. I am sorry to give you this trouble, but I assume that the manual labour of packing can be done downstairs.

1–The sequence of TSE's Norton Lectures was to run: (i) 'Introduction: The Relation of Criticism and Poetry', 4 Nov.; (ii) 'Apology for the Countess of Pembroke', 25 Nov.; (iii) 'The Age of Dryden', 2 Dec.; (iv) 'Wordsworth and Coleridge', 9 Dec.; and then, following the Christmas break: (v) 'Shelley and Keats', 17 Feb.; (vi) 'Matthew Arnold', 3 Mar.; (vii) 'The Modern Mind', 17 Mar.; (viii) 'Conclusion', 31 Mar.

2–TSE, *John Dryden: The Poet The Dramatist The Critic* (New York: Terence & Elsa Holliday) – a reprint of the BBC broadcasts – was published on 18 Oct. 1932 (1,000 copies).

I have written to Malraux c/o the N.R.F. I have not written to Mauron, and should be glad to have his address.

It is mysterious that J. S. Barnes has not yet sent the essay he wanted me to read, but I prefer to let the sleeping dog lie.

I return the proof of the verses herewith.[1] I have the Commentary in mind, or rather on my mind, but have not yet thought of anything to say.[2]

I have written to Mrs Culpin (Regina Temunovitch) about her ms., and Mr Morley should be hearing from her. Will you please [tell] him also that I have spoken to Professor Lowes about the Dunbar book, and he is very much interested; so that I should like to hear as soon as Professor Craigie has come to a decision. Only, if the book should be available, I want to know the name of the editor, as that is not on the proof which I have.[3]

Will you please tell Mr Faber that 6 copies of the Dibblee book reached me safely; that I will write to Mr Dibblee as soon as I have distributed them; and that I had to pay 65 cents duty on one copy, and nothing on the rest.[4]

If the December number threatens to be large I think Poncins might be postponed. There were 14 reviews arranged before I left, so I do not see how any more could be included except shorts. I have heard from Cournos, who says that he has not had any periodicals from Moscow; but I have asked him to do a notice of *émigré* periodicals by themselves. As the Randall notice[5] is usually not long the Cournos could go into December if it arrives in time, unless the number is otherwise inflated. Unless you have otherwise disposed of the book, I should like the Grierson *Letters of Walter Scott* to go to Mr Blake for a short notice, *if* there is room for it – and if not, it would not be too late in March.[6]

1–TSE, 'Five-Finger Exercises', C. 12 (Jan. 1933), 220–2.
2–TSE's 'A Commentary' (ibid., 244–9) tackled Trotsky's *Literature and Revolution* (1925) and V. F. Calverton's *The Liberation of American Literature* (1932). 'What faith in life may be I know not; I might inform Mr Calverton that, for the Christian, faith in death is what matters.'
3–In the event, WHA reviewed *The Poems of William Dunbar*, ed. W. Mackay Mackenzie, in C. 12 (July 1933), 676–8.
4–G. B. Dibblee, *Instinct and Intuition* (1929).
5–Untitled review of Sir Rennell Rodd, *Rome of the Renaissance and To-day*, C. 328–9. Alec (later Sir Alec) Randall (1892–1977), diplomat and writer, entered the Foreign Office in 1920. In the early 1920s he was Second Secretary to the Holy See. He ended his career as Ambassador to Denmark (where he was awarded the Grand Cross, Order of Dannebrog), 1947–52. He wrote on German literature for C. and *TLS*. Later works include *Vatican Assignment* (1956) and *The Pope, the Jews and the Nazis* (1963).
6–J. McN. R., untitled review of *The Letters of Sir Walter Scott, 1787–1807*, Vol. I, ed. H. J. C. Grierson, C. 12 (Apr. 1933), 325–7.

If you find any possible story within the next six months, that might do for the June number, I wish you submit it (or them) to Mr Morley.

I took a copy of the current number which arrived the day before I left.

The hospitality here is considerable, but I can usually have most of the daytime to myself. I am very sorry to hear such news of your Peter; I trust that your not mentioning him in your second letter means that he is on the way to recovery.

Yours sincerely,
T. S. Eliot.

There seem to be very few dogs in this country.

I have also written to Mirsky (his address is c/o the *Moscow News*) to ask him again to intercede for periodicals, which should come to the *Criterion* office.

TO *Mr Griffith*   Photocopy of TS

18 October 1932   B-11 Eliot House, Cambridge

Dear Mr Griffith,

Thank you very much for your kind letter of the 14th.[1] I am much honoured by the kind invitation of the Authors' Club which you convey. It would give me very great pleasure to be able to accept; but unfortunately, I find that I have so much to do here, even apart from outside engagements in the neighbourhood, that I have had to make up my mind that I cannot expect to get to New York before the Christmas vacation. I am sorry to have to defer the pleasure, as there are many people in New York whom I am anxious to see, as well as many whom I do not yet know and should like to meet; and I am still more sorry because it is impossible for me to be the guest of the Authors' Club on such an important occasion. I hope you will kindly convey my sincere expression of regret to the Council.

Yours very sincerely,
T. S. Eliot

1 – Not found.

20 October 1932   B-11 Eliot House, Cambridge

Dear Miss Manwaring,

Thank you for your two letters,[1] and for the punctual cheque for $125.00 of which, I suppose, this acknowledge[ment] is sufficient.

Of course, the Yorkshire Terriers are only a makeshift; when I retire to the country I intend to breed Blue Bedlingtons.[2] Tell that to Miss Straw.

You write as if you thought I had purposed to break our engagement for the 31st with Mr Tinker. Nothing was further from my thoughts; if I was doubtful about anything, it was about the concert; and it seems that I must take for my Norton lectures what evenings I can get; but I have entered Paderewski in my diary, and pray that the evening may be allowed me. It is very kind of you to take so much trouble.

And I must tell you how keenly I appreciated your hospitality and that of your colleagues. I enjoyed every moment, after the reading was over.[3]

With grateful thanks,
Yours very sincerely,
T. S. Eliot

---

1 – Not preserved.

2 – The Eliots had a Yorkshire terrier called Polly – see photo in John Harding's biography of Hodgson. See too TSE's 'Lines to a Yorkshire Terrier', written 1932. Cf. TSE's Harvard report, as if emulating Hodgson: 'I cannot afford yachting, but I should like to breed bull terriers.'

3 – TSE gave Manwaring a TS of 'Lines to Ralph Hodgson Esqre' inscribed 'With the author's compliments to Miss Elizabeth Manwaring. T. S. Eliot. 18. 10. 32.' (Beare to TSE, 9 Apr. 1955.)

Loucks ('The Exile's Return', 19) reports too that TSE attended a dinner at Wellesley in honour of W. B. Yeats, 'who had come to New York to see the Abbey Theatre Players' performance of his play *The Words Upon the Window Pane* ('Dublin Dramatist' 52) and had begun a lecture tour (Jeffares, 310). Richard Ellmann remarks, in *Eminent Domain: Yeats among Wilde, Joyce, Pound, Eliot and Auden* (1967), on the 'long, languid incompatibility' of Yeats and Eliot: 'Among their various mild collisions none was more defined than the dinner at Wellesley College when Yeats, seated next to Eliot but oblivious of him, conversed with the guest on the other side until late in the meal. He then turned and said, "My friend here and I have been discussing the defects of T. S. Eliot's poetry. What do you think of that poetry?" Eliot held up his place card to excuse himself from the jury' (89). *Pace* Ellmann, that story is surely apocryphal, and is belied by TSE's later comments in his *Paris Review* interview (1959): 'Yeats was always very gracious when one met him and had the art of treating younger writers as if they were his equals and contemporaries. I can't remember any one particular occasion.'

TO *Paul Elmer More*   TS Princeton

26 October 1932   B-11 Eliot House, Cambridge

My dear More,

Many thanks for your letter of the 18th – for the honour you do me in writing about me at all, and second your courtesy in letting me see it.* No, you may be sure that there is nothing I object to in the way of personalities. You are putting a problem – which you find – and not settling one. And I don't know the answer. I dare say it will all seem very simple when people are no longer interested in either my prose or my verse; *capo ha cosa fatta.*[1]

Please give me warning if you are unlikely to be in Princeton at the time of my visit in the spring; so that I may try to see you somehow before you go abroad. It would be very nettling to miss you both here and in London, this year, and I see you very seldom.

> Yours ever sincerely,
> T. S. Eliot

* More sent an article entitled 'Mr Eliot's Return', subsequently published as 'The Cleft Eliot', *The Saturday Review of Literature* 9: 17 (12 Nov. 1932), 233, 235. TSE's comments in the margin are given here as footnotes: 'It is pretty well known by now that T. S. Eliot has come from London to Harvard as Professor of Poetry for the year on the Charles Eliot Norton Foundation. The selection will be generally applauded, though a few may ask cynically what Mr Norton himself, with his kinship to the old preaching Eliots of Massachusetts and his uncompromising notions of arts, would have thought of such an appointment.[2] The significant fact is that the present scion of the family is perhaps the most distinguished man of letters today in the English-speaking world, and that his homecoming will be the occasion of much comment, favorable and unfavorable, and of much searching of our critical principles. For myself I have this personal interest, that his grandfather, a cousin, I believe, of the former President of Harvard, was Chancellor of the little university (at that time little) in St Louis to which I owe my academic allegiance, and that I had the privilege of teaching one of the grandsons in a school conducted under the charter of the University, though that office has not been extended in any form to my pupil's brother.

'As for the distinguished position of Mr Eliot, no one is likely to dispute the fact who is familiar with the English press and knows with what frequency and respect his name occurs. More significant even is his following among

1 – 'A thing done has an end': *Inferno*, XXVIII, 107
2 – 'Not quite clear why he should think that – tho' I dare say he would!' (TSE).

the younger thinking men of England, especially in the universities. Nor is this following confined to his adopted country. I can well remember the furor of enthusiasm roused among the youthful intelligentsia of Princeton a few months ago when I proposed that he should be invited to lecture here. Whatever the more sober part of the world may think of him, his name acts, or certainly has acted, like a spell upon the forward pushing minds of two countries.

'The fact of Mr Eliot's reputation is indisputable. But if one asks the reason for it, the answer is not so quickly at hand. As a critic he stands high. For myself I have been going through the volume of his *Selected Essays* (it is so comprehensive as almost to justify the title "collected"). Undoubtedly the author comes well through this ordeal of continuous reading. There is capable scholarship in these essays, particularly in those that deal with the Elizabethan and Jacobean dramatists; there is a play of alert and penetrating thought, and above all a certain unassumed gravity of judgment, a certain note of authority, not readily defined but instinctively felt. The "metaphysical" poets, from whom Mr Eliot rightly draws his spiritual lineage, will have a new value for any one who has read his analysis of their method. Yet there are sides to his critical work which are not so easily reconciled with his reputation. His apparent blindness to the real greatness of Milton[1] may be explained by the fact that Milton stands at the head of the line of development which to Mr Eliot's disciples, if not to Mr Eliot himself, has acted like a damper on English poetry until the advent of the modern 'metaphysicals'; but that cavalier judgment will not please many whose taste was formed in an older school, nor those younger advocates of a return to Milton of whom Professor Elliott, of Amherst, is a leader. And, on the other hand, the critic's pages are sprinkled with pungent sayings that must shock and sting the complacent enthusiasts of modernism. Who then are the authenticators of his critical renown, the conservatives or the modernists?

'But Mr Eliot is a poet as well as a critic, or, more precisely, a poet primarily; and it might be presumed that the source of his great reputation could be found in his verse rather than in his prose. And this in a sense is true. Yet here too difficulties arise, which perhaps may be best exhibited by relating a bit of personal experience. I am myself a staunch admirer of his Ash Wednesday, though the poem has been pretty harshly judged by certain narrow champions of his earlier style. Well, I have read the poem aloud five or six times to variously composed groups of listeners (and reading aloud is about the final test of a poet), with invariably the same result. Without exception, whether their taste was of the older or the newer model, the auditors have been deeply impressed. For one thing they have felt the sonority of the lines and have been stirred by the cadences of a music which is extremely rare in our free verse.

1 – 'I have considerably changed my mind here, but it is quite right to hold me to what I have said, until I say something else!'

And this is not the melody of merely prettily selected and adroitly adjoined words, independent of their sense, but suggests the profounder harmony – if one could only find it – of an organically constructive genius behind the superficial disarray of the phrases. Yet without exception also the poem – and generally if was read aloud two or three times consecutively to the same group – failed to see any clear meaning.[1] Regularly the comment was the same: This is beautiful, this holds our attention; but we[2] have the vaguest notion, if any notion, of what it is all about. Ordinarily the complaint was made by way of disparagement, whether of the poet's intelligence or the hearer's capacity. But not always. On one occasion the poem selected for reading was "The Hippopotamus", which ends, as will be remembered, with this rather startling comparison:

> He shall be washed as white as snow,
> By all the martyr'd virgins kist,
> While the True Church remains below
> Wrapt in the old miasmal mist.

At the conclusion of the reading I turned to one of the most attentive auditors, an enthusiast to whom Mr Eliot is the sublimest poet since Milton (the concession to Milton being, I suspect, of the lips only), with the query: Now this has the ring of poetry; but what in the name of sense *is* the hippopotamus? "Does it make any difference," cried he, almost jumping out of his chair at the indignity of such a question.[3] And his answer, if it did not elucidate Mr Eliot, explained several things to me in the taste of the younger generation. (I may add that on a later occasion the poet himself, with his sly ironic smile, put me off by intimating that possibly the writer could not – he meant would not – expound my riddle.)[4]

'Now all this points to a curious discrepancy in Mr Eliot's position. I find a good many poetry-lovers of the older tradition simply neglecting him as unintelligible and unimportant; and this indifference I can understand, though I do not share it. A few also of the ultra modern type repudiate him with equal finality, but with an added note of supercilious contempt which is rather characteristic of the fully emancipated mind. Miss Rebecca West, for instance, ridicules his "flustered search for coherence", and a preposterous contributor to the *Boston Transcript* ends a long diatribe with the complaint: "He still is lost in his Waste Land and, whether with malice or not, is still pointing out

---

1 – 'What is the *clear* meaning of Hamlet, or Measure for Measure? I feel that this question of obscurity is still an obscure question. We are on the edge of very deep waters.'
2 – 'Have "we", usually, a very clear notion of what the Vita Nuova means? You are of course entitled to say that our difficulties are chiefly of place & time. And you wouldn't admit "*Un coup de Des*".'
3 – More had written to TSE in an undated letter (? Mar. 1932): 'What in the devil is that Hippopotamus, anyway? I almost came to blows over him the other day with one of your young admirers.'
4 – 'I meant what I said.'

false roads to the oasis to those travelers who seek from him the way" – rather than from Mr Calverton. Other radicals distinguish for their own satisfaction between the poet of the past and the critic of the present. I once asked a young student of very advanced ideas about art and life how he, as an admirer of Mr Eliot, reconciled the *Waste Land* with the programme of classicism and royalism (i.e. the divine right of kings) and Anglo-Catholicism announced in a recent preface. His reply was quick and decisive: "I don't reconcile them; I take the one and leave the other." And to this rebuke I had nothing to say, since it pointed to a cleft in Mr Eliot's career to which I am myself sensitive, though my young friend's order of values is the reverse of my own.

'There it is, the dilemma that confronts those who recognize Mr Eliot's great powers; somehow they must reconcile for themselves what appears to be an inconsequence between the older poet and the newer critic, or must adjust their admiration to what cannot be reconciled. It is not that we have to do with an author who is strong in one phase of his work and weak in another, but that this power is so differently directed here and there. The writer of the *Waste Land* and the other poems of that period appeals to us as[1] one struck to the heart by the confusion and purposelessness and wastefulness of the world about, and as dismayed by the impoverishment of our human emotions and imagination in a life so divested of meaning and so dull of conscience. And to that world his verse will be held up as a ruthlessly faithful mirror. The confusion of life will be reflected in the disorganized flux of images; its lack of clear meaning in the obscurity of language; its defiance of authoritative creeds in a license of metrical form; its dislocated connection with the past in the floating débris of allusion; while its flattened emotions will be reproduced realistically, without comment. If there be any salvation from such a whirligig of chance and time it is only into the peace of utter escape – "*shantih, shantih!*"

And now against this lyric prophet of chaos must be set the critic who will judge the world from the creed of the classicist, the royalist, and the Anglo-Catholic, who will see behind the clouds of illusion the steady decrees of a divine purpose, and who has gone so far at least in that program as to compose a long pamphlet (included in the *Selected Essays*) of *Thoughts after Lambeth*. And what is the young rebel who rejoices in the disillusion[2] of the *Waste Land* to do with the Bishops of the Church assembled in solemn conclave to unravel the purposes of Deity? In one sense it would be easy to reconcile such a volte face of saying simply that the author has undergone a deep conversion; and that explanation is in a way true. But the embarrassing fact remains that somehow the poet contrives to carry on the old shop into

---

1 – 'You should say *as if*. I may not have been aware of anything but my own private grouse.'
2 – 'I believe in only a particular & personal disillusion. A self-styled "disillusioned age" seems to me merely one whose illusion is that it has no illusions – and we are producing plenty. I am sorry to have contributed (unintentionally) to the spread of this illusion.'

the new market. I think, for instance, that a sensitive mind cannot read Ash Wednesday without an uneasy perception of something fundamentally amiss in employing for an experience born of Anglo-Catholic faith a metrical form and a freakishness[1] of punctuation suitable for the presentation of life regarded as without form and void. Such a discord manifestly was felt by those to whom I have read the poem, though one and all they responded to the mere magic of the language in itself. And I am sure it is this same disharmony between subject and mode of expression that drives a friendly critic like Mr McGreevy to complain of being fairly disconcerted by "the distinct falling off in vigour and vividness, in pregnancy, suggestiveness of words, in technical adequacy to the subject, not only from the quality of the *Waste Land* but from that of the much earlier *Prufrock*." I am sure it is not inadequate technique that disconcerts Mr McGreevy, for there is no falling-off in adequacy, but wrong technique, which is quite another thing.

No, it is not the revolution in Mr Eliot's views of life, his conversion if you prefer the word, that troubles his true admirers, but the fact that his change on one side is complicated and disrupted by lack of change on the other side. And here I would like to recall a bit of conversation with him, trusting that I may do so without any breach of confidence or betrayal of the intimacies of friendship (if Mr Eliot will allow me the honour of calling myself a friend). It was in his London home; I was lauding the audacity of the critical conversion announced in the preface to his *Lancelot Andrewes*, then recently published, and I concluded with the query: "And now, when you have completed this heroic programme and have returned, as your intention is, to verse, will your form and style show any signs of this conversion, or will you cling to the old impossible (so I expressed it) manner of the *Waste Land*?" "No," he exclaimed, losing for a moment his armor of placid irony, and shaking a defiant fist in the air, – "No; in that I am absolutely unconverted!"

'I am not at all confident that I have interpreted Mr Eliot correctly, or that, in particular, I have grasped his state of mind when he composed the earlier poems; his is an elusive, though an unmistakable genius. But my perplexity over some unreconciled paradox, at once provocative and baffling, in his attitude towards life and letters has been confirmed by too many witnesses to leave me in doubt of its justification. Mr Eliot, I am sure, would disavow any ambition to pose as a leader of men; but he is a leader, and a very influential leader. Our difficulty is that he seems to be leading us in two directions at once.[2]

---

1 – 'I deny this.'
2 – '?? *What* directions ??'

TO *Ronald Bottrall*

TS Texas

26 October 1932   B-11 Eliot House, Cambridge

Dear Bottrall,

I was glad to get your letter of the 24th.[1] I had heard nothing about your accident in motoring. I sincerely hope that it will leave no permanent results? I am interested in what you tell me about 'Festivals of Fire', and should be very glad to see the revised version and the notes; I have not got the original text with me.

I am sure to be here throughout November and until about the 20th December. Please let me know when you are coming; I should like to get you to have a meal with me.

Yours sincerely,
T. S. Eliot

<Since closing this letter and stamping it I have learned that there are guest rooms in the House. So I can get you a room (given notice) unless you have been offered more desirable quarters.

T. S. E. >[2]

TO *Frank Morley*

TS Berg

26 October 1932   This address is correct . . . . .
                                   B-11 Eliot House, Cambridge

Dear Franck [*sic*],

Thanks for yours of the 13/14ths,[3] but I think it would have been better if I had drunk that Sherry instead of you; I had a bottle of Oloroso but it is gone, and I am making Do on a bottle of Western Reserve until my friend's home-made matures. But if you go on cultivating the Haveth Childers style you will not only be quite unintelligible (you are that already, please write again from Pike's Farm) but will get abscesses in your under & above your teeth (see enc.).[4] As it is, as things are, my brother wants me to have my teeth exrayed & I have rewritten my first lecture (delivery Nov. 4th) four times to make it pellucid. Boston Man Falls from Great Pyramid, Girl in Death Dive from Back Bay Skyscraper, party of young People held up by police in Roxbury had two cases of what they

1–Not found.
2–Added by hand.
3–Not found.
4–Enclosure not found.

said was Beer, and explained that they had been to a wedding; beer taken to police station to be analysed. My sister just recovering from a Parent Education Conference which she organised, and resuming work on her book. David McCord,[1] a friend of G. Blake's who says he knows you also, is very keen on young American Novelist named Edward Walters or Walter Edmunds; do you know anything about him or shall I look into the matter; *Erie Water* is his next, and is to be dramatised as a new *Show Boat*;[2] McC. thinks we ought to interest ourselves.[3] We had a dance in the Hall the other afternoon after the Dartmouth game (Harv. 10 Dart 7). Peters[4] is stalled at Balboa, Panama Canal Zone, on the yacht Pilgrim, if you want him; he has made some interesting remarks about the efficiency of the pumps; if the vessel can be made less like a sieve they are starting for Southampton via the Galapagos and Tahiti. The other members of

1 – David McCord (1897–1997), poet and writer of poetry for children, was Executive Director of the Harvard College Fund. His writings include *Oddly Enough* (poems, 1926); and he later won the National Council of Teachers of English Award for Excellence in Poetry for Children.

2 – Walter Edmunds (1903–98), prize-winning American author of *Erie Water* (1933) and of *Drums Along the Mohawk* (1936), which remained in the bestseller lists for two years and was made into a film (1939) directed by John Ford and starring Henry Fonda and Claudette Colbert.

3 – FVM replied, 25 Nov.: 'One matter not answered in your previous is about David McCord's young novelist friend who has written ERIE WATER. I have a notion that I read a novel of his, a sort of New York State WATER GIPSIES, but if he didn't write that, and there is no particular trouble attached I would be willing to look at ERIE WATER without prejudice and without hopes. David is an amiable lettuce with a heart too tender for words.'

4 – Harold Peters had been TSE's closest friend at Harvard. Samuel E. Morison said of Peters (whom he had known slightly) in a letter to TSE of 27 Aug. 1964: 'he was one of the best amateur sailors on the N.E. coast.' Corresponding in the last months of his life with Morison about the meaning and history of the Dry Salvages (see 'The Dry Salvages and the Thacher Shipwreck', *The American Neptune* 25: 4 [1965], 233–47), TSE was to recall something of the adventure of his youth: 'I cruised with Harold Peters several times up and down that coast and one of the most picturesque spots I remember was Roque Island which is really two islands with a kind of lagoon in between. Harold and I were once storm-bound there for a couple of days and lived chiefly on lobster.' Richard Walworth Hall characterised Peters and TSE, in an obituary notice for TSE, as 'an odd pair': 'It was Peters who chided [Eliot] about his frail physique, which led to his regular attendance at August's Gymnasium, which was in the basement of Apley Hall. He took this work seriously and developed into quite a muscular specimen. It also led to some boxing lessons somewhere in Boston's South End. He took up rowing in a wherry, and finally worked up to a single shell. Peters also introduced him to small-boat cruising and they made many cruises between Marblehead and the Canadian border. On one of these trips, in a nineteen-foot knockabout, before the days of power, they rounded Mt. Desert Rock in a dungeon of fog, a rough sea and a two reef breeze. The log book, the next day, shows a sketch of Tom in the tender in a heavy wind unmooring from an enormous pile mooring at Duck Island. The title of the sketch is "Heroic work by a swab", and beside this title, "Yes, and I never worked harder. T. S. E."'

the Nature Men's Association are flourishing, except that one has had his leg fractured at a horse show and one has married a self-educated lady in Havana. Willie Carver is beginning to recover from his jakey feet and has a grandson; all the other folks in Jonesport Me. are fine. Do you say Miss W.[1] is going to be married; well next time I want a real plain one of an Old Catholic Family, that can be trusted. I suppose that accounts for the fact that my Private & confidential English Church papers I asked her to send me have never turned up. The Dean of the Theological School here is a Congregationalist and has some good brandy; his daughter was at Lady Margaret and is studying psychiatry. I don't know Robert Frost and I haven't seen any elves; there are fairies at Wellesley but they call me Sir. Miss W. doesn't give me much information about the *Criterion*, and I wish you would be a Man and take the matter up. Meanwhile I will try to make as much money as I can, but the whisky is 3.75 a bottle. Send photo of Sukey.

Yrs. etc.
faithfully,
T. S. E.

TO *Louis Zukofsky*[2]   TS Beinecke

28 October 1932   B-11 Eliot House, Cambridge

Dear Mr Zukofsky,

Thank you for your letter of the 25th[3] enclosing a cheque for $3.00, but I am afraid I have not the slightest recollection of the *Objectivist Anthology* or of having given poems to it. Would you be so kind as to

---

1–Pamela Wilberforce.

2–Louis Zukofsky (1904–78), son of Lithuanian Jewish parents, grew up speaking Yiddish and was educated at Columbia University (being taught by Mark Van Doren and John Dewey). In 1927 he sent to EP 'Poem Beginning "The"' – a parody of *TWL* – which EP put out in his review *The Exile*, no. 3 (Spring 1928), 7–27. He worked for the Works Projects Administration, 1934–42, and in the English Department of the Polytechnic Institute of Brooklyn, 1947–66. A leader of the 'Objectivist' group (associates included William Carlos Williams), his works include '*A*' (published in full in 1978); *All: The Collected Short Poems, 1923–1964* (1971); and *Autobiography* (1970). See *Selected Letters of Ezra Pound and Louis Zukofsky*, ed. Barry Ahearn (1987); Mark Scroggins, *The Poem of a Life: A Biography of Louis Zukofsky* (2007). In a later reference to the Guggenheim Memorial Foundation, Jan. 1939, TSE was to reckon Zukofsky (who wished to write part 9 of his long poem '*A*') 'a minor follower of Ezra Pound'.

3–Not found.

remind me of the occasion and tell me for the republication of what poems I gave permission? I am sorry to trouble you.[1]

Yours very truly,
T. S. Eliot

TO *Bonamy Dobrée*

TS Brotherton

S.S. Simon & Jude [28 Oct.] 1932   B-11 Eliot House, Cambridge

Dear Bumbaby,

Here is my full & correct address (tel.: Porter 4117) and I have received your Penn.[2] Well I am That pleased although I haven't had the time to read it yet, but I will, Bonamy, I will. However I envy you the leisure which the perusal, however cursory, of my collected Prose Works implies.[3] I also envy you yr. beehive chair and your prospect over the mellow fields & mists of Norfolk. The New England landscape is very beautiful in autumn, with its beeches and maples in full blaze and clamour over the rugged hills; but the *paysage* is, after all, not humanised. Vermont: a beautiful and austere desert (*gaste lande*) which human beings seem to have scratched at for three hundred years and then given up in despair; except for a few nasty little towns set down on the surface here and there, wild nature has reclaimed its own. The bird life of New England is the most wonderful in creation, except that since my time the countryside has become infested with Starlings, a sordid and squalid immigrant who is driving out the natives.[4] Yes, I think I ought to relimn my portrait of Marlowe[5] with

---

1–'Marina' appeared in An 'Objectivists' Anthology, Edited by Louis Zukofsky (1932), 160–1. Zukofsky had asked for contributions on 24 Aug. 1931: 'In case these are not yet to be seen, may I have your permission to reprint Marina?' TSE's secretary Pamela Wilberforce wrote, 8 Oct., 'Mr T. S. Eliot has asked me to tell you that he has no objection to your reprinting Marina in the Objectivist's Anthology, nor to the terms mentioned in your enclosed card.'
2–Not found. BD had published William Penn: Quaker and Pioneer (1932).
3–See BD, 'A Major Critic' (on TSE's Selected Prose), The Listener, 5 Oct 1932, supp., xi.
4–At a talk given later in Chicago TSE remarked: 'When I returned to give a course of lectures at Harvard in 1932, after seventeen years' absence from America, I looked out of my window and saw a bird which arrested my attention because it looked like a starling. As a boy I had been an eager bird-watcher, and I know most of the resident and migratory birds of New England, and I knew no bird with that peculiar stumpy tail. On enquiry, I found that it was a starling: that bird had arrived and multiplied in that part of America while I wasn't looking' (Critic, Apr.–May 1960). HWE would confirm that TSE 'could identify some 70 birds at Gloucester' (carbon copy of letter to Donald Gallup, 25 Feb. 1937: Houghton).
5–'Notes on the Blank Verse of Christopher Marlowe' (1919): repr. in SE (Sept. 1932) as 'Christopher Marlowe'.

more care, but life is short and art shorter. I am immersed in refined and intellectual society, and Heaven knows what will come of it. I have forebodings I can't keep the pace. Of course the word 'caricature' is only an analogy;[1] one feels with Marlowe that the whole scale of emotion is in a different key (n.b. I am no musician, and dont vouch for this metaphor, but you will take it as meant). Do you ever go to London? I can tell you more accurately about this country after my whirlwind tour of the West at Christmas tide. Meanwhile, keep the faith and drink my health in your best hippocras.[2]

With greatful thanks, and I SHALL read it,[3]

Tom

TO *Sally Cobden-Sanderson*   Copy by Donald Adamson

SS. Simon & Jude [28 Oct.] 1932[4]   B-11 Eliot House, Cambridge

Dear Sally,

It has been upon my Mind to write to you ever since I arrived, but have been Obstructed by Obstacles, such as Social Engagements & the necessity of writing lectures & Participating in the Corporate Life of this College. What I wished to tell You was. That I am very grateful for your facilitation of my voyage & journey. The voyage was eventless & blameless, the cabin I had to Myself just as you Said I would. There was a young lady Said would I walk round the Deck with her as it was Dark & Slippery and she was afraid of Falling over Board. So I said Yes you Keep on the inside there is a Rail along it. So after twenty minutes she said I am going in to Listen to the music You don't give me any feeling of Support she said I don't mean Moral Support she Said. So after that I had no more Trouble. I arrived at Montreal at 8:40 on Sunday evening and the Train left at 8:30 but that was not Your fault; and by that time the Bar was closed You didnt warn me of That. So Mr Cox the Publicity

---

1 – The account of the Sack of Troy in *Dido, Queen of Carthage* – 'a hurried play' – was written in Marlowe's 'newer style', said TSE: 'this style which secures its emphasis by always hesitating on the edge of caricature at the right moment' (123–4).

2 – *Vinum Hippocraticum*: wine mixed with sugar and spices and heated

3 – FVM, who was looking after the *Criterion* in TSE's absence, would write to TSE on 3 Jan. 1933: 'After glancing through Bonamy's book on William Penn, I decided, against his several reminders, not to have it reviewed. It has had plenty of attention, and it is a sweet book and very fox-hunting, but we need the space for such as don't get such attention in other places.'

4 – Postmarked 28 Oct. 1932.

Manager of the Cunard Line came aboard and said you had told him he was to look after me, so with that he helped me get my luggage Through the customs and got my Ticket stamped and so on and then he said Do you mind It would be a great Favour but its for the Montreal Press I have a man with a camera all Ready in the Smoking Room and we should like your photograph, so with that he hustled me into the Smoking room & they got a photograph isnt it terrible (enc.) And so then he said I am the President of the Montreal Authors Club of Course its only a small affair but if you are coming back this way we should like to give you a reception and I said Thank you I Will; and now he has sent me a book of his Poems. So I gave tips just as you Said & it seemed right and the next day I got the bus to the Bonaventure Station and got aboard the train with mingled feelings & said to the Porter here is twentyfive cents don't show me any of your Poems. On the train was a nice old Gentleman in a khaki uniform too small for him & he wanted to see my passport he was very decent about it and extended my permission to stay in United States from six to eight months I expect you wrote to him too only he didnt give me his Poems. Then I had lunch on the Train there was tomato juice and fried pineapples and aspirin is a Beverage if you wanted it but I didnt because as I said the bar Was closed the night before and you hadnt warned me of that. So I got to Boston that evening and they said there is a Customs Officer we remember seeing him about sometimes but the most likely time to find him is tomorrow. (So I went back to the Station the next day and Sure enough there was a nice old Gentleman in Spectacles did you write to him too He said What's in that Box I said Books they are the tools of my trade for I am a professor and I promise to take them out of the country again next spring. Well he said the box looks just plumb ready to drop to Pieces I guess we better not monkey with it that will be five dollars and the Express Company will take your baggage out to Cambridge.

Since then I have met many folks the President of this University did you write to him about me I guess not because he didn't know who I was and said have you ever been in this country before but he didn't say anything about Poetry that was decent of him. I have met some of the Clergy too one of them has some very good brandy. So now my dear Sally I must Close I hope you are well and all the family & Richard able to play the concertina with his Feet now at the Doves remember me to all there including the Colonel. Yours respectfully,

TOM

[Envelope]

O Postman, will you quickly run
To house of *COBDEN-SANDERSON*
Minding in measures metrical
The address: *15, UPPER MALL*;
Or row and tie your little skiff
Hard by the DOVES at *HAMMERSMIFF*,
This house is neatly built of bricks
And stands in <u>*LONDON*</u> at *W.6.*
ENGLAND.

TO *Pamela Wilberforce*   TS Valerie Eliot

31 October 1932   B-11 Eliot House, Cambridge

Dear Miss Wilberforce,

Thank you for your letter of the 21st, which I have this morning. I enclose the Commentary. It is shorter than usual, but I think that these are bigger sheets than I ordinarily use. It proves rather difficult to think of anything to say, at a distance.

I have received the Lear, the *T.L.S.* and five Miscellany pamphlets. But, please where is the file of E.C.U. papers which I asked you to send?

Will you please ask Jones & Evans to send me the *Weekly Manchester Guardian* until May 1st.

I was mistaken about Cournos. He is not providing an émigré chronicle, but wanted to write an article upon émigré literature. So we must make do with the German periodicals.

It is quite right only to allow Miss Lion a short letter. It will probably be a long letter. We do not really want her very cordially as a contributor.[1]

If there is a copy of Augustine's *City of God* in the revolving book-case, I should like to have it. I find that the books which I asked you to send out have gone to Curtis Brown New York, not London; so that you will not be bothered.

---

1 – Wilberforce had written that Aline Lion had been 'roaring in a rather disturbing way. She is frantic at the misrepresentation of her theories by A. L. Morton and is out for his blood. She is quite hysterical about it – "I would do anything in the world for you if I may answer him as he deserves" – and of course there is neither room for nor interest in her to justify a full-dress answer. We have allowed her a short Letter to the Editor, and hope she won't have to be disentangled, like Rowse in the Smyth controversy.'

The *Criterion* list looks very presentable. I note that Rowse has come to life again (or has he?). If the Lowes Dickinson is in the form of a review it should be the first review.[1]

If there is time, I should like a galley of my commentary; but I leave that to your discretion.

I am not surprised to learn that you are engaged, though I do not know your future name.[2] I had meant to speak to you on the subject before I left; I mean, to express the hope that you would not get married before my return (in time for the Derby). However, if you must, I must trust you to train your successor, whoever she may be, thoroughly before you leave, and also train Mr Morley as far as he is trainable. And I hope that I may receive an invitation to your wedding.[3]

Yours sincerely,
T. S. Eliot

1 – Nathaniel Wedd on Lowes Dickinson (Jan. 1933).
2 – 'It may surprise you to know that I am engaged to be married, but it doesn't look as though I shall have to desert the *Criterion* yet.'
3 – Wilberforce's letter in reply (18 Nov.) included this gossip: 'There has been a battle royal with Miss [Aline] Lion who has spent the last twenty years of her life preparing for this affray with Communism (in the person of A. L. Morton), and now that the crisis has arrived – to use her own words – she is not going to fail. The affray is to take the shape of a libel action against A. L. M. in which her cause is to get world-wide publicity, and the forces of Communism are to be routed. I tried to point out to her that there is not one single point on which she could possibly have a case against A. L. M. but she is so convinced of the rightness of her cause and of her plan of action that nothing would move her. Her proposed Letter to the Editor was appallingly weak, rambling and unconvincing, as it obviously would be. So, primed with quotations from your famous letters to Rowse over the Smyth review, I lectured her for three quarters of an hour on the style and methods of English controversy. I must say that she took it very well, coming as it did from a mere chit like me. The result of the lecture was another letter, equally long, which Mr Morley declares to be good. My own judgement was absolutely crushed by the daily receipt of minute postcards from Miss Lion, crossed and re-crossed . . . Anyhow I hope it is all right now.

'N. Wedd's article on Lowes Dickinson is very good, and we are setting it up as an article not as a review . . .

'I wish very much that you might be able to come to my wedding. Matters have been precipitated by my fiancé's future employers who wish him to start work on March 1st. That means that we must be married and settled down before then, and the date of the wedding has now been fixed as January 14th . . . I shall very much dislike leaving 24 Russell Square, especially the *Criterion*. I do so wish that by next September you would find that you could not get on without me, and would urge Faber & Faber to let me come back perhaps as half-time secretary to you. I will do all I can to get the Criterion into a nutshell by the time I leave which will be in about three weeks' time, but I am afraid that there are a great many ins and outs which will have to remain unexplained . . . I am going to tea with your wife next week, and am looking forward very much to seeing her.'

TO *Louis Zukofsky*   TS Beinecke

31 October 1932   B-11 Eliot House, Cambridge

Dear Mr Zukofsky,

Thank you for your letters of the 28th and 29th.[1] While I did not doubt
that the matter was quite in order, it had left a complete gap in my memory.
I return the enclosures with thanks. I am sorry to hear that the books
have done so poorly; but my experience of similar ventures has made me
pessimistic, and I am not surprised. I have no doubt that the copies of
the Anthology reached London; my secretary does not ordinarily forward
books to me here, though she might have mentioned their receipt. I should
be very glad to have a copy, if it is not too much to ask.

I am sorry that I left London without giving a decision on your poems
– or on a great many others less worthy. I was very pressed, and out of
the poetry which took precedence I had selected all we could use in the
next few numbers. What I will do is to ask my secretary to send yours on
to me here, and I will then write to you again. I hope that I may meet you
in New York, but am hardly likely to be coming down before Christmas.
Have you heard anything about the publication of Pound's cantos in this
country?

> Yours sincerely,
> T. S. Eliot

TO *Frank Morley*   Telegram TS Faber

2 November 1932

PERMISSIONS MUST BE GIVEN I SUPPOSE STOP TITLE SWEENEY AGONISTES
FRAGMENTS OF AN ARISTOPHANIC MELODRAMA DONT MAKE IT ARTY
ELIOT[2]

1–Not found.
2–On 1 Nov. 1932 Richard de la Mare posted the text to the printer, Messrs R. MacLehose
(The University Press, Glasgow), describing it roughly as 'T. S. Eliot Book': 'Here is yet
another small book which we think may do for Christmas – this time two fragments by
T. S. Eliot 1) Fragment of a "Prologue" and 2) Fragment of an "Agon".' On 2 Nov. Hamish
MacLehose acknowledged de la Mare's order, referring to the work as 'Two Fragments –
T. S. Eliot'. FVM must have cabled TSE the same day, when he realised that a more suitable
title was urgently needed. On 3 Nov. de la Mare despatched to the printers R. MacLehose
& Co. 'The T. S. Eliot Fragments', giving the title as *Sweeney Agonistes: Fragments of an
Aristophanic Melodrama*.

TO *Henry Eliot* TS Houghton

2 November 1932 B-11 Eliot House, Cambridge

My dear Henry,

I have two postcards as well as previous letters to acknowledge from you.[1] I was distressed to hear of the death of Eliot Wilbur;[2] and I should like to know what his parents are going to do. I hope that they will feel able to stay in Poland until Earle[3] has completed his work; as that would probably be the best thing for both of them. If you can give me their address I will write to them.

I was invited to a dinner at the Authors' Club, certainly, but I am surprised that it should appear in the paper, as I declined. I don't like big dinners, and I haven't the time for them anyway, and I don't see why one should take all that trouble without being paid for it, and I thought it would be folly to accept. I have got to go to a small dinner at the St Botolph Club,[4] and a Class Dinner which I dread in December, and that is enough for the present. I should like very much to come down to stay with you, but I don't think I shall get away from Cambridge till Christmas. I have not settled my plans for the holidays, as they are rather complicated: I shall go to St Louis, and farther West, but I do not know in what order. I may have to come back earlier to spend a week in Baltimore at the end of January. I shall pass through New York at least once then; and shall come down again in February to lecture at Yale and Vassar; and I may be coming several times during the second half year to the New School of Social Studies. In any case I shall expect you here at Thanksgiving, and I hope Theresa will come too, though I cannot put her up; and I should like to know whether you have any intentions for Christmas.

1–Not found.
2–Thomas Lamb Eliot Wilbur (b. 1912), a fourth cousin, died at Pomona College, Claremont, Calif., 15 Oct. 1932.
3–Earl Morse Wilbur (1866–1956), father of Eliot Wilbur.
4–At the St Botolph Club dinner in TSE's honour on 15 Nov., another guest, Robert Frost, considered that TSE was taking himself too seriously and hit upon a prank. '[TSE] offered to read a poem ["The Hippopotamus"] if I would read one. I made him a counter-offer to write one while he was reading his. Then I fussed around with place-cards and a borrowed pencil, pretending an inspiration. When my time came I said I hadn't finished on paper but would try to fake the tail part in talk when I got to it. I did nine four-line stanzas on the subject "My Olympic Record Stride." . . . Several said "Quite a feat." All were so solemn I hadn't the courage to tell them that of course I was lying"' (Lawrance Thompson, *Robert Frost: The Years of Triumph 1915–1938* [1970], 402, 661; Loucks, 'The Exile's Return', 20).

My first lecture falls on this Friday, and I feel very nervous about lecturing.[1] I suppose by the end of the year I shall be at least habituated to it, and I hope more proficient. Meanwhile most of my evenings are engaged, but the days I have mostly to myself. I could easily spend weekends away or fill them up with meals if I wished.

Affectionately your brother,

Tom

I have not seen much of Margaret[2] – only that one occasion; and I am going to supper and to a concert with her on the 20th. I had lunch with Ferris Greenslet and he expressed himself as very well pleased with the success of *The Rumble Murders*, though he felt that the second book did not quite hit the detective audience.

One of my time-wasters is having to write so many business letters; it takes up time that I should like to give partly to writing to friends.

I hope Chardy[3] is recovered.

1–Loucks ('The Exile's Return', 19–20) reports of TSE's first lecture, 'The Relation of Criticism and Poetry', given in the New Lecture Hall at Harvard: 'R. P. Blackmur recalled TSE as "mild, serious, nervous, very tall, very white, smiling uncertainly in round cheeks, with smooth-slick parted hair – displayed but undisplaying – altogether, I think, in an agony which he had to make serene"' (Fraser, 104). Henry Regnery, who found TSE's 'Oxford English' accent 'hard to follow', was surprised to learn that the man was a Midwesterner like himself (*Memoirs of a Dissident Publisher* [1979], 213). See too Joel Roache, *Richard Eberhart: The Progress of an American Poet* (1971), 96: 'In November [Eberhart] sent a long, grandiloquently diffident request for Eliot's attention. Eliot replied, more cryptically, "Don't be so self-conscious about it," and suggested that Eberhart ring him up to arrange a meeting. Apparently, however, Eberhart remained self-conscious, for it was not until February [1933] that he wrote . . . "I called on T. S. Eliot this morning, found him dry and most sympathetic, a true human being." In another letter he was more graphic, remarking that Eliot "had a Renoir on his wall and a cold sore on his lip." Eliot apparently kept himself more or less available; in April, for example, Eberhart told Richards,

> Mr Eliot was kind enough to help me read [Eliot's] Triumphal March recently; it was a wonderful pleasure for me. I had missed the Husserl, the Aristophanic and phallic connotations of the sausage. I read Christ into Caesar, which he said was not intended; but one could have it if one liked.'

2–Margaret Dawes Eliot.
3–Charlotte Stearns Smith Talcott, a cousin (b. 1911).

FROM *Henry Eliot* TO *Abigail Smith*[1]   Photocopy of TS

3 November 1932

[Extract]

I spent four days in Cambridge, living in Tom's rooms where he has two bedchambers and is very comfortable, one window looking out on the quadrangle and the other out onto the river, quite Cantabrigian. Tom is very tired, and I think it is restful for him to be in a place where (to his family at least) he is just 'Tom'. And he is more like the lad of 1910 than he has ever been since he left this country. I don't mean lively, for he is grave enough, but I think he is grateful for personal affection after so much distant veneration. He speaks of going out to St Louis, but I don't know whether that means an engagement or not. I should be exceedingly thrilled if he would lecture at the university and cannot but feel that he would be much affected himself by the situation. I have an idea that one of his main objects is to visit Mother's and Father's graves. He has a very deep feeling about St Louis.

Eliot House, where Tom lives (B-11) is a huge dormitory, the biggest of any of those new big ones on the Charles River, with a luxurious lounge and library for students, and a beautiful dining commons where there is a life size Sargent portrait of C.W.E.[2] To see the elephant head over the doorway, and the Eliot coat of arms (without elephant, however) on chairs, and 'Eliot House' over all entries would, I think (at least it did me) give you the feeling of being in a house full of mirrors and just a trifle embarrassing.[3]

1–Abigail Eliot Smith (1900–84), daughter of Holmes and Rose Eliot Smith, graduated from Wellesley College in 1922, and took her MD at Washington University School of Medicine, 1927. She was Assistant Resident in Medicine, Barnes Hospital, St Louis, 1930–2; Instructor in Medicine, Washington University School of Medicine, 1932–4; Physician to out-patients, Washington University Dispensary, 1936–42; Cardiologist, Out-Patient Department, St Louis County Hospital, 1942; and Assistant Physician, Wellesley College, from 1942.

2–John Singer Sargent's portrait of Charles W. Eliot, President of Harvard College, 1869–1909, dates from 1907.

3–The elephant, which features four times at Eliot House, comes from the Eliot coat of arms.

TO *John Cournos*   Photocopy of TS

3 November 1932   Eliot House, Cambridge, Mass

Dear Cournos,

I have just fixed Friday February 23d as the date for my Yale lecture
– subject to the provision that I do not have to give one of my Norton
lectures on that date.[1] That I shall take [up] with Lowes shortly, but I do
not believe that there will be any difficulty. Is that convenient for you and
Mrs Cournos?[2]

I will notify London about your receipt of the books, so don't bother.

Yours ever,

T. S. Eliot

TO *Frank Morley*   TS Berg

6 November 1932   B-11 Eliot House, Cambridge

Dear Franck [*sic*],

I received your telegram *ainsi concu*:

PUBLISHING TWO JOYCE TALES AS XMAS HALFCROWN BOOK WANT
SAME TIME PRICE PUBLISH FRAGMENTS PROLOGUE AGON TOGETHER
CABLE PERMISSION TITLE STOP NOT TIME SEND PROOFS WOULD
COLLATE CRITERION TEXT MORLEY[3]

to which I replied as follows

MORLEY FABBAF WESTCENT LONDON

PERMISSION MUST BE GIVEN I SUPPOSE STOP TITLE SWEENEY

---

1 – Only portions of TSE's Yale lecture, 'Poets as Letter Writers', survive: 'The desire to
write a letter, to put down what you don't want anybody else to see but the person you are
writing to, but which you do not want to be destroyed, but perhaps hope may be preserved
for complete strangers to read, is ineradicable. We want to confess ourselves in writing to a
few friends, and we do not always want to feel that no one but those friends will ever read
what we have written.'

2 – Cournos and his wife were living at 242 West Elm Street, New Haven, Conn.

3 – FVM wrote again on 8 Nov.: 'To elaborate my cable, it occurred to us that it would be very
helpful to rake in some badly needed cash by producing the Two Fragments of SWEENEY
AGONISTES as a 2/6 item simultaneously with the two SHEM AND SHAUN tales which
will also be sold for 2/6. Paterson was enthusiastic, and we all think the Fragments will sell
and help the Christmas list. So I was glad to get your cable permission, though I anticipated
that it might not be without lugubriosity. Perhaps that was in part due to the effort of re-
writing your inaugural lecture. If you have any copies of the lectures I am in a position
to state that future issues of *The Criterion* might be enlivened by bits.' F&F brought out
Sweeney Agonistes and JJ's *Two Tales of Shem and Shaun* on 1 Dec. 1932.

AGONISTES FRAGMENTS OF AN ARISTOPHANIC MELODRAMA STOP DONT
MAKE IT ARTY ELIOT.

I don't know what you mean by collating texts as there is only one text, that in the *Criterion*, however, collate it if you can and emend it if you will.[1] I should have liked a short preface something like this:

The author has decided to reprint these two fragments, originally published in two numbers of *The Criterion*, only because such a long time has elapsed since the work was designed, that he has become reconciled to the probability that it will never be completed. Had the drama ever been continued, he is sure that the first fragment, which he recognises to be inferior, would have been much altered or even superseded. He reprints it only because it may help to give some notion of the original scheme, which was based upon the account of Aristophanic drama by F. M. Cornford in his *Origins of Attic Comedy*. At the close of the second scene, after the expulsion of three *Intruders* (two ticket-sellers and the tenant of the flat below) Mrs Porter was to have appeared.

The Lectures will not be ready until the autumn season, as the last will not be delivered till the end of March. First one last Friday night; large hall and big crowd, moderate applause; nobody tried to kiss me but Lowes seemed satisfied. I want to know about Chaucer, I mean Dunbar; but am going to see Dr Murdock of the University Press shortly anyway. Have attended a Republican Rally; whisky good but rallying below par. I think I had some other business point to mention but have forgotten so will now Close. Please speak to Miss W. about that file of papers.

Yours,

T. S. E.

TO *Mrs McKenna*   TS Churchill College Cambridge

11 November 1932   B-11 Eliot House, Cambridge

Dear Mrs McKenna,

Thank you very much for sending me your book of Michael, to which I had been looking forward for some months. Had the matter of it left me indifferent I should have taken you at your word and not acknowledged its receipt. I turned first of course to the poems, of which Ralph [?Hodgson]

1–FVM responded to this passage on 25 Nov.: 'I believe you wrote another letter casting aspersions on my use of the word collate. Had I been sending the cable correct [*sc.* collect] you may be sure that I would have been more expensive [*sc.* expansive], but for a single parsimonious expression you cannot beat that word in its context.'

had often spoken to me. He had shown me a copy of the *Rose*. They fully deserve, in my opinion, all that he has said of them, and of the author, in his prefatory note. They are not, certainly, achievement in the usual sense of poetry; and your son very likely would have found other interests in his life with a stronger claim upon him than literature – which besides has less satisfaction to offer to honest men than people usually think. But they have an intense purity and *solitariness* which is most uncommon, both in poetry & in people. It seems to me that to have had such a son might be better than whatever other satisfactions the world has to give.

Yours sincerely,
T. S. Eliot

TO *Gerald Graham*[1]

TS Gerald Graham

14 November 1932   B-11 Eliot House, Cambridge

Dear Graham,

I stupidly forgot to ask you at lunch. I am giving a lecture to the Radcliffe Club at Agassiz House, Radcliffe, tomorrow (Tuesday) evening at 8:15.[2] There are refreshments afterwards. I do not know whether your wife is up to going out in the evening, or, if so, whether she would care for an evening of that kind.[3] But Radcliffe is not very far from where you live, so I am enclosing two guest tickets (which I should not otherwise use, so don't bother about them) on the chance. In case your wife should feel able to go, and cared to go, and was also up to staying for a few minutes afterwards, I hope you will come and find me, as I should like to introduce

1–Gerald S. Graham (1903–88), a graduate of Trinity College, Cambridge, was instructor in History at Harvard, 1930–6. After a period as Assistant Professor of History at Queen's University, Kingston, Ontario, he was a Guggenheim Fellow, 1940–1; and during WW2 he served in the Canadian Army. He was to be Rhodes Professor of Imperial History at King's College, London, 1949–70; Life-Fellow and Vice-President of the Royal Commonwealth Society, and general editor of the Oxford *West African History* series. A world authority on naval power and the British Empire, his many publications include *Sea Power and British North America, 1783–1820: A Study in British Colonial Policy* (1941) and *The Politics of Naval Supremacy* (1967). See further *Perspectives of Empire: Essays presented to Gerald S. Graham*, ed. J. E. Flint and Glyndwyr Williams (1973). TSE was to tell Mary Trevelyan, 15 June 1949, he was 'giving dinner to Professor Graham, the very meritorious Professor of Canadian History at London University whom I knew when he was tutor at Eliot House'.

Graham wrote to EVE, 28 July 1984: 'T. S. E. was a most compassionate man. That is why he "picked me up" in Eliot House in 1932. We were brought close to each other because (unbeknownst to me at the time) we shared a common misery.'

2–TSE addressed the Radcliffe Club on 'The Experience of Poetry'.

3–Graham had married in 1929 (Winifred) Emily Ware (1907–90).

her to two of my sisters who will be there. If you don't go, please don't trouble to thank me.

Sincerely,
T. S. Eliot

TO *Gerald Graham*

TS Gerald Graham

14 November 1932[1]   B-11 Eliot House, Cambridge

Dear Graham,

Thank you for your invitation;[2] but I am engaged for supper, and I was on the point of writing to you anyway to say that I had stupidly forgotten that Wednesday is my At Home to students (I suppose I wanted to forget it). This happens to be a very full week, but I could come Wednesday (tomorrow) either to lunch or could come in after lunch for a little while. Perhaps as it is such short notice it had better be the latter; but please will you ring me up (Porter 4117) and let me know if either is possible?

With apologies,
yours,
T. S. Eliot

TO *Milton Abernethy*[3]

TS House of Books

18 November 1932   B-11 Eliot House, Cambridge

Dear Mr Abernethy,

Thank you for your letter of the 11th. I have only one copy of *Animula* by me, but when I can get the time I will copy it out for you as it is very short. I have been puzzling over the matter for a week, as not by the maddest imagination could one find anything censorable in this poem.[4] I finally asked a friend to exercise his wits upon it; and he pointed out,

---

1 – Probably misdated: ?Tues. 15 November 1932.
2 – Not found.
3 – Milton A. Abernethy (d. 1991), journalist, magazine editor, businessman, stockbroker; proprietor of the Intimate Bookshop, Chapel Hill, N. Carolina; co-editor of *Contempo: A Review of Books and Personalities*, (Chapel Hill, N. Carolina), 1931–4. See Jim Vickers, 'A Week or Three Days in Chapel Hill: Faulkner, *Contempo*, and Their Contemporaries', *North Carolina Literary Review* 1: 1 (1992), 17–29.
4 – On 28 Oct. 1932 the United States Customs Service had officially notified Abernethy's Intimate Bookshop that a single copy of *Animula*, imported from London, England, had been seized as being 'in violation of Section 305 of the Tariff Act of 1930'.

what I should never have thought of for myself, that the trouble must be with the illustration. It is a perfectly irrelevant decorative drawing by Gertrude Hermes, somewhat in the manner of Blake, depicting a naked man with normal genitalia.[1] I suppose that this must be the cause of offense, though I should never have thought of it.

In the circumstances I don't think that the matter can be treated as anything but a joke, but I shall certainly retail it as such to my acquaintance.

Yours sincerely,
T. S. Eliot

TO *Ronald Bottrall*   TS Texas

18 November 1932   B-11 Eliot House, Cambridge

Dear Bottrall,

Thanksgiving Day I must spend among relatives, and the day after is very crowded and I have to lecture in the evening.[2] If you came at almost any other time I could offer you a room; but my brother will be staying with me for that weekend. But if you come then will you dine with me on Saturday or Sunday night, or do you prefer lunch? Please let me know as soon as you can.

Yours sincerely,
T. S. Eliot[3]

1–Gertrude Hermes (1901–83), printmaker, sculptor and wood engraver, studied at the Beckenham School of Art, and from 1921 to 1925 at the Leon Underwood School of Painting and Sculpture, where fellow students included Blair Hughes-Stanton (later her husband), Eileen Agar and Henry Moore. Co-founder in 1925 of the English Wood Engraving Society, she was a member from 1932 of the Society of Wood Engravers. Among her works of architectural decoration were the mosaic floor and curved stone fountain in the foyer of the Shakespeare Memorial Theatre at Stratford-on-Avon. In 1963 she was the first woman to be elected an Associate of the Royal Academy; and she became a Royal Academician in 1971. She made many illustrations – 'decorations', she called them – for books including *Animula* (Oct. 1929).

2–Note from Bottrall not preserved.

3–Bottrall claimed in a letter to the *TLS* (24 Oct. 1980) that he 'became intimate friends' with TSE. 'I stayed with him at Harvard in 1932 and saw him frequently until his second marriage.' See also letter from Bottrall to Hugh Kenner, 4 June 1961 (Texas).

TO *Harry Levin*[1]   TS Houghton

18 November 1932   B-11 Eliot House, Cambridge

Dear Mr Levin,

It is a good many years, I am afraid, since I have even read Skelton's poems, but it might be worth your while to come to see me on the off chance of my being of some use. Will you please ring me up and we will fix an appointment? It is Porter 4117. Tomorrow <Saturday> morning from 9.30 – 10.00 or just before lunch would probably catch me.

Yours sincerely,
T. S. Eliot

TO *John Livingston Lowes*[2]   TS Houghton

18 November 1932   B-11 Eliot House, Cambridge

Dear Professor Lowes,

There are several small matters I have wanted to consult you about.

(1) You will have heard from a young man named Morrison who was at that very pleasant dinner the other evening. When he approached me about a contribution to the Graduates' Magazine, I told him that I had nothing to offer, and that I should be too busy writing lectures all the year

1 – Harry Levin (1912–94) graduated *summa cum laude* from Harvard in 1934. An authority on Renaissance literature, and nineteenth- and twentieth-century American, English and French literature, he rose to become Irving Babbitt Professor of Comparative Literature; author of *James Joyce: A Critical Introduction* (1941). Levin was to recall: 'I had written a senior essay for Theodore Spencer, who showed it to TSE. Though it had taken issue with his views on Metaphysical Poetry, he responded by expressing a willingness to publish it in his distinguished journal . . . Discussing my first article with him over a cup of tea in his rooms on the River Charles, I encountered that helpful benignity which so habitually graced his relations with younger and minor writers' ('Old Possum at Possum House', *T. S. Eliot: Essays from the 'Southern Review'*, ed. James Olney [1988], 154). At a symposium on TSE held at the University of Kent, Canterbury, 8 May 1983, Levin remarked too that Eliot's 'stateliness' at Harvard had been 'mitigated by shyness' (Ackroyd, *T. S. Eliot*, 195). See too Levin, 'T. S. Eliot: A Reminiscence', *The Harvard Advocate* 100: 3–4 (Fall 1966), 34–5. TSE told the Master of Eliot House on 27 June 1950, of Levin: 'I always liked him, and have a keen respect for his intellect, but I had sometimes wondered whether he liked me. It occurred to me at one time, that possibly he was one of those in America (I have never met with such here), who entertained the mistaken belief that I was in some way anti-Semitic. This, of course, is confidential.'

2 – John Livingston Lowes (1867–1945), American scholar of English literature – author of the seminal study of Coleridge's sources, *The Road to Xanadu: A Study in the Ways of the Imagination* (1927) – had taught for some years, 1909–18, at Washington University, St Louis, where he had become known to TSE's family. He later taught at Harvard, 1918–39.

to write anything else; and that I could not 'release' any of my outside lectures until the latter part of the year, because I might wish to use them more than once. He then proposed using one of the Norton Lectures. I told him that so far as I was concerned there was no objection whatever; but that I thought that these Lectures were the property of the University, and that he should consult both yourself, as acting Chairman of the Norton Committee, and the syndics of the University Press.[1]

(2) I have not yet heard whether Craigie[2] has made up his mind about the Dunbar. But there are one or two other publishing matters (including the Marston, in which my interest is quite unselfish) mostly connected with my own firm, which I should like to discuss with Dr Murdock. Could you please arrange for me to meet him at some time? I know that you are more busy than you ought to be, and this might be done without the necessity of your being present.

(3) I should like, if it is now possible, to fix the dates for four Norton lectures in February and March. I have one or two tentative engagements to speak on Fridays, and I should like to be able either to confirm or alter these.

(4) I should like to fix the date of my visit to Baltimore. I do not conceal from you (privately) that it would be to my advantage if these lectures could be arranged for some time during term, as my mercenariness is only limited by prudential considerations of health. 'Mercenariness' means in this context that I am in arrears with only one, but that the most formidable of creditors: the Inland Revenue Commissioners in Somerset House. It would mean that I could extend my lecture tour in the West during the recess. But on the other hand I do not wish to receive the slightest concession beyond what is usual for this and similar foundations; therefore the most to which I wish the President to agree is that I may be absent from Cambridge during the recess until the end of January.

Beyond that, I take it that during the term I may make any engagements which do not disturb my duties here. That is, I shall give four more Norton lectures (perhaps five), lecture on Tuesdays and Thursdays at 9 a.m., be at home to all the world for tea on Wednesdays, put myself at the disposal of students who have any justification at all for wanting conferences (I ought to see each of my 15 class students individually several times during the term, talk to such student bodies as want me, e.g. the Modern Language

1–TSE's 'Apology for the Countess of Pembroke' was to appear in *Harvard Graduates' Magazine* 41: 2 (Dec. 1932), 63–75; repr. *The Use of Poetry and the Use of Criticism* (1933).
2–Sir William A. Craigie, Professor of English, University of Chicago, 1925–36.

Conference) etc. Apart from carrying out such duties competently, I suppose that I may go for the night to New York, Brunswick Maine, or such places.

I hope that Mrs Lowes is making progress.

Sincerely yours,
T. S. Eliot

TO *Christopher Morley & Henry Seidel Canby*[1]

TS Haverford College

18 November 1932   B-11 Eliot House, Cambridge

Dear {Morley,
      {Canby,

I am extremely sorry that I could not come down for the Authors' Club Dinner – there was no warrant at all for the rumour that I was coming. I was very cordially pressed to come, but I simply could not have managed it at the time; and I am sorry that the rumour got about.[2] Now it is possible that I may come down for a couple of days and stay with my brother just before Christmas on my way to St Louis; and in that event I should be glad to know whether there may be the happy conjunction of yourselves, a copious supply of BEER (not the synthetic article made by the Harvard chemists, but Real Beer, whether British, German, Dutch or the original American variety), together with a Limburger cheese and a quiet corner with no women in it.

Yours sincerely, and
Sincerely yours,
T. S. Eliot

1–Christopher Morley (1890–1957), journalist, essayist, poet and novelist – esteemed eldest brother of TSE's Faber colleague FVM – was a founding editor of the *Saturday Review of Literature*, along with Henry Seidel Canby (1878–1961), who also taught at Yale University.
2–The Authors' Club Dinner in New York named WBY as an honorary member (Loucks, 19).

TO *J. Leslie Hotson*[1]   TS Valerie Eliot

22 November 1932   B-11 Eliot House, Cambridge

Dear Hotson,

Thank you very much for your letter of the 20th.[2] I should like very much to give a lecture at Haverford, at that fee; it is a place that I have always wanted to visit, and I should like to be able to tell Morley that I have been there.[3] At some time during the second half year I am going to Bryn Mawr and to Princeton; do you think that a visit to Haverford could be combined with either of those? I shall be rather straitened for times, as I shall have to take a course here on Tuesday & Thursday mornings at 9;

1–Leslie Hotson (1897–1992), Canadian-born Shakespearean researcher and controversialist. Educated at Harvard, he taught at Harvard and at New York University before joining Haverford College in 1931. Works include *Shakespeare versus Shallow* (1931), *Shakespeare's Sonnets Dated* (1949), *The First Night of Twelfth Night* (1954) and *Mr W. H.* (1964).

In a later year, when Hotson applied for a visiting fellowship at King's College, Cambridge, TSE wrote of him on 1 Nov. 1953: 'I . . . have known him for a good many years, and like him. I was of course unaware what qualifications, other than those of scholarly achievement, would be sought for in making the appointment to this Special Fellowship.

'Dr Hotson's eminence in the special field of literary-historical research is indisputable, though his conclusions have sometimes been disputed. Cambridge scholars in English Literature will be well acquainted with the nature of his studies and the results he has obtained; and King's will decide for itself whether this is the sort of work it wishes to advance. Dr Hotson is a man of immense industry; and I have no doubt that this appointment would be highly advantageous for labours that he pursues with the greatest zeal; nor do I doubt that the results of his investigations, during the tenure of the Fellowship, would be as remarkable as his previous discoveries.

'Dr Hotson's character is above reproach: he is a man of great integrity. I believe that the reason for his resignation from a Professorship at Haverford College, Pennsylvania, during the war, was due to a conflict between his outspoken pro-British sympathies and the views of the President (at that time) of the College, who was a somewhat authoritarian Isolationist. This is what I have been told. He has spent much time in England, for as long as two years at a stretch, carrying on his research in the Record Office and elsewhere. He is a member, I believe, of the Unitarian branch of the Society of Friends in America, and a member of the Athenaeum.

'Dr Hotson is also a person of considerable charm: talkative, a good raconteur and excellent mimic, and [has] some proficiency on several minor musical instruments. His wife [Mary] is a member of the well-known and very numerous Boston family of Peabody, and is herself a person of great activity . . .

'I can only add, that I feel sure that, within his own province and according to the standards of that province of scholarship, he would in the course of his tenure produce a really important piece of work.'

2–Not found.

3–Frank Morley had been a student at Haverford College, Pennsylvania (where his father, also Frank, was a distinguished professor of mathematics). Hotson taught at Haverford, 1931–42.

which means practically that I have only from Thursday over the week end for lectures afield. But if I could arrange Haverford & Bryn Mawr for Thursday & Friday evenings (Would I have time to get down for an evening lecture, after 10 a.m. on Thursday?) I should very much like to have a look at Philadelphia over the weekend.

Please give my kindest regards to Mary; I look forward to seeing both of you. I will not accept the responsibility of having deprived Harvard of you.

Yours cordially,
T. S. Eliot

TO *Geoffrey Faber*

TS Valerie Eliot

24 November 1932   B-11 Eliot House, Cambridge
Thanksgiving Day, in fact

Dear Geoffrey,

Many thanks for your letter of the 9th, which cheered me.[1] Not that I feel as dismal as I did when I first wrote to you: I was quite aware when I wrote that it was a passing mood, but putting it down on paper was a help. The time passes very quickly, and I am beginning already to wonder what my sensations and thoughts will be when the time comes to return. Very mixed, no doubt: relief in leaving, pleasure in getting back to London, and anxiety as to how to deal with my private affairs when I get there. Apparently, V. has settled down with this Mrs Nelson as a companion, who seems to be a good person – there was an Interim in which an old friend from here was staying with her, but the friend could stand it only for a fortnight. I am wondering whether Mrs N. might not suitably become a permanency, as her terms are very modest indeed; it would at least release me for visits and evening engagements, and might possibly be a complete substitute for me. V. seems to be hopelessly infantile, but so far as her last letters indicate, in a well-behaving mood.

I manage to keep my days fairly free, and they are consumed in writing lectures. In this year I shall probably have typed out more pages than in any normal five years at least; not only the 8 Norton lectures, but other lectures for delivery elsewhere. The Norton lectures, by the way, should be ready for the autumn list. I am lunching with Dr Murdock, of the University Press, next week. I should be glad if you would let me

1 – Not found.

know officially whether the firm will prefer to set it up in England or take sheets; in any case I want publication to be simultaneous, and one edition (if you do not take sheets) could be set up from the galleys of the other. I shall also take up with him the question of the Languages series (I have collected the proof from New York); I am still waiting to hear from you or Frank whether Craigie is taking the Dunbar or not. Lowes is very keen about it, but says he is not the specialist in that literature, and some specialist would have to read it carefully.

My first lecture was well attended – some hundreds I suppose – people sitting on the floor in the aisles and on the steps of the platform; apparently a very mixed audience, including Fashion, Professors & wives, under-graduates and undergraduettes. I do not expect so many tomorrow. There is some extremely pleasant society here and in Boston, with an intelligence and even sometimes learned interest in things of the mind; but one is very conscious that the pleasant society is always in an oasis, and without is the desert. I eat in Hall here, except when I dine out, which is nearly every evening – or I go to my sister Mrs Sheffield, who is the most congenial person here, and has all the Brains of the family.[1] I have fallen in with a delightful old Mrs Wolcott, a daughter of the historian Prescott, who is very intelligent and charming.[2] The 'tutors' with whom I eat are partly Cambridge men (Trinity) a mixture of English, American and Canadian; with a sprinkling of Oxford – Rhodes scholars, and a rather sad creature from Magdalen named Terence O'Brien. As the 'Master', Merriman, was at Balliol the picture is complete. You must imagine however a Hall with waitresses, with hours for meals (dinner is from 5.30, and you have to get in before 7 to be fed) and a dais but no high table on it. The tutors eat at a humble table down the hall, and even their eating together is considered undemocratic. But everything is very comfortable; my rooms overlook the river; and the house library, which is practically adjacent to my rooms, is comfortable and well stocked, and I have so far used it exclusively. There are arm chairs, and you can smoke; it compares favourably with the Merton Library. Only, it is, like every other room and building, torridly overheated.

I don't know that the election means very much. I think that most folk voted for Roosevelt because he seemed more positively Wet than Hoover;

1 – See FVM to Herbert Read, 23 June 1965, apropos Ada: 'I believe she felt in somewhat a motherly way that [TSE] was doomed by Dante . . .' (Berg).
2 – Edith Wolcott (1853–1934) was the widow of Roger Wolcott (1847–1900), a governor of Massachusetts. TSE was, however, mistaken about her ancestry: her father was William Gardiner Prescott (1826–1895), not the historian William H. Prescott (1796–1859).

but perhaps still more because they felt that Hoover had not done much to alleviate misery, and they might as well have a change.[1] The vote was distinctly a 'depression' vote; when times are very bad, people are always ready for a change of government. One could see no interesting and important differences of principle between the two parties. There *might* be a change of foreign policy, but there is no reason to assume that there will be. The people, even quite educated individuals, know nothing about foreign affairs, still assume that there is something 'normal' about prosperity – in America, at least, and refuse to admit that there are any new and permanent problems which did not exist fifty years ago. They seem conservative to a degree unknown in England, which, in contrast, appears a country inclined to rash experimentation. I think that one of the bad effects of prohibition is that it has prevented the mass of people from applying their minds to the real political issues and it is perhaps the only bad effect that will be removed when prohibition goes. The habits acquired during this period will not easily disappear, for they are social habits; and the cocktail (which means from two up, apiece) is not likely to disappear. Week before last I went to a cocktail party, an 'after church cocktail party', at the house of a Professor here, on a Sunday morning.[2] Whether any but myself had been to church I did not discover, but they all got there before I did; and a fashionable young woman entertained us with an account of a conversation she had had with a couple of gunmen and their 'molls' in a speakeasy.

This letter has gone on long enough, and I have my eye on my watch to see that I get in to Hall before the doors shut at 7; so with love to the

1 – In the Presidential Election held on Tues. 8 Nov. 1932 – the 'Depression Election', with national unemployment running at over 20 per cent – Franklin D. Roosevelt (1882–1945), Democratic Governor of New York, won an overwhelming majority of both popular vote and Electoral College with his promise of a 'New Deal'. Herbert Hoover (1874–1964) was the 31st President.

2 – Kenneth Paul Kramer, *Redeeming Time: T. S. Eliot's 'Four Quartets'* (2007), notes (10): 'Confirming the depths of Eliot's spiritual life, Wallace Fowlie [*Journal of Rehearsals* (1977), 138] provides a rare and privileged eye-witness account of Eliot's devotional practice. He writes that in the early 1930s, when Eliot was the Charles Eliot Norton lecturer at Harvard University, he often attended Mass at the Episcopal church of St John the Evangelist on Beacon Hill in Boston. Eliot was drawn there in part because the church was served by the Cowley Fathers, whose monastery was in Cambridge. During his time at Harvard, Eliot was a daily communicant at the monastery chapel. At one Mass, attended by Eliot and only two others (including Fowlie), after Eliot received the Eucharist and returned to his place, he seemed to fall "flat on his face in the aisle, with his arms stretched out." But Fowlie adds, "it was obvious at a glance he had not fallen." Indeed, when Fowlie helped Eliot to his feet, almost no physical effort was required. Fowlie continues, "I realized that Eliot had just undergone a mystical experience."'

children – and tell Enid that I shall write to her to thank her for her letter,
I remain

Yours,

T. S. E.

P.T.O.

I expect that you know a *great* deal more about the Oxford Movement,
and theology in general, than I do, now. No! my dear Geoffrey, I did
not expect these studies to alter your feelings about theological matters;
nevertheless, I look forward with the greatest interest to the result.[1]

I was interested to hear of the All Souls' elections, and am glad that Berlin
is among them. I hope to meet him when I get back. Richard Wilberforce
I met once at your house; Reilly I never heard of.[2] Which reminds me
that if it comes to the point of electing a successor to Miss Wilberforce[3]
before I return – may I be permitted to remark that the first qualification
from my point of view is discretion & incuriosity; you know that the
more important part of my private correspondence passes through Russell
Square, and some is very private. Miss W. has been excellent. I am sorry
that her fiancé is penniless – I seem to have heard his name somewhere
– perhaps he offered a contribution at some time – but I suppose that
something will be found to make marriage possible.

1–GCF dedicated *Oxford Apostles: A Character Study in the Oxford Movement* (F&F,
1933) to TSE 'with affection and respect'.

2–On 2 Nov. 1932 the Governing Body of All Souls College, Oxford, elected to the
Fellowship: Isaiah Berlin (1909–97), author, philosopher, founding President of Wolfson
College, Oxford; Richard Wilberforce (1907–2003), who was made a life peer in 1964
and served as Lord of Appeal in Ordinary in the House of Lords, 1964–82; Patrick Reilly
(1909–99), diplomat: he was to be Ambassador to the Soviet Union and to France, knighted
in 1957.

3–Pamela Wilberforce left F&F's employ in the second week of Dec. 1932. When VHE
wrote to FVM (letter not found), evidently to say she would be happy to help out, FVM
replied to her, 24 Nov.: 'Many thanks indeed for your letter about "The Criterion". It is a
very helpful suggestion, and we won't hesitate to let you know if occasion arises. So far I
have found that T. S. E. has planned everything with such care that there has been nothing
for me to do. We are, of course, sorry to lose Miss Wilberforce, but she will not go before she
has instructed her successor in the routine work.' He added: 'I am sending complimentary
advance copies, for your own interest, of SWEENEY AGONISTES and TWO TALES OF
SHEM AND SHAUN. I have sent T. S. E. his copies to Harvard. We plan to publish these
on December 1st.'

TO *Pamela Wilberforce*

TS Valerie Eliot

24 November 1932   B-11 Eliot House, Cambridge

Dear Miss Wilberforce,

I owe you an apology, first for cabling, as the documents arrived of course the following morning, and then for not writing immediately on receipt to tell you so. It is sometimes difficult to remember how long it takes, though I ought to know as well as anyone, and I had not made a carbon of the letter in which I had asked for them.

I presume that the November number will be off your hands by the time you receive this letter. I am sorry that I was not in time to have a galley of my commentary, as I should like to have improved what I think was a very feeble composition. The main point of this letter is to remind you that from about Christmas Day – or possibly a day or two beforehand, I shall be away from Cambridge, in the Far West, Middle West, and Baltimore, until the end of January; so that any communications from Russell Square during that period had best be sent to my sister Mrs Sheffield at 31 Madison Street.

Will you please have one copy of my Essays sent to me here. I have received two proof copies of Dunbar,[1] and expect to be seeing Dr Murdock, of the Harvard University Press, next week about the Languages Series; I am still awaiting word whether the Dunbar is free or not.

> With all best wishes,
> Yours sincerely,
> T. S. Eliot

TO *Ronald Bottrall*

TS Texas

26 November 1932   B-11 Eliot House, Cambridge

Dear Bottrall,

I expect to be back by 6:30 and I understand that we are to dine at 6:45 with the Master of Leverett House. Your bedroom is the one facing the river. There is some gin in the sitting room cupboard. If the room is too cool for you turn the radiator tap.

> T. S. E.

1–W. Mackay Mackenzie, *The Poems of William Dunbar* (F&F, 1932). TSE later wrote of Dunbar that he seemed to him 'a much bigger poet than Burns' (letter to Gerald Barry, Director-General, Festival of Britain 1951, 13 Feb. 1951).

Monday 29 November 1932   68 Clarence Gate Gardens

My dear Mary,

This is for a sample of my typewriting, and to tell you how very happy it has made me that I am to be your Secretary. I may really consider myself your Secretary from now on, may I not?

One point that I omitted to mention is that perhaps you would prefer to *dictate* your articles, and so not have to write them out in longhand at all? In that case I can take them down for you straight on to the typewriter, as I have done for Tom. Only, of course, it would mean that I should have to come to your house, or you to my flat.

The whole thing has made me so very happy, and I am going to write and tell Tom.

Do hurry up with your notes for this next article, I am impatient to begin.

I will ring you up about coming to tea with me on either Monday, Tuesday, or Wednesday of next week, and I do look forward to your coming.

With very much love, and many *thanks*.

Yours ever,
Vivienne Haigh Eliot

TO *W. R. Castle*[1]   Photocopy of TS

29 November 1932   B-11 Eliot House, Cambridge

Dear Bill,

That is very kind of you, and if I possibly can get over to Washington while in Baltimore I shall do so.[2] I mean to come to Baltimore during the last week of January; I shall probably have come straight from the West; and the only uncertainty is whether I shall have the time either before or

1–William R. Castle, Jr (1878–1963) graduated from Harvard College in 1900 and stayed on as instructor in English: he was Assistant Dean in charge of Freshmen, 1904–13 – he met TSE at that time – and edited the *Harvard Graduates' Magazine*, 1915–17. He was US Ambassador to Japan for a while in 1930; Assistant Secretary of State, 1927–30; Under Secretary of State, 17 Dec. 1931–5 Mar. 1933. He was elected to the American Academy of Arts and Sciences, 1932. See too William R. Castle, '00, *Fifty Years* (Printed Privately for the Fox Club, 1949) – which includes the first printing of TSE's 'Ballade of the Fox Dinner' (15 May 1909), 12–13.
2–Castle's letter not found.

after, as I have to start a Course here at the beginning of February. Your invitation is peculiarly inviting; I like strong waters but not in the form of the cocktail; and I like my Tea. I will let you know in January, and if when and if the time comes, it is not convenient, you will have the opportunity to say so; but I hope that I may come and also meet Mrs Castle.

With many thanks,
Yours ever sincerely,
T. S. Eliot

TO *Gilbert Seldes* TS Timothy and Marian Seldes

29 November 1932 B-11 Eliot House, Cambridge

My dear Seldes,

I did receive your first letter as well as your second;[1] but I have been infernally busy; this is my twentyfirst letter to-day, and I have half a dozen more that I must write. I shall look forward to seeing you in New York. The rumour that I was to come early in this month was false; and I shall now be there, for the first time, during or rather at some time during the Christmas holidays.

I really cannot see why my being in America should affect the question of your Chronicle at all. In the first place, such a chronicle requires more background than I can acquire in the time; secondly I am so immersed in the academic world at present and for most of my stay, that I shall still be very one-sided when I leave; thirdly I am much too busy with this sort of work; and finally I think you would do it better than I. So I have written to Miss Wilberforce to ask what number can take it best; I hope the March.

Looking forward to seeing you again,

Yours sincerely,
T. S. Eliot

1 – Letters not found.

FROM *Vivien Eliot* TO *Mary Hutchinson*   MS Texas

Wednesday 30 November 1932   68 Clarence Gate Gardens

My dear Mary

I have now heard from Mrs De La Mare that they can come to dinner here on Wednesday *14th* at 7.30. So I *do* hope that will suit you & Jack? You remember I mentioned it to you on Monday, & you said you would be free that night.

May I expect you both? Do say yes.

In the meanwhile, Mary dear, will you come to tea on Monday 5th & meet Mrs James Stephens[1] – or on Thursday or Friday (8th or 9th)? Do let me know.

Are you getting on with *the article?* I am so *looking forward* to *beginning work.*

> Yours ever,
> Vivienne Haigh Eliot

TO *Ford Madox Ford*   TS Cornell

1 December 1932[2]   B-11 Eliot House, Cambridge

My dear Ford,

I don't think that the publication of Ezra's *Cantos* in this country, needs any word from me, or from anybody else: it is rather an impertinence. There was a time when it did not seem unfitting for me to write a pamphlet, *Ezra Pound, his Poetry and Metric.*[3] But Ezra was then known to only a few; and I was so completely unknown that it seemed more ~~fitting~~ decent that the pamphlet should appear anonymously. I owe too much to Ezra to be a critic (I wish that the manuscript of *The Waste Land,* with Ezra's criticisms and still more important his excisions (Thank God he reduced a mess of some 800 lines to about half its size) might some day be exhumed (John Quinn had it) as a masterpiece of critical literature) (what can you do about these brackets?) I have preached the *Cantos* for some years now to young practitioners, as well as tried to tell them what I owed to Pound

---

1 – James Stephens (?1880–1950), Irish novelist and poet, had married his mistress, Millicent Josephine Gardiner Kavanagh – called 'Cynthia' – in 1919 (she had recently been widowed).

2 – This letter was to be reproduced, with small changes, in *The Cantos of Ezra Pound: Some Testimonies by Ernest Hemingway, Ford Madox Ford, T. S. Eliot, Hugh Walpole, Archibald MacLeish, James Joyce and Others* (1933), 16–17.

3 – *Ezra Pound: His Metric and Poetry* (1917); repr. *To Criticise the Critic* (1965).

in London, Paris, ~~on the ramparts of~~ Excideuil and Rapallo (it shall not all be told). One result is that (I blame no one) my copy of the *Cantos* has disappeared; and I want them to be republished so that I may have another copy. I find that with the exception of ~~Moberley~~ *Mauberley* there is no other contemporary (with disrespect to none (for I include myself)) whom I ever want to re-read for *Pleasure*.

Ever yours,
T. S. Eliot

TO *Theodore Spencer* TS Harvard Archives

1 December 1932[1]

Two selections suitable for a Christmas (or Yuletide) Reading:

> Stanzo 124.
> 'Twas Christmas on the Spanish Main!
> The wind it up and blew hard;
> The vessel gave an Awful lurch
> And heeled right down to leeward.
> The Chaplain was so very scared
> His breeches he manured,
> And Columbo slid along the deck
> And raped the smoke-room steward.

> Stanzo 34.
> 'Twas Christmas at the Spanish Court!
> They dined on roast flamingo.
> Columbo gave an Awful belch
> That broke a stained-glass window.
> The King at that was so perturbed
> He nearly was struck dumb (Oh!)
> But the Queen exclaimed, with perfect tact,
> 'You son of a bitch, Columbo!'

1 – In envelope, unmailed.

TO *Wilbur A. Nelson*   TS Alderman Library Virginia

3 December 1932   B-11 Eliot House, Cambridge

Dear Professor Nelson,

I have been considering your and Acting President Newcomb's very tempting invitation to deliver three lectures on the Barbour-Page [*sic*] foundation.[1] The University of Virginia is one of those in America which I should most like to visit. The only time possible for me would be during the week of May 8th–13th. Is that a feasible time or not?

I may mention that I shall be leaving for the West directly after Christmas; and any message to me after that should be direct to me care of A. D. Sheffield, 31 Madison Street, Cambridge, and marked 'urgent'.

I must apologise for my delay in answering.

Yours very sincerely,
T. S. Eliot

TO *John Livingston Lowes*   TS Houghton

5 December 1932   B-11 Eliot House, Cambridge

Dear Professor Lowes,

I am sorry to be such a nuisance. But I have three questions to put.

(1) I have been discussing the arrangement for my Turnbull lectures with Lovejoy.[2] Would it be permissible to fix them for Jan. 30 (Monday),

---

1–Wilbur A. Nelson (1889–1969), Professor in the School of Geology, 1925–59; Chairman, Committee on Public Occasions, Virginia, wrote: 'On behalf of the University of Virginia, I have the honor to invite you to deliver a series of lectures sometime during the spring of 1933 under the Page-Barbour Foundation. This Foundation was established in 1907 by the late Mrs Thomas Nelson Page (née Barbour) and the late Honorable Thomas Nelson Page, with a view to bringing to the University of Virginia eminent men from various fields of endeavor. I am enclosing a list of the former lecturers on this Foundation, with the titles of their lectures.

'The conditions of the Foundation are that the lectures, at least three in number, shall be prepared for the occasion, and that after being delivered at the University, they become the property of the University, the University having them published in the Page-Barbour series. The honorarium for these lectures is five hundred dollars . . .

'Acting President Newcomb and the members of my committee heartily join me in expressing the hope that you will find yourself able to accept this invitation.'

John Lloyd Newcomb (1881–1954), Dean of Engineering, was second president of the University of Virginia, 1931–47.

2–Arthur O. Lovejoy (1873–1962), historian of ideas, philosopher of science – author of *The Great Chain of Being: A Study in the History of an Idea* (1936) – was Professor of Philosophy at Johns Hopkins University, 1910–38. In 1940 he founded the *Journal of the History of Ideas*.

February 1st and February 3d (Friday) returning to Cambridge on Saturday? This is a week later than I had intended, but it would give me more time to get about the country, and I could fill two or three more engagements which otherwise I must drop. My English 26[1] opens on Tuesday the 7th, and the first Norton on the 17th.

Otherwise, I shall have the embarrassing duty of withdrawing from engagements in St Paul and Buffalo.

(2) I have learned that the Dunbar is free, and have lunched with Mr Murdock and given him a copy, with a copy of another book in which I should like to interest the Press. I did not feel, candidly, that matters would proceed very rapidly if left only in Mr Murdock's hands: he could hardly be expected to be a Dunbar enthusiast. I have another Dunbar copy: may I hand it to you to examine, or to pass on to whoever else (if there is anyone else) might be regarded as an expert; or if not may I have the name of someone to show it to?

(3) Delighted as I am that you will not be present to hear me play the fool about Coleridge, I should like to ask you to read the lecture – *afterwards*. And criticise it as brutally as possible. May I submit a copy to you after Friday?

Yours sincerely,
T. S. Eliot

TO *Horace Gregory*

TS Syracuse University Library

6 December 1932 — B-11 Eliot House, Cambridge

Dear Mr Gregory,

I can manage the evening of Dec. 21st (Wednesday) if that suits you[2] – if it does, call here at 6.30 and dine with me.

Can you tell me anything about Dahlberg?[3] He wired me several days before Thanksgiving; I had to wait a day to reply, in order to be sure of

---

1 – TSE's notes for 'English 26: Literature from 1890 to the Present Day' are at Houghton.
2 – Gregory's letter not retained.
3 – Edward Dahlberg (1900–77), novelist and essayist, was born in Boston to a single mother, and spent most of his teenage years in the Jewish Orphan Asylum in Cleveland. He went on to the University of California at Berkeley and to Columbia University. In the late 1920s he lived in Paris and in London, where his autobiographical novel *Bottom Dogs* (1930) was published with an introduction by D. H. Lawrence. After visiting Germany in 1933, he was for a while a member of the Communist Party, and in later years was a writer and college teacher. Other works include *Do These Bones Live* (essays, 1941) and *The Confessions of Edward Dahlberg* (1971).

my plans; and my wire to the address he gave in his wire was returned to me with the statement that the addressee had moved.

Yours sincerely,

T. S. Eliot

TO *Henry Eliot*

TS Houghton

6 December 1932   B-11 Eliot House, Cambridge

My dear Henry,

Thank you for your letter of the 4th, enclosing copy of the Norton pedigree.[1] I had referred in my lecture to his French origin, so I wanted to verify that.

Thank you also for the dress coat. I wore it at my last lecture out of sentiment, but I shall not keep it unless you will let me pay you the $25.00 as well as swapping coats. And you are not to pay it back to me in the form of a Christmas present either; I shall come on the 23d and stop over Christmas with you on condition that there are no presents exchanged. But with Theresa's advice, I must get a wedding present for Chardy when I get to New York.[2]

I think I could easily lecture to N.Y. University on one of the occasions when I come down to lecture at the New School. On one occasion I am to address Columbia, I believe. Will you tell him?

If I find that it seems *uncomfortable* for you to have me, I shall go to some hotel nearby, if there is one, and take meals with you. The only people I must try to see, if they are about, are Morley and Canby, and Harcourt & Brace.

Affectionately,

Tom

1–Not found.

2–Charlotte ('Chardy') Stearns Smith (b. 1911) had married Agnew Talcott on 30 Oct. 1931.

TO *Mary James Power*[1]   TS[2]

6 December 1932   B-11 Eliot House, Cambridge

Dear Sister,

In reply to your letter of December 1st,[3] perhaps the simplest account that I can give is to say that I was brought up as a Unitarian of the New England variety; that for many years I was without any definite religious faith, or without any at all; that in 1927 I was baptised and confirmed into the Church of England; and that I am associated with what is called the Catholic movement in that Church, as represented by Viscount Halifax and the English Church Union. I accordingly believe in the Creeds, the invocation of the Blessed Virgin and the Saints, the Sacrament of Penance etc.

Yours faithfully,
T. S. Eliot

TO *Jack Holmes Smith*[4]   Photocopy of TS

11 December 1932   B-11 Eliot House, Cambridge

Dear Uncle Jac,

Thank you very much for your wire and letter of the 7th.[5] I must say that I very warmly appreciate the kindness and patience of yourself and the Chancellor in this matter. It has proved a much more difficult jigsaw puzzle than I anticipated to fit in my various intentions and engagements, though I believe that by the end of the year I shall be qualified to act as a lecture agent for anyone. But it must have been very trying to put up with my delays and also with my stupidity about dates. If I had re-read the Chancellor's letter before wiring I should have spared you some trouble.

I will give then a lecture on the 17th January; if a rather more scholarly than popular subject is required I propose one on 'The Study of Shakespeare Criticism'.

---

1 – School Sisters of Notre Dame, Baltimore.
2 – This typescript letter – addressed to 'Sister Mary James, Couvent de Notre Dame, Fellaway East, Malden, Mass.' – was published in Sister Mary James Power, SSND, *Poets at Prayer* (1938), 124–6.
3 – Letter not found.
4 – Jack Holmes Smith (1862–1936), TSE's uncle-in-law.
5 – Not found.

As for anything in the nature of a reception, I think that I should leave that to yourself and the University authorities to arrange whatever suits best. I have to lecture in St Paul on the evening of the 19th, so I shall try to arrive in St Louis on the 15th. All else that I want to do is to visit Bellefontaine first,[1] and to have half a day or so just to wander about the city by myself. I look forward with great pleasure to staying with you and Aunt Rose.[2]

Yours always cordially,

Tom

I am writing to the Chancellor tomorrow.

TO *Lincoln Kirstein*[3]

TS Beinecke

16 December 1932   B-11 Eliot House, Cambridge

My dear Kirstein,

Thank you for your letter of the 14th.[4] I really did not expect to be paid for 'Difficulties' at all, and the cheque was a pleasant surprise.[5] As for the Norton lectures, I have told people that I do not feel that I ought to sell them separately anywhere; they are the property of the University under the terms of the Foundation. (One appears in the Graduates Magazine,

---

1–Many of his forebears, including father and mother, were buried in Bellefontaine Cemetery.

2–Rose Greenleaf Eliot (1862–1936). The schedule for TSE's visit had him arriving on Sun. 15 Jan. 1933, at 5440 Maple Avenue, followed by supper with the family; the following day, 16 Jan., he was to give a lecture on 'The Study of Shakespeare Criticism' in the Graham Memorial Chapel, Washington University, at 4 p.m., and go on to a University Reception in the Women's Building at 5 p.m. On Tues. 17 Jan. he was to have lunch with Mrs Greenfield Sender at 1 p.m.; take tea with the St Louis Women's Club between 4 and 5 p.m., and then attend dinner with Dr Throop at the Chancellor's Residence, 7 p.m.

3–Lincoln Kirstein (1907–96), writer, impresario, connoisseur of art, was born into a wealthy and cultivated Jewish family (his father was chief executive of the Boston department store Filene's). At Harvard he set up, with a contemporary, Varian Fry, the periodical *Hound & Horn: A Harvard Miscellany* – specifically modelling it on *C.* – which ran from 1927 until 1934. Smitten by what he styled 'balletptomaine', he launched in 1933, with his friend M. M. Warburg, the School of American Ballet, and then the American Ballet, which became the resident company of the Metropolitan Opera in New York. In 1946, he founded, with George Balanchine, the Ballet Society, later the New York City Ballet, of which he was General Director, 1946–89. In the 1960s he commissioned and helped to fund the New York State Theater building at the Lincoln Center. In 1935 he published *Dance: A Short History of Classic Theatrical Dancing*. See Martin Duberman, *The Worlds of Lincoln Kirstein* (2007).

4–Not found.

5–TSE, 'Difficulties of a Statesman', *Hound & Horn* 6: 1 (Oct./Dec. 1932), 17–19.

but I don't get paid for that, and I consulted Lowes about it first.)[1] I am sorry.

I shall be away from Christmas until February 4th. I wish that we might meet more often, and I hope that there will be opportunities in the New Year.

> Yours very sincerely,
> T. S. Eliot

TO *Eva Le Gallienne* Photocopy of TS

16 December 1932 B11-Eliot House, Cambridge

Dear Miss Le Gallienne,

I had hoped to see 'Dear Jane' on my way through New York directly after Christmas, but I learn from Miss Hinkley that it is not to be played that week.[2] Is it too much to ask you to let me know, when the programmes are settled, on what dates it will be played about the end of January and the beginning of February? And I do hope that when I do see it I may see you afterwards, and you might even have supper with me? I am delighted with some of the reviews, and congratulate you on what I hear of the production.

> Yours very sincerely,
> T. S. Eliot

FROM *Vivien Eliot* TO *Henry Eliot* TS Houghton

Friday, 16 December 1932 68 Clarence Gate Gardens

Dear Henry,

It was nice to get a letter[3] from you at last, after so long, and after Tom has been in America for just three months. Your letter arrived this morning, the day after Maurice['s] son's first birthday.[4] I was going to have lunch with the wife of Tom's chief of the Firm, Mrs Faber, who is very nice and a good friend to me. I took my American mail with me,

---

1 – 'Apology for the Countess of Pembroke', *Harvard Graduates' Magazine* 41: 2 (Dec. 1932), 63–75; repr. *TUPUC* (1933).
2 – Eleanor Hinkley's *Dear Jane*, a romantic comedy in three acts, was produced at the Civic Repertory Theatre from 13 Nov. 1932.
3 – Not found.
4 – Charles Warren Haigh-Wood was born on 15 Dec. 1931.

and told her all the news. The Fabers, as Tom will perhaps have told you live in a very large house up in Hampstead. A beautiful house with a very large garden.[1] They have three very nice children, Richard, Anne, and Tom. Tom, (your brother), has a photograph with him of them, I think, and can show it to you.

I sent a Christmas card to you and Theresa a week ago, on December 10th. But I sent it to 244, or 344, West 72nd Street, which was the address which Tom wrote down for me in my diary in the train on the journey to Southampton, when he was leaving England. I am therefore glad to have a letter from you, and to know your *actual address*.

You say that you gather from Tom that I am getting along pretty well without him. Well, if I am, it is only thanks to the united, and very strong efforts of all who know me here. I have never seen such team work in my life. Beginning with our firm of solicitors, Messrs James & James, (my Father's old friend and solicitor) and my doctor, who you will remember very well, Dr Miller, and on through all my family and all my old friends, as well as newer friends, I do not think anyone has ever received more kindness, and more actual help, as well as tact, consideration and understanding. I should never have believed it possible.

For nearly a year before Tom was to leave I was practically in a state of collapse. I looked so ill that many people spoke very severely about it, and many insisted that I should consult my doctor, when I did not want to. It was a terrible year to go through, and the worst sort of preparation for going to America to lecture that Tom could have had, for he was entertained and sought after very much indeed, and every attention and kindness was shown to him. It was all very kind, but of course it did tire him. Poor Tom, I did feel so awful for him. The time going on, and not a single lecture written. I nearly went mad, and so did he.

We shall never know until afterwards if all this has been for the best, but if harm of any kind should come out of it *to Tom*, you and I, Henry, will see to it. *I count on you for that.*

I am of course intensely interested in every detail you can write to me of Tom's doings, and his health, and his success. If he goes to Saint Louis, as he told me he should, I trust you will go with him. Had you written to me before, I should of course have written to you. But Tom left an accumulation of correspondence and papers, and much to see to and to attend to, and much to tidy up and put right, and I have been very very hard at work ever since he left, and indeed I still am, and am very tired

1 – The Fabers lived at 7 Oak Hill Park, Hampstead, since Sept. 1925.

indeed. Every night I sit up writing until midnight or after. Like Tom, I find it almost impossible to clear my mind for writing, until very late at night. Up till 11 p.m. there is nothing but disturbance of one kind or another.

Yes, I have had very great difficulties with tribes of useless and expensive servants who had gathered about us like birds *of prey*, and who it took some courage to dislodge. I have never seen people collect so many retainers as we seem to have done. But now I have one young woman, who Tom knows, who is doing her very best for me and she does well. Here we have a *large* flat, of five rooms, bathroom and kitchen, and a long corridor. It is absolutely full of furniture, and thick carpets, and lots of everything, and it takes immense energy to keep it clean. We have enough *belongings* to fill a fair sized *house*, and it will be a pity if we cannot move into a decent house within the next few years. I think Tom thought I should be removing while he was away, but I do not think I can. I do not feel up to it at present, and I should be afraid of the responsibility of choosing, and doing all the business while he is out of the country. I do not think I could manage it. I wish I could.

I feel that you and Theresa ought to return to England with Tom. I hope you will do this. Please do. I should love to see you both again, and it would be very comforting to me, and so good for him. I want Marion to come on a visit, and I hope she will.

I must not write more now, or I shall be up all night. But please write more to me. I wish you and Theresa all the best wishes for Christmas and the New Year. I *understood* that Tom would be with *Ada*, but you say he will be with you. I shall *now not know where to cable*.

I think *you* might *send me a cable, at Christmas*, saying exactly where Tom is, and how you all are.

Affectionately,
Vivienne Haigh Eliot
Saturday, December 17th 1932

P.S. I am just writing another piece to this now. I was writing this letter up till late last night.

You will have heard from Tom that Miss Lucy Ely Thayer came to England, to be here during his absence. She arrived two weeks *after* he left, so she did not see him at all. We understood that she would be staying in England until he returned. The whole business was a great worry to me, but I cannot go into details. You will see from this letter that I have *plenty to do*.

However, I was greatly astonished and upset, to hear, at two o'clock this afternoon, *that she had left England for America* this morning. She had not given me the slightest intimation. I understand from her hotel that she only told them yesterday. I had expected her to be staying with me here for Christmas, and had made preparations. She had left her trunk here all the time, and only fetched it away two days ago.

I am sending you a stupid little present. Please tell Tom that all his things have gone to *Ada's* – 31, Madison Street, Cambridge, Mass.

Yrs.

V. H. E.

TO *E. W. F. Tomlin*   TS Lady Marshall

17 December 1932   B-11 Eliot House, Cambridge

Dear Tomlin,

I am sorry that I did not acknowledge your ms. at once, as I should have done, as it is a manu- and not a typescript.[1] It seems to me a very able piece of work, and quite what I should expect; but I have had my hands too full to give it the detailed criticism that it merits. I hope to be able to attend to it soon after my return from a lecture tour in January. Meanwhile, with most cordial good wishes for Christmas,

I am,

Yours very sincerely,

T. S. Eliot

TO *Henry Eliot*   TS Houghton

19 December 1932   B-11 Eliot House, Cambridge

My dear Brother,

I had been hoping up to the last minute that I could assure you that I would come for Christmas. During the last week I have written two lectures for delivery, but I have still, before I start my travels, to revise parts of the Clark lectures into a series of three lectures on metaphysical poetry to deliver at Baltimore at the end of January. So I have been working under some strain and against time. I think that I can just finish them by Sunday, and indeed I *must*. I want, for reasons that I will explain later, to be in California by the 31st, and have a few days rest before my

---

1 – 'Some Implications of the Materialist Theory of Art' – 'chiefly inspired', as Tomlin wrote in a memoir, 'by Trotsky's *Literature and Revolution*' (*T. S. Eliot: A Friendship* [1988], 29).

first lecture, at Los Angeles, on the 4th January. I am going to see about tickets in the morning. What I shall do is come to New York on Monday, spend the night with you, and go on to California the next evening, if there is an evening train by the Santa Fé. This I should like to do even if, in the changed circumstances, you decide to come up and spend Christmas with me, as I have not yet seen Theresa; and if you come up we can return together. I shall see you in either case. I am very disappointed, but shall be thankful if I can do my work properly. From California I go to St Louis, where I lecture on the 17th, and in St Paul on the 19th; then I may spend a night or so with the Furnesses in Chicago without lecturing; go on to Ann Arbor and then to Buffalo for lectures; then back here for a night and then to Baltimore and perhaps Washington for a week. My class here begins on Feb. 7th, and the Norton lectures on the 17th.

I have heard from Wesleyan, but on reflection I have had to write to say that I have taken on as many outside lectures as I dare to do for the present; but that if they care to re-open the matter in March, when I know just how arduous my second half year will be, I shall be glad to reconsider. That is only the plain truth. I hope however that I can get there finally.

You will please collect this cheque immediately, otherwise I shall not keep your coat. I will bring the old one with me. And you are not to spend this on Christmas gifts for me; I have been much too busy to take the time to buy Christmas gifts for anyone, and therefore I do not want to receive any.

Your affectionate brother,
Tom

TO *Frank Morley*   TS Berg

20 December 1932   B-11 Eliot House, Cambridge

Dear Frank,

I suppose that the Fabers are at Ty Glyn Aeron Ciliau Aeron until the end of January – I am wondering whether a new secretary has been installed or put into training yet, and what will happen to the *Criterion*; but I have not had the time to wonder very much. I have bought a small camera for myself (the only Christmas present I am giving this year) and am off to Southern California on Monday (see enclosure). I shall not be settled here again until February 4th. Queer things do happen. I must now dress in order to dine at the Lodgings of the Master of Eliot, known to his friends and most of his pupils as Frisky. I have an undeserved reputation for limericks which I must live down. I went to a Christmas Dinner at my club (undergraduate) here and was presented to the company with the words 'Tom Eliot is a member we are all proud of, but I want to say that he is really just a good old Fart like the rest of us'. Odd things occur. What I meant to say was, that I should like to have a copy of the weekly list of books placed, to be placed, or irreplaceable in America sent to me regularly. I hope after all the touting I am doing for Auden & Spender that their volumes may be placeable here; and there may be others you wd. like me to talk about. I have had a letter from Ezra offering his support for the Presidency of Harvard. With love to Christina & Sukey, I am

the irreplaceable
T. S. E.

P.S. I still miss the Wensleydale & the Russian Stout.

TO *Alida Monro*   TS Texas

26 December 1932   B-11 Eliot House, Cambridge

My dear Alida,[1]

I am writing in a great rush: after writing five lectures in the last 3 weeks I am off tonight via New York for Los Angeles, San Francisco, St Louis, St Paul, Chicago, Detroit, Buffalo and back here to start for Baltimore. Look at the map! I expect to get about a week's rest in California before lecturing, and am taking Harold's mss. with me to do the introduction there. I have been trying to get hold of Greenslet of Houghton Mifflin, and when I get back (Feb. 4th) will go to see him. No news of aquaria yet, but I shall write to the Ministry of Agriculture in Washington, who most likely know. Thank you very much for your reports. V. had not mentioned Mrs Turner to me at all. Who is Mrs Wilson? I. Lockyer[2] speaks of a party there. I think you are right about choosing of acquaintances. A mysterious cable from V. says that Lucy Thayer left suddenly for N.Y. but I have no news from the latter. While away I shall put these things out of mind. A Happy New Year to you.

Yours ever,
Tom

1–Dominic Hibberd relates, in *Harold Monro*, 260: 'Vivien told Ottoline [Morrell] that Tom was doing a great deal for Alida, and that Alida understood him because he was so like Harold.'

2–VHE, in a letter to Aurelia (Hodgson) dated 27 Mar. 1932, refers to 'Mrs & Miss [Isobel] Lockyer, friends of my Mother's & mine' (Beinecke GEN MSS 245, box 9, folder 172).

TO *Ellen Fitz Pendleton*[1]   TS Wellesley College Library

26 December 1932   B-11 Eliot House, Cambridge

My dear Miss Pendleton,

   Your kind letter of the 21st[2] only reached me just before Christmas, and gave me a problem to resolve over the holiday. I am deeply sensible of the honour of being asked to be the speaker of a commencement address, especially at Wellesley where I have such pleasant associations, and the temptation is therefore considerable. But, in the first place, I am very doubtful whether my affairs in London will suffer me to remain away for so long, and it would therefore not be proper, at least, for me to commit myself so far ahead to an engagement of such importance. Second, if I do find that I am able to stay until the middle of June, it will be, I hope, for the purpose of taking a much needed rest in the country, after an arduous, though very pleasant year, and before resuming my normal work which will probably keep me in London throughout the summer. So I feel with very sincere regret that I must decline; and express with my regret at being unable to accept, my pleasure at the honour conferred by being asked.

                                        I am,
                                        Yours very sincerely,
                                        T. S. Eliot

TO *Scott Buchanan*   TS Houghton

26 December 1932   B-11 Eliot House, Cambridge

Dear Mr Buchanan,

   Thank you for your letter of the 19th.[3] You need not worry about the misinformation! I am coming anyway, the second week in May, and look forward to some conversation with you. It is a University I much want to visit.

   I have not yet chosen a subject. I shall be away, on holiday and lecturing, until February 4th. If you cared to write to me then and make some suggestion – I infer from your letter that you might have something vaguely in mind – it would be a helpful starting point, even if I did not accept it.[4]

1–Ellen Fitz Pendleton (1864–1936), President of Wellesley College from 1911.
2–Not found.
3–Not found.
4–TSE was scheduled to deliver the Turnbull Lectures at Johns Hopkins University,

Yours very sincerely,
T. S. Eliot

I hope that your mother is as well as possible. This letter conveys my wishes for the New Year.

TO *Wilbur A. Nelson*   TS Alderman Library Virginia

26 December 1932   B-11 Eliot House, Cambridge

Dear Professor Nelson,

Thank you for your letter of December 21st. It would really be possible for me to fix any three days in that week, but if it makes no difference, I suggest Wednesday, the 10th, and the Thursday and Friday following. The decision of a subject is more difficult, when it is a matter of three consecutive lectures: you would not want me to repeat my three Turnbull lectures on Three Varieties of Metaphysical Poetry. May I let you know at the beginning of February, as I am just leaving? [1] My address for the next fortnight will be c/o Scripps College, Claremont, California. [2]

Yours very sincerely,
T. S. Eliot

Baltimore, in May 1933: see *The Varieties of Metaphysical Poetry*, ed. Ronald Schuchard (1993).

1 – Nelson said that any three consecutive dates in the week of 8–13 May would be suitable. Replying on 14 Jan., Nelson said that TSE's suggested dates were 'entirely satisfactory', and reiterated: 'The Page-Barbour lectures must, in accordance with the grant which is used for this purpose, be lectures given for the first time at the University of Virginia, and these lectures, as stated in my first letter to you, are the property of the University of Virginia and are to be published by them through the Page-Barbour Foundation. The subject of your three lectures is left entirely to you, but we would like to know as soon as convenient what the subject will be.'

2 – A primary purpose of TSE's visit was to see Emily Hale, who taught classes in theatre and in diction at Scripps College from 1 Sept. 1932 to June 1934 (her letter of resignation is dated 19 Feb. 1934). See Kay Koeninger, 'Search for Eliot's Claremont Connection', *Los Angeles Times*, 18 Nov. 1982, 39 (Part V). For details of Hale's work, and of TSE's visit, see Gordon, *T. S Eliot: An Imperfect Life*, 247–52. While visiting Hale, TSE inscribed a copy of *Sweeney Agonistes* (1932) 'for Emily Hale from the author T. S. Eliot', 1 Jan. 1933: see William Baker, 'T. S. Eliot and Emily Hale: Some Fresh Evidence', *English Studies* 66: 6 (Oct. 1985), 434. TSE gave a lecture on 5 Jan. 1933 (in Balch Hall, Scripps College) on 'Edward Lear and Modern Poetry': see William Baker, 'TSE on Edward Lear', *English Studies* 64 (1983), 564–6.

26 December 1932   B-11 Eliot House, Cambridge

Dear Rabbitt,

I have forwarded your letter re ABC to Frank Morley in London (he is allright in spite of his brother) and trust he will go into the matter with you.[1] But I forgot to take down the name of your agent in N.Y. who has a copy, so shd. be grateful [if] you wd. let me have it again.[2] I am off for Los Angeles, Baltimore & other places tonight, but am Back here on February 4th.

The proper New Year's Salutations to you and D.

T.

This country is a very good place to Visit. I shall ask F. & F. to send you copy of Fragments (SWEENEY AGONISTES).[3]

Ezzum Pound, Sir, what I forget to say was, as well as I can reclect, I don't believe anybody worth noticeing learned anything from Bosschère.[4] No that tha's anything against him; its just a Fact. I was a Green & Bitter Child etc.

1 – EP wrote on 14 Dec.: 'I have done an ABC of economics // a bit longer than How to Read / but necessary eviceration and clarification of the subjekk.

'It may be yr/ sacred or scared jewty to print it in Crit.

'My economics are sound enough to pass the edtr/ of the Revista di Diritto Commerciale, who has a kid on the Cambridge faculty of econ. and I have been axd/ to deliver ten lectures in a inschooshum of learnin here.'

2 – EP's agent was V. Rice of New York City.

3 – 'I have asked Faber to send Sweeny Ag/ for rev. in Il Mare.' FVM confirmed, in a letter to EP (16 Dec.), that he would be sending him a copy of *SA* (YCAL MSS 43: Box 35, folder 1480). He added: 'I hear fairly regularly from Eliot at Harvard. He is reasonably chirpy and is being uncommonly industrious, but the rewards of industry must be seriously encroached on by the horrible rise in the price of liquor which, I understand, is going up from 3.75 a bottle to 8$.'

4 – 'Picked up old SympoZZZeum yester/ and noted admirable essay by Taup/ trad/ Z. (from Taup's Inf. Sym.) only one point to queery.

'T/ sez you owe something to Bosschere. Very surprisin' to me. I thought "we" thought Bosch/ unsatisfactory. At least I did.

'I at once typed a contradiction . . . but possibly better to have yr/ memories on the subject. I don't want to raise the issue if I am wrong.'

(Jean de Bosschère [1878–1953]: Belgian writer and painter.)

TO *Frank Morley*   TS Faber

St Stephen Protomartyr [26 Dec.] 1932   B-11 Eliot House, Cambridge

Dear Cheesemite,

Thanks for yours of the 6th instant from Pike's Farm with the Cheerful news from London.[1] I know several good Limericks now. The news from this Side is no better. I have had Mr Horace Gregory to spend the night here. In my pyjamas, I mean in another Pair. Have not yet seen Ed. Dahlberg or most of the East Side pals. I am glad the Party went off scessfully. This is a Business letter, as I shall now correspond with You instead of the Secretary as Miss Wilberforce has left. Miss Wilberforce was a good secretary, and I don't like the next one's name.[2] I expect you are a Bum secretary. As there is some question about a poem, I was going to use a section of Roditi's Lament of somebody Abravanell, but I cant remember which; but if there is a good bit of Read, shove that in. Remember that the price of *Five Finger Exercises* is to be added to Joyce's pay without comment.[3] Shall try to have a Commentary in time, but it will be a squeak;[4] have written 5 lectures in three weeks, dined out a bit too (the last dinner given by the Master of this house was a rouser, and the champagne was not bad, but he shouldn't have given me Benedictine and then Chartreuse, no he shouldnt; am off tonight for New York (but only there 12 hours this time, so shall miss Christopher [?Morley] again, but I am having another Xmas dinner to-day with my Uncle Christopher) thence to St Louis (stay 4 hours) thence to Claremont Cal., Los Angeles, Berkeley, St Louis (several days with my Aunt Rose who is stone deaf) St Paul (with my cousin Frederick who is a parson) St no I mean just Chicago to stay with Cousin Ruth, Ann Arbor with Professor Oscar James Campbell,[5] Buffallo or is it Buffalo Bufallo Bufaloo to stay with Professor Henry Ten

---

1 – Letter not found.

2 – The new secretary was Tacon Gilbert – who was to write to L. C. Knights on 9 May 1933: 'No, you are quite right; I am dear Madam. But I am quite accustomed to being Sir-ed: it is my own fault for having such an improbable name!'

3 – FVM replied, 3 Jan. 1933: 'The price of Five Fingers went to Jimmy Jay without so much as a word'.

4 – FVM (3 Jan.): 'I don't know what you mean in saying you will try to have a commentary in time; you damn well are to have a commentary in time or I'll gum the works entirely. My enthusiasm for *The Criterion* is being severely tested by the number of poems and essays, to say nothing of personalia with which I am having to deal. My education proceeds apace.'

5 – Oscar James Campbell (1879–1970), Professor of English, State University of New York at Buffalo; author of *Shakespeare's Satire* (1943) and *The Reader's Encyclopedia of Shakespeare*.

Eyck Perry,[1] then back here for a night, then to BALLTIMORE. So I shall be rather busy as I have to write a preface for Harold's Collected Works in the chinks. Must try to read The Theology of Crisis and Rethinking Missions on the Train. *Sweeney Agonistes* is nicely printed, I like the type; please send SIX more copies and debit my account. I hope I draw some royalties. Mem. to return 3 empty gallon jars to Ted Spencer before I leave tonight – can be done any time as no undergraduates about. I had lunch with D. McCord and Walter Edmunds at the Signet[2] – the latter a very likeable boy – the point is that *Erie Water* is to be turned into a musical show (Showboat); I trust you have received a copy of the book by now, but Edmunds was to have rung me up to say whether Little Brown had committed him to Sampson Low or not.

> There was a young lady named Ransome
> Who surrendered 5 times in a hansom,
> When she said to her swain
> He must do it again
> He replied: 'My name's Simpson, not Samson'.

I shall tackle that damn Murdoch again when I get back February 4th. Meanwhile I enclose two letters. I hope O'Conor[3] is not going to spoil a good story by antiquarian accretions; it may need your learned pruning knife. Will you deal with Ezra? I suppose it will be absolutely unsaleable, but there is always a chance of Ezra's turning out something good, so it ought to be looked at, and G.C.F. is not the man to do it.[4] The portraits of Sukey are capital, and suggest that she may develop some of the paternal physique. I have a small camera and will send her one of me if I can get anyone to look me in the eye and take it. Note that Ezra has another proposal as well. If you must cable about anything cable c/o Sheffield. So no more for the moment I will close.

Yours respectfully, & wishing yr family a Happy New Year,

T. S. E.

1 – Henry Ten Eyck Perry (1890–1973), Professor of English, University of Buffalo.
2 – The Signet Society, Harvard, founded in 1870.
3 – Norreys Jephson O'Conor, who had written a letter which TSE forwarded to FVM.
4 – FVM (3 Jan.): 'I have already been in correspondence with Ezra about the A.B.C. of Economics, and have written him about the armament companies, and French newspapers. Neither seems a certain gold mine, but naturally I am not sneezing at whatever he may care to send.'

TO *John Hayward*   TS King's

26 December 1932   B-11 Eliot House, Cambridge

My dear John,

God bless you for your Christmas message, which was cheering[1] – the
only one I got by cable, as my immediate connexions were not sure where
I was, but I was here; am leaving in a few minutes for New York, thence
to California, Maryland, and other places. I have been so busy, what with
turning out lectures – this typewriter will be a wreck by the time I have
finished, and hospitality, that I have written only business letters since I
got here. It is very pleasant, but one couldnt go on like this for ever, and
I shall be glad to return to the peaceful village life of London. I have just
returned from Ted Spencer's – whom I have seen a good deal of, and like.
He is aiding me in a course in Modern English Literature which I have
to give upon my return (February 4th).[2] I hope that I may write more
sensibly later: this is only to wish you the best of New Years, and to say
that you have been often in my thoughts.[3]

Affectionately,

T. S. E.

1 – Not found.
2 – It was almost certainly during one of the lectures he delivered at this season – HWE
stayed with TSE at Harvard for the first days of October 1932 – that Theodore Spencer
quoted certain remarks made by TSE about *The Waste Land* that the poet's brother took
note of: 'Various critics have done me the honour to interpret the poem in terms of criticism
of the modern world, have considered it, indeed, as an important bit of social criticism. To
me it was only the relief of a personal and wholly insignificant grouse against life; it is just
a piece of rhythmical grumbling' (*The Waste Land: a facsimile and transcript of the original
drafts including the annotations of Ezra Pound*, ed. EVE [1971], 1). EVE told Leonard Unger
on 29 May 1972: 'It is fairly certain that the "rhythmical grumbling" passage was said to
Spencer, and quoted by him, during my husband's tenure of the Charles Eliot Norton chair
in 1932–3. Henry Eliot noted the words at Spencer's lecture, but gave no date.' Moreover,
EVE wrote to John Press, 5 June 1973: 'I quoted the piece about a "personal and wholly
insignificant grouse against life" because my husband told me he was tired of being called
the voice of a generation, and that he would never have written the poem except for his
domestic unhappiness.'
3 – JDH had written to OM, 16 Dec. 1932: 'By the way Vivien rang me up yesterday – mad,
quite mad – to ask me to dinner at a few hours' notice; I couldn't go, and she now proposed
to pay me a visit alone in a new motor-car which she can't drive! And she insists on coming
alone. What will happen?' (Texas). And again on 21 Dec. 1932: 'I have read Tom's book
[*John Dryden* (New York, 1932)]: dull, and, I thought rather elementary. He had said it all
before, and so much better, in his "Hogarth Press" pamphlet on Dryden. He's too dry in his
prose: no passion, scarcely any feeling at all. It's odd, because his poetry is quite otherwise.
Sometimes he makes me feel that he is frightened of giving himself away, or something away
– I don't know what. I have felt as much in his conversation. Has Vivien killed him, do you
suppose?' (Texas).

FROM *Vivien Eliot* TO *Mary Hutchinson*   MS Texas

28 December 1932   68 Clarence Gate Gardens

My dear Mary

We have all had a shock. Lucy Thayer, you know who I mean, sailed for New York – yesterday, without saying good-bye to any of us. She was to have come to me *today*, & to have spent the Christmas holiday with me. I only found out, by ringing up the hotel, that she had gone. Vanished, flown. (Sailed on the *Europa* – yesterday.)

It is *frightfully upsetting*, because you see *Tom* will be so upset. She has a flat in New York, & *Tom* is to be *lecturing* in New York. She is vile to have done this – because she made her plans *gradually*. I never *guessed* what she was *up to*, but now I see it *all*. She kept asking about Tom, & she made everything *as* uncomfortable *here* for *me* as she *could*, but I was too well *protected* for her to do me any serious harm (*I think*). But now she goes back to New York, full of information about everything she wished to find out, here. Oh Mary – I am most horribly sick. Will you tell Jack? Tom never asked her here at all. He left *that* to my family – & they did invite her.

I am *really* worried, & wish you will please, dear, *ring me up*.

This has really been a very vile thing to do, I think.

Yours ever,
Vivienne

I have *cabled to Tom*.[1]

FROM *Vivien Eliot* TO *Mary Hutchinson*   MS Texas

Thursday 29 December 1932   68 Clarence Gate Gardens

My dear Mary & Jack

Thank you so very very much for your 3 beautiful presents. I do think it was sweet of you to give them to me. I like *each one* particularly, & I think they have so [much] meaning.

1–TSE was to visit Lucy Thayer's cousin Scofield Thayer (1890–1982) – his old school friend from Milton Academy and Harvard, later editor of *The Dial* – in a sanatorium during this visit: Scofield had been certified in 1930 and was to spend the remainder of his long life in care. It was the last time that TSE would see Scofield, as he told Alyse Gregory, 17 Dec. 1948. See John Richardson, 'The Madness of Scofield Thayer', *Sacred Monsters, Sacred Masters* (2001), 17–29; Alex Beam, *Gracefully Insane: The Rise and Fall of America's Premier Mental Hospital* (2001), 100–6; James Dempsey, *The Tortured Life of Scofield Thayer* (2014).

It was very dear of you to bring them yourselves, on Christmas evening – just when my family were here having dinner with me. It was a great surprise, to me.

I thought you were going to telephone the next day but you never did. Had you any news from *Tom*?

I still have my *Christmas tree* here, & I want you, Mary, to come in & see it before I take it down. Will you come, Mary, tomorrow afternoon, *to tea* – or if not *when*?

Again thanking you, very much indeed for the lovely presents –

Yours ever, with love,
Vivienne

TO *Ezra Pound*   PC¹ MS Beinecke

[?1933]

Podestà² have you had any communications from a Mrs A. Bladdar who says she is widow of Bap. Preacher in S. Wales. She has a theory about token money that is to lose value if you hoard it. If not, may I put her on to you. Please give me name address of Fr. Coghlin & particulars of his published works if any please

TP

TO *Geoffrey Faber*   PC³ MS Valerie Eliot

[Postmark illegible: ?January 1933]

En route to California. The train has been all day passing through Kansas (like this in season). Tonight we reach New Mexico, which is largely Spanish. There is a barbershop on the train. Back in Cambridge Feb. 4.

T. S. E.

FROM *Vivien Eliot* TO *Frank Morley*   TS Faber

5 January 1933   68 Clarence Gate Gardens

Dear Mr Morley,

Thank You very much for your letter of to-day.⁴ I am very glad you have written to Routledge. I hope the book they wish to bring out is a

---

1–The PC shows monkeys clustered round a mirror (a piece of mirrored glass set into the cardboard), with the caption: 'The one in the centre is you.'

2–*Podestà*: from the Latin *potestas* ('power'), this title is sometimes accorded to a high official, such as a magistrate, in an Italian city.

3–The PC depicts wheat harvesting in Kansas.

4–Routledge had requested a photograph to go with the entry on TSE in a forthcoming reference book. FVM wrote to VHE, 5 Jan.: 'I have written to Routledge this morning asking them to let me know exactly what the proposed reference book is. Quite likely it is merely something that I shall be able to handle without bothering you or T. S. E. further . . .

good one. I can tell you anything I know about portraits and photographs of my husband when you want me to.

I am sorry the Cambridge Methodist had to be snubbed.

Thank you very much indeed for the two copies of *Sweeney Agonistes*. I do not *know* how to act in that matter, and I must think it over.

About the notice for the newspapers. I am sure that Dr Miller is right, and I am sure it is necessary to insert a notice, such as he drew up, in the papers.[1]

I enclose herewith a letter from *Methuen*, which seems to prove the point. *Methuen*'s have not even got Tom's private address correct, – you see they put 98 instead of 68.

Of-course Faber & Faber know which Bank Tom's royalties are paid into. I do not.

I do hope I did not do wrong in opening this letter.

~~I should think I had better write and mention these~~

I shall be very pleased to come to tea with you at the Office again before long.

Yours very sincerely,
Vivienne Haigh Eliot[2]

TO *Frank Morley*

PC MS Faber

11 January 1933

PC postmarked Berkeley
[Printed address on PC:
The Brown Derby, Vine Street,
Hollywood, California]

I have just consumed a stack of wheats & a mug of mocha in this place. The weather is very hot: yesterday went out in a motor boat from Balboa

---

'I have also written to the Cambridge Methodist snubbing him politely.

'I hope to let you know about the item for the newspapers in a day or two . . .

'I am enclosing two complimentary copies of SWEENEY which you may care to send on to the dramatic people.'

1–See VHE's letter to Henry and Theresa Eliot, 11 Jan. 1933, below.

2– FVM replied to this letter, 6 Jan.: 'Dear Mrs Eliot, / I am sure you did quite right in opening and sending on the Methuen letter for instructions had been left that our accountant was to deal with royalties. He has written to Methuen asking that they shall be paid in to Lloyds Bank. The matter has, therefore, been all attended to, but I return the letter in case you wish to keep it . . .

'I am sending out the notice to the newspapers. I quite agree with Dr Miller that it would be good to have the notice inserted; but the only difficulty not envisaged is whether the newspapers will regard it as news, but at any rate I am trying.'

harbour.[1] Have lectured 3 times & addressed several classes;[2] have driven a Ford and got stuck in a snow drift. The trees are full of oranges.

T. S. E.

FROM *Vivien Eliot* TO *Henry & Theresa Eliot* TS Houghton

Wednesday 11 January 1933   68 Clarence Gate Gardens

Dear Henry and Theresa,

This is just to thank you very very much for your awfully nice Christmas present. It did arrive after Christmas, but that was all the better, as getting presents late make[s] the Christmas season last longer. I do like the collar so much, the colours are so nice and bright, it very much improves a dull dark brown dress I have got.

I must not write much now, because it is late, and I am very tired. I have had a kind of chill for the last few days, and the weather is very

1–Loucks, 'The Exile's Return', 22: 'Scripps student Marie McSpadden (later Sands) drove TSE and Emily Hale to [McSpadden's mother's cottage on] Balboa Island for a sailing excursion, "primarily so that they could have [un]interrupted hours together" (Sands). By way of thanks, TSE sent her an inscribed copy of "Marina" (Koeninger, "Search" V–34).'
2–Loucks, 'The Exile's Return', 21–2: '*January 6, 1 p.m.* At the University of California, Los Angeles, Eliot gave a lecture and poetry reading in Royce Hall auditorium on "The Formation of Taste" (Brown: "Dr Eliot to Lecture"). TSE identified four stages in the development of poetic taste, from childhood to maturity, the final phase involving the whole person. Characterizing his own taste as capricious and limited, he admitted he had never been able to appreciate Goethe and some of Wordsworth. "I do not affirm that what I like in poetry is good. If one is sincere, he will not enjoy a thing because he is told it is great. He must be true to his own feelings. Self knowledge is the most important factor in knowing what we really feel."' HWE reported, directly from TSE's lecture-notes, these remarks: 'For at no point has our development been merely a development of *Taste*, that is, an approximation to a discerning, appreciative enjoyment of all of the poetry worth reading, in its proper kind and degree. Such an ambition is a phantom, the pursuit of which we may leave to those whose aim in life is to be "cultivated" or "cultured" – I do not know which is the right word to use. Such people treat art as a luxury, and commonly end by becoming themselves luxury articles. The ideal is unattainable, and I think is in some sense even undesirable.' Immediately after his lecture, TSE read Part V of *The Waste Land*, a section of *Ash-Wednesday*, and "Triumphal March". Loucks records further: '*January 9.* In Mudd Hall of Philosophy at the University of Southern California, TSE gave a public lecture on "Edward Lear and Modern Poetry" (Hikida; "What's Doing" I–1) . . . *January 11, evening.* TSE lectured in Wheeler Auditorium at the University of California, Berkeley, on "The Development of Taste in Poetry" and read from his poetry (Roberts; "Poetic Taste").' He was introduced by Walter Morris Hart, chair of the Dept of English. He presented a copy of *Selected Essays 1917–1932* (1932): 'Gratefully inscribed to Mrs W. M. Hart by the author T. S. Eliot 12.i.33.' (Peter Harrington cat. 68, 2009, item 81.) He was never again to visit California.

trying. One day it is cold and foggy, and the next it is warm and damp. One of my Aunts is very very ill with congestion of the lungs, and has two nurses, and there is a terrible lot of illness of all kinds about, particularly influenza.

It was a complete surprise to me, and I must say, rather a shock, to hear that Tom had gone on a tour in California. He did not tell me in advance, so that I did not know. I feel very very worried, it is much more worrying than when he is safely living in Eliot House. I am sure that you feel the same, and will be glad to see him back. I suppose that he will visit you in your flat in New York on his way back to Cambridge.

I had to go to the Offices of Messrs. Faber & Faber last week because there were several matters of business that came here to this flat which I could not deal with by myself. It is very unfortunate that Tom cannot be got at directly in these matters at this moment. However, Mr Morley, of whom I am quite sure Tom has often talked to you about, had taken them in hand, and has promised to attend to them, and I am sure he will. All the same, it is a pity that Tom cannot be got at just now, it is really unfortunate. Mr Morley is putting a Notice in the Newspapers, giving Tom's address in America, and the reason of his absence, and the approximate date of his return. This was considered advisable by all. I will send you the notice when I see it. Tom's book *Sweeney Agonistes* is having a good deal of publicity here, and many people are very interested in getting it staged. In fact there is a great deal of talk about it, and to-day I saw Mrs James Stephens, the poet's wife, and she has promised to interest Leon M. Lion in it. He is of course the only person in England who would have the intelligence to really appreciate it. I think it will certainly be staged here.

I keep very busy, and there is always more than I can do, and so the time passes. Everyone is very kind, and they do not let me get too lonely, but all the same it is a very long time, and now it seems much too long a time to wait until May.

My family all appreciated the Christmas card that you sent, and also *very much appreciated* the reproduction of Theresa's drawing of Tom, lecturing at Trinity, Cambridge.[1] It is really very good indeed.

Now I must stop, or I shall be killed by the neighbours. With much love to you both,

Your affectionate sister-in-law,
Vivienne Haigh Eliot

1–Reproduced in *L* 3.

TO *Theodore Spencer*   MS Houghton

17 January 1933[1]   St Louis[2]

Dear Spencer

I think in the circumstances I must leave this to you to complete. I have made a few suggestions in pencil, but you can rub 'em out.

I have enjoyed myself very much – I leave tomorrow for the Twin Cities, and am sorry to leave my Native City, though glad to escape from Mrs Florence Noonan Gemmer, poetess and daughter of the Hon. J. J. Noonan, democratic Mayor of St. L. in what she calls 'the gay nineties'. Here is a sample.

1–Mistyped '1932'.

2–TSE lectured on Mon. 16 Jan., at the Graham Memorial Chapel, St Louis, on 'The Study of Shakespeare Criticism', remarking *inter alia*: 'We are . . . getting over our antiquated ideas of dramatic poetry, having no longer one dramatic and one poetic point of view. The poetry of the next period will, I hope, have more of a dramatic quality and in the light of that Shakespeare will be criticized anew' ('TSE Discusses Shakespeare's Critics' 3-B, cited in Loucks, 'The Exile's Return', 22). He remarked to a local newspaper reporter: 'I don't think I like writing . . . it's not a regular occupation. Thank God, I have a regular job . . . Then, too, one is never satisfied with what one does. I think a certain amount of pressure in not having quite enough time is a necessary stimulant. But for that, I couldn't write' ('T. S. Eliot Discusses Outlook for Poetry', *St Louis Post-Dispatch*, 16 Jan. 1933, 3-B; cited in Loucks, 22–4).

He was to write to Otto H. Shwarz (who had been a classmate at Smith Academy), 20 Apr. 1950: 'I was last in St Louis in 1933; when, to my pleasure and exasperation, I was rung up by Laurence Post, who suggested a meeting of ourselves and yourself. I say exasperated, because my good uncle-in-law, with whom I was staying (he is dead now) had arranged such a full programme for me (beyond the address at Washington U[niversity] which paid my rail fare) including meals with Old Family Friends, that I had no time for the two things I had come for: to ramble round the City by myself, and to look up Smith Academy friends. (There are others I should like to know about: Walter Donnell, Pat Griffin [. . .] Milton Hellman (the big good-looking one, there was another M. H. whom I didn't like so much – Charley Campbell (not Jim Campbell, who claimed to be the Heir Presumptive of the Duke of Argyll, but he doesn't seem to have got there yet – I liked Jim too, and he was a good footballer, and Millard Prunier Kayser; also Freddie Garrison Lake. (You see I haven't lost my memory yet, not quite) . . .

'You are right about Smith: I think we were well taught. I remember Jackson and Robinson with particular affection (I was Jackson's pet, and Laurence Post was Robinson's). Also Mme. J. Jouvet-Kauffman. I never got on so well with Rowe (Roe???) who taught us mathematics; or with Miss Chandler who tried to teach us German. (One wonders, in retrospect, whether one didn't get on with the teachers because one wasn't gifted for the subject, or whether one was bad at the subject because one disliked the teacher. Jerry Lambert was Rowe's favourite. As for Miss Chandler, I remember vividly the occasion on which *you* told her that you couldn't see any difference between *schiessen* and *scheissen* – a subtlety which caused Miss Chandler to blush (the only known occasion) and which earned you the reverence of the few in the class who knew enough German to appreciate the difference' (King's).

In the land of hearts' ease
Neath blossoming trees
Here each heart shall find a true mate.

I arrive in Cambridge on the 27th for a couple of nights. I shall be very THIRSTY as I have not had a drink for a month.

Yours ever,
T. S. E.

TO *Mary Hutchinson*   PC TS Texas

Postmarked 15 January 1933

Affectionate greetings for 1933; on my way I took in St Louis, Mis[1] and St Paul Minn. I have just been to California.

T. S. E.

TO *Ottoline Morrell*   PC MS Texas

15 January 1933

Your letter arrived just as I was leaving for California. I will answer it as soon as I get back to Cambridge. I don't like California much: no *country*, only *scenery*.

Aff.
T. S. E.

1–TSE recalled in a letter (1 Sept. 1939) to the Revd W. A. Gerhard, SJ, that in Jan. 1933 he had spent 'a very delightful afternoon' with the Fathers of St Louis University (the oldest university west of the Mississippi). To the Revd Walter J. Ong, SJ, 2 Sept. 1959: 'I remember with pleasure having tea with the Fathers at St Louis University in 1933.'

FROM *Vivien Eliot* TO *Frank Morley*   TS Faber

Wednesday, 18 January 1933   68 Clarence Gate Gardens

Dear Mr Morley,

Thank you very much for your letter of 17th inst.[1]

I am glad you have heard from Routledge and hope their book will be a good one.

I think the press cutting which you enclose from the 'Publishers' Circular' is a very good one. I only wish it could appear in *The Times* and other morning papers.

I am of course still thinking all the time about getting 'Sweeney Agonistes' staged, but I feel so worried just now by this tour my husband seems to be taking, and the fact that one cannot communicate directly with him, that I do not feel capable of doing anything much about it at present. But I shall feel much better when I know that he is safely back at Eliot House.

I am very glad that you enjoyed your visit to the Fabers in Wales.

> Yours very sincerely,
> and with many thanks,
> V. H. Eliot

FROM *Vivien Eliot* TO *Frank Morley*   TS Faber

Sunday, 22 January 1933   68 Clarence Gate Gardens

Dear Mr Morley,

I now have a feeling the *Sweeney Agonistes* would be safer in the hands of an Agent, and I intend to see to it. I feel sure you will agree.

My last news from Tom is dated January 11th.[2] I feel anxious, and have cabled, but had no reply.

> Yours very sincerely,
> Vivienne Haigh Eliot

1–FVM reported that Routledge had abandoned the idea of having photographs in their planned reference book. He wrote too, 'The only result which I have so far been able to trace of the paragraph that we sent to the press is the enclosed clipping from the *Publishers' Circular*.'

2–TSE's letter not found.

30 January 1933   [Faber & Faber Ltd]

Dear Mr Roberts,

Thank you for your letter of January 28th,[2] addressed to Mr Eliot, which I have opened in his absence – he is at present in America, and will not be returning for several months.

I am sure Mr Eliot will be interested to see your letter on his return, when I will lay it before him. No decision has yet been reached about whether or no we will review *Paul Valéry*, but in the event of our wanting you to review it, we will certainly let you know.[3]

Yours faithfully,

For the Editor.

1 – Michael Roberts (1902–48), critic, editor, poet, was educated at King's College, London (where he read chemistry), and at Trinity College, Cambridge (mathematics). In the 1930s he was a schoolmaster (in London and at the Royal Grammar School, Newcastle upon Tyne). After WW2, during which he worked for the BBC European Service, he became Principal of the Church of England training college of St Mark and St John in Chelsea, London. He edited the watershed anthologies *New Signatures* (1932) and *New Country* (1933); and *The Faber Book of Modern Verse* (1936). Other writings include *The Modern Mind* (1937), *T. E. Hulme* (1938), *The Recovery of the West* (1941). In 1935 he married the critic and biographer Janet Adam Smith. See further *A Portrait of Michael Roberts*, ed. T. W. Eason and R. Hamilton (1949).

TSE wrote soon after Roberts's death: 'His scientific bent and training were supplemented and corrected by a philosophical cast of mind; by critical abilities of a very high order; and by an imaginative gift which expressed itself in poetry of a meditative type. Such a combination of powers is unusual; and among men of letters of his generation it was unique. His first notoriety was due to the volume *New Signatures*, a presentation of the poetry which was beginning to attract attention in the late nineteen-twenties; a book which seemed to promise him the place of expositor and interpreter of the poetry of his generation. This book was followed in 1934 by *Critique of Poetry*, a collection of essays ranging between literary criticism, aesthetics and philosophy; then by *The Modern Mind*, a more coherent and profound examination of the age; by a study of T. E. Hulme, which remains the essential piece of bibliography for a man who occupied for his generation something like the place to which Roberts was entitled for his own; and finally, in 1941, by *The Recovery of the West*, an important essay in moral and sociological criticism . . . A little earlier . . . appeared *Orion Marches*, which contains, I think, some of the best of his poems.'

TSE noted too, of Roberts's 'isolated superiority' (a Dostoevskyan phrase he had once used of EP): 'He would have made an admirable editor of a review of ideas: indeed, had the *Criterion* continued, he was the only man junior to myself of whom I could think for the editorship' ('Introduction', *A Portrait of Michael Roberts*, x–xii; 'Views and Reviews: Michael Roberts', *The New English Weekly* 34 [13 Jan. 1949], 164).

2 – Not found.

3 – Evidently Roberts had asked in his letter to review Theodora Bosanquet's *Paul Valéry* (1933): 'His poetry compels attention but his "metaphysic" is intolerable . . . I know the sterility (in the strict sense) of a symbolic logic, but with Valéry, even after you have removed the inconsistencies, his terminology itself is unreal, inadequate. He fails, like Wittgenstein, because there are huge tracts of human experience of which he cannot speak at all.'

5 February 1933   B-11 Eliot House, Cambridge

My dear Alida,

Here it is.[1] First, I find it extraordinarily difficult to say anything about a contemporary (even if I had not known him). Second, I underestimated the fatigues and occupations of a lecture tour: this was begun in California, scrapped, and not written till now. Last weekend I hoped to do it; but I caught a cold on the way from Buffalo,[2] and had to spend two days in bed preparing for a lecture week in Baltimore, whence I have just returned.[3]

1–See TSE's note on the poetry of Harold Monro – 'Monro, with his amiable, but uncritical capacity for admiring other people's verse, gives me the impression of having tried, in some of his earlier work, but probably unconsciously, to be more like other writers than he really was . . . And his difficulties in expression must have been considerable. He is at the same time very intimate and very reticent. He does not express the spirit of an age; he expresses the spirit of one man, but that so faithfully that his poetry will remain as one variety of the infinite number of possible expressions of tortured human consciousness . . . I always feel that the centre of his interest is never in the visible world at all, but in the spectres and the "bad dreams" which live inside the skull, in the ceaseless question and answer of the tortured mind . . . To get inside his world takes some trouble, and it is not a happy or sunny world to stay in, but it is a world which we ought to visit. The external world, as it appears in his poetry, is manifestly but the mirror of a darker world within . . . Monro's work is so manifestly honest and bitter that we may be sure he would have cared for no praise that was not just and moderate . . . I think that his poetry, as a whole, is more nearly the real right thing than any of the poetry of a somewhat older generation than mine except Mr Yeats's' – in *The Collected Poems of Harold Monro* (1933), xiii–xvi.
2–Loucks, 23: 'Sponsored by the Fenton Lecture Series, TSE lectured on "Edward Lear and Modern Poetry" at the University of Buffalo (Basinski).'
3–Loucks, 23: '*January 30, February 1 and 3, 5 p.m.* TSE presented a series of lectures, "The Varieties of Metaphysical Poetry", in Latrobe Hall at the Johns Hopkins University on the occasion of the 29th Percy Graeme Turnbull Memorial Lectures ("TSE on Puritan Poets"; Schuchard, vii, 234). Individual lecture topics were "Toward a Definition of Metaphysical Poetry"; "The Conceit in Donne and Crashaw"; and "Laforgue and Corbière in our Time" (Schuchard, vii) . . . *February 2, evening.* Appearing before the Poetry Society of Maryland, TSE lectured on the charge of obscurity in modern poetry, then read from his work (Schuchard, 236).'
   The *Baltimore Sun* reported on Tues. 31 Jan. 1933, 20: 'T. S. Eliot Asserts Advantage Of Being Critic Is That It Pays: American-Born Poet, Who Became British Citizen, Gives First Of Three Percy Turnbull Memorial Lectures at Johns Hopkins:
   'It pays better to criticize poetry than to write it, T. S. Eliot has learned.
   'The eminent poet and leader of a reactionary movement in poetry said as much while discussing his calling yesterday after a lecture at the Johns Hopkins University. He gave the first of the three Percy Turnbull Memorial Lectures for this year. Speaking on The Metaphysical Poets, he will complete the season with lectures at 3 P.M. Wednesday and Friday in Latrobe Hall.
   'When asked how he could account for his success as both poet and critic, in view of the general rule that a great poet is seldom a great critic, he said:

If you don't like it, don't use it; I shan't be offended; if you want it altered in any way it can be altered. I should like to have done a good job.

I hope that I have not held up the book too long.

I learnt something about acquaria [*sic*] in St Louis and am sending you a catalogue. If you want any of the books mentioned in the catalogue send me the name and the publisher's name and I will get them for you. There is also the Department of Agriculture which I have not yet consulted.

I hope that the Bookshop is going fairly well, and that you are comfortable and that the Animals do not consider the life too confined. I should be glad for any more information or opinion you can give me about Vivienne; I have no letter from her for some days, which I consider a good sign.

California is a horrible place.

Yours ever,
Tom

'"Well, I don't know about that. My chief reason for being a critic at present is the fact that you can make a little money out of an essay on criticism."

'It was the second time this month that a poet from the British Isles visiting Baltimore has intimated that writing poetry is not a lucrative profession. Several weeks ago William Butler Yeats, leader of the renaissance of Irish literature, said that the Irish were great "appreciators of poetry, if not readers of it." They honored him as a personality, he admitted, even though they did not read his books.

'Mr Eliot, born in St Louis, aroused much speculation when he became a British citizen in 1927. Some said at the time that it was the case of a thinker seeking seclusion, like a mediæval monk going into the monastery.

'Asked if he found London conducive to the contemplative life, he replied:

'"Perhaps so. I think that London, being the largest city in the world, is the best place in the world to lose yourself . . . New York is not even second best. It is too noisy . . . In London you can always find some place where you can be alone. There people don't go out of their way to find you when you want quiet."

'For his lecture Latrobe Hall was packed with well over 400 persons. Prof. H. C. Lancaster, chairman of the department of romance languages, introducing the speaker, said, "Our English cousins are generous in sending us poets and other lecturers to help us in our war against Philistines and other barbarians. We are indebted to them, but we ask for no cancellation nor moratorium. Our debt is well paid, for we have given them Henry James and T. S. Eliot."'

TSE told John Quentin Feller, Jr (Baltimore), 22 Dec. 1960: 'Do you know, I have completely forgotten the subject of the Turnbull lectures which I gave in 1933, and I must have destroyed the text. I gave a great many single lectures, as well as the series at Harvard and the series at the University of Virginia, during the nine months of my stay in America because, to tell the truth, I was badly in arrears with payment of income tax and had to earn all the money I could in order to pay off my debts to the Inland Revenue. It seems very odd now that I should have given three lectures, preserved no copy, and forgotten the subject, but there it is.'

FVM wrote to EP, 23 Feb. 1933: 'Our Mr Eliot was publicly presented with an icosahedron in Baltimore. I suppose he will just the same come back in June.'

I am keeping the ms. to show to Greenslet.[1] I have been away since Christmas. I wish this note was better; but this is a sort of thing which one can never do satisfactorily to oneself.

TO *Elizabeth Manwaring*   TS Wellesley College Library

8 February 1933   B-11 Eliot House, Cambridge

Dear Miss Manwaring,

Thank you for your note of reminder, and for asking me to dine with you. It will be a great pleasure. I think the Sheffields will bring me out. I am looking forward to the evening with keen anticipation.

Yours sincerely,
T. S. Eliot

TO *Ottoline Morrell*   TS Texas

9 February 1933   B-11 Eliot House, Cambridge

My dear Ottoline,

I am ashamed not to have written to you before to thank you for your two letters and the Diary. I was afraid that this absence might make a break in the happy succession of diaries – I am so glad that it has not. But I was very hardworked up to Christmas, and immediately after left for a prolonged tour – to New York, California, Missouri, Minnesota,[2] Chicago, Buffalo and Baltimore; and I have only been back at work here since last Saturday; I am now lecturing to undergraduates (on Contemporary English Literature, a subject with which I have very little acquaintance) twice a week, as well as continuing my public lectures.[3]

1–Ferris Greenslet, Houghton Mifflin Co., Boston.
2–'*January 19, 11:30 a.m.* TSE addressed an all-university convocation in Northrop Memorial Auditorium at the University of Minnesota on "The Tendency of Some Modern Poetry". He predicted that future poetry will take two new forms: in the first, satire will be seriously developed; in the second, a new kind of poetic drama will emerge. The modern poet serves no essential function; only the worst and best poets are known; the former are published in newspapers, while the latter are appreciated only by the cultured minority ("Only best").' (Loucks, 23)
3–Loucks, 24: 'February 7. TSE and Theodore Spencer began teaching English 26b, "Contemporary English Literature (1890 to the present time)." An undergraduate course limited to 15 students with at least a B-plus average, it met "Tu., Th. and (at the pleasure of the instructor) Sat., at 9 [a.m.] . . . While preparing for this course TSE re-read Yeats's poetry; subsequently, he gave two lectures on Yeats and a third on the Irish Theatre.'

It has been pleasant and interesting to travel so much. Most of the country I do not like; California is a nightmare. Boston is the most agreeable; and it is strangely comfortable, after so many years, to be among a society which consists largely of one's own relatives. Certainly this break in my life will be very significant for me, and will perhaps alter my life somewhat. Not that I have not been very homesick for London, and for the smell of a country lane on a wet day! It is in fact in the country, or what passes for the country, that one feels least at home here. The English countryside will be a wonderful sight again. And I am already tired of seeing so many people – all very kind and friendly, but to see too many people makes me misanthropic. I have no 'private life', and I miss the anonymity which one can enjoy in London.

I understand why you have not seen Vivienne, but I cannot help regretting it for my own sake; simply because I am anxious to have trustworthy reports of her mental and physical condition. If you do see her, I shall be grateful for a line of description. And even the briefest word to show that I am remembered is very welcome.

Affectionately,
Tom

C. L. Sulzberger, who was to become a noted journalist and author, recalled: 'Eliot accepted me in a special course for fifteen pupils. We were illumined by his brilliant mind. Even in 1933 he forecast that Hemingway would be regarded as the Kipling of his time. Kipling was then seen as "square". Ultimately, Eliot predicted, both would find equal literary rank. Timid and withdrawn as Eliot was in class, he had a talent for banging the piano and singing a huge number of limericks, some of which I suspect he had written himself. I liked him despite the fact that he gave me a poor mark on my term paper. Its subject was "The Undergraduate Poetry of T. S. Eliot"' (*A Long Row of Candles: Memoirs and Diaries 1934–1954* [1969], 20–1).

Loucks, 19–20: 'After the fourth Norton lecture, a *New Yorker* reporter commented that TSE's material was "abstruse" and that the "adult listeners had a hard time keeping up" ("Error" [*New Yorker*, 21 Jan. 1933], 12).' '*February 17, evening*. Attending TSE's fifth Norton lecture, "Shelley and Keats", William Burroughs heard TSE deplore the excesses of English Romantic poets and question the Romantics' notion that people ought to be taught to think for themselves. Although he disagreed with TSE's views, he thought the lecture was humorous and well delivered (Morgan, 57).'

TO *Margaret Thorp*[1]   TS Princeton

14 February 1933   B-11 Eliot House, Cambridge

Dear Mrs Thorp:

Thank you very much for your kind invitation. I do not know yet whether Dr More will be in Princeton when I come, and I must write to him to inquire. In any case I shall do my best to save a meal to take with you, so that I may give you news of Emily, whom I saw in California.[2]

With best wishes to yourself and your husband,

Yours very sincerely,

T. S. Eliot

1–Margaret Thorp, née Farrand (1891–1970), educated at Smith College (AB, AM) and Yale (PhD, 1934), was a distinguished author and biographer: her works include *Charles Kingsley, 1819–1875* (1937), *America at the Movies* (1939), *Female Persuasion: Six Strong-Minded Women* (1949), *Neilson of Smith* (1956), *Sara Orne Jewett* (1966). She and Willard Thorp were married in 1930 and had spent a year in England on a travelling fellowship.

2–Emily Hale: see Biographical Register. TSE had arrived in Claremont, California, on 29 Dec. 1932. Loucks, 21: 'Stepping off the train at 6.20a.m., he was greeted by Emily Hale and Paul Havens, a former Rhodes Scholar who had met TSE at Oxford (Havens). His visit was "primarily a private one to Emily Hale," who described it as "a quiet rest between heavy lecture engagements" (Havens; Hale). Hale, then forty-one, was Head of House, Eleanor Joy Toll Hall, and Assistant Professor of Oral English (Sahak, 1992); she remained there for only two years, 1932–4 (Havens). A former student recalled "the weekly letters that came to her in blue envelopes with British postage from the great poet. She had a leather folder in her room with two pictures of Mr Eliot, autographed to her" (Hume).' Loucks reports too that in advance of TSE's visit, Emily Hale had given a talk on TSE and read from his poetry. '"Miss Hale . . . presented him not only as a well-known literary figure, but as a man, and a product of many influences . . . A man of extremes, a man of undoubted faults and highest virtues."' ('Campus Acquaintance'). Havens relates too that Hale 'spoke of him often, always as "Tom", and was obviously much in touch with him, and wore a ring that he had given her . . . [T]here was much excitement when Emily announced that he would visit her shortly after Christmas.' Loucks adds: 'Staying at the home of Miss Mary B. Eyre, near the college campus, TSE was entertained by Nathaniel Wright Stevenson and by Paul and Lorraine Havens. The latter recalls TSE's imbibing numerous cups of tea in her home during an animated discussion of Shakespeare, Donne, Milton, Dryden, and other English poets (Havens).' In early January, 'Lorraine Havens escorted TSE to Ellen Browning Hall at Scripps for tea. TSE seemed "somewhat reserved and formal, but very courteous, and obviously devoted to Emily [Hale]" (Havens). He inscribed a copy of Sweeney Agonistes "For Emily Hale / from the author / T. S. Eliot / Claremont / California. / January 1933" (Sahak, 1994).' On another day, 'TSE attended one of Paul Havens's seventeenth-century literature classes and joined in the discussion (Havens). During an informal evening meeting with students in the Tall Hall browsing room at Scripps, TSE discussed English humor, drawing mainly upon Lewis Carroll and Edward Lear. "His voice was pleasant, modulated and with little noticeable accent. (He admitted to impatience with having been born in St Louis instead of New England)" (Sands).'

TO *Walter de la Mare*   TS Estate of Walter de la Mare

14 February 1933   B-11 Eliot House, Cambridge

My dear de la Mare:

I was glad to get your letter of December 16th, and to hear from you.[1]

I shall be very happy to look up your friend Mrs Ladd, if I possibly can, and should like to meet both her and her husband. I expect to be giving one lecture in New Haven at the end of this month, but can only be there over one night, and from my experience, I imagine that I shall have no time to myself. But possibly I may be going to New Haven without lecturing at a later date.

I find myself very busy here, – indeed, very much busier than I normally am in London. I am now trying to make up arrears of letters unanswered during a tour of the West of this country at Christmas time.

I hope that I may see you when I get back, and compare experiences. With all best wishes to Mrs de la Mare and yourself.

Yours sincerely,
T. S. Eliot

TO *William Rose Benét*[2]   Photocopy of TS

14 February 1933   B-11 Eliot House, Cambridge

Dear Mr Benet:

I must apologize for my delay in answering your letter, and accordingly giving you the trouble of writing me again.[3]

I have thought the matter over, and my conclusion is that I have no poem which I should care to have presented to the public as my favorite. I am very sorry, but I am afraid there is nothing to be done about it.

Yours regretfully,
T. S. Eliot

1 – Letter not found.
2 – William Rose Benét (1886–1950), poet and editor, was associate editor of the *New York Evening Post Literary Review*, 1920–4; co-founder and editor of the *Saturday Review of Literature*, 1924–9. His works include the Pulitzer Prize-winning *The Dust Which Is God* (autobiography in verse, 1941), and *The Reader's Encyclopedia* (1948).
3 – Benét was gathering contributions for *Fifty Poets: An American Auto-Anthology* (1933), a collection of favourite single poems.

TO *Elinor Nef*[1]   TS University of Chicago

14 February 1933   B-11 Eliot House, Cambridge

Dear Mrs Nef:

Thank you very much for your kind letter of February 3. It would be a great pleasure to revisit Chicago, and meet you and your husband, and speak in that city.

I was in Chicago for a very brief time in January, but only to visit relatives and not to speak. And I am afraid that it will be impossible for me to get to Chicago again during my visit to America.

In any case I cannot take on any more lectures than those I have already promised to give.

> With many regrets and thanks,
> Yours sincerely,
> T. S. Eliot

TO *Ronald Bottrall*   TS Texas

15 February 1933   B-11 Eliot House, Cambridge

Dear Bottrall:

Your letter of the 14th of January[2] arrived while I was still away on a visit to the West, and since my return I have been overwhelmed with work. I assume that you are now back in Princeton. I am very sorry indeed to hear that you are not yet out of medical hands.

I look forward to your sending me shortly the section three of *Festivals of Fire*. Grigson's new venture seems very commendable, and you will be, I think, in quite good enough company.[3] I should hardly imagine that any periodical of the kind was likely to last long.

1–Elinor Castle Nef (1894–1953): first wife of John Ulric Nef (1899–1988), economic historian. A prolific diarist and letter writer, she corresponded with numerous artists and intellectuals. John Nef, a native of Chicago, graduated from Harvard in 1920, and received his PhD in 1927 from the Robert Brookings Graduate School, Chicago, 1927. He taught at Chicago from 1929, becoming Professor of Economic History in 1936; and in 1941 he underwrote the establishment of the celebrated interdisciplinary graduate department, the Committee on Social Thought, and served as its chairman, 1945–64. Publications include *The Rise of the British Coal Industry* (2 vols, 1932), *The United States and Civilization* (1942), *The Conquest of the Material World* (1964). See also Elinor Castle Nef, *Letters and Notes Volume I* (Los Angeles, 1953).
2–Not found.
3–Geoffrey Grigson (1905–85) – poet, author, critic; editor of the influential periodical *New Verse*, 1933–9 ('the new venture') – had first proposed himself to F&F in a letter to FVM

By all means mention my name in your application at Cambridge. If the electors refer to me, I shall put my best foot forward.

Now about the poem. I should like Faber and Faber to consider it for publication in the autumn. I am not, of course, in very close touch with the business while I am here, and I know little of the publishing situation now in general. But they have done Stephen Spender's poems just recently, and I should like them to consider your poems either for the autumn or for the end of January next, which is a pretty good time for poetry. I will write to them about the matter in my next letter, which ought to be within a few days. Of course, it is possible that they may have accepted some other book of poems without consulting me, but I do not think that this is likely.

Yours sincerely,

T. S. Eliot

TO *William Force Stead*[1]

TS Beinecke

15 February 1933   B-11 Eliot House, Cambridge

My dear Stead,

I have two letters to thank you for, and was indeed more than pleased to hear from you. I am simply run off my feet here with work and hospitality, and do not know when I can scrape the time to write you a reply worthy of your letters. I haven't even had the time to open your book yet, but I am going to read it and write and tell you what I think.

I shall be trying to see Ferris Greenslet of Houghton Mifflin & Company here in a week or two about several other publishing matters, and I will raise the question with him about *Uriel*.[2] I do not know that I can do anything more at the moment better than what could be done from

---

of 12 Nov. 1930 (when he was working as a reviewer for the *Yorkshire Post* and for the *Saturday Review*): he was venturing, he wrote, to compile an anthology of American and English poetry; and he added: 'Such an anthology would cover new ground, and might do good, and might pay (it seems to me) . . . Of my own powers of criticism, I have at least a humble, if confident opinion. If I have said things (of some of Mr Eliot's work, for instance) of which I ought to be ashamed, I am at least prepared to admit my shame to myself. Of the mechanical spade work of anthologists I am ignorant, but I suppose that it can be learnt at no great cost.'

1–William Force Stead (1884–1967), poet and clerhyman: see Biographical Register.
2–*Uriel: A Hymn in Praise of Divine Immanence* (1933).

London, as I shall not be visiting New York until April or May, but I will do what I can.

> In haste,
> Yours ever affectionately,
> T. S. Eliot

TO *Ezra Pound*

TS Beinecke

15 February 1933   B-11 Eliot House, Cambridge

Dear Rabbit:

Thanks for your letter of January 4.[1] I am not quite sure what you want me to do at the moment, but I see no reason why I should not act in the vague capacity indicated, especially if Yeats were in the same position. I agree as to the suitability of diverting Guggenheim money in that direction, but is there any other influence I can use except the rather feeble influence which an article might exert?

> Yours in haste,
> T. S. E.

TO *Alida Monro*

TS BL

16 February 1933   B-11 Eliot House, Cambridge

Dear Alida,

Thank you very much for cabling me that you like the Preface. I [am] never certain now [*sc.* how] anything I write about a friend (I mean about the work of a friend) will strike anyone else; but if you like this, I am quite happy over it. I trust you received the goldfish catalogue. Can I do anything further? I am, alas, too busy now for letters. I telephoned Greenslet but was unable to make an appointment; if I do not hear this week I will try again. I shall be grateful for news, and shall answer.

> Yours,
> T. S. E.

1 – Not found.

FROM *Vivien Eliot* TO *Henry Eliot*   TS Houghton

Sunday, 19 February 1933   68 Clarence Gate Gardens

Dear Henry,

This will be just a short letter about business. I do hope you are better than you were when Theresa wrote to me. She said you had a bad cold, and were in bed, and she had to come into the room to ask you how to spell propinquity. I hope I have spelt it right, myself.

My last letter from Tom is not cheerful, and he sent me a few snapshots, among them one of himself, and he did not look to me very well.

There has been a very great deal of illness here. And now there is snow, and sleet on the ground, and it is very bad weather.

I have not been feeling at all well for some weeks, and so I spent a good deal of time last week in draughting out a new Will. In this Will I have appointed you as Executor, together with my brother Maurice, and also George Lawrence Smith.[1]

It is my urgent wish that you will undertake this duty for me, although I am aware that it will cause you a good deal of inconvenience. I do not believe, however, that you will seriously object and I feel sure that you will see, and agree with me that in the interests of all concerned it is essential to have American Executors. There is no need to give reasons why I have chosen you, being as you are, Tom's elder and only brother. And you will understand my choice of George Smith, as I have so much affection for Theodora.

My solicitor's are Messrs. James & James
(Alfred E. James Esq.,)
23, Ely Place,
Holborn Circus,
E.C.1

I signed the Will yesterday, Saturday, February 18th, morning, at their Office.

I must not write more now, as I am very tired. But please write in reply to this at your earliest convenience. And let me know how *you* think Tom is, and how you are yourself, and Theresa, to whom please give my best love.

Your affect. sister-in-law,
Vivienne Haigh Eliot

1–George Lawrence Smith (1873–1962) – son of Professor Clement Lawrence Smith (1844–1909), who taught Greek and Latin at Harvard from 1870 – was widower of TSE's sister Charlotte (1874–1926). His daughter was Theodora Eliot Smith (1904–92) – 'Dodo' – beloved of TSE and VHE.

26 February 1933   B-11 Eliot House, Cambridge

My dear Alida,

Thank you for your letter of the 8th.[1] I will reply as frankly. I have formed some designs for the future, but rather different from what you suggest. Your alternative has made me think for a week, but I will put my objections.

You say that you wish that I might never put my feet over the threshold of my flat again. So do I. I feel sure that once I get in it will be much more difficult to get out than it will be to stay out if I don't go in. But your suggestion does not seem to me quite to fit with this. No matter how long I delay returning, or how gently I put it, it seems to me that if I go somewhere else – as I hope to do – on alighting from the ship, that will surely be an obvious break. I do not believe that there is any affection deep enough to consider, but there will be the emotion of fear, and of course very eminently that of Vanity; and it seems to me that it will be better to have a sharp sudden break and get it over with than allow matters to drag on for months until she becomes reconciled to the fact that I do not mean to return. It would mean months of anxiety and constant conversations on the subject (furthermore, there is the necessity of having a legal financial settlement in order to protect myself from being bankrupted). I have of course no feeling of affection myself to wound; this is a step which I have contemplated for many years; I should feel nothing but relief, and should prefer not to see V. again. (I have no doubt that all sorts of ulterior motives will be alleged in order to discredit my real, only and obvious motive of getting peace for work and throwing off the poison of uncongeniality and pretense).

My design had been to go straight to my club on arriving (concealing the date so as not to be met at the train or boat) and then find a furnished room in some quiet and retired quarter. I have written to two persons (Faber & the Dean of Rochester[2]) for their opinion and to ask the name of a suitable solicitor – it is important to get a really firm and tactful one. Then I should consult the solicitor *before* announcing my plans; I should certainly not make public or tell V. or anyone what I intended to do until I had the solicitor's advice as to when to do so – or whether to leave it until I arrived. I should certainly prefer to have the solicitor act as far as

1 – Not found.
2 – Francis Underhill (appointed Dean of Rochester in 1932) – TSE's 'Spiritual Director'.

possible in order to avoid painful interviews (and useless interviews) with V. and her family, who in all probability would try very hard to prevent the realisation of my plans.[1]

You may, when you wrote, have felt that you did not know how I felt about the matter – or you may simply have thought that I didn't know myself how I felt – probably you did not know that the whole history has been from the beginning a hideous farce to me; you wrote as if you were tentatively putting forward what I had never dared to think. I wonder if now you will be of the same opinion, in favour of [a] more gradual procedure? It will be some time before I can take any step, so I should be very grateful if I might know.

I had all this in mind, indeed, when I accepted the appointment here. America has not made any difference, except in making more real to me the fact that I can be comparatively happy *solely* by being away from V., that I am getting old – I mean that my years of activity can be counted, and I have no time now to waste, and that I cannot face the prospect of dragging on again the same futile life that I have been leading in London. It is odd to have such feelings combined: the happiness (if it may be called that) I have had here combined with a real dislike of America as a habitat and home-sickness for the quiet routine of London, and my friends there.

Ever yours,

T. S. E.

1–Giles Evans, *Wishwood Revisited: A New Interpretation of T. S. Eliot's 'The Family Reunion'* (1991), 128: 'If Robert Sencourt is reliable, Eliot was aware of the cruelty of his manner of separating. Ackroyd relies on Sencourt when he writes: ". . . when Maurice Haigh-Wood . . . asked Eliot if there were any other, less cruel, way than of writing through solicitors, he replied, "What other way can I find?"' Maurice Haigh-Wood was to write to Donald Adamson, 1 May 1970: 'When Tom returned from America in 1932 or 1933 & sent his solicitor with the letter to Vivienne, I don't remember using the word "cruel" when I spoke to Tom. I think I said how could he have broken off in such a harsh & abrupt way, instead of trying to prepare her for the separation. But I perfectly understood his point of view when he explained how any other way would have been worse.

'I regarded Tom almost as an older brother for 50 years, right up to his death, & I was delighted when eventually he married Valerie, with whom he was so happy, after all those years of loneliness' (Donald Adamson Collection).

TSE told Mary Trevelyan, 20 Aug. 1950: 'I didn't realize for a long time what was happening and I thought it was my fault for a period. I got away by going to America and not coming back. The difficulty is that you either suffer too much or too little with the sufferer' ('The Pope of Russell Square' [1950], 11).

TO *Virginia Woolf*   TS Berg

5 March 1933   B-11 Eliot House, Cambridge

My dear Virginia,

   After you have been a Time in America, Nothing can surprise you. To
begin with, that blue rubber soap dish I talked about, the Blue comes
off, and the soap dish is Wearing away.[1] That is the sort of thing that
happens. In Los Angeles (I have learnt how to pronounce Los Angeles and
Albuquerque, but Terre Haute is beyond me) they have a skyscraper and
it is bright green, but you hardly notice that, and they have a restaurant
called the Brown Derby which is built of concrete to look like a Brown
Bowler Hat, and you go there and eat Buckwheat Cakes & Maple Syrup
and Coffee at Midnight, and it seems just as normal as an A.B.C.[2] I have
four thousand dollars in the bank, and actually five dollars and thirty five
cents *disponible*,[3] and that seems normal too. I have been to Providence
(Rhode Island state)[4] and met a lady at dinner in the best society of the
place, the First Woman who has really ever made Eyes at me, I kept
dodging her Eyes for three hours, she seemed a trifle tipsy, and to any
remark of mine she always replied 'My! what a line you've Got!' She was
a bit too Plump, but said her age was 45. I have just been to Mt Holyoke
College, which is said to turn out more female missionaries than anywhere
else, but some were very Attractive.[5] Last night I dined with Lily Norton,

1 – TSE had written to VW on 20 Nov. 1932 (letter not traced), and she replied on 15 Jan.
mentioning *inter alia*: 'Your letter told me all I can absorb of life at Harvard. The Cabots
and the Sedwicks and the Wolcotts and the soap. And the sponge shaped like a brick . . . [O]
f course we go on reading MSS; and of course they are mostly about a man called Eliot, or
in the manner of a man called Eliot – how I detest that man called Eliot! Eliot for breakfast,
Eliot for dinner – thank God Eliot is at Harvard. But why? Come back soon; and write
again, to your old humble servant Virginia.' VW's letter (Denison Library) is quoted in full
and discussed in M. J. Dunbar, 'Virginia Woolf to T. S. Eliot: Two Letters', *Virginia Woolf
Miscellany* no. 12 (Spring 1979), 2.
2 – A.B.C. (Aerated Bread Company Ltd): a popular chain of self-service tearooms launched
in 1864. See TSE's 'A Cooking Egg' (1919): 'Over buttered scones and crumpets / Weeping,
weeping multitudes / Droop in a hundred A.B.C.'s.'
3 – *disponible*: available.
4 – Loucks, 24: '*February 19*. TSE participated in Brown University's second annual series
of modern poetry readings . . . TSE said he would comment between poems, as he had
not written enough verse for an hour of continuous reading; indeed, he added, "I feel
ignominious in reading it at all" (Mitchell; "TSE's Poems" 1).'
5 – Loucks, 25–6: 'February 25, evening. In North Mandelle Parlor at Mount Holyoke, TSE
dined with members of the honorary literary society, Blackstick, and gave an informal talk
followed by a poetry reading. The critic's task, he said, is to bring works of real merit to
the attention of the public. He confessed his inability to enjoy Goethe and Milton's *Paradise
Lost* bur said he expected to appreciate them in future. Major and minor poets differ in that
with the latter, the reader must be in the proper mood; with a major poet, however, one can

whom you may Remember; tonight with some people named Sears, and a young nincompoop named Henry Cabot Lodge who is a congressman.[1] There was cocktails, & champagne, and 3 kinds of liqueurs; also beer and whisky. So I was able to talk to a lady named Mrs McKean, who is remarkable. I have given a lecture at Yale University on English Letter Writers.[2] I only found out that I had to lecture on English Letter Writers

---

even be in the wrong mood. Literary greatness remains constant, though greatness can be attributed to different factors in different eras ("TSE Entertained").'

TSE would write to J. McG. Bottkol, 8 June 1964: 'I remember it was during the winter and Mount Holyoke seemed very remote from Cambridge, Mass., but I also remember that the undergraduates seemed to me a very nice lot of girls then.'

1 – Possibly 'some people' included Phyllis (Sears) Tuckerman, Bostonian heiress, who in 1916 married Bayard Tuckerman Jr (1889–1974), jockey, businessman, politician; or Eleanor Randolph Sears (1881–1968), champion tennis player and athlete; daughter of a Boston businessman – and cousin of Henry Cabot Lodge (1902–85), who was to become Senator for Massachusetts; a distinguished, much-decorated soldier in WW2; vice-presidential running-mate to Richard Nixon; and later Ambassador to the United Nations, West Germany, Vietnam. HWE had written to TSE, 15 May 1932: 'When you come to New York, I should like to have you go to tea at the Tuckerman ladies'. They are charming representatives of the old regime; you would almost think yourself back in London. They have been most cordial to us.'

2 – TSE spoke on 'English Poets as Letter Writers', under the auspices of the Lamont Memorial Foundation, to an audience of 500 in Sprague Memorial Hall, Yale University, 23 Feb. 1933.

The full lecture (Gallup C341) has not survived; but HWE copied out this opening paragraph: 'I am really the last person who ought to be talking to you about letter writers, even within the frame to which I have restricted myself. To begin with, I am almost illiterate, although not analphabetic. I am an extremely ill-educated and ignorant man. I have been trying for some years, indeed, ever since I provided one of my own poems with notes, to shatter the notion that I was a man of vast erudition. I have denied this at every opportunity, at first rather diffidently, finally rather querulously, and I have found that no one believes me. Sherlock Holmes, you will remember, when he remarked that his brother Mycroft's powers of observation were superior to his own, denied with what was for him unusual warmth, that his judgment was in any way biassed by modesty. So do I. I am genuinely sorry for my illiteracy; I have a great respect for educated men. I have certainly made use of the few scraps of learning that I possess, I see no reason why I should not use any quotation if it is apposite; but by quoting an author I do not delude myself into believing that I am perfectly acquainted with his works. Nor, until I woke up and found myself burdened with the weight of learning which I disclaimed, did I suppose that any one else would believe it either. I am merely a smatterer in a very few narrow fields. But I know what will happen. My words will fall on deaf ears, and everybody will go on believing in my incredible learning until I am dead. I mean, until a few days or a few weeks after I am dead; for critics are always very polite to you while you are still in the obituary state. And then one clever critic will have a new idea, and observe that in spite of this and that it must be said that Eliot was an ignorant man who had read very little. Then they will all take it up; until some other critic has the originality to remark that it is really the most significant thing about me; that it is, in fact, the clue to Eliot. Opinion will, I hope, be divided as to whether I know how ignorant I was, or whether I was justified in making use of learning which I did not possess, or whether I was a mere impostor. And in all the discussion no one will give me the credit of never having made

5 days before the lecture; that was trying. So I did. I gather that the serious people thought me very frivolous: but I met Mr Thornton Wilder at lunch.[1]

---

any pretensions to learning. For the moment I have been speaking, you see, not so much to the present audience as to posterity; for I have an apprehension that the importance of my ignorance is going to be, some years hence, grossly exaggerated. And if I ever print this lecture, you will know the reason why.'

The lecture was reported in *Yale Daily News* 56: 3 (24 Feb. 1933), 3 (Gallup C341): '"No other form of communication can ever supplant the letter," Mr Eliot said. "Letters in the future will be different from those in the past because they will be typed, but no good letter can be dictated; there must be no third person. Letter-writing permits us to forget ourselves and to express the worthwhile things that come spontaneously. It can be a provocation of and a consolation for solitude. Our minds should be left to wander when writing a letter, and a good letter will focus the reader's attention on what the letter is getting [at], rather than the letter itself."

'An ideal correspondence, according to Mr Eliot, will be with a person of the opposite sex, not one with whom the writer is in love, for love letters are monotonous. The recipient of the letter should be a mature friend, sufficiently understanding so that a good deal need not be said, but not to the point where the letters will be obscure to others. There should be sufficient sentiment to release the writer's mind to speak freely, without fear of betrayal, for the greatest pleasure derived from letter-writing is being indiscreet. The two correspondents should have interests in common and should be able to be brutally frank.

'"A poet can be judged by his letters," Mr Eliot said. "To me, the letters of Keats are the finest letters in existence of English poets, for Keats could express great truths and yet be frivolous. Shelley's letters, however, are dull." Other poets whose letters appeal to Mr Eliot are D. H. Lawrence and Virginia Woolf, whose epistles he termed "masterpieces of the letter-writing art".'

HWE noted: 'T. S. E. quoted from this passage from a letter of D. H. Lawrence dated 1916 [to Catherine Carswell, 11 Jan. 1916]: "The essence of poetry with us in this age of stark and unlovely actualities is a stark directness, without a shadow of a lie, or a shadow of deflection anywhere. Everything can go but this stark, bare, rocky directness of statement, this alone makes poetry, today". T. S. E. repeated this last sentence with approval, and continued: "This speaks to me of that at which I have long aimed, in writing poetry: to write poetry which should be essentially poetry, with nothing poetic about it, poetry standing naked in its bare bones, poetry so transparent that we see not the poetry, but that which we are meant to see through the poetry, poetry so transparent that in reading it we are intent on what the poem points at and not the poetry, this seems to me the thing to try for."' And HWE took particular note (when he read over TSE's lecture notes in June 1933) of this passage: 'The desire to write a letter, to put down what you don't want anybody else to see but the person you are writing to, but which yet you do not want to be destroyed, but perhaps hope may be preserved for complete strangers to read, is ineradicable. We want to confess ourselves in writing to a few friends, and we do not always want to feel that no one but those friends will ever read what we have written.'

See also F. O. Matthiessen, *The Achievement of T. S. Eliot* (3rd edn, 1958), 89–90.

Also on 23 Feb., TSE was entertained to lunch by Professor William Lyon Phelps, who noted: 'We talked a good deal about Paul Elmer More, whom we both admired. Mr Eliot gives one the same impression in conversation that one receives in reading him – intense sincerity' (*Autobiography with Letters* [1939]).

1–Thornton Wilder (1897–1975), playwright and novelist, author of the Pulitzer Prize-winning *The Bridge of San Luis Rey* (1927), also attended a poetry reading by TSE at Yale: see Gilbert A. Harrison, *The Enthusiast: A Life of Thornton Wilder* (1983), 133.

I also have Met Mr Mencken in Baltimore[1] – did I mention that I went to Baltimore after I left Buffalloo; and I met Mr Milliken in Pasadena,[2] but Einstein arrived after I left. So did a person described sometimes as the Hon. Lady Victoria Sackville West;[3] I saw the announcement of her coming to Buffalloo: with the names of the 40 ladies composing the Reception Committee. I hope she liked the Reception. In this country, as my friend St Leger Leger says in his *Anabase*: Doubt is Cast on the Reality of Things.[4] I am wondering whether I shall return to England my England[5] poorer than I left it: swindled to make a Bankers' Holiday. I should not ask How Stands England?[6] for I get the weekly *Manchester Guardian* two weeks late; but if I had been invited here one year earlier

1–H. L. Mencken (1880–1956), American author, editor, journalist, polemicist and autobiographer, was from 1908 editor of *Smart Set*, and of the *American Mercury* until 1933; his works include *Prejudices* (essays in 6 vols, 1919–27) and *The American Language* (1936). At TSE's request, Simone Boas invited Mencken and his wife Sara to meet TSE; but because his wife was ill, Mencken popped in for a while after dinner. Mencken wrote in his diary, 2 Feb:

'Eliot turned out to be a tall, somewhat ungainly fellow, looking more like an Oxford man than any Englishman. He said that he was having a quiet but tolerable time at Harvard. He lectures once a week, has a weekly tea-party open to undergraduates, and also gives a course in modern English literature – that is, since 1890. He told me that he found the last somewhat difficult, for he seldom reads modern literature, and in the main dislikes it. He said that one of the undergraduates brought a pretty girl to tea one day, and almost broke up the party. Eliot served notice that he'd prefer to have no female guests . . .

'An amiable fellow, but with little to say. He told me that his father was a brick manufacturer in Missouri. No talk of religion. We discussed magazine prices . . . I drank a quart of home-brew beer, and Eliot got down two Scotches. A dull evening' (*The Diary of H. L. Mencken*, ed. Charles A. Fecher (1989) 55).

2–Presumably Robert A. Millikan [*sic*] (1868–1953), experimental physicist; winner of the Nobel Prize for Physics, 1923, who worked at the California Institute for Technology (Caltech).

3–Vita Sackville-West (1892–1962), only child of the 3rd Baron Sackville; writer, poet, and landscape gardener (famous for her development of the gardens at her house near Knole and at Sissinghurst Castle, Kent), wrote novels including *The Edwardians* (1930) and *All Passion Spent* (1932), and works of poetry, non-fiction and biography. Sustaining an unorthodox relationship with her husband, the diplomat and writer Harold Nicolson (1886–1968) – both being essentially homosexual – she had love affairs with Violet Trefusis (1894–1972), daughter of Mrs Alice Keppel (mistress of Edward VII) – her relationship with Trefusis earned the tribute of Virginia Woolf's fantasy-fiction *Orlando* (1928) – with the poet Dorothy Wellesley, and with others, as well as a close relationship with Woolf herself, 1925–8. See Nigel Nicolson, *Portrait of a Marriage* (1973); Victoria Glendinning, *The Life of Vita Sackville-West* (1983); Suzanne Raitt, *Vita and Virginia: The Work and Friendship of V. Sackville-West and Virginia Woolf* (1993); *The Letters of Vita Sackville-West to Virginia Woolf*, ed. L. De Salvo and M. A. Leaska (1984).

4–See *Anabasis*, trans. TSE: 'And doubt is cast on the reality of things' (*Et le doute s'élève sur la réalité des choses*).

5–See D. H. Lawrence's collection of stories, *England, My England* (1922).

6–'And England – how stands England?' wrote Conan Doyle on the death of Queen Victoria in 1901.

and were back in England now consuming a dozen of Whitstable Natives[1]
and a Pint of Guinness I should be heaps happier.

Your deserving servant,
T. S. E.

TO *Donald S. Klopfer*[2]

TS Columbia University Libraries

7 March 1933

B-11 Eliot House, Cambridge

Dear Mr Klopfer,

Thank you very much for your interesting letter of the 23rd February.[3]
Your suggestion is an attractive one but requires considerable deliberation.
The question is whether the inclusion of my works in the Modern Library
would not completely kill the ordinary edition, and I certainly do not
want to let Harcourt Brace and Company down. It is, furthermore, a
matter which concerns Faber and Faber also, and I am writing to them
about it and will let you hear later.

Yours sincerely,
T. S. Eliot

TO *Edmund Wilson*[4]

TS Beinecke

7 March 1933

B-11 Eliot House, Cambridge

Dear Mr Wilson,

Thank you very much for your kind note.[5] I should be delighted to
come to stay with you. I shall be in New York on the 20th, but then must

1–Excellent native oysters from Whitstable, Kent.
2–Donald S. Klopfer (1902–86): publisher; founder with Bennett Cerf of Random House.
3–Not found.
4–Edmund Wilson (1895–1972): influential literary critic, social commentator and cultural
historian; worked in the 1920s as managing editor of *Vanity Fair*; later as associate editor of
The New Republic and as a prolific book reviewer. Major publications include *Axel's Castle:
A Study in the Imaginative Literature of 1870–1930* (1931) – which includes a chapter on
TSE's work, sources and influence – *The Triple Thinkers: Ten Essays on Literature* (1938),
and *The Wound and the Bow: Seven Studies in Literature* (1941). TSE was to write to
Geoffrey Curtis on 20 Oct. 1943: 'Edmund Wilson is a very good critic except that, like
most of his generation in America, he has mixed his literary criticism with too much political
ideology of a Trotskyite variety and perhaps he is also too psychological, but I have a great
respect for him as a writer and like him as a man.' See too Wilson, 'T. S. Eliot and the Church
of England', *The New Republic*, 24 Apr. 1929, 283–4; 'T. S. Eliot', *The New Republic*, 13
Nov. 1929, 341–9.
5–Not found.

stay with my brother; and again on the 27th, but then I must lecture at the New School and go to Bryn Mawr the next day.[1] That would be an unsatisfactory visit; but I want to meet you. I shall be in New York again in May; perhaps you would rather wait till then. I should have tried to see

1 – TSE lectured at the New School for Social Research, New York (where his friend Horace Kallen was on the faculty). On 21 Apr. he talked on 'The Verse of John Milton' in the McMillin Academic Theatre, Columbia, under the auspices of the Institute of Arts and Sciences. The *Evening Sun* (23 Apr.) reported his judgement that the most promising of the young British poets were Auden, Spender, MacNeice and Ronald Bottrall. William Carlos Williams passed on to Louis Zukofsky on 7 May 1937 this anecdote about TSE's lecture, as recounted by Professor Erdmann: 'In the character of a perfect Oxford Englishman Eliot first proclaimed, in drawling accent, that he didn't think he had ever before in public expressed his opinion of the poet Milton. The profs were by this time sitting openmouthed on the edge of their seats. Lycidas is, to be sure, a beautiful lyric poem. But Paradise Lost, exclaimed Mr Eliot, I consider a failure! The audience collapsed. It is the first time I have ever admired Eliot.' (*The Correspondence of William Carlos Williams & Louis Zukofsky*, ed. Barry Ahearn [2003], 253.)

On 27 Apr. he spoke again at the New School for Social Research. On at least one of those visits he gave a poetry reading, preceded by a dinner party hosted by Kallen. One of the other guests, Horace Gregory, related: 'Eliot arrived, in white-tie evening dress, ten minutes late: he was flushed and bright, and looked supremely exhilarated: he bowed to all of us and said, "Forgive me, if I seem a bit post-war, but I'm rather tight. I have to prepare myself to face all those people. I always drink before reading poetry' (Gregory, 205). Loucks, 'The Exile's Return', 27–8, relates further: 'Henry Eliot told Gregory that their mother "did not quite approve of some of Tom's more 'dangerous' poems, his Sweeney poems; they made her wonder what kind of company he kept." TSE prefaced his reading of "Sweeney Among the Nightingales" by saying that the poem was as abstract and impersonal as a modern painting, a remark seemingly addressed to Henry "in mock reassurance that he was only half as wicked as his family supposed him to be. I thought I saw him turn a bright flicker of a smile in Henry's direction." Gregory noticed that some had come to heckle TSE, "but he met the occasion with such well-poised levity that his enjoyment of the moment became contagious"' (206).

Harold Clurman reported of TSE's reading at the New School for Social Research: 'He had fine, regular features, he was tall and thin, wore a long black frock coat, and was strikingly pale-faced. There was something condescending, almost mocking, in his attitude toward the audience. He intoned the verse, a disagreeable mode of reading common among poets and especially wrong for Eliot's poetry. He looked for all the world like a highly bred Anglican cleric' (*All People Are Famous (instead of an autobiography)* [1974], 250).

Edmund Wilson related to John dos Passos: 'I heard Eliot read his poems the other night. He did them extremely well – contrary to my expectation. He is an actor and really put on a better show than Shaw . . . He gives you the creeps a little at first because he is such a completely artificial, or rather, self-invented character . . . but he has done such a perfect job with himself that you often end up admiring him' (*Letters on Literature and Politics 1912–1977*, ed. Elena Wilson (230) – cited in Gordon, *T. S. Eliot*, 253; Loucks, 28).

TSE spoke at Bryn Mawr on 28 Apr. on 'Modern Poetry', making the claim that his own poetry was 'very simple and straightforward' – some of the audience laughed at this good joke – and characterizing *TWL* as 'a piece of rhythmical grouching' (Loucks, 28; 'TSE Compares', 1).

you sooner; but I have had my nose to the grindstone, and have only had twelve hours in New York since my arrival.

Yours sincerely,
T. S. Eliot

TO *Frank Morley* TS Faber

7 March 1933 B-11 Eliot House, Cambridge

Dear Frank:

Many thanks for your admirable letter which I exhibited to my sister in giving her the photograph. Both letter and photograph were received with the greatest pleasure.

This is merely a hurried note to enclose a letter from Donald S. Klopfer, whom I do not know. I am not favorably disposed to this suggestion. It seems to me that it would kill the ordinary edition, and that Harcourt Brace would have legitimate grounds of complaint. Furthermore, I should say that I do better myself out of the Harcourt Brace edition than I should by dealing with these people. I should like your opinion.[1]

By the way, beside my Norton Lectures there will probably be a small volume of three lectures which I shall have to prepare for the University of Virginia in May. I don't want to flood the market, but will you let me know whether Faber and Faber want to publish it in England or whether they think it had better not go on the English market at all. I don't even know the title yet.

I am feeling rather meek at the moment as I was on the point of transferring most of my savings to London when the bank holiday caught me. I hope it will turn out all right in the end, as otherwise I shall be done pretty brown. I don't suppose I shall ever get as much for it in sterling as I should have done a week ago.[2]

1–FVM responded on 21 Mar.: 'Donald Klopfer. I take it he wants to put THE SELECTED ESSAYS in the Modern Library. The low down is as follows: if the sale of an ordinary edition is exhausted, the Modern Library reprint is worth while, but if an ordinary edition is selling 100 copies or more, the Modern Library reprint is probably not worth while. In this instance it is far too early to contemplate cutting in to Harcourt's edition with such a reprint. In your line you should say that you are all against the suggestion; but you should send him Klopfer's request because it is always well to ginger everybody with suggestions of competition. You should, I think, simultaneously write to Klopfer to say nothing doing yet awhile.'

2–FVM (21 Mar.): 'Your meekness as to not transferring your cash at the right time is understandable; your not having transferred it is inexcusable in a commentator who has ventured to discuss economics; and is one more instance of the absent minded professor.'

With love to Christina and Susanna,
Yours in haste,
T.

P.S. There is a young friend of mine from Jesus, Cambridge, who wants to review a book by James Agate, called *The English Dramatic Critics*. He says it is published by somebody named Barker whom I never heard of. Unless the book has been out too long, or something else has been done about it, or perhaps it isn't worth reviewing at all, I should like this fellow to have it. His name is Alistair Cooke, and his address is 953 Yale, New Haven, Connecticut.[1]

TO *John Cournos*   Photocopy of TS

7 March 1933   B-11 Eliot House, Cambridge

Dear Cournos,

I am sorry I haven't had a chance to read your tec yet;[2] but it got on my nerves knowing that you wanted it and fearing that if I waited I would forget; and so I posted it today. I shall read it when it is published. I am ashamed to have been so busy and tired that I have written no breadandbutter letter to Mrs Cournos – I hope for the moment that this will do – for I truly enjoyed very much being with you, and very much regretted that my stay was so flitting. I do hope to come to see you again before the end of the year.

Yours ever,
T. S. Eliot

TO *Harold G. Arnold*[3]   Photocopy of TS

7 March 1933   B-11 Eliot House, Cambridge

Dear Mr Arnold:

I must apologize for my delay in answering your kind invitation of the 20th February. I should be very glad to oblige the Boston Association of

---

1–FVM (21 Mar.): 'Your young friend from Jaggers is being taken care of by Miss Gilbert who is sending him the *English Dramatic Critics*. I am astounded that you haven't heard of Barker as publisher. Tut, tut, where have you been these months past? Come back to the hub and I'll tell you a lot of things you don't know yet.'
2–No letter found.
3–The Revd Harold Arnold, West Roxbury, Mass.

Ministers in any way that I can. I think that the date of April 10 will be possible for me, although a later date might be more convenient.

I confess, however, that my real difficulty, as, if I may say so, a rather fanatical Catholic, is what subject I could talk about to such an Association. A purely literary subject seems entirely out of place for such an occasion. If you have anything in mind, we might discuss the matter further.

Yours very sincerely,
T. S. Eliot

TO *Ottoline Morrell*   TS Texas

14 March 1933[1]   B-11 Eliot House, Cambridge

My dear Ottoline,

Your long and interesting letter is one for which I am very grateful. My impressions of America need to be clarified by a return to England, and I shall not try to put them down yet. I am quite sure that nothing here smells right; especially the countryside lacks that deep damp earthy smell of England. Of course, I have been very happy, for me; primarily because of being near my sisters, and not very far away from my brother – I have three sisters in Cambridge, and it is wonderful to be surrounded by such affection. Second, it is a pleasure to be among secondary relatives – aunts, uncles, cousins, nieces etc. – thirdly to be among so many other relatives, fourthly, to be where people know who I am: of course, outside of Boston I am simply T. S. Eliot, but here I am an Eliot. There is a pleasure in anonymity – and that I am better able to enjoy in London than here, where I am still a news item; but after eighteen years of being merely oneself there is a pleasure in being just a member of one's family. I don't know whether you can appreciate that. I like to be with people who were fond of me before the malady of poetry declared itself. Perhaps as one grows older one longs for family – perhaps one reverts to type, if the type is a strong one. I had rather revert to my type than to Bertie's, however. Bertie, because at first I admired him so much, is one of my lost illusions. He has done Evil, without being big enough or conscious enough to Be evil. I owe him this, that the spectacle of Bertie was one contributing influence to my

1 – TSE read his poetry after dinner at Eliot House on this day. F. O. Matthiessen commented: '[T]he excruciating poignancy of his voice brought tears springing to my eyes' (Louis Hyde, *Rat and the Devil: Journal Letters of F. O. Matthiessen and Russell Cheney* [1988], 223).

conversion. Of course he had no good influence on Vivienne. He excited her mentally, made her read books and become a kind of pacifist, and no doubt was flattered because he thought he was influencing her. (I have tried to subdue the desire to influence anyone). Unfortunately, she found him unattractive.[1]

I don't think that your notion of V. and I living in neighbouring flats is possible; but I am very glad to hear that she was not displeased. I entirely agree with you that she would flourish better without me. I also think that the present time, after my absence, is the best time for a break. For my part, I should prefer never to see her again; for hers, I do not believe that it can be good for any woman to live with a man to whom she is morally, in the larger sense, unpleasant, as well as physically indifferent.[2] But I am quite aware of putting my own interests first.[3] I will ask you not to give any indication of what I have said, not only to her, but to anyone else. I want to arrange matters in such a way as least to injure her vanity.

Affectionately, and in haste,
Tom[4]

---

1 – VHE wrote in an undated letter ('Monday') to OM, from 39 Inverness Terrace, W.2: 'My dear Lady Ottoline . . . About Bertie [Bertrand Russell], you know he was *extraordinarily generous* to me, I mean in *giving* things. So much so that it will always make me feel very mean for talking against him. I know you understand perfectly. But I think he was more generous to me than he has ever been to anyone. He really made a sacrifice . . . I have really suffered in the complete collapse of our relationship, for I was fond of Bertie (I think I still am). But it is of course *hopeless*, I shall never try to see him again . . . It is so bad for me to be always cautious & mistrustful. I think one often gossips in self-defence, knowing the other person will. But I shall not feel that way about you, if you won't about me?' (Texas TXR – A17: Morrell, O [recip.]: from Eliot, Vivienne).

2 – EVE told SS, 8 Oct. 1974, apropos a draft of his *T. S. Eliot* (1976): 'You imply, tactfully, that Tom was sexually a poor husband to Vivien. This is not true. He told me she had only one emotion: fear, and was terrified of having children. On medical advice they ceased relations.' VHE wrote to her brother MHW, 14 May 1936: 'that I never had any children in my life, I thank God, and never wished to, since I was a little girl of about twelve' (Bodleian MS Eng. lett. c. 383). John Worthen comments, in *T. S. Eliot: A Short Biography* (2009), 170: 'He found her "unpleasant" not (as has been suggested) because of her affair with Russell, but because she was "unpleasant as woman": morally unclean. Vivien in her turn was "physically indifferent" to him: she no longer wished to sleep with him.'

3 – This sentence, and the final phrase of the preceding sentence (from 'in the larger sense . . .'), are added in TSE's hand, replacing a typed phrase that is so heavily deleted as to be illegible.

4 – OM commented on this letter in a letter to JDH, 28 Mar. 1933: 'I had a very strange letter from T. S. E. this morning . . . He is obviously very happy in America & rejoices in being one with his family . . . He just loves being one of his family & that to us is very alien & foreign isnt it? . . . I long to congratulate him on his influence with Roosevelt about Beer – but I darent attempt any joke with Tom, would you?' (King's OM/JDH/19).

Friday, 17 March 1933   68 Clarence Gate Gardens

My dear Henry,

Thank you very much for your letter of March 7th, which I received yesterday, Thursday March 16th. I was very glad to have a letter from you, and all your news.

Following your suggestion, I wrote at once to my solicitor, Mr Alfred E. James, and put it to him that you suggested that a Copy of the Will should be sent over to you to get the opinion of American Solicitors. It seemed to me a reasonable suggestion.

I am now awaiting his reply.

I should have started by thanking you for agreeing to become my Executor. *I do thank you very much indeed.* It takes a great deal *off my mind.*

I notice that you use the word *Executor*, whereas I used the word *Trustee*.

In my letter to Mr James, *of February 14th*, of which I have the Copy, here with my Will, I say — 'I wish to appoint as my Trustees, my brother Maurice Haigh Haigh-Wood, my brother-in-law, Mr Henry Ware Eliot, and also Mr George Lawrence Smith.[']

I found that Mr James made the alteration of the word 'alternatively' in regard to Mr George Lawrence Smith.

I had thought it a good thing to have *three, (3) Trustees*, and I still do.

I am taking a third copy of this letter, and am sending it to *Tom himself.* And I doubt if I shall have time to write any other letters at all by this mail.

Tom has a typed Copy of the Instructions in the Event of my death during his absence in America, drawn up by my solicitor himself.

If anything should happen to me before you hear from me again, I wish you to know, Henry, that in my Will, which I purposely made as *simple and as brief as possible, I have left everything to Tom*, with the sole exceptions of three articles of furniture. These being the piano, and two family portraits in the dining room.

I have left the whole of my income, capital, and Securities, *and property, to Tom, for his whole lifetime. To be held in trust by* Tom for My nephew, Maurice's Son. I mean by this that Tom has everything for his *whole lifetime,* . . . .

Tom has had a hard and terrible experience. All his *friends* here know that.

I wish to make it certain that the rest of Tom's life is happier and easier and more secure than his life has ever been up till now.

I have also put in my Will that it is my earnest hope that Tom will make his permanent home in England.

I must stop now. I hope all is clear up to this point.

This evening I am expecting here to dinner with me, Mr and Mrs Geoffrey Faber, the head of Faber & Faber.

I understood from Tom that he has appointed Geoffrey Faber as Executor and Trustee of his Will, jointly with me, *I think*. But I may be wrong in this *last* point.

With best wishes to you and Theresa.

Yours very sincerely,
Vivienne Haigh Eliot

TO *Frank Morley*

TS Faber

18 March 1933   B-11 Eliot House, Cambridge

Dear Frank,

Paul More – Doktor Paul Elmer More – I am going to stay with him on Thursday, then on Friday to stay with the Haverfords to lecture at Hotson[1] – Paul More wants

> Paul Shorey: *What Plato Said*
>
> Cornford: *Before & After Socrates* (Camb. Univ. Press)

and pretty damn quick; could you please have them ordered and sent direct to him at 59 Battle Road Princeton N.J.[2] Ezzra (Brer Rabbit) seems pleased with himself at the moment.[3] I liked your letter from Shoreditch.[4] I have got to go tonight to a Dinner where Pres. Lowell is to be presented with a bowl. One more Norton lecture to give. Have been asked to make the Prize Day speech at my old school. *Sweeney Agonistes* is to be given

---

1 – TSE messes about: he was to stay with the Hotsons at Haverford College, where he lectured on 'The Development of Shakespearean Criticism', in Roberts Hall on 24 Mar.

2 – Paul Elmer More reviewed Paul Shorey, *What Plato Said*, and F. M. Cornford, *Before and After Socrates*, in C. 13 (Apr. 1934), 472–8. FVM wrote to More, 31 Mar. 1933: 'With his accustomed innocence Eliot mentioned that you also need Shorey's *What Plato Said*. I say innocence because this is published by the University of Chicago Press and it is much quicker, and considerably cheaper, to get it direct from them.'

3 – EP had written to FVM, 24 Jan. 1933: 'The level of britshit is almost incredibly low. Such OBVIOUSLY shoddy scribbling can NOT possibly last five years, even with Squire, Murry and all Eliot's snotty little criterion contributors obfuscating the thames foggs.'

4 – Not found.

at the Experimental Theatre at Vassar College, so no More from [*sic*] the Present, from the faithful

T. S. E.

TO *Hallie Flanagan*[1]   TS Lincoln Center

18 March 1933   B-11 Eliot House, Cambridge

Dear Miss Flanagan:[2]

I must apologise for the delay. I have no objection to your doing *Sweeney*, what there is of him, though I cannot imagine what anybody can do without me there to direct it. The action should be stylised as in the Noh drama – see Ezra Pound's book[3] and Yeats' preface and notes to *The Hawk's Well*.[4] Characters *ought* to wear masks; the ones wearing old masks ought to give the impression of being young persons (as actors) and vice versa. Diction should not have too much expression. I had intended the whole play to be accompanied by light drum taps to accentuate the beats (esp. the chorus, which ought to have a noise like a street drill). The characters should be in a shabby flat, seated at a refectory table, facing the audience; Sweeney in the middle with a chafing dish scrambling eggs (see 'you see this egg'). (See also F. M. Cornford. *Origins of Attic Comedy*,[5] which is important to read before you do the play.) I am talking about the *second* fragment of course; the other one is not much good. The second should end as follows: there should be 18 knocks like the angelus, and then ENTER an old gentleman. He is in full evening dress with a carnation, but otherwise resembles closely Father Christmas. In one hand he carries an empty champagne bottle, in the other an alarm clock.

1–Hallie Flanagan (1890–1969), American theatre producer and director, playwright, author, taught from 1927 to 1935 at Vassar College, Poughkeepsie, New York, where she built up the Vassar Experimental Theatre. She was to be National Director of the Federal Theater Project, 1935–42; and she ran the Theatre Department at Smith College, Northampton, Mass., 1942–52.
2–This letter was reproduced in Hallie Flanagan, *Dynamo* (1943), 82–4; and in Carol H. Smith, *T. S. Eliot's Dramatic Theory and Practice* (1963), 62–3.
3–'Noh' or Accomplishment: A Study of the Classical Stage of Japan. From the manuscripts of Ernest Fenollosa, ed. Ezra Pound (1917).
4–*At the Hawk's Well*, in *The Wild Swans at Coole* (1917). TSE to Patricia Greacen, 26 May 1961: 'My recollection of that drawing-room performance of *The Hawk's Well* is that Lady Cunard was occupying a house in Grosvenor Square, not Cavendish Square, but that could possibly be checked and I may be mistaken. I have only a dim recollection of everything except that marvelous [*sic*] performance by Ito, the Japanese dancer in the role of the Hawk.' The masks and costumes were designed by Edmund Dulac.
5–F. M. Cornford, *The Origin of Attic Comedy* (1914).

The Old Gentleman: Good evening. My name is Time. The time by the exchange clock is now nine-forty-five (or whatever it is). I come from the vacant lot in front of the Grand Union Central Depot, where there is the heroic equestrian statue of General Diego Cierra of Paraguay. Nobody knows why General Cierra is there. Nobody knows why I am there. Nobody knows anything. I wait for the lost trains that bring in the last souls after midnight. The time by the exchange clock is now 9:46.

Sweeney:	Have you nothing else to say?
The O.G.:	Have you nothing to ask me?
Sweeney:	Yes.
The O.G.:	Good.
Sweeney:	When will the barnfowl fly before morning?
	When will the owl be operated on for cataract?
	When will the eagle get out of his barrel-roll?
The O.G.:	When the camel is too tired to walk farther
	Then shall the pigeon-pie blossom in the desert
	At the wedding-breakfast of life and death.
Sweeney:	Thank you.
The O. G.:	Good night.

(As the O.G. leaves the alarm clock in his hand goes off).

I shall let you know if I can possibly come on May 6th.[1]

Yours very sincerely,

T. S. Eliot

---

1 – Joanne Bentley relates, in *Hallie Flanagan: A Life in the American Theatre* (1988), 137: 'On the morning of May 6, Philip [Davis, a member of the Vassar faculty, later Flanagan's husband] drove to Cambridge to pick up Eliot. On the way back they stopped at several bars. Hallie was frantic by the time they arrived [at Poughkeepsie]. "Oh, I thought you'd miss it!" she exclaimed. "I wish I had," Eliot murmured, but he took his seat. The audience ... was riveted by *Sweeney*.' *Vassar Miscellany News*, 10 May 1933, reported TSE's opinion of Flanagan's production (which formed part of the programme of the Vassar Experimental Theatre's spring season): 'Yes, *Sweeney* was entirely different from my previous conception of it ... But I liked it very, very much. In fact, I am inclined to think that Mrs Flanagan's way of presentation was better than my own might have been. *Sweeney* is still a fragment to me, I can only see it as part of a longer play, but Mrs Flanagan successfully produced it as a complete dramatic unit ... The first option on the dramatic performance of the finished work will go to Mrs Flanagan' ('World Premiere', 1).

F. O. Matthiessen commented in *The Achievement of T. S. Eliot* (1935; 3rd edn, 1948), 159: 'The songs in Eliot's play, "Under the bamboo tree" and "My little island girl", found their stimulus in American jazz, as did the syncopation of the dialogue. As a result Eliot's verse here seemed less novel than usual to American ears.'

In the summer of 1953, when a setting by Richard K. Winslow was staged at Columbia University, TSE told Winslow, 7 Dec. 1953: 'I thank you for sending me both the photographs and the recording of your short opera. The setting and choreography look to me very interesting, and I don't think that for a production of a fragmentary work like this, any more realistic setting would have been desirable. As for the music, it seems to me in places very interesting, and in other places not quite so successful. That perhaps is to be expected when a composer makes use of a text already written, and not originally intended for a musical setting. (It is true that my original design had been to have a good deal of accompaniment on percussion instruments).

'Your interpretation, like all the stage interpretations that I have seen of this fragment, gives me some surprises, but that is inevitable, in the first place because it is a fragment, and in the second place because I did not at that time clearly work out in my mind any scheme for the whole play. For that reason, the interpretations of the meaning of the play – the meaning of a play which was never written – are in a sense original creations of the interpreter. I think that if I had been able to finish, it would have turned out very differently from any interpretations of the fragment that I have seen, but I must confess that I simply don't know what it would have been like, and what the thing as a whole would have meant.'

On 11 June 1958 TSE was to write to Edward F. D'Arma (Program Associate, The Ford Foundation) – who had been Klipstein in Flanagan's production ('my first and only appearance on the stage, but it was a lot of fun') – 'I enjoyed that production of *Sweeney Agonistes* which was, I am sure, the world premiere. You may be interested to know that the B.B.C. have been enquiring about the possibility of a production with the same music of Quincy Porter.'

TSE later minimised the importance of the additions to *Sweeney Agonistes* represented by the second half of this letter to Flanagan – from 'ENTER an old gentleman' – and never sought to publish them. At one time he seemed even to forget them: when Flanagan cabled, out of the blue, on 28 Nov. 1941 – 'PRODUCING AT VASSAR MURDER IN THE CATHEDRAL DECEMBER SIXTH THINKING OF SWEENEY AND SCRAMBLING EGGS WITH YOU IN LONDON WISH YOU COULD FLY OVER PLEASE CABLE MY EXPENSE ANY ADDITIONS RE FATHER TIME' – he replied: 'CANT IDENTIFY FATHER TIME KINDEST REGARDS ELIOT.' On 2 Jan. 1958 he wrote to Alfred Weber, Berlin, of 'the fanciful continuation of *Sweeney Agonistes* which was written only for the entertainment of undergraduates on a specific occasion' – and which he did not wish to be published. (But see David Galef, 'Fragments of a Journey: The Drama in T. S. Eliot's *Sweeney Agonistes*', *English Studies* 69: 6 (Dec. 1988), 481–96; Randy Malamud, *Where the Words Are Valid: T. S. Eliot's Communities of Drama* (1994), 23–4.)

In a lecture, 'Shakespeare Criticism', at the New School for Social Research, New York, TSE remarked: 'I have attempted a *croquis* of a play (*Sweeney Agonistes*) to indicate that our tragic feelings are best expressed not through "tragedy" but through farce' (noted by HWE).

On 22 Mar. 1954 TSE told Erik Chisholm: 'It remains a fragment, and I have not the slightest idea what the play would have been like if I had ever completed it.'

The day after the performance (7 May 1933), in the same venue (Avery Hall at Vassar), TSE read some of his poetry and discussed it. *Vassar Miscellany News*, 10 May 1933, reported: 'He read two sections from *Ash-Wednesday*, the second and the fifth. "The three white leopards of the first," he explained, "are of course, the World, the Flesh and the Devil." The second borrowed John Donne's pun of "world" and "whirled", and introduced "word" into it. It was a protest against spiritual blindness, spiritual deafness, and it made use of a refrain from the Mass for Good Friday. *Ash-Wednesday* celebrated Mr Eliot's conversion to the Anglo-Catholic faith.'

Flanagan recalled, in her memoirs:

> Roaming about the setting of his own play he talked about poetry with impersonal lucidity.

TO *Paul Elmer More*   TS Princeton

26 March 1933   B-11 Eliot House, Cambridge

My dear More,

This is the first, and will probably be the last attempt of mine to write anything like a bread & butter letter during my stay.[1] The rare evenings which I have had with you are all memorable; but as one gets older (you cannot at least deny me the attainment of a little more than precise 'middle age') one's solitude in life becomes more and more evident to oneself – I hope that still more age will eventually bring me to complete Christian acceptance of the fact; but so far I am at least increasingly appreciative of the rare contacts in which one does not speak a wholly different language from the other person.

I had meant to catch a moment to inform you, in entire confidence, that upon my return to London I may be seeking some form of *private* but

---

'My poetry is simple and straightforward,' he declared; and when the audience laughed he looked pained. 'It is dubious whether the purpose of poetry is to communicate anyway. Poetry ought simply to record the fusion of a number of experiences.' Later when asked about *Sweeney Among the Nightingales*, he said, 'I'm not sure it means anything at all.' And he went on to develop the point that a poem may be like a still life, the meaning of which we do not formulate – 'We merely estimate the way the painter has used planes and angles.'

To student questions from the crowded house he was painstakingly exact, though sometimes cryptic.

'Was the production what you expected?'

'The moment expected may be unforeseen when it arrives.' (This line he later used in *Murder in the Cathedral*.)

And to the student who asked why he did not write Sweeney differently, he said thoughtfully, 'To be a different poem a poem would either have to be written by the same poet at a different time, or by a different poet at the same time.'

One questioner, referring to the lines,

> Every man has to, needs to, wants to
> Once in a lifetime do a girl in,

asked hopefully, 'Mr Eliot, did you ever do a girl in?' Mr Eliot looked apologetic and said, 'I am not the type.' (*Dynamo*, 84–5; cited in Bentley, *Hallie Flanagan*, 138–9.)

His audience for the reading included the students Elizabeth Bishop, Mary McCarthy and Muriel Rukeyser.

TSE may have written to Flanagan at a later date (in a now lost letter), questioning the character of her production of *Sweeney*, for she wrote to him on 17 May 1933: 'If you saw the play done against a realistic background, I have a feeling that you would be disappointed, because after all, isn't the realistic background as obsolete as arbitrary rhyme in poetry?' (quoted in Bentley, *Hallie Flanagan*, 137).

1 – On 23 Mar. TSE had given the Spencer Trask Foundation Lecture, 'The Bible and English Literature' in McCosh Hall, Princeton University.

definitive marital separation. (I have, by the way, taken spiritual as well as practical advice).[1] You might as well know this in advance – I have so far mentioned it to no one except those few consulted. It is possible that my summer may be made pretty unpleasant for me, but I hope to see you in July nevertheless. Please regard this as entirely private information.

Yours very gratefully,

T. S. Eliot

FROM *Vivien Eliot* TO *Ottoline Morrell*   MS Texas

31 March 1933   68 Clarence Gate Gardens

Dearest Ottoline,

Thank you for your letter of March 22. I am very *glad* you are better. But it is very cold again. Yes I <u>do</u> think it *might* be a good thing for me to go to the Sanatorium de la Malmaison for a time, as I am of course – *as you <u>know</u> – absolutely worn out* & run down and anaemic & really in a most terrible state of health – it is *obvious*. I look so *awful*. I have only had 2, or 3, baths since Tom went away. I have only washed my hair *twice*. I have the most *filthy* old clothes. And my hair is *grey* & my nails are *thick* with dirt & my hands are red & rough. My teeth are all

---

1–TSE was to disclose on 25 Mar. 1934 to Aurelia Hodgson: 'I might mention (as perhaps you may not have heard it otherwise) that I have been living alone since my return and expect to do so for the rest of my natural life. Vivienne is not yet very pleased about it and it has been very difficult, but I think in the end it will prove to be the best for both.' Much later, to another friend, Professor Gerald S. Graham, he would write on 13 Aug. 1945: 'According to my tenets I don't hold that divorce is "wrong": I am obliged to hold that is is *impossible*, that it isn't real. For those inside my church this has to mean the permanence of the legal form of marriage: for those outside it is rather different. They can ask themselves "was it a *real* marriage, or *only* the form without the spirit?" If they have to admit to themselves that it was real, but has merely ceased, that is one thing; if they can honestly say that it was n̶o̶t̶ never real, that is another. Of course this does not get us the whole way, because it is so terribly difficult to be honest, and in these matters above all others. I suppose one approach is to try to compare the first experience of love with the second, and decide for oneself, whether the experience of the second shows us something which was *always* lacking in the first . . .

'It is only about the question of separation that I am clear – assuming you to know, and I *am* making this assumption, going back to my recollections of thirteen years ago, that something interferes with your real existence. It is certainly not that I think the mere disappearance of "love" is enough to justify people separating; but when co-habitation involves any pretence, on one side or both, when there is not complete understanding and acceptance of the situation on both sides (and I do not see how there can be, here) then it is probably as bad for one as for the other, though the more conscious person suffers more consciously.'

broken away. It is *frightful*. Shocking. Children in the street do not look so dreadful.

But yet how miserable for me to go to any Nursing Home without *Tom* to *visit* me. No. I still have Liberty. But at what *cost*.

I send you my love dearest Ottoline.

Yrs. ever,
Vivienne Haigh Eliot

TO *Spence Burton*[1]

TS Colby College

3 April 1933   B-11 Eliot House, Cambridge

Dear Father Burton,

I should be grateful if you would give me an appointment for confession at any time during Holy Week. I say 'at any time', because I have made no engagements, except the three lectures that I must give on Tuesday, Thursday and Saturday at 9 a.m., and the offices.

Yours sincerely,
T. S. Eliot

TO *Ezra Pound*

TS Beinecke

5 April 1933   B-11 Eliot House, Cambridge

Rabbitt my Babbitt,:.

Owing to the Obsxurity of yr. episstlary stile I had done nothing about anything and owing to my being very busy what with receiving an obscure letter-in-French from the secretary of the Michael Mullins Marching & Chowder Club[2] (this evening the waitress at the Faculty Club has been Teaching me how to eat Clams clambs) and addressing the Clergy of Mussuchussetts at a Caferteria Lunch in the Crypt of the Cathedral and what with Going to address the Boston Assn. of Unittarrian Clergymen Inc. in Jammaica Plain me ead was dizzy & when I got yr. Letters I come over all of a Hoo Ha.[3] & I aint done nothink well what you Think I got

---

1 – The Revd Spence Burton, SSJE (1881–1966), Anglican priest, was Father Superior of the Church of St John the Evangelist (later Suffragan Bishop of Haiti and the Dominican Republic).

2 – A Harvard undergraduate club.

3 – See TSE's 'Fragment of an Agon' (1927), *SA* (1932): 'When you're along in the middle of the bed and / you wake like someone hit you in the head / You've had a cream of a

571

a letter from Harriett to Say. Dont do nothink Ezra dont understand its impppossible, Im (she said) a Guggenheimer Auslese myself & I know Dont imbarrass me by doink anythink so I says I aint done nothink because I didnt know what Ezra wanted me to do I would av done it if I ad known but as things was I was just waiting in a manner of speaking. Maybe Auden was born Dead but my nose tells me most of your friends Zuk and Bunt[1] et al. was born in putrifaction; the palin truth, the simpel truth and nothing but it: My Gawd aint you got no one to tell you the strait trewth but poor this? If you think that I could Get a Pres. Lowell to support anythink that anybody named Eliot wanted you aint Familiar with Local Politics, thats all. We aint on spooking terms. An dont suppos for a momen that there is any Harvard culture & refinement except what is provided by me & the Nortons. I am hoping to mix with the publishing world in N.Y.: both Plebeian & Yiddish. Report wuite true that I was too Refined for Boston audience: they dont always get Irony I find. As for yr. debunkin me there aint much you can teach me there; you will probably debunk the wrong places anyhow. Wot cynicism that is. Attack in any case is worth 1,000,000,000 of Praise in the way of Sales, so do all you can as I desperately need the Money.[2] Re the corpus, I shd, say you need my advice much less as to Whom to Include as to whom to Exclude, but you wdnt take it so I Shant give it. Guide yrself by Louise [sic] Untermeyer, and God destroy you. I have waxen tired proving to my Boys here that McLeesh[3] is a feeble imitation of Cantoes, and reading to them <u>Mauberley</u>,[4] & Damn you. Havnt seen ABC of OEconomics[5] yet,

---

nightmare dream and / you've got the hoo-ha's coming to you.' TSE would explain to Erik Mesterton, 16 Nov. 1948: 'As for "hoo-ha's", it is merely intended to be an inarticulate noise suggesting terror and impending doom. I seem to remember in Cockney speech some such phrase as "that gives me the 'hoo-ha's" meaning, in more modern and general terms, the jitters, otherwise shivers of nervousness and apprehension, but for my purpose you need take it only as a noise.'

1 – Louis Zukofsky and Basil Bunting.
2 – EP wrote accordingly to FVM, 12 May 1933: 'Brer / Possum dun say attack is worf mo'n laudashun, as 'strument ov pubcty / to himself az orthur. so we may consider several limes in dat prefashum az authorized by the Revrund hisself. Tenny rate I aint dun a sneek on 'im.'
3 – Archibald MacLeish.
4 – EP, *Hugh Selwyn Mauberley* (1920).
5 – EP's *ABC of Economics* was published by F&F on 6 Apr. 1933. The blurb (by FVM) reads: 'Mr Ezra Pound was asked to deliver ten lectures in an Italian University – on economics, not on the mummified muses. This is his necessary evisceration and clarification of the subject; a concise introduction to "volitionist economics".' EP had told FVM on 22 Jan. 1933: 'name is sometimes very useful and "volitionist" covers my difference from [C. H.] Douglas without opening me to confusion with any other brand. / If any body wants a definition you can say it means "to hell with Keynes, Salter and Hoover."'

but fear that Morley has been foolish in my Absence. so with that I must close hoping you are the same and in the maelstrom, (mushroom);[1]

Yrs. etc.
T. S. E.

Signature confirmed:

for the First National Bank of Boston:

F. X. Sweeney

for the Michael Mullins Marching & Chowder Club of Tufts College:

Michael Mullins Jr.

God be Praised! I may be harried out of England in July. And then may come to Rapallo, the Moral Bankrupt's Paradise.

TO *Ronald Bottrall*   TS Texas

10 April 1933   B-11 Eliot House, Cambridge

My dear Bottrall,

I wrote to the Colonial Office, of course, but I'm afraid it was impossible to catch the *Europa*. I found your letter on Thursday morning early just as I was leaving to lecture at Bowdoin College in Maine;[2] read it on the train; but was unable to write until I got back on Friday night. I fervently hope that my letter will reach London in time to be of help.

Yours ever,
T. S. Eliot

TO *Ottoline Morrell*   TS Texas

10 April 1933   B-11 Eliot House, Cambridge

My dear Ottoline,

I have a letter from Vivienne, in which she mentions that your comment upon my jingle about Hodgson was that Hodgson must be a very Cruel Man.[3] Of course I know how effectually V. can garble reports, but to be quite sure, I write to say that I have found Hodgson one of the gentlest

---

1 – 'The Rev. Possum flourishing in Masserchewzits,' remarked EP to FVM, 17 Apr. 1933.

2 – Loucks, 27: 'April 6–7. With Theodore Dreiser and others, TSE participated in an event at the Institute of Modern Literature at Bowdoin, lecturing on "The Poetry of Edward Lear" and joining in a round table conference ("Bowdoin College Program").'

3 – 'How Delightful to Know Mr Hodgson!': quoted in full in letter to Hodgson, 16 Aug. 1932.

of men, and the stanza was meant to indicate that. There have been mis-understandings before, I think.

Affectionately,
Tom

TO *Marianne Moore* TS Rosenbach Museum

11 April 1933 B-11 Eliot House, Cambridge

Dear Miss Moore,

I must apologise for my unpardonable delays in answering your letters, but I have had so much more to do here than I expected, or perhaps I can do so much less than I expected, that I have been quite unable to cope with *Criterion* matters at all. I did like 'The Plumet Basilisk' very much, and should have liked to print it. But I had filled up the *Criterion* in advance through the June number. I think you had best use the poem in the way suggested; but perhaps you could let me have something else to use in the autumn?

I hope that I may have a chance of making your acquaintance during one of my visits to New York.

With many apologies,
Yours very sincerely,
T. S. Eliot

TO *Henry Eliot* TS Houghton

16 April 1933 B-11 Eliot House, Cambridge

My dear Henry,

I should like to spend one night with you in New York, if T. will not worry about the cost.[1] But suppose I go to Arthur's this Thursday, and come to you the following Thursday, when I think I have no dinner engagement? Anyway, that seems to me the best. Will you tell Arthur that I shall be pleased, and am coming by the 12 o'clock on Thursday? I shall come back by the Friday midnight, but hope for a few days in New York, at a hotel, in May, when I can have no engagements and enjoy your company in peace.

1–TSE stayed with Henry and Theresa at their apartment at 315 East 68th Street, New York City, on a number of occasions through the spring and early summer of this year.

Affectionately,
Tom

TO *A. L. Rowse*   CC

18 April 1933   [Cambridge, Mass.]

Dear Rowse,

I am in difficulty over your note on Keynes. It is, as you intimate in your covering letter, not really a *Criterion* review at all. We can't run it as a separate note, and I can't cut it to short review length. I pondered it over Easter and came to the conclusion that the right thing would be to send it to you right away hoping that you can place it elsewhere.

With what you say in the review I am personally sympathetic; my difficulty is the diffuseness.[1]

Yours,
[T. S. Eliot]

TO *Virginia Woolf*   TS Berg

25 April 1933   B-11 Eliot House, Cambridge

My dear Virginia,

Very grateful thanks I proffer for your letter.[2] If I had more such letters it would help me to preserve my sense of the Reality of Things. Such queer things do happen. If I have not already told you the Adventure of the Wild Woman of Providence and the Curious Sequel, remind me to tell you upon my return. There is also the Clerical Cafeteria, and the Twenty Unitarian Clergymen; the Strange Case of Mrs McLean. The Blue of the Soap Dish comes off. There is the Episode of Shakespeare's Birthday and the Singing Dean. I have visited New York, Buffalo, Pasadena, Minneapolis, there is the Incident of the Peculiar Microphone in St Louis;[3] to Princeton have I been, and Haverford; to Yale, to Smith;[4] was Snowed in at Mt Holyoke

1–ALR, review of J. M. Keynes, *Essays in Biography*: C. 12 (July 1933), 674–6.
2–Not found.
3–Stunned at his Washington University lecture on 16 Jan. to find the audience ran to more than 600 – he had expected a modest turnout of English Faculty members – TSE joked about having to use a microphone: 'It's the first time I've talked to so many people at once by telephone.'
4–Loucks, 25: 'February 24, evening. In Sage Hall at Smith, Eliot presented "Edward Lear and Modern Poetry" ("TSE Sets"; "TSE, Poet" 11). His concluding comments were:

Ladies' Seminary, and still it does my heart good, except that 'Guests are Requested not to Smoke in the Dormitories'. Last night I addressed the Classical Club[1] in the Tower of Lowell House (there is also the Adventure of the Imperative Master); today I lectured twice (once to the male, once to the female college) on Joyce. The best paper offered in my course (English 26b)[2] was one on Virginia Woolf. The Student turns out to be an Englishman, named Peel. 'John?' said I; 'No', he replied, 'the other'. Robert the Peeler.[3] My assistant, Young Theodore[4] is to lecture on you on

'All modern poets attempt to write in such a way that the meaning reaches us in ways not distinctly traceable by the understanding! But what exactly is the meaning? Here my intellect fails and I must leave the question to others (qtd. in "TSE Sets").'

1–Harry Levin was to recall, 'Since he took a friendly interest in the activities of the Harvard Classical Club, we invited him to be a guest of honour at its annual banquet. This was a springtime relaxation after a studious year, a symposium in the convivial sense of the term; and, though we were still in the last months of Prohibition, through the good offices of a Greek bootlegger there was plenty of real – if not mellow – wine. By way of *jeu d'esprit* the programme featured a modern version of Aristophanes' *Frogs*, reduced to the dimensions of a puppet show and adapted to the festive occasion by substituting Shakespeare for the Old Poet, Aeschylus, and Eliot himself for the New Poet, Euripides. The Aristophanic put-down developed into somewhat more of an agon than we had naively intended, with our Eliotic ironies contrasting a heroic past and a decadent present. But the author of *Sweeney Agonistes* bore it with characteristic patience and charity' (*T. S. Eliot: Essays from the 'Southern Review'*, 154–5). See also Levin, 'T. S. Eliot and Harvard', *Harvard Advocate* 100: 3–4 (Fall 1966), 34–5.

2–TSE's lecture notes for English 26 ('English Literature from 1890 to the Present Day') are in Houghton. TSE gave them in June 1933 to Spencer – 'having no further use for them' – who gave them to the Eliot House Library. See also Ronald Bush, '"As if You Were Hearing it from Mr. Fletcher or Mr. Tourneur in 1633": T. S. Eliot's 1933 Harvard Lecture Notes for English 25 ("Introduction to Contemporary Literature")', *American Notes & Queries* 11: 3 (Summer 1998), 11–20.

3–Robert Peel was to write to TSE from Cambridge, Mass., 6 July 1933: 'May I say . . . what a great pleasure it has been knowing you personally and being a student in English 26. The last half-year has been one of the most stimulating that I have had and will sooner or later, I hope, bear fruit in writing that has something *positive* to say – with a core of spiritual conviction, that is, in addition to outward sensitiveness. That is what I particularly appreciated about your lectures and criticism: even where one disagreed with the judgments, one recognised them as three-dimensional and was consequently led to question all sorts of values other than purely literary ones. I don't know that my fundamental convictions have changed at all, but at least I know my reasons for them better than before, and that's somethink [*sic*]!' See Peel, 'Virginia Woolf', *C*. 13 (Oct. 1933), 78–96. Peel (1909–92), who was born in England and lived in Brookline, Mass., had already published his undergraduate dissertation, *The Creed of a Victorian Pagan* (on George Meredith), in 1931; a Christian Scientist, he went on to publish *Christian Science: Its Encounter with American Culture* (1958) and a three-volume life of Mary Baker Eddy – the fruit of twenty years of research – *The Years of Discovery* (1966), *The Years of Trial* (1971), *The Years of Authority* (1977). He taught English and Philosophy at Principia College and was Chief, Editorial Section, Christian Science Committee on Publication. TSE's other students included the distinguished journalist and author Cyrus Sulzberger (1912–93).

4–Theodore Spencer.

Saturday: two reasons (1) I feel incapable (2) I shall be among the young ladies of Bryn Mawr College, Philadelphia, on that date. Next week I go to Poughkeepsie N.Y. where the young ladies of Vassar College are to perform *Sweeney Agonistes* in treble pipe;[1] thence to Virginia (University of) to find out whether Virginians are as barbarous as Lady Astor. I believe they paint themselves with Woad, like the folk in Notting Dale. I have got to address the Oxford Centenary in Elizabeth, New Jersey, and give the Prize Day Oration at my old school. I have already been out there and done the Old Boy properly: 'now in my time it was quite easy to turn these beds upside down'; 'so it still is, Sir' etc. I have not yet attended a Big League Baseball Match, to sit on the Bleachers as I used to do, and hear Germany Schafer kidding the batter.

Yrs. in haste, distractedly,
T. S. E.

I will give your Kind Regards to Lily Norton when next I see her. May I also to Ellery Sedgwick (a Norton connexion) and to Ellen Bullard?

TO *Frank Morley*

3 May 1933   B-11 Eliot House, Cambridge

Dear Franck (Levy) &

Goddamb it if Herbie[2] had made Up his mind last autumn I cd. have got him a job at Xmas in St Louis for a year or probably longer if he wanted it; not that anyone wants to live in that climate more than a year; but its now pretty late in the season, and I couldnt do anything without permission to mention his name. I sensed this combing as they say the very 1st time I met H. & Mrs R. together; my suspicions grew stronger when I read his essay on Personality & Charakter; & you gave me a strong hint in a prior epistle. I gather from a feeler I put out that his Divorce wouldnt make any difference in this goddam pagan country so long as he doesnt bring the Lady with him before he marries her; Conrad Aiken made that mistake. Could he maybe stage a Lexture tour with an Agent? that is Hell; but there is still some money about the Womens Clubs, esp. if Herbert has by now developed a little Sex Appeal; but he would do better and save more money if he came without Miss Limburger (I always thought H. had

---

1 – Treble: the highest vocal range; soprano. *As You Like It*, II. vii. 164–6: 'his big manly voice, / Turning again toward childish treble, pipes / And whistles in his sound.'
2 – Herbert Read.

a Teutonic Drang[1] and now hes got his *Aufklärung*.[2]) I dont know how much of a draw his name wd. be here, and dont dare ask as this is all so private at present. I dont know what else to Say.

I think a coupla rooms in Surrey wd. do me a fair treat; give you & Xtina carte blanche to commit me to anything, or 1 room in that vicinage, wd. pay for it from July 1st and wd. stay 3 months at least, forever if really comfortable; but my acceptance or committal subject only to the discovery of unallowed for nuisances, bugs, fleas, jiggers or the village band; mice, bats, earwigs, or dangerous Cows, friendly bagmen etc. It Might suit me to live a country life permaniently more or less if I cd. commute comfortably. The more I think of it the better I think of not stopping in London a moment longer than necessary to confer with Ernest Bird of Bird & Bird and then lay low. There may be Hell popping; and I dont at all like having to expose myself at the Albert Hall even once. However, I am more Seasoned than Herbert. The no I wont quote Scripture. Ill wire you from Glasgow, if I go there. I had lunch with Chris,[3] my brother & H. Seidel also, but no Beer in speakeasies now. I hope to take a day off with Chris when I come to stay with Edm. Wilson jr and address the Anglo-Catholics at Elizabeth N.J. I liked the young ladies at Bryn Mawr. What a world it is; but theres always the Michael Mullins Marching & Chowder Club of Tufts College. Go to Vassar on Saturday to hear the Chickens recite *Sweeney Agonistes* in the Experimental Theatre. What you need now is a Pig, A pig, tell Sussanna that his name is Mr Pugstyles:[4] the way to pick a good pig; the ones that look like Stanley are better pigs than the ones that look like Winston;[5] get one of Stanley's pigs. Whent to a dinner last night where all talked French and gosh you know how I dew talk frensh; but Cousin Ethel has a Remarkable Yankee drawl, 'those folks down Cape Cod sound unusual' I said; 'Unusual?' she said, 'they are *able*. I bought some melons off one of em. Are these good melons? I said. Good? he said, I wouldnt be hired to eat em. So I took em home; and they were rotten. So I went back and I said to him: those melons you sold me were bad, I said. Bad? he said; waal, I told you I wouldnt eat em. Yes, they are *able*.' Made a gramophone record (5 in

1 – Yearning.
2 – *Aufklärung*: 'enlightenment'.
3 – Christopher Morley.
4 – See TSE's uncollected verses 'Mr Pugstyles: The Elegant Pig' (written by July 1934).
5 – I.e. Stanley Baldwin and Winston Churchill.

fact) at Barnard College; well I never heard such a voice; if *thats* my voice, well it *is* rich & fruity.[1]

Eager to hear about those logdiggings.

T.

TO *Horace Gregory* TS Syracuse University Library

15 May 1933 B-11 Eliot House, Cambridge

Dear Mr Gregory,

Of course I have no objection to your using my name as a reference – I trust you have already done so.[2] I shall be about for another three weeks; so I hope that if these people are going to apply to me they will do so in that time: I'll do my best.

I hope you will send me your reviews of Pound and Auden etc. I thought that you might like Spender. I shall be in New York once or twice more; I hope we may meet again before I return.

Yours ever,
T. S. Eliot

TO *Waldo Peirce*[3] TS Colby Colleg

18 May 1933 B-11 Eliot House, Cambridge

Dear Waldoo Peirce Pierce or Pearse

Waal that all right Im goin to have That Framed so as to Exhibit to my friends in the Rising Sun the Duek of Wellington the Friend at Hand[4] & Other Houses but what they wont reconise that effect of exhausted eunuch wich you Pourtray Its almost too Objective Lacks that Bolovian Touch and Careless Cora Also if There ad been a Parrett and a Bulll Terrierr that

---

1 – TSE recorded *The Hollow Men* and *Gerontion*, for the Department of English, Harvard University.
2 – Gregory had applied for a job lecturing in poetry at Sarah Lawrence College, New York – which he secured.
3 – Waldo Peirce (1884–1970): painter, sometimes styled 'the American Renoir'; friend of John Reed and of Ernest Hemingway. He had probably met TSE at Harvard some time before TSE first journeyed to England.
4 – The Rising Sun pub, Tottenham Court Road; the Duke of Wellington, University Street (subsequently renamed); the Friend at Hand, Herbrand Street (just round the corner from the Russell Square Tube station): all were in reach of the offices of Faber & Faber, Russell Square.

would have been better Wen they say They miss Me dawn the Pimlico Road of a Sattaday Night or wat Ho dawn the New Cut and Hoxton Way thats Serious Id like to get you towards the Doves in Hammersmiff[1] and try the O.B.E. five times is asking that wd. even soften an East Manxman what no tails[2] hoping you are. the Same yrs, respectfully

T. S. Eliot

You cant Have a good public House without a Parrett think about aht Parrett in the Angel Islington waht said to the barman Who's Been robbin the Till? That Parrett never told a Lie Yet. Those Birds Know, theyre artful.[3]

TO *Mrs J. C. [Edith] Perkins*   TS Donald Gallup

18 May 1933   B-11 Eliot House, Cambridge

Dear Mrs Perkins,

Thank you for your kind letter.[4] I shall be very happy to dine with you on Sunday at 6:30. I have been away every weekend since Lent, but I hope to get to King's Chapel, if not this Sunday, then the Sunday after.

Thank you for telling me your summer plans. Two of my friends are looking for quiet lodgings for me in Surrey, where I can keep in touch with my office without being in London.

I have no news from Emily for three weeks, and only learned of this Padua escapade yesterday from Miss Galitzi.[5] It seemed to me quite mad – after the neuritis and the fatigue of the Dragon – but I don't know what the provocation was – and there is no way of preventing these imprudences anyway.

Sincerely yours,

T. S. Eliot

1 – See TSE's letter to Sally Cobden-Sanderson, 28 Oct. 1932.
2 – The Manx cat, which originated on the Isle of Man, has no tail, or none to speak of.
3 – In 1939 TSE was to publish some light verses entitled 'Billy M'Caw: The Remarkable Parrot' (*The Queen's Book of the Red Cross*, 1939). Nearly ten years later, he wrote to his friend Jack Isaacs: 'I am pleased that you liked the Parrot . . . I daresay it was composed about the same time as *The Rock*, or a year or so later . . . [T]he episodes in the Life of Bill M'Caw are entirely my own invention. His figure was inspired by a very gifted parrot which used to belong to the licensee of a bar in Islington. The adventures of the real parrot were just as incredible as those of mine!' (29 Dec. 1948). The public house in question, the Prince Albert, Angel, Islington, London, is now the Charles Lamb.
4 – Not traced.
5 – Dr Christine Galitzi (b. 1899); author of *Romanians in the USA: a study of assimilation among the Romanians in the US* (1968). The nature of the Padua escapade is not known.

TO *Allen Tate*

TS Princeton

18 May 1933   B-11 Eliot House, Cambridge

Dear Tate,

I have just returned from Charlottesville, where I opened my series of lectures by referring touchingly to the Nashville Group (rehash of my commentary on *I'll take my Stand*). I have brought back a strong desire to see more of the South, and a still stronger sympathy with local aspirations. I hope to return in 1935 and visit Richmond, Charleston, Savannah, and so on via Tennessee to New Orleans and then up the River to St Loouss. If it were possible to come to Nashville during my remaining time I'd jump like a trout. An Hundred Dollars wd. suffice. But it aint possible. I'm sorry yr. Guggenheim dont extend another year. We must leave it to '35. My respects to Mrs Tate whose stories interest me very much.[1] If in '35 you can use any polliticle stumping by a dambyankee call upon me. But communicate to 24 Russell Square meanwhile.

Yours ever,
T. S. Eliot

TO *John Livingston Lowes*

TS Houghton

18 May 1933   B-11 Eliot House, Cambridge

Dear Mr Lowes,

It would give me particular pleasure to dine with you and Mrs Lowes, without company. Would either Thursday or Friday, the 25th and 26th, be convenient? If not, I shall probably be here over the following weekend.

Sincerely yours,
T. S. Eliot

TO *Paul Elmer More*

TS Princeton

18 May 1933   B-11 Eliot House, Cambridge

My dear More,

Thank you for your letter of the 7th which reached me today.[2] I expect to be in London about July 1st for a very few days (Oxford & Cambridge

---

1 – Caroline Gordon.
2 – Not preserved.

Club) and then to retire as quickly as possible to the country: some friends are looking for lodgings for me. I think that it is more convenient for my friends not to know the date and boat on which I sail. I have to take the chair at one of the Albert Hall meetings of the Oxford Centenary: I have no great stomach for this sort of thing in the best of times, and less than ever now, but my adviser (the Dean of Rochester) urged me to accept. And I have to speak in Oxford on the 24th July. I will write to you when I get settled. If I find myself in a comfortable place, I shall try to persuade you to spend a night or two in Surrey with me.

I should thank you also for your letter before leaving. I quoted it (anonymously) to the Clerical Association of Massachusetts (who behaved like a very amiable tar-baby:[1] the Unitarians, on the other hand, did not discuss my paper at all, but attacked me for not being a Papist[2]).

1–The Tar-Baby, which features in the second of the *Uncle Remus* stories (1881) by Joel Chandler Harris, is an effigy made of tar and turpentine used to entrap Br'er Rabbit; by extension, 'tar-baby' has come to denote any situation in which further struggle is useless.
2–TSE concluded his recent address, 'Two Masters', to the Boston Association of Unitarian Clergy: 'And the suggestion may be added, that the Church, in setting very high standards up to which it must know that the majority of its communicants will not live, is practising a certain hypocrisy. Would it not be better, people may ask, if the standard set were not that of an ideal asceticism, but rather that of the highest natural human life; for then, perhaps, more people would live up to it? An unattainable ideal, they may say, makes for dishonesty, and compels laxity in the treatment of the weaker members. Such a criticism, I think, is no more valid than the criticism of celibacy which maintains that celibacy cannot really be the highest life because if it were, the human race ought to come to an end. Perhaps the simplest retort is to ask what is the alternative. What happens when you trim your ideals down to fit the behaviour of the nicest people? Instead of compromising practice you have compromised the ideal, and that is a more serious matter. When you think that you are getting rid of hypocrisy, you are merely descending to complacency and self-conceit: an ideal which can be attained is one of the most dangerous of booby-traps, for its attainment leads to spiritual pride. The Catholic is alone in affirming *humility* as the greatest and first of the Christian virtues: humility, purity, charity, as Dr Paul More puts it. And apart from Christianity, humility is not a virtue; it has its significance only in the Christian setting. We must have an ideal so high that measured by it the purest and most devout feels that he is indistinguishable from the greatest sinner. We can have no ideal, for all human beings, lower than that of saintliness – in the exact sense. And this is the ideal which the world has repudiated, as being inhuman. Ideals *are* inhuman, but we are only human, instead of being animals, by our capacity to transcend humanity. It does not matter, that Christian heresiarchs have often proved themselves only petty human beings; it does not matter that ecclesiastical policy has often been politics; it does not matter that the mass of Christians should be lecherous, stupid, brutal, lazy and dirty. What matters is that the mass of humanity, in their naughty as well as their good behaviour, confess the true faith, the right ideal, and admit from what path it is that they have erred and strayed like lost sheep, by their own fault, their own fault, their own most grievous fault. The world, on the contrary, insists on being right. It insists on being virtuous. It is right, it is virtuous, and it is damned. Between the Catholic and the world there can be an indefinite compromise on behaviour; but there can be no compromise on ideal. There are Two Masters, and each of us has the power of choice. To whom ye yield

I liked what you said about solitude. (By the way, I quoted your Proust[1]
in a lecture at the University of Virginia, while pitching into Hardy and
D. H. Lawrence – one paragraph, with the exception of the last sentence
possibly, applied admirably to Lawrence[2]). My life seems like Alice and

---

yourselves servants to obey, his servants ye are to whom ye obey; whether of sin unto death,
or of obedience unto righteousness.'

1 – Paul Elmer More, 'Proust: the two Ways', *The American Review*, Apr. 1933, 50–75.

2 – From 8 May TSE stayed in Charlottesville as a guest of Scott Buchanan, Professor of
Philosophy, and his wife. (On 12 Sept. 1946, he would tell Dorothy Pound: 'I was very well
impressed fourteen years ago by the University of Virginia, which is only a short journey
from Washington. It is not only beautiful (designed by Thomas Jefferson, its founder, which
would please Ez) but it was rather backward – that is to say, not being progressive, it still
nourished the classics and preserved the remains of real education' [Beinecke].)

On three successive days from 10 May he delivered the Page-Barbour lectures, under the
working title 'Tradition and Contemporary Literature', in Madison Hall at the University
of Virginia: the individual lecture titles were 'The Meaning of Tradition', 'Modern Poetry'
and 'Three Prose Writers' – much of the last lecture being devoted to negative criticism of
Thomas Hardy and D. H. Lawrence – to be published in 1934 as *After Strange Gods*.

TSE was to write to H. L. Adlerstein (who was writing a doctoral thesis on D. H. Lawrence
at New York University), 29 Sept. 1949: 'I consider that I was unfair to Lawrence, and
probably to Thomas Hardy and perhaps others, in my lectures called *After Strange Gods*,
and as I was dissatisfied with this book, I have allowed it to go out of print in this country.
I agree with you that Lawrence's style is slovenly and that his philosophy is muddled, but
then one must remember that Lawrence was a self-taught man and was, therefore, liable to
be carried away by enthusiasms to which anyone better educated would be less exposed.

'I think Lawrence is an important writer, and I should say that what the reader has to do,
is to read Lawrence with his own eyes, and not worry about what one writer or another now
living, says about him.'

He reiterated, in a further letter to Adlerstein (30 Dec. 1949), that he felt he had been
unfair to both Lawrence and Hardy – 'though I must admit that of the two men, I find
Lawrence much more sympathetic. But, nevertheless, I think that my criticism of Hardy was
intemperate.'

In a memo on Northrop Frye's *T. S. Eliot*, TSE wrote on 20 June 1963: 'It should be
mentioned somewhere that I became dis-satisfied with *After Strange Gods*, which I came to
consider rather intemperate, especially in speaking of Thomas Hardy, and no longer keep
in print in this country.'

In 1960 TSE consented to be a witness for the defence in the trial of *Lady Chatterley's
Lover*, though in the event he was not called upon to give evidence. He wrote to Sir
William Emrys Williams (a director of Penguin Books), 19 Aug. 1960: 'I do not regard
Lady Chatterley's Lover as obscene, and I should regard its suppression as deplorable . . .
Although I was bored by the book, and in spite of a strain of cruelty which I thought I
detected in it, I am sure that the author's intentions were wholly serious. The book is in no
particular pornographic. It is on the ground of the author's serious intention as evinced in
this and in all of his works, that I should object to its suppression. I regard the question of
its "literary merit" as secondary.'

He wrote to Helen Gardner, 8 Dec. 1960: 'My feelings toward Lawrence remain
ambiguous and my desire to give witness was really rather as a protest against other books,
such as *Lolita*, which struck me as really evil, which much more deserve censoring. The great
pity is that the Crown chose Lawrence's book for prosecution. One knows what will happen:

the glass table:[1] there is something I want here (domestic affection) and something I want in England, and I can't have both; fortunately the time of choice is long since past. One side of life suffers from dullness, the other from nightmare – the last eighteen years like a bad Dostoevski novel. One of my most constant temptations is to a feeling of exasperation with human beings – not for their faults & vices, I can sympathise with those – but for their tepidity; their pettiness is somehow more awful than their evil – not many are alive enough to be evil. The materialism of the virtuous is what baffles me especially in this country. But I have nothing to complain of: I think that (so long as I can keep free of any illusions about my own importance) that I have got about what I deserved, both ways, and (to put it romantically) the vulture on the liver.

---

once a book has been under the charge of obscenity not even a jury can give absolution, and the book will be bought by thousands out of curiosity who are quite incapable of understanding what Lawrence was after. And I feel pretty sure that I should have disliked Lawrence personally if I had known him!' When Gardner responded that unlike him she admired *Lolita*, TSE wrote again on 13 Dec. 1960: 'How very curious that we should differ so widely about *Lolita*! It did seem to me a book which would make anyone in which such a perverse tendency was latent more conscious of his craving. And it seems to me a peculiarly undesirable book at a time when so many little girls have been abducted and strangled. As for Durrell's Alexandria novels I must confess that I have never looked into them. I very seldom read modern fiction, and my distaste for novels has at least the precedent of Paul Valéry . . . I only read *Lolita* because I had read about it and wanted to see how it compared to my mind with *Lady Chatterley's Lover*. And it did seem to me that the latter book came out as something very much more decent.'

He wrote to Roy Morrell, 15 May 1964: 'The book in which I criticised Thomas Hardy severely is one which I have subsequently regretted, and I regret in particular what I said about Hardy. Since publishing that book, which by the way I no longer keep in print, I have come to the conclusion that I do not find it worthwhile to write about any author, especially one who is no longer alive, merely to express antipathy, nor do I feel that dislike of Hardy's novels which I then felt. I particularly admire *The Mayor of Casterbridge* and parts of *Far From the Madding Crowd*. There are scenes in both which remain permanently in my memory, such as that when the mayor of Casterbridge looks over the bridge and sees his own effigy floating in the water.

'I entirely agree that some of Hardy's poems are very moving indeed. My only complaint against them is that there are too many of them, and the effect would be more impressive if he had pruned down his collection to the best. There is, however, at least one story in the volume *A Group of Noble Dames* which seems to me quite horrific (horrible)' (TS Waring-Jones).

EVE would write to Dr W. H. Toppen (Amsterdam) on 28 Sept. 1967: 'Hardy never meant much to my husband, and I doubt if he would have changed the views that he expressed in that book [*After Strange Gods*], although he might have phrased them differently.'

See also Roger Kojecky, 'Knowing Good and Evil: T. S. Eliot and *Lady Chatterley's Lover*', *ANQ: A Quarterly Journal* 11: 3 (Summer 1998), 37–50; Jeffrey Meyers, 'T. S. Eliot and Thomas Hardy', *Notes on Contemporary Literature* 42: 3 (May 2012): Literature Resource Center.

1–Lewis Carroll, *Alice in Wonderland*.

Yours affectionately,
T. S. Eliot

I am beginning to crave the anonymity that one enjoys in England.

TO *William Mortlock*   PC MS Ian Bonner

Postmarked 19 May 1933   [New York City]

This fake photograph gives only a feeble idea of the horror of New York.[1]
I don't like to talk about it on a postcard. America has two great mistakes:
New York and California; I have seen both. I hope to see you in July.
                                            T. S. Eliot

TO *Edmund Wilson*   TS Beinecke

21 May 1933   B-11 Eliot House, Cambridge

My dear Wilson,

    I have got to spend the night of May 29th in Elizabeth New Jersey;
would the night of May 30th be convenient for me to stop with you in
New York? Please tell me frankly if it is convenient or not; I am coming
to New York again on June 5th.
                                        Sincerely yours,
                                        T. S. Eliot

TO *Henry Eliot*   TS Houghton

21 May 1933   B-11 Eliot House, Cambridge

Dear Henry,

    That's all right, but Ada tells me you wrote to the wrong hotel, i.e. the
more expensive one; but she says its all in the family, so can easily be put
right. I shall do my best to get everything wound up here so that I can
come straight through with you to New Hampshire, stopping anywhere
you like en route. I will bring my lectures; but you must not take them too
seriously, as I want a holiday. I am looking forward to it eagerly; also to
staying with you on the 5th and 6th (did you get the tickets to distribute
to suitable relatives?) I dont know whether I shall see you on the 30th –

1 – The postcard is a sketch of the Waldorf-Astoria Hotel, then under construction.

shall spend the 29th in Elizabeth N.J. and the 30th with Edmund Wilson
if he can have me (314 E. 53d Street).

I enjoyed my last visit very much. Love to Th.

Affectionately,
Tom

FROM *Vivien Eliot* TO *Henry Eliot*   TS Houghton

Sunday 21 May 1933   68 Clarence Gate Gardens

Dear Henry,

This is in reply to your letter of May 9th. (My Father's birthday).

I am so very glad you were able to give me such good news of Tom,
and that you had seen him and that he looked well. This typewriter is
having a fit, and the ribbon keeps crumpling up so I really dont know if I
shall be able to finish this letter. It is exciting to hear that Tom is making
Gramophone records, but it is a horrible thing for a man to have to do.
Musicians hate to have to do it. Fancy Aldous Huxley turning up in New
York. Was Maria with him? I always liked them.

It is *worrying* to hear that Tom had not yet booked his passage when
you wrote. You know that he is booked to speak here in London at the
Albert Hall, *on July 13th at 2.30*. There is a great deal of excitement here
about this Anglo-Catholic Congress. It will be an immense affair. I am
very interested, and am wearing the Badge, and am selling tickets for
Thursday July 13th at 2.30. I wish that you and Theresa could be here,
but perhaps you will. You say things are very bad, financially, in America,
and we here realise that. I do not think they are so universally bad here,
and there are not such signs of depression that there used to be. I do think
you and Theresa might scrape up the money to come, for you could stay
with us here. We have the space for you. It would be a delight to us all.

I saw Maurice today. He looked splendid. He is doing very well in the
City, and is making a big name for himself in the world of Finance.

The little glass cigarette holder looks too sweet on the mantelpiece of
Tom's study, and now I have a most beautiful arrangement, with a special
electric lighting underneath the Rothenstein portrait of Tom. *If only you
could see it*. His room is a picture.

About the Ford car that I sold. I was mortified to have to do it, for there
is no doubt that it is the smartest small cheap car on the roads today, but
as you know I have no strength, I am hardly strong enough to drive any
car at all. The Ford was absolutely impossible for me to drive. It nearly

pulled me to peices [pieces]. It would have been perfect for Tom. But if I was to have a car at all, I had to go back to a Morris Minor. It is so light, that I can really drive it, when I can drive at all, and that is very seldom now.

All these points, however, are minor matters.

The two main points are,

1.) That I cabled to Tom, on May 7th, having obtained my doctor's permission,

'Will come America like a shot remainder of your visit cable yes or no Eliot.'

and that he replied

'Your proposal quite impossible very busy and shall be travelling about until middle June Eliot'

which I received on May 10th from a place called Charlottesville.

2.) That I cabled to Marion, on May 8th,

'Have cabled Tom will gladly come America remainder his visit await his answer love V. H. E.'

and that she replied

'I am (Tom) travelling about from now on Marion'

I showed these cables to my doctor, and reported fully to my Solicitors.

3.) With regard to my Will. You say you have not received Copy. That is because I have not sent it.

I wrote to Tom and explained fully to him, that having taken further advice, I was obliged to give up the idea of having any American Trustees. So I found four Trustees, Tom himself being one, and the other three being Englishmen, and friends of Tom's and of mine, middle-aged men of definite position in whom I have confidence. That being done I was told that it was not advisable to send a Copy of my Will to America. But should there be any question arising from American law, it could be taken to American solicitors here In London.

When I had done all this and made everything as perfect as I could and *Informed Tom*, I was extremely exhausted by the whole business, and hoped that there would be no further correspondence. And if there is any more correspondence I shall be reluctantly obliged to ask either our solicitor or one of my Trustees to undertake It.

4.) And here is the main point of all. When I cabled to Tom that I would gladly join him in America, had he agreed, I should of-course, have brought a Copy of my Will for you both to see. As, however, Tom does not want me in America, I think it will be less complicated to leave matters as they are.

5.) The longer Tom lingers in America now, when all obvious reasons for his being there at all are over, the more difficult does he make his, and all our positions here. I need not mention the firm of Faber & Faber.

With love to Theresa, and very best wishes to yourself,

> I am,
> Yours sincerely,
> Vivienne Haigh Eliot

TO *Ezra Pound*   TS Beinecke

Vigil of Ascension Day   B-11 Eliot House, Cambridge
[?24/25 May 1933]

Dear Rabbit,

I dont think I can figger out to meet you in Cherbourg. But I might let on to get you into England somb time in July, only you must come incognito, as I shall be the same, and cd. meet you at some predetermined sequestered spot like Cliftonville or Reigate. I expect to be livin in the country, but could meet you at some Where out of London if you cd. stand a short villegeature. This Being for your PRIVATE Ear alone. I think the U.S.A. has done me some good.

The asses have not sent *A.B.C.* yet, so must now wait. If you write to me at 24 Russell Square about July 1st it will reach me.

> Yrs. in bisto
> T.

TO *Edmund Wilson*   TS Beinecke

24 May 1933   B-11 Eliot House, Cambridge

Dear Mr Wilson,

Thank you for your letter – the first evidently crossed mine. I am afraid it is impossible for me to get back from Elizabeth N.J. until dinner time, as I am billed to speak at about 3. But I think I can stay over to take the midnight train on Wednesday. I have an engagement on Wednesday morning to make a gramophone record, but otherwise I am quite free. I should very much like to meet Marianne Moore.

Yours sincerely,
T. S. Eliot

TO *J. C. Perkins*   TS Donald Gallup

25 May 1933   B-11 Eliot House, Cambridge

Dear Mr Perkins,

Thank you for sending me the 'Humanist Manifesto'. It is an astonishing document, but not refreshing for the weary & heavy-laden. I have filed it for reference, and it will probably turn up one day in one of my jeremiads. I met that young Adams, the minister from Salem, on the street this morning, and he told me that he and another had prepared a rejoinder for next Saturday's *Transcript*.[1] He struck me as a man of some intelligence.

May I take this opportunity of saying how keenly I have appreciated your and Mrs Perkins's kindness to me during this year. It has been of much help to me, and I feel that it has been fortunate for me that your retirement did not take place a year ago.

Gratefully yours,
T. S. Eliot

TO *Geoffrey Faber*   TS Faber

26 May 1933   B-11 Eliot House, Cambridge

Dear Geoffrey,

This is only to tell you – I had forgotten it – that the University of Virginia agrees to Fabers publishing my three lectures 'Tradition & Contemporary Literature' if you want them. I have stipulated that they must come out a season after the Norton lectures, which should be ready for the late autumn. (I shall not have time to polish up the Norton lectures until I get to England, but will have that done by the middle of August). You must drive a hard bargain, because three lectures is a very small book. I dont know that they are worth publishing at all, only they have to be published in America by the terms of the foundation. You need not commit yourself until you have seen me and the lectures. I intend to pad it out however with Appendices made out of odd lectures on irrelevant subjects, chiefly education & religion. This case differs from the Norton, in that I get

1 – *The Boston Evening Transcript*, a daily newspaper.

no royalties, they all go to the University of Virginia, so make the best bargain you can. You will have to bargain with Prof. Wilbur Nelson, Dept. of Geology, University of Virginia, Charlottesville, Virginia. It is a beautiful place. Anyway, you can be considering it till I come, but you might drop a line to Wilbur to keep him reminded.[1]

Yrs ever,

T. S. E.

TO *Allen Tate*   TS Princeton

26 May 1933   B-11 Eliot House, Cambridge

Dear Tate,

Thank You for yrs. of the 23d inst.[2] what you say Put me all of a Hoo-Ha, I always did Say that Somethink before breakfast was wot did you Good, Here we Are all Scisters under the Sink in a manner Of speaking. I dont Hold with these newfangled Burriels any more than wat You said. If theres talk of juleps before breakfast I says there wheres theres juleps before Breakfast theres my spuurrettual home in a manner of speaking. Mean wile If theres a chace of seein You Hereabouts that is I Mean to say dahn the Pimlico Road or Up Holborn dont forget the Friend at Hand neitherwise the Risin Sun were You will always find, hopin you the best

yrs, respecfully

T. S. Eliot

TO *Waldo Peirce*   TS Colby College

26 May 1933   B-11 Eliot House, Cambridge

Dear Waldo Peirce,

I have just Run out of gin and am able to spell cerrectly. Thank you for yours of the 22nd inst, or Thereabouts Well sir I thank you for yr, kind letter Things is much the same with me You wd, ave ad a couple of laughs

1–FVM wrote on behalf of GCF to Wilbur Nelson, 8 June 1933: 'I have had a note from T. S. Eliot mentioning that the University of Virginia agrees to our publishing his three lectures on "Tradition and Contemporary Literature". I shall have to leave discussion of terms until Eliot returns, when I hope to see the lectures. If there are only three lectures they will make a very small book, and there may not be much margin to work with. However, as soon as Eliot returns we shall be able to make an estimate and I will then, if I may, write to you again.'
2–Not found.

Had you bin at Vassar well I thought Why am I alwys a Bridesmaid and never a blushin Bride? But Some fine Day Oh my it be Soon Well Heres the Dificulty Nothink wd, please me more that to inspect pete's Syphitic Mice and say tata to the lads at Jonesport etc. and Visit at Bangor which is a very fine Place I Hope the Dahneasters aint forgot wat I thaught em ahabt Chris. Columbo specly that abaht the same bein the Habits of the Religious in Malta & You cant beat than in Wiscasset no nor in Cutler wich Gawd help me is Rough place But wat Ho must take the smooth with the Rough after Eucharistic Congoress in Elizabeth N.J. then stay with Edm. Wilson jr, and Marianne to see, then back to say farewell to kinscousin here aBouts, then to N.Y. again then to new Amphire then to Montreal that the reminds me of one poem about

According to the sleuths of Reuter

The Bishopp of Gibraltar

has just arrived at Malta

My God! with Mrs Hicks![1]

and I Dont think as shall Have time for other Excurssions till my return in 1935 when Hoping You will be the same Or no worse I cant remember wether I Leave from Monreal for London or from Boston for Liverpool or from some Wheres else for southampton but its wherever my boxes have been sent to so wishin you always the same or a little Less or more as the case May be watever takes your fancy I will Close yrs. respectfully

T. S. Eliot

Hoping to see you in Rapallo in Jan. 1934 –

TO *Faber & Faber* Telegram TS Valerie Eliot

27 May 1933 Faber & Faber Ltd

POSTING COMMENTARY TOMORROW PLEASE WAIT IF POSSIBLE ELIOT

TO *Alida Monro* TS Valerie Eliot

1 June 1933 B-11 Eliot House, Cambridge

My dear Alida,

I have been very neglectful of your affairs, as well as of those of Faber & Faber; but I never knew before what complete absence of leisure was

---

1 – Nugent Hicks (1872–1942) was Lord Bishop of Gibraltar, 1927–33.

like. When do or did Harold's poems appear? I had been hoping to receive a copy. But it is not worthwhile asking questions now. I shall be back about July 1st; I think it is more convenient for people *not* to know what boat I am taking; and I shall probably get lodgings outside of London.

I have finally found time to go in and talk to Greenslet. He is not disposed to set up any book of English poetry at the present time, and I doubt whether any American publisher would. He would like to consider sheets, and wants quotations for 250, 500 and 750 with the usual specifications. I dont myself consider 250 worth noticing, but I think he could be induced to take 500. It would be worth while trying Harcourt, Brace & Co., my publishers, I think. I wish I could talk to Harcourt about it. But my visits to New York have all been filled in advance: I go on Monday to get an honorary degree; and I shall not have a moment of my own; but I will write to them.

Please forgive my inefficiency. It will be good to be again in a position to have time to do properly what I want to do. 24 Russell Square will always reach me after July 1.

Yours ever,
Tom

TO *Frank Morley* TS Berg

2 June 1933[1] B-11 Eliot House, Cambridge

Dear Frank,

O Boy say that Good. I'll be seein' yuh. That lodging with Mrs Eames sounds very Practical, and I thank you Both from the Bottom of my heart. I propose to spend one night at O. & C. and see Bird to whom I shall wire (have just wired him as he has sent me no news).[2] You will be

---

1–Certain letters in this strand of correspondence have not been traced: they must have included TSE's announcement to FVM that he had decided to separate from VHE and his request for help with securing secret lodgings on his return to England. On a handwritten list of letters dated 20 May 1972, FVM noted: 'intimate correspondence involving Vivien, solicitors, TSE's personal turmoil, worries & arrangements about coming to Pikes Farm was clearly never meant for publication and was destroyed by FVM'. On another page: 'What I've tried to get together here are specimens of earlier correspondence. Letters of course are relatively rare when for the most part we were in daily contact. Few of these are in themselves important except for incidental sidelights. Some letters I destroyed (I think rightly) at the time and some I don't think should be released.'

2–FVM, 'A Few Recollections of Eliot', 107–8: 'He was to have a bed and working-room and such meals as he might wish to have by himself at the house of Mrs Eames, wife of the foreman of the immediately adjacent brickworks. That was Uncle Tom's Cabin, a matter of

hearing from me. I can't begin to tell you about all the Fun lately, what with Virginia and the mint julep and Professor FitzHugh talking about the Tripodium his 2nd wife is Trudy she is German so you know how I talk German with a couple of mint juleps well she doesnt like Hitler thats a good place Virginia only they didnt have time to take me down to Sugar Hollow where they make the corn whisky which makes the mint

---

thirty paces to the open doors (front or back) of the farmhouse [occupied by the Morley family], where he could have at any time company, or crossword games, or anything. He wirelessed from his ship; I met the train and took his heavy luggage to the country. He spent one night at his London club [Oxford & Cambridge Club]; we met him next morning at our local station with the dog-cart, which at once reminded him of Sherlock Holmes and appeared to please him very much.'

Mrs Doris Eames (49 Shepherds Way, Horsham, W. Sussex) wrote to EVE, 14 Jan. 2010: 'Many years ago my husband's late uncle Jack Eames told us that he had Mr Eliot to stay for several months in 1933. Mr Eliot was in fact a guest of Mr Morley of Faber and Faber who lived next door. He dined with the Morley family but otherwise lived with Uncle Jack and his family. He chose this because it was quiet and he was not disturbed by the Morley children.

'However he must have enjoyed the childrens' company because I have a photocopy of a drawing of their house (Pikes Farm) drawn by Mr Eliot, showing his many "adventures" in the garden, and its surroundings . . .

'Uncle Jack described Mr Eliot as "a funny man really. He was very quiet and so engrossed in what he was doing that you could almost touch him and he wouldn't realise that you were there." Uncle Jack was foreman of the adjacent Brickworks and Mr Eliot called his home "Uncle Tom's Cabin". The drawing I have referred to shows all the exciting things that happened to "Uncle Tom". I believe that the original was sent to his godson Tom Faber.

'By coincidence my husband John Eames became manager at Crowhurst Brickworks and we lived in "Uncle Tom's Cabin" for about ten years. It is now derelict.'

FVM recalled elsewhere: 'In re TSE's letters to solicitors, Bird & Bird, he had consulted GCF and me before the letter S. [Sencourt] speaks of on 151; at TSE's request I went to discuss problems personally with Bird; GCF & Enid were also closely involved, Enid to help V. . . . TSE wrote to me from Harvard [letter not found] asking if we could find country quarters for him; was glad to accept arrangements we suggested at Pikes Farm. I met him with the Ford V8 on his arrival (Euston I think) put his luggage in it, drove him to O & C Club; after a drink there, left him with overnight case to have dinner at the club with Bird (solicitor) and spend the night there; I took the luggage to Pikes Farm, met him again at Lingfield next morning. There were no histrionics.' ('Notes on Sencourt's T. S. Eliot: A Memoir': Morley/Eliot Papers Box 95, Berg).

FVM informed Helen Gardner, 28 June 1978: 'When Tom on his return to England came to seclude himself with us at Pikes Farm . . . Ada (and of course Henry) expected occasional confirmations from me that Tom's health and spirits were not other (i.e. in any way worse) than his letters to them reported. Physical health was ostensibly what Ada enquired for. Now it happened that when I met Tom's boat-train, in the midst of other concerns to be discussed, Tom mentioned his hair – whether the same barber at our club . . . could be looking after it, for he expressed worry that it might be thinning. In writing presently to Ada I made some incidental comment to the effect that if a man's greatest worry were thought of baldness, his health otherwise couldn't be too bad. Silly or not, within the family references to Tom's general condition were sometimes indicated by saying the hair was kept on' (Berg).

juleps but I saw Monticello[1] thither taken by Prof. F. Stringfellow Barr (yes sir Col. Stringfell was an aide to Robt. E. Lee) who edits the *Virginia Quarterly*[2] I dropt a Pansy on WM. Force Stead's tomb he wrote a good poem while there all I remember is

> We has two men that worked Like Hell
> Pullin the corks of the bright Moselle.
> When we went tuh Washin'ton on trips
> We had two niggers to carry our grips;
> But we came back so full of stuff,
> That two pore niggers was not enough . . .

You ask him about it. Its a dizzy world this. I motored up to Kittery Maine last Saturday with the young Ellery Sedgwicks to visit Matthiessen; then we came down to Topsfield in the morning and I spent an afternoon in a canoe on the Ipswich River with Max Foster we both saw a longbilled marsh wren plain as print we saw him and heard him also chestnutsided warbler Foster says it was a baybreasted warbler anyhow there were Baltimore Orioles Galore (in Virginia there are plenty mocking birds and cardinals and indigos) after dinner some of them drank too much and talked about art and history but I finally got back as Mrs Sedgwick insisted on driving; that was right; Lily Norton once said that young Ellery smelt of Gin, on Beacon Hill too. So I got back and then took the Yankee Clipper next day and went to Elizabeth N.J. to speak at for an Eucharistic Congress what a congress the boys was lettin off firecrackers outside in Jersey Place it beining [*sic*] Memorial Day however I got off my speech a stirring one (that kind) laughter and tears and many ladies stopped me on the street afterwards to say Mr Eliot thank you for your words and I sat at Lunch at the Elizabeth Carteret Hotel beside the Bishop of Liberia all in Crimson and the man the other side whispered the reason why the Bishop wears a goatee is that the niggers in Liberia don't respect any man in authority who doesnt wear a Beard. Had two bottles of inferior Pabst at the Elizabeth Carteret Hotel and a shower and went to New York to spend the night with Edmund Bunny Wilson you know the communist well he is a good scout but his speakeasy gave us a bottle of bad wine the next afternoon my legs wobbled not fore and aft as usual but port to

1 – The plantation home of Thomas Jefferson, 3rd president of the USA, Charlottesville, VA.
2 – Stringfellow Barr (1897–1982), author, historian – editor of *Virginia Quarterly Review*, 1931–7 – was ultimately to become President of St John's College, Annapolis, Maryland, 1937–46. Benjamin Stringfellow (1816–1891), Missouri-born lawyer and Attorney General, and vehement anti-abolitionist, served as a Confederate officer and a spy for General Robert E. Lee.

starboard and vice versa thats what you call a funny feeling Bunny was no better He shares his house with one Barrry Griffin or Grifin Barry you know the father of Dora Russell's 3d child or is it 4th or 2nd and we were up in time to tea in came Mr & Mrs Gilbert Seldes and who do you think Marianne Moore well Marianne is a real Gillette blade she doesn't skip anything and she talks all the time but I love her the more for that.[1] Afterwards to *Of Thee I Sing* which is Quite praiseworthy[2] and to the Algonquin where who was there but Eva Le Gallienne and Josephine Hutchinson[3] well I got back to Boston on the Owl getting the last Upper Berth dined that night at the Somerset Club with Roger and Barbara then to a play *Dinner at 8* not good[4] then out here to a party for the Senior Tutor and there was Fred Robinson by the way his edition of Chaucer is the best yet[5] we ought to publish it this morning I decided to be useful so I girded myself and went in to see Ferris Greenslet as you told me to do on February 6th well I cdnt have chosen a worse day the moment I got out at Park Street there was a tremendous procession of High School Cadets I looked at Houghton Mifflin 15 minutes before I could Cross. So Greensalt wnt have Sitwell salted on him and I dont blame him, you know those Sitwells are Sharks and Dick de la Mare you know hasnt got those Rubber legs which are so useful when you swim in tropical waters I hope F. & F. dont get done down by those moneygrubbers. But Gruenschitt is interested rather mildly in Spender and Auden, I told him I was selling their stock and would let him in at 20 the ordinary Public to buy at 40 so he would like to see some of Auden works I had a Spender to

1–TSE told Marion Dorn, 3 Jan. 1944, that he met Marianne Moore 'once . . . in New York, but I took a great fancy to her: she and Bunny Wilson were the two people I liked best of those whom I met in New York in 1933. She is a very unusual person, as well as a good poet.' Charles Molesworth, *Marianne Moore: A Literary Life* (1990), 262: 'She was also able to confess to [her brother] Warner that she had met T. S. Eliot at a party, but she felt somewhat abashed, since their conversation was trivial and discreditable. She had had plans to meet Eliot and Wilson for dinner, but Wilson called at the last minute to say they couldn't come and would she attend a party with Eliot instead. Mrs Moore objected to what she called such rudeness, but Moore went anyway, drawn by Eliot's reputation, but finally was unable to say much to him beyond small talk.'

2–*Of Thee I Sing* (1931): musical by George Gershwin which opened on Broadway in 1931 and ran for 441 performances, winning the Pulitzer Prize for Drama, 1932; revived in 1933.

3–Josephine Hutchinson (1903–98) – American actress – was a member of the Civic Repertory Company, directed by Eva La Gallienne.

4–*Dinner at Eight*: play by George S. Kaufman and Edna Ferber; adapted for the screen with Jean Harlow and John Barrymore, directed by George Cukor, produced by David O. Selznick.

5–Fred Norris Robinson (1871–1966) edited *The Complete Works of Geoffrey Chaucer* (1933).

give him (not inscribed) but he would like to talk about this. He tried to sell things too I told him we werent sitting in on a Life of Jno. Greenleaf Whittier which he wants to get rid of[1] but might consider a Mexican yarn which he will be sending yuh. Would you call those Sitwells parashoots or parashitts they are charming people but I didnt enjoy talking to Greensnot with the High School cadets running outside; I had a Chat with Roger Scaife[2] too but mostly about old school days at Milton where Damnit I have to deliver the Prize Day Oration on June 17th.[3] Well I will send you a Wire from the Boat. Allen Tate is in good form. I hope to see Chris again but dont know I take this Columbia degree on Tuesday[4] then leave for the Presidential Range back on the 16th then what.

Yours etc,
T. S. E.

FROM *Vivien Eliot* TO *Henry Eliot*   Telegram TS Houghton

4 June 1933

DID YOU RECEIVE MY LETTER TWENTYFIRST CABLE REPLY GIVING DATE TOMS SAILING AND NAME SHIP VIVIENNE HAIG ELIOT

TO *Ronald Bottrall*   TS Texas

4 June 1933   B-11 Eliot House, Cambridge

Dear Bottrall,

I dont know quite what to say on a blanket testimonial, and this sounds rather meagre, but in most cases the people would have time to write to me. I hope that one of these things will materialise. I dont think Dobrée

---

1–Albert Mordell, *Quaker Militant: John Greenleaf Whittier* (1933).

2–Roger L. Scaife (1875–1951), a Harvard graduate, worked for Houghton Mifflin from 1898; for Little, Brown from 1934; and in 1943, aged sixty-eight, he became the fourth Director of Harvard University Press, retiring in 1947. See Max Hall, *Harvard University Press: A History* (1986).

3–Gordon, *T. S. Eliot*, 255; *Imperfect Life*, 250: 'The final glimpse of Eliot and Emily Hale at this time is on 17 June when, with Dorothy Elsmith and members of the Eliot family, she attended his address at his old School, Milton Academy.' The address was published in the *Milton Graduates' Bulletin*, Nov. 1933. You must develop solid convictions, he told the boys, since at some time you will have to stand 'quite alone' (cited in Ackroyd, *T. S. Eliot*, 203).

4–TSE was awarded the honorary degree of Doctor of Letters from Columbia University, New York, on 6 June.

found Cairo too bad, but most of his colleagues were Belgians, and he came to detest the natives. He was there in George Lloyd's regime; I dont know what Egypt may be like now.[1]

I am in such a mess here at the end that I dont know whether I have your complete poem in its final form here or not. Can you tell me? I am having to take dozens of manuscripts and letters back to England which I have not had time to deal with here.

Let me hear from you at 24 Russell Square early in July.

Yours ever,
T. S. Eliot

TO *Geoffrey Faber* TS Valerie Eliot

12 June 1933 Randolph N.H.

My dear Geoffrey,

- where I am spending a week in the mountains with my family.[2] I have a letter from Bird saying that he has had two interviews with you which have been very useful to him – for these I am very grateful to you – that he will see (now a wire to say that he has seen, satisfactorily) James; and beyond this I yet know nothing of what has happened. In the dark, I am considering whether it would not be wiser to go straight through London with my boxes to the lodgings which Frank has found, rather than stop over at the club, and then come up directly, free-footed, to see Bird. Unfortunately, I and two other people have had cables from Vivienne asking boat and date; and have finally been obliged to cable: *Toscania,*

1–Bottrall was to write to TSE on 5 Aug. 1933: 'I have heard little from Cairo, and I am afraid that my chances there are small. I hear that Graves and Dobrée cured them of a wish for young men. The last holder was an octogenarian, I believe.'

2–Gordon, *T. S. Eliot*, 255; *Imperfect Life*, 249–50: 'In the midst of family, in a bookish city [Cambridge, Mass.] where Eliot was a celebrity, he and Emily Hale were less free than in California. Dorothy Elsmith, a friend who lived in Woods Hole, provided a retreat, as she recalled: "Emily and Mr Eliot made several visits to the anonymity of my home here [Olcotage], where they walked the beach, in quiet retreat from Cambridge publicity." . . . Then, in early June, there was a family vacation, which included Emily Hale, at Mountain View House in Randolph, New Hampshire. Eliot's poem "New Hampshire" is patently autobiographical.' Lyndall Gordon, *Eliot's New Life* (1988), 79: 'There are photographs of a family vacation in rural New Hampshire, Eliot in a cloth cap, his sisters comfortable in their rockers on the porch of Mountain View House.' (Theresa Eliot did a drawing in red pencil of TSE during this visit to New Hampshire.) HWE of his brother at this time: 'A most lovable person.'

leaving Boston 25th, which is a fake.[1] I might as well tell you now that I am taking the *Laetitia* from Montreal on the 23d for Liverpool. It might be best for me to stay on the boat and get off at Glasgow, or alternatively while away a day or two at Chester; I do not know whether such elaborate precautions are necessary; but I have a feeling that V. will assume that I have been beguiled and seduced by evil counsellors here, and that if she could see me at once she could bring me to my senses; and I especially wish to avoid a private and unexpected interview. (Failing this, of course, she may try to get hold of me at the Albert Hall Meeting on July 13, where I shall be conspicuous enough as chairman – I shall try to get the Dean of Rochester to be present).[2]

1–VHE would write in her diary, Sun. 24 June 1934: 'Today is the *Anniversary of the day – one year ago* – when T. S. Eliot, *my husband*, was to have *sailed from Boston*, in the TUSCANIA (see cables) arriving at Glasgow . . . In this one year – June 24 1933 – June 24 1934 there has been more serious damage & *evil* & abomination in my life than I should have thought *possible* in England in 1934 to go *unpunished*. This is a black document.' Two days later, on 26 June, she added: 'The *19th* (nineteenth) Anniversary of Thomas Stearns Eliot & Vivienne Haigh Eliot. And what an exhibition of Puritan morality, New England culture & tradition & the value of learning & education on highly civilised man. What an example to hand down from generation to generation, & what an *invaluable* gift I have made to the *Bodleian* Library Oxford. I must make a note to my Will that the papers & M.S.S. & Diaries are *not to be used* in *any biography* & not to be paraphrased – but published, if published at all, *without alterations*.' On 27 June: 'Starving & fasting & fasting & prayer. That is all my life now & I am *not* complaining.'

2–VW had written to OM as early as 6 Sept. 1932: 'I had meant to discuss Tom and Vivienne Eliot with you; but its now an old subject and stale . . .: I hope the separation is complete and final, as it promised to be when I last had news'; so a separation was widely rumoured even in the autumn of 1932. Robert Sencourt would tell JDH on 9 Sept. 1965: 'Tom had no plan of separating from her [VHE] till well on in 1932' (King's HB L/12/16). TSE informed GCF and FVM, his solicitors, and possibly others, well in advance of his return to England; and – as is apparent from the letters to OM and Alida Monro above – he was making known his wishes to certain confidantes by at least the early part of the year. However, he had evidently hoped for some while that a formal communication from the solicitors to VHE might obviate the need for him to write directly to her; but after various consultations he had been advised that he would need to write a personal letter to her. The letter to VHE has not been traced, but it would seem that he ultimately supplied that necessary letter in June or early July.

See Gordon, *T. S. Eliot*, 283: 'In the spring of 1933 he had sent a letter to his London solicitor to prepare a Deed of Separation. He enclosed a letter for Vivienne, and then had to face his return to England in June. He told a friend that the interim was like "a phantasma, or a hideous dream" (Sencourt, *A Memoir*, 151).' Gordon notes, p. 617: 'It is still unclear whether TSE sent this letter in February or after 14 May (the latter date is given by Ronald Schuchard in *VMP*). Miranda Seymour notes in her biography of Lady Ottoline Morrell that Vivienne did not appear to hear of the intended separation until June, though she was increasingly distressed by her husband's silence. The June date seems to be confirmed by Virginia Woolf's diary.'

Would you show this letter to Frank; as the landlady ought to be warned to have my rooms ready by July 1st. I should be grateful if you would send me a short cable (which will refund) to the *Laetitia* before she lands, suggesting which course I had best pursue.

I return to town on Friday to give my school Prize Day Address, the last of my duties, and shall then be busy packing and saying farewells. I suppose other business might as well wait till my return.

Yours ever affectionately,
Tom

FROM *Vivien Eliot* TO *Mary Hutchinson*   MS Texas

Sunday 18 June 1933   68 Clarence Gate Gardens

My dear Mary

I hear you will be back on Tuesday morning. *Please* ring me up at your *first* convenient moment.

Thank you for the post card of the Eiffel Tower. I have been missing you badly – & have enquired several times. Was obliged to apply to Jack for news. I am glad you have been having such a lovely time but I shall be very very glad to know that you are at home again. All this wandering about. I dont approve of it. My love dear Mary, & *welcome* home – from your stay-at-home-sister

Vivienne

His solicitors, Bird & Bird, would in due course send him an account covering the period Apr. to Dec. 1933, itemised as follows: 'Professional charges in relation to your matrimonial affairs including correspondence with and cables to you whilst you were in America and also attendances upon and correspondence with Mr Faber conferring with him on the situation when he gave us certain information and on your instructions interviewing Mr James, your Wife's Solicitor, intimating to him your intention not to return to your Wife and discussing the best means by which this could be conveyed to her when after considering the matter and consulting your Wife's relations [presumably Rose Esther Haigh-Wood and MHW] he informed us that neither he nor they were prepared to acquaint her with your decision. Further interviews with Mr Faber and Mr James as to the various alternative ways suggested of dealing with the matter and ultimately reporting to you the result of our deliberations when you sent us a letter addressed to your Wife which you requested us to deliver. Perusing and approving the letter, conferring with Mr Faber thereon, making arrangements with Mr James for the delivery thereof so that whatever precautions were necessary could be taken and attending to deliver the letter.'

FROM *Vivien Eliot* TO *Ottoline Morrell*   MS Texas

Friday 7 July 1933   68 Clarence Gate Gardens

Dearest Ottoline

I feel that I ought to write to tell you that I am very anxious *indeed* about Tom.

As you have always been fond of him, & as you were *so* good to me in my trouble when my *Father died*, I feel I must let you know – without further delay – that I believe that Tom is in *danger*.

I have been nearly insane with anxiety for 2 weeks. I do not know *where he is*, and *no-one* knows where he is.

I have gone through 2 weeks of absolute terror.

I get enquiries all day long. *No-one* knows where he is, & everything is terrible. If you think you can help in this matter I should be most grateful. I am *sure* he *is in danger*.

Yours as always affectionately,
Vivienne Eliot[1]

TO *Henry Eliot*   TS Houghton

8 July 1933   *The Criterion*

My dear Henry,

I was very glad to get your letter of the 26th. My present, after all, was only a slight reciprocation of a similar present from you in 1922. I am grateful to you for not mentioning it to others, as I have not done the same by everybody. I am very glad that my wedding present to Chardy comes opportunely for the new flat, and am glad that I made it in that convertible form. One of the greatest, the greatest, satisfaction after slaving to make money is to be able to give a little of it away as one chooses. My year in America, however, was the happiest I can ever remember in my life; even though I am glad to be able to discard the public role, which sits uncomfortably on me, and return to private life.

My real address is c/o Mrs Eames, the East Surrey Brick Co., Lingfield, but I am uncertain of future movements – I shall pay several visits this summer – and 24 Russell Square is always the best address; but mark letters PERSONAL. For the moment I am in concealment; only three

---

1–OM wrote to JDH, 11 July 1933: 'I had a despairing letter from Vivienne & she rings up everyone' (King's OM/JDH/22).

people know where I am. I hope to get the official interview with Vivienne over quite soon, as this concealment is intolerable. Of course I dread it. She rang up Geoffrey Faber in an attempt to find out something about me, and offered three conjectures (1) that I was dead (2) that I was insane (3) that I had been kidnapped. Of course she does not really believe any of these alternatives. She has of course been officially notified of my decision. Meanwhile her mother and brother have left town for a time. I will write to you in a week or so when there is something more definite to report.[1]

I am very pleasantly in the country, have two rooms, am looking out on a rose garden where two magpies are looking for worms, and only pay 25 shillings a week for rooms and board; dinner at night I take with friends who live near by with 3 children and numerous animals; yesterday I assisted at a sheep-dipping for the first time in my life.[2]

I was glad to get the photographs: if mine come out well I will send you them; I have only just sent the roll to be developed. I shall write to Cousin

---

1 – TSE's cousin Abigail Adams Eliot was to say in her memoirs: 'Once when Anna [Holman] and I went to England in the summer, after he had been here for lectures and I had understood that he had gone back to England, I went to visit him and his wife in their apartment. I found only his wife, and she said to me, "Where is Tom?" I said that I did not know but that I would find out. I knew that I could do so through his publishers, Faber and Faber. They gave him the message that I wanted to see him, and we met at a restaurant, and he told me that he was separated from his wife. He had become an Anglo-Catholic and therefore would not consider divorce. When I told him that I had promised her to go back and see her to tell her where Tom was, he said I must not go because it was dangerous. However, I did go, and Anna stood outside and waited until after about ten or fifteen minutes, I reappeared at the front door. I had confirmed to her that Tom would not come back to live with her. She made no aggressive move toward me but accepted what I said. We had always been good friends' (*A Heart of Grateful Trust: Memoirs of Abigail Adams Eliot*, transcribed and ed. Marjorie Gott Manning [n.d.], 61). See further Cynthia Grant Tucker, *No Silent Witness: The Eliot Parsonage Women and Their Unitarian World* (2010), 225–9.
2 – FVM, 'A Few Recollections of Eliot': 'At Pikes Farm there were no large animals – no cows, of which Tom was scary [*sic*]. Tom wrote about the many small animals and small doings to his brother and sisters in America . . . The battered seventeenth-century brick farmhouse, with a very wavy ancient red-tiled lichened roof which architects said would fall in, contained a thousand inconveniences. Lighting and cooking were done by petrol-gas; the rickety and dangerous machine in an outside shed was worked by compressed air which had to be pumped by a long lever, backward and forward. Pumping was a chore Tom liked to do: he said it gave him more regular exercise than he had had since as an undergraduate at Harvard he and his classmate [A. D.] Peters had persuaded themselves to take Sandow's instructions. Emergency pumping was a frequent occupation. The life of Pikes Farm was a ramshackle life, many things homespun, homemade, improvised; not a neat and tidy life . . . But Tom knew that beforehand. There were retainers inside the house and outside who knew Tom and he knew them.'

Jenny to thank her for the Revd Andrew, whom I am very glad to have by me.[1]

> With much love to both,
> Tom

TO *Elizabeth Manwaring*   TS Wellesley College Library

11 July 1933   B-11 Eliot House, Cambridge
                                            [actually Pike's Farm, Lingfield]

Dear Miss Manwaring,

Thank you very much for your kind and considerate letter,[2] which has just reached me from Cambridge; I infer from the date that you sailed within a day of me, but from a different port.

I very much appreciate your generosity, and am especially pleased by your suggestion of a visit to my wife. I have not yet seen her, but there may be an official meeting tomorrow.[3] I am sure that she would be glad indeed to hear from you; and I myself am anxious that she should not lose the best of the acquaintances which she has made through me. I do not know how long you are to be in England; but I think that in a week or two of time she would probably be delighted to see you. If, after seeing her, I judge otherwise, I will let you know what the situation is. Most people in these circumstances are I imagine anxious to avoid both parties, lest they be bruised *entre le marteau et l'enclume*;[4] the more I appreciate your generosity.

I am staying in the country, and my present address is known only to those few who have to know it; if I am able to be in London and meet people I will let you know; and I want to restore Robinson into your hands before you leave.[5] Any letter to me at 24, Russell Square marked

1–A portrait of the Revd Andrew Eliot (1718–78), Congregational Minister of the New North Church, Boston; was elected President of Harvard College, but declined, preferring to minister to his parish.
2–Not found.
3–Over two years later, in her diary for Nov. 1935, VHE recorded that she had just had photos taken of herself wearing the same clothes in which she had 'met Tom on his historic return from the United States of America on July 12th 1933 – .' TSE was to write to Violet Schiff, 28 Jan. 1947, of VHE: 'I had not seen her since 1933' (BL).
4–*entre le marteau et l'enclume*: 'between the hammer and the anvil'.
5–In Feb. 1933 TSE had given her a copy of *The Swiss Family Robinson*, ed. J. R. Wyss (Everyman, 1929), inscribed: 'A poor edition, but apparently the only available. Miss Elizabeth Manwaring will please not write her name in it until she has read it *from cover to cover*. T. S. Eliot. 28. ii. 33.' Manwaring signed the book on 22 Mar. 1933 (Wellesley College Library).

PERSONAL will reach me, though the staff there in general do not know of my presence in England.

With very grateful thanks,
Yours ever sincerely,
T. S. Eliot

TO *Mary Hutchinson* TS Texas

13 July 1933   B-11 Eliot House, Cambridge
[postmark 14 July]   [postmark London s.w.1.]

My dear Mary,

Thank you very much for your kind note. I am very sorry that you and Jack have had such a bad time – I did not anticipate this, and I do not know how else I could have managed.[1] The letter I sent in advance must have made clear my reasons for concealing my movements. I fear that it

---

1–Mary Hutchinson's letter not found. St John Hutchinson gossiped to VW, who noted in her diary on 10 July: 'It seems possible that Tom has finally deserted Vivienne. Jack Hutch. . . . told us how V. has heard by cable that Tom sailed [on the *Tuscania* bound for Greenock, Scotland] on 26th & he has not arrived. She has by today worked herself into frenzy – in bed, with a nurse; & then Jack telephoned to Faber – L's idea – & they say mysteriously that they cannot discuss the matter on the telephone, but if V. will pull herself together she will realise that there is no reason for anxiety. This we interpret to mean that Tom is back; has told Faber that he is parting from her; but it is kept secret, until he gives leave – which he may do today. Anyhow, V. is clearly concealing something. J[ack] read one of Tom's last letters, & describes it as a very cold & brutal document, saying that he has made no money. I should expect that after his 6 months thought & absence he has decided to make the break here: has warned V. & provided for her. But she shuts the letters in the cupboard with the sealed string. L. is made her executor. So I go up to lunch with her' (*The Diary of Virginia Woolf 4: 1931–1935*, ed. Anne Olivier Bell, 167).

By 20 July VW knew more of the situation: 'This was quite a correct statement of the Eliot position. He has left her "irrevocably"; & she sits meanwhile in a flat decorated with pictures of him, & altars, & flowers. Sometimes she prevails on a stranger – like E. Bowen to believe her story, at others lapses into sense. We dine with the Hutchinsons tonight, & shall I expect found some sort of Vivienne fund' (ibid., 167–8). And she learned from the Hutchinsons that evening: 'Vivi. E[liot] said of the scene with Tom at the solicitors: he sat near me & I held his hand, but he never looked at me' (ibid., 169).

VW wrote to Elizabeth Bowen, 20 July 1933: 'Yes, Vivienne seems to have gone crazy poor woman. Tom however is back and safe, but I dare not write down the story as I dont know if its public yet. But I daresay you can guess' (*Letters 5*, 205). To Quentin Bell, 26 July 1933: 'Have you heard that Mrs Eliot is on the war path, said to have a carving knife with which first to skin Tom; then Ottoline; finally me? For she says Ott and I are Tom's mistresses; now as I never had a favour from that man its rather hard to give my life on the pavement' (ibid., 207).

See also TSE's next letter to VW, 16 Aug. 1933.

may take some time to make V. realise that my decision is irrevocable. She is very tenacious. I may have to remain in obscurity for some little time. Nevertheless I am glad to be back – though I had a successful and amusing year. All best wishes to both of you until we can meet.

Ever yours,
Tom

TO *Tacon Gilbert*[1]

16 July 1933 Faber & Faber Ltd

Dear Miss Gilbert,

Thank you for your letter of the 14th with enclosures. The Plekhanov [*sc.* Pudovkin] and the Hoffmansthal [*sic*] can be used in the next number.[2] I will bring them up later in the week when I see Mr Faber, together with *Wild Goose Chase* and a communism book (Pringle); I am, by the way, against publishing either of these books, if any question is raised at the committee. It is true that I promised to use part iii of *Festivals of Fire*.[3] The material seems skimpy, but the Hoffmansthal is long, rather too long in both senses. I shall choose another piece of verse.[4] What is needed is a story and it is a pity that the Lawrence is so monotonously like other stories of his: I dislike it. I should like to see Mrs Tate's story as she has some talent.[5] I should also like to see Mr Mairet's article.[6] I am afraid that I shall have to print the Knights essay.[7]

1–Tacon Gilbert wrote to Montgomery Belgion, 16 Dec. 1932: 'Miss Wilberforce has suddenly decided to get married, and I have taken her place at short notice.'

2–'The first three articles were placed in the "indefinitely accepted drawer" by you before you left England; the Hoffmansthal letter has been read by both Mr Morley and Mr Read, who both like it; the latter has suggested that if it were not suitable for the *Criterion* it might be published in the Hogarth Letters series.' V. I. Pudovkin, 'Acting – The Cinema v. The Theatre', trans. M. Seton, C. 13 (Oct. 1933), 1–6. Marta Karlweis, 'Hugo von Hofmannsthal: A Letter to a Doctor about a Poet', trans. M. D. Hottinger, 25–50. Frau Jakob Wassermann-Karlweis's article about Hofmannsthal, who had been an intimate of the Wassermans, grew out of a letter addressed to Dr Katzenstein of Zurich.

3–'"Festivals of Fire" was to have been published in the last issue, but was held over: Mr Bottrall says that he has had a talk with you about it, and he is definitely expecting it to go into this issue. He tells me that if the whole poem is not published this autumn by Faber and Faber, Capes have agreed to take it, and that it will have appeared in book form before the January issue of the *Criterion*.'

4–Robert Fitzgerald, 'Two Poems: Winter Quarters, Petit Jour', C. 13 (Oct. 1933), 113–14.

5–Caroline Gordon, 'Old Red', C. 13 (Oct. 1933), 51–73.

6–'[A]n article . . . was left, to await your arrival, at this office by Philippe Mairet:- 'The Moral Dilemma of the Age of Science.' This appeared in C. 13 (Jan. 1934), 196–201.

7–L. C. Knights, '17th Century Melancholy', C. 13 (Oct. 1933), 97–112.

604 TSE at forty-four

The *Criterion* is ordinarily fed chiefly by articles which I have solicited.

I should like, please, a list of review books on hand, and of any which have been asked for or sent out to reviewers. You sent me a full list of material before I left America, but I seem to have mislaid it since I got here. And I should like to know if any chronicles and periodical-reviews are ordered or in hand.

Yours sincerely,
T. S. Eliot

FROM *Vivien Eliot* TO *Mary Hutchinson*   MS Texas

Sunday 16 July 1933   68 Clarence Gate Gardens

My dear Mary

It *was* nice of you to send me your brother's book. I had no idea you were going to give it to me. I am very glad you have, as it adds to a little collection of books you have given to me, & to Tom. Which I value very much.

I am reading it with *great* interest, & a feeling of definite sympathy with the author.

I could say more, but will not. But hope to discuss it with you later. His *portrait* of you is *vivid*.

With love,
Yours affectionately,
Vivienne H. Eliot

TO *Theodore Spencer*   TS Houghton

19 July 1933   *The Criterion*

My dear Ted,

It was jolly to hear from you.[1] No need to worry about Aunt Katie on my account: stay away from Cambridge and let her worm what she can out of my sister Marian. This is not of course my address: but letters addressed there reach me the following day, wherever I am; and if anyone asks you you can say that it is my address; but for your private ear I am living at the East Surrey Brick Company, and a very pleasant place it is, though by the time you get this I shall be somewhere else. I should have

1 – Letter not found.

written ere now, but the first two weeks were the most exhausting, and I am only just beginning to feel my oats. I have still to address the Anglo-Cathollege I mean the Anglo-Catholic Summer School of Sociology at Oxford on Monday,[1] and shall while away a few days there with Paul More on the banks of the Ilyssus;[2] and this last public appearance is one too many. I am curious however to meet that man whose name I cant spell, Berdiayev you know.[3] Here I live in distinguished solitude. My friends and neighbours have gone to Norway by the Svenska Lloyd (Captain, Sir P. Spens) to perform feats on the fjords. Except for the landlady's loudspeaker, and that of the nurse next door who sits in the garden with it, and an occasional train from East Grinstead, and passing motorcycles, and the express-planes from Paris and Cologne passing over, you are in the Heart of the Country, more Kentish than Surrey: the house opposite has an imitation oast to it.[4] Still, I think that the English countryside is

1–TSE, 'Catholicism and International Order', *Christendom: A Journal of Christian Sociology* (Oxford) 3: 11 (Sept. 1933), 171–84: the text of TSE's address at the Summer School held at Keble College, Oxford (see Roger Kojecky, *T. S. Eliot's Social Criticism* [1971], 155).

2–TSE and Elmer More lodged for several nights at the Isis Private Hotel, Iffley Road, Oxford.

3–Nikolai Berdyaev (1874–1948): Russian religious and political philosopher; author of *The End of Our Time* (1933).

4–FVM, 'A Few Recollections of Eliot', 108–9: 'When he had been installed in Uncle Tom's Cabin, and knew the running of the whole caboodle . . . my wife and I just left him (nominally in charge) and went for three weeks to Norway . . . Whether this is the right treatment for a man who is climbing his private mountain of Purgatory, I don't know – you never know . . . We were back from Norway . . . on 7 August. The estate was in good heart, and so was Tom. He was sunburnt, but, more important, he had been in touch with people he had thought of, and was planning to write *The Rock* . . . Correspondence had been flowing; now people began to come down for days and nights. Geoffrey Faber, Donald Brace from New York, to see what he was doing. He was keeping up with business . . . [H]e was also learning to bake bread. We did our own baking, and Tom was very proud of the first loaf he made – insisted on a photograph with him holding it well forward to make it appear bigger. In odd moments we invented various kinds of crossword games, in different languages.' In an interview for a BBC TV 'Omnibus' programme (8 June 1970), FVM said: 'The intellectual activities [at Pikes Farm] were very considerable; we spent a great deal of time doing crosswords – I mean making them up in most languages. Hebrew we had some difficulty in completing but Greek and Latin and French and German and Italian we passed these things' (ref. 6349/1079: 141 Take 1: CC in Morley/Eliot Papers, Berg box 95).

Michael Tippett would recall in his memoirs that TSE 'was to become my spiritual and artistic mentor and his advice in the early stages of writing *A Child of Our Time* proved absolutely crucial. I met him through Francis Morley . . . Morley's younger son, Oliver, then about six, while musically very talented, was almost inarticulate verbally. He confined himself to a few remarks like "That dog barks in B flat." Morley asked W. H. Auden for advice [and WHA] recommended me as a trained musician with an interest in psychology and in the education of children. Morley thus stopped off at my Oxted cottage, on his way

as beautiful as any; there is nowhere else where the forms of *individual* trees are so lovely, and the tracery of a hedge-top against the sunset. Parts of southern France smell just as good, I admit; but the English sky is the most beautiful, and thank God not too much sunlight, and the weather is variable and mostly bad.[1] I have had a letter from John Hayward: he has slightly altered his calligraphy, but it is just as fine and Jacobean as ever, so I hope he himself is no worse; in a few weeks I hope to go to see him. I can say for Old England that she is working just as hard at turning out Literature as ever; the bulldog breed hangs on tenaciously to Russell Square. Two typical letters: one from a boy of 17 who says his friends tell him he is mad (they are merely untrained in psychological discrimination, that's all) and one from a Lady from whom I had not heard for some years but who now believes that her boy at Eton has Talent: whether she expects him to be a Poet or a Publisher or both I am not sure; but she has her teeth in my coattails anyway. And most of the old lunatics are rallying up too: Irish, Scots, Singhalese, Sudanese etc. all writing poetry. If the next world war enlisted only Poets, I believe the British Empire would win inside the time required to mobilise. I am sorry you are playing Golf at the Haven, where the Proper sport is dinghy-racing in Fox Island Thoroughfare, and your willingness to get back to Cambridge is a bad sign too. Say can ye tell me naught of Jonesport, and how fare they of East Machias? how bite the lobster off Roque Island? do they still fight with knives at Cutler? and is canibalism still practised on the Wolves? where now be all those seafaring

---

home to Crowhurst, and discussed the possibility of my teaching Oliver music, as a way of tempting him to speak. Meanwhile, mooching about on the grass outside I could see Eliot, wearing his famous clerical hat. My sessions with Oliver brought me some vicarious family life with the Morleys and with Eliot . . . This was the domestic Eliot, helping in the kitchen and studiously picking blackcurrants in the garden. We also played Monopoly, at which Eliot was quite good. Oliver always caused a scene if he lost, which Eliot bore with good humour' (*Those Twentieth Century Blues: An Autobiography* [1991], 50–1).

1–Curiously, FVM would later write to HR (23 June 1965): 'Tom's whole life at Pike's Farm was observably a mental one. I don't think he *saw* country things . . . And perhaps as he got older . . . the sphincter muscles closed tighter and he began to lose feeling, even repress feeling, for individual people' (Berg). 'A Few Recollections of Eliot', 115: 'I don't believe he saw country things with direct sensuous appreciation. In his Town diversions his eye was perhaps quicker for the object; in the country he tended not to look. With the children at Pikes Farm he was never otherwise than kindly and avuncular, but I am not sure how clearly he *saw* them.'

HR to FVM, 29 June 1965: 'Tom's attitude to children, which you do bring in obliquely, perhaps deserves more attention. You know better, but my feeling is that they were among the things he never *saw*. Oh yes, he could be nice and avuncular towards them, but I don't think he felt any real affection for them. This may have been the self-protection of a childless man, but I've known childless men who behaved differently' (Morley Papers, Berg, folder 16).

folk of the Haven, Cobbs and Saltonstalls, notable men of yore? these are the matters you should report of.

My wits are still hardly better than those of a frozen frog, but they will come back, I hope, along towards the end of the year; if I dont spend too much time dozing after lunch in the smoking room. The man who wanted to lecture is now living in Hampstead with the Lady Musician, I hear; she is said to be a devout Catholic, which is interesting; but until my other friend comes back from Norroway I dont know whether I may divulge the name, though he appears to have been divulging it himself pretty freely. Believe that the quondam Buffoon of Eliot House is long since inoculated against such carryings on; 'what strange behaviourism'! as I heard a lady say. I drink a small drink of gin to your health, for in this country, gin is good gin but is 12s. the small bottle; and 12s. is 12s. when you spend it, and only 9s. when you earn it. Love to everybody.

Affectionately yours,
T. S. E.

I must begin seriously studying British Birds. And Chess. I am to be taught bricklaying. In the intervals I visit Deans. The worst of the country is that I am terrified of Cows. How does one get over that?[1]

TO *Susan Hinkley*[2]   TS Houghton

19 July 1933   *The Criterion*

Dear Aunt Susie,

Thank you very much for your letter of the 9th.[3] No action of this sort, of course, is worth taking until one is prepared to take it whatever anyone thinks (except of course for ecclesiastical advice) but après coup it is a help to know that one's relatives are not censorious. But once such a train is started, one has to carry it out to the end in a kind of anaesthesia. At the moment I am fortunately able to feel very little.

I am at present living in seclusion in the country, and very lovely English country too, of varying sky and delicate lights, and beautifully formed trees on horizons, and hedgerows and newmown hay. I expect to make a small round of visits in the country, but to see little of London until as late in the year as possible.

---

1 – See TSE's poem 'The Country Walk' published, as 'Cows', in *The Times*, 6 June 2009.
2 – Susan Heywood Hinkley, née Stearns (1860–1948): TSE's maternal aunt.
3 – Not found.

With much love to both,
Affectionately your nephew,
Tom

TO *John Hayward*

MS King's College Cambridge

19 July 1933

Oxford & Cambridge Club,
Pall Mall, s.w.1.

Dear John

I found your letter today on coming up from the country.[1] Thank you very much and for previous messages unanswered from America. Where I found my time very fully occupied: I never before realised how completely social engagements can fall into the category of 'work'. I think that I spoke in public (to be comprehensive) between 70 and 80 times, ending with a Prize Day address at my old school – where I believe that I surpassed myself. I saw much of Ted Spencer, of whom I became very fond. We fell into the habit of gin & bitters every weekday at 12.50. I took some photographs to prove it.

You have been constantly in my thoughts. I am at present in the country. As soon as I am in town again I will write or ring up & am anxious to see you.

Ever affectionately,
Tom

When I am more settled, say by September, I shd like to lunch with you alone, preferably. I have seen no one yet. Meanwhile, I am paying various country visits.

TO *Tacon Gilbert*

TS Valerie Eliot

23 July 1933

Faber & Faber Ltd

Dear Miss Gilbert,

I shall see Mr Faber in town tomorrow and will give him the following papers for you.

1. Proof of *Bedoyere*, Mss. of Peel, Knights, Fitzgerald, Bottrall, and Mrs Tate (Catherine [Caroline] Gordon).[2]

---

1 – Not found.
2 – Caroline Gordon's story 'Old Red' would appear in C. 13 (Oct. 1933), 51–73.

Bottrall's Section III is to be set up for the *Criterion*, although like everything else after a year's time, it is not as good as I thought it was. His *Complete Poem* should go back to him, with the remark, that as our possibilities are so uncertain, we advise him to close with Cape at once. Mrs Tate's *Old Red* can be set up, as it appears to be the only story available (but I should like to see the stories by the man you mentioned). The other can be returned to her: having appeared in the *Hound and Horn* it is of no use to us. The others listed above are to be set up. There will not be time to send proof to Peel & Fitzgerald, as they are in America.

2. D. H. Lawrence Story *A Modern Lover*. I should not think of using this in the *Criterion*, but if they want to use it as a Christmas cheap I will not object.

3. Letters to the Editor from Dobrée and Pound, to be set up.

4. Matter relating to Lord Clonmore and the Dean of Westminster, with memorandum.

5. A folder of dead correspondence. You may not know where to file much of this, so you may leave it till I see you. I want it out of the way here.

6. Catalogue advt. for my book, with carbon to be sent at once to the Harvard University Press, Cambridge, Mass.

7. Advts. of two Pound books, which Mr Morley left with me.

As for the price to be set on my book, it consists of 127 <u>large</u> typed quarto pages: I should think it could make 148 to 160 printed pages. There will not be much in the way of footnotes, so it should be pretty straightforward.

As for reviews, I shall try to review Housman's lecture myself (I have it here). I should think that there ought to be enough.[1] I do not want the Russian books sent to Muggeridge,[2] as I do not know what his abilities are; but if there is time, I wish you would offer Penty and Saintsbury

1–TSE, review of A. E. Housman, *The Name and Nature of Poetry*: C. 13 (Oct. 1933), 151–4.
2–Malcolm Muggeridge (1903–90), journalist and broadcaster, graduated from Selwyn College, Cambridge, and taught in India, 1925–7, then for three years in Cairo. From 1930 he wrote for the *Manchester Guardian;* and from 1932 he lived for a while in Russia; later in Switzerland. Later still, he wrote for the *Calcutta Statesman* and the *Evening Standard.* His work for the Intelligence Corps in WW2 earned him the Légion d'honneur and the Croix de Guerre with Palm. In 1945 he became a leader writer for the *Daily Telegraph* (he served too as Washington correspondent, 1946–7); and he edited *Punch*, 1952–7. From the 1950s he won fame as a TV presenter. In 1982 he was received into the Roman Catholic Church. Works include a biography of Samuel Butler (1936), *The Thirties* (1940), and autobiographies. See also Richard Ingrams, *Muggeridge: The Biography* (1995), and G. Wolfe, *Malcolm Muggeridge: A Biography* (1995).

and Wood to Professor MacMurray. Kemp Smith should certainly have Barth's Romans.[1] Read should review Santayana.[2]

James Jeans's book should be offered to Sykes Davies.[3] *New Country* you may offer to Pound, but that would probably have to be for December.[4] Anyway, the books mentioned above are important enough to review in the winter number if there is not time to get reviews for the autumn number.

We will use the German periodicals in September. Sykes had better keep on the American periodicals until he gets tired of it, or until I have had a chance to discuss it with him.

I leave tomorrow for Oxford: my address Monday night, Keble College, Tuesday and Wednesday nights, c/o P. E. More, Isis Hotel. I return here on Thursday, but my address over the weekend will be The Deanery, Winchester. These addresses are of course confidential, and you probably will not have to use them. From Monday week (the 31st) I shall be here again until further notice.

Yours sincerely,
T. S. Eliot

TO *Ronald Bottrall*   CC

25 July 1933   [London]

Dear Mr Bottrall,

Thank you for your letter of July 11th, giving me your address.[5] I am just writing to say that the third Part of 'Festivals of Fire' will duly appear in the forthcoming number of *The Criterion*. As regards the whole poem, however, Faber & Faber feel rather worried. The market for poetry is so bad just now that almost anything is a risky proposition to publish, and the general depression makes us unwilling to take risks which in normal times we should not hesitate over. In the circumstances we feel that perhaps it would be wisest for you to close with Cape's offer for the

---

1–Norman Kemp Smith (1872–1958), Professor of Logic and Metaphysics at Edinburgh, 1919–45; noted for his translation of Immanuel Kant's *Critique of Pure Reason* (1929). Karl Barth, *The Epistles to the Romans*, was reviewed by Norman W. Porteus: C. 13 (Jan. 1934), 342–4.
2–Not done.
3–Not done.
4–In the event, the anthology *New Country: an Anthology of Prose and Poetry* (Hogarth Press), ed. Michael Roberts, was reviewed by T. C. Wilson, C. 13 (Apr. 1934), 485–7.
5–Bottrall wrote from Cornwall.

book, so I am returning your MS. herewith. We are all very sorry that it is not appearing under Faber's imprint.

Yours sincerely,

[T. S. Eliot]

TO *Philip Radcliffe*[1] CC

28 July 1933   [as from *The Criterion*]

My dear Sir,

Mr J. B. Trend, who as you know has just been appointed to a Professorship at Cambridge, has for ten years supplied a Music Chronicle to the *Criterion*. He tells me that his new duties will make it impossible for him to continue this Chronicle. It is a regular item of the *Criterion* which has proved very successful, and I do not wish to abandon it; therefore I am writing to you in the hope that you will consider undertaking it regularly as Mr Trend's successor.

I must say that Mr Trend himself suggested your name; but I should naturally have asked him to nominate his successor; and I warmly endorse his nomination. The emolument is small: we pay the same rate throughout, two guineas per thousand words, and the length has to be limited. On the other hand I know that the readers of the *Criterion* pay great attention to the Chronicles and Reviews, and that a good deal of influence can be exerted by a regular contributor.

I should be glad to have a Chronicle every quarter; but if that did not suit your convenience I would compound, though regretfully, on a half-yearly chronicle.

I am assuming that you have read some at least of Mr Trend's chronicles, which have suited the purposes of the *Criterion* to perfection. If I am mistaken, I shall be glad to send you a number of copies containing his contribution. I must explain that I should not expect Mr Trend's successor to model his chronicles any more closely than he wished to do. In fact the word 'chronicle' suggests something more impersonal and arid than I wish for the *Criterion*. What I seek in these chronicles is the continuity of one man saying exactly what he thinks on one subject at any one moment. I do not want anyone to try to recount everything that

---

1–Philip Radcliffe (1905–86), Fellow of King's College, Cambridge, from 1931; University Lecturer from 1948. J. B. Trend wrote, in a letter to Tacon Gilbert (20 July), that Radcliffe had 'the rare combination of being both a learned, scholarly musician and an acute critic of contemporary music, who goes to International Festivals'.

has happened in any one art during the past three months; sometimes recent books rather than recent performances, may be the subject; and I should ordinarily send you all the books on musical subjects that came in for review, or order any others that you wished to see; or the 'chronicler' is at liberty, when nothing has taken place, and no books have appeared, that interest him, to take the opportunity to expound his views on any musical subject.

I hope very much that you will accept in principle, and we will then discuss any further details.

Yours very truly,
T. S. E.

TO *Tacon Gilbert*   TS Valerie Eliot

28 July 1933   B-11 Eliot House, Cambridge

Dear Miss Gilbert,

I have written to Mr Faber about *Die Judenfrage* and shall send him the book.[1]

I enclose a letter from Mr J. B. Trend and carbon of a letter which I have written to Mr Philip Radcliffe, which explains itself.

I find that I have here three stories by Mr Guy Dent, which I believe Mr Morley brought down. I have now read them, and will keep one called

---

1 – Gilbert had written to TSE (27 July) to stress that GCF was about to leave for Wales and was hoping for a decision on *Die Judenfrage* ('The Jewish Question') before he left London.

On 1 June 1933, Gerhard Kittel (1888–1948) – a New Testament professor and Christian theologian at the University of Tübingen (founder and co-editor of *Theologisches Wörterbuch zum Neuen Testament*, 5 vols, 1933–79) – gave a speech he called *Die Judenfrage* ('The Jewish Question'), which was presently published as a 78-page booklet. Kittel's text was candidly anti-Semitic, recommending among other measures that Jews should be designated 'guest people' (non-citizens), that mixed marriage between Jews and Christians in Germany should not be permitted, and that professions including law, medicine and teaching should be closed to them.

How this vicious tract came to F&F's notice is not known; nor whether TSE actually ever read it. GCF's appalled reaction to the booklet can be gathered from the following extract from a letter that he sent to Erich Alport three days later (it was primarily concerned with SS's novel *The Temple*), on 31 July 1933: 'I am also reading a curious MS. about the Nazis, written by a German Jew, who is *mirabile dictu* not unfriendly to the movement. But how I loathe this ideal of the authoritarian state! I become more and more of a Liberal. Will England go down, too, into this wild beast pit of dogmatic dictatorship?' TSE's thoughts on the text are not known, but he normally agreed with GCF's opinions – his enthusiastic response to Djuna Barnes's novel *Nightwood* in 1936 was to be a rare exception – and *Die Judenfrage* was not published by F&F.

'The Accessory' which I will send you for future use.[1] I want 'Old Red' (Catherine [*sc.* Caroline] Gordon) set up for the next number.

Yours sincerely,
T. S. Eliot

TO *Gerald Graham*

MS Gerald Graham

31 July 1933   Oxford & Cambridge Club,
Pall Mall

My dear Graham

Owing to my unfortunate private affairs I have thought best to be in the country. I should like to see you before you return, however. If you would drop me a line to 24, Russell Square ('Personal') & let me know your plans, perhaps you could lunch with me one day soon?

I should have to ask you, however, not to divulge either place or date to anyone until after the event.

Please give my respects to your wife. I hope she is in the best of health.

Yours ever,
T. S. Eliot

I hear Sykes has got his fellowship at John's.[2]

TO *Tacon Gilbert*

TS Valerie Eliot

2 August 1933   Faber & Faber Ltd

Dear Miss Gilbert,

I duly received your envelope of ms. from Mr Stokes's book.[3] I am in principle in favour of publishing a section in the *Criterion*, provided that one short enough can be found. But let me first recapitulate the mss. which I have so far sent you, by Mr Faber, for the next number.

PUDOVKIN   on Films[4]
HOFFMANSTHAL [*sic*]   REMINISCENCES (this may have to be cut in proof; it could well stand it).

1–Guy Dent, 'The Accessory', C. 13 (Jan. 1934), 203–15.
2–Hugh Sykes Davies (1909–84): author and critic; see also TSE to him, 11 Dec. 1933.
3–Presumably Adrian Stokes, *The Stones of Rimini* (F&F, 1934).
4–V. I. Pudovkin, 'Acting – The Cinema v. The Theatre', trans. Marie Seton, C. 13 (Oct. 1933), 1–6. The article was submitted by John Grierson, Film Dept., Empire Marketing Board, on 8 May 1933.

MRS. TATE (C. Gordon)	'Old Red'.
BOTTRALL	Fest. of Fire Section III
PEEL	on Virginia Woolf
BEDOYERE	Censorship
Knights	On Melancholy
FITZGERALD	Two Poems

If Mr Stokes can select a passage of about 20 to 25 pages, not more, we will use it in this number. If the number should then threaten to be too long the PEEL can be held over in galley, as I did not promise to use it at once. It is always a good habit to have a few contributions in galley several months ahead.

I shall post you the Stokes mss. and ask you to settle with him if you can upon a section of the right length. I shall include also the DENT mss. of which you will retain 'An Accessory', returning the rest to him. 'An Accessory' can go into the December number. Will you please write to Mrs Tate to tell her that 'Old Red' is to appear. There will hardly be time to send proof out to her, or to Fitzgerald who is probably in Europe somewhere. If Peel is postponed to December galley proof should be sent to him. Will you please acknowledge receipt of his ms. to him and say that it will be published either in September or December, and that in the latter event he will receive proof?

It is allright for Mr Porteous, whom I do not know, to have the Barth Romans; though I think I could have done better if the book had not been offered to Mr Kemp Smith in the first place. Mr Read knows a good deal more about Mr Aurousseau than I do; I did not know that he reviewed economic works. The lot seems puzzlingly miscellaneous, but I have not seen the books. I am rather in the dark, but I will ask you to ask Mr Aurousseau to cut to 1500.

On your list of 'Books in Hand' you include several rather important books (Penty, Wood, Saintsbury) with the name of Mr Muggeridge (whom again I do not know much about) after them. Does this mean that they have been definitely promised to him? If not, I think that I could find someone I am surer of – I think Maurice Reckitt might be the man – but it is very difficult to decide on reviewers without glancing at the books.

I hope that the Demant book which Mr Aurousseau has reviewed is not merely a reprint of a book which came out a couple of years ago and which I discussed in a Commentary at the time.[1]

1–TSE had written about the Revd V. A. Demant, *This Unemployment*, in 'Commentary', C. 11 (Jan. 1932), 268-75. Aurousseau did not review Demant; but TSE gave brief mention

You had better let me know how much time I may have for my Commentary and for the Housman review. And please send me a copy of Pound's *ABC of Economics*, which I have never had, and a proof of his letter as soon as you have one. The Commentary may be concerned partly with that and partly with the death of Irving Babbitt.[1]

Yours sincerely,
T. S. Eliot

If there should be anything really urgent, you could telephone to me tomorrow at the Oxford & Cambridge Club at lunchtime; but please, in that event, put the call through yourself as there is no need for Miss Swan to be aware of my movements at present.

Wd. you please let me know What Book the Revd. Mr Box (enclosed) is talking about? I have no recollection of him.

I should object distinctly if it turned out that the two reviews were closely similar. But I prefer to be quite sure. Will you please retain the enclosed cutting (as it is safer in your hands) and send it back to me *with* a copy of the proof when it comes in. In any case, I may write to Mr Grant Watson when he next asks for a book, to say that we prefer that he should choose books for the *Criterion* that he is not reviewing elsewhere. Probably he got this one from the *Criterion* first.

TO *Stephen Spender*   TS Northwestern

2 August 1933   Faber & Faber Ltd

Dear Spender,

I am back in England, but for private reasons not yet back in London. I am occasionally there for the day. Please let me know something of your plans for this month, so that we can arrange a day for lunch. I should much like to see you.

Yours ever,
T. S. Eliot

---

to Demant's 'important' *God, Man and Society* in his Commentary in C. 13 (Jan. 1934), 277.
1–Babbitt had died on 15 July 1933.

TO *Ronald Bottrall*   TS Texas

2 August 1933   Faber & Faber Ltd

Dear Bottrall,

I am sorry to learn your news, because I am not very hopeful about the prospects of our undertaking any poetry this autumn. But the information you give is useful, and if you will return the text (I think the copy restored to you was in the final form?) I will do everything I can. I am not at present in London, nor likely to be for some time, and just at this period my colleagues are never all there at once. But please return a copy.

I shall be interested to know whether your application for Cairo is likely to bear fruit. Do keep me informed of your plans.

Yours ever,
T. S. Eliot

TO *Gerald Graham*   TS Gerald Graham

2 August 1933   Faber & Faber Ltd

Dear Graham,

(There is no need for Mr I think). I was glad to get your letter. Unfortunately I can only be up in town the one day this week (Thursday) and doubt whether I have time to lunch as I [am] engaged up to and after. So I suppose we must leave it until you return. Will you let me know as soon as you get back? It is just possible that I may be in Wales about that time, but I should only be away for a week. I should be much disappointed not to see you at all.

With best wishes for your holiday in Spain. Of course, if you shouldn't go away quite so soon, I could lunch one day early next week.

Yours ever,
T. S. Eliot

TO *Ottoline Morrell*   TS Texas

9 August 1933   Faber & Faber Ltd

My dear Ottoline,

Gordon George forwarded me the letter which you wrote to him and asked him to send me. He has however no greater facilities than anyone else: my letters are forwarded from Russell Square, as I have not wished to inconvenience any friends by entrusting them with an address which they would be expected to conceal.

I am afraid that my impressions of Alida have got altered in the process of transmission. I did not suppose for a moment that she had said disagreeable things about Vivienne, nor had I heard any reports at all. I have not turned against her in any way, nor have I the slightest criticism to make of her conduct towards V. or otherwise. I only felt that – perhaps partly owing to her own unhappy life, but perhaps partly instinctive – she had a certain antipathy to V. which she had tried in vain to overcome. Perhaps I am wrong; but even if I am right, what I had in mind was something that Alida could not help. Now, I have something of this feeling myself, and recognise it as due largely to fundamental differences about which there is no arguing. But in the circumstances, I have felt – you can call it merely pride, I suppose – rather on guard against everyone, however admirable and however good friends, whom I might suspect to be inclined to be 'against' V. in any way. In my position one is perhaps over-anxious to avoid sympathy, from any quarter whatever. And it seems to me better that I should be socially invisible for as long as is practicable.[1]

Affectionately yours,

Tom

I am glad to hear that Hope Mirrlees has been able to help.[2]

1 – OM wrote to Alida Monro (undated: 'Monday morning') about that '*cat* Sencourt' who had 'made mischief. I don't believe Tom is as bad only he wants to hide & to salve his conscience. It may have been a dig at *me* really. For I havent been good to V. as you have & I havent been nice about her. I wrote a very stiff letter to him' (MS BL Add MS 83366).

2 – Hope Mirrlees (1887–1978), British poet, novelist, translator and biographer, became a close friend of TSE; author of important works including *Paris: A Poem* (1918) and *Lud-in-the Mist* (novel, 1926); see also *Collected Poems of Hope Mirrlees*, ed. Sandeep Parmar (2011). She would recall in 1971, of VHE: 'Fear, that's it. Because she gave the impression, you see, of absolute terror. Of a person who'd seen a hideous ghost; a goblin ghost, and was always seeing a goblin in front of her. Her face was all drawn and white; and wild, frightened, angry eyes, and an over-intensity over nothing, you see; over some little thing you'd say. Suppose you were to say to her: "Will you have some more cake?"; and she'd say (in a wild voice): "What's that, what's that, what d'you mean, what did you say that for?" She was terrifying. At the end of an hour, when she used to come and see me, I was absolutely exhausted, sucked dry; and I felt to myself, poor Tom this is enough. But – she was his Muse all the same' ('The Mysterious Mr Eliot', BBC TV, 1 Jan. 1971: see too 'Eliot's Life', *The Listener* 85 [14 Jan. 1971], 50; cited in Gordon, *Eliot's New Life*, 55–6; Seymour-Jones, 479).

FROM *Vivien Eliot* TO *Mary Hutchinson* MS Texas

Thursday 10 August 1933 68 Clarence Gate Gardens

My dear Mary

I have never thanked you for the *lovely* set of clothes. This certainly does not mean that I was not intensely pleased with them. I was enchanted with them all. The *gloves* & the *coat* are so lovely.

I have just been *terribly* ill & queer ever since you last telephoned. I have felt so stressed [?stunned] & at the same time so *weak*. I can scarcely walk, & cannot *think* at all. So I have not attempted to write any letters.

It is not surprising that I feel so strange, for I have had 2 years of terrible strain – ending with a very great shock.

So forgive me [?more]. Believe I *love* the clothes, & thank you truly, & [I] think about you very often.

I read a little bit of Jim's book each night, very slowly.

With love
Yours ever [?always]
Vivienne

I am sure Tom never wished to go back to America – but was put in a position where he could not refuse. This *all* works out clearly for years back. Poor *poor* Tom.

V. H. E.

TO *Ottoline Morrell* TS Texas

14 August 1933 Faber & Faber Ltd

My dear Ottoline,

I was glad to get your letter, but must write again at once as I do not seem to have made myself at all clear. Though it may have been unnecessary for you to defend someone whom I had not attacked, I was not in the slightest degree annoyed with you; and it would surely be unreasonable to be vexed with anyone merely for being misinformed. I was a little annoyed with Gordon George for chattering to you about what he thought I thought of Alida, that is all. I should be extremely sorry not to be on terms of friendship with her. Nor had anyone intimated to me that she had said unkind things about either V. or myself.

I am anxious to be able to feel that Vivienne will not lose any friends through my action, or cease to see any of the people whom I have liked

her to see in the past; but I quite understand your not wanting to try to
see her at this moment.

Yours always affectionately,
Tom

TO *Theodore Spencer*   PC MS Houghton

Postmarked 15 August 1933

Your ltr. forwarded to here in Gloucestershire.[1] (Wm Morris' tomb or
gravestone in foreground). Shall be back in London on 17th, away from
31st to Sep. 4, and again Sep. 8–17. John Hayward (22, Bina Gdns s.w.7)
knows of a place in Lowndes Sqre. wh. wd. *just suit you*. Write to him at
once.

Aff.
T. S. E.

TO *Hoffman Nickerson*[2]   cc

16 August 1933   [Faber & Faber Ltd]

My dear Hoffman,

You must not blame the apparently unbusiness-like methods of Faber
and Faber: the fault & delay was entirely my own fault.[3] To begin with,
I have been, and am, in the country, deprived of the assistance, and what
is still more important, the perpetual reminding of things undone which
is a large part of a secretary's function. In such circumstances I am very
disorderly – I can also plead a good deal of work on hand, lassitude and
preoccupation with private affairs – however, nothing excuses.

We all liked your book very much – were cordially in accord with the
doctrines of common sense inculcated. The only deciding factors were the
state of the market and the lack of public interest in such matters (alas)
and finally the American angle of view. I don't mean, of course, that the

1–Letter not found.
2–Hoffman Nickerson (1888–1965), journalist and historian, had been a friend of TSE at
Harvard.
3–Nickerson had written on 8 June, 'Up to the time I left England a week ago, Faber and
Faber had not received my script from you and had had no correspondence from you about
it, so I suppose you still have it. I therefore wired you this afternoon "Please wire collect
whether you have read manuscript and how long you will remain in Cambridge. Letter
follows."' The book in question was *Can We Limit War?* (1933).

last at all diminishes its value for the serious reader, English or of any other nationality, but, especially when the subject is not a popular one at the moment anyway, it very much restricts the market.

I meant to follow up my wire with a letter, explaining that I thought best to hold the ms. for your instructions. I suggested Eyre & Spottiswoode, because I thought that some of the people there would be sympathetic to your views (they also run *The English Review* which I think, by the way, you might sometimes find a good vehicle for articles). If you like, I should be glad to write to Jerrold[1] there about it. I should much like to see the book published here, though we can't do it ourselves.

I am sorry to have missed you altogether; it is a pity that you could not have been in London in July instead of June: there were some interesting public occasions. I hope you will be over again next year.

Yours ever cordially,
[T. S. Eliot]

TO *Ezra Pound* TS Beinecke

16 August 1933 Faber & Faber Ltd

Dear Rabbett,

Well heres a long time, since much water has Flowed under many bridges has they say well I Dont know hardly where to begin but here one point for immediet attention.

In Cantos Page 106 I query Palgrave's Golden Treasury. On one hand identity of MacMillan hardly concealed, second allegation cant be proved and cannot be literally true and might be resented & possibly libellous. I regret that this point was not noticed before. *Might* do to put Cohen's Thesaurus instead but perhaps spoils the point, which does not seem to me very important or telling especially as no one will believe it in that form. I suggest leaving out those lines or if you prefer dotting them. As time is short will you send at our expense (collect, if possible, but otherwise will refund on presentation of claim) Wire to Morley (see telegraphic address above), giving assent or making suggestion, as the book should be through the press immediately.[2]

1–Douglas Jerrold, editor of *The English Review*.
2–In the event, EP's *A Draft of XXX Cantos* was to be published by F&F on 14 Sept. 1933 with the reference in Canto xxii, p. 106 (which TSE found problematical) phrased as follows:

Several other points but mainly that communications to me at address above will eventually reach me in my Retreat.

yrs. etc.

T.

TO *Christina Chapin*[1]   CC

16 August 1933   [Faber & Faber Ltd]

Dear Miss Chapin,

I am very sorry for the delay in reporting on your poem, 'Sanctuary'. I have been out of London ever since my return to this country, and not always in one place for very long, so that my business methods are not what they should be. I regret very much any anxiety and inconvenience that I may have caused you.

> The whole fortune of
> Mac Narpen and Company is founded
> Upon Cohen's Thesaurus.

As TSE noted, EP had originally made – in the first edition of *A Draft of XXX Cantos* published by the Hours Press, Paris (1930), p. 100 – a specific reference to 'Palgrave's Golden Treasury', as published by Macmillan & Co – the publisher being 'hardly concealed' under the nonce-name 'Mac Narpen'. The allusion to 'Cohen's Thesaurus' is explained by a letter from FVM to EP, 11 Aug. 1933: 'Have you had a letter from The Deacon [TSE] abaht the two lines in your Cantos where you remark upon Macmillan and the Golden Treasury? He had some notion, which seemed to have a germ of [truth] within it, that it might be amusing to refer to the family name of Palgrave, which was Meyer Cohen. It was the unpleasant Francis T.'s grandfather who was Meyer Cohen and changed the name. The Deacon was a-going to write to you about it.'

EP assented to the alteration by cable, 19 Aug. 1933: 'PUTT COHENS THESAURUS'; and the emendation was passed on to the printers by Richard de la Mare two days later.

The Golden Treasury of the Best Songs and Lyrical Poems in the English Language (1861, 1897) – edited by Francis Turner Palgrave (1824–97), English poet and critic, and Oxford Professor of Poetry, 1885–95 – was a bestseller for decades into the twentieth century. Francis Turner Palgrave's father, Sir Francis Palgrave, FRS (1788–1861), archivist and historian, born Francis Ephraim Cohen, was the son of Meyer Cohen, a Jewish stockbroker.

EP had already published the story of how he had in an earlier year in London applied to a literary agent to handle his works and received 'a hasty summons' to meet the man in person:

'I found him awed, as if one had killed a cat in the sacristy. Did I know what I had said in my letter? I did. Yes, but about Palgrave? I did. I had said: "It is time we had something to replace that doddard Palgrave." "But don't you know", came the awestruck tones, "that the whole fortune of X & Co. is founded on Palgrave's *Golden Treasury*?"

'From that day onward no book of mine received a British imprimatur until the appearance of Eliot's castrated edition of my poems.' ('How To Read', *New York Herald Tribune Books*, 13 Jan. 1929, 1, 6; *Literary Essays*, ed. with an Introduction by TSE [1954], 18)

1 – Editor of *The Bird-Lover's Book of Verse* (1937).

We have read and considered your poem carefully; and while I am impressed by its excellence and great accomplishment in a difficult stanza, I am afraid that as a publisher I cannot hold out much hope for it under present conditions. In the present state of the market we have to consider and restrict our list very carefully; and as a publisher inevitably produces poetry at a loss, I am compelled to say that we cannot undertake the poem.

With many regrets,
I am,
Yours sincerely,
[T. S. Eliot]
Director.

TO *Elizabeth Manwaring*   TS Wellesley College

16 August 1933   [Faber & Faber Ltd]

Dear Miss Manwaring,

Thank you for letting me know of your plans.[1] I had just written, but not posted, a letter to say that I hoped you would go to see my wife when you got back to London, as I was now of the opinion that a visit from you would do her good, and I am sure that she would have been very glad to see you, as she was indeed attached to you. I am very sorry that you cannot see her, and especially sorry that your visit has had to be cut short, and for such a reason. I very much hope that Miss Stearns will be fully recovered before the autumn term. Please give her my sympathy. I shall ask the Sheffields for further news.

So I must post *Robinson* back to America after all. I had hoped to present it into your hands. But I trust that you will return next summer as usual.

With many regrets,
Yours very sincerely,
T. S. Eliot

1 – Manwaring's letter not found.

TO *Virginia Woolf*

TS Berg

16 August 1933   Faber & Faber Ltd

My dear Virginia,

I have since my return been living quietly in the country, playing Patience, observing the habits of finches and wagtails, composing nonsense verses, and worrying not at all about public affairs. If, as I hope, you are well and are to be at Rodmell for the usual season, it would give me great solace and gratification to spend a night there at any time in September. If this suggestion is an impertinence, please excuse it, and remember that I have had no news of you & Leonard since you went to Italy.

> Your obedient servant,
> T. S. E.

(now Honorary Member of the Michael Mullins Marching & Chowder Club).[1]

TO *Antonio Marichalar*[2]

TS Real Academia de la Historia

17 August 1933   Faber & Faber Ltd

Cher Ami,

Votre lettre du 7 août m'a trouvé en villégiature.[3] Je serais très content d'être présenté au public espagnol sous votre égide. Quant à mes essays, si vous voulez en choisir deux, je proposerais 'Tradition and the Individual Talent', à condition que vous y mettiez une note pour appeler l'attention du lecteur au date (1917). Pour l'autre, je choisirais le 'Dante', si ceci n'est pas trop long. Qu'en pensez-vous? Les dramaturges elisabethéens sont peut-être trop méconnus pour que le lecteur pût former une opinion de mon oeuvre d'après mes propos à ce sujet. Est-ce que le 'Lancelot Andrewes' aussi serait trop eloigné de l'esprit du public que vous enviseagez?

1–VW noted of this letter, on 24 Aug.: 'Tom is all artifice & quips & querks. A defence. One of these days perhaps he'll give up the trick, with marriage, or perhaps religion' (*Diary* 4, 174).
2–Antonio Marichalar, Marquis of Montesa (1893–1973): author, critic, biographer, journalist; contributor to the newspaper *El Sol* and the periodical *Revista de Occidente* (on subjects including Claudel, JJ, Valéry, and VW). Works include *Mentira desnuda*: 'The Naked Lie' (essays on European and American culture, 1933); *Riesgo y ventura del duque de Osuna* (1932): *The Perils and Fortune of the Duke of Osuna*, trans. H. de Onís.
3–Not found.

En espérant vous serrer la main un de ces jours, je vous envoie mes amitiés sincères.

T. S. Eliot[1]

TO *George Bell*   CC

17 August 1933   [Faber & Faber Ltd]

My dear Lord Bishop,

I am writing a line to acknowledge your letter of the 18th May, which was kept here against my return.[2] I have been back now for some weeks, but have been in the country, and only gradually working through my arrears. I am extremely sorry that we could not see any possibility of publishing Dr Box's able treatise; but such a book would, in these times, be a luxury for any publisher to consider.

Please remember me to Mrs Bell. As I am now settling down after my travels, I hope that I may look forward to seeing you again.

I am, My Lord,

Yours very sincerely,

[T. S. Eliot]

---

1 – *Translation:* Dear Friend, Your letter of the 7th August came when I was on holiday. I should be very pleased to be introduced to the Spanish public under your aegis. As regards my essays, if you wish to choose two, I would suggest 'Tradition and the Individual Talent', provided you add a note to call the reader's attention to the date (1917). For the other, I would choose *Dante*, if it is not too long. The Elizabethan dramatists are perhaps too little known for the reader to form an opinion about my work from what I say about them. Would *Lancelot Andrewes* also be too far removed from the mentality of the public you have in mind?

With the hope that I shall be able to shake your hand some day soon, sincere and friendly greetings. T. S. Eliot

2 – 'The Rev. H. S. Box has written a thesis which won him his D.D. at London University on dealing with certain aspects of the Thomist philosophy. I have recommended him to send the MS. to your firm for consideration. Dr Box is a clever man, about 40, very clear-headed.'

to *Hubert S. Box*[1]   CC

17 August 1933   [Faber & Faber Ltd]

Dear Sir,

Your manuscript was held at this office against my return.[2] I was very glad to have the opportunity of examining it, as it struck me as an admirable piece of work, in a field in which the more [that] can be published the better. It was with great regret, therefore, that I came to [the] same conclusion already arrived at tentatively by my colleagues. In the present state of affairs, we, like other publishers, must be very hesitant in publishing books which can have only a small public, unless we are sure that they are quite in our line, and that we are probably the most suitable firm for marketing them. A book like yours is really, I think, one which Longmans', for instance, if not the S.P.C.K. could handle better than we.

Thanking you for letting me see the manuscript, and with renewed regrets, I am,

Yours very truly,
[T. S. Eliot]

to *W. H. Auden*   CC

17 August 1933   [Faber & Faber Ltd]

My dear Auden,

I am sending this to your Birmingham address as probably the quickest way to reach you during the holidays.

A year ago, in November, we brought out the two small books enclosed, Joyce's and mine – you have probably seen them, but here are two extra copies – at half a crown for the Christmas trade – at a flat ten per cent royalty, as I remember – and they did fairly well: I mean they paid for themselves with a small profit for publishers and authors. We propose to produce a few in a similar style and size and at the same price. The question therefore is asked: whether you have anything you would care to

---

1–The Revd Dr Hubert S. Box was to be author of *A Thomist Apologist: God and the Modern Mind* (1937), *Spiritual Exercises: A Handbook for Directors of Souls* (1938) and *The Principles of Canon Law* (1949).

2–Box (Hurstpierpoint College, Sussex) had submitted on 12 May 1933 the manuscript of his PhD thesis, which he hoped might be published by F&F under the title 'God and Philosophy'.

let us bring out in this way, and whether you think that this would be a good step to take.[1]

Your *Poems*, you know, are out of print.[2] Had we anticipated this, we should of course have made a larger printing; but the early sales gave no reason to expect such an uncommon event, and the type was distributed. I don't think that this is a bad thing; it makes you a collectors' item and stimulates interest in future books. As you know, I consider it always the best policy for a poet's output to be sparse and small; in the long run it pays best from every point of view. Whether you want to turn out anything this autumn or not depends therefore not only on what you have in hand in the way of parerga but on what you are working on and how big a thing it is and when you want to have it finished. Assuming that you have the suitable material, I should think however that it might be a good plan to bring out a small book like this and wait at least until next autumn before launching anything else.

I can't remember whether *The Fronny* is too long or not;[3] and of course I don't know what you have been working on during this last year.

I have not been in town, but am recuperating from America in the country and paying visits; so if you should be passing through London at any time it would be as well to give me as long notice as possible so that we could arrange to meet. Let me know what you think of this suggestion, and if you like it what you have in the way of material; I should be glad to have your news in any case.

Yours ever,
[T. S. Eliot]

---

1 – Tacon Gilbert advised TSE, 16 Aug.: 'At Book Committee today it was suggested that a "Christmas Extra" by W. H. Auden might be a good thing, and the committee felt that you would be the best person to write to Mr Auden if you would do so. I am enclosing a stamped addressed envelope, and copies of *Sweeney Agonistes* and *Shem and Shaun*, as the committee felt that you might like to send these to Mr Auden, to give him an idea of the length etc. required.'

2 – FVM would write to Geoffrey Grigson, 19 Oct. 1934: 'Our notion of ceilings for our kind of poets is best indicated by our first printings which for Auden and Spender were 2,000. This was for their first books, and they have both justified the faith and have been reprinted.'

3 – See W. H. Auden and Christopher Isherwood, *Plays, and Other Dramatic Writings by W. H. Auden 1928–1938*, ed. Edward Mendelson (1989).

TO *F. O. Matthiessen*[1]   TS Donald Gallup

20 August 1933   Faber & Faber Ltd

Dear Matty,

Many thanks for your letter of August 8th. There has been considerable, and sometimes heated, discussion about your manuscript. In the first place, I haven't been allowed to see it, but both of the directors who have read it, speak of it with the highest praise. In the second place, I raised very strong objections to our publishing a book about myself, however good. This is not pure modesty, but the belief that it would be better all round, and much better publicity for me, if some other firm undertook it. Your first version is now, I understand, in the hands of the Oxford University Press, and I have heard from a friend of mine whom they asked to report on it, that he has recommended them to publish it. If they do not want it, I dare say we shall in spite of my personal protests. I look forward to seeing the revised version.[2]

1–F. O. Matthiessen (1902–50), author and academic, graduated Phi Beta Kappa from Yale University in 1923 and was thereafter a Rhodes Scholar at New College, Oxford, before gaining his PhD at Harvard in 1927. After two years at Yale, he taught for twenty-one years in the English Department at Harvard, where he specialised in American literature and Shakespeare, becoming Professor of History and Literature in 1942. The first Senior Tutor at Eliot House (where he became a good friend to TSE in 1932–3), he was a Resident Tutor there from 1933 to 1939. His publications include *The Achievement of T. S. Eliot* (1935) and *American Renaissance* (1941).

The Master of Eliot House, Harvard, was to write to TSE on 24 Apr. 1950, following Matthiessen's death by suicide on 1 Apr.: 'He had increasingly cut most of his immediate ties with active life . . . [H]is increasing isolation seemed to spring from some necessity in him and was self-imposed. Sometimes I think that what was wrong was, so to speak, the narrowness of the American ideal of Tom Sawyer – in the sense that certain promptings in Matty . . . inclined him to a gregarious and energetic ideal of conventional success, while he discovered in himself other and opposite promptings which did not jibe with the former . . . The terrifying and most moving thing was that Matty's very virtues of effort, sincerity, and will-to-do were in some way related to this sense of strain.'

TSE replied to the Master, 5 Apr. 1950: 'I always thought him a person of a kind of repressed excessive intensity. I think that Matty was, in his way, a very religious man. Perhaps that was part of the trouble – I mean that he had a capacity for religious fanaticism, without the discipline and control of a dogma or a church.'

See further *F. O. Matthiessen (1902–1950): A Collective Portrait*, ed. Paul M. Sweezy and Leo Huberman (1950); George Abbott White, 'Ideology and Literature: *American Renaissance* and F. O. Matthiessen', in *Literature and Revolution*, ed. George Abbott White and Charles Newman (1972), 430–500; *F. O. Matthiessen: The Critical Achievement*, ed. Giles B. Gunn (1975); Kenneth S. Lynn, 'Teaching: F. O. Matthiessen', *The American Scholar* 46: 1 (Winter 1976–7), 86–93; Harry Levin, 'The Private Life of F. O. Matthiessen' (review article), *New York Review of Books*, 20 July 1978, 42ff.

2–Matthiessen's first chat with TSE took place on 24 Oct. 1932, and he recorded on 3 Nov.: 'Ted [Spencer] and I had our first real talk with Eliot last night, and got him going on

I am glad to hear that you liked Charlottesville. I was enchanted with the place. I intend to propose myself for a visit to Kittery next summer.[1]

With best wishes for the Mathias cat and yourself.

Yours ever sincerely,
T. S. Eliot

TO *Ottoline Morrell*   TS Texas

21 August [?1933]   Faber & Faber Ltd

My dear Ottoline,

Thank you for your further note. I only want to add that I cannot for the life of me remember giving Robert[2] a message for you: perhaps he said 'may I tell Lady O. that you will be writing to her' or something like that. I should be very unlikely to convey any important message in that way – Robert is very sweet and good and has been kind to both V. and me at every opportunity; but he is something of a chatterbox – likes to know everybody, and it pleases him to give people news about each other etc.

Affectionately,
Tom

TO *Henry Eliot*   TS Houghton

21 August 1933   Faber & Faber Ltd

My dear Brother,

I was very glad to get your letter of August 5th. The Bears went to Tom (acknowledgement enclosed) and the stamps on the letter to Donald

---

his poetry. A very interesting experience.' Loucks (*The Exile's Return*, 18–19) notes: 'On November 14 Matthiessen invited TSE to tea, heard the poet praise Joyce, and concluded that he was both warm and kindly (Hyde, 223).' *The Achievement of T. S. Eliot* was to be published two years later by OUP. TSE would write to Charles Williams, 22 July 1944: 'Matthiessen's book was, I think, a very good book of its date (1933 [*sic*]): and he had the inestimable advantage, while working on it, of having me in daily view, at breakfast, lunch and dinner, and sometimes for bootleg evenings, in Cambridge Mass. It is the work of a Professor of English Literature, and I was rather overawed by it; for he showed such an appalling consistency of philosophy and purpose, and such consistency between essays written at different times and under the spur of the need of money, that I felt I had been merely the trance medium for some intellectual giant of the spirit world. The notes are the most amusing part of the book.'

1 – Matthiessen's summer retreat at Kittery, Maine.
2 – Robert Sencourt.

Morley (age 7½) who is beginning to collect. I am glad that you had such a successful holiday; and I hope that the subsequent heat in New York has not destroyed the good effects. There was a spell of intense heat here, during which I was very glad to be out of London and not living too active a life; at present the usual English summer weather, with alternations of cloud and sun. I have been up to London two or three times for the day – also visited Paul More in Oxford, and spent a weekend at Winchester – am going to Rochester for tonight; next week go for ten days to the Fabers' in Wales; from there I think to the Society of the Sacred Mission at Kelham for a week;[1] then back here for a few weeks which will take me into October; and after that have no plans.

This Surrey country is very lovely. We drove out yesterday afternoon for a picnic tea – through Penshurst with Sidney's (or was it the Pembrokes') fine castle[2] – a very lovely village named Chiddingstone, and some of the most delightful country in Kent. Henry VIII's Hever Castle is nearabouts, now inhabited, alas, by one of the Astors.[3] Beyond the current work for the *Criterion* I have worked chiefly on getting my Norton lectures ready for press, an uninspiring task – they were good enough as lectures, but will look pretty poor in print – for this autumn; after that I must set to work on re-writing my Virginia lectures for the spring. A certain amount of correspondence, without a secretary, takes up the rest of the time. I sit out of doors when it is fine; and I think my health is improving: the first fortnight or so in England was a great strain.

The lawyers are all away on holiday, so nothing much happens until the end of the month; but it would appear that V. is now somewhat more

1–According to George Every, SSM, who entered the Society in 1930, 'liturgical activity was understood as the expression of our will to live and work together in obedience to Christ and in accordance with traditions derived from monasticism. Each student participated in manual labor in one of these departments: the house department (i.e. sweeping, polishing, dusting); the chapel department (i.e., cleansing, polishing); and the grub department (i.e., preparing food, washing dishes, setting tables). Much of this work was done in silence' (interview, 27 May 1989, cited in Kenneth Paul Kramer, *Redeeming Time: T. S. Eliot's 'Four Quartets'* [2007]), 11. TSE's enthusiasm for visiting Kelham so often over the next few years may be understood in part from these words from his address 'Two Masters', delivered to the Boston Association of Unitarian Clergy in the spring of 1933: 'It is imperative that the next generation shall see to the restoration of the monastic life in society, especially that of the more contemplative orders. Their value is not only for the work that they do, or for those who have the vocation to join them; it is also for the standard and ideal of life that they set for the layman, as well while he is doing his work in the world as when he uses them for retreat and meditation.'
2–Penshurst Place, nr. Tonbridge, Kent, was the birthplace of Sir Philip Sidney (1554–86).
3–The thirteenth-century Hever Castle, Edenbridge, Kent, was purchased in 1903 and restored by the American millionaire William Waldorf Astor.

reconciled; and a statement of her private income is being prepared so that the lawyers may discuss terms of allowance. When I can avoid it, I don't think about these matters. I have to work out a new way of life: even when the change is a blessed relief, it is difficult to start life afresh – with a very limited amount of freshness even – at forty five.

I think that V. has dropped all those fictions, for the present; of course it is possible that she may invent new ones. I cannot think at all what is to become of her; and I have to force myself to consider that that is not my business any more, beyond providing the necessary and possible funds.

I am very glad to hear about Chardy's baby.[1] I hope she will have several more. There will be money enough in time, from the various sources, if there is any money at all by that time. I should [like] to know what you think of the future of the present policy in America.

With much love to both,
Affectionately your brother,
Tom

FROM *Vivien Eliot* TO *Ernest Bird*[2]   TS Copy

Tuesday, 22 August 1933   68 Clarence Gate Gardens

Dear Sir,

I am writing to tell you – and I should have done so long ago but that it never occurred to me that such a question might be raised – that my only wish is that my husband returns to me under any conditions, and in whatever state of health, and on any condition or conditions *he wishes to make.*

And that he has been and always will be my only interest and reason for existence; and that I should always do the best I could for him.

His staying away from his home is not of my choosing, and I am in absolute disagreement with it, and it is doing me every possible kind of *harm and damage.*

Will you please be so kind as to see that my husband reads this letter, as I wish him to see it. I am sending a copy of it to Messrs James & James.

1–Charlotte Stearns Smith (b. 1911) was to have a child, Priscilla Stearns Talcott, on 19 Feb. 1934; and so presumably 'baby' refers to the announcement of her pregnancy.
2–Of Bird & Bird, TSE's solicitors.

I sent Messrs James & James a letter on August 3rd, and suggested that a copy of it should be sent or delivered to you. I have a copy of it here of course as well, and it can be seen here.[1]

I am,
Yours faithfully,
V. H. Eliot.

TO *Donald Brace*   CC

27 August 1933   [Faber & Faber Ltd]

Dear Mr Brace,

University of Virginia Lectures.

I have not written to you about these before, because I was very uncertain as to what promises I could make. Until now, I have had to give all my spare time to rewriting my Harvard lectures: these have to appear this autumn, as it is essential that the two sets of lectures should not appear in the same season. In about ten days time – as I have now finished my work on the others – I expect to settle down seriously to rewrite these. They were originally prepared under considerable pressure, and I shall want to do a good deal of documentation to make them reasonably water-tight. I am sorry; but I am especially interested in these lectures, and am anxious to make a good job; so I cannot promise them to you before the

---

1–VHE's letter to A. E. James of James & James (3 Aug.) reads, in part: 'With regard to the settlement of financial affairs, the kindest thing you can do for me, being as you are my Father's old friend, is to inform my husband immediately, through whatever channel is the quickest, that what I ask is for him to assume complete control over my income and personal property, and to arrange for us to have a joint Banking account. Of course, taking it for granted that he would in any case give me all the usual and customary protection of a husband.

'That is what I want, and it is the only thing I have got to suggest.

'Living alone costs me double in every way.

'I have to pay for paid attendants, where my husband has always acted as my Nurse, as well as my friend and companion not to speak of chauffeur.

'I have to take twice the amount of medicines, therefore my chemist's bills are doubled – not only because of the increase in the amount but because of the enormous charges they make to make up the prescribed doses which my husband did for me himself.

'If my husband is kept away from me it is everybody's loss.

'I will stand on this point, as if you can do me that great kindness, and arrange with my husband to assume the control of all my affairs, no further figuring and argument is necessary.

'This is the only thing I have to suggest.

'Perhaps a copy of this letter had better be sent to Mr Ernest Bird.'

latter part of November. If I can get them to you in October so much the better.

'Poems 1909–25': Anthology Permissions

I think that the most convenient arrangement for both sides would be for me to give a general authority to you – not to your firm generally, but to you personally – to use your discretion.[1] My stipulations are that only a reasonable small amount of my verse should be used in any one anthology; second, that permission should never be granted without a reasonable fee; third, that *The Waste Land* should not be used in this way either whole or in part. For other poems, not in this volume, anthologists should of course apply direct to me.

Yours always sincerely,
[T. S. Eliot]

TO *F. Stringfellow Barr*   CC

27 August 1933   [Faber & Faber Ltd]

Dear Mr Barr,

I must apologise for letting you down over the lecture.[2] What happened was, that on re-reading the set I found that they need very much more re-writing than they should, and that I was unwilling to let even one appear in periodical form until I had been able to revise it; and until now I have had to concentrate on preparing my Harvard lectures for press for this autumn. I hope to get to work on the Page-Barbour lectures in about ten days; I will send you a revise of number III as soon as ready and hope that there will be time, if it fits your editorial plans, to have it appear in the *Quarterly*.

Meanwhile, as a peace-offering, I enclose two small songs – if you don't want them for the *Quarterly* return them. I am not likely to use them elsewhere; some day I may add a few more, or else tear them up. I may add that they have no political significance whatever: but if you don't care to use them, I shan't mind in the least.[3]

---

1 – Brace wrote on 10 Aug. that Ludwig Lewisohn was compiling an anthology to be called *Creative America* (Harper and Brothers), and wished to print three poems by TSE. 'I don't know what you would like to have us do about requests of this sort. Do you want us to refer all such requests to you?'

2 – Stringfellow Barr, editor of *The Virginia Quarterly Review*, had asked TSE on 5 June to send him a carbon copy set of his Page-Barbour Lectures: he hoped that the third lecture might be slightly refashioned as an article for his review.

3 – 'Words for Music: New Hampshire; Virginia', *Virginia Quarterly Review* 10: 2 (Apr.

With best wishes and pleasant memories,

Yours ever sincerely,

[T. S. Eliot]

My colleague, Frank Morley, would like to be remembered to you.

TO *George Bell*   CC

27 August 1933   [Faber & Faber Ltd]

My dear Lord Bishop,

Thank you for your note. I should not have bothered you with this further communication, but that your mention of the *Life of Davidson* stimulates a publisher's responses.[1] I have very little doubt that publication has already been arranged – but if it had not, I feel sure that we should be much interested. Of course I am writing quite personally, and should not mention it to any of my firm unless there were some prospect of the book being available. And if, as I suppose, the book is already bespoken, then do not bother to answer this enquiry.

Yours very sincerely,

[T. S. Eliot]

I have had a very interesting suggestion from Martin Browne, which I have been considering.[2]

1934), 200. Barr replied (19 Sept.): 'Morally, you are entirely justified: your peace-offering sees to that. I like "Words for Music" and am intending to publish it . . . Are you sure it has no "political significance"? Do let it have a little. There is some much better history in it than in the work of historians; and, you know, I am supposed to be a historian and am supposed therefore to know.'

1–Bell had written (24 Aug.): 'At the moment I am working hard on my "Life" . . . a hard thing.' See G. K. A. Bell, *Randall Davidson, Archbishop of Canterbury*, 2 vols (Oxford University Press, 1935).

2–Presumably the suggestion was that TSE might become involved in writing the words of the proposed pageant *The Rock*, to be staged on behalf of the churches of the City of London.

27 August 1933   [Faber & Faber Ltd]

Dear Auden,

I was glad to get your letter (undated).[1] From what you say of your play-ballet I see no reason why it should not be suitable; if it is to be produced early in the new year, so much the better. Can you send a copy quite soon? Better address it to F. V. Morley personally, as I may not be available for a fortnight.

Another matter has been brought up. General opinion is now in favour of re-publishing your *Poems*; and the notion is to produce them at 5/- in boards in similar format to Spender's *Poems*. My advice would be strongly, not to include any new matter, but to put this out simply as a second edition. Of course there will not be anything like the sale, immediately, that there would be for a new work; but we think that on the whole it would be wise to keep this in print. Will you drop a line to Morley and tell him what you think about it?

I enclose a letter from Mrs Hallie Flanagan, who produced *Sweeney Agonistes* very well indeed at Vassar (I can show you some photographs. The male parts are taken by men). She is an enterprising person, and seems to have considerable liberty; I regard her as a very intelligent producer. Perhaps you would write to her, if you have any ideas on the subject.[2]

Yours ever,

[T. S. Eliot]

1 – WHA wrote: 'As to myself, I have a sort of play-cum-ballet which I understand that some people called the Group Theatre are going to produce at the Westminster Theatre in March. It is about the right length, I think, but I dont know how it will read without the music or the dancing, nor whether it would be better to wait until it has been performed. I haven't a copy at the moment, but I will get one back and send it to you as soon as possible, and perhaps you would be kind enough to give me your advice.'

He added: 'Couldnt you drop a kind word of advice to whoever at Faber's does the Puffs; they are getting worse and worse.'

The Dance of Death was to be published on 9 Nov. 1933, with this blurb, almost certainly by TSE: '"We present to you this evening a picture of the decline of a class, of how its members dream of a new life, but secretly desire the old, for there is death inside them. We show you that death as a dancer."

'These are the introductory words spoken by the Announcer in *The Dance of Death*. This new poem by the author of *The Orators* and *Poems* is in dramatic form, parts being taken by performers both on the stage and in the auditorium. Satirical in character, it will extend the reputation of its author, who is already recognized as one of the four or five living poets worth quarrelling about.'

2 – 'I will write to Mrs Flanagan,' replied WHA (30 Aug.)

TO *Frank Morley*   TS Faber

?31 August 1933[1]   Ty Glyn Aeron, Ciliau Aeron,
                                      Cardiganshire

I forgot to say that I am not keen on the Jaeger for us.[2] My idea was
philanthropic in resuming discussion with Woods – I thought if Harvard
wd. share cost possibly Oxf. or somebody might take it up here. Have
spoken to G. F. who thinks as I do that we cd. only consider it if it meant
no outlay on our part, which wd. be unlikely. I hope however that you
found out how long Woods is likely to be loose round the place, as I
should like to see him. Nothing has been done with Jaeger direct.

                             T. S. E.

Re enclosed from Auden.[3] G.F. says Auden gave the same reply some time
ago. I see no objection myself to Auden changing a few poems, so long as
he leaves the charade in. Whats your opinion £¾%?? [*sic*][4]

1 – According to a note on the letter, this was written at some time between 15 June and 29
Aug.

2 – Werner Jaeger's *Aristotèles: Grundlegung einer Geschichte seiner Entwicklung* (1923) had
been recommended to F&F; see *Aristotle: Fundamentals of the History of His Development*,
trans. Richard Robinson (1934). Jaeger (1888–1961) was Professor of Classics, Berlin
University, 1921–36; Professor of Classics, Chicago, 1936–9; Harvard, 1939–61.

FVM wrote on 30 Aug.: 'A pleasant old bustard named Woods came to take up the midst
of the morning. I told him whatever I could, but I wasn't sufficiently Jaeger. He wants me
to write him at wonst to apprise his professional mind whether 1. we should still like to do
Jaeger's Aristotle if we can get a substance. 2. whether a boyd called Robinson is the right
man to translate. 3. whether anything or nothing has been done with Jaeger direct.

'Woody was anguished because you hadn't reported in full whether you have achieved a
support for Jaeger from the bored [*sic*] at Harvard.'

James Houghton Woods (1864–1935) was Professor of Philosophy at Harvard, 1913–
34; Chair of the Department of Philosophy and Psychology, 1914–16. TSE studied Greek
Philosophy with him in 1911–12, and 'Philosophical Sanskrit' in 1912–13.

3 – WHA replied on 30 Aug. to TSE's of the 27th: 'As to a republication of my *Poems*, I am
quite willing as long as I am allowed to remove about seven of them. If you think that this
would make the book too short I could put in a certain number of poems written between
it and the composition of the *Orators*. I don't mind as long as I can suppress the ones I
particularly dislike.' (FVM had written to WHA, 27 Jan. 1933: 'We should like to consult
you about your *Poems*. The stock of the 2/6 edition is running low, and it does not seem
practicable to do a reprint at that price. We have been wondering whether it would not
be better to print a new edition in the same format as THE ORATORS at 5/- or 6/-. Here
though, it would be easier to justify the increased price if the volume were definitely a new
edition with some new poems included.')

4 – FVM answered TSE on 4 Sept.: 'OK about Auden. We see no objection to his changing a
few poems. Am writing him to that effect.'

FVM wrote to WHA on the same day: 'First of all many thanks for the DANCE OF
DEATH which I find on my desk this morning. I think this will be just right for separate
publication in November. As soon as I have read it, and talked with de la Mare about
production, we will write again.'

TO *Virginia Woolf*   TS Berg

31 August 1933   Ty Glyn Aeron, Ciliau Aeron

My dear Virginia,

Just in case, I expect to be free on either the 8th (Friday) or the 9th or
the 10th or the 11th, whichever night suits you best if any. After that I go
North for a week or so, and could come probably any night after the wO I
mean 29 no I mean the 20th thats what I mean excuse unfamiliar machine.
(*Happy Thought*: Not to ask the Lord Lieutenant of the Country to Tea
when I come). And Please do not divulge to a soul either my present
address or the date (if any) on which you invite me.[1]

                                    Yours obediently,
                                    T. S. E.

'About your *Poems*, we can see no objection to your changing a few of them in the new
edition, so long as you leave the charade in. Could you prepare a copy for us at your earliest
convenience? I cannot send you a copy to work on because we are sold right out; but if you
have not one of the first edition to spare, perhaps you could indicate which poems are to be
deleted, and send the substitutes, and indicate the order clearly.'

FVM to WHA, 7 Sept. 1933: 'Very many thanks for the POEMS. The alterations were
quite clear. I am giving them, and THE DANCE OF DEATH, to de la Mare to make
estimates of production costs. Did Eliot say anything about terms? If not, I will be writing
again after our Committee Meeting to-morrow.'

1 – VW noted on 2 Sept., 'Tom wrote yesterday, telling me, in his jaunty uneasy manner, to
conceal his address, & the date of his visit. The mystery I imagine flatters him' (*Diary* 4,
177).

TSE visited Monk's House on 9 Sept., and VW took stock the next day: 'why am I sitting
here at 10.30 on a Sunday morning, rather stiff in the back, rather sore of the lips, writing
diary, not novel? Because of dear old Tom largely. 24 hours (short interval for sleep) solid
conversation . . . He is 10 years younger: hard, spry, a glorified boy scout in shorts & yellow
shirt. He is enjoying himself very much. He is tight & shiny as a wood louse (I am not
writing for publication). But there is well water in him, cold & pure. Yes I like talking to
Tom. But his wing sweeps curved & scimitar like round to the centre himself. He's settling in
with some severity to being a great man. Keats wasn't that. We talked about Keats's letters.
Tom said that letter writing was a form he preferred to *Times* leader writing. I think this
hints some change in his views. He said that he no longer <thought> felt quite so sure of a
science of criticism. He also said that people exaggerate the intellectuality & erudition of his
poetry. "For example Ross Williamson in his book on me [*The Poetry of T. S. Eliot* (1932)]
. . ." He says that very seriously. I couldnt quote Holtby [Winifred Holtby, *Virginia Woolf:
A Memoir* (1932)] with the same candour. Ross apparently attributed the dog, in Tom's
quotation from Webster, to profound associations with the dog star. Not a bit of it says Tom:
I was having a joke about Webster. I connect all this with his bubbling up of life. At 46 he
wants to live, to love; even seeing Rochester is an event to him. He has seen nothing, nobody,
for the last 10 years. We had it out about V. at breakfast. Some asperity on Tom's part. He
wont admit the excuse of insanity for her – thinks she puts it on; tries to take herself in;
for this reason, mystified Eth Bowen. I thought him a little resentful of all the past waste &
exaction. I gather he will see a good deal of us: & if I had time, & if I could move the heavy
stone of his self esteem an inch or two higher, I should like to talk out to Tom about writing.

2 September 1933[2]   [as from Faber & Faber Ltd]

Dear Janes,

I have been meaning to write to you for some time. But I have been staying at various places in the country and it is difficult in these circumstances to get everything done that one wants to do. I expect to go to stay in the Midlands early during this month. I am very well indeed, and have enjoyed the hot weather. I hope that you have not found the heat troublesome; I know you always preferred cold weather. I am sure that Polly is very well under your care. I hope that Mrs Eliot has some good woman to do for her now; and I am sure that you will look after her as well as anyone can. Please give my best regards to Mrs Janes; I hope that she is keeping up and not troubled by her cough.

Yours always sincerely,

T. S. Eliot

Only there's always the reservation – I cant talk about "my writing"; so that talk about his writing palls[?]. But I am to find him 2 rooms in Somers Town. And we agreed about the infamy of teaching English; the idiocy of lectures; the whole hierarchy of professor, system & so on: at any rate I got him to go some way with me in denouncing Oxford & Cambridge. He learnt (1) self confidence at Oxford; (2) how to write plain English – thats all. I daresay though he will become Prof. of Poetry at Oxford one of these days.

    'His father was a brick merchant in St Louis; & they lived in the slums among vacant lots. & his father always gave away money; & died, alas, in 1919 before Tom had become – well happily his mother lived to see him what she called (& I daresay Tom too) a great man. What a queer naïve vanity all this is! But of course, when you are thrown like an assegai into the hide of the world – this may be a definition of genius – there you stick; & Tom sticks' (*Diary* 4, 177–9).

    Gordon, *Eliot's New Life*, 70: 'Virginia Woolf found her [VHE] in September 1933 sitting "under a crowned effigy", Eliot's photograph by Elliot Fry with a wreath of daisies' – citing VW, *Letters* 5, 222.

1–William Leonard Janes (1854–1939) was an ex-policeman who had worked as general factotum for TSE since 1924. 'If I ever write my reminiscences, which I shan't,' TSE reminisced to Mary Trevelyan, 2 Apr. 1951, 'Janes would have a great part in them' ('The Pope of Russell Square'). TSE told Adam Roberts, 12 Dec. 1955: 'I . . . knew a retired police officer, who at one period had to snoop in plain clothes in the General Post Office in Newgate Street – he caught several culprits, he said' (Adam Roberts).

2–Envelope dated 28 Sept. 1934 – but presumably not the envelope that carried this letter.

TO *Frank Morley*

TS Faber

6 September 1933   Ty Glyn Aeron, Ciliau Aeron

Dear Frank,

Enclosed proof.[1] Which I said at the time was not to be sent to Fitzgerald, and could not have been because his address is unknown. It was to have been sent to me.

It is Stewart's business to get the endorsed certificates from Blake and the cheque from me.[2] G.F. believes the transfer has to be passed by the board first.

G says we will be in ample time to catch the 6.10 and wishes you to remind Lister that he is staying at Russell Square and wants the bedroom ready.

I must come up with you on Friday to lunch with Bonamy and go down to Rodmell for that night.

> Yrs etc.
> Tom

TO *Alida Monro*

MS Texas

12 September 1933   Society of the Sacred Mission,
                                     Kelham Theological College,
                                     House of the Sacred Mission,
                                     Kelham, Newark, Notts.

Dear Alida,

I would have written before, but I thought that you (and others) would find it less embarrassing if in ignorance of my movements. I shall be

1–FVM had written, 4 Sept.: '[Robert] Fitzgerald is a case in point as to the anguish of sending proofs to authors . . . Postman may have pinched his proof out of the unsealed letter, so I am sending you another. If we don't get Fitzgerald's proofs back, we will probably have to go to press with your corrections to his poems, if any.'

2–FVM (4 Sept.): 'I meant to ask before whether you had actually sent George Blake his yellow boys? I haven't heard from you or him about the matter, and have been wondering how it stands.' FVM wrote to GCF, 8 Aug. 1933: 'I had the advantage of discussing the matter with Eliot last night, and naturally it was discussed with the others this morning . . . You will have heard from Eliot that he is willing to take up 200 of George Blake's shares, provided that we can offer him £100. 0. 0. advance, should he need it, on his next book; and that he would be able to cough up the £200. 0. 0. immediately. Dick said that he had not answered your letter, as yet, because he did not feel himself in a position to cough; but Eliot's offer is at once magnanimous and reliable, and I should like to ease George's anguish with it so soon as I have word from you. I expect such word is on the way; if it isn't here tomorrow I may, greatly daring with linguistic difficulties, ring you up.'

out of town certainly through October, by which time I hope matters will be more settled. I gather that by now most of my friends have some knowledge of the situation, after inevitable alarums. I have *never received* a copy of Harold's poems. I am going to buy several anyway, but would like to have one direct. I expect it is an oversight of Cobden's. How are you? 24 Russell Square will always reach me.

Yours always,

Tom

TO *Mary Hutchinson* TS Texas

20 September 1933   Faber & Faber Ltd

My dear Mary,

Until now I have wished not to bother my friends with my affairs; but since an interview with Ernest Bird yesterday afternoon which left me very much puzzled about my next step, I think that I should like you to know the present position. And I should be very grateful if you or Jack cared to express any opinions about it.

It would seem that Vivienne adopts the attitude that I have simply and unaccountably chosen to absent myself, leaving her in suspense and very much in the dark.[1] On the contrary, it is she who is holding matters up. It has been made clear to her that I insist upon a permanent separation; though naturally I have so far thought it fruitless and unnecessary to give her any reasons for my decision, beyond that I am convinced that it will be in the long run the best thing for both of us. The following extract from a letter written by her solicitors to mine will go towards explaining the situation:

'To induce her to regard the separation as final is quite impossible . . . She asks that her husband shall return to her and manage her affairs and is ready to accept any conditions he may impose. She writes that she is staying at the flat until she has had another and more satisfactory interview with her husband and that this interview should be at the flat . . . If only

---

1 – TSE's sister Ada Sheffield would write to him, 14 Jan. 1934: 'Marion, Margaret, and Miss Manwaring have each of them had a note or letter from V. written as if she had only just taken it in that you are in earnest. To Marion she says that it is the influence of your family over here, and to Margaret implies it. This was to be expected, and no one here minds it at all.'

Mrs Eliot could be given some hope, however faint, of occasional visits by her husband and of eventual re-union it would help enormously.'[1]

Of course I cannot approve the last sentence. But her policy of refusing to admit the situation may make matters very difficult for me. I do not know what step can be taken to induce her to give up hope that obstruction and cajolery may make me surrender my position. I cannot help feeling that a certain passivity on the part of her family and advisers has done something to prolong the delay. I hardly need to add that I cannot think of returning to a situation to which I have already given the best years of my life.

If you should see her, I do not know whether you could say anything towards convincing her that this attitude is useless and that she has finally met with a decision that cannot be altered; but at least I now want you, and presently a certain number of other people, to know what the position is. I have not yet written to anyone else.[2]

Affectionately yours,

Tom

Russell Sq. is my best address. Letters marked '*Personal*'.[3]

1–James's letter to Bird & Bird reads more fully: 'I have done my best to persuade Mrs Eliot to accept the position if only for a time but without success. To induce her to regard the separation as final is quite impossible. The letter she wrote to you on the 22nd August and the letter of which I sent you an extract on the 8th ult. show the attitude she has taken up and from this nothing that her relations or I can urge will move her. She asks that her husband should return to her and manage her affairs and is ready to accept any conditions he may impose. She writes that she is staying at the flat until she has had another and more satisfactory interview with her husband and that this interview would be at the flat. Will you kindly convey this message to Mr Eliot and urge him to consent to a meeting at an early date? I feel, as does her mother, that the only person who can influence her at all is her husband and I venture to suggest that to mitigate in some measure the sudden blow of his refusal to return he should write to her a letter in kindly terms assuring her that although for some time at any rate it is impossible for him to return he is most anxious for her well-being and it would be a great comfort to him if she would go for a time to the Hindhead Home [in Hampshire] where he knows she would be well nursed and cared for. Meanwhile an effort could be made to find a more cheerful flat to which she could go on leaving Hindhead and the financial question could be discussed between us. If only Mrs Eliot could be given some hope, however faint, of occasional visits by her husband and of ultimate re-union it would help enormously. Is not this possible? It seems to me that without some such hope nothing short of force will make her leave the flat or discuss the terms of a separation.'

2–Ernest Bird, to whom TSE sent a copy of this letter to Mary Hutchinson (Bird approved it), wrote to TSE, 22 Sept.: 'I confess to a certain feeling of despair as to what can be done and as to the next step in connection with your Wife . . . It is not a question of law but of persuading your Wife to accept the inevitable. No one is more difficult than an individual – especially a lady of your Wife's temperament – who simply sits still and does nothing. I think that the only possible course is that which we discussed on Tuesday of endeavouring to bring external pressure to bear. You have already embarked upon it and one can only hope for success.'

3–Added by hand.

21 September 1933   [Faber & Faber Ltd]

My dear Henry,

I enclose herewith a deed of Trust for my remaining free property in America, which I had drawn up by Charles Curtis of Choate, Hall & Stewart in Boston, and which is approved by my London solicitor, Ernest Bird of Bird & Bird. Curtis suggests that I send it to you for your seal and signature, and that you then forward it to the Old Colony (that is A. H. Macintyre, the Trust Officer, whom I consulted in the first place).

You will see that the purpose of the Trust is to secure the property after my death, whilst leaving me free to realise any of it in case of need during my lifetime. In effect, this property and any that I may add to it, is eventually secured to Theodora and Chardy. I am sure that you will approve of this step. If Hydraulic ever appreciates to the point of being saleable, I should like you to sell my remaining shares and add the proceeds for investment to this Trust.

I am still living in the country. The first part of this month I spent in visits to Wales and Nottinghamshire, and I have returned indefinitely to my former lodgings. My affairs at the moment are in a state of deadlock. After a period of apparent capitulation, Vivienne again begs that I return to her 'on any conditions that I may impose' – which is of course a meaningless phrase. The next step is to try to find people who can convince her that I mean what I say and do not propose to go back on my intentions. As her lawyer himself remarked in conversation, I have had my fair share; and I'll never get those seventeen years back.

On the whole, however, this summer, with visits and a quiet country life, has been the pleasantest I have ever had. My hair does not improve. I enclose a few photographs; most I have sent to Ada; but I will have prints made of some of the ones I have taken about England to send to you. I should like to hear from you as often as possible. I look back on my past year with satisfaction: it was lovely to be surrounded by so much affection.

> With much love to both of you,
> [Tom]

TO *Allen Tate*   TS Princeton

21 September 1933   Faber & Faber Ltd

Dear Tate,

I am certainly pleased to hear from you and to learn about your sympossum, and I callate you are about right this time not to make it so local and I think it would be pretty cute to have one or two simon-pure Yankees in the show.[1] I aint quite certain from what you say yet what its all about, and whether I have anything to say or know anything about anything that would fit in. Furthermore I am not right certain yet whether I shall have the time to do anything decent in the time. But I would certainly like to hear some more about this matter.

I will try to get a look at Agar's book.[2] I have heard of him and seen reviews etc. by him; but I don't rightly know where he was born and raised. Has Mrs Tate been informed about the publication of 'Old Red' in the forthcoming *Criterion?* I have not been in London and don't know whether anything has been overlooked. There wasn't time after I got back and read it, to send her proof, for which I apologise; I read it pretty carefully myself. It seems to me a right good tale.[3]

---

1 – Tate wrote on 9 Sept. that he and his colleagues were aiming to put together another symposium on the subject of reactionary regionalism – along lines not unlike those of *I'll Take My Stand* – and hoped TSE might be willing to contribute to it. 'Our purpose this time will be more general with respect to geography, and more specific in objective. I suppose the essays might be called Essays in Definition of a Conservative Revolution in the United States.'

2 – Tate (9 Sept.) recommended a 'remarkable popular book' – 'short history of the United States' – *The Peoples' Choice*, by Herbert Agar. 'It fits beautifully into a genuinely reactionary scheme. 'One thing that he does is to argue your case for J. Q. Adams, who was the last hope for this country: a thesis that I have come to accept in the last few years more and more.'

3 – Delmore Schwartz, in 'The Criterion, 1922–1939', *Purpose*, Oct.–Dec. 1939, felt able to praise only two of the stories that had appeared in C. throughout its entire run: 'a story by Miss May Sinclair which may have suggested a passage in "Sweeney Agonistes" to Mr Eliot, and a very fine story by Miss Caroline Gordon' (236). TSE agreed with Schwartz in a letter of 26 Oct. 1939: 'As for the fiction, I was always at a loss where to turn for good stories; what were offered were usually appalling; and I didn't like to beg from people who could command a higher price elsewhere. You must have gone through the files with a fine tooth comb, for you picked out what I remember, myself, as two of the best stories I had' (Beinecke).

On 27 Oct. 1933 TSE wrote for the F&F Book Committee this report on *Penhally*, by Caroline Gordon: 'Mrs Tate seems to me a very interesting writer, not at all profound, but very exact; knows how to observe sensitively and get it down in words. I think she will even deserve a permanent place as an historian of the semi-barbarous society of Virginia and Kentucky. The trouble that I find with this book is a lack of organisation and construction. It is a succession of shots of the history of a rural, slave-owning, very much intermarried (they are all related to each other and to their negroes) society during the last hundred years;

Yours ever,

T. S. Eliot

I shd. be grateful for any news you cd. give me of Fletcher; & wd. like to send him my best.

TO *Ezra Pound*

ᴛꜱ Beinecke

21 September 1933   Faber & Faber Ltd

Dear Rabbett Well Ive got to do something about somethink sooner or later and well to-day its Raining. so Here goes Well I think that anthology is Tripe[1] Well the only think in it worth printing is the preface Goodness

---

but there are so many people about, and the generations follow each other so confusingly, that I constantly lost the thread. There is no plot to speak of; the book is decidedly a study of a society rather than of individuals; and it seems to me that you have to know the people. I cannot see any prospect for such a book here; but Mrs Tate is worth watching.

'But as I do not trust my own opinion on fiction I think that the book ought to have another reading.'

1–EP's *Active Anthology* (Oct. 1933) included selections of work by poets including William Carlos Williams, Basil Bunting, Louis Zukofsky, E. E. Cummings, Ernest Hemingway, Marianne Moore, George Oppen and D. G. Bridson, as well as from TSE ('Fragment of a Prologue', from *SA*), along with a cento of passages from EP's *Cantos*. The blurb pronounced: 'In this volume he [EP] presents an assortment of writers, mostly ill-known in this country, in whose verse a development appears, or in some instances we may say "still appears", to be taking place; in distinction from contemporary poets in whose work Mr Pound finds no such activity or further develoopment . . . Mr Pound's introduction is itself a provocative and exciting document.' EP's 'Praefatio' included the remarks that TSE's 'contempt for his readers has always been much greater than mine, by which I would indicate that I quite often write as if I expected my reader to use his intelligence, and count on its being fairly strong, whereas Mr Eliot after enduring decennial fogs in Britain practically always writes as if for very very feeble and brittle mentalities, from whom he can expect neither resilience nor any faculty for seeing the main import instead of the details or surfaces . . . Mr Eliot's misfortune was to find himself surrounded by a horrible and microcephalous bureaucracy which disliked poetry, it might be too much to say "loathed" it. But the emotion was as strong as any in the bureaucratic bosom . . . That there is a percentage of bunk in the *Selected Essays* [of TSE] Mr Eliot will possibly be the last to deny, but that he had performed a self-analysis is doubtful.

'This kind of essay assumes the existence of a culture that no longer subsists [*sic*] and does nothing to prepare a better culture that must or ought to come into being. I say "better", for the new paideuma will at least be a live paideuma not a dead one.'

EP maintained too, in glancing at C.: 'Such essays are prepared NOT for editors who care about a living literature or a live tradition, or who even want the best of Eliot's perceptions applied to an author of second or third or fourth category (per ex. Seneca), they want to maintain a system wherein it is possible to receive fifteen guineas for an article of approximately 3000–4000 words, in a series to which Mr Eliot's sensitivity and patience will give lustre and wherein his occasional eminence will shed respectability on a great mass of inferior writing.'

knows where you swept Up all those jossers from Well I think poetry gests Worse every year now thats the long and the Short of it if you take my Meaning.[1] I know my lectures ('What is Poetry? No!') are tripe too but I did that for money god damb it well the job was well Paid but there Goes 33% in taxes and the rest here and there The Cantoes is all right but here & there a little humanitarian pus might aye been squeesed out you need a canto or two with a REAL hell in it somebody feeling something but I know I know 300 years of Calvinism from Calvin to Cooledge makes it come hard[2] Well now has to this Mystere Laic I might say in a manner of Speaking Whats the Game?[3] this book as been out some five years or more And I dont believe that anybody his going to buy an English translation now I dropped some of the firms money on one Cocteau book in 1926[4] and I cant allow that again Well now to get down to business I am to see it myself the Jefferson Muss. I mean as soon as Pollinger gets round to it:[5] but I must explain that in this as in some other in fact all matters relating to publishing I am Hampered. at present. Everysince I returned from the states I have been living alone in the country that means moving around more or less and leaving no address until my wife gets used to it and convinced that I have no intention of ever returning Well I should

However, EP did at least allow that TSE was England's 'most accurate critic'.

EP responded to this letter, 24 Sept.: 'The Agon ['Fragment of a Prologue'] is not tripe.'

1 – EP wrote again (undated: Sept.): 'I agree that the preface [to A. A.] was well worth printing & deny that the anthology is exclusively Tripe = several good things in it.'

2 – EP replied on 24 Sept., of the Cantos: 'Mebbe 38 which Mr O'Rage [Orage] izza kindly printin this week, will sa'zisfy yr/ craving for a really theological HELL. I've got a few more details for the preliminary round of that distrist, cantos whatever XIV and XV but judging by Morely's prudence re/ names, purrhaps I am doing well to reserve 'em for later editions.

'so long as the pus is humanitarian and not Babbity humanism, praps that also can pass/ it is extractable, it don't so infect all the circumjacence . . .

'That Calvinical work . . . etc.

yr/ sentence lacks definition/// are my protagonists or protozoists to have just emotions in general or some partikkeler BRAND of ditto??'

In a slightly later letter (n.d.), EP asserted that TSE's 'half baked Theology' made him muddle Hell and Purgatory. 'I'm dealin with mental rot . . . besides my hell is what I see – I am not postulatin post mortem vengeance.'

See too EP, 'Hell', C. 13 (Apr. 1934), 382–96.

3 – EP (11 Sept.): 'Desirability of bringing out extant eng/ version of Cocteau's Mystere Laic.' Jean Cocteau, Le Mystère Laïc: Essai d'étude indirecte, avec cinq dessins de Giorgio de Chirico (1928).

4 – Cocteau, A Call to Order: written between the years 1918 and 1926 and including 'Cock and Harlequin', 'Professional Secrets' and other critical essays (F&G, 1926).

5 – EP (11 Sept.): 'I really want the Jefferson/Mussolini to go to press. Morely [sic] liked it.' (Jefferson and/or Mussolini: L'Idea Statale: Fascism as I have seen it, by EP, was eventually published in London in July/Aug. 1935 by Stanley Nott; in the USA by Liveright in Jan. 1936.)

like to visit rapallo though I much prefer frogs to wops and which I cant
talk the language;[1] but first I have to be round where my solicitor is etc.
and then there IS the *Criterion* and other business something has to be
done about but as I Say its Difficult, furthermore I must live cheap until I
can get things settled and know how much I shall have for myself to live
upon then my Hair started coming off of one side just before I left for
America thats over a year ago and I dont know is there a good wiggmaker
in Rappalo Well this leads up to explaining that I cant lay my hands on
Pavannes or Instigations etc.[2] (Harvard pays 10,000 dols. I forgot to put
that in, the deduct 8% income tax at source)[3] until I can break up my
home properly and I dont suppose London Lib. has them as they was
Published not in London Do you know anybody about who could lend
copies I think my Guido is at office unless somebodys pinched it. But I
think this 'Slected Essayes?' is a good idea I may be able to come out to
your ribiera later by the way that Mexican painter is a bum one[4] you can
get 500 dols. for lectures (3) in Virginia and 750 dols. in Baltimore (3) you
can get 225 dols at Yale but there you have to talk about English Letters
Writers and I got away with it but I think they will tar & feather the next
jonny who tries to talk about English letter Writers without having read
any of them And when I came we cd. discuss the Selectet Essays work in
progress You will be glad to hear that the Pullman Porter is still on the
job you dont need to send any subscription to Nancy for him hes about
the only thing left after the Great White Uprush the other coons are all
actors and stockbrokers I guess. Your general ideas about Essays seem
sound and coolheaded Where's your List of matter from P. & D.and Inst.?
Im not sure about French poets until I see it again because as I remember
it was mostly French poets and not much E.P. and publikum might not
think they was getting good EP value out of that but there was a good
one once on Hy James (that N. England climate is not what it once was
but with a fur coat and a punkah coolee you can get through the winter)
Please elucidate following sentences:

    "Re/ new material. The elimination from
    "that can be made after I know what Pos-
    "sum etc/ etc/"

1 – EP (11 Sept.): 'cant you take a vacashun on the woptalyan Riviera . . . wd. be pleased to
see yuh, AN we are goin tuh have smore lllovely muzik.'
2 – EP, *Pavannes and Divisions* (New York: Alfred A. Knopf, 1918); *Instigations of Ezra
Pound* (New York: Boni and Liveright, 1920).
3 – EP (11 Sept.): 'Wotter they PAY at ole Ha wvud, tuh dwive away dull ca/uh??'
4 – EP responded, 24 Sept.: 'Dunno nowthink erbout no Mexican painter. Wot mex pynter?'
TSE was presumably referring to Diego Rivera.

Well well Life is like that anyway this will Do to Start of. Address me 24, Russell Square and wherein matter is contained of nature personal please mark envelope PERSONAL

molti distinti/etc/etc
T.

Solicitors *are* expensive.

TO *Hoffman Nickerson* CC

22 September 1933

Dear Hoffman,

Many thanks for yours of the 29th August: I too have been away until recently. I am glad to know that the War Book will appear; and will you ask Arrowsmith to send the *Criterion* a copy for review?[1]

If you will send on the article on the Republican Party I will forward it to Jerrold with a note. I should think that even if this article were not suitable, he might well have something in mind on which he would like to have your views for publication.

I should like to have an article from you on Babbitt; there should be more said about him beyond my personal obituary. Could you let me have it by the latter part of October, so that I could get it into the next number? I should say up to 6000 words (not more) and we pay a flat rate to everybody of £2 (say two pounds) a thousand. If you can't do it in the time I should appreciate a short deferred cable!![2]

Yours ever,
[T. S. Eliot]

TO *E. W. F. Tomlin* TS Lady Marshall

23 September 1933 Faber & Faber Ltd

Dear Mr Tomlin,

I should have answered your letter of the 25th June, which awaited my return;[3] but I did not see any immediate prospect of meeting, as I have spent the summer out of London. I should be glad to hear from you.

1–*Can We Limit War?* was to be published by Dial Press (NY), and by Arrowsmith in London.
2–Nickerson, 'Irving Babbitt', C. 13 (Jan. 1934), 179–95.
3–Not found.

When do you go up again? It might be possible to fix a meeting on some day when I was coming to town.[1]

I should be interested to know whether you have done any writing, and have written anything since your essay on 'Materialist Art'.

Yours sincerely,
T. S. Eliot

TO *James Joyce*   TS National Gallery of Ireland

25 September 1933   Faber & Faber Ltd

My dear Joyce,

I returned from America in early July, but have been in the country all the summer. I should be very glad if I might have news of you – how your eyes have fared since I heard from you nearly a year ago, how your work is progressing, and where you are. I hope that I may get over to Paris for a brief visit before the end of the year.

Please give my kind regards to Mrs Joyce.

Yours always sincerely,
T. S. Eliot

TO *Mary Hutchinson*   TS Texas

26 September 1933   Faber & Faber Ltd

My dear Mary,

Thank you very much for your kind letter, and for being willing to see V.[2] I do not of course expect that any individual can do much. I have had a talk with her doctor, since I wrote to you, and he has written her an explicit letter.

1–Tomlin replied, 25 Sept.: 'I return to [Brasenose College] Oxford on Oct. 5th, and am free any time from now until Oct. 4th. I should very much like to see you sometime before I go up, and if this is possible, I will bring with me another essay which I have been preparing, entitled "D. H. Lawrence and his Critics".'

2–MH had replied on 22 Sept. to TSE's letter of 20 Sept.: 'I will see Vivienne but I doubt if I can make any impression! I have noticed that since I told her that I knew the truth and compared it with her stories she has not wanted to see me – and I believe she only likes to see people who will accept that unreal world of hers.

'Of course you could not return – Won't you come and dine with us on Monday or Wednesday – quietly – or if you cannot be in London in the evening shall we lunch together? but then you would not see Jack. I should like you to come here at any time you can and let us talk things over. I will see V. before you come.'

I did not get your letter to be able to dine tomorrow. Wednesday is my best evening, because I can get a train back, but I have already made an engagement for tomorrow. I could probably arrange to dine some other Wednesday at your choice, and I should very much like to see Jack; and I could be in town for lunch almost any day. I will ring you up when I am next in town and hope that I may catch you.

Gratefully,
Tom

TO *Alida Monro*

TS Valerie Eliot

26 September 1933   Faber & Faber Ltd

My dear Alida,

Thank you for your letter of the 22nd,[1] and for sending me the Book, which I think is very nicely produced. I suppose that the first copy was treated by my new secretary as a review copy: one or two other books have gone astray in the same way.[2]

I hope that your projected anthology will be a success and help the Bookshop. I imagine that the labour of editorship involved is immense. Of course you may have the four poems you mention.[3] Is there anyone whom you would like me to approach also?

While in America I made a gramophone record of 'The Hollow Men' and 'Gerontion'. Some copies were promised me for July, and I have just written to ask why they have never turned up. If they come, I will give you one; if you have a gramophone and if you want it.

I wonder if you have seen anything of V. I rather fancy not. Someone else to whom I wrote recently to enquire has just replied: 'I have noticed that since I told her that I knew the truth and compared it with her stories

1 – Alida Monro wrote in response to TSE's letter of 12 Sept.: 'I was glad to have your letter & to know that most of your friends now know of your separation. It is so unpleasant to hear all sorts of rumours & to be without the power to contradict them. I am glad that things are going well & I shall look forward to seeing you when you feel you can venture into the world again.'
2 – 'I sent you a copy of Harold's poems. I hope you were pleased with it. R. C-S says he sent you a copy to Faber & Faber. What do you suppose happened to it?' *The Collected Poems of Harold Monro*, ed. Alida Monro, with a biographical sketch by F. S. Flint and a critical note by T. S. Eliot (Cobden-Sanderson, 1933).
3 – Monro asked to include in a projected anthology entitled *Recent Poetry 1923–33*, four poems by TSE: 'Prufrock', 'La Figlia che piange', *The Hollow Men* and *Triumphal March*. 'Please consent to their appearing in it,' she pleaded, 'because without you the book wouldn't exist.'

she has not wanted to see me – and I believe she only likes to see people who will accept that unreal world of hers.'

The unreal world is being a nuisance, because V. refuses to face the situation and therefore we do not come to a settlement. She insists (through a rather feeble family solicitor) that she is waiting for me to return 'on any terms I may impose' and that she wishes me to 'manage her affairs for her'. Both of which phrases seem to me meaningless. I wish that she might have the counsel of firm and clearheaded people who would refuse to dramatise the matter and insist calmly that this was the most sensible thing for both of us, instead of an irrational betrayal. I want to get the position regularised and a financial settlement come to so that I may return peaceably and live somewhere in London.

Yours ever,
Tom

TO *Bonamy Dobrée* TS Brotherton

26 September 1933   Faber & Faber Ltd

My dear Bumbaby,

I have to acknowledge gratefully the receipt of your book *As Their Friends Saw Them*;[1] to thank you for the inscription; and to express my pleasure in the anticipation of reading and partly re-reading your learned, witty & polite dialogues, in which the most weighty matter is communicated with a sprightliness suited to the most fashionable society; in which just criticism conspires with <u>livliness</u> of stile to capture the attention of the least attentive, and to excite the faculties of the most indolent minds; and throughout which the most scintillant gems of thought are scattered with so lavish a hand, as to exhibit upon every page your accurate observation, and ponderate judgement of men & manners; and in such a way as to arouse the envy of your detractors, and the admiration and applause of your devoted friends: amongst whom I am proud to subscribe myself,

Your most obliged, obedient servant,
T. S. Eliot

P.S. I may be going to York for 2 days on the 10th October. Is that anywhere near Mendham? And how far is Walsingham?[2]

---

1 – *As Their Friends Saw Them: Biographical Conversations* (1933).
2 – The Shrine of Our Lady, Walsingham, Norfolk – one of the great medieval Christian shrines.

26 September 1933

My dear Bird,

Thank you for your letter of the 25th, just received.[1] I am writing, not because yours needs a reply, but to put you in possession ~~with~~ of the following letter from my brother-in-law (~~the relevant part of it~~) so that, as soon as possible on your return, you may advise me as to the way in which I should meet him:

'My dear Tom,

I have written you a long business letter and addressed it to Faber & Faber.

This is just to say that I want very much to see you as soon as you can possibly manage it. I believe that it would help enormously in getting things straightened out. I also believe that it will be easier to get matters settled in a manner satisfactory to both V. & yourself, than it would appear on the face of things.

Only, *until* matters are definitely settled you will realise that the situation at 68 C.G.G. is very bad and must get worse.

I hope to see Mr James next week. It appears that he is away at the moment.

By the way, I don't know whether your last letter to me was intended to be confidential, but I have treated it as such, & therefore I do not officially know your present address. This, however is one of the chief points that is making the situation so extremely difficult & upsetting, I mean the ignorance of your address.

I do hope that you will be able to see me next week – as early as possible.

　　Yours affectionately,

　　Maurice.'[2]

---

1 – Bird had heard from Dr Miller. 'In saying that if he [VHE's solicitor James] "could adopt a firmer attitude something might be accomplished" Dr Miller is only emphasizing a state of affairs of which you and I are both painfully aware – indeed, it would almost be true to say that his [James's] weakness is one of our chief difficulties. I agree that in default of some settlement we shall have to state our own terms and adhere to them but naturally one would prefer to arrive at an amicable agreement . . . I entirely concur with Dr Miller's view that you should decline to see her until the financial position is settled and it may be that the prospect that you might then do so will prove the strongest inducement in bringing her to reason.'

2 – MHW's letter was dated 22 Sept. 1933.

EVE told Alida Monro, 31 Aug. 1965, that MHW called on her soon after TSE's death 'and wept as he said, "My sister gave him hell"' (BL Add MS 57752).

The reference to my address is due to my writing to him from Kelham on their notepaper. I did not mention to him that I was leaving the next day: this letter to me was forwarded from there to Russell Square. I cannot myself quite see why the question of my address should take so much importance in the situation.

I should be glad to hear from you on this matter as soon as convenient, as I do not like to keep him waiting.

I have also a reply from Mrs Hutchinson, who says that she will see my wife, but adds:

'I will see Vivienne but I doubt if I can make any impression! I have noticed that since I told her that I knew the truth and compared it with her stories she has not wanted to see me – and I believe she only likes to see people who will accept that unreal world of hers.'

Yours sincerely,
[T. S. Eliot]¹

TO *Conrad Aiken*

MS Houghton

27 September 1933   Oxford & Cambridge Club

Dear Conrad,

? ? ? I got a mysterious message here this afternoon.

Unfortunately I do not come to town regularly, and don't expect to be up on Friday. I'd like very much to see you. My affairs are rather complicated at present: wheels within etc. Please write me at 24 Russell Sq. & tell me something of yourself, & I'd like you to lunch with me at the first opportunity. I might be able to manage a day next week. Any letter to Russell Sq reaches me within 24 hrs.

Yours ever,
T. S. E.

1–Bird responded to this letter, 30 Sept.: 'I think you should accept [Maurice's] invitation to see you and, on the whole, I incline to the view that in the first instance you should do so alone.'

28 September 1933   Faber & Faber Ltd

Dear Miss Gilbert,

I will clear up as many matters as I can remember.

1. 'Silent Show [*sic*]' is a brilliant piece in its queer and rather useless way, but our reason for rejecting it is that it has already appeared about a year ago in the *Virginia Quarterly*, where I read it.[1]

2. 'Old Play' is not worth the space.[2] Please suggest to Professor Renwick that it is not quite suitable for the *Criterion* and ought to be published in a technical periodical.

3. The review of *The Greek Language* should be unset. Please hold the article on Joyce for the moment: I fear that it was definitely accepted and therefore must be paid for anyway (except that the text of The Mookse & the Gripes[3] should not be counted in). Can you look up the correspondence for me? The others are to be as you have marked them.

4. I will write to Gurian.[4]

5. Mr Scott Moncrieff may have the two books he wants.[5] I should like to have his address.

6. The books not marked on your list may be sold. I know that Foyle does not pay as well as some, but he is reliable. Some enquiry ought to be made about the status of the other applicant. You might take this up with Mr Morley.

7. I cannot find any recent book that appears to have any special appropriateness for Mr Spender, but the Reminiscences of George ROBEY might be worth a review. (Constable: *Looking Back on Life*). Try it.[6]

8. Mr A. L. Morton may have Sir James Frazer's new book.[7] Not more than 1000 words. Please get Elliot Smith's *The Diffusion of Culture* for Mr Codrington (800 words).

---

1 – Gilbert asked on 27 Sept.: '"Silent Snow, Secret Snow" [by Conrad Aiken] has been in our hands for some time, but was borrowed back for some weeks by the agents, and has recently come back here. They would like a prompt decision if possible.'
2 – Submitted by Prof. W. L. Renwick (Stocksfield, Northumberland) on 9 May 1933.
3 – 'The Mookse and the Gripes': from *Finnegans Wake*, 152–9.
4 – See next letter.
5 – Gilbert (27 Sept.): 'May Mr [George] Scott Moncrieff review the *Way of All Women* and *Psychology and Social Progress*?'
6 – SS on George Robey's reminiscences *Looking Back on Life*: C. 13 (Jan. 1934), 345–6.
'I remember Queen Mary sitting in a box and laughing at something of George Robey's, and Robey wagged a finger at her and said: "I don't mean what you mean . . .!"' (quoted in John Barber, 'Love & Mr Eliot', *Daily Express*, 16 Aug. 1958).
7 – Frazer, *The Fear of the Dead in Primitive Religion*.

9. A German Chronicle should be the next thing, but I cannot for the life of me remember who does it now. It may be Max Rychner still.[1]

Please look up the last German Chronicle that we had; and then I fear you will have to look up the correspondence to find Rychner's present address (if it is he). I want an American Chronicle by Gilbert Seldes in the March number, but I must look up his address for you first.

So far as I know Sykes Davies is still responsible for American Periodicals. Will you please ask him for one for this number.

Unless the correspondence has already been definite enough to make it unnecessary, I suggest your writing to Philip Radcliffe to make sure of a Music Chronicle for the next number.[2] Will you please write to Mr Orlo Williams and ask him how soon he feels inclined to do another Fiction Chronicle, and whether there are any books he would like us to get for him for it.[3]

10. Dont bother about Mr Richards's books; they have been out too long.[4] I should be obliged however if you would drop him a line to Magdalene College and ask him to let me know as soon as he gets back from America.

11. I enclose a copy of the page signature of *The Use of Poetry*, corrected, which please send to the Harvard University Press calling their attention especially to the alterations in the Preface and the correction of a quotation from Byron.

12. Miss Mackay's verse is not interesting.[5] Return with polite regrets.

13. I return Mesterton correspondence.[6] I shall be glad to see him; so please make a note to let him have an appointment as soon as I am back regularly.

This is all that I can think of at the moment.

Yours sincerely,
T. S. Eliot

1 – Max Rychner, 'German Chronicle: Germany and the West', trans. Marjorie Gabain, *C.* 13 (Jan. 1934), 300–6.
2 – Philip F. Radcliffe, 'Music Chronicle: Beethoven', ibid., 294–9.
3 – OW, 'Fiction Chronicle', ibid., 279–86.
4 – Gilbert (27 Sept.): 'Mr Richards has had two books for review since, I understand, last November. I have written several times to remind him of them, but the review has not yet reached me. Should I do anything further?'
5 – Gilbert (27 Sept.): 'Miss Mackay brought in the enclosed poem for you some time in January; I hoped she might forget about it, but she has called. She says that you expressed interest in her work earlier, and she particularly wants you to see this poem.'
6 – Erik Mesterton (24 Sept.) was visiting London (from Sweden) 'for a long time' – 'probably . . . till December at least' – and wished to meet TSE.

TO *Waldemar Gurian*[1]   CC

28 September 1933   [*The Criterion*]

My dear Sir,

I read with great interest the English translation of your book on Bolshevism when it appeared; and having recently been given your address, I am writing to ask you whether you would consider offering a contribution to the *Criterion*, a Quarterly Review of which I am the Editor.[2] I imagine that you would find the general attitude of this review one which you could endorse. I am having a specimen copy sent to you.

We have the same rates for all contributors: £2 for each 1000 words; and when articles have to be translated, the translator's fee of 15s. per 1000 words must be deducted. My friends, Jacques Maritain and Henri Massis, who have been contributors, could tell you something about the review.[3]

I am, Yours very truly,
[T. S. Eliot]
Editor.

TO *Ezra Pound*   TS Valerie Eliot

28 September 1933   Faber & Faber Ltd

Dear Rebet well well wed better not argue too long about the relative merits (?) of the inferior because that Sort of discussion tends to lower ones critical pressure but Here having just had my 45 birthday[4] its hard to Think theres no living poets under the age of 45 but there it is[5] and

1 – Waldemar Gurian (1902–54), German-Armenian political scientist and journalist; commentator on Catholicism and Communism; author of *Bolshevism: Theory and Practice*, trans. E. I. Watkin (1932).
2 – TSE had been tipped off that Gurian, who was a friend of Maritain and Massis, was 'in great straits'. The informant, with whom TSE was not acquainted, added: 'He is a Catholic Jew and writers of Jewish *blood* are not encouraged in Germany today . . . He has written a large number of articles on philosophical, political & general subjects . . . He is particularly well informed about Germany and France.'
3 – Gurian did not contribute to C.
4 – In celebration of TSE's forty-fifth birthday, FVM planted a circle of forty-five acorns at Pikes Farm; but the oaks were destroyed during WW2 when the field had to be ploughed for food. See Morley, *Literary Britain: A Reader's Guide to Writers and Landmarks* (1980), 118.
5 – EP responded to this statement, 15 Oct.: 'Meditatin' on yr/ wail that there be no poETS under 45 and thence to a meditated essay / on what shits we were riz among/ and the footling idiocy of the Georgian milieu and how NOBODY ever even heard of technique . . .'

at the other end Binyon with death before & after and night below & above his life is a watch and/or a vision betwixt a Sleep & a Sleep. Of course I except Marianne[1] she is a Contemporary and worth the price of a visit to Brooklyn captivating creetur and can dress in the style of 1900 that must cost her something and gets away with it too. As a Eye like a Auk and a brain like a Gimblet is in the front row of Remarkable females as I ave met. Yes that a good Idea. about Unttermeyer cd. you Untertake him Cremation is the only thing for a corps in that state and let me get to windward. I said what I could both publicly & privately in America after all Palgrave's harm is done & done and Louie goes marchin On hes done more to discredit poetry in U.S.A. than anybody in or out of N.Y. Ghetto. As for Babet I dont Kno you two have a Lot in common Babet & Rabet Inc. Jess & Muff not yet to hand it dont matter Much what you says about Uncle John we was never so proud of him has That. Now then

1. Preface.
2. Troubadours
3. Arnaut
4. Elizab. classicists
5. Translattors of Greek
6. French Poets revised & maybe rebreviated: note that Edith Sitwell & a few people in Sydney N.S.W. have been reading Rimbaud since You was Last in London; young folk mention Laforgue & Corbière but I dont believe have read them and have no idea of relative Perportions.
7. Henry James. Shd. certainly be included but does it need any revision due to Passage of Time. Dont kno not havin it to Hand, but was thinking that the young nowadays get bogged by a pertickler Anglo-Am.situation which is Over and fail to grasp essentials. Very few will think of going back just that far to learn anythink about how to WRITE. I shd. be intempted to say something about emotional deterioration of our time influence of Cambridge & N.Y. Ghetto. But that if I was saying anything, which I aint.
8. Cavalcanti. Yes. Shd. be copy available.

1–EP wrote, 24 Sept.: 'Marianne [Moore] has got to a particularness, and god damn precision ... etc. from which the illuminatus might learn. In fact the contributors are unsatisfactory when you compare 'em to us, but NOT when set against the circumjacent pewkosity.'

9. Harold Monro. F.V.M. & self think this should be followed by (or preceded?) by your excellent lumbagoration re Housman (Boulevard).[1]

How many pages to you reckon this makes? I dont want folk to get the Impression you write less than I do. What about How to Read? This is a good Piece and might be included; and I could write something somewhere sometime to warn people against it. I SHOULD LIKE TO SEE STUDIES IN CONTEMPORARY MENTALITY:[2] want to be sure whether is still CONTEMP. enough; it isnt so much that London has changed since your time exe. perhaps more Jews one got in yesterday according to the Times; it is rather that the Ygr. Genration always THINK things have changed and may miss the point unless driven right through the Skull. Yes I reclect Eliza. Classcists well Enough for Practicle purposses.

Yrs. for the present
T.

TO *Ezra Pound*

TS Beinecke

Michaelmas [29 September] 1933   Faber & Faber Ltd

Dear BRabet dont worry about fountpens at your age stick to the Instrument you have mastered[3] Well well thats just it there aint anythink real about blokes like Rothermere Beaverbrook Mellon and Henri Deterding[4] I dont know who Lawrence is[5] No matter and you cant make them real Its beyond Shakesp. etc. to give them individuality there are just types politicians profiteers financiers newspapersprops. & pressgangs, Calvin, the English, Vicecrusaders, liars, stupids pedants preachers bishops lady golfers fabians conservatives imperialists & people who dont

---

1 – EP (11 Sept.): 'The frivolity re/ Housman oughtn't to be "too good for" yr/ readers.' See EP, 'Mr Housman at Little Bethel' (on A. E. Housman's *The Name and Nature of Poetry*), C. 13 (Jan. 1934), 216–24.

2 – EP (24 Sept.): 'the only copy of "Studies in Contemporary Mentality" is in London, and cd. more easily go straight to Fabers.'

3 – EP had written (undated: Sept.): 'I'm learning to write wif a fountain pen.'

4 – Harold Sidney Harmsworth, first Viscount Rothermere (1868–1940): newspaper proprietor. Max Aitken, 1st Baron Beaverbrook (1879–1964): Canadian-born business tycoon, politician, press baron. Andrew W. Mellon (1855–1937): banker, businessman, industrialist, philanthropist, art collector; 11th United States Ambassador to the UK; US Secretary of the Treasury, 1921–32; co-founder of Carnegie Mellon University. Henri Deterding (1866–1939) – 'the Napoleon of Oil' – executive of the Royal Dutch Petroleum Company; chairman of combined Royal Dutch/Shell oil company, 1900–36.

5 – EP had protested in his previous (undated) letter: 'Hen. Deterding worry? or is Herbie [D. H.] Lawrence on the rack??'

believe Major Douglas etc. I dont see what you can do with Hell without Sin & sinners This is not a theologgical argument its just the way it seems to me thing hang together or dont It may be allright just as an interlude in Limbo but it wants to be supported by a real Hell underneath with real people in it Put me in if you Like Anyway without that it just Oh well no more for the present from yours etc.[1]

T.

TO *Ralph & Aurelia Hodgson* telegram Bryn Mawr

[Sept/Oct. 1933]

CONGRATULATIONS FROM ELIOT AND MORLEY[2]

TO *E. W. F. Tomlin* TS Lady Marshall

7 October 1933 Faber & Faber Ltd

Dear Mr Tomlin,

I am extremely sorry that I could not arrange a day in town free enough from other engagements to be able to ask you to come and see me. I hope that it will be easier by the time of the Christmas vacation.

Could you send me the Lawrence article to read? I should very much like to see it. I am of course considerably in accord with your views in 'Some Implications of the Materialist Conception of Art'; nevertheless, and in spite of its admirable exposition, I did not feel sure that this was

---

1–EP hit back on 2 Oct.: 'Homer got on O/K/ without very much hell. There is an wuz shades (Ah dont mean buck niggush) but indefinite an wafty dark shadows etc.

'There is SHIT, and what the god damn prots/ have lost is the good ole cawflik concept of mind-shit rottenness and STINK of the mind or soul or pussYYchee or wotever . . .

'As fer makin the bustuds real/ you git the current New Eng/ Weekly sept. 28 an read my 38 epistle to the gophesians . . .

'I dunno wot I'd do with you in hell/ purgatory you have wafted abaht in/ I daresay . . .

'If I had anything to do about you or any other dam possum I shd/ christlikely try to pull you out.

'What the hell / aint there no yap about atonement in any of yr halfmasted, but orderly=sentence=producing bloody theologians?? . . .

'To return to my poem / the idea that they suffer might be one thing, but their STINK is a fact. I smell'zum.

'As for the theology of the CANTOS / I dont spect a dod damn low down Christianly perverted animal or in fact anyone to git ANY idea of it furr years and yearrrs.'

2–Ralph Hodgson and Aurelia Bolliger were married in Yokohama, Japan, on 24 Oct. 1933. This telegram was sent to the Imperial University, Sendai.

the right piece to start you off with. There is plenty of time. I think I had better send it back to you now, as it is your only copy, and we will discuss it again when we meet.

Yours sincerely,
T. S. Eliot

TO *L. C. Knights*   TS Texas

8 October 1933   Faber & Faber Ltd

Dear Mr Knights,

I should [be] very glad to review Murry's *Blake* for *Scrutiny*, but I have several rather difficult jobs on hand just now, and I find it quite impossible to take on anything new.[1] I might be able to review something for you in the spring. Anyway, I have been in the ring so often with Murry, that perhaps it is just as well that this book should be taken on by some younger man who has not yet tackled him: I have made it clear enough what I think of Murry.

With best wishes,
Sincerely yours,
T. S. Eliot

TO *Stephen Spender*   TS Northwestern

8 October 1933   Faber & Faber Ltd

Dear Spender,

Mrs Monro of the Poetry Bookshop, the widow of Harold Monro, has asked me to ask you if you would allow her to reprint, in a contemporary anthology that she is preparing, three poems from our volume: 'He will watch the hawk', 'Oh young men oh young comrades' and 'The Express'. The book is to be published by Gerald Howe in conjunction with the Poetry Bookshop at 5s., and I understand that a royalty of 20% is to be divided between the authors.[2]

I have given her permission to use the poems of mine that she wants, and I hope that you can see your way to consenting, as the book will help

---

1–Knights (29 Sept.) invited TSE to review JMM's *Blake*. 'We should be very glad and grateful to be able to publish something by you in *Scrutiny*, the more so as we have published criticisms of you.'
2–Alida Monro asked on 29 Sept. to print Spender's poems in *Recent Poetry 1923–33*.

the Bookshop. But if there are other poems by which you would prefer to be represented, do tell her so. Will you write to her in any case: Mrs Monro, The Poetry Bookshop, 38, Great Russell Street, w.c.1.?

I hope it may not be long before we meet now.

Yours ever,
T. S. Eliot

TO *Tacon Gilbert*   TS Valerie Eliot/?Faber

8 October 1933   Faber & Faber Ltd

Dear Miss Gilbert,

I enclose to be set up for the next number
  Philippe Mairet: 'Moral Dilemma of the Age of Science'.
  Louis MacNeice: Four Poems.
  John Cournos: Myth in the Making.

I also enclose 'Ben Jonson's Lyric Poetry' which the author was so querulous about. Will you please write to him to say that it will be used in one of the next two numbers.[1]

I enclose Mr Vijayatunga's Poem.[2] Why I ever accepted this I cannot understand; I expect it was because he was hard up, as I remember advancing him ten shillings out of pocket. Would you please arrange to have a cheque for a guinea drawn for him, and send it to him saying that the editor is unable to state when the poem can be published, but as it has been so long delayed the payment is enclosed herewith.

I may still use the article on Joyce, so it should not be unset; but I should not in any case use the long quotation from the Mookes & Gripes, and possibly not the glossary.

The material for the next number so far is accordingly: Bedoyere, Willey,[3] Dent, Cournos, Mairet, MacNeice, and the article on Irving Babbitt by Hoffman Nickerson if it comes in time.

Could you tell me if we have on hand some verse mss. by Edouard Roditi called the Lament (or something like that) of somebody Abravanell

---

1–Ralph S. Walker, 'Ben Jonson's Lyric Poetry', C. 13 (Apr. 1934), 430–48.
2–'Reply', a rhyming poem by J. Vijaya-Tunga, a journalist based in London (soon to be winner of a King's award): submitted in Feb. 1932 and accepted by TSE at an unknown date.
3–Basil Willey, 'Wordsworth's Beliefs', C. 13 (Jan. 1934), 232–51. (An essay from a forthcoming book to be published by Chatto & Windus.)

or Abarbanell.[1] I had a special folder for Roditi, as for some other poets. There should also [have] arrived during the summer an essay on John Cleveland by one Harry Levin in America, which I should be curious to see.[2]

I will write to Sampson when I can think of some book for him.[3]

The Pound on Housman should also be set up, but I should like to see a proof copy before it is sent to him.

Yours sincerely,
T. S. Eliot

TO *John Cournos* CC

8 October 1933   [*The Criterion*]

Dear John,

You can abuse me as much as you like for my delay;[4] I shall have plenty of apologies but no valid excuses – torpor, being in a muddle, and having a variety of distracting matters to claim my attention. Well, I am having the 'Lenin' set up, but as you have had to wait so long and patiently about it I am enclosing a cheque on Boston (which will be more convenient for you and if the dollar collapses meanwhile we will adjust later).[5] So that postpones any other contribution of the chronicle kind until March – so meanwhile I should like any fresh or repeated suggestions you care to make.

I wish that you could get over here again. Let me know how things are with you, and please give my regards, with very pleasant memories of hospitality, to Mrs Cournos.

Yours ever sincerely,
{T. S. E.]

---

1 – 'The Complaint of Jehudah Abravanel'. Roditi's next contribution was to be 'Trafalgar Square', C. 13 (Apr. 1934), 449–50.
2 – 'John Cleveland and the Conceit', C. 14 (Oct. 1934), 40–53.
3 – Ashley Sampson on Paul Claudel's *Ways and Crossways*: C. 13 (July 1934), 678–80.
4 – Cournos's letter has not survived. Alfred Satterthwaite wrote to EVE, 2 Sept. 1976: 'The vast majority of originals that are missing was sold by John Cournos to rich young students at Yale College during the Depression, when Cournos was very hard pressed for money. No record of these sales was kept; therefore, I cannot say who possesses the letters.'
5 – Cournos, 'Myth in the Making', C. 13 (Jan. 1934), 225–9.

TO *H. Carter*   CC

8 October 1933

Dear Sir,

Thank you for your letter of the 30th ultimo.[1] I am troubled by not yet
have [*sc.* having] been able to accept the repeated invitation to address the
Double Crown Club, and distressed that I do not yet feel free to accept.
I have taken on several pieces of work which will take the best of my
attention until the spring, and I do not believe that meanwhile I could
prepare a paper worthy of the occasion. I hope that it may be possible at
a later date.

> With renewed regrets,
> Believe me,
> Yours very truly,
> [T. S. Eliot]

FROM *Janet Adam Smith*[2]   TS Valerie Eliot

11 October 1933   *The Listener*, Broadcasting House,
                                         London w.1

Dear Mr Eliot,

I am very pleased to hear from Herbert Read that you might be willing
to look through the poems we have printed in the *Listener* and give some
sort of opinion on them.[3]

1–Carter (Imperial Chemical House, Millbank, London) invited TSE to address the Double
Crown Club on 9 Nov., or else in Dec. or Jan.

2–Janet Adam Smith was Assistant Editor of *The Listener*, 1929–35; then worked for the
NS&N, 1949–60: for the last eight years as Literary Editor. In 1935 she married Michael
Roberts, and TSE was to become godfather to Adam, one of their three children.

3–Smith recalled in a memoir, 'Tom Possum and the Roberts Family': 'Later in my *Listener*
career I approached him, at the suggestion of Herbert Read, when the poetry we published
– particularly a poetry supplement [12 July 1933] whose centrepiece was Auden's "The
Witnesses" with woodcuts by Gwen Raverat – was under attack, and we thought the best
defence would be to commission a report from an outside authority. Mr Eliot agreed to write
such a report; though it was not as appreciative as I had naively hoped, it silenced the critics
within the BBC' (*Essays from the 'Southern Review'*, 213). She recalled too, in 'Auden and
the Listener', that it was Auden's 'The Witnesses' – 'a startling and compelling poem' in
29 verses of six lines each – that had 'shocked many a reader': 'It is hard now to recapture
the sense of outrage that the poets of the early Thirties could provoke. The impact of Eliot
had been deep rather than widespread. Many readers of the *Listener* who sincerely loved
poetry, and – because they had been brought up on the anthologies of *Georgian Verse* and
the English Association's *Poems of Today* – thought they loved "modern" poetry, simply

The situation leading to our request to you is this: on the publication of a Poetry Supplement and an Editorial leader on Modern Poetry on July 12, Sir John Reith sent for me and wished to know more about the poetry in the *Listener* – how it was chosen, why there was so much which seemed odd, uncouth, 'modernist', etc. I think he was particularly concerned with the long poem in the Supplement by W. H. Auden, 'The Witnesses'. We had some talk on modern poetry in which I mentioned your name; and he later suggested it would be interesting to have your opinion of the poetry we publish. I don't think he objects to modern poetry as such any more than he does to the modern music broadcast by the B.B.C.; but I think he is anxious that it should be recognised as having some merit by responsible persons outside the B.B.C.

For myself, I would make no great claims for the poems we publish. It would be difficult to find fifty-two good short poems in one year, and we have certainly printed some that are by no means good – though in my opinion they are better than the hundreds we have rejected. They are for the most part chosen from the mass of verse submitted, in the ordinary way; though some poets have been directly invited to send in work – e.g. instructions came to us to ask Sir Henry Newbolt and Mr de la Mare for poems for our last Christmas number. One or two poems have also, I fear, found their way in for irrelevant reasons. Some of the more simple and traditional ones were so chosen deliberately: knowing our rather peculiar position as an official organ of the B.B.C. and our wide and very varied circle of readers I thought it best occasionally to print something more likely to be understood by most of them than the poems which I myself set store by. Most of these, and a good many others for which I have only my bad choosing to blame, are now as dead as mutton; you will see that from the book. But it is, I imagine, precisely *not* these that concern Sir John Reith; I should rather think he is concerned with those which I am glad to have chosen – most of the poems in the Supplement, the four Spender poems, the Herbert Reads, the Auden poem, those by C. Day-Lewis, Conrad Aiken, Charles Madge, John Pudney, John Lehmann, A. S. J. Tessimond, Michael Roberts, Philip Henderson, George Barker,

---

could not see early Auden or Day-Lewis as poetry at all.' In consequence of the 'commotion' caused by 'The Witnesses', TSE was commissioned to report on the poetry published in the *Listener*: 'In his report, Auden and Spender were commended as the most promising of the younger poets: this imprimatur greatly eased my situation. From that time till I left the *Listener* in 1935 there was no question of R. S. Lambert [Editor of *The Listener*] vetoing any Auden poems: he grumbled a bit, and begged me (as with poems by Dylan Thomas or David Gascoyne) to provide him with a prose crib so that if there were questions from higher up he could give some kind of an answer' (*The Listener*, 18 Oct. 1963, 532, 534).

etc., etc. And what he wishes is an opinion on their poetic respectability (and thus on the handling of the poetry in general) – to know that the appearance of such poems is not simply the result of one person's queer taste, and that by printing them *The Listener* has not made the British Broadcasting Corporation look a fool. I myself feel we have been all too respectable, and can far more justly be condemned, on the evidence of the poems as a whole, for stodginess than for revolutionary or extremist tendencies.

I should be extremely interested to read what you have to say and show it to Sir John. Would you suggest a suitable fee for giving this specialist's opinion?

I am sorry the book should be rather untidy, with marks made when there was some question of publishing a selection in book form.

Yours sincerely,
Janet Adam Smith
Assistant Editor.

TO *Vivien Eliot*

TS Valerie Eliot

16 October 1933[1]

c/o Messrs Bird & Bird,
5 Grays Inn Square, W.C.1.

My dear Vivienne,

I have now been back in England for three and a half months, and it becomes necessary for us to come to a definite financial arrangement. The present arrangement is not only indefinite, but is positively beyond my means to keep up. As we are to be living apart, it is obvious that we must have separate incomes, and that I cannot be responsible for anything beyond the fixed allowance to be settled upon. You must obviously have a definite income upon which you can fix your scale of living.

After very careful consideration, this is what I am prepared to do. I will give you £5 a week out of which, with your private income, to defray

---

1 – TSE sent the draft of this letter to his solicitor Ernest Bird on 15 Oct., and Bird responded, 18 Oct.: 'With some diffidence I venture to submit the accompanying alternative based very much on your own. I do not know that there is really any difference between the two but I am anxious to make it abundantly clear that these terms, which I regard as generous, are final and that they are not, so to speak, open to criticism by your Wife. Please do not hesitate to alter my draft in any way that may commend itself to you. I just send it for your consideration. In the circumstances I return your own letter in the envelope that contained it.' Thus the letter, incorporating Bird's suggestions – dated 23 Oct.? and reproduced below – is presumably the one TSE sent to VHE.

all expenses. In addition, I will continue to pay the rent of 68, Clarence Gate Gardens until the expiry of the lease in June next 1934, after which you will have of course to find other accommodations for yourself. The furniture and fittings are your property, with the exception of course of my books and bookcases and my family photographs etc. This income of £5 a week is to remain fixed during your mother's lifetime; upon her death I propose that the financial arrangement should be reviewed with consideration to our respective incomes thereafter, by two persons one to be appointed by you and one by me; and if these two cannot come to an agreement as to what will be a fair division of income, they will leave the decision to a third and impartial party, such as the President of the Law Society.

This seems to me a fair arrangement, and I am not prepared to go farther. I wish indeed that I was in a position to do so. You will receive a confirmation of the terms from Mr James, and I earnestly hope that you will accept them. As I say, it is beyond my means to continue the present arrangement, which will have to cease in any case.

Affectionately your husband,
T. S. Eliot [signature crossed out]

TO *I. A. Richards*

TS

17 October 1933   Faber & Faber Ltd

Dear Richards,

I was glad to get your card, because I had been thinking that you must be back, but meant to wait until you were settled before writing to you. I only had a letter from my sister a few days ago saying how much they had enjoyed seeing you and Mrs Richards.

As I believe you know, I have not yet returned to London, and may not do so for some little time. But I am fairly free to move about, and I should like very much to spend a night or two in Cambridge as soon as you find it convenient. There is much to talk about – you will think my Norton lectures lamentable, but the Preface may amuse you – and we have not had a satisfactory meeting for years.

We will forget about those two books, but you must do something else for me as soon as you can; the *Criterion* needs freshening up.

Yours ever,
T. S. E.

17 October 1933   [*The Criterion*]

My dear Herr Gurian,

I thank you for your letter of the 5th instant. For your suggestions, I cannot say anything about your article *Der katholische Publizist*[1] without knowing more about the subject matter; the other two suggestions seem to me very suitable; but I would suggest that as you are at present best known here by your book on Soviet Russia, the second, *Der bolschevistische Mensch*,[2] might be the best title to use first.

Articles for the *Criterion* should not be longer than 6000 words; and the payment is £2 per 1000 words, less the expense of translation which is 15s. per 1000 words.

As for your further remark, I would say that the *Criterion* is not concerned with topical and practical political affairs, especially not with the domestic affairs of foreign nations; but that it is very much concerned with political and social theory.

Awaiting your further news, I am,
Yours very sincerely,
[T. S. Eliot]
Editor.

TO *Hugh Gordon Porteus*[3]   TS Beinecke

17 October 1933   Faber & Faber Ltd

Dear Mr Porteus,

Thank you for your letter of the 3d instant, which has been passed on to me.[4] I am grateful to you for your appreciation of my fragments, and also

---

1 – *Der katholische Publizist*: 'The Catholic Journalist'.
2 – *Der bolschevistische Mensch*: 'The Bolshevistic Man'.
3 – Hugh Gordon Porteus (1906–93), literary and art critic; literary editor of *The Twentieth Century* (magazine of the Promethean Society), 1931–3; advertising copywriter; author of *Wyndham Lewis: A Discursive Exposition* (1932) – supplemented by his essay 'A Man Apart' in *Agenda* magazine (1969–70) devoted to Lewis – and *Background to Chinese Art* (1935). See obituary in *The Times*, 20 Feb. 1993; 'Forgotten man of the Thirties', *TLS*, 26 Mar. 1993, 13–14.
4 – Porteus, who addressed his letter 'Dear Sir', wondered *inter alia* if there might be an opportunity for him to do some reviewing. 'At a recent *Criterion* meeting, Mr Read suggested to me, in conversation, that there might be a possibility of my doing some . . . I should particularly like to write notices of books on art – such e.g. as Mr Brodzky's study of Gaudier-Brzeska [*sic*].' He enclosed as a 'specimen', a review of *Sweeney Agonistes* – 'I believe it happens to be one of the only fair expositions of Mr Eliot's verse drama.'

for your remarks about the *Criterion*. The answer to the price is, that it is commonly found that reductions in the price of a review of this character are very far from increasing the sale in proportion; its immediate public must always be very small and its circulation can never make ends meet. Of course another editor might be able to make it more popular; so long as I edit it I must recognise my limitations and work within them. Besides, we do pay contributors.

I should be very glad if from time to time you would make suggestions of books you care to review. In the ordinary way, however, books on art and books on music go to the regular contributors of the respective chronicles.

Yours very sincerely,
T. S. Eliot

TO *Hoffman Nickerson* CC

17 October 1933 [*The Criterion*]

Dear Hoffman,

I am sorry you can't do the Babbitt in time – thanks for your cable – but as it is, take your time over it and I will expect it definitely in time for the following issue.[1] Meanwhile I hope that you will have time to let me have a review for the December number.[2]

I have not yet seen your book, but am out of town and perhaps there is a copy waiting at the office. I have forwarded your article on the Republican Party to Jerrold with a letter[3] – I am not sure that he will think it suitable material for an English periodical, but I suggested that he should get in touch with you in any event.

By the way, I recommend getting hold of a book called *Northern Catholicism* and reading a brilliant article in it by N. P. Williams on the

---

1–Nickerson wrote, 29 Aug.: 'I was fond of him and thought him a magnificent thinker on the negative side, i.e. in his critique of modernism.' Nickerson submitted his article on 27 Oct.: 'Irving Babbitt', C. 13 (Jan. 1934), 179–95.
2–Presumably Nickerson had been sent Guglielmo Ferrero's *Peace and War* (a translation of *Fin des aventures*), and Liddell Hart's *The Ghost of Napoleon* (published by F&F on 21 Sept.).
3–Not found.

Theology of the Oxford Movement.[1] If you should come across Will Spens during his visit, remember me to him.

Yours ever,
[T. S. Eliot]

TO *E. L. Grant Watson*   cc

17 October 1933

Dear Mr Grant Watson,

I must apologise for not having written to you sooner; but I have been out of London, there was some delay in getting your address, and so I formed the mistaken impression that I had already written.

I should have explained that the reason why I was unable to use your review in question[2] was that it was brought to my notice that this review resembled very closely one that you had contributed to the *Observer* – so closely in my opinion, as to render it superfluous. I know that a reviewer cannot always avoid the accident of receiving the same book for review from different quarters. But when this happens, I would ask reviewers not to review the book for the *Criterion* as well as for some other periodical, unless the book is such that they find they have a great more to say about it than can be confined within the limits of one review.

Yours very truly,
[T. S. Eliot]

TO *Frederick C. Packard, Jr*[3]   cc

17 October 1933

My dear Dr Packard,

I am sorry to learn from your letter of the 6th instant that we have been at cross purposes.[4] I trust that it will have been immediately clear to you

---

1–N. P. Williams, 'The Theology of the Catholic Revival', in *Northern Catholicism: Centenary Studies in the Oxford and Parallel Movements*, ed. Williams (Lady Margaret Professor of Divinity, Oxford) and Charles Harris (1933). The term 'Northern Catholicism' was used to designate all non-Roman, Western European high church movements including the Church of England.

2–A review of *The Way of All Women*.

3–Frederick C. Packard, Jr (1899–1985): Instructor at Harvard University who in due course became Professor of Speech and Dramatics.

4–Packard, who had recorded TSE reading 'The Hollow Men' and 'Gerontion' for the 'Harvard Vocarium', said he had not heard from TSE since TSE's letter of 25 June (not

that I never received your letter which crossed mine. I judged from your having cashed the cheque that you had received mine; my letter did not require any answer, but as you had said that the records would be ready within a few weeks I wondered what had gone wrong.

Neither I nor my firm have any objection to the record being 'published' (if that is the right word – I was going to say 'uttered') by the Harvard University Press. I do not see how such circulation could do anything but benefit the sale of my books. I also confirm our verbal understanding that I should receive 10% royalty on all sales in America and 5% on all sales in Britain and foreign countries; but I should like to stipulate that Faber & Faber should have the agency for British sales if they desire it.

This last point is perhaps one for discussion. It occurs to me that in time the Harvard University Press should build up a very interesting list of records; there is no similar undertaking here; and I think that we could handle them as well as any publishing firm here, and perhaps more advantageously than older firms which might not be easily interested in anything so unusual. I should like to hear from you about this. Meanwhile please go ahead with your plans for 'publication'.

I have no objection at all to your approaching Professor Greet with a view to securing his assent to my reproducing the same poems for you, when and if this becomes possible. I do not of course admit that I have conceded to his undertaking any monopoly of these poems, but I should not like to reproduce them without consulting him first.

Thank you very much for going ahead and having made for me the records for which I asked. I hope that my cheque covered postage amply. I look forward with interest to hearing the record again.

With most cordial wishes to yourself and Mrs Packard,

Yours very sincerely,

[T. S. Eliot]

---

found) containing the list of individuals whom he wished to receive copies of his gramophone record, together with his cheque for 10 dollars. 'I also asked for your written agreement confirming our verbal understanding that you would receive ten per cent royalty (five per cent in England) of all sales . . . Besides this, I wanted your approval of my asking Professor Greet if he would have any objection to our recording some of the poems you did for him, when and if the opportunity arose. Did the letter not reach you?' He went on: 'Having despaired of hearing from you, and not wishing to keep your friends waiting, I followed the course which I thought you would desire: I ordered the requisite number of records to be printed "Privately", and these are now being shipped to me here. As soon as they arrive I shall distribute only those for which you sent me addresses in America, and the remaining six will reach you eventually at 24 Russell Square.'

TO *Edith Sitwell*[1]

17 October 1933 [*The Criterion*]

My dear Edith,

I have your letter of the 14th instant, and am extremely sorry to hear that anything in the *Criterion* should have been a cause of annoyance to you.[2]

1–Edith Sitwell (1887–1964): poet, biographer, anthologist, novelist; editor of *Wheels*, 1916–21. Her collection, *The Mother and Other Poems* (1915), was followed by *Clown's Houses* (1918) and *The Wooden Pegasus* (1920). In 1923, her performance at the Aeolian Hall in London of her cycle of poems, *Façade* (1922), with music by William Walton, placed her briefly at the centre of modernistic experimentation. Other writings include *Collected Poems* (1930), *Fanfare for Elizabeth* (1946), *The Queens and the Hive* (1962), *Taken Care Of* (memoirs, 1965). She was appointed DBE in 1954. See John Pearson, *Façades: Edith, Osbert and Sacheverell Sitwell* (1978); *Selected Letters of Edith Sitwell*, ed. Richard Greene (1997); Richard Greene, *Edith Sitwell: Avant-Garde Poet, English Genius* (2011). TSE remarked to Mary Trevelyan on 16 Oct. 1949: 'Edith and Osbert [Sitwell] are 70% humbug – but kind – and cruel' (Trevelyan, 'The Pope of Russell Square').

2–ES complained from Renishaw Hall, Derbyshire (country seat of the Sitwells), of Geoffrey Grigson's review of her brother Sacheverell's *Canons of Giant Art; Twenty Torsos in Heroic Landscape*, in *C.* 13 (Oct. 1933), 138–40. Grigson had written: 'Like a man swallowing his false teeth, [Sitwell] chokes with a muddle of cancelling epithets and images . . . Not one of these long poems (except the well told story of Hercules and Pholus) is properly designed. The limpness of each line of blank verse permits no total organization. There seems no reason why these poems should end and not continue towards infinity . . . His reactions form the whole material – a snobbish cultural material – of these "canons of giant art", and beyond them it is possible to discover of Mr Sitwell only that he goes to "culture" because he hates noise and speed, and approves of Fascism and Mussolini because Italy (to him) is the birthplace of the arts.'

And so Edith Sitwell complained to TSE: 'I have been much distressed to see, in the new *Criterion*, a very impertinent notice of Sachie's new poems, by a person named Grigson, and I would like to call your attention to this, for I am certain that you, who have been away for so long, cannot have seen it, or you would never have allowed it to appear under your editorship.

'I am convinced of this, since you were one of the first to recognise Sachie's great gifts as a poet, when he was still a boy, and, as well, the rule of the *New Criterion* is that reviews shall be courteous. This review is not only exceedingly stupid, it is also very discourteous, as you will see, if you will look at it. Mr Grigson – whoever he may be – has made a practice for some years of being as impertinent as possible to me, and he is evidently now going to carry on this impertinence to Sachie. I wish to protest most strongly. As far as I know, Mr Grigson is utterly uninstructed with regard to poetry – (I can, of course, only judge by his reviews, which are invariable silly and insensitive, otherwise I know nothing of him.) It seems to me a pity, as well as unfair, that poetry, and especially such fine poetry as Sachie's, should be judged by a person of this kind.

'I am sure the review was inserted during your absence. But I do wish that the crowds of silly little people like this, would take to brick-laying or something useful, instead of airing their valueless opinions about an art of which they are ignorant.'

It is true that the books given to Mr Grigson to review were given to him without my knowledge and in my absence; that I know him only very slightly, though I believe him to have a serious zeal for poetic standards; and that this is the first occasion on which he has written for the *Criterion*.[1] It is also true however that I returned in time to read the proof of the current number, with a view to detecting any improprieties.

It has always been my own endeavour to select reviewers for books with an eye to fitness between reviewer and reviewed; but once the book is assigned I do not pretend to any censorship, though I sometimes offer suggestions, in the reviewer's interest, towards moderating intemperance or exaggeration. Beyond that, I am only concerned with libellous matter, or with personal remarks which seem definitely in bad taste. You will understand that I should always be still more scrupulous to exert no influence, in the case of books which have been published by my own firm. In the review in question I found nothing to which I think an editor could justifiably take exception.

I do not consider the *Criterion* as a personal organ, and the contributions frequently express views which are wholly alien to my own.

I am very sorry to hear such bad news of Helen. Please convey her my sympathy. I had heard that you now spend most of your time in Paris, but I hope for an opportunity of seeing you this winter.[2]

Yours ever sincerely,

[T. S. Eliot]

1 – Grigson claimed in later years that he had first met TSE and VHE (presumably in 1932) at 'a formal summertime tea in the upstairs flat in South London of an elderly friend of Eliot's, a novelist': 'Through Alice Herbert's drawing-room window . . . we had . . . watched the arrival of the Eliots. He emerged from an Austin Seven, or rather there first emerged a little Pomeranian lap-dog and then the eccentric Mrs Eliot, who proved to be uncommonly like a difficult irritable Pomeranian herself, given to yapping and sudden pointless incursions into the tea-time conversation about St Louis and other matters which polite thin Eliot was carrying on with this pink and pretty daughter of a foolish Tom Galt. [Grigson's first wife, who was present at the tea-party in question, was Frances Galt, daughter of Tom Galt who was known to TSE from his early years in St Louis and who had for a while gone to school with TSE.]

'"Why?" she would suddenly say, "Why?", and balancing his tea-cup or his thin bread-and-butter or cucumber sandwich Eliot would patiently explain why. That this Englishwoman was Eliot's cross was true unquestionably' ('Meeting T. S. Eliot', *Recollections: Mainly of Writers and Artists* [1984], 10–11).

2 – 'I live in Paris, for most of the year now. Poor Helen [Rootham – ES's companion], who is there too, with her sister, has just had another terrible operation.'

18 October 1933   [Faber & Faber Ltd]

Dear Miss Smith,

I enclose a report on *The Listener* poems which you have sent me to examine. I would ask that it be considered as confidential and for the inspection only of those who need to see it for the purpose for which it was written. I do not wish to hurt any feelings.

I should be willing to revise it if the form is unsuitable, or if anything is irrelevant. It seems to me that a fee of ten guineas would be reasonable for putting some of my professional secrets at the disposal of *The Listener*. I should be glad to answer any further questions which are pertinent and which I may have overlooked.[1]

                              Yours very truly,
                              [T. S. Eliot]

I have been asked to give my opinion of a series of short pieces of verse by contemporary writers which have appeared in *The Listener* between February 1931 and the present time. As the terms of reference are rather large it might be well to consider first upon what grounds a weekly periodical is justified in publishing specimens of contemporary verse, and with what frequency, and on what principles it should choose verse to publish.

A weekly may allocate space either for publishing a little of as many writers as possible, or a good deal of a few authors of exceptional merit. There are two objections to the latter plan. One is formal: in a periodical appearing so frequently, it is much more practical to allot a little space every week than a good deal of space at rare intervals. The other is material: there are not enough good poets of established reputation; and the poets of established reputation are those who have nothing to gain by periodical – especially *weekly*-periodical – publication. While I believe that periodicals should pay as much for poetry as they can, and that poetry should be better paid than prose, yet it would remain certain that the amount of money to be made in this way by serious poetry is

---

1 – Janet Adam Smith responded to TSE's letter and report: 'You request that it should be kept confidential shall be most scrupulously observed. If I may say so, I think your general remarks about the place of poetry in a weekly periodical will be extremely helpful and valuable to us long after this immediate occasion for them is over.' She wrote again on 31 Oct.: 'Sir John Reith was most appreciative of the report and of the trouble you took for us. He considered it very complete and has no supplementary questions to ask.'

derisible, and that the one strong motive is advertisement. It is only the younger poets to whom a weekly can appeal on this ground; when the best older poets give you contributions, you may regard it as an act of charity on their part. For the first ten years of his working life a poet has something to gain by having his verse seen occasionally in weeklies; later, he has nothing to gain and indeed something to lose. On both moral and practical grounds therefore a weekly, if it publishes poetry at all, should look to the younger writers, which implies publishing a larger number of small pieces by many writers, rather than a small number of large pieces by few writers.

I am inclined to believe also that the public for an intelligent weekly prefers to have its small weekly dose of poetry, rather than occasional larger doses. The format adopted by *The Listener*, of having the poem inset in a surround on the same page of every number, seems to be excellent. The readers know where to look for the Regular Feature, and the form discountenances the suspicion, aroused by most weeklies, that the verse is there only to fill a vacant space at the foot of a column. And the quantity seems to me right: most verse is of such mediocrity that no reader can read much at a time, and take it in, without fatigue.

The question now arises as to the principle of choice. An editor may aim at choosing 'anthology' pieces, that is the occasional *trouvailles* of authors the bulk of whose work may be worthless. (It is only the most completely unqualified writers of verse who cannot have the luck to strike out one or two such pieces in a lifetime). But such pieces are not so easily come by as one might think: I speak from ten years' experience in reading masses of manuscript verse of Britain, Ireland, America and the Dominions and Colonies. I suspect that the inferior poet is more likely to submit his more pretentious, rather than his more honest pieces. There is happily another aim that we may pursue. We may take up the young poets who seem to have any *promise*, and give each of them a number of chances, over a period of several years, until we are forced to the conclusion that his promise has not been fulfilled. I must affirm my belief that even the most gifted poetry editor must be content to have a great many more failures than successes, and that it is impossible to be sure of genius at first sight. Poetic greatness requires a certain moral stamina which cannot be proved by his first writings.

In taking up and nursing young writers in this way a periodical can justify its publication of verse. A weekly has advantages over periodicals appearing at less frequent intervals. It can give a little help – in this way of Advertisement of which I spoke – to a much larger number of writers;

and accordingly the odds, so to speak, are not nearly so long against the editor as in the case of a Quarterly. I have myself followed the practice of keeping a *dossier* for each young poet in whom I discerned any promise; not with the expectation of drawing upon it for publication, but in order to compare his writing over a period of several years, in the hope of coming to some conclusion about him. I have found this often helpful. It must also be borne in mind that a larger number of young writers are worth encouraging than those who will ultimately devote themselves usefully to poetry: among these beginners are some who have talent, but have not yet discovered the exact direction in which that talent ought to be exercised; for whom poetry is only a transitional mode of expression, but who through their verse essays come to learn their true vocation. These also are to be encouraged.

From the point of view of a service to the reading public, as well as that to the young writers, it seems to me that – I judge from the character of the other contents – a consistent policy of this kind should appeal to readers of *The Listener*. This weekly seems to aim at a public which is curious and avid of information about the latest facts, ideas and discoveries in contemporary art and thought; its readers, so far as they are interested in poetry, must want to know what sorts of verse are being written. From this point of view, whether the verse is of the highest quality does not matter much: what you want to be able to say confidently to your readers is that this is representative of the best that is being written by men and women of their generation. At least, it will serve as a document upon the time, and if the time should not produce any poetry worth preserving, that would be an interesting fact in itself. By publishing verse in this way, you should have every hope of publishing something by the one or two poets who will be recognised ten or twenty years hence, and thus building up a future reputation for the paper.

I should not however recommend pursuing this method to the entire exclusion of the other. What I have just outlined is what seems to me the only *aim* that an editor can justifiably and consistently follow; but at the same time he should keep his eyes open for the occasional charming piece, of some positive accomplishment and no promise whatsoever, which may now and then turn up from unexpected sources. It is also a good thing, now and then, to publish some small piece by one of the few elder poets of deserved reputation, most of whom from time to time produce trifles which they might be willing to print in this way.

I have examined the collection of poems published in *The Listener* from early in 1931 to the present time. The great majority of the contributors are known to me in one way or another; some have appeared in *The Criterion*, and more have several times offered contributions to *The Criterion*. Except for the absence of American writers – English and American poetry at the present time are fundamentally very much alike, and equally good and bad – it seems to me very representative. One could, no doubt, think of some equally good writers who are absent; and no doubt one could pick out a few poems included which are below the possible level: but both of these attempts seem to me irrelevant to the opinion which I am asked to give. For good or bad, the collection seems to me representative of the verse of its time. As one must expect of any time, the great majority is mediocre and conventional: it reveals the occasional influence of myself, Mr Yeats, Mr Pound and Gerard Hopkins, and some other more discredited originals. (I am not concerned with the small number of already known poets who are represented, but with the younger rank and file). But while not encouraging for poetry, the selection is on the whole very creditable to *The Listener*. I do not say that the poetry is positively better than the kind that Sir John Squire would select; but there is this great difference: that Squire's kind of poetry is now completely out of date, and this is not. In short, I do not believe that *The Listener* could be any *more* conservative without making itself ridiculous. It is I think the one London weekly (with the possible exception of *The New English Weekly*) in which I would not dissuade any promising young poet from seeking to appear.

A few of the writers have appeared in *The Criterion*; two of them, W. H. Auden and Stephen Spender, have had volumes published on my recommendation by Faber & Faber. Of all the younger poets, Auden is the one who has interested me the most deeply, though I feel that it is impossible to predict whether he will manifest the austerity and concentration necessary for poetry of the first rank, or whether he will dissipate his talents in wit and verbal brilliance.

It may be irrelevant to mention my belief that beyond a point it becomes nullifying for an editor to try to give the public the *sort* of poetry it likes. Those who like poetry at all do not like sorts of poetry, but the work of individual poets. It is a good thing, I believe, to give the 'public' from time to time poems by individual poets whom it already likes; but it can never serve any purpose to give it imitations of the poetry it already likes. A poem by Kipling is a good thing to have, if you can get it; but not an imitation of Kipling. Imitations of certain more recent poets are bound to creep in: because it is often almost impossible to tell whether a young poet is cleverly imitating or whether he is being *influenced*. To be influenced by *any* earlier poet is justifiable; imitation, on the other hand, is only just pardonable when the poet imitated is himself fairly new. It is natural for a young writer to be carried away by anything good and new, but he may outgrow it.

TO *Tacon Gilbert*   TS Valerie Eliot

18 October 1933   Faber & Faber Ltd

Dear Miss Gilbert,

The Pound on Housman is to be set up as an article (if I have not let you know before).[1] But I should see a galley *before* it is sent out to him.

It was quite right to set up Mr Read's poem for the next number: I notice that his name has been accidentally omitted.[2]

Nor can I find that I told you that I don't know Fitzgerald's address.[3] He is an American, but he intended to be in France this autumn, and promised to let me have his address. You might drop him a line c/o Harvard University in the hope that it will reach him.

Spender may have the Soviet Anthology – no, stop, I had rather he did the Robey, if that appeals to him.[4] Primarily I should like to know whether all the people whom I suggested to you for reviews some time ago, have accepted or not. I presume Mr Morley gave you the *New Statesman* in which I had checked the books I want. Of course at this time of year there is a glut; but half of the reviews of books that come in now have to go into the March number, as after the beginning of November there will be comparatively few appearing.

Let Mr Penty do the article he suggests.[5] I dont suppose he expected to get it done in time for this number.

Please send a copy of CCC Cantoes to Miss Marianne Moore, 260 Cumberland Street, Brooklyn, New York, and ask her if she will be so kind as to review it up to 1500 words. If she can't do it in time (and that

1–EP, 'Mr Housman at Little Bethel', C. 13 (Jan. 1934), 216–24.
2–HR, 'A Short Poem for Armistice Day', C. 13 (Jan. 1934), 202.
3–F. Scott Fitzgerald.
4–SS, review of George Robey's memoirs *Looking Back on Life*: C. 13 (Jan. 1934), 345–6.
5–See Arthur J. Penty's reply to Eric Gill, 'Beauty Does Not Look After Herself', C. 13 (Apr. 1934), 353–70.

would hardly be possible) give her the date for the March number.[1] Will you also please say that I should be glad to publish a new poem of hers, if she has one to offer.

Please send *The Winding Stair* to Hugh Gordon Porteus – or rather, write and ask him, whether he would like to review it – but say that I suggest that it is not worthwhile unless he happens to be specially interested in Yeats's poetry. He could in that case have Aldington's poems instead.[2]

Is Mr Orlo Williams doing anything for this number?[3]

I enclose the Barth review. It is tolerable, but I think I could have got it better done, and we need not keep Mr Porteus [sc. Porteous] in mind for the future.[4]

With you ask the Revd Victor Demant whether he will review *The Philosophy of Communism*? Failing him, I should like you to ask Maurice B. Reckitt.[5]

I return an article on *Logan P. Smith*, which is of no use.

I return *The Dictatorship of Things* which please to offer to Montgomery Belgion for review.[6]

Can We Limit War? will have to be reviewed, but I can't think of anyone but Liddell Hart at the moment, and as Nickerson reviews him I must find someone else.[7]

Could you give Mr Morley *The Spirit of the Oxford Movement* for me to see.[8]

Could you give me a new list of (1) material gone to press (2) material confidently expected, for the next number.

I should like to have some more flimsies (sheets for copies) and a good lot of continuation sheets.

Yours sincerely,

[T. S. Eliot]

1 – Moore, review of EP's *A Draft of XXX Cantos* (F&F, 1933): C. 13 (Apr. 1934), 482–5.

2 – Porteus on W. B. Yeats, *The Winding Stair*: C. 13 (Jan. 1934), 313–15.

3 – Williams, 'Fiction Chronicle' – on Arthur Waley's translations of Lady Murasaki – C. 13 (Jan. 1934), 279–86.

4 – Norman W. Porteous – (1898–2003) Scottish theologian – on Karl Barth, *The Epistle to the Romans*: C. 13 (Jan. 1934), 342–4.

5 – V. A. Demant on John Macmurray, *The Philosophy of Communism* (F&F): C. 13 (July 1934), 686–9.

6 – Belgion on Geoffrey Sainsbury, *The Dictatorship of Things*: C. 13 (Jan. 1934), 321–3.

7 – GCF wrote on 24 Oct. to Major General Sir Ernest Dunlop Swinton to ask him to review Hoffman Nickerson's *Can We Limit War?* Swinton's review: C. 13 (July 1934), 657–9. Nickerson reviewed Liddell Hart's *The Ghost of Napoleon* (F&F): C. 13 (Apr. 1934), 513–15.

8 – Christopher Dawson's book was not reviewed in C.

TO *Marcel Aurousseau*   CC

19 October 1933

Dear Mr Aurousseau,

   Mr Morley has shown me your letter, and I am writing to apologise for
my ineptitude in addressing you – for I suppose it was I who addressed
the letter in question.

   I have never previously had to write to you since I took over here, and I
am afraid that I assumed from your name that you were French (of course
I ought to have known better); the address was the one in my file, but it
has now been duly altered.

   I am sorry about the proofs.[1] The review proofs were none of them sent
to their authors this issue, as they were held up at the printer's, and did
not come in until it was too late to send them out. As things turned out,
the *Criterion* was so late that it would not have mattered, but we could
not foretell that.

   Mr Read's address is now 3, The Mall, Parkhill Road, N.W., and his
telephone number Gulliver 4538.

                                                    Yours truly,
                                                    [T. S. Eliot]

TO *Vivien Eliot*

[?23] October 1933   c/o Messrs Bird & Bird,
                                           5 Gray's Inn Square, W.C.I.

My dear Vivienne,

   It is now some three and a half months since I returned to England
and it is essential that we should without further delay come to a definite
financial arrangement. We are in future to live apart which obviously
involves separate incomes. The present plan under which Mr James
makes payments to and for you is beyond my means. On the other hand,
you should know upon what income you can rely so that you can settle
your scale of living. You have said in effect that the matter is one for my
decision. After careful consideration therefore I set down the provision
that I am prepared and can afford to make for you. For the sake of
convenience I do so under the following heads:–

1–Aurousseau had reviewed C. Delisle Burns, *Leisure in the Modern World*; John Martin,
Corner of England; and F. R. Leavis and Denys Thompson, *Culture and Environment: The
Training of Critical Awareness*: C. 13 (Oct. 1933), 134–7.

(a) I will give you £5 a week which with your own income should be amply sufficient for your reasonable needs. I propose that this allowance shall remain fixed during your Mother's lifetime but that on her death the situation shall be open to review according to our respective circumstances at that time. Should we <at that time> be unable to agree the matter had best be left to the determination of two persons to be nominated by each of us respectively or should they fail to agree to an independent individual.

(b) I will continue to pay the rent of No. 68, Clarence Gate Gardens until the expiration of the lease at Midsummer next after which you must, of course, find accommodation for yourself out of your own income.

(c) On the completion of this arrangement which must be embodied in a formal agreement my present instructions to Mr James will be cancelled.

These conditions seem to me in the circumstances to be generous and, in any event, I can do no more. I am in fact advised that having regard to my own income I shall be paying you more than by law I could be compelled to do. Mr James will no doubt confirm what I have written and I must leave it to him to settle with Mr Bird such document as may be necessary.

In conclusion let me emphasize again that the present arrangement must cease if only for the reason that, on the one hand, I cannot afford to continue it and that, on the other, you should know definitely how you stand.

Affectionately,
your Husband,
[T. S. Eliot][1]

1–Ernest Bird of Bird & Bird wrote to TSE on 26 Oct. (having been absent for a while with illness). 'Upon my arrival I received your letter of the 20th inst. and immediately sent to Haigh-Wood by hand a copy of your letter to your Wife, of which incidentally I entirely approved. The original was posted to her on the same evening so that your brother-in-law's request was duly carried out.'

Alfred E. James wrote to Bird, 3 Nov. 1933, that he had finally met with his client and discussed with her the subject of TSE's letter:

> For the first time she has shown herself willing to deal with the matter in a practical way and I think I am justified in saying that subject to the points mentioned below she has, with reluctance, decided to accept her husband's proposals. The points I have referred to are these: –
>
> 1. Mrs Eliot tells me that a sum of about £300 was in June 1930 paid by her out of her own capital in respect of the premium paid on taking over the lease of 68, Clarence Gate Gardens and she considers that the amount should be repaid to her.
>
> 2. The question of the furniture should be dealt with. I understand that the bulk of the furniture belongs to Mrs Eliot but there must be many things belonging to Mr Eliot, in particular the books which are numerous and stacked on shelves running round one of the rooms. Without the books the empty shelves would

make the room impossible. If the shelves as well as the books are removed the room would be equally uninhabitable without redecoration.

The latter point may not be of great importance but ought to be arranged between the parties before an agreement is signed.

I ought perhaps to mention that Mrs Eliot still hopes and believes that with the passage of time her husband's views will change and that this separation which he alone asks for will come to an end.'

James wrote again on 6 Nov. with regard to two new points raised by VHE:

(1) the advisability of her going to the French Sanatorium where she was some years ago, and

(2) the extension of the present tenancy of the flat for two years. She writes that unless she goes to this Sanatorium there is not the slightest chance of her getting any stronger. Possibly the doctor may have suggested this as advisable. The reason for extending the lease is her familiarity with the flat and the difficulty of a move in her state of health. Of course the suggested income would not justify the rent of £225 and the question therefore is whether your client would increase his allowance for the next two years.

Ernest Bird's response on behalf of TSE (10 Nov.) included the following points:

Mr Eliot is not prepared to bind himself to pay to his wife the sum of £300 which you say she found for the premium on taking over the lease of the flat. May be she is correct in her statement but, on the other hand, it must not be forgotten that my client has from time to time given his wife sums of money to the extent of some £600 or £700 which have been invested in her name. I am desired to add that if Mr Eliot finds himself able to do so – it is really a question of what he can afford – he will endeavour to meet his wife's wishes. The payment, however, would be entirely voluntary and must not be embodied as a condition in the deed of separation . . . The advisability or otherwise of Mrs Eliot going to a French Sanatorium does not appear to be material to the matter with which we are dealing. Should she wish to do so and the Doctor so advises there can obviously be no objection, but her husband certainly cannot bear the additional expense if that is the suggestion. In a word, he has gone to the limit of what he can do . . . Mr Eliot will certainly not agree to any extension of the tenancy of the flat. One of the main points is that this liability shall be brought to an end at the earliest possible moment – quite apart from the question of expense which Mr Eliot is not prepared and unable to meet . . .

We really have arrived at the stage when this matter must be brought to a conclusion. I therefore propose to submit to you a draft deed based on the conditions which I have already laid down and if your client declines to execute it I shall be left with no alternative but to advise Mr Eliot to act upon the conditions in question. May I suggest that you should get into touch with her brother with a view to persuading her to look at the matter reasonably.

TSE was told by Bird, as late as 22 Jan. 1934: 'Mr James writes that your Wife declines to sign any separation agreement and persists in her demand for your return. I have in reply once again pointed out to him that if she desires to do so she can take proceedings for restitution of conjugal rights.' (As far as is known, VHE never took any such proceedings.)

TO *Charles Davies*   CC

23 October 1933   [*The Criterion*]

Dear Sir,

I return herewith the manuscript enclosed with your letter of the 9th instant. It is, to begin with, inconveniently long for the *Criterion*. But the chief trouble is that, though I have read it with interest and amusement, I remain very much in the dark as to what is being satirised; so that I am left with a feeling, perhaps due to my own ignorance of successful novelists etc., that it does not seem to have been worth satirising. Still, I like the form of it, and should be interested to see any more of your work of the same kind.

Yours very truly,
[T. S. Eliot]

TO *Hugh Gordon Porteus*   TS Beinecke

24 October 1933   Faber & Faber Ltd

Dear Mr Porteus,

Thank you for sending me your drypoint, which interests me very much.[1] When I am settled in London again you must show me some more of your work.

I think, as you are interested in Yeats (as I had hoped) that you might take on two prose books of his, which I have not yet seen, but which are announced – if that is they are out in time to put them into the same review. I will ask my secretary to let you have them.[2]

To revert to your point – I don't think that you would find that the cost of good paper and a good printer makes so much difference in the cost of a review like the *Criterion* as you think. We have been into these

---

1–Porteus wrote, 21 Oct.: 'I regret my rash reference to the price of *The Criterion*: I realise that the demand for a cheaper issue (I mean cheap-paper edition, not "more popular" version) is not yet quite so wide as it is in other ways real.' He went on: 'Thank you, too, for offering me some reviewing work. I am particularly grateful for the opportunity to notice *The Winding Stair* . . . At the moment I am extremely interested in Yeats's work, because what he is doing with words as symbols I am trying to do plastically.' He enclosed a specimen of his 'proper work': 'The drypoint "proof" herewith is a design based on a Chinese radical – itself a root-image – and I have tried to intensify its force as a symbol by giving it overtones of "meaning" as well as plastic significance.'
2–In the event, Porteus did not review Yeats's *The Words Upon the Window Pane* and *Letters to the Other Island*; he did review Yeats's *The Winding Stair* in C. 13 (Jan. 1934), 313–15.

questions in the past. I fear that only altering the form, reducing the size and sweating the contributors would make much difference.[1]

Yours sincerely,
T. S. Eliot

TO *Ronald Bottrall*

TS Texas

24 October 1933   Faber & Faber Ltd

Dear Bottrall,

I am sorry to have kept you waiting so long, but my absence from London slows up the machinery in these matters.[2]

We should be glad to do your poems in the Spring at 5s. – similar format I imagine to Spender's, on a straight 10% royalty. So it is now really for you to choose which avenue of publication you prefer; and as Fraser offers certain advantages – publication before Christmas and a lower price – I don't think that I ought to try to influence you – especially as he has been interested for so long (excuse my vile typing). There are some advantages, of course, in appearing in a London perspective.

In any case, I dare say you would like to have the copy back for the time, as you say it is the only perfect one in existence. I am inclined to suggest omitting the dramatic bit at the end. It is a useful exercise, but I do think that if one is seriously interested in dramatic possibilities, that one must search for a simplified idiom. I fear that its effect at the end of a volume would be lost, at best; and I think that in a volume like this, especially when one long poem leads off, one must be on guard against giving the impression of having added anything to 'fill up'.[3]

1 – Porteus replied (25 Oct.) that he would be 'extremely interested' to review the Yeats. He added, 'I may mention that in pleading for a cheaper edition I meant an alternative issue – *de luxe* at 7/6, and on cheap proof-paper at (say) 2/6. But I know nothing about these things.'
2 – Bottrall wrote, 3 Oct., that he had been appointed to the Singapore professorship for a three-year period, and would be leaving the UK in two or three weeks: 'Before I leave I should like to make certain about the position of *Festivals of Fire*. The Minority Press has again approached me and [Gordon] Fraser is very anxious to publish the book. But I do not want to get so closely mixed up with the *Scrutiny* group. On the other hand, if Faber's cannot promise to bring out my book in the spring I must close with Fraser.' On 19 Oct.: 'Gordon Fraser has now offered to bring out my book of poems before Christmas in cloth with large page format and a new type, at 3/6, which is attractive. Unless you feel that Faber's can publish me in the spring, please let me have the typescript as soon as possible – it is the only complete one in existence.'
3 – *Festivals of Fire* carried this blurb, probably by TSE: 'Ronald Bottrall's first book, *The Loosening and Other Poems*, established him as one of the very small number of

Would you be free to lunch on November 9th (Thursday)? I think I can be up on that day.

Yours ever,
T. S. Eliot

P.S. Could you give me Empson's address, and do you know when he returns? I have been wanting to write to him for some time.[1]

TO *Tacon Gilbert* TS Valerie Eliot

24 October 1933 Faber & Faber Ltd

Dear Miss Gilbert,

I return herewith the payments sheet for October. I notice that you have knocked off odd shillings, but that is all to the good. I have only two alterations: (1) I never take payment for the reviews I write, but for regularity they should be entered, as I have done, and subtracted at the end. (2) I have always paid Periodicals contributors at the same rate as body article contributors, because it is hard and thankless work. So for 2340 words Randall should have say £4:10:- which brings the total up to about the same.

I return your list of books ordered, because I think it premature to indicate them for reviewers until I know which have come in – they may not all come, or some may be delayed. Would you kindly let me know, say at the end of the week, what books are actually in hand which I have not allocated? The two other Yeats books,[2] which should have come, should go directly to Porteus (see enclosed carbon).[3]

Yours sincerely,
T. S. Eliot

----

contemporary poets of impressive achievement and promising futures. Since then he has become well known to all who, in England and America, take an intelligent interest in modern poetry. Although critics anxious to "place" him have commonly related him to Mr Eliot, actually it is Mr Pound – the Pound of *Mauberley* and the *Cantos* – who has influenced his technique. But his poetry is his own and highly individual, for his attitude to the problems of the contemporary world, his interests and his sensibility are as unlike Mr Pound's as his technique is unlike Mr Eliot's.

'The present volume registers a remarkable development, and contains also the decided intimation of a new and most interesting phase.'

Presumably by prearrangement (since Bottrall was in Singapore), the proofs of *Festivals of Fire* were read and corrected by FRL and returned by him to F&F on 18 Jan. 1934.

1 – Bottrall promised (27 Oct.) to send Empson's address as soon as he returned to Cambridge.
2 – *The Words Upon the Window Pane* and *Letters to the Other Island*.
3 – Porteus asked Gilbert on 21 Oct. for W. B. Yeats's *The Winding Stair*.

Please send a market copy of Oct. number with review of *The Romantic Agony* to Mr Mario Praz.[1]

TO *James Joyce*

MS Buffalo

26 October 1933

Oxford & Cambridge Club,
Pall Mall

Dear Joyce,

There is a possibility of my being in Paris for a few days about the 13th or 14th November, so I should very much like to know whether I am likely to find you there. I gathered from Morley that there was a possibility of your being in Zurich.

I should be grateful if you could let me know what your plans are in this respect – I mean, that if I find that some of the people I want to see in Paris are away, including yourself, I might postpone my visit till later. In any case, your news would be very welcome.[2]

Yours ever,
T. S. Eliot

FROM *Vivien Eliot*

TS Valerie Eliot

26 October 1933

68 Clarence Gate Gardens

My dear Tom,

I have your letter of October 23rd, and have noted the contents.

Will you please write and arrange for me to meet you as soon as possible in order for me to *hand* you certain papers etc which you *must have*. Any time and place which is convenient to you.

I am sorry I have not enough stamps and so must owe you 2d.

Hoping you are *well* and with much love,

Affectionately, your wife,
V. H. Eliot

1–Praz wrote to TSE on 20 Oct. with a request for a copy of this issue.
2–FVM wrote to Paul Léon, 1 Nov. 1933: 'Mr Eliot is contemplating a short visit to Paris on the 13th November. Will Mr Joyce be in Paris then? I understand that Mr Eliot wrote to him care of you, but I am afraid that the letter may have gone to 21 Rue Casimir Perier, not to 27; and therefore may have been delayed. I'm very tempted to come to Paris with Mr Eliot.' He wrote again to Léon, 21 Nov. 1933: 'May I express our very great gratitude to you and Mr Joyce for your hospitality; in particular, I would be most grateful if you would thank Mr Joyce for the evening we had together.'

28 October 1933   Faber & Faber Ltd

Dear Ezzum They never consulted me about reprinting yr. Selected Poems at 3s. 6d. or I shd. have Protested against including the Introduction that was all very well at the first publication but had served its purpose if any and is now An impertinence. However I have just heard from a Lady unknown to me in Philadelphia she says She as just bought the Poems to read my introduction but She finds she likes your poems bettern Mine so There you are. Now here is what it is F/V/M as persuaded me to ackompny Him to Scotland on business and he Says Well wile were in Inverness Wy not Hop over the Paris? Well I dont know and maybe Donald Brace is going too[1] He thinks he would feel safer in Paris that Way and the Long

---

1–FVM wrote to George Blake (who was working for Associated Scottish Newspapers, Glasgow), 26 Oct. 1933: 'There is a grand chance of a real junket, for I propose to bring with me Eliot as well as Brace. As you know, Eliot is very interested in affairs in Scotland, though he knows comparatively nothing of the country; and Brace . . . is greatly tempted by the thought of the expedition. Of course it is rather a large army to bring, but if it does sound manageable, it would be a really fine trip for all concerned. Could you and Ellie endure three of us (I admit it is a tall order, and we won't be disgruntled if she says no) for breakfast at your flat on Armistice Saturday? We shouldn't be able to come up before the Friday night train, but we should appear ravenous by breakfast time on Saturday. The next question is if the famous car and its magnificent driver (I hope to God you had the wheels stuck on) be respectively able and willing to trundle across to Inverness at the firm's expense. The next question is about dinner at Inverness. It would seem to me a terrible load to plant on Mrs Gunn; and what I would hope to arrange, if this would be taken in good part and not upset the good lady's pride, would be supper for the four us and the Gunns at the appropriate Inverness hotel. If, then, the Gunns would let us spend the evening at their house, and allow you and me to spend the night there, Brace and Eliot ought to snuggle down contentedly at the aforesaid hotel . . . If you feel strong enough on the Sunday, and haven't run out of petrol as you did before, could we get back to Glasgow in time to take you and Ellie out to dinner and to one of the Sunday theatres? There is just this snag, that if there is a Sunday night train back to London, we must catch it for the most complicated plans are set whereby Brace and Eliot and I have to leave London at 11 o'clock Monday for Paris . . . I am going to dress Eliot up to look like Brace, and Brace to look like Eliot, and I shall wear my wig which make[s] me look like A. G. Street.' When Blake warned on 1 Nov., 'it would be well to be decently clad, for we have after all to cross three 1200ft. passes', FVM responded, 3 Nov.: 'Eliot has a bearskin coat which will keep him warm on any Crampion, and I shall try to get a deer-stalker hat for Brace. Be prepared for surprises in the shape of disguises.'

Neil M. Gunn (1891–1973), novelist, worked for many years as a clerk in the Civil Service and as an officer in the customs and excise before becoming a full-time writer. An active Scottish nationalist, he helped to establish the Scottish National Party in 1934. He and his wife Jessie (Daisy) lived in a bungalow they had built at Inverness. Works include *Hidden Doors* (1929), *Morning Tide* (published in 1931 by Porpoise Press: see TSE to George Blake, 9 Aug. 1932), *Highland River* (1937). See further *Selected Letters*, ed. J. B. Pick (1987); F. R. Hart and J. B. Pick, *Neil M. Gunn: A Highland Life* (1981).

& the Short of it is: would you care to run up to Paris about the 13 or 14 of this next month of November? That might Just tilt the ballence so far as I am concerned if you take my meaning so I will not confuse the Issue by mentioning other affairs but will close yours truly

T. S. E.

TO *John Hall Wheelock*

TS Princeton

31 October 1933 Faber & Faber Ltd

Dear Mr Wheelock,

I am interested to hear from you about Scott Fitzgerald's new novel, of which he told me something when I saw him in Baltimore in the spring.[1]

1–John Hall Wheelock (Charles Scribner's Sons) wrote on 20 Oct. 1933: 'We hope to publish in the spring Scott Fitzgerald's new novel [*Tender is the Night: A Romance*] – the one he has been working on for some time. It is still a secret, but I am writing to you in connection with a paragraph in Mr Fitzgerald's letter to us in which he speaks of a letter you wrote him sometime ago about his "Great Gatsby". He was so tremendously pleased by what you said. It has occurred to me that you might be willing to send us a word or two about that book or about his work in general, which we could use as an endorsement on the dust-cover of his new and extraordinarily interesting novel. We shall probably quote also from the review of Rebecca West and, from Gertrude Stein's autobiography, the passage in which she gives such high praise to "Great Gatsby" and "This Side of Paradise".'

Matthew Bruccoli related in *The Life of Scott Fitzgerald*, 404: 'When T. S. Eliot lectured on the metaphysical poets at Johns Hopkins University in February 1933, the Turnbulls invited Fitzgerald to a dinner they gave for Eliot. Fitzgerald regarded him as the greatest living poet and had been gratified by his praise of *The Great Gatsby*. On this occasion Fitzgerald was asked to read Eliot's poems [including a section of *TWL*] aloud, which he did effectively.' Fitzgerald wrote to Edmund Wilson (*c.* Feb. 1933): 'T. S. Eliot and I had an afternoon + evening together last week. I read him some of his poems and he seemed to think they were pretty good. I liked him fine. Very broken and sad + shrunk inside' (*F. Scott Fitzgerald: A Life in Letters*, ed. Bruccoli [1994, 2005], 227). See also Bruccoli, *Some Sort of Epic Grandeur* (1981), 345; Arthur Mizener, *The Far Side of Paradise: A Biography of F. Scott Fitzgerald* (1965), 249.

T. S. Matthews adds (*Great Tom*, 115): 'On the afternoon of Eliot's arrival at the Turnbull House Fitzgerald came to see him, and the two went off for a long walk. Mrs Turnbull remembers seeing them start off across the lawn . . . When Eliot returned from his walk, Mrs Turnbull showed him her copy of *The Divine Comedy*, and told him with some pride that she had read it. "*Begun* to read it," he corrected her.'

On 30 Oct. 1958 TSE wrote to Andrew Turnbull (son of Mr and Mrs Bayard Turnbull), who was at work on a biography, *Scott Fitzgerald* (1962): 'Fitzgerald seemed to me a very sick man at the time I saw him in Baltimore. I liked him and enjoyed our conversation, though I cannot now remember what topics were discussed. I *can* remember the carboy of gin which he produced from a cupboard toward my refreshment, very similar indeed to a carboy of gin which one of my friends at Harvard provided for me <regularly! $\$3^{00}$ a gallon> during that period. I also remember that you paid me a sort of compliment, or so I was told afterwards. Someone said that you had remarked about me that I had the manners

Before answering your question may I show my interest in another way by asking whether the British rights are still open; and if so, whether Faber & Faber might have the first view of the book? and if so, how soon? I know nothing of the subject of the book; but I start with a strong predisposition, with which I think I could infect my colleagues, in favour of it.

---

of a titmouse and the strength of a lion. I do not know quite what the manners of titmouse would be and I have certainly never felt myself to be very leonine, but the impression made by the remark was rather pleasant.'

TSE wrote on 22 Sept. 1960 to John Quentin Feller. Jr.: 'I did go to see Scott Fitzgerald and his wife in 1933 when I went down to Baltimore to deliver the Turnbull lectures there and was a guest of the Turnbulls. Fitzgerald and his wife were then living in a house on the Turnbull Estate which had been put at their disposal by Miss Turnbull. I called on them one afternoon. It was the first and only occasion of my meeting with Scott Fitzgerald in person. I remember that he looked a very sick man and I remember that he produced from a cupboard the usual prohibited carboy of bootlegged gin for my entertainment. But what we talked about I do not remember. It was a friendly occasion and I liked the man, but I retain a strong impression of sadness. And I have never read *Tender is the Night*, though I am proud to possess a copy inscribed to me by him. I still regard *The Great Gatsby* as a very fine and remarkable novel' (Bauman Rare Books Catalogue, 1996).

Fitzgerald inscribed a copy of *Tender is the Night: A Romance* (New York, 1934):
'T. S. Eliot from F. Scott Fitzgerald
   with all admiration
      all respect
      all – –
All everything from one who believes that Dr Johnson's sneer at "reciprocal courtesy between authors," must have been tossed off in a bitter moment' (TSE library).

TSE's copy of *The Great Gatsby*, which Fitzgerald sent him in Dec. 1925, is inscribed: 'For T. S. Elliott [*sic*] / Greatest of Living Poets / from his enthusiastic / worshipper / F. Scott Fitzgerald. / Paris. / Oct. / 1925.' But TSE lamented to Jack L. Morris (Tallahassee, Fla.), 3 Sept. 1959: 'Oh dear, I wish I knew what had become of the copy he inscribed for me, but – like so many of my books – it has vanished.' TSE's secretary told Jeffrey Hart, 26 Mar. 1964: 'Mr Eliot does not think that his copy of *The Great Gatsby* was inscribed by Scott Fitzgerald. In fact he is almost certain that he bought it for himself, but he cannot verify this because unfortunately he has mislaid it.' (See too Jeffrey Hart, 'Scott Fitzgerald's America', *National Review*, 19 Nov. 1963, 443–4.) EVE wrote to a Swiss researcher, Eugen Huonder, 17 Mar. 1970: 'Alas, I am sorry to say that my husband's inscribed copy of *The Great Gatsby* disappeared many years ago and there is no record of the inscription.' See Daniel G. Siegel, 'T. S. Eliot's Copy of Gatsby', *Fitzgerald/Hemingway Annual 1971*, 291–3. TSE's copy of *The Great Gatsby*, inscribed by FSF, was donated in Dec. 2007 to the John Hay Library, Brown University, by Daniel Siegel of M & S Rare Books Inc., Providence, RI.

TSE told Marie P. Harris (19 Feb. 1952) likewise: 'I liked Fitzgerald personally, and rated *The Great Gatsby* very high indeed.'

On 3 Feb. 1933 TSE wrote in a copy of *Ash-Wednesday* (1930) on the title page: 'Inscribed to Scott Fitzgerald with the author's homage T. S. Eliot' (Matthew J. Bruccoli).

TSE would later inscribe his copy of Fitzgerald's posthumous collection *The Crack-Up* (1945), for Valerie Eliot: 'I met S. F. only once: in Baltimore in 1933.'

TSE told John Quentin Feller, 22 Dec. 1960: 'You can tell Miss Turnbull, who I have no doubt is a very charming lady, that I am as shocked by her intolerance of Scott Fitzgerald's weakness [for alcohol] as she is by Scott Fitzgerald himself.'

I have never seen any of Fitzgerald's novels except *The Great Gatsby* – I seem to have heard that it is the best.

I read *The Great Gatsby* when it first appeared. At the time I knew nothing about the author; but I remember saying that it interested me more than any American novel I had read since Henry James's. Since then I have been waiting impatiently for another book by Mr Scott Fitzgerald; with more eagerness and curiosity than I should feel towards the work of any of his contemporaries, except that of Mr Ernest Hemingway.

Is the foregoing paragraph of any use to you?[1]

Yours sincerely,

T. S. Eliot

TO *Herbert Read*

TS University of Victoria

31 October 1933   Faber & Faber Ltd

Dear Herbert,

Many thanks for your letter. Your reception of my lectures is more favourable than I could have hoped.[2] As you say, they break no new ground. I had no opportunity to work on them until I reached America, and had not made up my mind what to lecture about: so I obviously had to choose some subject for which I should need to do as little new thinking and reading as possible.

---

1 – Wheelock responded to this letter, 14 Nov.: 'We now plan to bring it out in the spring under the title "Tender Is the Night". The author had originally in mind for the title "Richard Diver: A Romance", but later changed it.

'We are delighted to have the paragraph which you have so kindly sent us and will, with your permission, use it on the jacket of the book. I'm sure that this endorsement will be of great help to the book's career.

'Unfortunately another English publisher has an option on this novel and is now considering it.'

2 – HR wrote, 29 Oct. 1933: 'Morley sent me a copy of your book, and . . . I had to set everything aside and read yours straight through, with the interest and excitement you always give. You were very deprecating of the book when I saw you last, but I don't think you have any cause to be. Perhaps you break very little new ground, but what you have to affirm cannot be affirmed too often. In some directions I seem to be parting company with you – not willingly. I felt, when I sent it to you, that you would find a good deal to disagree with in *Form in Modern Poetry* [1932]. Perhaps I find my independence slowly, but I don't think there is any undue illogicality in the development of my ideas. I may seem to get nearer an acceptance of the romantic attitude, but that is only because I am attempting to include it in something wider. As for pouring out the baby with the bathwater, perhaps I just forgot all about him.'

I think the subject you suggest might be a fruitful one.[1] But it may be that any judgement between, say, Milton and Wordsworth, must be largely guided by one's outside preferences; in any case between two poets of the second order I find it very difficult to be sure just *what* is guiding me. All I can be sure of, perhaps, is that Milton is of more use to *me*!

I think that it is quite likely that I am too complimentary to Richards's sensibility, and I agree that the 'Landor' is lamentable.[2] Probably one unconsciously – in anything controversial – inclines to be very complimentary to that side of an opponent's work which one is not at the time concerned with attacking. Also it appears to strengthen one's case etc. – kind of unconscious hypocrisy of fairness. I dare say that the Five Points give away his taste: but my concern was with the religious flapdoodle; and hereafter am more concerned with (a) his explicit theory of value (b) his implicit theory of education – or perhaps the absence of any theory of education; I mean he has erected an elaborate superstructure of how to teach poetry without having really examined the question whether it ought to be taught at all.

Anyway, you will find more to query in my Virginia lectures.

I am sorry you have to do so much reviewing. No able man ought to *have* to review books after he is 35. I do hope that some better supplement to the *Burlington* will appear.[3]

I may be living in London before very long; then I hope to see you.

Yours ever,

T. S. E.

1 – 'I have never yet faced up to the problem of Milton. I want to some day – I want to write a book on Rhetoric and Poetry, and then I think I can be clearer about what I mean by the gap between Milton and Wordsworth. Actually I don't think such gaps are so impossible as you seem to think. Painting, for example, got into a wrong track in the sixteenth century from which it is only just emerging, and if painting, why not poetry? The track, in both cases, was an interesting one – lovely scenery on both sides of the lines – but it wasn't the royal road.'

2 – 'I think you have too high a regard for Richards's *sensibility*. The Landor article [IAR, 'Fifteen Lines from Landor', C. 12 (Apr. 1933), 355–70] was rather a giveaway. I don't think a man of real poetic sensibility would use such a method. It seems to me to betray a lack of confidence in his direct apprehensions. "There is no mystery about meaning", says Alexander in his new book on *Beauty and other Forms of Value*; Richards is mainly a mystery-making man.'

3 – HR was editor of the *Burlington Magazine*, 1933–9.

TO *Ronald Bottrall*   TS Texas

31 October 1933   Faber & Faber Ltd

Dear Bottrall,

I have your letter of the 27th.[1] You don't say whether you want to have
the mss. back meantime; but I think at least that you had better remove
the fragmentary play with your own hands, so the manuscript will be at
the office in my secretary's charge.

I will expect you at 1 o'clock on Thursday the 9th at the Oxford &
Cambridge Club.

Yours ever,
T. S. Eliot

TO *Geoffrey Curtis*   TS Houghton

31 October 1933   Faber & Faber Ltd

My dear Curtis,

I know that I have owed you a letter all the summer, which ought to be
on my conscience; but I had been waiting until there might appear some
possibility of my paying you a visit. I have been, for private reasons, living
in the country – I may be returning to town in a few weeks time – and
have only come to London at irregular intervals for business engagements.
At the moment, I have been laid up with a cold; but I have one or two
engagements in London on Thursday, and if I am well enough to come,
I shall try to ring up your nursing home and see if you are visitable.
I trust that your ailment is no more serious than the word 'tonsils' usually
implies.

I have been very busy re-writing lectures for publication, and have
undertaken to cooperate in a kind of play – I call it a *revue* – to be given
for the benefit of the 45 Churches Fund.[2]

If I do not see you on Thursday – or later during your stay – I still hope
that later, when I am settled in London in November, you will invite me
down to Shropshire for a weekend, or a night during the week if more
convenient, so that we may talk at leisure.

---

1 – Bottrall had replied: 'I am quite certain that it will be best for me to publish with Faber's.
My reason for mentioning Fraser's offer was that, should you have been unable to promise
anything until next autumn, it might have been wise to accept it.'
2 – *The Rock* (1934), the pageant-play which TSE wrote while residing in Surrey.

With best wishes for your convalescence and for your future work and happiness,

Yours affectionately,

T. S. Eliot

TO *Virginia Woolf*   TS Berg

31 October [1933]   Faber & Faber Ltd

My dear Virginia,

Enclosed the more pleasing of the two photographs. Except that Leonard's costume rather belies it, I should say that you were off for a day on the grouse moors; a shotgun under your elbow would look just right. You should also, by now, have received a copy of my Voice, of which there is very little at the moment, as I have been in bed with a cold.

I have not done much more about lodgings; but my present intention is to look at a room in Kensington (a district which I dislike) on my next visit to town, and if it is possible, take it temporarily while I am looking about elsewhere. This one is 3 gns. a week for one room with breakfast and dinner; but I think I ought to get two rooms, for that price or less, in some other part of London. I have got the address of a vicar in Clerkenwell who is said to know about such things. Richmond advises Camberwell, Blackheath or Greenwich. Dont want Balham: have just been reading about the Bravos.[1]

Yrs

T. S. E.

TO *Frederick C. Packard, Jr*   CC

31 October 1933

Dear Dr Packard,

Many thanks for your letter of the 20th.[2] I trust that you received my previous letter and now feel able to go ahead with your designs. I quite

---

1–Charles Bravo (1845–76) a lawyer resident in Balham, London, was fatally poisoned with antimony: the case has never been solved, but the culprit was possibly his wife Florence.

2–'I have mailed to you today six copies of your recording of "Gerontion" and "The Hollow Men" . . . I thought it best that you distribute them to those on your list abroad – as you suggested. For your convenience, the list was: yourself, Mr Faber, Mr Morley, Mrs Woolf, The Lady Morrell, and la Principessa de Bassiano [Marguerite Caetani].

agree with you that even if the returns are negligible, it is in the public interest, and can hardly be to any author's detriment, to make such records as you are producing available, and at a reasonable price. Especially for poetry, the future of this sort of thing is incalculable; and I think that the Society of Authors, and the Publishers' Associations, would do well to elaborate some international scheme of copyright and system of royalties etc. while the industry is still in its infancy. Our present arrangement however seems to me quite satisfactory for our purposes; and from my point of view it is more desirable that the records should be marketed cheaply, than that I should draw larger royalties.

I enclose my cheque for $2.15 with grateful thanks. I will write again on receipt of the records, and also hope to hear from you in reply to my previous letter. I am very much obliged for the trouble you have taken.

Yours sincerely,
[T. S. Eliot]

TO *Tacon Gilbert*   TS Valerie Eliot

31 October 1933   Faber & Faber Ltd

Did Dobrée's *As Their Friends Saw Them* come in for review? If so, John Hayward should be asked to do it. If not, please leave it alone.[1]
I NEED SOME MORE ENVELOPES
Dear Miss Gilbert,

I enclose, to clarify my own mind, a list of the material for the next number. Will you please check and let me know of any omissions. Note that this list is not in final order of publication.

'I have mailed copies to H. W. Eliot, New York, and Emily Hale, Seattle, and I have delivered copies personally to Miss Hinckley, Dr Spencer, and the Eliot House Library. This completes the list you sent; but I took the liberty of turning my copy over to your sister – I knew you would want her to have one.

'Unfortunately, the records cost a dollar apiece . . . So that the actual cost of the records was a dollar more than the amount of your cheque. The cost of shipping-containers and postal charges totaled $2.15 more . . .

'I most earnestly urge you to confirm in writing our verbal agreement that your records be included in the "Harvard University Phonograph Records" now being marketed by the University Press, under my editorship . . . I think they would sell well; but even if you received negligible royalties, the records are a dignified way of conveying the correct interpretation of your work to your readers. In fact, I should like to effect an arrangement with your publishers for selling them with the volume which contains the same poems.'

1 – Not reviewed.

I take it that you wrote to Rychner (in Frankfurt?) and that you have had no reply?

I have not received M. Millet's article (I do not know him) but I will make enquiries.

Mr Williams should have the Mansfield book. He should always let you know in good time whether the books are all wanted for the Chronicle, or whether he is reviewing them separately.

I am under the impression that you told me McEachran was reviewing Berdaiev's [Berdyaev] [*The*] *End of our Time*. If it is not too late, he should be offered *Christianity and Class War* as well.

Miss Phare's book on Hopkins, and *The Later Wordsworth* should be offered to Mr Read for short reviews. The trouble is now that he is reviewing a good deal, and it is difficult to find books that he has not reviewed elsewhere.

Mussolini's pamphlet and (if it comes) *The Italian Co-operative State* should go to Penty for short notices. *Plough & Tithe* should be for Viscount Lymington. But some of the books in the *N.S.* list may not appear till after Christmas.

Will you please try to persuade Mr Morley to bring me 3 more copies of my lectures, 1 of my Essays and 1 Poems (large paper) for me to inscribe for people.[1]

I shall probably use Demant's, Wood's and Penty's books in my commentary; and I may do a short notice of Dawson's *Oxf. Movement*.[2]

Rowse may have Strachey's book (850 words) although his letter was damned impertinent.

I will try to let you have the proofs by Thursday morning.

Yours sincerely,
T. S. Eliot

McKerson reviews enclosed.

1–FVM was to write to HR, 23 June 1965: 'On Guy Fawkes night, 1933 . . . before he said goodnight he handed me an advance copy of *Use of P. and Use of Criticism*, with an inscription he had written beforehand: "to FVM, for counsel, penance, and absolution. TSE" . . . He was a disturbed, tormented fellow at that moment' (CC in Berg, folder 15). FVM's copy is now in TSE's Library: the inscription is dated 4 Nov. 1933.

2–In the event, TSE did not write on Christopher Dawson, *The Spirit of the Oxford Movement* (1933).

TO *A. L. Rowse*[1]   TS Exeter

All Saints, 1933 [1 November]   Faber & Faber Ltd

Dear Rowse,

Thank you for your letter. I have asked that Strachey should be sent to you.[2] It seems to me that Wells can be left quiet for a time; after a few more books we can see whether he has a new phase or not. I doubt whether he will ever again be worth dealing with at length.

The proofreading was as much my responsibility as anybody's; the number was delayed owing to my absence, and at the end there was not time to send a number of things to the authors; so the proof read was read by myself and by my secretary. I am sorry.[3]

Yours ever sincerely,
T. S. Eliot

TO *Mary Hutchinson*   TS Texas

3 November 1933   Faber & Faber Ltd

My dear Mary,

I was horrified to get your card of the 25th last night,[4] and to discover that you had expected me on Tuesday – it was an odd combination of misfortunes – I don't know whether it was my Miss Gilbert or somebody else in the office responsible for the letter being delayed – ordinarily there is only a few hours delay – I wish that I had given you my address, it was only that I have not been giving it to anyone lest it might be an inconvenience to them to know it. Furthermore, I had never really grasped the fact that you expected me definitely on the 31st – I had been waiting to hear from you what date it should be – and had been looking forward with great pleasure. Finally, I was in bed anyway on Tuesday! with a cold from which I am just recovering. I am very much disappointed. May we not meet again soon. I am hoping to find a *temporary* abode in London within the next fortnight, from which to conduct a search – I hope to look

---

1 – 'I remember Eliot coming back from his year professoring at Harvard, saying in his quiet voice, "But no-one to talk to! Just no-one to talk to." If he found that – and after all he was a native – I might reasonably complain' (*The Diaries of A. L. Rowse*, ed. Richard Ollard [2003], 273).
2 – Rowse on Lytton Strachey, *Characters and Commentaries*: C. 13 (Apr. 1934), 518–20.
3 – ALR's review of Fr. David Mathew, *The Celtic Peoples and Renaissance Europe*: C. 13 (Oct. 1933), 154–6.
4 – Not found.

at a place on Monday – on Friday I am going to Inverness for a couple of days, and thence possibly to Paris for a day or two; then I want to settle in London. I will try to get you on the telephone when next in town. I am waiting to hear whether V. is prepared to sign the agreement. Please my dear Mary accept my humble apologies for the accident.

Yours,
Tom

I read of Barbara's engagement in the *Times* – please give her my felicitations.[1]

TO *John Hayward*   MS King's

6 November 1933   Oxford & Cambridge Club,
                                    Pall Mall

Dear John

Don't be silly.[2] You have been constantly in my mind. I have been in London very rarely & only for the day. In about a fortnight I expect better opportunities and will ring you up.[3]

I might have sent you a copy of the Lectures: *but* I am not proud of them. They contribute nothing new, and are lacking in structure & purpose. Please attach no importance to them.

Always affectionately,
T. S. E.

1 – The Hutchinsons' daughter Barbara was engaged to be married, on 28 Dec. 1933, to Victor Rothschild (1910–90), who would become a Fellow of Trinity College, Cambridge, 1935–9. In 1937 he succeeded his uncle as 3rd Baron Rothschild.

2 – No communication found.

3 – Smart, *Tarantula's Web*, 99: 'On the morning of 17 November there was a surprise visitor to Bina Gardens. It was Eliot, looking much healthier and happier than when he had left England. He appeared as from nowhere, invited himself to lunch and stayed all afternoon. A delighted Hayward reported that all was now well between them. He did not ask Eliot about his plans, but another visit was promised in ten days' time. Both men had had to endure the bitterness of broken relationships and now, in autumn 1933, they retreated into the familiar safe world of male camaraderie. Eliot began to have supper or dinner at least once a week at Bina Gardens.' JDH to OM, 18 Nov. 1933: 'Tom invited himself to lunch and stayed all the afternoon. I thought he looked well and he certainly appeared to be more happy than when I saw him a year – more than a year ago. I didn't ask him what plans he was making: I thought it wiser to let him tell me if he wanted to. But he promised to come and see me again in ten days' (Texas). TSE next visited 22 Bina Gardens on 26 Nov., to play chess; and again on 12 Dec., in company with BLR.

TO *G. B. Harrison*   CC

7 November 1933

Dear Harrison,

I should rather have an essay about Marston from you than from anyone else,[1] but unfortunately I accepted, about a year ago, an essay on him by a young Ph.D. in America, which I have not yet published, and which I must publish. This sort of thing is very annoying to an editor; but I am afraid there is nothing to be done about it.

I will ask my secretary to send you the book you want if it comes in.[2] If not, let me know of anything else you would like.

I have not been able to be in town much, but in a fortnight's time I will endeavour to get hold of Harris and clear up the bibliography for that unfortunate contribution.[3]

Yours always sincerely,
[T. S. Eliot]

TO *Theodore Spencer*   TS Harvard

7 November 1933   Faber & Faber Ltd

Dear Ted,

A short note to thank you for yours of the 21st, which was very welcome.[4] I must also write to Graham[5] – I was delighted with the menu – with the printed side, to think that I was not eating that food; and with the inscribed side, which made me regret afresh that I was not among that company. A few names I missed, and a few were new to me. The London

---

1 – Harrison proposed (4 Nov.) an essay to mark the tercentenary of John Marston in June 1934.

2 – Harrison hoped to review E. D. Ross, *Sir Anthony Shirley and His Persian Adventure* (1933).

3 – The contribution cannot be identified: presumably not used.

4 – Spencer thanked TSE for sending him *The Collected Poems of Harold Monro*. 'Your preface seems extremely good in print, particularly the end, which is almost terrifying. I find that sentence about there being no way out haunting me as I walk the streets, and I quoted it the other day, not using the name of the author, at the end of my lecture in the extension courses I am giving, and it kept the audience frozen in their seats for a minute after I had stopped talking. Monro's poems, as I read them, seem fragmentary, as if he never got out what he wanted to say, or perhaps never had really quite enough to get out; they don't stay in my head very long.'

5 – Graham had sent a menu card from Eliot House.

edition of the Nortons shd. have reached you[1] – mind you, when you read them, I am not proud of that piece of work – nothing new in it, and no conclusion that amounts to anything – only a *few* good things by the way; I am sure that they will disappoint you.[2] It was a grind re-writing them against time, and a worse grind to have to turn directly to do the same to my Virginia lectures – which I am not pleased with either, but they may appear a little more sensational – they break new ground anyway. Now (after a hurried visit to Inverness and Paris this week) I am to start work seriously on the text of the Revue for the 45 Churches,[3] and am working myself up into the temper of a Prophet of Israel –

> Men! polish your teeth on rising and retiring;
> Women! polish your finger-nails:
> You polish the tooth of the dog and the talon of the cat.

If they don't mind my writing that sort of thing I believe I can do it –

> Remembering the words of Nehemiah the Prophet: the trowel
> in hand, and the gun rather loose in the holster.

I have not yet seen Richards, but have passed a few notes with him – says he is very busy, but will invite me to Magdalene later.[4] I do wonder

1 – *The Use of Poetry and the Use of Criticism* was published by F&F on 2 Nov. 1933. TSE drafted, on paper printed 'T. S. Eliot / B-11 Eliot House / Cambridge', this blurb: 'This volume consists of a series of eight lectures delivered by the author in 1932–33 as Charles Eliot Norton Professor of Poetry at Harvard University. It considers the relation of the criticism of poetry to the poetry of its time, in examining several typical critics from the Elizabethan age to our own. When these critics are themselves poets, the author is concerned with the relation between each poet's theory and practice, but larger issues are raised in the historical survey. The causes which give rise to critical theory, the changes in the questions asked and in the standards posited by criticism, the changes in the function of criticism in relation to a changing social and religious background: these and other related problems are considered in the course of the book. It constitutes Mr Eliot's most explicit and most mature statement so far, on matters touched upon in his previous essays on poets and poetry.'

2 – In a preface written for the 1953 impression of *The Use of Poetry and the Use of Criticism*, TSE remarked: 'I did not find leisure to prepare the lectures until I arrived in Cambridge, Massachusetts, in the autumn of 1932, and so they had to be composed, under considerable pressure, during the period of my residence there. Nevertheless, after re-reading them twice, I found to my surprise that I was still prepared to accept them as a statement of my critical position . . . The eight lectures in this volume, in spite of the fact that some of them were written in the course of delivering the series, seem to me still valid. At least, I am ashamed neither of the style nor of the matter. Not having looked at them for many years, I found them, after two readings, acceptable enough for me to hope that republication in the present form may justify itself.'

3 – *The Rock* (1934).

4 – TSE visited the Richardses on Sun. 3 Dec. 1933. Dorothea Richards's diary: 'Eliot arrived at 4, stayed till 7. Strangely ill at east at first – mellowed fairly steadily, sat in the Peacock chair, smoking his own Turkish cigarettes. Talked about English teaching at Harvard & how the young don't now get anything out of *Ulysses* now its notoriety has gone – more

about all that basic business.[1] Between Ourselves, I don't feel very happy about his Landor analysis in the *Criterion* last spring – did you see it?[2] Aiken I missed: his novel seems very well done, if that sort of thing is worth doing, which I question; and I don't feel hopeful about him as an analyst.[3] I do hope that your private affairs are going to work themselves out in the right way.

Ever affectionately,

T. S. E.

PS. Tell Nock that Maurice Child gave me a very good dinner, with [runs off the page].

TO *Paul Elmer More*   TS Princeton

7 November 1933   Faber & Faber Ltd

My dear More,

I should have written before, but am writing now because, on re-reading your letter of September 27,[4] I discover that the copy of the English edition of my Norton lectures for you was directed to 45 Battle Road – I don't know why. So if it has not reached you will you please let me know, and I will send another.

I am not pleased with the book. The lectures themselves were prepared not under the most favourable conditions; and my choice of subject was directed by the necessity of finding one which would demand the minimum of new reading and new thinking. So there is nothing new in the book, and I fear a lame conclusion.

---

interested in Lawrence, Teaching a limited class English 26 – at 9 a.m.' (Magdalene College Cambridge).

1–Spencer wrote, 21 Oct.: 'Richards [who had stayed at Eliot House, Harvard, for a few days before sailing] seems to be getting less and less interested in literature, and more and more caught up in establishing symbols for universal communication; at the moment he is anxious to study Egyptian, Chinese, and I believe Eskimo, in the hope of reducing all language to a series of about 70 symbols, which, as far as I can gather, are not to be spoken at all, but played as tunes on little pipes constructed for the purpose. How seriously he takes all that, I don't know.'

2–'Fifteen Lines from Landor', C. 12 (Apr. 1933), 355–70.

3–'Aiken turned up last week . . . [H]is novel [*Great Circle* (1933)], he says, has interested the psycho-analysts and he is hoping to get later on a session with Freud himself, provided the old gentleman recovers from a set of rather complicated physical disorders from which he is now suffering.'

4–Not found.

The revision of these lectures, however, required pretty concentrated attention during the first part of the summer, as I was working against time so that they might be published this autumn. Since then I have had to turn to the revision of my Virginia lectures which have to be published in the spring. Again, an unsatisfactory piece of work. A good subject, I think: fundamentally a criticism of the lack of moral criteria – at bottom of course religious criteria – in the criticism of modern literature. But the treatment is very sketchy, and I cannot do anything satisfactory to myself in the time. I should have liked to ask permission to dedicate the small book to you, as I think that you would find most of it acceptable; but as I had occasion to touch upon Babbitt's Confucianism, I thought that (even if you did not wholly disapprove of what I said) you might find such incrimination embarrassing. I hope that the book (it is only three lectures) will not let me in for a great deal of controversy – not merely that Hardy is condemned – or that Lawrence appears as a *suppôt de Satan*[1] – but that on a fundamental matter like this I seem to take up an isolated position, and dissociate myself from most of my contemporaries, including Pound, Yeats, Richards, Read.

Now that these two bad jobs are off my hands, I am working on something which amuses me more: the writing of some verse choruses and dialogues for a sort of play to be given to advertise the campaign for raising money for 45 new churches in London diocese. If I have a free hand I shall enjoy it. I am trying to combine the simplicity and immediate intelligibility necessary for dramatic verse with concentration, under the inspiration of, chiefly, Isaiah and Ezekiel.

I wish that earnest people would not continually get up volumes of essays by various hands about some important subject: it is very difficult to keep out of them.

If my brother is representative, everyone in America seems to be in an intellectual fever on the subject of sound money and inflation at present. I follow the NRA (I think it is called) with interest but without understanding.[2]

I will try to get the book of Dora Greenwell, of which I had never heard before, but I gather from what you say that it is out of print.[3]

---

1 – 'Limb of Satan.' See TSE's poem 'Petit Epître' (*c.* 1917), l. 37: '*Mais c'est un suppôt de Satan!*'
2 – The National Recovery Administration, a New Deal agency set up by President Franklin D. Roosevelt to help control prices and unfair competition, and set a minimum wage, lasted only until 1935.
3 – The English poet Dora (Dorothy) Greenwell (1821–82) wrote poems on Christian themes.

Christopher Dawson's *Spirit of the Oxford Movement* is worth reading:[1] oddly enough, from this book Hurrell Froude really appears as the central figure, though I don't think Dawson quite meant him to be; and one also gets the impression (not new, but interesting from an R.C.) that Froude and Pusey were much more 'English' fundamentally than Newman, and that there is a profound difference between the Anglican and the Roman mind. I fear that Dawson's accusations of modernism against the Anglican theological mind of today are not altogether without foundation; I look forward all the more eagerly to your book, which might, I believe, date a new phase in our theology. I am not sure from what I have read that Gore was always sound, but I don't really know his work well. I look forward especially to reading your introduction.

My tedious business may reach the point of a written and signed agreement before long. It has been a great strain, and I don't know whether my mind will ever be at peace about it; nevertheless this has been the happiest summer I remember. I have been in the country, and have made visits – including Gordon Selwyn who is very able, and William Temple who is almost too able. My plans are to take a room in London in a fortnight's time, and from there look about for furnished lodgings; in a year's time, I hope to be in a position to furnish two rooms for myself as a permanent abode; but that means not only choosing a neighbourhood but knowing exactly what my financial resources will be.

I hope you will write whenever you have time.

Yours ever,
T. S. Eliot

TO *William Temple*[2]   CC Houghton

7 November 1933   [Faber & Faber Ltd]

My Lord Archbishop,

I return herewith Your Grace's memorandum of the 2nd instant, together with a few scattered comments. I fear that they are random and

---

1 – Christopher Dawson had written, 2 Oct. 1933, of his new book *The Spirit of the Oxford Movement*: 'I am afraid that it has come out too late to catch the centenary market, but I believe it is the first book to explain the precise origins of the Tracts for the Times – even Church [R. W. Church, *The Oxford Movement: Twelve Years 1833–1845* (1891)] is not wholly satisfactory there. He was writing too near to the events.'
2 – William Temple (1881–1944) – son of Frederick Temple (1821–1902), Archbishop of Canterbury – taught Classics at Oxford; was ordained in 1908; served as Headmaster of Repton School, Derbyshire, 1910–14; and was Bishop of Manchester until translated in 1929

not very helpful, but I am just going away for a week, and feared that any further delay might render them completely useless.

So far as the immediate effect, in relation to the measure before the House, is concerned, it seems to me that while any greater relief for the unemployed is unlikely, and will be said by politicians to be impossible – as in the present state of things it may be – the important point is to gain an admission of the fact that the unemployed *ought* to be better looked after than they are.

My only other point, perhaps, is that it seems to me that as the paragraphs on possible lines of advance (14–17) occupy a large proportion of the statement, they might perhaps be placed elsewhere, so as to avoid any possibility of giving the impression that the manifesto is only concerned with immediate alleviation.

I remain,
Your Grace's obedient Servant,
[T. S. Eliot]

[Enclosure]

I should be inclined to draw a sharper distinction (partly for tactical reasons, to avoid an anti-climax) between immediate relief and the ultimate goal. It is the duty of the Christian citizen to interest himself in forwarding everything comprised under 14–17. And it is also his duty to face the fact that the present assumptions of society will not do. Unless he is prepared for drastic changes in the social structure, all his efforts of an immediate practical kind can aim only at alleviation.

I do not feel satisfied with the gospel of leisure as preached for instance by the disciples of Major Douglas. It seems to me that the proportion of time that the vast majority of human beings can well occupy in amusement, games, hobbies, self-education etc. is very limited; and that we need a new conception of 'work'. What everyone needs, surely, is to be able to feel that his activity is of a special character: that his work has some other function, from his own point of view, than merely to support him; and that, if he has much spare time, that time may be spent for some larger purpose than merely to occupy his own body and mind. What the unemployed need is not merely occupation, but occupation useful to society. Under the present conditions it is not by any means

---

to the Archbishopric of York. In 1942 he became Archbishop of Canterbury. Writings include *Christus Veritas* (1924), *Nature, Man and God* (1934), *Christianity and Social Order* (1942). In the 1920s he won authority as a leader of the movement for international ecumenism – 'this world-wide Christian fellowship', as he proclaimed it.

all of those who are fully employed, even, who can feel that they are *usefully* occupied. I am a publisher myself, and I have grave doubts of the usefulness of this industry.

My point is supported, I think, by the occasional signs of discontent amongst persons who have enough private income for their needs, and who have had the education which should fit them to use leisure profitably, but who suffer from the inability to find occupation which they can believe to be useful. E.g. young Chetwynd who killed himself the other day. I mean, to extend the conception of unemployment to cover merely the 'blackcoated' as well as the labourers does not seem to me enough: this is not a disease of the less-privileged classes only, but pervades the whole of society.

Para. 13. 'Redistribution of power'. As it stands, this suggests merely more democracy, profit-sharing etc. What is really called in question is the whole joint stock limited company system, compound interest, multiplication of shareholders and employees neither of them having any power or real interest. I think that when one speaks of power, economic and financial power cannot be too clearly distinguished from political power.

With regard to occupations for the unemployed, should not emphasis be put upon their being given the opportunity to produce for consumption – have not experiments in self-contained communities been made in a small way.

While Christianity (par. 19) does not offer itself as an alternative to Communism, in that it admits the possibility of a variety of social organisations, and is primarily concerned only in so far as they may conflict with the practice of the Christian life by all, it must assert the absolute incompatibility of communism and Christianity. It must regard communism only as the completion of the actual order, and whereas communism finds this to be partly good, to Christianity they are subject to the same condemnation. I should, I confess, like to see a more positive condemnation both of communism and of the modern world than I find in this statement. I admit that I find it a little colourless.

Also, if it could be observed that when a situation is admitted by all thinking people, yet evaded by political leaders and denied by the press, except when it happens to represent the opposition, the result is apathy or a dangerously growing contempt for all political activity as at present practised by any party.

To be made clear that a statement about unemployment is not primarily a call to charitable activity, but a call to recognise that society is diseased.

TO *Customs & Excise Office*   CC

7 November 1933   [Faber & Faber Ltd]

Dear Sirs,

Referring to your form of the 2nd instant announcing the arrival of six gramophone records for me, your forms do not seem to be applicable to this importation, which comes rather under the head of 'Private Importations'. The facts are as follows.

In June of this year I made a record of my own voice, in New York, for the benefit of some phonetic studies at Harvard University. Besides such copies as the University required, twelve copies were made for me, six of which I presented to friends in America, and six of which have now been sent to me here for presentation to friends in England.

I believe that Harvard University has the intention of having more copies made for public sale, but the only copies made so far are for private distribution. I have paid $6.00 (six dollars) for the six copies which you have, the sum of a dollar each representing the cost of manufacture.

There is nothing on your forms to indicate what duty, if any, is payable on this consignment which is valued at $6.00. I should be obliged if you would make your assessment, and kindly deliver the parcel to this address, where I am giving instructions that the duty required shall be paid to the postman.

Yours faithfully,
[T. S. Eliot]

TO *F. Stringfellow Barr*   TS Virginia

7 November 1933   Faber& Faber Ltd

Dear Mr Barr,

I apologise humbly for my delay.[1] I only finished re-writing my lectures two days ago, and even now I am very dissatisfied with them for being so sketchy and rambling. However, here is the third, and I hope that it arrives in time for you. Originally I thought that the third would do for periodical publication in the form in which I delivered it; but the more

---

1 – Barr wrote in a 'panic-stricken fashion' on 17 Oct. to ask TSE to submit his article by 1 Nov.

carefully I looked at it the more defects I saw. Incidentally I have changed the title of the book: at present it is *After Strange Gods*.[1]

With sincere apologies and regrets, and best wishes,

Yours sincerely,

T. S. Eliot

TO *Messrs James & James*   CC

7 November 1933   [Faber & Faber Ltd]

Dear Sirs,

I enclose another Income Tax application which I had overlooked.

I should be very grateful if you could let me know that you have made progress with my assessments up to date. A settlement of my Income Tax arrears would considerably facilitate the settlement of my other problems.

Yours faithfully,

[T. S. Eliot]

P.S. I shall be out of town for about a week, but after that expect to be available.

1–*After Strange Gods: A Primer of Modern Heresy: The Page-Barbour Lectures at the University of Virginia 1933*, was to be published by F&F on 22 Feb. 1934 (3,000 copies, with a further 1,500 copies in Dec. 1934); and by Harcourt, Brace and Company, New York, on 19 Apr. 1934 (1,500 copies). Barr responded, 22 Nov.: 'We have had to make some small changes in it in order not to have it appear as a printed lecture. (It is against our editorial practice to publish lectures . . .) I wish you had been able to get the essay to me in time for me to secure your approval of the very minor changes we have made; but I do not believe you will object to them when you see the essay in print.'

TSE was to write to JDH (who had been asked by GCF to edit a selection of TSE's critical prose), 10 Dec. 1940: 'The two books of American essay-lectures [*TUPUC* and *ASG*] . . . were potboilers prepared under great difficulty, with no time for replenishing my mind by reading, with the motive of averting bankruptcy: the circumstances being of a domestic nature which I could not present in public extenuation. I should never have published them if publication had not been required by the foundations. They are therefore largely drivel, but amongst them, I am still persuaded (but I cannot bring myself to read them) are imbedded a few paragraphs in which I was talking about what I knew and saying something fresh. If any such paragraphs can be exhumed I shall be indeed grateful: and that is an operation I could never perform for myself.'

TO *A. C. Ellis*   CC

8 November 1933   [Faber & Faber Ltd]

Dear Sirs,

I have your letter of the 25th ultimo asking for permission to reprint certain of my poems in Braille.[1] It is not quite clear to me which poems you wish to print. In any case I am perfectly agreeable in principle, but I should like to know the names of the poems before I give my formal consent.

Yours faithfully,
[T. S. Eliot]

TO *Ezra Pound*   TS Beinecke

8 November [19]33   Faber & Faber Ltd

Respected Remus & Limb of Satan,

Re Jeff & Mutt[2] what the ell can i do about it when I avnt never yet seen that corpussle? why dont you get Round to tellin somebody to show it to me?[3] What? No, I dont know Adelphi Co, in Amerika nor does F/V.M/ but I dont like the name. Well Heres it I cant spare the money to get to Rapelow just now thats a pity besides I have Got to move into London lodgings presently and must be on and for legal-domestic affairs So am sorry you cant move north for a Bit. I ought to be able to get through more work when in London with secretary etc. and Turn towards editin your literary parerga & paralipomena so no more for the Present[4] I hope you are enjoying this nice weather yours

---

1 – Ellis, Superintendent, American Printing House for the Blind, was producing in braille *The Book of Living Verse*, ed. Louis Untermeyer.

2 – In referring to EP's forthcoming *Jefferson and/or Mussolini*, TSE jokes on the title of the popular newspaper comic strip *Mutt and Jeff*, syndicated from 1907 to 1983. *Jefferson and/or Mussolini* was ultimately to be published in London in summer 1935 by Stanley Nott and by Boni & Liveright, New York, 1936. EP wrote in a foreword, '40 publishers have refused it . . . It is here printed verbatim . . . as record of what I saw in February 1933.'

3 – EP replied, 11 Nov.: 'Oh yuss/ Polinger will send you the J/muss unless Routledge nabs it.'

4 – FVM wrote to EP, 8 Dec.: 'The Rt. And Rev. Prelate has full possession of a typewriter, and part-time of a "Type-writer", and there is no reason at all why he shouldn't be one of the cheerfulest and activest of correspondents. If he isn't, will you please to tell me so and I will go upstairs and prod him.' EP to FVM, 12 Nov.: 'A DANGEROUS departure from his usual conservatism shows in an "urgent" letter from the Reverendissio ElYot/ he offers to "DO" something to right matters.'

'I can not encourage this / in first place it is agin his natr/ (better or worse).'

T. S. E.
My Wigg won't be ready till the Spring[1]

TO *Ezra Pound*   TS Beinecke

8 November 1933   Faber & Faber Ltd

Dear Child of Satan,

   In yr. last Epistle to the *New English Weekly* you refer to 'episcoaple slum owners'.[2] Not clear from syntax whether past or present. Please let me know by return which bishops and what slums, and any usefull details, so that I may do what I can to right matters.

                                Yrs. etc.
                                T. S. E.

TO *Stephen Spender*   TS Northwestern

8 November 1933   Faber & Faber Ltd

Dear Spender,

   I have been meaning to write to you for some time, but have hardly been in London, and there has been no possibility of a meeting. In about ten days time I hope to be more in town, and hope that I can get hold of you for a meal.

                                Yours ever,
                                T. S. Eliot

1–Added by hand. EP (11 Nov.): 'Sorry about the wig// wd/ have liked you here, even without.'
2–EP had commanded on 2 Oct.: 'As fer makin the bustuds real/ you git the current New Eng/ Weekly sept. 28 an read my 38 epistle to the gophesians.'
   'that will putt a bit of solid under the lyric disgust of XIV and XV.'
   EP, '"Selfless Service"', *The New English Weekly* 4: 4 (9 Nov. 1933), 96:
   'Sir, – Miss Margaret Shaw's attack on Miss Jameson drags in the "ideal of selfless service."
   'This is the old ticket to heaven swindle and it won't wash. The dirtiest episcopal slum-owners and poverty-maintainers have been dangling this bag of vomit for too many centuries.
   'A little honest knowledge of Anything ought to cure a contemporary literate. (A) The thing is bunk in itself, – "Selfless service," – as you can't benefit mankind without ultimately sharing in the benefit. (B) The cheque is on the non-extant bank, or on one whose existence is not subject to proof.'

TO *Allen Tate*   TS Princeton

8 November 1933   Faber & Faber Ltd

Dear Tate,

I will write something for you if I can in the time,[1] but I have taken on
a spare time job of a sort with which I am unfamiliar, so that I have no
idea how much time it will take: i.e. writing the choruses and dialogues
for a sort of play to be given in the spring; and they will want to start
rehearsing in February.

The only thing I am doubtful of in your programme for a book is its
looseness. It seems to me that you, as editor, should be something of a drill
sergeant – if there are enough contributors near enough to get together for
a preliminary meeting so much the better – but so many of these books
are just collections. If you could think of some more precise niche for me
to fit myself into, so much the better again. Here's wishin you, anyhow,
and hoping I can get down to your territory in a year or two. I had a fairly
cheerful letter from John G. the other day, thanks to your mentioning me
to him.[2]

Yours ever,
T. S. Eliot

TO *Geoffrey Curtis*   MS Houghton

10 November 1933   Oxford & Cambridge Club,
                                  Pall Mall

My dear Curtis,

Alas! I came up for the first time yesterday, & rang up your nursing
home, to be told that you had left the day before. In so far as it implies

1 – Tate endeavoured to explain (3 Oct.) that his proposed symposium was to 'support the
need of what I called a Conservative Revolution': 'This kind of revolution seems to me to
depend solely upon restoring the land to something of its old autonomy: if this is to happen
in "western civilization", it will have to happen here, because we are the only people left
who have an abundance of land . . . We shall probably have to say somewhere that society
in modern times is a focus of interests that cannot be served equally; that somebody has got
to suffer; that it is time for concentrated capital to suffer; that, in short, the liberal pretense
of serving all interests in the end serves none, but rather paves the way of communism, etc.'
2 – John Gould Fletcher wrote to TSE, 23 Oct., from Little Rock, Arkansas (where he
expected to remain): 'I'm glad I came back, as Europe has very little to offer me now – I
hope to be more generally useful over here . . . I experience a remarkable joy in living in a
country so agrarian as this – where no one gets excited over anything more subtle than the
price of foodstuffs and cotton.'

that your recovery was rapid, I am glad, but for myself very disappointed.

At any time between the beginning of December and next summer I should like to spend a night with you – especially if you are unlikely to be in London. Let me hear in any case.

Affectionately,
T. S. Eliot

TO *Virginia Woolf*

MS Berg

10 November 1933   Oxford & Cambridge Club

Dear Virginia

I was sorry, extremely sorry, missing a good dinner in the best company, but through a hitch at 24 Russell Sq. I didn't get Mary's confirmation of the date till 2 days after the event.

Yes 3 gns. is far too much, with the dollar disappearing; so if you *should* take a walk in Islington I should be grateful to your discriminating eye.[1] Within the fortnight I should be able to lunch with Clive, if he were still in town: and shd. like to have tea with you.[2]

Yours ever,
T. S. E.

1–VW wrote in an undated note ('Saturday', *c.* Nov. 1933): 'I am sorry to have been so long answering your letter; and to have no contribution to make even when I do. I asked a friend of mine who lives in Great James Street about rooms in that quarter (which has great advantages); but he says theyre all let in flats; but he is enquiring among neighbours who might be ready to turn out for a year. Then Argylle Square; near Kings Crosss. An admirable square, but sunk low, so that baths are shared and the lodgers are transitory and dubious – I'm afraid thats no good. On the whole Leonards hotel plan seems most feasible. His mother tells me that in her hotel, by Earls Court station, single rooms high up are to be had with all meals, fire, service and light – everything – for 5 guineas weekly. This is a respectable quarter, and I think up in the Islington or Holborn district the charge should be lower. I'll look for hotels as I take my afternoon walk. I'm very sorry to be so inconclusive, but that seems to be the sum of my observations. And perhaps by now you have found something suitable elsewhere' (EVE).

2–TSE went to tea with VW on Wed. 29 Nov.

17 November 1933   Oxford & Cambridge Club,
                                    Pall Mall

My dear Spender

I have been away, so waited to answer your letter till I had read your review.[1] Excuse the writing, as a pen is painful for me.

Your criticisms are much milder than my own; in fact you give me the impression of having gone as far as possible to be generous, perhaps too far. The lectures were written under great difficulties, from hand to mouth: I was indeed forced to pick my way carefully so as to produce what I could with the minimum of new reading & new thinking. I am keenly aware of their lack of direction and conclusiveness. I was quite sincere in my preface in saying that I would not have published them had I been free not to.

There are, I think, two misunderstandings. I have not got my book here, but I believe that in saying that I was not concerned with politics,

1 – Spender apprised TSE, 11 Nov.: 'I have just written a review of your book for the *New Statesman*. It is too long, so they may cut it about. I hope you wont think it impertinent, I have tried very hard not to be.'

Spender's review, 'The Use of Poetry', *NS&N*, 6: 143 (18 Nov. 1933), 637–8, opened with the comment that TSE 'certainly does succeed in making us all think; nonetheless, there is no very strong thread of argument running through these lectures':

'Where one may wish that Mr Eliot were a little more positive is in his attitude to political morality, and in his occasional references to religion. He explains on the first page of his first lecture "the present lectures will have no concern with politics." Yet frequent references to what I understand to be (in the widest sense) politics are made; indeed, if one discusses Trotsky's *Literature and Revolution*, and at the same time declares that one is not interested in politics, it seems to me that one is striking a political attitude – an attitude of superiority . . . Now I believe that Eliot is a true poet, and I believe he has "walked through hell"; I think also that he is a writer of genuine humility, and often a writer of great frankness: there are plenty of examples of such writing in this book. Therefore it seems the more surprisingly inconsistent that he often gives the impression of being snobbish and superior . . .

'One of Mr Eliot's gambits is this habit of making a loosely expressed phrase, even where its meaning is clear, seem meaningless. But what are we to think when he himself speaks thus of Arnold: "It is a pleasure, certainly, after associating with the riff-raff of the early part of the century, to be in the company of a man qui sait se conduire"? Who are the riff-raff? We ask in the manner that he himself has taught us . . .

'The violent prejudices which stick out of this book are apparently the symptoms of an extreme self-consciousness. Eliot often makes generous judgments, as in his lecture on Coleridge. In a lecture on Shelley and Keats, however, he exhausts himself in trying to overcome his dislike of Shelley's poetry, and he cannot restrain his dislike of the man . . . D. H. Lawrence was generous in his dislike of Shelley, and also of Goethe (which he shared with Mr Eliot), but Mr Eliot is not . . . He shares with Flaubert the dislike of anyone not staying in his pigeon-hole.'

I was referring quite simply to the quotation with which I opened – i.e. merely reminding the audience that that was only a topical joke, & that the lectures had nothing to do with immediate affairs. The lecture was delivered three days before the Presidential Election. Had I meant more, your stricture would be quite just.

The second point is less vital. My joke about the 'riffraff' was partly ironic – i.e. was intended partly as a caricature of Arnold's own attitude. Arnold is such a bloody gentleman.

In short, your only weakness consists in taking the lectures too seriously.

I must wait till tomorrow when I am back at my typewriter, to write about your story. G.C.F. told me you thought I might be offended by the review – possibly in its complete form it is more severe – if so, it does the *N. Statesman* no credit to have toned it down – but, as it stands – I should not think well of anyone so thinskinned as to be offended by that![1]

I hope to see you in a week or so.

Yours sincerely,
T. S. Eliot

TO *Theodore Spencer*   PC MS

[November] 1933

I should have posted this from Pitlochry but had no time. I tried to get you a P.C. with a distillery on it: they are all working overtime, you will be

---

1–Spender was to recall, in 'Remembering Eliot' (1966): 'In 1933 I published a review attacking some of his views in *The Use of Poetry and the Use of Criticism*. I felt miserable in doing so, and wrote to him apologizing' (*The Thirties and After* [1978], 255). In his early autobiography he elaborated in a way that goes beyond the evidence of TSE's letter: 'Quite early in our relationship I wrote a review of Eliot's essays, criticizing his political attitudes and certain implications of his traditionalism. After this had been published, it grieved me, and I sent a copy of the review to him, together with a letter of explanation. Eliot wrote back an answer which, while disagreeing with one or two points in my review, was gentle. He ended by saying that I must always write exactly what I felt when I criticized his work and that our public relationship had no connection with our private one' (*World Within World* [1951], 148). TSE told Anne Ridler, 26 Nov. 1943: 'I was, once, more annoyed by his expressing concern (later in conversation) lest I might have been annoyed by something he wrote about me, than by what he had written; because he didn't seem to grasp the difference between one's being irritated by unfavourable criticism, and one's being annoyed at misrepresentation.'

glad to hear. The whisky gets better the farther north you go, & is superb in Inverness.[1]

T. S. E.

TO *James Joyce*

TS Buffalo

19 November 1933   Faber & Faber Ltd

My dear Joyce,

 I did not have the opportunity, amongst so many people, to [inform] either you or Mrs Joyce, that I am arranging a private separation, and have not been living with my wife since my return from America. I am writing at once, because I feared that you might meanwhile hear this information from some other source, and would wonder why I had not told you myself.

 I was very sorry to have to leave so early the other evening, violating all my instincts; but the next time I come we will arrange it differently. Please let me know whether you find anyone to go to Zurich with you.

Yours ever,
T. S. Eliot

TO *Tacon Gilbert*

TS Valerie Eliot

21 November 1933   Faber & Faber Ltd

Dear Miss Gilbert,

 I forgot to add this note on Dandieu to the Commentary which I gave Mr Morley to hand you.[2] Will you please give it at once to the printers and ask them to set it up as the last paragraph of my Commentary.

1–FVM, *Literary Britain: A Reader's Guide to Writers and Landmarks* (1980), 463: 'Neil Gunn . . . was living at Inverness in the years between the two world wars when George Blake and I, and on one occasion T. S. Eliot, were privileged to stay . . . One item I remember from that between-wars drive from Glasgow to Inverness with Eliot was the pause we made on Rannoch Moor. It was some weeks later that Eliot handed me his short poem, one of the few *Landscapes* that he cared to preserve, called "Rannoch, by Glencoe".'

2–Arnaud Dandieu, who had died in Aug. 1933, aged thirty-five, was co-author with Robert Aron of 'Back to Flesh and Blood', C. (Jan. 1933). His works included *Marcel Proust: sa révélation psychologique* (1930), and (in collaboration with Aron) *Décadence de la nation française* (1931), *Le cancer américain* (1932) and *Le révolution nécessaire* (1933). Also with Aron he founded in 1933 a quarterly review, *L'Ordre nouveau*; and he had been working (with a young mathematician, Claude Chevalley) on a metaphysical essay. TSE remarked: 'I regret having had no personal acquaintance with M. Dandieu, of whose personal

And will you please put in a slip with each record you send off, informing the recipient that it is to be played with a wood or thorn, not a metal needle?

Yours sincerely,
T. S. Eliot

TO *R. Webb-Odell*[1]   CC

21 November 1933   [Faber & Faber Ltd]

Dear Mr Webb-Odell,

I can now write more fully in reply to yours of the 9th instant.[2]

---

charm and conversational powers I had heard much. The direction and the quality of his thinking struck me as a most promising symptom among the younger generation in Paris; and his death is a loss to *The Criterion* as well as to the intellectual life of Paris' (*C.* 13 [Jan. 1934], 278).

Montgomery Belgion, who had become a friend of Dandieu, had told TSE on 15 Aug. that 'quite apart from his work, he was a very remarkable human being'; and he was in addition a great conversationalist and a kind man.

1 – The Revd Rosslyn Webb-Odell, MA (1879–1942), Rector of St Anne's, Soho; Organising Director of the Forty-five Churches Fund for the Diocese of London; editor of *The Christian Faith: a series of essays . . .* (1922) and *Church Reform* (1924).

2 – Looking back in 1959, TSE was to consider the year 1933 'good . . . as that is the year in which I broke into Show Business. In that year I was commissioned to write the text for a mammoth Pageant to advertise the need for 45 new churches in the outer suburbs of London' ('Class of 1910: Fiftieth Anniversary Report, 1960', Harvard University; written 29 Nov. 1959).

Webb-Odell wrote, 9 Nov. 1933: 'As for the fee for your invaluable service, I should like to know if the sum of a hundred guineas, tentatively mentioned, may be taken as agreed upon. As to the publication of your work: – (1) quite clearly the ultimate copyright must be yours; (2) we should certainly wish to sell it at the Theatre, and to print it in such a form that the price would not be prohibitive, but would yield some profit on sale. I think, as we shall have to bear the expenses of that printing, we should have some good share of the profits of the sale *there and then*, while leaving all subsequent sales to you, as well as the rights of production afterwards in another form. . . . Also, is there any possibility that would be advantageous to either party, of a dearer edition, issued at the same time at 2/6 or 3/- and with some illustrations – to be carried off as a *souvenir*?' (Bodleian: MS. Don. D. 44 f. 1 & 1[R]).

The Three Voices of Poetry (1953): 'Twenty years ago I was commissioned to write a pageant play to be called *The Rock*. The invitation to write the words for this spectacle . . . came at a moment when I seemed to myself to have exhausted my meagre poetic gifts, and to have nothing more to say. To be, at such a moment, commissioned to write something which, good or bad, must be delivered by a certain date, may have the effect that vigorous cranking sometimes has upon a motor car when the battery is run down. The task was clearly laid out: I had only to write the words of prose dialogue for scenes of the usual historical pageant pattern, for which I had been given a scenario. I also had to provide a number of choral passages in verse, the content of which was left to my own devices: except

We agree upon the fee of one hundred guineas for my share of the work. I suggest that the profits of the first edition of the play should go entirely to the Fund. It should of course embody descriptions of the pageantry etc., and so many other persons will have contributed to the whole that I could not think of it as a personal production. In fact I think that the current edition should be as impersonal as possible, giving the names of everyone concerned, with no emphasis upon my name as the author of the text. If, after say three months, I should wish to bring out my own contributions, either as a separate whole or in a collected volume of verse, I should be free to do so. There remains the technical question of the name in which the first copyright should be taken out – I will consult my colleagues on this point.

In consideration of forgoing any profits, however, I should ask that my firm have the job of publishing the booklet of the play. It ought to be done in paper, I should think, at a shilling. I think there is a good deal to be said for a smaller printing of an edition with illustrations: for this type of performance, I should expect that many persons would like to have photographs of the scenes, as well as the text, as a souvenir. The details of this might be worked out between Mr Browne and our production manager, Mr de la Mare.

It is, in fact, a term in my contract with Faber & Faber, that they have the option on all my work in book form; so that their publishing the book would avoid this complication; and I am sure that they can do it as cheaply and efficiently as anyone. It is a matter for you to decide, but I should think it would be well – for advertisement, to have the book on sale at some bookstalls as well as at the theatre, from the opening day on, or perhaps shortly before.

For a publication of this kind, I suggest that the arrangement between the Fund and my firm should be on a commission basis; but if you are in accord in principle I should like to put you in touch with our Chairman, Mr Geoffrey Faber, for definitive arrangements.

Yours sincerely,
[T. S. Eliot]

---

for the reasonable stipulation that all the choruses were expected to have some relevance to the purpose of the pageant, and that each chorus was to occupy a precise number of minutes of stage time . . . This chorus of *The Rock* was not a dramatic voice; though many lines were distributed, the personages were unindividuated. Its members were speaking *for me*, not uttering words that really represented any supposed character of my own.'

TO *Tacon Gilbert*

TS Valerie Eliot

21 November 1933   Faber & Faber Ltd

Dear Miss Gilbert,

I enclose Cover Order for the January number. I am sorry that I did not get this to you sooner; but I mislaid the list of contributions which you sent me. I also cannot lay my hand on a proof of Bedoyère,[1] so that I cannot estimate the length exactly; but I make it to be about 148 pages without Commentary and Bedoyère: so that it should be about 170 pages in all.

I understand that six gramophone records have arrived for me. Will you please give one to Mr Faber and one to Mr Morley. Three should be sent to (1) Mrs Woolf, 52 Tavistock Square, (2) Mrs Hutchinson, 3 Albert Road, Regents Park (3) Mrs Monro, 38 Great Russell Street. The two in Bloomsbury could be delivered by hand; if the one in Regents Park cannot be delivered in the same way, it had better perhaps wait for me rather than risk the post. The sixth please hold for me.

Please do not send me anything here after tomorrow.

Yours sincerely,

T. S. Eliot

The short notices in the order you gave them, with correct initials.[2]

TO *Montgomery Belgion*

CC

21 November 1933   [Faber & Faber Ltd]

Dear Belgion,

This paper has got very smutty because I turned the ribbon upside down after I started, but it doesn't seem to type any more clearly than before.

I am sorry that I could not answer your letter of the 10th at once; but I was already away when it arrived. I went first to Scotland, and had only two days in Paris; but I hope to be able to go again within a couple of months. I saw Massis, and got Maulnier's address from him; but was unable to look up any new people. I shall certainly try to see both Aron and Daniel-Rops on the next occasion.[3] Which reminds me that I wished

---

1 – Michael de la Bedoyère, 'Censorship: More or Less?', C. 13 (Jan. 1934), 252–69.
2 – Sentence added by hand.
3 – Belgion had written on 10 Nov.: 'It will be nice if you can mention Dandieu in your next Commentary, as – it is not my doing – the bereaved mother is looking forward to your doing so.

to ask you to let me know whenever you had any interesting enough material to write about to make another French Chronicle, please let me know.[1]

My book is not one of which I am proud.[2] Owing to circumstantial difficulties, I was unable to do any work on the lectures until I reached America; several of them were only finished on the very morning before delivery. I re-wrote them this summer, again under pressure of time, but there was not very much that could be done without scrapping them completely and writing another book. I was forced to choose some subject on which the minimum of new reading and new thinking would be necessary for me; I am painfully aware of lack of structure and coherence, still more of any conclusion – so that I think any reader may well wonder whether the book has any justification. All that it can offer is in occasional passages and scattered remarks.

I am very sorry if I have misrepresented you. I am away from my books, but as soon as I can get hold of a copy of *The Human Parrot* I will look up the passage. It is the more regrettable because a disagreement with you played no vital part. My difference with Read is more important, still more so my difference with Richards – whom I do not think I have misrepresented, but whose own opinion on the point I have not yet

---

'In Paris you should, I suggest, see Robert Aron, Dandieu's collaborator, who is carrying on their formerly joint work. He can put you in touch with [Thierry] Maulnier. He is to be found at the *NRF*, where he deals in the foreign rights the firm has to sell.'

1 – 'French Chronicle', *C.* 13 (July 1934), 642–55.

2 – 'On p. 126 of your new book, it seems to you that I make my own mistakes. Isolated, the remark is no doubt unimpeachable. But in the context it appears as if you found that I had not realized how "what the poet experienced is not poetry but poetic material", how "the writing of poetry is a fresh 'experience' for him", and how "the reading of it, by the author or any one else, is another thing still", and it happens that I have said precisely this in *The Human Parrot* and elsewhere and in talking with you.

'You may accuse me of exaggerating the importance of what you say, but the consequences of such an unjustified criticism are not, it seems to me, purely literary . . . Already plenty of illiterate and half-baked people are only too disposed to believe that I am a bletherer, and that adds to my very great difficulty of making a living . . . It is one thing unnecessarily to disparage a man you do not know and one thing unnecessarily to disparage [I. A.] Richards, whose reputation is established, and another thing unnecessarily to disparage me or, say, [John Gould] Fletcher, whose position is not assured and who is "up against it" . . .

'Your book I have tried to review for the *Dublin* . . . Broadly, it seems to me that when in these lectures you theorize you raise hopes you do not satisfy and that your real virtue as a critic lies in what you have to say of particular poems, only you have so little so say of that kind. And I think it is a pity such an overwhelming share in the book falls to Richards. [Herbert] Read tells me he has the same objection and apparently he does not approve of what you say about him.'

Belgion concluded: 'I have not made £30 this year, and I have nothing but what I earn.'

heard – no doubt he will think that I have: I fear that the difference of temperament is too wide there for any currence to be arrived at.

It seems to me, of course, that you exaggerate my possible influence, especially as I only refer to one passage in passing, and am not attacking any principal position. I do not see how anyone could get the impression from my remark that your book is negligible; and surely anyone who was at all interested in the subject, and was unacquainted with your work, would merely be induced to look it up for himself. (And by the way, have I ever written anything disparaging about Fletcher?).

I don't know what can be done except, if you are reviewing the book for the *Dublin* or elsewhere, for you to call attention to any misrepresentation, and for me to write a letter to the Editor for publication to make amends, in so far as I find that I have gone astray. Or you could write to the *Criterion*, and I could reply in the same number. It seems unlikely that the ordinary reviews will say enough about the book to hang a letter on: those I have seen have been quite futile – (why are reviewers so much less interested in what one says than in the nasty way in which one says it? they seem to make their reviews the pretext for airing some almost personal grievance).

One point – I can't feel that I have given too much space to Richards – though I admit that the lectures have no form or proportion whatever. You say yourself that he is 'established'; well, and except for your own essay, I don't think that anyone has questioned his work seriously; I dare say most people are frightened by his apparatus. That's the way in England. And I do think that it is more important to question writers who are still young, than decrepit ones like Russell and Wells. I think you might accomplish something if you would turn your attention to the philosophy of Herbert Read, and John Macmurray – the latter has a most questionable philosophy which looks to me as if it might have a certain vogue.

I expect to be in town shortly – I could lunch on Tuesday or Wednesday next, I am fairly sure, if you should be in town. And from [the] week after next, almost any day would do.

Yours ever,
[T. S. Eliot]

TO *Maurice Haigh-Wood*   CC

22 November 1933   [Faber & Faber Ltd]

My dear Maurice,

I am very sorry for the delay in answering your letters (of the 13th, 15th, and 18th) but after a hurried trip I found several matters which had to be cleared away at once. I will try to answer all your points herewith.[1]

(1) I am in favour of taking up the Metropolitan Electric new shares. This amounts, I gather, to £20.

(2) I concur in the desirability of realising the corporation stocks already agreed upon; and I await your suggestions for re-investment. But especially if we re-invest the £400 from N.S.W. in industrials, I think that the sum realised by sale of corporations should be reinvested as nearly as possible in stocks of the same kind.

(3) Of the suggestions in your letter of the 16th I like the idea of Imperial Chemicals best. The reports of Spillers and Enfield Cables did not seem very optimistic. But I have no objection to your suggestion of the 18th, North Eastern Electric, if you are still in favour of that. I do not think that £400 more of Electrics would be injudicious.

I am sorry that you have met with so much and various difficulty; but it was rather as I expected. If you think fit to go ahead with Imperial Chemical or North Eastern I agree.

Yours ever,
[Tom]

I return reports herewith.

FROM *Vivien Eliot*   MS Valerie Eliot

Wednesday 22 November 1933   68 Clarence Gate Gardens

My dear Tom,

I am ill. Will you come and see me.
Please come, at once.

Your wife, with *love*
Vivienne Eliot

1–TSE and MHW were executors of the estate of Charles Haigh-Wood, father of MHW and VHE, who had died in 1927.

TO *Virginia Woolf*   PC MS Berg

25 November 1933   Oxford & Cambridge Club,
                                          Pall Mall

I do think this is rather scurvy of you! Besides, I should have been able to
guide your tottering footsteps back to Tavistock Square. However, I *shall*
come to tea nevertheless (is nevertheless pleonastic here?), on Tuesday,
and tipsily, too.

                                                        T. S. E.

TO *I. A. Richards*   PC MS Magdalene

27 November 1933   Faber & Faber Ltd

Should like to very much, but am only there for weekend & KP[1] seems to
have filled the time up. We still [*sc.* shall] have to see when the time comes.
Are you ever likely to spend a night in London?

   Wd. you be willing to write something about Jesperson for me? I have a
big new book for review. Cd. provide some of his earlier works –[2]

                                                        T. S. E.

TO *Vivien Eliot*   MS Valerie Eliot

27 November 1933   Faber & Faber Ltd

                              (Copy)[3]

My dear Vivienne
   I am very sorry to learn that you have not been well: I hope that you are
being well looked after. I do not feel, however, that it would be suitable
for me to come to see you, or for us to meet until these legal arrangements
are completed.

                              Affectionately your husband,
                              T. S. Eliot[4]

---

1 – Kenneth Pickthorn.
2 – Otto Jespersen (1860–1963): Danish linguist. IAR did not write about him for C.
3 – Written in TSE's hand.
4 – Nearly two years later, in mid-July 1935, VHE pasted into her diary 1935 – Bodleian MS.
Eng. misc. e. 878, fol. 127 – this statement: 'I have not seen Tom's *signature* for 2 *years*, nor
received any letter from him *since Nov. 27th 1933*. This seems to me a very important point.'
Ernest Bird (Bird & Bird) wrote to TSE, 28 Nov. 1933: 'I am much obliged to you for telling
me yesterday of the communication received from your Wife. Frankly, I think it is another

TO *Messrs Monro, Saw & Co.*   CC

28 November 1933   Faber & Faber Ltd

Dear Sirs,[1]

I understand from Mr James Joyce that you are his solicitors in this country, and we are now his English publishers. We shall be publishing his *Work in Progress* when it is completed, and are meanwhile exploring the possibility of bringing out a new edition of *Ulysses*. I am therefore writing to you to ask you to be so kind as to provide us with such facts in the history of the case as may be in your possession, and as would be relevant to this venture.

First of all, I am told categorically by Mr Joyce that *Ulysses* is copyright in this country, and in his own name. I should be obliged if you could confirm this statement from your own knowledge. If this is so, the situation is materially different from that in America.

Together with my colleague Mr Morley, I went to Paris last week and discussed matters with Mr Joyce and with his Paris solicitor, M. Paul Léon. Subsequently M. Léon sent us a memorandum of the relevant facts in his possession, but these leave gaps which must be filled before we can proceed further.[2]

------

attempt to get you to the flat and I therefore entirely approve of the reply that you had made a copy of which has reached me this afternoon.'

1 – First published in James Joyce, *Letters*, ed. Ellmann, III, 292

2 – Paul Léon wrote to FVM, 19 Nov. 1933: 'I cannot refrain from thinking that it would be time to do something about bringing out ULYSSES in England. I am sure (and I am not talking without reasons) that should the H. O. be approached you will find the authorities (though naturally unwilling to commit themselves or promise anything) less difficult to be talked to on the matter than they ever have been. In fact I think that unofficially they would hint that personally they will not start a case and ban the book. Of course the Director of Public Prosecution is at the mercy of letters from private persons who will complain but I am sure that he will think twice before starting a case himself.

'Obviously the winning of the case in America will constitute a strong card in our game but I do think that even independently of this something should be done in England. From the cuttings concerning L. Golding's book you will see how public opinion is being prepared independently from us. Unless something is actually started right away it will mean a terrible amount of time wasted for you must not forget that there is a constant stream of copies going to England which take away the readers of the eventual British publication.

'I hope you will find your way in devising some scheme; it will not mean great investment of capital since a case can be provoked following the American precedent of having a copy of the current edition seized by the Customs authorities.'

In a postscript: 'Mr Joyce, whom I have just seen, wishes me to tell you that in view of the lack of courage which he had met with up to now, he is strongly advised to undertake the publication of Ulysses in G. B. himself.'

Léon's memo, 'Notes on the circulation of the English edition of *Ulysses* in England':

1). In the last week of April or in the first week of May 1932 there appeared in the *Evening Standard* an interview with one of the keepers of the British Museum. This gentleman is quoted as saying (the question he was interviewed on was "banned books") and emphasizing that *Ulysses* was not a banned book, that they took it off their catalogue at their own discretion and that they never made any difficulty in giving it to the reading public in fact to any person who had a valid reason to alledge [*sic*] for reading it. In fact *Ulysses* had been read so much that they had to acquire several copies and had them bound. Their proceedings would naturally have been different if *Ulysses* had been under a ban of a decision taken by a Court.

2) I do not know the details of the seizure of the 499 copies of the second edition of *Ulysses* by the Custom Authorities at Folkestone (the entire edition was of 500 copies). You may obtain the entire correspondence between the customs and the then editor of *Ulysses* Mr John Rodker from this gentleman (whose address can be found in the P.O. Directory). The Customs at the time refused to send the copies back to France and the Chief of the Folkestone Customs Office is supposed to have destroyed them all. As a matter of fact, there are strong reasons (among which words said by the Customs Officers themselves) showing that this was not done and a copy of this edition can, I am sure be found on sale in London. It is an open secret that *Ulysses* is sold in London. Mr Stuart Gilbert at the time in India had a copy sent to him from Oxford from Messrs Blackwell to Burmah – This copy bears the imprint: Printed for the Egoist Press by John Rodker, Paris.

3) Finally last year *Ulysses* was placed as a text book in Cambridge on the list of a young professor's [FRL] lectures on Modern English Litterature. The course actually took place and it is an open secret that a copy of *Ulysses* is easily obtainable (though expensively) at any bookseller of the University cities. In fact the course would have passed unnoticed had not this young lecturer applied to the Home Office to obtain a copy officially. As a result his course and his private life were investigated by the H.O. authorities and the Director of Public Prosecution went so far as to warn the Vice Chancellor of the unheard of thing that was going on in the Cambridge University. The Vice Chancellor showed this letter to several persons including the incriminated professor. It contained amidst vehement protests about the indecency of *Ulysses* the humorous offer to forward a copy of *Ulysses* for the Vice-Chancellor's private and personal edification.

4) The BBC censor refused to allow Mr Harold Nicholson's [*sic*] lecture discussing *Ulysses* over the Radio. Only after three weeks of continued tergiversation and under the threat of Mr Nicholson's resignation did he finally give way with the condition that the title of *Ulysses* would not be mentioned.'

The following details of the publication history of *Ulysses* were supplied:

'1st Printing	(Shakespeare and Company, Paris) (1000 numbered copies)	February 1922.
2nd Printing	(Egoist Press, London): (2000 numbered copies, of which 500 burned by New York Post-Office Authorities).	October 1922
3rd Printing	(Egoist Press, London); (500 numbered copies, of which 499 seized by Folkestone Customs Authorities).	January 1923
4th–11th Printing	(Shakespeare and Company, Paris) First issued by the Odyssey Press:	January 1924–May 1930. December 1932.

'A copy of the 2nd printing was sent to the British Museum in accordance with the

We are anxious to find out all the facts about the publication of the first edition of *Ulysses*. It seems that after vain attempts by Miss Harriet Weaver to persuade a British publisher to produce the book for her, she had it printed in Paris as published by the Egoist Press Limited, of London, of which she was proprietor. I have the impression that it was this edition of 499 copies which was seized by Customs authorities at Folkestone. According to M. Leon's memorandum, however, the consignment seized at Folkestone was a second edition, and he tells me nothing about the first edition. I presume that it was shortly after this seizure that Miss Weaver abandoned her attempt, and the book passed into the hands of Miss Sylvia Beach in Paris. In my own acquaintance with the case there is a complete gap between Miss Weaver's first attempts to get the book printed in this country, and Miss Beach's production of the book in Paris. Miss Beach sent me by post a copy of her first edition, which some years later I unfortunately lost: that is to say, it was borrowed or stolen.

We are most anxious to know through whose intervention this book was first brought to the attention of the Customs or any other civil authorities in Britain, and to what legal process of condemnation it was submitted. I should like to be quite clear as to the legal differences between this case and that of books which have been condemned, or, according to newspaper slang, 'banned', after being printed and published in this country. Not until we are thoroughly acquainted with the case shall we be in a position to conjecture in what way, if in any, proceedings against a new publication of the work in this country after more than ten years' lapse of time, might be instituted.

There are possibly some gaps in the history of the case which could be completed by Miss Weaver, or possibly Mr John Rodker, but I am sure that you will agree that it is best that we should first obtain all the information possible from yourselves, as Mr Joyce's legal representatives here, before enquiring elsewhere.

English Copyright laws. It was not catalogued but can be seen by special request. (See note of Mr Léon's).

'The above particulars as to Printings are copied from the first Odyssey Press edition and the date (January 1923) given for the 3rd printing is incorrect. I cannot remember the exact date (Mr Rodker had the particulars) but it was certainly later in the year than January. Nearly 1500 copies had been sold (in Paris and London) before a ban was heard of.

'The title page of the 2nd and 3rd editions bore the impress: Published for the Egoist Press, London by John Rodker, Paris.'

See further Kevin Birmingham, *The Most Dangerous Book: The Battle for James Joyce's 'Ulysses'* (2014).

I think that my name will be known to Mr Monro, as I had some communication with him a year and a half ago, on quite a different matter.

Yours faithfully,

[T. S. Eliot]

Director.

TO *Max Plowman*[1]

CC

28 November 1933

Dear Sir,

Thank you for your letter of November 26th about Miss Petre's book on D. H. Lawrence.[2] We shall be very much interested to read the manuscript if you will be kind enough to send it to us.

Yours faithfully,

[?T. S. Eliot]

Faber & Faber Ltd

FROM *Vivien Eliot*

MS Valerie Eliot

28 November 1933   68 Clarence Gate Gardens

My dearest Tom

Thank you for writing. I have been *quickly* losing all my health, *since June 24th*. People are kind of course, but I can't say I am well looked after. And being *alone* here *so much* & such *long* hours of isolation wear me down & I see *no* chance of recovery, now, *until* you do *feel that you can come in & out, freely* to see me.

1–Max (Mark) Plowman (1883–1941): British poet, editor, pacifist (he endured terrible active service in WW1 and was treated for neurasthenia at Craiglockhart Hospital). Plowman took to poetry and journalism after working for ten years in his father's brick business; worked for JMM at *The Adelphi* from 1930, becoming editor in 1938; a disciple of William Blake (on whom he wrote a book) and D. H. Lawrence, he was also a friend of George Orwell. Other publications include *A Lap Full of Seed* (poems, 1917), *The Right to Live* (anonymous pamphlet, 1917), *A Subaltern on the Somme* (by 'Mark VII', 1927), *The Faith Called Pacifism* (1936). See further *Bridge into the Future: Letters of Max Plowman*, ed. Dorothy Lloyd Plowman (1944).

2–'Miss M. D. Petre, who is perhaps known to you as George Tyrrell's biographer, has entrusted me with the MS. of a *Short Study of the Work of D. H. Lawrence* by her, and I should be glad to know if you would care to consider it.'

I am *sure* that you are not *intentionally* cruel, but it *is* cruel not to come now that you *know* that I am ill & know that I cannot go out & know that *anything* might happen.

I promise you it *would help* you in whatever arrangements they are that you want to make, & it WOULD make me feel *so much better* & *happier* – & there is nothing *'unsuitable'* in going to see your *ill wife*, at *any* time. Why *shouldn't* you? Please come, dear, I want to *hand* you these things & I *long* to see you. I will *NOT lock* the *front door tomorrow* Wed. night so please just come in & don't hesitate. Polly will swoon for joy, & so will Whiskuscat.

Please come directly you receive this tomorrow *Wed. 29th* – by 1 p.m. – or telephone or else write.

Your loving wife,
Vivienne

But *COME – COME. Quickly.*
God bless you dear . . . keep you *safe.*

TO *Herbert Read*   CC

28 November 1933   [Faber & Faber Ltd]

My dear Herbert,

To my great regret, my colleagues are of [the] opinion that we ought not to attempt the Haecker book, as the probability is that we should not cover expenses on it for a long time to come, if at all.[1] The great stumbling block in the case of a book like this, which one expects to publish at a loss, is, of course, the translator's fee. I think myself that the book is very much more in Sheed & Ward's line than anyone else's, and I think that they could probably sell it better than we could. If Tom Burns has not yet had an opportunity of considering this book, I think that he ought to see it at once.

Many thanks, however, for letting me read the book. I am writing to Haecker to ask him to contribute to the *Criterion*.

Yours ever,
[T. S. Eliot][2]

1–HR had sent on 21 Nov. the proof of a new book *Was Ist Der Mensch?* by Theodor Haecker, Catholic apologist and authority in Germany on Kierkegaard. Alexander Dru, in London, had translation rights.

2–HR, in his letter to TSE of 3 Dec. 1933, refers to a postscript to this letter, praising HR's *End of a War*.

TO *Theodor Haecker*[1]   CC

28 November 1933   [*The Criterion*]

My dear Sir,

I have read with the greatest interest and sympathy such of your works as I have been able to obtain during the last few years, and I am therefore writing to ask you whether you would be interested to contribute to the *Criterion*, a Quarterly Review, of literary and general ideas, of which I am the editor. I think that you would find the *Criterion* the most suitable vehicle in England through which to convey your views; and I think that through it you would reach a new and sympathetic public in this country.

I have no doubt that you are acquainted with my friend Jacques Maritain, who has been a contributor, and you could inform yourself fully of the character of this periodical from him. Amongst your compatriots, my friend Ernst Robert Curtius has been an old and valued supporter.

I am sending you the current issue for examination. We prefer contributions to be from 4000 to 6000 words in length. Our rate of payment, which is the same for all contributors, is £2.0.0. for a thousand words. When contributions are submitted in another language than English, we are obliged to deduct 15/- per 1000 words as the translator's fee.

If you have nothing suitable on hand that you would care to contribute, I should be very glad if you would make any suggestions for articles which you might care to write.

I hope very much that we have the honour and distinction of your collaboration.[2]

I am, my dear Sir,
Yours faithfully,
[T. S. Eliot]
Editor

1–Theodor Haecker (1879–1945): author and cultural critic; translator into German of Newman and Kierkegaard. A Catholic convert from 1921, he became a prominent opponent of the Nazi regime, and his journals give witness to his resistance to National Socialism: see *Journal in the Night*, trans. Alexander Dru (1950). Other works include *Virgil, Father of the West*, trans. A. W. Wheen (1934).
2–Haecker, 'Theodicy and Tragedy', trans. Alexander Dru, C. 13 (Apr. 1934), 371–81.

TO *E. Martin Browne*   CC

28 November 1933   [Faber & Faber Ltd]

Dear Browne,

I spent Sunday with a couple of books on the Crusades, which, so far as they go, confirm my difficulty about bringing Peter the Hermit into that episode. As you know, I was already doubtful of its appropriateness. If Peter the Hermit ever came to London, he couldn't have made very much stir here, but apparently he never did; and that means going outside of the London frame altogether to get your scene, which I am rather loth to do. I should like to know your views on this subject, and whether you are dead set on the Crusades. If not, can you think of any other appropriate local episode to represent that general period? I have thought of Thomas a'Becket, of course, but even that takes us further from London than I like.

                                        Yours in haste,
                                        [T. S. Eliot]

TO *Thierry Maulnier*[1]   TS Valerie Eliot

30 November 1933   [*The Criterion*]

Monsieur,

Depuis qu'est paru 'La Crise est dans l'homme' j'ai eu l'intention de demander votre collaboration au *Criterion*, revue trimestrielle de letters et d'idées, don't je suis le rédacteur. Je ne sais pas si notre revue vous est connue; je vous envoie sous pli séparé le numéro actuel; vous pourriez aussi vous renseigner chez notre ami Henri Massis. *Le Criterion* a aussi publié – la seule, je crois, entre les revues de l'Angleterre – des choses de Maurras, de Maritain et d'autres écrivains français du premier rang. Les noms que je viens de citer vous sonneront aussie une idée des tendences politiques et sociologiques du *Criterion*.

Nous solicitons un article d'entre 4000 et 6000 mots; nous les payons toujours £2 les 1000 mots, moins les frais de traduction – 15 shillings les 1000 mots. Si nous pouvons nous entendre, en principe, je serai heureux de recevoir ou un inédit, ou un choix de sujets. Je peux vous assurer que vous trouveriez, parmi les lecteurs du *Criterion*, un public instruit et sympathique; et je tiens beaucoup à l'honneur d'inscrire votre nom entre nos collaborateurs.

---

1 – Thierry Maulnier (1909–88): journalist, essayist, literary critic and dramatist.

Je vous prie, monsieur, de croire à mes sentiments les plus distingués.[1]
T. S. Eliot[2]

TO *A. G. Hebert*[3]   CC

5 December 1933   [Faber & Faber Ltd]

Dear Father Gabriel,

I have your letter of November 30th, enclosing a prospectus of the forthcoming *Oecumenica*.[4] I should be very glad to assist such a project, both by subscribing to the periodical and in any other way in my power, and I have no objection to appearing as a future contributor. I do not know, however, of any subject on which I am competent to write, but perhaps at a future date you will have some suggestions to make. I should prefer, in any case, not to be called upon for a contribution until the

1 – Maulnier responded with enthusiasm on 24 Dec., proposing essays on either '*La littérature de l'action dans la France d'aujourdhui*,' or '*Un sentiment tragique du monde nait en France*', or else to write on the revival of nationalism in France.

2 – *Translation*: Sir, Since *The Crisis is in Man* appeared I have been intending to ask you to write something for the *Criterion*, a quarterly review of literature and ideas, of which I am the editor. I do not know if you know of our review; I am sending the current issue under separate cover; you could also get information from our friend Henri Massis. The *Criterion* has also published – the only one, I believe, of the English reviews – pieces by Maurras, Maritain and other French writers of the first rank. The names I have just quoted will also give you an idea of the *Criterion*'s political and sociological leanings. We are looking for an article of between 4000 and 6000 words; we always pay £2 a thousand words, less the cost of translation – 15 shillings a thousand words. If we can agree in principle, I will be delighted to have from you either an unpublished article or a choice of subjects. I can assure you that you would find, among the *Criterion*'s readers, an informed and sympathetic public; and I look forward to the honour of placing your name among our contributors. Please believe me, Sir, with the highest esteem, T. S. Eliot.

3 – The Revd (Arthur) Gabriel Hebert (1886–1963), monk and theologian; member of the Society of the Sacred Mission, the Anglican theological college at Kelham Hall, Newark-on-Trent, Nottinghamshire, where he had tutored since 1913. Crucially concerned with liturgical evangelism, he was author of *Liturgy and Society* (F&F, 1935); *The Throne of David* (1941); *The Authority of the Old Testament* (F&F, 1947); *Fundamentalism and the Church of God* (1957); *The Christ of Faith and the Jesus of History* (1962); *Apostle and Bishop: a study of the Gospel, the ministry, and the Church-community* (F&F, 1963). See further Christopher Irvine, *Worship, Church and Society: an exposition of the work of Arthur Gabriel Hebert* (1993).

4 – Hebert invited TSE to contribute an article 'some time in the future' to an adventurous new Anglican theological journal in French, *Oecumenica: revue anglicane de synthèse théologique*, which was to be launched, with the approval of the Church of England Council on Foreign Relations, in Jan. 1934. This quarterly was 'most urgently needed, and . . . has got to be run so as to be at once comprehensive and catholic – catholic as the Lambeth Conference is catholic'.

spring, as most of my spare time meanwhile will be taken up with work connected with the Forty-Five Churches Fund.

I look forward to seeing you again, and visiting the Society at the end of January.

Yours sincerely,

[T. S. Eliot]

TO *Serge Bolshakoff*[1]

5 December 1933

Dear Sir,

I must apologise for my delay in answering your letter of the 19th November.[2] I thank you for your invitation. I should like very much to

---

1 – Serge (Sergius) Bolshakoff (1901–90), Russian-born ecumenist; educated in St Petersburg and in Tartu, Estonia, he lived for a while in France and then in England, 1928–51, where he resided for his first ten years at the Anglican Benedictine community of Nashdom, at Burnham in Berkshire. An oblate rather than a monk, he committed his extraordinary personal energies to working towards an Anglican–Orthodox rapprochement: he set up an International Academy of Christian Sociologists: a confraternity with the object of Christian unity. His many publications include *The Christian Church and the Soviet Union* (1942), *The Foreign Missions of the Russian Orthodox Church* (1943) and *Russian Mystics* (1976). On 14 Dec. 1933 the Revd V. A. Demant was to ask TSE, in confidence: 'Sergius Bolshakoff tells me that you are standing in with him over some project to form a Christian International, and he has for a long time worried me to come in too. I should be very grateful if you are able to tell me what you really think about him and his project. I understand him to be an able man with a most synthetic philosophy, but frequent requests to expound it have brought only enthusiastic proposal for a strong movement to express it. So frankly, I am a little suspicious that he may be little else than an unconscious charlatan. I am putting it at its strongest, and I shall be glad if you can tell me that you think differently.' TSE seems to have replied to Demant's enquiry in a (now lost) letter dated 15 Dec. – 'I find from other sources', wrote Demant on 16 Dec., 'that Bolshakoff has told a number of people that others have accepted his invitation, including myself, who have declined' – and thereafter TSE tended to hold himself at a distance from Bolshakoff's project.

2 – Bolshakoff – 'a Russian, a journalist and a clergyman in minor orders', as he described himself; and author of a book, written in Russian and due to be published in Poland, entitled *The Religious Communities of the Anglican Church* – had approached TSE in the late spring of 1933, to invite him to be formally associated with an 'International Centre of the Christian Social Studys' based at the Anglican Benedictine community of Nashdom Abbey. 'The object of this center', he ventured in his first (undated) letter, 'will be the study of the various social problems from the Christian point of view and also the defense of the Christian religion and civilization by the study of the methods of work of antichristian forces.' He was hoping to attract a 'small circle' of like-minded individuals – 'the reception into this center must be only by the cooptation' – to participate in lectures, conferences and international congresses, and to publish a magazine. The Marquis of Tavistock (President of the National Credit Association of Great Britain and a member of the Anglican Industrial

come to Nashdom from the 19th to the 21st, and so far as I can see there will be no obstacle to my doing so. I should very much like to meet Daniel Rops, of whom I have heard from a mutual friend, and some of whose work I know. I should be grateful if you would let me know anything further that there is to say about the characters of the meeting, and the trains and other material conditions.

Yours sincerely,
[T. S. Eliot]

TO *Algar Thorold* CC

5 December 1933   [*The Criterion*]

My dear Thorold,

I was very glad to get your letter, but I am distressed to hear of your continued ill-health, and to learn that there is no immediate prospect of a meeting in London.[1] If you are still confined to The Gravel Pit[2] by that time, I should like very much to run down to Beaconsfield and see you some time at your convenience after Christmas.

Would you let me know whenever there is a chance of another contribution or review from you? I am more or less settled in London, and, as I say, would very much like to come and see you as soon as the Christmas rush is over.

Yours ever,
[T. S. Eliot]

Fellowship) had already committed himself. Others who expressed interest included figures known to TSE such as V. A. Demant, Algar Thorold (who was to publish an article by Bolshakoff in the *Dublin Review*), and Kenneth Ingram; as well as Professor Daniel Rops from Paris. In his second letter Bolshakoff told a little more about himself: 'I am an orthodox clergyman and a professor, at least nominally . . . in Bulgaria.' He hoped above all, he said, for collaboration between 'various Anglican, catholic and orthodox social groups'. He explained too: 'Economically my doctrine is near to that of Major Douglas.'

In his letter of 19 Nov. he invited TSE to spend three days, 19–21 Dec., at Nashdom Abbey in company with the Marquis of Tavistock and Daniel Rops: they would hold preliminary discussions with a view to the formal opening of the Centre in the spring of 1934.

1 – Thorold, aged sixty-eight, had undergone 'a slight operation in the spring'; he was now suffering from a weak heart which gave him bouts of pain, and he was leading a sedentary life at home.

2 – Thorold's home address: The Gravel Pit, Chalfont St Peter, Bucks.

TO *Michael de la Bedoyère* CC

5 December 1933

Dear de la Bedoyère,

I hope you will not be put out of countenance by finding that your paper on Censorship is to appear after all.[1] I think that you were informed in my absence that it would definitely appear in some issue, but considerations of make-up prevented it being published sooner. I trust that there were no further corrections or alterations you wanted to make, as you had had proofs some time ago.

I am afraid that I cannot use your article on Berdiaev, for the reason that we have published in the last number a longish review of this book.[2] That is the trouble with submitting articles based on some recent publication – that the subject is likely to have been dealt with by a reviewer. Another time I suggest that you should write to me in advance, to make sure that the book has not been given out for review, and I shall be glad to let you have it if it is suitable.

With all best wishes,
Yours very sincerely,
[T. S. Eliot]

TO *Mary Hutchinson* TS Texas

5 December 1933 Faber & Faber Ltd

My dear Mary,

I am sorry to learn that the record does not work.[3] I think that I can get you another one, but I may take some time, because the few copies which I gave away were made specially for me, and I do not think that any market supply has yet been undertaken. Meanwhile, however, I suggest your trying it over, if you have the patience, with a steel needle. I imagine that ordinary records when you buy them have been played over in this way. On the one of the records which I tried myself, I found the same trouble of duplication of voices when played with a fibre or soft needle;

1–De la B. wrote (1 Dec.), 'I wonder whether you would care to take the enclosed article in place of the dreadful one I once sent on 'Censorship" and which you set up, but have not printed.'

2–F. McEachran on Berdyaev's *The End of Our Time*: C. 13 (Jan. 1934), 307–10.

3–MH (30 Nov.) was excited to have TSE's record, but it seemed to have 'flaws': 'the voice gets stopped and there are continuous repetitions.' Could it be exchanged for another copy?

but by using an ordinary steel needle this was avoided. Probably after they are worked in a bit they can be played with fibre needles. And no record is at its best until it has been played several times. I am sorry if this condemns you to hearing the record more than you want, but perhaps you could persuade Deal to carry out this exercise in the kitchen.

I don't think our Sadlers Wells secretary can be very efficient, because I wrote to him several weeks ago to say I wanted to renew my subscription for this season, and I have had no reply. I wanted to get this done quickly, so as to try to get good seats for ourselves and the Woolfs for *Measure for Measure* as we suggested. I shall trust you to let me know when there is a meeting of the Committee, as I should like to come.

I don't seem to have received the invitation to Barbara's party. I should very much have liked to come and make the acquaintance of Victor, but in the present circumstances I don't go to parties, and I hope you will excuse me to Barbara.[1]

Yours very affectionately,
Tom

P. S. I see from your letter that *Measure for Measure* is apparently this Thursday, but I can't at the moment lay my hand on the programme. May I leave it to you to secure the seats for me, for ourselves and whomever else you have it in mind to ask?[2]

TO *A. H. Macintyre*[3]   CC

7 December 1933

Dear Mr Macintyre,

I must apologise for my long delay in answering your kind letter of admonition about the proposed trust. I have been unsettled until recently, and my business habits have, I fear, deteriorated. It is true that I had quite overlooked the point about the high proportion of commission to income. In the circumstances, I have finally decided to scrap the new trust altogether, with your concurrence, and make other dispositions in my will – which will I think make matters simpler in the end for my executors and trustees, including yourselves. I shall write to explain the position to Curtis.

---

1 – MH had sent TSE c/o F&F an invitation to an engagement party for her daughter Barbara and Victor Rothschild.
2 – TSE was not giving his full attention to MH's letter, which made it clear that she had already acquired two seats in the Stalls: she invited him to go with her.
3 – Trust Officer, Old Colony Trust Company, Boston.

With many thanks for your consideration, and with the season's good wishes.

Yours very sincerely,
[T. S. Eliot]

TO *John Cournos*   CC

7 December 1933   [*The Criterion*]

Dear John,

I have just realised that I ought to have answered your letter of November 2nd long before this.[1] The point is to let you know that I shall be delighted to use any slight prestige I may have with the Guggenheim people on your behalf, but I have not yet heard from Moe, and I am beginning to wonder whether his communication may not have gone astray. If he is supposed to have written to me, I think you would be well advised to drop him a line to say that I am still waiting, and that any letter should be posted to this address.

With all best wishes to yourself and your family for Christmas,

Yours in haste,
{T. S. E.]

TO *T. F. Burns*   CC

7 December 1933   [Faber & Faber Ltd]

Dear Burns,

Thank you very much for sending the latest *Essay in Order*, which I am sure I shall enjoy reading.

I am sorry that I did not answer you immediately about MacNeice.[2] I think it is now two years since I saw his *Collected Poems*, and I do not

---

1 – Cournos asked TSE to support his application to the Guggenheim Memorial Foundation: he had applied for a fellowship to Europe, where he proposed to write a two-volume study of Russian literature – 'The Golden Age of Russian Literature' and 'The Twilight of Russian Literature'. 'I must beg you to answer their letter and toot my horn for all you are worth!' Henry Allen Moe (1894–1975) worked for the National Endowment for the Humanities.

2 – Burns had enquired (14 Nov.) after MacNeice's poems – was F&F going to do anything with them? He ventured too: 'I was wondering whether F. would publish if, say, Hague & Gill printed them in a small edition: I mean, possibly the fact of its being limited & rather "special" would help the sales just to the extent of making them pay for the job. I couldn't handle the book, it's right out of my line.' Burns asked again in a short note of 6 Dec.

know whether he has added to, or altered, them in any way since. I am doubtful whether we should be prepared to produce a new poet in any but our usual way, although I might be prepared to propose it. I think that, if you have the MS. at your office, it would be a good thing if you would send it along for me to refresh my mind about. As you know, MacNeice is one of the people in whom I have taken some interest.

Yours ever,
[T. S. Eliot]

TO *E. W. F. Tomlin*   CC

7 December 1933   [Faber & Faber Ltd]

Dear Mr Tomlin,

I have been meaning to write to you about your very interesting Lawrence essay, but a talk would be more satisfactory. This is just a line to acknowledge your note, and to ask you to let me know whether I shall find you at your Purley address after this?[1] I should then be glad if you would lunch with me on the first day that we can both arrange.[2]

Yours in haste,
Pp T. S. Eliot

TO *E. Martin Browne*   CC

7 December 1933   [Faber & Faber Ltd]

Dear Browne,

I recalled yesterday with consternation that I had not made out the extra copies which I promised to send you. I hope that this has not caused you any delay; in any case, here they are. I also add a couple of pages of the Workmen's dialogue, for your consideration. There is a gap to be filled in with a few bricklayers terms, which I shall obtain from an expert.

1–Tomlin wrote from Oxford (5 Dec.) to say he would be free for the vacation – between 8 Dec. and 13 Jan. – and hoped 'to get something done . . . – from what I remember of my Lawrence essay I am far from satisfied'. (His home address was in Purley, Surrey.)
2–Tomlin said he learned from Fr. M. C. D'Arcy at Oxford that TSE had mentioned him in a footnote to *After Strange Gods*; and TSE told Tomlin in person what he thought of his work at lunch in the Oxford & Cambridge Club, London, on 23 Feb. 1934: 'He considered the Lawrence essay to be a much more mature piece of work than "The Younger Generation and Politics". He even said it was "good stuff". The trouble was that it was a good deal too long' (Tomlin, *T. S. Eliot: A Friendship* [1988], 46).

Oddly enough, I met last night by accident a lady who appears to be Miss Fogerty's assistant in charge of these choruses.[1] She is large, dark, and has a slight cast in one eye, but I did not catch her name.

I will come on Tuesday morning to the Albert Hall at ten. I have not yet had any inspiration about the title, but pray that one will come before I see you. I am sufficiently impressed by what you say about the crusades, and will have another shot at it.

You will find me at this office on Friday afternoon, if you would care to look in, and if you come at the proper time, I should be delighted to give you a cup of tea.

Yours ever,
[T. S. Eliot]

P.S. I find I have left the copies behind as an additional piece of stupidity. I am very sorry, but I will post them to you in the morning.

TO *Virginia Woolf*   TS Berg

7 December 1933   *The Criterion*

My dear Virginia,

To revert to a familiar and tedious matter.[2] I have been tramping Clerkenwell this afternoon, and while there is much to be said for it geographically I mean topographically and also it is said to be very healthy the trouble is bathrooms. I took one name and address as the rooms were rather attractive (I mean well built with bookcases) but the bath is in the basement and very poor at that. I imagine that the society of East Bloomsbury (I mean between Southampton Row and Grays Inn Road) is less congenial and less respectable but perhaps some houses have decent bathrooms. I suppose geysers are the rule. So if you should hear of

---

1–Elsie Fogerty, CBE, LRAM (1865–1945), teacher of elocution and drama training; founder in 1906 of the Central School of Speech and Drama (Laurence Olivier and Peggy Ashcroft were favourite pupils), was to train the chorus for the Canterbury premier in 1935 of TSE's *MiC*. Her assistant was Gwynneth L. Thurburn (1899–1993), who was to succeed Fogerty as Principal of the Central School, 1942–67.

2–VW had been househunting for TSE, and reported in an undated note (?14 Nov. 1933): 'We took an afternoon walk through Islington & found Percy Circus, very nice: Holford Square excellent. I expect rooms are to be had, but you would have to ring the bell to ask. Then we found a nice Georgian baywindowed house in Frederick Street, off Kings X Road to be let. I believe you'd find it cheaper, cleaner, roomier & better to take a little house like this –. But come & see us, & we might take the car & look round – but let me know the day beforehand.'

anything thereabouts well recommended (furnished bed and sitting room) I should be grateful for the information. Standard rates in Clerkenwell for that accommodation seem to be: rooms one guinea per week, breakfasts four and six a week, suppers eighteenpence each, and half a crown a week for coals.

Yrs
T. S. E.

TO *Thomas McGreevy*[1]

TS TCD

7 December 1933   *The Criterion*

Dear Tom,

I don't think that I took your remark any more seriously than it was intended, so there is no harm done.[2]

1–Thomas McGreevy (1893–1967) – the family name was 'McGreevy', but by the 1930s he would assume the more Irish spelling 'MacGreevy' – poet, literary and art critic, and arts administrator – worked for the Irish Land Commission before serving in WW1 as a 2nd lieutenant in the British Royal Field Artillery: he fought at Ypres and the Somme, and was twice wounded. After reading History and Political Science at Trinity College, Dublin, he moved in 1925 to London, where he met TSE and started to write for the *Criterion*, *TLS* (with an introduction from TSE) and *N&A*. His poem 'Dysert' appeared in *NC* 4 (Jan. 1926) under the pseudonym 'L. St. Senan' (the title was later changed to 'Homage to Jack Yeats'). In 1927 he took up teaching English at the Ecole Normale Supérieur in Paris, where he became friends with Beckett and JJ (to whom he had been introduced in 1924) and with RA. (His promotional essay on JJ's *Finnegans Wake* – 'The Catholic Element in Work in Progress' – appeared in *Our Exagmination round his Factification for Incamination of Work in Progress*, 1929.) In addition, he journeyed through Italy with WBY. Back in London in 1933, he lectured at the National Gallery and wrote for *The Studio*. Ultimately he was appointed Director of the National Gallery of Ireland, 1950–63. He was made Chevalier de la Légion d'Honneur, 1948; Cavaliere Ufficiale al merito della Repubblica Italiana, 1955; and Officier de la Légion d'Honneur, 1962. In 1929 he published a translation of Paul Valéry's *Introduction à la méthode de Léonard de Vinci* ('Introduction to the Method of Leonardo da Vinci'); and in 1931, two short monographs, *T. S. Eliot: A Study* and *Richard Aldington: An Englishman*; and his *Poems* would appear in 1934. Publications on art include *Jack B. Yeats: An Appreciation and an Interpretation* (1945) and *Nicolas Poussin* (1960). See also *The Collected Poems of Thomas MacGreevy: An Annotated Edition*, ed. Susan Schreibman (1991).

2–McGreevy wrote, 5 Dec.: 'One shouldn't leave misunderstandings about important things.

'I didn't mean seriously what I said about not accepting converts as Catholics this afternoon. And if it *should* happen that some day you feel you must jump the fence I could, and would be glad to, put you in touch with a holy father who knows the exact blend of humility and lightheartedness that constitutes the second of the virtues, the most Catholic one.

'Which sounds as if I were going very solemn indeed. Tant pis.'

Would you be willing to undertake for me short notes as well as long ones – I mean notes on books, each about half a page in length? I used to attach a good deal of importance to the short notices, but they have rather lapsed for a long time, inasmuch as I could not find anyone to do them satisfactorily except myself. Any fool can write a long review, but it does take some skill to say anything worth saying in a paragraph. I can't say that it is remunerative; you get 5/- per half-page. If any book appears to be just trash, you don't review it.

Here are a few titles, which I should be glad to send along to you: *Ernest Psichari,* by Henriette Psichari; *François Mauriac* by Charles du Bos; *Le Pari,* by Ramon Fernandez; *George Moore,* by Humbert Wolfe; *James Joyce,* by Louis Golding.[1]

And how would you feel about reviewing *Conversions to the Catholic Church*, with an introduction by Martin d'Arcy, in the same way?[2]

Yours ever,
T. S. E.

TO *A. J. Penty*   CC

7 December 1933   [*The Criterion*]

Dear Penty,

I shall be glad to use your article 'Beauty does not look after Herself' in the April number, and you will get proofs in due course.[3]

Yours in haste,
[T. S. Eliot]

TO *Messrs Monro, Saw & Co.*   CC

8 December 1933   [Faber & Faber Ltd]

Sirs,

With further reference to my letter of the 28th ultimo, I should like to draw your attention to the statement in the Paris edition of the *New*

---

1 – McGreevy reviewed all five books in C. 13 (Apr. 1934).

2 – Not done.

3 – Penty's piece was a challenge to Eric Gill's book *Beauty Looks After Herself* (1933): C. 13 (Apr. 1934), 353–70. 'I propose to include it and "Tradition and Modernism in Architecture" in a volume of architectural philosophy which will outline the various problems confronting architecture to-day.'

735

York Herald of the 7th December to the effect that Mr Joyce's *Ulysses* has successfully passed the tribunal of Judge Woolsey of New York. It would appear from this decision that the book is now legally importable and publishable in America.

I do not propose that this has any direct bearing on the situation in this country; nevertheless, it might have some usefulness at a later stage.

I await with interest your further reply to my letter.[1]

Yours faithfully,
[T. S. Eliot]

TO *Alistair Cooke*   CC

8 December 1933   [Faber & Faber Ltd]

Dear Cooke,

I owe you, and indeed my own firm, a serious apology. When I received your letter of October 9th, I was in the country, and after thinking it over, sent it up to my office to be considered by the other directors. Unfortunately, I put it with a number of other papers, all of which were intended for filing, so that this letter was not drawn to the attention of the directors until my return to London some days ago.[2]

I hope that this delay has not caused you great inconvenience and annoyance. You mention some other publishers to whom you propose to offer the book, but I gather that you were waiting to hear from us before going further.

---

1 – Monro, Saw & Co. replied, 13 Dec.: 'With reference to your letters of the 28th ult. and 8th instant, it is true that we have the pleasure of acting as Mr Joyce's Solicitors in this country, and we have been informed that you are publishing his *Work in Progress*.

'We have no instructions to provide you with facts in the history of this case, but there appears to be no doubt that the work in question is copyright in the country, and we may say that we are fortified in this view by the opinion of leading Counsel.'

2 – Cooke wrote in connection with a series of seven articles he was writing for the *Observer*, which it had been suggested to him would make up a book with the title *Hollywood Prospect*. '[I]t is a summary of Hollywood's prospects for a niche in the history of the cinema . . . [A] commercial despotism has forced good cinema out of circulation completely and left us only Hollywood . . . I should try and keep it light and alternate the subjective, whimsical accounts of Hollywood . . . with serious discussion of film technique. There would be an additional talk with Chaplin on Form.' He would include as a frontispiece a photograph he had taken – 'head and shoulders simply' – of Chaplin. He therefore hoped F&F might be interested in his volume. 'I am going to offer it also to Jonathan Cape, Wishart, Geoffrey Bles, and Peter Davies. But your offer, if any, would come first . . . I can have the script ready within a few days of your answer.'

The trouble is that it is very difficult to say anything definite about any book of this kind without seeing some (if not all) of it in a finished state, and a more detailed scheme of the rest. I think that the best thing that you can do, if you have so far done nothing, is to finish the manuscript as soon as you can, and send it on for us to consider. I can only say at this point that the scheme strikes us as interesting, and that we have in principle no practical objection to such a book.

If, however, it proved that the book was not one which we felt we could do well by, or fit in suitably with our list, you would want to send it at once to someone else. In that case, rather than hand it direct from publisher to publisher, I should suggest that you gave us the name of one of the literary agencies in London, whom you would nominate to handle this book, and let us pass the book on to him if we could not publish it. You could then tell him to what publishers you would like to have it sent. In this way, if the book were suitable for our list, you would not have to bother with an agent; but if not, the agent could take off your hands the negotiations with other publishers.

Do please accept my humble apologies for the oversight, which was entirely my own fault.

The new company at the Old Vic have made an extremely good job of *Measure for Measure*, which I saw last night. Charles Laughton is not yet a perfect Shakespearean actor, and apologises for not knowing how to speak blank verse, but he is extremely keen, and I think may be really first-rate in time.

I should be very glad to have your news, and meanwhile offer best wishes for Christmas and your holidays.

Yours very sincerely,
[T. S. Eliot]

P.S. Can you tell me what Richard Riddle is doing at present? I have not seen his name anywhere.[1]

TO *Bonamy Dobrée*   CC

8 December 1933   [Faber & Faber Ltd]

Dear Bonamy,

I have received yours of the 7th. I should be delighted to lunch with you on either Monday or Tuesday at the Spanish restaurant in Swallow

---

1–See TSE to Susan Hinkley, 9 Dec. 1933.

Street. In obeying your instructions as well as I can, I am not sure whether you will get this letter. May I suggest that you need an efficient secretary? Your letter enclosed.

Yours ever,

[T. S. E.]

TO *Paul Elmer More*

TS Princeton

8 December 1933   *The Criterion*

My dear More,

I write in haste to thank you for your letter of the 17th November – if I do not write now it may get left till after Christmas. I consider what you say about my lectures very flattering: especially as the reception has been mixed and at a low temperature. My reputation is at the dangerous age at which what I write is compared (unfavourably) with something I wrote earlier. I am ready to concede fully your points about Addison and Saintsbury: these were lecture-hall attitudes, capricious and unperpended. As for Richards, that is a more delicate and complicated matter. I incline more, the last year or so, to your opinion. The man is fundamentally a Liberal: the sort of person who refuses to make *moral* judgements (because one must be tolerant in such matters) but is always ready to make intellectual judgements. I am beginning (since his Landor remarks) to question even his perceptions. But I doubt whether it would have been effective, (and I certainly was not prepared) to go further in these hasty lectures, which are only a skirmish anyway. Of course I am nearer to Babbitt.

My aim now is to avoid *controversy* with people with whom I am fundamentally in disaccord. It seems to me that controversy is only possible between people who have not only formulations, but more important, fundamental moral attitudes and emotional organisations (if that is not too psychological a phrase) in common. Nowadays one has nothing fundamental in common with the serious enemies. Therefore one can only try to *state* as clearly and thoroughly as possible, and leave argument to debaters. I don't find it profitable, for instance, even to discuss in conversation most modern writers with most of the people whom I know. But I am aware that I want to bring to the light of day the differences between my views and those of people with whom I have been (superficially) associated like Read and Richards.

My affairs have only got to the point of presenting a Deed of Separation for signature. I shall write again about Christmas time and hope to have something more definite to say, as well as to be able to write at greater length.

Yours ever sincerely,
T. S. Eliot

TO *Marianne Moore*   cc

8 December 1933   [London]

Dear Miss Moore,

In my gradual attempt to go through and put in order all my papers of the last year, I have found a series of poems called *The Plumet Basilisk*. My impression is that this was the poem which you withdrew from the *Criterion* for publication in the *Hound and Horn*, but anything of yours interests me so much that I am writing to ask, on the remote possibility that the poem may yet be published. If it has been published, may I hope to have something else from you soon?[1]

I look forward with much interest to your review of the *Cantos*, wondering whether you will find the same strong and weak points in them that I do.

With all best wishes,
Yours sincerely,
[T. S. Eliot]

TO *Ezra Pound*   TS Beinecke

8/10 December 1933   Faber & Faber Ltd

Resp. Ezzum,

I remain of the same opinion, in some respects.

30Cantoes30 has gone to Marianne to review at length. Havnt told her what to say. That's a bright girl.[2]

1–Moore replied on 25 Dec. that 'The Plumet Basilisk' was in the Oct. issue of *Hound & Horn*. 'If I could give you something that would really please you, it would be a great pleasure to me.'

2–EP replied (11 Dec.): 'I have no doubt whatever Marianna sez will be perfectly unintelligible and ergo acceptable to the memebrs of the Athenaeum and other London clubs.' See Moore's review of EP, *A Draft of XXX Cantos* (F&F, 1933): C. 13 (Apr. 1934), 482–5.

As for me, I can't help it. My great-grandfather was on same witch jury with Nat Hawthorne's great-grandfather; and I just naturally smell out witches etc.

Don't know about what you say about frogs.[1] Always assumed civilisation extended, thinly, from Thames to Loire. To the eastward: Skowegians. To west: Welsh, Irish and Connecticut Crooners.

But all the same admit that London tubeman knows he's a fool to be punching tickets: whereas people in Paris Metro take it SERIOUSLY.

What is is that I don't feel altogether happy about rewarmed contemporanea of London periodicals.[2] Can't feel convinced that war-time periodicals of London (enlapping much idiocy that can be parallelledelled elsewhere) will search the vitals in 15 minutes today like Geronimo's Snake Oil Purgative. Not presuming to interfere after all it is your book not mine especially after what Judge Wooolley says, only I am topocraphically nearer to the Old Bull & Bush than you are.

The only trouble with wops is that they are wops.

I MAY or may NOT get my expenses paid to lecture or read in Rome next spring (per Bassiano) if so I might just be able to breathe long enough to take a day off at Rappalo.

The only objection to Italy is the Climate. Clerkenwell is all right but there arent any bathrooms there. I have just been looking into the matter. It contains, curiously enough, Little Italy. They have swell funerals. Where to live? Highbury Barn, perhaps. Canonbury. Don't say Belsize Park, I couldn' stand that from You.

All this indicates that I am on the Job again from 10 to 6 daily except most Saturdays, and earneastly desirous of reopening communications. Have a secretary for plain correspondence and wrapping up parcels etc.

I could get a house with grounds on the banks of Loch Lomond for £10 per annum. But I dont like the climate. We cant live farther south than Paris or farther north than Wiltshire, and the latter is really too exposed.

Yrs etc. P for

Possum

1–EP had written, in an undated letter: 'I think it is time to deal with god damn frogs/ whose racial inferiority has been deepening for some time.

'I fergit the name of the pimp on the Figaro, who was well known and who got paid by authors to write shitiques of their pukes. died a few years back /

'L abominable venalité de la press.'

2–EP (11 Dec.): 'As I havent seen the "Contemporary Mentality" for a couple ov years/ I wunt argue till I have another chance.'

9 December 1933   Faber & Faber Ltd

My dear Henry,

I have been meaning to write for a long time; but I am a poor correspondent. This letter is to convey my Christmas greetings to you and Theresa, and to express the wish that I might be with you. How jolly that day in New York after Christmas was! I shall never forget it. You will receive an envelope containing Christmas cards to the New York relatives who entertained me, and to Horace Kallen, will you please put the addresses on, which I don't remember?

And I should have let you know that we will gladly take seven dollars and fifty cents for a subscription to the *Criterion*. And if you will let me know where your subscription stopped I will send all the back numbers as a bonus: we are grateful for subscriptions.

My affairs drag along, but ought to be near their termination. A Deed of Separation Settlement has been drawn up and presented to V.'s lawyers. I have not seen her since that once at the solicitor's office. She writes now and then to say that she is ill and would I come to see her; but no good could come of that; and if she was really ill I should hear in other ways. I sometimes see people who have seen her, but she does not know this. It is impossible, as it always has been, to gauge the amount and rate of mental deterioration; but it is possible that eventually – perhaps not for years – she will have to be looked after in a home.[1]

I fear that the NRA has kept you in a state of worry. Do you think that Roosevelt will ultimately be frozen out? Tell me whether you are doing any writing at present. I am at present in a polite boarding house in South Kensington, and am having difficulty deciding where to look for more permanent quarters. I want to get two furnished rooms for the rest of the winter; perhaps spend the summer in the country near London; and next winter, when things are more settled, take two rooms and furnish them simply.

---

1 – Tomlin, *T. S. Eliot*, 171: 'Theresa Eliot, his sister-in-law, told me that on the few occasions when he discussed his first marriage, he ventured to suggest that Vivien might have been a victim of demonic possession. For there had come a point when mental disturbance had seemed to give place to something more horrible and intractable.' Reporting a talk with TSE on 23 Sept. 1958 (following TSE's marriage to Valerie Fletcher), Tomlin says: 'As to the earlier alliance, he summed it up, not so much in bitterness as though trying to get across what it had in fact amounted to: "*Seventeen* years of married misery!" This was said with an almost bewildered emphasis on the final word, by way of pointing to his present happiness' (210).

I wish you and Theresa could get over next summer; but I hope to visit you in 1935!

> Ever your affectionate brother,
> Tom

TO *Susan Hinkley*   TS Houghton

9 December 1933   Faber & Faber Ltd

Dear Aunt Susie,

Thank you for your letter of the 26th ultimo and for letting me know about young Barbara's babies.[1] It must be bewildering to have so many descendants! And I suppose that Francis will be getting married in the spring. I sincerely hope that the twins will live and flourish, and shall be glad if you will write again later and let me know how they are, and their mother. I imagine it was fortunate that young Barbara did not begin with twins, but presumably was better fitted for the strain because of previous experience. No doubt the spare parts such as finger nails will arrive in due course. Please give my felicitations to young Barbara (and everybody else who has any direct or indirect responsibility for this event) and tell her that I forgive her for not inviting me to her house, but nothing less than the same circumstances will induce me to forgive her a second time.

I thought of you this summer while staying with the Archbishop of York at Bishopthorpe, where, amongst all his predecessors and successors from James I's time to the present, the portrait of Richard Sterne hangs over the dining table. I had always understood from mother that he was an ancestor; but I fear that mother was a little weak in chronology, as Richard was not Archbishop until the Restoration, and your ancestors arrived in America, I believe, much earlier. That makes me begin to doubt the descent from Colonel Blood, of whom I have always boasted (pretending, what hitherto could not be disproved, that the name of Thomas comes to me eventually from him). I should be very grateful for your reassurance on this point: I have never seen a Blood pedigree. There are Bloods about still – a well-known general (whom I don't know) is Sir Bindon Blood.[2]

---

1 – Letter not found; babies not identified.
2 – General Sir Bindon Blood, GCB (1842–1940), a military commander who served in Egypt, Afghanistan, India and Africa, was descended from Thomas Blood (1618–80) – a self-styled 'Colonel' – who had attempted to steal the Crown Jewels from the Tower of London in 1671.

By the way, I do not think that I wrote to Eleanor (so will she please take this paragraph instead) about a young man from Jesus (Cambridge) named Alistair Cooke, at present residing at 420 Memorial Drive. He is a Commonwealth Student, and was last year at Yale under G. P. Baker, and is now doing research at Harvard. His special interest is dramatic criticism, but also every aspect of the drama and stage, and he can talk about all that, and so far as I know, about nothing else. He is a pleasant enough fellow. I met him first through Richard Riddle, to whose sister he was said to be engaged. Richard Riddle and his sister are the children of one of Henry Ainley's wives, I don't know which, but I think it was a Baroness Bunsen, but that sounds wrong, Baroness somebody.[1] I give the introduction in this way, rather than send Cooke a letter; because people sometimes present letters of introduction at inconvenient moments; and in this way you can ask him when you like, or not at all. I have not mentioned you, or anyone else, to him.

I am delighted to hear that *Aphra Behn* is finished, and burn with curiosity to read it. Now that Judge Woolsey has declared *Ulysses* to be a proper enough book, there is perhaps less risk of censorship;[2] and I

TSE told the Librarian, St Andrews, Mar. 1941: 'My mother's family, the name of which is really Stearne, comes from Suffolk, whence three brothers emigrated to America in 1632.'

But in Oct. 1954 TSE's cousin Eleanor Hinkley would send him a family tree she had compiled that exploded (as he acknowledged in a letter to her, 22 Oct. 1954) 'two myths which I think were dear to my mother's heart (i) that the Bloods were descended from Col. Blood who tried to steal Charles II's Crown Jewels (2) that we are nearly related to Laurence Sterne. I am sure my mother would not have wanted either the Restoration underworld character, or the rather unsavoury 18th Century parson in her house (she certainly didn't admit Laurence Sterne's works into the library) but she was rather proud of the connexion all the same. But the coat-of-arms that you show is totally different from that in the *Sentimental Education*, which we had always supposed to be ours as well: that one has a starling for a crest, and you know that the name Sterne or Stearne comes from the Old Danish word for starling – the Stearnes's came from Dedham Essex, and Laurence's family from Suffolk (just across the border – so they were obviously descended from Danes of the Danelaw. Why did you get *your* Stearns coat?

'I have somewhere a Chauncy pedigree that Henry had, going back to the 11th century. It is sad to think that the only Stearns's left (and I know they are numerous as the sands of the sea) are so remote that one can take no interest in them. There were I believe three brothers, who came over in the *Arbella*; and they must all have had large families' (Houghton bMS Am2244).

1 – The Irish-American novelist Bettina Riddle (1874–1957), later Baroness von Hutten zum Stolzenburg. Her daughter, to whom Cooke was briefly engaged in 1932, was Henrietta Riddle.

2 – Judge John M. Woolsey ruled in the United States District Court for the Southern District of New York that *Ulysses* was not obscene, and that therefore copies of the book could be published and sold without fear of legal reprisal: his decision was upheld on appeal. Bennett Cerf thereupon printed the judge's opinion in all copies of *Ulysses* published by Random House.

shouldn't think there was much you couldn't do on the American stage, compared to the English. (I am now conducting legal investigations to revive the *Ulysses* question here). How does Eva feel about taking on new plays at present? I should imagine that everyone in America was all of a hoo-ha, if you take my meaning.

I suppose that Uncle Rob never goes out now, and will not be able to be with you for Christmas? Please give him my love and Christmas wishes; this carries the same to yourselves, which should also have reached you on a plain card by the previous mail.

Affectionately your nephew,
Tom

TO *Hugh Sykes Davies*[1]

CC

11 December 1933 [*The Criterion*]

Dear Sykes Davies,

It is true that I have had no communication with you since we met for a moment in the summer, but on the other hand the *Criterion* has heard nothing from you. Are you willing to go on with the American Periodicals, which you had been doing? If so, it would be not only a convenience to me in saving me the trouble of scratching about for another editor of that department, but also a satisfaction, as I always enjoy reading your reviews. I should be glad to be clear on this point, and should also like to know how you are fixed with regard to other work, for (a) book reviewing for the *Criterion*, and (b) a longer contribution of some kind. I do wish you would make some suggestion for an article on one of your numerous subjects of interest.

My secretary tells me you don't answer her letters.

I spent last Sunday in Cambridge with the Pickthorns, but did not have time to see anyone else except Richards. I hope I may see you either there or here before long.

Yours ever,
[T. S. Eliot]

1–Hugh Sykes Davies (1909–84): author and critic. Educated at St John's College, Cambridge – where he edited, with William Empson, the magazine *Experiment*, and where he took the Jebb Studentship and the Le Bas Prize, 1931 – he became University Lecturer and Fellow of St John's. In the 1930s he was a Communist and Surrealist, and co-created the London Surrealist Exhibition, 1936. Novels include *Full Fathom Five* (1956); other writings include the posthumous *Wordsworth and The Worth of Words* (1986).

TO *Algar Thorold*   CC

11 December 1933   [*The Criterion*]

My dear Thorold,

Many thanks for your letter. As soon as I can make the time in the
new year, I shall certainly propose myself one day for a call upon you at
Chalfont-St-Peter.

By all means go ahead with Malebranche so far as I am concerned,
but of course when the time comes, it will be all the better if I can have
a little notice before it turns up. I am afraid that I never had more than
a smattering undergraduate acquaintance with that philosopher at best.[1]

Yours ever,
[T. S. Eliot]

TO *Gilbert Seldes*   TS Timothy and Marian Seldes

11 December 1933   *The Criterion*

My dear Seldes,

After being completely disorganized all this summer with a year's
supply of unfiled letters and papers, I have at last unearthed the address
you gave me, and I am therefore writing to ask how you feel about an
American Chronicle for the April number of the *Criterion*. When I say
'how you feel', I am alluding to the fact that in order to cover theatres
etc., I know you may incline to one season rather than another, so it is
a question of whether enough has happened to interest you to make a
Chronicle for the next number. If so, please go ahead with it, but please
let me know at once.

With all best wishes to yourself and Mrs Seldes,

Yours ever,
T. S. Eliot

1 – Thorold wrote on 6 Dec. that he had 'recently been discovering Malebranche who excites
me so much as to be bad for my heart. (I conceal this symptom from my doctor who has
no philosophy.) I shd like to write on him for you . . . provided I cd take my own time
about it.' Nicolas Malebranche (1638–1715) was a French Oratorian priest and rationalist
philosopher.

TO *James Joyce*   TS Buffalo

11 December 1933   Faber & Faber Ltd

My dear Joyce,

Many thanks for your letter.[1] It does not now look as though I should
be able to get over to Paris again this year, but I hope to come during
January or February. I will not fail to let you know in advance, so that we
may have an evening together. Meanwhile, if you should leave Paris for
Zurich, I hope you would be able to get word to me.

I am delighted to hear that the censorship of *Ulysses* in America appears
to have lifted. I do not suppose that this will have any direct influence on
the situation here, nevertheless it is a useful parallel to be able to draw. A
few days after I got back from Paris, I wrote to Monro, Saw & Co. to ask
them to be so kind as to let me have an account of the history of *Ulysses*
so far as they have knowledge of it. I have had an acknowledgement of my
letter, but no reply: after I hear from them, I shall also try to get in touch
immediately with Miss Weaver and with Rodker, to find out if they have
any material facts to add to the dossier.

Yours very sincerely,
T. S. Eliot

TO *James Boyle*   CC

11 December 1933

Dear Mr Boyle,

I have not yet thanked you for your letter of October 23rd, but I was
out of London until rather recently.[2] Please accept my assurance that I am
very much honoured by your invitation to contribute an introduction to
a book. I dare say that by this time your book has been published, and in
any case I can do nothing but wish it well. Had I written at once, I should

---

1–JJ had replied on 5 Dec. to TSE's previous letter: 'No, I had heard nothing at all [of TSE's
separation from VHE] though some of your replies at lunch struck me. As you wrote me
through your office I prefer to wait till I see you over here again to allude to the matter.'
    VHE was to send a copy of *Marina* to JJ, inscribed 'To James Joyce / *from Vivienne Haigh
Eliot. / February 2 1933*' (Peter Grogan catalogue 1 [2015], item 25).
2–Boyle was working at the periodical *Harvard Advocate* and trying to revive the Harvard
Poetry Society. He asked, 'We intend publishing at the end of the year one of the thin things
the University Press does very well. Would you be absolutely against giving the child a name?
that is, a really quite brief introduction. I suppose it's cheek to ask . . . And you'd want to
see the mss if you were willing.'

have said that I had no objection in principle but that I didn't see how I could accept definitely without having a clearer idea of the book. So, if the book is not yet in existence, please tell me more about it; if it is in existence, I should like to get a copy.

As for your enquiry about Faber & Faber books, we can always send you books on receipt direct of their value in sterling.[1] There would be some postage at this end, but unless your orders were really immense, I could guarantee your postage, and collect it from you afterwards. It is also probable that you would have some small duty to pay when you got them – never a round sum, but always odd cents.

Please express, if you get the opportunity, my regrets to Michael Mullins Marching and Chowder Club at having been unable to attend their annual Chowder in Lowell House; I think, however, that they might have held it in a better place.[2]

Yours very sincerely,
[T. S. Eliot]

TO *The Editor of* The Times[3]

11 December 1933   24 Russell Square

'Measure for Measure' at the Old Vic

Sir, – If I am not too tardy, and if you have the space for this type of brief communication, I should like to endorse Mr John Gielgud's appeal in your issue of December 8 on behalf of the current production of *Measure for Measure* at the Old Vic.[4] The opportunity to see this play – and a

1 – Boyle asked in his letter, 'If one sent one of those exchange orders would Faber & Faber oblige with books at English prices? I haven't the last Sweeney yet, and that's near a year old.'

2 – 'On Michaelmas Dean Leighton read a special Chapel for the ever-glorious Michael Mullins Marching & Chowder Club whose Chapter attended in full force save for you . . . The M.M.M. & C.C. held a chowder in Lowell [House], too, and it was all immense and preposterous with side-arms and chasse-pots, chapeaux bras, cricket caps, the halberd and the flagellum Dei &c.' (Manifestly, TSE thought it would have been better to have held the chowder at Eliot House.)

3 – Published in *The Times*, 14 Dec. 1933, 10.

4 – Gielgud regretted the lack of attendance at the production of *Measure for Measure*. 'Let me assure any who, like myself, may feel hesitant about going to see this play, which is usually unfamiliar and unpopular, that they will miss seeing, unless they go quickly, a most beautiful and satisfying production, which makes me very proud to belong to the English theatre. The production only runs for two and a half weeks. Surely many will miss it unless they go immediately. I wish it might be shown to the English provincial towns and to New York, for it seems to me quite complete and perfect in its way, entirely original, and modern

very great play – of Shakespeare which is too rarely produced should be enough of an attraction; but it has been also an opportunity to see some very fine acting and, apart from a few minor blemishes, as satisfactory a presentation as one is likely ever to find. As the blame for any lack of popularity cannot be laid upon the players, it must be attibuted to Shakespeare; but even those whose principles prevent them from approving either the subject-matter or the profoundly Christian spirit of the play might profit be seeing it so very well performed.

> I am, Sir,
> Your obedient servant,
> T. S. Eliot

TO *Emma Healing* CC

11 December 1933   [Faber & Faber Ltd]

Dear Madam,

I thank you for your letter of November 27th, and have read with much interest your son's poems, which disclose genuine feeling and fineness.[1] It is a matter of great regret from every point of view that such a career was so prematurely ended, and anyone who reads the poems must sympathise with your loss.

It is very difficult to say from a publisher's point of view what should be done with such a volume of verse. Many, probably the majority, of the poems are, as you are probably aware, very immature, and interesting only as the work of a very precocious youth. They show, as such work always does, evidence of influences and enthusiasms. I think that the book is more likely to be acceptable to a publisher who brings out a larger proportion of poetry, than it could be to us. We can undertake so little poetry that we are obliged to concentrate either on poets of established reputation, or on young men from whom much may be expected in the future: that is to say, we have to select on the principle of authors rather than on that of individual books.

---

in conception, and yet executed with a sureness and power worthy of the best and oldest traditions of our stage.'

1 – Arnold Cuthbert Healing (grandson of Thomas Healing, Inspector of Schools; colleague and friend of Thomas Arnold), who graduated in modern languages from Cambridge and taught for five years at Watford Grammar School, had died at the age of twenty-eight. His mother collected about fifty of his poems, which she thought distinctive, to submit on 27 Nov. 1933 for TSE's judgement.

I hope you may be able to see your son's poems published in some form.

Yours sincerely,

[T. S. Eliot]

TO *Darsie R. Gillie*[1]   CC

11 December 1933

My dear Gillie,

I must apologise for never having answered your postcard of this summer.[2] I was not at all in London this summer, and although your card was forwarded to me, I was at that moment away from where I was, so to speak, and did not get it until after you had left.

I am now in London again, and I shall be delighted to hear from you, and still more to see you, on your next visit to London.

If you ever have any publishing ideas, I hope that you will let me know of them.

Yours sincerely,

[T. S. Eliot]

TO *John Kaestlin*   CC

12 December 1933   [Faber & Faber Ltd

Dear Sir,

Thank you for sending me the copy of *Contemporaries*, including your article on the work of T. F. Powys, which I shall read with interest.[3] I am afraid that it is impossible for me to express any opinion on Mr Powys's work in general, since all I know of it is two short stories which he has submitted at different times to the *Criterion*. The first of these appeared

---

1–Darsie R. Gillie (1903–1972): Berlin correspondent of *The Morning Post*; later in the 1930s he reported from Warsaw, and as Paris correspondent of the *Manchester Guardian*. During WW2 he worked for the BBC as French News Editor; and in 1944 he returned to the *Guardian*; ultimately, he would be the BBC's representative in Paris.

2–Gillie had sent a PC on 2 Oct., hoping to see TSE on his way through London.

3–Kaestlin (1914–63) wrote from St John's College, Cambridge (where he edited the periodical *Contemporaries*), 7 Dec.: 'There are many who have expressed their desire to hear your opinion on the subject of a man, whom I at any rate consider, with your permission, infinitely more important than he is commonly held. I should be very interested to hear your comments & would be pleased, if you should so wish, to print your criticism in our next issue.'

several years ago, and the second is in my hands, and will be published. The fact is that I am very imperfectly acquainted with contemporary literature, except what I meet with as editor and publisher. I have recently, however, read some volumes of the late D. H. Lawrence's work, but that was in connection with lectures in America.

Yours sincerely,
[T. S. Eliot]

TO *V. A. Demant* cc

12 December 1933   [Faber & Faber Ltd

Dear Father Demant,

Thank you for your letter of the 8th December.[1] I am not, to tell the truth, by any means anxious to lecture or speak in public, after having had so much of it in America, and I am afraid that I may be very busy during the month of April. However, if I accept your invitation, I shall be in a stronger position to decline others, and I feel a certain debt of gratitude to you of which you are probably unaware. I will therefore accept your invitation for April 17th.

Will you please send me a reminder about a month ahead? I shall be interested to hear who your other speakers are to be.

I have written a short note about your book in the forthcoming *Criterion*, but it is very scrappy, and inadequate; it could hardly be called more than a kind of small puff.[2]

Yours sincerely,
[T. S. Eliot]

1–Demant, who wished to make his new parish 'a centre of Religious Education in the district', was planning a course of public lectures: he hoped TSE might lead off with a talk on 'Religion and Literature', on Tues, 17 Apr. 1934. Other lecturers (including perhaps Evelyn Underhill) would speak on politics, economics, and philosophy.

2–'I have suggested that the Christian social philosopher may legitimately, so long as he is careful to distinguish between that which is essential and that which is merely desirable, make use of associated ideas . . . But the Christian social philosopher of our time can only follow such a course safely if he is equally prepared for a *dis*sociation of ideas. He must be able to consider the ideas of class, of property, of nationality not according to current or local prejudices, but according to permanent principles. The Reverend V. A. Demant's *God, Man and Society* . . . possesses, among other excellences, this merit of contributing to the dissociation of ideas' (C. 13 [Jan. 1934], 276–7).

TO *Louis Zukofsky*   TS Beinecke

12 December 1933   *The Criterion*

Dear Mr Zukofsky,

I am afraid that I have let some time elapse without answering your
letter of the 30th November, which I see is somewhat urgent.[1] Of course I
have no objection to your reprinting the part of your essay which appeared
in the *Criterion* – indeed you had no need to ask my permission as the
Criterion only asks for the first serial publication rights.

I shall hope to write to you further about your MS. shortly. I know that
it has been in my hands for some time.

Yours very truly,
T. S. Eliot

TO *Brian Coffey*[2]   CC

12 December 1933

Dear Mr Coffey,

I had delayed writing to you in the hope that I might have time to read

---

1 – Zukofsky had written, 13 Nov.: 'The *Observer* (Memphis, Tenn.) has accepted my essay
E.P.: His Cantos, section 3 of which appeared in the *Criterion*, April, 1931. I should be
grateful for your permission to reprint that section.

'Also, I should vastly appreciate word from you – favorable or unfavorable – on my
MSS. which you have had for some time: some poems, and the third part of an essay on
[Guillaume] Apollinaire by M. René Taupin and myself – due to appear shortly as a volume,
in French.' (Taupin had submitted the essay on Apollinaire on 7 Jan. 1933.) See Zukofsky
and Taupin, *Le Style Apollinaire* (1934).

2 – Brian Coffey (1905–95), poet, critic, educator and publisher, attended Clongowes Wood
School and University College, Dublin, where he read medicine and then mathematics,
physics and chemistry; from 1930 he studied in Paris, where he befriended Samuel Beckett
and Thomas MacGreevey; and in 1933 he enrolled at the Institut Catholique where he
studied philosophy under Jacques Maritain. During WW2 he worked as a teacher in England,
and he then emigrated to the USA where he became Assistant Professor of Philosophy at St
Louis University, Missouri, 1947–52. From 1954 to 1972 he taught sixth-form mathematics
in London (he taught among others the young Haffenden). His collections of poetry include
Poems (co-written with his friend Denis Devlin, 1930); *Three Poems* (1933); *Third Person*
(1938); a much-anthologised long poem called 'Missouri Sequence' (*University Review*,
1962); *Selected Poems* (1971); and translations from Paul Éluard, Stéphane Mallarmé and
others. See further *Brian Coffey Special Issue, Irish University Review* 5: 1 (Spring 1975);
Donal Moriarty, *The Art of Brian Coffey* (2000). TSE wrote to Edith Sitwell on 28 Aug.
1945: 'Brian Coffey always seemed to me a nice, sensible young man and I have not the
slightest recollection of his writing any poems. He is really a philosopher but the Irish haven't
very much use for philosophers who are not in Holy Orders and he has been teaching in a

M. Raymond's book first, but so far I have not been able to do so.[1] I shall certainly look at it as soon as possible, both with a view to publication and for its own interest. I am very much obliged to you for making the suggestion, and will give the book serious attention, though I am doubtful whether there would be a large enough public to justify its translation into English.

I should be very much interested to see the essay which you are writing, and should be grateful if you could let me know how to obtain it when it is published. I am very much obliged to you for your kind and encouraging remarks.[2]

Yours sincerely,
[T. S. Eliot]

TO *Alexandre Marc*[3]   CC

12 December 1933

My dear Sir,

I must apologise for not replying more quickly to your letter of the 25th September, enclosing a chapter of *Jeune Europe*, but I knew that it was quite out of the question to consider it for immediate publication, as your book was to be published so soon, and I therefore put it aside to read at more leisure. I am extremely interested, and, of course, very sympathetic to your general conclusions. If I were considering this chapter for publication in the *Criterion*, I should suggest that there is a certain amount in it which covers much the same ground as has already been covered by persons writing in England; and I should have suggested

---

Roman Catholic school near Sheffield.' TSE to Charles Monteith, internal memo, 15 May 1964: 'I knew Brian Coffey, whose father, Dr Coffey, was my host once in Dublin. He was the head of University College, if I remember rightly, and had something to do with the "rising" which was suppressed by the Black-and-Tans during the first world war.'

1–Coffey wrote from Paris (15 Nov.) with the hope that F&F should be interested in a book by Marcel Raymond entitled *De Baudelaire au Surréalisme* which everyone was praising in Paris. 'The calm and sound judgement of M. Raymond has above all pleased the poets.'

2–Coffey was working on an article, '*La jeune poésie anglaise*', for a French review, and proposed to say 'a lot' about Auden and Spender and others. 'But it seems to me that their work has been made possible only by the numerous suggestions and hints that you have given in your critical work. Besides there is your poetry without which they are lost.' Coffey wrote again on 29 Dec. that it was his friend Maritain who asked him to write on the young English poets – 'but where he intends to publish my work I do not yet know'. He asked to see TSE on his way through London on 10 Jan.

3–Alexandre Marc (1904–2000), Russian-born French Jewish writer.

that we should be much more interested in your own observations and statement of principles, than in a summary of the situation.

I am writing now, however, to express the hope that you will have some other suggestion to make of a subject within the frame of your social and political philosophy which I could use in the *Criterion*. I should be very glad indeed to be able to publish something by you, and would welcome the receipt of anything which you have on hand which you consider suitable, or else suggestions towards articles which you have in mind to write.

I am,
Yours sincerely,
[T. S. Eliot]
Editor.

TO *Benjamin Bissell* CC

12 December 1933

Dear Mr Bissell,

I must apologize for the delay in answering your letter of November 11th. It is difficult to tell, merely from the titles of papers, whether they are suitable for the *Criterion* or not, but I should be very glad to see the ones which you suggest, if you would forward them to me here.[1]

I hope that you enjoy your work in Cambridge, and that I may see you there on some future visit.[2]

Yours sincerely,
[T. S. Eliot]

---

1 – The Revd Bissell's proposed titles were 'The Problem of Leisure' and 'Newman and the Problem of Authority'.
2 – Bissell (a friend of Austin Warren) had written on 11 Nov., 'I am now working on a parish here (St Andrew's, Chesterton) and hope to remain for a time.'

TO *T. F. Powys*[1]

CC

12 December 1933

Dear Sir,

I wish to keep your story 'The Gong' for publication in the *Criterion* as soon as possible, and I am therefore returning herewith the other story which you sent me at the same time, entitled 'They were my Fields'.[2]

Yours faithfully,

[T. S. Eliot]

TO *Stephen Spender*

TS Northwestern

12 December 1933   Faber & Faber Ltd

My dear Spender,

I must apologise for keeping your story 'By the Lake' so long.[3] I am not, in fact, quite sure what I think about it, but very likely would have wanted to use it if it had been of a possible length. It is twice too long for use in the *Criterion*, and I am afraid that you will have the same difficulty anywhere. As to serialization, it might possibly be run in two parts in a periodical appearing at more frequent intervals than the *Criterion*, but I think myself that it would be spoilt by breaking it up in that way. Have you any other stories or sketches on hand?[4]

I have been meaning to write and suggest a day for lunch, but I find my time pretty well filled up till Christmas. Almost any day after Christmas, including Sundays, but not the following one, the 31st, will do for me. Will you suggest a day?

Yours ever,

T. S. Eliot

Can you come to a *Criterion* evening on Jan. 3d? Full notice [to follow].[5]

1–T. F. Powys (1875–1953), novelist and short-story writer: author of *Mr Weston's Good Wine* (1927) and *Unclay* (1931).

2–Powys had submitted the stories on 31 Oct. 1933, and wrote to ask for them back on 7 Dec. Powys, 'The Gong', C. 13 (Apr. 1934), 397–406.

3–Submitted by Spender on 11 Nov.

4–Spender replied, 14 Dec.: 'I have no other stories at present, as all my work of that sort is held up by the work I am doing on a book about Henry James.'

5–Added by hand.

TO *Edouard Roditi*

TS UCLA

12 December 1933   Faber & Faber Ltd

Dear Roditi,

I have been meaning to write to you for some time. First of all about the new poems that you enclose with your letter of the 22nd. Their format of typing, by the way, sometimes makes it a little difficult to know where one poem stops and the next one begins. I like best one called 'Trafalgar Square', which I believe includes two pages. I also like the next page after that, beginning 'No man is master of the land', which appears to be a separate poem. I should like to use these instead of Jehudah Abravanel.

These poems seem to me on the whole to show an improvement in management, although I still have to complain of a lack so to speak of imagery that I can bite my teeth into. In this respect Jehudah Abravanel seems to me to be much stronger.

I am very sorry that we cannot see our way to doing your book of verse, but we can undertake very little in the way of poetry at the present time. I have the MS. here, and will not forward it to your Paris address until I have your instructions.

It is possible that I may be in Paris again for a few days in January or February, & will let you know in the hope of a meeting.[1]

Yours sincerely,
T. S. Eliot

TO *Michael Roberts*

TS Janet Adam Smith

12 December 1933   *The Criterion*

Dear Mr Roberts,

I must apologise for my delay in answering your letter of the 5th November.[2] It was not lost from my mind, however, and the other day

---

1 – Roditi replied, 19 Dec.: 'The poems which I sent you are seven in all, that is to say one poem on each page, so that what you understood to be a second page of "Trafalgar Square" is, as a matter of fact, a distinct poem although much on the same theme.

'As you say, I have concentrated in these poems, particularly on the construction and management and neglected imagery, which might have diverted my attention and which, I feel, I can always fall back on whenever I want. I had scarcely hoped that these last poems would interest you for the *Criterion* and I had already given them to someone else.'

Roditi, 'Trafalgar Square', C. 13 (Apr. 1934), 449–50.

2 – Roberts had been talking to Charles Madge – 'whom I have known for some time as a young poet of considerable originality & force. The width of his reading & the temper &

I was in Cambridge and had the opportunity of a few words with Mr Richards about your friend Charles Madge. I think the best thing would be for him to come and see me here one day, and I should be very much obliged if you would convey the invitation to him. It would be most certain, if he would ring up first and make an appointment with my secretary.

Yours very sincerely,
T. S. Eliot

TO *Harry Levin* TS Houghton

13 December 1932   *The Criterion*

Dear Levin,

Thank you for your letter of the 27th November, enclosing the long-delayed essay on Cleveland.[1] I shall be very glad to use it, though I am afraid that I may have to keep it for six months or so, the reason being that I have had on hand for some time an essay on Crashaw which must take precedence, and it wouldn't do to publish both in the same number.

If you are going to be in London, will you not come and see me here one day? The best way is to ring up and make an appointment with my secretary beforehand.

Yours sincerely,
T. S. Eliot

TO *Hugh Gordon Porteus* CC

13 December 1933   [*The Criterion*]

Dear Mr Porteus,

Would you care to review Lewis's *One-Way Song*[2] for the next number of the *Criterion*? I daresay that you have already reviewed it elsewhere,

---

balance of his judgment would be exceptional in a man of any age. He was telling me that he would like to read Mr Murry's new book on Blake, and it occurred to me later that, if you have not already sent out the book for review, no more suitable reviewer than Mr Madge is likely to be found, for he has done some remarkable work on Blake himself, and, as a member of the Communist Party who has some inkling of that which the Christian means by religion, he is qualified to examine Mr Murry's thesis. I think Mr Richards would very willingly confirm my judgment.'

1–Letter not found. Levin was visiting London at this time.

2–TSE wrote in his 'Foreword' to a reissue (Methuen, 1960) of *One-Way-Song* (F&F, 1933): 'The question for the reader to ask who reads *One-Way Song* without any knowledge

but if not in too conspicuous a periodical, that might not matter. It is difficult to think of anyone who knows and understands Lewis's work well enough to do the job satisfactorily.[1]

Yours sincerely,

[T. S. Eliot]

TO *Mario Praz*　　　　TS Galleria Nazionale d'Arte Moderna, Rome

13 December 1933　　　　　*The Criterion*

My dear Praz,

I must apologise for having left your letter of the 20th October so long unanswered. What happened was that I was away in the country. I gave your letter to another director to attend to your protest about review books. He agreed with me that the books you mentioned, especially *The Quattro Cento* should certainly have been sent to you.[2] I hope that you will have no trouble in the future in getting the books you want, but if you do, please let me know.

Your letter left my hands in this way before I had answered it, and therefore, I am sorry to say, left my mind. I am not quite sure whether you

---

of [Wyndham] Lewis's other writings, is not "Is this poetry?" The first question is simply: "Does this writing attract or repel me?" After we have acquainted ourselves with a few of Lewis's principal prose books, we may return to *One-Way Song* and draw comparisons, finding perhaps some similarity to the "snarling satirists" of the Elizabethan age – an age of writers of a vigour, opulence of diction and careless abundance which make them congenial to the genius of Lewis. If we then decide that *One-Way Song* is *verse* rather than *poetry*, we shall find that it belongs with that body of high-ranking verse which is more important than most minor poetry; and it would be only the very obtuse who could dismiss this verse as *doggerel*. You will have to admit that it has style . . . Lewis is unto the "intellectuals" a stumbling-block, and unto the multitude foolishness. The latter indeed are hardly aware of his name. The more respectable of the former, being unable to stomach his work, treat Lewis for the most part to an uneasy silence; the less respectable vociferate the cry of "fascist!" – a term falsely applied to Lewis, but flung by the *massenmensch* at some who, like Lewis, choose to walk alone' (9–10).

1–Porteus, who had written an unsigned notice of *One-Way Song* for the *Listener*, replied on 15 Dec. that he felt keen to write 'at greater length' about Lewis's volume. 'Perhaps I have too much sympathy with Lewis to be a good critic of his work; but the poem is not likely, I think, to get any justice done to it by persons familiar with his work but out of sympathy with him.'
Porteus on *One-Way Song*: C. 13 (Apr. 1934), 492–4.
2–'Some time ago I reviewed in the *Stampa* Adrian Stokes' book on the *Quattro Cento*: I sent a copy of my review to the Publicity Dept. of Faber & Faber, and asked for a copy of the reviewed book (I had read a friend's copy), wch I would have liked to possess . . . I had no reply. So that I do not venture to ask now for a copy of E. Pound's *XXX Cantos* or H. Read's

are still in England. If so, I hope that I may see you before you leave; if not, I am very sorry.

I have learned from other sources that I have to congratulate you on two events; the first is your appointment to Rome, which, I understand, is the most distinguished professorship of its kind in Italy, and the second is your marriage.[1]

It is just possible that I may be invited, through the offices of the Princess di Bassiano, to give a lecture in Rome in the Spring, and if so, I shall certainly look forward to meeting you, and, I hope, making the acquaintance of your wife.

I hope, finally, that your duties in Rome will not be so arduous as to prevent you from occasionally contributing to the *Criterion*, and reviewing books for it.

With all best wishes,
Yours ever sincerely,
T. S. Eliot

<Could you let me have, or tell me how to obtain, a copy of your translation of *The Waste Land*, which may have gone astray in America?>[2]

TO *Norman W. Hester*   CC

14 December 1933   [Faber & Faber Ltd]

Dear Mr Hester,

Thank you very much for your letter enclosing your new design of the Creation, which I shall accept with pleasure as a Christmas gift, and for the pleasant memories which it recalls.[3] It seems to me that you have made a very great improvement over the original design as I recall it, and I am very happy to have it in its new form. It seems to me on the whole very successful.

Art Now. Apparently Faber & Faber does not think that foreign reviews help to the selling of books. Still, no Italian would have known of A. Stokes' *Quattro Cento* but for my article.'
1 – Praz had been appointed Professor of English at the University of Rome, with effect from Nov. 1934; and he was engaged to be married in London in Mar. 1934 before leaving for Rome.
2 – Added by hand. Praz's translation of *TWL* had first appeared in *Circoli* with additional notes.
3 – Hester wrote (n.d.) from Kelham Theological College: 'This attempt is the final of several that I have done since you were here, and personally I think it is the most satisfactory. I tried several other ideas for the chaos, including geometric forms expressing light and darkness. But I could not get it right to my satisfaction, and finally I conceived the idea of making the chaos into a "vortex" . . . I shall be interested to hear what you think of it.'

I am afraid that I don't know either the play which you have just produced, or the one you are to produce next year.[1] I have heard the latter praised, and hope that I may have the opportunity of coming to see your performance.

Thanking you for your news, and looking forward to seeing you again in January.

Yours very sincerely,
[T. S. Eliot]

TO *Serge Bolshakoff*

CC

14 December 1933   [Faber & Faber Ltd]

Dear Mr Bolshakoff,

Thank you very much for your very full letter of instructions.[2] I am very sorry indeed that I cannot join you first at Farnham in the morning, as I had hoped; I find that I have an important appointment at 10.0 o'clock that morning, so I shall have to come in the afternoon, taking a train which leaves Taplow at 4.9. I am sorry to be unable to see Farnham under your guidance, and hope that I shall have some later opportunity.

Yours sincerely,
[T. S. Eliot]

---

1 – 'One reason for my delay in writing is that we have been quite busy this term with a play which we presented . . . at a small private theatre near here. I had quite a large part . . . The play was "The Berg", by Ernest Raymond. Do you know it? Is it by no means a great play, and some of the "theology" in it aroused great opposition in the House. Next year, if all is well, I hope to produce "Richard of Bordeaux" by Gordon Daviot, which is now running in London at the New Theatre. Have you seen it? It is certainly a fine play.' *Richard of Bordeaux*, which ran for over a year in the West End, made a star of John Gielgud; 'Gordon Daviot' was a pseudonym of Elizabeth Mackintosh (1896–1952), playwright and novelist, who also wrote as 'Josephine Tey'.

2 – Bolshakoff's directives included the instruction that TSE should arrive by the Southern Railway at Farnham, Surrey – because he wanted first of all to show delegates the 'remarkable Community of the Servants of Christ the King' at Mount Olivet Monastery in Frensham.

14 December 1933   [Faber & Faber Ltd]

Dear Browne,

Thank you for your letter of the 15th, enclosing useful information for the Crusades and the Dedication.[1]

By some odd delusion, I had formed the impression that our meeting with Miss Fogerty was to be last Tuesday, instead of next. I did not come to my senses until I arrived at the Albert Hall, and finding no one there, pulled out your letter, where the date was clearly *enough* shown.

I have to go down to Rochester for the night on Monday, but trust that I will catch an early enough train back to be with you at 10 o'clock next Tuesday. I expect to have the whole morning free at all events.

Yours ever,
[T. S. Eliot]

TO *Stephen Spender*   TS Northwestern

14 December 1933   *The Criterion*

Dear Spender,

There is a postscript which I should have added to my last letter. When I sent you that book of Asquith's letters, I had hardly glanced at it, and thought that it was merely something which it would be slightly amusing to cut up. Since then, I have talked with somebody about it, and have more information about the lady to whom the letters are addressed. It seems to me on second thoughts best that a book of this kind should be allowed to sink to the bottom without comment, so please scrap it.[2]

Please let me know if there is anything else you would like to review for the *Criterion*.

Yours sincerely,
T. S. Eliot

---

1 – Historical information to be deployed in the theatrical pageant, *The Rock*.
2 – *H. H. A.: Letters of the Earl of Oxford and Asquith to a Friend*, ed. Desmond MacCarthy (1933). The Liberal Prime Minister H. H. Asquith (1852–1928) penned some 560 letters to Venetia Stanley (1887–1948) during the period 1910–15: he took care to destroy her letters to himself.

TO *Thomas McGreevy*   TS Trinity College Dublin

14 December 1933   Faber & Faber Ltd

Dear Tom,

My time seems to be pretty well filled up to the end of the year, and I shall be going away for the New Year's weekend. Would you care to lunch with me on Sunday the 24th? If that won't do, I will suggest a day after Christmas, but I am not at present sure which.

Yours ever,

T. S. Eliot

TO *Richard Rees*   CC

14 December 1933   [*The Criterion*]

Dear Rees,

Mr R. P. Blackmur of Cambridge, Massachusetts, has sent me the enclosed essay on the work of Ezra Pound, which he says is to appear in the January number of the *Hound and Horn*.[1] He has offered it also to me, but unfortunately our January, or rather December, number is already through the press, and I could not use it until March at the earliest. He suggested, in the letter he wrote me, that if I could not use it, he would like me to send it to Middleton Murry, but I presume he is thinking of the *Adelphi*, and in that case it seems to me best to send it direct to you. If you can not use it, I should be very grateful if you would be so kind as to send it on to *Life & Letters*, for which it is perhaps more suitable than for the *Adelphi*.[2]

Yours very sincerely,

[T. S. Eliot]

1 – Presumably 'Masks of Ezra Pound' (written 1933), *Hound & Horn* 7: 2 (1934).
2 – Rees (19 Dec.) said he would send the essay on to *Life & Letters*. 'P.S. I wonder if Herbert Read ever showed you some poems by Dylan Thomas?'

15 December 1933   Faber & Faber Ltd

Exc. Podesta Rumpuscat/[1]
   Lorsque les loups vivent de vent:[2] in reply to yours of the 24th
September.[3] What about
        Preface
        Roubadours (PD)
        Arnaut (Inst)
        Eliz. Classics (PD)
        TRANSLATORS OF Greek
        French Poets revised
        H. James
        Reme de Gourmont
        Cavalcanti
        Fenellosa

1 – Cf. TSE, 'Of the Awefull Battle of the Pekes and the Pollicles: Together with some Account
of the Participation of the Pugs and the Poms, and the Intervention of the Great Rumpuscat'
– whose eyes (perhaps not unlike Ezra Pound's) 'were like fireballs fearfully blazing'.
2 – In his early, anonymous essay on EP's verse, *Ezra Pound: His Metric and Poetry* (1918),
TSE compared EP's early work with that of Mallarmé, and with these lines from *Le
Testament* of François Villon: '*Sur le Noël, morte saison, / Lorsque les loups vivent le vent*'
(*TCC*, 171).
3 – EP (24 Sept.) had sketched the contents of his proposed volume of selected essays –
utimately published as *Make It New* (F&F, 1934):
        1. Preface
        2. Troubadours / Quarterly Rev. 1912   (Pavs)
        3. Arnaut Daniel (Instigations)   Instig.
        4. Eliz/ Classicists (Egoist)   Pav.
        5. Translators of Greek (Egoist)   Inst.
        6. French Poets/ revised.   Inst.
        7. H. James,
        8. Cavalcanti   general criticism Marsano edtn. And
                                               Guido's Relations. Dial 1928.
        9. Harold Monro   Criterion 1932
appendices. Studies in Contemporary mentality as
I. (documents pour servir, and to prevent any gay allusions in the Harold, from
seeming to be merely launched by fancy in to pissing air)
II. Strife and contention / i: e. the Don't's without the 'of an Imagist'.
Matter of ACT/ there must be a Cavalcanti somewhere in London. IF I send you
an Instig/ that wd/ leave only the Eliz/ Classicists / which I think you vaguely
remember.
and the Stud/ Contemp / Ment / the sottisier pubd/ in New Age. showing god
damn it SHOWING the shit eaten by Brit. Reader during that pee/ree/yod.'
   A postscript, penned by EP at the head, notes too: '9 Essays of a vermiform appendix.'

Noh – or yes? Havent got the volume available.

Houseman

Monro

I must ask you to put these in chronological and topographical order; you know I havnt any Head for figures.

What about 'In the Vortex' just to remind public what a good tipster you was – with the DATES in large letters?[1]

With your last ejection of bile at the end as you suggest.

I presume you wish to keep your literary criticism clear from parerga on economics, American history, religion, music etc. and think its just as well: this vol. lit. crit. only.

Please give actual PAGES of Cavalcanti you wish include: I have the volume here.

Contemporanea now under scrutiny of Morley.

What else have you written, is the question. Goddamb it I cant keep track of my own published works, let alone yours. If I had complete files of all American periodicals for last 20 years it would be diffrent. Dont believe you ever said anything important about Corneille, Goethe or Appolonius Rhodius. Have you got copy of *Dial* with that other Arnaut thing you want in?

Please give list of contributions selected from

Pavannes

Instigations

Cavalcanti

which can be set up WITHOUT alterations. But I have my copies of Pavannes & Inst. and can send them out to you if helpful.[2]

Nothing heard yet about Jeff/Mutt.

Goddamb it.

What do you know about a man named Lowenfels. I dont generally like foreigners. He iss very proliffic.

Your Brideson piece in anthology is the best of him that I have seen, but I dont think it is any more Essential literature than Auden.[3]

Goddamb it.

T.

---

1 – 'In the Vortex' was collected in EP's *Instigations* (New York: Boni and Liveright, 1920), incorporating EP's review of TSE's *POO*, from *Poetry* 10: 5 (Aug. 1917), 264–71.
2 – EP (24 Sept.): 'I take it there is no call for me to send up Pavs/ and Insts? ???'
3 – See EP on D. G. Bridson, *Active Anthology* (1933).

TO *Horace Gregory*   TS Syracuse University Library

19 December 1933   Faber & Faber Ltd

My dear Gregory,

It seems that I never answered your letter of October 22nd about your Lawrence book.[1] I am deeply sorry for the delay; I have been under the impression for a long time that I had written to you after the matter was brought up before our directors. I was away from London most of the time: hence several oversights on my part.

I think your book is an interesting and a good book, but we came to the conclusion that, from a publisher's point of view, it was not worthwhile to attempt the Lawrence market with a small critical essay like this. My own feeling in fact was that, as we have not published anything by or about Lawrence except his two pamphlets, it was too late to be wise for us to take any notice. We thought that this was distinctly a book for Secker to handle, and I trust that something has been accomplished by the Viking in this direction, and that the book has not been held up through my negligence. If Secker doesn't take it, I should think it might appeal to a firm like Wishart. Probably it is best to leave the matter to the Viking.

Do let me see some more poems of yours with a view to the *Criterion*.
With all good wishes for the Christmas season,

Yours ever sincerely,
T. S. Eliot

TO *Serge Bolshakoff*   cc

19 December 1933   [Faber & Faber Ltd]

Dear Mr Bolshakoff,

I was extremely grieved to find myself obliged to send you a wire yesterday to say that I should be unable to join you after all, but I found that some important private legal business required my presence in London tomorrow. It is a disappointment not to meet the other guests whom you have invited, and to make the acquaintance of Nashdom Abbey, but

---

1 – Viking Press published *Pilgrim of the Apocalypse: A Critical Study of D. H. Lawrence* (1933), by Gregory, who asked if F&F might be interested in securing the British rights. 'I'd be very grateful for your opinion of the Lawrence book, for some parts of it, I think, are effectively written.'

I hope you will let me know when you come to London, and give me the opportunity of a talk with you then.

With many regrets,
Yours sincerely,
[T. S. Eliot]

TO *Alida Monro*   CC

20 December 1933   [Faber & Faber Ltd]

Dear Alida,

Some days ago, a lady named Mrs Healing sent me the collected poems of her son, who died at the age of 28. I returned them with the most sympathetic note I could write, as they were the usual sort of thing. She now writes to me that, having seen your anthology, she intends to send you the poems, or some of them, with a view to your including them in some future edition, and asks me to send her a word of commendation which she could enclose to you.

I can't honestly do this, so I shall send word to her that I am writing directly to you, and this is the best that I can do. However, I trust that you will give the poems a conscientious glance. She writes very nicely indeed about them, and I wanted to be as kind as possible.[1]

Yours ever,
[T. S. Eliot]

TO *David G. Peck*[2]   CC

20 December 1933   [Faber & Faber Ltd]

My dear Sir,

I thank you for your letter of the 16th instant, inviting me to address a meeting in Oxford on Wednesday January 24th.[3] I am honoured

---

1–Monro replied on 6 Jan. 1934, after reading the poems by Healing: 'I entirely agree with you regarding their merits.'

2–David G. Peck (b. 1911) was to be author of *Faith* (1939), *Catholic Design for Society* (1940), *Earth and Heaven: the theology of the countryside* (1947), *Living Worship – The Archbishop of Canterbury's Lent Book* (1944) and *Eulogy on William Barnes* (1951).

3–Peck (St John Baptist Rectory, Manchester) invited TSE to address a meeting organised by Anglo-Catholic ordinands and undergraduates, with the assistance of the Dean of Oriel and others. 'Those of us who heard your speech at the last A. C. Summer School, or have since read it in "Christendom", ['Catholicism and International Order', *Christendom: A*

by the invitation, and flattered by what you say of my remarks at the summer school, and would willingly come to address such a meeting, but unfortunately I have to address the students at Kelham during the course of the same week, and it is impossible for me, with all the other work that I have to do, to deliver two public addresses so close together. I hope that we may be able to arrange another day at some future time.

Yours very truly,

[T. S. Eliot]

TO *H. A. Moreton*   CC

20 December 1933   [Faber & Faber Ltd]

Dear Mr Moreton,

Thank you for your letter of the 18th December.[1] I had already heard fairly fully about *Oecumenica* from Father Gabriel, and had signified my willingness to contribute, although warning him that I might not have the time to do so before next summer. As for what you ask, Jacques Maritain is a friend of mine, and I am quite willing to write and ask him to give his name, though I am not sure whether he is at the moment in Paris or in Toronto. It is impossible to say whether a French Roman Catholic would be prepared to contribute or not. Ordinarily, as you probably know, it is likely to be easier to get Continental Romans to contribute to an Anglican venture than it is to get English Romans. But whether it might not be more difficult to get [him] to contribute to a review published on the Continent and in French, I do not know. But before I write to him, I wish you would let me know whether there are any other Romans in any European country, and preferably clerics, whose collaboration is assured. If I could mention the names of one or two Roman clergy, it might be reassuring to Maritain. Do you know, for instance, a certain Father Péret, whom I have come across at one or two Anglican or interdenominational affairs in London. There might be a few Belgians who would be well-disposed, and I dare say Father Gabriel's friends at Marienlach.

Journal of Christian Sociology 3: 11 (Sept. 1933), 171–84], feel that you could do us an immense service if you could speak somewhat upon the same lines . . . I can assure you that our movement in Oxford is full of promise. It is in touch with the University Church Union, & its direction is in the hands of practicing Catholics.'

1–Fr. Moreton, Pencombe Rectory, Herefordshire, wished to promote the periodical *Oecumenica: Revue Trimestrielle de Synthèse Théologique*.

I cannot think of any other Continental friends of mine, except Maritain, who would be important to you.

Yours sincerely,
[T. S. Eliot]

TO *Leon M. Little*   CC

20 December 1933   [Faber & Faber Ltd]

My dear Leon,

I have your letter of November 25th, but I don't know any more of the whereabouts of Tinckom-Fernandez than you do.[1] As a matter of fact, you wrote to me giving an address in Chiswick, but I did not find out anything about him, and I am afraid I did not take the trouble to investigate personally at that address. I don't see what I could do except to call Scotland Yard, and I don't suppose they would know anything about him there; and they would certainly not be pleased at being bothered by such an enquiry. I am afraid there is nothing to be done about it.

Best wishes to you and Eleanor for Christmas and the new year.

Yours ever,
[T. S. Eliot]

TO *Theodor Haecker*   CC

20 December 1933   [Faber & Faber Ltd]

My dear Herr Haecker,

Thank you very much for your letter of the 15th instant. I should certainly suppose, judging from the title and from what I have read of your work, that the essay you suggest would be, if anywhere near the proper length, quite suitable.

1–Class of 1910, Harvard College. 'Our classmate, Tinckom-Fernandez has got himself lost again from my records. I believe you knew him in college. The last I heard of him he was a newspaper correspondent in Constantinople . . . Have you any idea how to address him?' William George Tinckom-Fernandez had been a good friend of TSE's at Harvard: see his memoir 'T. S. Eliot, '10, an Advocate Friendship', *Harvard Advocate* 125: 3 (Dec. 1938); repr. in *The Harvard Advocate Anthology*, ed. Donald Hall (1950), 317–27. 'I used to descend on him at his summer home in East Gloucester . . .' wrote Tinckom-Fernandez. 'He used to take me sailing in his catboat, and he could handle a sheet with the best in Gloucester.' TSE called him 'a crony of mine' (*Paris Review*, 1959).

May I suggest, however, that the safest plan would be for you to send me the German text to read first, and I can then give it to Mr Dru to translate for us. I should be glad to have the essay as soon as possible, and look forward to reading it with the keenest interest.[1]

With the most cordial good wishes of the season,

Yours very sincerely,

[T. S. Eliot]

FROM *Vivien Eliot* TO *Ottoline Morrell*   MS Texas

26 December 1933   68 Clarence Gate Gardens

My dearest Ottoline

Thank you so very much for your two presents, & for not forgetting me this terrible Christmas. Both your presents mean a great deal to me, and I am very pleased indeed to have them.

I have felt frightfully being quite cut off from you all these terrible months, and I do not see why it is necessary.

I should have been thankful for an opportunity to speak to you, or to have a message, even.

I live now in a state of siege. How long it will be I dont know. I had such a terrible shock in the summer, & then since then an increasing nightmare, with more & more *attacks*, & complete *bewilderment*. If one had the *strength* of 2 or 3 *strong men* one would have been worn down to nearly death by now.

I am pleased to think my strength *cannot* last much longer.

What appalled [?appals] & amazes & completely bewilders me is that I was expected to *agree* with & aquiesce in a *wicked plot*. And *still* am – ! *Bombarded. Threatened.*

I had no little presents for anyone this year. I had to stay in bed nearly all of the last 3 months, & can only dress for a few hours, some days . . . and have had to *type*, and *write* day after day without ceasing.

Do let me have a word, *soon*.

My love to you.

Vivienne – Haigh – *Eliot*

1 – 'Theodicy and Tragedy', trans. Alexander Dru, C. 13 (Apr. 1934), 371–81.

TO *Serge Bolshakoff*   CC

27 December 1933   [Faber & Faber Ltd]

Dear Mr Bolshakoff,

Thank you for your very copious letter of the 21st instant, which reached me this morning.[1] I was indeed sorry to be obliged to miss your conference. As a matter of fact, I was not even able to fulfil the engagement on account of which I remained in London, as I contracted a bad cold, and had to keep my bed most of that week.

I have not had time fully to digest your letter, but I think that I had better write at once and say frankly that I cannot give my name to be used publicly in connection with any project until I am a little clearer in mind as to what the project is. I think that I understand better the scheme of organization of your academy than I understand the purposes which the academy is to serve. For this reason it seems to me desirable that I should have the opportunity of discussing the whole matter in conversation before I proceed any further.

I must say, however, that I disagree emphatically from the views of Lord Tavistock about including Quakers and Unitarians.[2] Of course I cannot speak with any finality on this point until I understand the aims better, but it is my conviction that any organization of Christians so wide as to include these parties, is not likely, with all due respect, to have any concern with any purposes in which I am personally interested.[3]

                                        Yours very sincerely,
                                        [T. S. Eliot]

1 – Bolshakoff's long letter reported on the initial discussions held the previous week, including details of the proposed 'Statutes of the International Academy of the Christian Sociology'.

2 – Bolshakoff reported among many other things Lord Tavistock's view that 'the Quakers and the Unitarians are also the Christians but not baptised and they do very serious social work'.

3 – Bolshakoff returned on 29 Dec.: 'As you state that you understand the organisation but not the purpose clearly I shall try to restate you that more extensively [*sic*]. The projected Academy is a body of Christian thinkers, social workers or statesmen discussing periodically together various social problems.' Apropos TSE's specific reservation: 'I am in perfect accord with you about Quakers and Unitarians because . . . I doubt if they are Christians. I believe they are not.'

TO *Jean de Menasce*[1]   TS Archives Dominicaines, Paris

St John the Evangelist   Faber & Faber Ltd
[27 Dec.] 1933

My dear Menasce,

I was very happy to find your card this morning, and to learn that you think of me from time to time. At some time or other – next spring or summer if you are there – I should like to visit you for a day or two at Le Saulchoir.[2] Perhaps you will let me know if this is permissible. I think one of our S.S.M. (Kelham) men, Father Gabriel Hebert, visited the monastery last year. I have no ties now other than business, and am much alone.

I shall send you a small book of three lectures which pleases me (so far) more than *The Use of Poetry*, as soon as it is published. I have just given the proof to D'Arcy to look over. I should love to see Cattaui again, if he is about.

Ever yours affectionately, and in Christo,

T. S. Eliot

TO *Ottoline Morrell*   TS Texas

27 December 1933   Faber & Faber Ltd

My dear Ottoline,

Thank you very much for the Diary, which I found here this morning. It was really kind of you – I did not expect that you would remember me in this accustomed way. Like the previous editions, it will go with me everywhere throughout the year.

---

1 – Jean de Menasce (1902–73), theologian and orientalist (his writings include studies in Judaism, Zionism and Hasidism), was born in Alexandria into an aristocratic Jewish Egyptian family and educated in Alexandria, at Balliol College, Oxford (where he was contemporary with Graham Greene and took his BA in 1924), and at the Sorbonne (Licence es-Lettres). In Paris, he was associated with the magazines *Commerce* and *L'Esprit*, and he translated several of TSE's poems for French publication: his translation of *TWL* was marked '*revuée et approuvée par l'auteur*'. He became a Catholic convert in 1926, was ordained in 1935 a Dominican priest – Father Pierre de Menasce – and went on to be Professor of the History of Religion at the University of Fribourg, 1938–48; Professor and Director of Studies, specialising in Ancient Iranian religions, at the École Pratique des Hautes Études, Paris. TSE came to consider him 'the only really first-rate French translator I have ever had' (letter to Kathleen Raine, 17 May 1944).
2 – A French Dominican study house in the French-Belgian town of Le Saulchoir.

I should like very much to come to see you, if you care to have me; but not, of course, when you are having other people.[1]

> Yours ever affectionately,
> Tom

TO *James Joyce*

TS National Gallery of Ireland

28 December 1933

Faber & Faber Ltd

My dear Joyce,

Many thanks for your letter of the 18th. I am very glad to have further news about the early publication of *Ulysses* in New York.[2]

I am sorry that your solicitors do not seem to have understood the nature of my enquiry, as I wrote very fully. They could get a little more enlightenment, I hope, if they would write to me; so far, I have had nothing from them but an acknowledgement of my letter, but I suppose that they quite correctly applied to you first for your authorisation to communicate with me. The major point was certainly not the matter of copyright, as I understood from you quite clearly in conversation that *Ulysses* is copyright in this country, and that it is copyright in your name. The point is simply that in going ahead with the matter, we should wish to have a lawyer of our own at hand who was completely conversant with the whole history of the case, from Miss Weaver's first attempts to get the book printed here, down to the Customs prohibition. The data which M. Léon provided are not adequate for the first part of this history. All

1–OM wrote from 10 Gower Street to VW, 5 Dec. 1933: 'I have not laid eyes on the Frozen Rev. T. S. Eliot since he left for U.S.A. – He has dropt me – but I survive – I dare not read his book – as I should feel so angry with it I know. Also his sort of criticism bores me – It is arid – like dry stale biscuits . . . But I see how good Toms own Poetry is' (Berg). And OM was to write to JDH on 9 Jan. 1934, after seeing TSE: 'And he was so charming, & simple & interesting & friendly that I felt quite elated by seeing him. He really is remarkable. It is nice to see him in a reasonable way. Not always *watching* Vivienne & worried by her' (King's OM/JDH/34).

2–'Thanks for your letter [11 Dec.] but the U.S. ban does not "seem" to be lifted. It is lifted . . . Three-fourths of the text [of the judge's ruling] was published in the *N. Y. Herald Tribune* of 7 December. The U.S. attorney-general, immediately after the decision, stood up and said he accepted the judge's ruling with great satisfaction and that the state would not appeal from it to a higher court. The defendant, Cerf, then said he would publish the book with an account of the proceedings (I suppose like the *édition définitive* of *Madame Bovary*) on 19 January next.

'My solicitors don't understand very clearly what [?why] they were written to. No more do I. I told you I am the absolute owner of the copyright and property rights in England' (*Selected Letters of James Joyce*, ed. Richard Ellmann [1975], 367).

I wanted from Monro Saw & Co. was that they should tell me all they knew of the history of the case, just as Léon wrote to Morley to give him all that he knew of it. I hope that they are willing to do so, and then, as I said, I propose to pick up what details I can from Miss Weaver and John Rodker.

Hoping to see you early next year, and with best wishes for the new year to you, to Mrs Joyce, and to your family,

Yours ever sincerely,
pp T. S. Eliot

TO *F. Stringfellow Barr*   TS Virginia

28 December 1933   Faber & Faber Ltd

Dear Mr Barr,

Thank you for your very interesting letter of December 12th, and also for your kindness in sending me a cheque for the essay, which having received, I will gratefully cash.[1] I am very glad that my paper reached you in time to appear in the *Virginia Quarterly*.

I shall write to you again about your suggestion for an article on censorship.[2] This is a very difficult matter to write about, and only to be treated

---

1 – 'Personality and Demonic Possession', *The Virginia Quarterly Review* (Jan. 1934), 94–103. TSE later (2 Dec. 1962) commented on his copy of the periodical: 'I have completely forgotten this draft of what became a chapter of *After Strange Gods* but on re-reading I think it's good enough to inscribe . . . to Valerie.' The fee was $50. Barr wrote, 'I remember your objecting to payment for this essay on the grounds that it was the property of the Page-Barbour Foundation. I must merely repeat that there is no connection between the Foundation and the *Virginia Quarterly*; that it was with the Foundation's full permission that we secured the essay from you; and that therefore we should feel very badly if you declined the payment which is due you.'

2 – 'Our audience, perhaps like most audiences of today, is so drenched with Protestantism in religion, liberalism in politics, and – despite our apocalyptic New Deal – with laissez faire in economics that the notion of censorship would be, I think, extremely unfriendly to it. For that reason I should like to bring it to their attention, and I do not know to whom else besides yourself we could turn. [Lambert] Davis has therefore asked me to beg you to consider such a discussion for him. It seems to us that within the past few years the protestant-liberal laissez faire ideology is cracking up. People apparently begin to suspect that what Americans call rackets actually run things. Could one say that authority can never cease to exist, that it can merely be dispersed and remain unrecognized? This seems to us to make it very dangerous . . . I take it that Fascism, in no matter what field and no matter how blindly and clumsily it may work, is our present response to this discovery. Am I jumping a cog when I conclude from what I have just said that some regulation (the word censorship is still unpleasant to my own ears) of our ideas is desirable if we can persuade ourselves of the legitimate sovereignty of some great tradition? I don't doubt I have stated my case very

with the greatest care. All I can say at the moment is that the subject is one of perennial interest to me, an interest both speculative and practical, and that I should like to tackle it. The only thing I am sure of is that I could not possibly make the time to give it the attention it needs before next summer. Perhaps, however, that is as well, inasmuch as the recent legalisation of *Ulysses* in America gives the subject too great a topicality for quite dispassionate treatment at the moment.

This is really only a note of acknowledgement and thanks, and to return the enclosed proof of my verses.[1]

With best wishes for the new year to Mrs Barr and yourself, and for the future of the *Quarterly* under its new editor.[2]

Yours sincerely,
T. S. Eliot

TO *F. S. Oliver*[3]　　　　　　　　　　　　　　　　　　　　CC

28 December 1933　　　　　　　*[The Criterion]*

My dear Oliver,

Thank you very much for your letter of the 26th, which reached me this morning. I had had no news about you for a long time, which made your letter all the more welcome, but had not expected you to bother to acknowledge my poor book at all, fearing that you probably were not very robust. It is very good to have news of you, but I am sorry that your news is not better. It is something to be able to look forward to the continuation of your history, even if I may not look forward to seeing you in this part of the world.[4]

---

obscurely, but it is my humble hope that it will arouse in your own mind a train of ideas which you would be willing to develop for us.'

1 – 'Words for Music: New Hampshire; Virginia', *Virginia Quarterly Review* 10: 2 (Apr. 1934), 200.

2 – Barr was giving up as editor of *Virginia Quarterly Review*; Lambert Davis was taking over.

3 – F. S. Oliver (1864–1934), businessman and polemicist, was educated at Edinburgh and Trinity College, Cambridge, before joining forces in 1892 with Ernest Debenham in the firm of Debenham and Freebody (drapers, wholesalers, manufacturers), which they caused to flourish and expand (buying up Marshall and Snelgrove and Harvey Nichols); Oliver, who had become a wealthy man, retired as managing director in 1920. A radical Tory, he engaged himself in many public issues. His publications included *Alexander Hamilton* (1906), *Ordeal by Battle* (1915) and *The Endless Adventure* (3 vols, 1930–5).

4 – Oliver, who had a bad heart, thanked TSE for *The Use of Poetry and the Use of Criticism*. 'My chief pleasures are (a) breakfast & (b) writing each day a few lines of my posthumous

I thought of you particularly this summer, during a very short tour in the highlands – my first visit to your romantic and beautiful country. I wished that I could have stopped in and called upon you at Edgerston. I still hope that we may meet in that way.

With most cordial good wishes for the new year to yourself and Mrs Oliver.

> Yours sincerely,
> [T. S. Eliot]

TO *L. C. Knights*

TS L. C. Knights

28 December 1933   Faber & Faber Ltd

Dear Knights,

I presume that the letter of the 21st December, on *Scrutiny* letter paper, comes from you, because most previous letters have come from you, but this letter is not signed.[1] I am afraid that it is too soon for me to contemplate reviewing anything for *Scrutiny*. I don't really expect to have time for anything of the sort until next May. I admit that I have agreed to review one book for the *Spectator*, but that was only under extreme temptation, as it is my favourite book – that is, Malory's *Morte d'Arthur*, and I could not resist the opportunity of having this new edition.[2] As for Leavis's book, I should like to think that over for a little, and I will run through the book again with your suggestion in view. I am not sure that I am an appropriate person to review that, as I am, and the *Criterion* is, to a considerable extent involved in Leavis's criticisms. If I think I can do anything about it, I will let you know.

If I have not yet renewed my subscription to *Scrutiny* it is simply through the unbusinesslike methods of my private life. May I please have a new form, or at least the address to which subscriptions are to be sent?

> Yours sincerely,
> [signed for] T. S. Eliot

---

work. With my one very dicky lung & my broken heart it isn't a life I lead at all, at all!'

1–Knights invited TSE to review for *Scrutiny* either John Sparrow's *Sense and Poetry* or a new edition of Marlowe's *Edward II*. 'If neither of these should attract you, it has occurred to me that you might have some criticism to make of Leavis's *For Continuity*. In the normal way, for fairly obvious reasons, the book would not be mentioned in *Scrutiny*. But the issues raised are certainly fundamental (so that the question of indelicacy hardly arises) and if you should wish to discuss them from your own standpoint there seems every reason why this should be done in *Scrutiny* itself. Needless to say, we should publish any criticism that you cared to make. I do not imagine that Leavis will object when I tell him of my proposal.'

2–'Le Morte Darthur', *Spectator* 152: 5513 (23 Feb. 1934), 278.

TO *J. McG. Bottkol*[1]   CC

28 December 1933   [*The Criterion*]

Dear Bottkol,

Many thanks for your letter of the 7th. I am glad of your reminder to do what I should have done immediately on my return to England. I have now put Eliot House Library on the free list for the *Criterion*, and have arranged to have the four 1933 numbers sent.

I trust that you received the copy of my Norton lectures, which I had sent to the library?

If it is possible, I should be glad if you could let me have a couple of the library book-plates, as a pleasant souvenir.

With all best wishes for the new year both to Eliot House and to yourself personally.

Yours sincerely,
[T. S. Eliot]

TO *S. C. Carpenter*[2]   CC

28 December 1933   [Faber & Faber Ltd]

Dear Carpenter,

I was very glad to get your letter of the 23rd, which reached me this morning.[3] I am obliged to you for expressing your opinion about the episode in question, as it is a welcome support to my own views. The scenario was originally prepared by Webb-Odell, and subsequently revised by Martin Browne. I have been conforming to it as closely as possible, and

---

1 – J. McG. Bottkol was librarian of Eliot House, Harvard University.

2 – S. C. Carpenter, MA, DD (1877–1959): Master of the Temple, London, 1930–5; Chaplain to the King, 1929–35; Dean of Exeter, 1935–50. His works include *The Anglican Tradition* (1928).

3 – Dr Carpenter – having been advised that the episode in *The Rock* proposed for St Martin's Church was to take the topic 'During an Air Raid' – wrote: 'I cannot refrain from venturing to suggest that this might be reconsidered. It seems that the Church does not particularly mind, but ... to me alas it seems very unfortunate.

'Do you feel able to say that for your part you would prefer something else? Such a scene would call up many bitter anti-German war memories, from which the [illegible] people have for the most part escaped, & it could [?anger] the young people who take part in the acting to represent emotions of terror & panic which seem at the least unnecessary.

'There are plenty of other things done at St Martin's which might serve, e.g. their Christmas tree, or even the mighty dossing of the down and out.

'Please forgive me if I have taken a liberty, but . . . I am exercised about it.'

merely supplying the words.[1] I had already demurred somewhat to this episode, but as I had not yet actually tackled it, I was waiting until I had some alternative to offer. Some sort of cataclysm seems to be needed at that point, but I quite agree with you that any reference to the late War, or, for the matter of that, to any war not waged on religious grounds, is both irrelevant and in bad taste.

When I have thought of some alternative, we might discuss the matter further.

Yours sincerely,   ·
[T. S. Eliot]

TO *St Clair Donaldson* CC

30 December 1933   [Faber & Faber Ltd]

My dear Lord Bishop,

Thank you for your letter of the 28th. I am still more doubtful of being able to speak for you than when we met. Meanwhile, however, I think that I should be hard put to know what to make of the subject suggested. I should have thought that the 'Message of Christianity' was always fundamentally the same, and that it was the business of 'these days' to make themselves relevant to Christianity, rather than the other way about. But perhaps I am stupid. In any case, I do not think that you sent me a list of the subjects. Might I see them, before the decision has to be made?[2]

I am, my Lord Bishop,
Your obedient servant,
[T. S. Eliot]

1 – TSE stressed in a prefatory note to the text of *The Rock* (1934): 'I cannot consider myself the author of the "play", but only of the words which are printed here. The scenario, incorporating some historical scenes suggested by the Rev. R. Webb-Odell, is by Mr E. Martin Browne, under whose direction I wrote the choruses and dialogues, and submissive to whose expert criticism I rewrote much of them. Of only one scene am I literally the author: for this scene and of course for the sentiments expressed in the choruses I must assume the responsibility.'

2 – Donaldson (Bishop of Salisbury) responded, 1 Jan. 1934: 'My idea about the revelancy [*sic*] of the Message of Christianity was in relation to the modern objection that Christ's teaching as recorded in the New Testament . . . is out of date now. F. R. Barry in his book [*Christ in University Life: Addresses given in St Mary-the Virgin, Oxford*, ed. Barry (1931)] shows that in once sense this is true, Our Lord's Relation to His Fellow men during His life time, was that of a citizen of the Roman Empire . . . The divine and eternal element in His teaching is found in His fundamental relation to God. In this sense His teaching is the only possible basis of a right view of the modern world.' He enclosed with his letter a list of proposed subjects.

TO *Martin Shaw*[1]   TS Houghton

30 December 1933   *The Criterion*

Dear Shaw,

Here is a draft of a theme song. If the metre does not suit you you have only to say so. Also, if the slightly different length and pattern of the six stanzas is bothersome I will trim them into equal sizes and shapes. Also, if you want more stanzas. At your command.[2]

With cordial wishes for the New Year in Christo,

T. S. E.

<Awaiting your opinion of my opening –

<Perhaps the *last* stanza should come at the beginning too. The order can be changed, of course.

<I am arranging to see your Dr Coomaraswami. Cant remember the exact name and have been in bed with a germ until today.>[3]

TO *Stephen Spender*   TS Northwestern

30 December 1933   *The Criterion*

Dear Spender,

I have been in bed, but expect to be quite out and about by Tuesday, so the lunch engagement stands: Oxford & Cambridge Club, 1:15.

I am afraid that my secretary did not word her invitations properly, and I shall have to look into the matter – it isn't a Dinner on Wednesday – we haven't accommodation for that – half a dozen dine first, but the

---

1–Martin Shaw (1875–1958), composer of stage works, choral pieces and recital ballads; associate of Edward Gordon Craig, Ralph Vaughan Williams and Percy Dearmer (with whom he put together *The English Carol Book* (1913); Director of Music, Diocese of Chelmsford, 1935–44. Other works include *Anglican Folk Mass* (1918); *Songs of Praise* (co-ed., 1925); *The Oxford Book of Carols* (co-ed., 1928). He was writing the music for TSE's *The Rock* (1934).

2–See *The Builders: Song from 'The Rock'* (J. B. Cramer, 1934).

> Ill done and undone,
> London so fair
> We will build London
> Bright in dark air,
> With new bricks and mortar
> Beside the Thames bord
> Queen of Island and Water
> A House of Our Lord.
> A Church for us all and work for us all and God's world for us all even unto this.

3–Additions written in pencil (as is the signature).

invitations are merely for the evening, *from* 8:30 – wine, beer, biscuits etc. Come as soon as convenient after dinner.

Yours ever,
T. S. E.

FROM *Vivien Eliot* TO *Ottoline Morrell* MS Texas

31 December 1933   68 Clarence Gate Gardens

My dearest Ottoline

Thank you for your letter & this is to wish you a very happy New Year, & good health in 1934.

All *I* want is my *own* husband, & to be able to look after him and take *care* of him again.

I am afraid I cannot be persuaded, *again*, into what I think is wrong, or converted to cruelty –

But the truth will come out, if not in *our* life – *then after it* –

Meanwhile I am sure you will be able to imagine my constant fear & *anxiety* for Tom's *safety*. That is the *only* aspect in which I can see it –

I will write again when I have anything new to say –

Yours ever affectly.
Vivienne Haigh Eliot

APPENDIX

Two Letters to Emily Hale[1]

These letters were inadvertently left out of Volume 5; thanks to Lyndall Gordon for the reminder. These are the only letters to Hale that are not under embargo: we must wait until 2020 before the cache of Eliot's letters held at Princeton University (1,130 letters and related enclosures) becomes available.

TO *Emily Hale*   TS Princeton

17 September 1930   Faber & Faber Ltd

Dear Emily,[2]

I must warn you that the Taupin book is only about a certain *current* of modern poetry; also that Flint feels strongly – more strongly than I do – that Taupin is too much under the influence of Ezra Pound – and he tells me that he has accordingly made a few marginal notes for your benefit.[3] No book on contemporary verse is – or for that matter, can be – comprehensive and fair all round: they are usually written by people who are hopelessly old-fashioned, or else who have rather narrow prejudices.

It is rather difficult to talk about the 'poetry' of D. H. Lawrence, although he has to be reckoned with in case anybody asks a question. I mean that it is not technically very important, and it is much more related to his other work than it is to other people's poetry. Another (living) poet who ought to be mentioned is Roy Campbell, whose last book you will receive in Boston: I don't think it is anything that will affect the future, and find it too wordy for my own taste; but it is good of its kind, and has a

---

1 – Emily Hale (1891–1969): see Biographical Register.
2 – Hale was staying c/o Mrs R. H. Gretton, 'Calendar's', Burford, near Oxford.
3 – René Taupin (1905–1981), French translator and critic who moved in the 1920s to the USA, where he lectured in Romance Languages at Columbia University, New York. A friend of Louis Zukofsky and correspondent of EP, he was author of *L'Influence du symbolisme français sur la poésie américaine, de 1910 à 1920* (1929): *The Influence of French Symbolism on Modern American Poetry* (rev. edn 1981) – the work to which TSE refers in these remarks. See TSE's letter to Taupin, 12 Apr. 1928.

flamboyant vigour which is uncommon.[1] I am afraid that I find the Sitwells hopelessly dull, although they are very nice people.

yours in haste,

T. S. E.

TO *Emily Hale*

6 October 1930   Faber & Faber Ltd

Dear Emily,

I said that I might send a few more notes about the poets. You may wonder particularly why I sent a big book of prose by Hulme with only five little poems at the end.[2] The reason is that these little poems have been a kind of symbol of the whole of the first phase of modern poetry in England: say from about 1909. Hulme was an extraordinary man, who has had a great *stimulating* influence on many of us (his views on Humanism and Original Sin are the starting point for Herbert Read and myself, and Ivor Richards and Ramon Fernandez know his work etc.) He wrote the poems as a tour de force, among a group of friends, Monro, Flint, Pound and others, as a kind of illustration of 'Imagism' and they should be read in connexion with what he says about modern poetry in the prose text. I think 'Conversion' is very beautiful, though I do not understand it.[3]

1–Roy Campbell (1901–57), South African-born poet, satirist, and translator, arrived in England in 1918 and was taken up by the composer William Walton and the Sitwells, and by Wyndham Lewis. He made his name with the long poem *Flaming Terrapin* (1924). Later poetry includes *Adamastor* (1930) – the volume to which TSE refers in this letter – *The Georgiad* (1931), and *Talking Bronco* (1946). See Peter F. Alexander, *Roy Campbell: A Critical Biography* (1982). In a letter to the American publisher Henry Regnery, 26 Dec. 1953, TSE volunteered this endorsement for the US edition of Campbell's *Poems*: 'I am astonished that no collection of Roy Campbell's poems should have hitherto been published in the United States, since he has been for many years one of the most conspicuous figures in English poetry in my time. His work is unclassifiable: it cannot be defined in terms of any movement. But the best of his work will surely be included in whatever assemblage of the poetical remains of our time, later generations will consider of permanent worth.'

2–T. E. Hulme, *Speculations: Essays on Humanism and the Philosophy of Art*, ed. Herbert Read (1924).

3–'Conversion', by T. E. Hulme:

> Light-hearted I walked into the valley wood
> In the time of hyacinths,
> Till beauty like a scented cloth
> Cast over, stifled me. I was bound

I agree with Read about Owen[1]: he belonged to no group, and his interesting technical innovations are all his own, though he may have known the work of Gerard Hopkins. Look at Auden's 'Paid on Both Sides', which has an interesting new metric based on Pound's 'Seafarer' and on original study of Anglo-Saxon. It is people like these, and partly Macleod,[2] and also young Stephen Spender (see the last *Criterion*)[3] who are making new verse; and not those like the Sitwells, who contribute nothing new except a rather gaudy sense of visual beauty. I cannot see anything very big about Robert Graves.

I hope that you will have had a good crossing. I hope that I may, in some way or another, see the text of your lecture and of anything you write.

Sincerely yours,
T. S. Eliot

Motionless and faint of breath
By loveliness that is her own eunuch.

Now pass I to the final river
Ignominiously, in a sack, without sound,
As any peeping Turk to the Bosphorus.

1 – Wilfred Owen (1893–1918), soldier and war poet, was killed in France one week before the end of WWI. See Jon Stallworthy, *Wilfred Owen: A Biography* (1974).

2 – Joseph Macleod (1903–84), poet, playwright, actor, theatre director, historian and BBC newsreader, was educated at Balliol College, Oxford (where he was friends with Graham Greene), and in 1929 joined the experimental Cambridge Festival Theatre, of which he became director, 1933–5 (his productions included Chekhov's *The Seagull* and Ezra Pound's Noh plays, and five of his own plays). In 1938 he joined the BBC as announcer and newsreader, retiring to Florence in 1955: it was during the BBC period that the poetry he produced under the pseudonym 'Adam Drinan' became sought-after in Britain and the USA: he was much admired by writers including Basil Bunting and Edwin Muir. His first book of poems, *The Ecliptic* (1930), was published by TSE at F&F. His plays included *Overture to Cambridge* (1933) and *A Woman Turned to Stone* (1934). See *Selected Poems: Cyclic Serial Zeniths from the Flux*, ed. Andrew Duncan (2009); James Fountain, 'To a group of nurses: The newsreading and documentary poems of Joseph Macleod', *TLS*, 12 Feb. 2010, 14–15.

3 – Spender, 'Four Poems' – dedicated to W. H. Auden – C. 10 (Oct. 1930), 32–4.

BIOGRAPHICAL REGISTER

Conrad Aiken (1889–1973): American poet and critic. Though he and Eliot were a year apart at Harvard, they became close friends, and fellow editors of *The Harvard Advocate*. Aiken wrote a witty memoir of their times together, 'King Bolo and Others', in *T. S. Eliot: A Symposium*, ed. Richard Marsh and Tambimuttu (1948), describing how they revelled in the comic strips of 'Krazy Kat, and Mutt and Jeff' and in 'American slang'. In the 1920s he settled for some years in Rye, Sussex. His writings include the Eliot-influenced *House of Dust* (poems, 1921) and *Selected Poems* (1929), which won the Pulitzer Prize; *Modern American Poets* (ed., 1922) and *Collected Criticism* (1968). His eccentric autobiographical novel *Ushant: An Essay* (1952) satirises TSE as 'Tsetse'. On 7 Nov. 1952 TSE thanked Aiken for sending him an inscribed copy: 'It is certainly a very remarkable book. After the first few pages, I said to myself, this is all very well for a short distance, but can he keep it up through 365 pages without the style becoming oppressive? Anyway, you have done it, and I have read the book through with unflagging interest and I hope that it will have a great success.' Asked in Feb. 1953, by the editor of *The Carolina Quarterly*, if he would contribute to a symposium on *Ushant*, TSE replied on 17 Feb. that he had no time to prepare a critical piece but that '*Ushant* fully deserves such extended and varied critical treatment'. However, TSE was to write to Cyril Connolly on 17 Apr. 1963: 'Aiken is an old & loyal friend – I don't think he is a booby, though *Ushant* is a curiously callow work.' Stephen Spender noted in 1966 that Eliot 'once told me that he always felt disturbed and unhappy that . . . Aiken had had so little success as a poet. "I've always thought that he and I were equally gifted, but I've received a large amount of appreciation, and he has been rather neglected. I can't understand it. It seems unjust. It always worries me"' ('Remembering Eliot', *The Thirties and After* [1978], 251). See too *Selected Letters of Conrad Aiken*, ed. Joseph Killorin (1978); Edward Butscher, *Conrad Aiken: Poet of White Horse Vale* (1988).

W. H. Auden (1907–73): prolific poet, playwright, librettist, translator, essayist and editor. He was educated at Gresham's School, Holt, Norfolk, and at Christ Church, Oxford, where he co-edited *Oxford Poetry*

(1926, 1927), and where his friend Stephen Spender hand-set about thirty copies of his first book, a pamphlet entitled *Poems* (1928). After going down from Oxford with a third-class degree in English in 1928, he visited Belgium and then lived for a year in Berlin. He worked as a tutor in London, 1929–30; then as a schoolmaster at Larchfield Academy Helensburgh, Dunbartonshire, 1930–2; followed by the Downs School, Colwall, Herefordshire, 1932–5. Although Eliot turned down his initial submission of a book of poems in 1927, he would presently accept 'Paid on Both Sides: A Charade' for the *Criterion*; and Eliot went on for the rest of his life to publish all of Auden's books at Faber & Faber: *Poems* (featuring 'Paid on Both Sides' and thirty short poems, 1930); *The Orators* (1932); *Look, Stranger!* (1937); *Spain* (1936); *Another Time* (1940); *New Year Letter* (1941; published in the USA as *The Double Man*); *The Age of Anxiety* (1947); *For the Time Being* (1945); *The Age of Anxiety: A Baroque Eclogue* (1948); *Nones* (1952); *The Shield of Achilles* (1955); *Homage to Clio* (1960); and *About the House* (1966). Eliot was happy too to publish Auden's play *The Dance of Death* (1933), which was to be performed by the Group Theatre in London in 1934 and 1935; and three further plays written with Christopher Isherwood: *The Dog Beneath the Skin* (1935), which would be performed by the Group Theatre in 1936; *The Ascent of F6* (1936); and *On the Frontier* (1937). In 1935–6 Auden went to work for the General Post Office film unit, writing verse commentaries for two celebrated documentary films, *Coal Face* and *Night Mail*. He collaborated with Louis MacNeice on *Letters from Iceland* (1937); and with Isherwood again on *Journey to a War* (1939). His first libretto was *Paul Bunyan* (performed with music by Benjamin Britten, 1941); and in 1947 he began collaborating with Igor Stravinsky on *The Rake's Progress* (performed in Venice, 1951); and he later co-wrote two librettos for Hans Werner Henze. Other works include *The Oxford Book of Light Verse* (1938); *The Enchafed Flood: The Romantic Iconography of the Sea* (1951); *The Dyer's Hand* (1963); and *Secondary Worlds* (1968). See further Humphrey Carpenter, *W. H. Auden: A Biography* (1981); Richard Davenport-Hines, *Auden* (1995); Edward Mendelson, *Early Auden* (1981) and *Later Auden* (1999); David Collard, 'More worthy than Lark: a television tribute to T. S. Eliot, by W. H. Auden and others', *TLS*, 9 Mar. 2012, 14.

Montgomery ('Monty') Belgion (1892–1973), author, was born in Paris of British parents and grew up with a deep feeling for the language and culture of France. In 1915–16 he was editor-in-charge of the European edition of the *New York Herald*; and for the remainder of WW1, 1916–18, he served first as a private in the Honourable Artillery Company and was then commissioned in the Dorsetshire Regiment. Between the wars he worked for the Paris review *This Quarter* and then for newspapers including the *Daily Mail* and *Daily Mirror*, and for a while he was an editor for Harcourt, Brace & Co., New York. In WW2 he was a captain in the Royal Engineers, and spent two years in prison camps in Germany. In 1929 Faber & Faber brought out (on TSE's recommendation) *Our Present Philosophy of Life*. Later writings include *Reading for Profit* (1945) and booklets on H. G. Wells and David Hume.

Marguerite Caetani, née Chapin (1880–1963) – born in New London, Connecticut, she was half-sister to Mrs Katherine Biddle, and a cousin of TSE – was married in 1911 to the composer Roffredo Caetani, 17th Duke of Sermoneta and Prince di Bassiano (a godson of Liszt), whose ancestors included two Popes (one of whom had the distinction of being put in Hell by Dante). A patron of the arts, she founded in Paris the review *Commerce* – the title being taken from a line in St-John Perse's *Anabase* ('*ce pur commerce de mon âme*') – see Sophie Levie, *La rivista Commerce e il ruolo di Marguerite Caetani nella letteratura europea 1924–1932* [1985]); and then, in Rome, *Botteghe oscure*, 1949–60, a biannual review featuring poetry and fiction from many nations – England, Germany, Italy, France, Spain, USA – with contributions published in their original languages. Contributors included André Malraux, Albert Camus, Paul Valéry, Robert Graves, E. E. Cummings, Marianne Moore.

John Cournos (1881–1966) – Johann Gregorievich Korshune – naturalised American writer of Russian birth (his Jewish parents fled Russia when he was ten), worked as a journalist on the *Philadelphia Record* and was first noted in England as an Imagist poet; he became better known as novelist, essayist and translator. After living in England in the 1910s and 1920s, he emigrated to the USA. An unhappy love affair in 1922–3 with Dorothy L. Sayers was fictionalised by her in *Strong Poison* (1930), by him in *The Devil is an English Gentleman* (1932). Other works include *Miranda Masters* (a *roman à clef* about the imbroglio between himself, the poet HD and Richard Aldington, 1926), and *Autobiography* (1935).

In 1934 TSE wrote in support of Cournos's application for a fellowship from the Guggenheim Memorial Foundation: 'He has for some years contributed regularly to the *Criterion*, on the subject of Russian literature; and he is a personal friend of mine. I have a very considerable respect for his abilities, and regard him as a sound and judicious critic. I cannot recall any candidate about whom my opinion has been asked, of whom I could speak with more assurance and approval.' See further David Ayers, 'John Cournos and the Politics of Russian Literature in *The Criterion*', *Modernism/modernity* 18: 2 (Apr. 2011), 355–68.

Ernst Robert Curtius (1886–1956), German scholar of philology and Romance literature. Scion of a family of scholars, he studied at Strasbourg, Berlin and Heidelberg, and taught at Marburg, Heidelberg and Bonn. Author of *Die Französische Kultur* (1931; *The Civilization of France*, trans. Olive Wyon, 1932); his greatest work was *Europäische Literatur und Lateinisches Mittelalter* (1948; trans. by Willard R. Trask as *European Literature and the Latin Middle Ages*, 1953), a study of Medieval Latin literature and its fructifying influence upon the literatures of modern Europe. In a letter to Max Rychner (24 Oct. 1955) Eliot saluted Curtius on his seventieth birthday by saying that even though he had met him no more than twice in thirty-five years, he yet counted him 'among my old friends', and owed him 'a great debt': 'I have . . . my own personal debt of gratitude to acknowledge to Curtius, for translating, and introducing, *The Waste Land*. Curtius was also, I think, the first critic in Germany to recognise the importance of James Joyce. And when it is a question of other writers than myself, and especially when we consider his essays on French contemporaries, and his Balzac, and his Proust, I am at liberty to praise Curtius as a critic . . . [O]nly a critic of scholarship, discrimination and intellect could perform the services that Curtius has performed. For his critical studies are contributions to the study of the authors criticised, which must be reckoned with by those authors' compatriots. We cannot determine the true status and significance of the significant writers in our own language, without the aid of foreign critics with a European point of view. For it is only such critics who can tell us, whether an author is of European importance. And of such critics in our own time, Curtius is one of the most illustrious.' Eliot praised too 'that masterly work, *Europäische Litteratur und Lateinisches Mittelalter*, on which he had been at work during the years when freedom of speech and freedom of travel were suspended. It bears testimony to his integrity and indomitable spirit . . . Curtius deserves, in his life and in his work, the gratitude and admiration of his fellow writers of every European nation' (Eliot's letter is printed in full in 'Brief über Ernst Robert Curtius', in *Freundesgabe für Ernest Robert Curtius zum 14. April 1956* [1956], 25–7.) See too Peter Godman, 'T. S. Eliot and E. R. Curtius: A European dialogue', *Liber:*

A European Review of Books, 1 (Oct. 1989), 5, 7; J. H. Copley, '"The Politics of Friendship": T. S. Eliot in Germany Through E. R. Curtius's Looking Glass', in *The International Reception of T. S. Eliot*, ed. Elisabeth Däumer and Shyamal Bagchee (2007), 243–67.

Martin D'Arcy (1888–1976), Jesuit priest and theologian, entered the novitiate in 1906, took a first in Literae Humaniores at Pope's Hall – the Jesuit private hall of Oxford University – and was ordained in 1921. After teaching at Stonyhurst College, in 1925 he undertook doctoral research, first at the Gregorian University in Rome, then at the Jesuit House at Farm Street, London. In 1927 he returned to Campion Hall (successor to Pope's Hall), where he taught philosophy at the university. He was Rector and Master of Campion Hall, 1933–45; Provincial of the British Province of the Jesuits in London, 1945–50. Charismatic and influential as a lecturer, and as an apologist for Roman Catholicism (his prominent converts included Evelyn Waugh), he also wrote studies including *The Nature of Belief* (1931) and *The Mind and Heart of Love* (1945). Louis MacNeice, in *The Strings Are False: An Unfinished Autobiography* (1965), wrote of Fr D'Arcy: 'He alone among Oxford dons seemed to me to have the glamour that medieval students looked for in their masters. Intellect incarnate in a beautiful head, wavy grey hair and delicate features; a hawk's eyes.' Lesley Higgins notes: 'Five of his books were reviewed in *The Criterion*, some by Eliot himself; his twenty-two reviews and articles in the latter certainly qualify him as part of what Eliot termed the journal's "definite . . . [and] comprehensive constellation of contributors".' See further H. J. A. Sire, *Father Martin D'Arcy: Philosopher of Christian Love* (1997); Richard Harp, 'A conjuror at the Xmas party', *TLS*, 11 Dec. 2009, 13–15.

Christopher Dawson (1889–1970), cultural historian. An independent and erudite scholar of some private means (he would inherit estates in Yorkshire on the death of his father in 1933), he taught for a while, part-time, at the University College of Exeter, 1925–33; and, though not a professional academic, was ultimately appointed at the good age of sixty-eight to a Chair of Roman Catholic Studies at Harvard, 1958–62. A convert to Roman Catholicism, he devoted much of his research and published output to the idea of religion as the driver of social culture. His works include *Progress and Religion* (1929), *The Making of Europe* (1932) and *Religion and the Rise of Western Culture* (1950); as well as a series entitled *Essays in Order*, which he edited from the 1930s for the Catholic

787

publishers Sheed and Ward: his own contributions were *Enquiries into Religion and Culture* (1934), *Medieval Religion* (1934), *The Judgement of Nations* (1943). For TSE he wrote Criterion Miscellany pamphlet no. 13: *Christianity and Sex* (1930). See Christina Scott – Dawson's daughter – *An Historian and His World: A Life of Christopher Dawson, 1889–1970* (1984); Bradley H. Birzer, *Sanctifying the World: The Augustinian Life and Mind of Christopher Dawson* (2007); and James R. Lothian, *The Making and Unmaking of the English Catholic Intellectual Community, 1910–1950* (2009). See too Dawson, 'Mr T. S. Eliot and the Meaning of Culture', *The Month* ns 1: 3 (Mar. 1949), 151–7.

Bonamy Dobrée (1891–1974), scholar and critic, was Professor of English Literature at Leeds University, 1936–55. After service in the army during WW1 (he was twice mentioned in despatches and attained the rank of major), he read English at Christ's College, Cambridge, and taught in London and as a professor of English at the Egyptian University, Cairo, 1925–9. His works include *Restoration Comedy* (1924), *Essays in Biography* (1925), *Restoration Tragedy, 1660–1720* (1929), *Alexander Pope* (1951). On 8 Sept. 1938, TSE would write to George Every, SSM, on the subject of the 'Moot': 'I think [Dobrée] would be worth having . . . He has his nose to the grindstone of the provincial university machine . . . but he is not without perception of the futilities of contemporary education. His mental formation is Liberal, but he has the rare advantage of being a man of breeding, so that his instincts with regard, for instance, to society, the community and the land, are likely to be right. He is also a person of strong, and I imagine hereditary, public spirit.' In Feb. 1963, TSE urged his merits as future editor of Kipling's stories: 'He is far and away the best authority on Kipling . . . I have often discussed Kipling with him, and know that we see eye to eye about the stories. As for Dobrée's general literary achievements, they are very high indeed: his published work is not only very scholarly, but of the highest critical standing, and he writes well . . . If this job is ever done – and I should like to see it done during my lifetime – Dobrée is the man to do it.' See also Jason Harding, *The 'Criterion': Cultural Politics and Periodical Networks in Inter-War Britain* (2002).

Henry Ware Eliot, Jr (1879–1947), TSE's elder brother, went to school at Smith Academy, and then passed two years at Washington University, St Louis, before progressing to Harvard. At Harvard, he displayed a gift for light verse in *Harvard Celebrities* (1901), illustrated with 'Caricatures and

Decorative Drawings' by two fellow undergraduates. After graduating, he spent a year at Law School, but subsequently followed a career in printing, publishing and advertising. He attained a partnership in Husband & Thomas (later the Buchen Company), a Chicago advertising agency, from 1917 to 1929, during which time he gave financial assistance to TSE and regularly advised him on investments. He accompanied their mother on her visit to London in the summer of 1921, his first trip away from the USA. In February 1926, he married Theresa Anne Garrett (1884–1981). It was not until late in life that he found his true calling, as a Research Fellow in Near Eastern Archaeology at the Peabody Museum, Harvard, where his principal publication was a discussion of the prehistoric chronology of northern Mesopotamia, together with a description of the pottery from Kudish Saghir (1939): see his posthumous publication *Excavations in Mesopotamia and Western Iran: Sites of 4000 – 500 B.C.: Graphic Analyses* (1950), prefaced by Lauriston Ward: 'It was a labor of love, of such magnitude as to be practically unique in the annals of archaeology . . . a monument to his scholarship and devotion . . . Eliot had all the qualities of the true scholar, which include modesty as well as ability.' In 1932 he published a detective novel, *The Rumble Murders*, under the pseudonym Mason Deal. He was instrumental in building up the T. S. Eliot collection at Eliot House (Houghton Library). Of slighter build than his brother – who remarked upon his 'Fred Astaire figure' – Henry suffered from deafness owing to scarlet fever as a child, and this may have contributed to his diffidence. Unselfishly devoted to TSE, whose growing up he movingly recorded with his camera, Henry took him to his first Broadway musical, *The Merry Widow*, which remained a favourite. It was with his dear brother in mind that TSE wrote: 'The notion of some infinitely gentle / Infinitely suffering thing' ('Preludes' IV).

Vivien Eliot, née Haigh-Wood (1888–1947). Born in Bury, Lancashire, on 28 May 1888, 'Vivy' was brought up in Hampstead from the age of three. After meeting TSE in company with Scofield Thayer in Oxford early in 1915, she and TSE hastened to be married just a few weeks later, on 26 June 1915. (TSE, who was lodging at 35 Greek Street, London, was recorded in the marriage certificate as 'of no occupation'.) She developed close friendships with Mary Hutchinson, Ottoline Morrell and others in TSE's circle. Despite chronic personal and medical difficulties, they remained together until 1933, when TSE resolved to separate from her following his academic year in America. She was never to be reconciled to the separation, became increasingly ill, and in 1938 was confined to a psychiatric hospital, where she died (of 'syncope' and 'cardiovascular degeneration') on 22 January 1947. She is the dedicatee of *Ash-Wednesday* (1930). She published sketches in the *Criterion* (under pseudonyms with the initials 'F. M.'), and collaborated on the *Criterion*. See Michael Karwoski, 'The Bride from Bury', *Lancashire Life*, Mar. 1984, 52–3; Carole Seymour-Jones, *Painted Shadow: The Life of Vivienne Eliot* (2001); Ken Craven, *The Victorian Painter and the Poet's Wife: A biography of the Haigh-Wood Family* (e-book, 2012); Robert Crawford, *Young Eliot: From St Louis to 'The Waste Land'* (2015).

Geoffrey Faber (1889–1961), publisher and poet, was educated at Malvern College and Christ Church, Oxford, where he took a double first in Classical Moderations (1910) and Literae Humaniores (1912). He was called to the Bar by the Inner Temple (1921), though he was never to practise law. In 1919 he was elected a prize fellow of All Souls College, Oxford, which he went on to serve in the capacity of Estates Bursar, 1923–51. Before WWI – in which he served with the London Regiment (Post Office Rifles), seeing action in France and Belgium – he spent eighteen months as assistant to Humphrey Milford, publisher of Oxford University Press. After the war he passed three years working for Strong & Co., brewers (there was a family connection), before going in for publishing on a full-time basis by joining forces with his All Souls colleague Maurice Gwyer and his wife, Lady Alsina Gwyer, who were trying to run a specialised imprint called the Scientific Press that Lady Gwyer had inherited from her father, Sir Henry Burdett: its weekly journal, the *Nursing Mirror*, was their most successful production. Following protractedly difficult negotiations, in 1925 Faber became chair of their restructured general publishing house, which was provisionally styled Faber & Gwyer. After being introduced by Charles Whibley to T. S. Eliot, Faber was so impressed by the personality and aptitude of the 37-year-old American that he chose both to take on the running of the *Criterion* and to appoint Eliot to the board of his company (Eliot's *Poems 1909–1925* was one of the first books to be put out by the new imprint, and the firm's first best-seller), which was relocated from Southampton Row to 24 Russell Square. By 1929 both the Gwyers and the *Nursing Mirror* were disposed of to advantage, and the firm took final shape as Faber & Faber, with Richard de la Mare and two additional Americans, Frank Morley and Morley Kennerley, joining the board. Faber chaired the Publishers' Association, 1939–41 – campaigning successfully for the repeal of a wartime tax on books – and helping to set up the National

Book League. He was knighted in 1954, and gave up the chairmanship of Faber & Faber in 1960. His publications as poet include *The Buried Stream* (1941), and his works of non-fiction were *Oxford Apostles* (1933), *Jowett* (1957), and an edition of the works of John Gay (1926). In 1920 he married Enid Richards, with whom he had two sons and a daughter.

Frank Stuart ('F. S.') Flint (1885–1960), English poet and translator, and civil servant, grew up in terrible poverty – 'gutter-born and gutter-bred', he would say – and left school at thirteen. But he set about to educate himself in European languages and literature (he had a deep appreciation of the French Symbolists and of Rimbaud), as well as in history and philosophy. In 1908 he started writing articles and reviews for the *New Age*, then for the *Egoist* and for *Poetry* (ed. Harriet Monroe). Swiftly gaining in reputation and authority (his influential piece on 'Contemporary French Poetry' appeared in Harold Monro's *Poetry Review* in 1912), he became associated with T. E. Hulme, Ezra Pound, Richard Aldington and Hilda Doolittle; and he contributed poems to the *English Review* (ed. Ford Madox Hueffer) and to Pound's anthology *Des Imagistes* (1914). In 1920 he published *Otherworld Cadences* (The Poetry Bookshop); and with TSE and Aldous Huxley he was one of the contributors to 'Three Critical Essays on Modern English Poetry', in *Chapbook* II: 9 (March 1920). Between 1909 and 1920 he published three volumes of poetry, though his work as essayist, reviewer and translator was the more appreciated: he became a regular translator and reviewer for the *Criterion* from the 1920s – and a member of TSE's inner circle – even while working full-time in the statistics division of the Ministry of Labour (where he was Chief of the Overseas Section) until retiring in 1951. See also *The Fourth Imagist: Selected Poems of F. S. Flint*, ed. Michael Copp (2007).

E. M. Forster (1879–1970), novelist, was educated at King's College, Cambridge, where he gained a second in the classics tripos (and where he was elected to the exclusive Conversazione Society, the inner circle of the Apostles). Though intimately associated with the Bloomsbury group in London, where his circle of friends and acquaintances came to include Edward Garnett, Duncan Grant, Roger Fry, Lytton Strachey, and Leonard and Virginia Woolf, he derived much from visits to Italy, Greece, Egypt and India – where he worked for a while as private secretary to the Maharaja of Dewas: that experience brought about one of his most acclaimed novels, *A Passage to India* (1924), which sold around one million copies during his lifetime. His other celebrated novels include *Where Angels Fear to Tread* (1905), *A Room with a View* (1908), *Howards End* (1910) and the posthumous *Maurice* (1971, written 1910–13), a work that addressed his homosexuality. He gave the Clark Lectures at Cambridge in 1927 – in succession to TSE – which were published as *Aspects of the Novel* (1927). He turned down a knighthood, but in 1953 he was appointed Companion of Honour; and he received the OM in 1969. See also Forster, 'Mr Eliot and His Difficulties', *Life and Letters*, 2: 13 (June 1929), 417–25; P. N. Furbank, *E. M. Forster* (2 vols, 1977, 1978); *Selected Letters of E. M. Forster*, ed. Mary Lago and P. N. Furbank (2 vols, 1983–5); Nicola Beauman, *Morgan: A Biography of E. M. Forster* (1993).

Maurice Haigh-Wood (1896–1980): TSE's brother-in-law. He was eight years younger than his sister Vivien, and after attending Ovingdean prep school and Malvern School, trained at Sandhurst Military Academy before receiving his commission on 11 May 1915 as a second lieutenant in the 2nd Battalion, Manchester Regiment. He served in the infantry for the rest of the war, and on regular visits home gave TSE his closest contact with the nightmare of life and death in the trenches. After the war, he found it difficult to get himself established, but became a stockbroker, and he remained friendly with, and respectful towards, TSE even after his separation from Vivien in 1933. In September 1968 he told Robert Sencourt – as he related in a letter to Valerie Eliot (2 Sept. 1968) – 'I had the greatest admiration & love for Tom whom I regarded as my elder brother for fifty years, & I would never think of acting against his wishes.' In 1930 he married a 25-year-old American dancer, Ahmé Hoagland, and they had two children.

Emily Hale (1891–1969) came from a similar Bostonian milieu to the Eliot family. Her father was an architect turned Unitarian preacher who taught at Harvard Divinity School, and her uncle was a music critic for the *Boston Herald*. Eliot met Emily at the home of his cousin Eleanor Hinkley in 1912, and in an unpublished memoir wrote that he fell in love with her before leaving for Europe in 1914. However, after his marriage in 1915, he did not see her again for many years. Although she did not go to college, a fact which handicapped her career, Emily was a passionate theatre-goer, amateur actor and director, and was to forge a career as a drama teacher. In 1921 she took a post as administrator and drama tutor at Milwaukee-Downer College, a private women's school, and later taught at Scripps College, Smith College, Concord Academy, and Abbott

Academy. During the 1930s and 1940s, Eliot once again took up his relationship with her, and they saw a lot of one another both in England, where they visited Burnt Norton together in 1934–5, and during his trips to the USA. Following Vivien's death in 1947, Emily was disappointed that Eliot did not want to marry her, and there was a cooling of their friendship. Towards the end of his life Eliot apparently ordered her letters to him to be destroyed, while his letters to her are at Princeton University, where they are sealed until 2020. See Lyndall Gordon, *T. S. Eliot: An Imperfect Life* (1998); Robert Crawford, *Young Eliot: From St Louis to 'The Waste Land'* (2015).

John Hayward (1905–65), editor, critic, anthologist, read modern languages at King's College, Cambridge. Despite the early onset of muscular dystrophy, he became a prolific and eminent critic and editor, bringing out in quick succession editions of the works of Rochester, Saint-Évremond, Jonathan Swift, Robert Herrick and Samuel Johnson. Other publications included *Complete Poems and Selected Prose of John Donne* (1929), *Donne* (1950), *T. S. Eliot: Selected Prose* (1953), *The Penguin Book of English Verse* (1958) and *The Oxford Book of Nineteenth Century English Verse* (1964). Celebrated as the learned and acerbic editor of *The Book Collector*, he was made a chevalier of the Légion d'honneur in 1952, a CBE in 1953. Writers including Graham Greene and Stevie Smith valued his editorial counsel; and Paul Valéry invited him to translate his comedy *Mon Faust*. Hayward advised TSE on various essays, poems, and plays including *The Cocktail Party* and *The Confidential Clerk*, and most helpfully of all on *Four Quartets*. See further Helen Gardner, *The Composition of 'Four Quartets'* (1978); John Smart, *Tarantula's Web: John Hayward, T. S. Eliot and Their Circle* (2013).

Mary Hutchinson, née Barnes (1889–1977), a half-cousin of Lytton Strachey, married St John ('Jack') Hutchinson in 1910. A prominent Bloomsbury hostess, she was for several years the acknowledged mistress of the art critic Clive Bell, and became a close, supportive friend of TSE and VHE. TSE published one of her stories ('War') in *The Egoist*, and she later brought out a book of sketches, *Fugitive Pieces* (1927). She wrote a brief unpublished memoir of TSE (Harry Ransom Humanities Research Center). See David Bradshaw, '"Those Extraordinary Parakeets": Clive Bell and Mary Hutchinson', *Charleston Magazine* 16 (Autumn/Winter 1997), 5–12; 17 (Spring/Summer 1998), 5–11.

James Joyce (1882–1941): Irish novelist, playwright and poet. Having lived in Zurich and Trieste, Joyce moved to Paris in 1920, where he became a centre of expatriate writers, including Pound and Gertrude Stein. Wyndham Lewis, in *Blasting and Bombardiering* (1937), recounts his and Eliot's first encounter with Joyce, in Paris in August 1927, when bringing him a parcel of shoes. Joyce's *A Portrait of the Artist as a Young Man* was serialised in the *Egoist*, and *Ulysses* in the *Little Review* up to 1920. When *Ulysses* first appeared in book form in 1922, the same year as *The Waste Land*, TSE called it 'the most important expression which the present age has found' – 'a book to which we are all indebted, and from which none of us can escape' ('Ulysses, Order and Myth', *Dial* 75: 5, Nov. 1923). TSE published in the *Criterion* a number of pieces by and about Joyce, and at Faber – having failed to secure British rights to *Ulysses*, despite his best efforts in 1933–4 – he was responsible for the publication of *Finnegans Wake* (1939).

F. R. Leavis (1895–1978): literary critic; Fellow of Downing College, Cambridge, 1927–62, Reader from 1959; founding editor of *Scrutiny*, 1932–53. His works include *New Bearings in English Poetry* (1932), *The Great Tradition* (1948), *The Common Pursuit* (1952) and *D. H. Lawrence: Novelist* (1955). See further Ian MacKillop, *F. R. Leavis: A Life in Criticism* (1995); Christopher Hilliard, *English as a Vocation: The 'Scrutiny' Movement* (2012).

On 23 July 1942, TSE wrote to Sir Malcolm Robertson, British Council, to recommend a subsidy for *Scrutiny*: 'Some of us are privately not very happy when we see so many émigré periodicals cropping up mostly of dubious ephemeral value – copies are sent to me and I wonder who reads them – while it is such a struggle to keep any serious indigenous magazines alive.' To Desmond McCarthy, 14 Nov. 1947: 'I think that Leavis deserves some encouragement for having carried *Scrutiny* under considerable difficulties; for, with all its limitations and tiresomeness, it is the best academic periodical we have, and indeed almost the only serious periodical of a literary kind that is readable at all. He knows that I regard the establishment of English Schools at Oxford and Cambridge as a great mistake.' To the Rockefeller Foundation, 25 May 1948: 'I have always taken a keen interest in the work of Leavis, both in his theory and practice in the teaching of English, and in the extension of cooperative study through *Scrutiny*. I regard *Scrutiny* (even without allowing for its explicit limits) as the most valuable periodical (excepting of course weeklies and dailies, with which it cannot be compared in kind) that we now have in

England. May I take the opportunity of saying that I should welcome anything that could be done to forward and facilitate Dr Leavis's work.' To the Revd M. Jarrett-Kerr, CR, 20 Aug. 1951: 'I have been increasingly distressed in the last year or two, to observe that Leavis is abandoning criticism in favour of invective. A great deal of his spleen takes the form of innuendos and sneers at a number of writers in passing. It is all a very great pity.'

Harold Monro (1879–1932): poet, editor, publisher and bookseller. In 1913 he founded the Poetry Bookshop at 35 Devonshire Street, London, where poets would meet and give readings and lectures. In 1912 he briefly edited *The Poetry Review* for the Poetry Society; then his own periodicals, *Poetry and Drama*, 1913–15, and *The Chapbook* (originally *The Monthly Chapbook*), 1919–25. From the Poetry Bookshop, Monro would put out a remarkable mix of publications including the five volumes of *Georgian Poetry*, ed. by Edward Marsh (1872–1953), between 1912 and 1922, the English edition of *Des Imagistes*, and first volumes by writers including Richard Aldington, F. S. Flint and Robert Graves, along with some of his own collections including *Children of Love* (1915) and *Strange Meetings* (1917). TSE was to accept *The Winter Solstice* for publication by Faber & Gwyer as no. 13 of the Ariel Poems. Though a homosexual, Monro was to marry the sister of a friend, 1903–16; and in 1920 he wed Alida Klemantaski (daughter of a Polish-Jewish trader), with whom he never cohabited but who was ever loving and supportive to him: both of them endeared themselves to Eliot, who would occasionally use the premises of the Poetry Bookshop for meetings of contributors to the *Criterion*. After Monro's death, TSE wrote a critical note for *The Collected Poems of Harold Monro*, ed. Alida Monro (1933), xiii–xvi; and on 21 Jan. 1947 he told Marvin Magalaner (who was writing a dissertation on Monro during the period 1912–14): 'I think that Monro did play a role of importance and value during the period of several years up to 1914. He cared passionately though not always quite discriminately about poetry and was one of the few poets of whom it can be said that they care more for poetry in general than for their own work. He not only helped in giving publicity to what have been called the Georgian Poets but to the work of poets of a more advanced type. People like Pound, Flint, Aldington and the other "Imagists" made, I believe, something of a centre of his bookshop and Flint's chronicles and reviews of contemporary French poetry which were published in Monro's magazines did a great deal, I believe, to arouse an interest in French poetry in this country. As for American poets, Monro was certainly as ready to forward the interests of Americans as of his fellow countrymen and anyone whose poetry he liked was sure of his support.' See Joy Grant, *Harold Monro and the Poetry Bookshop* (1967); Dominic Hibberd, *Harold Monro: Poet of the New Age* (2001).

Marianne Moore (1887–1972), American poet and critic, contributed to *The Egoist* from 1915. Her first book, *Poems*, was published in London in 1921. She went on to become in 1925 acting editor of *The Dial*, editor 1927–9, and an important and influential modern poet. Eliot found her 'an extremely intelligent person, very shy . . . One of the most observant people I have ever met'. Writing to her on 3 April 1921, he said her verse interested him 'more than that of anyone now writing in America'. And in Eliot's introduction to her *Selected Poems* (F&F, 1935) he declared that her 'poems form part of the small body of durable poetry written in our time'. See too Moore, 'A Virtuoso of Make-Believe', in *T. S. Eliot: A Symposium*, ed. Richard March and Tambimuttu (1948), 179–80; *The Selected Letters of Marianne Moore*, ed. Bonnie Costello (1998); Linda Leavell, *Holding On Upside Down: The Life and Work of Marianne Moore* (2013).

Paul Elmer More (1864–1937), critic, scholar and prolific writer, had grown up in St Louis, Missouri, and attended Washington University before going on to Harvard; at one time he had taught French to TSE's brother Henry. Initially a humanist, by the 1930s he assumed an Anglo-Catholic position not unlike that of TSE (who appreciated the parallels between their spiritual development). See also 'An Anglican Platonist: the Conversion of Paul Elmer More', *TLS*, 30 Oct. 1937, 792. At the outset of his career, More taught classics at Harvard and Bryn Mawr; thereafter he worked as literary editor of *The Independent*, 1901–3, and the *New York Evening Post*, 1903–9, and as editor of *The Nation*, 1909–14, before finally turning to freelance writing and teaching. TSE keenly admired More's many works, in particular *Shelburne Essays* (11 vols, 1904–21), *The Greek Tradition* (5 vols, 1924–31), and *The Demon of the Absolute* (1928); and he took trouble in the 1930s to try to secure a publisher for *Pages from an Oxford Diary* (1937), which More stipulated he would only publish in anonymity.

In 1937, TSE wrote in tribute: 'The place of Paul More's writings in my own life has been of such a kind that I find [it] easiest, and perhaps most effective, to treat it in a kind of autobiographical way. What is significant to me . . . is not simply the conclusions at which he has arrived, but the fact that he arrived there from somewhere else; and not simply that he came from somewhere else, but that he took a particular route . . . If I find an analogy with my own journey, that is perhaps of interest to no one but myself, except in so far as it explains my retrospective appreciation of the *Shelburne Essays* . . .

'It was not until my senior year [at Harvard], as a pupil of [Irving] Babbitt's, that More's work was forced on my attention: for one of the obligations of any pupil of Babbitt was to learn a proper respect for "my friend More". But while one was directly exposed to so powerful an influence as Babbitt's, everything that one read was merely a supplement to Babbitt.

'It was not until one or two of the volumes of *The Greek Tradition* had appeared, that More began to have any importance for me. It was possibly Irving Babbitt himself, in a conversation in London, in 1927 or '28, during which I had occasion to indicate the steps I had recently taken, who first made me clearly cognizant of the situation. In the later volumes of *The Greek Tradition*, and in the acquaintance and friendship subsequently formed, I came to find an auxiliary to my own progress of thought, which no English theologian <at the time> could have given me. The English theologians, born and brought up in surroundings of private belief and public form, and often themselves descended from ecclesiastics, at any rate living mostly in an environment of religious practice, did not seem to me to know enough of the new world of barbarism and infidelity that was forming all about them. The English Church was familiar with the backslider, but it knew nothing of the convert – certainly not of the convert who had come such a long journey. I might almost say that I never met any Christians until after I had made up my mind to become one. It was of the greatest importance, then, to have at hand the work of a man who had come by somewhat the same route, to <almost> the same conclusions, at almost the same time: with a maturity, a weight of scholarship, a discipline of thinking, which I did not, and never shall, possess.

'I had met More only once in earlier years – at a reception given by the Babbitts to which some of Babbitt's pupils had the honor of invitation and that remained only a visual memory. My first meeting with him in London, however, seemed more like the renewal of an old acquaintance than the formation of a new one: More was a St. Louisian, and had known my family' (*Princeton Alumni Magazine* 37 [5 Feb. 1937], 373–4).

See further Arthur Hazard Dakin, *Paul Elmer More* (1960) – of which TSE wrote on 29 Mar. 1960: 'What the author says about Paul More and myself seems to me very accurate . . . [W]e did see very nearly eye to eye in theological matters.'

Frank Vigor Morley (1899–1980), son of a distinguished mathematician – his brothers were the writer Christopher, and Felix (editor of the *Washington Post*) – was brought up in the USA before travelling as a Rhodes Scholar to New College, Oxford, where he earned a doctorate in mathematics. After working for a while at the *Times Literary Supplement*, he became London Manager of The Century Company (Publishers) of New York. In 1929 he became a founding director of Faber & Faber, where he would be a close friend of TSE: for some time they shared a top-floor office at Russell Square. Morley would remark that TSE's 'great skill' as a publisher was that he 'had an unerring gift for spotting talent, but he would never fight for people. I used to watch, and know him so well that if he quietly suggested publishing the poetry of Marianne Moore, whom nobody knew, I would take up the cudgels and be the loud hailer' ('The time when Eliot lit the fuse', *Sunday Times*, 8 June 1980).

In 1933 when TSE separated from Vivien, Morley arranged convivial temporary accommodation for him near his farmhouse at Pike's Farm, Lingfield, Surrey. In 1939 Morley moved to the USA, where he became Vice-President of Harcourt Brace and Company (and during the war he served on the National War Labor Board in Washington, DC). In 1947 he returned with his family to England to take up the post of Director at Eyre & Spottiswoode. A large, learned, ebullient figure, he earned the sobriquet 'Whale' – though not merely on account of his corpulence: in his youth he had spent time aboard a whaling ship (he was revolted by the slaughter), and subsequently wrote (with J. S. Hodgson) *Whaling North and South* (1927) – which was reviewed in the *Monthly Criterion* by his friend Herbert Read. His other publications include *Travels in East Anglia* (1923), *River Thames* (1926), *Inversive Geometry* (1933), *My One Contribution to Chess* (1947), *The Great North Road* (1961), *The Long Road West: A Journey in History* (1971) and *Literary Britain* (1980); and contributions in verse (together with TSE, Geoffrey Faber and John Hayward) to *Noctes Binanianae* (privately printed, 1939).

Morley Kennerley told *The Times* (25 Oct. 1980) that 'one of [Morley's] hobbies was to work out complicated problems for his friends, and for those baffled there were amazing practical jokes. Convivial lunches with interesting people were a joy to him . . . He found jobs for many and squeezed me into Fabers where he generously put up with my sharing a corner of his room for some years. I was present all day during his interviews, dictation, visitors and often lunch. How he put up with all this I do not know. His correspondence with Ezra Pound was quite something, and I think he out-Pounded Pound. As his family say, he was a compulsive letter writer and was rarely without a pencil in his hand or pocket.'

In 1939, when Frank Morley was on the point of returning to the USA, Geoffrey Faber wrote of him to the editor of *The Times*: 'Morley is a quite outstanding person ... [His] first obvious quality is that he is a born "mixer", with an extraordinary range of friends in different walks of life. He is a very good talker, though rather fond – like many Americans – of spinning the yarn out. But he never spins without a purpose. As a negotiator he is in a class by himself. His judgment of men and situations is first rate. He knows the personnel of both the English and American publishing and journalistic worlds. As for his mental equipment, he took a doctorate at Oxford with a mathematical thesis. The story is that nobody in Oxford could understand it, and help had to be got from Cambridge. But he is at least as good a man of letters as he is a mathematician.'

On 2 July 1978 Morley wrote to Helen Gardner, of Eliot: 'I loved him, as I think you know, near to the side of idolatry.'

Lady Ottoline Morrell (1873–1938): daughter of Lieutenant-General Arthur Bentinck and half-sister to the Duke of Portland. In 1902 she married Philip Morrell (1870–1941), Liberal MP for South Oxfordshire 1902–18. A patron of the arts, she entertained a notable literary and artistic circle, first at 44 Bedford Square, then at Garsington Manor, nr. Oxford, where she moved in 1915. She was a lover of Bertrand Russell, who introduced her to TSE, and her many friends included Lytton Strachey, D. H. Lawrence, Aldous Huxley, Siegfried Sassoon, the Woolfs and the Eliots. Her memoirs (ed. by Robert Gathorne-Hardy) appeared as *Ottoline* (1963) and *Ottoline at Garsington* (1974). See further Miranda Seymour, *Life on the Grand Scale: Lady Ottoline Morrell* (1992, 1998).

Edwin Muir (1887–1959): Scottish poet, novelist, critic; translator (with his wife Willa) of Franz Kafka. TSE was to write to Leonard Woolf on 22 Aug. 1946: 'I am anxious to do anything I can for Muir because I think highly of his best poetry and I think he has not had enough recognition.' To Eleanor Hinkley, 25 Dec. 1955: 'Edwin is a sweet creature, who never says anything when his wife is present, and only an occasional word when she isn't. An evening alone with him is very fatiguing. But he is a good poet, and I believe, what is even rarer, a literary man of complete integrity. He is not really Scottish, but Orcadian – in other words, pure

Scandinavian.' On 1 Jan. 1959, when pressing the claims of Muir upon the Royal Literary Fund, TSE wrote to Alan Pryce-Jones: 'I have a very high opinion indeed of Edwin Muir as a poet, and admire him particularly because his poetry has gone on gaining in strength in later years. And I think that both he and Willa deserve recognition because of their work in translation. It is through them, you remember, that Kafka became known in this country, as they translated, I think, all his novels.' In a tribute: 'Muir's literary criticism had always seemed to me of the best of our time: after I came to know him, I realised that it owed its excellence not only to his power of intellect and acuteness of sensibility, but to those moral qualities which make us remember him, as you say justly, as "in some ways almost a saintly man". It was more recently that I came to regard his poetry as ranking with the best poetry of our time. As a poet he began late; as a poet he was recognised late; but some of his finest work – perhaps his very finest work – was written when he was already over sixty . . . For this late development we are reminded of the later poetry of Yeats; and Muir had to struggle with bad health also: but in the one case as in the other (and Muir is by no means unworthy to be mentioned together with Yeats) we recognise a triumph of the human spirit' (*The Times*, 7 Jan. 1959). Willa Muir commented on TSE's plaudits: 'Eliot, in his desire to present Edwin as an orthodox Christian, overdid, I think, the desolations and the saintliness. Edwin's wine could never be contained in any orthodox creed' (letter to Kathleen Raine, 7 Apr. 1960). TSE would later say of Muir: 'He was a reserved, reticent man . . . Yet his personality made a deep impression upon me, and especially the impression of one very rare and precious quality . . . unmistakable integrity'; and of his poems: 'under the pressure of emotional intensity, and possessed by his vision, he found almost unconsciously the right, the inevitable, way of saying what he wanted to say' ('Edwin Muir: 1887–1959: An Appreciation', *The Listener*, 28 May 1964, 872). Writings include *First Poems* (1925) *An Autobiography* (1954); *Selected Poems of Edwin Muir*, preface by TSE (1966); *Selected Letters of Edwin Muir*, ed. P. H. Butter (1974).

John Middleton Murry (1889–1957), English writer, critic and editor, founded the magazine *Rhythm*, 1911–13, and worked as a reviewer for the *Westminster Gazette*, 1912–14, and the *Times Literary Supplement*, 1914–18, before becoming editor from 1919 to 1921 of the *Athenaeum*, which he turned into a lively cultural forum – in a letter of 2 July 1919, TSE called it 'the best literary weekly in the Anglo-Saxon world'. In his 'London Letter', *Dial* 72 (May 1921), Eliot considered Murry 'genuinely studious to maintain a serious criticism', but he disagreed with his 'particular tastes, as well as his general statements'. After the demise of the *Athenaeum*, Murry went on to edit *The Adelphi*, 1923–48. In 1918, he married Katherine Mansfield (d. 1923). He was friend and biographer of D. H. Lawrence; and as an editor he provided a platform for writers as various as George Santayana, Paul Valéry, D. H. Lawrence, Aldous Huxley, Virginia Woolf and Eliot. His first notable critical work was *Dostoevsky* (1916); his most influential study, *The Problem of Style* (1922). Though as a Romanticist he was an intellectual opponent of the avowedly 'Classicist' Eliot, Murry offered Eliot in 1919 the post of assistant editor on the *Athenaeum* (which Eliot had to decline); in addition, he recommended him to be Clark lecturer at Cambridge in 1926, and was a steadfast friend to both TSE and Vivien. Eliot wrote in a reference on 9 Sept. 1945 that Murry was 'one of the most distinguished men of letters of this time, and testimony from a contemporary seems superfluous. Several volumes of literary essays of the highest quality are evidence of his eminence as a critic; and even if one took no account of his original contribution, his conduct of *The Athenaeum*, which he edited from 1919 until its absorption into *The Nation*, should be enough to entitle him to the gratitude of his contemporaries and juniors. His direction of *The Adelphi* should also be recognised. Since he has devoted his attention chiefly to social and religious problems, he has written a number of books which no one who is concerned with the same problems, whether in agreement with him or not, can afford to neglect. I am quite sure that no future student of these matters who wishes to understand this age will be able to ignore them, and that no future student of the literary spirit of this age will be able to ignore Mr Murry's criticism.' He wrote to Murry's widow, 29 May 1957: 'The friendship between John and myself was of a singular quality, such that it was rather different from any other of my friendships. We did not often meet. We disagreed throughout many years on one point after another. But on the other hand, a very warm affection existed between us in spite of differences of view and infrequency of meetings. This affection was not merely, on my part, a feeling of gratitude for the opportunities he had given me early in my career during his editorship of *The Athenaeum*, but was something solid and permanent. He was one of the strangest and most remarkable men I have known, and no less strange and remarkable was the tie of affection between us.' See F. A. Lea, *The Life of John Middleton Murry* (1959); David Goldie, *A Critical Difference: T. S. Eliot and John Middleton Murry in English Literary Criticism, 1919–1928* (1998).

Kenneth Pickthorn (1892–1975): historian and politician; Fellow of Corpus Christi College, Cambridge, from 1914; Dean, 1919–29; Tutor, 1927–35; President, 1937–44. From 1950 to 1966 he was Conservative MP for a Midlands constituency; an outspoken parliamentarian, critical of cant, he was made a baronet in 1959, Privy Councillor in 1964. His writings included *Some Historical Principles of the Constitution* (1925) and *Early Tudor Government* (2 vols, 1934).

Ezra Pound (1885–1972), American poet and critic, was one of the prime impresarios of the modernist movement in London and Paris, and played a major part in launching Eliot as poet and critic – as well as Joyce, Lewis and many others. Eliot called on him at 5 Holland Place Chambers, Kensington, on 22 Sept. 1914, with an introduction from Conrad Aiken. On 30 Sept. 1914, Pound hailed 'Prufrock' as 'the best poem I have yet had or seen from an American'; and on 3 October called Eliot 'the last intelligent man I've found – a young American . . . worth watching – mind "not primitive"' (*Selected Letters of Ezra Pound*, 40–1). Pound was instrumental in arranging for 'Prufrock' to be published in *Poetry* in 1915, and helped to shape *The Waste Land* (1922), which Eliot dedicated to him as '*il miglior fabbro*'. The poets remained in loyal correspondence for the rest of their lives. Having initially dismissed Pound's poetry (to Conrad Aiken, 30 Sept. 1914) as 'well-meaning but touchingly incompetent', Eliot went on to champion his work, writing to Gilbert Seldes (27 Dec. 1922): 'I sincerely consider Ezra Pound the most important living poet in the English language.' He wrote an early critical study, *Ezra Pound: His Metric and Poetry* (1917), and went on, as editor of the *Criterion* and publisher at Faber & Faber, to publish most of Pound's work in the UK, including *Selected Shorter Poems*, *The Cantos* and *Selected Literary Essays*. After his move to Italy in the 1920s, Pound became increasingly sceptical about the direction of TSE's convictions and poetry, but they continued to correspond. TSE wrote to James Laughlin, on the occasion of Pound's seventieth birthday: 'I believe that I have in the past made clear enough my personal debt to Ezra Pound during the years 1915–22. I have also expressed in several ways my opinion of his rank as a poet, as a critic, as impresario of other writers, and as pioneer of metric and poetic language. His 70th birthday is not a moment for qualifying one's praise, but merely for recognition of those services to literature for which he will deserve the gratitude of posterity, and for appreciation of those achievements which even his severest critics must acknowledge' (3 Nov. 1955). TSE told Eaghor G. Kostetsky on 6 Jan. 1960 that the

Cantos 'is unquestionably the most remarkable long contemporary poem in the English language'. After TSE's death, Pound said of him: 'His was the true Dantescan voice – not honoured enough, and deserving more than I ever gave him.' See *The Selected Letters of Ezra Pound 1907–1941*, ed. D. D. Paige (1950); Humphrey Carpenter, *A Serious Character* (1988); A. David Moody, *Ezra Pound: Poet: A Portrait of the Man and his Work*, I: *The Young Genius 1885–1920* (2007); II: *The Epic Years 1921–1939* (2014).

Mario Praz (1896–1982): scholar and critic of English life and literature; author of *La Carne, la Morte e Il Diavolo nella Letteratura Romantica* (1930: *The Romantic Agony*, 1933). Educated in Bologna, Rome and Florence, he came to England in 1923 to study for the title of *libero docente*. He was Senior Lecturer in Italian, Liverpool University, 1924–32; Professor of Italian Studies, Victoria University of Manchester, 1932–4; and Professor of English Language and Literature at the University of Rome, 1934–66. His many other publications include *Il giardino dei sensi* (1975). In 1952 he was conferred by Queen Elizabeth II with the title of Knight Commander of the British Empire (KBE). In 'An Italian Critic on Donne and Crashaw' (*TLS*, 17 Dec. 1925, 878), TSE hailed Praz's study *Secentismo e Marinismo in Inghilterra: John Donne – Richard Crashaw* (1925) as 'indispensable for any student of this period and these authors'. In 'A Tribute to Mario Praz', 15 Apr. 1964, he noted: 'My first acquaintance with the work of Mario Praz came when, many years ago, the *Times Literary Supplement* sent me for review his *Secentismo e Marinismo in Inghilterra*. I immediately recognized these essays – and especially his masterly study of Crashaw – as among the best that I had ever read in that field. His knowledge of the poetry of that period in four languages – English, Italian, Spanish and Latin – was encyclopaedic, and, fortified by his own judgment and good taste, makes that book essential reading for any student of the English "metaphysical poets" . . . I tender these few words in testimony to my gratitude and admiration, not wishing my name to be absent from the roster of men of letters who, as well as more learned scholars of the period, owe him homage' (*Friendship's Garland: Essays presented to Mario Praz on His Seventieth Birthday*, ed. Vittorio Gabrieli [1966]).

See Praz, 'Dante in Inghilterra', *La Cultura*, Jan. 1930, 65–6; 'T. S. Eliot e Dante', *Letteratura* 15 (July 1937), 12–28; 'T. S. Eliot and Dante', *Southern Review* no. 3 (Winter 1937), 525–48; *The Flaming Heart* (1958).

Herbert Read (1893–1968): English poet and literary critic, and one of the most influential art critics of the century. Son of a tenant farmer, Read spent his first years in rural Yorkshire; at sixteen, he went to work as a bank clerk, then studied law and economics at Leeds University; later still, he joined the Civil Service, working first in the Ministry of Labour and then at the Treasury. During his years of service in WWI, he rose to be a captain in the Green Howards, a Yorkshire regiment (his war poems were published in *Naked Warriors*, 1919); and when on leave to receive the Military Cross in 1917, he arranged to dine with TSE at the Monico Restaurant in Piccadilly Circus. This launched a lifelong friendship which he was to recall in 'T. S. E. – A Memoir', in *T. S. Eliot: The Man and his Work*, ed. Allen Tate (1966). Within the year, he had also become acquainted with the Sitwells, Ezra Pound, Wyndham Lewis, Richard Aldington and Ford Madox Ford. He co-founded the journal *Art & Letters*, 1917–20, and wrote essays too for A. R. Orage, editor of the *New Age*. In 1922 he was appointed a curator in the department of ceramics and glass at the Victoria and Albert Museum; and in later years he was to work for the publishers Routledge & Kegan Paul, and as editor of the *Burlington Magazine*, 1933–9. By 1923 he was writing for the *Criterion*: he was to become one of Eliot's regular leading contributors and a reliable ally and adviser. In 1924 he edited T. E. Hulme's posthumous *Speculations*. His later works include *Art Now* (1933); the introduction to the catalogue of the International Surrealist Exhibition held at the New Burlington Galleries, London, 1936; *Art and Society* (1937); *Education through Art* (1943) and *A Concise History of Modern Painting* (1959). In 1947 he founded (with Roland Penrose) the Institute of Contemporary Art; and in 1953 he was knighted for services to literature. Eliot, he was to recall (perhaps only half in jest), was 'rather like a gloomy priest presiding over my affections and spontaneity'. According to Stephen Spender in 1966, Eliot said 'of the anarchism of his friend Herbert Read, whom he loved and esteemed very highly: "Sometimes when I read Herbert's inflammatory pamphlets I have the impression that I am reading the pronouncements of an old-fashioned nineteenth-century liberal"' ('Remembering Eliot', *The Thirties and After* [1978], 251). Joseph Chiari recalled TSE saying of Read: 'Ah, there is old Herbie, again; he can't resist anything new!' See Herbert Read, *Annals of Innocence and Experience* (1940); James King, *The Last Modern: A Life of Herbert Read* (1990); and *Herbert Read Reassessed*, ed. by D. Goodway (1998). Jason Harding (*The 'Criterion'*: see citation under Dobrée) calculates that Read wrote 68 book reviews, 4 articles and 5 poems for the *Criterion*.

I. A. Richards (1893–1979): theorist of literature, education and communication studies. At Cambridge University he studied history but switched to moral sciences, graduating from Magdalene College, where in 1922 he was appointed College Lecturer in English and Moral Sciences. A vigorous, spell-binding lecturer, he was to the fore in the advancement of the English Tripos. His early writings – *The Foundations of Aesthetics* (with C. K. Ogden and James Wood, 1922), *The Meaning of Meaning* (also with Ogden, 1923), *Principles of Literary Criticism* (1924), *Science and Poetry* (1926), *Practical Criticism: A Study of Literary Judgment* (1929) – are foundational texts in modern English literary studies. After teaching at National Tsing Hua University in Peking, 1929–30, he repaired for the remainder of his career to Harvard University, where he was made a university professor in 1944. His other works include *Mencius on the Mind* (1932), *Coleridge on Imagination* (1934), *Basic in Teaching: East and West* (1935), *The Philosophy of Rhetoric* (1936), *Interpretation in Teaching* (1938) and *Speculative Instruments* (1955), as well as translations from Plato and Homer. He was appointed Companion of Honour in 1963, and awarded the Emerson–Thoreau medal of the American Academy of Arts and Sciences, 1970. Out of the teaching term, he enjoyed with his wife Dorothea (1894–1986) an adventurous life of travel and mountain-climbing. See *Selected Letters of I. A. Richards, CH*, ed. John Constable (1990); John Constable, 'I. A. Richards, T. S. Eliot, and the Poetry of Belief', *Essays in Criticism* (July 1990), 222–43; *I. A. Richards and his Critics*, ed. John Constable – vol. 10 of *I. A. Richards: Selected Works 1919–1938* (2001) – and John Paul Russo, *I. A. Richards: His Life and Work* (1989).

Bruce Richmond (1871–1964), literary editor, was educated at Winchester and New College, Oxford, and called to the Bar in 1897. However, he never practised as a barrister; instead, George Buckle, editor of *The Times*, appointed him an assistant editor in 1899, and in 1902 he assumed the editorship of the fledgling *Times Literary Supplement*, which he commanded for thirty-five years. During this period, the 'Lit Sup.' established itself as the premier academic and critical periodical in Britain. He was knighted in 1935. TSE, who was introduced to Richmond by Richard Aldington in 1919, enthused to his mother that year that writing the leading article for the *TLS* was the highest honour 'in the critical world of literature'. In a tribute, he recalled Richmond's 'bird-like alertness of eye, body and mind . . . It was from Bruce Richmond that I learnt editorial standards . . . I learnt from him that it is the business of an editor to know his contributors personally, to keep in touch with them and to make suggestions to them. I tried [at the *Criterion*] to form a nucleus of writers (some of them, indeed, recruited from *The Times Literary Supplement*, and introduced to me by Richmond) on whom I could depend, differing from each other in many things, but not in love of literature and seriousness of purpose . . . It is a final tribute to Richmond's genius as an editor that some of his troupe of regular contributors (I am thinking of myself as well as of others) produced some of their most distinguished critical essays as leaders for the *Literary Supplement* . . . Good literary criticism requires good editors as well as good critics. And Bruce Richmond was a great editor' ('Bruce Lyttelton Richmond', *TLS*, 13 Jan. 1961, 17).

Edouard Roditi (1910–92): American-Jewish poet, critic, biographer, translator and essayist. With a background that was partly Spanish-Portuguese and partly Greek, he attended schools in England, and went up (for a single year, 1927–8) to Balliol College, Oxford. Precocious as both poet and translator, by the age of twelve he had translated into Latin and Greek a good deal of the poetry of Byron; and at fourteen he put Gerard Manley Hopkins into French. His adult works included *Prison Within Prison: Three Elegies on Jewish Themes* (1941); the prose poems of *New and Old Testaments* (1983); collections of essays including *The Disorderly Poet* (1975) and a treatise, *De L'Homosexualité* (1962); as well as translations into English, German and French. The *Times* obituary remarked (18 May 1992): 'In 1926 he was sent to a Swiss clinic, where he set himself the task of translating the French poet Saint-John Perse's *Anabase* into English. A little later he discovered that T. S. Eliot was engaged in the same project, and so sent him his version, from which, he claimed, Eliot took up more than a few interpretations. But Eliot also made encouraging comments about some of the boy's original verse.'

Roditi wrote to *The Jewish Quarterly*, no. 142 (38: 2, Summer 1991), 72: 'I was barely eighteen when I first met Eliot in 1928 because I too had undertaken a translation of Saint-John Perse's *Anabase* without knowing that its French author had already granted Eliot the right to translate and publish it in English.

'Eliot then proved to be very cordial and almost paternal in his typically reserved manner. After discussing our different interpretations of some of the more cryptic passages in *Anabase*, Eliot invited me to submit to him some of my own poems. From some of these he was soon able to conclude that I was of Jewish origin and attempting somehow to discover my Jewish identity in a few of my poems. Very kindly, he suggested corrections to these somewhat immature poems and encouraged me to continue submitting my poetry to him for guidance. After a while, he even suggested publishing in *The Criterion* one of my most overtly Jewish poems – in fact one of the sections of my long elegy entitled "The Complaint of Jehuda Abravanel"; but this particular section of my poem had already been accepted for publication either in *The Spectator* or *The Jewish Review*. I then submitted a group of shorter poems and Eliot published three of these in *The Criterion*.

'I continued to see Eliot fairly regularly in London between 1928 and 1937 and can testify to the fact that he expressed to me on several occasions after 1933 his horror of the anti-Semitic outrages which were already occurring in Nazi Germany. My personal impression is that, after writing *The Waste Land*, Eliot had become a much more devout Christian, before writing the so-called "Ariel Poems" and *Ash Wednesday*. As a Christian he no longer felt or expressed the kind of somewhat immature and snobbish anti-Semitism that can be detected in the earlier poems and letters.'

See also Roditi, 'T. S. Eliot: Persönlichkeit und Werk', *Der Monat* 3 (1948), 86–9; 'Corresponding with Eliot', *London Magazine* 28: 5/6 (Aug./Sept. 1988), 33–44.

William Rothenstein (1872–1945), Bradford-born son of Jewish immigrants, painter and administrator, was Principal of the Royal College of Art from 1919; knighted in 1931. See *Twelve Portraits* (F&F, 1928); *Men and Memories: Recollections of William Rothenstein* (2 vols, 1931–2); *Since Fifty: Men and Memories, 1922–1938* (1939); Robert Speaight, *William Rothenstein: The Portrait of an Artist in His Time* (1962).

A. L. Rowse (1903–97), Cornish historian, was educated at Christ Church, Oxford, and elected a Prize Fellow of All Souls in 1925. He was a lecturer at Merton College, 1927–30, and taught also at the London School of Economics. His many books include *Sir Richard Grenville of the Revenge* (1937), *William Shakespeare: A Biography* (1963), *Simon Forman: Sex and Society in Shakespeare's Age* (1974), *All Souls in My Time* (1993), and volumes of poetry gathered up in *A Life* (1981). Though he failed in 1952 to be elected Warden of All Souls, he was elected a Fellow of the British Academy in 1958 and made a Companion of Honour in 1997. See Richard Ollard, *A Man of Contradictions: A Life of A. L. Rowse* (1999), and *The Diaries of A. L. Rowse* (ed. Ollard, 2003). TSE wrote to Geoffrey Curtis, 1 May 1944: 'Rowse is an old friend of mine, and a very touching person: the suppressed Catholic and the rather less suppressed Tory (with a real respect for Good Families), the miner's son and the All Souls Fellow, the minor poet and the would-be politician, the proletarian myth and the will-to-power, are always at odds in a scholarly retiring mind and a frail body. He is also very patronising, and one likes it.' Rowse hailed Eliot as 'nursing father to us all'.

Robert Esmonde Gordon George – Robert Sencourt (1890–1969): critic, historian, biographer. Born in New Zealand, he was educated in Tamaki and at St John's College, Oxford. By 1929 – perhaps to avoid confusion with Professor George Gordon (President of Magdalen College, Oxford) – he was to take the name of Robert Sencourt. He taught in India and Portugal before serving as Vice-Dean of the Faculty of Arts and Professor of English Literature, University of Egypt, 1933–6. The *Times* obituarist noted that he was 'born an Anglican [but] was converted to Roman Catholicism which alone could inspire him with the spiritual dimension of the life of grace . . . [He] was the most fervent and devout of religious men, with the same personal mysticism which makes his life of St John of the Cross a joy to read. Never fearing to speak his mind in religious matters, even when (as often) his view ran counter to the Church's, he was intolerant of any form of ecclestiastical cant or humbug.' His books include *The Genius of the Vatican* (1935), *Carmelite and Poet: St John of the Cross* (1943), biographies of George Meredith, the Empress Eugénie, Napoleon III and Edward VIII, and the posthumous *T. S. Eliot: A Memoir*, ed. Donald Adamson (1971). EVE wrote to Russell Kirk, 15 May 1973: 'Sencourt's memoir is, to put it mildly, unfortunate, and leaves a nasty taste. As you say, the whole background is both strange and malicious. He had nothing whatsoever to do with Tom's conversion – this long, slow process had come to fruition before they met.' See too Sencourt, 'T. S. Eliot: His Religion', *PAX: A Benedictine Review*, no. 312 (Spring 1965), 15–19.

In 1938, when Sencourt applied to be Professor of English at Raffles College, Singapore, TSE urged the Universities Bureau: 'I am eager to add my recommendation, as I am sure that no more suitable incumbent could be found: Mr. Sencourt is qualified for such a position to an unusual degree, both by his academic and literary attainments, by his experience of teaching, and in particular by his experience in teaching Orientals. He has furthermore all the social and personal qualifications – such as patience, tactfulness, and a cosmopolitan experience which gives him a sympathy with foreign minds.'

Sencourt wrote to TSE in Oct. 1930, after staying for a few days with him and VHE: 'I could hardly imagine a spirit more congenial and refreshing than yours.'

Charles Arthur Siepmann (1899–1985), radio producer and educator, was awarded the Military Cross in WWI. He joined the BBC in 1927, and became Director of Talks, 1932–5; Regional Relations, 1935–6; Programme Planning, 1936–9. He was University Lecturer, Harvard, 1939–42; worked for the Office of War Information, 1942–5; and was Professor of Education, New York University, 1946–67. Works include *Radio's Second Chance* (1946), *Radio, Television and Society* (1950), *TV and Our School Crisis* (1959). See Richard J. Meyer, 'Charles A. Siepmann and Educational Broadcasting', *Educational Technology Research and Development* 12: 4 (Winter 1964), 413–30. TSE told HWE on 9 Mar. 1937: 'In spite of his name he is in all appearance a perfectly English person, and was educated at Rugby and Oxford. I think his father or grandfather was German. Siepmann is an extremely serious, not to say solemn, young man, of about 36, who has been in the British Broadcasting Corporation longer than anyone I have ever heard of except Sir John Reith himself . . . [H]is political sympathies are rather liberal and left. He is a very nice fellow, although somewhat humourless.'

Stephen Spender (1909–95), poet and critic, won a rapid reputation with his first collection *Poems* (F&F, 1933), following an appearance in Michael Roberts's anthology *New Signatures* (1932). He cultivated friendships with some of the foremost younger writers of the period, including W. H. Auden, Christopher Isherwood, John Lehmann and J. R. Ackerley. For a brief while in the 1930s he joined the Communist party and went to Spain to serve the Republican cause. With Cyril Connolly he set up the magazine *Horizon* in 1940. In the postwar years he was to be a visiting professor at a number of American universities, and he undertook trips on behalf of the British Society for Cultural Freedom, the Congress for Cultural Freedom, and PEN. He served too as poetry consultant to the Library of Congress, 1965–6. For fourteen years from 1953 he was co-editor of the magazine *Encounter*, which – as it was ultimately proven – was from the start the beneficiary of funding from the CIA (just as writers including William Empson had suspected). Spender's other works include *Vienna* (1934), *The Destructive Element* (1935), *Forward from Liberalism* (1937), *World within World* (autobiography, 1951), *The Creative Element* (1953), *Collected Poems* (1955), *The Struggle of the*

Modern (1963), *The Thirties and After* (1978), *New Selected Journals 1939–1995*, ed. Lara Feigel and John Sutherland with Natasha Spender (2012), and *The Temple* (novel, 1989). He was instrumental in setting up Index on Censorship in 1971, and worked as Professor of English at University College, London, 1970–5. He was awarded the CBE (1962), elected a Companion of Literature by the Royal Society of Literature (1977), and knighted in 1983. See further John Sutherland, *Stephen Spender: The Authorized Biography* (2004); Matthew Spender, *A House in St John's Wood: In Search of My Parents* (2015).

William Force Stead (1884–1967), poet, critic, diplomat, clergyman, was educated at the University of Virginia and served in WW1 as Vice-Consul with the American Foreign Service in Liverpool. After working for a while in Florence, he was appointed in 1927 Chaplain of Worcester College, Oxford, where he became a Fellow. While in England, he befriended literary figures including W. B. Yeats, John Masefield and Robert Bridges, as well as TSE – whom he was to baptise into the Anglican Church in 1927. In later years, after living through WW2 in Baltimore, he taught at Trinity College, Washington, DC. Publications include *Uriel: A Hymn in Praise of Divine Immanence* (1933), and an edition of Christopher Smart's *Rejoice in the Lamb: A Song from Bedlam* (1939) – a work which he discovered.

TSE wrote a testimonial on 4 Dec. 1938 (sent to the University of Cairo, on 9 Dec.): 'I have known Mr. William Force Stead for over eleven years and count him as a valued friend. He is, first, a poet of established position and an individual inspiration. What is not so well known, except to a small number of the more fastidious readers, is that he is also a prose writer of great distinction: his book [*The Shadow of*] *Mt. Carmel* is recognised as a classic of prose style in its kind. And while the bulk of his published writing on English literature is small, those who know his conversation can testify that he is a man of wide reading and a fine critical sense.

'Mr. Stead is, moreover, a man of the world in the best sense, who has lived in several countries and is saturated in European culture. By both natural social gifts and cultivation, accordingly, he has a remarkable ability of sympathy with all sorts and conditions and races of men.

'I would say finally that I know from several sources, that Mr. Stead was most successful as a teacher of young men at Oxford; that he gained both the affection and the respect of his students; and that he exercised upon them a most beneficial influence. He has the scholarship necessary

810

to teach English literature accurately, and the personal qualities necessary to make the subject interesting to his pupils; and I could not recommend anyone for the purpose with more confidence' (Beinecke).

See 'Mr Stead Presents An Old Friend', *Trinity College Alumni Journal* 38: 2 (Winter 1965), 59–66; George Mills Harper, 'William Force Stead's Friendship with Yeats and Eliot', *Massachusetts Review* 21: 1 (Spring 1980), 9–38; David Bradshaw, '"Oxford Poets": Yeats, T. S. Eliot and William Force Stead', *Yeats Annual* 19: *Special Issue: Yeats's Mask*, ed. Margaret Mills Harper and Warwick Gould (2013), 77–102.

Allen Tate (1899–1979), poet, critic and editor, grew up in Kentucky and attended Vanderbilt University (where he was taught by John Crowe Ransom and became associated with the group of writers known as the Fugitives). He taught at various universities before becoming Poet-in-Residence at Princeton, 1939–42; Poetry Consultant to the Library of Congress, 1944–5; and editor of *The Sewanee Review*, 1944–6; and he was Professor of Humanities at the University of Minnesota (where colleagues included Saul Bellow and John Berryman), 1951–68. Eliot wrote of him in 1959: 'Allen Tate is a good poet and a good literary critic who is distinguished for the sagacity of his social judgment and the consistency with which he has maintained the least popular of political attitudes – that of the sage. He believes in reason rather than enthusiasm, in wisdom rather than system; and he knows that many problems are insoluble and that in politics no solution is final. By avoiding the lethargy of the conservative, the flaccidity of the liberal, and the violence of the zealot, he succeeds in being a representative of the smallest of minorities, that of the intelligent who refuse to be described as "intellectuals". And what he has written, as a critic of society, is of much greater significance because of being said by a man who is also a good poet and a good critic of literature' (*Sewanee Review* 67: 4 [Oct.–Dec. 1959], 576). Tate's works include *Ode to the Confederate Dead* (1930), *The Mediterranean and Other Poems* (1936), *Reactionary Essays on Poetry and Ideas* (1936) and *The Fathers* (novel, 1938).

Harriet Shaw Weaver (1876–1961), English editor and publisher, whom Virginia Woolf described as 'modest judicious & decorous' (*Diary*, 13 April 1918). In 1912, Weaver began by giving financial support to *The Freewoman*, a radical periodical founded and edited by Dora Marsden, which was renamed in 1913 (at the suggestion of Ezra Pound) *The Egoist*. Weaver became editor in 1914, turning it into a 'little magazine' with a big influence in the history of literary Modernism. TSE followed in the footsteps of Richard Aldington and H.D. to became assistant editor in 1917 (having been nominated by Pound), and remained so until it closed in 1919. When Joyce could not secure a publisher for *A Portrait of the Artist as a Young Man*, Weaver in 1917 converted *The Egoist* into a press in order to publish it. She went on to publish TSE's first book, *Prufrock and Other Observations* (1917), Pound's *Dialogues of Fontenelle* and *Quia Pauper Amavi*, Wyndham Lewis's novel *Tarr*, and Marianne Moore's *Poems*, and other notable books. (She played a major role as Joyce's patron and confidante, and went on to be his literary executor and to help put together *The Letters of James Joyce*.) TSE wrote to Patricia Lloyd, 4 Oct. 1951: 'She was a generous and enlightened patron of letters, and I believe was of very material assistance to James Joyce.' And he paid tribute in 1962: 'Miss Harriet Shaw Weaver . . . was so modest and self-effacing a woman that her generous patronage of men of letters was hardly known beyond the circle of those who benefited by it . . . Miss Weaver's support, once given, remained steadfast. Her great disappointment was her failure to persuade any printer in this country to take the risk of printing *Ulysses*; her subsequent generosity to James Joyce, and her solicitude for his welfare and that of his family, knew no bounds . . . [Working for her at *The Egoist*] was all great fun, my first experience of editorship. In 1932 I dedicated my *Selected Essays* to this good, kind, unassuming, courageous and lovable woman, to whom I owe so much. What other publisher in 1917 (the Hogarth Press was not yet in existence) would, I wonder, have taken *Prufrock*?' See also Jane Lidderdale and Mary Nicholson, *Dear Miss Weaver: Harriet Shaw Weaver, 1876–1961* (1970).

Orlando (Orlo) Williams (1883–1967): Clerk to the House of Commons, scholar, critic; contributor to the *TLS*; Chevalier, Légion d'honneur. Publications include *The Clerical Organisation of the House of Commons 1661–1850* (1954); *Vie de Bohème: A Patch of Romantic Paris* (1913); *Some Great English Novels: The Art of Fiction* (1926).

Edmund Wilson (1895–1972): influential literary critic, social commentator and cultural historian; worked in the 1920s as managing editor of *Vanity Fair*; later as associate editor of *The New Republic* and as a prolific book reviewer. Major publications include *Axel's Castle: A Study in the Imaginative Literature of 1870–1930* (1931) – which includes a chapter on TSE's work, sources and influence – *The Triple Thinkers: Ten Essays on Literature* (1938), and *The Wound and the Bow: Seven*

Studies in Literature (1941). TSE wrote to Geoffrey Curtis, 20 Oct. 1943: 'Edmund Wilson is a very good critic except that, like most of his generation in America, he has mixed his literary criticism with too much political ideology of a Trotskyite variety and perhaps he is also too psychological, but I have a great respect for him as a writer and like him as a man.'

Leonard Woolf (1880–1969): writer and publisher; husband of Virginia Woolf, whom he married in 1912. A friend of Lytton Strachey and J. M. Keynes at Cambridge, he played a central part in the Bloomsbury Group. He wrote a number of novels, including *The Village and the Jungle* (1913), and political studies including *Imperialism and Civilization* (1928). As founder-editor, with Virginia Woolf, of the Hogarth Press, he published TSE's *Poems* (1919) and *The Waste Land* (1923). In 1923 he became literary editor of *The Nation & Athenaeum* (after TSE had turned it down), commissioning reviews from him, and he remained a firm friend. See *An Autobiography* (2 vols, 1980); *Letters of Leonard Woolf*, ed. Frederic Spotts (1990); Victoria Glendinning, *Leonard Woolf: A Life* (2006).

Virginia Woolf (1882–1941), novelist, essayist and critic, was author of *Jacob's Room* (1922), *Mrs Dalloway* (1925) and *To the Lighthouse* (1927); *A Room of One's Own* (1928), a classic of feminist criticism; and *The Common Reader* (1925). Daughter of the biographer and editor Leslie Stephen (1832–1904), she married Leonard Woolf in 1912, published her first novel *The Voyage Out* in 1915, and founded the Hogarth Press with her husband in 1917. The Hogarth Press published TSE's *Poems* (1919), *The Waste Land* (1923) and *Homage to John Dryden* (1923). TSE published in the *Criterion* Woolf's essays and talks including 'Kew Gardens', 'Character in Fiction' and 'On Being Ill'. Woolf became a friend and correspondent; her diaries and letters give first-hand accounts of him. Woolf wrote to her sister Vanessa Bell, 22 July 1936: 'I had a visit, long ago, from Tom Eliot, whom I love, or could have loved, had we both been in the prime and not in the sere; how necessary do you think copulation is to friendship? At what point does "love" become sexual?' (*Letters*, vol. 6). Eliot wrote in 1941 that Woolf 'was the centre, not merely of an esoteric group, but of the literary life of London. Her position was due to a concurrence of qualities and circumstances which never happened before, and which I do not think will ever happen again. It maintained the dignified and admirable tradition of Victorian upper middle-class culture

– a situation in which the artist was neither the servant of the exalted patron, the parasite of the plutocrat, nor the entertainer of the mob – a situation in which the producer and the consumer of art were on an equal footing, and that neither the highest nor the lowest.' To Enid Faber, 27 Apr. 1941: 'she was a personal friend who seemed to me (mutatis considerably mutandis) like a member of my own family; and I miss her dreadfully, but I don't see her exactly as her relatives see her, and my admiration for the ideas of her milieu – now rather old-fashioned – is decidedly qualified.' See further Hermione Lee, *Virginia Woolf* (1996).

William Butler Yeats (1865–1939): Irish poet and playwright. According to TSE, he was 'one of those few whose history is the history of their own time, who are part of the consciousness of an age' (*On Poetry and Poets*). TSE met Yeats soon after arriving in London, but despite their mutual admiration of Pound, they had little contact until 1922, when TSE told Ottoline Morrell that Yeats was 'one of the very small number of people with whom one can talk profitably of poetry'. In his review of *Per Amica Silentia Lunae*, he said 'One is never weary of the voice, though the accents are strange' ('A Foreign Mind', *Athenaeum*, 4 July 1919). He was keen to publish Yeats in the *Criterion*: see 'A Biographical Fragment', in *Criterion* 1 (July 1923), 'The Cat and the Moon', 2 (July 1924), 'The Tower', 5 (June 1927). Yeats was instinctively opposed to TSE's work, but discussed it at length in his Introduction to the *Oxford Book of Modern Verse* (1936), and declared after the publication of *The Waste Land* that he found it 'very beautiful' (Jan. 1923). EVE wrote to Professor John Kelly, 24 Oct. 1995: 'I feel that the Yeats/Eliot relationship should have been more fruitful, and that the admiration of my husband was not reciprocated.' See further Roy Foster, *Yeats: A Life*: I *The Apprentice Mage* (1997), II *The Arch-Poet* (2003).

INDEX OF CORRESPONDENTS
AND RECIPIENTS

Gregg, Frances Wilkinson, 237
Gregory, Horace, 260, 516, 579, 764
Grieve, Christopher Murray (Hugh MacDiarmid), 14, 101, 117
Griffith, Mr, 478
Gurian, Waldemar, 655, 666

Haecker, Theodor, 724, 767
Haigh-Wood, Maurice, 346, 717
Hale, Emily, 779, 780
Halifax, Charles Lindley Wood, 2nd Viscount, 124
Hamilton, G. Rostrevor, 313
Harmsworth, Desmond, 7
Harris, Charles, 132, 365, 443
Harris, E. M., 426
Harrison, G. B., 35, 106, 258, 696
Harrison, Ruth, 296, 326, 393
Havens, Raymond D., 323
Hayward, John, 293, 413, 441, 457, 531, 609, 695
Healing, Emma, 748
Hebert, A. G., 726
Henderson, Ian L., 409
Henson, Herbert, 239
Hester, Norman W., 758
Higham, David, 74, 355, 356, 449
Hinkley, Eleanor, 167, 377, 465, 468
Hinkley, Susan, 608, 742
Hodgson, Aurelia (*earlier* Bolliger), 109, 127, 168, 185, 242, 259, 269, 314, 355, 368, 377, 385, 386, 658
Hodgson, Ralph, 23, 154, 169, 225, 242, 259, 347, 368, 385, 406, 658
Holliday, Terence A., 417
Holter, Betty, 390
Hopkins, Gerard, 361
Hotson, J. Leslie, 505
House, A. Humphrey, 365
Hudson, Revd Cyril E., 349
Hutchinson, Mary, 11, 200, 215, 273, 277, 299, 346, 367, 386, 425, 458, 511, 513, 532, 539, 599, 603, 605, 619, 640, 648, 694, 729

Ingram, Kenneth, 153

James & James, Messrs, 190, 301, 426, 704
James, J. L. Beaumont, 217
Janes, W. L., 638
Jerrold, Douglas, 29, 87, 222

Jones, P. Mansell, 241, 246
Joyce, James, 13, 79, 93, 107, 114, 121, 144, 150, 180, 196, 207, 304, 316, 375, 648, 684, 711, 746, 771
Judson, M., 176

Kaestlin, John, 749
Kapur, R., 451
Keynes, John Maynard, 177, 292, 366, 422
Kirstein, Lincoln, 519
Klopfer, Donald S., 558
Knight, G. Wilson, 204, 295, 388, 427
Knights, L. C., 289, 447, 659, 774
Kreymborg, Alfred, 206
Kurath, Gertrude P., 312

Lacey, J. de, 250
Lawson, Terence, 401
Leach, H. G., 61
Leavis, F. R., 45, 104, 111, 256, 265, 371
Leeds, University of, The Vice Chancellor, 244
Le Gallienne, Eva, 520
Lehmann, John F., 42
Leippert, James G., 238, 293
Léon, Paul, 92, 369
Levin, Harry, 502, 756
Lion, Aline, 133
Listener, The, The Editor, 226
Little, Leon M., 767
Lloyds Bank, The Manager, 416
Lowenfels, Walter, 360
Lowes, John Livingston, 502, 515, 581

Macdonald, Hugh, 34, 342
McEachran, F., 43, 74
McGreevy, Thomas, 734, 761
MacIntyre, A. H., 402, 730
McKechnie, Alexander, 95
McKenna, Mrs, 498
McKerrow, R. B., 213
MacNeice, Louis, 249, 341, 363
Madge, Charles, 383
Manent, Marià, 261
Manning, Frederic, 52
Manwaring, Elizabeth, 15, 466, 479, 544, 602, 623
Marc, Alexandre, 752
Marichalar, Antonio, 624
Maritain, Jacques, 330
Massingham, Harold John, 102
Massingham, Hugh, 191

GENERAL INDEX

Burlington Magazine, 689

Burns, Tom F., **64n**; and Gurian's
  Bolshevism, 264; on Kierkegaard, 315,
  317; and Ruth Harrison's Book on Péguy,
  326; and Haecker's *Was Ist Der Mensch?*,
  723

Burroughs, William, 465n, 545n

Burton, Revd Spence, SSJE, **571n**

Butts, Mary, **6n**; marriage to Atkin, 227n;
  Ashe of Rings, 6n

Byron, George Gordon, 6th Baron, 150

Cabot, Mabel (Mrs Ellery Sedgwick), 403n

Caetani, Marguerite (*née* Chapin; Princess
  di Bassiano), **785**; acquires Grand
  National lottery tickets, 94; proposes
  opening picture gallery in London, 116;
  and Paulhan, 133; considers house in
  London, 171; unpaid account with Jones
  and Evans Bookshop, 275; receives
  recording of TSE's poetry readings, 691n;
  and TSE's lecturing in Rome, 740, 758

California, 523–4, 539, 543, 545, 585

California, University of, 536n

Campbell, Charley, 538n

Campbell, Jim, 538n

Campbell, Oscar James, 529

Campbell, Roy, **280n**, 779

Canadian Pacific Railway, 256

Canby, Henry Seidel, **348n**, 396n, 504n,
  517

Cape, Jonathan, Ltd (publishers), 415

Carpenter, Humphrey, 186n

Carpenter, S. C., **775n**

Carroll, Lewis, 252, 546n; *Alice in
  Wonderland*, 583–4

Carswell, Catherine, 565n

Carver, Willie, 487

Cassell, Professor, 410

Castle, William R., Jr, **511n**

Catholic Literature Association, 416

'Catholicism and International Order'
  (address), 606n

Cattaui, Georges, **68n**; translates *A Song
  for Simeon*, 373n

Cavalcanti, Guido, 62–3, 656, 763; *Rime*,
  252n, 297, 318

Cecil, Lady Beatrice Ethel Mildred, 215n

Cecil, Lord David, **324n**

Cerf, Bennett, 93, 144n, 181n, **285n**, 743n,
  771n

Chambers, Sir Theodore, 90n

Chandler, Miss (St Louis teacher), 538n

Chandos group, 394n

Chapin, Christina: 'Sanctuary' (poem), 622

Chaplin, Charlie, 338n, 736n

Charles I, King, 29

Charles II, King, 100n

Charlottesville *see* Virginia, University of

Chatto & Windus (publishers): publish
  Virginia Woolf, 8

Chester Terrace, London, 301

Chesterfield, Philip Dormer Stanhope, 4th
  Earl of: *Letters*, 151, 196, 211n, 212

Chesterton, G. K., 199

Chetwynd (suicide), 702

Chevalley, Claude, 711n

Chiari, Joseph, 15n

Chicago, 548

Child, Maurice, 698

Chisholm, Erik, 568n

Choate, Hall & Stewart (Boston), 642

*Christendom: a Quarterly Journal of
  Christian Sociology*, 195n, 210n, 211,
  765n

'Christianity and Communism', 157

Church, Richard W., **395n**; on C. M.
  Grieve (MacDiarmid), 15n; *The Oxford
  Movement: Twelve Years 1833–1845*, 700

Churchill, Winston, 578

Claremont, California, 546n; *see also*
  Scripps College

Clarence Gate Gardens, London, 82, 345,
  415–16, 679

Clark, Harry H., **77n**; 'The Literary
  Theories of Thomas Paine', 280

Clark, Kenneth: reviews Adrian Stokes's
  The Quattro Cento, 237, 252, 297

Clarke, Revd C. P. S., 271n

Clarke, Lowther, 365

Claudel, Paul: *Ways and Crossways*, 661n

Clemen, Wolfgang H., **362n**

Clemens, Cyril Coniston, **29n**

Clerical Association of Massachusetts, 582

Cleveland, John, 661, 756

Clifton, Mrs, 446

Clonmore, William Forward-Howard,
  Baron (*later* 8th Earl of Wicklow), 610

Clurman, Harold, 559n

Cobden-Sanderson (publishing house), 157,
  640

Cobden-Sanderson, Richard, **329n**; TSE
  invites to joint Sadler's Wells Society,
  284; TSE recommends Richard Marriott

to, 329; TSE hopes to lunch with, 430;
and Rexi Culpin's manuscript, 474n;
publishes Monro's *Collected Poems*, 649n
Cobden-Sanderson, Sally, **284n**; arranges
TSE's travel to Boston, 284, 300, 328,
342, 357, 430, 453; TSE reports on
voyage to, 489
Cocteau, Jean: *A Call to Order*, 645;
Le Mystère Laïc, 645
Codrington, K. de B., 653
Coffey, Brian, **751n**
Coghlin, Fr, 534
Cohen, Francis Ephraim *see* Palgrave,
Sir Francis
Cohen, H. M., 396n
Cohen, Meyer, 622n
Coleman, Emily Holmes, 365n, 399
Coleridge, Samuel Taylor, 516, 709n;
Unpublished Letters, 332
Colhoun, Charles K.: TSE requests
translation of Mauron from, 302;
translates Poncins article, 455
Colonial Society, 251
Colum, Padraic, **187n**, 304
Columbia University, New York: awards
honorary doctorate to TSE, 596
'A Commentary', 477
Commerce (magazine), 116, 194n, 233,
274
Communism: Murry on, 78, 183n;
Macmurray on, 277; TSE on, 292n; Aline
Lion on, 492n; and Christianity, 702; *see
also* Marxism
'The Conceit in Donne and Crashaw'
(lecture), 542n
Conservative Party, 87–8
Constable & Co. (publishers), 32n, 36n
Contemporaries (collection), 19, 749
Cooke, Alistair, **338n**, 561, 736, 743;
'A Preface to Theatrical Criticism', 364
'A Cooking Egg', 554n
Coomaraswamy, Ananda K., 777
Corbière, Tristan, 656
Cork, W. Edmund, **85n**
Cornford, F. M.: *Before and After Socrates*,
565; *The Origin of Attic Comedy*, 498,
566
Cornford, John, 12
Correspondent, Le, 94
Courage, James F., **108n**
Cournos, John, 785; complains of
inadequate payment, 353; TSE requests

address, 456; proposes Chronicle for
Criterion, 462; fails to receive Russian
periodicals, 477; writes on émigré
literature, 491; applies for Guggenheim
fellowship, 731; in New Haven, Conn.,
437, 497n; *Myth in the Making*, 660
Craigie, Sir William A., 477, 503, 507
Crane, Grace Hart: collects son's
unpublished poems, 335
Crane, Hart, 335
Crankshaw, Edward, **334n**; submits
fragments of novel to TSE, 388
Crashaw, Richard, 408–9, 442, 455
Crewe, Robert Offley Ashburton Crewe-
Milnes, Marquis of, 288
Criterion (later *New Criterion*): editorial
meetings, 10, 40–1, 105, 173, 203,
212, 267n, 273, 310, 320–1, 326, 331;
supposed clique, 46; French Chronicle,
322; fees for contributors, 353n, 655,
683; Fiction Chronicle, 381, 654, 677,
693; reviews during TSE's absence in
USA, 413–14; TSE edits during absence,
423, 470; TSE resumes editing on return
from USA, 604–5; Music Chronicle, 612,
656; TSE designates contributors, 653–4;
price, 667; American Chronicle, 745
Criterion Miscellany: sections of *Ulysses*
published in, 93, 121; audience, 257
Crofton, H. C., **140n**
Crofton, John, 140n
Crosby, Caresse (*née* Jacob), **82n**
Crosby, Harry, 82n
Cukor, George, 595n
Culpin, Rexi (*née* Regina Temunovich):
The Dead Image, 414–15, 456, 474n,
477
Cunard, Maud Alice (Emerald), Lady, 566n
Curry, William Burnley, **272n**
Curtis Brown (agents), 449n
Curtis, Charles, 642
Curtis, Revd Geoffrey, **30n**; sends poems
to Evelyn Underhill, 128; illness, 690–1;
'Lyra Subapostolica', 31, 79
Curtius, Ernst Robert, **786**; and translation
of *TWL*, 38, 40; TSE cites to Haecker,
724; *The Civilisation of France*, 59–60;
Deutscher Geist in Gefahr, 43, 60

Dahlberg, Edward, 107n, 516, 529
Dandieu, Arnaud, 236, 711n, 714n
Daniel-Rops, Henry (pseud. of Henri

Donnell, Walter, 538n
Doolittle, Hilda *see* H. D.
Dorn, Marion, 595n
dos Passos, John, 559n
Double Crown Club, 145, 145n, 662
Doughty, Charles, 117
Douglas, ('Major') C. H., **119n**, 572n, 658, 701, 728n; *The Monopoly of Credit*, 53
Doyle, Sir Arthur Conan, 557n
Drake, Lawrence, 19
Dreiser, Theodore, 573n
Drinkwater, John, 314, 395
Dru, Alexander, 723n, 768
Dryden, John, 232, 342n, 355
Dublin, 404
Dublin Review, 219
du Bos, Charles: diary, 25, 97n, **149n**; *Approximations*, 230; *Byron*, 150; *François Maurois*, 735
Duff, Charles, 94, 121n, 151
Dukes, Ashley, 98n
du Maurier, Daphne, 59n
Dun Laoghaire, Ireland, 181
Dunbar, M. J., 554n
Dunbar, William, 507, 510, 516
Duncan-Jones, Austin, 73n, 99n
Duncan-Jones, Elsie *see* Phare, Elsie Elizabeth
Dunster House Bookshop, Cambridge, Mass., 250n, 251
Durrell, Lawrence, 108n; *Alexandria Quartet*, 584n

Eames, Doris, 592, 593n
Eames, Jack, 593n
Eames, Mrs Jack, 592, 593n, 600
Earle, Mr (Eleanor Farjeon's friend), 335n
Eastman, Max, *The Literary Mind*, 32, 84n, 343
Eberhart, Richard, 495n
Echanges (magazine), 218
Edman, Irwin, 293n
Edmunds, Walter: *Erie Waters*, 486, 530
'Edward Lear and Modern Poetry' (lecture), 527n, 542n, 575n
Edward, Prince of Wales, 101
Edwards, Harold Llewelyn Ravenscroft, **411n**
Egoist Press, 720n
Eliot House *see* Harvard College
Eliot, Abigail Adams, 214, 601n
Eliot, Revd Andrew, 602

Eliot, Charles W., 496
Eliot, Charlotte Champe (TSE's mother): death, 13
Eliot, Revd Christopher Rhodes (TSE's uncle), **213n**, 529
Eliot, Elizabeth Berkeley (*née* Lee), 129n, 209, 253n
Eliot, Revd Frederick May (TSE's cousin), 129n, 214
Eliot, Henry Ware (TSE's father): death, 13
Eliot, Henry Ware, Jr (TSE's brother), **788**; TSE writes to on Barnes, 89n; sees TSE in USA, 471, 496; letter to VHE, 520; stays at Harvard with TSE, 531n; letters and telegrams from VHE, 536, 551, 564, 586, 596; on TSE's lecture on taste, 536n; VHE appoints executor of will, 551, 564; TSE stays with, 574, 585; praises TSE, 597n; TSE sends deed of Trust to, 642; receives recording of TSE's poetry readings, 692n; *Rumble Murders*, 230, 495
Eliot, Margaret Dawes (TSE's sister), 231, 408, 411, 595, 640n
Eliot, Marion Cushing (TSE's sister), 461, 605, 640n
Eliot, Martha May (TSE's cousin), 214
Eliot, Minna (*née* Sessinghaus), 136
Eliot, Richard ('Ricky'; Frederick May/Elizabeth's adopted son), 129
Eliot, Rose Greenleaf *see* Smith, Rose Holmes (TSE's aunt), 17
Eliot, Theresa (HWE Jr's wife): TSE stays with, 574n; drawing of TSE, 597n; and TSE's view of VHE's mental state, 741n
Eliot, Thomas Dawes (TSE's cousin), **130n**; arranges lecture engagements for TSE in USA, 253; invites TSE to visit in Chicago, 253
Eliot, (Esmé) Valerie (TSE's second wife), 181n, 186n, 531n, 553n, 584n, 651n, 687n, 741n
Eliot, Vivien (TSE's first wife; *née* Haigh-Wood), **789**; ill-health, 11, 17n, 185, 275n, 521, 570, 619, 717, 722; unable to accompany TSE to USA, 17; friendship with Aurelia Bolliger (Hodgson), 23, 109, 127, 168, 355, 377, 385; and TSE's absence at Harvard, 50, 68, 215, 232, 275, 277, 386, 476; and TSE's cat poem, 134n; TSE informs of Harvard appointment, 136; and Mrs Dixon

Co., 114; and TSE's financial investments, 346; sees TSE off to Montreal, 464n; appointed VHE's executor, 551, 564; and TSE's separation from VHE, 553n; success in City, 586; letter to TSE on settlement with VHE, 651; Bird forwards TSE's proposals for financial settlement with VHE, 679n; as father's executor, 717

Haigh-Wood, Rose Esther (VHE's mother), 68, 599n

Haldane, J. B. S., 62–3

Hale, Emily, **792**; introduces Dilys Bennett's work to TSE, 76n; TSE visits in USA, 460, 546, 597n; TSE inscribes copy of *Sweeney Agonistes* to, 527n; TSE loses touch with, 580; attends TSE's address at Milton Academy, 596n; TSE sends Dobrée's *As Their Friends Saw Them* to, 692n

Halifax, Charles Lindley Wood, 2nd Viscount, **124n**, 518; *The Good Estate of the Catholic Church*, 124

Hall, Richard Walworth, 486n

Hamilton, (Sir) George Rostrevor, 313

Hamilton, James, 450n

Hamilton, W. K., 387

Hanbury, Dom Michael, 96n

Harcourt, Alfred, 432n, 433n, 517, 558

Harcourt Brace (US publishers), 232, 261, 408, 560, 592

Harding, D. W., 265

Hardy, Thomas, 583, 699

Harlow, Jean, 595n

Harmsworth, Desmond, 6n, **7n**, 94, 415

Harris, Revd Charles, **132n**

Harris, Dr, 426

Harris, Marie P., 687n

Harris, Reginald, 174

Harrison, G. B., **35n**, 359, 696n

Harrison, Ruth: writes on Péguy, **296n**, 315n, 361, 393

Harrisson, Tom, 383n

Hart, Basil Liddell, 677; *The Ghost of Napoleon*, 667n

Hart, Jeffrey, 687n

Hart, Walter Morris, 536n

Harton, Fr F. P.: *The Elements of the Spiritual Life*, 132, 365, 372

Harvard Classical Club, 576n

Harvard Club, New York, 3

Harvard College: TSE elected Charles Eliot Norton Professor of Poetry, 3n, 13,

15–16, 25n, 29n, 49–50, 67n, 70, 100n, 136–8, 387; TSE's accommodation in Eliot House, 5n, 50, 70, 81, 137, 147, 321–2, 333, 404, 419, 457, 459, 467, 496; TSE early impressions of, 459; TSE entertains at, 465; life at, 475, 507–8

Harvard University Press, 669, 692

Hassall, Christopher, 57n, 58n

Havens, Lorraine, 546n

Havens, Paul, 546n

Havens, Raymond D., 323n

Haverford College, Pennsylvania, 505, 565n

Hayward, John Davy, **793**; TSE disparages Bowra to, 125n; and TSE's relations with sister Ada, 146n; proposed as reviewer of *Chesterfield's Letters*, 151; TSE's testimonial for, 293; TSE requests reviews during absence in USA, 414; TSE confides in, 441n; VHE invites to TSE's farewell party, 441; on VHE's proposal to meet, 531n; handwriting, 607; asked to review Dobrée's *As Their Friends Saw Them*, 692; TSE visits, 695; and TSE's published lectures, 704n

H. D. (Hilda Doolittle), 22, 237–8

Healing, Arnold Cuthbert, 748n, 765

Healing, Thomas, 748n

Hebert, Revd (Arthur) Gabriel, **726n**, 766, 770

Hellman, Milton, 538n

Hemingway, Ernest, 545n, 688

Henderson, Ian L., 392n, 409

Henn, T. R., 5n

Henson, Herbert, Bishop of Durham, **239n**, 241

Herbert, Alice, 671n

Herbert, George, 54n, 127n, 161n, 166n

Hermes, Gertrude (*later* Hughes-Stanton), 501

Hester, Norman W.: design for Creation, 758

Hever Castle, Kent, 630

Hibberd, Dominic: *Harold Monro*, 155n, 525n

Hicks, Nugent, Bishop of Gibraltar, 591n

Higham, David, 74n; revises Jerrold's 'Authority, Mind and Power', 222; and US publication of TSE's *John Dryden*, 355–6; and Spender's *The Temple*, 436n, 449

Hiller, Revd Frank, 53n

Lion, Leon M., 378

Listener, The (magazine), 24, 157, 169n, 335; TSE reports on poems in, 662–4, 672–6

Little, Brown *see* Blanchard, Little, Brown & Company, 196

Little, Eleanor (*née* Wheeler), 475n, 767

Little, Leon M., 231n, 475

Liveright, Horace, 286

Lloyd, George, 87n, 91

Lloyds Bank: Aylward employed at, 33n

Lockyer, Isobel, 525; *Collected Poems*, 731

Lockyer, Mr & Mrs, 169

Lodge, Henry Cabot, 555

London Play Company, 167

Lossky, N. O.: *Freedom of Will*, 219

Loucks, James F.: 'The Exile's Return', 465n, 479n, 495n, 536n, 538n, 544n, 546n, 559n, 575n, 639n

Lovejoy, Arthur O., 515n

Low, Elias, 63

Lowell, Abbott Lawrence, 458, 565

Lowenfels, Walter, 107n, 360n, 763

Lowes, John Livingston, 502n; letter from FVM on Porpoise Press, 396n; and Mackenzie's book on Dunbar's poetry, 477, 507; and TSE's Norton lectures, 497–8, 520; TSE invites to dine, 581

Lunn, Arnold, 294

Lymington, Gerard Wallop, Viscount (*later* 9th Earl of Portsmouth): reviews *Plough and Tithe*, 693; *Horn, Hoof and Corn*, 306, 349

Macaulay, Thomas Babington, Baron, 391–2, 409

MacCarthy, Desmond, 113n, 468

McCarthy, Mary, 569n

MacColl, Dugald S., 305

McCord, David, 486, 530

Macdonald, Hugh, 34n; compiles Dryden bibliography, 342; divorce and remarriage, 342n; 'Church and Empire in Dante', 43

McEachran, Frank, 43n, 434, 693, 729n

MacEwen, Sir Alexander: *The Thistle and the Rose*, 390

McGreevy, Thomas, 484, 734n, 751n

MacIntyre, A. H.: misdirects remittances to TSE, 402–3; TSE sends deed of Trust to, 642

Mackay, Miss, 654

McKean, Mrs, 555

McKechnie, Alexander, 95

McKenna, Michael, 498

McKenna, Reginald, 395

Mackenzie, W. Mackay: *The Poems of William Dunbar*, 510n

McKerrow, R. B., 213n

Mackie, Albert, 14n

Maclagan, Eric, 50, 70, 100, 147

Maclaren, Moray: *Return to Scotland*, 390n

MacLehose, Hamish, 282n, 493n

MacLehose, Messrs R., 493n

MacLeish, Archibald, 572; *Conquistador*, 97n, 333

Macleod, Joseph ('Adam Drinan'), 781

Macmurray, John, 23, 72, 611; *The Philosophy of Communism*, 677

MacNeice, Louis, 149n; translates *Agamemnon*, 162n; TSE publishes poems in *Criterion*, 341, 363, 660; and Henderson's essay on Macaulay, 409; TSE praises, 559n

McSpadden, Marie (*later* Sands), 536n

M'Taggart, John M'Taggart Ellis, 461n

Madge, Charles, 383n, 755n, 756

Maeztu, Ramiro de, 192

Maine de Biran, François Pierre Gonthier, 96, 219, 266, 420

Mairet, Philippe: 'The Moral Dilemma of the Age of Science', 604, 660

Malebranche, Nicolas, 745

Mallarmé, Stéphane, 762n

Malmaison Sanatorium, Rueil, 275, 317

Malnik, Bertha, 308

Malory, Sir Thomas: *Morte d'Arthur*, 774

Malraux, André, 223, 235, 266, 477

Manchester Guardian, 100

Manent, Marià, 261n

Manning, Frederic, 52n, 59, 225; *Her Privates We*, 52n

Mansfield, Katherine, 83n, 693

Manwaring, Elizabeth, 15n; and TSE's poetry readings at Harvard, 466; offers to visit VHE, 602, 623; letter from VHE on separation from TSE, 640n

Marc, Alexandre: *Jeune Europe*, 752

Mare, Il (magazine), 438, 528n

Marichalar, Antonio, Marquis of Montesa, 624n

'Marina', 488n, 536n, 746

Maritain, Jacques, 329–30, 330n, 374,

835

Morrell, Philip, 171n, 368, 439
Morris, Howard, 3n
Morris, Jack L., 687n
Morris, William, 620
Morton, A. L., 130n, 491n, 492n, 653;
  'Property and Poetry in a Communist
  Society', 281
Mosley, Sir Oswald ('Tom'), 90n, 91n, 105
Mount Holyoke College, Mass., 554
Mount Olivet Monastery, Frensham, 759n
Muggeridge, Malcolm, 610, 615
Muir, Edwin, 337n, 781n, 799; translates
  Kafka's 'He', 45
Muir, Willa (née Anderson), 337n, 445n
Mumford, Lewis, 66; Herman Melville: a
  Study of His Life and Vision, 66n, 437
Munson, Gorham B., 66–7, 390
Murder in the Cathedral, 98n, 569n
Murdock, Kenneth B., 49n, 137, 251n,
  498, 503, 506, 510, 516
Murphy, James M., 56
Murray, J. Tucker, 138n
Murray, Leonora Eyles, 44n
Murry, John Middleton, 800; protests
  at Smyth's review of Rowse, 26n, 78;
  criticises Russian Communism, 78;
  reviews Wilson Knight's The Imperial
  Theme, 205; and Plowman, 722n;
  and Richard Rees's article on Pound,
  761; Blake, 659, 756n; The Fallacy of
  Economics, 30, 69; The Necessity of
  Communism, 183
Mussolini, Benito: friendship with J. S.
  Barnes, 89n; pamphlet, 693
Myron, Herbert B., Jr, 460n

Nabokov, Vladimir: Lolita, 583n
Napoleon I (Bonaparte), Emperor of the
  French, 319
Nashdom Abbey, Berkshire, 727n, 728n
Nashville, Tennessee, 581
National Recovery Administration (USA),
  699, 741
Neagoe, Peter: edits Anthology of American
  Artists Abroad, 247n
Needham, Joseph, 129n; Oldham proposes
  for religious group, 71; on religious
  experience, 161n; 'Laudian Marxism',
  201
Nef, Elinor Castle, 548n
Nelson, J. H.: edits anthology of prose and
  verse for Macmillan, 245, 312, 370

Nelson, Mabel, 463, 506
Nelson, Wilbur A., 515n, 590
the new broom (magazine), 238
New English Weekly, 675, 706n
'New Hampshire', 597n
New Statesman & Nation (journal), 163,
  676, 709n, 710
New York, 3, 558–9, 585, 595
New York City Ballet, 519n
New Yorker (magazine), 545n
Newcomb, John Lloyd, 515
Nichols, Robert, 361n; Wings Over Europe
  (with Maurice Browne; play), 259
Nickerson, Hoffman, 620n; TSE invites
  article on Babbit from, 647, 660, 667;
  writes on Republican Party, 647, 667;
  Can We Limit War?, 621, 647, 677
Nicolls, Basil E., 145n
Nicolson, Harold, 45, 90n, 91n, 257,
  427n, 557n, 720n
Nizan, Paul: Les Chiens de Garde, 266
Noonan, J. J., 538
Norton, Katherine, 391
Norton Lectures, 100n, 233, 441n, 476n,
  479, 497, 503, 506, 519, 524, 560, 589,
  630, 665, 698, 775; see also The Use of
  Poetry and The Use of Criticism
Norton, Lily, 577, 594
Norton, W. W., 398n
'Notes on the Blank Verse of Christopher
  Marlowe', 488
Nott, Stanley, 705n
Nouvelle Revue Française, 194
Nowell-Smith, Simon, 33n
Noyes, Penelope, 320
Nuova Antologia, La (magazine), 197, 280

Objectivist Anthology, 487
O'Brien, Terence, 507
obscenity laws, 164n
O'Conor, Norreys Jephson, 67n; and
  Weston book, 418; invites TSE to lunch,
  438; alters text, 530
Odyssey Press, 721n
Oecumenica (journal), 726, 766
Ó Faoláin, Seán, 110n
Old Colony Trust Company, Boston,
  Mass., 327, 416, 642, 730n
Old Possum's Book of Practical Cats, 219n
Old Vic and Sadler's Wells Society, 229,
  251, 258, 284, 730
Oldham, Joseph H., 71n, 99n, 117, 162,

'Poets as Letter Writers' (lecture), 497n
Poets on Poets series, 117n
Poncins, Léon de, 234n; 'La France contre l'Americanisme', 234, 470, 477
Ponsonby, Colonel Sir Charles Edward, 84
Porpoise Press, 118, 396n, 397
Porteus, Hugh Gordon, 666n; reviews Yeats's *The Winding Stair*, 677, 681n, 683n; suggests cheap edition of *Criterion*, 682n; asked to review Wyndham Lewis's *One-Way-Song*, 756-7
'Portrait of a Lady', 312
Post, Laurence, 538n
Postgate, Raymond, 214n
Pound, Dorothy, 583n
Pound, Ezra, 802; TSE writes introduction to selection of poems, 6; supports Basil Bunting, 65n; Leavis on, 104-5; on Harold Monro, 180n, 222, 224; reviews Stokes's *The Quattro Cento*, 252, 325, 358; influence on Bottrall, 254-5n, 683n; and TSE's supposed anti-Semitism, 287n; edits Cavalcanti *Rime*, 297, 318n, 319, 321, 763; TSE writes on metrics and poetry, 312, 762; Richard Church questions TSE's sponsoring of, 395n; letter from VHE on seduction by Lucy Thayer, 463; letter from Morley on TSE in USA, 543n; disparages British writing, 565n; on Noh drama, 566; Gregory reviews, 579; TSE proposes meeting in England, 588; letter to *Criterion*, 610; and Palgrave, 622n; differences with TSE, 655-8; on TSE's 45th birthday, 655n; on Housman, 661, 676; influence, 675; Marianne Moore reviews, 676, 739; proposed volume of essays, 762-3; influence on Taupin, 779; and Hulme, 780; *ABC of Economics*, 528, 572,, 588, 616; *Active Anthology* (ed.), 644; *Cantos*, 254, 371, 421, 513-14, 645n, 676, 757n; *A Draft of XXX Cantos*, 621n; 'Hell', 645n; *Hugh Selwyn Mauberley*, 255n, 371, 397, 514, 572; 'In the Vortex', 763; *Instigations*, 646; *Jefferson and/or Mussolini*, 70, 645n, 656, 763; 'Mr Housman at Little Bethel', 676n; *Pavannes and Divisions*, 646; 'Seafarer', 781; *Selected Poems*, 685; 'Selfless Service', 706n
Powell, Dilys, 75n
Powell, Lawrence Clark, 340n

Power, Sister Mary James: *Poets at Prayer*, 518n
Powys, T. F., 749; 'The Gong', 754
Praz, Mario, 758n, 803; translates *TWL* into Italian, 197, 373n, 758n; on metaphysical poetry, 270; translates TSE's poetry, 279-80, 373; sends Ungaretti poem to TSE, 373; *The Romantic Agony*, 684
Prescott, William Gardiner, 507n
Press, John, 531n
Princeton University, 102-3, 131-2, 184, 232, 362, 569n
'Prufrock', 649n
Psichari, Henriette: *Ernest Psichari*, 735
Publishers' Circular, 540
Pudovkin, V. I.: 'Acting – The Cinema v. The Theatre', 604n, 614
Pusey, Edward Bouverie, 102, 191n, 700

Quennell, Peter, 48n; 'Climacteric', 48
Quiller-Couch, Sir Arthur, 112n, 387n

Radcliffe Club, Boston, 397, 499
Radcliffe, Philip, 612n, 654
Rafferty, Seán, 396
Ragg, T. M.: 'The Pond', 311
Raine, Kathleen, 770n
Randall, (Sir) Alec, 477, 683
'Rannoch, by Glencoe', 711n
Rattray, R. F., 309n
Raven, Charles Earl, 71
Raymond, Ernest: *The Berg* (play), 759n
Raymond, Marcel: *De Baudelaire au Surréalisme*, 752n
Read, Herbert, 804; introduction to Duff's book on Joyce, 151; attends *Criterion* meetings, 246, 267, 273, 303, 310; financial difficulties, 273; and publication of Kierkegaard, 351; judges poems for TSE, 365; and Mrs Clifton, 446; proposed post in St Louis, 577; on TSE's attitude to children, 607n; reviews Santayana, 611; on Aurousseau, 615; suggests TSE look through poems in *Listener*, 662; recommends Porteus as reviewer, 666n; praises TSE's published lectures, 688; reviews for *Criterion*, 693; Belgion criticises, 715n; differences with TSE, 738; and poems of Dylan Thomas, 761n; influenced by Hulme, 780; on Wilfred Owen, 781; *Art Now*, 757-8n;

End of a War, 723n; *In Retreat*, 460;
The Innocent Eye, 203, 447; 'Personality
in Literature', 303; 'A Short Poem for
Armistice Day', 676
Reckitt, Maurice B., **195n**, 615, 677
Reed, A. W., 411
Reed, Revd D. V., 111n
Reed, Marjorie, 121n
Rees, Goronwy, 125n
Rees, Sir Richard, **358n**; 'Masks of Ezra
Pound', 761
Reeves, Father (Dominican), 169
Regnery, Henry, 495n, 780n
Reilly, Patrick, 509
Reith, Sir John: approves 'The Modern
Dilemma' talks, 48n; admires Bishop Bell,
100; praises TSE's broadcast talks, 184;
and poems in *Listener*, 664, 672n
'The Relation of Criticism and Poetry'
(lecture), 495n
Rendall, Richard A., 56n, **185n**
Renwick, W. L.: 'Old Play', 653
Review of English Studies, 213
Rhondda, Margaret Haig Thomas,
Viscountess, 363n
Rhys, Ernest, **223n**; 'Rhymes and
Unrhymes', 223n
Rice, V., 528n
Richards, I. A., 805; reviews Eastman's
Literary Mind, 32, 343; and TSE's
lecturing at Harvard, 69; recommends
Elsie Elizabeth Phare's novel to TSE, 73;
and Belgion on Belief, 115, 135, 140n;
and TSE's visit to USA and Canada,
255–6; suggests Madge submit essay
on Blake and Dryden to TSE, 383n;
delays reviews for *Criterion*, 654, 665;
sensibility, 689; TSE visits at Magdalene,
697; growing interest in language, 698n;
TSE on disparaging, 715n; TSE questions
judgement, 738; discusses Charles Madge
with TSE, 756; influenced by Hulme, 780;
'Fifteen Lines from Landor', 689, 738;
'Science Value and Poetry', 84n
Richards, P. S., 295
Richmond, Bruce L., 805; TSE recommends
Grieve to, 15; TSE addresses on Curtius's
The Civilisation of France, 59–60; and
foreign reviewing, 267
Ricketts, Charles, 98n
Rickword, C. H., 431n
Riddle, Bettina (*later* Baroness von Hutten

zum Stolzenburg), 743n
Riddle, Henrietta, 743n
Riddle, Richard, 737, 743
Ridler, Anne, 710n
Rimbaud, Arthur, 656
Rivera, Diego, 646n
Robbins, Lionel: *An Essay on the Nature
and Significance of Economic Science*,
322
Roberts, Adam, 638n
Roberts, Michael, **541n**; (ed.) *New
Country*, 611
Roberts, Richard Ellis, **163n**
Roberts, S. C., 304
Robertson, Sir Malcolm, 113n
Robey, George: *Looking Back on Life*, 653,
676
Robinson, Fred, 595
The Rock (pageant), 634n, 690n, 697, 698,
712–13, 732–3, 769n, 775–6n, 777n
Rodd, Sir Rennell: *Rome of the
Renaissance and To-day*, 477n
Roditi, Edouard, 806; translates Spender
poems, 7–8; and Thoma's unsigned copy
of TSE's *Dante*, 389; on Abravanel,
529; submits poems to TSE, 755; 'The
Complaint of Jehudah Abravanel', 340n,
661n, 755
Rodker, John, 6n, 720n, 721, 746, 772
Rodmell, Sussex, 276n, 637, 639
'Le roman anglais contemporain', 194n
Ronsard, Pierre de, 246
Roosevelt, Franklin D., 508n, 563n, 699n,
741
Rootham, Helen, 671
Rosenfeld, Paul, 80
Rosenstock, Eugen: *Die Europaeischen
Revolutionen, Volkskaraktere und
Staatenbildung*, 199n
Ross, E. D.: *Sir Anthony Shirley and His
Persian Adventure*, 696n
Rothenstein, William, 807; portrait of TSE,
586; *Memoirs*, 283
Rothermere, Harold Sidney Harmsworth,
1st Viscount, 657
Rothschild, Victor (*later* 4th Baron), 695,
730
Routledge (publishers), 534, 540
Rowse, A. L., 807; protests at review of
Politics and the Younger Generation,
26–8, 78, 491n; essay on Keynes, 173,
575; answers TSE's criticisms of eassy on

Keynes, 175n; contributes to symposium on H. G. Wells's *The Work, Wealth and Happiness of Mankind*, 218, 241; recommends Bishop Henson to review Wells, 239; Tomlin criticises *Politics and the Younger Generation*, 351n; withdraws from TSE, 440; reviews Lytton Strachey's *Characters and Commentaries*, 693–4; reviews David Mathew, 694n

Rubin, Nathan Harold, **141n**, 196, 271n; *Brick and Mortar*, 270, 357

Rubinstein, Helena, 19n

Rukeyser, Muriel, 569n

Russell, Bertrand, 339n, 442n, 562–3

Russell, Dora, 595

Russell, George William (Æ): *Song and its Fountain*, 110

Rutherford, Margaret, 57n

Rychner, Max, 362, 654, 693

Rylands, George ('Dadie'), 18n

Sackville-West, Vita (Victoria), 557

Sadleir, Michael: and Tudor Translations, 32, 36

Sadler's Wells Society *see* Old Vic and Sadler's Wells Society

Sainsbury, Geoffrey: *The Dictatorship of Things*, 677

St Botolph Club, Boston, 25, 494

St Louis, Mo., 496, 519, 524, 538–9, 575

St Margaret's school, Bushey, 189n

Saint Paul *see* Minnesota, University of

Saintsbury, George, 610, 615, 738

Salt, W. E., 350n

Sampson, Ashley, 350n, 661

Santayana, George, 380, 611

Sargent, John Singer: portrait of Charles W. Eliot, 496

Sassoon, Siegfried, 227n, **262n**, 269, 395

Satterthwaite, Alfred, 661n

Saturday Review of Literature, 348

Saunders, Olivia (*later* Mrs James Agee), 465n

Sautoy, Peter de, 121n

Sayers, Dorothy L., 99n

Sayers, Michael, **123n**, 404

Scaife, Roger L., 596

Scheler, Max: *Die Idee des Friedens und der Pazifismus*, 46

Schiff, Sydney, **12n**, 144

Schiff, Violet (*née* Beddington), 12n, 602n

Schuchard, Ronald, 598n

Schwartz, Delmore, 643n

Schwarz, Otto H., 538n

Scotland: nationalism, 390n, 396n; TSE visits with Morley, 685, 695, 697, 774

Scott Moncrieff, George, 653; *Café Bar*, 382

Scripps College, Claremont, Calif., 460n, 527, 546n

Scrutiny (magazine), 113n, 265, 289, 419, 774

'The Search for Modern Sanction' (broadcast talk), 226n

Sears, Eleanor Randolph, 555n

Sedgwick, Ellery, 70n, 403, 577, 594

Seide, H., 578

Selden, Anna, 461n

Seldes, Gilbert, **202n**, 595, 654

Selected Essays 1917–1932, 232, 348, 409, 481, 483, 536n, 560n, 644n

Selwyn, Revd Edward Gordon, **148n**, 179, 700

Selznick, David O., 595n

Sencourt, Robert *see* George, Robert Esmonde Gordon

Sender, Mrs Greenfield, 519n

Seward, A. C., 112n

Seymour, Miranda, 598n

Shahani, Ranjee G., **75n**

Shakespeare Association, 35, 106, 258

'Shakespeare and the Stoicism of Seneca', 35

Shakespeare, William: *Measure for Measure*, 730, 737, 747

Shapcott, Mr (of James & James), 452

Shaw, George Bernard, 174

Shaw, Margaret, 706,

Shaw, Martin, **777n**

Sheed & Ward (publishers), 326, 723

Sheffield, Ada (*née* Eliot; TSE's sister), **146n**; and TSE's accommodation at Harvard, 137, 146–7; TSE stays with, 411, 458, 465n, 466, 507; and VHE's acceptance of separation, 640n

Sheffield, Alfred Dwight, **146n**; introduces Elizabeth Manwaring to TSE, 15n

Shelley, Percy Bysshe, 383, 709n

Sheppard, (Sir) John Tressider, 422n, **430n**, 470

Shorey, Paul: *What Plato Said*, 565

Sidney, Sir Philip, 630

Siepmann, Charles Arthur, **809**; proposes BBC talks, 48; forms committee on religious broadcasting, 228; and Gurian's *Bolshevism*, 264; overwork, 448

Silverstein, Theodore, 247n

Simon, Sir John, 101, 116, 708n

Simpson, Canon Sparrow: *History of the Anglo-Catholic Revival*, 345

Sitwell family, 595–6, 780–1

Sitwell, (Dame) Edith, **670n**; on VHE's health, 17n; at Harold Monro's funeral, 155n; reads Rimbaud, 656; complains of Grigson's review of Sacheverell poems, 670n; TSE writes to on Brian Coffey, 751n

Sitwell, Georgia, 17n

Sitwell, Sacheverell: *Canons of Giant Art*, 670n

Skelton, John, 502

Smart, John: *Tarantula's Web*, 441n, 695n

Smith, Abigail Eliot (TSE's niece), **496n**

Smith, Charlotte (*née* Eliot; TSE's sister), 551n

Smith, Charlotte Stearns ('Chardy') *see* Talcott, Charlotte Stearns Smith

Smith, Elliot: *The Diffusion of Culture*, 653

Smith, George Lawrence, 551, 564

Smith, Jack Holmes (TSE's uncle-in-law), **518n**

Smith, Janet Adam, 51n, **662n**; 'Tom Possum and the Roberts Family', 662n

Smith, Jordan, 121n

Smith, Logan P., 677

Smith, Rose Holmes (Rose Greenleaf Eliot; TSE's aunt), 17, 232, 519, 529; *Complementarities*, 84

Smith, Theodora Eliot ('Dodo'; TSE's niece), 68n, 551, 642

Smyth, Revd Charles, **51n**; broadcast talk, 24, 48–9, 85; reviews A. L. Rowse's *Politics and the Younger Generation*, 26–8, 491n; and Sencourt's *Spanish Crown*, 193; moves to St Clement's parish, Barnsbury, 201n; Needham praises, 201; on Divine Right of Kings, 277; reviews Dibdin, 321; expertise on Tudor period, 412; 'The Education of an Officer Class', 52n, 208

Smyth, Ethel, 276n

Society of the Sacred Mission, Kelham, 630, 639, 726n, 727

Sollory, Ellen (*née* Kellond), 189n

Sollory, William L., **189n**, 190, 216 & n

Song for Simeon: French translation, 374

Sophocles: *Oedipus Rex*, 162n

Spaeth, J. D., 102n, 131n, 184

Sparrow, John: *Sense and Poetry*, 774n

Spectator, The (journal), 166n, 198, 340, 774

Spencer, Katherine, 5n

Spencer, Theodore, **5n**; and TSE's accommodation at Harvard, 69, 70n, 81, 137, 147; teaches at Radcliffe, 378n; article on Marston, 456; welcomes TSE to Harvard, 457, 465; and Harry Levin, 502n; TSE sends stanzas to, 514; friendship with TSE at Harvard, 530–1, 609; teaching, 544n; lectures on Virginia Woolf, 576–7; visit to London, 620; and Matthiessen, 628n; poems in *Listener*, 663n, 675; receives recording of TSE's poetry readings, 692n; lunches with TSE, 777; 'John Marston', 451; 'The Poetry of T. S. Eliot', 403

Spencer-Trask Foundation (and lecture), 102, 131, 569n

Spender, Stephen, **809**; Roditi translates, 8; in Germany, 16, 384; poems published in Hogarth Press anthology, 42, 77; reviews, 152n, 157; homosexuality, 158; delays sending poems to TSE, 384; returns to London, 417; TSE promotes in USA, 525, 559n; Faber publishes, 549; TSE recommends to Gregory, 579; on George Robey, 653, 676; Alida Monro asks to print poems, 659; reviews TSE's lectures in *New Statesman*, 709; Coffey on, 752n; writes on Henry James, 754n; and Asquith letters to Venetia Stanley, 760; new verse, 781; 'By the Lake' (story), 754; 'Four Poems', 781n; *Poems*, 450n, 627n, 635; 'Remembering Eliot', 711n; *The Temple* (novel), 152n, 156–7, 290, 384, 417, 435, 449, 471, 613n; *World Within World*, 291n

Spens, (Sir) Will, 148n, **179n**, 668

Springarn, Jake, 95n

Squire, Sir John C., 87n, 91, 675

Stamp, Josiah, 72

Standley, Commander Hugh and Mary, 134n

Stanhope, Charles, 3rd Earl, 455

Stanley, Venetia, 760n

Stead, William Force, 810; visits TSE, 263, 288; tomb, 594; *Uriel*, 549

Stein, Gertrude, 686n

Tomlin, E. Walter F., 350n; on TSE's first marriage, 741n; 'D. H. Lawrence and His Critics', 648n, 658, 732; 'Some Implications of the Materialist Theory of Art', 523, 648, 658; 'The Younger Generation and Politics', 350–1, 732n

Tonks, Henry, 283n; paintings, 305

Toppen, W. H., 584n

Torrence, Ridgley, 432n

'Toward a Definition of Metaphysical Poetry' (lecture), 542n

'Tradition and Contemporary Literature' (lectures), 583n, 589, 590n

'Tradition and the Individual Talent', 624

Trask, Sherwood, 310n

Trefusis, Violet, 557n

Trend, J. B., 4n, 212, 388, 434, 612

Trevelyan, Mary, 499n, 553n, 638n

Trevelyan, Robert C., 395–6

Tribe, Revd Reginald, 369n

'Triumphal March', 280, 373, 495n, 649n

Trotsky, Leon: Literature and Revolution, 709n

Tuckerman, Bayard, Jr, 555n

Tuckerman, Phyllis (Sears), 555n

Turnbull, Andrew, 686n

Turnbull, Mr and Mrs Bayard, 686n

Turnbull Lectures, Johns Hopkins University, 323, 515, 526n, 527, 542n, 686n, 687n

Turnbull, Miss, 687n

Turner, Miss J., 236

Tustain, Philippa: The Gate of Heaven (morality play), 412, 420, 455, 469–70

Twain, Mark, 66

'Two Masters' (talk), 429n, 582n

Tyrrell, George, 722n

Underhill, Evelyn (Mrs H. S. Moore), 54n, 365

Underhill, Revd Francis (later Bishop of Bath and Wells), 111n; as Evelyn's spiritual director, 54n; appointed Dean of Rochester, 279; TSE seeks advice from on breakdown, 552

Ungaretti, Giuseppe: 'Moammed Sceab' (poem), 352, 373

Unger, Leonard, 531n

Untermeyer, Louis (ed.): The Book of Living Verse, 705n

Upcott, Lewis E.: on John Ford's The Broken Heart, 282

Upward, Edward: 'The Colleagues', 9n, 16

The Use of Poetry and the Use of Criticism (published Norton lectures), 654, 693n, 697n, 699, 704n, 709–10, 770, 773n

Vail, Laurence, 82–3n

van Doren, Mark, 86, 293n

Vansittart, Sir Robert, 89n

'The Varieties of Metaphysical Poetry' (lecture), 527, 542n

Vassar College, Poughkeepsie, 494, 566, 577–8, 635

Vaucher, Paul, 298n

Verschoyle, Derek, 198n

Victoria, Queen: death, 557n

Vigée, Claude see Strauss, Cyril

Vijaya-Tunga, J.: 'Reply' (poem), 660

Viking Press, 764

Villon, François: Le Testament, 762n

Vinogradoff, Igor, 171n

Vinogradoff, Julian see Morrell, Julian

Virginia, University of, 515, 543n, 560, 583n, 589; see also Page-Barbour lectures

Vogt, Professor (ophthalmologist), 369n, 375n, 376

Waley, Arthur: translations of Lady Murasaki, 677n

Walker, Ralph S.: 'Ben Jonson's Lyric Poetry', 660

Waller, Robert, 229n

Walsingham, Norfolk, 650

Walton, William, 780n

Warburg, M. M., 5119n

Ware, Martin, 398n

Warner, Francis, 181n

Warner, Rex E., 424n; The Wild Goose Chase, 424

Warren, Austin, 442, 442n

Washington University, 575n

Wassermann-Karlweis, Frau Jacob, 604n

The Waste Land: Swedish translation, 37–40; Italian translation, 197, 373n; Hugh Ross Williamson on, 251n, 252n; as model for Bottrall's 'Festival of Fire', 254n; Ash Wednesday compared with, 313; P. E. More on, 483; Pound's revisions and comments on, 513; Theodore Spencer on, 531; TSE restricts anthologising, 633

Watson, E. L. Grant, 436n, 616, 668

Wayment, H. G., 278n

recordings of poetry readings to, 691, 714; and TSE's search for lodgings, 691, 708n, 733; *Orlando*, 557n

Woolsey, Judge John M. (New York), 736, 740, 743

'Words for Music: New Hampshire; Virginia', 633n, 773

Wordsworth, William, 536n, 689

Worthen, John, 563n

Wyon, Olive, 60n

Wyss, J. R.: completes *The Swiss Family Robinson*, 602, 623

Xavier, Sister Mary, 54n

Yale University, 474–5, 494, 497, 547, 555

Yeats, William Butler, 814; TSE seeks introductions from, 181–2; given dinner at Wellesley College, 479n; made honorary member of Authors' Club, 504n; on Irish as appreciators of poetry, 543n; TSE re-reads for teaching English course, 544n; and Pound, 550; influence, 675; friendship with McGreevy, 734n; *At the Hawk's Well*, 566; *Letters to the Other Island*, 683n; *The Winding Stair*, 677, 681n, 683n; *The Words Upon the Window Pane*, 683

Zaturenska, Marya (Mrs Horace Gregory), 260n

Zukofsky, Louis, 487n, 559n, 572; 'Ezra Pound: His Cantos', 751n